THE WORLD'S HISTORY

HOWARD SPODEK

THE WORLD'S HISTORY

FIFTH EDITION

PEARSON

Boston   Columbus   Indianapolis   New York   San Francisco
Hoboken   Amsterdam   Cape Town   Dubai   London
Madrid   Milan   Munich   Paris   Montréal   Toronto   Delhi   Mexico City
São Paulo   Sydney   Hong Kong   Seoul   Singapore   Taipei   Tokyo

Vice-President of Product Development:
Dickson Musslewhite
Senior Acquisitions Editor: Billy J. Grieco
Program Manager: Emily Tamburri
Project Manager: Gail Cocker
Senior Operations Supervisor: Mary Ann Gloriande
Media Director: Sacha Laustsen
Media Editor: Michael Halas
Media Project Manager: Elizabeth Roden

Printed and bound by Times Offset, Malaysia

Credits and acknowledgments borrowed from other sources
and reproduced, with permission, in this textbook appear
on the appropriate page within text or on the credits pages
in the back of this book.

Front cover: *La Gran Tenochtitlán*, Diego Rivera (detail).
1945. Palacio Nacional, Mexico City. © 2013 Banco de
Mexico Diego Rivera & Frida Kahlo Museums Trust,
Mexico D.F./Artists Rights Society (ARS), New York.
Photo © 2003 Schalkwijk/Art Resource/Scala, Florence

This book was designed and produced by
Laurence King Publishing Ltd, London
www.laurenceking.com

Every effort has been made to contact the copyright holders,
but should there be any errors or omissions, Laurence King
Publishing Ltd would be pleased to insert the appropriate
acknowledgment in any subsequent printing of this
publication.

Commissioning editor: Kara Hattersley-Smith
Senior editor: Melissa Danny
Production: Simon Walsh
Designer: Nick Newton
Picture researcher: Peter Kent
Text permissions editor: Julie Kemp
Copy editor: Rosanna Lewis
Proofreader: Jessica McCarthy
Indexer: Pauline Hubner

Library of Congress Cataloging-in-Publication Data

Spodek, Howard
  The world's history / Howard Spodek. -- Fifth edition.
    pages cm
  Includes bibliographical references and index.
  ISBN 978-0-205-99612-4 -- ISBN 0-205-99612-4
  1. World history. I. Title.
  D20.S77 2015
  909--dc23
                          2014010924

10 9 8 7 6 5 4 3 2 1

PearsonSchool.com/Advanced

ISBN 10: 0-13-395267-3
(High School Binding)
ISBN 13: 978-0-13-395267-4
(High School Binding)

BRIEF CONTENTS

CONTENTS

CHAPTER THIRTEEN
The Opening of the Atlantic and the Pacific
Economic Growth, Religion and Renaissance, Global Connections

CHAPTER FOURTEEN
The Unification of World Trade
New Philosophies for New Trade Patterns

CHAPTER FIFTEEN
Migration
Demographic Changes in a New Global World

PART SIX
TURNING POINT: REVOLUTION
1640–1914
Coping with Western Revolutions

CHAPTER SIXTEEN
Political Revolutions in Europe and the Americas
The Birth of Political Rights in the Age of Enlightenment
1649–1830

CHAPTER SEVENTEEN
The Industrial Revolution
A Global Process
1700–1914

CHAPTER TWENTY-TWO
China and India
Into the Twenty-First Century 770

China and India: A Comparison 771
China's Revolutions 772
Chiang Kai-shek and the Guomindang 773
Mao Zedong and Peasant Revolt 774
Gender Issues in the Revolution 775
The Long March and the Communist Triumph 776
   The Yan'an Soviet 776
   Cooperation with the GMD 776
   The GMD Retreats to Taiwan 777
The People's Republic of China 779
Revolutionary Policies 779
   "Let a Hundred Flowers Bloom" 780
   The Great Leap Forward 781
   The Cultural Revolution 781
   Recovery 782
Women in the People's Republic of China 782
China's International Relations 783
   The United States 783
   China's Neighbors 784
   India 785
Postrevolutionary China 785
India's Struggle for Independence 786
First Steps Toward Self Rule 786
Mohandas Gandhi and Civil Disobedience 786
   Gandi Develops Satyagraha in South Africa 787
Gandhi and the Independence Movement 789
   Cultural, Social, and Economic Policies 789
   Congress Campaigns for Independence 790
   Gandhi's Leadership 792
Independence and Partition 793
Hindu–Muslim Separation/Partition 793
Unifying the Nation 795
Democracy and Its Challenges 796
Indian Politics 796
   Indira Gandhi 796
Gender Issues 797
   Legal Changes 797
   Social Changes 798
   Economic Changes 798
Economic and Technological Development 799
   Revolutions in Agriculture 799
   Challenges of Population and Poverty 799
   Industrialization and Its Consequences 800
International Relations 800
Comparing China and India:
What Difference Does It Make? 801

PART EIGHT
TURNING POINT: FROM PAST TO PRESENT TO FUTURE
1979– 806

CHAPTER TWENTY-THREE
Contemporary History
Evolution, Settlements, Politics, and Religion 810

On Evolution 811
The DNA Code and Its Discoveries 811
   Cloning and Genetic Engineering 812
The Evolution of Diseases 814
On Settlements 814
The Growth of Cities 815
Cities as Systems 817
   Urban Slums 817
On Politics and Empire 819
The Former Soviet Union 819
The United States Stands Alone 820
   Terrorism 820
China: An Emerging Superpower? 822
   Poverty 824
   Corruption 824
   The Environment 825
   Population Control 825
   The Road to Democracy? 826
   Transparency 827
   Global Recognition 827
The Unification of Europe 828
On Religion 829
Theocracy in Iran 830
Islamic Militants in Afghanistan 832
Islam, Secularism, and Christianity 833
Religious Strife in Yugoslavia 834
Hinduism and Islam in India 836
Buddhists in Tibet 837
Judaism 837
Christianity 837
   Roman Catholicism 838
   Evangelical Christianity 839
The Thematic Approach:
What Difference Does It Make? 841

CHAPTER TWENTY-FOUR
Contemporary History
Trade, Revolution, Technology, Identity 844

On Trade 845
The Institutions of Globalization 845
   The Internet, the World Wide Web, and
      Containerization 845
Globalization and Its Critics 847
Setting Goals for Globalization 850

MAPS

Engage your students beyond the classroom . . .

. . . with MyHistoryLab and
THE WORLD'S HISTORY, Fifth Edition

Would your students get more out of their history course if you could engage them with history *beyond* the classroom? Would class discussion go farther if they were reading and writing more, working with primary sources, studying maps, and mastering key topics . . . *before* class meetings begin?

If your answer to these questions is yes, then it's time to consider how MyHistoryLab can help you meet these challenges. MyHistoryLab offers immersive content, tools, and experiences to engage students and help them succeed, enabling you to craft a better learning experience for them.

Prepare students on key topics with the MyHistoryLab Video Series

Are your history students ready and eager to contend with a college textbook narrative? If not, help them get up to speed with the new MyHistoryLab Video Series: Key Topics in Western Civilization. Correlated to the chapters of *The World's History*, each video unit reviews key topics of the period, readying students to get the most from the text narrative. These engaging videos feature seasoned historians reviewing the pivotal stories of our past, in a lively format designed to demonstrate the power of historical narrative.

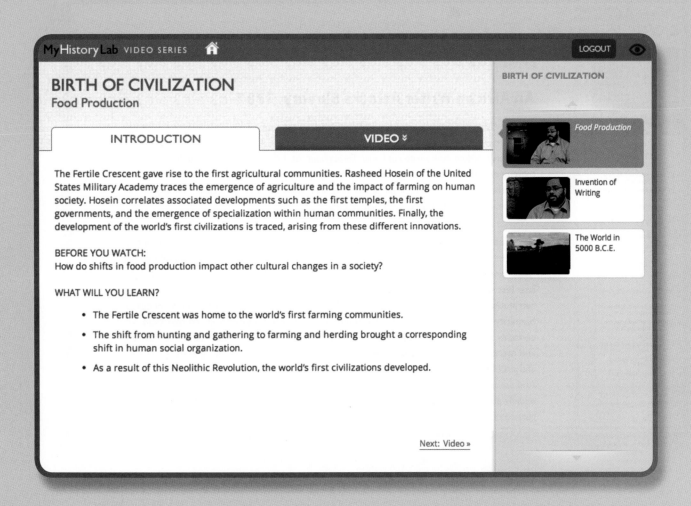

MyHistoryLab VIDEO SERIES   LOGOUT

BIRTH OF CIVILIZATION
Food Production

INTRODUCTION   **VIDEO ⌄**

The Fertile Crescent gave rise to the first agricultural communities. Rasheed Hosein of the United States Military Academy traces the emergence of agriculture and the impact of farming on human society. Hosein correlates associated developments such as the first temples, the first governments, and the emergence of specialization within human communities. Finally, the development of the world's first civilizations is traced, arising from these different innovations.

BEFORE YOU WATCH:
How do shifts in food production impact other cultural changes in a society?

WHAT WILL YOU LEARN?

- The Fertile Crescent was home to the world's first farming communities.

- The shift from hunting and gathering to farming and herding brought a corresponding shift in human social organization.

- As a result of this Neolithic Revolution, the world's first civilizations developed.

Next: Video »

BIRTH OF CIVILIZATION

Food Production

Invention of Writing

The World in 5000 B.C.E.

Drive your students into primary sources with the new MyHistoryLibrary

Now your students can read dozens of the most commonly assigned primary-source documents, specially formatted in Pearson's powerful new eText. Students also have the option of listening to each reading in the accompanying Chapter Audio. Either way, students may access the text or the audio with various devices anytime they have access to the Internet.

An African Writer Attacks Slavery, 1787

Quobna Ottobah Cugoano was born in West Africa in the late 1750s. Sold into slavery at age thirteen, he was eventually taken to England by his owner in 1772. At some point after that, he gained his freedom, how we do not know. Throughout the 1790s, he was active in the abolitionist movement, speaking at meetings, writing to newspapers, and publishing two books on the slave trade. The excerpts from his writings included here come from his first book, Thoughts and Sentiments on the Evil of Slavery, *published in 1787.*

But whereas the people of Great-Britain having now acquired a greater share in that iniquitous commerce than all the rest together, they are the first that ought to set an example, lest they have to repent for their wickedness when it becomes too late; lest some impending calamity should speedily burst forth against them, and lest a just retribution for their enormous crimes, and a continuance in committing similar deeds of barbarity and injustice should involve them in ruin. For we may be assured that God will certainly avenge himself of such heinous transgressors of his law, and of all those planters and merchants, and of all others, who are the authors of the Africans' graves, severities, and cruel punishments, and no plea of any absolute necessity can possibly excuse them. And as the inhabitants of Great-Britain, and the inhabitants of the colonies, seem almost equally guilty of the oppression, there is great reason for both to dread the severe vengeance of Almighty God upon them, and upon all such notorious workers of wickedness;

Immerse your students in a powerful eText deeply integrated with MyHistoryLab

Teachers have long struggled to get students engaged in traditional textbooks. Now Pearson's MyHistoryLab offers a deeply immersive eText that transforms how students experience history. With a new pedagogically driven design, it highlights a clear learning path through the material and offers a visually stunning learning experience in print or on a screen. With the Pearson eText, students can transition directly to MyHistoryLab resources such as primary-source documents, videos, and Closer Look features. At last, history students can experience the eText they have been waiting for—one that comes alive on the screen.

PEARSON

Welcome SSA history   Print | Settings | Help | Sign Out

Browse   My Searches   Search...   Go

Page 89   125%

4 A Polycentric World

Cities and States in East Asia, the Americas, and West Africa

1700 B.C.E.–1000 C.E.

This chapter completes the survey of the seven areas of primary urbanization. It covers the four areas that developed primary urbanization somewhat more recently: the Yellow River valley of China; two regions of the western hemisphere—Mesoamerica and the South American Pacific coastal plain with the adjacent Andes Mountains that tower above it; and the Niger River valley of West Africa. The first cities in these regions date from as early as 1700 B.C.E. in China to as late as 400 C.E. in the Niger valley. They include cities that were not in major river valleys as well as some that were. They all show at least some evidence of state formation, long-distance trade, and religious practices. But they include settlements that did not have written languages and records. In at least one of them—West Africa—the settlement pattern is so different from urbanization elsewhere that we are asked to stretch our definition of urbanization and challenge our value system in assessing its significance.

Writing Space

Better writers make great learners—who perform better in their courses. To help you develop and assess concept mastery and critical thinking through writing, we created the Writing Space in MyHistoryLab. It's a single place to create, track, and grade writing assignments, provide writing resources, and exchange meaningful, personalized feedback with students, quickly and easily. Plus, Writing Space includes integrated access to Turnitin, the global leader in plagiarism prevention.

Key Supplements and Customer Support

Annotated Instructor's eText

Contained within MyHistoryLab, the *Annotated Instructor's eText* for your Pearson textbook leverages the powerful Pearson eText platform to make it easier than ever for you to access subject-specific resources for class preparation. The *AI eText* serves as the hub for all instructor resources, with chapter-by-chapter links to PowerPoint slides, content from the Instructor's Manual, and *MyHistoryLab's* ClassPrep engine, which contains a wealth of history content organized for classroom use.

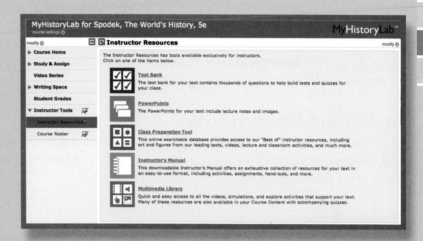

Instructor's Manual

The Instructor's Manual for *The World's History* contains learning objectives, a list of important themes discussed in the chapter, an annotated chapter outline with summaries of each section's content, suggestions for class activities, discussion questions, and suggestions for additional print and online resources for instructors. At the end of each chapter, MyHistoryLab Media Assignments catalog all of the MyHistoryLab resources for the chapter. The Instructor's Manual also contains a MyHistoryLab syllabus and suggestions for integrating MyHistoryLab into your course.

PowerPoint Presentations

Strong PowerPoint presentations make lectures more engaging for students. Correlated to the chapters of *The World's History*, each presentation includes a full lecture outline and a wealth of images, maps, and time lines from the textbook.

MyTest Test Bank

Containing a diverse set of multiple-choice, short-answer, and essay questions, the MyTest test bank supports a variety of assessment strategies. The large pool of multiple choice questions for each chapter includes factual, conceptual, and analytical questions, so that instructors may assess students on basic information as well as critical thinking.

IRC Access

Most of the teacher supplements and resources for this text are also available electronically to qualified adopters on the Instructor Resource Center (IRC). Upon adoption or to preview, please go to **www.pearsonschool.com/access_request** and select Instructor Resource Center. You will be required to complete a brief one-time registration subject to verification or educator status. Upon verification, access information and instructions will be sent to you via e-mail. Once logged into the IRC, enter 9780133952674 in the "Search our Catalog" box to locate resources.

1
2
3
4
5
6
7

MyHistoryLab™

MyHistoryLab with Pearson eText is an online homework, tutorial, and assessment system that improves results by helping students better master concepts and by providing educators with a dynamic set of tools for gauging individual and class performance. Its immersive experiences truly engage students in learning, helping them to understand course material and improve their performance. And **MyHistoryLab** comes from Pearson—your partner in providing the best digital learning experiences.

Preview and Adoption Access

Upon textbook purchase, students and teachers are granted access to **MyHistoryLab** with Pearson eText. High school teachers can obtain preview or adoption access for **MyHistoryLab** in one of the following ways:

Preview Access

- Teachers can request preview access by visiting **PearsonSchool.com/access_request**. Select Initial Access then using **Option 2**, select your discipline and title from the drop-down menu and complete the online form. *Preview Access* information will be sent to the teacher via e-mail.

Adoption Access

- With the purchase of a textbook program that offers a media resource, a *Pearson Adoption Access Card*, with student and teachers codes and a complete Instructor's Manual, will be delivered with your textbook purchase. (ISBN 978-0-13-354087-1 / 0-13-354087-1)
- Ask your sales representative for an *Adoption Access Code Card/Instructor Manual package* (ISBN: 978-0-13-354087-1 / 0-13-354087-1)

OR

- Visit **PearsonSchool.com/access_request**. Select Initial Access then using **Option 3**, select your discipline and title from the drop-down menu and complete the online form. Access information will be sent to the teacher via e-mail.

Students, ask your teacher for access.

PREFACE

Why History?

The professional historian and the student of a history course often seem to pass each other on different tracks. For the professional, nothing is more fascinating than history. For the student, particularly one in a compulsory course, the whole enterprise often seems a bore. This text is designed to help the student to understand and share the fascination of the historian. It will also remind teachers of their original attraction to history, before they began the specialization that has almost certainly marked their later careers. Furthermore, it encourages student and teacher to explore together the history of the world and the significance of this study.

Professional historians love their field for many reasons. History offers perspective and guidance in forming a personal view of human development. It teaches the necessity of seeing many sides of issues. It explores the complexity and interrelationship of events and makes possible the search for patterns and meaning in human life.

Historians love to debate—the challenge of demonstrating that their interpretations of the pattern and significance of events are the most accurate and the most satisfying in their fit between the available data and theory. Historians also love the detective work of the profession, whether it is searching through old archives, uncovering and using new sources of information, or reinterpreting long-ignored sources. In recent years historians have turned, for example, to oral history, old church records, files of photographs, cave paintings, individual census records, and reinterpretation of mythology.

Historical records are not simply lists of events, however. They are the means by which historians develop their interpretation of those events. Because interpretation differs, there is no single historical record, but various narrations of events each told from a different perspective. Therefore the study of history is intimately linked to the study of values, the values of the historical actors, of the historians who have written about them, and of the students engaged in learning about them.

Professional historians consider history to be the king of disciplines. Synthesizing the concepts of fellow social scientists in economics, politics, anthropology, sociology, and geography, historians create a more integrated and comprehensive interpretation of the past. Joining with their colleagues in the humanities, historians delight in hearing and telling exciting stories that recall heroes and villains, the low-born and the high, the wisdom and the folly of days gone by. Increasingly, history also includes the history of science—its discoveries, its methods, and its implications for philosophy, technology, and human life. This fusion of the social sciences, humanities, and natural sciences gives the study of history its range, depth, significance, and pleasure. Training in historical thinking provides an excellent introduction to understanding change and continuity in our own day as well as in the past.

Why World History?

Why specifically world history? Why should we teach and study world history, and what should be the content of such a course?

First, world history is a good place to begin for it is a new field for teacher and student alike. Neither its content nor its pedagogy is yet fixed. Many of the existing textbooks on the market still have their origins in the study of Western Europe, with segments added to cover the rest of the world. World history as the study of the interrelationships of all regions of the world, seen from the many perspectives of the different peoples of the earth, is still virgin territory.

Second, for citizens of multicultural, multiethnic nations such as the United States, Canada, South Africa, and India, and of many other countries, such as the United Kingdom, Australia, and most nations of the European Union, which are moving in that direction, a world history course offers the opportunity to gain an appreciation of the national and cultural origins of all their diverse fellow citizens. In this way, the study of world history may help to strengthen the bonds of national citizenship.

Third, as the entire world becomes a single unit for interaction, it becomes an increasingly appropriate subject for historical study. The new reality of global interaction in communication, business, politics, religion, culture, and ecology has helped to generate the new academic subject of world history.

Organization and Approach

The text, like the year-long course, links *chronology*, *themes*, and *geography* in eight units, or Parts, of study. The Parts move progressively along a time line from the emergence of early humans to the present day. Each Part emphasizes a single theme—for example, urbanization or religion or migration—and students learn to use them all to analyze historical events and to develop a grasp of the chronology of human development. The final chapter employs all the themes developed in the first seven Parts and adds an additional one, identity—personal, group, national, and global—as tools for understanding the history of our own times. Geographically, each Part covers the entire globe, although specific topics place greater emphasis on specific regions.

New to the Fifth Edition

Each chapter of the book has been reviewed and revised for this new edition, to accommodate new scholarship and in response to reviewer comments. The final two chapters, dealing with the contemporary world, have been extensively revised.

The pedagogical features have been carefully examined, and a completely new design makes it easy for students to find special features, such as the How Do We Know? boxes. The Turning Point boxes and Part openers have been revised, rewritten, and combined into one for all Parts.

Content Changes

Within each Part, material has been updated, revised, and added. Examples of some of the more notable changes and additions include: Substantial additions to the discussion of the DNA genetic record; additional material on the Aryans and the Indus valley settlers; discussion of recent archaeological discoveries in China; expanded coverage of agricultural villages; new material on Theodora, wife of the emperor Justinian; updated scholarship on the history of the Jewish people; new scholarship on the slave trade to the Americas; consideration of Russian migration to the west coast of the New World, via the Bering Straits and Alaska.

In updating the book to cover the events of contemporary history, we have added new materials to reflect new developments. These include: Breakthroughs in genetically modified crops; new ideas about the morality of using animals, especially chimpanzees, in research; coverage of the world economic collapse of 2008 and the nature of the recovery that began about 2012/13; discussion of the so-called Arab Spring; information on the Naxalite revolts in the tribal (*adivasi*) areas of India; material on globalization; updates in ecological technology and reliance on petrofuels; material on WikiLeaks, Julian Assange, Bradley Manning, and Edward Snowden; the public humanitarian activism of rock stars such as Bono; and the significance of the early influence of Pope Francis I on the Roman Catholic Church.

Chapter-by-Chapter Revisions

Chapter One, on human origins, substantially modifies and adds to the discussion of the DNA genetic record.

Chapter Two expands coverage of agricultural villages. Material has been added on family life, village life, treatment of graves, and the role of women. The discussion of Hammurabi's Code has been enhanced.

Chapter Three clarifies the significance of the New, Middle, and Old Kingdoms with additional information. Material has been added explaining the relationship between the Aryans and the Indus valley settlers.

Chapter Four adds material on recent archaeological discoveries at Huanbei and in the Anyang region of China. Coverage has been added on Eurasian immigrants to the New World and on the peoples in and urbanization of the Andes Mountains. A new excerpt from the *Popol Vuh* has been included.

Chapter Six includes new information on Theodora, wife of Emperor Justinian.

Chapter Ten includes updated scholarship on the history of the Jewish people and material on early Christian attitudes to sexuality, beginning with Jesus' early follower Paul, and leading to the later ban on priests marrying.

Chapter Eleven's section on the Crusades has been expanded and updated to reflect recent scholarship.

Chapter Twelve has been reorganized chronologically and geographically, and now moves from the general introduction to the specifics of trade in the Indian Ocean and Asia, then to Africa, and finally to the Americas. The section on the Mongol Empire has been revised and expanded, and indicates the reasons that many historians now call the Mongol Empire, and its trade routes, the marker of the beginning of the modern world.

Chapter Fourteen adds material on the inflation caused by the trans-Pacific silver trade. A new section discusses the Thirty Years War. Coverage has been added of the St. Bartholomew's Day Massacre and Cardinal Richelieu. Material has been added on the rule and achievements of Catherine the Great. The section on the Ottoman Empire has been expanded, and material has been added on the *millet* system.

Chapter Fifteen adds material on Russian expansion across the Bering Straits and into "Russian America." New scholarship has been included relating to the number of slaves transported to the Americas. New material covers the *janissary* system in the Ottoman Empire.

Chapter Sixteen expands on *Candide* and adds more coverage of the ideas of Adam Smith. Additional material is included on the "American school" of ethnography, as described by Samuel George Morton. The chapter now includes a discussion of the salons of Paris and an excerpt from Rousseau's *Emile*. Historiography of the French Revolution has been expanded with new scholarship.

The **Part Seven opener** and the **Turning Point** are restructured into one, reframing the discussion of the Olympics as a case study of what was happening in international relations at the time.

Chapter Eighteen now includes coverage of the German historian and philosopher Heinrich von Treitschke. The chapter covers the modernization program in Egypt, including *Aida*, the new opera commissioned from Verdi.

Chapter Nineteen has been restructured to show that while Latin America and China did not get involved in World War I, the war and the Great Depression did affect them, and the effects came about because of their decisions not to industrialize effectively.

Chapter Twenty contains an expanded discussion of the Italian preference for fascism over communism. Coverage of the Nuremberg Trials has been expanded, and material has been added on the Tokyo Tribunal.

Chapter Twenty-one has been tightened and reorganized. More has been added to the discussion of the beginning of the ecology movement.

Chapter Twenty-two shows a more comprehensive discussion of the importance of Mohandas Gandhi.

Chapter Twenty-three includes updated material on chimpanzee research, genetically modified plants, and infectious diseases that are transmitted from animals to humans. It includes coverage of China's plan, now being implemented, to move millions of people to cities built by the government for that purpose. Material on migration to cities has been added throughout, along with updated material on urban slums and the UN's Conferences on Human Settlements, Habitats I and II. Coverage of terrorism and world terrorist organizations and actions has been updated, with a section added on Boko Haram in Nigeria. The coverage of Barack Obama's presidency has been expanded, as has the discussion of China's economy and its rise as a superpower. Discussion of world poverty has been updated with new research. The chapter includes coverage of the economic crash of 2008 and the global recession. The Arab Spring is analyzed and information brought up to date. In religion, there are updates on internal tension between secular and religious Israelis; on the Catholic Church and Pope Francis I; and on the significance of evangelical Christianity and of the religions of new immigrants in the United States.

Chapter Twenty-four has been much updated, with new data on population levels, the value of the global economy, the amount of goods shipped globally, and so on. New material covers globalization and the protests against it; social media; poverty and efforts to eradicate it worldwide; and growing income disparity. A new section covers the financial crisis that began in 2008 and the recovery that began in 2013. The chapter includes expanded coverage of nationalist and separatist movements from Ireland to Spain, to Canada, to Belgium, to several African nations. The Arab Spring is discussed for its political ramifications, somewhat distinct from its religious ramifications covered in Chapter Twenty-three. Gender issues, and especially changing family relationships, have gained expanded coverage. Coverage of the Naxalite revolts in India has been added, and that of migration and of refugees has been thoroughly updated with new facts and statistics. Updates to the cultural coverage include the additions of Kiran Ahluwalia and Bono. A new section discusses Bradley Manning, WikiLeaks, and Edward Snowden. Material has been added to update the information on ecological technology and reliance on petrofuels.

Special Features

• Learning Objectives now appear at the beginning of each chapter, and are repeated in question form under the relevant section headings and in tabs down the side of each page as reminders, before being answered at the end of each chapter, to encourage students to consider their own reading of the chapter.

LEARNING OBJECTIVES

8.1 ((	8.2 ((	8.3 ((	8.4 ((
Describe the important literature of the Aryan immigrants.	Understand the philosophy of the Maurya and Gupta Empires.	Describe the consequences of the Hunas invasion of India.	Compare India's empires with those of China and Rome.

((Listen on **MyHistoryLab**

8.1	
8.2	What were the philosophies of the Maurya and Gupta empires?
8.3	
8.4	

A Golden Age of Learning
erature and Hindu philos
composed two epic poer
Shakuntala, the first Sans
times. Much of the impor
transcribed into writing, i
emendations were made t

The Gupta Empire bega
spondence. Panini (*fl. c.* 40
Astadhyayi (perhaps the m
but the Mauryas and mos
that was closer to the com
as the *Laws of Manu*, and r
studied, revised, and furl

Despite its military and cultural achievements, the Gupta dynasty's power began to wane in the late fifth century C.E. The subcontinent was once again politically divided and subject to one wave of invader-rulers after another. These internal divisions and conquests by outsiders—notably the Mughals in the sixteenth century and British in the eighteenth—continued until the modern independence of India and Pakistan in 1947 and of Bangladesh in 1971.

Huna Invasions End the Age of Empires

| 8.3 | What were the consequences of the Hunas' invasion of India? |

In the fifth century, new conquerors came through the passes of the nor throwing the Gupta Empire and establishing their own headquarters Afghanistan. These invaders were the Hunas, a branch of the Xiongnu Mongol tribes that roamed the regions north of the Great Wall of Chi times invaded. In previous expansions, they had driven other group into the Roman Empire, as we saw in the chapter "Rome and the Domino-fashion, these groups pushed one another westward. The

• The Introduction to the book describes the key themes of the text and the methods historians use to practice their craft.

• The introductions to each of the eight Parts now include more specific key references to the chapters that follow.

• **MyHistoryLab** links, to primary sources, videos, images, and maps, appear throughout the chapters.

was theirs. In the next 20 years they captured the Yucatán and most of Central America, although revolts continued in the region. Cortés became ruler of the Kingdom of New Spain, reorganized in 1535 as the Vice-Royalty of New Spain.

View the **Closer Look: The Meeting of Cortés and Moctezuma** on **MyHistoryLab**

Read the **Document: Excerpt from The Broken Spears, an Indian account of the conquest of Mexico** on **MyHistoryLab**

Read the **Document: Anonymous (Aztec): The Midwife Addresses the Woman Who Has Died in Childbirth** on **MyHistoryLab**

In South America, Vasco Nuñez de Balboa found a portage across the Isthmus of Panama in 1513. Now the Spanish could transport their ships from the Atlantic coast overland across the Isthmus and sail south along the Pacific Coast to Peru. Rumors of great stores of gold encouraged these voyages to the Inca Empire. Like the Aztecs, the Inca were divided. In 1525,

• Key Terms are listed at the end of each chapter for easy reference, and collected in the Glossary at the end of the book.

KEY TERMS

blood and iron Bismarck's policy of using warfare against enemies as a means of unifying his new nation. Subsequently the term has been used to designate the policy of any government committed to foreign warfare as a means of internal unification.

pogrom A murderous attack on a group of people—usually based on their ethnicity or religion—that is sanctioned by the government, either officially or unofficially.

• Turning Point essays, some completely new for this edition, illustrate visually the connections between one Part and the next. In some cases, the Turning Points tell their own story as well, notably in the bridge into the twenty-first century that uses the modern Olympic Games to illustrate and introduce many of the issues that are to follow. Turning Point Questions ask students to consider the material that has been presented.

PART SEVEN

TURNING POINT: EXPLODING TECHNOLOGIES
1914–1991

For Death and Life

The twentieth century began with great promise. The political and industrial revolutions of the previous two centuries encouraged Western Europeans to believe that they were mastering the secrets of securing a long, productive, comfortable, and meaningful life for the individual and the community. They believed that they were transmitting these benefits around the globe through their colonial policies, and that their colonial possessions would continue long into the foreseeable future. The Polish poet Wislawa Szymborska (1923–2012) captured this optimism in the opening of her poem "The Century's Decline" of 1986:

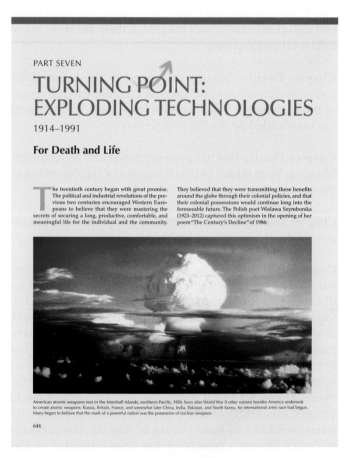

American atomic weapons test in the Marshall Islands, northern Pacific, 1950. Soon after World War II other nations besides America undertook to create atomic weapons: Russia, Britain, France, and somewhat later China, India, Pakistan, and North Korea. An international arms race had begun. Many began to believe that the mark of a powerful nation was the possession of nuclear weapons.

644

- The How Do We Know? features help the student to understand how historians use evidence, both textual and visual, to interpret the past.

Evaluating the Legacy of Colonialism

As the colonial era ended, historians divided sharply in assessing the impact of colonial rule. Leften Stavrianos, who spent most of his career at the University of California, San Diego, presented a Marxist, primarily economic, critical perspective. Colonial rule created "an unprecedented increase in productivity" in commerce and industry, but no corresponding increase in pay for the workers nor in distribution of wealth to the colony. In many colonies, white settlers and plantation owners seized the best lands. Rural communities were disrupted as

> private property arrangements displaced the former communal ownership and cultivation of land ... Land now became a mere possession, food a mere commodity of exchange, neighbor a mere common property owner and labor a mere means of survival. (Stavrianos, p. 9)

As the Industrial Revolution matured into industrial capitalism, exploitation became more severe. The results were unfortunate and long-lasting:

> All these global economic trends combined to produce the present division of the world into the developed West as against the underdeveloped Third World. But underdevelopment did not mean nondevelopment; rather it meant distorted development—development designed to produce only one or two commodities needed by the Western markets rather than overall development to meet local needs. In short, it was the familiar Third World curse of economic growth without economic development. (p. 11)

Theodore Von Laue, on the other hand, who studied Westernization, said very little about economic inequality. Deeply influenced by Judeo-Christian perspectives, he emphasized the cultural upheaval of colonialism and the paradoxical introduction by force of Western values of freedom: "The world revolution of Westernization, in short, carried a double thrust. It was freedom, justice, and peace—the best of the European tradition—on the one hand; on the other hand (and rather unconsciously) raw power to reshape the world in one's own image" (Von Laue, p. 16). The transformation to Western values was not complete, however:

> Underneath the global universals of power and its most visible supporting skills—literacy, science and technology, large-scale

organization—the former diversities persist. The traditional cultures, though in mortal peril, linger under the ground floors of life. Rival political ideologies and ambitions clash head on. The world's major religions vie with each other as keenly as ever. Attitudes, values, life-styles from all continents mingle freely in the global marketplace, reducing in the intensified invidious comparison all former absolute truths to questionable hypotheses. (p. 7)

Von Laue looked forward to the day when all people "will be ready to fuse their personal egos with the egos of billions of other human beings, even in intimate matters like procreation and family size" (p. 9). It would appear that the common values on that day would be the Western values of the Enlightenment.

Dipesh Chakrabarty questioned this assumption that Western values would win out. Born in India after independence, trained in Australia and the United States, and later teaching there as well, Chakrabarty argued that the greatest (self-)deception of the colonizers was to project European values as the appropriate goals for the entire world, and to see history moving in that direction: "First in Europe, then elsewhere." He rejected the idea that the rest of the world exists in Europe's "waiting room." He did appreciate European, Enlightenment values, but he did not think they were the only valid ones, nor that they ought to or necessarily would become universal. Chakrabarty did not address economic issues. On cultural transformations brought by colonialism, however, he was not prepared to accept Von Laue's celebration of exclusively Western values, nor to look forward to the day when they alone would triumph.

- Which effects of colonialism do you think were more important, the economic and technological effects, or the cultural effects? Please be specific about the effects you are discussing.
- To the extent that the Cold War from the mid-1940s to the mid-1980s represents in part the values of the West, what values do you think colonized countries learned from the West?
- Do you think it is a good idea that some day the peoples of the world may share a similar set of values? Why or why not? If it is a good idea, then what should those values be? To what extent are they technological values?

- This edition also continues the emphasis on the use of primary sources, for this is the kind of material from which the historical record is argued and fashioned. Most chapters have two or more Source boxes, which have been colored purple in this edition to stand out.

The Journal of Columbus' First Voyage to the Americas

Columbus kept a day-by-day journal of his first voyage. The original has been lost, but fortunately the priest Bartolomé de Las Casas (1474–1566) prepared an abstract, which he used in writing his own *Historia de las Indias* (1875). Columbus' leading biographer in English, Samuel Eliot Morison, calls the abstract "The most important document in the entire history of American discovery." This account of what Columbus saw and how he related to it is written sometimes in the first person of Columbus, and sometimes in the third person, as the voice of Las Casas. Note especially the overwhelming importance given to religion:

Prologue: Your Highnesses, as Catholic Christians and Princes devoted to the Holy Christian Faith and the propagators thereof, and enemies of the sect of Mahomet and of all idolatries and heresies, resolved to send me, Christopher Columbus, to the said regions of India, to see the said princes and peoples and lands and the disposition of them and of all, and the manner in which may be undertaken their conversion to our Holy Faith, and ordained that I should not go by land (the usual way) to the Orient, but by the route of the Occident, by which no one to this day knows for sure that anyone has gone ...

12 October 1492: At two hours after midnight appeared the land, at a distance of two leagues ... Presently they saw naked people, and the Admiral went ashore in his barge, and [others] followed. The Admiral broke out the royal standard, and the captains [displayed] two banners of the Green Cross, which the Admiral flew on all the vessels as a signal, with an F and a Y, one at one arm of the cross and the other on the other, and over each letter his or her crown ... and said that they should bear faith and witness how he before them all was taking, as in fact he took, possession of the said island for the King and Queen ...

15 October: It was my wish to bypass no island without taking possession, although having taken one you can claim all ...

22 October: All this night and today I was here, waiting to see if the king here or other people would bring gold or anything substantial, and many of this people came, like the others of the other islands, as naked as as painted, some of them white, others red, others black, and [painted] in many ways ... any little thing I gave them, and also our coming, they considered a great wonder, and believed that we had come from the sky ...

1 November: It is certain that this is the mainland and that I am before Zayto [Zaytun] and Quisay [Hangzhou] [two great port cities of China], 100 leagues more or less distant the one from the other ...

6 November: If they had access to devout religious persons knowing the language, they would all turn Christian, and so I hope in Our Lord that Your Highnesses will do something about it with much care ... And after your days (for we are all mortal) ... you will be well received before the eternal Creator ...

12 November: Yesterday came aboard the ship a dugout with six young men, and five came on board; these I ordered to be detained and I am bringing them. Afterwards I sent to a house which is on the western bank of the river, and they brought seven women, small and large, and three boys. I did this because the [Indian] men would behave better in Spain with women of their country than without them ...

27 November: Your Highnesses ought not to consent that any foreigner does business or sets foot here, except Christian Catholics, since this was the end and the beginning of the enterprise ...

22 December: The Indians were so free, and the Spaniards so covetous and overreaching, that it was not enough that for a lace-tip or a little piece of glass and crockery or other things of no value, the Indians should give them what they asked; even without giving anything they [the Spaniards] wanted to get and take all, which the Admiral had always forbidden ...

23 December: In that hour ... more than 1000 persons had come to the ship, and that all brought something that they owned, and that before they come within half a crossbow shot of the ship, they stand up in their canoes with what they brought in their hands, saying "Take! Take!" (cited in Morison, pp. 41–179)

- The Suggested Readings for each chapter have been thoroughly revised, updated, and expanded to reflect current scholarship. Films, videos, and online assets have been added. Each item in the bibliography is annotated to direct students with their reading.

- Each chapter text ends with a discussion of legacies to the future, namely, What Difference Does It Make?

- Each chapter concludes with a Chapter Review, where the reader is given answers to the Learning Objectives, essentially a summary of the most important material covered in each main heading.

THE MEIJI RESTORATION AND INDUSTRIALIZATION IN JAPAN	
1853	Commander Perry sails into Edo Bay, ending 250 years' isolation
1854	Treaty of Kanagawa gives United States trading rights with Japan
1860s	Series of "unequal treaties" gives United States, Britain, France, Russia, and Netherlands commercial and territorial privileges
1868	Daimyo force Tokugawa shogun to abdicate. Executive power vested with emperor in Meiji restoration
1871	Administration is overhauled; Western-style changes introduced
1872	National education system introduced, providing teaching for 90 percent of children by 1900
1872	First railway opened
1873	Old order changed by removal of privileges of samurai class
1876	Koreans, under threat, agree to open three of their ports to the Japanese and exchange diplomats
1877	Satsuma rebellion represented last great (unsuccessful) challenge of conservative forces
1879	Representative system of local government introduced
1884	Western-style peerage (upper house) created
1885	Cabinet government introduced
1889	Adoption of constitution based on Bismarck's Germany
1889	Number of cotton mills has risen from three (1877) to 83
1894–95	War with China ends in Japanese victory
1895	Japan annexes Taiwan and Pescadores Islands
1902	Britain and Japan sign military pact
1904–05	War with Russia ends in Japanese victory
1910	Japan annexes Korea
1914	Japan joins World War I on side of Allies

AT A GLANCE: THE AGE OF REVOLUTIONS			
DATE	EUROPE	NORTH AMERICA	LATIN AMERICA
1640	• Galileo dies; Newton is born (1642) • Civil wars in England (1642–46; 1647–49; 1649–51) • Execution of King Charles I of England (1649) • Hobbes' *Leviathan* (1651) • Restoration of English monarchy (1660) • Royal Society of London founded (1662)		• Portugal takes Brazil from the Dutch (1654)
1670	• The "Glorious Revolution" in England (1688) • The English Bill of Rights (1689) • John Locke's *Second Treatise on Government* (1689) • *Philosophes*: Diderot (1713–84); Voltaire (1694–1778); Rousseau (1712–78); Montesquieu (1689–1755)		
1760	• Tennis Court Oath (June 20, 1789) • French Revolution (1789–99) • "March of the Women" (1789) • "Great Fear" (1789)	• British levy taxes on Americans in the Stamp Act (1765) • American Declaration of Independence (1776); War of Independence (1775–81) • Constitution (1789)	• Revolts against European rule in Peru, Colombia, and Brazil (1780–98) • Tupac Amarú revolt, Peru (1780)
1790	• "Second French Revolution" (1791–99) • "Reign of Terror" (1793–95) • Napoleon seizes power (1799); Emperor (1804) • *Concordat* between Napoleon and Pope Pius VII (1801) • Napoleon issues Civil Code (1804) • Napoleon invades Russia; finally defeated (1812)	• Bill of Rights ratified (1791) • Louisiana Purchase from France (1803)	• Toussaint L'Ouverture leads slave revolt against French in Saint-Domingue (Haiti) (1791) • Haiti proclaims independence (1804) • Joseph Bonaparte, king of Spain (1808) • Bolívar and San Martín lead revolts against Spain (1808–28) • Paraguay declares independence (1810–11)
1820	• Congress of Vienna (1814–15) • Reform Act extends voting franchise in Britain (1832) • Britain abolishes slavery in its empire (1833)	• President Andrew Jackson evicts Cherokee Indian Nation: "Trail of Tears" (1838) • Warfare with Mexico ends in victory for America (1848) • United States abolishes slavery (1863, 1865)	• Mexico wins independence (1821) • Prince Pedro declares Brazil independent (1822)

New Layout and Design

Readers will notice cleaner design of box features. The format has reverted to the original taller page size so that the text and pictures have a little more room to breathe.

Maps and Illustrations

To aid the student, extensive, clear, and informative charts and maps represent information graphically and geographically. A wide range of illustrations, most in color, supplements the written word. For the fifth edition we have added more than 50 new illustrations.

Acknowledgments for the Fifth Edition

Each edition, each evolution of the text, brings new, indispensable colleagues who make the enterprise what it continues to become. This revision began once again at Laurence King Publishing in London, under the guidance of Kara Hattersley-Smith, and then Melissa Danny and, under her supervision, the illustrators, designers, proofreaders, and other personnel who have added their suggestions, based on a wealth of experience, and kept the project on track. Freelance editor Margaret Manos of New York and New Hampshire once again read the text—old and new—with great sensitivity and worked wonders in reorganizing, clarifying, streamlining, and improving readability. She sifted through the many external reviews and focused their key comments and criticisms into improving the revision process. She frequently sharpened perspectives, especially on issues of feminism and European and American history. In some important cases she helped to select artwork that added insight and aesthetics to the arguments of the book. At Pearson, Billy Grieco exercised overarching supervision of the entire project.

Kara Hattersley-Smith, Editorial Manager, assures me that this transoceanic venture has proceeded smoothly, aided by Melissa Danny, Senior Editor, Nick Newton, Designer, and Peter Kent, Picture Researcher. Without them, there would be no fifth edition, and I am grateful for their patient and firm guidance and wise diplomacy.

I have also benefitted immensely from the kindness of the many students (especially my own students at Temple University), colleagues, and teachers who have used this book and taken time to share with me their advice and suggestions. A surprising number of high-school teachers and students, who use this book as their text for AP World History, have written to me over the years with interesting questions that have kept me on my toes, and suggestions that have benefitted the text. I thank them all and hope that they will see the effects of their good counsel in this edition.

One element that has not changed in this new edition is the mental image I keep before me of my own children—albeit at a younger age, since by now their knowledge in so many fields far surpasses my own—and of my students. I write for them.

Grateful acknowledgments are also extended to the following reviewers of the fifth edition: Raymond Hylton, Virginia Union University; Robert Haug, University of Cincinnati; Cynthia Stephan, South Florida Bible College; Bruce Strouble, Bainbridge College; Walter Roberts, University of North Texas; James Brodman, University of Central Arkansas; Robert Hendershot, Grand Rapids Community College; Adrianna Lozano, Purdue University; Michele Louro, Salem State University; Maxim Matusevich, Seton Hall University; Jared Krebsbach, University of Memphis; Joseph Sramek, Southern Illinois University; Eleanor Aronstein, Marist College; Mark Tauger, West Virginia University; Faith Childress, Rockhurst University; Dandan Chen, Wells College.

About the Author

Howard Spodek received his B.A. degree from Columbia University (1963), majoring in history and specializing in Columbia's newly designed program in Asian Studies. He received his M.A. (1966) and Ph.D. (1972) from the University of Chicago, majoring in history and specializing in India. His first trip to India was on a Fulbright Fellowship, 1964–66, and he has spent a total of some twelve years studying and teaching in India. He has also traveled widely throughout the United States, Latin America, Asia, Africa, and Europe. He has been a faculty member at Temple University since 1972, appointed Full Professor in 1984. He was awarded Temple's Great Teacher designation in 1993.

Spodek's work in world history began in 1988 when he became Academic Director of a comprehensive, innovative program working with teachers in the School District of Philadelphia to improve their knowledge base in world history and facilitate a rewriting of the world-history program in the schools. Immediately following this program, he became principal investigator of a program that brought college professors and high-school teachers together to reconsider, revise, and, in many cases, initiate the teaching of world history in several of the colleges and universities in the Philadelphia metropolitan area. Those projects led directly to the writing of the first edition of the current text (1997).

Howard Spodek has published extensively on urbanization in India, including *Urban-Rural Integration in Regional Development* (1976); *Urban Form and Meaning in South-East Asia* (editor, with Doris Srinivasan, 1993); *Ahmedabad: Shock City of Twentieth-Century India* (2011); and a wide array of articles, including analyses of working women's organizations. In addition, he wrote and produced the documentary film *Ahmedabad* (1983), and was the executive producer and subject specialist for the documentary film *The Urban World: A Case Study of Slum Relocation in Ahmedabad, India* (2013). He organized and served on the three-person team that translated the six-volume *Autobiography of Indulal Yagnik* from Gujarati to English (2011). He has written on his experiences with world-history faculty at the college and high-school levels in articles in *The History Teacher* (1992, 1995). He has received funding for his research, writing, teaching, and film from Fulbright, the National Endowment for the Humanities, the National Science Foundation, the American Institute of Indian Studies, the Smithsonian Institution, and the World Bank.

Howard Spodek

INTRODUCTION:
The World Through Historians' Eyes

Themes and Turning Points

Most readers of this textbook have probably not taken many courses in history. Few are (thus far) planning to major in history, much less become professional historians. A lot therefore rides on this single text. It must present a general introduction to world history that interests, engages, and even fascinates the reader through its subject matter, its narrative, and its analysis. It must open the eyes, minds, and hearts of students who come to this course believing that history is only about the past, and mostly a matter of learning names, dates, and places. It must introduce them to the methods and "habits of mind" of the historian. It must demonstrate how knowledge of the contents and methods of world history—and of this book in particular—will broaden their horizons and also have practical usefulness.

"Usefulness" is a word not always associated with the study of history. Indeed, in everyday conversation, the phrase "that's history" means that an event is no longer significant. It may once have been important, but it is not now. From that point of view, "history" is a record of people and events that are dead and gone. For the historian, however, the opposite is true. The past has made us who we are, and continues to influence who we are becoming. In this sense, the past is not dead, just as people whom we have known personally and who have influenced our lives are not "dead," even though they may no longer be with us. This text will highlight ways in which the past continues to have a profound effect on the present and future. It will help us to understand who we have become.

History does not provide specific answers to today's problems, but it does provide examples and case studies that help us to improve our thinking. Generals study past wars to understand how modern battles may be fought; economists study past periods of growth and recession to understand how we can encourage the former and avoid the latter. Understanding the ways in which families and relationships have functioned in the past helps us find ways to make our own families and relationships more satisfying today.

World history gives us the largest possible canvas on which to carry out these studies. We cannot, however, study everything that ever happened. We must choose what to include and what to exclude. We must choose strategies that maximize our ability to understand our lives today in the context of the whole range of human experience.

In this text we choose two fundamental organizing principles as our framework for the study and teaching of world history. First, we choose a series of eight chronological turning points, each of which changed the patterns of human life. Second, we explain the importance of each of these changes in terms of the new themes they introduced into human experience. These two elements—chronological turning points and interpretive themes—go together.

This text is organized around eight turning points and themes. Others might also have been chosen, but these turning points represent some of the most important transformations in human life. The thematic analysis of these turning points encourages students to grapple with the origins and continuing presence of eight of the most significant themes in life: the biological and cultural qualities that make humans the special creatures we are; the settlements we create and live in; the political power we assemble and sometimes oppose; the religious systems through which many individuals and communities find meaning; the movement of trade and people that has linked the peoples of the world ever more closely, sometimes in cooperation, sometimes in competition, and sometimes in conflict; the political, industrial, and social revolutions, especially of the seventeenth through the twentieth

Learning about silkworms, from a book on the silk industry. Gouache on paper. Chinese school, nineteenth century. This painting suggests some of the concerns of modern world history that have previously received less attention: non-Western regions presented in their own right, and not only in their relationship to the West; daily activities and ordinary people; the human conditions of production and trade; the activities of women. Also, the use of art and illustration is a powerful tool in our becoming acquainted with the peoples of the world throughout time.

centuries, the era we now call "modern"; the technological developments that continue to reshape our world; and the quest for personal and group identity, so prevalent in our own times.

Because real life does not fit neatly into exact chronological periods, there will be significant overlap among the turning points. Readers may argue that the themes are also not limited to single chronological periods. For example, political regimes, religious systems, and economic organizations appear at all times in history. This argument is, of course, correct: "Everything is related to everything else," and in reality each chronological period will include several themes. We have chosen, however, to highlight particular themes in particular historical periods so that students will understand these themes more thoroughly and learn to employ them as tools of analysis in forming their own understanding of our world.

Chronological Turning Points and Part Themes

PART ONE Turning Point: Human Origins
To 10,000 B.C.E.

The emergence of the first humans. Biological and early cultural evolution.

THEME: Historians and anthropologists search for and interpret fossils, DNA biological materials, and artifacts to determine what is human about humans.

PART TWO Turning Point: Settlement Patterns
10,000 B.C.E.–1000 C.E.

Creating settlements, first agricultural villages and then cities.

THEME: Settlements—villages, towns, and cities—are created to meet community needs and, in the process, create new communities and new needs.

PART THREE Turning Point: From City-states to Empires
2000 B.C.E.–1100 C.E.

Creating empires, from Sargon of Assyria through Alexander the Great, Republican and Imperial Rome, Qin and Han China, and India of the Mauryas and Guptas.

THEME: Imperial political power is generated, expanded, consolidated, and resisted.

PART FOUR Turning Point: Creating World Religions
2500 B.C.E.–1500 C.E.

Creating global religions: Judaism, Christianity, Islam, Hinduism, and Buddhism.

THEME: Spiritual feelings are mobilized into powerful religious systems, some of which attain global scope.

PART FIVE Turning Point: Trade
1300–1700

The global movement of goods and people bridges the seas and links the continents.

THEME: The flow of goods and people is channeled into global networks, creating new knowledge, inspiring new outlooks, and challenging existing political and economic structures.

PART SIX Turning Point: Revolution
1640–1914

Revolutions: political, industrial, and social.

THEME: Vast, abrupt changes in political and economic systems create new social values and institutions, transforming the lives of individuals, families, and communities.

PART SEVEN Turning Point: Exploding Technologies
1914–1991

Technological change and its human control.

THEME: New technological systems, both simple and complex, are instituted that improve—and threaten—human life.

PART EIGHT Turning Point: From Past to Present to Future
1979–

The application of historical themes to an understanding of contemporary events.

THEME: A brief review of the seven themes developed until now, and an exploration of their applicability to the understanding of our own times, the last 30 to 40 years. Includes a final consideration of ways in which individuals and groups form their own identities in the space between past and future.

Global Scope

The scope of this text, and of each turning point and theme within it, is global. Often the method is comparative, especially in early times, as we compare early cities, early empires, and early global religions across regions of the world. For more recent times, the method is more interactive. For example, the study of the Industrial Revolution in Europe includes its funding—in part—from the wealth that poured into Europe from its New World conquests of people, land, gold, and silver, and from African slave labor; its global extensions in the form of imperialism in Asia, Africa, Australia, and Latin America; and the interaction of colonizers and colonized in response to the new opportunities and challenges.

Social Science Methods, Comparative History, and the Study of Values

Comparative History and the Methods of the Social Sciences

The global, interactive, and comparative format of this text provides also an introduction to social science methodology. The methods of the social sciences are embedded in the structure of the book. Because each part is built on relationships among different regions of the world, the reader will become accustomed to posing hypotheses based on general principles and to testing them against comparative data from around the world.

This method of moving back and forth between general theory and specific case study, testing the degree to which the general theory and the specific data fit each other, is at the heart of the social sciences. For example, in Part Two we will explore the general characteristics of cities, and then examine how well these generalizations hold up through case studies of various cities around the world. In Part Three we will seek general theories of the rise and fall of early empires based on comparisons of China, Rome, and India. In Part Four we will search for commonalities among religious systems through a survey of five world religions. In Part Eight we begin with an analysis of new issues of political and cultural identity and then examine their significance in a series of brief case studies in different regions of the world. These comparisons enable us more clearly to think about and understand the workings of cities, empires, and religions not only of the past, but also of our own time and place.

Multiple Perspectives

The text highlights the importance of multiple perspectives in studying and interpreting history. The answers we get—the narrative histories we write—are based on the questions we ask. Each Part suggests a variety of questions that can be asked about the historical event that is being studied and a variety of interpretations that can emerge in the process of answering them. Often there is more than one "correct" way of understanding change over time and its significance. Different questions will trigger very different research and very different answers. For example, in Part Five we ask about the stages and processes by which Western commercial power began to surpass that of Asia. This question presupposes the fact that at earlier times Asian power had been superior, and raises the additional questions of why it declined and why European power advanced. In Part Six we ask how the Industrial Revolution affected and changed relationships between men and women; this question will yield different research and a different narrative from questions about, for example, women's contributions to industrialization, which is a useful question, but a different one.

Through the systematic study of the past in this thematic, comparative framework, students will gain tools for understanding and making their own place in the world. They will not only learn how the peoples of the world have gotten to where we are, but also consider the possibility of setting out in new directions for new goals.

Assessing Values

This form of analysis will also introduce a study of values. In order to understand the choices made by people in the past, we must attempt to understand the values that informed their thinking and actions. These values may be similar to, or quite different from, our own. In order to understand the interpretation introduced by later historians, we must understand the historians' values as well. These, too, may be similar to, or different from, our own. Historians usually had personal perspectives from which they viewed the past, and these perspectives influenced their interpretation. Finally, in order for student-readers to form their own understanding of the past, and to make it more useful in their own lives, they must also see how their own values influence their evaluation of past events.

For most of the past century, social scientists spoke of creating "value-free" disciplines. Today, most scholars believe that this is impossible. We cannot be "value-free." On the contrary, we must attempt to understand the values that have inspired historical actors, previous historians, and ourselves. Coming to an understanding of the values of others—historical actors and the historians who have studied them—will help readers to recognize and formulate their own values, a central part of a liberal arts education.

History and Identity

History is among the most passionate and bitterly contentious of disciplines because most people and groups locate a large part of their identity in their history. Americans may take pride in their nationality, for example, for having created a representative, constitutional democracy that has endured for more than 200 years (see Part Six). Yet they may be saddened, shamed, or perhaps incensed by the existence of 250 years of slavery followed by inequality in race relations continuing to the present (see Part Five). Christians may take pride in 2,000 years of missions of compassion toward the poor and downtrodden, yet they may be saddened, shamed, or even incensed by an almost equally long record of religious warfare and of persecution of those whose beliefs differed from their own (see Part Four).

As various ethnic, religious, class, and gender groups represent themselves in public political life, they seek not only to understand the history that has made them what they are, but also to persuade others to understand that history in the same way, to create a new consciousness.

Feminist historians, for example, find in their reading of history that patriarchy, a system of male-created and male-dominated institutions, has subordinated women. From available data and their interpretation of them, they attempt to weave a persuasive argument that will win over others to their position.

Some will not be persuaded. They may not even agree that women have been subordinated to men, but argue that both genders have shared in a great deal of suffering (and joy) throughout history (see Parts One and Seven). The historical debates over the origins and evolution of gender relationships evoke strong emotions because people's self-image, the image of their group, and others' perceptions of them are all at stake. And the stakes can be high.

Control of Historical Records

From earliest times, control over historical records and their interpretation has been fundamental to control over people's thoughts. The first emperor of China, Qin Shi Huangdi (r. 221–210 B.C.E.)—the man who built the concept of a united China, an idea that has lasted until today—attempted to destroy all knowledge of the past:

> He then abolished the ways of ancient sage kings and put to the torch the writings of the Hundred Schools in an attempt to keep the people in ignorance. He demolished the walls of major cities and put to death men of fame and talent. (de Bary, I: 229)

So wrote Jia Yi (201–168? B.C.E.), poet and statesman of the succeeding Han dynasty. Qin Shi Huangdi wished that only his interpretation of China's past, and his place in it, be preserved. Later intellectuals condemned his actions—but the lost records were irretrievable (see Part Three).

In similar fashion, the first great historian of the Christian Church, Eusebius of Caesarea (c. 260–339), in his accounts of the early Christians in the Roman Empire, chose carefully to include elements that he considered of "profit" to his mission, and to exclude those that were not:

> It is not for us to describe their miserable vicissitudes [in persecution] … just as it is not a part of our task to leave on record their faction-fights and their unnatural conduct towards each other, prior to the persecution. That is why we have decided to say no more about them than suffices for us to justify God's Judgment … We shall rather set forth in our whole narrative only what may be of profit, first, to our own times, and then to later times. (MacMullen, p. 6)

Historical Revision

The interpretation of events may become highly contested and be revised even after several centuries have passed.

Colonial governments seeking to control subject peoples sometimes argued that the conquered people were so backward that they benefitted from the conquest. Later historians, with more distance and more detachment, were often less kind to the colonizers. Some 1,900 years ago, the historian Tacitus was writing bitterly of the ancient Romans in their conquest of England: "Robbery, butchery, rapine, the liars call Empire; they create a desolation and call it peace." (*Agricola*, p. 30)

In our own era, the many nations that have won their freedom from colonialism display similar resentment against their foreign rulers, and set out to revise the historical record in keeping with their newly won political freedom. Jawaharlal Nehru, the first prime minister of independent India (1947–64), wrote in 1944 from the prison cell in which he had been incarcerated for his leadership of his country's independence movement:

> British accounts of India's history, more especially of what is called the British period, are bitterly resented. History is almost always written by the victors and conquerors and gives their viewpoint; or, at any rate, the victors' version is given prominence and holds the field. (Nehru, p. 289)

Philip Curtin, historian of Africa and of slavery, elaborates an equally critical view of European colonial accounts of Africa's history:

> African history was seriously neglected until the 1950s … The colonial period in Africa left an intellectual legacy to be overcome, just as it had in other parts of the world. … The colonial imprint on historical knowledge emerged in the nineteenth and early twentieth centuries as a false perspective, a Eurocentric view of world history created at a time of European domination … Even where Europeans never ruled, European knowledge was often accepted as modern knowledge, including aspects of the Eurocentric historiography. (Curtin, p. 54)

Instead, Curtin continues, a proper historiography must

> … show the African past from an African point of view … For Africans, to know about the past of their own societies is a form of self-knowledge crucial to a sense of identity in a diverse and rapidly changing world. A recovery of African history has been an important part of African development over recent decades. (p. 54)

Religious and ethnic groups, too, may seek to control historical records. In 1542, the Roman Catholic Church established an Index of Prohibited Books to ban writings it considered heretical. (The Spanish Inquisition, ironically, stored away many records that later scholars used to recreate its history and the history of those whom it persecuted.) More recently, despite all the evidence of the Holocaust, the murder of six million Jews by the Nazi government of Germany during World War II, a few people have claimed that the murders never took place. They deny the existence

Indians giving Hernán Cortés a headband, from Diego Duran's Historia de las Indias, 1547. Bent on conquest and plunder, the bearded Spaniard Cortés arrived on the Atlantic coast of Mexico in 1519. His forces sacked the ancient city of Tenochtitlán, decimated the Aztec people, and imprisoned their chief, Moctezuma II, before proclaiming the Aztec Empire "New Spain." By stark contrast, this bland Spanish watercolor shows local tribesmen respectfully paying homage to the invader as if he were a god; in ignoring the brutality exercised in the colonization of South America, the artist is, in effect, "rewriting" history. (Biblioteca National, Madrid)

of such racial and religious hatred and its consequences, and ignore deep-seated problems in the relationships between majority and minority populations.

The significance of the voyages of Columbus was once celebrated uncritically in the United States in tribute both to "the Admiral of the Ocean Sea" himself and to the courage and enterprise of the European explorers and early settlers who brought their civilizations to the Americas. In South America, however, where Native American Indians are more numerous and people of European ancestry often form a smaller proportion of the population, the celebrations have been far more ambivalent, muted, and meditative.

In 1992, on the 500th anniversary of Columbus' first voyage to the Americas, altogether new and more sobering elements entered the commemoration ceremonies, even in the United States. The negative consequences of Columbus' voyages, previously ignored, were now recalled and emphasized: the death of up to 90 percent of the Native American Indian population in the century after the arrival of Europeans; the Atlantic slave trade, initiated by trade in Indian slaves; and the exploitation of the natural resources of a continent until then little touched by humans. The

ecological consequences, which are only now beginning to receive more attention, were not all negative, however. They included the fruitful exchange of natural products between the hemispheres. Horses, wheat, and sheep were introduced to the Americas; potatoes, tomatoes, and corn to Afro-Eurasia. Unfortunately, the spread of syphilis was another consequence of the exchange; scholars disagree on who transmitted this disease to whom (see Part Five).

Thugs sometimes gain control of national histories. George Orwell's satirical novel *Animal Farm* (published in 1945) presented an allegory in which pigs come to rule a farm. Among their many acts of domination, the pigs seize control of the historical records of the farm animals' failed experiment in equality, and impose their own official interpretation, which justifies their own rule. The rewriting of history and suppression of alternative records by the Communist Party of the former Soviet Union between 1917 and 1989 reveals the bitter truth underlying Orwell's satire (see Part Seven).

Although the American experience is much different, in the United States, too, records have been suppressed. Scholars are still trying to use the Freedom of Information Act to pry open sealed diplomatic archives. (Most official

Lenin addressing troops in Sverdlov Square, Moscow, May 5, 1920. The leaders of the Russian communist revolution crudely refashioned the historical record to suit the wishes of the winners. After Lenin's death in 1924, his second-in-command Leon Trotsky (pictured sitting on the podium in the top picture) lost to Joseph Stalin the bitter power struggle that ensued. Not only was Trotsky banished from the Soviet Union, but also his appearance was expunged from the official archives (see doctored picture, bottom).

archives everywhere have 20-, 30-, or 40-year rules governing the waiting period before certain sensitive records are opened to the public. These rules are designed to protect living people and contemporary policies from excessive scrutiny.)

What Do We Know? How Do We Know It? What Difference Does It Make?

So, historical records are not simply lists of events. They are the means by which individuals and groups develop their interpretation of these events. All people develop their own interpretation of past events; historians do it professionally. Because interpretation differs, there is no single historical record, but various narrations of events, each told from a different perspective. Therefore the study of history is intimately linked to the study of values.

To construct their interpretation, historians examine the values—the motives, wishes, desires, visions—of people of the past. In interpreting those values, historians must confront and engage their own values, comparing and contrasting them with those of people in the past. For example, they ask how various people viewed slavery, or child labor, or education, or art and music in societies of the past. In the back of their minds they compare and contrast those older values with values held by various people today, and especially with their own personal values. They ask: How and why have values changed—or remained the same—over the passage of time? Why, and in what ways, do my values compare with values of the past? By learning to pose such questions, students will be better equipped to discover and create their own place in the continuing movement of human history. This text, therefore, consistently addresses three fundamental questions:

What Do We Know?
How Do We Know It?
What Difference Does It Make?

Even when historians agree on which events are most significant, they may differ in evaluating why those events are significant. One historian's interpretation of events may be diametrically opposed to another's. For example, virtually all historians agree that part of the significance of World War II lies in its new policies and technology of destruction: nuclear weapons in battle and genocide behind the lines. In terms of interpretation, pessimists might stress the continuing menace of this legacy of terror, while optimists might argue that the very violence of the war and the Holocaust triggered a search for limits on nuclear arms and greater tolerance for minorities. With each success in nuclear arms limitation and in toleration, the optimists seem more persuasive; with each spread of nuclear weapons and each outbreak of genocide, the pessimists seem to prevail.

The study of history is thus an interpretation of significance as well as an investigation of facts. The significance of events is determined by their consequences. Sometimes we do not know what the consequences are; or the consequences may not have run their course; or we may differ in our assessment of the consequences. This play between past events and their current consequences is what the historian E.H. Carr had in mind in his famous description of history as "an unending dialogue between the present and the past" (Carr, p. 30).

Tools

The study of history requires many tools, and this text includes most of the principal ones:

- Primary sources are accounts that were produced at the time an event occurred. Those who produced them were eyewitnesses with direct knowledge of what happened. The core of historical study is an encounter with primary materials, usually documents, but including other artifacts—for example, letters, diaries, newspaper accounts, photographs, and artwork. Every chapter in this text includes representative primary materials.
- Secondary sources are interpretations of past events by later historians who re-examine the primary sources either from new perspectives, or with the addition of primary sources that had been lost or overlooked.
- Images, a strong feature of this book, complement the written text, offering non-verbal "texts" of the time. These are often central pieces of evidence. For example, in Chapter Nine we illustrate the influence of Hinduism and Buddhism in Southeast Asia through the temple architecture of the region.
- Maps place events in space and in geographical relationship to one another.
- Chronological time lines situate events in time and sequence.
- Brief charts supply summaries as well as contextual information on such topics as religion, science, and trade.

Suggested Readings

Basic, Comprehensive, Introductory Materials

Carr, E.H. *What Is History?* (Harmondsworth, Middlesex: Penguin Books, 1964). A classic introduction to the study of history and historiography from the point of view of a master.

Budd, Adam, ed. *The Modern Historiography Reader: Western Sources* (New York: Routledge, 2009). Presents 55 essays from about 1700 to the present, discussing major forms of historical inquiry and writing.

Cannadine, David, ed. *What is History Now?* (New York: Palgrave Macmillan, 2002). Revisits the question asked by Carr and presents nine different answers, each by a master of some form of history today: social, political, religious, cultural, etc.

Tosh, John. *The Pursuit of History: Aims, Methods, and New Directions in the Study of Modern History* (London: Longman, 4th ed., 2006). Excellent, comprehensive introduction to the study of history, with discussions of many different kinds of historical study, their methods and purposes.

——, ed. *Historians on History: Readings* (Harlow, England: Pearson, 2nd ed., 2009). Excellent selection of brief extracts from major historians who have given new direction to the field, mostly practicing in the last half-century.

For World History specifically, see the three volumes edited for the American Historical Association

Adas, Michael. *Agricultural and Pastoral Societies in Ancient and Classical History* (Philadelphia, PA: Temple University Press, 2001).

——. *Islamic and European Expansion: The Forging of a Global Order* (Philadelphia, PA: Temple University Press, 1993).

——. *Essays on Twentieth Century History* (Philadelphia, PA: Temple University Press, 2010).

More Specialized Materials

Bennett, Judith M. "Medieval Women, Modern Women: Across the Great Divide," in David Aers, ed., *Culture and History, 1350–1600: Essays on English Communities, Identities, and Writing* (New York: Harvester Wheatsheaf, 1992), pp. 147–75. Discusses continuity, in contrast to change, in women's history.

Curtin, Philip D. "Recent Trends in African Historiography and Their Contribution to History in General," in Joseph Ki-Zerbo, ed., *General History of Africa, Vol. I: Methodology and African Pre-History* (Berkeley: University of California Press, 1981), pp. 54–71. An excellent introduction to this fine series commissioned by the United Nations.

Dunn, Ross. *The New World History: A Teacher's Companion* (Boston, MA: Bedford/St. Martin's, 2000). Excellent selections both on what the new world history ought to be, and what it is as major historians write it.

de Bary, William Theodore, et al., comps. *Sources of Chinese Tradition*, 2 vols. (New York: Columbia University Press, 2nd ed., 1999, 2000). The anthology of materials on the subject.

Lerner, Gerda. *The Creation of Patriarchy* (New York: Oxford University Press, 1986). A controversial study of patriarchy in ancient Mesopotamia by a distinguished historian of the United States. Lerner retooled to study this fundamental feminist question.

MacMullen, Ramsay. *Christianizing the Roman Empire (A.D. 100–400)* (New Haven, CT: Yale University Press, 1984). Excellent analysis of the factors leading to Christianity's success in the Roman Empire. Gives a major role to government support.

Manning, Patrick. *Navigating World History: Historians Create a Global Past* (New York: Palgrave Macmillan, 2003). A major historian presents a magisterial, somewhat dense survey of the field.

Nehru, Jawaharlal. *Glimpses of World History* (New York: Penguin, 2004). A history of the world, written in jail during the struggle for freedom by the man who became India's first prime minister.

Orwell, George. *Animal Farm* (New York: Harcourt, Brace, 1946). A classic satire on government by thugs; aimed at the USSR.

Tacitus, Cornelius. *Tacitus' Agricola, Germany, and Dialogue on Orators*, trans. Herbert W. Benario (Norman: University of Oklahoma Press, 1991). One of ancient Rome's great historians who understood the cruelty underlying the power of empire.

THE WORLD'S HISTORY

FIFTH EDITION

PART ONE

TURNING POINT: HUMAN ORIGINS

To 10,000 B.C.E.

Humankind Begins

Historians ask some very big questions. Of course, the stereotype of the historian as a person who searches in dusty archives for tiny, concrete bits of data is often correct. Detail and accuracy are important. Beneath this search for details, however, lie profound questions of fundamental importance. In this chapter we address some of the biggest questions of all: Where did humans come from? How did our collective life on earth begin? How are we similar to other living species, and how are we unique?

When and where should we begin our search? This is one of the hottest questions in the study of world history today. It was not always so. (For non-historians it may be surprising, but historical questions are not settled once and for all.) Until the mid-nineteenth century, stories, often in the form of religious traditions, provided the answers to our questions about human origins and the meaning and purpose of human life. Then a reevaluation of religious and narrative traditions invited a search for alternative explanations.

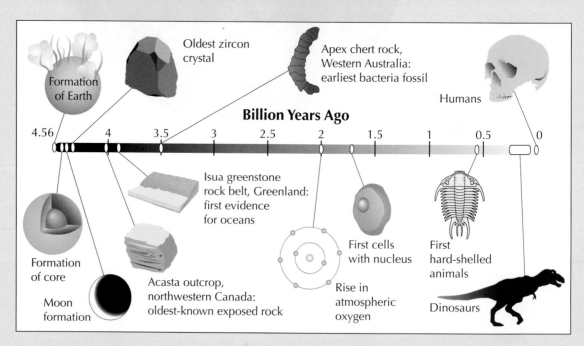

The timeline of Earth. Scientists now believe that the universe came into existence about 13.7 billion years ago, the earth about 4.5 billion years ago, cellular life forms about 1.7 billion years ago, and humans—*Homo sapiens*—only about 100,000 years ago.

Nevertheless, until perhaps fifty years ago, most historians would have begun their accounts of world history with Mesopotamia and Egypt, the first civilizations which created writing and written records, a little more than 5000 years ago. For these historians, "history" requires writing, for only with writing can we determine people's ideas and motives. Only with writing can we discover how we humans have understood our world. The study of the past without written records – through archaeology, for example – is "prehistory," less important and less valuable than the real thing.

At another extreme, in the last two decades, some historians have begun to speak of "big history"; these historians begin their accounts with the creation of the universe, perhaps 14 billion years ago, and continue on with the formation of the planet Earth, about 4.5 billion years ago, and the emergence of the first single-celled life forms, about 3.7 billion years ago. This perspective usually begins with the study of science and of the basic chemical, physical, and biological building blocks of the universe. Since modern humans appear very late in the history of the universe, only about 100,000 years ago, in these accounts, humans appear correspondingly late. Modern times may occupy only a very small proportion of these accounts.

We choose a middle path. We are concerned with human life, so we begin our account with the evolution of the first modern humans from their origins as primates, about 100,000 years ago, much later than the creation of the universe as a whole, but much earlier than the first writing. We ask: "What does it mean to be human?" This profound question leads us to the study of human creativity. Humans are what humans do. We travel and migrate, often out of sheer curiosity as well as to find food and shelter. As we shall see, by about 15,000 B.C.E., humans had traveled, mostly over land, and established themselves on all the continents of the earth except Antarctica. We also create and invent tools. Our account in this chapter begins with the simplest stone tools dating back millions of years and continues up to the invention of pottery and of sedentary farming some 10,000 years ago. Finally, we humans also express our feelings and ideas in art, music, dance, ritual, and literature. In this chapter we examine early evidence of this creativity in the forms of sculptures and cave paintings from 20,000 years ago.

For time periods more recent than 20,000 years ago, we usually adopt the notation "B.C.E." (Before the Common Era) and "C.E." (Common Era). These designations correspond exactly to the more familiar "B.C." (Before Christ) and "A.D." (Anno Domini, "in the year of our Lord"), but remove the specific reference to a single religion. For dates more than 20,000 years ago, "B.P." (Before the Present) is sometimes used.

A skeleton from Herculaneum, Italy, 2001. An archaeologist excavates the skeleton of an inhabitant from the Roman city of Herculaneum, which was buried by the eruption of Mount Vesuvius in 79 C.E.

1 The Dry Bones Speak

To 10,000 B.C.E.

The study of the earliest development of humans advances very quickly and often in sudden leaps forward. Because we know so little to begin with, each new discovery has a profound impact. Before Darwin, the entire religious and mythological literature of the Judeo-Christian-Islamic world assumed that humans had been created directly by God about 6,000 years ago. (Hindu and Buddhist mythology had a much deeper time frame, but little interest in exploring the distant past as history.) Darwin's theories, and a continuing array of fossil finds which supports them, propose a vastly longer time frame and a different interpretive framework for understanding human origins and early development. The discovery in 1953 of the structure of the DNA molecule, and our subsequent understanding of its role in determining the nature of each species and each individual, have further enriched our understanding of the evolution of humans. Discoveries of human cultural achievements beginning 35,000 years ago—sophisticated toolkits, cave paintings and small sculptures, long-distance migrations by land and sea—have added to our appreciation of the accomplishments of our ancestors, and of the people who study them so assiduously.

A skeleton from Herculaneum, Italy, 2001. An archaeologist excavates the skeleton of an inhabitant from Herculaneum.

LEARNING OBJECTIVES

 1.1

Understand how myths explain creation.

 1.2

Describe the evolution of human beings.

 1.3

Discuss the cultural creations of early humans.

((• **Listen** on **MyHistoryLab**

Human Origins in Myth and History

1.1	How do myths explain the origins of human beings on the earth?

How do myths explain the origins of human beings on the earth?

1.1

1.2

1.3

Where did we come from? How did humans come to inhabit the earth? These questions are difficult to answer because the earliest human beings left no written records or obvious oral traditions. For more than a century, we have sought the answer to these questions in the earth, in the records of the fossils that archaeologists and **paleo-anthropologists** have discovered and interpreted. But before the diggers came with their interpretations, human societies from many parts of the world developed stories based on popular beliefs to explain our origins. Passed from generation to generation as folk wisdom, these stories give meaning to human existence. They not only tell how humans came to inhabit the earth, they also suggest why. Some of these stories, especially those that have been incorporated into religious texts such as the Bible, still inspire the imaginations and govern the behavior of hundreds of millions of people around the world.

Early Myths

As professional history developed, many historians dismissed these stories as **myths**, imaginative constructions that cannot be verified with the kinds of records historians usually use. However, myth and history share a common purpose—trying to explain how the world came to be as it is. Many historians and anthropologists now accept myths as important aids in understanding how different societies have interpreted the origins of the human world. Myths often contain important truths, and they can

KEY TERMS

paleoanthropology The study of the earliest humans and their environments.

myth An interpretive story of the past that cannot be verified historically but may have a deep moral message.

AT A GLANCE: EARLY HUMANS AND THEIR ANCESTORS

YEARS AGO	PERIOD	HOMINID EVOLUTION	MATERIAL CULTURE
6.5 million		• Toumai	
5 million	• Pliocene	• Fragments found in northern Kenya; possibly *Australopithecus*	
4.5 million		• *Ardipithecus ramidus*	
3.75 million	• Pleistocene	• *Australopithecus* genus, including Lucy (East and southern Africa) • *Homo habilis* (eastern and southern Africa) • *Homo erectus* (Africa) • *Homo erectus* thought to have moved from Africa into Eurasia	• Tools • Stone artifacts • Use of fire
500,000		• *Homo sapiens* (archaic form) • Remains of Beijing Man (*Sinanthropus*) found at Zhoukoudian	
130,000–80,000		• *Homo sapiens* (Africa and western Asia)	• Stone artifacts
100,000–33,000		• Neanderthals (Europe and western Asia)	
40,000	• Aurignacian		• Tools include long blades • First passage from Siberia to Alaska
30,000	• Gravettian	• Human remains of the Upper Paleolithic type, *Homo sapiens sapiens* (remains from 25,000) found in China	• Venus figures (25,000–12,000)
20,000	• Solutrean		• Chauvet cave, France (18,000)
17,000	• Magdalenian		• Lascaux cave paintings (c. 15,000) • Altamira cave paintings (c. 13,550)

1.1 How do myths explain the origins of human beings on the earth?

1.2

1.3

have powerful effects on people's values and behavior. Shared myths give cohesion to social relationships and provide people with a sense of shared community.

For thousands of years, various creation stories have presented people with explanations of their place in the world and of their relationship to the gods, to the rest of creation, and to one another. The narratives have similarities, but also significant differences. Some portray humans as the exalted crown of creation, others as reconfigured parasites; some depict humans as partners with the gods, others as their servants; some suggest the equality of all humans, others stress a variety of **caste**, race, and gender hierarchies. To some degree, surely, people transmit the stories as quaint tales told for enjoyment only, but they also provide guidance on how people should understand and live their lives.

One of the earliest known stories is the *Enuma Elish* epic of the people of Akkad in Mesopotamia. This account probably dates back to almost 2000 B.C.E. It tells of wars among the gods. Tiamat mates with Apsu and gives birth to younger gods. Later the parents seek to kill off this new generation of their children-gods. To save the god-children, the god Ea slays Apsu while Ea's son Marduk rallies the younger gods, and kills and dismembers Tiamat and her new husband, Kingu. From the blood of Kingu, Marduk creates humans (and all of earth's creatures), on condition that they are to be his servants. Written at a time when the competitive city-states of Mesopotamia were constantly at war, this myth elevated the importance of Babylon, the city that Marduk chooses as his capital; affirmed the authority of its powerful priests and rulers; and assigned purpose and direction to human life.

KEY TERM

caste A hierarchical ordering of people into groups, fixed from birth, based on their inherited ritual status and determining whom they may marry and with whom they may eat.

India, vast and diverse, has many different stories about the origin of humans. Two of the most widespread and powerful illustrate two principal dimensions of the thought and practice of Hindu religious traditions. The ancient epic *Rigveda*, which dates from about 1000 B.C.E., emphasizes the mystical, unknowable qualities of life and its origins:

> Who verily knows and who can here declare it, whence it was born and whence comes this creation?
>
> The Gods are later than this world's production. Who knows then whence it first came into being?
>
> He, the first origin of this creation, whether he formed it all or did not form it, whose eye controls this world in highest heaven, he verily knows it or perhaps he knows not.

In contrast to this reverent but puzzled view of creation, another of the most famous hymns of the *Rigveda*, the Purusha-sakta, describes the creation of the world by the gods' sacrifice and dismemberment of a giant man, Purusha:

> His mouth became the Brahmin; his arms were made into the Warrior, his thighs the People, and from his feet the Servants were born.
>
> The moon was born from his mind; from his eye the sun was born. Indra and Agni came from his mouth, and from his vital breath the Wind was born. (Ch. 10; v. 129)

In this account, humans are part of nature, subject to the laws of the universe, but they are not born equal among themselves. Several groups are created with different qualities and in different castes. This myth of creation supports the hierarchical organization of India's historic caste system.

Shiva Nataraja, or Dancing Shiva. Bronze from the Chola Dynasty, southern India, thirteenth century. The cosmic dance of the Hindu Lord Shiva brings about destruction, crushing evil underfoot, and prepares the way for rebirth in the cycle of existence. The bronze sculptures of the Cholas, and the architecture of their temples, are striking in their beauty and power. (Museum of Fine Arts, Houston)

Perhaps the most widely known creation story is told in the Book of Genesis in the Hebrew Bible. Beginning from nothing, in five days God created heaven and earth; created light and separated it from darkness; created water and separated it from dry land; and created flora, birds, and fishes, and the sun, moon, and stars. God began the sixth day by creating larger land animals and reptiles, and then humans "in his own image."

The Book of Genesis assigns humans a unique and privileged place as the final crown and master of creation. Humans are specially created in God's own image, with dominion over all other living creatures. When the creation of humans is complete and their exalted position in nature is specified, God proclaims the whole process and product of creation as "good." Here humans hold an exalted position within, but also above, the rest of creation.

Until the late eighteenth century, these kinds of story were the only accounts we had of the origins of humans. No other explanations seemed necessary. In any case, no one expected to find actual physical evidence for the processes by which humans came to exist.

How do myths explain the origins of human beings on the earth?

1.1
1.2
1.3

The Evolutionary Explanation

During the eighteenth century, some philosophers and natural scientists in Europe, who were most familiar with the creation story told in the Bible, began to challenge its belief in the individual, special creation of each life form. They saw so many similarities among different species that they could not believe that each had been created separately, although they could not demonstrate the processes through which these similarities and differences had developed. They saw some creatures change forms during their life cycle, such as the metamorphosis of the caterpillar into the moth, or the tadpole into the frog, but they could not establish the processes by which one species metamorphosed into another. They also knew the processes of breeding by which farmers encouraged the development of particular strains in farm animals and plants, but they lacked the conception of a time frame of millions of years that would allow for the natural evolution of a new species from an existing one.

Challenging the authority of the biblical account required a new method of inquiry, a new system for organizing knowledge. By the mid-eighteenth century, a new intellectual environment had begun to emerge. Scientific method called for the direct observation of nature, the recording and analysis of observation, and the discussion and debate of findings throughout an international community of scholars. It rejected the authority of religious texts that asserted truths without presenting substantiating evidence.

Charles Darwin (1809–82) and Alfred Russel Wallace (1823–1913), separately, formulated the modern theory of the biological evolution of species. They saw the mounting evidence of biological similarities among related species; they understood that these similar species were, in fact, related to one another, not separate creations; and they allowed a time frame adequate for major transformations of species to take place. They then went on to demonstrate the method by which small differences within a species were transmitted from generation to generation, increasing the differentiation until new forms were produced.

Both Darwin and Wallace reached their conclusions as a result of extensive travel overseas. Darwin carried out his observations on a scientific voyage around the world in 1831–36 aboard the British warship *Beagle*, and especially during his stay in the Galapagos Islands off the equatorial west coast of South America. Wallace traveled for many years in the islands of Southeast Asia. In 1855 he published a paper suggesting a common ancestor for primates and man. In 1858 Wallace and Darwin published a joint paper on the basic concepts of evolution.

In the isolated Galapagos Islands, Darwin had found various kinds of finches, all of which were similar to each other except in their beaks. He rejected the idea that

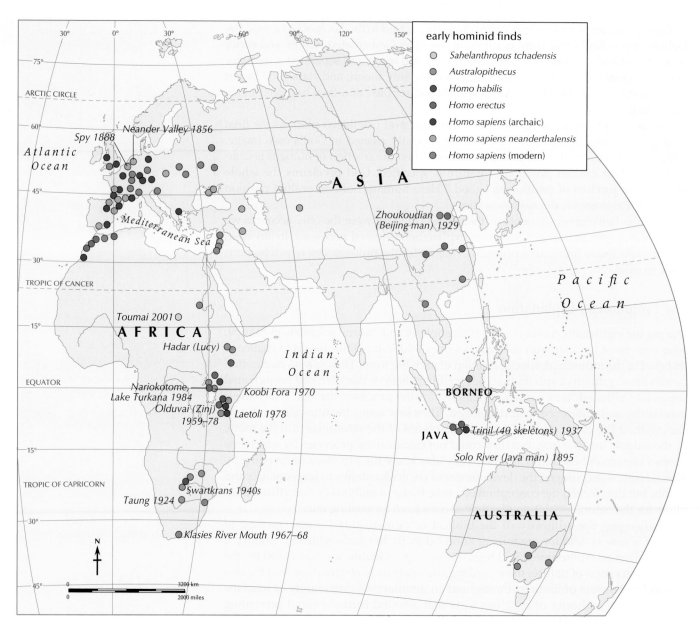

early hominid finds

- ○ *Sahelanthropus tchadensis*
- ○ *Australopithecus*
- ● *Homo habilis*
- ● *Homo erectus*
- ● *Homo sapiens* (archaic)
- ○ *Homo sapiens neanderthalensis*
- ● *Homo sapiens* (modern)

Human ancestors. Fossil remains of the earliest direct human ancestors, *Australopithecus* and *Homo habilis*, dating from one million to five million years ago, have been found only in tropical Africa. The unique soil and climatic conditions there have preserved the fossils. *Homo erectus* remains, from 1.5 million years ago, are the earliest to be found outside Africa. They, along with *Homo sapiens*, have been found throughout Eurasia.

1.1
1.2
1.3

How do myths explain the origins of human beings on the earth?

each kind of finch had been separately created. Rather, he argued, there must have been an ancestor common to them all throughout the islands. Because each island offered slightly different food sources, different beaks were better suited to different islands. The different ecological niches on each separate island to which the birds had immigrated had evoked slightly different evolutionary development. From a single, common ancestor, new species had evolved over time on the different islands.

Darwin compared natural selection to the selection process practiced by humans in breeding animals. Farmers know that specific traits among their animals can be exaggerated through breeding. Horses, for example, can be bred either for speed or for power by selecting those horses in which the desired trait appears. In nature the act of selection occurs spontaneously, if more slowly, as plants and animals with traits that are more appropriate to an environment survive and reproduce while others do not.

In 1859 Darwin published his findings and conclusions in *On the Origin of Species by Means of Natural Selection*, a book that challenged humankind's conception of life on earth and of our place in the universe. Darwin explained that the pressure for each organism to compete, survive, and reproduce created a kind of natural selection. The population of each species increased until its ecological niche was filled to capacity. In the face of this population pressure, the species that were better adapted to the niche survived; the rest were crowded out and tended toward extinction. Small differences always appeared within a species: some members were taller, some shorter; some more brightly colored, others less radiant; some with more flexible hands and feet, others less manipulable. Those members with differences that aided survival in any given ecological setting tended to live on and to transmit their differences to their descendants. Others died out. Darwin called this process "natural selection" or "survival of the fittest."

The New Challenges. Darwin's argument challenged two prevailing stories of creation, especially the biblical views. First, the process of natural selection had no goal beyond survival and reproduction. Unlike many existing creation myths, especially biblical stories, evolutionary theory postulated no **teleology**, no ethical or moral goals and purposes of life. Second, the theory of natural selection described the evolution of ever more "fit" organisms, better adapted to their environment, evolving from existing ones. The special, separate creation of each species was not necessary.

For Darwin, the process of natural selection of more complex, better adapted forms also explained the evolution of humans from simpler, less well-adapted organisms. Perhaps this was "the Creator's" method. Darwin concluded *On the Origin of Species*:

> Thus, from the war of nature, from famine and death, the most exalted object which we are capable of conceiving, namely, the production of the higher animals, directly follows. There is grandeur in this view of life, with its several powers, having been originally breathed by the Creator into a few forms or into one; and that, whilst this planet has gone cycling on according to the fixed law of gravity, from so simple a beginning endless forms most beautiful and most wonderful have been, and are being, evolved.

Note, however, that the words "by the Creator" did not appear in the first edition. Darwin added them later, perhaps in response to criticisms raised by more conventional Christian religious thinkers, who continued to find the biblical story a credible explanation for the origins of human beings.

Within a decade, Darwin's ideas had won over the scientific community. In 1871, in *The Descent of Man*, Darwin extended his argument to the evolution of humans, concluding explicitly that "man is descended from some lowly organized form." Humans are a part of the order of primates, most closely related to great apes and chimpanzees.

The search now began for evidence of the "missing link" between humans and apes, for some creature, living or extinct, that stood at an intermediate point in the

"That Troubles Our Monkey Again." Cartoon of Charles Darwin from *Fun*, November 16, 1872. As scientists and theologians struggled to come to terms with the implications of evolutionary theory, popular reaction was often hostile and derisive. In this cartoon from a contemporary British weekly, Darwin is caricatured as an ape checking the pulse of a woman—or, as the cartoonist ironically refers to her, a "female descendant of marine ascidian" (a tiny invertebrate).

How do myths explain the origins of human beings on the earth?

1.1

1.2

1.3

KEY TERM

teleology The philosophical study of final causes or purposes. Teleology refers especially to any system that interprets nature or the universe as having design or purpose. It has been used to provide evidence for the existence of God.

1.1

1.2 What do we
know about the
1.3 evolution of
human beings?

evolutionary process. In this search archaeology, and the adjunct field of paleoanthropology, flourished.

Fossils and Fossil-hunters

1.2 What do we know about the evolution of human beings?

The search for the "missing link" began in Europe, because that is where the major scientific researchers lived and worked. Later, the search led to Java, Indonesia, and Beijing, China. Still more recently, Africa has yielded the earliest specimens of the human species, fulfilling Darwin's prediction of an African origin of human evolution, based on the abundance of nonhuman primates—apes and chimpanzees—living on that continent.

As archaeologists discovered a variety of kinds of **hominid**—creatures that exhibited some characteristics of humans as well as of earlier primates—they concluded that there was no single missing link, but rather a variety of evolutionary paths that led to the emergence of humans.

The Puzzling Neanderthals

In August 1856, workers quarrying for limestone in a cave in the Neander Valley near Düsseldorf, Germany, found a thick skullcap with a sloping forehead and several skeletal bones of limbs. Some speculated that it was a deformed human. Others thought it was a soldier lost in a previous war. Similar skeletal remains had been found before, but without any clearer understanding of their meaning.

In 1863, Thomas Henry Huxley (1825–95), a leading advocate of Darwin's theory of evolution, argued that the skull was part of a primitive human being who stood between nonhuman primates and **Homo sapiens**, our own species. He claimed that it was the "missing link." In 1864, scholars gave the fossil a name that signified this intermediate position: *Homo neanderthalensis*.

One of the first questions archaeologists asked themselves was: What did *Homo neanderthalensis* look like? Reconstructing the appearance of Neanderthals was difficult, because soft tissue—hair, flesh, and cartilage—does not survive as fossils. Scientists had to use their imaginations.

The earliest efforts to reconstruct the appearance of Neanderthals showed them walking like apes, with a spine that had no curves, and hunchbacked, with their heads pushed forward on top of their spines. Showing muscular but clumsy-looking creatures, with heavy jaws and low, sloping foreheads, these pictures strongly suggested that *Homo neanderthalensis* was brutish and lacking in intelligence. For many years this interpretation, and others similar to it, carried great weight. Museum representations carried the message to the general public. Over the years, however, archaeologists have discovered more about Neanderthals' ability to make tools and survive in challenging environments. Impressed with these accomplishments, anthropologists now create reconstructions that show Neanderthals looking much less "primitive" and more like modern humans.

Moving beyond the individual skeleton in isolation, teams of experts from such disciplines as biology, geology, and climatology cooperate to reconstruct the natural settings of human and hominid development. As Neanderthal skeletons have been found from northern Europe to Africa, from Gibraltar to Iran, these natural settings vary greatly. Remains from caves near Gibraltar suggest that Neanderthals in that area lived in a nuclear family. Elsewhere, evidence shows that many Neanderthals lived in larger bands of up to 20 to 30 individuals.

One recent discovery suggests that at least some Neanderthals were cannibals. The evidence comes from a cave in southern France. A total of 78 bones from at least

KEY TERMS

hominid Any of a family (*Hominidae*) of erect bipedal (two-legged) primate mammals, which includes humans and humanlike species.

Homo sapiens *Homo*, "human," is the genus in which modern humans are placed; *sapiens* means "wise."

Diorama of "bovine" Neanderthals. Displayed for decades in the Field Museum of Natural History in Chicago, this reconstruction suggests that Neanderthals were unintelligent and clumsy. More recent interpretations portray a more intelligent, more graceful creature.

Alternate reconstructions from Neanderthal skull. Because soft tissues—hair, flesh, cartilage—do not survive as fossils, archaeologists must use their imaginations in adding these elements to the solid bone of excavated skeletons.

two adults, two teenagers, and two children aged about seven show that the flesh from all parts of the bodies was carefully removed. Bones were smashed with rocks to get at the inside marrow, and skulls were broken open. The Neanderthal bones and the bones of deer were tossed together into a heap and show similar marks from the same stone tools. On the other hand, there are many other examples of Neanderthals burying their dead carefully, suggesting that their cultural behavior differed from group to group.

Homo erectus: A Worldwide Wanderer

The next of these prehistoric hominid species to be unearthed—the most widespread, and the closest to modern humans—was *Homo erectus* ("upright human"). Examples of this species were discovered in widely dispersed locations throughout the eastern hemisphere and first named according to the locations in which they were found. Later, anthropologists recognized the similarities among them, named them collectively *Homo erectus*, and traced their migration patterns from their earliest home in Africa to new habitats across Asia.

1.1

1.2

What do we know about the evolution of human beings?

1.3

KEY TERM

Homo erectus The most widespread of all prehistoric hominids, and the most similar to humans. Evolved about two million years ago and became extinct 100,000 years ago.

11

LANDMARKS IN EARLY LIFE

Years ago (millions)	Geological period	Life form
2,500	Archaean	earliest living things
590	Cambrian	first fossils
505	Ordovician	first fish
438	Silurian	first land plants
408	Devonian	first amphibians
360	Carboniferous	first reptiles
286	Permian	reptiles expanded
248	Triassic	first mammals and dinosaurs
213	Jurassic	first birds
144	Cretaceous	heyday of dinosaurs
65	Cretaceous	mammals flourished; dinosaurs extinct
25	Tertiary	first hominoid (ancestor of apes and humans)
5	Tertiary	first hominid (human ancestor)
0.1	Quaternary	modern humans appeared

In 1891, Eugène Dubois (1858–1940), a surgeon in the Dutch army in Java, Indonesia, was exploring for fossils. Employing the labor of convicts in Dutch prisons, along the bank of the Solo River, he discovered a cranium with a brain capacity of 900 cc (compared to the modern human average of 1,400 cc), a molar, and a femur. Dubois claimed to have discovered *Pithecanthropus erectus,* or ape-man. This find, widely referred to as Java Man, was the first early hominid discovered outside Europe. Dubois' Java Man forced scholars to consider the theories of the evolution of humans more seriously and to understand the process in a global context.

In 1929, in the vast Zhoukoudian cave, 30 miles from Beijing, Chinese archaeologists discovered a 500,000-year-old skullcap. In the next few years, in this fossil-rich cave, they discovered 14 more fossil skulls and the remains of some 40 individuals, whom they dated to 600,000 to 200,000 years ago. The cave seems to have been the home of a band of hunters, who lived in a forested, grassy, riverine area and who ate plants as well as animals, such as bison and deer. Remaining bones and ash indicate their ability to use fire for light and cooking. With a brain capacity ranging from 775 to 1,300 cc and a height up to 5 feet 6 inches, anatomically Beijing Man was almost identical to Java Man. About a decade later, further excavations in Java turned up the nearly complete skull of one hominid and the skeletons of some 40 others who had lived 100,000 to 900,000 years ago. Anthropologists soon recognized similarities between Java Man and Beijing Man, and classified them collectively under the name *Homo erectus.* The 40 skeletons from Java represent one-third of all the *Homo erectus* skeletons uncovered to this day in the entire world. Those in the Zhoukoudian cave represent another third. The most complete skeleton we have of *Homo erectus* was discovered, however, in Africa, in 1984, on the shores of Lake Turkana, Kenya.

The Search Shifts to Africa

In 1924, a medical student in South Africa called the attention of his professor, Raymond Dart, to some fossils in a quarry near Taung. Dart investigated and proclaimed the Taung skull to be *Australopithecus africanus,* "southern apelike creature of Africa," a two-million-year-old ancestor of humans. Another medical doctor, Robert Broom, discovered additional hominid fossils, including some of *Homo erectus,*

1.1

1.2

What do we
know about the
evolution of
human beings?

1.3

similar to those discovered in Java and China. Between 1945 and 1955, Dart and his colleagues began to discover bone tools among the hominid fossils, as well as evidence of the first controlled use of fire, about a million years ago. Their research extended beyond the archaeology of individual hominid skeletons to paleoanthropology. Their ecological analyses included, for example, the fossils of hundreds of animals discovered near the hominids.

Archaeologist Louis Leakey (1903–72) began his excavations in East Africa in the 1930s, although his most important discoveries were achieved with his wife, Mary (1913–96), after 1959 in the Olduvai Gorge, where the Great Rift Valley cuts through northern Tanzania.

The Great Rift Valley runs from the Jordan River valley and the Dead Sea southward through the Red Sea, Ethiopia, Kenya, Tanzania, and Mozambique. The Rift is a fossil-hunter's delight. From at least seven million years ago until perhaps 100,000 years ago, it was a fertile, populated region; it is geologically still shifting and, therefore, has covered and uncovered its deposits over time. Rivers that run through the Rift Valley further the process of uncovering the fossils, and it is volcanic, generating lava and ash that preserve the fossils caught within it and provide the material for relatively accurate dating.

At Olduvai in 1959, the Leakeys discovered a hominid they called *Zinjanthropus boisei*, soon nicknamed "Zinj." At first they hoped that Zinj might be an early specimen of *Homo*, but its skull was too small, its teeth were too large, its arms were too long, and its face was too much like an ape's. Zinj, who was 1,750,000 years old, was another *Australopithecus*, a hominid closer to apes than to modern humans. The *Australopithecus* clan was thus extended to include a new cousin, *Australopithecus*

Louis and Mary Leakey examining the palate of the "Zinj" skull, 1959. This husband-and-wife team revolutionized our understanding of anthropology. Their excavations in the Olduvai Gorge in East Africa led to the generally accepted belief that hominids originally evolved in Africa.

13

boisei. The australopithecine family tree—or "bush"—by now showed a number of branches, although the relationship among them and to us is not always clear. The chart later in this chapter represents these branches and relationships.

📖 **Read** the **Document: The Long Journey (5M BCE)** on **MyHistoryLab**

Homo habilis. The Leakeys' continued excavations at Olduvai turned up skull fragments of creatures with brain capacities of 650 cc, between the 400–500 cc of australopithecines and the 1,400 cc of modern humans. The Leakeys named this new type of hominid *Homo habilis,* "handy person," because of the stone tools they made and used in scavenging, hunting, and butchering food. Dating suggested that *Homo habilis* lived at about the same time as Zinj, demonstrating that *Homo* and *Australopithecus* had lived side by side about two million years ago.

The Leakeys' discoveries at Olduvai furthered the search for the ancestors of modern humans in several directions: they pushed back the date of the earliest known representative of the genus *Homo* to 1.5–2 million years ago; they indicated the extent of the tool-using capacity of these early *Homo* representatives; and they reconstructed the ecology of the region 2.5–1.5 million years ago, placing *Homo habilis* within it as hunter and scavenger. Together with earlier discoveries, the findings enabled the Leakeys to identify Africa as the home of the earliest hominids and the earliest representatives of the genus *Homo.*

In the 1970s, Louis and Mary's son, Richard Leakey (b. 1944), discovered additional bones of the species *Homo habilis* at Koobi Fora on the east side of Lake Turkana in Kenya. The finds confirmed the size of its brain at about 650 cc; its opposable thumb, which allowed it to grip objects powerfully and manipulate them precisely, and thus to make tools; and its upright, bipedal (two-legged) walk, evident from the form of its hip and leg bones.

Australopithecus afarensis. In 1974, at Hadar, Ethiopia, near the Awash River, Donald Johanson (b. 1943) discovered "Lucy," the first known representative of

"Lucy" skeleton, *Australopithecus afarensis,* found at Hadar, Ethiopia. "Lucy" is thought to have lived about 3.2 million years ago, and was at the time of her discovery in 1974 the earliest known hominid ancestor of modern man. She had humanlike hands and could walk upright; however, there is no evidence that she made or used tools, and her sturdy, curved arms are still consistent with tree-climbing. Until the discovery of *Ardipithecus* in 1994, Lucy was the most complete hominid skeleton from the period before two million years ago. (Natural History Museum, London)

Australopithecus afarensis, named for the local Afar people. (Lucy herself was named for the Beatles song "Lucy in the Sky with Diamonds," which was playing on a tape recorder just as the Johanson team was realizing the importance of their find.) This discovery pushed back the date of the earliest known hominid to about 3.2 million years ago.

Lucy's overall height was between 3 feet 6 inches and 4 feet, and Johanson and his team estimated her weight as 60 pounds. The archaeologists were able to uncover about 40 percent of her skeleton, making Lucy the earliest and most complete hominid skeleton known at the time. She had humanlike hands, but there is no evidence that she made or used tools, and her sturdy, curved arms are still consistent with tree-climbing. Later excavations at Hadar revealed numerous additional skeletons of *Australopithecus afarensis*, including the first complete skull, discovered by Johanson in 1992.

The cranial capacity of Lucy and her fellow *Australopithecus afarensis* was only 400 cc, too small for her to be a *Homo*. Her pelvis was too small to allow the birth of offspring with a larger skull, but the form of that pelvis and the fit of her knee joints characterized Lucy as a two-legged hominid. Lucy had walked upright. She was a kind of bipedal ape, and, in her bipedalism, an ancestor of modern humans.

Further evidence of the bipedalism of these apelike creatures came from Laetoli, Tanzania. There, in 1978, Mary Leakey discovered the footprints of two *Australopithecus afarensis* walking side by side. In volcanic ash, she found 70 footprints walking a distance of 80 feet. The ash provided material for dating the prints; they were 3.5 million years old. The tracks suggest that *Australopithecus afarensis* had a slower, more rolling gait than modern man, although the prints reveal well-defined feet. Mary Leakey saw in them a slight sideward turn, a hesitation in direction, which she interpreted as the first evidence of human doubt.

In 1994, some 17 fossils of a new genus, *Ardipithecus ramidus*, "ground ape," were discovered in Aramis, Ethiopia, in the bed of the Awash River, not far from the Lucy find. An international team of archaeologists analyzed them. Ten of the fossils were teeth, two were cranial fragments, and the remainder were bones from the left arm. Later, the team recovered about 80 percent of an *Ardipithecus ramidus* skeleton. It dated to 4.4 million years, pushing back the date of the earliest apelike hominid by half a million years.

Then, in 2001, a team working in Chad, Africa, under the French paleoanthropologist Michel Brunet (b. 1940), discovered a six- to seven-million-year-old skull, nicknamed "Toumai," which means "hope of life" in the Goran language. Toumai is at least 2.5 million years older than any previously discovered hominid skull, and, remarkably, it is nearly complete. On the cusp between ape and human, it displays human characteristics that include a relatively thick and continuous brow ridge, a relatively flat nose and face, and canine teeth that are shorter and more thickly enameled than those of chimpanzees. On the other hand, its cranial capacity is about the size of a chimp's, about one-fourth of a modern human's. It is not clear if Toumai was bipedal, but its spine entered its cranium in a pathway consistent with bipedalism.

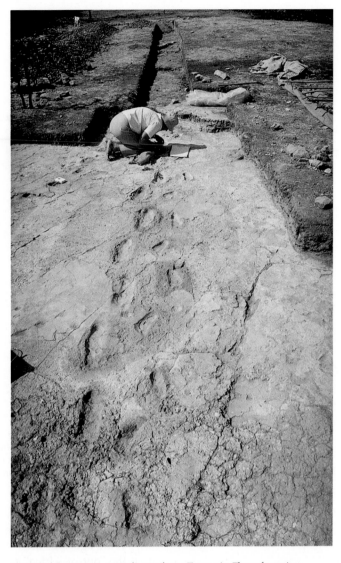

Hominid footprints, Laetoli, northern Tanzania. These footprints in ash at Laetoli confirmed that hominids were walking upright 3.5 million years ago. The tracks reveal well-defined feet and suggest that *Australopithecus afarensis* had a slower, more rolling gait than modern man. Mary Leakey (pictured) discovered the prints.

1.1

1.2

What do we know about the evolution of human beings?

1.3

15

"Toumai," the oldest prehuman fossil, Chad, Africa, 2001. This skull was discovered in Chad by an international team of paleoanthropologists. It is from the earliest member of the prehuman family so far discovered, dating back six to seven million years. "Toumai" is the name given to children in Chad born near the dry season.

"Toumai" fits the dominant theories of evolution as to the time at which and the pattern by which the hominid line of evolution separated from the chimpanzee line, taking on its own distinct characteristics. It challenges most current beliefs, however, in suggesting that hominids evolved not only in the difficult, harsh, arid climate of the Rift Valley, where all the earlier hominids had been uncovered, but also in the more accommodating lush forests that covered western Chad six million years ago.

As paleoanthropologists assembled this record of the earliest human ancestors, they also found more recent skeletons that more closely resemble our own. The earliest known anatomically modern *Homo sapiens* fossil also appeared in Africa. It was discovered in 1967–68 in caves at the Klasies River mouth on the coast of South Africa. These fossil remains of the oldest known example of the species *Homo sapiens* date to 75,000 to 115,000 years ago. They include lower and upper jaws, skull fragments, teeth, and bones of limbs. With them fossil-hunters found thousands of stone quartzite tools, an abundance of bones from numerous land mammals, and the remains of hundreds of thousands of shellfish, suggesting a diet rich in meat and seafood. The Klasies River mouth discovery raised most provocatively the question of where the first *Homo sapiens* emerged, and how they spread.

The Debate over African Origins

Almost all paleoanthropologists and archaeologists now believe that *Homo erectus* appeared first in Africa and spread from there to Asia and, perhaps, to Europe between one and two million years ago. But then the scholars split into two camps: the "multiregionalists" and the "out-of-Africa" camp. The multiregionalists argue that *Homo erectus* evolved into *Homo sapiens* in each region of migration. The out-of-Africa group argues that *Homo erectus* evolved into *Homo sapiens* only once—in Africa. Then, about 100,000 years ago, the new humans emigrated to the rest of the world from Africa.

Both groups of scholars agree that the varieties of racial development—differences in physical characteristics such as skin color, characteristics of hair, bone structure, and minor genetic modification—are responses to different ecological niches. They differ, however, on the time and place of the development. If the evolution from *Homo erectus* to *Homo sapiens* began in several different locations up to two million years ago, then racial differentiation is very old. Even so, the groups did not remain entirely separate from one another, and over time substantial interbreeding took place among the different regional groups despite their geographic distances. No race remained "pure." If, according to the alternative theory, all modern *Homo sapiens* share a common origin until just 100,000 years ago, and began to differentiate by race only after emigrating from Africa to new locations, then these differences are much more recent and even more superficial.

At present, the supporters of the "out-of-Africa" theory are in the majority. They point out that it is more common for just one branch of any particular species to evolve into another and ultimately to displace all the other branches than for all the different branches to evolve simultaneously. They minimize the biological significance of race based on skin color as a relatively recent, and only "skin-deep,"

1.1
1.2 What do we know about the evolution of human beings?
1.3

Homo sapiens sapiens
present day

Homo (sapiens) neanderthalensis
50,000 B.P.

Homo erectus
1.4 million B.P.

Homo habilis
1.8 million B.P.

Australopithecus boisei
1.9 million B.P.

Australopithecus africanus
2.7 million B.P.

difference among the peoples of the earth. The advocates of both the multiregional and the out-of-Africa schools of thought agree that at deeper levels, such as blood types and the ability to interbreed, race has no significance.

Reading the Genetic Record

In the search for the time and place of the origins of *Homo sapiens*, a different kind of discovery, based on genetics rather than fossils, on laboratory research rather than field excavations, emerged in the 1960s. Scientists began to study the DNA (deoxyribonucleic acid) record of human and animal genes. DNA is each cell's chemical code of instructions for building proteins, and the DNA research reveals the degrees of similarity and difference among the creatures studied. While the fossil record relied on comparing form and function among the relatively few specimens that have been discovered, DNA research relied on comparison of the arrangement of the basic building blocks of existence from the single-cell organism through the most complex animal form.

Because DNA is inherited, differences and similarities in the proteins and DNA of animals (including humans) living today suggest the date up to which they might have shared common ancestors before separating into different streams of evolution.

Skull reconstructions of some of the ancestors of modern man in chronological order. The generalized dates attached to each species imply that one followed the other, but actually some earlier species lived on for some time alongside more recent ones. By about 35,000 B.C.E., however, all except *Homo sapiens* were extinct. (Natural History Museum, London)

1.1

1.2

What do we know about the evolution of human beings?

1.3

The human "bush." Popular thought usually imagines a straight-line development from apes to humans, but anthropologists speak of a human "bush," a variety of interacting and interbreeding species that finally produced *Homo sapiens*. Most anthropological models see *Ardipithecus ramidus* and *Australopithecus afarensis* as the first steps in the branching-apart of humans from apes about five million years ago. One line of further evolution led toward modern *Homo sapiens*. All the other hominid forms, those in our own line and those in other lines, subsequently became extinct.

1.1

1.2 What do we know about the evolution of human beings?

1.3

1.1

What do we
know about the
evolution of
human beings?

1.2

1.3

In 1970, for example, biochemists first analyzed the protein albumin and the DNA of apes and humans and found that, genetically, modern humans are 97 percent the same as chimpanzees and 96 percent the same as gorillas. These data suggest that chimpanzees, gorillas, and humans shared common ancestors until five to seven million years ago, when evolutionary separation occurred. This genetic dating matches and reinforces the fossil record.

Extending the method further, researchers have analyzed the mitochondrial DNA (genetic material found outside the cell nucleus and passed only from mother to daughter) of thousands of women living today, and conclude that *Homo sapiens sapiens* emerged solely from Africa around 120,000 years ago, and that all of us today are descendants of a single woman living in Africa about 200,000 years ago. They often call her "mitochondrial Eve" or "the African Eve." This does not mean that she was the only woman alive at the time, but she is the only one who has descendants still living today in an unbroken female line: that is, in every generation there was a mother who gave birth to at least one daughter. Similarly, analysis of the Y-chromosomes (structures containing DNA, and passed only from father to son) of thousands of men living today shows that the earliest ancestor who contained this chromosome lived in Africa about 150,000 years ago, "Y-chromosomal Adam" or "the African Adam." Again, he was not the only man alive at the time, but the only one who has descendants alive today in an unbroken male, father-to-son, line.

The Theory of Scientific Revolution

We have given a lengthy introduction to various explanations for the emergence of the first humans. Many historians would choose to move more quickly toward the present, although, of course, in covering six million years in one chapter we are moving swiftly! We have chosen to elaborate this account not only for its intrinsic interest but also because it helps to demonstrate most clearly our concern with "how we know" as well as with "what we know," since we believe that historians and paleoanthropologists share in the traditions of social science.

Paleoanthropologists maintain a lively debate about each of their findings and interpretations. They present their views and situate them within the ongoing debates in their field. They present the historical record as an ongoing search and argument. Existing data may be reevaluated; new data may be added; interpretations may be revised; new questions may arise. The historical record is never complete.

Amendments to the historical record, however, are usually minor additions to, or revisions of, a pattern already well known. Thomas Kuhn, in his path-breaking study of the history of science, *The Structure of Scientific Revolutions*, wrote that

> normal science [like history] ... is a highly cumulative enterprise, eminently successful in its aim, the steady extension of the scope and precision of scientific knowledge. Normal science does not aim at novelties of fact or theory and, when successful, finds none. (Kuhn, p. 52)

The history of the evolution of hominids usually follows this pattern of "normal science." Thus the discoveries of 4.5-million-year-old *Ardipithecus ramidus* in 1994, of six- to seven-million-year-old Toumai in 2001, and of *Homo floresiensis*, discovered in 2003 and dating to as recently as 13,000 years ago, did not surprise paleoanthropologists. The new fossils fit neatly into the expected time frame for the process of evolution from apes to hominids (although the geographical location of Toumai in Chad was unexpected, and *Homo floresiensis* was a very late survival of pre-*Homo sapiens sapiens*). This was normal science filling in an existing model, or paradigm, with new detail.

Sometimes, however, new discoveries challenge existing paradigms. At first the new discoveries are discounted as exceptions to the rule. But when the exceptions

1.1

1.2

1.3   What do cultural
         creations tell us
         about the lives of
         early humans?

KEY STAGES IN HUMAN DEVELOPMENT

4.5 million B.P.	First appearance of bipedalism. (First clear appearance; Toumai of Chad, 6 million B.C.E., was apparently bipedal.)
2 million B.P.	Change in structure of forelimbs—bipedalism is perfected. Gradual expansion and reorganization of the brain. Hunting, scavenging, and gathering cultures stimulate production of stone tools.
500,000 B.P.	Rapid brain growth.
120,000 B.P.	*Homo sapiens sapiens*, anatomically modern humans. Fire now in use.
40,000 B.P.	Interglacial period. Existence of modern humans, with fully developed brain and speech. Tools constructed from component parts. Cave art and portable art in Europe. Human migration begins from Asia into America.
10,000 B.C.E.	Invention of bow and arrows. Domestication of reindeer and dog (north Eurasia). Settled food production.
8000–4000 B.C.E.	Increase of human population by 1,500 percent. Domestication of sheep and goats (Near East). Earliest pottery (Japan). Farming spreads to Western Europe. Rice cultivation starts in Asia.
3000 B.C.E.	Writing, metals.

increase, scientists seek new explanatory paradigms. Darwin's breakthrough followed this second pattern of scientific revolution. His discoveries on the voyage of the *Beagle* and his subsequent analyses of his findings challenged the existing concepts of creation that were based on biblical narratives. Darwin provided a radically different scientific explanation of the mechanisms of evolution that displaced the biblical paradigm. Both Darwin's scientific analysis and the Book of Genesis in the Bible, however, postulate the creation of an entire cosmos and world, replete with flora and fauna, before humans achieve their place in the universe and begin to name the other species.

Major revisions of the historical record often follow this trajectory. A general pattern of explanation is followed, until new research raises new questions and new theoretical paradigms provide more fitting explanations for all the available data and information. Throughout this text we shall continue to see changes in historical explanation over time. A "paradigm shift" may occur not only as a result of the discovery of new data, or of new interpretations that better fit the available data, but also as a response to new questions being raised that may not have been asked before. The historical record, like the scientific record on evolution, is always subject to reevaluation. Readers of this textbook may want to keep up with the latest research through such popular journals as *Archaeology* or *Scientific American*, or the online record of the Human Origins project at the Smithsonian Institution in Washington, DC. More specialized journals include *Nature* and *Science*. For example, see on the Smithsonian website the record of the discovery in 2003 and the continuing interpretation of the fossil *Homo floresiensis*, sometimes known as "The Hobbit" because of its small size. Or see the research on the presence of Neanderthal genes in modern *Homo sapiens sapiens* on the online version of *Archaeology*.

Humans Create Culture

1.3   What do cultural creations tell us about the lives of early humans?

Until now we have been examining biological evolution, "natural selection." Those organisms best able to survive did survive. By the time of *Homo habilis*, the *Homo* biological genus was creating simple tools through which it could shape nature to meet its needs. *Homo habilis* sculpted stone tools of increasing sophistication. They apparently hunted, scavenged, gathered in groups, and shared their booty. Throughout the intervening two million years, up to our own day, *Homo* has continued to increase its sophistication in creating tools, art, rituals, settlements, concepts, and language, and in domesticating plants and animals—the basic elements of what anthropologists call culture. By the time *Homo sapiens* had evolved, cultural creativity had superseded biology as the principal method by which humans coped with nature. Humans were no longer content to exist in nature. They sought to control it.

Cultural evolution seems to have been encouraged by biological evolution. As the *Homo* brain continued to develop and get bigger, it became impossible for the genus *Homo*, with its relatively narrow birth canal, to give birth to a child with a fully formed brain in a fully formed cranium. The brain capacity of human young must continue to develop for some time after birth (in fact, the brain of a human reaches its adult size only at the age of six or seven). Within the genus *Homo*, therefore, parents must devote significant time to nurturing and teaching their young children. In addition, in female *Homo sapiens* the *oestrus* cycle, the alternating period of fertility and infertility, occurs each month rather than seasonally, allowing them to bear children more frequently than other primates. Increased childbearing further increases the time and energy devoted to nurturing the young. Because of the greater attention to nurturing, cultural life could flourish—and it did.

Our species has not changed anatomically since the earliest known appearance of *Homo sapiens* in the archaeological record about 200,000 years ago. The skeletons unearthed at the Klasies River mouth are no

Two Aurignacian implements, France, Mesolithic era (c. 30,000 B.P.). Stone Age cultures first appeared in Western Europe in 33,000 B.P. and underwent constant changes in technology—implying a gradual evolution in human behavior. By the Aurignacian era, flint-end scrapers (right) were employed in processing skins, woodworking, and carving artifacts like this bone spearpoint (left). (Natural History Museum, London)

different from our own. About 120,000 years ago, however, a new creativity appeared in the cultural and social life of *Homo sapiens*, perhaps the result of a modification in the internal structure of the brain. The people who lived before this development are called "archaic" *Homo sapiens*; those with the new cultural capabilities are considered a new subspecies, **Homo sapiens sapiens** (wise, wise human). They are us. Unlike their predecessors, *Homo sapiens sapiens* developed forms of symbolic expression, apparently spiritual and cultural in nature, including burial rituals and artwork that is sometimes stunningly beautiful and creative.

Seven creative behaviors mark the arrival of *Homo sapiens sapiens*. First, we persisted. We are the lone survivor from among all the hominids of the last six million years. Second, we continued to spread to all parts of the globe in waves of migration that had begun even earlier. Third, we built small, temporary settlements to serve as base camps for hunting and gathering. Fourth, we continued to craft more sophisticated tools. Fifth, we elaborated more sophisticated use of language. Sixth, by about 25,000 B.C.E., on cave walls and in stone, we began to paint and sculpt magnificent works of art and symbolism. Seventh, by 15,000–10,000 B.C.E., we began to domesticate plants and animals, introducing the art and science of agriculture.

How Did We Survive While Others Became Extinct?

While Neanderthals appeared to be *a* link between apes and humans, continuing excavations demonstrated that they were not *the* link. In fact, as researchers have

1.1

1.2

1.3

What do cultural creations tell us about the lives of early humans?

KEY TERMS

B.P. Before the Present. Archaeologists frequently use this notation, especially for dates before about 20,000 B.C.E.

Homo sapiens sapiens The first human being of the modern type.

HOW DO WE KNOW?

Dating Archaeological Finds

Continuous improvements in dating techniques have changed our understanding of the relationships among the early *Homo sapiens*, and even among the earlier hominids, and their relationships to their environment. The most common technique, since its discovery in 1949, is radiocarbon dating, sometimes called the carbon 14 (C14) method. Living organisms breathe in air, and so they contain the same percentage of atoms of radioactive carbon as the earth's atmosphere. When an organism dies, its radiocarbon atoms disintegrate at a steady, known rate. By measuring the amount of radiocarbon remaining in a fossil skeleton, scientists can calculate backward to the date of death. Because the total amount of radiocarbon in any organism is small, little is left after 40,000 years, and the method does not work at all beyond 70,000 years into the past.

For a broader spectrum of dates, scientists use a technique called thermoluminescence, developed in 1987. This technique was applied to burned flints discovered in the caves where early humans had lived. Radioactivity occurring in nature releases electrons in flint and clay, but they can finally escape only when the substance is heated. When the flints were first burned by the people of the caves, the electrons freed up to that time were released. Reheating the flints in the laboratory today releases the electrons stored up since the first burning. Scientists calculate the date of the first burning by measuring the light of those electrons.

This technique works not only for burned flint of 50,000–300,000 years of age, but also for burnt clay, enabling scientists to date pottery from the last 10,000 years.

For much earlier dates, such as those of the earliest hominid fossils that go back as much as six million years, scientists measure the decay of the radioactive element potassium 40 into argon 40, a process that takes place in volcanic rocks and soils. Potassium-argon dating, in use since the 1950s, was invaluable in estimating the age of the soil in which stone tools and hominid remains were found in the Olduvai Gorge. This dating method was the clue to determining the deep antiquity of these fossils, and in shifting the search for the earliest hominids to Africa.

- Biochemists and physicists have their contribution to make in understanding—and dating—the evolution of the earliest humans. What have been the contributions of other academic specialists encountered in this book?
- What are the similarities between radiocarbon, thermo-luminescence, and potassium-argon dating? Why is each limited to a particular time period?
- Which of these methods directly dates fossil remains? Which dates the soil in which fossils are found? What might be the problems with dating fossils by the soil in which they are found?

1.1

1.2

1.3 What do cultural creations tell us about the lives of early humans?

continued to find additional examples of early hominids all over the world, it has become increasingly clear that there is no single chain leading directly from apes to humans. Rather, anthropologists now believe that many hominids contributed to a formation better described as a "bush" of various hominids, with many branches, and that our species evolved from the various interbreedings of these hominids. All the other intervening species died out. As a result, it might appear that first there were apes and then, in a direct chain, there were humans. But the fossils of many different species in between show that the evolutionary path was not so direct.

For example, from our first appearance in the archaeological record, about 120,000 years ago, until about 35,000 years ago, anatomically modern *Homo sapiens sapiens* seem to have coexisted alongside Neanderthals and other archaic *Homo sapiens* in several sites. The best studied are in the Middle East. Caves near Haifa, Israel, have yielded skeletons and tools of both Neanderthals and modern humans from almost that entire time period. They shared similar types of tool. Neanderthals seem to have used slightly simpler, smaller Mousterian stone tools (named for the village of Le Moustier in southwestern France, where they have been most clearly documented). Their modern human neighbors used the thinner, longer, more precisely crafted Aurignacian tools (named for another hunter-gatherer site in southern France). The differences were marked but not huge.

How, then, did modern *Homo sapiens sapiens* eventually displace all other hominids? Three principal interpretations, in various combinations, have been suggested. The first is that modern humans defeated all the other hominids through warfare and murder. This theory suggests a violent streak in the earliest humans. The second theory suggests that modern humans successfully filled up the ecological niche available, outcompeting archaic *Homo sapiens* for the available resources. Modern humans did not directly confront the archaic forms but displaced them—in a sense, we ate them out of house and home. The third, related theory argues that in some cases,

Early humans in the Ice Age. By 20,000 years ago, when ice covered much of Europe and much of Canada, almost the whole world (except Polynesia) had been colonized. Early humans were able to spread north because water frozen into ice sheets reduced sea levels so much that land bridges appeared, linking most major areas. The cold was intense, and the migrants' survival depended on their ability to stitch together animal hides into primitive clothing, control fire, and hunt large mammals.

1.1

1.2

1.3

What do cultural creations tell us about the lives of early humans?

modern humans and Neanderthals mated. Research published in 2010, using DNA from Neanderthal bones dating from 45,000 to 34,000 years ago, discovered in caves in Croatia, argues that the genes of human beings today are composed of between 1 and 4 percent Neanderthal genes. At least once, and presumably more frequently, our immediate ancestors made love, not war, and we contain a Neanderthal heritage. Because *Homo sapiens sapiens* was better adapted to nature as the ice ages ended, it was mostly their (our) genes that survived and persisted.

Global Migration

Homo sapiens sapiens appeared in Africa no later than 120,000 years ago, evolving from *Homo erectus*. Within 30,000 years the species began to appear throughout Europe and Asia. Anthropologists suspect that early human migrations were not aimless wanderings, but were purposeful and specific. From earliest prehistory, people weighed their options and opportunities and then chose appropriate actions. Global migration was the ultimate outcome.

Changes in climate may have been one of the main reasons for migration. The Sahara, now a desert, provides one example. Until about 90,000 years ago, when the earth was in a warm, wet stage, the Sahara region was fertile and attractive to human settlement. People and animals from southern Africa migrated there. But then began an "ice age," one of the periods of global cooling that have affected the

The colonization of the Pacific. The land bridges of the last Ice Age enabled early humans to spread south from China to Java and Borneo. There, some knowledge of navigation was required to cross the Banda Sea to New Guinea and Australia. The most spectacular voyages were undertaken by the Polynesians, who journeyed hundreds and thousands of miles by canoe into the uncharted Pacific waters.

View the **Interactive Map: Intercontinental Migration Patterns in Pre-History** on **MyHistoryLab**

View the **Map: The Spread of Human Populations** on **MyHistoryLab**

1.1

1.2

1.3 What do cultural creations tell us about the lives of early humans?

earth's climate over millions of years. Much of the earth's water froze. The Sahara dried up, turning to desert, and people and animals emigrated. Some may have turned back to southern Africa; some may have journeyed toward the North African coast; still others may have followed the Nile valley into western Asia. So began one wave in a global process of migration.

To reach the most distant areas, such as Australia, the islands of the Pacific, and the Americas, took tens of thousands of years. These migrations required changes in climate as well as in the skills of *Homo sapiens sapiens*. The successive ice ages of 90,000–10,000 years ago froze much of the water of the oceans, reducing sea levels, extending the coasts of the continents, and creating land bridges that linked modern China with Japan, Southeast Asia with the Philippines and Indonesia, and Siberia with Alaska.

"Navigation in Van Diemen's Land," Charles Alexandre Lesueur, plate 14 from *Voyage of Discovery to Australian Lands*, 1807. Engraving. When Europeans began settling Van Diemen's Land, now called Tasmania, in Australia, they found people who had arrived there some 40,000 years before, having crossed over from southeastern China.

People reached Southeast Asia apparently via land bridges about 50,000 years ago. Reaching Australia, however, required the sailing knowledge and skill to cover hundreds of miles of open water, and the continent was reached only about 45,000 years ago. The Pacific islands known as Polynesia, thousands of miles from any major landmass, were peopled only thousands of years later. Only in 1000 B.C.E. did New Guineans, performing extraordinary feats of navigation in simple canoes, colonize Polynesia.

North America was reached about 14,000–16,000 years ago. Until then, Siberia and the north of the continent may have been too cold for human passage. But by about 16,000 years ago, the last of the great ice sheets had retreated. Despite the rising sea levels brought about by the melting of the ice, a land bridge remained, and the climate was warm enough for people to cross over into North America. In the 1920s, stone tools were discovered near Clovis, New Mexico. Similar tool kits were subsequently discovered across North America, suggesting that the Clovis immigrants were the first humans to inhabit the Americas, about 13,000 years ago. In the 1970s, however, discoveries at Monte Verde, Chile, suggested an arrival 1,000–1,500 years before that. It also raised the question—not answered—of how a settlement so far south could precede those in North America: could the immigrants have used ships for at least part of their journey? Beginning in about 2008, findings relating to mastodon hunts in what is now Washington State, and tool kits in what is now Texas and elsewhere, and the DNA testing of remains of human feces in several additional locations suggest three waves of arrival slightly earlier, perhaps 15,000 years ago. The search for even earlier settlements continues, although none are expected before about 16,000 years ago, the end of the last major ice age.

View the **Closer Look: Mammoth Hut** on **MyHistoryLab**

1.1
1.2
1.3

What do cultural creations tell us about the lives of early humans?

What do cultural
creations tell us
about the lives of
early humans?

Increased Population and New Settlements

Gradually, as human population expanded, so, too, did the number of human groups and the closeness or "density" of their relationships to one another. Such increasing density and population pressure became a staple of human history. Frequently, the result was conflict among groups for the best lands and resources. Some groups chose to stand and fight for their territory, others reached accommodation with newcomers, and yet others emigrated, either by choice or by force, following losses in battle. (These patterns have repeated themselves for tens of thousands of years. Today there are some 17 million refugees in the world.)

How large were these groups? They had to include enough members to provide security in defense and cooperation in work, yet be small enough to subsist on the natural resources available and to resolve the interpersonal friction that threatened the cohesion of the group and the safety of its members.

Calculated from the experience of modern hunter-gatherers, such as the Khoisan of the African Kalahari Desert, and theoretical mathematical models of group process, a five-family group of 25 people seems the ideal balance. Mating and marriage rules

HOW DO WE KNOW?

Man the Hunter or Woman the Gatherer?

Every human society has established its own patterns of gender relationships between males and females. In recent years especially, historians have turned their attention to discovering and analyzing these patterns. Their research is often determined both by the historical materials available and, to some degree, by their own biases.

In 1971 anthropologist Sally Slocum, writing under the pseudonym Sally Linton, published one of the first feminist critiques of the current understanding of hominid evolution. She was responding to a set of papers published in 1968 entitled *Man the Hunter*. One of the papers asserted: "The biology, psychology, and customs that separate us from the apes—all these we owe to the hunters of time past." This argument, Slocum replied, put too much emphasis on aggressive behavior, the tools and organized planning required for hunting, the importance of fresh meat in the hominid diet, and male activities generally.

In "Woman the Gatherer: Male Bias in Anthropology," Slocum pointed out that gathering contributed more to group nutrition than hunting, as studies of modern hunter-gatherers showed. She also pointed out that tools usually linked to hunting might have been used for gathering instead, and she urged anthropologists to look afresh at the whole idea of tools:

> Bones, sticks, and hand-axes could be used for digging up tubers or roots, or to pulverize tough vegetable matter for easier eating. If, however, instead of thinking in terms of tools and weapons, we think in terms of cultural inventions, a new aspect is presented. I suggest that two of the earliest and most important cultural inventions were containers to hold the products of gathering, and some sort of sling or net to carry babies.

Further, Slocum argued, the skills of raising and nurturing young children, usually women's tasks, evoked more innovation and perhaps more development of the brain than did hunting:

I suggest that longer periods of infant dependency, more difficult births, and longer gestation periods also demanded more skills in social organization and communication—creating selective pressure for increased brain size without looking to hunting as an explanation. The need to organize for feeding after weaning, learning to handle the more complex social-emotional bonds that were developing, the new skills and cultural inventions surrounding more extensive gathering—all would demand larger brains. Too much attention has been given to the skills required by hunting, and too little to the skills required for gathering and the raising of dependent young.

Slocum concluded that anthropologists needed to confront their own assumptions about male dominance. As she put it, "The basis of any discipline is not the answers it gets, but the questions it asks."

- Sally Slocum suggests that our historical searches are determined by the questions we ask. Are there questions about the paleoanthropological record that you want to ask that have not been addressed thus far? Can you suggest methods to find answers to these questions?
- Sally Slocum wrote of "Male Bias in Anthropology." Do you think that the different experiences of men and women influence the questions they ask in historical time as well as in prehistory? Give examples. Keep this list at hand as you read this book to determine whether you seem to be correct.
- How do the resources available for answering questions—such as stone tools as compared with fibers and cloths, or tools for hunting compared with tools for child-raising—determine the agendas for scholarly research?

1.1

1.2

1.3

What do cultural creations tell us about the lives of early humans?

might well have required, as they often do today, choosing a mate from outside the immediate band. For such an exogamous, or external, marriage pattern to function, a tribe would theoretically require at least 19 bands of 25 members each, a total of 475 people, a figure reasonably close to the 500 found in modern hunter-gatherer societies.

How much territory did such bands require to support themselves? Anthropologists have calculated that an individual using the technology of Upper Paleolithic times (150,000–12,000 years ago) would have required 77 square miles of relatively unproductive land or 7–8 square miles of fertile land to meet survival needs. At such densities, the area of the United States (excluding Alaska and Hawaii) might have supported a maximum of 600,000 people; and the entire world ten million at most, although actual populations were less. As populations grew, bands began to stake out their own territories and to mark out boundaries. They began to work out formal relationships with the occupants of neighboring areas.

Groups began to establish small settlements. The Neanderthals had occupied upland sites, but the later Cro-Magnons (named for the region in France where this subspecies was originally discovered) moved down into the more valuable valleys and riverbeds. About half their sites are within 1,100 yards of a river, and all are near fords or shallows. These sites not only allow easy crossing, but also are at the points of animal crossings and therefore good for hunting. Tools took on regional patterns both in processes of manufacture and in styles of aesthetic appearance. These local patterns differentiated each group from its neighbors. Each group may have begun to develop a language, or a dialect, of its own.

Changes in the Toolkit

Even as the pace of exploration, migration, and trade increased, the clearest changes in human development appeared in our stone toolkits. The steady improvements in tool technology give this period its archaeological names. The entire period is called the Paleolithic or Old Stone Age. Tools show a slow progression from the Lower Paleolithic, ending about 150,000 years ago, to the Upper Paleolithic, which continued to about 10,000 B.C.E.

From about 2.5 million years ago until about 150,000 years ago, the dominant technology of *Homo erectus* had been Acheulian hand-held axes and cleavers made of stone (named for St. Acheul in northern France, but actually developed first in Africa and only later throughout Europe and Asia). Some sites from about 250,000 years ago reveal a more sophisticated technique, the Levallois (named for a suburb in Paris where the first examples were discovered). The Levallois technique produced more precise tools, including side-scrapers and backed knives, fashioned by more consistent patterns of preparing flakes from the stone, and a more standardized final shape and size. This technique marked the emergence of archaic *Homo sapiens*.

The technology of *Homo sapiens sapiens* developed much more rapidly. By about 40,000 years ago, Aurignacian tools were being produced in or near a cave close to the present-day village of Aurignac in the Pyrenees. This technology included narrow blades of stone as well as tools crafted from bone, ivory, and antler. Four additional styles followed, each named for the region in France in which it was discovered. Gravettian styles appear about 30,000 to about 20,000 years ago. Then came Solutrean styles, 20,000–17,000 years ago, which included the production of the first known needles. Magdalenian tools, about 17,000–12,000 years ago, included barbed harpoons carved from antlers. Finally, Azilian tools, 12,000–8000 B.C.E. (from the border between France and Spain), completed the Paleolithic sequence. Each location and time period had its own aesthetic style, and each produced an increasing variety of tools. Tool patterns began to differ from one region to another, suggesting the formation of new communities among small hunter-gatherer bands, and a greater sense of separation and distinction between groups.

What do cultural creations tell us about the lives of early humans?

Not all tools were directly related to food production, nor even to work. As early as 35,000 B.P., flutes made from the bones of birds, reindeer, and bears suggest that creating and performing instrumental music had already become part of the human repertoire. Aesthetics and play already had their roles.

The tools we have found represent only a small fraction of the daily objects that early humans probably made and used. Tools made of stone have endured; those of wood have not. Those made from natural fibers have, of course, disintegrated, which means we know little about clothing or basketry or food preparation. In most hunter-gatherer societies, making clothing and preparing food are usually women's work. So a whole area of technological development, most likely in the hands of women, was long overlooked through the focus on stone tools.

Language, Music, and Communication

Language is an intangible innovation, invisible in the archaeological record. It must be inferred from more solid evidence: global migration, fixed settlement sites, new tools and new materials, regional differences in production, trade across long distances, social hierarchies often marked by personal adornment and ritual burials, and the creation of art and instrumental music. Many of these activities would have been difficult, if not impossible, without some kind of language.

Exactly when a system of spoken language emerged is much debated, especially because we can only infer the answer. The craniums of archaic *Homo sapiens* were as large as, or even larger than, our own, and they seem to have indentations indicating

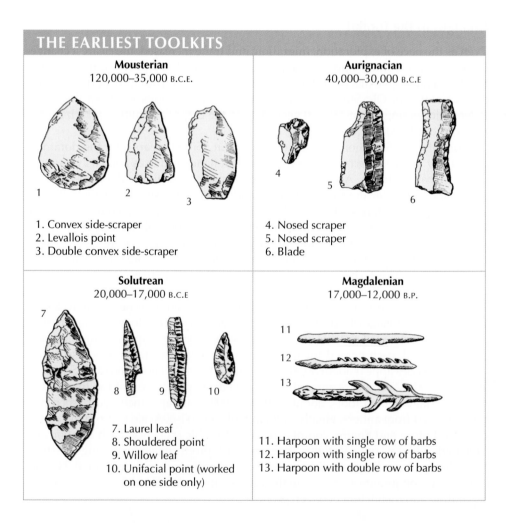

THE EARLIEST TOOLKITS

Mousterian
120,000–35,000 B.C.E.

1. Convex side-scraper
2. Levallois point
3. Double convex side-scraper

Aurignacian
40,000–30,000 B.C.E

4. Nosed scraper
5. Nosed scraper
6. Blade

Solutrean
20,000–17,000 B.C.E

7. Laurel leaf
8. Shouldered point
9. Willow leaf
10. Unifacial point (worked on one side only)

Magdalenian
17,000–12,000 B.P.

11. Harpoon with single row of barbs
12. Harpoon with single row of barbs
13. Harpoon with double row of barbs

Early tools. Many of the earliest human tools were crafted from stone and show increasing sophistication. The "toolkits" shown here are named for the four different locations in which they were found. At first, humans simply chipped away at stone until edges and points were exposed. Later, they began to carve the stone to meet more specific needs. The development took 100,000 years.

1.1

1.2

1.3

What do cultural creations tell us about the lives of early humans?

Bone flute, found in the Dordogne, France, *c.* 35,000 B.P. Simple wind instruments like this 4½-inch-long flute were made from the hollowed-out bones of birds, reindeer, and bears. They date back to as long ago as 35,000 B.P. (British Museum, London). To hear a 9,000-year-old flute from China actually played, go to: http://www.bnl.gov/bnlweb/pubaf/pr/1999/bnlpr092299.html.

(a)

(c)

(d)

(e)

(b)

(f)

Tools and artifacts, Western Europe, 30,000–18,000 B.P. (a) Bone used to make needle blanks; (b) Bone needle; (c & d) Harpoon head and barbed point carved from antler; (e & f) Two heads carved in mammoth ivory. (Natural History Museum, London)

Spearthrower, Montastruc, France, 12,000 B.C.E. More than 14,000 years ago, beauty was an integral part of purely functional objects. Spearthrowers allowed hunters to propel their missiles with a surer aim and added leverage, as is symbolized by the streamlined and powerful figure of this leaping horse. Did the shape of the bone suggest the animal, or did the artist search for a bone to match his (or her) preconceived idea?

1.1

1.2

1.3   What do cultural
      creations tell us
      about the lives of
      early humans?

the presence of areas in the brain that influence speech capacity. Archaic *Homo sapiens* probably possessed a larynx that had descended sufficiently low in the throat to produce the sounds of modern human language.

The dispute arises here. Some anthropologists believe that with this biological equipment, humans began to develop modern language and speech slowly, through cultural evolution. Others, notably the linguist Noam Chomsky (b. 1928), believe that a change took place within the organization of the brain that gave humans a new capacity for language. Chomsky draws his conclusion from analyzing similarities in the "deep structure" of languages around the world. These universal similarities suggest that the rules of syntax of human language are embedded in the brain. Chomsky argues that just as humans are born to walk, so they are born to talk. Bipedalism is not a learned cultural capacity, but has evolved biologically; talking, too, is not culturally learned but has biologically evolved. (The use of individual languages is, of course, culturally specific.) The archaeologist Steven Mithen goes farther, and argues that before there was language, there was music and rhythm, also "hardwired' into the genus *Homo* as a natural means of expressing emotion. Speech, including the ability to express thoughts, evolved, in part, from this capacity to express and experience musical sound. There is, unfortunately, no way to provide evidence for this engaging and persuasive theory.

However language emerged, the sophisticated psychological and social relationships that make us human became possible only with its development. Modern language allowed the emergence of increasingly elaborate social structures and greater complexity in human relationships. With language, humans could become more introspective as well as more communicative with others, deliberating over increasingly sophisticated thoughts and reflections.

Cave Art and Portable Art

Cave paintings and portable art suggest both individual creativity and group process. They may represent the sharing of information, hope, and feelings, and serve as a means of transmitting them to subsequent generations. Finds of artwork from before 35,000 B.P., such as beads, pendants, and incised animal bones, are rare, and the purpose of such items is disputed. Cave paintings and statuettes dating from as early as 40,000 years ago have been found in sites around the world. At Kundusi, Tanzania, Mary Leakey discovered stylized ocher paintings of human beings dating back perhaps 25,000 years. On the southern coast of Australia, in the Koonalda Cave, a flint mine at least 20,000 years old, a crisscross of abstract finger patterns was engraved into the soft limestone. In eastern Australia at about the same time, people stenciled images of a hand and a pipe and stem onto the walls of Kenniff Cave. And at Kakadu, in northern Australia, a series of rock paintings was begun about 20,000 B.P. Local peoples continued to paint new ones almost to the present.

More than 200 decorated caves and more than 10,000 decorated objects (portable art) have been discovered in Europe, 85 percent of them in southern France and northern Spain. Many of the tools from the Magdalenian period (17,000–12,000 B.P.), as noted above, were fashioned to be beautiful as well as practical. Many of the figurines include delicately carved features, such as the face and hair on the figurine from about 22,000 B.P. discovered at Brassempouy, France, and only about 1½ inches high (illustrated on the previous page). Many others pay scant attention to face and personal features, but accentuate and exaggerate sexual organs and buttocks, such as the 25,000-year-old figurine discovered at Dolní Vestonice, Moravia. The portable art represents a desire to create and enjoy beautiful objects. The exaggerated forms of the female "Venus" objects that appear throughout Europe and in northwestern Asia suggest also a desire for human fertility.

The first of the cave art was rediscovered only in 1868, at Altamira, Spain. It was not recognized as prehistoric until 1902, but now we recognize that the simplest of

1.1

1.2

1.3

What do cultural
creations tell us
about the lives of
early humans?

the paintings—red disks, lines, dots—date back 40,000 years. They probably evolved from an artistic tradition 10,000 years older than that. We do not know if the tradition began in Africa and was brought to Europe, or if it originated in Europe, shortly after the first humans arrived. By now, 200 caves decorated with artworks have been discovered in Europe, most of them in the river valleys of southwest France and the adjacent Pyrenees and the Cantabrian Mountains of northern Spain. The most recent discoveries, stunning in the variety of animal life depicted and the artistry employed, include the Cosquer Cave in 1991 and the Chauvet Cave in 1994, both in southern France.

The painters used natural pigments, such as ocher, that produced reds, browns, and yellows, and manganese oxides that made black and violet. (So far, blues and greens have not been found.) Over time, the subject matter—which began as simple abstract forms—became more figurative. The depiction of humans is rare in the European caves. The usual representations are of large animals, such as bison, deer, wild oxen, and horses. Occasionally there are mammoths, lions, and fish, as well as fantasy figures, such as unicorns. Clay sculptures of bison have been found at caves such as Le Tuc d'Audoubert, France. In many caves, the outlines of human hands have been stenciled onto the walls by projecting pigment around the hands. No one knows how the pigments were applied, but the most common guess is that they were chewed and then either spat directly or blown through a pipe onto the walls.

Some of the cave art was abstract, some representational, some painted, some in relief. This rich artistic tradition did not continue past the Magdalenian period, about 12,000 B.P. Many of the techniques of the cave paintings, such as perspective and the feeling of movement, did not reappear in Western art until the Renaissance, about 1400 C.E.

Clay bison, from Le Tuc d'Audoubert, Ariège, France, after 15,000 B.C.E. Most cave art owes its survival to the very particular atmospheric conditions formed in the limestone caves in which it was sealed thousands of years ago. Only a very small number of sculptures have survived. The one reproduced here—in high relief—shows a female being pursued by a male bison.

"Venus" figurine, found at Dolní Vestonice, Moravia, c. 23,000 B.P. Several hundred early female figures have been recovered, but no male figures. This seems to support the thesis that these statuettes were created not so much as representations of ideal feminine beauty, but as fertility charms Notice how the breasts, buttocks, and thighs are emphasized to the exclusion of any individualizing facial traits. (Moravian Museum, Brno)

📖 Read the Document: Early Art: Religion and Worship? (25,000 BCE) on MyHistoryLab

1.1

1.2

1.3 What do cultural creations tell us about the lives of early humans?

Ever since the cave art was rediscovered, people have wondered about its function and meaning. The first interpretation to gain widespread acceptance argued that the paintings represented a kind of magic designed to bring good fortune to the hunters of the animals represented on the cave walls. The seemingly abstract geometrical patterns, some said, represented hunting equipment, such as traps, snares, and weapons. The mural paintings of animals may represent a hope for their fertility so that the hunters might find abundant prey. Another interpretation suggested that the caves were meeting grounds to which neighboring bands of people returned each year to arrange marriages and to cement political and social alliances. The different styles of painting in each cave represent the artistic production of many different groups.

The art is often located not at the mouth of the cave, where it would have been in daily view of the campsites, but deep in the inner recesses. Why were so many images—about one-third of the total—painted so deep inside the caves? Some scholars of prehistoric art have suggested that they were not simply decorative, but were links to ancient spirits, which were remembered and invoked in the dark depths of the cave through shamanistic rituals. Among the San people of the Kalahari Desert, **shamans** are thought to communicate with spirits by means of trances induced through the use of drugs, breathing exercises, singing, dancing, and rhythmic clapping. They enter into trance states of increasing intensity in which they "see" first geometric patterns, then images from nature, and finally creatures not found in nature at all. Sometimes they see these various images as projections on the wall. Supporters of this theory believe that the Upper Paleolithic cave paintings represent such shamanistic hallucinations or visions from trance states.

The cave art and portable art of 25,000–10,000 B.P. begin the known record of human aesthetic creation. For the first time we have examples of what humans regarded as beautiful and therefore worth creating and preserving. From this time onward, the desire to create and appreciate beauty is part of the human story. The cave creations also give us insight into their creators' search for meaning and purpose in life. Our art gives outward expression to our understanding of, and our deepest feelings about, our place in the world. In our art we express our fears and our hopes for ourselves, our loved ones, our communities, our world. Through our art we attempt to connect with larger forces in the world and to communicate with one another. By studying the form and meaning of ancient art, historians attempt to understand the external aesthetics and the inner world of the people who produced it.

Agriculture: From Hunter-gatherer to Farmer

Some hunter-gatherers began to stay for longer periods at their temporary campsites. They noted the patterns of growth of the wild grains they gathered and the migration habits of the animals they hunted. They began to experiment with planting the seeds of the largest, most nutritious cereals in the Middle East and Europe, maize in the Americas, and root crops in Southeast Asia. In addition to pursuing animals as prey, people may have tried to restrict their movements to particular locations, or hunters may have built their own campsites at points frequented by the animals, adjusting human movements to those of the animals. They learned to domesticate dogs, and domesticated dogs may have accompanied the first Americans on their travels across Beringia (the land bridge between easternmost Asia and westernmost North America, today the Bering Strait). In the Middle East, the sheep was the first species to be domesticated, perhaps 10,000 years ago.

Chauvet Cave, Rhône-Alpes region, France, 18,000 B.C.E. On Christmas Day 1994, a team of archaeologists led by Jean-Marie Chauvet discovered a cave 1,640 feet deep in the Ardèche River Canyon. The cave's 300-plus Paleolithic wall paintings of horses, buffalo, and lions are the earliest known examples anywhere in the world.

📖 Read the Document: A Need to Remember (13,000 BCE) on MyHistoryLab

1.1

1.2

1.3

What do cultural creations tell us about the lives of early humans?

By 15,000–10,000 B.C.E., humans had the biological and cultural capacity to farm and raise animals. But first they had to want to do so. Otherwise why give up hunting and gathering? Why settle down? Perhaps the transformation took place at sites with especially valuable and accessible natural resources, such as the fishing sites of the Jomon people of Japan, or the quarries of obsidian stone, used for making sharp cutting tools, around Çatal Hüyük in modern Turkey. A permanent source of food to eat or materials to trade might have outweighed the desire to shift with the seasons and travel with the herds.

Perhaps rising population pressures left no alternative. The press of neighbors may have restricted scope for travel. On limited land, hunter-gatherers would have found that planting their own crops and domesticating their own animals could provide them with more food than hunting and gathering. Despite the risks of weather and of plant and animal diseases that left agricultural settlements vulnerable, some groups began to settle. Ten thousand years ago, almost all humans lived by hunting and gathering. Two thousand years ago, most were farmers or herders. This transformation created not only the first agricultural villages, but also cities. Cities grew up as the central administrative, economic, and religious centers of their regions. A new era was beginning. It is the subject of the next chapter and Part Two.

📖 Read the Document: From Hunter-gatherers to Food-producers—Overcoming Obstacles on MyHistoryLab

KEY TERM

shaman In the religious beliefs of some African, Asian, and American tribal societies, a person capable of entering into trances and believed to be endowed with supernatural powers, with the ability to cure the sick, find lost or stolen property, predict the future, and protect the community from evil spirits. A shaman may act as judge or ruler, and, as a priest, a shaman directs communal sacrifices and escorts the souls of the dead to the next world.

The Story of Prehistory: *What Difference Does It Make?*

The materials of this chapter, which are largely based on the research of paleoanthropologists, make us aware of different ways of knowing and their different kinds of usefulness. They lead us to be open-minded, yet skeptical, for example, of the uses of creation stories as a way of explaining the significance of human life, and to note that different myths and stories encourage different behaviors. Myths that are widely accepted within a society are not merely quaint stories; they are powerful explanatory messages that speak deeply to people's understanding of the world.

Similarly, these materials lead us to be open-minded, yet skeptical, of the powers of science to explain the world. Scientific research does not exist in a vacuum, but responds to the questions we ask. The process of evolution was not immediately evident until scientists began asking the right questions; the role of women in cultural evolution was not considered until feminist researchers began asking questions that had not been asked before; Africa as a location for the earliest hominids and humans was ignored until racial prejudices were put aside. Scientific enquiry is an enormously powerful tool in unlocking the mysteries of the world, but it addresses only those questions that we ask.

We have also learned to distinguish between "ordinary" science, which builds on what is already known and accepted, and revolutionary science, which puzzles over new information and anomalies, elements that do not fit into already existing patterns, until it may create "paradigm shifts," new ways of understanding the world.

We have seen that from the very earliest times human behavior has been characterized by migration; the creation of tools; the formation of ever-larger groups, which nevertheless apparently create distinctions between members and "others"; communication through language; self-expression through art; and oscillation between accepting nature as it is and trying to control it. These are the principal legacies of the earliest hominids and humans, and they are the record of our success in finding methods of understanding our world more clearly through historiography and through paleoanthropology.

CHAPTER REVIEW

HUMAN ORIGINS IN MYTH AND HISTORY

1.1 How do myths explain the origins of human beings on the earth?

Each culture has its own myths and creation stories that it passes down from generation to generation. Such narratives tell us a great deal about the values of the culture that created them.

FOSSILS AND FOSSIL-HUNTERS

1.2 What do we know about the evolution of human beings?

Beginning in the mid-1800s, fossil-hunters sought a "missing link" between human beings and apes. Today, DNA analysis demonstrates a wide variety of evolutionary paths that led to the emergence of human beings. Evolutionary biologists join paleoanthropologists in studying the relationship between humans, Neanderthals, chimpanzees, and apes.

HUMANS CREATE CULTURE

1.3 What do cultural creations tell us about the lives of early humans?

From the earliest times, humans have migrated from place to place, crafted tools, organized into groups, communicated through language, and expressed themselves in art. Today we examine their creations to understand how they survived, flourished, and understood their place in the universe.

Suggested Readings

PRINCIPAL SOURCES

Adas, Michael, ed. *Agricultural and Pastoral Societies in Ancient and Classical History* (Philadelphia: Temple University Press, 2001). Ten diverse, expert, readable essays provide invaluable guides to relatively recent research.

Barber, Elizabeth Wayland. *Women's Work: The First 20,000 Years: Women, Cloth, and Society in Early Times* (New York: W.W. Norton & Co., 1994). Fascinating account of the earliest known production of cloth, and women's role in producing it.

Charlesworth, Brian and Deborah. *Evolution: A Very Short Introduction* (New York: Oxford University Press, 2003). Excellent. Covers theories, fossils, and DNA.

Darwin, Charles. *Darwin*, ed. Philip Appleman (New York: W.W. Norton & Co., 2nd ed., 1979). Excellent anthology of works by and about Darwin.

Fagan, Brian M. *People of the Earth* (Upper Saddle River, NJ: Prentice Hall, 13th ed., 2010). Outstanding textbook introduction to prehistoric human life around the globe.

Johanson, Donald, Lenora Johanson, and Blake Edgar. *Ancestors: In Search of Human Origins* (New York: Villard Books, 1994). An account of the work of one of the greatest paleoanthropologists, and of its significance.

Leakey, Richard, and Roger Lewin. *Origins Reconsidered* (New York: Doubleday, 1992). A great paleoanthropologist, continuing and expanding the accomplishments of his even more famous parents, presents his account of the fossil record of evolution.

Lewin, Roger. *The Origin of Modern Humans* (New York: Scientific American Library, 1993). Remarkably lucid presentation of the story of evolution and early humans.

Mithen, Steven. *After the Ice: A Global Human History, 20,000–5000 B.C.* (Cambridge: Harvard University Press, 2004). A global tour emphasizing patterns of living, with special emphasis on the effects of climate.

Past Worlds: The (London) Times Atlas of Archaeology (London: Times Books Ltd., 1988). Text, maps, pictures are all superb on all aspects of archaeological understanding and accomplishment.

Renfrew, Colin. *The Making of the Human Mind* (New York: Modern Library, 2007). A scholarly review of archaeological and anthropological studies of early *Homo sapiens*, especially on the evolution of the mind.

Stringer, Chris, and Peter Andrews. *The Complete World of Human Evolution* (London: Thames and Hudson, 2nd ed., 2012). Brief, clear, concise, authoritative account of human evolution, beautifully illustrated, presented in neatly packaged, readable, discrete topical sections.

Tattersall, Ian. *The World from Beginnings to 4000 B.C.E.* (New York: Oxford University Press, 2008). Brief, clear, concise, authoritative account from the genetic and fossil study of earliest humans through the beginning of agriculture.

——. *Masters of the Planet: The Search for Our Human Origins* (New York: Palgrave Macmillan, 2012). Emphasizes more recent discoveries and lays out the framework for understanding the theory of a "bush" of human ancestors rather than a linear progression.

ADDITIONAL SOURCES

Brown, Judith. "Note on the Division of Labor by Sex," *American Anthropologist* LXXII (1970), pp. 1075–76. Argues that, historically, women's work has been compatible with child-care responsibilities.

Chauvet, Jean-Marie, Eliette Brunel Deschamps, and Christian Hillaire. *Dawn of Art: The Chauvet Cave, the Oldest Known Paintings in the World* (New York: Abrams, 1996). Gorgeous presentation of this recently discovered cave art.

Darwin, Charles. *The Origin of Species by Means of Natural Selection or the Preservation of Favored Races in the Struggle for Life*, reprinted from the Sixth Edition, ed. Edmund B. Wilson (New York: Macmillan, 1927). The classic, revolutionary work.

——. *On the Origin of Species 1859* (New York: New York University Press, 1988). The first edition, without mention of "the Creator."

Dawkins, Richard. *The Selfish Gene* (New York: Oxford University Press, 30th anniversary edition, 2006). Classic work identifying genes as the units "selected" by nature to survive and reproduce.

Fedigan, Linda. "The Changing Role of Women in Models of Human Evolution," *Annual Review of Anthropology* XV (1986), pp. 22–66. Comprehensive introduction to feminist perspectives on evolution.

Gamble, Clive. *Timewalkers: The Prehistory of Global Colonization* (Cambridge, MA: Harvard University Press, 1994). Ponders the migrations of humans from earliest times to all corners of the earth.

Gould, Stephen Jay. *The Structure of Evolutionary Theory* (Cambridge, MA: Harvard University Press, 2002). A comprehensive summary of all that we know of evolution today, by a master scholar-writer, published just months before his death.

Holm, Jean, with John Bowker, eds. *Myth and History* (London: Pinter Publishers, 1994). Analysis of the functions of myth and of history in human understanding.

Kuhn, Thomas S. *The Structure of Scientific Revolutions* (Chicago, IL: University of Chicago Press, 1970).

Lewis-Williams, David. *The Mind in the Cave: Consciousness and the Origins of Art* (London: Thames and Hudson, 2002). Argues that in prehistoric caves "image-making," religion, and social discriminations were a "package deal," as humans realized a new capability for higher-order thought.

Lewontin, Richard. *It Ain't Necessarily So: The Dream of the Human Genome and Other Illusions* (New York: New York Review of Books, 2000). Social nurture is more important than genetic nature argues this leading evolutionary biologist.

Linton, Sally (pseud. for Sally Slocum). "Woman the Gatherer: Male Bias in Anthropology," in Sue-Ellen Jacobs, ed., *Women in Perspective: A Guide for Cross-Cultural Studies* (Urbana, IL: University of Illinois Press, 1971). Asking new questions from a feminist perspective, Linton demonstrates a much enhanced role of women in early cultural evolution.

McNeill, William H. *Mythistory and Other Essays* (Chicago, IL: University of Chicago Press, 1986). A master historian discusses the difference between myth and the professional study of history, and how the two perspectives intersect in the public mind.

Mithen, Steven. *The Singing Neanderthals: The Origins of Music, Language, Mind and Body* (Cambridge, MA: Harvard University Press, 2006). Differentiates between the evolution of the emotional, musical capacities of humans, and of our linguistic, informational abilities.

Nature. Interdisciplinary scientific journal related to biological concerns. Volume 418 (2002) contained numerous articles on the discovery of Toumai, and reprinted several classic articles on earlier archaeological discoveries, from Dart's in 1925 to the present.

The New English Bible (New York: Oxford University Press, 1976). For clarity and simple, basic annotation, my favorite edition.

Pfeiffer, John. *The Creative Explosion* (Ithaca, NY: Cornell University Press, 1982). Argues for a dramatic leap in human intellectual and artistic capacities about 35,000 years ago in Europe. Very well written. Now more controversial than ever.

Scott, Joan W. "Gender: A Useful Category of Historical Analysis," *American Historical Review* XCI (1986), pp. 1053–76. A classic article in helping to bring feminist perspectives into mainstream historical research.

Stearns, Peter. *Sexuality in World History* (New York: Routledge, 2009). The understanding and regulation of sexuality in various societies around the world through time.

Wilson, E.O. *Sociobiology* (Cambridge, MA: Harvard University Press, 25th anniversary edition, 2000). Classic presentation of the importance of genetic inheritance in human behavior.

FILMS

Video on molecular evolution by Prof. Robert Weinberg of MIT (2004; 50 minutes) http://ocw.mit.edu/courses/biology/7-012-introduction-to-biology-fall-2004/video-lectures/lecture-32-molecular-evolution

Video on the ethics of using genetics to determine the future of individuals by Prof. Robert Weinberg of MIT (2004;50 minutes) http://ocw.mit.edu/courses/biology/7-012-introduction-to-biology-fall-2004/video-lectures/lecture-35-human-polymorphisms-and-cancer-classification

TURNING POINT: SETTLEMENT PATTERNS

10,000 B.C.E.–1000 C.E.

Settling Down: Villages and Cities

As human populations grew, hunting and gathering alone could not produce enough to feed them all. People had to travel ever greater distances, which brought them into direct conflict with their neighbors—who were also hard pushed to hunt and gather adequate food and were also expanding in number. Settled agriculture was the solution. Careful attention to plant and animal patterns on the part of hunter-gatherers had already set the stage.

The Agricultural Village

As they settled down, humans began to domesticate not only food crops but also animals, which served for food, for power and energy in carrying goods and pulling plows, and for products such as milk, wool, fur, and leather. Village dwellers produced tools that were increasingly sophisticated in usefulness and aesthetic beauty. Some of these tools were made of organic materials, such as bone and fiber, but many were made of stone. Villagers became skilled at grinding and polishing the stone tools, and this new era is called the Neolithic or New Stone Age.

Settled agriculture began about 12,000 years ago in the Fertile Crescent—that is, Mesopotamia, the valley between the Tigris and Euphrates rivers—and in the Nile valley. However, one of the best preserved early villages was discovered in China at Banpo, near Xi'an. The residents of Banpo cultivated millet and domesticated pigs and dogs. They practiced slash-and-burn agriculture, and pollen samples show distinct alternating periods of cultivation and fallow.

Farming in China, c. 5000 B.C.E. Evidence of the earliest established agriculture in East Asia is found in the arid but fertile regions of north central China, along the central reaches of the Huang He (Yellow River). Villages such as Banpo grew up on the flood plain, rich in alluvial and loess deposits, where drought-resistant plants such as millet could be cultivated. (Xi'an and Luoyang are included for placement purposes.)

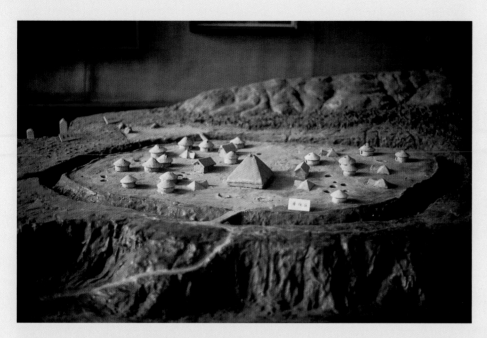

Model reconstruction of Banpo. The Banpo site has been made into a museum open to the public. Visitors can walk on special paths through the ancient ruins. This on-site model provides an archaeological reconstruction of what the entire village looked like in its time.

Agriculture was the basis of most early villages, but there were exceptions. In southern Japan, the Jomon people supported themselves by fishing and hunting deer and wild boar with bows and arrows, and by gathering and storing acorns, nuts, and seeds. Some of the Jomon lived in caves, but others built villages with individual pit-houses and central, communal buildings. They may have also cultivated root crops and cereals, but they were not primarily agricultural. They created stone tools but they are most famous for their distinctive pottery, some of the world's earliest and most beautiful, dating to as early as 10,500 B.C.E. It was made by forming clay into cords and wrapping the cords by hand into pots. Their pots were both functional and artistic (see image of a Jomon vase in the chapter entitled "From Village Community to City-state").

Another non-agricultural development in villages occurred in eastern Anatolia (modern Turkey), on the shores of Lake Van. The presence of volcanic obsidian stone gave

The most ancient layers of the excavation, which date to about 6000 B.C.E., give a clear idea of the physical form of an early agricultural village.

Immediately adjacent to the excavation, archaeologists have reconstructed a model of the entire prehistoric village. It represents Banpo's three housing styles: square, round, and an oblong, split level, part underground and part above. Banpo villagers stored their grain in some 200 underground pits, which were dug throughout the village. A moat surrounds the entire residential settlement.

North of the village was a pottery production center with six kilns, and next to them was a public cemetery where some 250 graves have been excavated. The bodies of children were placed in urns and buried in the main residential area. Archaeologists do not know why adults and children were buried separately.

In the center of the settlement was a large square building. What was its function? Presumably it had political and social significance for the entire village. Was it a ruler's palace? A priest's shrine? A place for the Banpo inhabitants to discuss public affairs? We do not know.

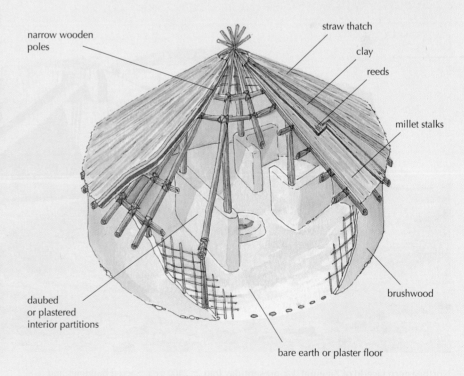

narrow wooden poles

straw thatch

clay

reeds

millet stalks

daubed or plastered interior partitions

brushwood

bare earth or plaster floor

Typical Banpo dwelling. Three forms of residence have been reconstructed at Banpo—round, square, and oblong with part underground. Here, archaeologists provide an illustration of the round form.

Obsidian blades, Çatal Hüyük, c. 3000 B.C.E. Çatal Hüyük carried on trade in these obsidian tools, exchanging them with villages near and far for food and agricultural commodities. It was taking on the commercial characteristics of a small town.

Northeastern façade of Ziggurat, Ur, present-day Iraq, c. 2100 B.C.E. Sacred buildings and temples dominated the center of Ur and this three-story-high ziggurat was the most famous of them. Each major Mesopotamian city had a ziggurat dedicated to its deity. Ur's was dedicated to Nanna, the moon God.

villagers a substance they could craft into blades of extraordinary sharpness, which they used themselves and also traded to villages hundreds of miles away on the eastern shores of the Mediterranean and the Persian Gulf. For most of these Anatolian villages, the trade in obsidian was complementary to agriculture. But one site, Çatal Hüyük, grew into a 32-acre town, with an economy based on the manufacture and trade of obsidian tools. Çatal Hüyük stands out as a new kind of settlement, one that combined agriculture with industry and trade. It was a transitional form in the development of early cities.

The First Cities

The construction of cities, with impressive buildings and crowds of inhabitants, along with other, less tangible, developments, brought a revolution in human settlement patterns. Cities were nodes in the regional networks of exchange of goods and culture, and they encouraged the production of sophisticated arts, the specialization of labor, and the elaboration of a social hierarchy. Most significantly, cities signaled the emergence of a state organization for guiding and administering the city and its surrounding area. The new state, hand-in-glove with the new city, provided leadership, organization, and official control of armed power. It governed the people of the city, sometimes with their consent, often without it. The state enforced and helped to create the conditions of hierarchy that emerged among the people of the new cities. In all these characteristics, the ancient city reminds us of our own.

Unlike modern cities, however, almost all early cities were relatively small. The largest contained perhaps 100,000 people in eight square miles; most had only a few thousand inhabitants. Until the Industrial Revolution in the late nineteenth century, a few thousand people concentrated in 100 acres might have constituted a city, for cities held only a tiny percentage of the total population of any region.

Most of the world's population were farmers or hunter-gatherers when the first cities developed. The multiplication of cities and urban residents that we see today took place only after the Industrial Revolution created new urban factories, transportation hubs, and mass labor forces. Moreover, many of the early cities, although small, were centers of independent city-states; most cities today are single points in much larger national and even international networks. Finally, the earliest cities emerged in each of seven regions around the world. Mostly, they took root along the banks of great rivers, reflecting the importance of water, irrigation, and agriculture to their development. The world's earliest cities emerged between the Tigris and Euphrates rivers in what is now modern Iraq. They developed along the Nile River in Egypt and in the Indus valley of modern Pakistan. In China the earliest cities flourished in the flood plain of the Yellow River. Finally, early cities appeared in West Africa near the great bed of the Niger River. The Americas provide some exceptions, with the growth of great civilizations in the valleys and jungles of Mexico and on the heights of the Andes Mountains.

Many of these early cities were dedicated to gods and were built on the foundations of existing shrine centers. As the cities grew, the shrines grew with them, providing a more profound meaning to the lives of their inhabitants by linking their mundane existence to transcendent and powerful supernatural forces.

Evolution of maize. The steady evolution of maize, from the rather stunted cob of wild corn from the valley of Mexico (about 5000 B.C.E.) to the more productive and nutritious plant of about 1 B.C.E., reveals the benefits that came with the creation of agricultural villages.

Turning Point Questions

1. Why was the development of agriculture essential to the growth of the city?
2. What is the difference between a village and a city?
3. In what ways did settling down and abandoning nomadism change people's lives?
4. Cities brought together larger numbers of people in a relatively smaller geographic space than villages had. In addition, they marked the creation of political states. What was the significance of the new states to the way people lived?

2 From Village Community to City-state

Food First: The Agricultural Village

10,000 B.C.E.–750 B.C.E.

Until about 12,000 years ago humans hunted and gathered their food, following the migrations of animals and the seasonal cycles of the crops. They established temporary base camps for their activities, and caves served them for homes and meeting-places, but they had not established permanent settlements. They had begun to domesticate some animals, especially the dog and the sheep, but they had not yet begun the systematic practice of agriculture. Then, about 10,000 B.C.E., people began to settle down, constructing the first agricultural villages.

Sumerian ruins, Uruk, present-day Iraq, c. 2100 B.C.E. A man and child stand amid what is left of the ancient city of Uruk.

LEARNING OBJECTIVES

2.1 ((•	2.2 ((•	2.3 ((•	2.4 ((•
Describe the world's first villages.	Discuss the creation and contributions of the earliest cities.	Tell the story of the world's first urban revolution.	Distinguish between cities and villages in size and organization.

((• Listen on MyHistoryLab

Why did they do it? Is food production through agriculture easier than hunting and gathering? Surprisingly, the answer seems to be "no." Research suggests that, with the technology available at that time, adult farmers had to work an equivalent of 1,000–1,300 hours a year for their food, while hunter-gatherers needed only 800–1,000 hours. Moreover, agricultural work was more difficult.

Why did they change? An appealing, although unproved, answer is that increasing population pressure, perhaps accompanied by centuries of unfavorable climates, such as the droughts in Mesopotamia, forced people to take on the more productive methods of irrigated agriculture. Scientists estimate that even in a lush tropical environment, 0.4 square miles of land could support only nine people through hunting and gathering; under organized, sedentary agricultural techniques, the same area could support 200–400 people. In the less fertile subtropical and temperate climates into which the expanding populations were moving at the end of the last ice age, after about 13,000 B.C.E., hunting and gathering were even less productive. For humankind to survive, sedentary agriculture became a necessity.

The memory of this transition survives in myth. For example, the myth of Shen Nung, whom the ancient Chinese honored as the inventor of agriculture and its wooden tools (and of poetry), captures the transformation:

> The people of old ate the meat of animals and birds. But in the time of Shen Nung, there were so many people that there were no longer enough animals and birds to supply their needs. So it was that Shen Nung taught the people how to cultivate the earth. (Bairoch, p. 6)

In addition to increasing agricultural productivity, villages facilitated an increase in activities of all kinds. It may have taken longer to raise food than to hunt and gather it, but the sedentary farmers did not stop work when they had secured their food supply. In their villages they went on to create textiles, pottery, metallurgy,

AT A GLANCE: VILLAGE COMMUNITIES AND CITY-STATES

DATE	POLITICS	RELIGION AND CULTURE	SOCIAL DEVELOPMENT
4500 B.C.E.	• Ubaid people in Mesopotamia		
3500 B.C.E.	• Sumerians (3300–2350) • Ziggurats built	• Cuneiform writing • Sumerian pantheon	• Urbanization in Mesopotamia
3000 B.C.E.	• Hereditary kings emerge		• Invention of the wheel • Bronze casting • Sumerian city-states (2800–1850)
2500 B.C.E.	• Ur, First Dynasty (2500–2350) • Akkadian kingdoms (2350–2150); Sargon of Akkad (2334–2279) • Third Dynasty of Ur (c. 2112–2004)	• Akkadian language used in Sumer • *The Epic of Gilgamesh* (c. 2113–1991)	• Sumerian Laws
2000 B.C.E.	• Semitic rulers gain control of Mesopotamia • First dynasty of Babylon (c. 1894–1595) • Hammurabi (1792–1750) • Hittites in Asia Minor		• Mycenaean traders in Aegean 1800–1000 B.C.E. • Hammurabi's Code of Law
1500 B.C.E.	• Hittite Empire (c. 1460–1200)	• "Golden age" of Ugarit	
1000 B.C.E.	• Assyrian Empire (900–612)	• Hebrew Scriptures recorded	
750 B.C.E.	• Sargon II (d. 705) • Sennacherib (c. 705–681) • Ashurbanipal (d. 627) • Fall of Nineveh (imperial capital) (612) • Nebuchadnezzar (605–562)	• *Gilgamesh* (complete version) • Homer (*fl.* 8th century) • Hesiod (*fl.* 700)	
600 B.C.E.	• Neo–Babylonian Empire	• Library at Nineveh	
500 B.C.E.	• Persian Empire in control of Mesopotamia		

architecture, tools, and objects of great beauty, especially in sculpture and painting. Did agriculturists work harder than hunter-gatherers simply to survive under greater population pressure, or because they craved the added rewards of their extra labor, or both? We can never know for sure, but the agricultural village opened new possibilities for economic, social, political, and artistic creativity. The very act of domesticating plants and animals put humans in charge of directing evolution. The village changed forever humanity's concepts of life's necessities and potentials.

The Agricultural Village

2.1 What was life like in the world's first agricultural villages?

The first agricultural villages that archaeologists have discovered date to about 10,000 B.C.E. They are located in the "Fertile Crescent," which curves from the Persian Gulf and the Zagros Mountains in the east and south, on the border of today's Iraq and Iran, northwest into present-day Turkey, and then turns south and west through present-day Syria, Lebanon, and Israel on the Mediterranean Sea, and on into the Nile valley. In this region, wild grasses—the ancestors of modern wheat and barley—provided the basic grains, first for gathering, and later for cultivation. By 8000 B.C.E. the Natufians, named for their valley in northern Israel, and the peoples immediately to the south, in the Jordan River valley near Jericho, were growing fully domesticated cereals. Peas and lentils and other legumes followed. Irrigation enabled this agriculture. Villagers developed additional new skills: sewing, basket weaving, textile manufacture, pottery making. Some trade linked the villages, and small boats began to appear on the Nile, the Tigris, and the Euphrates by about 3500 B.C.E. There had already been some limited sea-borne trade in the Aegean Sea, off the coast of modern Greece, by 6000 B.C.E.

The peoples of the Fertile Crescent hunted gazelles and goats. Later, they domesticated the goat and the sheep. (Dogs were domesticated three millennia earlier, in several different regions of the world.) In Turkey they added pigs; around the Mediterranean, there were cattle. Life in settled villages, with domesticated animals living as neighbors, or even residing in villagers' homes, brought new problems of sanitation and hygiene. New diseases flourished, including smallpox, flu, measles, mumps, whooping cough, bubonic plague, malaria, yellow fever, tuberculosis, and rabies. Diseases became increasingly endemic as villages grew in size and density, and, later, as cities emerged. Nevertheless, birth rates were high and population continued to increase.

In other parts of the world, agriculture and animal domestication focused on other varieties. In the western hemisphere, these included maize, especially in Mesoamerica, and root crops such as manioc and sweet potatoes in South America. Amerindians domesticated the llama, the guinea pig, and the turkey. Domesticated dogs probably accompanied their migrant masters across the Bering Strait about 15,000 years ago. Perhaps the process of domestication was then repeated with the dogs found in the Americas.

In Southeast Asia and tropical Africa, wild roots and tubers, including yams, were the staple crops. In the Vindhya Mountain areas of central India, rice was among the first crops to be cultivated, about 5000 B.C.E. Anthropologists are uncertain when rice was first cultivated in Southeast and East Asia, rather than just being harvested from the wild, but a date similar to India's seems likely. From earliest times, as today, China's agriculture seems to have favored rice in the south and millet in the north. Some crops, including cotton and gourds, were brought under cultivation in many locations around the globe.

Our knowledge of early agriculture continues to grow as the archaeological record is expanded and revised. European sedentary agriculture, for example, which was

What was life like in the world's first agricultural villages?

2.1
2.2
2.3
2.4

once thought to have been borrowed from the Near East, may have been a local response to changing climate conditions.

The era in which villages took form is usually called **Neolithic**, or New Stone Age, named for its tools rather than its crops. Farming called for a different toolkit from hunting and gathering. For cutting, grinding, chopping, scraping, piercing, and digging, village artisans fashioned new tools from stone. Archaeological digs from Neolithic villages abound with blades, knives, sickles, adzes, arrows, daggers, spears, fish hooks and harpoons, mortars and pestles, and rudimentary plows and hoes.

As villages expanded their economic base, these stone tools became valued as items of trade. Obsidian—a kind of volcanic glass with very sharp edges—was traded from Anatolia and is found in hundreds of digs from central Turkey to Syria and the Jordan valley. Among other items of trade, recognized by their appearance in digs a long distance away from their point of origin, are seashells, jade, turquoise, and ceramics. Metallurgy in bronze formed one of the major technological accomplishments that would later usher in the transition from village to city. By 7000 B.C.E., craftsmen were working with raw copper in southeastern Turkey; three thousand years later, craftsmen with far more experience learned to smelt the copper with alloys and transform it into bronze.

Although ceramics occasionally appear among nomadic populations, the weight and fragility of clay make pottery essentially a creation of the established Neolithic village. As a vessel for storage, pottery further reflected the sedentary character of the new village life. The fine designs and colors decorating its pottery became the most distinctive identifying mark of the Neolithic village, and archaeologists often designate eras, locations, and groups of people by descriptions of their pottery—the "grayware," the "red glazed," or the "cord-marked," for example.

Simple pottery is easy to make and accessible to anyone, but specialized craftspeople developed ceramics into a medium of artistic creativity. Fine ceramic jewelry, statuary, and figurines attained great beauty and were frequently used in religious rituals.

Village life created and required several new social adaptations that paved the way for later urbanization. Increased size and stability of residence required more organizational leadership and brought about some degree of hierarchy, as leaders and followers sorted themselves out. The Natufians, for example, a people of the eastern Mediterranean, buried their dead in cemeteries with stone slab grave covers and mortar markers. Seashells and stone bowls found in some of the graves suggest an early hierarchical ranking system. Sedentary life also led to demarcating possessions, especially possessions of land. In place of the shared community responsibilities of the roaming bands of hunter-gatherers, newly settled villagers staked their claims on their own fields, and the idea of private property was born.

Family life also underwent a transformation. Settling down led to the development of more formalized family structures in both nuclear (father-mother-children) and extended families (including also grandparents, spouses of married children, and their children). Before the advent of writing, it is difficult to know how women were valued as compared to men, but most scholars now agree that women were decisive in the transition to agriculture in most regions:

> On the basis of anthropological evidence for societies still living traditional foraging lifestyles and those living by simple, non-mechanical farming, taken in conjunction with direct archaeological evidence, it seems probable that it was women who made the first observations of plant behavior, and worked out, presumably by long trial and error, how to grow and tend crops. (Ehrenberg, p. 78)

Women probably also had the major responsibility for cooking, carrying water, producing clothing—weaving is the most studied of their early arts—and, of course, most important of all, they gave birth to children and probably had the major responsibility for nurturing and raising them. Still, we do not know the degree to which agricultural,

KEY TERM

Neolithic "New Stone Age," the last division of the Stone Age, immediately preceding the development of metallurgy and corresponding to the ninth to fifth millennia B.C.E. It was characterized by the increasing domestication of animals and cultivation of crops, established agricultural communities, and the appearance of such crafts as pottery and weaving.

Jomon vase, Kanto province, Japan. Earthenware. Jomon pottery dates to as early as *c.* 10,000 B.C.E., making it (among) the oldest in the world. Jomon means "cord marking" because the village potter formed the work from the bottom, without the use of a wheel, adding coil upon coil of soft clay. (Musée Guimet, Paris)

village societies valued women as compared to men. As we shall see below, once societies became literate and urban—and we have written records—we find women valued less than men.

Some villages did form on an economic base of hunting and gathering. In southern Japan, for example, a non-agricultural village society appeared among the Jomon people along with some of the earliest and most beautiful pottery (see the introduction to Part Two). Jomon pottery, which is marked by distinctive cord lines, dates back to 10,500 B.C.E. and spread from the southern island of Kyushu northward through Honshu, reaching Hokkaido by 6500 B.C.E. The Jomon villagers supported themselves by fishing, hunting deer and wild boar, and gathering and storing nuts. They created stone tools and lived in caves and in pit-houses in settled villages with central, communal buildings. Yet the Japanese did not develop agricultural cultivation for another several thousand years. Similar villages without agricultural bases were established in a few other regions with similar availability of food supplies in nature. The native Americans of the Pacific coast, from today's California to Canada, found abundant fish; deer, elk, and bear; and berries, acorns, and hazelnuts. They ate well with no need for farming. Seafood from the Pacific also enabled the area of Norte Chico, not far from modern Lima, Peru, to establish villages without an agricultural base. In Denmark and southern Sweden, too, the sea provided adequate food, so while the people along these coasts did build villages, they did not begin farming until about 3200 B.C.E.

Read the **Document: A Visitor from the Neolithic Age: The Iceman (3300 BCE)** on **MyHistoryLab**

What was life like in the world's first agricultural villages?

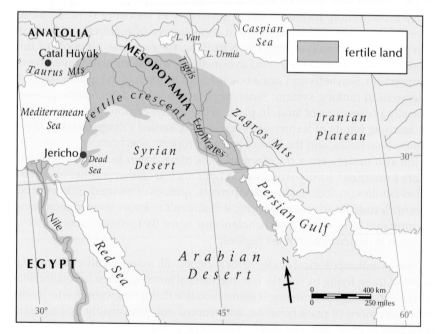

The Fertile Crescent. The Tigris and Euphrates rivers gave life to the first known agricultural villages, about 10,000 years ago, and the first known cities in human history, about 5000 years ago. Fertile land extended to the Mediterranean and some contact apparently continued to the Nile valley. Its borders were defined to the south by arid regions receiving less than 10 inches of rainfall per year, and to the north by mountains and semi-arid plateaux.

The origins of agriculture and domestic animals. The development of agriculture and the domestication of animals took place independently in different parts of the world, but the Near East, Mesoamerica, Southeast Asia, and China were among the first and most significant regions.

The First Cities

| 2.2 | In what way were cities new creations, different from villages? |

The first cities were constructed on the economic base of sedentary village agricultural communities. In excavating these earliest cities around the globe, archaeologists ask which city forms were invented indigenously, by their own inhabitants, and which were borrowed from earlier examples or, perhaps, imposed from outside on local rural populations. Technically, the question is one of **innovation** versus **diffusion**. Thus far, most experts agree that innovative primary urbanization, not borrowed or imposed from outside, occurred in seven places: five river valleys in the eastern hemisphere—Mesopotamia, the Nile, the Indus, the Huang He, and the Niger—and, in the western hemisphere, in Mexico and in the Andes Mountains. The birth of primary urbanization took place in these seven locations at very different times, with Mesopotamia the oldest, at about 3300 B.C.E., and the Niger the most recent, at about 400 C.E.

2.1
2.2
2.3
2.4

In what way were cities new creations, different from villages?

KEY TERMS

innovation The explanation that similar cultural traits, techniques, or objects found among different groups of people were invented independently rather than spread from one group to another.

diffusion The spread of ideas, objects, or traits from one culture to another.

2.1

2.2

2.3

2.4

In what way
were cities
new creations,
different from
villages?

Cities transform human life, as the physical form of the early cities shows vividly. Even today we can trace on the surface of the earth the 5,500-year-old designs of the first cities and the irrigation systems that supported them. Remnants of walls and fragments of monuments still rise from their sites. From under the surface archaeologists salvage artifacts: bricks; pottery; tools of wood, bone, stone, and metal; jewelry; and skeletons of citizens and slaves. The technology of the early cities included new means of transportation; we find the remains of wheeled vehicles and of sailboats. The earliest city dwellers advanced their skill in metallurgy, and products of their craftsmanship in copper, tin, and their alloys abound in the archaeological excavations. In recognition of these technological breakthroughs, we often call the era of the first cities the Bronze Age.

But cities are more than bricks and mortar, metal and artifacts. They require institutions for their larger scale of organization and administration. As society and economy became more complex, new class hierarchies emerged. Professional administrators, skilled artisans, long-distance traders, local merchants, and priests and kings enriched the diversity and sophistication of the growing cities. External relations with other cities required skilled negotiations, and a diplomatic corps emerged. Armies mobilized for defense and attack. In short, with the growth of the city the early state was also born, with its specialized organization, centralized rule, and powerful armies.

To keep track of business transactions and administrative orders, the proclamations of rulers and the rituals of priests, the legends of gods and the history of the city, new methods of record-keeping were developed. At first these were tokens, pictures, seals, personalized markings, and, in the Andes, *quipu*, knots made in special

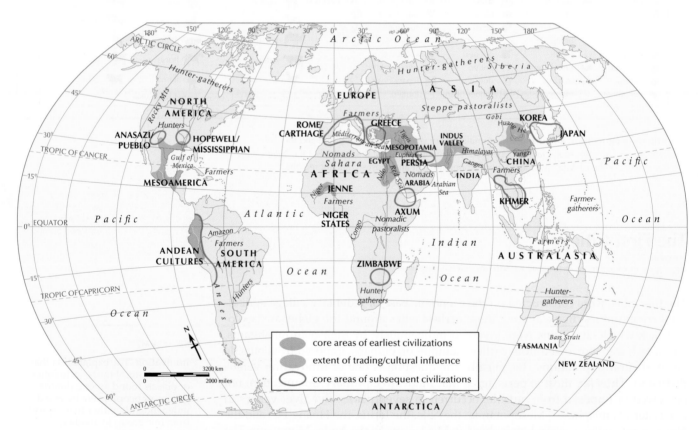

The spread of civilizations. The first civilizations developed where unique local climatic and soil conditions, favorable to settled agriculture, occurred, mostly in major river basins. With the development of an agricultural surplus came the growth of urban centers, trade, and population. Related civilizations tended to develop in regions adjacent to these heartlands, or along trade routes between them.

2.1

2.2

2.3

2.4

Who pioneered
the world's first
urban revolution
and how did it
change human
life?

lengths of string. By about 3300 B.C.E., in Sumer, which is geographically equivalent to today's southern Iraq, the world's first system of writing had evolved. This was one of the most revolutionary inventions in human history. The prestigious occupation of scribe was born, and schoolteachers soon followed.

📖 **Read** the **Document: Redefining Self—From Tribe to Village to City (1500 BCE)** on **MyHistoryLab**

Sumer: The Birth of the City

2.3   Who pioneered the world's first urban revolution and how did it change human life?

A people called the Sumerians pioneered the world's first urban revolution in Mesopotamia, literally "between the rivers"—that is, the region between the Tigris and Euphrates rivers, approximately modern Iraq. They migrated into southern Mesopotamia about 4000 B.C.E., perhaps from around the Caspian Sea, but no one knows for sure. They faced uncertain odds. While the area between the Tigris and Euphrates became known as the Fertile Crescent for its high agricultural productivity, high temperatures and unpredictable floods constantly challenged the Sumerians. To succeed in building cities in the region, peoples had to construct irrigation ditches and intricate canals.

The Sumerians were not the first to inhabit this land. Archaeological excavation of pottery shows the earlier presence in Mesopotamia of the Ubaidians, a people who spoke the Semitic languages of northern Africa and the Middle East, and spread throughout Mesopotamia from south to north, from about 5300 B.C.E. to about 4000 B.C.E.. The Ubaidians drained marshes, developed an early irrigation system, domesticated plants and animals, and settled into agricultural villages, which show marks of social hierarchy. The Ubaidian village societies came to an end about 3800 B.C.E., apparently because the water levels of the Mesopotamian rivers and lakes dropped, and the land became too arid for farming.

Several centuries later, the Sumerians began to dominate the region, supplanting the Semitic-speaking populations. They dug better canals for irrigation, improved roads, and expanded urban developments. For a millennium, from 3300 B.C.E. until 2350 B.C.E., the Sumerians lived in warring city-states—Kish, Uruk, Ur, Nippur, Lagash, Umma, and dozens of smaller ones. Each of these city-states included a central city with a temple, and the agricultural region surrounding it. The city controlled and protected the fields of grain, orchards, and land for livestock, which, in turn, provided enough food to support the cities' growing populations.

With the city-states constantly at war with one another, their leaders began to think in terms of conquering others to create large empires. In *c.* 2350 B.C.E., Sargon, king of the city of Akkad, conquered the Sumerian cities one by one, allowing the Semitic-speaking Akkadians to overshadow the Sumerians. Calling himself the "king of Sumer and Akkad," Sargon was the first to unite the city-states under a single, powerful ruler. After some 200 years under Akkadian rule, the Mesopotamian city-states regained their independence under the third dynasty of Ur (2112–2004 B.C.E.), but they resumed their inter-urban warfare, which weakened them. Eventually, Hammurabi (1792–1750 B.C.E.), king of "Old Babylonia," launched a series of aggressive military campaigns. He extended his control over much of Mesopotamia, including Sumer and Akkad, and Sumerian influence

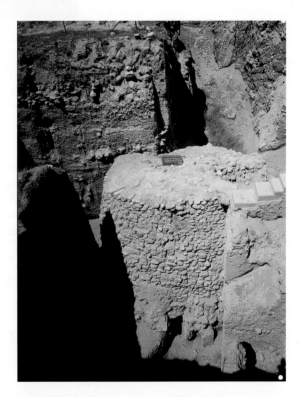

Stone tower and wall, Jericho, c. 8000 B.C.E. Before Sumer, a Neolithic community based at Jericho in the Jordan valley, Palestine, was the first to develop cereals of a fully domesticated type. In 8000 B.C.E. these farmers, keen to secure their settlement in the arid environment, constructed a stone perimeter wall 10 feet thick that was strengthened at one point by a circular stone tower more than 30 feet high. This wall is one of the earliest such defenses known.

How did the
first cities in
Mesopotamia
differ from earlier
villages?

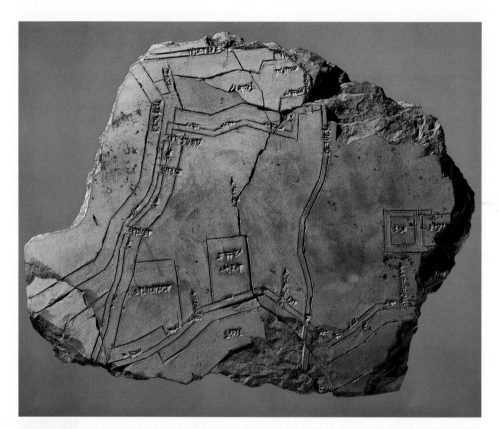

Map of Nippur, 1500 B.C.E. This plan of Nippur, the ancient cultural center of Sumer, is the oldest known
city map. Inscribed in a well-preserved clay tablet, 8¼ by 7 inches in size, the map is drawn accurately
to scale and shows several of the city's key temples and buildings, its central park, its rivers and canals,
and especially its walls and gates. The script is mostly Sumerian with a few words of Akkadian, the
language of the Semitic people who eventually conquered the Sumerians. (Hilprecht Collection,
Friederich-Schiller University, Jena)

waned. The cities they had built died out, having fought one another to exhaustion.
A series of foreign powers—Hittites, Assyrians, Babylonians again, Achaemenid Persians, and Greeks under Alexander the Great—variously conquered and controlled
Mesopotamia. The Sumerian culture lived on, however, assimilated into their conquerors' literature, philosophy, religion, law, and patterns of urbanization.

📖 View the **Map**: **The Ancient Near East** on **MyHistoryLab**

📖 View the **Closer Look**: **A Board Game from Ancient Sumer** on **MyHistoryLab**

The Growth of the City-state

2.4 How did the first cities in Mesopotamia differ from earlier villages?

What were the characteristics of the urban revolution in Mesopotamia? How did its
cities differ from the earlier villages? The most obvious feature was that the scale
of the city-state—its physical size, population, and territorial control—was much
greater than that of the village.

The Neolithic village housed a few dozen or a few hundred residents on a few
acres. The largest Neolithic site in the Near East, Çatal Hüyük in Anatolia, grew by
5500 B.C.E. to occupy slightly more than 30 acres. It became a town. By comparison,

2.1

2.2

2.3

2.4

How did the
first cities in
Mesopotamia
differ from earlier
villages?

SUMER: KEY EVENTS AND PEOPLE

c. 3300 B.C.E.	Sumerians invent writing.
c. 3000	Sumerians become dominant power in southern Mesopotamia.
c. 2800–2340	Sumerian city-states: early dynastic period sees spread of Mesopotamian culture to the north.
c. 2350	Sargon captures Sumer and establishes Semitic dynasty at Akkad, the new capital.
c. 2112–2004	Third dynasty of Ur.
c. 1900	Ammorites at Babylon.
1792–1750	Reign of Hammurabi; Babylon is the new capital of Mesopotamia.
c. 1600	Invasion by Hittites and Kassites, destroying Hammurabi's dynasty.

the first cities of Mesopotamia were ten times larger, accommodating about 5,000 people.

Over time, the larger cities reached populations of 35,000–40,000 and covered more than 1,000 acres or 1½ square miles. The major cities were walled. The ramparts of Uruk (modern Warka, Biblical Erech), the city of the king-god-hero Gilgamesh, stretched to a circumference of 6 miles, engirdling a population of 50,000 by 2700 B.C.E. By 2500 B.C.E., the region of Sumer held 500,000 people, four-fifths of them in its cities and villages! Urbanism in Sumer became a way of life.

To support these growing urban populations, the range of control of the Sumerian cities over the surrounding countryside, and its agricultural and raw material resources, continued to expand. For example, the total sway of Lagash, one of the major cities, probably extended over 1,200 square miles. The king, priests, and private citizens controlled the fields of this area.

Networks of irrigation canals supported agriculture in this arid region and expanded Sumerian control over the land and its productivity. Irrigation permitted settlement to extend southward to central Mesopotamia, where cities would later emerge about 3300 B.C.E. The construction and maintenance of the canals required larger gangs of workers than the work teams that were based on family and clan alone. Loyalties that had been limited to blood relatives now extended beyond kinship to civic identity. Through the organizing of these public works projects, a sense of citizenship, based on a shared space rather than on blood kinship, was born. It was enshrined in legal principles that made geographical residence the basis of citizenship. These new loyalties and laws marked the beginning of city life.

Organizing the canal systems required more powerful leaders than villages had known. At first, this leadership appears to have been exercised by councils of respected elders, who worked closely with religious leaders. In times of crisis, especially during warfare with other cities, the council appointed a temporary single leader, but after about 2800 B.C.E., these men began to assume the position of hereditary kings and to rule in conjunction with temple priests. Political power and organization were both centralized and sanctified. Thus was the **state** born and consolidated.

Religion: The Priesthood and the City

Considerable power rested with the priests of the many deities of Sumer, because residents believed that survival in the harsh environment of ancient Mesopotamia depended partly on the will of the gods. In contrast to modern patterns, in which

KEY TERM

state Several definitions; here used for the total political organization of a group of people controlling their own territory.

How did the
first cities in
Mesopotamia
differ from earlier
villages?

the countryside is often considered more sacred and the city more secular, in ancient times the authority of the temple community vested enormous religious prestige and power in the city, and urban ritual practice was more fully elaborated than was its rural counterpart.

To consolidate their temporal and supernatural influences, the city priests built great temples, called **ziggurats**. Found throughout the region, ziggurats were a form of stepped temple built on a square or rectangular platform of small, locally produced sunbaked bricks. The baked bricks were covered by glazed bricks, which may have had religious significance. A small sanctuary rested atop the structure, which could reach as many as ten stories high. The ziggurat lacked internal chambers, and worshipers probably reached the sanctuary via external ramps. The walls themselves were more than seven feet thick to support the weight of the massive edifice. (Ziggurats are probably the model for the Bible's Tower of Babel, which was depicted as a challenge to the power of the God Jehovah.) The ziggurats dominated the fields that the priests controlled and farmed, rented out, or turned over to their servants and favorites. As their power increased, the priests built the ziggurats ever taller and more massive. From within these vast temple complexes, they controlled huge retinues, including artisans and administrators, and retained gangs of field workers to farm the temple's estates. Temples employed and fed multitudes. The chief temple in the city of Lagash in Mesopotamia, for example, provided daily food and drink (ale) to some 1,200 people by about 3000 B.C.E. The leading temples became virtual cities within cities.

Rituals, especially those of the priests and kings, suggest further the significance of religious thought in the minds of Sumerians. On New Year's Day, for example, the king of Ur in Sumer proceeded to the top of the city's major ziggurat, where he was symbolically married to the goddess of fertility, Inanna. The entire population witnessed this affirmation of his divinity.

Royal burials also asserted the divinity and authority of the king. Royal tombs were elegant. Their arches, vaults, and domes, suggesting new levels of architectural

KEY TERM

ziggurat A temple tower of ancient Mesopotamia, constructed of square or rectangular terraces of diminishing size, usually with a shrine on top built of blue enamel bricks, the color of the sky.

Standard of Ur, from Iraq. Sumerian, Early Dynastic II, c. 2800–2400 B.C.E. In Sumer the city-state was created as strong kings came to rule over walled cities and the surrounding countryside. This banqueting scene, found in a tomb in the royal cemetery at Ur, shows the court drinking the health of the king. The boxlike "standard" is thought to have rested on top of a long pole during festive processions. (British Museum, London)

How did the
first cities in
Mesopotamia
differ from earlier
villages?

skill, were built of brick and stone, and many of the funeral objects interred with the dead were of gold and silver. As in the other ancient civilizations we shall encounter in later chapters, some of the royal dead were accompanied by attendants who might have been sacrificed for the purpose and were buried nearby. They, too, were adorned with jewelry of gold and silver. The British archaeologist Sir Leonard Woolley (1880–1960) described the death pit adjacent to the royal burial place in Ur, which he excavated in the 1920s:

> Six men servants carrying knives or axes lay near the entrance lined up against the wall; in front of them stood a great copper basin, and by it were the bodies of four women harpists, one with her hands still on the strings of her instrument. Over the rest of the pit's area there lay in ordered rows the bodies of sixty-four ladies of the court. All of them wore some sort of ceremonial dress … Clearly these people were not wretched slaves killed as oxen might be killed, but persons held in honor, wearing their robes of office, and coming, one hopes, voluntarily to a rite which would in their belief be but a passing from one world to another, from the service of a god on earth to that of the same god in another place. (pp. 70–72)

In contrast to these elaborate royal burials, most common people were buried in small brick vaults in basement chambers of their own houses, and some were interred in cemeteries outside the city walls.

Occupational Specialization and Class Structure

The priests and the political-military rulers were only the most powerful of the new classes of specialists that emerged in the complex, large cities. Managers, surveyors,

Mesopotamian trade, c. 2000 b.c.e. The Sumerian trading network, revealed by the wide range of valuable and exotic materials used by Mesopotamian craftsmen, was both extensive and sophisticated, drawing on resources often well over 2,000 miles distant. Egyptian tomb paintings show Semitic merchants with donkey caravans, while some of the earliest writing is found on Sumerian clay tablets recording commercial transactions.

How did the
first cities in
Mesopotamia
differ from earlier
villages?

artisans, astronomers, brewers, warriors, traders, and scribes—all in addition to the farmers working their own fields and those of the temples and landowners—gave the cities a far more sophisticated hierarchical class structure than villages possessed.

Arts and Invention. Creativity flourished. Artisans crafted works of art in terra cotta, copper, clay, and colors surpassing village standards in their beauty and complexity. Cylinder seals (small cylinders of stone engraved with designs, for stamping clay tablets and sealing jars) became a common form of practical art in Sumer and spread as far as Anatolia and Greece. Astronomers established an accurate calendar based on lunar months that enabled them to predict the onset of seasons and to prepare properly for each year's planting and harvesting. Musicians created, designed, and played the lyre and composed and chanted songs, often dedicated to gods. Designers and architects, supervising armies of workers, built the canals of the countryside and the monuments of the cities.

Engraved cylinder seal (left) and impression (right). Seals were first used as signatures before the invention of writing. The cylinders produce continuous patterns that are repetitive, but the figures themselves are remarkably naturalistic.

Sumerians apparently invented the first wheels: the potter's wheel for ceramics and wagon wheels for transportation. They dramatically improved the plow, learning how to harness it to oxen. Metallurgists, smelting their new alloy of copper and tin, ushered in the Bronze Age. From the new metal they fashioned tips for the plow and an array of new tools: hoes, axes, chisels, knives, and saws. They turned their attention to weapons and produced lance points and arrowheads, swords, daggers, and harpoons. They made bronze vessels and containers, as well as smaller items such as nails, pins, rings, and mirrors.

Trade and Markets: Wheeled Cart and Sailboat. Trade was central to urban life. Sumerian traders carried merchandise by land, river, and sea, in the world's first wheeled carts and sailboats, as well as by donkey caravan. Rich in agricultural commodities and artisan production but poor in raw materials, Sumerians traded with the inhabitants of hilly areas to the north for wood, stone, and metal. They sailed into the Persian Gulf to find copper and tin, and continued along the Arabian Sea coast as far east as the Indus valley for ivory and ceramics. They traveled east overland through the passes of the Zagros Mountains to bring back carnelian beads from Elam. Shells from the Mediterranean coast that have been found in Sumer indicate trade westward, probably overland, as well.

2.1

2.2

2.3

2.4

How did the
first cities in
Mesopotamia
differ from earlier
villages?

Lady Pu-abi's headdress. The splendor of this gold ornament, discovered in the 1920s in the royal burial place of Ur, reflects the wealth of this Mesopotamian urban society, the skill of its craftsmen, the hierarchy of its people, and the anticipation of some form of future life. (University of Pennsylvania Museum)

In the city marketplace, merchants sold locally produced foodstuffs, including vegetables, onions, lentils and beans, more than fifty varieties of fish taken from the Tigris and Euphrates rivers, milk, cheese, butter, yogurt, dates, meat—mostly mutton—and ale. In vats in their homes, women, especially, brewed up to 40 percent of the barley and wheat harvest into ale for home use and for sale. For taste, effect, and storage purposes the Sumerians preferred ale to grain. (Hops had not yet been introduced to enable the processing of ale into beer.)

Thus, from king and priest through professionals, artisans, craftsmen, farmers, and laborers, specialization and division of labor and a hierarchical class structure marked the city's social and economic life as far more complex than that of the smaller, simpler village.

He-Goat and Flowering Tree. Offering stand for fertility god. Sumerian, from Ur, *c.* 2500 B.C.E. This offering stand was created with a magical as well as a functional purpose in mind, being intended to work as a fertility charm too. The goat, an ancient symbol of male sexuality, is shown rearing up against a flowering tree, emblem of nature's fecundity. (British Museum, London)

2.1
2.2
2.3
2.4

How did the first cities in Mesopotamia differ from earlier villages?

Monumental Architecture and Adornment

For the Sumerians, the size and elegance of their cities and monuments were a source of great pride. The earliest introduction to Gilgamesh, hero of the greatest surviving Sumerian epic, proclaims his excellence as city builder: "In Uruk he built walls, a great rampart, and the temple of blessed Eanna for the god of the firmament Anu, and for Ishtar the goddess of love. Look at it still today: the outer wall where the cornice runs, it shines with the brilliance of copper; and the inner wall, it has no equal."

Artwork adorned the city, especially the temple precincts. Sculptures, murals, mosaics, and especially stone bas-reliefs not only provided beauty and elegance, but also represented pictorially key scenes in the history of the cities and their rulers. The magnificence of this monumental architecture and art defined the image of the city, impressing residents and giving warning to enemies.

Writing

The Sumerians invented writing, thereby altering human history. Indeed historians so value writing as a means of communication and of recording events that they often call all the events prior to the invention of writing **prehistory**. For these historians, only when events are recorded in writing can they be called history, since without writing we cannot know directly what people thought and said.

The earliest Sumerian scribes first used writing, beginning about 3300 B.C.E., for business purposes, to note the contents of commercial packages, the names of their owners, and to catalog this information into lists. They employed styluses made of bone or of hollow reed stems to incise **pictograms**, picture representations of the objects of their writing, onto clay tablets. By 3000 B.C.E. they were representing the key features of the pictures in wedge-shaped signs that we call **cuneiform**. Some cuneiform signs represented whole words, but others represented individual phonetic sounds based on words.

KEY TERMS

prehistory Everything that occurred before the invention of writing.

pictogram (alternative: pictograph) A pictorial symbol or sign representing an object or concept.

cuneiform A writing system in use in the ancient Near East from around the end of the fourth millennium to the first century B.C.E. The earliest examples are in Sumerian. The name derives from the wedge-shaped marks (Latin: *cuneus*, a wedge) made by pressing the slanted edge of a stylus into soft clay.

THE EVOLUTION OF WRITING

Pictographic c. 3000 B.C.E.										
Early cuneiform representation c. 2400 B.C.E.										
Late Assyrian c. 650 B.C.E.										
Sumerian phonetic equivalent and meaning	k eat	mŭsen bird	sag head	gu ox	še barley	ud day	sŭ hand	ku fish	a water	b cow

The origins of writing. Writing was invented in west Asia in the fourth millennium B.C.E. and developed from the need to keep a record of business transactions. From the wedge-shaped marks formed by a hollow-shaped reed, or stylus, cuneiform script evolved gradually. In this pictographic script, stylized drawings are used to represent words: each pictograph stands for a syllable, and abstract concepts are conveyed by using concrete notions that are close in meaning (e.g. "open mouth" for "eat").

As the cuneiform became more sophisticated, so too did the subject matter, and by *c.* 2400 B.C.E. Sumerian writing began to take over the oral tradition, recording tales of heroes, proclaiming political and military victories, singing the poetry of lovers, praising the glories of gods, and lamenting the fall of cities. Written literature took form and flourished. Archaeologists have excavated tens of thousands of Sumerian clay tablets, containing literature as well as business notations, and transferred them to research institutions around the world.

Many later peoples in the region—Elamites, Babylonians, Assyrians, and Akkadians—adopted cuneiform to write their own languages. The conquests of Alexander the Great in the fourth century B.C.E., however, helped to introduce alphabetic writing—of the Aramaic language—and cuneiform died out. The last known cuneiform text was written in 75 C.E.

Although some of the earliest town dwellers in other parts of the world—the settlers of the Niger valley of West Africa, the Olmec and Teotihuacános of Mesoamerica, and the Chavin and Inca of the Andes Mountains of South America—achieved urban form and size without the use of any form of writing, most of the earliest cities did invent some system of recording. As in Sumer, these systems moved "from token to tablet"— that is, from a simple recording of business transactions and

Clay tablet with cuneiform, Jemdet Nasr, Iraq, 3000 B.C.E. This example of writing from Mesopotamia is among the earliest known anywhere in the world. (British Museum, London)

HOW DO WE KNOW?

Decoding Sumerian Writing

The Sumerians wrote no historical interpretive accounts of their accomplishments, but at least five kinds of written material help us to reconstruct their past. King lists give us not only the names and dates of many of the principal kings of the major cities, but also some chronology of their continuing warfare. Royal correspondence with officials illuminates relations with neighbors. Epics transmit Sumerian values and their sense of the heroic, and lamentations recount the continuing devastation wrought by their inter-city religious warfare. Finally, legal codes suggest the principles and hierarchies of their everyday life.

Despite Sumerian accomplishments, historians lost access to the Sumerians and their literature for at least 2,000 years. The locations of even the grandest of the historic sites passed from memory. Biblical scholars, however, kept alive an interest in the region, searching for locations mentioned in Scripture, and British officials arriving at the British East India Company's outpost in Baghdad revived this interest. They began to investigate the ruins of Babylon and its artifacts, and they dispatched their finds, including written tablets, back to London. Still, no one knew what the wedge-shaped symbols meant.

Then, in the 1830s and 1840s, at Behistun, near Kermanshah in Persia, a British army officer began to copy a huge inscription that had been incised into a 300-foot-high cliff to announce the military victories of the Persian king Darius I about 500 B.C.E. The officer, H.C. Rawlinson, had a scaffolding constructed so that he could reach the ancient writing, sometimes while suspended from a rope 300 feet above the surface of the earth. Rawlinson and other scholars found that the inscription actually included

three scripts that represented different but related languages: Old Persian, Babylonian, and Elamite. The Old Persian and Elamite were written in cuneiform scripts; the Babylonian in alphabetic script. The stone had probably been prepared to publicize Darius's triumphs in three of the major languages of his empire. The three inscriptions were translations of one another, enabling linguists who could already read the alphabetic script to crack the cuneiform—although it took several generations before scholars completed this task.

Later archaeological digs in Mesopotamia uncovered tens of thousands of tablets and fragments. One especially rich cache was the royal library of the Assyrian king Ashurbanipal (r. 668–627 B.C.E.) at Nineveh. Through texts and digs, scholars resurrected the Sumerian economy, belief systems, and culture. Most of the texts deal with practical, everyday business transactions and administration. One contains the first known recipe for the ale that Sumerians enjoyed so much. Others recorded the world's first written literature.

- Why do you think the ancient language and literature of Sumer, like those of Egypt, were lost for 2,000 years?
- How might the written records, once deciphered, complement the archaeological record known from excavations?
- How do the five kinds of record discovered in Sumerian writing differ from "historical interpretive accounts"? How do they contribute to an understanding of history even though they themselves may not be "historical interpretive accounts"?

How did the
first cities in
Mesopotamia
differ from earlier
villages?

The stela of vultures. This limestone tablet, or stela (sometimes spelt stele), depicts in **bas-relief** Lagash's victory over Umma, in about 2450 B.C.E. Some 3,600 of the enemy were slaughtered by King Eannatum of Lagash and his soldiers, who are seen here marching into battle. (Louvre, Paris)

KEY TERM

bas-relief In sculpture, relief is a term for any work in which the forms stand out from the background. In bas- (or low) relief, the design projects only slightly from the background and the outlines are not undercut.

ideogram (alternative: ideograph) A character or figure in a writing system in which the idea of a thing is represented rather than its name. Languages such as Chinese use ideograms.

registration of ownership through designated tokens, often marked with individual notations, through picture writing, to **ideograms**, and finally to phonetic, alphabetical writing.

Not all civilizations followed this sequence. In China, for example, the first writing seems to have been symbols inscribed on oracle bones. They seem to have been an attempt to divine the future. To this day Chinese writing is still ideographic and maintains a visible connection to its most ancient forms. The Chavin and Inca developed a form of recording transactions and chronology through knots made in strings, called *quipu*, but they did not develop an independent system of writing. Nor did the people of the Niger valley.

Writing facilitated communication, commerce, administration, religious ritual, and, later, the recording and transmission of literature. It enabled society to enlarge to a scale never seen before, and it encouraged a self-consciousness and historical analysis previously unknown. It created a "knowledge industry," transmitted through systems of formal education and headed by scribes. By 2500 B.C.E., Sumerians had apparently established a number of schools where students could master the skill of writing. In a sense, this textbook had its origins in Sumer some 5,000 years ago.

Achievements in Literature and Law

Much of what we know about the ancient Sumerian imagination and world vision comes from its literary works. *The Epic of Gilgamesh*, the most famous of the remaining literature, weaves together a series of tales about the hero Gilgamesh. Its most complete version comes from various shorter stories found in the library at Nineveh from about 750 B.C.E., but earlier fragments in the Sumerian excavations corroborate the antiquity of the core legends going back to the time when Gilgamesh ruled Uruk, about 2600 B.C.E.

How did the first cities in Mesopotamia differ from earlier villages?

SOURCE

The Epic of Gilgamesh

Like all epics, *Gilgamesh* recounts the deeds of a larger-than-life hero. The Sumerian epic introduces the first hero in written literature:

I will proclaim to the world the deeds of Gilgamesh. This was the man to whom all things were known; this was the king who knew the countries of the world. He was wise, he saw mysteries and knew secret things. … When the gods created Gilgamesh they gave him a perfect body. Shamash the glorious sun endowed him with beauty, Adad the god of the storm endowed him with courage, the great gods made his beauty perfect, surpassing all others, terrifying like a great wild bull. Two-thirds they made him god and one-third man.

Aruru, the goddess of Uruk, who had also created Gilgamesh, created Enkidu, a forest dweller, who became Gilgamesh's friend and played a central role in the epic. *Gilgamesh* highlights the suggestive myth of Enkidu's seduction by an urban harlot who lures him from the wilderness to the pleasures of the city as well as to his wrestling match with Gilgamesh. The implication is that sexuality is experienced very differently in the city—more intensely and in more sophisticated fashion—than in the countryside. So, too, is friendship:

The harlot and the trapper sat facing each other and waited for the game to come … on the third day the herds came; they came down to drink and Enkidu was with them … The trapper spoke to her: "There he is. Now, woman, make your breasts bare, have no shame, do not delay but welcome his love. Let him see you naked, let him possess your body. When he comes near uncover yourself and lie with him; teach him, the savage man, your woman's art, for when he murmurs love to you the wild beasts that shared his life in the hills will reject him." She was not afraid to take him, she made herself naked and welcomed his eagerness; as he lay on her murmuring love she taught him the woman's art.

For six days and seven nights they lay together, for Enkidu had forgotten his home in the hills; but when he was satisfied he went back to the wild beasts. Then, when the gazelle saw him, they fled. Enkidu would have followed, but his body was bound as though with a cord, his knees gave way when he started to run, his swiftness was gone. And now the wild

creatures had all fled away; Enkidu was grown weak, for wisdom was in him, and the thoughts of a man were in his heart. So he returned and sat down at the woman's feet, and listened intently to what she said. "You are wise, Enkidu, and now you have become like a god. Why do you want to run wild with the beasts in the hills? Come with me. I will take you to the strong-walled Uruk, to the blessed temple of Ishtar and of Anu, of love and of heaven: there Gilgamesh lives, who is very strong, and like a wild bull he lords it over men." When she had spoken Enkidu was pleased; he longed for a comrade, for one who would understand his heart. "Come, woman, and take me to that holy temple, to the house of Anu and of Ishtar, and to the place where Gilgamesh lords it over the people. I will challenge him boldly."

With Enkidu's first encounter with Gilgamesh in the city, the epic also recounts the first example of male bonding, forged through a test of physical strength. When Gilgamesh and Enkidu first meet, they engage in a mighty wrestling match:

They broke the doorposts and the walls shook, they snorted like bulls locked together. They shattered the doorposts and the walls shook. Gilgamesh bent his knee with his foot planted on the ground and with a turn Enkidu was thrown. Then immediately his fury died … So Enkidu and Gilgamesh embraced and their friendship was sealed.

The epic also unveils the hero's driving ambition for fame and glory, both for himself and for his city, as Gilgamesh courageously chooses to enter the strongholds of Humbaba, guardian of the forest, and, with Enkidu, to fight him.

I will go to the country where the cedar is cut. I will set up my name where the names of famous men are written; and where no man's name is written I will raise a monument to the gods … I, Gilgamesh, go to see that creature of whom such things are spoken, the rumor of whose name fills the world. I will conquer him in his cedar wood and show the strength of the sons of Uruk; all the world shall know of it.

The importance of metallurgy and metals, especially for weapons, is highlighted:

(continued)

SOURCE (continued)

The Epic of Gilgamesh

[Gilgamesh] went to the forge and said, "I will give orders to the armorers: they shall cast us our weapons while we watch them." So they gave orders to the armorers and the craftsmen sat down in conference. They went into the groves of the plain and cut willow and box-wood; they cast for them axes of nine score pounds, and great swords they cast with blades of six score pounds each one, with pommels and hilts of thirty pounds. They cast for Gilgamesh the axe "Might of Heroes" and the bow of Anshan; and Gilgamesh was armed and Enkidu; and the weight of the arms they carried was thirty score pounds.

The victory of Gilgamesh and Enkidu over Humbaba parallels the massive assault by urbanites on the natural resources of the world, turning the products of nature into objects of trade and commerce, and using them to build cities.

Now the mountains were moved and all the hills, for the guardian of the forest was killed. They attacked the cedars,

the seven splendors of Humbaba were extinguished. So they pressed on into the forest … and while Gilgamesh felled the first of the trees of the forest Enkidu cleared their roots as far as the banks of Euphrates.

Lower Mesopotamia has no stone, wood, or metal. To obtain these raw materials, Sumerians had to send parties over long distances to quarry, cut, and dig; to trade; and to conquer. The mixed responses of the gods to the murder of Humbaba suggest the deep ambivalence of the Sumerians to their own increasing power:

[Gilgamesh and Enkidu] set [the corpse of] Humbaba before the gods, before Enlil; they kissed the ground and dropped the shroud and set the head before him. When he saw the head of Humbaba, Enlil raged at them, "Why did you do this thing? From henceforth may the fire be on your faces, may it eat the bread that you eat, may it drink where you drink."

The Epic of Gilgamesh presents a world of many gods before whom humans are passive and frightened subjects. Gilgamesh, however, defers neither to human nor to god. Devastated by the death of his closest friend, Enkidu, he sets off to the underworld in search of eternal life. Along the way he encounters the Sumerian prototype of Noah. This man, Utnapishtim, tells him of a flood that destroyed all human life except his family. A god who counseled him to build a boat had saved them. In the bleak underworld of the dead, Gilgamesh obtains a plant that will give eternal youth, but on his return voyage a snake rises from the water and snatches it from him. Gilgamesh recognizes a fundamental truth: Misery and sorrow are unavoidable parts of human life. Resigned to his losses, Gilgamesh returns to Uruk. Finally, he dies at a ripe old age, honored and mourned by his fellow citizens.

A second form of written document that marks the evolution to a more complex society is the legal code. Archaeologists discovered at Ur fragments of a legal code that dates to the twenty-first century B.C.E., and legal systems must have existed even before this. Legal systems remained crucial for all Mesopotamian urban societies. The post-Sumerian code of the Babylonian King Hammurabi, formulated *c.* 1750 B.C.E. (but rediscovered only in 1901–02), seems to have been based on the earlier concepts.

The First Cities:
What Difference Do They Make?

We do know that early cities facilitated some of the accomplishments that people then and now considered vitally important: increases in human population (a questionable asset under today's conditions, but not then); economic growth; effective organization for common tasks; creative breakthroughs in technology, art, and, perhaps most significantly, in writing, record-keeping, and literature; the inauguration of a rule of law; and the formation of a non-kin-based community with a sense of purpose and humanity.

SOURCE

The Code of Hammurabi

As states grew larger, formal, written law codes replaced the customs and traditions of the farming villages. By the time of his death, around 1750 B.C.E., the Babylonian ruler Hammurabi had conquered Mesopotamia, uniting its warring city-states under his rule. To reinforce that unity he carried out many works of public service and set forth in the name of Shamash, the sun god, a code of laws that covered many aspects of daily life and business. The prologue set forth noble goals: "To make justice appear in the land, to destroy the evil and the wicked that the strong might not oppress the weak … to give justice to the orphan and the widow."

The code provides a marvelous insight into the problems and nature of urban life at the time. It provides a detailed insight into property rights and urban crime, as well as social and gender divisions in the society. Finally, it gives students and scholars some idea of how justice was perceived in Hammurabi's world. The code is a list of 282 laws; only some of them are reproduced here. In the original list, they are not particularly organized; we have reorganized some of them here into three categories.

Property

Property laws incorporated laws of consumer protection for house buyers, boat renters, and contractors for services. In one case, a brutal punishment for faulty workmanship indicates that common people, too, were viewed as commodities. The sins of the fathers may be taken out on the children. The specific laws included:

- If [the collapse of a building] has caused the death of a son of the owner of the house, they shall put the son of that builder to death.
- If any one steal the property of a temple or of the court, he shall be put to death, and also the one who receives the stolen thing from him shall be put to death.

Urban Crime

Many laws provided for punishment for robbery and for personal injuries. Many

Stela of Hammurabi, from Susa, Iran, c. 1760 B.C.E. Hammurabi, the great king of Babylon, is the first known ruler to have created a detailed legal code; other societies with unknown rulers developed much earlier codes. On this commemorative stone slab, Hammurabi, standing, is receiving the Babylonian laws from the sun god Shamash. The laws themselves are inscribed below on the stela. (Louvre, Paris)

of the latter varied according to the social class of the person inflicting the injury as well as of the person suffering the injury:

- If anyone is committing a robbery and is caught, then he shall be put to death.
- If a gentleman has destroyed the eye of a member of the aristocracy, they shall destroy his eye.
- If he has broken another gentleman's bone, they shall break his bone.
- If he has destroyed the eye of a commoner or broken the bone of a commoner, he shall pay one mina of silver.
- If he has destroyed the eye of a gentleman's slave or broken the bone of a gentleman's slave, he shall pay one half his value.

Gender in Ancient Babylonia

Numerous laws governed marriage, bride-price, dowry, adultery, and incest. Although women did own the dowries given them, their rights of ownership were limited. Marriage is presented in large part as a commercial transaction, in which the groom's family pays a bride-price to the bride's father, while the bride's father gives her a dowry. Childlessness is grounds for divorce, but the husband must return his wife's dowry. Behavioral restraints in marriage are unequal: if the husband "has been going out and disparaging her greatly," the wife may leave, taking her dowry; if the wife is "a gadabout, thus neglecting her house [and] humiliating her husband," he may have her drowned.

- If a woman quarrels with her husband, and says: "You are not congenial to me," the reasons for her prejudice must be presented. If she is guiltless, and there is not fault on her part, but he leaves and neglects her, then no guilt attaches to this woman, she shall take her dowry and go back to her father's house.
- If she is not innocent, but leaves her husband, and ruins her house, neglecting her husband, this woman shall be cast into the water.

📖 **Read** the **Document**: "Hammurabi's Law Code" (1700s BCE) on **MyHistoryLab**

Some Modern Critiques of Early Urbanization

Sumer's city-states had many accomplishments to their credit, but some historians have pointed out that their civilization came at the cost of increasing warfare, growing social inequality, and the oppression of women. These modern critiques reflect the importance of studying the past in order to understand the present more fully.

Politically, each of the major cities of Sumer was also a state, ruling over the contiguous agricultural areas and often in conflict with neighboring city-states. The artwork of the city-states often depicts royal armies, military expeditions, conquests, and a general appreciation, even an exaltation, of warfare. The fighting seems to have been frequent, and the main combatants were the largest of the city-states. Battles were fought hand-to-hand and also from donkey-drawn chariots.

The warfare was especially destructive because the kings and soldiers believed that they were upholding the honor of their gods. When cities are sacred, conflicts between them mean holy war, fights to the finish. The "Lamentation over the Destruction of Ur," which was addressed to Ningal, goddess of the Ekushnugal Temple, describes that city's utter destruction after the Elamites sacked it, exiled its ruler, and destroyed the temple c. 1950 B.C.E.:

> After your city had been destroyed, how now can you exist!
> After your house had been destroyed, how has your heart led
> you on!
> Your city has become a strange city; how now can you exist!
> Your house has become a house of tears, how has your heart
> led you on!
> Your city which has been made into ruins—you are no longer
> its mistress!
> Your righteous house which has been given over to the
> pickax—you no longer inhabit it,
> Your people have been led to slaughter—you are no longer
> their queen. (Kramer, p. 142)

Lewis Mumford, one of the most respected modern commentators on the history of cities, regarded this early union of power, religion, and continuous warfare as a permanent curse of urban life. "War," he wrote, "even when it is disguised by seemingly hardheaded economic demands, uniformly turns into a religious performance; nothing less than a wholesale ritual sacrifice." (p. 42)

The first Sumerian cities fostered division of labor into occupational categories. We have noted the roles of kings, priests, landowners, architects, scribes, long-distance traders, local merchants, artisans, cooks, farmers, soldiers, laborers—the whole panoply of occupational categories absent in villages but forming the backbone of a sophisticated urban economy and society. Priests and kings held great wealth and power and largely controlled the means of production, but it is not clear that they formed an exclusive category of "haves" versus "have nots." The spectrum seems to have been more varied, including a substantial group of middle classes. But there is, nevertheless, much evidence of the enormous power of the aristocracy.

At the bottom of the economic hierarchy were slaves. People entered slavery in four ways: some were captured in battle; some were sentenced to slavery as punishment for crimes; some sold themselves (or their family members) into slavery to cope with poverty and debt; and some were born into slavery. We have no record of the number or proportion of slaves in the general population of Sumer and its cities. The law codes' extensive regulations of slaves and slavery suggest, however, their widespread existence.

The socialist philosopher-historian Karl Marx argued in *The German Ideology* that the rise of cities brought about "the division of the population into two great classes." Marx's formulation was too stark, ignoring the broad range of classes in the city, but he does force us to think about the class structure in our own cities, including the relationship between rich and poor, and its implications for the health of society.

Finally, the transformation of society from a rural, egalitarian, kin base to an urban, hierarchical, territorial, class base may have provided the entering wedge for the subordination of women. Some women in Sumer had great power. Several seem to have held independent high administrative posts in major temples controlling large land holdings. The high status of Lady Pu-abi (c. 2500 B.C.E.) was revealed in her burial. She was adorned with gold (see illustration above) and buried with several other bodies, presumably those of servants, suggesting a woman of high rank, perhaps a queen. Shagshag, wife of King Uruinimgina (also known as Urukagina), c. 2300 B.C.E., held great power in the name of her husband.

Women in Sumer generally had certain basic rights, including the rights to hold property, engage in business, and serve as legal witness. Nevertheless, it is clear that women's legal rights were limited by their husbands. Even powerful women were often only pawns in the power struggles of men.

The feminist historian Gerda Lerner argues that before the evolution of city-states, with their warfare and hierarchical class structures, the status of women had been more equal to that of men. Kin groups had been the basic economic units of society, and women had had more power in these family groups than they did in the city-states that displaced them. Lerner claims that inequalities between men and women are not products of unchanging biological differences. Rather, the inequalities have been created by humans—and they can be altered by humans.

- What did Lewis Mumford learn about warfare from his study of ancient cities? How did this affect his view of modern warfare?
- What did Karl Marx learn about class relations from his study of ancient cities? How did this affect his view of class relationships in modern (nineteenth-century) cities?
- What did Gerda Lerner learn about gender relationships from studying ancient cities?

They did not always succeed, however. The city-states could not work out a system of government and regulation that would enable them to live in peace. At the same time powerful and vulnerable, oscillating between psalms of victory and lamentations of defeat, they seemed to fall into one of two painful alternatives: inter-state warfare or conquest by imperial rulers. Their shortcomings cost them dearly. As long as each political entity was a law unto itself—as were the city-states of Sumer, pre-Han China, classical Greece, medieval Europe, and India during much of its history—war was likely. This problem of warfare among competitive states persists to our own day, although the scale has escalated from the city-state to the nation-state.

The evolution of the large, complex city implies the evolution of a state capable of organizing and administering it. In aristocratic and monarchical Sumer, much depended on the disposition of the king. The legendary Gilgamesh ended his royal career devoted to, and honored by, his people, but it had begun differently. The epic tells us that in Gilgamesh's youth, "the men of Uruk muttered in their houses" about his faults:

> His arrogance has no bounds by day or night. No son is left with his father, for Gilgamesh takes them all, even the children … his lust leaves no virgin to her lover, neither the warrior's daughter nor the wife of the noble.

They realized that it should have been different—"The king should be a shepherd to his people"—but they apparently had to submit. The only recourse they saw was muttering in their houses and praying to their gods. They "tamed" the wild Enkidu and lured him to Uruk in hopes that he would befriend and "tame" Gilgamesh (see Source, above).

From the time of Sumer, the political questions, questions of how to organize and administer the city-state to achieve a good life, have been central to the process of urbanization. In modern times, scholars ask how well Sumer did, and many call attention to its shortcomings (see How Do We Know? box, opposite). They caution us to learn from the past so as not to repeat what they see as the mistakes of Sumer in our own cities: not to make warfare into a religious obligation; not to isolate the city from the countryside; not to establish oppressive class distinctions; not to institutionalize the patriarchal suppression of women.

Underlying these warnings, however, is yet another myth, the myth of the pre-urban agricultural village as an egalitarian, peaceful settlement well integrated into its natural surroundings. We do not know if this was so. Pre-urban villagers produced no written records, and their artifactual remains are thin, inconclusive, and subject to widely divergent interpretation. Scholars draw many of their conclusions concerning pre-urban life from observing isolated groups in today's world, such as the !Kung people (! implies a clicking sound) of the African Kalahari Desert of a generation ago. But here, too, interpretations vary, and are equally subject to debate.

THE EARLIEST URBAN SETTLEMENTS

3500 B.C.E.	Rise of Sumer, southern Mesopotamia.
3100	Emergence of Egyptian state; new capital at Memphis.
2500	Development of Mohenjo-Daro, urban civilization on the Indus plain.
1800	Urban growth after Shang dynasty established in northeast China.
1200	Formative period in Mesoamerica, marked by first shrine centers, especially the Olmec.
c. 400 B.C.E.	City-states in Mesoamerica and South America.
400 C.E.	Urbanization of Jenne-jeno, Mali, sub-Saharan Africa.

Sumer evolved in accord with the edicts of its kings and its priests. In the next two chapters, we shall examine the evolution of other primary cities and city-states around the world.

CHAPTER REVIEW

THE AGRICULTURAL VILLAGE

2.1 What was life like in the world's first agricultural villages?

The development of agriculture and the domestication of animals took place independently in different parts of the world, with the earliest agricultural villages forming in Mesopotamia's Fertile Crescent. There, people gathered wild grasses and eventually cultivated them. They domesticated animals, fashioned tools from stones, and began to make pottery and woven cloth. In other parts of the world, villages sometimes took on different forms.

THE FIRST CITIES

2.2 In what way were cities new creations, different from villages?

The first cities grew out of agricultural villages and developed in seven different regions of the world. The development of an agricultural surplus enabled the growth of urban centers with monumental architecture, social hierarchies, specialization of labor, trade, writing, and new organizational power that could be used in peace and war.

SUMER: THE BIRTH OF THE CITY

2.3 Who pioneered the world's first urban revolution and how did it change human life?

The Sumerian people gradually began to dominate Mesopotamia. They created dozens of warring city-states each with its own king, its own god(s), and its own powerful elites. Sargon, king of the Mesopotamian city of Akkad, first united these city-states under a single, powerful ruler, about 2350 B.C.E.

THE GROWTH OF THE CITY-STATE

2.4 How did the first cities in Mesopotamia differ from earlier villages?

Over time, the cities of the Fertile Crescent grew in size and population. Networks of irrigation canals supported agriculture and expanded productivity, requiring more workers and strong leadership. Powerful kings came to rule over walled cities and the surrounding countryside, and a sophisticated hierarchical class structure developed. Architecture and adornment, writing and literature grew, and a law code was introduced to give structure to this urbanizing world.

Suggested Readings

PRINCIPAL SOURCES

Adas, Michael, ed. *Agricultural and Pastoral Societies in Ancient and Classical History* (Philadelphia: Temple University Press, 2001). Excellent introductions to the history and historiography of this period. Especially useful are John A. Means, "Agricultural Origins in Global Perspective," pp. 36–70, and Sarah Shaver Hughes and Brady Hughes, "Women in Ancient Civilizations," pp. 116–50.

Diamond, Jared. *Guns, Germs, and Steel: The Fates of Human Societies* (New York: W.W. Norton, 1997). Now classic work on why some societies succeeded economically, while others did not. Fate seems determined by ecology; this argument is both a strength and a weakness of the book.

Fagan, Brian M. *People of the Earth: An Introduction to World Prehistory* (Upper Saddle River, NJ: Prentice Hall, 13th ed., 2010). Excellent general textbook introduction to prehistory.

Gilgamesh, The Epic of, trans. and ed. N.K. Sandars (Harmondsworth, Middlesex: Penguin Books, 1972). Very readable edition of the classic epic.

Kramer, Samuel Noah. *The Sumerians: Their History, Culture, and Character* (Chicago, IL: University of Chicago Press, 1963). A masterful, accessible summary by one of the greatest scholars in the field.

Kurlansky, Mark. *Salt: A World History* (New York: Random House, 2002). Lively history of salt as food, commodity, and object of struggle.

Lerner, Gerda. *The Creation of Patriarchy* (New York: Oxford University Press, 1986). Lerner brings a critical feminist perspective to studies of Sumer, although many scholars have criticized her scholarship here; her main field is American history.

Mithen, Steven. *After the Ice: A Global Human History, 20,000–5,000 B.C.* (Cambridge, MA: Harvard University Press, 2004). Travels the world, providing views of developments through the eyes of a mythical tourist, with clear analyses as provided by today's scholarship. Engaging and readable.

Ponting, Clive. *A New Green History of the Earth: The Environment and the Collapse of Great Civilizations* (New York: Penguin, 2007). An ecological history of the ancient world, arguing that most "improvements" in productivity actually harmed the ecology and ultimately backfired.

Pritchard, James B., ed. *Ancient Near Eastern Texts Relating to the Old Testament* (Princeton, NJ: Princeton University Press, 3rd ed. with supplement, 1969). Excellent compendium of primary source materials. Presentation is very scholarly and painstaking.

Reader, John. *Potato: A History of the Propitious Esculent* (New Haven, CT: Yale University Press, 2009). Scholarly and fascinating history of the potato and its global travels.

Roaf, Michael. *Cultural Atlas of Mesopotamia and the Ancient Near East* (New York: Facts on File, 1996). Another in the excellent Facts on File series, copiously supplied with maps and pictures as well as readable, scholarly, introductory text materials.

Trigger, Bruce. *Understanding Early Civilizations: A Comparative Study* (Cambridge: Cambridge University Press, 2003). Very scholarly. Stresses methods of comparative study, selection of parameters for study.

ADDITIONAL SOURCES

Aristotle. *Basic Works*, trans. and ed. Richard McKeon (New York: Random House, 1941). Aristotle's *Politics*, in particular, presents very early, very thoughtful concepts of urban governance.

Bairoch, Paul. *Cities and Economic Development: From the Dawn of History to the Present*, trans. Christopher Braider (Chicago, IL: University of Chicago Press, 1988). Comprehensive presentation of the importance of cities in economic history. Europe is the main focus.

Cohen, Mark. *The Food Crisis in Prehistory* (New Haven, CT: Yale University Press, 1977). Asks why people began to settle into farming and continue it.

Ehrenberg, Margaret. *Women in Prehistory* (Norman: University of Oklahoma Press, 1989). Fascinating mixture of data and speculation, from a feminist perspective.

Hudson, M., and B. Levine. *Privatization in the Ancient Near East and the Classical World* (Cambridge, MA: Peabody Museum of Archaeology and Ethnology, 1996). Papers from two conferences focusing on Hudson's view of the importance of private enterprise in the ancient world.

MacNeish, Richard. "The Origins of New World Civilization," *Scientific American*, (November 1964), pp. 29–37. Macneish looks at the agricultural origins. His analysis of the evolution of maize, under human guidance, is classic.

Marx, Karl. *Capital: A Critique of Political Economy*, trans. Ben Foulkes (New York: Vintage Books, 1977). Writing at the height of the Industrial Revolution in Western Europe, Marx explores the history of urbanization as part of his larger work.

Marx, Karl, and Friedrich Engels. *The German Ideology* (New York: International Publishers, 1939). Includes a critical examination of the capitalist city.

Mumford, Lewis. *The City in History* (New York: Harcourt, Brace and World, Inc., 1961). The master examines the history of all cities, urging his readers to see the importance of social life and community as the key to the good city.

Postgate, Nicholas. *The First Empires* (Oxford: Elsevier Phaidon, 1977). Comparative presentation of early city-states that preceded empires.

Sjoberg, Gideon. "The Origin and Evolution of Cities," *Scientific American* (September 1965), pp. 19–27. Sjoberg, a sociologist, stresses the differences in political life and technological sophistication between pre- and postindustrial cities in this general introduction.

Wheatley, Paul. *The Pivot of the Four Quarters* (Chicago, IL: Aldine Publishing Company, 1971). For this enormously learned geographer, early cities were primarily concerned with their relationship with the gods and the cosmos, as reflected in their structure and leadership.

Woolley, C. Leonard. *Excavations at Ur* (London: Ernest Benn, Ltd., 1954). One of the greatest of the excavators describes his expeditions and their results. Well illustrated and very accessible.

FILM

Guns, Germs, and Steel (2005; 1 hour). Jared Diamond's book represented in film. Excellent for classroom use in introducing early villages and agriculture. The presentation is in three parts of one hour each. The first one-hour part is excellent and germane to this chapter.

3 River Valley Civilizations

The Nile and the Indus

7000 B.C.E.–750 B.C.E.

The urban civilization of Mesopotamia was flanked by two other such civilizations: the Nile valley to the southwest and the Indus valley to the southeast. Scholarly opinion is divided as to whether these two cultures learned to build cities and states from the Mesopotamian example or invented them independently. Whatever the source of inspiration, the peoples of these three river valleys created separate and distinct patterns of urbanization and political life.

Mohenjo-Daro, present-day Pakistan, c. 2600–1800 B.C.E. When it flourished, Mohenjo-Daro held some 40,000 inhabitants in its carefully laid-out precincts, and it continued to exercise an attraction for thousands of years. The round stupa, or burial mound, that now crowns the settlement was built as part of a Buddhist monastery some 2,000 years after Mohenjo-Daro had ceased to be a city.

LEARNING OBJECTIVES

3.1 ((	3.2 ((
Describe the characteristics of Egypt's early cities, and how we know about them.	Tell what we know about the Indus valley civilization, and how we know.

((Listen on MyHistoryLab

In Mesopotamia's Tigris–Euphrates valley, development of the physical city and the institutional state went hand in hand. In the Nile valley, the creation of the Egyptian state had greater significance than the growth of individual cities. In the Indus valley, we have extensive archaeological information on the individual cities, but we know next to nothing about the formation of the state. Until scholars learn to decipher the script and language of the Indus civilization, our knowledge of its institutional development will remain limited.

What were the characteristics of Egypt's early cities? How do we know?

3.1

3.2

Egypt: The Gift of the Nile

3.1 What were the characteristics of Egypt's early cities? How do we know?

Egypt has been called the "Gift of the Nile" because outside the valley of that great river the country is a desert. An immense, flowing ribbon of water, the Nile runs the length of the country from south to north, branching finally into an extraordinary delta as it approaches the Mediterranean. The river provides natural irrigation along its banks and invites further man-made irrigation to extend its waters into the desert to the east and west. Unlike the unpredictable floods of Mesopotamia, a more or less predictable flood of water poured through the Nile valley every July, August, and September, not only providing natural irrigation, but also carrying nutrient-rich silt that fertilized the land. (As we shall see, twentieth-century dam construction brought more control over the annual flood, and hydroelectric power, but also stopped the flow of silt.) Meanwhile, increased population filled in marshlands adjacent to the riverbed.

The vital significance of the Nile appears in this 4,000-year-old Egyptian poem:

Food bringer, rich with provisions,
  himself the author of all his good things,
Awe-striking master, yet sweet the aromas rising about him
  and, how he satisfies when he returns!—
Transforming the dust to pastures for cattle,
  bringing forth for each god his sacrifice.
He dwells in the underworld, yet heaven and earth
  are his to command, and the Two Lands he takes for his own,
Filling the storerooms, heaping the grainsheds,
  giving his gifts to the poor.   (Foster, p. 113)

The desert flanking the Nile valley protected Egypt from external invasion from the east and west; cataracts—precipitous, impassable waterfalls in the river—provided

AT A GLANCE: ANCIENT EGYPT

DATE	POLITICS	RELIGION AND CULTURE	SOCIAL DEVELOPMENT
4000–3600 B.C.E.	• Nagada I		
3500 B.C.E.	• Early Dynasty (c. 3000–2700)	• Narmer Palette (c. 3200) • Hieroglyphics in use	• Villages in Nile valley
3000 B.C.E.	• Old Kingdom (c. 2700–2181)	• Ruler of Egypt becoming godlike	• First use of stone in building
2500 B.C.E.		• Step pyramid at Saqqara • Pyramids at Giza, including Great Pyramid (of Khufu)	• Irrigation programs along Nile
2000 B.C.E.	• First Intermediate Period (c. 2200–2040) • Middle Kingdom (c. 2030–1640) • Second Intermediate Period (c. 1640–1540)	• Golden age of art and craftwork (1991–1786)	• Social order upset; few monuments built (2181–1991) • Country divided into principalities (1786–1567)

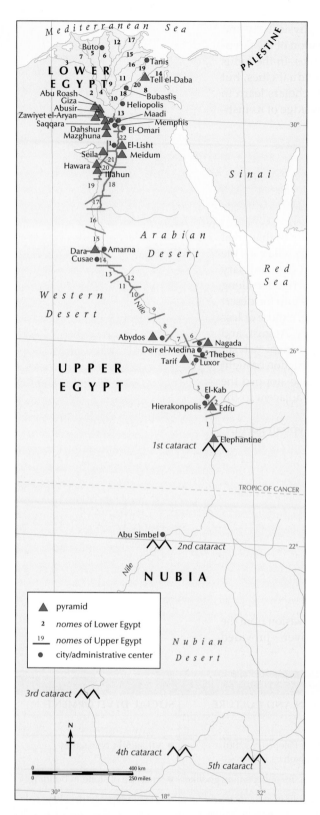

Land of the Nile. Stretching over 1,000 miles along the Nile River, ancient Egyptian civilization depended on a strong government. The kingdom was divided into Lower and Upper Egypt, and further subdivided into *nomes* (tax districts).

a buffer against Nubia to the south; and the Mediterranean provided a defensible northern border. As a result, for most of the first half of its 5,000 years of recorded history, Egypt was ruled by indigenous dynasties. The rule of the kings began about 3100 B.C.E. and continued with few exceptions for nearly 2,600 years, an unparalleled stretch of cultural and political continuity. These kings were later called pharaohs after the palaces they constructed, and gradually, pharaoh became the generic name for all Egyptian kings.

Monumental structures—such as the pyramids and Sphinx at Giza near modern Cairo in the north of Egypt, the temples at Karnak and Thebes in the south, and the pharaohs' tombs nearby in the Valley of the Kings—make clear the wealth, skill, and organizational capacity of ancient Egypt. However, we know less about the physical form of Egypt's ancient cities than about those of Mesopotamia. The Nile has washed away many ancient structures and eroded their foundations. On the other hand, we know much more about the Egyptian state than about almost any other. The written records of ancient Egypt, once they were deciphered, provided the institutional information.

Earliest Egypt: Before the Kings

In Egypt, as in Mesopotamia, agriculture provided the underlying sustenance for city life. By 12,000 B.C.E., residents of Nubia and Upper Egypt were using stones to grind local wild grasses into food, and by 8000 B.C.E. flour was being prepared from their seeds. (Upper or southern Egypt and Lower or northern Egypt derived their names from the flow of the Nile River, which originates south of Egypt and flows north to the Mediterranean Sea.) By 6000 B.C.E. the first traces appear of the cultivation of wheat and barley, grasses and cereals, and of the domestication of sheep and goats. To the west, the Sahara was becoming drier and some of its inhabitants may have moved to the Nile valley, bringing with them more advanced methods of cultivation.

By 3600 B.C.E. a string of villages lined the Nile, at intervals of 20 miles or so. The village economies were based on cereal agriculture. They were linked by trade along the river, although, since they mostly produced the same basic foodstuffs, trade was not central to their economy. The villages show little evidence of social stratification. These settlements characterized the "Nagada I" period (c. 3500 B.C.E.).

Gradually, population increased, as did the size of the villages, and by 3300 B.C.E. the first walled towns appeared in the upper Nile, at Nagada and Hierakonpolis. Tombs for rulers and the elite were built nearby, suggesting new levels of social stratification.

View the **Map: The Spread of Agriculture** on **MyHistoryLab**

The Written Record

Writing began early in Egypt, almost simultaneously with ancient Mesopotamia, about 3500–3000 B.C.E. Egyptians may have learned the concept of writing from Mesopotamia, but in place of cuneiform, they developed their own script based on tiny pictographs called **hieroglyphs,** a word based on the Greek for "sacred carvings." Some scholars believe that hieroglyphic writing in Egypt was completely independent of the Mesopotamian invention, and possibly preceded it.

Scribes, an important and highly regarded occupational group in ancient Egypt as in Mesopotamia, later invented two shorthand transcriptions of hieroglyphs: first, the more formal script, called hieratic; later, the more abbreviated, shorthand, demotic script. They wrote on stone tablets, on limestone flakes, on pottery, and on papyrus—a kind of paper—made by laying crossways strands of pith from the stalk of papyrus plants and pressing it until it formed sheets.

As in Mesopotamia, some of the earliest Egyptian writing is notation for business and administration. Over the millennia it grew into a rich literature, including chronological lists of kings, religious inscriptions, spells to protect the dead, biographies and autobiographies, stories, wisdom texts of moral instruction, love poems, hymns to gods, prayers, and mathematical, astronomical, and medical texts. From this literature, scholars have reconstructed a substantial picture of the history of Egypt.

For the earliest 500 to 1,000 years, until about 2400 B.C.E., the written records are thin. They do, however, provide a list of *nomes*, or administrative districts, suggesting the geographical organization of the Egyptian state as early as 2900 B.C.E. They also provide lists of the earliest kings of Egypt.

King lists written on stone about 2400 B.C.E., and on papyrus about 1200 B.C.E., combined with lists compiled in the third century B.C.E. by the Greek historian Manetho,

> What were the characteristics of Egypt's early cities? How do we know?
>
> 3.1
> 3.2

KEY TERMS

hieroglyphs The characters in a writing system based on the use of pictograms or ideograms. In ancient Egypt, hieroglyphics were largely used for monumental inscriptions. The symbols depict people, animals, and objects, which represent words, syllables, or sounds.

nome An administrative district in ancient Egypt.

HOW DO WE KNOW?

Written Texts and Archaeological Excavations

Few modern Egyptian scholars had been interested in recovering the ancient past of their country, apparently because its pharaonic, polytheistic culture did not connect with their own monotheistic Islamic and Christian cultures. In Europe, however, scholars and researchers were attempting to understand the early history of the civilization. The interest in this scholarship was so great that when Napoleon Bonaparte led a French military invasion of Egypt in 1798, he brought along with his armies a contingent of scientists, literary scholars, and artists.

In 1799 one of Napoleon's officers working at a fort on the western, Rosetta branch of the Nile delta discovered a large, black basalt stone slab. This "Rosetta Stone" (see overleaf) carried an inscription from the year 196 B.C.E. issued by the Greek ruler of Egypt and written in three languages: the most ancient Egyptian script, hieroglyphs, at the top; demotic Egyptian, a simplified script based on the hieroglyphs, in the middle; and Greek at the bottom. The French dispatched copies of the inscription back to Europe, where scholars were working on deciphering the Egyptian hieroglyphs. Until this time, their efforts had not been successful because they mistakenly believed that all the hieroglyphs were ideographs, a kind of picture writing in which each symbol stood for a word or a concept. Now, however, a young French scholar of linguistics, Jean-François Champollion (1790–1832), using the Rosetta Stone to compare the ancient Egyptian forms with the Greek, which he knew, recognized that hieroglyphic writing combined several forms—ideographic, syllabic, and alphabetic. Once he made this discovery, he was prepared to crack the script. In 1822, after 14 years of research, which he had begun at age 18, he published the results of his work.

Champollion himself made only one trip to Egypt, in 1828–29. With an Italian student, he produced the first systematic survey of the history and geography of Egypt as revealed in its monuments and inscriptions. He earned the informal title "Father of Egyptology," and in 1831 a chair in Egyptian history and archaeology was created for him at the Collège de France.

Archaeological excavations, primarily in search of monumental objects, began in 1858, although tomb-robbing and the theft of ancient artifacts had been continuous from earliest times. The annual expeditions of the British Egyptologist W.M. Flinders Petrie (1853–1942), beginning in 1880, introduced more scientific archaeological studies of Egypt and of Nubia, immediately to the south. By about 1900, scholars had identified the basic outlines of Egypt's history from 3600 B.C.E. to their own time. Working with both text and artifacts, they could produce a doubly rich historical record.

- Why were modern Egyptian scholars no longer interested in the ancient past of their own country? Do you find this surprising? Why or why not?
- The earliest known alphabetic writing dates to about 1900 B.C.E. Its use in place of hieroglyphic writing has been described as revolutionary, "comparable to the invention of the printing press much later." Why?
- How do written accounts and monumental architecture complement each other in giving us a more complete understanding of ancient civilizations?

3.1   What were the
       characteristics
3.2   of Egypt's early
       cities? How do
       we know?

The "Rosetta Stone," ancient Egyptian, 196 B.C.E. The inscription is transcribed in
three different forms: hieroglyphics, a later Egyptian shorthand called "demotic,"
and Greek. By comparing the three, scholars were able to decipher the ancient
hieroglyphs. (British Museum, London)

give the names of the entire sequence of Egypt's kings from about 3100 B.C.E, all
the way through the Persian conquest in 525 B.C.E. and the victory of Alexander the
Great in 332 B.C.E. After that event we have many sources for constructing the basic
chronology of Egypt's political history.

📖 Read the Document: An Egyptian Folk Tale on MyHistoryLab

📖 Read the Document: Elders' Advice to Their Successors (2250, 2450 BCE) on MyHistoryLab

Unification and the Rule of the Kings

The king lists, records of the *nomes* of Upper Egypt, and inscriptions and designs
on pottery suggest strongly that Egyptian national life and history began with the
unification of the kingdom about the year 3100 B.C.E. This unity was forged from the
diversity of peoples who came to inhabit Egypt. Semites from the desert to the east,
Phoenicians from the sea coast, Blacks from Nubia and the heart of Africa, and Europeans from across the Mediterranean immigrated and amalgamated into a common
national stock. They recognized one another and intermarried without apparent reference to race or ethnicity. Paintings of ancient Egyptians show them sometimes

What were the characteristics of Egypt's early cities? How do we know?

3.1
3.2

pale in color, sometimes black, very often red, perhaps reflecting their mixed ethnicity. Many historians believe that the colors may also be related to gender—women, mostly relegated to household chores, were usually depicted as pale; men, assumed to be outside the household, were often painted much darker.

Who first unified the upper and lower Nile into the single kingdom of Egypt? Most king lists mention Menes, but some cite Narmer. Some scholars believe that these were two different names for the same person. The event took place about 3100 B.C.E., but tombs of kings excavated at Abydos predate it by about 200 years. Perhaps these were kings of local regions, or perhaps unification was actually accomplished under a "predynastic" king before Menes, or unification may have been a long process and "Menes" simply symbolizes the whole process.

As Egypt became unified, the kings grew steadily more powerful, finally gaining a position as gods, who lived on earth and were responsible for maintaining *ma'at*, justice and order, throughout the kingdom. They were responsible for keeping the forces of nature balanced and for inviting the annual flooding of the Nile River that made Egyptian agriculture possible. An increase in monumental tombs and funerary objects suggests an increasing hierarchy and an uneven distribution of wealth, two common characteristics of state building. A more or less unified artistic style in both pottery and architecture after that time mirrors the unification of Egyptian politics. This era, called the Early Dynastic period, lasted about 400 years, from *c.* 3100 to *c.* 2686 B.C.E. By this time Egypt exhibited the cultural complexity associated with early civilizations, including a national religious ideology and the centralized control of political administration and even of artistic productivity.

Read the **Document**: **Two Accounts of an Egyptian Famine** on **MyHistoryLab**

The Gods, the Unification of Egypt, and the Afterlife

Egyptian religious mythology gives great prominence to the political unification of the country. The triumph of Isis, Osiris, and their son Horus—three of Egypt's most important gods—over disorder and evil represents in mythic terms the significance of the unification of Egypt. Osiris represented order and virtue; his brother, Seth, disorder and evil. Seth tricked Osiris into lying down inside a box that was to be his coffin, sealed it, and set it floating down the Nile. Isis, Osiris' wife and sister, found the box and brought Osiris back home. Seth, however, recaptured the body and cut it into 14 separate pieces, which he scattered throughout Egypt and the eastern Mediterranean. Isis tracked down all the parts, brought them back to Egypt, reattached them, and briefly restored life to them. From the restored body, she conceived a son, Horus. Horus defeated Seth in battle and gave Osiris new life, this time as king and principal god of the underworld. In some representations Horus and Seth are seen in reconciliation, binding Egypt into a single state. Seth represents southern areas around Nagada and Thebes; Horus, less specifically, represents the north.

GODS OF THE EGYPTIANS

Belief in one god (Aten, represented by the sun) was promoted during the reign of Akhenaten (r. 1353–1335), when the capital of Egypt was moved from Thebes to Amarna. At other times, the Egyptians worshiped a pantheon, whose main gods and goddesses are listed below.

God	Description
Amon-Re	The universal god, depicted as ram-headed
Anubis	The jackal-headed god of funerals, son of Nephthus and Osiris. He supervised the weighing of souls at judgment
Hathor	The goddess of love, represented either as a woman with a cow's horns or as a cow with a solar disk
Horus	The falcon-headed god of light
Isis	Goddess of magic and fertility; sister and wife of Osiris; as mother of Horus, she was mother goddess of all Egypt
Nephthus	Sister of Isis; a funerary goddess who befriended dead mortals at judgment
Osiris	Ruler of the underworld and chief judge of the dead; normally depicted mummified or as a bearded man wearing the crown of Upper Egypt and with a flail and crook in his hands
Ptah	Magician and patron of the arts and crafts; later became judge of the dead. Normally represented as a mummy or holding an *ankh* (looped cross)
Seth	The god of evil and the murderer of Osiris
Thoth	The supreme scribe, depicted either with the head of an ibis or as a dog-headed baboon

3.1
3.2

What were the
characteristics
of Egypt's early
cities? How do
we know?

Horus became the patron god of the Egyptian kings, the first Egyptian god to be worshiped nationally. In painting and sculpture he is often depicted in the form of a falcon, sometimes perched on the head or shoulder of the king, sometimes atop the double crown that symbolized the unity of Upper and Lower Egypt. The kings believed that if they lived proper, ordered lives they would be united with Osiris after they died.

This belief in the afterlife inspired the mummification of the dead—at least of those who could afford it—and the construction of Egypt's most spectacular monuments, the pyramids, as a final resting place for the dead kings until their soul and life force emerged for their journey through the afterworld. After passing through the ordeal of judgment in the next world, the souls might also revisit these elaborate tombs.

At first believed to be a preserve of the kings alone, later the afterworld was seen as a destination for important officials as well and, still later, for a larger proportion of the population. The belief in a utopian afterlife seems to have made optimists out of most Egyptians. Even those who may not have shared this belief were urged to enjoy life in this world to the full, as this 3,100-year-old song suggests:

> All who come into being as flesh
> pass on, and have since God walked the earth;
> and young blood mounts to their places.
> The busy fluttering souls and bright transfigured spirits
> who people the world below
> and those who shine in the stars with Orion,
> They built their mansions, they built their tombs—
> And all men rest in the grave. …
> So, seize the day! Hold holiday!
> Be unwearied, unceasing, alive,
> you and your own true love;
> Let not your heart be troubled during your sojourn on earth,
> but seize the day as it passes! …
> Grieve not your heart, whatever comes;
> let sweet music play before you;
> Recall not the evil, loathsome to God,
> but have joy, joy, joy, and pleasure!   (Foster, pp. 181–82)

Cities of the Dead

Burial sites, shrines, and sometimes towns were based on the need to provide final, collective resting places for the bodies of the most prominent Egyptians. As early as 3100 B.C.E., kings and members of the court were buried at Abydos, a 300-mile boat trip upriver, south of Memphis. Their tombs, called *mastabas*, were made of sun-baked mud bricks, with flat roof and sloping sides, designed to last forever. Inside the structure were the food, weapons, tools, and furniture that the king might need in the afterlife. His body was mummified and buried in an underground chamber. Abydos later became the center for the worship of Osiris.

Another group of high officials was buried in the north, close to Memphis, near Saqqara, in mud-brick tombs. Their funerary goods included copper objects and stone vessels. Over the centuries a series of burial sites grew up nearby, stretching some 45 miles along the Nile. At the beginning of the second dynasty, 2770 B.C.E., the royal necropolis, the city of tombs, was sited at Saqqara itself.

Women of elite families were usually buried in simple pyramid tombs, but in 1998 the more elaborate pyramid tomb of Ankhesenpepi II was uncovered at Saqqara and explored. She was the wife of two Egyptian kings of the sixth dynasty (c. 2345–c. 2181)—Pepi I followed by his nephew Merenre—and she was the mother

KEY TERM

mastaba A low, rectangular, benchlike structure that covered a grave. The architectural forerunner of the pyramid.

of a third king, Pepi II. Although her name means "she lives for Pepi," Ankhesenpepi II seems to have gained power also for herself. She is the first female known to have magical, biographical, hieroglyphic text—a format found frequently in the tombs of kings—inscribed in her tomb to facilitate her access to the afterworld.

Adjacent to the burial sites were the towns of the workers who built the increasingly elaborate tombs for the kings and aristocrats. Several of these workers' towns have been excavated, most notably Deir el-Medina, opposite Thebes in the south of Egypt, near the Valley of the Queens, although it dates to a later period. Mummification was also carried out in workshops in these towns.

The Growth of Cities

Unlike Mesopotamia, Egypt has almost no existing record of independent city-states. In Egypt, thousands of small, generally self-sufficient communities seem to have persisted under a national monarchy, but within a generally decentralized economy for the local production and consumption of food and basic commodities. Gradually, among the villages along the Nile, somewhat larger market towns must have grown up. Because administration, business, and transportation require some centralization, some of the villages began to house those functions. These selected villages, spaced strategically at larger intervals in the landscape, grew into larger settlements, and perhaps even into fully fledged cities.

In early dynastic Egypt, the siting of the administrative headquarters of the *nomes* would have given just such a boost to the towns in which they were located. Some settlements also hosted additional functions, including irrigation control and religious observance. The consolidation of villages into towns and towns into cities marks the beginning of "Nagada II" culture (c. 3300 B.C.E.), and the development of the site of Hierakonpolis along the Nile in Upper Egypt illustrates the process. Stretching for 3 miles along the banks of the river, Hierakonpolis ("Nekhen" in ancient Egyptian) did not have the form of a compact city, but it exercised many urban functions.

Archaeological excavations showed that the population of Hierakonpolis grew from a few hundred in 3800 B.C.E. to 10,500 by 3500 B.C.E. At least two cemeteries served the city: one for common people, another for the wealthier traders and more powerful administrators.

What precipitated the population growth, occupational specialization, and social hierarchy? One possibility is that local leaders introduced and implemented irrigation systems that saved agriculture and even enriched it during a period of severe drought. These changes enhanced the economy of the region and created subsequent growth and change. Indeed, Hierakonpolis seems to have been the capital from which King Menes, or Narmer, unified Egypt. The Narmer palette, a slate tablet illustrating this unification, was discovered there.

Political/administrative leaders continued to create irrigation systems along the Nile. These projects began in Old Kingdom Egypt, c. 2700–2200 B.C.E. They were expanded with the development of the Fayyum Lake region and the transfer of

Stela from the tomb of Djet (the "Serpent King"), Abydos, c. 3000 B.C.E. Horus, in the form of a falcon, is pictured above a serpent representing Djet, the "Serpent King," and the façade of a palace ("pharaoh" literally meant "great house" or "palace"). (Louvre, Paris)

What were the characteristics of Egypt's early cities? How do we know?

3.1

3.2

71

population to it during the Middle Kingdom, c. 2030–1640 B.C.E. New technology arose during the New Kingdom, c. 1550–1050 B.C.E., with the beginning of *shaduf* irrigation, which used buckets attached to a huge, turning wheel to dip into the river, bringing up water that then poured into man-made irrigation channels. The general predictability of the Nile's constant flow and annual flood meant that Egypt had fewer problems with its water supply than did Mesopotamia, but even here control of water resources influenced the formation of cities and the state.

Egypt's cities, like those of other early civilizations, had a religious base as well as an administrative one. Hierakonpolis, for example, housed a temple and prominent tombs as well as a ruler's palace. Perhaps the city flourished because its temple community and worship became especially attractive to surrounding villages. The combination of irrigation, administration, and worship built the city.

Earlier archaeological reports seemed to suggest that after unification under a single king, Egyptian cities were not usually walled. The central government may have suppressed the kind of inter-city warfare that characterized Mesopotamia, rendering defensive walls unnecessary. Also, although invasions occurred from time to time and required defensive precautions, the desert to the east and west of the Nile valley usually provided an adequate natural shield.

More recent excavations, however, question this view of open cities. The walls of some cities have been uncovered, and archaeologists are beginning to suspect that walls of other cities may have been removed and the materials used for other purposes. Excavations at El-Kab, across the Nile from Hierakonpolis, revealed a city enclosed in a wall, 1,600 feet square, dating to 1788–1580 B.C.E. This wall, in turn, seems to have intersected a more primitive town, of circular or oval shape surrounded by a double wall.

Largest of all the Nile towns were the political capitals, first in the north at Memphis, later in the south at Thebes, and occasionally at other locations. Most of the spectacular temples and monuments at Thebes today, for example, date only to the eighteenth and nineteenth dynasties, 1550–1196 B.C.E. This was a period of substantial population growth in Egypt, rising from 1.5 million to between 2.5 and 5 million people. Archaeologists cannot excavate below these monuments to reach older urban levels, and the residential buildings of that older city are probably below the current water table. They are irrecoverable.

Other types of city completed the urban network. Trade cities, especially in the Nile delta, linked Egypt internally and to the outside world. As early as 3650 B.C.E., the city of Buto in the Nile delta near the Mediterranean served as the port of landing for shipping from the Levant (modern Syria, Lebanon, and Israel) and Mesopotamia. Further south but still in the delta, at El-Omari, many goods imported from the Mediterranean

The palette of King Narmer, c. 3200 B.C.E. This slate palette, used for ritual purposes, shows the power of King Narmer, who had just united Upper and Lower Egypt. In the top register, Narmer (left), wearing the double crown of authority over both Upper and Lower Egypt, inspects the bodies of dead enemies (right); at the bottom, the strength of the king is symbolized by the bull shown destroying the walls of a city. (Egyptian Museum, Cairo)

SOURCE

The Egyptian Book of the Dead and the "Negative Confession"

Many ancient Egyptian texts concern the attempt to secure eternal happiness after death.

A selection from these mortuary texts has been collected by modern scholars and titled *The Book of the Dead*. A segment of these texts presents the "negative confession" of a deceased person in the court of judgment of the dead, protesting his innocence of evil and crime:

I have not committed evil against men.
I have not mistreated cattle.
I have not committed sin in the place of truth.
I have not tried to learn that which is not meant for mortals.
I have not blasphemed a god.
I have not done violence to a poor man.
I have not done that which the gods abominate.
I have not defamed a slave to his superiors.
I have not made anyone sick.
I have not made anyone weep.
I have not killed.
I have given no order to a killer.
I have not caused anyone suffering.
I have not cut down on the food or income in the temples.
I have not damaged the bread of the gods.
I have not taken the loaves of the blessed dead.
I have not had sexual relations with a boy.
I have not defiled myself.
I have neither increased nor diminished the grain measure.

I have not diminished the measure of land.
I have not falsified the land records.
I have not added to the weight of the balance.
I have not weakened the plummet of the scales.
I have not taken milk from the mouths of children.
I have not driven cattle away from their pasturage.
I have not snared the birds of the gods.
I have not caught fish in their marshes.
I have not held up the water in its season.
I have not built a dam against running water.
I have not quenched a fire at its proper time.
I have not neglected the appointed times and their meat-offerings.
I have not driven away the cattle of the god's property.
I have not stopped a god on his procession.
I am pure: I am pure: I am pure: I am pure. …

Behold me—I have come to you without sin, without guilt, without evil, without a witness against me, without one against whom I have taken action. I live on truth, and I eat of truth.

I have done that which men said and that with which gods are content. I have satisfied a god with that which he desires. I have given bread to the hungry, water to the thirsty, clothing to the naked, and a ferry-boat to him who was marooned. I have provided divine offerings for the gods and mortuary offerings for the dead. So rescue me, you; protect me, you.

(Pritchard, pp. 34–36)

What were the characteristics of Egypt's early cities? How do we know?

3.1

3.2

Wooden model of a sailing boat from Meir, Egypt, *c.* 2000 B.C.E. The presence of a mummy on board this twelfth-dynasty model boat indicates that it was intended as a funerary artifact, used to symbolize the journey of the dead into the afterlife. We recognize important elements of early Egyptian vessels— from the large central sail to the figures on deck, representing the pilot, the owner, and sailors working the halyards. (British Museum, London)

3.1

3.2

What were the
characteristics
of Egypt's early
cities? How do
we know?

coast have also been found. In these ports, goods must have been offloaded for trans-shipment in smaller boats or by donkey caravans to Maadi, near Memphis. Maadi was the trade link between the delta and Upper Egypt.

👁 **Watch** the **Video**: **The Temple of Karnak** on **MyHistoryLab**

Monumental Architecture of the Old Kingdom: Pyramids and Fortresses

As in Mesopotamia, the increasing power of the Egyptian state inspired the construction of monumental architecture. In the third dynasty (2649–2575 B.C.E.), King Djoser's architect, Imhotep, elaborated the rather simple *mastaba* into a series of stepped stone slabs, one on top of the next, built to house the king's remains at death. This forerunner of the pyramids demonstrated an astonishing royal control over labor, finances, and architectural and building techniques. The administrative organization and economic productivity of government continued to increase, until,

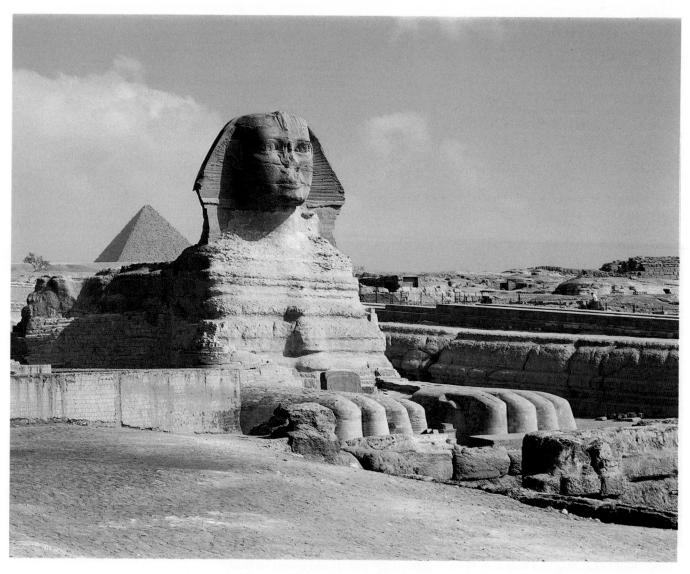

The Sphinx and the Pyramid of Khefren, Giza. The greatest of all the pyramids, the burial tombs of the kings, are at Giza, near modern Cairo, and date to around 2600–2500 B.C.E. The face of the sphinx—a mythological creature with a lion's body and a human head—is thought to be a likeness of King Khefren, who ruled Egypt some time after 2600 B.C.E.

Step pyramid of King Djoser, Saqqara, Egypt, *c.* 2700 B.C.E. This step pyramid, forerunner to the ancient architectural masterpieces at Giza, developed from the *mastaba*, a low, rectangular, benchlike structure that covered a grave. The purpose of this early pyramid, effectively a 200-foot-high ziggurat without a temple on top, was to mark and protect the underground tomb chamber 90 feet below.

What were the
characteristics
of Egypt's early
cities? How do
we know?

3.1

3.2

by the end of this dynasty, Egypt had extended its control of the Nile valley as far south as the first cataract, its classical southern frontier. At the same time, Egypt's artistic genius continued to develop the sculpture of its tombs and the sophistication of its script. Old Kingdom rulers (*c.* 2686–*c.* 2160 B.C.E.) spent fortunes constructing pyramid tombs to preserve their mummified bodies for the afterlife.

Within a half-century, architects realized the beauty of filling in the steps of the multi-storied *mastaba* to create the simple, elegant, triangular form of the true pyramid. Kings of the fourth dynasty, 2575–2465 B.C.E., supervised the construction of the greatest pyramids in history. The 450-foot-high pyramids of Khufu (Cheops; r. 2551–2528 B.C.E.) and Khefren (r. 2520–2494 B.C.E.), and the smaller pyramid of Menkaure (r. 2490–2472 B.C.E.), all arranged in a cluster with the Sphinx, proclaim creative vision, organizational power, and aspirations to immortality. The sculpture, reliefs, paintings, and inscriptions in the pyramids and in the many tombs of court officials and other powerful men of the time express the highest artistic achievements of the era. Tombs of queens and officials are situated in proximity to the kings' pyramids in accordance with their inhabitants' power and rank. (Tomb-robbing was, however, so common that we have no idea how long any of them lay undisturbed in their tombs.) All these architectural, spiritual, political, and military accomplishments date to the millennium we now call the predynastic, early dynastic, and Old Kingdom.

Following Menkaure, however, whose pyramid was already smaller than those of Khufu and Khefren, the size and quality of these enormous monuments decreased, suggesting that Egyptian power generally was diminishing. At the height of the Old Kingdom, for example, Egyptian trading, raiding, and mining initiatives had extended southward into Nubia, above the first cataract of the Nile. These expeditions were protected and consolidated through the construction of the Buhen fortress at the second cataract, probably at about the time of the building of the great

roof support

outside covered in white limestone

air shaft or the soul's exit

unused burial chamber

king's chamber

main shaft

mortuary temple

stepped construction can be clearly seen here

causeway from the Nile

original burial chamber

escape shaft

Cutaway of Great Pyramid of Khufu, Giza. The rectangular plan and stepped form of Djoser's pyramid were gradually modified to become the colossal, smooth-faced monuments with which we are familiar. This pyramid is some 450 feet high on a square base occupying 13 acres, and was built using forced labor.

3.1

3.2

What were the characteristics of Egypt's early cities? How do we know?

pyramids. That fortress, however, also seems to have declined after about 2400 B.C.E., although trading and raiding expeditions continued.

The Disintegration of the Old Kingdom

Lists of the kings of ancient Egypt record a 3000-year chronology, beginning about 3200 B.C.E. The first dynasty, including King Narmer, succeeded in unifying upper and lower Egypt. The 32nd, and last, dynasty (330–305 B.C.E.) was imposed from outside by Alexander the Great after he conquered Egypt. (Some scholars refer to the rule of Ptolemaic, Greek, kings, 305–30 B.C.E., ending with Cleopatra, as a 33rd dynasty.) Within these three millennia, scholars today identify the three "Kingdoms," Old, Middle, and New, as unified, prosperous, and powerful eras in Egyptian history. In between them came periods of dissolution and instability.

For example, after the height of the era of pyramid building in the Old Kingdom, central authority began to weaken and provincial officials in each *nome*, called nomarchs, asserted their powers. They collected and kept the taxes for themselves, and their private armies ruled locally. Based on the size and records of cemeteries, the death rate seems to have increased at this time. Famine was prevalent. Apparently the Nile did not reach optimal flood heights for agriculture, and weak rulers could not create adequate irrigation works to compensate for the shortfall. Finally, in 2181 B.C.E. the Old Kingdom fell. At first, several nomarchs held independent local power. Then two separate centers began to stand out in the contest for power:

Herakleopolis in the north and Thebes in the south. This period of disunity, the First Intermediate Period, lasted for almost a century and a half.

What were the characteristics of Egypt's early cities? How do we know?

3.1

3.2

The Rise and Fall of the Middle Kingdom

In about 2040 B.C.E., King Mentuhotep of Thebes defeated his rivals in the north and reunited the kingdom, initiating the Middle Kingdom, *c.* 2030–1640 B.C.E. Trade revived, with two patterns achieving special prominence. One was the local caravan trade in spices, resins, and minerals across the northern Sinai desert, between the Nile delta and Palestine. The other—the long-distance trade carried by ship throughout the eastern Mediterranean—was commanded by royal families to bring in timber and resins, lapis lazuli, copper, and ivory for official construction and for adornment.

The fine arts and literature flourished. Among the finest literary gems of the Middle Kingdom was "The Autobiography of Si-nuhe," the narrative of a high-ranking court official who went into self-imposed exile until, in his old age, he was recalled to the capital and awarded great honors. The story reveals not only the intrigues of the court and the royal family, but also the sharp contrast between the life of the elite of the capital and the harsh rigor of the surrounding desert.

Most importantly, the Middle Kingdom saw the state develop more organization and power than ever before. Egypt was administered efficiently and spread its power aggressively into Nubia and the Middle East. Egypt became an empire, ruling over more distant, foreign peoples. From this time onward, Egypt's fate would be intertwined with that of its empire. The Middle Kingdom ended in part because

SOURCE

The Autobiography of Si-nuhe and the Glorification of Court and Capital

Si-nuhe, a high-ranking official and royal attendant, fled from the Egyptian court when a new king came to the throne. Apparently he feared that his loyalty to the new ruler was suspect and his safety endangered. A skilled warrior and administrator, even in self-imposed exile he earned high positions in several Asian kingdoms. In Si-nuhe's old age, however, the king of Egypt and his family invited him back to the court so that he could spend his last years "at home" in comfort and be buried with appropriate rites.

This personal tale of reconciliation is almost certainly based on reality. Its glorification of Egypt over other countries, of the city, and especially of the royal capital and the royal court over the countryside represented the beliefs of the Egyptian elite. This account of the career and moral personality of a court official, and of the excellence of the reigning king, is an outstanding example of the autobiographies inscribed in ancient Egyptian tombs. Si-nuhe's story became one of the most popular classics of Egyptian literature, and manuscripts that include it began to appear about 1800 B.C.E. and continued to about 1000 B.C.E. One modern scholar refers to it as "the crown jewel of Middle Egyptian literature." (Lichtheim, vol. I, p. 11)

Si-nuhe returned to the capital, then in the city of Lisht, near the Faiyum Lake.

So I went forth from the midst of the inner chambers, with the royal children giving me their hands. Thereafter we went to the Great Double Door. I was put into the house of a royal son, in which were splendid things. A cool room was in it, and images of the horizon. Costly things of the Treasury were in it. Clothing of royal linen, myrrh, and prime oil of the king and of the nobles whom he loves were in every room. Every butler was busy at his duties. Years were made to pass away from my body. I was plucked, and my hair was combed. A load of dirt was given to the desert, and my clothes to the Sand-Crossers. I was clad in fine linen and anointed with prime oil.

I slept on a bed. I gave up the sand to them who are in it, and wood oil to him who is anointed with it. I was given a house which had a garden, which had been in the possession of a courtier. Many craftsmen built it, and all its woodwork was newly restored. Meals were brought to me from the palace three or four times a day, apart from that which the royal children gave, without ceasing a moment.

There was constructed for me a pyramid-tomb of stone in the midst of the pyramid-tombs. The stone-masons who hew a pyramid-tomb took over its ground-area. The outline-draftsmen designed in it; the chief sculptors carved in it; and the overseers of works who are in the necropolis made it their concern. Its necessary materials were made from all the outfittings which are placed at a tomb-shaft. Mortuary priests were given to me. There was made for me a necropolis garden, with fields in it formerly extending as far as the town, like that which is done for a chief courtier. My statue was overlaid with gold, and its skirt was of fine gold. It was his majesty who had it made. There is no poor man for whom like has been done.

(Pritchard, pp. 18–22)

3.1

3.2   What do we
know about the
Indus valley
civilization? How
do we know?

the Nubians drove out their Egyptian conquerors, but more importantly because of the invasions of the Hyksos, or "princes of the foreign lands," who spoke a Semitic language and probably came from the north and east of the Sinai desert. The New Kingdom (*c.* 1550–1050 B.C.E.) would rise again as an empire by once more asserting its authority over Nubia and over large regions of Palestine and adjoining segments of Syria. These issues of empire and its significance for Egypt are discussed in the chapter entitled "Dawn of the Empires." One fascinating event from the New Kingdom period—the construction and destruction of the city of Akhetaten—belongs here, however, because it highlights the symbolic importance of capital cities.

Akhetaten, Capital City of King Akhenaten

Modern excavations at Amarna on the east bank of the Nile unearthed the ruins of an ancient Egyptian capital that owed its entire existence to the idiosyncratic vision of one ruler—King Amenhotep IV, better known as Akhenaten.

Within a few years of coming to the throne, Amenhotep IV (r. 1353–1335 B.C.E.) challenged the order of ancient Egypt by adopting a new monotheistic religion. Instead of worshiping a whole pantheon of gods, he offered his devotion to a single deity—Aten, god of the solar disk (or sun). Amenhotep appointed himself mediator between his people and the god. He abandoned his official dynastic name in favor of Akhenaten ("he who serves Aten"). The name of Amon, principal god of the old religion, was swiftly erased from inscriptions throughout Egypt, as were the words "all gods" in certain texts.

To bolster the new order and escape the power of the hostile priesthood, Akhenaten moved his capital 200 miles north from the established center, Thebes, to an untouched site in the desert. The city he built was named Akhetaten ("horizon of Aten"; present-day Amarna), and it was there that Akhenaten, the Great Royal Wife Queen Nefertiti, and their six daughters practiced the new religion.

The eccentricity of Akhetaten's ruler was reflected in the city's architecture, sculpture, and wall painting. Solid statements of eternity gave way to a freedom of expression that emphasized the here and now. Aten was worshiped in an open temple that ushered in the sun's rays, rather than in one of the dark, austere sanctuaries usually designated for worship. Residential buildings included spacious villas with large gardens and pools to house wealthy officials. In artistic expression, solemnity gave way to an unprecedented liveliness and invention. Artists showed the royal parents playing with their children or dandling them on their laps. Curious depictions of Akhenaten's drooping jaw and misshapen body capture his individuality, marking a departure from the highly stylized representations of previous pharaohs.

Akhenaten's isolated position, both geographically and intellectually, threatened the stability of Egypt's empire. When he died, Akhenaten's successors abandoned Akhetaten. The capital returned to Thebes, where the old religious and political order could resume. Subsequent pharaohs so hated Akhenaten's religion that they razed the city to the ground and used its building materials on other sites.

From this discussion of the varied cities of the Nile valley, with their abundance of archaeological and textual material, we move eastward about 2,500 miles to explore the earliest cities of the Indus valley with their very different structures and materials.

The Indus Valley Civilization and its Mysteries

3.2   What do we know about the Indus valley civilization? How do we know?

The civilizations of ancient Mesopotamia and Egypt never disappeared completely. Hebrew and Greek accounts and surviving artifacts, such as the spectacular pyramids, kept them alive in the popular imagination. Intermittent discoveries of tombs, and the thefts of their contents, added concrete evidence. Nevertheless, systematic excavating of sites and deciphering of texts did not occur in modern times until the mid-1800s.

The civilization of the Indus valley was lost almost entirely, so it is no surprise that its excavation did not begin until the 1920s and that its script is still not deciphered. The accidental discovery and systematic exploration of this long-lived and far-flung civilization is one of the great stories of mid- and late twentieth-century archaeology.

3.1

3.2

What do we know about the Indus valley civilization? How do we know?

The Roots of the Indus Valley Civilization

In 1856, the British colonial rulers of India were supervising construction of a railway between Lahore and Karachi, along the Indus River valley. As they progressed, construction workers discovered hundreds of thousands of old fire-baked bricks in the semi-desert area and used them to lay the road bed. Scattered among the old bricks, workers discovered steatite stone seals marked with artistic designs. These seals and bricks were the first clue that the area had been home to an ancient and unknown civilization. Some were passed along to officers of the Archaeological Survey of India, and they took note of them, but formal systematic excavation began only in 1920 when John Marshall, Director General of the Archaeological Survey, commissioned his staff to survey a huge mound that rose above the desert floor where the seals had been found.

These excavations soon revealed a 4,500-year-old city. Archaeologists named the site Harappa, and they often used this name to designate the entire Indus valley civilization. Two years later, R.D. Banerji, an Indian officer of the Survey, recognized and began to excavate a twin site 200 miles to the southwest, later named Mohenjo-Daro, "Hill of the Dead." The two cities had many urban design and architectural features in common. Both were about 3 miles in circumference, large enough to hold populations of 40,000. With these two excavations, an urban civilization that had been lost for thousands of years was uncovered.

Before these excavations, scholars had believed that the civilization of India had begun in the Ganges valley with the arrival of Aryan immigrants from Persia or central Asia *c.* 1250 B.C.E. and the construction of their first cities *c.* 700 B.C.E. The discovery of the Harappan cities pushed the origin of Indian civilization back an additional 1,500 years and located it in an entirely different ecological zone.

As archaeologists explored more widely in the Indus valley, they found that civilization there began earlier, lasted longer, and spread farther than anyone had suspected. Some of its roots seem to lie in a settlement called Mehrgarh, in the foothills of the Bolan Pass, that has yielded early settlement artifacts going back to 7000 B.C.E. and, with ever-increasing sophistication, coming forward to 2500–2000 B.C.E. At its

AT A GLANCE: THE INDUS VALLEY

DATE	POLITICS	RELIGION AND CULTURE	SOCIAL DEVELOPMENT
7000 B.C.E.			• Traces of settlements; trade with Mesopotamia
3000 B.C.E.			• Cotton cultivated
2500 B.C.E.	• Height of Harappan civilization in northern India (2500–2000)		• Cities of Harappa and Mohenjo-Daro
2000 B.C.E.	• Collapse of Harappan civilization (2000–1900)	• Evidence of decline in standards of architecture	
1500 B.C.E.	• Immigration of Aryans into India (*c.* 1250)		
1000 B.C.E.	• Aryan immigrants reach west Ganges valley (*c.* 1000) and build first cities (*c.* 750)		• Iron tools used to clear Ganges valley for agriculture (*c.* 1000)

What do we
know about the
Indus valley
civilization? How
do we know?

height, it had major settlements as far west as the Makran Coast toward Iran, north and east into Punjab and even the upper Ganges River valley, and south and east to Dholavira in Kutch, and on to the banks of the Narmada River.

What was the relationship between this civilization and that of Mesopotamia? At first, many scholars assumed that the Indus valley people learned the art of city-building from the Sumerians and other peoples of Mesopotamia. But later scholars have argued that Harappa was not a derivative of Mesopotamia but grew up independently. It is conceivable that the civilizations of both Mesopotamia and the Indus had a common ancestor in the settlements of the hills and mountains between them.

Written records, the key that reopened the civilizations of ancient Mesopotamia and Egypt, are scarce in the Indus valley. The only written materials so far discovered are seal inscriptions, which give only limited information. In addition, scholars have not succeeded in their attempts to decipher the script; they differ substantially in their interpretations. As a result, our understanding of Indus civilization is limited. Artifactual remains give a good representation of the physical cities and settlements, but not of their institutions. Moreover, while we can make educated guesses about the function and meaning of the remaining artifacts and physical structures from our own perspective, we do not have the words of the Harappans themselves to explain their own understanding of their civilization.

The Design and Construction of Well-planned Cities

Archaeological evidence to date reveals an urban civilization with its roots as early as 7000 B.C.E. in simple settlements, such as Mehrgarh in the hills. Over the millennia, people moved down into the plains and river valley. At first, they may have practiced **transhumance**, moving into the forested river valley only in the colder months, and

KEY TERM

transhumance The practice of shifting residence and livestock between mountains and valleys according to the season of the year.

Cities of the Indus. Confined to the north and west by mountains, and to the east by desert, the Indus valley had, by 2500 B.C.E., developed a sophisticated urban culture based on individual walled cities sharing common patterns of urban design. In terms of geographical extent this civilization was the largest in the world in its time.

CHAPTER THREE: RIVER VALLEY CIVILIZATIONS 7000 B.C.E.–750 B.C.E.

3.1

3.2
What do we
know about the
Indus valley
civilization? How
do we know?

herding their flocks of sheep and cattle, including the humped zebu, back to the hills for the summer. Over time they may have decided to farm the river-watered alluvial lands of the valley and to settle permanently. They began to trade by boat along the Indus and even down the river into the Arabian Sea and, further, into the Persian Gulf and up the Tigris and Euphrates into Mesopotamia. Goods from the Indus valley have been found in Mesopotamia and vice versa.

Crafts and the Arts. Crafts of the Indus valley included pottery making, dyeing, metalworking in bronze, and bead making. Bead materials included jade from the Himalayas, lapis lazuli from Afghanistan, turquoise from Persia, amethyst from Mewar in India, and steatite, which was found locally. All these items suggest an active interregional trade. Small sculptures in stone, terra cotta, and bronze appear to represent priestly or governmental officials, dancing girls, and, perhaps, mother goddesses. Since there are no accompanying texts to explain exact identities, these can be only guesses. Dice and small sculptures of bullock carts were probably used as toys and games. The first known use of cotton as a fiber for weaving textiles occurred in the Indus valley, introducing one of India's, and the world's, most enduring and important crops and crafts.

Limestone dancing figure from Harappa, *c.* 2300–1750 B.C.E. This dancing figure displays a grasp of three-dimensional movement and vitality rare in the arts until much later periods. Human sculptures in contemporary Mesopotamia and Egypt are, by contrast, symbols of pure power, either immutable ideals of divinity or semidivine kingship. Indeed, this Harappan accomplishment is so extraordinary that some scholars have cast doubt on its early date. (National Museum of India, New Delhi)

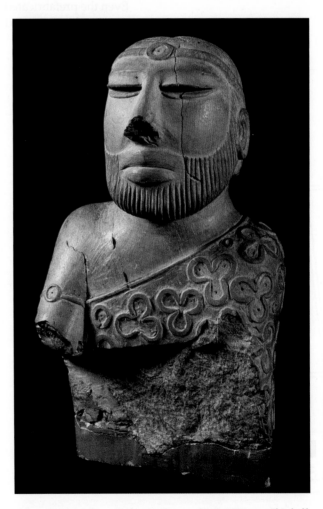

Limestone bust from Mohenjo-Daro, *c.* 2300–1750 B.C.E. This half-figure with horizontal slits for eyes, flat, thick lips, and fringes of beard is thought to have represented a priest or shaman because of the way the robe is hung over its left shoulder. Despite its monumental appearance, the figure is only seven inches high. (National Museum of Pakistan, Karachi)

3.1

3.2

What do we
know about the
Indus valley
civilization? How
do we know?

Carefully Planned Cities. By about 2500 B.C.E., a thriving civilization encompassing 1,000 known sites reached its apex and maintained it for about 500 years. Each of the two largest settlements, Harappa and Mohenjo-Daro, had a core area of about 3 miles in circumference, and Mohenjo-Daro also had a suburb—residential or industrial—about a mile away. Each city accommodated about 40,000 people.

The two cities share similar features of design. To the northwest is a citadel, or raised area; to the south is a lower town. In Mohenjo-Daro, the citadel is built on an architectural platform about 45 feet above the plain, and it measures 1,400 by 450 feet. On the summit was a vast communal bath 8 feet deep and 23 by 29 feet in area. Numerous cubicles—perhaps small, individual baths—flanked it. Adjacent to the large bath was a huge open space, identified as a granary, where food was stored safe from possible flood. Other spaces may have been used for public meetings. Fortified walls mark the southeast corner, and it appears that the entire citadel was walled.

The lower city was laid out in a gridiron, with the main streets about 45 feet wide. Here were the private houses, almost every one with its own well, bathing space, and toilet, consisting of a brick seat over a drainage area. Brick-lined drains flushed by water carried liquid and solid waste to sumps, where it was collected and carted away, probably to fertilize the nearby fields. The town plan was orderly and regular. Even the prefabricated, fire-baked bricks were uniform in size and shape. A uniform system of weights and measures was also employed throughout.

Excavation of the two largest cities has now reached severe limits. The city of Harappa was vandalized for thousands of years before, as well as during, the railroad construction, and few artifacts remain to be discovered. Mohenjo-Daro sits on a high water table, and any deeper excavation threatens to flood the site. It is impossible to dig down to the foundation level of the city.

Further exploration of Mohenjo-Daro's surface, however, continues to yield fascinating results. A recent survey revealed an outlying segment about a mile away from the known city. Was it part of an industrial area or a residential suburb? It is impossible to determine. The discovery, however, identifies Mohenjo-Daro as a larger city than Harappa. Perhaps it was the capital city of the civilization. The regularity of plan and construction suggests a government with great organizational and bureaucratic capacity, but no truly monumental architecture clearly marks the presence of a palace or temple, and there is little sign of social stratification in the plan or buildings. Those burials that have been discovered are regular, with the heads pointing to the north, and with some grave goods, such as pots of food and water, small amounts of jewelry, simple mirrors, and some cosmetics. These were not the extravagant royal burials of Egypt or even Mesopotamia.

In more recent years, additional Indus valley cities have been discovered and excavated, giving a fuller idea of the immense geographical extent of this civilization. The new excavations generally confirm the urban design patterns of the earlier finds, but they add some new elements. The excavations at Dholavira, in Kutch, India, for example, begun in the late 1980s, revealed immense, ornamented gates at the principal entrances to the city, and playing fields in the area between the upper and lower cities. Dholavira was not located on a river, but in the elevated center of a small region that may have formed an island during the monsoon,

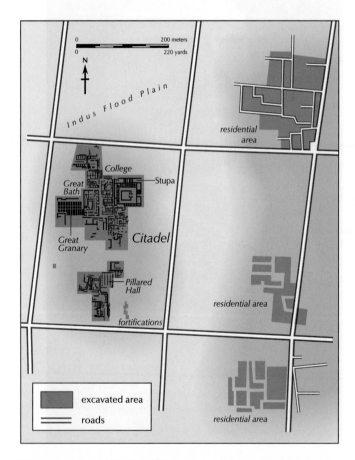

Planned cities. With an area of 150 acres and about 40,000 inhabitants, Mohenjo-Daro was a thriving Indus city. Excavations reveal a raised citadel area, containing ceremonial and administrative buildings, and a residential quarter centered on boulevards about 45 feet wide, with grid-patterned streets, an underground sewerage and drainage system, and a range of brick dwellings.

3.1

3.2

What do we
know about the
Indus valley
civilization? How
do we know?

EARLY SCIENCE AND TECHNOLOGY (7000–1000 B.C.E.)

7000–6000	Pottery made in Middle East
c. 5500	Copper, gold, and silver worked in Mesopotamia and Egypt
c. 4000–3500	In Asia and Africa, potter's wheel and kiln invented; mud bricks used; spindle developed for spinning; basketmaking begins
c. 3500–3000	Plow and cart invented; bronze cast and cuneiform writing developed in Sumer
3100	Reed boats in Egypt and Assyria; appearance of hieroglyphs in Egypt
3000	Cotton cultivated in the Indus valley
c. 2500	Wooden boats used in Egypt; ink and papyrus writing material used
2050	First glass in Mesopotamia
1790	Mathematics and medicine practiced in Babylon
1740	War chariots introduced from Persia to Mesopotamia (and later Egypt)
1370	Alphabetic script used in western Syria
1000	Industrial use of iron in Egypt and Mesopotamia

when water levels around it were highest. Huge cisterns were cut into the rock of the upper city for collecting rainwater in this extremely arid area. Dholavira also demonstrates a stark contrast between the relatively spacious quarters of the upper city and the more modest accommodations of the lower. Among the 20,000 artifacts uncovered, however, the extraordinary extremes of wealth and poverty of Egypt and Mesopotamia do not appear.

Questions of Interpretation. Interpretations of Indus valley artifacts stress the apparent classlessness of the society, its equality, efficiency, and public conveniences. Some interpreters view these qualities negatively, equating them with oppressively rigid governments and drab lives. While some scholars emphasize that the Harappans apparently survived and prospered for centuries, others argue that the cities changed little over long periods of time and lacked the dynamism of the cities in Mesopotamia and Egypt. With no contemporary literature to guide us, interpretation of what is found is in the eyes, and the value system, of the beholder.

We also do not know if this uniform, planned civilization had a single capital city, or several regional capitals, or no centralized political system at all. We see careful planning in the urban forms, but we do not know if the Indus valley civilization developed urban institutions for governance, trade, religion, or worship, much less the quality of any such institutions. While Egypt had a state but, perhaps, few cities, the Indus valley had cities but no clearly delineated state. Indeed, some scholars argue that the Indus valley did not create state structures at all. Was it like Egypt before unification or after unification? Was it like Mesopotamia, with numerous city-states all participating in a single general culture? All three suggestions have been made.

Until the Harappan language is deciphered, its civilization will remain mysterious: How was it organized? Why did it disperse? How did it move eastward? In what ways did it enrich its successor, the Aryan civilization of the Ganges River valley?

Legacies of the Harappan Civilization

Waves of immigrants entered India from Persia and central Asia beginning around 1250 B.C.E. Our understanding of these immigrants, called Aryans in Sanskrit (a name related to Persians or Iranians), has changed with recent archaeological and linguistic scholarship. We used to believe that the Aryans came in one major military invasion,

3.1

3.2

What do we
know about the
Indus valley
civilization? How
do we know?

but we now think they came more peacefully, in waves of immigration over centuries. As they entered India through the mountain passes, and continued eastward toward the Ganges River basin, they encountered the already settled Harappans of the Indus valley. Interchange between the resident Harappans and the invading Aryans produced new, hybrid cultural forms that we know primarily from the Aryan records. Ironically, these records are almost entirely literary and artistic. Reversing the Harappan pattern, the early Aryans have left a treasure of literature, but virtually no architectural or design artifacts.

Four legacies of Harappa stand out. First, the Aryan invaders were a nomadic group, who must have adopted at least some of the arts of settlement and civilization from the already settled residents. Second, as newcomers to the ecological zones of India, the Aryans must also have learned methods of farming and animal husbandry from the Harappans. Later, however, as they migrated eastward into the Ganges valley, they confronted a new ecology based on rice cultivation and the use of iron. Here, Harappan skills were useless. Third, a three-headed figure frequently appearing in Harappan seals resembles later representations of the Aryan god Shiva. Perhaps an earlier Harappan god was adopted and adapted by the Aryans.

Finally, the Aryan caste system—which ranked people at birth according to family occupation, color, and ritual purity, and prescribed the people with whom they might enter into social intercourse and marry—may reflect the need of the Aryans to regulate relationships between themselves and the Harappans. To claim and maintain

HOW DO WE KNOW?

The Decline of Harappan Civilization

By about 2000 B.C.E. the architecture of the Indus civilization began to decline. New buildings and repairs to existing structures lacked attention to quality and detail. Residents began to leave the cities and towns along the Indus and to relocate northeastward into the Punjab to towns such as Kalibangan, and southeastward to towns such as Dholavira in Kutch and Lothal in Gujarat. Meanwhile, newcomers—squatters—seem to have moved into the old cities.

Archaeologists suggest a variety of reasons—most of them ecological—for the decline in the cities and the geographical redistribution of their populations: perhaps the river changed course or became erratic; perhaps the soil became too saline; perhaps the forests were cut down and the topsoil eroded. An older opinion—that the Indus civilization was destroyed by the invasion of Aryan peoples from somewhere northwest of India—is now less widely held. It rested on Harappan archaeological evidence and Aryan literature. Several sets of skeletal remains in Mohenjo-Daro indicate violent deaths, while Aryan religious texts suggest that the invaders burned and destroyed existing settlements. The *Rigveda*, one of the earliest and most important of these texts, tells of the destructive power of the god Indra:

With all-outstripping chariot-wheel, O Indra, thou far-famed,
   hast overthrown the twice ten kings of men
With sixty thousand nine and ninety followers …
Thou goest on from fight to fight intrepidly, destroying castle
   after castle here with strength. (i, 53)
… in kindled fire he burnt up all their weapons,
And made him rich with kine and carts and horses. (ii, 15)

The Aryan god of fire, Agni, is still more fearsome:

Through fear of you the dark people went away, not giving battle, leaving behind their possessions, when, O Vaisvanara, burning brightly for Puru, and destroying the cities, you did shine. (7.5.3)

Newer archaeological evidence, however, suggests that the decline, deurbanization, and dispersal of the Indus civilization seem to have preceded the Aryan invasion. Further evidence suggests that the Aryans may have swept into the region not in a single all-conquering expedition, but in a series of smaller waves of immigration. The arrival of the Aryans may have only completed the Harappan decay.

- Why does the formation of new cities such as Kalibangan and Lothal suggest the decline of the Indus valley civilization?
- Why did scholars once believe that Aryan invasions destroyed the Indus valley civilization? Why do they now question that belief?
- What is the range of alternative explanations that have been offered? Why are scholars uncertain about the accuracy of these explanations?

their own supremacy, the Aryans may have elaborated the social structures of an early caste system and relegated the native inhabitants to permanent low status within it.

The Aryan groups grew increasingly skilled and powerful as they moved east. The first known archaeological evidence of their urban structures dates to about 700 B.C.E. and is found in the Ganges valley. We will read more about it in the chapter entitled "Indian Empires."

The Cities of the Nile and Indus:
What Difference Do They Make?

To what extent do the river valley civilizations of the Indus and the Nile confirm or alter our views of the significance of cities? They do show us that cities come in very different forms and networks. In Mesopotamia they had appeared as warring city-states. Along the Nile they were parts of a single state that was first unified by about 3000 B.C.E. By 2000 B.C.E., following foreign conquests, they formed the core of an imperial state, and they continued to be unified through most of the next 2,500 years. In the Indus valley we do not know if the cities were independent city-states or parts of a unified state; it is apparent, however, from their design and cultural products that they comprised a single cultural unit. In all three areas, then, life in cities created the state and gave concrete form to its value system.

We also learn of the significance of archaeological and textual study in unearthing and recovering all these early civilizations. To greater or lesser degrees, all had been lost to history for thousands of years before being exhumed by scholars in the nineteenth and twentieth centuries. In the task of reconstruction, written records have been critical to understanding the social structures and value systems of these cities. In both Mesopotamia and the Nile valley, excavations and written records enable us to see clearly the presence of religious elements, alliances between rulers and priests,

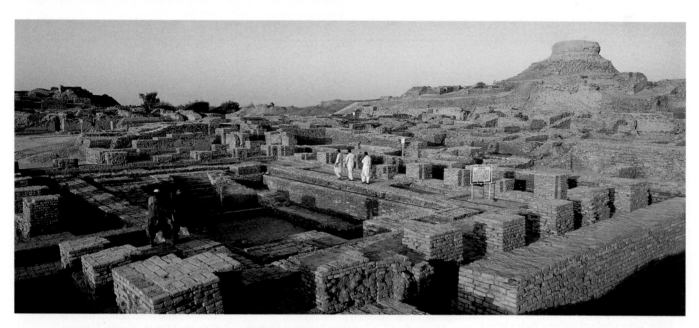

The citadel of Mohenjo-Daro, c. 2300 B.C.E. and later. The citadel at Mohenjo-Daro, a massive, mud-filled embankment that rises 43 feet above the lower city, was discovered by the archaeologist Daya Ram Sahni while investigating the second-century C.E. Buddhist stupa (burial mound) that can be seen in the distance. The citadel's summit houses the remains of several impressive structures, of which the most prominent is the so-called Great Bath (foreground).

extensive temple complexes and, in Egypt, burial complexes as well, and, in both civilizations, extensive specialization of labor and social stratification. But before we take these characteristics as the normal ancestry of city life, we pause at the Indus valley excavations, for here we see no record of such intense occupation with the otherworldly or the afterlife. We see no record of such extensive specialization of labor nor of such extreme social stratification—although the more recent excavations at Dholavira exhibit significant differences between the richest and poorest residential areas. We also see little evidence of the levels of artistic accomplishment of Mesopotamia and Egypt. And, of course, without texts, we have no written record of religious, philosophical, legal, or administrative systems in the Indus valley.

To explore further the global legacy of city and state formation, we now turn to four other regions of indigenous, early city and state formation in places far from those we have studied and far from one another: the Yellow River valley of China, Mesoamerica, South America, and the Niger River valley of West Africa. We are in for some surprises.

CHAPTER REVIEW

EGYPT: THE GIFT OF THE NILE

3.1 What were the characteristics of Egypt's early cities? How do we know?

Egypt's early cities in the Nile River valley have left us a wealth of archeological and textual materials. Often dedicated to specific gods, these early cities had a religious base as well as an administrative one. The Egyptians introduced monumental architecture and extensive specialization in social, political, and economic life. Trade networks of goods and ideas flourished. With the invention of writing, bureaucrats, businessmen, and scholars had new means of recording transactions, biographies, and philosophical principles.

THE INDUS VALLEY CIVILIZATION AND ITS MYSTERIES

3.2 What do we know about the Indus valley civilization? How do we know?

Written records of the Indus valley are scarce and we have not been able to decipher them. Thanks to archaeology, however, we know that a reasonably consistent Indus valley civilization extended over an immense space, the most dispersed of any early civilization, over thousands of years. Cities were exceptionally well laid out on a grid pattern with channels for water and sewerage. They seem to have been less hierarchical than the cities of Egypt or Mesopotamia. The people of the Indus valley made the first known use of cotton fiber for textiles. Waves of immigrants later implanted some of their own practices in the valley even as they transplanted some Indus agricultural practices eastward.

Suggested Readings

PRINCIPAL SOURCES

Fagan, Brian. *People of the Earth: An Introduction to World Prehistory* (Upper Saddle River, NJ: Prentice Hall, 13th ed., 2010). The best available textbook introduction to prehistory.

Foster, John L., trans. and ed. *Ancient Egyptian Literature* (Austin, TX: University of Texas Press, 2001). A fine anthology of varied forms of literature, culled from the translator/editor of many previous collections, plus a few new pieces.

Hawass, Z. *Silent Images: Women in Pharaonic Egypt* (New York: Harry N. Abrams, 2000). A study of the female form in Egyptian art.

Kenoyer, Jonathan M. *Ancient Cities of the Indus Valley Civilization* (New York: Oxford University Press, 1998). Lavishly illustrated accompanying volume to museum exhibit.

Lesko, Barbara. "Women of Egypt and the Ancient Near East," in *Becoming Visible: Women in European History*, ed. Renata

Bridenthal, Claudia Koonz, and Susan Stuard (Boston, MA: Houghton Mifflin, 2nd ed., 1998). Interpretive survey of current issues and existing literature.

——, ed. *Women's Earliest Records: From Ancient Egypt and Western Asia* (Atlanta, GA: Scholar's Press, 1989). Primary sources.

Manley, Bill. *The Penguin Historical Atlas of Ancient Egypt* (New York: Penguin Books, 1996). Through maps and pictures, an excellent review of Egyptian history from predynastic times through Alexander's conquest. Special sections include coverage of foreign relations and warfare, urbanization, and women. Special emphasis on trade.

Nashat, Guity. "Women in the Ancient Middle East," in *Restoring Women to History* (Bloomington, IN: Indiana University Press, 1999). Interpretive survey of current issues and existing literature.

Possehl, Gregory L. *The Indus Civilization: A Contemporary Perspective* (Lanham, MD:

AltaMira Press, 2003). One of the final works of this great scholar before his death.

Spodek, Howard, and Doris Meth Srinivasan, eds. *Urban Form and Meaning in South Asia: The Shaping of Cities from Prehistoric to Precolonial Times* (Washington, DC: National Gallery of Art, 1993). The papers of an international conference by some of the leading archaeologists working in South Asian urbanization.

ADDITIONAL SOURCES

Hassan, Fekri A. "The Predynastic of Egypt," *Journal of World Prehistory* II, No. 2 (June 1988), pp. 135–85. Careful and comprehensive account of the research.

Lichtheim, Miriam. *Ancient Egyptian Literature: A Book of Readings* (Berkeley, CA: University of California Press, 3 vols., 1973). Wide-ranging, comprehensive account of 3,000 years of literature.

Mumford, Lewis. *The City in History* (New York: Harcourt Brace, and World, 1961). Mumford looks only at cities of the Western world, but he is thoughtful, opinionated, and persuasive on what makes a good city.

Noble Wilford, John. "Egypt Carvings Set Earlier Date for Alphabet," *The New York Times* (November 14, 1999), A–1, p. 16. Records the discovery of the earliest alphabetic writing yet found.

Pritchard, James B., ed. *Ancient Near Eastern Texts Relating to the Old Testament* (Princeton, NJ: Princeton University Press, 3rd ed., 1969). The most comprehensive and accessible anthology of texts. Presented with full scholarly annotation.

Shaw, Ian., ed. *The Oxford History of Ancient Egypt* (New York: Oxford University Press, 2004). Brings together experts on many aspects of ancient Egypt. Well illustrated and comprehensive.

Wheeler, Mortimer. *Civilizations of the Indus Valley and Beyond* (London: Thames and Hudson, 1966). Head of the Archaeological Survey of India presents a clear view of its early findings in layman's terms.

FILMS

Ancient Egypt, in particular, is the subject of a constant flow of documentaries of all types from sources, such as *National Geographic,* The History Channel, Time Life, the BBC, etc. These are often (over-) dramatized, but they usually include some scholarly comments and interesting perspectives. Many are easily available on YouTube. Search and choose. Among recent ones, see:

Ancient Egypt: Life and Death in the Valley of the Kings (2013; 59 minutes). Attempts to reveal daily life in ancient Egypt through texts and art found in Upper (southern) Egypt.

Sex in the Ancient World: Egyptian Erotica (2009; 45 minutes). Reveals erotica from ancient Egypt, especially the Turin Papyrus (*c.* 1150 B.C.E.) and various tomb paintings and graffiti. The filmmakers claim that the Turin Papyrus may have been a kind of men's magazine.

Ancient Egypt's Greatest Warrior (2005; 52 minutes). Calls Thutmosis III (r. 1479–1425 B.C.E.) "Egypt's Napoleon," and describes his battles to create an Egyptian empire from Syria to Nubia, and also his relationship to his stepmother, Hatshepsut.

The Egyptian Book of the Dead (2006; 1 hour 30 minutes). The ethical and moral principles expressed in *The Book of the Dead* show that while the Egyptians wrote of death, and prepared for it, they loved life.

Films on the Indus valley civilization are comparatively few, and they borrow footage from one another. Because the civilization's script is not deciphered, there is less to relate; also, the ancient civilization straddles the modern, hostile, border of India and Pakistan, so filming is difficult. Try:

Indus: The Unvoiced Civilization (2000; 1 hour). Produced by Japanese NHK, with others with whom it shares footage. Goes to both Pakistan and India, as well as the Gulf region. Good for visuals and some scholarly commentary. Not, however, a scholarly production.

4 A Polycentric World

Cities and States in East Asia, the Americas, and West Africa

1700 B.C.E.–1000 C.E.

This chapter completes the survey of the seven areas of primary urbanization. It covers the four areas that developed primary urbanization somewhat more recently: the Yellow River valley of China; two regions of the western hemisphere—Mesoamerica and the South American Pacific coastal plain with the adjacent Andes Mountains that tower above it; and the Niger River valley of West Africa. The first cities in these regions date from as early as 1700 B.C.E. in China to as late as 400 C.E. in the Niger valley. They include cities that were not in major river valleys as well as some that were. They all show at least some evidence of state formation, long-distance trade, and religious practices. But they include settlements that did not have written languages and records. In at least one of them—West Africa—the settlement pattern is so different from urbanization elsewhere that we are asked to stretch our definition of urbanization and challenge our value system in assessing its significance.

Warrior ear ornament, cleaned and reconstructed (tomb 1), Moche Royal Tombs, Sipán, Peru, first to sixth centuries C.E. The warrior armed for battle suggests a culture dominated by powerful warrior priests. (Bruning Archaeological Museum, Lambayeque, Peru)

LEARNING OBJECTIVES

4.1 ((	4.2 ((	4.3 ((
Describe the characteristics of early Chinese cities.	Describe the differences between East Asian and American cities.	Explain the urban pattern of West African settlements.

((**Listen** on **MyHistoryLab**

China: The Xia, Shang, and Zhou Dynasties

4.1   What were the characteristics of early Chinese cities?

What were the
characteristics
of early Chinese
cities?

4.1

4.2

4.3

The Earliest Villages

As early as the eighth millennium B.C.E., Neolithic pottery decorations marked the transition from hunting and gathering to the culture of farming and village life. This Yangshao culture, first excavated in 1921, was named for the location where it was discovered in China's western Henan province. Among other fascinating finds, in late 1999 archaeologists uncovered a set of tiny flutes carved some 9,000 years ago from the wing bones of a large bird. Three thousand years older than the next known musical instruments, from Sumer, one of them is still playable.

The Yangshao lasted to *c.* 2700 B.C.E. Farmers of this era grew millet, wheat, and rice, and domesticated pigs, dogs, goats, and perhaps horses. They lived mostly in river valleys, and the villages were often surrounded with earthen walls for defense. Ban Po is the best excavated village of the Yangshao culture. From archaeological evidence, it appears that individual nuclear families occupied these dwellings, while a larger building in the center of the village may have housed clan meetings.

Slightly later and slightly to the northeast, a more sophisticated Neolithic culture, the Longshan, grew up. The people of the Longshan made their pottery on wheels, whereas the Yangshao had coiled or molded their pots by hand. The Longshan people domesticated sheep and cattle, which were not seen in Yangshao sites. Longshan graves were dug under their own homes, while the Yangshao had buried their dead in graveyards far from their villages. Sometimes Longshan funeral urns were cemented into foundation walls, suggesting ancestor worship.

Several hundred miles to the east, somewhat further down the Yellow River in Shandong, and one or two centuries later, yet another branch of Longshan culture developed, with another distinct type of pottery, often characteristically reddish-brown and gray in color, quite different from the black pottery of the Longshan of Henan. Although the high points of Yangshao and the western and eastern Longshan cultures appeared at successively later times, they overlapped one another to a considerable extent.

Headless skeletons of human sacrificial victims, tomb 1001, Anyang, China, *c.* 1495–1122 B.C.E. The royal tombs discovered at Anyang testify to the wealth and power of the Shang rulers. Numerous servants and prisoners-of-war gave their lives willingly or unwillingly to accompany their masters to the grave. The heads of the decapitated figures shown here were located elsewhere in the tomb.

4.1
4.2
4.3
What were the
characteristics
of early Chinese
cities?

The Henan Longshan culture seems to have been a harsh one. Excavations reveal the burials of victims of killing, some decapitated and showing signs of struggle, suggesting warfare between villages. The defensive walls of pounded earth that encircle some of the villages support this hypothesis, as does the presence of bronze knives.

The Beginnings of State Formation

Out of these struggles among villages, larger political units gradually emerged. Ancient Chinese historical texts tell of three early dynasties—the Xia, the Shang, and the Zhou—that ruled over large regions of China. In its time, each ruled over the most powerful single kingdom among the embattled states of northern China. All were based primarily around the Huang He (Yellow River) valley in northern China. State formation may have begun under the Xia, c. 2205–1766 B.C.E., although records are too sparse to recreate its cities and institutions. The archaeological record on urbanization under the Shang, c. 1600–1046 B.C.E., is far more revealing and reliable. The Zhou, c. 1046–256 B.C.E., consolidated both city and state, and left extensive archaeological remains and written records. None of the three dynasties succeeded in annexing all its enemies and building a single unified empire. That process would come later.

The traditional dating suggests that the states succeeded one another, but recent evidence indicates that there may, in fact, have been considerable overlap. For centuries, they may have coexisted in neighboring regions, with first one, then another, having comparatively greater power and prestige.

By the time of the Shang, if not already in the Xia dynasty, people had founded cities in northern China as centers of administration and ritual. State formation was well under way, and cities served as capitals and administrative centers. An urban network ruled the entire dynastic state. Capitals were frequently shifted, suggesting that new rulers wanted to make their mark through new construction, or that confrontation with neighboring, enemy states required strategic redeployments for improving offensive or defensive positions. Kings frequently entrusted the administration of regional cities to their blood relatives. It appears that rulers performed productive economic functions for their subjects, especially in the control of water. The ability to organize huge work gangs to construct irrigation channels and dikes for flood control confirmed their power and status. As a result, the lineages on top

AT A GLANCE: CHINA 800–100 B.C.E.

DATE	POLITICS	RELIGION AND CULTURE	SOCIAL DEVELOPMENT
8000 B.C.E.		• Neolithic decorated pottery	• Simple Neolithic society established
5000 B.C.E.	• Yangshao culture in China (5000–2700)	• Marks on Yangshao pottery possibly writing	• Penal code; defensive structures around villages
3500 B.C.E.	• Longshan late Neolithic culture	• Delicate Longshan ceramics	• Farming, with domesticated animals
2000 B.C.E.	• Xia dynasty (2205–1766) • Shang dynasty (c. 1600–c. 1046) • City of Zhengzhou (c. 1600) • Under Shang, bronze vases found in ceremonial burials	• Oracle bones • The "sage kings" in China known from legend; first known use of writing in this area	• Agricultural progress • Cities (by 1700) under control of Shang kings
1100 B.C.E.	• Zhou dynasty (c. 1045–256)	• Poetry extant from Zhou period	• Under Zhou, iron, money, and written laws in use
500 B.C.E.	• Warring States period (480–222) • Qin dynasty (221–206)	• Confucius (d. 479) • Great Wall of China begun (214) to keep out Xiongnu	• Crossbow invented (c. 350)
100 B.C.E.		• Sima Qian (d. 85)	

What were the
characteristics
of early Chinese
cities?

4.1

4.2

4.3

lived lives of considerable wealth while those on the lower levels had little, as sharp class differences emerged in the early dynastic states. The cemeteries of different classes were segregated into different neighborhoods within the city and its suburbs, and were of different quality.

In common with primary cities in other parts of the world, the Chinese cities were also religious centers, with the kings presiding over rituals as well as administration and warfare. Indeed, the warfare was necessary to supply the human and animal sacrifices that were central to the rituals.

Early Evidence of Writing. One of these early rituals has left us evidence of a crucial development in Chinese civilization: the invention of writing. Oracle bones—bones of birds, animals, and especially the shells of turtles—were inscribed with markings and writing for use in predicting the future. After they were marked, these bones were placed in a fire and tapped lightly with a rod until they began to crack. The cracks were then interpreted by specialists in predicting the future. A poem from the later Zhou dynasty noted the use of oracle bones in deciding the location of a new city:

> The plain of Chou was very fertile,
> Its celery and sowthistle sweet as rice-cakes.
> "Here we will make a start; here take counsel,
> Here notch our [turtle]."
> It says, "Stop," it says, "Halt.
> Build houses here."

> (Chang, *Shang Civilization*, pp. 31–32)

Some of the oracle-bone inscriptions confirm the names and approximate dates of Xia and Shang rulers. Other bones suggest that their purpose was to communicate with the gods. The location of the bones and the content of their inscriptions encouraged archaeologists to search further in the north-central Chinese plains, near the point where the Yellow River flows out of the mountains, for evidence of China's early dynastic period.

Historical Evidence of the Xia Dynasty. Chinese legend long spoke of three ancient dynasties—the Xia, the Shang, and the Zhou. While many written records exist on the Zhou dynasty, historians were skeptical of the existence of the earlier dynasties until relatively recently. At Erlitou, east of Luoyang, in western Henan, archaeologists found a culture in precisely the areas described by ancient texts as the site of the legendary Xia dynasty. The pottery at Erlitou seemed intermediate in style and quality between the earlier Longshan and the later Shang. Although the link is not certain, many archaeologists took Erlitou to be representative of the Xia dynasty.

The Xia, like the later Shang and Zhou, seems to have been ruled by specific family clans, each with its own king. As in many cultures, kingship and kinship were linked. As head of both his biological clan and his geographical realm, the king performed rituals, divinations, and sacrifices; waged war; constructed irrigation and flood-control works; and administered his government. The king mediated between the world of the spirits and the world of humans. He was thought to be descended from the god of the spirits, who controlled human health, wealth, agriculture, and warfare. The king's assertion of his right to perform sacrifice in a particular place was, in effect, his assertion of his right to rule over that place. Rights over ritual implied rights over land and people.

Another critical task of the ruler was to tame the waters of the mighty, and hazardous, Yellow River. China's first settlements had avoided the immediate flood plain of the river, one of the most treacherous in the world. Its bed filled with the silt from the mountains, the Yellow River has jumped its course 26 times in recorded history, wreaking untold devastation. As early as the Longshan culture, people built great

HOW DO WE KNOW?

Ancient China

Three kinds of sources provide most of our direct information about early Chinese cities and dynasties: written texts, oracle bones, and artifacts uncovered archaeologically. (Scholars also sometimes take records, such as poetry, from later eras and infer that they may represent earlier conditions as well, as we shall see in the next pages.)

Texts

We have no literary texts from the Xia and Shang dynasties. Some scholars believe that the Zhou dynasty destroyed those that did exist. Much later texts ascribed to the Chinese teacher Confucius (551–479 B.C.E.) refer to the Xia and Shang dynasties, but give little detail. Later, Sima Qian (Ssu-ma Ch'ien; c. 145–85 B.C.E.), court historian of the Han dynasty, wrote the first of China's official historical annals. Sima, who had access to many texts that have not survived, devoted a chapter to the Shang royal house, beginning with its legendary founder, Xie, who moved his capital to a town called Shang, now believed to have been in eastern Henan. Successive rulers moved this capital eight times. Xie's fourteenth successor, Tang, established the hereditary dynasty of Shang. Sima's sources of information were limited, however, and his chapter mostly outlined the genealogy of the rulers, recounted moralistic tales of their rule, and briefly noted their capital cities.

Oracle Bones

A new source of information came to light in the 1890s and early 1900s. Numerous oracle bones—some apparently hidden away for many years, others recently uncovered—appeared in antiques markets in China. Over the decades more than 10,000 were discovered, mostly in the central plains of north China. These bones of birds and animals, and shells of turtles, were inscribed with symbolic notation, placed in a fire, and tapped with a rod until they began to crack. Specialists then "read" the cracks to predict the future. Some of the oracle-bone inscriptions confirmed Sima Qian's accounts of early Shang rulers. The location of the bones and the content of their inscriptions encouraged archaeologists to search further for additional oracle bones and other artifacts in the area around the ancient Shang capital of Anyang.

Archaeology

Archaeology was in fashion in China in the 1920s. Beijing Man had been discovered at Zhoukoudian, and in the process a new generation of Chinese archaeologists had received on-the-job training. Meanwhile, the new "doubting antiquity" school of Chinese historiography began to question the dating and to challenge the authenticity of many ancient Chinese historical events. In response, the newly established National Research Institute of History and Philology dispatched the young archaeologist Dong Zobin to explore the Anyang region. Dong recommended excavating for oracle bones. These excavations, mostly under the direction of Li Ji, uncovered not only bones but also sites from the Shang dynasty. These led to the discovery of artifacts from earlier eras as well. Scholars understood these to be evidence of the existence of the Xia dynasty. Ancient texts, bronzes, oracle bones, and excavations reinforced one another in recounting parts of ancient China's urbanization and state formation. Civil war in China, beginning in 1927, and war with Japan, beginning in 1937 (see "World War II"), interrupted excavations until 1950, but since then continuous archaeological research (except in 1966–74) has yielded new understanding.

- What historical evidence enabled the Xia dynasty to emerge from the realm of legend to its current status as the accepted first dynasty of ancient China?
- Politics and fashion as well as scholarly motives influence the kind of research that archaeologists can and do undertake. Discuss this assertion in terms of the excavation of the sites of early Chinese cities and dynasties.
- What kinds of skill do you think a "reader" of oracle bones must have had to be successful? What would have been considered success in this profession?

4.1 What were the characteristics of early Chinese cities?

4.2

4.3

levees and canals for flood control, drainage, and irrigation. Chinese legend credits the first success in taming the Yellow River to one of the cultural heroes of ancient history, Yu the Great of the twenty-third century B.C.E., legendary founder of the Xia dynasty. The legend reflects the idea of a royal house's gaining power through its ability to organize great gangs of laborers to construct a system of water control.

The Xia dynasty, according to mythology that is steadily being validated by archaeological finds, went further with human organization. It assembled armies, built cities, carved jade, cast and worked bronze into both weapons and ritual vessels, created the pictograms that would evolve into Chinese script, and may have designed China's first calendar.

Similarities Among the Three Dynasties. All three of these earliest dynasties, the Xia, Shang, and Zhou, built walled towns. Indeed, in written Chinese the same character, *cheng*, represents both city and city wall. At times these towns were loosely connected to one another, forming a network of rule and trade. At other times, when a single

CHAPTER FOUR: A POLYCENTRIC WORLD 1700 B.C.E.–1000 C.E.

What were the
characteristics
of early Chinese
cities?

4.1

4.2

4.3

powerful king headed the dynasty, a single capital city predominated. Archaeologists see many similarities among the towns and the political structures of all three dynasties.

In the absence of earlier written records, scholars sometimes use literary evidence from later dynasties as evidence for patterns in the earlier dynasties. For example, in arguing for the supremacy of royal rule during the Shang dynasty, they find supporting proof from "Pei shan," a poem of the Zhou dynasty:

Everywhere under Heaven
Is no land that is not the king's.
To the borders of all those lands
None but is the king's slave.

(trans. Waley)

There is some evidence that women could wield power in the earliest of Chinese dynasties, but it is otherwise difficult to say much about gender relations in ancient China. By the time of the Shang dynasty, however, all evidence points to China as a patriarchal society wherein women had many fewer options than men.

City and State under the Shang and Zhou

By the time of the Shang dynasty, the ruler directly controlled a growing network of towns. The king ruled from his capital city. He apportioned regional cities to his designated representatives, who were usually blood relatives. These relatives received title to land, shares in the harvests, and rights to build and control the regional capital cities. In exchange, they represented and served the king and his interests in the provinces.

Territorially, the Shang dynasty was based in northern and central Henan and southwestern Shandong. At its most powerful it extended as far south as Wucheng, south of the Yangzi River; east to the Pacific, incorporating the Shandong Peninsula; north into Hebei and southern Manchuria; and west through Shanxi into the

Shang China. Centered where the Huang He (Yellow River) enters its flood plain from the mountains of northeast China, the Longshan farming communities of about 2500 B.C.E. benefited from rich alluvial soils and extensive metal ore deposits. By 1800 B.C.E., a powerful, highly organized, urban metalworking culture, the Shang, had developed.

4.1

4.2

4.3

What were the
characteristics
of early Chinese
cities?

Inscribed oracle bone, China. Shang kings
communicated with their ancestors through
both sacrificial rituals and divination. Diviners
would pose questions—about health, harvest,
or politics—by applying a red-hot poker
to animal bones or turtle shells and then
analyzing the resulting heat-induced cracks.
(Royal Ontario Museum, Toronto)

📖 Read the Document: Inscribed
Oracle Bone and Chinese Characters
on MyHistoryLab

mountains of Shaanxi. At its greatest extent it may have controlled 40,000 square
miles. In addition, recent archaeological finds suggest that Shang cultural influence
extended to regions and cities far away from this center of its political control. On the
fringes, Shang territories were interspersed with those of other rulers, and warfare
between them was apparently frequent.

Early Royal Capitals. Oracle bones identify a city named Yinxu, established about
1384 B.C.E., about 50 miles north of today's city of Anyang, as the seventh and final
capital of the Shang dynasty. Some archaeologists believe that Luoyang was the first,
but it has been difficult to excavate because it lies directly under a modern city. Today,
most believe that Zhengzhou, about 100 miles southwest of Anyang, was the first
dynastic capital, and it has been excavated extensively. Founded *c.* 1700 B.C.E., its core
covered about 1¼ square miles and it was enclosed by a wall 4½ miles long and, in
places, still surviving to a height of 30 feet.

What were the
characteristics
of early Chinese
cities?

4.1

4.2

4.3

Shang-dynasty bronze wine vessel, fourteenth to eleventh century B.C.E. The thousands of Shang bronze vessels that survive today continue to astonish us with their technical mastery and elegance. They testify to the elite's willingness to devote huge quantities of a precious resource to ritual purposes. During times of war, such bronzes were often melted down to produce weapons, but once peace resumed, they were recast into ritual objects. (British Museum, London)

Inside the walled area lived the royal family, the nobility, and their retainers. Outside this palace/ritual center was a network of residential areas; workshops making bone, pottery, and bronze artifacts; and cemeteries. The class divisions written into this spatial pattern were reinforced by the geography of the suburbs: to the north were the dwellings and graves of the wealthy and powerful, marked by ritual bronze vessels and sacrificial victims; to the south were the dwellings of the commoners and their burial places in trash pits. Occupations tended to be inherited within specific family units (compare the caste system of India discussed in the chapters entitled "Indian Empires" and "Hinduism and Buddhism," below). Many *zu*, or lineage groups, corresponded to occupational groups.

Capital of the Middle Period: Huanbei. In the intermediate years, between Zhengzhou and Yinxu, Huanbei (meaning 'north of the Huan River') seems to have served as a capital of the Shang dynasty, dating to about 1400 B.C.E. Discovered in excavations conducted by a joint team from the Chinese Academy of Social Sciences and the University of Minnesota, beginning in 1996, it stands within a two-square-mile enclosure surrounded by rammed-earth walls. In the center stood a palace/temple complex, the largest ever excavated from Shang times, and within the palace an enormous courtyard—the first ever discovered in China. Around the temple were 43 sacrificial pits, many containing human skulls, apparently the result of human sacrifices. Some were buried with pieces of jade, suggesting that they were people of some substance. An abundance of bronze objects have also been uncovered.

4.1

4.2

4.3

What were the
characteristics
of early Chinese
cities?

EARLY CHINESE CULTURE

5000 B.C.E.	Rice cultivation, basketry, weaving, use of wooden tools, primitive writing
3000	Domestication of sheep, cattle, water buffalo
2000	Human grave sacrifices
1900	Metalworking, class system, domestication of horse
1200	Chariots in warfare

Anyang: The Last Shang Capital. The final, most powerful, and most elaborate capital of the Shang dynasty was at Anyang itself. Shang texts report that the nineteenth king, Pan Gieng, moved his capital to Yin, and that the dynasty remained there until its fall 273 years later. Archaeologists identify that site as Anyang. This capital was the center of a network of sites stretching about 200 miles from northwest to southeast. The core area around Anyang is difficult to excavate fruitfully. The city burned to the ground, and farmers have been plowing the area, and robbers pillaging it, for 3,000 years. Remains of royal graves and of buildings that appear to be royal palaces hint at the greatness of the ancient city, but they do not yield many secrets. Nonetheless, scholars have found bronze treasures in royal graves.

The Shang excelled in crafting bronze. They produced bronze axes, knives, spears, and arrowheads as well as bronze utensils, ritual vessels, and sculptures. They also used horse-drawn chariots, which may have been derived from those of Indo-Europeans who migrated into China. The ability to use bronze in their weapons gave Chinese kings and warriors a decided advantage over their enemies, but it appears that most bronze was crafted for ritual use.

Cultural Outposts. The excavations in the Anyang region and the discoveries of the oracle bones gave evidence that the mythical Shang dynasty had been real, and that the area around Anyang had been its heartland. More recent excavations have shown that the cultural influence of the Shang reached far distant regions: massive bronzes discovered in the Yangzi River valley, more than 500 miles from Anyang; pits with hundreds of artifacts including elephant tusks, cowrie shells, and objects of jade, gold, and bronze at Sanxingdui, in Sichuan province, 700 miles to the west, dating to about 1200 B.C.E.; and at Jinsha, also in Sichuan, more bronzes cast in human forms. The objects were too different from those of Anyang for anyone to claim that all these regions formed a political unity, but they were similar enough to allow the claim of cultural unity.

The Zhou Dynasty. The Shang dynasty fell to the Zhou around 1122 B.C.E., but it did not disappear, just as the Xia had not disappeared when it had fallen to the Shang. Instead, in defeat, these kingdoms continued to exist, albeit with diminished territory and power. Until the Qin dynasty unified China in 221 B.C.E., the defeat of a dynasty did not mean that it completely disappeared. Rather, it became one of the many smaller kingdoms competing for power in continuous warfare in northern China.

The Zhou survived for more than 600 years, making it one of the longest-lasting Chinese dynasties. The Zhou made several important conceptual contributions to Chinese thinking about culture, politics, and military strategy. Moreover, with the advent of substantial written sources, we know much more about the Zhou than about the earlier Chinese dynasties.

One of the most important written sources for Zhou political thought is the *Book of Documents*, which describes the Zhou conquest of the Shang. As is often true, such a book is written from the perspective of the winners. In this case, the Zhou portrayed their victory as one of heroic soldiers over decadent forces led by a corrupt and

SOURCE

The Cosmo-magical City

In his classic and convincing *Pivot of the Four Quarters*, Paul Wheatley argues that ancient Chinese cities, like most ancient cities, began as ritual centers. He calls these cities "cosmo-magical." Archaeological and textual records support this interpretation for China. Consider, for example, this Zhou poem illustrating the siting of a royal capital. The process begins with reading the oracle shell of a tortoise to determine its location, and ends with sacrifices to mark the completion of construction:

Of old Tan-fu the duke
At coming of day galloped his horses,
Going west along the river bank
Till he came to the foot of Mount Ch'i.
Where with the lady Chiang
He came to look for a home.

The plain of Chou was very fertile,
Its celery and sowthistle sweet as rice-cakes.
"Here we will make a start; here take counsel,
Here notch our tortoise."
It says, "Stop," it says, "Halt.
Build houses here."

So he halted, so he stopped,
And left and right
He drew the boundaries of big plots and little,
He opened up the ground, he counted the acres
From west to east;
Everywhere he took his task in hand.

Then he summoned his Master of Works,
Then he summoned his Master of Lands
And made them build houses.
Dead straight was the plumb-line,
The planks were lashed to hold the earth;
They made the Hall of Ancestors, very venerable.

They tilted in the earth with a rattling,
They pounded it with a dull thud,

They beat the walls with a loud clang,
They pared and chiselled them with a faint *p'ing, p'ing*;
The hundred cubits all rose;
The drummers could not hold out.

They raised the outer gate;
The outer gate soared high.
They raised the inner gate;
The inner gate was very strong.
They raised the great earth-mound,
Whence excursions of war might start.

The rituals seem to have conferred worldly benefits. Potential enemies fled. The poem continues:

And in the time that followed they did not abate their sacrifices,
Did not let fall their high renown;
The oak forests were laid low,
Roads were opened up.
The K'un tribes scampered away;
Oh, how they panted!

Oracle records recognize more than 20 titles of officials grouped into three categories—ministers, generals, and archivists—"but the most important categories of officials insofar as our available data are concerned are the diviners ... and the inquirers. ... Jao Tsung-yi enumerated the activities of as many as 117 diviners and inquirers in the oracle records. Ch'en Meng-chia counted 120." (Chang, 1980, p. 192) Besides the diviners, a cadre of priests performed religious rituals, including human sacrifices.

Military force was needed to sustain these rituals, by providing the prisoners-of-war to be sacrificed when rituals demanded. Oracle records speak of Shang military campaigns of 3,000, 5,000, and even 13,000 troops. As many as 30,000 prisoners-of-war were claimed in one large battle, and 300 prisoners were sacrificed in a ritual of ancestor worship. Archaeological finds show that 600 humans were sacrificed at the completion of a single house; 164 for a single tomb.

debauched king. Nonetheless, they wanted to portray their strong connections and good relations with previous kings so that they would appear legitimate.

They also developed a heretofore unique explanation of why they should be considered the legitimate rulers of the region: the idea of the "**Mandate of Heaven**." The *Book of History* assumed a close relationship between Heaven and the king, but the king had the mandate to rule only if he acted in the interests of the people. If a king was weak, the theory argued that others had the right to remove him, with the "Mandate of Heaven." This doctrine would shape Chinese thinking on leadership for centuries.

While they were in power, the Zhou made several important contributions to Chinese culture. One of the most important was the *Book of Songs*, which includes a collection of China's earliest poetry, some of which appears to have been from earlier societies and transmitted orally until it was recorded. The poetry focuses on

KEY TERM

Mandate of Heaven A concept in China: the ruler had moral authority so long as the heavenly powers granted it to him on the basis of his good character. A well-functioning government was evidence that the ruler possessed the Mandate of Heaven. A poorly functioning government, especially when accompanied by such natural disasters as flood or drought, showed that the Mandate had passed away.

Burial pit, unearthed at Liulihe, Hebei province, Western Zhou period (1122–771 B.C.E.). Evidence for the centrality of ritual in ancient Chinese culture is found in this tomb, which contains the remains of horses and chariots. These important instruments of rule would have been regarded as valuable offerings to the gods and were thus buried along with their owner.

4.1

4.2 How did the first cities of the Americas differ from those of East Asia?

4.3

the exploits of kings and aristocrats, but also provides powerful insights into family life and gender relations in early China.

One poem, for example, describes the anxiety of a woman who became too old to marry. It makes clear that a man would pursue a woman in courtship and not the other way around, and that the woman would leave her family to join her husband's. Other poems speak of a deep distrust of women in politics and argue that men alone should be in the public sphere; women belonged at home. Challenging the notion of the Mandate of Heaven, at least one poem argues that women in politics, not Heaven, sowed disorder in dynasties. Still others deal with the give and take of seduction and love outside marriage.

The Zhou also transformed warfare, turning away from the chariots that seemed so useful earlier. They both developed cavalry, in which soldiers fought successfully with bows and arrows on horseback, and introduced infantry troops of draft foot soldiers who could effectively fight the cavalry with crossbows.

The Zhou expanded significantly, creating a much larger state than that ruled by the Shang. Recognizing the difficulty of ruling such a large state, the Zhou created a decentralized administration that left much power in local hands. In the end, this contributed to much instability, with the Zhou remaining in power at least nominally at the top, while facing competition from subordinates throughout China. Because of the chaos, by 480 B.C.E. a period subsequent scholars have named "the Warring States period" emerged, which lasted until the Qin dynasty unified the country in 221 B.C.E.

The Western Hemisphere: Mesoamerica and South America

4.2 How did the first cities of the Americas differ from those of East Asia?

The first cities of the Americas share several characteristics with those of East Asia. They began as religious shrine centers, linked by shamans, individuals who had special powers to communicate with the spiritual world on behalf of the community. They developed into city-states with important functions in politics and trade as well as in religion, and some even incorporated whole empires under their sway. Specific individual cities, most notably Teotihuacán, had enormous cultural influence over other settlements that were spread across great distances.

There were also great differences between the hemispheres. Geographically, the cities of the western hemisphere were built at the water's edge, usually near lakes or small rivers, but not on major river systems. Technologically, the people of the Americas did not use metals in their tools. In fact, they hardly used metal at all except for ornaments, jewelry, and artwork. They used neither wheels nor draft animals in transportation, perhaps because the Americas had no large, domesticable animals to use for pulling carts until horses and cattle were introduced by the Spaniards in the sixteenth century. Llamas served as pack animals for small loads in the Andes in South America, but otherwise goods were carried by hand, dragged, or shipped by canoe. Construction and transportation were therefore far more labor-intensive than

AT A GLANCE: THE EARLY AMERICAS

DATE	POLITICS	RELIGION AND CULTURE	SOCIAL DEVELOPMENT
6000 B.C.E.		• Stone tools in Mexico (6700 B.C.E.)	
5000 B.C.E.			• Plants (including maize) cultivated in Mesoamerica
3000 B.C.E.			• Villages established in Mesoamerica; gourds and beans grown
2500 B.C.E.	• Maya culture originated (2000)	• Pottery from Mesoamerica	
1500 B.C.E.	• Olmecs, Gulf of Mexico (c. 1500–400 B.C.E.) • Zapotecs, southern Mexico (1400 B.C.E.–900 C.E.)	• Olmec center of San Lorenzo; pottery, mirrors, ceramics	
1000 B.C.E.	• Chavín, northern Peru (c. 900–200 B.C.E.)		
200 B.C.E.	• Moche, north coast of Peru (200 B.C.E.–600 C.E.)	• First Teotihuacán buildings, valley of Mexico	
100 B.C.E.	• Nazca, Peru (1–600)		
500 C.E.	• Tiwanaku, Bolivia (c. 200–1200) • Maya culture (southern Mexico, Guatemala, Belize) at peak (325–900) • Huari, Peru (c. 650–1200)	• Teotihuacán population 100,000 • First fully developed towns in the Mississippi valley (c. 700) • Teotihuacán culture at peak (500–650)	
1000 C.E.	• Toltecs (c. 950–1170) • Chimú, northwest Peruvian coast (c. 1000–1470)		
1200 C.E.	• Aztecs (c. 1100–1521) • Inca, Andean South America (c. 1200–1535)	• Aztec pictographs and hieroglyphs • Aztec gold, jade, and turquoise jewels, textiles, and sculptures	• Aztec tribute empire over surrounding lands from capital of Cuzco

in most of Afro-Eurasia. Finally, except for the Maya, the Native Americans did not create writing systems. Some, such as the Zapotecs and Toltecs, used limited hieroglyphic symbols and calendar formats, but these did not develop into full, written languages. In Afro-Eurasia, only in the Niger River area did settlements grow into cities without developing writing systems.

In many respects, the cities of the western hemisphere still had one foot in the Stone Age. Urban society evolved much later in the Americas. Stone tools ground by hand first appeared in central Mexico about 6700 B.C.E.; the domestication of plants began about 5000 B.C.E.; villages were established about 3000 B.C.E.; pottery appeared about 2300 B.C.E.; and population suddenly increased about 500 B.C.E. These processes were much slower than in the river-valley civilizations of Eurasia, perhaps because humans arrived in the New World relatively recently. Also, the immigrants to the New World had longer journeys, from today's Alaska to the southern reaches of South America. Often, they seemed to found new towns and then abandon them for still newer ones, sometimes because they were defeated in battle; sometimes because the residents quarreled among themselves; and sometimes because they sought a better ecological niche. (See Source box, The Popul Vuh, below.)

Origins: Migration and Agriculture

Humans arrived in the western hemisphere across the Beringia land bridge (connecting Alaska and Siberia) about 15,000 years ago and then spread throughout both North and South America. By 5000 B.C.E., they were cultivating maize, at least in

4.1

4.2

4.3

How did the first cities of the Americas differ from those of East Asia?

Classic cultures of the Americas. Sophisticated urban cultures developed in two tropical regions of the Americas: humid southern Mexico and the more temperate valleys of the central Andes. Both regions witnessed a succession of distinctive cultural and political centers. The Maya civilization of the Yucatán emerged, by 250 C.E., as the outstanding power in Mesoamerica, while the Huari empire of the Andes prefigured that of the Inca. In South America, urban civilizations appeared both near sea level along the Pacific coast and in the Andes Mountains, at altitudes from 6,500 to 12,000 feet.

small quantities, as well as gathering wild crops and hunting animals. By around 3000 B.C.E., they also grew beans and gourds.

Archaeologists and botanists have documented the beginnings of domestication of maize in the valley of Tehuacán, 200 miles southeast of Mexico City. Beginning with wild corn cobs about 5000 B.C.E., farmers slowly bred larger and more nutritious varieties, producing an early form of modern corn about 2,000 years ago. Later excavations in Peru showed that the cultivation of maize began there by 4000 B.C.E., perhaps introduced from Mesoamerica. In both regions, at about the same time, the other two staples of the American diet, beans and squashes, also appear. Further, in the Andes Mountains, potatoes and other root crops were also grown. The valley of Mexico and the high Andes of Peru thus became incubators of much of the civilization of the Americas from an early date. Agricultural innovation, urbanization, and the foundation of empires originated in these regions and spread outward.

Mesoamerican Urbanization: The First Stages

By 2000 B.C.E., the agricultural foundations for an urban civilization were in place in Mesoamerica. Farmers throughout present-day Mexico and Central America were cultivating maize, gourds, beans, and other food crops. In addition to farming dry fields, their methods included "slash-and-burn agriculture," which kept them moving from place to place in search of new land; "pot irrigation," dipping pots into wells and simply pouring the water onto the fields; canal irrigation; and, in low-lying swamplands, the creation of *chinampas*, raised fields or so-called hanging gardens. *Chinampas* were created by piling up the mud and the natural vegetation of the swamps into grids of raised land crisscrossed by natural irrigation channels. When the Spanish arrived in 1519, they estimated that the *chinampas* could feed an impressive four persons per acre; more recent archaeological estimates of their productivity suggest eight people.

Olmec Civilization along the Gulf Coast. On the basis of these agricultural systems, localized permanent settlements that centered on religious shrines and were led by local chiefs began to emerge. Trade and shared cultural and ceremonial practices gave a common character to specific regions within Mesoamerica. Along the Gulf coast of Mexico, the earliest of these civilizations, the Olmec, took shape from about 1500 B.C.E.

The Olmec built raised platforms, settlements, and shrines above the low-lying woodlands. The first that we know of was built at San Lorenzo about 1150 B.C.E. Labor brigades constructed *chinampas*, and the population of the settlement may have reached 2,500. Olmec artwork—representations of animals and mythological creatures in sculpture and bas-relief—suggests a shared religious basis for the society. The Olmec also developed rudimentary hieroglyphics, but no one has yet been able to

4.1
4.2
4.3

How did the first cities of the Americas differ from those of East Asia?

CIVILIZATIONS FLOURISHING IN CENTRAL AMERICA BEFORE COLUMBUS	
Olmec	c. 1500–400 B.C.E. Gulf of Mexico. First complex society, or cluster of related societies, in region, with centralized authority. Known for carvings of giant stone heads and jade animals.
Maya	c. 2000 B.C.E.–900 C.E. S. Mexico, Guatemala, Belize. Most enduring of the Middle American civilizations, the Mayans had by 325 C.E. built many stepped pyramids and some astronomical observatories, smelted metal tools, and developed hieroglyphs.
Zapotec	c. 1400 B.C.E.–900 C.E. S. Mexico. Built ceremonial center of Monte Albán and peaked as a civilization around 200 C.E.

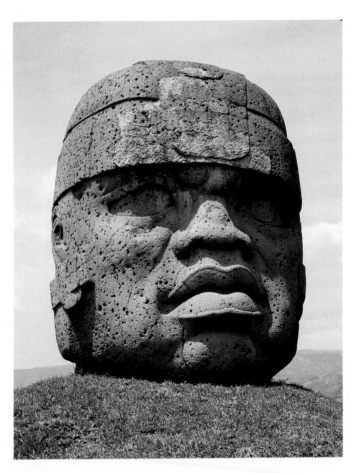

Colossal head from San Lorenzo, Veracruz, Mexico, before 400 B.C.E. Weighing around ten tons, this massive sculpted head is one of nine that were found at San Lorenzo. Made from basalt and carved with stone tools, the heads originally stood in rows on the site and are most probably portraits of Olmec rulers. All display the same full, resolute lips and broad, flat noses. Similar sculptures were found at La Venta. (Museo Regional de Veracruz, Jalapa, Mexico)

decipher them. About 900 B.C.E. the San Lorenzo site was destroyed, its artwork defaced. No one today knows why.

About a century later, some 100 miles to the northeast and closer to the Gulf of Mexico, Olmec peoples at La Venta built a small island in the middle of a swamp, and constructed on it an earth mound, half again as large as a football field and 100 feet high. Buildings atop the mound were probably used as temples. Monumental stone sculptures, including some of the giant stone heads typical of Olmec art, mark the space. Some of them probably served also as altars. The stone building materials were transported there from at least 60 miles away, the jade from much further. La Venta flourished for four centuries, until about 400 B.C.E. it, too, was destroyed and its monuments defaced. Again, no one today knows why.

Zapotec Civilization in the Oaxaca Valley. Olmec products—pottery, ritual objects, mirrors, and ceramics—appeared in the highlands around modern Oaxaca as early as 1150 B.C.E., along with natural products, such as obsidian and seashells from around the Gulf of Mexico. At first, therefore, scholars believed that the Zapotec culture of the Oaxaca valley was an offshoot of the Olmec. More recent finds in the village of San José Mogote, dating to 1400–1150 B.C.E., demonstrate, however, that the Zapotec settlements began as early as the Olmecs. The imported products reflected trading between the two groups.

Zapotec civilization peaked on the slopes of Monte Albán. By 400 B.C.E., ceremonial and public buildings dotted the summits of the hills. The settlement grew over the centuries, reaching its peak in the centuries after 200 C.E., when up to 50,000 people lived there. It was not entirely concentrated into a single city, but extended over 15 square miles, with some 2,000 terraces built into the hills, each with a house or two and its own water supply. Temples, pyramids, tombs, and an array of religious images suggest the importance of symbolism among the Zapotecs, too. Monte Albán peaked in population and creativity about 700 C.E. and then declined.

4.1
4.2 How did the first cities of the Americas differ from those of East Asia?
4.3

The Urban Explosion: Teotihuacán

Meanwhile, in the valley of Mexico, another civilization was coalescing, dominating the lands near it and finally creating a substantial empire. At its core, about 40 miles to the northeast of present-day Mexico City, stood Teotihuacán, one of the great cities of the ancient world. Teotihuacán represented a totally new kind of settlement in the Americas. It marked the beginning of a true urban revolution. At its peak, about 550 C.E., Teotihuacán accommodated about 100,000 inhabitants in some 8 square miles. Teotihuacán civilization had no system of writing, so, again, our knowledge is limited to the excavation and interpretation of physical artifacts.

The first buildings of Teotihuacán appeared about 200 B.C.E. One hundred years later, there were still only about 600 inhabitants. By 150 C.E., however, the population had grown to 20,000 and the area to 5 square miles. Then the population multiplied as the city exploded with religious, trade, artisanal, and administrative functions and personnel.

4.1
4.2
4.3

How did the
first cities of the
Americas differ
from those of East
Asia?

The city sat astride the major communication line between the valley of Mexico and the passes eastward to the Gulf of Mexico. Life in the city was a gift of the low-lying lake system of the valley of Mexico, especially of nearby Lake Texcoco. The lakes provided irrigation for the fields of the Teotihuacán valley, and salt, fish, and waterfowl. Basalt, limestone, and chert stone for building and clay for pottery were readily available in the valley, but other raw materials were imported, notably obsidian for tools and weapons from the surrounding mountains. Marine shells and copal (a tree resin used as incense) were imported from the Gulf region, and feathers of the quetzal bird came from the Maya regions of the southeast. Trading outposts of Teotihuacán appeared 700 miles south in Maya areas, and Teotihuacán ceramics have been found as far south as Tikal (see the discussion of Maya civilization, below). More than 400 workshops in the city produced pottery, obsidian manufactures, ornaments fashioned from seashells, and art and jewelry from jade and onyx.

A huge pyramid, the Pyramid of the Sun—at its base as broad as the great pyramid of Khufu in Egypt, though only half as high—dominated the Teotihuacán cityscape. The pyramid sits above a natural cave that early inhabitants enlarged into a clover-leaf-shaped chamber. The combination of natural cave and pyramid suggests that local people may have believed this cave to be the "navel of the universe." As Mircea Eliade (1907–86), the historian of religions, has demonstrated, the belief that all human life, or at least the lives of the local people, had emerged upward onto earth from a "navel," a single specific geographical point, was widely held in many civilizations of the ancient world. (The Garden of Eden story is a later variant of this belief.) Two additional massive shrines—the adjacent, smaller Pyramid of the Moon, and a central temple dedicated to the god Quetzalcoatl—enhance the religious dimensions of the city. Throughout its lifetime, and indeed even afterward until the Spanish conquest, Teotihuacán attracted multitudes of pilgrims from as far away as Guatemala.

The city was laid out on a monumental, geometric grid that centered on the 150-foot-wide Avenue of the Dead, the north–south axis of the city. More than 75 temples line this road, including the Pyramid of the Sun. The Pyramid of the Moon demarcated its northern terminal. The regularity of the city plan suggests a powerful government; indeed, a large administrative headquarters, the Ciudadela, dominates the southeastern terminus of the Avenue. The placement of the central Temple of Quetzalcoatl within the Ciudadela implies a close relationship between religion and administration.

At its peak, 500–650 C.E., Teotihuacán exercised a powerful imperial force over its immediate surrounding area and exerted spiritual, religious, cultural, economic, and military influence for hundreds of miles, especially to the south, into Maya areas. In 650, however, the city was deliberately burned down. Teotihuacán declined in significance. By 750 its power was broken, and its population scattered to smaller towns and rural areas. Several reasons have been suggested: the region may have become increasingly arid,

Teotihuacán. Between 400 and 750 C.E., high in the valley of Mexico, Teotihuacán was the dominant power in Mesoamerica. Covering around 8 square miles, with a population of 100,000, the city was laid out on a regular grid plan connecting the elements of a massive ceremonial complex. The residents thrived on agriculture, craftwork, and trade in ceramics and locally quarried obsidian.

🔎 **View** the **Closer Look**: **Teotihuacán Ruins in Mexico** on **MyHistoryLab**

4.1
4.2
4.3

How did the
first cities of the
Americas differ
from those of East
Asia?

Teotihuacán, Mexico, with the Pyramid of the Moon (foreground) linked to the Pyramid of the Sun by the Avenue of the Dead. By 200 B.C.E. in the valley of Mexico, the combined effects of intensified trading, growing religious activity, and huge surpluses of food led to the founding of this major city, which for centuries enjoyed religious, political, and economic dominance in the region. Teotihuacán reached an enormous size (8 square miles) and population (100,000) before eventually being deliberately, and mysteriously, burned down in 650 C.E.

incapable of supporting so large a population; increasing density of population, augmented by government programs for moving rural populations into the city, might have led to conflict and revolt from within; or neighboring city-states, pressured by the increasing militarization in Teotihuacán, may have attacked the city. These are, however, only educated guesses. In the absence of written records, no one knows for sure.

Cities interact with one another in networks of exchange, so advances or declines in one are usually echoed in the others. Teotihuacán and Monte Albán both declined simultaneously about 750 C.E., but smaller, nonurban centers kept the political, cultural, and religious legacies of Teotihuacán alive in the region. (Compare this with the experience of Western Europe after the decline of Rome, discussed in the chapter entitled "Rome and the Barbarians.") Three subsequent civilizations—the Toltec, the Aztec, and the Maya—absorbed and perpetuated its influence.

Successor States in the Valley of Mexico

When the Toltecs arrived in the valley of Mexico from the north and came to dominate the region from a new capital at Tula, about 900 C.E., they apparently ruled on Teotihuacán foundations and built their chief ceremonial center in honor of

4.1

4.2

4.3

How did the first cities of the Americas differ from those of East Asia?

Quetzalcoatl. Their rule, however, was short-lived. About 1170 C.E., still newer immigrants destroyed the Toltec temples and government.

After Tula fell, the Aztecs entered the valley. They established settlements on the southeastern shores of Lake Texcoco and built Tenochtitlán as their capital, only 40 miles from the earlier site of Teotihuacán. As the Aztecs built their large, militaristic empire, the population of Tenochtitlán grew to 200,000. Militarism and the demand of their gods for human sacrifice led the Aztecs into a constant quest for captives to sacrifice and, therefore, into constant warfare with their neighbors. When the Spanish conquistadores arrived in 1519, the neighboring peoples helped them to overthrow the Aztecs and their empire. The Spanish then razed Tenochtitlán to the ground and established their own capital, Mexico City, atop its ruins.

The Rise and Fall of the Maya

Teotihuacán's third legacy was to the Maya. The Maya lived where their descendants still dwell today—in the Yucatán Peninsula of Mexico, in Guatemala, and in Belize. The Maya built on Olmec and Teotihuacáno foundations as well as on their own practices. They began to construct ceremonial centers in Yucatán and central America by 2000 B.C.E. Between 300 B.C.E. and 300 C.E., they expanded their centers to plazas surrounded by stone pyramids and crowned with temples and palaces. The classic phase, 300–600 C.E., followed with fully fledged cities and monumental architecture, temples, extensive sacrifices, and elaborate burials; and the Olmec and Teotihuacán cultural influences are evident. Maya culture flourished in the southern lowlands, and major construction took place at Palenque, Piedras Negras, Copán, Coba, and elsewhere.

The Great City of Tikal. Tikal, in today's Guatemala, is one of the largest, most elaborate, and most completely excavated of these cities. In its center, Tikal holds five temple pyramids, up to 230 feet high and built between 300 and 800 C.E. (One appeared so massive, powerful, and exotic that the filmmaker George Lucas used it as a setting for *Star Wars*.) As the first modern archaeologists hacked away the tropical rainforest and uncovered this temple core, they concluded that Tikal was a spiritual and religious center. Later, they uncovered housing and water cisterns that accommodated up to 50,000 people outside the temple precincts. This led them to change their assessment of Tikal. Instead of viewing it as a purely religious shrine, they began to see it as a large city of considerable regional political and economic significance as well. At the height of its powers, Tikal's authority covered almost 1,000 square miles containing 360,000 people. Most Maya states held only 30,000–50,000 subjects. The number of states ruled by kings grew from perhaps a dozen in the first century B.C.E. to as many as 60 at the height of the lowland civilization in the eighth century C.E.

The Maya also created an elaborate calendar that recorded three related chronologies: dates and events

A bloodletting rite, limestone lintel from Yaxchilán, Mexico (Maya), c. 725 C.E. The king, Lord Shield Jaguar, in his role as shaman, brandishes a flaming torch to illuminate the drama that is about to unfold. His principal wife, Lady Xoc, kneeling, pulls through her tongue a thorn-lined rope that falls into a woven basket holding blood-soaked strips of paper cloth. These will be burned and thereby transmitted to the gods. Few works of art made by the Maya capture so completely the link between their political and religious ideas in an appropriately sacramental style. (Having deciphered the hieroglyphics of the Mayan calendar, scholars know that this event took place on October 28, 709 C.E.) (British Museum, London)

Great-Jaguar-Paw: Mayan King of Tikal

By deciphering, translating, and interpreting the stelae at Tikal, Linda Schele and David Freidel recreate an heroic moment of military victory in the life of the king Great-Jaguar-Paw and in the history of his kingdom. Their interpretation is based primarily on the stela illustrated below and on comparison with later stelae representing the same event:

jaguar paw ax blade

god dangling from the royal belt

Tikal location

captive

Despite the fact that he was such an important king, we know relatively little about Great-Jaguar-Paw's life outside of the spectacular campaign he waged against Uaxactun. His reign must have been long, but the dates we have on him come only from his last three years. On one of these historical dates, October 21, A.D. 376, we see Great-Jaguar-Paw ending the seventeenth katun [a ritual cycle of twenty years] … This fragmentary monument shows him only from the waist down, but he is dressed in the same regalia as his royal ancestors, with the god Chac-Xib-Chac dangling from his belt. His ankle cuffs display the sign of day on one leg and night on the other … He holds an executioner's ax, its flint blade knapped into the image of a jaguar paw. In this guise of warrior and giver of sacrifices, he stands atop a captive he has taken in battle. The unfortunate victim, a bearded noble still wearing part of the

regalia that marks his noble station, struggles under the victor's feet, his wrists bound together in front of his chest. He will die to sanctify the katun ending at Tikal.

Warfare was not new to the Maya. Raiding for captives from one kingdom to another had been going on for centuries, for allusions to decapitation are present in even the earliest architectural decorations celebrating kingship. The hunt for sacrificial gifts to give to the gods and the testing of personal prowess in battle was part of the accepted social order and captive sacrifice was something expected of nobles and kings in the performance of their ritual duties. Just as the gods were sustained by the bloodletting ceremonies of the kings, so they were nourished as well by the blood of noble captives. Sacrificial victims like these had been buried as offerings in building terminations and dedications from late Preclassic times on, and possibly even earlier …

The war waged by Great-Jaguar-Paw of Tikal against Uaxactun, however, was not the traditional hand-to-hand combat of proud nobles striving for personal glory and for captives to give to the gods. This was war on an entirely different scale, waged by rules never before heard of and for stakes far higher than the reputations or lives of individuals. In this new warfare of death and conquest, the winner would gain the kingdom of the loser. Tikal won the prize on January 16, A.D. 378 …

The subjugation of Uaxactun by Great-Jaguar-Paw and Smoking Fog [his commander-in-chief], which precipitated this new kind of war and rituals, survives in the inscriptional record almost entirely in the retrospective histories carved by later rulers at Tikal. The fact that these rulers kept commemorating this event shows both its historical importance and its propaganda value for the descendants of these conquerors. (Schele and Freidel, pp. 144–48)

- What are all the symbols through which this stela represents the power and strength of Great-Jaguar-Paw?
- What does the war between Tikal and Uaxactun tell us about the increasing power of the state?
- What do you think Schele and Freidel mean by "the propaganda value" of commemorating the victory of Tikal over Uaxactun?

4.1
4.2
4.3

How did the first cities of the Americas differ from those of East Asia?

in cosmic time periods of thousands of years; historic events in the lives of specific rulers and their states; and the yearly cycle of agricultural activity. Maya rituals were permeated by the sense of living at once in the world of the here and now, and in a spiritual realm connected with other worlds and gods. Their kings were shamans, bridges between the two worlds.

Maya Civilization in Decline. By 900 C.E., the great classical period of the Maya people in the southern lowlands ended. No one knows why. The most frequent hypotheses

How did the
first cities of the
Americas differ
from those of East
Asia?

include: excessive population pressure on natural resources, especially agriculture; climatic changes beyond the ability of the Maya to adjust; and excessive warfare that wore out the people and destroyed their states. No one knows for sure.

No one knows, either, why at the time of the Maya decline in the lowlands, new Maya cities and states grew up in the northern highlands of the Yucatán peninsula, notably at Uxmal and Chichén Itzá. These cities, in turn, declined by 1200; and the last Maya capital, Mayapán, was constructed between 1263 and 1283. It adapted many of the cultural monuments of Chichén Itzá, but grew only to some 10,000–20,000 inhabitants. Mayapán seemed militaristic, beleaguered, and possessed of tough sensibilities

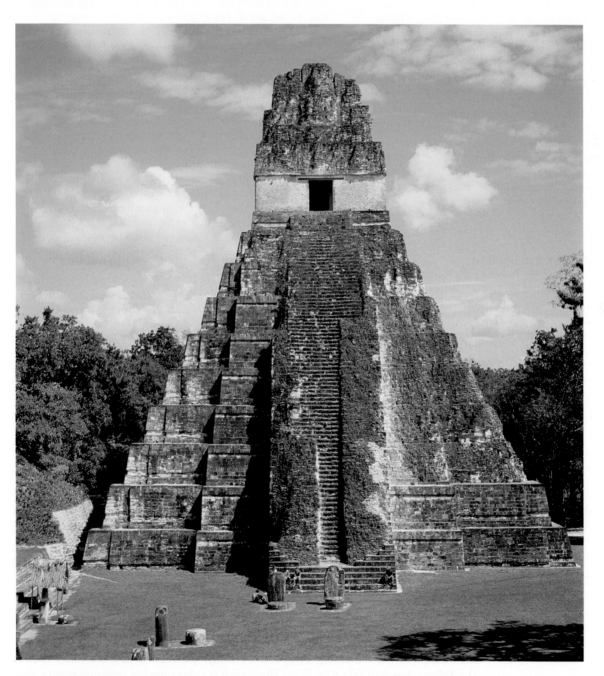

Temple I at Tikal, Guatemala (Maya), before 800 C.E. At its height, the city-state of Tikal covered almost 1,000 square miles and was home to 360,000 inhabitants. Its symbols of authority were centralized in its monumental shrines. This unusually steep stepped pyramid, about 154 feet high, would have been the backdrop for self-inflicted bloodletting and the sacrifice of prisoners-of-war as offerings to the gods.

SOURCE

The Popol Vuh ["Book of the People"]

The *Popol Vuh* is the most complete existing collection of creation myths and legends of early Maya history to survive the Spanish conquistadores. Originally written in Maya hieroglyphs, it was transcribed into Latin in the sixteenth century to confuse and escape the Church censors, who wanted to destroy the Maya culture. In the eighteenth century, a Dominican priest translated it into Spanish. The selection cited here captures the hunger for movement of the Quiché Maya, who repeatedly changed their location, building new towns and cities. It also speaks of the intense and lethal competition among various Maya groups leading to warfare and the subsequent human sacrifices of the defeated warriors to the gods of the victors.

Then they investigated the mountains near their citadel. They looked for a mountain on which to dwell, for they had become numerous. They who had received lordship in the East were now dead. They who had come to the peaks of each citadel had become aged grandfathers. But they were not content. They passed through numerous afflictions and misfortunes until at last they discovered the citadel of the grandfathers and the fathers.

This therefore was the name of the citadel that they came to:

THE FOUNDATION OF CHI IZMACHI

CHI IZMACHI, then, was the name of the mountain on which they dwelt as their citadel. There they settled and tested their glory. They ground their lime plaster and their whitewash in the fourth generation of lords. It is said that Co Nache and Beleheb Queh ruled then, along with the Lord Magistrate.

It was there at Chi Izmachi that Lord Co Tuha and Iztayul ruled as Ah Pop and Ah Pop of the Reception House. Under them it came to be a very fine citadel.

Only three great houses were built there at Chi Izmachi, not the twenty-four great houses of today. Yet there were three great houses:

Just one great house of the Cavecs;
Just one great house over the Nihaibs;
And just one of the Ahau Quichés.

There were only two swollen great houses, one each for the two lineage divisions at Chi Izmachi. Their hearts were united. There were no bad feelings or anger, only steadfast lordship. There was no contention or disturbance. There was only purity and a tranquil sense of community in their hearts. There was no envy or jealousy.

Yet their glory was still meager. They had not pulled together, nor had they become great. They attempted to strengthen their defenses there at Chi Izmachi. This act was surely a sign of their sovereignty. It was surely a sign of their glory, as well as their greatness.

However, this was seen by the Ilocab, who fomented war. They desired that Lord Co Tuha be murdered. They desired that there be but one lord over them. Thus the Ilocab wished to convince Lord Iztayul to murder him. But this plot against Lord Co Tuha did not succeed. Their envy merely fell on their own backs. This first attempt by the Ilocab to kill the lord failed. Yet it was the foundation of strife and the clamor for war.

Thus the Ilocab made a first attempt at invading the citadel, coming as killers. It was their desire that the Quichés be destroyed. They wished to exercise lordship in their own hearts. But when they came to seize it they were captured and despoiled, and few of them were ever set free again.

Then began the sacrifices. The Ilocab were sacrificed before the face of the god as payment for their offenses against Lord Co Tuha. Thus many were taken into captivity and enslaved. They became servants. They merely gave themselves up in defeat as a result of their clamor for war against the lord as well as his canyon-citadel. They had desired in their hearts to ruin and mock the lordship of the Quichés. But this was not accomplished. Thus they commenced to sacrifice these people before the face of the god.

Then they built their war defenses, and this was the beginning of the fortification of the citadel at Chi Izmachi. Thus they began to lay the foundation of their glory, because the sovereignty of the Quiché lord was surely great. Everywhere there were enchanted lords. None came to humiliate or mock them. They were but workers of greatness.

There they put down roots at Chi Izmachi, and there also their bloodletting god increased in greatness. And all the nations, the small and the great, became afraid. They witnessed the arrival of captive people to be sacrificed and killed by the glory and sovereignty of Lord Co Tuha and Lord Iztayul, in alliance with the Nihaib and Ahau Quichés. There were only three divisions of lineages there at the citadel named Chi Izmachi. …

These three lineages, and these three great houses, dwelt a long time there at Chi Izmachi. But then they looked for and found another citadel. And so they abandoned the peak of Chi Izmachi. (*Popol Vuh*, Christenson, pp. 249–50)

How did the first cities of the Americas differ from those of East Asia?

as evidenced by wholesale human sacrifice. The city was destroyed in civil wars in the mid-1400s.

By the time the Spanish conquistadores reached Mesoamerica in 1517, only a few small Maya towns remained. The period of Maya power and splendor had ended. The Toltecs, too, had fallen by then. The Aztecs had become the reigning power, and the Spaniards destroyed them.

📖 **Read** the **Document**: **(Maya): Victory Over the Underworld** on **MyHistoryLab**

HOW DO WE KNOW?

The Mysteries of Maya Writing

For centuries the connection between today's Maya—living an often impoverished existence—and the glories of their civilization in the third through the tenth centuries C.E. had been lost. Then, in 1839–41, a New York lawyer, John Lloyd Stephens, and a Scottish artist, Frederick Catherwood, discovered the remnants of the cities of Copán and Palenque in the rainforests of Mesoamerica, and the temples of Uxmal and Chichén Itzá in the Yucatán peninsula. Stephens and Catherwood wrote and painted what they saw and made rubbings of the designs they found on Maya stelae (stone marker tablets). Their research, published in 1841, opened the way for the modern academic study of the Maya at almost exactly the same time as H.C. Rawlinson and others were discovering the great archaeological sites of Mesopotamia and deciphering its language.

Stelae and other inscriptions demonstrated that the Maya had created a written language, but no one could read it. Even the Maya themselves, prevented by the Spanish from keeping their language alive, had forgotten the script. Scholars could read parts of the elaborate and sophisticated Maya calendar system, but they could not discern whether the events recorded were historical, mythical, or some combination of the two.

In the 1950s and 1960s, at Harvard University, Tatiana Proskouriakoff began to demonstrate that the Maya stelae recorded the reigns and victories of real kings who had ruled real states. Then the Russian scholar Yuri Knorozov demonstrated, against fierce opposition, that the Maya script included representations of phonetic sounds as well as of full words. By the 1970s a new generation of linguistic scholars began to decode the syntactical structure of the writing. They learned to distinguish the signs for nouns and those for verbs, and their place in the structure of the narrative. They were well on their way to discovering Maya history, and they were surprised by what they found.

The archaeologists Linda Schele and David Freidel finally mastered the hieroglyphs and scripts of the people of the city of Palenque. In contrast to previous beliefs that the Maya were peaceful and somewhat otherworldly in their concerns, as their massive temples seemed to indicate, Schele and Freidel found records of constant warfare among the local shaman kings and their profoundly religious local city-states. The Maya kingdoms fought in order to gain captives who would serve as slaves and human sacrifices to their demanding gods. The temples, it turned out, were the altars on which the sacrifices were performed. Schele and Freidel also discovered the exact lineage of the Palenque kings, and the picture of a tree used to symbolize the king, for the Maya represented their royal families as forests of trees and forests of kings.

- Why was it easier to decipher the cuneiform of Sumer and the hieroglyphs of Egypt than the symbols of Maya writing?
- Why had the Maya forgotten their own written language? Does the reason surprise you? Why or why not?
- In the How Do We Know box on Great Jaguar Paw, you can see an example of Maya writing. As you look at it, what seem to you to be the difficulties in deciphering the Maya written language?

Urbanization in South America

South America had few established trade links with Mesoamerica, but the two regions share many similarities. Both constructed religious shrine centers that seem to have dominated their general cultural foundations by about 1500 B.C.E. Both developed small city-states that defined local cultural variations from 300 to 200 B.C.E. Both created proto-empires throughout significant regions about 500–600 C.E.; and generated large, urban empires—the Aztecs in the valley of Mexico, the Inca in the Andes—and developed trading relationships between their coastal regions and their mountainous inland cores.

The contrast between coast and inland mountains is most dramatic in South America. The Pacific coast of Ecuador, Peru, and Chile is a desert in most places. The prevailing winds come not from the Pacific, but from the Amazon basin to the east. The Andes Mountains thus have little rainfall from the Pacific Ocean to trap on their western slopes, but they do intercept the precipitation from the Atlantic, making the eastern slopes fertile while leaving the west coast dry. The most spectacular urban civilizations of South America took root in the 10,000-foot-high plains and passes of the Andes rather than in the arid Pacific coast below. The contrast with the river-basin civilizations of Afro-Eurasia could not be more vivid.

Coastal Settlements and Networks

The Pacific coast is not, however, uninhabitable. It yields abundant quantities of fish, seaweed, and salt. Even today, these ocean products are traded to the mountain cities

4.1

4.2

4.3

How did the first cities of the Americas differ from those of East Asia?

How did the
first cities of the
Americas differ
from those of East
Asia?

CIVILIZATIONS OF SOUTH AMERICA

Chavín	c. 1200–200 B.C.E. Northern Peru. Farming society, comprising different regional groups, whose main town may have been a pilgrimage site.
Moche	200 B.C.E.–600 C.E. North coast of Peru. Modeled ceramics of animals in a realistic style. Religious and political life focused on the Huaca de la Luna (artificial platform) and Huaca del Sol (stepped pyramid).
Nazca	?1–600 C.E. Peru. Known principally for its series of water channels and causeways for irrigation. Seen from the air, their outlines, the "Nazca Lines," have appeared to be a mysterious symbol, perhaps a hummingbird 900 feet long.
Tiwanaku	c. 200–1200 C.E. Bolivia. Named for the ancient city, near Lake Titicaca, that was occupied by a series of five different cultures, then abandoned.
Huari	c. 650–1200 C.E. Peru. Empire whose style of architecture and artifacts, similar to Tiwanaku's, was dispersed throughout the region.
Chimú	c. 600–1470 C.E. Northwest coast of Peru. Large urban civilization (capital: Chan Chan) responsible for fine gold work, record-keeping, and aqueducts. Conquered by the Inca.
Inca	c. 1476–1534 C.E. Andean South America. Last and largest pre-Columbian civilization (capital: Cuzco) that was destroyed by Spanish conquistadores in the 1530s.

in exchange for their food crops. In some areas the cultivation of cotton is also possible, and coastal Peru rivals the Indus valley as the home of the first production of cotton textiles, about 4500 B.C.E. The quality of the textiles and the colorful designs dyed into the cotton show up most clearly in the burial cloths of semi-mummified bodies.

In addition, although climatically a desert, the coast does have some small mountain-fed rivers running through it. The same people who organized labor brigades to channel these rivers for irrigation also created ceremonial centers along the coast, beginning perhaps by 2000 B.C.E. The oldest of these shrine centers, and the one closest to the Pacific, is El Paraíso, near modern Lima, at the mouth of the Chillón River. Built in a typically U-shaped complex of buildings, El Paraíso appears to have been constructed by people from many separate villages and kin groups. Few lived at El Paraíso, but apparently the shrine served them all, and many used the location as a burial place.

The Moche. In the Moche valley of coastal northern Peru, settlements of up to 2,000 separate structures had grown up by 200 B.C.E. From about 200 B.C.E. to 600 C.E., in this and neighboring valleys, the Moche state established itself. The Moche created irrigation systems, spectacular monuments, and important tombs. In the late 1980s, at nearby Sipán, archaeologists discovered three royal tombs that demonstrate the social and political stratification of the society. Each tomb housed a lord, buried in shrouds, adorned with jewelry, some made of gold, and surrounded by servants and perhaps family members, and by animals—llamas, and at least one dog and one snake—that were buried with him. Paintings and ceramic designs within the tombs show priests engaged in warfare and performing human sacrifices of prisoners-of-war. The Moche built provincial centers in nearby river valleys from which they apparently ruled, traded, and introduced irrigation systems.

The Chimú. By about 600 C.E. the Moche had left the region, for reasons that are not entirely clear, and were succeeded by the Chimú kingdom which controlled twelve coastal river valleys. The Chimú built irrigation and water storage facilities, trade networks, and a powerful state that stretched some 1000 miles along the Peruvian coast. Their monumental capital, Chan Chan, built near the earlier Moche, was

CHAPTER FOUR: A POLYCENTRIC WORLD 1700 B.C.E.–1000 C.E.

4.1

4.2

How did the
first cities of the
Americas differ
from those of East
Asia?

4.3

surrounded by a 35-foot-high mud wall, and it covered nearly 4 square miles, with palaces, temples, administrative offices, and housing for the common people. Chan Chan contained ten royal compounds. Apparently each king in turn built his own center, ruled from it during his life, and was buried in it after his death.

In each area they dominated, the Chimú built subsidiary administrative centers that formed a network reaching as far south as modern Lima. The Chimú empire reigned until it was conquered by the Inca in 1470. Ironically, thanks to the Inca transportation and communication network, Chimú artwork influenced western South America even more after the Inca conquest than it had before.

Urbanization in the Andes Mountains

Despite these coastal settlements and networks, most scholars believe that the core areas of South American urbanization were in the Andes, the 20,000-foot-high mountain chain that parallels the Pacific coast for the entire length of South America. From earliest times to today, there has been considerable "vertical trade," linking coastal lowlands with high mountain areas in an exchange of the various products of their different ecologies. With the trade came networks of cultural, religious, and political communication, and some archaeologists have argued that the civilization of the Andes Mountains was developed from a prior foundation along the sea coast far below.

The Chavín. The first known civilization of the Andes, the Chavín, flourished for about a millennium, 1200–200 B.C.E. The civilization is named for its best-known and largest ceremonial center at Chavín de Huantar, in central Peru, which flourished from about 900 to about 200 B.C.E. Chavín temples include a pantheon of gods preserved in paintings and carvings, including jaguar-like humans with serpents for hair, eagles, caymans, and many mixed figures, part-human, part-animal, reminiscent of similar figures in China. Like El Paraíso and the coastal shrines, Chavín seems to have been built by the joint efforts of many nearby kin and village groups. At its height, it held only 2,000 inhabitants, but its culture and its gods inspired common religious forms in the vicinity, and carried them throughout the high Andes.

View the **Closer Look**: **The Raimondi Stela at Chavín de Huantar** on **MyHistoryLab**

The Tiwanaku, Huari, and Nazca. Some 600 miles to the south, south of Lake Titicaca, on today's border between Peru and Bolivia, at an elevation of 12,000 feet, lay the largest open, flat plain available for agriculture in the Andes. By 200 C.E., Tiwanaku (Tihuanaco) at the southern end of the lake, near the modern city of La Paz, became the capital of the region. Its rulers irrigated their high plains (*altiplano*) region to support perhaps 20,000 people and to create a ritual center of monumental structures and religious and spiritual practices that suffused the Andes and the coast. The people of the *altiplano* traded their fruit, vegetables, llamas, and lake-caught fish in exchange for the seafood and perhaps seashells of the Pacific coast 12,000 feet below. When Tiwanaku collapsed, for reasons now lost to history, other states in the region, notably at Huari and Nazca, kept alive many of their administrative and religious practices. The Huari lands stretched for 1,000 miles along the Pacific and up into the mountains, centered on a capital city, Huari, and a line of about a dozen administrative centers along the spine of the Andes. The Nazca, in particular, built causeways and channels to control irrigation. The "Nazca lines" (see illustration, overleaf) were apparently part of this system, but were long (mis)understood as some kind of symbolic, ritual formation, visible only from far above.

The Inca. These five states—Chimú, Chavín, Tiwanaku, Huari, and Nazca—established foundations on which the Inca built their powerful but short-lived empire,

4.1

4.2

4.3

How did the
first cities of the
Americas differ
from those of East
Asia?

Nazca lines, San José pampa, Peru desert, c. 500 C.E. A successor state of Tiwanaku, the Nazca, created great patterns of lines drawn with pebbles on the desert surface. The overall designs, like this 900-foot-long figure that looks like a hummingbird, are comprehensible only from the air. For a long time they were viewed as indecipherable, mystical symbols. More recently they have been seen as outlines of irrigation channels and causeways.

which stretched for 2,000 miles from north to south and as far as 200 miles inland from the Pacific, and lasted from 1476 to 1534. The Inca adapted many of the gods and religious symbols, artwork, ceramics, and textiles of these earlier states. They built a new capital, Cuzco, at a height of 10,000 feet, and connected it to all the mountain and coastal regions of their empire by an astonishing 25,000-mile system of roads, with tunnels, causeways, suspension bridges, travel lodges, and storage places. The roads were sometimes broad and paved, but often narrow and unpaved, especially because the Inca had no wheeled vehicles. Enforced, *mit'a* labor was exacted from local populations for the construction.

In 1438, Cusi Yupanqui was crowned "Inca," or king-emperor, after he won a victory over a neighboring tribe, and forged his quarreling peoples into a conquering nation. Thereafter, the whole nation was called Inca. Cusi Yupanqui established a hereditary monarchy, and his descendants built a great empire from his early conquests. They employed the *mit'a* system, demanding unpaid labor for public construction for part of each year from all adults in the empire. The Inca did not develop writing, but they did create an abacus-like system of numerical records through the use of knots tied on string. These *quipu* held the administrative records of the empire. (See photograph of a *quipu* in the chapter "Establishing World Trade Routes".)

In each conquered region, the Inca established administrative centers, from which tax collectors gathered two-thirds of the crops and the manufactured products (such as beer and textiles), half for the state, and half for the gods and their priests. They established state workshops to produce official and consumer goods, and they seem to have encouraged significant standardization of production, for Inca arts and crafts show little variation over time and place. Inca religion apparently encouraged different gods and worship for different people. The sun god was the chief deity, and the emperor was considered his descendant; the nobility worshiped the military god Viracocha, while the common people continued to worship their own indigenous spirits, along with the newer sun god. The organization and the study of empire, however, take us to the Part entitled "From City-states to Empires."

Agricultural Towns in North America

Agricultural settlements took root in many locations in continental North America in the first few hundred years C.E. Several grew into small towns, reaching their maximum size about 1000–1400 C.E., and some scholars see in them the signs of early urbanization. Nevertheless, these towns are not included among the seven sites of primary urbanization because few of them reached a population size that might be considered urban; nor do they demonstrate clearly a nonagricultural base to their economies. They may also be derivative of earlier settlements to the south. For example, those in the southwestern United States, such as the Hohokam, Mogollon, and Anasazi peoples, show evidence in their artwork and building patterns of influences from Mexico and even South America.

The first fully developed towns in the Mississippi River valley appeared about 700 C.E. Their inhabitants built temple mounds and left evidence of elaborate ritual funerals, suggesting a hierarchical social and political organization. The largest of the temple-mound towns, Cahokia, occupied land along the Mississippi, across the river from and a few miles east of present-day Saint Louis. Cahokia held a population of 10,000 in the city and 38,000 in the region in the twelfth and thirteenth centuries. Such a large population probably included many craft specialists. Around the town were sited some 100 mounds, which served as burial tombs or as platforms for homes of the elite. The mounds resemble those of Mexican cities and suggest interchange between the two regions. Evidence indicates that a strong central authority controlled the town. For reasons that are not entirely clear, Cahokia, like almost all the towns of North America, was in decline or even deserted before the arrival of European invaders in the early 1500s. Archaeologists continue active research into the towns of North America, their cultures, and their links to one another and to other regions.

📖 Read the Document: Nineteenth-century Description of Cahokia on MyHistoryLab

West Africa: The Niger River Valley

4.3   How did urbanization in the Niger River valley differ from urbanization elsewhere?

Until the late 1970s, all the cities in sub-Saharan Africa that were known to archaeologists had developed along patterns introduced from outside the region. Meroe and Kush on the upper Nile had adapted urban patterns from Egypt. Axum in modern Ethiopia had followed examples of urbanization from both the Nile valley and the trading powers of the Indian Ocean. Port cities along the East African coast, such as Malindi, Kilwa, and Sofala, had been founded by traders from across the Indian Ocean. The walled stone enclosures, called **zimbabwes**, built in the region of modern Zimbabwe and Mozambique to house local royal rulers, had been initiated through contact with Swahili traders from the coast.

In West Africa, the first known cities, such as Timbuktu, Jenne, and Mopti along the Niger River, and Ife and Igbo Ukwu deeper south in the Yoruba lands near the tropical forests, had been built as centers of exchange. They were thought to be responses to the arrival of Muslim traders from North Africa who crossed the Sahara southward after the seventh century C.E. Archaeologists believed that Africans, like Europeans, had learned about city building from outsiders. This viewpoint has now been challenged.

📖 Read the Document: Strabo on Africa (1st c. CE) on MyHistoryLab

KEY TERM

zimbabwe (zim-bahb-way) Stone-walled enclosure or building built during the African Iron Age in the region of modern Zimbabwe and Mozambique. The structures were the courts of local rulers. They have been associated with foreign trade, integrated farming and animal husbandry, and gold production. The Great Zimbabwe is the ruins of the former capital of the Monomatapa Empire, situated in Zimbabwe and occupied from around the thirteenth to the sixteenth century C.E.

AT A GLANCE: EARLY AFRICA

DATE	POLITICS	RELIGION AND CULTURE	SOCIAL DEVELOPMENT
500 B.C.E.		• Nok terra-cotta sculptures • Bantu adopting settled agricultural lives	• Iron smelting
250 B.C.E.	• Jenne-jeno founded	• Copper and semi-precious stone ornaments from Niger	
500 C.E.	• Ancient Ghana		
1000 C.E.	• Foundation of Benin (c. 1000)		
1200 C.E.	• Ghana falls; Kingdom of Mali founded		• Cities in Niger valley (400 C.E.) recorded by Arab visitors

4.1

4.2

4.3 How did urbanization in the Niger River valley differ from urbanization elsewhere?

West Africa Before Urbanization

The most important developments of pre-urban West Africa were iron smelting, apparently initiated by contact with North Africa; the development of new artistic traditions, especially by the Nok peoples; and the spread of agricultural civilization by the Bantu people. Iron smelting entered the archaeological record in West Africa suddenly about 500 B.C.E. In most places the technology jumped directly from stone to iron, with only a few examples of copper-work in between. Most archaeologists interpret this technological jump to indicate that iron working was introduced from outside, probably from the Phoenician colonies along the North African coast, and they find evidence for this idea in the rock art of the Sahara Desert. Along the routes

Trade across the Sahara, c. 500 C.E. Ivory, gold, hardwoods, and slaves were the magnets that drew trading caravans south across the arid Saharan wastes, often following routes established before the desert had formed. These routes linked the classical cultures of the Mediterranean and southwest Asia with an array of rich trading states strung along the Sahel/Sudan axis.

crossing the desert, rock engravings and paintings dating from between 1200 and 400 B.C.E. depict two-wheeled chariots that suggest trans-Saharan traffic.

In northern Nigeria, the Nok peoples were producing terra-cotta sculptures, especially of human heads, from about 500 B.C.E. Living in settlements along the Niger, near its confluence with the Benue in modern Nigeria, the Nok also built iron-smelting furnaces, dating to 500–450 B.C.E.

Meanwhile, also in the lower Niger, some Bantu peoples were giving up nomadic pastoralism for settled agriculture, although many remained nomadic for a long time. They began great, but gradual, migrations southward and eastward over thousands of miles, introducing their languages, their knowledge of iron production, and their experience with settled agriculture. In the thousand years between 500 B.C.E. and 500 C.E., the Bantu carried their languages, their new, settled way of life, and their metallurgical skills almost to the southern tip of Africa.

Jenne-jeno: A New Urban Pattern?

Neither the Nok nor the Bantu built cities. Other people of the Niger River, however, apparently did. In excavations that began in 1977 and continue today, archaeologists Susan and Roderick McIntosh uncovered Jenne-jeno, "Ancient Jenne," the first known indigenous city in sub-Saharan Africa. The Jenne-jeno settlement began about 250 B.C.E. as a small group of round mud huts. Its herding and fishing inhabitants were already using iron implements, and the village grew to urban size by 400 C.E., reaching its peak of settlement by about 900 C.E.

The physical form of the city was different from that of the other six centers we have studied. A central inhabited area of some 80 acres was surrounded by a city wall 10 feet wide and 13 feet high with a perimeter of 1¼ miles. Near this central area were some

The spread of Bantu. About 1500 B.C.E. an extraordinary cultural migration began to transform sub-Saharan Africa. From their homeland near the Niger delta, groups of Bantu-speaking farmers began to move east and south, spreading cattle domestication, crop cultivation, and iron-working. By about 500 C.E., they reached southern Africa, the original hunter-gatherers having been marginalized to remote regions such as the Kalahari Desert.

View the **Map**: **Bantu Migration** on **MyHistoryLab**

4.1

4.2

4.3

How did urbanization in the Niger River valley differ from urbanization elsewhere?

Two men with an ibex, Tanzoumaitak, Tassili Mountains, Sahara, 7000–6000 B.C.E. Rock painting. Rock art of the Sahara at first represented such wild animals as buffalo, rhinoceros, hippopotamuses, giraffes, and elephants. By 6000 B.C.E. it was representing domesticated animals, such as ibex or goats, dogs, horses, and camels, suggesting a transition from hunting to pastoralism and settled agriculture.

How did
urbanization in
the Niger River
valley differ from
urbanization
elsewhere?

forty smaller, but still substantial, additional settlements. They extended to a radius of 2½ miles. By the year 1000, the settled area may have contained 50,000 people.

Excavations through numerous levels have revealed that the people of Jenne-jeno ate fish from the river, rice from their fields, and beef from their herds. They probably drank the cows' milk as well. At least some wore jewelry and ornaments of imported copper and semi-precious stones. Dozens of burial urns, each up to 3 feet high, yielded human skeletons arranged in fetal position. The urns date from 300 to 1400 C.E., and their burial inside and adjacent to the houses suggests a reverence for ancestors. Statuettes in a kneeling position set into walls and under floors further suggest the probability of ancestor worship.

This part of the religious and cultural heritage of Jenne-jeno seems to have endured. Although not built primarily as a shrine center, Jenne-jeno included religious functions as an important part of its activities, as its modern counterpart does today. There are also similarities between the arrangement of the huts of Jenne-jeno 1,000 years ago and the grouping of family huts there today. In ancient times as in modern, it appears that the husband-father lived in one large central hut while his wives occupied the surrounding huts.

Jenne-jeno must have engaged in trade, because even in 250 B.C.E. its inhabitants were using iron and stone that had to be brought from at least 30 miles away. Sandstone for their grinding stones must have been imported from at least 60 miles away, while copper and salt came from hundreds of miles away. The McIntoshes have also discovered one gold earring, dating to about 750 C.E., in the region. The nearest site of gold mining was 500 miles away. Perhaps the people of Jenne-jeno traded the fish of the Niger and the rice of their fields for these imports. Some Jenne-jenoites may have become professional merchants.

Innovation in architectural concepts may also have come to Jenne-jeno from outside. By about 900 C.E., some rectangular houses began to appear among the circular ones, perhaps introduced through contact with northern peoples. Outside contact increased with the introduction of camel transportation across the Sahara about 300 C.E. and with the Muslim Arab conquest of North Africa about 700 C.E. Especially after 1200 C.E., Muslim traders crossing the Sahara linked the savanna and forest lands of the south to the cities of the Mediterranean coast. Most scholars have argued that these external contacts and trade possibilities encouraged the growing importance of such new cities as Timbuktu, Jenne-jeno, Niani, Gao, Kano, and, further south, Benin. The McIntoshes suggest an opposite perspective: that these cities predate the northern connections, and, indeed, their prosperity and control of the trade routes and the gold further to the south encouraged the northerners to dispatch their camel caravans across the Sahara. This debate remains unresolved.

By 1100, the settlements peripheral to Jenne-jeno began to lose population. Some of their inhabitants apparently moved to the central settlement. In another century the rural population also began to decline. By 1400, Jenne-jeno and its satellites were no more. Why? Perhaps warfare and slave-trading upset local stability. It is also possible that land rights and family structures shifted, reducing residents' interest in the region. Finally, it is possible that migration to other places along the Niger River simply allowed Jenne-jeno to decline slowly. We just do not know.

Head from Jemaa, Nigeria, c. 400 B.C.E. The Nok were a nonliterate farming people who occupied the Jos Plateau in northern Nigeria during the first millennium B.C.E. Their distinctive sculptures—of elephants, snakes, monkeys, people, and even a giant tick—are all boldly modeled and skillfully fired in terra cotta. This powerful life-size head probably formed part of a full-length statue. (National Museum, Lagos, Nigeria)

State Formation?

Could the settlements of the Middle Niger at Jenne-jeno be an example of early urbanism without a strong centralized government? Without a state? It is possible. The population at Jenne-jeno lived in neighboring clusters that were functionally interdependent, rather than in a single urban center with a prominent core marked by large-scale, monumental architecture, as was found in most other centers of primary urbanization. This kind of development might be viewed as "a precocious, indigenous, and highly individual form of urbanism" (R. McIntosh, p. 203). In this case, it is possible that Jenne-jeno rose on the basis of trade and expanded into neighboring, interactive settlements, but without a hierarchical social structure or a strong, central authority. In contrast to primary urbanization in all the other regions of the world we have examined, Jenne-jeno may have experienced relative equality and cooperation among its citizens, rather than competition, dominance, and coercion.

On the other hand, a comparative assessment might suggest that Jenne had developed only to about the stage of the Olmec settlements and had not yet created the kind of centralized authority that emerged clearly and powerfully among the later Maya. Had Jenne-jeno persisted longer and grown larger, perhaps centralization and stratification would have developed. Indeed, the presence of a central settlement surrounded by smaller adjacent settlements suggests that some hierarchy was already emerging. Did Jenne-jeno represent an alternative kind of urbanization, or was it a settlement that was on its way to full-scale conventional urbanization? These are the kinds of questions of comparison that archaeologists—and historians—love to debate.

The First Cities:
What Difference Do They Make?

With the creation of cities, humanity entered into many new forms of living. The first of these cities, in the river valleys of Mesopotamia and the Nile almost 5,500 years ago, introduced not only new scale and density in human settlement patterns but also new technology in the metallurgy of copper, tin, and bronze; monumental scale in architecture; and specialization and hierarchy in social, political, and economic life. These cities flourished also as nodes in networks for the exchange of goods and ideas. The invention of writing in these cities not only gave new life to cultural creativity, but also provided new means of record-keeping for the bureaucrat, businessperson, and scholar. These new cities allowed and demanded complex and hierarchical government to keep them functioning. Although we sometimes see cities today as homes of secularism and heterogeneity, these early cities were also religious in the sense that they often existed to promote dedication to specific gods through their physical and ritual organization. Differences in climate and culture separate Egyptian from Mesopotamian urbanization, but they also shared many similarities. We know somewhat less about Egyptian urbanization because the Nile itself washed away many of its foundations, but more recent archaeology has uncovered Egyptian as well as Sumerian city walls and residential structures, suggesting that they also needed to protect their inhabitants from outsiders.

Sumer and Egypt provide what scholars sometimes refer to as a "**master narrative**," a conventional, widely accepted view of historical transformation, suggesting that the historical process at other times and places will follow similar patterns. Each of our subsequent case studies has reinforced some dimensions of the "master narrative," while challenging others.

- Indus valley urbanization suggested that a generally consistent civilization could extend over an immense geographical space, over thousands of years. A few of its distinctive, planned cities stood out as capitals, but even after they were evacuated, other cities of the far-flung network kept the civilization alive.

Bronze kneeling figure, Jenne, Mali, c. 1100–1400. Archaeological activity since the 1970s has revealed Jenne-jeno, "Old Jenne," as a commercial center on the Niger River from about 250 B.C.E. Its traditions seem to have persisted through the centuries and into "new" Jenne, the city that now stands adjacent to the older excavation. Such statuettes as this one, produced in Jenne-jeno, may have been used in worship of and for ancestors. (Private collection)

KEY TERM

master narrative The conventional, widely accepted view of the historical record.

117

Moreover, Indus agricultural practices were adopted and adapted by invaders who transplanted some of them from the Indus valley to the Ganges valley.

• Early Chinese urbanization, represented in the historical record through oracle bones and through the geometrical design of city plans, placed added emphasis on the religious dimension of cities, although the rulers did not neglect to mobilize large and powerful armed forces.

• In the Americas, such cities as Teotihuacán and the later cities of the Maya demonstrated again the importance of monumental religious architecture, although each additional excavation reveals the extent of both long-distance trade and everyday, mundane activities. Urbanization in the Andes Mountains indicates that not all early cities needed riverbeds. Urban rulers could construct fabulous networks for trade, communication, and troop movement at forbidding altitudes. From their capital cities they could launch empires. They could also administer cities, and even empires, without having invented writing.

• In the Niger River valley of West Africa, the single primary urban settlement that has been excavated challenges the "master narrative," suggesting that cities may develop through the interrelationship of adjacent smaller settlements without the need for hierarchy, centralization, government structure, or written language. The data presented thus far may be, however, subject to different interpretations. Perhaps the central mound in Jenne-jeno does, in fact, represent some hierarchical structure. Or perhaps it is a collection of contiguous villages rather than an urban center. The interpretation depends in part on how far the definition of a city and its functions may be—and ought to be—stretched. Continuing excavation and interpretation will help to decide the degree to which the "master narrative" concerning early urbanization will hold up, and to what degree new, less rigid ideas of the role of urbanization in human history are yet be formulated.

CHAPTER REVIEW

CHINA: THE XIA, SHANG, AND ZHOU DYNASTIES

4.1 What were the characteristics of early Chinese cities?

The first cities in China were centers of administration and ritual, long-distance trade and religious practice. They were laid out according to priestly interpretations of oracle bone inscriptions. A king ruled from a capital and controlled a network of subordinate cities run by his representatives. He performed rituals, divinations, and sacrifices; waged war; saw to the construction of irrigation works; and administered the government. Cities contained bronze, pottery, and bone artifact workshops, and networks of residential areas. Archaeological evidence shows the class divisions in cities' spatial plans: the dwellings and decorated graves of the wealthy and powerful are in one area, and the dwellings of the commoners and their burial places are located in trash pits.

THE WESTERN HEMISPHERE: MESOAMERICA AND SOUTH AMERICA

4.2 How did the first cities of the Americas differ from those of East Asia?

Like the urban areas of East Asia, the first cities of the Americas began as religious shrine centers, then developed into city-states with functions in trade and politics as well as religion. They frequently made war with one another, and various groups succeeded one another as the most powerful.

Some cities wielded enormous influence over a wide area of settlements. The cities of the Americas were not built on major river systems as in East Asia. In Mesoamerica they emerged at water's edge, on lakes or small rivers; in South America they emerged on the shores of the Pacific below and in the Andes Mountains above. The Americans did not use metals for much of anything apart from jewelry and artwork. They did not invent the wheel nor use draft animals (except for llamas) for transportation. Only the Maya created writing systems.

WEST AFRICA: THE NIGER RIVER VALLEY

4.3 How did urbanization in the Niger River valley differ from urbanization elsewhere?

The first known cities in the Niger River valley of West Africa were built as centers of exchange. The people traded copper, sandstone, salt, and gold across the Sahara. It is possible that the people in Jenne-jeno, the only early city that has been found in this region so far, lived in clusters of interdependent communities, without a single core that included hierarchy, centralization, and government structure—the elements of urbanization found elsewhere. It may be that the people in the settlements of the Niger River valley experienced cooperation, rather than competition, equality rather than coercion.

Suggested Readings

PRINCIPAL SOURCES

Coe, Michael, Dean Snow, and Elizabeth Benson. *Atlas of Ancient America* (New York: Facts on File, 1986). One in the excellent series by this publisher, prepared by experts, with text, maps, pictures.

Fagan, Brian. *People of the Earth: An Introduction to World Prehistory* (Upper Saddle River, NJ: Prentice Hall, 13th ed., 2010). Outstanding anthropological textbook on prehistory.

Hessler, Peter. "The New Story of China's Ancient Past," *National Geographic* (July 2003), pp. 56–81. Journalist-scholar Hessler presents accessible, up-to-date information and illustrations of Shang urbanization, especially around Anyang, but also in southwest China, where it may not be Shang.

Loewe, Michael, and Edward L. Shaughnessy, eds. *The Cambridge History of Ancient China* (Cambridge: Cambridge University Press, 1999). The article by D.N. Keightley, "The Shang: China's First Historical Dynasty," pp. 232–91, is most relevant on the period and its archaeological finds, urban and other.

Mann, Charles C. *1491: New Revelations of the Americas Before Columbus* (New York: Vintage Books, 2006). Scholarly, accessible, a best seller. Summarizes much new scholarship; focuses more on the period just before Europeans arrived, but goes back even to before "Native Americans" arrived.

Mazurkewich, Karen. "Personal Journey: The Art of China; Unearthing a New History," *Asian Wall Street Journal*, May 14, 2004, p. 1. Report on the excavations at Huanbei, with discussion by the archaeologists.

McIntosh, Roderick James. *Ancient Middle Niger Urbanism and the Self-Organizing Landscape* (Cambridge: Cambridge University Press, 2005). The most recent book publication on Jenne-jeno by one of the two principal archaeologists involved in its excavation.

Murray, Jocelyn, ed. *Cultural Atlas of Africa* (New York: Facts on File, 1982). One in the excellent series by this publisher, prepared by an expert with text, maps, pictures, and time lines.

Schele, Linda, and David Freidel. *A Forest of Kings: The Untold Story of the Ancient Maya* (New York: William Morrow, 1990). Tells how the Mayan language was deciphered, by those who did it.

Smith, Michael E., and Marilyn Masson, eds. *The Ancient Civilizations of Mesoamerica: A Reader* (Oxford: Blackwell, 2000). Twenty-three outstanding scholars contribute. Several of the essays deal with urbanization. Classroom-tested by the editors.

Tang, Jigen, Zhichun Ding, and George Rapp. "The Largest Shang City Located in Anyang, China," *Antiquity* LXXIV:285 (September 20, 2000), p. 479. Brief account adding Huanbei Shang City, excavated since 1996, to the series of capitals established sequentially by the Shang dynasty.

The Times (London). *Past Worlds* (Maplewood, NJ: Hammond Inc., 1988). Excellent, comprehensive, scholarly introduction to archaeological prehistory, lavishly illustrated with maps and pictures.

ADDITIONAL SOURCES

Alva, Walter, and Christopher Donnan. *The Royal Tombs of Sipán* (Los Angeles, CA: Fowler Museum of Cultural History, University of California, 1993). Lavishly illustrated account of the excavation.

Chang, Kwang-chih. *The Archaeology of Ancient China* (New Haven, CT: Yale University Press, 3rd ed., 1977). The expert's account, somewhat dated, but still the standard.

——. *Shang Civilization* (New Haven, CT: Yale University Press, 1980). Comprehensive account by an archaeologist who participated in some of the most significant excavations.

Connah, Graham. *African Civilizations* (Cambridge: Cambridge University Press, 1987). Excellent, comprehensive textbook on prehistoric Africa. Covers the entire continent.

Curtin, Philip, Steven Feierman, Leonard Thompson, and Jan Vansina. *African History from Earliest Times to Independence* (New York: Longman, 2nd ed., 1995). A standard textbook by four distinguished experts.

de Bary, William Theodore, *et al.*, comp. *Sources of Chinese Tradition.*, Vol. 1. (New York: Columbia University Press, 1998). The best available anthology of classic writings. Good section on oracle bones.

Demarest, Arthur, and Geoffrey Conrad, eds. *Ideology and Pre-Columbian Civilizations* (Santa Fe, NM: School of American Research Press, 1992). Scholarly argument on the importance of ideas, both cosmo-magical and political, in the construction of pre-Columbian civilizations.

Ebrey, Patricia Buckley. *The Cambridge Illustrated History of China* (Cambridge: Cambridge University Press, 2nd ed., 2010). Only a short section on early urbanization, but places it in very accessible context, and the illustrations and maps are helpful.

Keightly, David N., ed. *The Origins of Chinese Civilization* (Berkeley, CA: University of California Press, 1983). An excellent account.

MacNeish, Richard S. "The Origins of New World Civilization," *Scientific American*, November 1964. Reprinted in *Scientific American, Cities: Their Origin, Growth, and Human Impact* (San Francisco, CA: W.H. Freeman and Company, 1973), pp. 63–71. Brief introduction, especially interesting on domestication of crops and animals.

McIntosh, Susan, and Roderick McIntosh. "Finding West Africa's Oldest City," *National Geographic* CLXII No. 3 (September 1982), pp. 396–418. Popular introduction based on early archaeological expeditions.

McIntosh, Susan Keech, ed. *Excavations at Jenné-Jeno, Hambarketolo, and Kaniana (Inland Niger Delta, Mali): The 1981 Season* (Berkeley, CA: University of California Press, 1995). Comprehensive, scholarly documentation on the excavations.

Millon, René. "Teotihuacán," *Scientific American*, June 1967. Reprinted in *Scientific American, Cities: Their Origin, Growth, and Human Impact*, pp. 82–91. Basic introduction to the early professional excavations of Mesoamerica's largest prehistoric metropolis.

Moseley, Michael E. *The Maritime Foundations of Andean Civilization* (Menlo Park, CA: Cummings, 1975). Argues that the Andean cities were founded on the basis of the Pacific coastal developments.

Popul Vuh: Sacred Book of the Quiché Maya People, translation and commentary by Allen J. Christenson (Norman: University of Oklahoma Press, 2007).

Scientific American, ed. *Cities: Their Origin, Growth, and Human Impact* (San Francisco, CA: W.H. Freeman and Company, 1973). Anthology of articles on urbanization culled from *Scientific American* articles. Still useful.

Waley, Arthur, trans. *The Book of Songs* (New York: Grove Press, 1996). Marvelous translation of poetry from the age of Confucius.

Wheatley, Paul. *The Pivot of the Four Quarters: A Preliminary Enquiry into the Origins and Character of the Ancient Chinese City* (Chicago, IL: Aldine, 1971).

FILMS

Legacy: The Origins of Civilization— China (1992; 1 hour). Michael Wood's idiosyncratic introduction to ancient China, with useful sections on the discovery of oracle bones and early cities. Good visuals.

Time-Life. *Lost Civilizations: China: Dynasties of Power* (2002; 1 hour). Also good visuals and interesting comments from experts explaining how the earliest cities functioned, and the role of regional rulers in establishing them.

National Geographic. *Megastructures: Machu Picchu* (2012; 46 minutes). Emphasizes the engineering and construction of this remote city in the Andes Mountains. Asks how the buildings functioned and how they were built.

Teotihuacán (2001; 27 minutes). Looks at the belief system that encouraged the Aztecs to build this huge and remarkable city, and at the engineering skill needed to build it.

West Africa (2009; 47 minutes). Includes a four-minute section on Jenne-jeno and its significance for later developments.

PART THREE

TURNING POINT: FROM CITY-STATES TO EMPIRES

2000 B.C.E.–1100 C.E.

What Are Empires and Why Are They Important?

From Gilgamesh onward, the rulers of city-states constructed city walls and mobilized armed forces. If situated at water's edge, they commanded ships and sailors as well. Their reputation rested on both military prowess and civilian administration. The literature from Mesopotamia, pre-imperial China, ancient Greece, and Mayan Mesoamerica abounds with tales of warfare among city-states. They fought incessantly.

Increasing military force transformed these city-states into empires. Sargon of Akkad (exact dates uncertain) set the example. His conquest of the quarreling city-states of Mesopotamia around 2250 B.C.E. created the first empire recorded in history.

After conquering the cities of the middle and upper Euphrates, Sargon marched into southern Anatolia. Then he turned eastward, capturing Susa, the capital city of the Elamites in western Iran. Sargon's empire lasted for only

A phalanx formation. The box-office success of the film *300* indicated the continuing power of Herodotus' history of the Persian Wars, and especially its story of the defensive strategy of Leonidas and his 300 men at Thermopylae. The film accurately shows the power of the phalanx, the company of soldiers protecting themselves and their fellows with the collective positioning of their shields.

about a century, but from his time onward Mesopotamia was usually ruled by a single empire, most frequently an invading force (like his own), but sometimes by an ambitious army arising from within. Sargon's rule ended the era of the Mesopotamian city-states and ushered in the era of empire.

The Meaning of Empire

New York proudly calls itself the Empire State. At least five states in the United States contain cities named "Imperial." California boasts an Imperial Valley and an Imperial County. Until recently, Britain maintained its "imperial gallon" as a measure of volume. Today, however, "empire" often carries negative connotations, and "imperialism" even more so. The demise within the past generation of many empires, most recently that of the Soviet Union, has met with general approval around the world. Why has the significance of "empire" changed so dramatically? What is an empire? How do empires rule?

The Assyrian army with its musicians, from the Palace of Ashurbanipal, Nineveh, seventh century B.C.E. Limestone relief. From earliest times armies included musicians whose horns and trumpets would encourage their own troops and frighten the enemies, and whose lyres, after battle, might bring some respite. (Louvre, Paris)

Empires grow from the conquest of one people by another. They have been as natural in human history as the desire of one people to exert control over other peoples and their resources, and they have arisen as frequently as rulers have been able to build military organizations capable of attaining those goals.

Scholars emphasize two forms of imperial rule: hegemony and dominance. The ruling powers themselves prefer hegemony, foreign rule that governs with the substantial consent of the governed people. Subjects in such an empire accept foreign rule willingly, if they can be persuaded that it is in their best interests. Subjects may benefit from the stability and peace imposed by imperial rule; the technological improvements it introduces; the more extensive networks it develops and opens for trade and profit; the cultural sophistication it exhibits and shares; and the opportunities for new kinds of advancement that membership in the empire may offer. If imperial membership is perceived to have such benefits, the subject peoples may welcome it peacefully, even eagerly. They may accept the ideology of the imperial power, its moral authority and its claim to legitimacy.

Should the imperial ideology not be acceptable, however, and should opposition arise, rulers will impose their government through dominance, the exercise of military force and sheer power. So the state expends vast sums on recruiting, training, and equipping its armies. It mobilizes its troops across the vast spaces of empire, dispatching them along the same roads that carry the imperial commerce. To subdue and overwhelm its enemies, the imperial government may deploy its power in acts of cruelty and arrogance.

Resistance to imperial rule is as normal as empires themselves. Sooner or later, the secrets of the imperial power spread among the conquered. Empires begin by using their superiority to rule, but eventually subject populations learn from the technology introduced by their conquerors: newer and more powerful weapons, materials, military formations, agricultural methods, administrative organizations, and techniques of production. They gain the capacity to challenge their rulers. Subject peoples, who may originally have felt some gratitude toward their imperial benefactors, may later grow resentful, restive, and finally rebellious.

The Dynamics of Empire

To inspire admiration and loyalty among allies, and caution among potential enemies, empires build monumental palaces for the emperor and the leadership cadre. They establish vast marketplaces stocked with exotic and luxurious goods, and they build highways and roads, ports and dockyards, to service them. Specific examples stand out, such as the grand canals linking the rich agricultural lands of southern China to the imperial capital in the north. Similarly, the phrase "All roads lead to Rome," the capital of an equally powerful empire, may have been an exaggeration, but its central idea was correct.

In order to function as a single political structure, empires create bureaucratic administrations with at least some uniformity in language, currency, weights, measures, and legal systems. Perhaps the most significant administrative task of all is the empire's collection of taxes from its subjects and tribute from the conquered. Such revenues provide the means to support armies and public works, and financial profits for the rulers.

Empires often encourage great creativity in the arts and in learning. They bring peoples of different languages, religions, ethnic origins, and cultural and technological levels under a single, centralized rule. Depending on the needs of the empire, some groups from among the subject populations are granted full citizenship; a few might even be invited to serve as local representatives of the distant imperial power. Those at the bottom, especially war captives, might be enslaved. A few—those who proved particularly dangerous or costly to the imperial rulers—might be executed as a warning to potential rebels.

Empires are not static: they rise and they fall. The causes of the decline and fall of empires include:

- Failure of leadership—the inability of the empire to produce or select rulers capable of maintaining the imperial structures;
- Overextension of the administration—the inability of the imperial rulers to sustain the costs of a far-flung empire while coping simultaneously with critical domestic problems;
- Collapse of the economy—the overextension of empire to territories so remote or so difficult to subdue and govern that costs outrun benefits;
- Doubts over the ideology—the end of belief in the justice or benefit of empire, which may occur either when cynical colonizers abandon the colonial enterprise, or when frustrated colonized peoples revolt, or both;
- Military defeat—external enemies and the colonized people combine in revolt.

The First Empires

Akkad provides the earliest example of empire-building, as we shall see in the chapter "Dawn of the Empires." Egypt provides the next example, and then we turn to the Persian Empire. In Persia's wars against the Greeks in the fifth

Battle of Til-Tuba between the Assyrian king Ashurbanipal and the king of Elam, from the palace of Ashurbanipal, 645 B.C.E. Stone relief. An Assyrian soldier holds the severed head of Teumann, king of Elam. (British Museum, London)

century B.C.E., we see a fundamental clash between monarchy and democracy, between a powerful consolidated empire and an alliance of independent city-states.

The great empires of the ancient world—Rome, China, and India—controlled vast areas, influenced tens of millions of lives, and have remained models even to our own time. They represent turning points in the history of most of humankind.

Rome, China, and India were so successful that their ideologies of empire—their explanations of why they should rule over others—prevailed for centuries. Indeed, the Roman Empire endured for almost a thousand years, from about 500 B.C.E. to almost 500 C.E.; if we include the Eastern Empire, based in Constantinople, Rome's duration is some 2,000 years. Moreover, Rome inspired an imperial image that was expressed throughout Europe centuries later in the so-called Holy Roman Empire. In the nineteenth and early twentieth centuries, many commentators compared the British Empire with Rome, and in the mid-twentieth century, many drew a similar comparison with the United States. The Chinese Empire, founded in 221 B.C.E., lasted more or less continuously until 1911 C.E., and some would argue that it persists even today in new, communist garb. The first emperor to rule almost all of the Indian subcontinent, Asoka (Ashok) Maurya (r. c. 265–238 B.C.E.), is still commemorated today on every rupee note printed in India. These three great empires, spanning almost all of Eurasia, maintained communication with one other and we include analysis of these links among them.

Turning Point Questions

1. How important are warfare and murder in the construction of empire?
2. What skills and powers, beyond the military, are necessary to consolidate and rule an empire?
3. What might be the tipping points that would turn a peaceful colony into a rebellious one?

Roman soldiers besieging a town, from *The History of the Nations*. Aquatint engraving by Antonio Nani. Rome's array of military devices—battering rams, equipment for scaling walls, catapults, and horses and chariots at the ready—facilitated its policy of the "new wisdom," namely, to defeat the enemy through patient, deliberate preparation, and the demonstration of overwhelming force. (Private collection)

5 Dawn of the Empires

Empire-building in North Africa, West Asia, and the Mediterranean

2000 B.C.E.–300 B.C.E.

O ur study of empires begins with the world's earliest known empires, in Mesopotamia and the Nile valley. We then discuss three warring empires that set new standards of empire-building, competition, and warfare: the Persian Empire consolidated its base of power in the Middle East and then attempted to conquer the independent Greek city-states of the Mediterranean. In response, the Greek city-states formed a successful coalition to fight off the Persians, but afterward, ironically, succumbed to the demands of Athens, which now proclaimed its own imperial power over its former allies. Throwing off Athenian domination, the Greek city-states squabbled and fought among themselves for a generation, until Alexander the Great swept down from his kingdom of Macedonia to the north, conquered them all, and turned eastward to defeat the mighty Persians. Alexander then established his own empire on foundations the Persians had built.

Abu Simbel. This temple (one of two) at Abu Simbel was built in the thirteenth century B.C.E. as a monument to Pharaoh Ramses II and his queen Nefertari. In 1968, to save them from being submerged when the Aswan High Dam was built on the Nile River, the two temples were removed and relocated at the edge of the newly formed Lake Nasser.

LEARNING OBJECTIVES

5.1	5.2	5.3	5.4
Describe the characteristics of early empires.	Discuss the long rule of Darius I.	Describe the political organization of the Greek city-state.	Explain how Greek culture spread throughout Alexander's empire.

Listen on MyHistoryLab

The Earliest Empires

5.1 What were the characteristics of early empires?

What were the
characteristics of
early empires?

5.1

5.2

5.3

5.4

The first empires were born in Mesopotamia and the Nile valley more than four thousand years ago, and we already see in them the characteristics of imperial rise and fall. Since many of the characteristics of imperial power expand upon a base in urban power, it is no surprise that the city-states of Mesopotamia provided fertile soil for the flowering of empires. Once established, the empire of Sargon inspired others to challenge and overthrow it, introducing a succession of empires in the region.

Egypt's empire began not in urban power but in state power. By 3000 B.C.E. Egyptian rulers had consolidated a single state unifying the Upper and Lower Nile. It took a thousand years before they successfully expanded their power over others, first over the Nubians to the south and later out of the Nile valley entirely, eastward into the Middle East and Mesopotamia. Egypt's imperial fates rose and fell with the shifting balance of strength between its own armies and administration, and those of its adversaries.

📖 **Read** the **Document**: **Suffering Explained (1800 BCE, 700 BCE)** on **MyHistoryLab**

Mesopotamia and the Fertile Crescent

Mesopotamia's independent city-states could not reach political accommodation among themselves. They fought one another constantly for land, irrigation rights, and prestige, and recorded their struggles in bas-relief artwork from third-millennium Sumer. This artwork and related cuneiform records enable archaeologists to reconstruct two main antagonists, the cities of Lagash and Umma, which, with their allied forces, dominated the Mesopotamian warfare of the time. Victory by any one of the city-states over any other, however, was frequently avenged in the next generation.

Sargon of Akkad. Geographically, the city-states of Mesopotamia were also vulnerable to immigrant groups crossing their territory and challenging their powers. About 2300 B.C.E., Sargon (r. *c.* 2334–2279 B.C.E.), leading an immigrant group of Semitic peoples from the Arabian peninsula, entered Sumer. The new arrivals settled in and around northern Sumer and called their land Akkad. Sargon led the Akkadians to victories over the leading cities of Sumer, over the Elamites to the east, over northern Mesopotamia, and over a swath of land connecting Mesopotamia to the Mediterranean. He founded his Akkadian capital at Agade, a city whose exact location is now unknown.

Historical records are skimpy, but those that do exist correspond to our assessment of the key characteristics of empire. First, the Akkadians conquered widely. Administrative tablets of the Akkad dynasty have been found as far away as Susa, several hundred miles to the east in Persia, suggesting a far-flung governmental administration. Second, after razing the walls of the major cities of Ur, Lagash, and Umma, Sargon displaced the traditional local civilian hierarchies with his own administrators, designated the "sons of Akkad." Third, the Akkadian language was used in administrative documents in Sumer. Fourth, measurements of length, area, dry and liquid quantities, and probably weight were standardized throughout the empire; indeed, people in the region used the Akkadian units of measure for more than a thousand years, far longer than the empire itself survived. Finally, Sargon imposed his own imagery and ideology of empire. Documents were dated from the founding of the Akkadian kingdom, legal oaths were taken in the name of the Akkadian king, and Sargon installed his own daughter as high-priestess of the moon god Nanna at Ur.

The empire of Sargon. During the third millennium B.C.E., Sargon established control over the city-states of southern Mesopotamia, creating the world's first empire. Building a capital at Agade, he founded the Akkadian dynasty, which for a century ruled the Fertile Crescent, from the Persian Gulf to the Mediterranean Sea.

Sargon's empire lasted for about a century and was followed by other outsiders, the Gutians, and then by a revival of internal Sumerian power under Ur-Nammu (r. *c.* 2112–*c.* 2095 B.C.E.). Culturally, Sumer was so advanced that it influenced even its conquerors, the Akkadians, the Gutians, and later arrivals. The Akkadian language, however, supplanted Sumerian by about 2000 B.C.E.

Waves of Invaders: The Babylonians and the Hittites. Throughout this time, waves of immigrants continuously entered the Fertile Crescent, attracted perhaps by empty land on its fringes, or perhaps by the presence in its heartland of already settled peoples on whom they could prey. Historians have not always been able to determine the specific origins of the immigrants, but two groups have stood out most clearly: Semites and Indo-Europeans. Each is designated by the family of languages that it spoke and (later) wrote; a common language probably indicates a degree of internal ethnic relationship as well.

Among the Semitic groups were the Amorites, who invaded and conquered Sumer about 1900 B.C.E. and founded their own new dynasty slightly to the north at Babylon. At first they employed Sumerian cultural and administrative forms, but over time they created new systems of their own. Their sixth ruler, Hammurabi (r. 1792–1750 B.C.E.), is most famous for his law codes, but he was also a skilled military leader who defeated the Sumerian city-states that had remained independent. He created the Babylonian Empire, imposing an administrative network that stretched from the Persian Gulf to Syria and endured for 250 years, until its defeat about 1500 B.C.E. by the Hittites, a new group of invaders.

While the Semitic Amorites had apparently immigrated from the south, the Hittites arrived as part of a vast movement of Indo-European peoples that originated in the north, apparently in the mountain regions of the Caucasus. This group of peoples

What were the
characteristics of
early empires?

5.1
5.2
5.3
5.4

spoke "Indo-European" languages, from which developed many of the principal languages of the lands to which they migrated and settled, from Britain in the northwest to Persia and India in the southeast.

In the course of their migrations, the Indo-Europeans also invented the decisive weapon of the age, the two-wheeled war chariot. Drawn by a horse, which bore part of the weight of the chariot, this new war machine had light wheels with a hub and spokes, and carried three warriors, at least one of whom could continuously shoot his wooden bow, reinforced with bone and sinew. Unlike the four-wheeled chariot, the Indo-Europeans' new design had great maneuverability.

The Hittites shared in this invention. When they settled in Anatolia, they also helped to usher in another innovation, iron-working technology that they developed in this iron-rich region. They established their capital in Hattushash, modern Bŏgaz-köy, Turkey, in the early second millennium B.C.E., extending their power over much of Anatolia and northern Syria. Much of what we know about them comes from some 25,000 cuneiform tablets that were discovered there. About 1590 B.C.E., they invaded and conquered Babylonia. About 1400–1200 B.C.E., during the New Kingdom of Egypt, the Hittites ruled as one of the most powerful nations of the Middle East. In *c.* 1274 B.C.E., in one of the greatest battles of the Middle East, they confronted the Egyptian armies at Qadesh, Syria. The two armies, each with about 20,000 men, and the Hittites with 2,500 two-wheeled chariots, fought to a draw. Within a few years these two great powers concluded treaties of peace and mutual defense, reaffirmed by royal marriages.

The Hittite Empire suddenly collapsed about 1193 B.C.E., perhaps under an onslaught from invaders, the "Sea Peoples," who arrived via the Mediterranean. City-state and regional outposts of Hittites survived until about 710 B.C.E., when they were defeated by the Assyrians and incorporated into their empire.

The Assyrians. Assyrians, descendants of the Akkadians, joined the other major participants in the continuous warfare in Mesopotamia. In the twentieth century B.C.E. they established an independent state and, through the trade of their private businessmen, achieved some prosperity. Then, after a period of subjugation by the Mitanni, they regained their independence in the thirteenth century only to lose it again to the Arameans *c.* 1000 B.C.E.

Around 900 B.C.E. a Neo-Assyrian (New Assyrian) kingdom began a series of conquests, sweeping westward to the Mediterranean coast, northward to Syria and Palestine, and southeastward into Babylon. Infantry provided their main force, while archers riding in chariots led the attacks, and battering rams and siege towers assaulted fixed positions.

More than most ancient empires, the Assyrians controlled conquered peoples through policies of terror and forced transfers of population. They tortured those they captured to instill fear. They also deported some peoples into exile from their homelands, including the "lost" ten of the tribes of Israel; that is, these tribes lost their sense of ethnic and religious identity and presumably assimilated to Assyrian culture, just as the conquerors had hoped. In other regions, the Assyrians imported their own people to settle among the defeated peoples and keep them under control.

Bronze head of an Akkadian ruler (?Sargon I), *c.* 2250 B.C.E. Exuding royal self-confidence, this near-life-size bronze head probably depicts Sargon I, founder of the Akkadian dynasty. For more than half a century, Sargon dominated one city-state after another until he had conquered most of Mesopotamia. After his death, his successors worshiped him as a god. (National Iraq Museum, Baghdad)

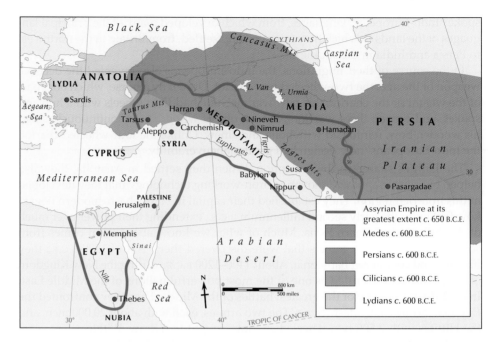

Assyria and its rivals. The shifting political map of southwest Asia was dominated between 850 and 650 B.C.E. by the powerful and martial Assyrians, who even occupied Egypt. Anatolia was fragmented into smaller states. To the north a powerful federation of Median tribes was a growing threat. In 614, in alliance with the Babylonians, they crushed Assyria.

King Esarhaddon (r. 680–669 B.C.E.) conquered Egypt in 671 B.C.E., making Assyria the greatest power of its day. His successors held the entire province, driving the Nubians from the southern regions and suppressing rebellions. Assyria finally withdrew from Egypt, defeated not primarily by the Egyptians but by internal dynastic struggles and by the combined forces of Babylonians, Arameans, the Medes of Iran, and Scythian invaders, who attacked Assyria's Mesopotamian heartland. The Assyrian capital, Nineveh, fell in 612 B.C.E.

Only the last of the Neo-Assyrian kings, Ashurbanipal (r. 668–627 B.C.E.), is known to have been literate, and he constructed a great library in his capital at Nineveh. Some 20,000 tablets are still preserved from that library, including the earliest complete version of *The Epic of Gilgamesh*.

The city-state political structures of Mesopotamia, and its geographical openness, had left the region very vulnerable. As the city-states fought destructively among themselves, they were repeatedly attacked by, and absorbed into, powerful foreign empires. The Mesopotamians had to expend their resources on warfare as their local units of government faced increasing challenges from ever-greater external powers.

Egypt and International Conquest

Egypt's empire was very different from Mesopotamia's. From early times Egypt was governed as a unified state. Geography had encouraged Egypt to become a single administrative unit, incorporating the entire Nile valley from the first cataract northward to the Mediterranean Sea. From 3000 B.C.E. to the present, Egypt has usually remained a single political unit, so we think of it as a kingdom with a single government ruling a single civilization rather than as an empire of one people ruling over others.

Egyptian forces did not always stay within their own borders. During the Middle Kingdom, *c.* 2030–1640 B.C.E., Egyptians conquered Nubia, the territory stretching southward some 900 miles from just above the first cataract in the Nile, at present-day Aswan in Egypt, to present-day Khartoum, capital of the Sudan. At first, this imperial conquest was only into lower Nubia, and Nubia's success in driving out the Egyptian conquerors was one of the factors that brought Egypt's Middle Kingdom to an end.

During the Second Intermediate Period (c. 1640–1540 B.C.E.), a time of disunity between periods of consolidation, immigrant Semitic groups, referred to in Egyptian texts as the Hyksos, ruled Lower Egypt. It is not clear if the Hyksos first came as traders or as nomadic immigrants, but as the Egyptian kingdom disintegrated they became rulers over large parts of the remains. Although later Egyptian rulers despised them, they are recognized as the legitimate 16th dynasty. A Semitic people, the Hyksos introduced bronze-making technology and horses and chariots to Egypt.

Under new leadership, Egypt became consolidated once again into the New Kingdom (c. 1550–c. 1050 B.C.E.), and the Hyksos were expelled. In pursuing the Hyksos into Palestine, the Egyptians began their active, direct involvement in Middle Eastern affairs. They remained an imperial presence in the region for several centuries. Thutmosis I (r. 1504–1492 B.C.E.) extended Egypt's control not only further south into Nubia than ever before (see "Middle and New Kingdom Egypt" map), but also northeast as far as the Euphrates River, creating Egypt's greatest historical empire. The small states of Syria and Palestine managed to remain self-governing, but Egypt stationed army units and administrative officials in the region and collected taxes. Egypt seemed more interested in access to these taxes, raw materials, and trading opportunities than in imperial governance.

The Art of Palace and Temple. The colonies of the New Kingdom enriched Egypt, helping to produce a period of great opulence and creativity. Because the pharaoh often traveled throughout the country, the Egyptians built a number of elegant palaces at various points along the Nile, from the delta all the way to the northern edge of Nubia. The state religion and the state administration were closely linked, so temple complexes dominated the towns that grew up around them. One of the greatest of these temples was constructed by Pharaoh Ramses II (r. c. 1279–1213 B.C.E.) at Abu Simbel, just north of the first cataract, and dedicated to the greatest gods of the New Kingdom and to Ramses II himself. (In the 1970s, the newly built Aswan dam threatened to flood the entire complex, including its grand sculptures, but the government saved them by relocating them.)

👁 **Watch** the **Video: Ramses II's Abu Simbel** on **MyHistoryLab**

In addition to Ramses II, another pharaoh calls for special note. One of the four female pharaohs, Hatshepsut (c. 1473–c. 1458 B.C.E.) was the widow of one pharaoh and served as regent to her stepson when he succeeded to the throne. For 15 years, however, until the boy grew up, Hatshepsut declared herself "king," since there was no official sanction for a female ruler. She encouraged artists to represent her as a man, wearing male clothing and with a king's beard. She built a temple at Deir

Middle and New Kingdom Egypt. By 2040 B.C.E. the unification of Egypt into a centralized, militaristic state was under way. Its hierarchic society focused on the priesthood and the dynastic succession of semi-god rulers, the pharaohs. The consolidation of power was reflected in the size and scale of royal building projects, including fortifications, new cities, temples, and grandiose tombs, and by conquests in Nubia.

Relief from the temple of Beit el-Wali (detail), Lower Nubia, c. 2000–1850 B.C.E. The rich variety of produce here presented to Ramses II after his conquest of lower Nubia—bags of gold, incense, tusks, ebony logs, ostrich eggs, bows, shields, fans, and wild animals—seems to mirror the ethnic diversity on display. Pale-, brown-, and black-skinned peoples coexisted in Egypt and Nubia. (British Museum, London)

5.1	What were the characteristics of early empires?
5.2	
5.3	
5.4	

Royal pyramids and adjacent iron slag heaps at Meroe, Sudan, c. 600 B.C.E. The rulers of Meroe and Egypt shared many artistic traditions, but often gave them a distinctive local interpretation, as can be seen in the forms of their pyramids and palaces.

What were the
characteristics of
early empires?

5.1
5.2
5.3
5.4

el-Bahri near Thebes, which was devoted to the worship of the traditional god Amon, but which she also hoped would promote her as a deity after her death.

The End of Empire. Egypt's imperial control over remote and diverse peoples met resistance from local powers within the Fertile Crescent. The Hittites, the Babylonians, and, especially, the Mitanni mounted frequent revolts. (Egyptian pharaoh Ramses II reported the great, but indecisive, battle against the Hittites at Qadesh, noted above, as a brilliant victory, neither the first nor the last time that a government would claim military honors it had not won.) Egyptian control ended by about 1200 B.C.E., although its trading interests and political and economic influence in the region continued for centuries.

After suffering defeats in the Levant, Egypt was pushed back within its river domains, but by now these once again included Nubia. Early in the New Kingdom, Egypt had reconquered the heartland of central Nubia, the core of the sophisticated,

The empires of southwest Asia. Toward the end of the second millennium B.C.E., three empires fought for control of the Fertile Crescent. Egyptians, Mitanni of northern Mesopotamia, and Hittites of Anatolia came into direct conflict. Building on strong political control over their core regions, each dispatched powerful armies with the most up-to-date weapons to seize territory from the others.

131

independent state and a source of gold, minerals, wood, and recruits for Egypt's army and police. It maintained its imperial power over this southern colony until *c.* 1050 B.C.E., when the colony broke free. The loss of empire, together with the loss of the gold, supplies, and slaves it had provided, helped to bring an end to the unified New Kingdom of the Egyptians and to usher in the Third Intermediate Period of divided rule (*c.* 1069–747 B.C.E.).

Three centuries later, Nubia marched northward to capture Egypt, reversing the relationship between colonizer and colonized. For half a century, 712–657 B.C.E., Nubia ruled over an empire of its own, which included all of Egypt. Thereafter Nubia remained strong, with its capital first at Napata and later at Meroe, while Egypt fell into decline.

In 671 B.C.E., while Nubians ruled southern Egypt, Assyrians conquered and occupied the north. Egypt could not regain its independence. The Persians conquered it in 525 B.C.E. Two centuries later, in 332 B.C.E., Alexander the Great captured Egypt from Persia, and in 30 B.C.E., Egypt passed to the next great Mediterranean empire, that of Rome. No longer an empire, Egypt had become a prize.

The Persian Empire

5.2 How did Darius I come to rule the Persian Empire?

Medes and Persians began to appear in the region east of Mesopotamia about 1300 B.C.E., bringing with them the use of iron. Written cuneiform records of the mid-ninth century B.C.E. confirm the archaeological evidence of their arrival. At first the Medes were more numerous and powerful, but later the Persians came to predominate. Like the Hittites, both groups were Indo-Europeans.

Cyaxares of Media (r. 625–585 B.C.E.) established an army; conquered the Scythians, another immigrant group in the region; sealed an alliance with the Babylonians by marrying his granddaughter to the son of their ruler; and, with them, captured Nineveh, the capital of Assyria. They destroyed Assyria as a major military force, and a new **balance of power** among the Egyptians, Medes, Babylonians, and Lydians emerged in western Asia.

Persian Expansion

Cyrus II, the Great, of Persia (r. 558–529 B.C.E.), however, broke the balance when he defeated the other three kingdoms of western Asia—the Medes, the Lydians, and the Babylonians—and incorporated them into his own empire. Under Cyrus, the Achaemenids (as this group of Persians called themselves, in honor of their legendary ancestor Achaemenes) dominated the entire region from Persia to the Mediterranean.

Cyrus II's eldest son, Cambyses II (r. 529–522 B.C.E.), expanded his father's conquests. Crossing the Sinai Desert, he captured Memphis, the capital of Egypt, and carried its pharaoh back to Susa in captivity, thus completing the conquest of all the major powers that had influenced the Middle East. Egypt frequently revolted, and large garrisons were required to keep it under control, so the Achaemenids under Darius I (r. 522–486 B.C.E.) completed a canal across the desert, connecting the Nile River and the Red Sea. This early "Suez Canal," first envisioned by the Egyptians as a trade route, became a troop supply line for Persian control over Egypt.

Darius also extended the Persian Empire farther into the Indian subcontinent, as far as the Indus River. The Achaemenids now controlled some of the most valuable trade routes in Asia; the **satrapy**, or province, of "India" submitted one-third of the annual cash receipts of the Achaemenids, and Indian troops served in the Achaemenid armies. From this time, Indian- and Persian-based powers would regularly confront one another across the borders of what are today Afghanistan and Pakistan.

KEY TERMS

balance of power In international relations, a policy that aims to secure peace by preventing any one state or alignment of states from becoming too dominant. Alliances are formed in order to build up a force equal or superior to that of the potential enemy.

satrapy A province or colony in the Achaemenid or Persian Empire ruled by a satrap or governor. Darius I completed the division of the Empire into provinces, and established 20 satrapies with their annual tributes. The term "satrapy" can also refer to the period of rule of a satrap.

Achaemenid Persia. The Medes and the Persians were united under Cyrus the Great in 550 B.C.E. to form the Achaemenid or Persian Empire. Cyrus and his successors, notably Darius and Xerxes, extended the empire to the Indus in the east and to Egypt and Libya in the west, and twice invaded Greece.

Meanwhile, in the west, Darius expanded to the fringes of Europe, capturing Thrace and Macedonia, and bringing the Persian Empire to its greatest extent.

Attempts to advance further were stymied. The Scythians to the north and west fought a kind of guerrilla warfare that the massed forces of the Persians could not overcome. To the south and west, the Greeks defeated Persian armies of invasion. As we will see later in this chapter, a confederation of small, democratic Greek city-states managed to repulse the mighty Persian Empire.

📖 Read the Document: Darius the Great: Ruler of Persia (522 BCE) on MyHistoryLab

Imperial Policies

The Persian imperial form of rule and administration changed in the three generations from Cyrus II, its chief architect, through his son and successor, Cambyses II, to Darius I, its most powerful emperor. The differences among the three emperors became especially clear in their policies for achieving a balance between the power of the central government and the desire of local, conquered peoples for some degree of autonomy. Under Cyrus and Darius, Persia respected local customs and institutions even as the empire expanded, providing a good example of an **hegemonic** empire, ruling with substantial consent of the conquered. Cambyses was more dictatorial, and met an early end, leaving an apt example of an empire based on more ruthless military **dominance**.

Cyrus II. Cyrus respected the dignity of his opponents. When he conquered the Medes, he allowed their king to escape with his life. He administered his newly

How did Darius I come to rule the Persian Empire?

KEY TERMS

hegemony The predominance of one unit over the others in a group, for example, one state in a confederation. It can also apply to the rule of an empire over its subject peoples, when the foreign government is exercised with their substantial consent.

dominance The imposition of alien government through force, as opposed to hegemony.

5.1

5.2 How did Darius I come to rule the Persian Empire?

5.3

5.4

acquired lands through the existing Median bureaucracy and army, allowing Median officials to keep their positions, though under Persian control. When Cyrus conquered Lydia, he spared its king, the fabulously wealthy Croesus, and even enlisted him as a consultant. In conquered Ionian cities he retained local rulers who were willing to work under Persian direction. On defeating Babylon, his most powerful rival, Cyrus chose to rule in the name of the Babylonian god Marduk and to worship daily in his temple, thus keeping the support of the priests. He continued to employ local bureaucrats and to protect the trade routes that brought wealth to the empire, securing the loyalty of the merchant classes.

Perhaps most strikingly, Cyrus allowed the peoples Babylonia had captured and deported to return to their homes. For example, he permitted the Jewish community of exiles in Babylon to return home to Judea and to rebuild their temple in Jerusalem. He also returned to them the gold and silver that had been taken from the temple. The 40,000 exiles who returned over 1,000 miles to Judea hailed Cyrus as their political savior and kept their renewed state loyal to the Persian Empire.

Cambyses II. Unlike his father, Cambyses II seems to have lost sight of the need for restraint in both the expansion and the administration of his empire. His conquest of Egypt and his use of Egyptians in his own administration of that land followed Cyrus' model, but then he overextended his reach. His attempted campaign against the Phoenician city of Carthage in distant North Africa failed when Phoenician sailors in his own navy refused to fight. An army sent south from Egypt to Nubia, attempting to capture its fabled gold supplies, failed to reach its destination and retreated from the desert in tatters. Cambyses may have been emotionally unstable; it was rumored that he kicked to death his pregnant wife/sister. It was further rumored that he committed suicide as he was returning to Persia to put down an insurrection. His seven-year rule had been costly to Persia in manpower, treasure, and the loss of support even among his own people.

Darius I. Darius, a general in the Persian army and prince of the Achaemenid dynasty, succeeded to the throne by murdering Bardiya (r. 522), who ruled briefly after Cambyses II. Darius ruled for 35 years. He was more deliberate, more balanced, and more capable as an administrator than Cambyses, and he became much richer as emperor than his predecessors. Like Cyrus, he used local administrators to staff local governments. He sought to create smaller, more efficient units of government by increasing the number of provincial administrative units, or satrapies, even faster than he expanded the empire. Some of the regional administrators, or satraps, were from the local elite; some were Persian. In each satrapy, loyalty to the empire was assured by the presence of Persian army units, which reported directly to the king, and by a secretary, who monitored the actions of the satrap and also reported back to Persia.

Darius commissioned the design of the first written Persian script. He established the tradition that royal inscriptions were to be posted in three languages—Old Persian, Babylonian, and Elamite. Among these trilingual inscriptions was a proclamation of Darius' ascent to power, inscribed on the "Behistun stone," a rock tablet that became the key to unlocking cuneiform writing 23 centuries later, when archaeologists discovered it in Behistun near Kermanshah, Iran. In the midst of the multitude of languages used across the empire, these three were to be the official written languages of administration. The most widely spoken public language was Aramaic, however, and this Semitic language of the common people throughout much of the eastern Mediterranean greatly influenced the development of formal Persian.

Legal codes varied among the satrapies to reflect local usage, and the Persian rulers frequently codified and recorded these laws. They rationalized tax codes. They evaluated, measured, and recorded the size and productivity of agricultural fields, and fixed the tax rate at about 20 percent. In each satrapy a Persian collector

5.1

How did Darius I
come to rule the
Persian Empire?

5.2

5.3

5.4

Homage rendered to Darius, bas-relief, Persepolis, Iran, 550–330 B.C.E. On New Year's Day, ambassadors of each of Persia's 20 and more satrapies presented themselves to the emperor in his audience hall at Persepolis. Darius, bejeweled and arrayed in royal robes of purple and gold, received them.

gathered the various taxes—on industry, mining, ports, water, commerce, and sales. The satraps remitted most of the revenues to Persia, but some were retained locally for administrative and development expenses.

Darius built, maintained, and guarded an imperial system of roads, the most famous of which was a 1,700-mile royal road stretching from his capital at Susa to Sardis across Anatolia (but not quite reaching the Mediterranean). Along these roads he established a series of inns for travelers and a royal courier service with stations about every 15 miles. He completed the construction of the Nile–Red Sea canal, which the Egyptians themselves had abandoned.

To increase agricultural production, Darius renewed the irrigation systems of Mesopotamia, and encouraged the introduction of new crops from one part of the empire to another. He standardized the empire's gold coinage, and permitted only his own imperial mints to strike the official coinage, the gold daric, in his name. Agriculture and commerce flourished, and not only for the benefit of the wealthy. Craftsmen produced goods for everyday use—leather sandals, cheap cloth, iron implements and utensils, and pottery—in increasing quantities.

Substantial sums of the enormous wealth of the flourishing empire went to the construction of four capital cities. The most sumptuous and lavish of them, and the one most Persian in style, was built by Darius and named "Parsa," Persia. The Greeks later called it "Persepolis," the city of the Persians.

Symbols of Power

Although the records of ancient Persia speak of painting as one of its arts, little has been found. Our greatest knowledge of Persian art comes from imperial architecture and design, most especially at Persepolis. The outstanding architectural monument

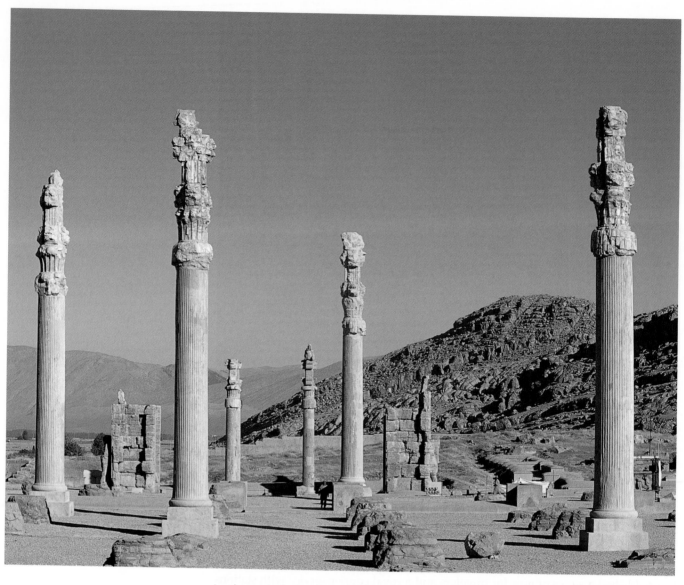

Apadana, principal audience hall, Persepolis, Iran, 521–486 B.C.E. Persepolis was destroyed by Alexander the Great. Still visible today are columns from the Apadana of Darius I.

5.1

5.2 How did Darius I come to rule the Persian Empire?

5.3

5.4

in this capital was a fortified citadel that held ceremonial and administrative buildings. Immediately below it was a large complex of residential palaces, probably the homes of the court.

Alexander and subsequent conquerors looted and burned the city, as we shall see, and the dominant remains today are forests of 60-foot-high columns, which have survived to indicate the grandeur of the city at its height. The largest and highest of all the remaining structures in the palace is the audience hall of Darius. Its façade is covered by creatures—lions, bulls, and griffins—asserting the power of the emperor and intimidating visitors. These visitors—many of them representatives from Persia's subject lands come to pay their respects in a procession before the emperor—are immortalized in bas-reliefs on the façades of the building and its stairways. The array of reliefs suggests the imperial power of Persia over its empire, and yet a place of honor seems to have been found for each of the delegates.

In accordance with the political theory that had evolved in imperial Persia, the emperor legally possessed all the property of the realm as well as the power of life and death over his subjects. Darius did not, however, choose to become a god. He

5.1

5.2

5.3

5.4

What was the nature of the Greek city-state political organization?

was probably a follower of the religion of the teacher Zarathustra, or Zoroaster as the Greeks called him. Zoroastrian scriptures date him to about 600 B.C.E., although modern scholarship places him as much as 1,000 years earlier. In a series of hymns, called *Gathas*, Zoroaster described a conflict between Ahuramazda, the god of goodness and light, and Ahriman, who embodied the forces of evil and darkness. Individuals had to choose between them, and they would be rewarded or punished for their choice on a final day of judgment. The *Avesta*, a later, fuller book of Zoroastrian scripture, further elaborated on the concept of an afterlife and the resurrection of the dead. Although, like Cyrus, Darius did not impose his own religious beliefs on the peoples he conquered, Zoroastrianism, with its roots in Persia, did spread rapidly under his rule. Darius also tried to soften the imposition of imperial administration and tax collection by maintaining local traditions and by enlisting members of the local elite to serve in his administration. Like Cyrus II, Darius managed to balance imperial majesty with local autonomy. At the western end of his empire, however, his neighbors and rivals, the Greeks, fought back against his attempts to rule over them.

The Greek City-states

| 5.3 | What was the nature of the Greek city-state political organization? |

The Greek historian Herodotus (d. *c.* 420 B.C.E.) has represented the warfare between Persians and Greeks as one of the great turning points in world history: a war between civilizations, between Asia and Europe, between empire and city-state, between tyranny and democracy. So, in the midst of our discussion of empire, we insert this flashback to consider the nature of Greek city-state democracy, its strengths and weaknesses in its warfare against the Persian Empire. At the end of our account, we will share in Thucydides' melancholy realization that, after their brilliant victory over the Persians, the freedom-loving Greeks fell victim to a new, home-grown imperialism imposed on them by Athens, their leader in the war against the Persians.

The Greek city-states had deep historic roots of their own. Long before the Persian Empire, civilizations had risen and fallen on the Greek peninsula, its neighboring islands, and the island of Crete in the eastern Mediterranean Sea. Archaeological excavations show that for some five hundred years in Greece and for a thousand in Crete, local, brilliant, urban civilizations had flourished.

🔍 **View** the **Closer Look: The Trireme** on **MyHistoryLab**

Early City-states of the Aegean

The Minoans. Immigrants began to settle on Crete about 6000 B.C.E. Scholars call these people Minoans after the legendary King Minos of ancient Crete. By 3000 B.C.E. they had built villages, and by 2000 B.C.E. they erected the first and largest of at least four major palace complexes on the island, at Knossos. The palaces combined three functions: they were elaborately furnished royal residences, centers for religion and ritual, and headquarters for administering the Cretan economy. The craftspeople of Crete produced bronze tools, gems, and extraordinarily fine pottery in the form of eggshell-thin vessels, which they exported throughout the eastern Mediterranean. As an island kingdom located at the crossroads of multiple trade routes, Crete excelled in commerce. Pictographic writing existed from at least 2000 B.C.E., and syllabic writing was introduced *c.* 1700 B.C.E. Known as Linear A, this script has not yet been deciphered.

About 1450 B.C.E., some, now unknown, disaster led to the destruction of three of the major palaces. (For a time scholars believed that eruptions of the volcano Thera might have caused the destruction, but deep-sea excavations show that the eruption

AT A GLANCE: ANCIENT GREEKS, PERSIANS, AND THEIR NEIGHBORS

DATE	POLITICS	RELIGION AND CULTURE	SOCIAL DEVELOPMENT
600 B.C.E.	• Cyaxares of Media (r. 625–585) • Age of Greek tyrants (657–570)	• Zoroaster (630–553)	• City-states in Greece
550 B.C.E.	• Cyrus II (r. 558–529); defeat of Medes, Lydia, Babylon • Peisistratus (d. 527) controlled Athens • Cambyses II (r. 529–522) conquered Egypt	• Pasargadae and Susa developed	• Nile–Red Sea canal
500 B.C.E.	• Darius I (r. 522–486); Persian Empire extended to Indus River; war against Greek city-states • Ionian revolt (499) • Battle of Marathon (490) • Xerxes I (r. 486–465) • War between Athens and Sparta: First Peloponnesian War (461–451)	• Pythagoras (d. c. 500) • Piraeus established as port of Athens • Persepolis built	• Athens at the height of its power. Acropolis built (c. 460); architecture, city-state democracy, political philosophy flourished
450 B.C.E.	• Pericles (c. 495–429) and Delian League • Second Peloponnesian War (431–404) and end of Athenian power	• Persian script written down • "Golden Age" of Athens • Aeschylus (525–456) • Herodotus (d. c. 420) • Sophocles (c. 496–406) • Euripides (480–406) • Thucydides (d. c. 401)	• Persian Empire: regional laws codified; roads built; centralized administration; irrigation systems extended
400 B.C.E.		• Socrates (c. 470–399)	
350 B.C.E.	• Philip II (r. 359–336) and Alexander the Great (r. 336–323) extended Macedonian Empire • Athens and Thebes defeated (338), ending Greek independence • Alexander conquered Asia Minor (334) and Egypt (332), and reached Indus (326)	• Aristophanes (c. 450–385) • Plato (c. 428–348) • Aristotle (384–322) • Demosthenes (384–322) • Alexandria (Egypt) founded (331) • Persepolis burned (331)	• Spread of Hellenistic culture
300 B.C.E.	• Ptolemies in Egypt • Seleucids in Asia		

5.1

5.2

5.3 What was the nature of the Greek city-state political organization?

5.4

was too early, c. 1625 B.C.E., and too distant to have caused such devastation.) Crete seems to have become more deeply enmeshed in the affairs of the Greek mainland at this time. A new script, known as Linear B, was created for transcribing Greek, suggesting that this had now become the language of Crete. In 1370 B.C.E. the palace at Knossos was also destroyed, and Crete came under the sway of Mycenae, the leading city-state of mainland Greece. The glories of Knossos were lost, preserved for thousands of years only in legend.

The Mycenaeans. The Greek poet Homer (c. 800–c. 750 B.C.E.), author of the *Iliad* and *Odyssey*, portrays the Mycenaeans as brave and heroic warriors as well as active sailors and traders. They carried on extensive trade and cultural exchange with Crete, including sharing the use of Linear B script. After 1450, when several of Crete's important towns were destroyed, Mycenae came to dominate the relationship.

Mycenae was home to several small kingdoms, each with its own palace or citadel and accompanying cemetery of beehive-shaped tombs. The greatest of the cities was Mycenae itself, capital of Homer's legendary king Agamemnon. This administrative center of the entire region was surrounded by a colossal wall up to 25 feet thick. Its massive entrance gate was adorned with huge stone lions looking down on all who entered and left. The site is rich in the evidence of warfare: weapons, armor, paintings of warriors, and, at the seashore a few miles distant, ships of war. Some of the kings, at least, were quite wealthy: one was buried with 11 pounds of gold, and the funeral "mask of Agamemnon" was a work of consummate craftsmanship in gold. Scholars have been unable to discover the reason for the fall of Mycenaean civilization; perhaps it was invaded, perhaps it imploded in internal warfare. By the end of the twelfth century B.C.E., all the palaces and towns of Mycenae had been destroyed or abandoned.

Their fall ushered in the Greek "Dark Ages," a period of general upheaval throughout much of the eastern Mediterranean. The Greeks even lost their knowledge of how to write. Apparently, additional waves of nomadic immigrants entered Greece from the north. By about 850 B.C.E. the peoples of Greece began to emerge from an age of darkness and once again to settle, to build towns, to trade overseas, to receive new waves of immigrants that increased their population, and to restore their written culture.

The Greek Polis: Image and Reality

The Greeks developed a very different form of political organization from that of the Persian imperial structure. The Greek city-state, or polis, was an intentionally small, locally organized government based on a single central city with enough surrounding land to support its agricultural needs. Most of the city-states had populations of a few thousand, with only the very largest of them exceeding 40,000 people.

Geography and topography played a large part in limiting the size of the Greek city-state. In and around the Greek peninsula, mountains, rivers, and seas had kept the units of settlement rather small and isolated. (To the north, where farmland was more expansive, as it was in Macedonia, geographically larger states developed within such centralized city capitals.) When a region could no longer support an expanding population, it hived off colonies to new locations. Most of the Greek city-states in Anatolia, for example, seem to have originated as colonial settlements of older cities on the Greek mainland, part of an array of Greek city-states that spread along the Mediterranean coast, extending as far west as present-day Marseilles in France and Catalonia in Spain. Although separate and usually independent politically, the city-states were united culturally by the use of the Greek language, a myth-history centered on Homer's *Iliad* and *Odyssey*, and such festivals as the Olympic Games, held every four years after 776 B.C.E.

Each polis developed its own form of government. Councils of nobles governed some cities, while others fell under the rule of a single powerful individual. Here we recount the fate of the city of Athens, in particular, for three reasons: it was a leader among the Greek city-states; it gave birth to the modern concept of political democracy; and it has left us the most historical records. Of all the major cities of Greece—for example, Sparta, Corinth, Thebes, and Syracuse—Athens seems to have moved farthest from rule by kings and oligarchies in the direction of rule by the people, democracy.

About 600 B.C.E., Solon (*c.* 630–*c.* 560 B.C.E.), who had risen to high office as a general and a poet, ended the monopoly over public office held by the Athenian hereditary aristocracy. Because the only surviving accounts of his administration date to at least 500 years after his death, Solon's accomplishments are not entirely clear,

Death mask ("Mask of Agamemnon"), gold, sixteenth century B.C.E. When archaeologists in the late nineteenth century discovered this brilliant death mask at Mycenae, the leading city-state of ancient Greece, they naturally claimed that it represented Mycenae's King Agamemnon himself, leader of the Greek forces in their war against Troy. Later judgments differed, because the date of the mask was too early. (National Archaeological Museum, Athens)

5.1

5.2

5.3

What was the nature of the Greek city-state political organization?

5.4

139

SOURCE

Homer and the Value System of Early Greece

Historical folk tales survived from the era of Mycenae through the Dark Ages. From these tales, which had probably circulated orally since the twelfth century B.C.E., the poet Homer (c. 800–c. 750 B.C.E.) wove his two great epic poems, the *Iliad* and the *Odyssey*. The *Iliad* tells of the Trojan War, which, Homer writes, a coalition of Greek city-states launched against the Trojans in retaliation for the seduction of Helen, the wife of the king of Sparta, by Paris, the son of the king of Troy. Just as the war begins in a personal vendetta, so, too, individual feuds during the war break out among the Greeks themselves, for personal more than for political reasons. The bitter personal quarrel between Agamemnon, brother of the king of Sparta and himself king of Mycenae, and Achilles, the mightiest of the Greek warriors, cripples the effectiveness of the Greek coalition and dominates the storyline of the *Iliad*. The *Odyssey* tells the still more personal postwar story of the ten-year struggle of Odysseus, king of Ithaca, to return to his home and of his ultimate reunion with his wife, Penelope, and son, Telemachus.

Although some literary critics believe that "Homer" was really more than one author, most today believe that just one person wrote, or dictated, the epics. The stories on which Homer bases his poetic accounts were probably well known among the Greeks of his time. Homer's lasting reputation and fame rest on his skill in crafting these stories into coherent narratives told in poetry of great power. Further, by focusing on personal stories within the national epics, Homer created images of human excellence (*arete* in ancient Greek) at levels of heroism that inspire readers to this day. He writes with equal power of excellence in war and in love.

Bravery in warfare is a cardinal virtue, and, in the *Iliad*, Homer portrays Hektor, the mightiest of the Trojans, praying that his son might inherit his own strength in battle, and even surpass it. The child's mother would apparently share this vision of her son as warrior:

> Zeus, and you other immortals, grant that this boy, who is my son,
> may be as I am, preeminent among the Trojans,
> great in strength, as am I, and rule strongly over Ilion;
> and some day let them say of him: "He is better by far than his father,"
> as he comes in from the fighting; and let him kill his enemy
> and bring home the blooded spoils, and delight the heart of his mother.
>
> (*Iliad*, VI: 476–81)

Praising excellence in warfare and combat, Homer portrays Odysseus, Telemachus, and their allies as fierce raptors swooping down upon the men who had spent years harassing Penelope and attempting to seduce her while Odysseus fought in Troy and struggled to return home:

> After them the attackers wheeled, as terrible as falcons
> from eyries in the mountains veering over and diving down

> with talons wide unsheathed on flights of birds,
> who cower down the sky in chutes and bursts along the valley—
> but the pouncing falcons grip their prey, no frantic wing avails,
> and farmers love to watch those beaked hunters.
> So these now fell upon the suitors in that hall,
> turning, turning to strike and strike again,
> while torn men moaned at death, and blood ran smoking over the whole floor.
>
> (*Odyssey*, XXII: 310–19)

Homer sang equally vividly, and far more sweetly and poignantly, of excellence in love. As the *Odyssey* moves toward its conclusion, the hero and heroine, Odysseus and Penelope, are reunited after a wartime separation of 20 years:

> Now from his breast into his eyes the ache
> of longing mounted, and he wept at last,
> his dear wife, clear and faithful, in his arms,
> longed for as the sunwarmed earth is longed for by a swimmer
> spent in rough water where his ship went down
> under Poseidon's blows, gale winds and tons of sea.
> Few men can keep alive through a big surf
> to crawl, clotted with brine, on kindly beaches
> in joy, in joy, knowing the abyss behind:
>
> and so she too rejoiced, her gaze upon her husband,
> her white arms round him pressed as though forever.
>
> (*Odyssey*, XXIII: 234–44)

> So they came
> into that bed so steadfast, loved of old,
> opening glad arms to one another,
> Telemachus by now had hushed the dancing,
> hushed the women. In the darkened hall
> he and the cowherd and the swineherd slept.
> The royal pair mingled in love again
> and afterward lay reveling in stories:
> hers of the siege her beauty stood at home
> from arrogant suitors, crowding on her sight,
> and how they fed their courtship on his cattle,
> oxen and fat sheep, and drank up rivers
> of wine out of the vats.
> Odysseus told
> of what hard blows he had dealt out to others
> and of what blows he had taken—all that story.
> she could not close her eyes till all was told.
>
> (*Odyssey*, XXIII: 298–313)

War and love, the bloody heroism of the battlefield and the warm intimacy of family life—Homer addressed both in imagery that has inspired readers, and listeners, to this day.

but he is always presented as having moved Athens towards democracy. It appears that Solon gave to all free men the right to participe and vote in the decision-making public assembly, although only those meeting certain income levels could be elected to high public office. The Council of Four Hundred, which he also created, represented the interests of the wealthy and noble factions, while the assembly balanced them with the voices of more common men. Perhaps more importantly, Solon canceled all public and private debts, and abolished the practice of enslaving people to pay off their debts.

Solon's reforms came under attack when he left office, leading to a decade or so of struggle between rich and poor and between men of different hereditary clans. About 550 B.C.E., Peisistratus seized control of the government as a "**tyrant**," the Greek term for a single autocratic ruler. Peisistratus fostered economic growth through loans to small farmers; export promotion programs; road construction; and public works, including major building programs for the beautification of Athens. On his death in 527 B.C.E., the city-state again fell into disarray and even civil war. In 510 B.C.E., at the invitation of a faction of Athenian noblemen, the king of Sparta, already Athens' greatest rival, invaded the city and deposed the descendants of Peisistratus.

Nevertheless, the ideals of Solon survived. A new ruler, Cleisthenes (*c.* 570–*c.* 508 B.C.E.), came to power as a tyrant and dramatically reorganized the city and its surrounding countryside. He did away with the aristocratic family centers of power by registering each Athenian as a citizen according to his geographical residence, or **deme**, in the city. Similarly, he reorganized the electoral districts of Attica, the region around Athens, into ten electoral units, creating new political identities and allegiances. The assembly resumed meeting about every ten days, and all male citizens were expected to participate; 6,000 were necessary for a quorum. Above the assembly, and setting its agenda, was a Council of Five Hundred, even more open than Solon's Council of Four Hundred had been, since members were selected from each deme for one-year terms by lottery, and members were not allowed to serve for more than two terms. In organizing themselves by deme, Athenians based their political identity on geographical residence in the city, not on heredity and kinship, nor on class and wealth.

A red-figure cup by the sculptor Douris, fifth century B.C.E. The figures depict scenes from the education of a young man: learning to play the flute, and learning to read and write, all under the watchful eye of a pedagogue. (Staatliche Museen zu Berlin)

What was the nature of the Greek city-state political organization?

KEY TERMS

tyrant A ruler with absolute power, sometimes granted through election in times of crisis, sometimes seized through force of arms.

deme A rural district or village in ancient Greece, or its members or inhabitants. The demes were a constituent part of the polis but had their own corporations with police powers, and their own cults, officials, and property.

5.1

5.2

5.3

5.4

What was the nature of the Greek city-state political organization?

This new concept of civic identity allowed the city to welcome new residents and the ideas they brought with them, regardless of their place of origin. It allowed people of different ethnic origins, even of enemy ethnic stock, to enter the city, although they were not eligible for full citizenship, which was restricted to free men born in the deme. The human interaction in the small Greek city-state nurtured the intellect of its citizens. Life in the polis meant constant participation in a kind of ongoing public seminar. As Socrates (c. 470–399 B.C.E.), the leading philosopher of fifth-century Athens, said: "I'm a lover of learning, and trees and open country won't teach me anything, whereas men in the town do."

When Darius I's Persian Empire challenged the Greek city-states, Athens took the lead in forming a coalition against it. The contrast between the combatants was stark: city-state versus empire; local administration versus imperial power; evolving, decentralized democracy versus established, centralized imperial control. Persia was a huge, centrally governed empire; each Greek city-state was independent, although many had joined into regional confederations and leagues for mutual assistance and trade. A single emperor who set policies for the entire empire headed Persia; an assembly of all its adult, free, male citizens, for the most part, governed each individual Greek city-state. These assemblies passed laws, judged criminal and civil cases, carried out administration and implementation of legislation, and arranged for military defense as the need arose. The Greek city-states were moving toward democracy; they understood their legal systems to be their own creation and responsibility, neither ordained by the gods nor imposed by a powerful external emperor.

War with Persia

Some of the Greek city-states in Anatolia had earlier fallen under Darius' empire. Although they were permitted to retain their own form of local government as long as they paid their taxes to Persia, some of them revolted and called on the Greek cities of the peninsula for help. Athens tried, half-heartedly and unsuccessfully, to assist its overseas relatives with ships and soldiers. According to the historian Herodotus (see below), Darius was furious at this interference. He ordered one of his servants to remind him, every day at dinnertime, "Master, remember the Athenians." In 490 B.C.E., Darius I dispatched a naval expedition directly across the Aegean to punish Athens for its part in the revolt in Anatolia.

War with the Persians tested the Greeks' fundamental mode of political organization. How could the tiny Greek city-states hold off Darius' imperial armies and keep their incipient democracies alive? First, they had the enormous advantage of being close to home, with a good knowledge of local geography and conditions. Second, the largest among them, especially Athens and Sparta, chose to cooperate in defense against a common enemy.

When the Persian fleet of 600 ships landed 48,000 soldiers at Marathon in 490 B.C.E., a force of some 10,000 Greek **hoplite** soldiers, joined by about 1,000 soldiers from Plataea and another 1,000 slaves, confronted them. The hoplite forces were deployed in solid phalanxes, columns of soldiers arrayed in tight lines, the left arm and shield of one man pressed against the right shoulder of the other, row on row. If a soldier in the front row fell, one from the next line took his place. (In these hoplite formations, each individual soldier is crucial to the welfare of all. Many analysts have seen in this egalitarian military formation the rationale for Athenian political democracy.)

The discipline of the Athenians defeated their enemy at Marathon: Persia lost 6,400 men, Athens 192. The Athenian general sent his fastest runner, Pheidippides, racing back to Athens to tell of the victory, to strengthen the resolve of the Athenians at home, and to hasten their preparations for battle against the surviving Persian forces. Pheidippides delivered the message, and died of exhaustion on the spot. (Today's marathon race is named for his 26-mile run.)

KEY TERM

hoplite A heavily armed foot soldier of ancient Greece, whose function was to fight in close formation, usually in ranks of eight men. Each soldier carried a heavy bronze shield, a short iron sword, and a long spear for thrusting.

What was the nature of the Greek city-state political organization?

Xerxes I (r. 486–465 B.C.E.), Darius' son, succeeded him and mounted a renewed attack on the Greek mainland by land and sea in 480 B.C.E. Courageous resistance by the Spartan general Leonidas and his troops at Thermopylae cost the lives of all the defenders, but won time for the Athenians to evacuate their city and regroup their forces. Xerxes continued to push onward to Athens, capturing, burning, and plundering the city and its Acropolis (its "city on high," as the religious citadel in an ancient Greek city was called), but the Athenian warriors had withdrawn to the nearby port of Piraeus and the Bay of Salamis. At Salamis, a force of some 1,000 Persian ships confronted a much smaller fleet of some 300 Greek triremes, a ship named for the three levels in which its approximately 170 rowers were arranged. One of Xerxes' most trusted naval advisers, Artemisia, a widowed queen among the people of Halicarnassus and a captain of one of the ships, counseled waiting and watching. Xerxes, however, followed the majority and sailed into battle. The Athenians maneuvered the Persians into a bottleneck in the Salamis Channel and destroyed 200 of their ships while losing only 40 of their own. Xerxes sailed for home, and Persia never again attacked Greece by sea.

The Persians did, however, continue to fight by land. In 479 B.C.E., in alliance with their subjects in Macedonia and some northern Greeks, they prepared an army of some 100,000 men on the edge of the plains opening southward to Athens and the Peloponnese. Sparta and Athens formed an alliance with other city-states to field an opposing army of about 40,000. Despite initial confusion in the ranks, the allied Spartan and Athenian forces destroyed the Persian armies and their camp, annihilated the elite guard, and killed the leading Persian general. At about the same time, the Greek fleet defeated the surviving Persian fleet at Mycale, on the Ionian coast of Anatolia.

In the face of these losses, and with weaker leadership at home, Persia left Europe, never to return in such force. The small Greek city-states, led by arch-rivals Athens and Sparta, had shown an ability to combine in the face of a common enemy. They had demonstrated the virtues of small-scale, local units of society and the resilience of popular, democratic forms of government. Conversely, the Persians had exhibited one of the great flaws of empire: the tendency to overextend its powers.

The Golden Age of Athenian Culture

Under the military and civic leadership of Pericles (c. 495–429 B.C.E.), Athenians took immense pride in their city-state, its democratic philosophy and artistic creativity. During the war years, the Persians had destroyed and burned much of Athens. When victory was secure, the Athenians began to rebuild.

Athens rose from a plain, and with each level upward its functions and architecture became more exalted. At the bottom were the houses of commoners, built simply from local materials of stone and mud, with little concern for architectural merit. Further up the hill was the **agora**, or civic and market center, with clusters of buildings for trade in goods, ideas, and political decision-making. These public buildings were more elegant, designed for greater comfort and show. In the splendor of the agora Athenians demonstrated the value placed on public life and on physical

KEY TERM

agora A central feature of ancient Greek town planning. Its chief function was as a town market, but it also became the main social and political meeting-place. Together with the acropolis, it normally housed the most important buildings of the town. Later, the Roman forum fulfilled this function.

Plan of Acropolis. The construction of the Acropolis (Greek for "high city"), beginning in c. 460 B.C.E. under the leadership of Pericles, signified the start of a Golden Age for Athens. The plan above indicates some of its most celebrated buildings—the Parthenon (1), the Erechtheum (2), the Propylaea (3), and the Temple of Athena Nike (4).

View the **Closer Look**: **The Erechtheum: Porch of the Maidens** on **MyHistoryLab**

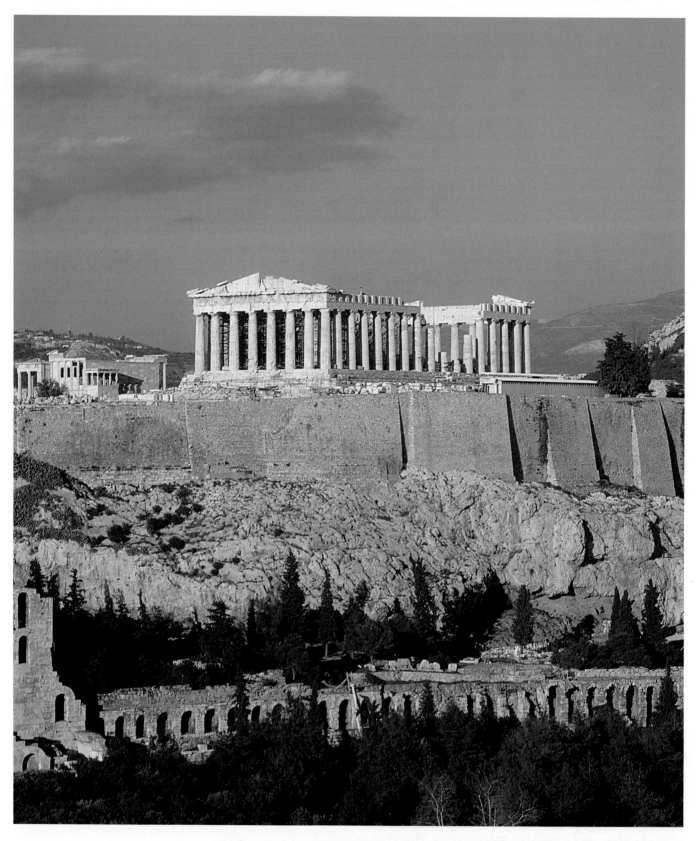

Parthenon, Athens, 447–432 B.C.E. The Parthenon on the Athenian Acropolis was a temple dedicated to the goddess Athena, the city's patron-deity. It was built at the initiative of Pericles as a symbol of Athens' growing importance, and represents, in architectural terms, the summit of classical Greek achievement.

SOURCE

Pericles' Funeral Oration

As political and military leader of Athens, 460–429 B.C.E., Pericles delivered this eulogy at a mass funeral of troops who had died in battle in the early years of the Peloponnesian War. As reported by Thucydides, it is one of the great proclamations of the civic, aesthetic, moral, and personal virtues of the Athenian city-state:

Our system of government does not copy the institutions of our neighbors. It is more the case of our being a model to others, than of our imitating anyone else. Our constitution is called a democracy because power is in the hands not of a minority but of the whole people. When it is a question of settling private disputes, everyone is equal before the law; when it is a question of putting one person before another in positions of public responsibility, what counts is not membership of a particular class, but the actual ability which the man possesses. No one, so long as he has it in him to be of service to the state, is kept in political obscurity because of poverty ...

We [obey] those whom we put in positions of authority, and we obey the laws themselves, especially those which are for the protection of the oppressed, and those unwritten laws which it is an acknowledged shame to break ...

When our work is over, we are in a position to enjoy all kinds of recreation for our spirits ... all the good things from all over the world flow in to us, so that to us it seems just as natural to enjoy foreign goods as our own local products ...

Our love of what is beautiful does not lead to extravagance; our love of the things of the mind does not make us soft. We regard wealth as something to be properly used, rather than as something to boast about. As for poverty, no one need be ashamed to admit it: the real shame is in not taking practical measures to escape from it. Here each individual is interested not only in his own affairs but in the affairs of the state as well: even those who are mostly occupied with their own business are extremely well informed on general politics—this is a peculiarity of ours: we do not say that a man who takes no interest in politics is a man who minds his own business; we say that he has no business here at all. We Athenians, in our own persons, take our decisions on policy or submit them to proper discussions: for we do not think that there is an incompatibility between words and deeds; the worst thing is to rush into action before the consequences have been properly debated ...

I declare that our city is an education to Greece, and I declare that in my opinion each single one of our citizens, in all the manifold aspects of life, is able to show himself the rightful lord and owner of his own person, and do this, moreover, with exceptional grace and exceptional versatility.

(Thucydides, *History of the Peloponnesian War*, Book II:37–41; pp. 145–48)

prowess and discipline. Nearby were gymnasia for exercise and competition. An amphitheater where plays were regularly performed was carved out of the hillside. At the top of the hill, on the Acropolis, surrounded by a wall, were the chief temples of the city. Pericles hired the architects and urban designers Ictinus and Callicrates to rebuild the Acropolis (plundered by the Persians) and build the Parthenon, the temple dedicated to Athena, the city's patron goddess. The sculptor Phidias carved the friezes on the Parthenon and created a 40-foot-high statue of Athena to reside within it.

As the architectural projects flourished, Pericles founded a colony in southern Italy and took a fleet into the Black Sea. More importantly, he encouraged naval battles against Sparta and Corinth, as well as Persia, in order to promote his radical egalitarian democracy at home. Rowers typically were poorer than hoplites, but benefited from regular salaries and the spoils of war and empire. Eventually, Pericles realized his strategy was flawed, concluding that his imperial ambitions threatened the very Athenian democracy he cherished.

Historians. The city's historians began to reflect on its origins and accomplishments, and the challenges it had faced. Indeed, the modern profession of history as a systematic attempt to understand the influence of past experience on the present began in Athens. Two of the most outstanding historians of the fifth century B.C.E. have given us the history of the city and its relationships with its neighbors. Herodotus wrote *The Persian Wars*, and in the narrative recaptured a general, if anecdotal, history of the whole eastern Mediterranean and eastward as far as Persia and India from a Greek perspective. Thucydides (d. *c.* 401 B.C.E.), far more systematically and carefully, recounted the subsequent *History of the Peloponnesian War*, the war between Athens and Sparta that lasted from 431 B.C.E. until 404 B.C.E.

5.1

5.2

5.3

What was the nature of the Greek city-state political organization?

5.4

SOURCE

Socrates on the Rights of the State over the Individual

Condemned to death on trumped-up charges of corrupting the political morals of youth and blaspheming against the gods of Athens, Socrates is offered the opportunity to escape and live out his life in another city-state. He refuses. He notes that the state has acted through formal legal process and has the right to execute him. He, in turn, has the obligation to accept the sentence.

Are you too wise to see that your country is worthier, more to be revered, more sacred, and held in higher honor both by the gods and by all men of understanding, than your father and your mother and all your other ancestors; and that you ought to reverence it, and to submit to it, and to approach it more

humbly when it is angry with you than you would approach your father; and either to do whatever it tells you to do or to persuade it to excuse you; and to obey in silence if it orders you to endure flogging or imprisonment, or if it sends you to battle to be wounded or to die? That is just. You must not give way, nor retreat, nor desert your station. In war, and in the court of justice, and everywhere, you must do whatever your state and your country tell you to do, or you must persuade them that their commands are unjust. But it is impious to use violence against your father or your mother; and much more impious to use violence against your country. (Plato, *Crito*, XII:51:b)

📖 **Read** the **Document: Thucydides on Athens (5th c. BCE)** on **MyHistoryLab**

Philosophers. Philosophers such as Socrates and his student Plato introduced questions, methods of analysis and of teaching, and examinations of the purpose of life that continue to command attention for their range and depth. Plato's prize student, Aristotle, later wrote that man is a "political animal," a creature of the polis, or city-state, and many of the key works in Greek history, drama, and philosophy explored the working of the city-state itself and the relationship of the individual to it.

For the philosopher Socrates, the Athenian state was father and mother; he derived his sense of self and purpose from the education the state gave him and from his continual debates with fellow citizens both in public and in private. Socrates argued for the supremacy of the city-state over the individual. The citizen had obligations to the state for all the benefits he received from it, but had no rights to claim against the power of the state.

Socrates took philosophy personally and seriously. He opposed and satirized the **sophist** philosophers of his day who earned their salaries by training future statesmen to argue any side of any question without necessarily staking any personal commitment. Through his incessant questions, he taught his students to be thoughtful but critical about the truths of others and about their own truths, and, after having reached their own conclusions, to live their own truths fully even if it meant their death, as it did for Socrates himself (see Source box "Socrates on the Rights of the State over the Individual," above).

Plato (*c.* 428–348 B.C.E.) was Socrates' leading pupil and the founder of the Academy, which endured for centuries as Athens' leading school of philosophy. His philosophical works dealt with many topics, including love, justice, courage, and the nature of the state. Plato conceived of ideal situations, whether realistic or not. The ideal state, according to Plato, would be administered by a philosopher-king, who by virtue of innate good character and intensive training would know and do what was best for all citizens in the state. Similarly, Plato saw love beginning with emotional and sexual passion between individuals and subsequently transforming into the contemplation of universal ideals.

Aristotle (384–322 B.C.E.) addressed an astonishing array of subjects—logic, physics, astronomy, metaphysics, religion, rhetoric, literary criticism, and natural science—but he, too, devoted some of his most important writing to ethics and politics. His analysis of the principal forms of constitutional government in his *Politics*

5.1

5.2

5.3   What was the nature of the Greek city-state political organization?

5.4

KEY TERM

sophist An itinerant professor of higher education in ancient Greece, who gave instruction for a fee. The subjects taught, which included oratory, grammar, ethics, mathematics, and literature, had the practical aim of equipping pupils for successful careers. The sophist professor taught his students to argue all sides of every question, regardless of their merit. **Sophistry** is this kind of clever argumentation, regardless of merit.

5.1

5.2

5.3

5.4

What was the nature of the Greek city-state political organization?

remains a useful introduction to the field even today. Aristotle later tutored Alexander the Great, although that world-conqueror seems to have thoroughly rejected his teacher's argument for small units of government like the city-state. Aristotle argued:

> If the citizens of a state are to judge and to distribute offices according to merit, then they must know each other's characters; where they do not possess this knowledge, both the election to offices and the decision of lawsuits will go wrong. When the population is very large they are manifestly settled at haphazard, which clearly ought not to be. (*Politics* VII:4, p. 326)

Alexander, clearly, was not persuaded.

Dramatists. Drama developed and flourished in the theaters of Athens. The pursuit of justice, morality, and equity was a core theme. Athenian playwrights invented the dramatic forms of tragedy and comedy, and their most important plays all include themes related to the evolution of their city and its institutions.

The *Oresteia* trilogy by Aeschylus (525–456 B.C.E.) follows three generations of murders within the royal family of Atreus, as one act of revenge provokes the next. Finally, in a trial at Athens, Athena, patron goddess of the city, acquits Orestes, suggesting that divinely ordained vengeance will be replaced by human justice and the cycle of murder will be ended.

Oedipus Rex by Sophocles (*c.* 496–406 B.C.E.), perhaps the most famous single play of ancient Athens, centers on the family tragedy of Oedipus' unknowing murder of his own father, the king of Thebes, and his subsequent marriage to his own mother. The play opens with the people of Thebes gathered around King Oedipus—before his tragedy is revealed—crying out for his help in arresting a plague that is afflicting the city. Oedipus' own moral corruption has brought the plague on the city, although that is revealed only later. Sophocles' *Antigone* confronts the conflict between loyalty to family and loyalty to the city-state, as Antigone chooses to bury her brother Polynices, despite the royal decree to leave his corpse unattended as an enemy of the state.

Euripides (480–406 B.C.E.) saw more clearly Athens' move toward imperialism, and criticized it in *The Trojan Women*. The hilarious, sexually explicit comedy *Lysistrata* by Aristophanes (*c.* 450–385 B.C.E.) portrays the women of Athens and Sparta agreeing to go on strike sexually until their men stop fighting the Peloponnesian Wars. As long as the men make war, the women will not make love! The best of the Athenian dramatists addressed directly the political and social issues that confronted their city.

📖 Read the **Document**: **Greek Poetry (800–400 BCE)** on **MyHistoryLab**

The Limits of City-state Democracy

Socrates' justification of the state demonstrates that even in the most democratic Greek city-state, government could exact respect and service from the citizen, but the citizen had few rights vis-à-vis the state. The citizen had the right, and indeed the obligation, to participate in the activities of the state and to serve the state, but not to have the state serve him.

For women, even the right of participation was absent. Women born of two Athenian parents were regarded as citizens, enjoyed some legal protection, and had responsibilities for performing certain religious rituals of great importance for the state. But, like slaves, they were excluded from attending the meetings of the assembly, holding annual public offices, serving as jurors, initiating legal cases on their own, or owning property in their own names. They had to have a man speak for them before judges and juries. Women's segregation from public life in ancient Greece perpetuated long-standing beliefs that there is a public sphere and

A second-century c.e. copy in marble of the statue of Athena Parthenos, dedicated in 438 b.c.e. Phidias' 40-foot Athena, the divine guardian of the city, dominated the central chamber of the Parthenon on the Acropolis. This miniature Roman copy of the destroyed statue hardly suggests the glittering magnificence of the enormous gold-and-ivory original, a powerful symbol of the might of the goddess and her city, Athens. (Acropolis Museum, Athens)

a private sphere, and that women should be confined to the latter. Pericles captured this belief in his famous funeral oration, when he delivered this advice to the widows of fallen warriors: "Great will be your glory in not falling short of your natural character; and greatest will be hers who is least talked of among the men, whether for good or for bad."

Since many Greeks believed that true friendship was possible only among equals, many Greek men sought relationships, including sexual relationships, with other men outside their households, even when they held their marriages in high esteem. Greek vases, especially those used in male drinking parties, often carried paintings that glorified the phallus. Given this evidence, some historians have concluded that this culture was misogynistic—hating women—and that the exaltation of masculinity could have been at the root of the constant warfare and militarism of ancient Greek society. (see How Do We Know? box, below).

Plato recognized the prejudice against women in his society. When he suggested in his visionary *Republic* that women should be treated equally with men in their access to the highest professional and civic responsibilities, and in the education needed to achieve them, he knew his ideas were revolutionary for Athens in his time and that they would be greeted with derision. Plato himself believed that men were generally more talented than women, but he argued that both should be offered equal access to political opportunity. On the subject of gender equality, he seemed to remain consistent with his general philosophy: the state should encourage each citizen to reach his or her educational potential, and should direct the most talented into governmental affairs. Plato wrote:

> There is no occupation concerned with the management of social affairs which belongs either to women or to men, as such. Natural gifts are to be found here and there in both creatures alike; and every occupation is open to both, so far as their natures are concerned, though woman is for all purposes the weaker ... Now, for the purpose of producing a woman fit to be a Guardian, we shall not have one education for men and another for women ... If we are to set women to the same tasks as men, we must teach them the same things. They must have the same two branches of training for mind and body and also be taught the art of war, and they must receive the same treatment.

Aristotle confirmed Plato's apprehensions, but not his optimism nor his sense of potential equality. Aristotle wrote of women: "The temperance of a man and of a woman, or the courage and justice of a man and of a woman, are not, as Socrates maintained, the same; the courage of a man is shown in commanding, of a woman in obeying." He quotes with approval the general view that "Silence is a woman's glory." In practice, Athens followed Aristotelian rather than Platonic views on the role of women in public life.

Even among males, only the sons of native-born Athenian mothers and fathers were eligible for citizenship. Slaves captured in war, and even allies, could not gain citizenship. When classical Athens reached its maximum population of 250,000, only about one adult Athenian in six qualified for citizenship. These limits on Athenian democracy increased domestic social strains.

From City-state to Small Empire. Ironically, the city-state of Athens, having led the Greek city-states in the struggle against the Persian Empire, subsequently set out to construct an empire of its own. Following major victories in the Persian wars, Athens assembled its principal allies into the Delian League, with its council and treasury situated in Delos. At first, membership was voluntary, but soon Athens forbade withdrawal. Some cities left the League, usually because they could not pay the tribute Athens demanded. Many found it difficult to supply triremes, because they lacked the shipyards of their larger ally. In response, Athens might declare war against them. As a result, "the Athenians as rulers," in the words of Thucydides, "were no longer popular as they used to be."

By 461 B.C.E., many of the Greek city-states turned to Sparta to help them to resist Athenian coercion. Although the two city-states had been allies in the war against the Persians, they had chosen very different political forms: Athens was ruled through a limited democracy, Sparta through a military elite; Athens proposed the

5.1
5.2
5.3
5.4

What was the nature of the Greek city-state political organization?

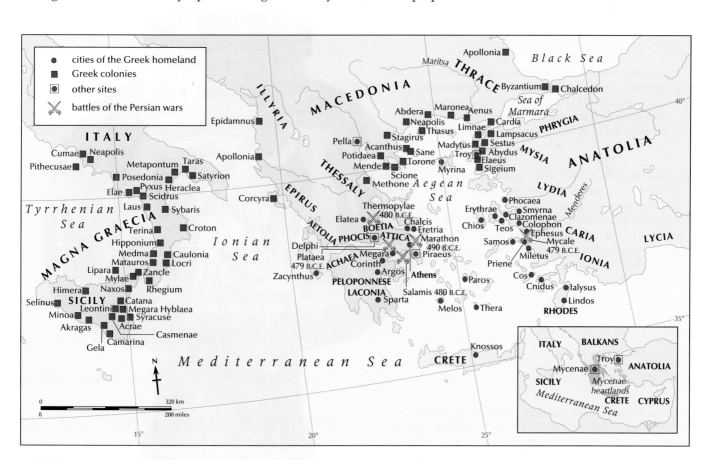

Classical Greece, *c.* 500 B.C.E. The hilly terrain and sea-boundaries of Greece discouraged the growth of large settlements, and Greek philosophers also stressed the importance of local community. When population grew too great, the citizens encouraged their younger cohort to establish new city-states of their own. The resulting spread of settlements established Greek influence all the way from Sicily to Anatolia.

Gender Relations in Ancient Greece: Voices from the Vases

Understanding and representing the quality of gender relations has become a central task of historians.

For ancient Greece, historians have reached consensus that women were second-class citizens. Indeed, legally they were not citizens at all. In ancient Athens, in most respects the most democratic of all Greek polities,

> They had no role in the political sphere. Women could not speak or vote in the Assembly, could not sit on juries in the law courts. Women's private lives were also relatively circumscribed, for example, in the choice of a marriage partner or the age at which to marry, which for Athenian girls was generally as soon as they were ready to bear children, at fourteen or fifteen. (Kaltsas and Shapiro, p. 13)

Within these general restrictions on women, however, scholars have staked out differing interpretations. Most fascinating, some of these scholars have used the paintings on Greek vases as their evidence. In *The Reign of the Phallus: Sexual Politics in Ancient Athens*, art historian Eva Keuls rages against Athens as both cruelly misogynist and aggressively militaristic, and suggests that these two characteristics were interrelated. Classical Athens, Keuls argues, was a phallocracy,

> A society dominated by men who sequester their wives and daughters, denigrate the female role in reproduction, erect monuments to the male genitalia, have sex with the sons of their peers, sponsor public whorehouses, create a mythology of rape, and engage in rampant saber-rattling. (Keuls, p. 1)

Keuls finds most of her evidence in the paintings on Greek vases, specifically of a type used in male drinking parties (see accompanying illustration), but she asserts that additional support for her claims is widespread and easily accessible. She then asks, and answers, the historiographical question: Why have we not heard more of these phallocratic elements previously?

The story of phallic rule at the root of Western civilization has been suppressed as a result of the near-monopoly that men have held in the field of Classics, by neglect of rich pictorial evidence, by prudery and censorship, and by a misguided desire to protect an idealized image of Athens. (p. 1)

This contrary view, of women enjoying their domestic and religious roles, permeated an art exhibition at the Onassis Cultural Center in New York in 2008–09, titled *Worshiping Women: Ritual and Reality in Classical Athens*, and in the accompanying catalogue of the same name. The curators of the exhibition argue that

> the focus on the exclusion of women from political life has obscured the important roles that women played in the religious life of the polis, often in very public and visible ways. Unlike modern Western societies, religious observance permeated every aspect of life in the ancient Greek city and was inseparable from "secular" affairs, which meant that

Psykter (wine cooler) painted by Douris with cavorting satyrs, 500–490 B.C.E. Feminist historian Eva Keuls argues that, contrary to the cradle-of-civilization clichés, Athenian society was excessively warlike and women-hating. She finds much of her evidence on Greek vases of the type used at male drinking parties. (British Museum, London)

women's activities in cults, rituals, and festivals marked a major contribution to the civic life of Athens.

The accompanying vase-illustration of a newly wed bride receiving gifts from her female relatives, probably in the female quarters of her new home, represents that perspective. Just in front of the bride's left hand, Eros, the god of love, presents his gift, a necklace. In this setting women reign supreme, although the exhibition catalogue reminds us that through marriage the bride passes "from the possession of her father to that of her husband" (Kaltsas and Shapiro, p. 318).

Another vase in the exhibition presents a third perspective: males and females cavorting freely in sport and play, without any indication of superiority or inferiority, of domination or suppression. Although these creatures are mythical male satyrs and female maenads, rather than humans, the message of equality between the genders seems clear.

Vase painting, no less than drama, poetry, philosophy, and formal historical studies, can provide insights into gender relations—and the insights are complex, varied, and subject to interpretation.

- Does the drinking vase support Keuls' overall viewpoint? Why or why not?
- What elements, if any, in the *Worshiping Women* exhibition might support Keuls' viewpoint? Who are the sponsors of the exhibit and catalogue?
- Do you believe that young men and women of Athens could have identified with the activities of the maenads and satyrs of the vase? Why or why not?

Attic red-figure nuptial lebes with lid, clay, 410 B.C.E. This vase depicts the day after the marriage ceremony, when gifts are presented to the bride. Eros himself, the god of physical love, personifying happiness and beauty, presents a necklace. The scene apparently takes place in the women's quarters of the house, and includes the mothers of the bride and of the groom. (National Archaeological Museum, Athens)

5.1

5.2

5.3

5.4

How did Greek culture spread from the Mediterranean to India, Afghanistan, Russia, and Egypt?

cultural development of all its citizens, Sparta stressed universal military service for its able-bodied male citizens; Athens prided itself on its cosmopolitan sea-borne trade and openness to outside influences, Sparta was an armed camp. For ten years, from 461 to 451, Athens and its allies confronted Sparta and its allies in intermittent warfare. During these wars, contradicting its own democratic traditions, Athens exploited its allies. In 454 B.C.E. Pericles moved the treasury of the Delian League to Athens and appropriated its funds in order to create at Athens a spectacular center of power and authority, particularly by building the Parthenon and expanding the fleet. A democracy at home, Athens was fast becoming an imperial power holding sway over its neighbor.

The Peloponnesian War

Relationships between Athens and its neighbors also deteriorated. Pericles' imperialistic policies encroached on its own allies as well as on those of Sparta. Fearful that the Athenians would use their navy to destroy Spartan control over its own alliance system, the Peloponnesian League, Sparta determined to destroy Athens' power. In 432 B.C.E. Sparta attacked Athens, and the Peloponnesian War began in earnest. The struggle was for power, not for higher ideals.

Thucydides, historian of the conflict, portrays Athens setting forth its claims increasingly bluntly. He reports the arrogant Athenian ultimatum ordering the people of the island of Melos to submit to Athenian authority:

> Our opinion of the gods and our knowledge of men lead us to conclude that it is a general and necessary law of nature to rule whatever one can. (V:105; p. 404)

Much weaker than Athens, Melos nevertheless chose to resist. When the Athenians finally conquered the Melians in 415 B.C.E., they killed all the men of military age whom they captured, and sold the women and children into slavery. Throughout Greece, admiration for Athens turned to loathing.

By 404 B.C.E. Sparta, supported by Persian funding, defeated Athens and captured the city. The Spartans may have benefited especially from the warlike spirit of their women. Although the Spartan women did not go into battle themselves, legend had it that they commanded their husbands and sons who were departing for battle to return either carrying their shields—victorious—or carried on their shields—dead.

The Peloponnesian War between Athens and Sparta and their allies had dragged on for a full generation. Both sides were exhausted. Nevertheless, warfare soon resumed among the Greeks, with Thebes and Corinth now entering the lists as major contenders. Each major city-state sought advantage over the others, and the stronger continued to force the weaker into subordinate alliances as intermittent warfare sputtered on.

📖 **Read** the **Document: Plutarch on Life in Sparta (1st c. BCE)** on **MyHistoryLab**

The Empire of Alexander the Great

5.4 How did Greek culture spread from the Mediterranean to India, Afghanistan, Russia, and Egypt?

To the north of the squabbling Greek city-states lay the rougher, less urbanized Macedonia, a borderland between Greece and the Slavic regions to the north and east. The principal language and culture of Macedonia were Greek, but other languages and cultures were also present. While the Greeks looked upon the Macedonians as semi-barbaric, the Macedonian kings, first Philip II (r. 359–336 B.C.E.) and then his son Alexander (the Great) (r. 336–323 B.C.E.), came to view the Greeks as undisciplined and ripe for conquest. The Macedonian conquest of Greece turned out to be only the beginning of one of the greatest, but very short-lived, of the empires that spanned Europe and Asia.

The Conquests of Philip

In 359 B.C.E., in the Macedonian capital of Pella, Philip II persuaded the Macedonian army to declare him king, in succession to his brother, who had died in warfare. After consolidating his power in Macedonia, Philip declared two goals. The first of these was to unify and bring peace to Greece; the second was to liberate the Greek city-states in Asia Minor from Persian control. Skillful as a diplomat and careful to introduce economic improvements in the lands he conquered, Philip nevertheless realized that his army was the real key to achieving his goals. He built up its phalanxes, armed the soldiers with spears up to 15 feet long, and augmented the foot soldiers with powerful and swift cavalry. Philip led the troops himself, suffering numerous, serious wounds in battle.

Between 354 and 339 B.C.E. Philip conquered the Balkans from the Danube to the Aegean coast and from the Adriatic to the Black Sea. To pacify and administer the area, he established new towns, which were populated by both Macedonians and local peoples. Similarly, he employed many local people in his administration. Within Greece proper, his accomplishments were more mixed. He won some allies, such as Thessaly; defeated the armies of several city-states; and mediated the end of a war between two coalitions of Greek city-states. He was honored with election as president of the Pythian Games at Delphi in 346 B.C.E., but Athens and Thebes bitterly opposed his overtures for greater power in Greece.

The orator Demosthenes (384–322 B.C.E.) delivered three "Philippics," public addresses calling Athens to battle against the Macedonian king and predicting the end of Athenian democracy if Philip defeated the city-state. In the face of this opposition, Philip met Athens and its allies in battle, defeating them at Chaeronea in 338 B.C.E. Philip now sought to create a self-governing league of Greek city-states, to accomplish his first goal, and to forge an alliance between Macedonia and the league to fight Persia, his second goal. But he was assassinated in 336 B.C.E. His 20-year-old son, Alexander, continued his father's mission.

The Reign of Alexander the Great

No stranger to warfare, Alexander had fought by his father's side just two years beforehand as he defeated Athens at the Battle of Chaeronea. Applauded by the army, Alexander succeeded to the throne without opposition and continued his father's career of conquest. Over the next 12 years, his disciplined army traversed some 22,000 miles, conquering lands that stretched from Egypt in the west to the Indus River in the east. Alexander's empire became the largest known up to his time, and in 324 B.C.E. he declared himself a god.

Like his father, Philip, and the Persian emperors Cyrus II and Darius I, Alexander followed a policy of benevolent despotism much of the time. But, also like them, he implemented this policy only after his power had been amply demonstrated. Unfortunate Thebes provided an early site for this demonstration. Soon after assuming the throne, Alexander had marched north to the Danube River to suppress revolts in Thrace. Mistakenly informed that Alexander had been killed in battle, Thebes revolted against his local forces. Alexander quickly marched his troops back to Thebes, captured and sacked the rebel city, killed 6,000 of its inhabitants, and sold into slavery 20,000 of those who survived.

In 334 B.C.E. Alexander was ready to cross into Asia, where his first major victory came at Granicus. From there he continued southward, forcing the Persians out of the Greek cities that lined the Ionian coast. To make sure that the Persians would not return, Alexander marched eastward through Anatolia with 35,000 Greek troops,

The empire of Alexander. In 338 B.C.E. the Greek city-states were defeated by Philip of Macedon. His son, Alexander, extended the imprint of Greek culture far beyond its Mediterranean homeland. In a series of whirlwind campaigns between 334 and 323 B.C.E., Alexander gained control of Syria and Egypt and then destroyed the might of Persia. He took his armies east to the Indus and north to central Asia, but died at age 33 in Babylon.

5.1
5.2
5.3
5.4

How did Greek culture spread from the Mediterranean to India, Afghanistan, Russia, and Egypt?

routing the 300,000-man army of the Persian emperor Darius III at Issus in 333 B.C.E. and forcing Darius himself into flight.

Alexander continued southward down the coast of the eastern Mediterranean. At Tyre, which held out in siege against him for seven months, he again demonstrated power and brutality, killing 7,000 men and selling 30,000 captives, mostly women and children, into slavery. Elsewhere, however, Alexander showed the velvet glove, respecting local religions, ruling through local hierarchies, and maintaining local tax rates. To drive Persia from the Mediterranean basin and to establish his own control, Alexander continued south and then west, conquering Egypt. He was welcomed as Egypt's liberator from Persian rule and treated as a god by the Egyptian priests of the god Amon, whose shrine he visited. At the western end of the Nile delta, Alexander laid the foundation of what would be for several centuries the most attractive and cultured city of the Mediterranean coast, Alexandria.

His appetite whetted (a common experience with empire-builders once they begin their careers), Alexander moved onward to conquests previously unplanned. He set out to conquer the Persian Empire and make it his own. He marched northeastward across the Fertile Crescent and through Mesopotamia. At Gaugamela in 331 B.C.E. he again faced the Persian emperor, Darius III, and again routed him. The historical capital cities of Babylon, Susa, Persepolis, and Pasargadae lay open to Alexander. He destroyed Persepolis, Darius' own capital, almost totally. Then, having captured the heartland of the Persian Empire, he set off to conquer the eastern half as well, finally reaching and capturing the Indus River valley in the east, and Sogdiana, across the Oxus River, in the northeast.

Although Alexander wanted to continue into India as far as the Ganges, his troops mutinied. They would go no farther. As he was returning from his new frontiers,

The "Alexander Mosaic," first-century B.C.E. mosaic copy from Pompeii of a painting by Philoxenos, c. 300 B.C.E. This mosaic portrays the Battle of Issus (333 B.C.E.) in terms of a personal duel between Alexander the Great and Darius III, emperor of Persia. Darius (right) is shown about to turn and flee in his chariot as the youthful Alexander (left), wild-haired and helmetless, charges toward him. (Museo Archeologico Nazionale, Naples)

View the Image: **Mosaic of Alexander the Great** on **MyHistoryLab**

5.1
5.2
5.3
5.4

How did Greek culture spread from the Mediterranean to India, Afghanistan, Russia, and Egypt?

Alexander contracted a fever. Weakened both by the hardships of war and by heavy drinking, he died in Babylon in 323 B.C.E., only 33 years old. Several accounts report that he was poisoned; some said the instigator was his own former teacher Aristotle. On his deathbed Alexander reputedly declared, "Let the job go to the strongest." In the battle for succession among his generals, Alexander's wife, Roxane, and their 13-year-old son were murdered.

The empire Alexander created did not survive two generations. In the east, local rulers regained power in India and Afghanistan. In the west, the Greeks returned to their internal warfare, finally breaking up once more into individual city-states, kingdoms, and leagues. Macedonia remained a separate kingdom and continued to meddle in Greek affairs.

Two major kingdoms emerged from the dissolution of Alexander's empire: Egypt under the dynasty of Ptolemy, which ruled through a Greek and Macedonian elite until the Roman conquest; and the empire established by Seleucus I Nicator (d. 281 B.C.E.), who was governor of Babylon when the empire split apart, and who added to his own domain Iran, Afghanistan, and Anatolia. But the Seleucid Empire, too, fragmented. Parthians reclaimed Persia in the east, and Anatolia divided into numerous local governments. By 200 B.C.E. the Seleucid Empire was limited primarily to the area around Syria.

The Legacies of Alexander

What were the legacies of the empire Alexander built? He made the language and culture of Greece dominant among the ruling intellectual and commercial elites from the Mediterranean east to India, Afghanistan, and the borders of Russia, and south as far as Egypt. A common dialect of Greek, known as Koine, spread as the language of educated people throughout the ancient western world.

Waves of Greek administrators, businessmen, and soldiers followed Alexander's conquests and helped to transmit Greek culture. At the same time, local customs, especially the imperial ceremonial forms of Persia, endured and transformed the simplicity of the earlier **Hellenic** culture into the more complex, elaborate, and cosmopolitan Hellenistic culture that flourished from the time of Alexander until the death of the last Macedonian queen of Egypt, Cleopatra, in 30 B.C.E. One striking example of the mixture of **Hellenistic** and local cultures—this time from India—can be seen in some of the first representations of the Buddha in sculpture from the area of India/Pakistan after it was conquered by Alexander. These sculptures represent the Buddha wearing a toga (illustrated in the chapter entitled "Indian Empires," below).

To facilitate travel and commerce, as well as conquest and administration, Alexander built roads, canals, and whole new cities, including at least 16 Alexandrias across the length and breadth of his conquests, using the gold and silver captured

KEY TERMS

Hellenic Having to do with Greek culture before the time of Alexander the Great.

Hellenistic Having to do with Greek culture after the time of Alexander, when Hellenic culture was influenced by Persian culture, with its greater emphasis on political empire, government power and centralization, and more ornate artwork.

HOW DO WE KNOW?

Evaluating Alexander the Great

Alexander remains a controversial figure. He was reputed to have murdered hundreds of thousands to achieve his power, yet his admirers see in him a creative genius who aimed at forging a unified Greco-Persian culture that extended into central Asia. By some he was called Alexander the Great; by others Iskander the Accursed. Subsequent historians and other scholars are unsure whether he was an innocent multiculturalist or an imperial monster. There seems to be no question that he believed in his own divinity, but much about this young man remains unknown.

By the end of his life, however, few sorrowed over Alexander's death. The historian Peter Green, who has written an historiographical sketch of Alexander's reputation through the ages, found that the conqueror's image has changed dramatically over time.

The earliest remaining accounts of Alexander's life date from the first century B.C.E., at least 200 years after his death, while the most reliable and fullest of the earliest biographies still extant, that written by Arrian Flavius Arrianus, dates to the second century C.E. For the most part, all historians work from these same basic records, but their assessments reflect the issues and conditions of their own day.

Arrian, who lived at the height of the Roman Empire, and approved of it, praises Alexander for his conquests. Alexander was the prototype of Rome's own Caesars. Closer to our own times, in the late eighteenth and nineteenth centuries, during the democratic era of the American and French revolutions, and of the Greek War for Independence (see the chapter entitled "Migration"), historical opinion turned against Alexander. George Grote's *History of Greece* (1888) represented both Philip and Alexander as "brutalized adventurers simply out for power, wealth, and territorial expansion, both of them inflamed by the pure lust for conquest" (Green, 1991, p. 482).

On the other hand, Johann Gustav Droysen, an ardent advocate of a reunified, powerful Germany (see the chapter entitled "The Industrial Revolution"), saw Alexander as a model. Droysen's scholarly biography *Alexander der Grosse* (1833)

praised Alexander for introducing Greek culture into large parts of Asia.

As the British Empire expanded in the nineteenth and early twentieth centuries, many British scholars also adopted a favorable view of Alexander. William Tarn's two-volume biography saw his conquests as instrumental in spreading a social philosophy of the Brotherhood of Man, bringing together Greeks and Persians, the conquerors with the conquered. Even in our post-imperial day, Cambridge University scholar N.G.L. Hammond agrees, citing the essay by the biographer Plutarch (c. 46–126 C.E.):

> He harnessed all resources to one and the same end, mixing as it were in a loving-cup the lives, manners, marriages and customs of men. He ordered them all to regard the inhabited earth as their fatherland and his armed forces as their stronghold and defense.

Nonetheless, Green remains critical, arguing that his own assessment is closest to that at the time of Alexander's death:

> His all-absorbing obsession through a short but crowded life, was war and conquest. It is idle to palliate this central truth, to pretend that he dreamed … of wading through rivers of blood and violence to achieve the Brotherhood of Man by raping an entire continent. He spent his whole life, with legendary success, in the pursuit of personal glory, Achillean *kleos*; and until very recent times this was regarded as a wholly laudable aim. The empire he built collapsed the moment he was gone; he came as a conqueror and the work he wrought was destruction. (Green, 1991, p. 488)

- What seems to be the basis for Green's interpretation of Alexander's career?
- Would you consider Alexander a hero or a villain?
- In light of America's increasing use of power overseas, how do you think scholarly interpretation of Alexander might change?

from Persia to finance much of the construction. The most famous and illustrious Alexandria was the metropolis in Egypt, which became the leading Mediterranean city of its day. Egyptian Alexandria housed palaces, administrative centers, theaters, stadia, the greatest library of Greek knowledge, containing 700,000 manuscripts, and the final resting place of Alexander himself.

At the eastern end of the empire, on the Oxus River in today's Uzbekistan, the Greeks constructed, on Persian foundations, Ai Khanoum, a small, well-defended city centered on a palace. Ai Khanoum was rediscovered and excavated only in the 1960s, and archaeologists believe it may prove to be Alexandria Oxiana, a lost city from the age of Alexander the Great.

Between Alexandria in Egypt and Ai Khanoum in central Asia were dozens of cities and small towns, which served as seeds of Greek culture throughout the empire. The Alexandrian Empire and its successors built a Hellenistic **ecumene**—that is, a unified urban culture, encompassing vast lands and diverse peoples. Some of its cities, which had long, independent Greek heritages, retained strong elements of their pre-Alexandrian culture and even their autonomy. These were the cities of the Greek heartland, such as Athens, Sparta, Thebes, Corinth, and Delphi. Others were cities of empire, built later by Alexander and his successors either from the ground up or on existing but relatively minor urban bases. These cities served as new regional capitals, to administer the new empire, extend its economy, and broadcast its culture.

Alexander and his successors also administered their empire through the existing indigenous urban framework, but added to it the principal institutions and monuments of Hellenistic culture: temples to Greek gods, frequently set on a walled acropolis; theaters; an agora; civic buildings, such as a council chamber and town hall; gymnasia; and stadia. Examples of this style of urban Hellenization in newly conquered lands included Susa, Damascus, Tyre, Kandahar, and Merv. Residents of these varied cities might feel themselves to be both citizens of the locality and participants in a semi-universal ecumene. A sharp division intensified between the cities with their high culture, now very much Hellenized throughout the empire, and the rural areas, which continued their traditional patterns of life without much change.

The empire encouraged the flow of trade and culture in many directions. Greek ships have been found as far west as the British Isles and as far east as the Indian Ocean. European, African, and Asian trade routes intersected at Taxila, Ai Khanoum, Begram, and Merv. The Persians had begun to create an Asian–African–European *ecumene*; Alexander carried the process further and deeper. Rome, already beginning to rise by the time of Alexander, would later extend a similar imperial mission throughout much of Europe to the west and north, although Rome would not control the east, as we shall see in "Rome and the Barbarians."

Empire-building:
What Difference Does It Make?

Mesopotamians, Egyptians, Persians, Greeks, and Macedonians launched their imperial ambitions from very different backgrounds. Mesopotamians and Greeks began as city-states; Egyptians and Persians as consolidated nations. Sargon conquered Mesopotamia, creating the first empire. Out of the fractious chaos of the Greek city-states Macedon built its small state to imperial dimensions under a father and son who ruled as ambitious and skillful kings. Although our coverage was necessarily sketchy, we have seen that each empire erected a central capital from which it could control the provinces; provided a uniform language, coinage, and legal system across the empire; constructed a road and communications network; articulated an ideology of empire that won the loyalty of many of its citizens and subjects; and created art and architecture to impress on friend and foe alike the power of the empire. Each assembled military forces to apply coercion where necessary.

KEY TERM

ecumene A word of Greek origin referring to the inhabited world and designating a distinct cultural-historical community.

A time finally came for each empire to rein in its ambitions and limit further expansion. Sometimes it reached the limit of its capacity to conquer and administer profitably; sometimes it was defeated in war; often it encountered a combination of both these humbling experiences.

The imperial armies of Alexander the Great refused to proceed to newer, more distant conquests beyond the Indus River. So he turned back toward home. Ironically, Alexander's school tutor had been the philosopher Aristotle, who had written: "To the size of states there is a limit." Aristotle's ideal political unit was the Greek city-state because it promoted the maximum personal participation in democratic government through intense social and political interaction among the citizens.

In choosing to build an empire, Alexander was neither the first nor the last student to disregard his teacher's advice. (Alexander wanted the city-states of Greece to be self-governing, but he did not want other areas to have such powers.) Nor was Aristotle the first or last to weigh the relative merits of small, local democratic government units against those of large, centralized bureaucracies. Similar debates still go on in our own day. Debates over the usefulness, limits, and legitimacy of empire were also central to the political thought of ancient Rome, China, and India, the three huge empires that are the focus of the chapters entitled "Rome and the Barbarians," "China," and "Indian Empires."

CHAPTER REVIEW

THE EARLIEST EMPIRES

5.1 What were the characteristics of early empires?

The world's first empires, like the first cities, arose in Mesopotamia and the Nile River valley. The emperor Sargon established control over Mesopotamia's far-flung independent city-states. He standardized measurements and the use of the Akkadian language in the empire's documents, and he replaced local leaderships with his own administrators. Mesopotamia's city-state structure and its geographical openness left the region vulnerable. After Sargon, outside empires continually attacked and absorbed the region's city-states.

The Egyptian empire, in contrast, began as a single unified state, which then slowly expanded its power over others. By about 2000 B.C.E. it conquered Nubia in the southern Nile valley; by about 1500 B.C.E. it conquered parts of Mesopotamia. (At other times, Egypt was conquered by the Nubians and by peoples of Mesopotamia.) The empire constructed enormous royal building projects, including new cities, elegant palaces, temple complexes, tombs, and fortifications. Egypt's hierarchical society was focused on the dynastic succession of its semi-god rulers, the pharaohs.

THE PERSIAN EMPIRE

5.2 How did Darius I come to rule the Persian Empire?

Darius I took over the Persian Empire that Cyrus II had established and ruled it for 35 years. He softened the imposition of imperial administration and tax collection by maintaining local traditions and bringing local elites into his administration. He created more efficient units of government by increasing the number of local governments. At the same time, he created an imperial system of roads, with a series of inns for travelers and a royal courier service along the roads. He built a new capital city, later called Persepolis. He renewed the region's irrigation systems, encouraged the introduction of new crops, and standardized the empire's coinage, called the daric after himself.

THE GREEK CITY-STATES

5.3 What was the nature of the Greek city-state political organization?

The Greeks developed a very different form of political organization from that of the Persians. The Greek city-state, or polis, was an intentionally small, locally organized government based on a single central city. With enough surrounding land to provide for its agricultural needs, each city-state had its own form of government and was individually independent. Athens, in particular, took pride in its government by all of its free, adult, male citizens (but not by its women or its slaves or newcomers to the city). These assemblies passed laws, judged criminal and civil cases, implemented legislation, and arranged for military defense as needed. The Greek city-states understood their legal systems to be their own creation and responsibility: not imposed by an emperor or decreed by the gods. Athens was proud of its ability to unify the Greek city-states in successful warfare against the Persian empire, and of the "golden age" of culture that followed. Its former allies, however, especially Sparta, accused it of imperial ambitions. The Peloponnesian War among the rival Greek city-states followed.

THE EMPIRE OF ALEXANDER THE GREAT

5.4 How did Greek culture spread from the Mediterranean to India, Afghanistan, Russia, and Egypt?

Alexander, who came from Macedonia, Greece's northern neighbor, made the language and culture of Greece dominant among the ruling elites all across his enormous empire. The waves of Greek administrators, soldiers, and businessmen who followed Alexander's conquests helped transmit Greek culture, although they permitted many local customs, and prior Persian practices, to remain. Alexander built roads, canals, and cities across the empire, at least 16 of them named Alexandria, and in the cities he and his successors built stadia, theaters, gymnasia, and temples, all in the Hellenistic style.

Suggested Readings

PRINCIPAL SOURCES

Baines, John, and Jaromir Malek. *Atlas of Ancient Egypt* (New York: Facts on File, 1980). Two noted experts continue the excellent books in this series with fine text, maps, pictures, time lines, and breadth of coverage.

Green, Peter. *Alexander of Macedon* (Berkeley, CA: University of California Press, 1991). An excellent, thoughtful biography with good historiographical coverage as well.

——. *The Greco-Persian Wars* (Berkeley, CA: University of California Press, 1996). A revision of a classic on the wars.

Hanson, Victor Davis. *The Wars of the Ancient Greeks* (London: Cassell & Co, 1999). A readable volume that incorporates recent scholarship on Greek warfare.

Kagan, Donald. *The Peloponnesian War* (New York: Viking, 2003). Distills the great scholarship, and increases the readability, of his earlier four-volume work. Based largely on Thucydides, but includes considerable additional scholarship and new perspectives.

Levi, Peter. *Atlas of the Greek World* (New York: Facts on File, 1982). The series continues its excellent, broad coverage with outstanding text, maps, pictures, and time lines.

Past Worlds: The (London) Times Atlas of Archaeology (Maplewood, NJ: Hammond, Inc., 1988). Beautifully produced, superbly researched atlas with fine text and excellent pictures as well.

Postgate, J.N. *Early Mesopotamia* (London: Routledge, 1992). Scholarly analysis and clear presentation.

Thucydides. *History of the Peloponnesian War*, trans. Rex Warner (Harmondsworth, Middlesex: Penguin Books, 1972). The definitive primary source, cynically philosophical about political motives, the product of bitter and cynical events.

Wycherley, R.E. *How the Greeks Built Cities* (Garden City, NY: Anchor Books, 1969). Excellent introduction to the urban plans of the Greek cities, with good attention to the significance of the buildings and designs, and to the variety of city-states.

ADDITIONAL SOURCES

Aristotle. *Basic Works*, ed. and trans. Richard McKeon (New York: Random House, 1941). Direct introduction to the work of the philosopher, whose works continued authoritative for at least 2,000 years.

Bernal, Martin. *Black Athena: The Afroasiatic Roots of Classical Civilization* (New Brunswick, NJ: Rutgers University Press, 1987). Bernal demonstrates the influence of Egyptian culture on ancient Greece. Because of the title the book became involved in racial debates, but the text does not concentrate on race.

Hamilton, J.R. *Alexander the Great* (London: Hutchison University Library, 1973). A standard biography.

Hammond, Mason. *The City in the Ancient World* (Cambridge, MA: Harvard University Press, 1972). A history of the ancient Western world through an analysis of its cities.

Hammond, N.G.L. *The Genius of Alexander the Great* (Chapel Hill, NC: University of North Carolina Press, 1997). A standard biography.

Herodotus. *The Persian Wars*, trans. George Rawlinson (New York: Modern Library, 1942). Some consider this the first secular book of history. Mixes myth with history in recreating the great clash of civilizations between the Greeks and the Persians.

Homer. *Iliad*, trans. Robert Fagles (New York: Penguin Books, 1998). The story that inspired the ancient Greeks in warfare, and gave us insight into their world.

——. *Odyssey*, trans. Robert Fagles (New York: Penguin Books, 1999). The great story of the journey of Odysseus through one trial after another from the Trojan war back to his home in Greece.

Hornblower, Simon. *The Greek World 479–323 B.C.* (London: Methuen, 1983). A standard historical survey.

Kaltsas, Nikolaos, ed. *Athens–Sparta* (New York: Alexander S. Onassis Public Benefit Foundation, 2006). Catalog of a 2006–07 museum exhibition comparing the two city-states, primarily through their art.

Kaltsas, Nikolaos, and Alan Shapiro, eds. *Worshiping Women: Ritual and Reality in Classical Athens* (New York: Alexander S. Onassis Public Benefit Foundation [USA] in collaboration with the National Archaeological Museum, Athens, 2008). Catalog of a 2008–09 museum exhibition of the same name.

Keuls, Eva C. *The Reign of the Phallus: Sexual Politics in Ancient Athens* (New York: Harper and Row, 1985). Opinionated, belligerent, engaging feminist critique of ancient Athens; evidence taken from painting on drinking vessels.

Mumford, Lewis. *The City in History* (New York: Harcourt, Brace and World, 1961). Classic history with a strong argument for small, manageable cities with a strong sense of community.

O'Brien, John Maxwell. *Alexander the Great: The Invisible Enemy* (London: Routledge, 1992). Critical biography.

Plato. *The Collected Dialogues of Plato*, ed. Edith Hamilton and Huntington Cairns (New York: Bollingen Foundation [distributed by Pantheon Books], 1961). The complete works of the classic philosopher of ideal types.

Plutarch. *The Lives of the Noble Grecians and Romans*, trans. John Dryden, revised by Arthur Hugh Clough (New York: Modern Library, n.d.). Writing from the height of the Roman Empire, this Greek historian preserves many materials that have otherwise been lost as he assesses the accomplishments of many of the Greek and Roman greats.

Robinson, Eric W., ed. *Ancient Greek Democracy: Readings and Sources* (Malden, MA: Blackwell, 2004). Very useful selection of primary documents on the function and limits of ancient Greek democracy.

Saggs, H.W.F. *The Might that Was Assyria* (London: Sidgwick & Jackson, 1984). Fine general survey.

Sophocles. *Oedipus Rex* and *Oedipus at Colonus*, trans. Robert Fitzgerald in *The Oedipus Cycle* (San Diego: Harcourt Brace Jovanovich, 1969). Two of the most famous plays from ancient Greece.

Tacitus. *The Annals of Imperial Rome*, trans. Michael Grant (Baltimore, MD: Penguin Books, 1959). Primary source by this government official and historian of Rome, often very critical of the growth of empire.

Tarn, W.W. *Alexander the Great* (Cambridge: Cambridge University Press, 2 vols., 1948). Laudatory biography.

FILMS

PBS Home Video. *Athens. The Dawn of Democracy* (2007; 2 hours). Superb analysis of the rhetoric, reality, and historic evolution of Athenian democracy. Excellent visuals; outstanding scholars. Recent research. Narrated by Bettany Hughes.

BBC Horrible Histories: *Wife Swap: Spartans and Athenians,* YouTube (2009; 4½ minutes). Hilarious parody of the family styles of the two city-states. Makes some telling points.

300 (2007; 1 hour and 57 minutes). Film based on the historical story of Leonidas, as related through the 1999 graphic novel of the same name, leading 300 Spartan warriors to their doom in a defense against Persian invaders which nevertheless inspired Sparta and other Greek city-states to unite and keep the Persians out. Testosterone-fueled violence. Single-dimensional characters. Huge box-office success. For the information and the fun of it, read the variety of perspectives on the film presented in Wikipedia.

6 Rome and the Barbarians

The Rise and Dismemberment of Empire

753 B.C.E.–1453 C.E.

All roads, by land and sea, led to Rome, the capital of one of the longest-lasting and most influential of empires. Situated on the Tiber River, not far from the sea, Rome served as the center of communication and trade for the entire Italian peninsula. To the surrounding sea the Romans gave the name "Mediterranean," the middle of the earth, for it is itself surrounded by the three continents that they knew: southern Europe, northern Africa, and western Asia. Later, as Roman armies conquered and ruled an empire that encompassed all these lands and many territories still more distant, they began to call the Mediterranean *Mare Nostrum* ("Our Sea").

Battle line formed with shields by the Romans against the Dacians, from Trajan's Column, Rome, *c.* 113 C.E. Plaster cast of marble original. The Romans adapted the Greek phalanx into a more maneuverable, but tightly configured, array of foot soldiers with shields, spears, and daggers. Victory memorials, such as Trajan's Column celebrated the resulting successes in battle. Compare with the Greek phalanx in the chapter opener entitled "From City-state to Empire". (Museo della Civiltà, Rome)

LEARNING OBJECTIVES

6.1 ((•	6.2 ((•	6.3 ((•	6.4 ((•	6.5 ((•	6.6 ((•	6.7 ((•
Describe the formation of the early Roman republic.	Understand the Roman republic as a military society.	Understand how the Romans won support from conquered peoples.	Trace the generals' power struggles and the end of the Republic.	Describe the achievements of Augustus and the Roman Principate.	Understand why the Roman Empire declined.	Discuss how the eastern empire survived after the end of the Roman Empire.

How did the early Republic take shape?

6.1
6.2
6.3
6.4
6.5
6.6
6.7

At its greatest extent, in the second century C.E., the Roman Empire ruled between 70 and 100 million people of vastly diverse ethnic, racial, religious, and cultural roots. Geographically, it sprawled over 2,700 miles east to west and 2,500 miles north to south, extending from Scotland to the Persian Gulf. At its most powerful, between 27 B.C.E. and 180 C.E., Rome enforced the *Pax Romana*, the Roman peace, a reign of stability and relative tranquility throughout all these vast regions.

From the first, this empire evoked both praise and condemnation. The Latin poet Virgil (70–19 B.C.E.) led one of the greatest choruses of praise, describing Rome as a gift of the gods, and praising its citizens for successfully carrying out their mandate: "Remember Romans/ To rule the people under law, to establish/ The way of peace." Virgil praised the sheer size of the empire, its roads, its cities, its trade, and its monuments. Most of all, however, he cited the *Pax Romana*, the peace and prosperity established through Rome's rule of law, enforced by Rome's armies.

The historian Tacitus (*c.* 56–*c.* 120 C.E.) mocked this praise of peace and prosperity: "Robbery, butchery, and rapine they call 'Empire.' They create a desert and call it 'Peace.'" Writing a century after Virgil, and viewing the empire through the eyes of a defeated Celtic chieftain, Tacitus characterized the *Pax Romana* as a policy of brute military conquest and destruction. This chapter will explore the conditions underlying both of these contradictory points of view.

From Hill Town to Republic, 753–133 B.C.E.

6.1 How did the early Republic take shape?

The legendary date for the founding of the city of Rome is April 21, 753 B.C.E., and although this is probably not exact, it is approximately correct. (Romans today still celebrate April 21 as the birthday of their city, with free concerts and public festivities.) According to this legend, beloved by the Romans, Romulus and Remus—twin sons of Mars, the god of war—founded the city at the site where they were rescued from the Tiber River and suckled by a nurturing she-wolf. (See the Etruscan statue illustration, below.)

KEY TERM

Pax Romana The "Roman peace," that is, the state of comparative concord prevailing within the boundaries of the Roman Empire from the reign of Augustus (r. 27 B.C.E.–14 C.E.) to that of Marcus Aurelius (r. 161–180 C.E.), enforced by Roman political and military control.

Capitoline wolf, c. 500 B.C.E. According to legend, Rome was founded by Romulus and Remus, twin sons of Mars, at the spot where they were rescued from the Tiber River and suckled by a she-wolf. The group of she-wolf with twins was adopted as the symbol of Rome, although the children in this particular statue were added almost 2,000 years later, during the Renaissance. (Museo Capitolino, Rome)

6.1
6.2
6.3
6.4
6.5
6.6
6.7

How did the early Republic take shape?

For two and a half centuries, the kings of neighboring Etruria, the land to the north of Rome, ruled the city. The Romans learned much from the Etruscans about city-building, art, religion, mythology, and even language. As Rome entered the Mediterranean trade networks of the Etruscans, merchants and craftworkers immigrated to the city. The Etruscan king Servius Tullius (578–534 B.C.E.) reformed the military, creating the *comitia centuriata*, a deliberative ruling council organized by hundreds (*centuriae*), representing the soldiers of Rome. This assembly of Roman citizens persisted for centuries after Etruscan rule had ended, reinforcing the connection between the armies of Rome and its government.

Patricians and Plebeians in the Early Republic

About 509 B.C.E., the wealthy, powerful citizens of Rome drove out the Etruscan kings. They declared Rome a **republic**, a government in which power resides in its citizens, who elect officials to represent them in decision-making. However, the new government perpetuated the class conflict that was already a staple of Rome's Etruscan history. Full citizenship under the early Republic included only seven to ten percent of the population: the wealthy, the powerful, and those with hereditary residential ties to Rome. These were the **patricians** (from the Latin *pater*, "father"). Patricians were also called "free men," to distinguish them from the overwhelming majority, the **plebeians**. Plebeians lacked long-standing hereditary ties to the state and usually lacked property as well, so they could not serve as officers in the military and were excluded from government, as were slaves (usually, men captured in war) and women.

The two classes, patricians and plebeians, had already become polarized under Etruscan rule. The patricians forbade intermarriage with the plebeians and monopolized for themselves not only membership in the Senate, but also the religious offices of the state. The plebeians had looked to the Etruscan king as their protector, and the fall of the monarchy further reduced their status.

The Struggle of the Orders. The first conflict between patricians and plebeians, the Struggle of the Orders, broke out 15 years after the fall of the monarchy and persisted through more than a half-century (494–440 B.C.E.) of the early Republic. The plebeians relied on their ultimate strengths: their bodies and their numbers. They were the foot soldiers of Rome, and their periodic boycotts of military service threatened the city of Rome itself. In 451 B.C.E., in an attempt to resolve the conflict, a commission of ten patricians codified Rome's existing customary practices into the Law of the Twelve Tables, so named because they were inscribed on 12 tables of ivory (or, perhaps, bronze).

The patricians, with their legal skills, outfoxed the plebeians, who were horrified when they recognized the severity of the laws that were imposed upon them. The laws were often written without explicit distinction between plebeian and patrician, but they were especially hard on the weak and the impoverished, and hardest of all on slaves. All these people were most likely to be plebeians. For example, after a 30-day grace period, debtors could be arrested and brought to court, held in chains or stocks, and, after 60 days, sold into slavery or even killed. The punishment for pasturing animals on someone else's land or for cutting crops from someone else's field secretly by night was death by hanging. Slaves had the fewest rights, and the lowest human value, of all. The financial punishment for bruising or breaking the bone of a free man was twice that for similar injuries to a slave. The punishment for theft by a free man was flogging and arranging some form of repayment; for theft by a slave it was flogging and execution by being thrown from the Tarpeian Rock on the Capitoline Hill in Rome (Lewis and Reinhold, I:109–13).

Slowly, under pressure, however, the patricians yielded power. For example, a series of laws that relieved debts were enacted, which helped plebeians especially,

KEY TERMS

republic A state that is ruled not by a hereditary leader (as in a monarchy) but by a person or persons appointed under the constitution.

patrician Born to a family with long-standing residence and prominence in Rome, a patrician was an aristocrat. About seven to ten percent of Rome's population were patricians.

plebeian A citizen of ancient Rome who was not a member of the privileged patrician class. Beginning in the later Republican period, the term "plebeian" implied low social class.

tribune In ancient Rome, a plebeian officer elected by the plebeians and charged to protect their lives and properties, with a right of veto against legislative proposals of the Senate.

magistrate An official elected by the Senate of Rome to administer the Republic under the supervision of the Senate. There were many different ranks of magistrate, serving different functions. At the end of their term of office they became senators themselves.

consul Under the Roman Republic, one of the two magistrates holding supreme civil and military authority.

How did the
early Republic
take shape?

6.1

6.2

6.3

6.4

6.5

6.6

6.7

although indebtedness continued to be a problem throughout Roman history. Plebeians gained representation along with patricians in Rome's Senate, and they gained the right to elect two **tribunes**, officers charged with defending their legal rights.

The Senate of Rome

The Roman Senate was the legislative and consultative body of the government. The Senate elected a variety of **magistrates** to carry out the administration of the Republic, sometimes under the control of the Senate, at other times with greater independence. As magistrates ended their one-year (renewable) term of office, they automatically became senators themselves. The Senate and the magistrates were part of the Etruscan heritage. The Etruscans had had a senate, composed of the elders of the society, which elected and advised the king. Similarly, the Roman Senate, in the days of the Republic, decided policy, especially concerning peace and war, and appointed and advised the magistrates. At the highest executive level, two **consuls** held power that extended over all the lands Rome ruled. Nominated by the Senate and elected by citizens in the *comitia centuriata* (the popular assembly of leaders of Rome's soldiers, another holdover from Etruscan rule), the consuls held office for one year. At first only patricians could serve as consuls, but in 360 B.C.E. the first plebeian consul was elected. In later years of the Republic the consuls usurped the power of the Senate and gained the power to appoint the senators.

AT A GLANCE: THE ROMAN EMPIRE 500–50 B.C.E.

DATE	POLITICS	RELIGION AND CULTURE	SOCIAL DEVELOPMENT
500 B.C.E.	• Rome independent of Etruscan rule (509); Republic founded		
450 B.C.E.	• Rome sacked by Gauls (390)		• Laws of Twelve Tables promulgated
350 B.C.E.	• Roman expansion into Italy south of Po (327–304)		
300 B.C.E.	• First Punic War (264–241)		• Earliest Roman coinage (280–275)
250 B.C.E.	• Second Punic War (219) • Hannibal invaded Italy • Roman conquest of Cisalpine Gaul (202–191)	• Stoicism—Zeno	
200 B.C.E.	• Rome annexed Spain (197) • Conquest of Macedon (167)	• Polybius (200–118)	
150 B.C.E.	• Third Punic War (149–146) • T. Gracchus tribune (133) • G. Gracchus tribune (123 and 122) • Gallia Narbonensis a Roman province	• Carthage destroyed • Corinth destroyed	• *Pax Romana* led to widespread trade throughout Empire; roads built
100 B.C.E.	• Sulla conquers Greece • Civil war in Rome (83–82) • Conquest of Syria (66) • First Triumvirate (60)		• Spartacus slave revolt (73–71)
50 B.C.E.	• Civil war (49) • Julius Caesar dictator (47–44) • Second Triumvirate (43) • Annexation of Egypt (31) • Augustus Caesar (63 B.C.E.–14 C.E.)	• Cicero (106–43) • Virgil (70–19) • Jesus (c. 4 B.C.E.–c. 30 C.E.) • Augustus deified on his death • Forum in Rome • Livy (59 B.C.E.–17 C.E.)	

AT A GLANCE: THE ROMAN EMPIRE 1–550 C.E.

DATE	POLITICS	RELIGION AND CULTURE	SOCIAL DEVELOPMENT
1 C.E.	• Christianity reaches Rome • Invasion of Britain (43)		
50 C.E.	• Trajan (r. 98–117)	• Seneca (c. 4–65) • Destruction of Temple in Jerusalem (70) • Pompeii and Herculaneum buried by eruption of Vesuvius (79)	• Jewish revolt (66–73) • Roman women gain new rights
100 C.E.	• Dacia conquered by Trajan • Hadrian (r. 117–138)	• Tacitus (c. 56–c. 120) • Trajan's column and forum (112–113) • Pantheon in Rome • Hadrian's Wall	
150 C.E.	• Marcus Aurelius (r. 161–180)		
200 C.E.	• Caracalla (r. 212–17) • Decius (r. 249–51)	• Baths of Caracalla	• Roman citizenship for all males
250 C.E.	• Gallienus (r. 253–68)	• Persecution of Christians	
300 C.E.	• Constantine (r. 306–37)	• Edict of Milan (313) • Constantinople inaugurated (330)	
350 C.E.		• St. Augustine (354–430) • End of state support for paganism (394)	
400 C.E.	• Sack of Rome (410)		
450 C.E.	• End of Roman Empire in West (476)		
550 C.E.			• Justinian codifies Roman law; with Theodora, beautifies Constantinople

6.1 How did the early Republic take shape?

6.2

6.3

6.4

6.5

6.6

6.7

KEY TERMS

centuries The smallest units of the Roman army, each composed of some 100 foot soldiers and commanded by a *centurion*. A legion was made up of 60 centuries. Centuries also formed political divisions of Roman citizens.

dictator A leader elected at a time of crisis by the Senate of Rome for a short term, usually six months, and vested with extraordinary powers to deal with the situation.

The early empire ruled by armed force, and all Rome's senators were veterans of military service. They could be either patricians or plebeians. However, because soldiers provided their own arms, only men with some wealth and property could command and rise in the ranks. They in turn were ordered by class, according to the quality and cost of the weapons they provided, and then divided into military units called **centuries**, or groups of approximately 100, as they had been under the Etruscans. The *centurions*, leaders of the centuries, met in assembly to elect the senators and the magistrates, including the consuls.

At each level of administration, the officials were paired, so that they would have to consult with each other and neither could seize excessive power. The power of the former Etruscan kings, for example, was now shared between the two consuls in this new system of checks and balances; each consul had the power of veto over the other. (In extraordinary emergencies, the Senate could appoint a **dictator**, a leader with absolute emergency powers, elected for the limited term of six months.)

Roman Military Power

From its beginning, Rome was a military state. Rome's armies were central to its life, and they excelled in organization and technology. When necessary, they adopted creative innovations. Although at first they copied the Greek hoplite phalanxes (see the chapter entitled "Dawn of the Empires") in their military deployment, later Roman armies were reorganized. Small, flexible units, armed with swords and throwing javelins in place of the older spears, lined up with less experienced, younger troops in front, more tested troops behind them, and then, as the final resort, veterans of courage and proven valor. If the front ranks could not hold and fell back into the rear lines, the advancing, overconfident enemy was suddenly confronted by a compact mass of soldiers of the greatest numbers and skill.

6.1

How did Rome build its empire on military expansion?

6.2

6.3

6.4

6.5

6.6

6.7

Although it had never previously possessed a navy, Rome built one that conquered Carthage, the greatest seapower of the day. The Romans learned to build sophisticated warships by capturing one from Carthage and copying it. Confronting great walled towns in the east, Rome developed unprecedented machinery to besiege the walls, catapult firepower into them, and batter them down. The Roman preference for massing overwhelming strength and their willingness to let time work on their side through siege warfare brought many victories with minimal losses of their own.

The Expansion of the Republic

6.2 How did Rome build its empire on military expansion?

The Roman Republic established alliances with other nearby city-states in west-central Italy, and began to challenge the Etruscans. In 396 B.C.E., after a siege of six years, the Romans captured Veii, a principal Etruscan city only 12 miles from Rome. Celtic invaders sacked Rome itself in 390 B.C.E., but the setback was brief, and Rome's expansion continued. By 264 B.C.E., Roman armies controlled all of Italy south of the Po valley.

The Roman Empire. Rome built its empire on military expansion, first within Italy by overthrowing its neighbors, then across the Mediterranean by defeating the Carthaginians, then northwest to Gaul and Britain and north to the Danube. Rome offered many benefits to the peoples it conquered, but finally its power rested in its armies.

6.1
6.2   How did Rome
       build its empire
6.3   on military
       expansion?
6.4

6.5

6.6

6.7

Rome became a society geared for war. Roman armies, and its new navy, continued to expand Roman rule. For the next 140 years its troops were almost constantly on the move. The most bitter and decisive of their battles were the three Punic Wars against Carthage.

The Punic Wars

Carthage, only 130 miles across the narrow waist of the Mediterranean from Italy, had developed as a major trade outpost of Phoenician seafarers. Just as Rome dominated Italy, the Carthaginians controlled the north-central coast of Africa and the western Mediterranean. One of their trade networks focused on the mineral wealth of Spain, especially its silver mines. To protect that route, Carthage developed ports and cities in Sicily and Sardinia. It even controlled trade outposts on the Italian mainland in Etruria. Carthage and Rome were set on a collision course.

The three wars that broke out are known as the Punic Wars after the Roman term for Phoenicians, *Punici*. The fighting opened in Sicily in 264 B.C.E. By 241 B.C.E., when the first Punic War ended, Rome was victorious both on land and at sea. It took control of Sicily and imposed taxes on the island. Four years later, Rome took advantage of a mutiny among Carthaginian troops in Sardinia to occupy Sardinia and Corsica. In 227 B.C.E., it annexed the islands. For the first time, Rome had provinces outside the Italian peninsula.

Carthage, however, rebuilt its forces, especially in Spain. When the Spanish city of Saguntum asked for Roman help, the Romans intervened, threatening Carthage's Spanish colonies. The brilliant 27-year-old Carthaginian commander Hannibal (247–183 B.C.E.) defeated Rome's troops in 219 B.C.E., and the second Punic War had begun. It continued for almost 20 years.

Hannibal unexpectedly took the offensive by land, marching tens of thousands of troops and 37 elephants 1,000 miles along the French coast, over the Alps, into the Po valley, and toward Rome. In two months he overran most of northern Italy and destroyed the armies sent against him. But Hannibal could not break the power of Rome. Most of Rome's allies remained loyal, and Rome raised new armies, as well as recapturing cities that had previously gone over to Hannibal. Hannibal did annihilate a Roman army at Cannae in southern Italy, but ultimately he was isolated there. Meanwhile, Rome won victories in Spain in 211–206 B.C.E., especially under the general Publius Cornelius Scipio. In 204 B.C.E. Scipio invaded Africa. Hannibal returned to defend his homeland, but Scipio, later named Scipio Africanus for his victory, defeated him at the Battle of Zama (202 B.C.E.). The war was over, and Carthage became a dependency of Rome.

The "New Wisdom." In its treatment of the rebellious city of Capua and its surrounding region of Campania, just to the south of Rome, the Romans exhibited what would become known as their "New Wisdom," a policy of brute force toward their enemies. Roman leaders executed 70 senators, imprisoned 300 Campanian aristocrats, and put others into the custody of trusted allies. They sold the mass of Campanian citizens into slavery, although they allowed resident aliens, former slaves, and petty tradesmen and artisans to continue to work.

A half-century later, Rome again responded with brute force after Carthage attacked Rome's African ally, King Masinissa of Numidia. Disregarding Carthage's legitimate claims that its land was being encroached upon, Rome sided with its ally and provoked the third Punic War (149–146 B.C.E.). With the aged Cato calling in the Roman Senate for the complete destruction of Carthage, Rome razed it to the ground, sold its survivors into slavery, and sowed salt into the soil so that it would never again flourish. The Romans annexed all of Carthage into the Roman province of Africa. Rome had become mistress of the Mediterranean.

SOURCE

Artifactual Records

Rome has bequeathed rich material artifacts. Much of the infrastructure of the empire—its roads, aqueducts, stadia, public baths, forums, temples, triumphal arches—as well as substantial parts of many of the military camps and cities it constructed still stand. Roman coinage and statuary are everywhere.

The cities of Pompeii and Herculaneum, comprising a total population of about 20,000, were buried in dust and cinders in the volcanic eruption of Mount Vesuvius in 79 C.E. Archaeologists uncovered these remains, forgotten for almost two millennia, in the late eighteenth century, providing an unparalleled view of the structure and furnishings of these provincial towns. Preserved like time capsules, they reveal their urban design, buildings, furniture, and household objects.

Pompeii was a walled town, with seven gates, a forum, a council chamber, offices of magistrates, temples dedicated to Apollo and Jupiter, market buildings, a stock exchange, a law court, a theater, auditoriums, an amphitheater for gladiatorial contests and wild beast hunts, three Turkish-style baths, workshops, shops, brothels, and homes. Carbonized food, preserved and sealed in hot volcanic mud, suggests that at least some of the inhabitants ate well. Walls, surviving to their full height, have preserved vivid murals from the residences and businesses. At least some Pompeiians had cultivated aesthetic sensibilities. Some of the art in the seven brothels indicates also a cultivated taste for pornography.

In the countryside, archaeologists have also been able to reconstruct *latifundia*, rural estates that were controlled by rich owners who bought up family farms and ran them as plantations. Offshore searches have uncovered sunken ships in the Italian Mediterranean that shed light on Roman trade missions and their cargoes.

Archaeological digs have also uncovered the history of the many Gothic, Celtic, and other groups of migrating peoples who lived on the fringes of the empire, later settled within its territories, and finally established their own states on those lands as the empire disintegrated. Their settlements, burial grounds, tools, and artwork yield significant information about their lives, even though they had no writing systems until they learned from the Romans.

With such extensive artifacts complementing the rich documentary record, scholars can reconstruct the rise and fall of the Roman Empire and its relationships with neighboring peoples. Relatively abundant materials provide the sources also to explore new topics, such as the extent of slavery, the treatment of women, and patterns of health and disease in ancient Rome.

The young Hercules wrestling with a snake, fresco, House of the Vettii, Pompeii.

The body of a man petrified by ash from the eruption of Mount Vesuvius, Pompeii, 79 C.E.

6.1
6.2 How did Rome build its empire on military expansion?
6.3
6.4
6.5
6.6
6.7

Rome's brutal use of military power served as a warning to potential foes. Roman generals were not pressed to win quick, brilliant victories, but to defeat the enemy through patient, deliberate preparation and decisive force. Ideally, the enemy would be so awed by Roman forces that it would never dare oppose them. Rome might prefer to rule by hegemony, with the consent of the people it conquered, but ultimately it did not flinch from the brute force of domination.

Further Expansion

After Rome had eliminated the Carthaginian threat with the end of the second Punic War, it turned to the conquest of the Gauls in northern Italy and annexed their territory, 202–191 B.C.E. It annexed Spain in 197 B.C.E. but treated that province so harshly that constant revolts simmered until Rome finally crushed them in 133 B.C.E. Rome then turned its power toward Gaul (modern France). In southern Gaul, Rome's ally Massilia (Marseilles) asked for help against Gallic tribes, and by 121 B.C.E. Rome had annexed most of the region.

The Eastern Mediterranean. The Romans were opportunists, seizing land wherever they saw weakness. Even as they conquered territory in the west, they expanded in the east as well. In the eastern Mediterranean, the Romans encountered Macedonians and Greeks, the proud heirs of Alexander the Great, who still ruled the lands that he had conquered and Hellenized. Rome's first battle on Greek soil came in 200 B.C.E., and it was the start of the complete restructuring of political power in the eastern Mediterranean.

At the death of Alexander the Great in 323 B.C.E., his empire had divided into three regional kingdoms. In 203–202 B.C.E. two of these kingdoms, Macedonia and Syria, where the Seleucid dynasty ruled, combined to threaten the third, Egypt, where the Ptolemaic family ruled. Neighboring Greek city-states encouraged Rome to use these divisions to establish its own balance of power in the region. Rome accepted the invitation. It warned Macedonia not to interfere in Greek affairs. When Philip V of Macedon (r. 211–179 B.C.E.) rejected this warning, the Romans attacked and defeated him. In victory, the Romans declared the Greek city-states of the eastern Mediterranean "free," granting them nominal independence, but, in fact, placing them under Roman control.

Rome had similarly warned Antiochus III, the Great, of Syria (r. 223–187 B.C.E.) to stay out of Europe and Egypt. When Antiochus ignored the warning, Roman forces crushed him, pushed him back to Syria, and forced him to pay a huge indemnity.

In the next generation, Rome decisively defeated Philip V's son Perseus in 168 B.C.E., ending the Macedonian monarchy. In the same year, Rome again protected Egypt from the Seleucids, asserting its own control of the eastern Mediterranean.

Here, too, Rome applied the brutal tactics of the "New Wisdom." In 148 B.C.E., when the Greek city-state of Corinth and its allies flouted Roman wishes, and even attacked Roman envoys, Rome razed Corinth to the ground, sold all its surviving inhabitants into slavery, and carried its artistic works to Rome. Recognizing Rome's power, the king of Pergamum, in Asia Minor, bequeathed his lands to Rome at his death in 133 B.C.E. Throughout the Mediterranean, Rome was now the dominant power.

In the east, the general Gnaeus Pompeius Magnus (Pompey the Great) (106–48 B.C.E.) added Syria and most of Asia Minor to the empire. In 63 B.C.E. he captured Jerusalem, the capital of Judea, allowing a Jewish king to rule as a client-monarch. Pompey favored such indirect rule through local potentates throughout the east, where sophisticated governmental structures had existed for centuries. He also founded some 40 cities as centers of Roman political influence.

View the **Closer Look**: Spoils from Jerusalem on the Arch of Titus in Rome on **MyHistoryLab**

The Politics of Imperial Rule

6.3 How did the Romans win support from the people they conquered?

6.1

6.2

6.3

How did the
Romans win
support from
the people they
conquered?

6.4

6.5

6.6

6.7

Empires are ultimately sustained by military force, but successful empires must also win at least some degree of support from among the conquered peoples. Beginning with its early conquests, Rome had often won such support through its political, cultural, economic, and ideological policies, but most importantly through the granting of citizenship. As it expanded, Rome frequently offered its opponents a choice between alliance and conquest. Subsequently it bestowed various levels of Roman citizenship throughout Italy to induce its residents to support Rome and join its armies.

Citizens of Rome

All free men from Rome were automatically citizens of Rome; the rest of the men of Italy, however, were not. In 381 B.C.E. the town of Tusculum, some 15 miles from Rome and surrounded by Roman territory, seemed poised to oppose Rome. The Romans won over the Tusculuns by offering incorporation into Rome and full citizenship, including voting rights, legal rights over property, legal enforcement of contracts, the right to marry Roman citizens, freedom from property taxes, and protection against arbitrary arrest and punishment. In 338 B.C.E. full citizenship was bestowed on four additional Latin cities, in the vicinity of Rome, while some other cities were granted partial citizenship.

In 91 B.C.E. Marcus Livius Drusus the Younger was elected tribune. Drusus proposed extending citizenship and the vote to all Rome's Italian allies, but the Senate rejected the proposal. Drusus was later assassinated, leaving the Italians frustrated and furious. So began the "Social War" or "War of the Allies." After two years, however, Rome did offer full citizenship to all Italians who had remained loyal, and even to those who agreed to put down their arms. It extended full citizenship north as far as the Po River, and partial citizenship up to the Alps. So, grudgingly, citizenship was offered as an inducement to loyalty. In newly annexed lands, the aristocrats, the group to whom Rome usually granted these rights and obligations, regarded even partial citizenship as attractive.

The Politics of Private Life

Asymmetrical power relationships characterized all of Roman life—private as well as public—under the Republic. The earliest enduring social structure in Rome was the **patron–client relationship**. Strong men acted as protectors of the weak; the weak, in turn, provided obedience and services for the strong, as requested.

In civilian life, patrons, usually patricians, would provide legal protection and representation for their clients, usually plebeians. In exchange, the client was expected to help to pay fines and public charges levied against his patron and to help to provide dowries for his patron's daughters at marriage. To mark the symbolism of the relationship, the client was to present himself periodically at the residence or office of the patron, and the patron was to give him a small gift at that time. The patron–client relationship was also protected by law, and a patron who defrauded a client was subject to execution, later commuted to exile and confiscation of property.

The relationship of ex-masters to ex-slaves was of patron to client, and it was frequently characterized by warm feelings, especially if freedom was granted by gift of manumission rather than by the slave's purchase. These relationships often endured through several generations. Similar patron–client relationships between strong and weak later characterized Rome's imperial control over conquered provinces.

KEY TERM

patron–client relationship In a patron–client relationship, the patron offers protection and, often, employment, while the client offers obedience, labor, and services in exchange. Sometimes these relationships are formalized under law. More frequently they exist in place of law, in situations where legal structures are weak or nonexistent. Patron–client relationships are common throughout world history.

169

Contemporary Historians Evaluate the History of Rome

During the later Republic historians began consciously to write the history of the city. Their accounts were often ambivalent, revealing a mixture of pride in the conquests and achievements of their empire with skepticism and even hostility toward the abandonment of the earlier republican ideals.

The most famous of the early historians was Polybius (c. 200–c. 118 B.C.E.), a Greek taken to Rome as a political captive. Polybius marveled at the overwhelming event of his own time, Rome's conquest of an empire through its victories over Carthage, Macedonia, and Spain:

> There can surely be no one so petty or so apathetic in his outlook that he has no desire to discover by what means and under what system of government the Romans succeeded in less than fifty-three years [220–167 B.C.E.] in bringing under their rule almost the whole of the inhabited world, an achievement which is without parallel in human history.
>
> (*The Histories* I:1, cited in Finley, p. 443)

Livy (59 B.C.E.–17 C.E.) praised the glories of Rome's imperial expansion, but he decried the resulting class conflict between Rome's aristocrats and its common people, which was currently ripping apart Rome's self-governing, elected, republican form of government.

Tacitus (c. 56–c. 120 C.E.) continued the story to the height of imperial power. He praised the heroism of the Roman conquerors, but he also understood the anguish and bitterness of the conquered peoples. In *Agricola*, Tacitus attributes to the Celtic chieftain Calgacus one of the most devastating critiques of imperialism ever articulated. In Tacitus' account, Calgacus condemns the Romans, whose tyranny cannot be escaped by any act of reasonable submission.

> These brigands of the world have exhausted the land by their rapacity, so they now ransack the sea. When their enemy is rich, they lust after wealth; when the enemy is poor, they lust after power. Neither East nor West has satisfied their hunger. They are unique among humanity insofar as they equally covet the rich and the poor. Robbery, butchery, and rapine they call "Empire." They create a desert and call it "Peace."
>
> (I:129)

As the empire began to decay, mainstream historians added more critical perspectives. Dio Cassius (c. 150–235 C.E.) nostalgically recalled the rule of Augustus as Rome's golden age and lamented the empire's subsequent decline "from a monarchy of gold to one of iron and rust." Like Tacitus, he cited and sympathized with the frustration and rage of those like Boudicca, the warrior-queen of the Celts, who led her armies in revolt against the Romans in 61 C.E.:

> We have been despised and trampled underfoot by men who know nothing else than how to secure gain.
>
> (Lewis and Reinhold, II:334)

Other historians illuminated the empire from its fringes rather than from its center, and they, too, were often critical of the effects of empire on its subjects. For Jewish historians, such as Philo of Alexandria (c. 13 B.C.E.–c. 45 C.E.) and Josephus (c. 37–c. 100 C.E.), and Christian theologians, such as Tertullian (c. 155–c. 225 C.E.) and St. Augustine, bishop of Hippo in North Africa (354–430 C.E.), the Roman Empire was not the central concern, but it was an inescapable presence. These historians, philosophers, and theologians had to take account of Rome's power in their own teaching, writing, and actions. From their marginal positions, they usually counseled realistic accommodation to Rome's power.

In addition to these formal histories, leading men of the empire left important documents that shed light on their times. The great orator and political leader Cicero (106–43 B.C.E.) left dozens of letters, 57 public speeches, and extensive writings on public affairs. Julius Caesar's account of the Gallic Wars describes his military organization and strategy, the Roman virtues that characterized his troops, and the lands and peoples against which he fought. It is the only account of a Roman war written by a participant that has endured to today. In part, Caesar was writing a propaganda piece, preparing the path for his later assertion of personal power in Rome.

Caesar's accounts are filled with great slaughter. For example, in 58 B.C.E., he reported that his armies slaughtered 226,000 Helvetii, with only some 110,000 surviving. In the same year he reports killing almost an entire German army of 120,000 men and, the next year, almost every soldier in a Belgic army of 60,000 men. He captured the region around Namur in northern France and sold all 53,000 inhabitants into slavery. In 56 B.C.E., he massacred two German peoples, killing as many as 460,000 people, including women and children. By the end of nine years of war in Gaul, Caesar reports a total of 1,192,000 enemy killed and another million captured.

- Which Roman authors and historians saw the expansion of the Roman Empire as unfortunate for the people of Rome? Why? Do you agree? Why or why not?
- Name Jews and Christians whose writings shed light on the Roman Empire. What topics did they address that are useful in understanding empires?
- If you could join archaeologists at a Roman site, which site would you like to explore? Why?

The Roman Family

Patron–client relationships also marked the structure of the family. The father of the family, the *paterfamilias*, had the right of life and death over his children as long as he lived. In reality, most fathers were not tyrants, and in exercising the right to choose their children's occupations and spouses, and to control their economic possessions, they would normally try to consider their children's needs and desires. Nevertheless, fathers had the legal power to act as they wished: they continued to have control over their daughters' economic lives even after their marriages, for this did not pass to the husbands. These rights were enshrined in the law of *patria potestas*, the right of the head of the household.

According to Roman custom and practice, a woman's role was subordinate to a man's. A woman was legally subject to her father as long as he lived. After his death, she was required to obey the advice of her husband or a legally appointed guardian in any kind of legal or business transaction. Actual practice was, however, more liberal. If a woman had reached adulthood, she usually gained her independence at the death of her father, as did her brothers. Also, at least as early as the fifth century B.C.E., a wife could block the legal powers of her husband by absenting herself from his home for three nights in a row each year.

The families of the bride and groom arranged their marriages. Motherhood was considered the most significant rite of passage for a woman. Freeborn women were exempted from the legal control of their father, husband, or guardian after giving birth to three children; women who had been freed from slavery were exempted after the birth of four.

Romans respected women if they lived chastely and more or less contentedly within these guidelines of family, motherhood, and domesticity. The feminine ideal was the faithful and loyal *univira*, the "one-man woman." A woman caught in adultery was banished from her home and might well be executed; men apprehended in adultery were not punished. Women found drinking wine could also be punished; men could not. These principles of behavior were, of course, fully applicable only to the upper classes. The masses of lower-class free women entered the working world outside the home, and slaves had little control over their lives. The prevalence of prostitution and brothels further indicate the limited applicability of the Roman female ideal.

Class Conflict: Urban Splendor and Squalor

Imperial expansion exacerbated class conflicts within Rome. The benefits of the conquests went mostly to the rich, while the independent small farmers who served as the troops were often bankrupted by the wars. After serving in the army for years, they would return home to find that in their absence their wives and children had not been able to maintain the family farms and might even have sold them to owners of large estates, called *latifundia*, and left for the city, impoverished.

Class divisions were most glaring in the capital. The city of Rome itself grew seemingly without limit and without adequate planning. As Rome came to control Italy and then the Mediterranean, the city's population multiplied, reaching one million by about the first century C.E.

Some of the newcomers were wealthy and powerful, and they adorned the city by adding new examples of Greek architecture and urban design to the earlier Etruscan forms. They replaced wood, mud, and local volcanic rock with concrete and finer

6.1

6.2

6.3

6.4

6.5

6.6

6.7

How did the Romans win support from the people they conquered?

KEY TERM

paterfamilias The head of a family or household in Roman law—always a male—and the only member to have full legal rights. The *paterfamilias* had absolute power over his family, extending to life and death.

Mosaic of Neptune and Amphitrite (detail), Herculaneum, before 79 C.E. Art sometimes seems to contradict the legal evidence concerning gender relationships in the Roman Empire. The artist responsible for this mosaic of the sea god Neptune and his wife, Amphitrite, has accorded the couple apparent equality.

6.1

6.2

6.3

6.4

6.5

6.6

6.7

How did the
Romans win
support from
the people they
conquered?

stone. Augustus himself would later boast that he had found Rome a city of brick and left it one of marble (see below). A modern urban historian has described the private homes of the wealthy patricians as models of comfort:

> The houses of the patricians, spacious, airy, sanitary, equipped with bathrooms and water closets, heated in winter by hypocausts, which carried hot air through chambers in the floors, were perhaps the most commodious and comfortable houses built for a temperate climate anywhere until the twentieth century; a triumph of domestic architecture. (Mumford, p. 220)

The poor also came streaming into the city, but from bankrupt family farms. For them, Rome was a nightmare. The contrast was shocking.

> Not only were these buildings unheated, unprovided with waste pipes or water closets, unadapted to cooking; not merely did they contain an undue number of airless rooms, indecently overcrowded: though poor in all the facilities that make for decent daily living, they were in addition so badly built and so high that they offered no means of safe exit from the frequent fires that occurred. And if their tenants escaped typhoid, typhus, fire, they might easily meet their death in the collapse of the whole structure. Such accidents were all too frequent …
>
> The main population of the city that boasted its world conquests lived in cramped, noisy, airless, foul-smelling, infected quarters, paying extortionate rents to merciless landlords, undergoing daily indignities and terrors that coarsened and brutalized them, and in turn demanded compensatory outlets. (Mumford, pp. 220–21)

Canopus, Hadrian's Villa, Tivoli, c. 135 C.E. Rome's wealthy and powerful elites commanded private luxuries beyond the imagination of the average Roman. The Villa of the emperor Hadrian comprised a series of buildings, gardens, and pools—this one representing a well-known Egyptian canal—laid out on the side of a hill in Tivoli. The complex was designed to bring the more sophisticated pleasures of city life to the country.

Attempts at Reform

The most exemplary of the leaders who tried to achieve equity for Rome's poorer citizens were the reforming Gracchi brothers, Tiberius Sempronius Gracchus (163–133 B.C.E.) and Gaius Sempronius Gracchus (153–121 B.C.E.). In 133 B.C.E., while serving as tribune of the people, the office established to protect the interest of the plebeians, Tiberius proposed distributing some public lands among the poor, especially among poor soldiers. Opposed to this liberal proposal, and fearing that Tiberius was attempting to gain too much political power for himself, a number of senators, supported by their clients, clubbed him and 300 of his supporters to death. This was the first political murder over a public policy issue in Rome in nearly 400 years; class conflict boiled over into violence within the Senate itself. Despite the murder, the redistribution of public land did take place.

In 123 B.C.E., Gaius Gracchus was elected tribune. He extended his brother's plan for land redistribution by establishing new colonies for the resettlement of some of the poor people of Rome in the regions conquered in the Punic Wars, including Carthage itself. He also introduced subsidized grain sales—later extended into a dole of free bread—to Rome's poor people. Gaius argued that citizenship should be granted to all Latins and to the local civic officials in all other communities.

He was not equally sensitive to the problems of non-Italians, however, for his legislation exploited the provinces by enabling Roman knights, the second tier of the military elite, to serve as "**publicans**," or **tax farmers**. These tax farmers struck an agreement with the state to turn over a fixed amount of net taxes from their region while retaining the right to collect as much as they were able and to keep the balance for themselves. Tax farming enabled the state to collect taxes without monitoring the process; it enabled the tax farmers to become wealthy; and it exploited the people who were being taxed, leaving them without protection. Gaius auctioned off the collection of taxes in Asia. While this profited the elite and helped to secure their loyalty to him personally, it impoverished the residents of the Roman province of Asia. Many senators became increasingly hostile to Gaius Gracchus, and in 121 B.C.E. he too was assassinated, along with his fellow tribune, Flaccus. Some 3,000 of his supporters were executed.

The reforms of the Gracchi brothers seemed blocked, but in fact they laid the foundations for the events that led to the end of the Republic a century later. They

KEY TERM

publicans or **tax farmers**
Collected taxes on behalf of the government, paying in an agreed sum but keeping for themselves any surplus they could extort. The system was extremely oppressive to those who were taxed.

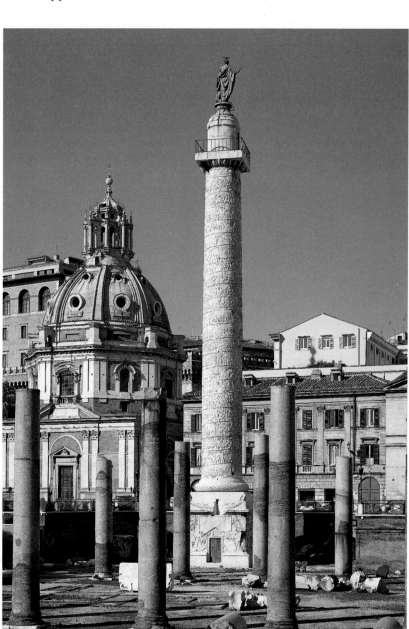

Column of Trajan, Rome, dedicated 113 C.E. The Romans built tall commemorative columns in order to celebrate the power and military might of the empire. The Column of Trajan is covered with a continuous strip of carving that tells the story of the emperor Trajan's victories over the barbarian tribes along the Danube.

6.1

6.2

6.3 How did the
Romans win
support from
6.4 the people they
conquered?

6.5

6.6

6.7

challenged the power of the Senate and exposed the problems of the poor and the war veterans, while their enemies employed violence, murder, and thuggery as tools for fashioning and implementing public policy.

"Bread and Circuses." A new method of coping with class conflict developed: "**bread and circuses.**" Rome bribed the poor, many of them former soldiers from its conquering armies, with a dole of free bread. Up to 200,000 people were served each day. The dole encouraged them to while away their time in public religious festivities, races, the theater, and gladiatorial contests of great cruelty, which pitted man against man and man against beast in spectacles witnessed by tens of thousands. The public arenas of Rome, including Rome's largest race-track and stadia, could accommodate about half of Rome's adult population. On days of gladiatorial contests of strength, endurance, and cunning, hundreds of men and as many as 5,000 animals, including elephants and water buffalo, might be slaughtered in a single day. This combination of free food and gory spectacle was offered to keep the unemployed urban masses compliant.

Later, emperors continued these policies without actually solving the problems of unemployment and lack of dignity. Until its final collapse, the empire was threatened by unrest and revolt, and one of the reasons for the later popularity of Christianity in Rome was its message of compassion and salvation for the poor and downtrodden (see the chapter entitled "Judaism and Christianity").

Slavery in Roman Life

As wealthy Romans assembled vast estates and Roman armies captured valuable underground mineral resources, they needed labor for farming and mining. Increasingly, they turned to the acquisition of slaves. Through military conquest, piracy, and raids in foreign regions, Rome accumulated slaves numbering perhaps in the millions. Short wars yielded thousands, longer conflicts hundreds of thousands. In his nine years in Gaul (see below), Julius Caesar may have captured nearly half a million slaves. As much as a quarter of Rome's agricultural labor force was slave labor. Among the one million residents of the city of Rome, as many as 400,000 were slaves.

"Every slave we own is an enemy we harbor," was a sardonic Roman proverb by the time of **Caesar Augustus** (Lewis and Reinhold, I:245). That emperor proclaimed in his epitaph that in successful campaigns against pirates, "I turned over to their masters for punishment nearly 30,000 fugitive slaves who had taken up arms against the state" (Lewis and Reinhold, I:569). Three great slave revolts grew into wars. During the Great Slave War in Sicily (134–131 B.C.E.), 70,000 slaves resorted to armed resistance. In 104–100 B.C.E., a second revolt broke out in Sicily when it seemed that Germanic tribes would invade Italy and keep the imperial troops occupied in the north. Finally, Spartacus, a runaway slave who had been forced into training as a gladiator, led a revolt among his fellow gladiators that continued for two years, 73–71 B.C.E. In the end, after suffering many defeats, the Romans crushed the Spartacus revolt mercilessly. Some 100,000 slaves were killed in the fighting, and 6,000 captured slaves were crucified along the roads leading into Rome, their torture and death serving as a brutal warning to any other potential rebels.

Slaves continued throughout the imperial centuries as a threat within the Roman Empire. When foreign armies later invaded Rome successfully, slaves often revolted and joined them. For example, when an army of Goths invaded in 410 C.E., "day by day almost all the slaves who were in Rome poured out of the city to join the barbarians, who now numbered about forty thousand" (Zosimus, *New History*, cited in Lewis and Reinhold, II:626).

Read the **Document**: **Slaves in Roman Law (2d c., 5th c. CE)** on **MyHistoryLab**

KEY TERMS

bread and circuses Provision by the government of free food and entertainment, designed to divert the masses, and especially the poor masses, from engaging in political action.

Caesar Augustus "Caesar" and "Augustus" are both titles of the emperor Octavian. Caesar means ruler or emperor, and the word comes down to the present in the title czar or tsar. Augustus means dignified, even majestic. It was sometimes used in place of Octavian's given name. The words could also be reversed as Augustus Caesar.

The End of the Republic

6.4 How did the generals' power struggles lead to the end of the Republic?

In the militaristic empire that was Rome, generals gained power. At first Rome's military leaders were constrained by the aristocratic Senate and the general assembly of Rome, but later they themselves began giving the orders. Eventually their struggles for power would lead to civil war and the end of the Republic.

6.1

6.2

6.3

6.4

How did the generals' power struggles lead to the end of the Republic?

6.5

6.6

6.7

Generals in Politics

General Gaius Marius campaigned to have himself elected consul in 107 B.C.E. He broke with the normal practice of recruiting only troops who owned property, and accepted soldiers who were indebted to him personally for their maintenance. Elected consul six times between 107 and 100 B.C.E., Marius restructured the armies

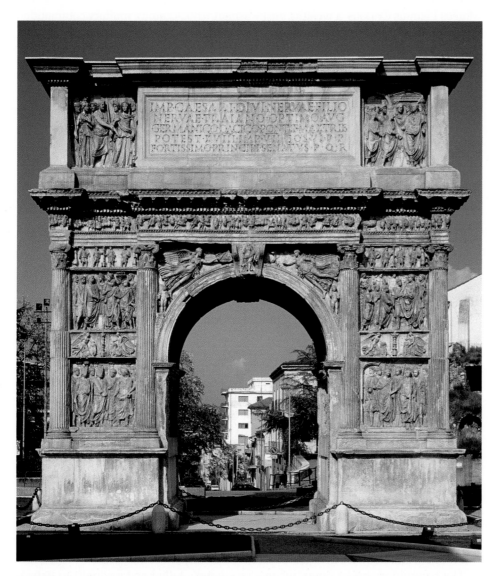

Arch of Trajan, Benevento, 114–117 C.E. Triumphal arches are another peculiarly Roman means of celebrating the power of the ruler and his empire. This particular arch, dedicated to Trajan, stands at the point where the road to Brindisi, a port on the east coast of Italy, branches off the Appian Way, the first major road in the Romans' strategic network.

6.1
6.2
6.3
6.4 How did the generals' power struggles lead to the end of the Republic?
6.5
6.6
6.7

to increase their efficiency. He arranged large allotments of land for veteran soldiers in North Africa, Gaul, Sicily, Greece, and Macedonia, a move that solved temporarily one of the great problems of Rome: how to accommodate soldiers returning home after long tours of duty. The armies now depended for their welfare on Marius rather than on the state.

The generals began to compete among themselves for power. At the highest level, the struggle between the generals Lucius Sulla and Gaius Marius precipitated civil war in Rome. To fight against Mithridates VI, king of Pontus (r. 120–63 B.C.E.), the Senate called Sulla. Marius, however, arranged to have the command transferred to himself. In response, Sulla rallied soldiers loyal to him and invaded Rome, initiating the first civil war (83–82 B.C.E.). He declared Marius an outlaw and left with his troops for Greece, where he defeated Mithridates. Meanwhile Marius, joined by another general, Lucius Cornelius Cinna, seized Rome and banned Sulla. Sulla returned with his army, invaded Italy and Rome, had himself declared dictator, a position he held for two years, and then abdicated.

Twenty years later, in 60 B.C.E., two great generals, Julius Caesar and Pompey, and Marcus Licinius Crassus, a wealthy businessman who became a military commander, formed a **triumvirate**, a ruling alliance of three men. The three competed among themselves, however, until Caesar defeated the others.

The Dictatorship of Julius Caesar

Born in Rome of an aristocratic patrician family about 100 B.C.E., Caesar felt the hand of the military dictator Sulla as a young man when Sulla ordered him to divorce his wife, Cornelia, daughter of Cinna, Sulla's great rival. Caesar refused. Biographers are not sure whether this was because of Caesar's love for Cornelia, exceptional personal pride, an assessment that the alliance with Cinna's faction would, in the long run, prove advantageous, or some combination of calculations. In any case, Caesar's refusal was unusual in a world where aristocratic marriages—and divorces—were usually contracted for political purposes. (Caesar, for example, later married his 17-year-old daughter to the 47-year-old Pompey.) No one else, not even Pompey the Great, refused Sulla's commands. It was also out of character for Caesar himself, a man who had already begun to earn a growing reputation for marital infidelity, including rumors of some homosexual activity (Grant, *Julius Caesar*, pp. 23–24, 33–39).

To escape Sulla's grasp, Caesar fled into exile in the Greek islands where he studied philosophy and oratory until he was pardoned and returned to Rome. He was elected magistrate in 65 B.C.E., with responsibilities for producing public games. Pouring his own money as well as public and borrowed funds into the task, he won widespread acclaim. His prominence increased when he was elected chief priest, *pontifex maximus*, of the Roman state in 63 B.C.E., a position of greater prestige and patronage than religious significance. Reaching toward the pinnacle of political power, Caesar was elected to the judicial office of **praetor** in 60 B.C.E. and to the highest executive office of consul in 59 B.C.E. A military man, he sometimes used strong-arm methods to intimidate the Senate, on one occasion having his fellow consul attacked and beaten.

In Rome, military prowess counted most, and Caesar was Rome's most successful general. In 58 B.C.E. he led his armies on a mission to dominate Gaul and protect it from invaders. (This move also got him out of Rome at the end of his term as consul, thus escaping legal prosecution for his abuse of power in office.) Nine years of military campaigns brought all of Gaul under Rome. Caesar also briefly crossed the Rhine River, to demonstrate that Rome had the capacity to invade the Germanic territories if it wished, and he twice invaded Britain, also briefly.

The triumvirate broke down when Crassus was killed as he sought to extend Rome's empire in the east. Pompey now saw Caesar as his direct rival, and Rome again dissolved into civil war. Pompey was defeated in a series of battles and was finally killed while seeking refuge in Egypt. Caesar ruled Rome alone, but only briefly.

KEY TERMS

triumvirate Literally, an association of three strong men. An unofficial coalition of Julius Caesar, Pompey, and Crassus formed in 60 B.C.E. After Caesar's murder in 44 B.C.E., a triumvirate including his heir Octavian (later Augustus), Mark Antony, and Marcus Lepidus was appointed to maintain public order.

praetor In ancient Rome, the term was originally applied to the consul as leader of an army. In 366 B.C.E. a further praetor was elected with special responsibility for the administration of justice in Rome, with the right of military command. Further praetors were subsequently appointed to administer the increasing number of provinces.

Jealous of, and frightened by, his extraordinary powers, Roman senators stabbed Caesar to death on the Ides of March (March 15), 44 B.C.E.

In his three years as dictator, Caesar revised the Roman calendar, creating the Julian calendar, which lasted for 1,500 years (and is still used by some churches); reorganized Rome's city government; extended citizenship to the peoples of many conquered provinces; continued the policy of free bread and circuses; and appointed many of his opponents to public office in an attempt at reconciliation. He resolved one of the most intractable problems of Rome's citizens: the debts that had piled up during the years of civil war. He forced creditors to accept payment in land and property valued at prewar prices, and he canceled all interest due since the wars began. Caesar selected his sister Julia's grandson, Gaius Octavius (63 B.C.E.–14 C.E.), later called Octavian, as his heir. Following Caesar's assassination, this adopted son avenged his death by murdering 300 senators and 2,000 knights; triumphed over Lepidus and Mark Antony, the two rivals who had been his colleagues in a second triumvirate; and became the unchallenged ruler of Rome for more than half a century.

To avert civil war, Octavian used his sister Octavia as a diplomatic and political tool, marrying her to his rival, Antony (83–30 B.C.E.), in 40 B.C.E. In 36 B.C.E., Antony openly married the alluring and seductive queen of Egypt, Cleopatra (r. 51–30 B.C.E.), even though he was already married to Octavia, and established his headquarters in Egypt, the richest state in the east. By sharing local rule with Cleopatra, Antony betrayed Rome's imperial policies. Eventually, Antony discarded and divorced Octavia, humiliating Octavian personally as well as infuriating him politically. The warfare between the two men became especially bitter. Octavian finally defeated Antony and Cleopatra in the decisive naval battle at Actium (31 B.C.E.), formally annexed Egypt, and seized the Egyptian treasury for himself. Octavian now controlled more wealth than the Roman state.

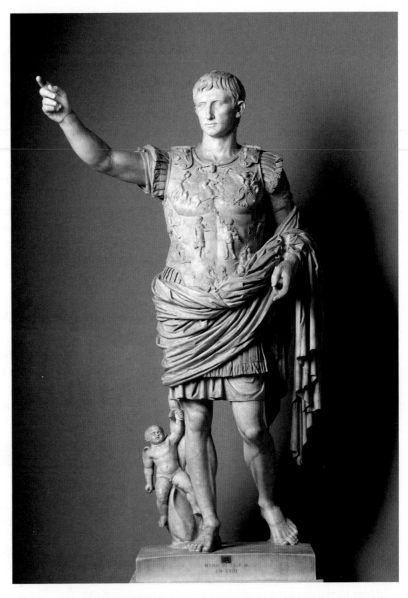

Augustus of Prima Porta, early first century C.E. With the gratitude of the Senate of Rome, which was weary of civil warfare among its generals, Augustus transformed Rome into an imperial monarchy under his control. (Musei Vaticani, Rome)

The Roman Principate, 30 B.C.E.–330 C.E.

6.5 What were the achievements of Augustus and the Principate?

By 30 B.C.E., following 14 years of civil war, Octavian had become master of a reunified Roman world. A grateful Senate, weary of seemingly endless civil wars, heaped him with honors, including, in 27 B.C.E., the title *Augustus*, meaning "sacred" or "venerable." His achievements were immense, and after his death the Romans designated him a god.

6.1

6.2

6.3

6.4

6.5

What were the
achievements of
Augustus and the
Principate?

6.6

6.7

6.1
6.2
6.3
6.4
6.5
6.6
6.7

What were the achievements of Augustus and the Principate?

With Augustus, Rome became an imperial monarchy, a territorial, political, and economic empire ruled by a single military commander, the *imperator* (from which the term "emperor" is derived), and his armies. For years generals had wanted this centralized power. Now, in gratitude for his ending the civil wars, the Senate was willing to turn it over to Augustus. Augustus rejected the title of monarch, preferring to be called *princeps*, or first citizen. This gesture of humility fooled no one. With Augustus' reign, even though the Senate and the consuls and other magistrates survived, the imperial form of government began. From Augustus on, all real power in the Roman state lay in the hands of the emperor.

Augustus ruled Rome for 56 years until his death in 14 C.E. He fought wars that stabilized the borders of the empire while ensuring peace and facilitating trade, commerce, and economic growth throughout the Mediterranean. He restructured imperial administration into a form that lasted for almost two centuries. He inaugurated public projects that beautified Rome and kept its workers employed. He pacified the Roman masses and won over the aristocracy. He patronized the arts and literature, which flourished in a "Golden Age." He built new roads and cities throughout the length and breadth of the empire.

Family Life in the Age of Augustus

Augustus instituted conservative policies concerning family life. The growth of urban life, especially in Rome itself in the first century B.C.E., offered new opportunities to a few upper-class Roman women to gain education and even to participate in public life, although usually behind the scenes. New marriage laws enabled them to live as equals of their husbands and gave them the right to divorce and to act without

SOURCE

The Legacy and Epitaph of Augustus Caesar

Primary sources on Augustus' life are limited, and almost all his autobiography has been lost. Therefore, the *Res Gestae Divi Augusti* ("Account of the Accomplishments of Augustus") has become a crucial text. Written for the people of Rome by Augustus himself shortly before he died, and inscribed on several temples throughout the empire, it is his own statement of how he wanted to be remembered. Its 35 paragraphs cover the honors bestowed on him; his personal donations for public purposes; and his accomplishments in war and peace:

1. At the age of nineteen, on my own initiative and at my own expense, I raised an army by means of which I liberated the Republic ... the people elected me consul and a triumvir for the settlement of the commonwealth ...

3. I waged many wars throughout the whole world by land and by sea ... and when victorious I spared all citizens who sought pardon ... About 500,000 Roman citizens were under military oath to me.

15. To the Roman plebs I paid 300 sesterces apiece in accordance with the will of my father [Julius Caesar]; and in my fifth consulship [29 B.C.E.] I gave each 400 sesterces in my own name out of the spoil of war, reaching never less than 250,000 persons ... And in my fifth consulship [29 B.C.E.] I gave out of the spoils of war 1000 sesterces apiece to my soldiers settled in colonies ... received by about 120,000 persons ... In my thirteenth consulship [2 B.C.E.] I gave 60 denarii apiece to those of the plebs who at that time were receiving public grain ... a little more than 200,000 persons.

19. I built ... the senate house and ... the temple of Apollo ...

22. I gave a gladiatorial show three times in my own name, and five times in the names of my sons or grandsons; at these shows about 10,000 fought ... Twenty-six times I provided for the people ... hunting spectacles of African wild beasts in the circus or in the Forum or in the amphitheaters ...

23. I turned over to their masters for punishment nearly 30,000 slaves who had run away from their owners and taken up arms against the state.

28. I established colonies of soldiers in Africa, Sicily, Macedonia, in both Spanish provinces, in Achaea, Asia, Syria, Narbonese Gaul, and Pisidia. Italy, moreover, has 28 colonies established by me which grew large and prosperous in my lifetime ...

31. Royal embassies from India, never seen before any Roman general, were often sent to me. (Lewis and Reinhold, I:561–72)

reference to a legal guardian. They could own and control wealth in their own name. Women did not have access to the professions or to public political office, but several exercised great influence over their husbands, brothers, and sons.

Augustus sought to restore the earlier family order. He made adultery a criminal offense, punishable by exile, confiscation of property, and even execution. Indeed, he exiled his own daughter and only child, Julia, a charming and intelligent woman who offended him with her frequent and publicly known affairs. He encouraged marriage and childbearing, and punished celibacy. These laws were widely opposed and disobeyed, but they reveal the link in Augustus' mind between a well-ordered family and a well-ordered empire, a link that was repeated in the official policies of many empires throughout history. (Compare China and India, Britain, Japan, and Germany.)

6.1
6.2
6.3
6.4
What were the achievements of Augustus and the Principate? **6.5**
6.6
6.7

The Military under Augustus

Within Italy, captured city-states were required to supply not gold and taxes but men for the armies. At the time of Julius Caesar, the average Italian male served seven years in the army. Under Augustus, soldiering became more professional: men enlisted for between 16 and 25 years and were paid regular wages. Conquered peoples outside Italy also contributed troops to Rome's armies, while invaders were often encouraged to settle in Roman territories and to enlist in Roman armies. An outward spiral of imperial expansion resulted. As Rome expanded, so did its armed forces; it then expanded further, in part to capture the wealth needed to pay its larger armies; this expansion, in turn, enlarged its armies once more.

In the field, the soldiers built their own support systems: military camps; administrative towns; strings of fortress watchtowers along the borders; roads; and aqueducts. Many of the walled military camps were kernels from which sprouted later towns and cities, one of Rome's most distinctive contributions. (See illustration of Timgad, below.) These urban outposts established Rome's military and administrative rule in the midst of remote rural regions. In the reign of Augustus, these nodes were linked by 50,000 miles of first-class roads and 200,000 miles of lesser roads. The roads facilitated commerce and communication, but their original and fundamental purpose was to enable the swift movement of troops throughout the empire.

The Roman Empire Expands

As the empire continued to expand through military conquest, Rome's generals demanded, and were granted, increasing powers until, with Augustus, they supplanted republican, civilian government with an administration headed by the military commander-in-chief. Before we analyze the significance of this political transformation, however, let us complete our account of the continuing geographical expansion of the empire.

Augustus annexed modern Switzerland and Noricum (modern Austria and Bavaria) in 16–15 B.C.E., and established Rome's historical frontier in central Europe at the Danube River. After an attempt to conquer central Germany failed in 9 C.E., the Rhine became the normal border in the northeast.

In the 40s C.E. the Romans conquered modern England and Wales, which became the Roman province of Britain. Some 2,000 miles to the east, the emperor Trajan (r. 98–117 C.E.) conquered Dacia (modern Romania), and briefly annexed Armenia and Parthia (Mesopotamia).

Trajan's successor, Hadrian (r. 117–138 C.E.), consolidated Roman gains. He permanently withdrew the Roman forces from Mesopotamia back to the Euphrates and built a wall, west to east, across the narrow neck of the northern part of Britain. Twenty-five years later, his successor, Antoninus Pius (r. 138–161 C.E.), built another wall some 50 miles further north. The limits of the Roman Empire had been reached.

6.1
6.2
6.3
6.4
6.5 What were the achievements of Augustus and the Principate?
6.6
6.7

The policy of granting citizenship to consolidate empire continued on a limited basis as Rome expanded. In 14 C.E. Augustus Caesar announced that there were 4,937,000 citizens in the empire, about two million of them in the provinces. At that time, the total population of the empire was between 70 and 100 million. In 212 C.E., the emperor Caracalla (r. 212–17) officially proclaimed citizenship for all free males in the empire, although ambiguous legal restrictions limited the effect. Provincials could occupy the highest offices in the empire: senator, consul, and even emperor. The emperor Trajan was from Spain; Septimius Severus (r. 193–211) was from North Africa; Diocletian (r. 284–305) was from Dalmatia (modern Croatia).

The development of international law, the *jus gentium*, the law of nations, also helped to unite and pacify the empire. After its victory in the first Punic War in 241 B.C.E., Rome interacted more than ever with foreigners and with subjects of Rome who did not have citizenship. To deal with legal cases between Romans and others, a new official, the foreign magistrate, was appointed. The *jus gentium* evolved from his judgments. Over time, this law was codified, first by Hadrian, and later, in the east, by the emperor Justinian (see box below).

Economic and Trade Policies

Imperial rule and the opening of imperial markets brought opportunities for economic development and profit in the conquered provinces, although most of these opportunities went to the local wealthy elite who possessed the capital and skills to take advantage of them. In general, Roman rulers were solicitous of the upper classes in the provinces, both because of a shared class position and because they believed that the loyalty of this elite was crucial to maintaining Roman hegemony.

The cost of this imperial role, however, could be heavy, and it eventually became oppressive. The Romans levied tribute, taxes, and rents, and recruited soldiers from

HOW DO WE KNOW?

Roman Law: Theory and Practice

Modern historians have generally praised Rome's incipient international legal system as:

> one of the most potent and effective ideas that the Romans ever originated … It demonstrated that a body of law could be established upon a foundation acceptable to the members of different peoples and races at any and every phase of social, economic, and political evolution; and so it brought the laws of the Romans nearer to universal applicability than any others that have ever been devised. (Grant, pp. 104–05)

Legal theory and practice, however, did not always coincide in ancient Rome (as they do not always coincide today). The poor did not receive the same protection and benefits as the rich; soldiers abused their authority; laws were not applied consistently. The satirist Juvenal (c. 55–c. 127 C.E.) ridiculed the inability of Rome's legal system to curb the violence of Roman soldiers:

> Your teeth are shattered? Face hectically inflamed, with great black welts? You know the doctor wasn't too optimistic about the eye that was left. But it's not a bit of good your running to the courts about it. If you've been beaten up by a soldier, better keep it to yourself. (cited in Boardman, *et al.*, p. 575)

In practice, the law was also not as universal as it claimed, and those challenging the empire might not reap its benefits. Jewish nationalist writers, for example, compared the hypocrisy of Rome's laws to the ambiguous associations of the unclean pig:

> Just as a pig lies down and sticks out its trotters as though to say "I am clean" [because they are cloven], so the evil empire robs and oppresses while pretending to execute justice. (cited in Boardman, *et al.*, p. 582)

Beginning about the second century C.E., preferential treatment for the wealthy and the powerful entered explicitly into the law, deepening class antagonisms and weakening the empire.

- On what basis do historians differ when evaluating the quality of the Roman legal system?
- The modern historian Michael Grant writes about Rome's system of international law while the satirist Juvenal lived in ancient Rome and wrote about its local criminal law. How is each author's perspective affected by his time and expertise?
- What do you think is the effect on society of a legal system that gives preferential treatment to one group over another?

the peoples they conquered. They settled their own soldiers in captured lands, turning those lands into Roman estates and enslaving millions of people to work on them. They exploited their political power for the economic advantage of their own traders and military and administrative elite. As the size and wealth of the empire grew, many Romans felt that they had conquered the world but lost their souls. They spoke not of victory, but of loss. The historian Livy, writing at the height of the age of Augustus, lamented the end of innocence:

> With the gradual relaxation of discipline, morals first gave way, as it were, then sank lower and lower, and finally began the downward plunge which has brought us to the present time, when we can endure neither our vices nor the cure. (cited in Lewis and Reinhold, I:8)

6.1

6.2

6.3

6.4

6.5   What were the achievements of Augustus and the Principate?

6.6

6.7

Eurasian trade. The commercial links that bound the ancient world were both extensive and sophisticated. Self-sustaining individual networks—the Saharan caravans, the Arab dhows plying the Indian Ocean, the fleets of Chinese junks coasting East Asia, and, most famously, the silk routes traversing central Asia—linked at key entrepôts such as Alexandria and Oc Eo by sea, and Ctesiphon and Kashgar by land, to form a truly intercontinental trading system.

ROMAN EMPERORS

	Augustus (27 B.C.E.–14 C.E.)
Julio-Claudian dynasty	Tiberius (14–37) Caligula (37–41) Claudius (41–54) Nero (54–68)
Flavian dynasty	Vespasian (69–79) Titus (79–81) Domitian (81–96)
Age of the Antonines	Nerva (96–98) Trajan (98–117) Hadrian (117–138) Antoninus Pius (138–161) Marcus Aurelius (161–180) Commodus (180–193)
Severan dynasty	Septimius Severus (193–211) Caracalla (212–17) Elagabalus (218–22) Severus Alexander (222–35)
The late empire	Philip the Arabian (244–49) Decius (249–51) Gallus (251–53) Valerian (253–60) Gallienus (253–68) Claudius (268–70) Aurelian (270–75) Tacitus (275–76) Florian (276) Probus (276–82) Carus (282–83) Numerianus (283–84) and Carinus (283–85) Diocletian (284–305)

6.1

6.2

6.3

6.4

6.5   What were the achievements of Augustus and the Principate?

6.6

6.7

Livy proclaimed the widely held myth of an older, golden age of simplicity, and lamented its loss:

> No state was ever greater, none more righteous or richer in good examples, nor ever was where avarice and luxury came into the social order so late, or where humble means and thrift were so highly esteemed and so long held in honor. For true it is that the less men's wealth was, the less was their greed. Of late, riches have brought in avarice, and excessive pleasures the longing to carry wantonness and license to the point of personal ruin and universal destruction. (cited in Lewis and Reinhold, I:8)

This nostalgia had two related but different versions. One drew on examples from the days of simple, rustic equality before the advent of the Etruscan kings. It condemned the maltreatment of the plebeians and the slaves at the hands of the patricians that had begun under Etruscan rule and intensified under the Republic. The other version wished to recreate the days of the oligarchic, patrician Republic, before the transfer of power from the Senate to the generals.

Supplying Rome. Feeding and provisioning the city of Rome, which had a population of about a million by the time of Augustus, called on vast resources throughout the empire. The most important requirement was grain, and Romans imported it from Sicily, Egypt and the North African coast, Spain, and the lands surrounding the Black Sea.

Merchants imported more specialized products from all parts of the empire: olive oil and wine came from within Italy, Spain, and the Mediterranean shores; pottery and glass from the Rhineland; leather from southern France; marble from Asia Minor; woolen textiles from Britain and northern France, Belgium, and the Netherlands; and slaves from many lands. For gladiatorial contests in the Colosseum, and for general display in Rome, lions were brought from Africa and Asia, bears from Scotland, horses from Spain, crocodiles and camels from Egypt, and leopards and rhinoceroses from northwest Africa. The transportation of bulk commodities, especially within the empire, was most often by sea.

Building Cities. A few other extremely large cities, such as Alexandria, also needed to import extensively to provide for their hundreds of thousands of inhabitants, but most of the empire was locally self-sufficient. Most people worked on the land, most production was agricultural, and people consumed most produce near the place of production, especially in the newly conquered and settled regions of Western Europe.

To incorporate these regions into the empire, the Romans constructed and promoted new cities as administrative, military, and financial centers. These included the cores of modern London, Paris, Lyons, Trier, Nîmes, Bruges, Barcelona, Cologne, Budapest, and many other European cities. In an empire that rested on agriculture, Rome laid the foundations of a small but potent ruling urban civilization.

At the height of its power, the empire contained more than 5,000 civic bodies. The orator Marcus Tullius Cicero (106–43 B.C.E.) referred to Narbonne, Rome's administrative capital in southern Gaul from about 118 B.C.E., as "a colony of Roman citizens, a watchtower of the Roman people, a bulwark against the wild tribes of Gaul" (cited in Mumford, p. 209). Roman rule especially attracted and benefited the urban upper classes in the conquered regions, and helped to urbanize some leaders of the newly arriving German settlers.

Engineering Triumphs. Cities are physical places as well as institutions, as we have argued earlier. Not only did the Romans build the institutional cores of their new and renovated administrative cities, but also they built their infrastructure: administrative and defensive fortresses, public buildings, temples, stadia, baths, markets, roads, and aqueducts. Rome itself was the greatest challenge. To build, garrison, and sustain the imperial capital required engineering skills beyond any known before. Several illustrations throughout this chapter, depicting examples of Roman architecture of stone and marble that still stand to this day, testify to its beauty, utility, and endurance. The architectural and engineering skills mastered in Rome were then applied throughout the empire. On the other hand, the Romans paid little attention to the needs of the poor, whose wooden and mud structures vanished long ago.

Luxury Trades. People of wealth and power could command specialty goods. Supplying their demands generated small but significant streams of intercontinental, long-distance, luxury trade. For this commerce to flourish, trade routes had to be protected and kept safe. The *Pax Romana* secured the Red Sea routes, which allowed the importation of frankincense, myrrh, and other spices from the Arabian peninsula and the Horn of Africa and spices and textiles from India, some of them transshipped from vessels coming from China. By the first century C.E., sailors had discovered that by sailing with the summer monsoon winds they could reach India from Egypt in about four months. They could then return with the winter monsoon, completing the round trip within a year.

Rome's repayment in this exchange was mostly precious metals. Hoards of gold coins from Rome have been discovered in southern India, with smaller treasuries in China, Southeast Asia, and East Africa. The historian Pliny the Elder (23–79 C.E.) complained that the trade drained Italy's precious metals, but the profits to be made back home were extraordinary: "In no year does India absorb less than 50,000,000 sesterces of our Empire's wealth, sending back merchandise to be sold with us at a hundred times its original cost" (cited in Lewis and Reinhold, II:120).

Overland routes were also vital. The need for safety and protection was most evident in the silk trade, which prospered when Augustan Rome, Parthian Mesopotamia and Iran, Kushan India, and Han China—the four empires that spanned the silk routes—were at their peak. Goods from Luoyang and Xian in China crossed the mountains of central Asia, connecting finally at one of the great trading emporia of Begram, Bactra, or Merv. From there, they continued onward into the Mediterranean.

Silk, light and valuable, was the principal export westward, but the caravans also carried lacquerware, bronzes, and other treasures. A storehouse discovered in 1938 in Begram, which stood at the crossroads of China, India, Persia, and the

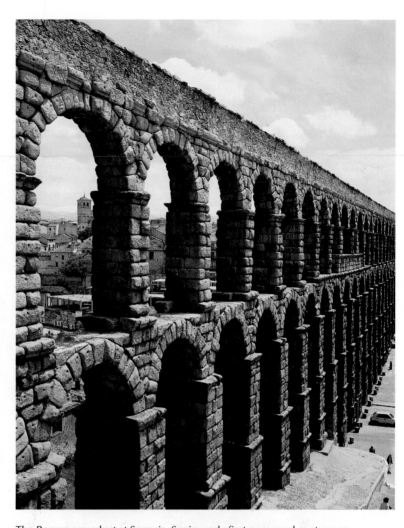

The Roman aqueduct at Segovia, Spain, early first or second century C.E. Unlike the Greeks, the Romans are remembered less for their art than for their great engineering feats. The need to improve the water supply to Roman settlements increased with urban population growth, and the popularity of the public bathing houses heightened the demand even more. The Romans developed a massive network of aqueducts to channel water into cities across uneven terrain.

6.1

6.2

6.3

6.4

6.5

What were the achievements of Augustus and the Principate?

6.6

6.7

183

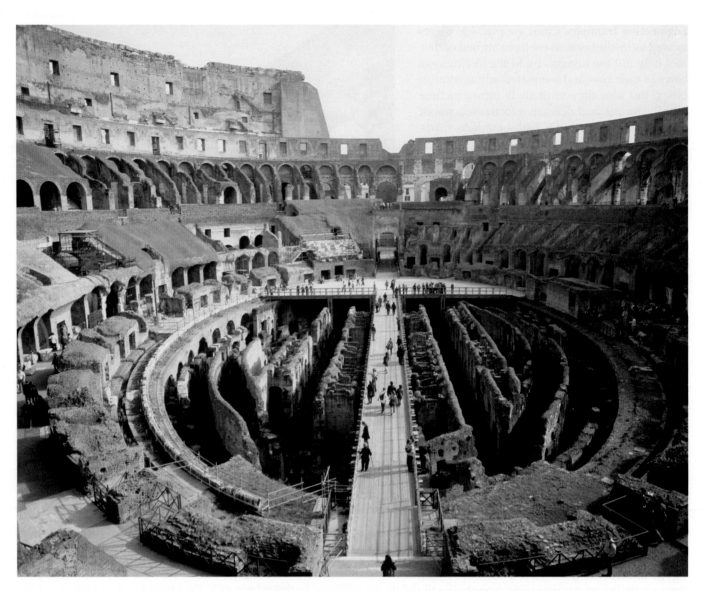

The Colosseum, Rome, c. 72–80 C.E. Built to house spectacular entertainments, such as mock sea-battles and gladiatorial combats, for audiences of up to 50,000 people, the Colosseum combined Greek decorative traditions with Roman engineering ingenuity, epitomized in the advanced use of concrete as a building material.

6.1
6.2
6.3
6.4
6.5 What were the achievements of Augustus and the Principate?
6.6
6.7

Mediterranean, revealed some of the principal luxury goods of this intercontinental trade: lacquerwork from China; ivory statues and carvings from India; alabaster, bronze, and glass works from the Mediterranean. Astonishingly, many of the carriers of these treasures seem to have been the steppe nomads of central Asia, the Huns and other peoples, who at other times attacked and plundered the empires across which they now traded.

Officially, the Roman upper classes scorned trade as beneath their status. Unofficially, they often entered into contracts with freed men, their own ex-slaves, to front for their commercial enterprises. Trade was lucrative, and the aristocrats did not wish to lose the profits. The preferred methods of earning a livelihood were from land ownership, tax collecting for the state, or military conquest, but even generals, such as Julius Caesar, profited from the sale of slaves captured in war.

Roman traders could be very exploitative. Especially when working in Rome's provinces, they often inspired great hatred. When Mithridates VI, king of Pontus in

CHAPTER SIX: ROME AND THE BARBARIANS 753 B.C.E.–1453 C.E.

6.1
6.2
6.3
6.4
6.5
6.6
6.7

northern Anatolia, invaded the Roman province of Asia in 88 B.C.E., he encouraged Asian debtors to kill their Roman creditors. Eighty thousand Italian and Italian–Greek businessmen were reported murdered (Grant, p. 184).

In the late second century C.E., internal revolts and external attacks by Germanic peoples brought an end to the *Pax Romana* and introduced major obstacles to this trade. Roads and markets were no longer secure, and only items that could be consumed locally were worth producing. For example, manufacturers cut back sharply the production of glass, metals, and textiles in northern Europe. Provisioning Rome and other cities became more difficult. The population of cities fell and the protection they could offer declined, as did their levels of consumption. They provided less opportunity for making a profit and less incentive to producers. Trade and productivity faltered. As the *Pax Romana* began to break down politically and militarily, trade declined and became more localized.

The Golden Age of Greco-Roman Culture

Roman cultural achievements had lagged far behind those of Greece, but as Rome conquered the Greek city-states, it began to absorb their culture. The Roman aristocratic classes adopted Greek language and literature as well as the architectural, sculptural, and painting traditions of the Greeks. The Romans now borrowed from the Greeks as they had earlier borrowed from the Etruscans.

Rome carried this polyglot culture outward in its conquests in Europe and Asia. Its schools in the provinces spread Greek as well as Latin among the tribal Goths and Gauls. Greek was the language of high culture. Latin, however, became the language of administration. Roman troops constructed amphitheaters, stadia, and baths wherever they went, the Roman invention of concrete making such construction feasible. In these settings Roman rulers provided theaters and spectacles modeled on those in Rome.

Rome's sense of its own superiority doubtless encouraged its conquest of other peoples, whom it deemed inferior, and was encouraged, in turn, by the success of those conquests. Rome's greatest epic poem, the *Aeneid*, written by Virgil during the reign of Augustus, sings the emperor's praises and celebrates Rome's superiority.

> … Behold the Romans,
> Your very own. These are Iulus' children,
> The race to come. One promise you have heard
> Over and over: here is its fulfillment,
> The son of a god, Augustus Caesar, founder
> Of a new age of gold, in lands where Saturn
> Ruled long ago; he will extend his empire
> Beyond the Indies, beyond the normal measure
> Of years and constellations, where high Atlas
> Turns on his shoulders the star-studded world.

At the same time, Virgil upholds the concept of *noblesse oblige*, the duty of the superior to help the inferior:

> … remember Romans,
> To rule the people under law, to establish
> The way of peace, to battle down the haughty,
> To spare the meek. Our fine arts, these, forever.
> (*Aeneid*, VI:822–31, 893–96; trans. Rolphe Humphries)

In the *Aeneid*, Virgil incorporates many of the forms of the earlier Greek epics, especially Homer's *Odyssey*, but he adds his own notes of an intensely imperialistic triumphalism.

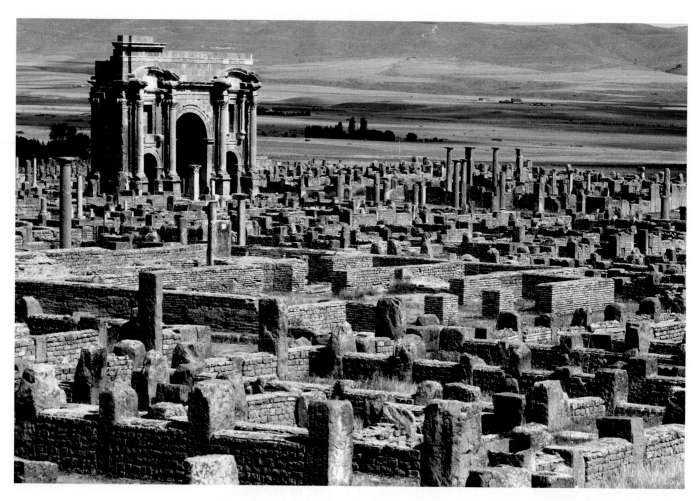

Timgad, North Africa. Timgad, in Algeria, was founded as a military and administrative fortress around 100 C.E. and designed as a perfect square with a grid plan for the streets. The Romans tended to adhere to standard templates of town construction, despite variations in local topography, and Timgad is one of the clearest surviving models of what a provincial headquarters looked like.

6.1

6.2

6.3

6.4

6.5   What were the
achievements of
6.6   Augustus and the
Principate?
6.7

Stoicism. Romans borrowed philosophical as well as literary ideas from the Greeks. Many thoughtful Romans were attracted to Stoicism, a philosophy founded by the Greek Zeno about 300 B.C.E. Stoicism took its name from the *stoa*, the covered walkway, in Athens where he taught. Zeno began with a cosmic theory of the world as a rational, well-ordered, and coherent system. Therefore humans should accept, without joy or grief, free from passion, everything that takes place in this world. Lucius Annaeus Seneca (*c.* 4 B.C.E.–65 C.E.), a Roman Stoic living three centuries later, elaborated:

> What is the principal thing? A heart … which can go forth to face ill or good daunt-less and unembarrassed, paralyzed neither by the tumult of the one nor the glam-our of the other. (Seneca, *Natural Questions*, cited in Lewis and Reinhold, II:165–66)

A corollary of Zeno's moral philosophy stated that people should treat one another with decency because we are all brothers and sisters. Cicero, one of Rome's most important orators, commentators, and statesmen, and much influenced by Stoic beliefs, wrote:

> The private individual ought first, in private relations, to live on fair and equal terms with his fellow citizens, with a spirit neither servile and groveling nor yet domineering. (Cicero, *On Duties,* cited in Lewis and Reinhold, I:273)

6.1
6.2
6.3
6.4
6.5
6.6
6.7

What were the achievements of Augustus and the Principate?

How, then, did Stoics address the conditions of slavery in Rome? Although Stoics did not advocate the end of slavery, they did propose more humane treatment. Writing on the treatment of slaves, Seneca proposed a kind of Golden Rule:

Treat those below you as you would be treated by those above you. (Seneca, *Moral Epistles*, cited in Lewis and Reinhold, II:180)

At this, however, Tacitus accused Seneca, one of Rome's richest citizens, of hypocrisy:

"By what wisdom, by what principles of philosophy had he acquired 300,000,000 sesterces within four years of [receiving Emperor Nero's] royal favor? At Rome the childless and their wills are snared in his nets, as it were; Italy and the provinces are drained by his enormous usury" (*Annals* XIII:xlii, cited in Lewis and Reinhold, II:165–6, n. 58).

Stoicism reached the height of its influence in Rome with the selection of Marcus Aurelius Antoninus as emperor (r. 161–180 C.E.). He ruled through two decades of almost continuous warfare, economic upheaval, internal revolts, and plague. Through it all, Marcus Aurelius remained courageous and Stoic. He recorded his thoughts in his *Meditations*, one of the most philosophically reflective works ever written by a man in a position of such power:

Keep thyself then simple, good, pure, serious, free from affectation, a friend of justice, a worshipper of the gods, and help men. Short is life. The universe is either a confusion, and a mutual involution of things, and a dispersion; or it is unity and order and providence … If the [latter], I venerate, and I am firm, and I trust in him who governs. (VI:30, 10)

📖 Read the **Document: Marcus Aurelius, The Meditations, Book Two (167 CE)** on **MyHistoryLab**

Religion in Imperial Rome

Officially, Rome celebrated a religion centered on the person of the emperor-god. Augustus, in particular, had rebuilt temples and encouraged the worship of ancestral gods. After the deification of Augustus at his death, the official priesthood offered animal sacrifices to him and later to his successors, adding these to the traditional sacrifices to the major pagan gods, especially Jupiter, Juno, and Minerva. People celebrated the birthdays and death anniversaries of the emperors as holidays.

Beyond these rituals, however, Roman religious policies allowed a great deal of flexibility. For the most part, as long as people venerated the emperor and did not question the legitimacy of the state, Roman emperors allowed diverse religious practices to flourish.

GREEK AND ROMAN GODS

In the second century B.C.E., Greece was absorbed by the Roman Empire. In the process the Romans adopted and adapted many Greek myths, linking their own gallery of gods to Greek legends and deities.

Greek	Roman	
Aphrodite	Venus	Goddess of love and beauty
Apollo, Phoebus	Apollo, Phoebus	Greek god of sun, god of music, poetry, and prophecy
Ares	Mars	God of war
Artemis	Diana	Virgin huntress, goddess of the moon
Asclepius	Aesculapius	God of medicine
Athena (Pallas)	Minerva	Goddess of wisdom and art
Cronus	Saturn	Father of the supreme god: Zeus or Jupiter
Demeter	Ceres	Goddess of the harvest
Dionysus	Bacchus	God of wine and fertility
Eros	Cupid	God of love
Hades	Pluto, Dis	God of the underworld
Hephaestus	Vulcan	God of fire
Hera	Juno	Queen of heaven, wife of Zeus/Jupiter, goddess of women and marriage
Hermes	Mercury	Messenger of the gods, god of roads, cunning, commerce, wealth, and luck
Hestia	Vesta	Goddess of the hearth
Hymen	Hymen	God of marriage
Irene	Pax	Goddess of peace
Pan	Faunus	God of flocks and shepherds
Persephone	Proserpina	Goddess of corn and the spring, goddess of the dead
Poseidon	Neptune	God of the sea
Zeus	Jupiter, Jove	Supreme ruler of gods and men, king of heaven, and overseer of justice and destiny

6.1

6.2

6.3

6.4

6.5 What were the
achievements of
Augustus and the
Principate?

6.6

6.7

Mystery Religions. Mithraism, a religion that worshiped the Persian sun god Mithra as mediator between god and man, emphasized discipline and loyalty. It was especially popular within the military, particularly among the Germanic and eastern troops who were attracted to its message of fighting vigorously against both internal passions and external military opponents. Two religions that were popular in early imperial Rome centered on goddesses, and were especially attractive to women. Like Mithraism, both were mystery religions—that is, they had rituals of initiation that defied rational understanding and that were unknown to outsiders. These could include orgies and baptisms. One such faith worshiped Cybele, the venerated earth-mother of Asia Minor. Another worshiped the Egyptian goddess Isis, with her annual promise of rebirth and a variety of dramatic rituals to be observed throughout the year.

Rome and the Jews. Rome did not, however, tolerate sects that challenged the authority of the empire or the emperor. The government cracked down on worship of the god Bacchus, for example, in 186 B.C.E., fearing that lower-class members of this cult might turn against the state. The same antagonism toward potential revolt put Rome on a collision course with the Jews of Judea, in the eastern Mediterranean.

After conquering the eastern Mediterranean from the Seleucid inheritors of Alexander the Great, the Romans turned their attention to Judea. For at least a century the region had been fragmented, and often in the throes of open warfare, among contending factions and people of a wide variety of beliefs and political commitments: Seleucids; pagans, who believed in many gods; and Jews. In the chapter entitled "Judaism and Christianity" we shall see how the Jews, from their roots in the seventeenth century B.C.E., developed a religion based on monotheism (the worship of one god) and a fierce sense of ethnic nationalism. Here, we note only that both of these qualities evoked strong opposition among the Roman rulers. The zealous monotheism of most of the Jews left no room for worship of the Roman emperor as a god, and the ethnic nationalism meant that a spirit of revolt against Roman authority was always simmering. From the time that Rome conquered Judea and turned it into a subject state, in 63 B.C.E., fighting broke out frequently, not only between Jews and Romans, but also among Jewish political and religious factions that differed on the proper behavior toward the Roman conquerors and toward one another. In response to three major revolts by the Jews, the Romans destroyed Jerusalem and its principal Jewish Temple, established the Roman colony of Aelia Capitolina on its site, destroyed Judea as a Jewish state, and exiled the Jews from this land, with repercussions that would last for centuries.

Rome and the Early Christians. One of the religious factions that grew up among the Jews in Judea venerated the preacher, exorcist, and miracle worker Jesus of Nazareth (c. 4 B.C.E–c. 30 C.E.). Many of Jesus' followers believed him to be divine and later called him Christ, or the Messiah (the anointed one of God). The discussion of his ministry and its emergence from Jewish roots will also wait for the chapter entitled "Judaism and Christianity" in the unit on religion. Here, suffice it to say that the Roman government clashed with the early Christians, followers of Jesus, much as it did with Judaism, on the grounds of its monotheism, resistance to emperor worship, and potential as a force for political revolution.

For the first three centuries of its existence, many Romans viewed Christianity as atheistic because it rejected the divinity of the emperor. Some Romans saw the new Christian religion as treasonable because it spoke of a kingdom of heaven that was distinct from the Roman earthly empire. Finally, the Roman governor of Judea, Pontius Pilate, tried and crucified Jesus, partly because he was a threat to the religious and political stability of the imperial colony. By the time of Marcus Aurelius, however, despite continued persecution, Christianity was making serious inroads into Roman thought. The Stoic philosophy was not far removed from the Christian

6.1

6.2

6.3

6.4

6.5

Why did the
Roman Empire
decline and fall?

6.6

6.7

concept of an orderly world and concern for social welfare. To these beliefs, Christianity added faith in a god actively intervening in human affairs, and, specifically, the doctrines of the birth, life, miracles, and resurrection of Jesus. At first it attracted the poor, who were moved by Jesus' concern for the downtrodden, but later, more powerful classes also joined, attracted by both the organization and the message of Christianity. The new religion promoted greater freedom for women, and it began to incorporate some of the sophistication of Greek philosophy, attracting a new intellectual leadership. By 313, when the joint emperors Constantine (272–337) and Licinius (263–325) issued the Edict of Milan, proclaiming equal toleration for Christians and non-Christians, estimates suggested that one in ten inhabitants of the Roman Empire was a Christian (Lewis and Reinhold, II: 553).

When Constantine ruled alone, after 324, he favored Christianity as a religion that had brought miraculous benefits to himself personally and to his empire, and he granted it official recognition and legal status. Christianity spread freely throughout the conquered lands and peoples of northwestern Europe. The network of roads and towns created to facilitate administration also served to transmit the Christian message, and members of the clergy frequently served as a bridge between the religious practices of Christian Rome and those of others. After emerging as the official state religion in 380, Christianity succeeded in having government support for polytheistic cults terminated in 394. Even the most widespread of these cults, Mithraism, with its message of loyalty to the emperor, died out. Christianity emerged triumphant. (For a fuller discussion of early Christianity and its relationship to the Roman Empire, see the chapter entitled "Judaism and Christianity.")

The Dismemberment of the Roman Empire

6.6 Why did the Roman Empire decline and fall?

Rome labeled many of its neighbors on its far-flung borders "barbarians," including the Celts of central Europe, the various Germanic groups of northern and eastern Europe, and the steppe nomads of central Asia. These "barbarians" spoke unknown foreign languages. They did not have cities, written languages, formal government structures, established geographical boundaries, codified laws, or labor specialization. Some, like the Celts and Germans, lived in villages and carried on settled farming. Nomadic steppe peoples spent their lives riding, herding, and often fighting among themselves in far-off central Asia. Such peoples, the Romans must have thought, could benefit from the civilizing influences of the empire. Perhaps Virgil had this in mind when he was writing the *Aeneid*.

Invaders at the Gates

The Celts had arrived in central Europe as early as 2000 B.C.E. Burial sites indicate their respect for horse-riding warriors and the slow development among them of iron technology in weapons and tools. The Hallstatt cemetery in Austria reveals a greater use of iron by the eighth century B.C.E. and includes items of Greek manufacture. A cemetery at La Tène in what is now Switzerland shows continuing Greek and then Roman influences from the fifth century B.C.E. to the first century C.E.

By 400 B.C.E., the Celts were expanding their territory. In 390 B.C.E. they managed to sack the city of Rome. By 200 B.C.E. Celtic groups had covered central Europe and were pushing out toward Spain, the British Isles, the Balkans, and Anatolia. Learning from Greek and Roman examples, they built fortified towns throughout their territories. The largest of these covered more than half a square mile. Celtic women enjoyed more freedom than did Roman women, which evoked the scorn of some Roman writers. Tacitus, who seemed to appreciate Calgacus' revolt in 83–84 C.E., was

6.1

6.2

6.3

6.4

6.5

6.6 Why did the
Roman Empire
decline and fall?

6.7

far more critical of the failed Celtic revolt of 61 C.E. in Britain led by the female army leader Boudicca. Ultimately, Rome conquered the Celtic peoples. They were killed, or assimilated, or fled to Ireland, Scotland, and Wales, where, to some degree, they continue today to preserve the Celtic language and culture.

The Goths—an array of Germanic peoples (primarily Visigoths and Ostrogoths), distinguished in part by their use of Germanic languages, in part through their residence in lands that later became Germany—settled at first in northern Europe outside the Celtic and Roman strongholds. Indeed, much of what we know of this early period comes from burials in the bogs of modern-day northern Germany and Denmark. By 600 B.C.E. these Germanic peoples had established small villages, and by about 500 B.C.E. they had begun working with iron. With the discovery of richer iron deposits and contact with Greek and Roman technology, the Goths developed more sophisticated tools and weapons.

Romans and Germans had faced each other along the Rhine since Julius Caesar had conquered Gaul, and along the Danube from the time Augustus had secured that border. They had skirmished, traded, and at times penetrated each other's territories. Recent archaeological excavations show that leaders of the Germans adopted for themselves many of the tools, weapons, and luxury goods of the conquering Romans. Roman goods, and some values, spread through imitation as well as by force.

In 370 C.E., steppe nomads began to invade across the thousands of miles from central Asia, bringing pressure to bear on the whole of Europe. In response to this pressure, the Goths began to migrate westward, pushing more vigorously into Roman territory. These massive Germanic invasions upset the rough balance of power that existed between Rome and the Goths, and threatened the stability of the empire. Ultimately, the Goths formed their own states within the imperial territories. A second Germanic emigration occurred about 500 C.E. as a response to floods in the areas of north Germany and Denmark. Among the emigrant Germanic groups, the Saxons sailed across the North Sea and the English Channel to Britain, where they came to form a substantial part of the population.

The Romans called all the steppe peoples who invaded Europe from central Asia in 370 C.E. "Huns." In fact, however, the Huns were only one of the many groups of warrior-nomads who inhabited the flat grasslands from European Russia to Manchuria. They virtually lived on their horses, herding cattle, sheep, and horses as well as hunting. They slept in tents and used wagons to transport their goods as they moved from place to place, especially in their annual shift between summer and winter locations.

Although they lived in tent encampments, the Huns' living arrangements and political structures were by no means haphazard. Many groups had chiefs and even governments, and their leaders lived in the most elaborate of the tents. When the Huns invaded Europe, Romans observed emissaries of various peoples enter the tent of Attila, their leader, to conduct political negotiations.

At the time Augustus ruled Rome, groups of steppe nomads engaged in battles that would ultimately help to topple the Han dynasty in China. They also launched the attacks on India that would make two of the groups the rulers of northern India: the Kushanas, 150–300 C.E., and the Hunas, 500–550 C.E. The Huns arrived in Europe in 370 C.E., defeating and displacing the Alans, Ostrogoths, and Visigoths, and pushing them in the direction of Rome. The "domino effect" that would ultimately destroy the empire had begun.

Decline and Dismemberment

Rome proved vulnerable to the invaders, especially after a plague that wiped out up to a quarter of the population of some areas in 165–180 C.E. Historians debate the exact severity and impact of this plague, but it diminished the numbers and

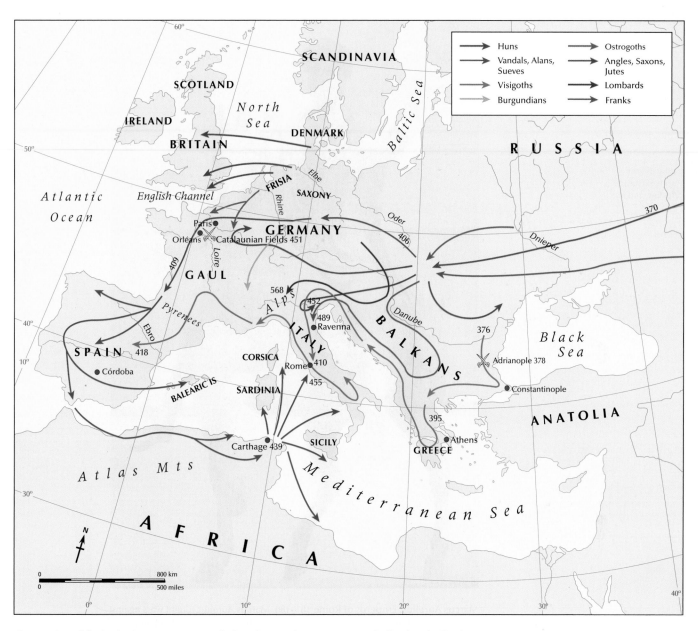

The coming of the barbarians. Rome's control of northern and Western Europe declined in the fourth century C.E. as successive waves of Germanic peoples began to migrate and colonize the outer reaches of the empire. When the Huns began to advance westward from central Asia they pushed before them additional Gothic peoples who increased the pressure on Rome. Other Huns were meanwhile pushing south into India and east into China.

undermined the self-confidence of the empire's population. During the reign of Marcus Aurelius (r. 161–180 C.E.), the Marcomanni, a Germanic tribe from Bohemia, began to invade the Danube basin. Some penetrated into Greece and across the Alps and into Italy. "Barbarian" invasions continued for hundreds of years, ultimately leading to the break-up of the Roman Empire.

For seven years, 168–175, Marcus Aurelius fought the invaders, but he also recognized that they could be assimilated into the empire for mutual benefit. The Marcomanni wanted to establish settlements, so he offered them land within the borders of the empire that they could farm; they were soldiers, so he also offered them positions in Rome's armies.

6.1
6.2
6.3
6.4
6.5
6.6
6.7

Why did the Roman Empire decline and fall?

Marcus Aurelius, Emperor of Rome 161–180. Marcus Aurelius fought wars against the Parthian Empire in Asia and Germanic tribes in northern and central Europe. He is equally famous as the philosopher/author of the *Meditations*, a classic Stoic text on duty and service, which remains influential today. His magnificent bronze statue, now housed in the Capitoline Museum at the center of modern Rome, is the only complete bronze equestrian statue to survive from antiquity.

Some of the Gothic groups also accepted assimilation into the empire. Some wished simply to plunder and withdraw; others wished to seize portions of the empire for themselves and settle.

The Crisis of the Third Century. Invaders repeatedly penetrated the borders represented by the Danube and the Rhine. In 248 the emperor Decius (r. 249–51) defeated an invasion of Goths in the Balkans but was himself killed by another Gothic group. The Goths continued into the Balkans and beyond into Asia Minor. They took to ships and attacked Black Sea commerce, in the process cutting off large parts of Rome's grain supplies. Meanwhile, further west, Franks and Vandals swept across the Rhine into Gaul and Spain, and as far south as North Africa.

The "Barbarians"

Roman and Chinese Sources

The steppe peoples had no written language, and their nomadic lifestyle left few archaeological remains. We know about them in part from burials, especially those of the Scythians, a group living in southern Russia and in the Altai Mountains of Mongolia. Mostly we know of them from the accounts of the peoples whose lands they invaded: Romans, Greeks, Chinese, and Indians. All these accounts report them as fierce, mobile, swift, and terrifying warriors on horseback, armed with powerful bows, swords, and lances. In more peaceful times, the Huns carried the goods of the overland silk routes through central Asia.

Latin histories did not mention the Huns until Ammianus Marcellinus (c. 330–95 C.E.) described them:

> They are without fixed abode, without hearth, or law, or settled mode of life, and they keep roaming from place to place, like fugitives, accompanied by the wagons in which they live; in wagons their wives weave for them their hideous garments, in wagons they cohabit with their husbands, bear children, and rear them to the age of puberty …
>
> This race of untamed men, without encumbrances, aflame with an inhuman desire for plundering others' property, made their violent way amid the rapine and slaughter of the neighboring peoples as far as the Halani [the Alans, on the river Don]. (cited in Lewis and Reinhold, II:623)

Five hundred years earlier, the Chinese historian Sima Qian had depicted them as coarse warriors:

> During the Ch'ien-yuan reign [140–134 B.C.E.] … the Son of Heaven made inquiries among those of the Hsiung-na [Xiongnu; Huns] who had surrendered and been made prisoners, and they all reported that the Hsiung-na had overcome the king of the Yueh-chih and made a drinking vessel out of his skull. The Yueh-chih had decamped and were hiding somewhere, constantly scheming how to revenge themselves on the Hsiung-na. (Sima Qian, p. 274)

Further elaboration by Sima delineates several groups of steppe nomads who frequently fought among themselves and sometimes invaded China itself. Both his description and that of Ammianus Marcellinus reflect the similar fear with which settled, imperial powers viewed their powerful, nomadic adversaries.

- What examples of barbarism does Ammianus Marcellinus cite from Rome? How do they compare with those cited by Sima Qian from China?
- What advantages did horse-mounted warriors with bows, swords, and lances have against the might of the empires of Rome and China?
- If we had records from the "barbarians" about the "civilized" peoples whose land they were invading, how do you think they would describe them?

The empire struck back. The emperor Gallienus (r. 253–68) created a mobile cavalry and moved the imperial military headquarters from Rome to Milan in the north, better to confront invaders into Italy. In a series of battles Roman armies preserved Italy for the empire. Aurelian (r. 270–75), an even more brilliant and energetic general, succeeded Gallienus as emperor after the latter died in a plague. In a series of battles, Aurelian protected Rome's western and northern borders, although he abandoned Dacia and pulled back to the Danube.

In the east, too, Rome defeated revolts. The greatest challenge came as the new, expansive Sassanid dynasty in Persia confronted Rome in Armenia and Syria. In 260 the Roman emperor Valerian (r. 253–60) was captured and held prisoner for the rest of his life in humiliating conditions. (Legend told that after his death he was stuffed and preserved in a Persian temple.) Nevertheless, Rome recaptured its eastern areas, partly because the Sassanians treated the inhabitants of these lands so badly that they revolted. In another revolt against Rome, Zenobia, the widow of the leader of semi-independent Palmyra, declared the independence of Syria and Mesopotamia, and annexed Egypt. Her revolt lasted only a few years, and in 273 Aurelian defeated her, took her back to Rome in chains, and put her on public display, fully bedecked in jewels.

The Fragmentation of Authority. Continuing warfare forced the decentralization of Rome's power from the capital to distant provincial battlefields, and from civilian control by the Senate in Rome to generals in the field. Soldiers in Gaul, Britain, and Spain declared their general Postumus (r. 259–68) the independent emperor of those

6.1
6.2
6.3
6.4
6.5
6.6
6.7

Why did the Roman Empire decline and fall?

6.1

6.2

6.3

6.4

6.5

6.6 Why did the Roman Empire decline and fall?

6.7

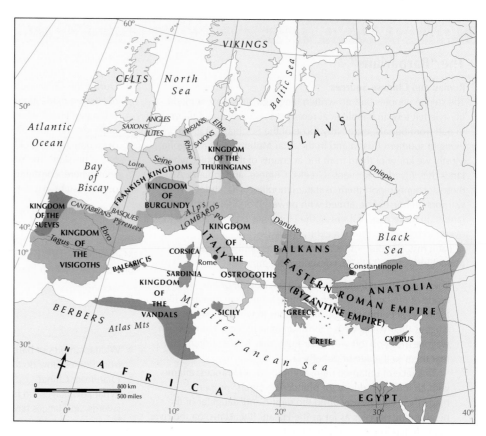

Rome's successors. Following the sack of Rome by the Ostrogoths in 455 C.E., a new map of Europe emerged. The Roman power base had shifted east to Constantinople, forming the Byzantine Empire. The steppe invaders, keen to emulate the Romans, had created new kingdoms in Italy, Africa, and Iberia, while Germanic peoples were struggling to create a new power balance in the north.

regions, but Aurelian defeated their mutiny in 274. Militarily, the empire staged an extraordinary comeback.

In the belief that an aura of pomp and majesty would be helpful in asserting central control, the emperor Diocletian (r. 284–305) claimed for himself a sanctity and splendor never before seen in Rome. The expense of his battles and the extravagance of his court bankrupted the empire and brought misery to its inhabitants. To cope with the attacks on distant borders, emperors established regional capitals. In 330 Constantine established Constantinople as a secondary capital for ruling the entire eastern region. After 395, one emperor in Rome and another in Constantinople formally divided the Roman Empire, west and east.

"Barbarian" tribes continued to breach the imperial borders and defenses. Valentinian I (r. 364–75) was the last emperor capable of driving them back effectively. From this time on, impelled by the invasion of the Huns, the Germans pushed against Roman defenses in increasing numbers. In 378 Valentinian's brother, the eastern Emperor Valens (r. 364–78), lost two-thirds of the eastern armies—and his life—in battle against the Visigoths at Adrianople. Valens' successor, Theodosius I (r. 379–95), who ruled from Constantinople, settled Visigoths within the empire, requiring them to provide soldiers and farmers for the imperial armies and lands. This "federate" status for Goths and other "barbarians" became a common pattern, with Goths, Franks, Alans, and Vandals settling within the imperial borders in increasing numbers. The empire was Roman in name, but was a mixed enterprise in terms of population, armies, and leadership. Increasingly, emperors avoided Rome and preferred to reside in such cities as Milan and Trier.

6.1
6.2
6.3
6.4
6.5
6.6
6.7

Why did the
Roman Empire
decline and fall?

Alaric the Visigoth (*c.* 370–410) invaded Italy in 401 and, in response, the emperor Honorius (r. 395–423) removed the capital from Milan to Ravenna, a more defensible city on the east coast of Italy. Alaric invaded Italy again in 407, and in 410 he sacked Rome. At the end of 406, combined armies of Goths, Vandals, Suevi, Alans, and Burgundians crossed the Rhine into Gaul and moved into Spain. At first they sacked, looted, and burned, but within a few years they established their own settlements and local kingdoms, displacing or merging with Roman landlords. The Vandal King Geiseric (r. 428–77) crossed into North Africa, seizing Carthage and its agriculturally rich hinterlands. Gaining control of a fleet, he challenged Roman control of the Mediterranean. The Romans could not defeat him.

The Huns were building up their own imperial confederacy in central Europe. Their most powerful leader, Attila (*c.* 406–53), commanded them from 434 to 453. His territory stretched from the Baltic to the Danube. He invaded Italy in 451, threatening Rome and withdrawing only on the intervention of Pope Leo I. After Attila's death, his armies dissolved and never again regained their power. In 476, the German general Odoacer deposed the last Roman emperor in the west. Odoacer became the first barbarian king of Italy (r. 476–93), and thus the five-centuries-old Roman Empire came to an end.

In the west, the Roman imperial system continued to function for at least two more centuries, but its leadership and its legions were in the hands of Germans and other invading groups. The groups carved up the empire into several distinct regions. There was no central government. Rome was no longer capital of an empire.

Read the **Document: Huns & Goths** on **MyHistoryLab**

Causes of the Decline and Fall

Structural problems had been visible in the Roman Empire even at the height of its power. Internally, the conflict between the elite and the masses continued, under different names, throughout the history of the Republic and the empire. The cost of sustaining the empire by military force overtaxed the imperial economy, impoverishing the middle classes and the remaining agricultural classes. The small, independent farmers, the class that had first built up the Roman Republic, were ruined. Although the rich continued to live off their estates in Italy and elsewhere and the senatorial classes continued to do well, popular support for the imperial ideal had disappeared. In earlier times, an ever-expanding frontier had brought new economic resources to support the empire, but expansion had come to an end in the second century. The empire was overextended.

In addition, the quality of the empire depended on the quality of its emperors, but Rome had no viable system of succession. In the century between Marcus Aurelius and Diocletian, more than 80 men assumed command as emperor, and many of these were assassinated. In the third century C.E., as fighting in the border regions decentralized the empire, competing armies fought to have their generals selected as emperor. The results were devastating to the economy, administration, and morale of the empire.

Rome could no longer win its frontier battles against invaders, but neither could it continue to assimilate Goths and others into its armies and settlements as subordinates. The Roman armies and vast territories of the empire had become heavily Germanic, and when whole tribes of Goths began to serve together in single units under Gothic commanders, questions arose concerning the army's loyalty to the empire. Romans and Germans saw each other as "other," alien, and the Romans even forbade intermarriage. As Germanic peoples began to take over leading positions, the empire effectively ceased to be Roman.

The rise of Christianity as the principal religion and philosophy of the empire also suggested that the Roman desire for earthly political power was evaporating.

6.1
6.2
6.3
6.4
6.5
6.6
6.7   What allowed
the eastern
empire to survive
after the end
of the Roman
Empire?

At first, Christianity was accepted by the poor, who used it as a means of expressing their disaffection toward the power of the Caesars. Later, when Constantine declared Christianity a legitimate state religion in 313, and the favored state religion in 324, more mainstream Romans also converted. Christianity offered an alternative focus for human energy. The eighteenth-century English historian Edward Gibbon argued, in his classic *History of the Decline and Fall of the Roman Empire*, that Christianity turned people against this-worldly attractions and power. Later historians regard this as an overstatement. They point to growing numbers of imperial administrators who converted to Christianity as evidence that the new religion and the Roman Empire were compatible. Christianity did, however, preach that eternal salvation was more important than fighting for the empire, and it siphoned energy toward more spiritual and humanitarian goals, and toward competition with other religious groups.

More recently, scholars have suggested that climate change reduced agricultural productivity and hurt the economy. Still others have noted that epidemics killed up to a quarter of the population in some imperial centers between 165 and 180 C.E. and again between 251 and 266 C.E. These diseases sapped the empire of manpower and left it more open to attack. Such biological and ecological arguments complement the more traditional explanations of Rome's fall: overextension; financial and military exhaustion; a failure of leadership; the rise of new, alternative value systems; and the infiltration of Germanic peoples, which fragmented the empire into new, separate, independent states that no longer wished to be subordinated to Rome.

The Eastern Empire, 330–1453 C.E.

6.7   What allowed the eastern empire to survive after the end of the Roman Empire?

On May 11, 330, Emperor Constantine inaugurated the "New Rome which is Constantinople," to share with Rome, as co-capital, the administration of his huge empire. From its inception three complementary elements characterized the new city: Greek language and culture; Roman law and administration; and Christian faith and organization. While the western half of the empire survived for only another century and a half, the eastern empire continued on its own until 1453. It became an empire in its own right, later called Byzantium after the name of the Greek city around which Constantinople was built.

Resurgence under Justinian

Like the west, the east had to withstand military attack. Germanic tribes crossed the Danube, but found Constantinople impregnable, defended behind huge walls built by the emperor Theodosius II (r. 408–50). Using German mercenaries, the eastern emperor Justinian I (r. 527–65) recaptured many of the western regions, including North Africa, southern Spain, Sicily, Italy, and even Rome itself, but the costs in wealth and manpower crippled his empire. After his death most of these western conquests were lost, while the Persians constantly warred with the remnants of the Roman Empire in the east.

Justinian's legal, administrative, and architectural initiatives produced more lasting results. He codified the system of law that had been developing in Rome over the centuries in four great works, known collectively as the Justinian Code, thus helping to perpetuate an administration of great competence. In time, the Code became the basis for much of modern European law. He adorned Constantinople with numerous new buildings, crowned by the Church of Hagia Sophia, the Church of Holy Wisdom. He had churches, forts, and public works constructed throughout the empire.

6.1
6.2
6.3
6.4
6.5
6.6
6.7

What allowed the eastern empire to survive after the end of the Roman Empire?

Justinian and Theodora. Emperor Justinian (top) expanded the eastern empire, codified the precedent-setting Justinian Code of law, and built lasting architectural monuments throughout the empire. His wife, the Empress Theodora (bottom), disagreed with him on religious issues, but inspired him to fight against his enemies, and argued for laws favorable to women in the Justinian Code. Here they are enshrined in the astonishing mosaics (c. 547 C.E.) of the St. Vitale Church, Ravenna, Italy.

Theology was closely intertwined with politics in the eastern empire. Disputes that appeared to concern only theology frequently had political consequences, and here Justinian seemed to overreach. When many Syrian and Egyptian Christians declared themselves Monophysites, believers that Jesus' nature was only divine, not human, Justinian oppressed them in the name of theological conformity and imperial authority. In his religious zeal, he created antagonisms that smoldered for centuries and contributed to the loss of these provinces to the Muslims in the seventh century. Theodora, the emperor's wife, was among the Monophysites; her father was a priest in the sect, and she often advocated for them even in the face of her husband's opposition.

6.1

6.2

6.3

6.4

6.5

6.6

6.7

What allowed the eastern empire to survive after the end of the Roman Empire?

Justinian had reason to allow this opposition. First, he must have loved her deeply. Theodora grew up, like her mother, as an actress and dancer, and some accounts say a prostitute (as these professions usually elided into one another). As heir to the throne, Justinian was not legally permitted to marry a woman of such a background; his uncle, the emperor Justin I, repealed the law for his nephew's sake. Moreover, in 532, when urban warfare broke out between factions in Constantinople, and Justinian was prepared to flee the city, Theodora persuaded him to remain and fight. He—and later historians—credited this decision with saving his throne. She is also considered responsible for introducing court practices that emphasized the supremacy of the royal couple over everyone else at court and in the military. Theodora and Justinian were both active sponsors of Christianity, although they promoted different, competitive, and often clashing sects. Theodora was Justinian's partner in beautifying Constantinople architecturally, and she contributed also to the legal system, which he was codifying. She was most concerned with laws affecting women, giving them greater rights in divorce settlements, including property ownership and guardianship rights over children. She advocated for the death penalty for rape, called for revoking the law sentencing adulterous women to death, and wanted an end to exposing unwanted children to their deaths. She is credited with enduring contributions to raising the status of women.

Read the Document: The Reign of Justinian from Secret History (558) Procopius on MyHistoryLab

Religious Struggles

Troops burst out of Arabia after 632, inspired with the religious zeal of Islam. Emperor Heraclius (r. 610–41) had defeated the Persian Empire, but he and his successors could not hold back these new invaders. The Arabs captured much of the land of the eastern empire, including Syria and Egypt, with their disaffected Monophysites.

By this time, so much had changed in the relationship between Rome and Constantinople that the eastern empire had taken on an identity of its own as the Byzantine Empire. For centuries, the Christian Byzantine Empire based in the Balkans and Asia Minor would confront Islam militarily and religiously. The Byzantine Empire organized its armies into **themes**, administrative districts and army units, in which peasants were given farms in payment for their military service. These themes and the impregnable fortifications of Constantinople were the empire's bulwark in confronting Arab armies.

The iconoclastic controversy, the bitter battle over the use of images, or icons, in Christian worship, began in 726, in large part as a response to the Arab invasions. Islam rigorously excluded religious imagery, and its armies were hugely successful. Some eastern clergy thought these two facts might be linked. They became **iconoclasts**, arguing that Christianity should enforce the Biblical commandment against the worship of idols by also banning icons. They campaigned to break and discard religious images, and the reigning Byzantine emperors supported them. For more than a century, until it was rescinded, this decision split what became known as the Eastern Orthodox hierarchy and positioned its mainstream in opposition to the western Church. It added to the strain in the political–religious relationship between the western Church and the Byzantine Empire.

The great leaders of the Byzantine Empire were known for their combination of military prowess and religious leadership. Basil I (r. 867–86), for example, kept control of the Balkans and crushed the Bulgar invaders; initiated a dynasty that reconquered Crete, Syria, southern Italy, and much of Palestine from the Arabs; and also healed the religious rift with Rome for a time.

Ultimately, however, beginning in the late eleventh century, a combination of religious and political antagonisms contributed to the decline of the Byzantine Empire. Battered from the north by invading Normans and Slavs, the Byzantine rulers turned

KEY TERMS

theme A theme was originally a military unit stationed in one of the provinces of the Byzantine Empire, but it later applied to the large military districts that formed buffer zones in the areas most vulnerable to Muslim invasion.

iconoclast An "image-breaker," or a person who rejects the veneration of icons, on the grounds that the practice is idolatrous.

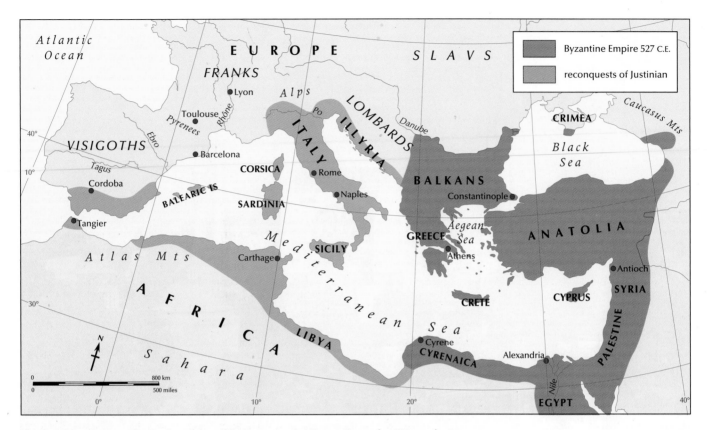

The Byzantine Empire. Despite the erosion of Roman power in Western Europe by 457 C.E., the East Roman or Byzantine Empire survived with varying fortunes for another 1,000 years—Greek-speaking and Orthodox Christian—until 1453. Centered on Constantinople, its heartland straddled the crossroads between Europe and Asia. Only briefly, under Justinian (r. 527–65), did it recover control of the western Mediterranean.

to the pope in Rome for help against the Islamic Seljuk Turks who had overrun Asia Minor from the east. In response, the pope called for crusades, military campaigns to recapture Jerusalem and the Holy Land from the Muslims. But, in 1204, crusaders en route to Palestine defied the pope's explicit orders. They conquered and sacked Constantinople, poisoning the relationship between the eastern and western churches for centuries. The Byzantines recovered the city in 1261, but their empire was irreparably weakened. In 1453 it finally succumbed to the Turks.

A Millennium of Byzantine Strength

How did the Byzantine Empire manage to survive for 1,000 years after Rome had fallen? The administrative system of the Byzantines deserves much of the credit, as a modern historian has explained:

> Consisting of a group of highly educated officials trained primarily at the university or, rather, "higher school" of Constantinople, the civil service was organized into a hierarchical system of considerable complexity even by today's standards. Taxes were collected regularly, justice was administered, armies were raised and put into the field, and the functions of the state in general were very adequately carried out. It may be said that in its period of greatest power (330–c. 1050) the Byzantine government, despite all its faults (excessive love of pomp and protocol, bureaucratic tendencies, and frequent venality), functioned more effectively, and for a longer period, than virtually any other political organism in history. (Geanakoplos, p. 3)

6.1

6.2

6.3

6.4

6.5

6.6

6.7

What allowed the eastern empire to survive after the end of the Roman Empire?

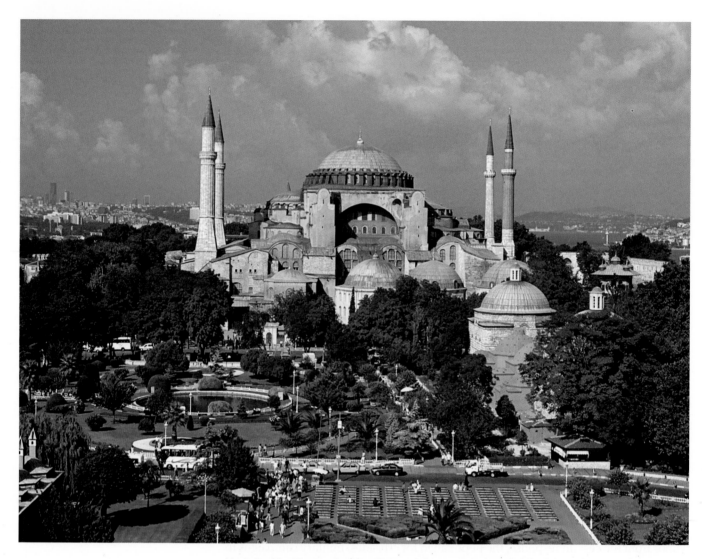

Hagia Sophia, Constantinople, 532–37 C.E. The Hagia Sophia (Church of the Holy Wisdom), built under the Emperor Justinian, is an imposing visual symbol of the power of the eastern empire. The dome, unusual in churches, represented the canopy of heaven. Later, Islamic mosques would often employ this form. The minarets, or pointed towers, at the four corners, were added in the fifteenth century when the Ottomans captured Constantinople and the church was converted into a mosque.

View the Image: The Interior of Hagia Sophia on **MyHistoryLab**

6.1

6.2

6.3

6.4

6.5

6.6

6.7 What allowed the eastern empire to survive after the end of the Roman Empire?

The ruling classes were never as isolated and alienated from the common people as in the west. The eastern empire was also less geographically overextended. Even when it lost its more distant territories, it could defend its heartland. Its sources of wealth and military manpower were in Thrace and Anatolia, geographically close to its center of political power in Constantinople, which remained an impregnable fortress for almost 1,000 years. In these settled lands, the Byzantine Empire had an older and stronger urban tradition than the west, and its cities remained viable centers of commerce long after most cities in the west had all but disappeared. The fiercest of the invading Germanic tribes turned away from these more settled regions and marched westward, toward the more open agricultural lands of the Roman Empire. In all these ways, the east was different from the west and was able to survive as an imperial state for another 1,000 years.

The Legacy of the Roman Empire:
What Difference Does It Make?

The Roman Empire laid foundations that have lasted until today in language, law, urban and regional development, and religious organization. Rome's language, Latin, was the official language of the empire, and it persisted as one of the two languages (with Greek) known by all educated Europeans until the seventeenth century. It survived until the mid-twentieth century as the language of ritual prayer for the Roman Catholic Church. It formed the base of the Romance languages (Italian, Spanish, Catalan, Portuguese, French, and Romanian) and contributed substantially to English.

Roman law, which developed and was codified over several centuries, inspired the transition to modern, codified law in much of Europe. It was the ancestor of the Napoleonic Codes that the French general and emperor institutionalized wherever he ruled in early nineteenth-century Europe.

The hundreds of towns that Rome founded and developed as administrative and military centers throughout the empire provided the nuclei around which the urban structure of much of modern Europe and northern Africa developed. The 50,000 miles of well-paved roads that connected the cities of the empire laid the foundation for much of modern Europe's land transportation patterns.

Even after its decline and fall, about 476, the Roman Empire continued to shape the vision and the administration of hundreds of millions of people. In 330 the emperor Constantine inaugurated Constantinople as an eastern, sister capital of the Roman Empire, and that city dominated much of the eastern Mediterranean until 1453.

Meanwhile in Western Europe, the Roman Catholic Church adapted the Roman imperial administrative organization for its own uses. This basic organization persists to the present. When the Emperor Constantine gave Christianity legal status throughout the empire and chose it as his own religion, he opened the gates for its unprecedented growth. What later became known as the Holy Roman Empire, which ruled much of central Europe for some 900 years from 800, also styled itself a successor to Rome, although the comparison was somewhat far-fetched.

Images of the Roman Empire remain powerful even to our own times. The British Empire, which girdled the globe from the eighteenth to the mid-twentieth century, proudly described itself as recreating and extending the imperial military power, administration, legal system, and technological superiority that had characterized Rome. They spoke of administering a "Pax Britannica." More recently, many political analysts have referred to the exercise of American political and military power around the globe as a "Pax Americana."

CHAPTER REVIEW

FROM HILL TOWN TO REPUBLIC, 753–133 B.C.E.

6.1 How did the early Republic take shape?

After driving out the ruling Etruscan kings, Rome's wealthy, powerful citizens declared Rome a republic, with power residing in a body of citizens and the representatives they elected. However, the early Republic was led by the small percentage of the population that was wealthy, powerful, and had hereditary residential ties to Rome: the patricians. The vast majority of people were in the plebeian class; they had no hereditary ties to the state and usually no property, which meant they were excluded from government. These two orders struggled for years in the early Republic, including armed struggles and political assassinations. Slowly, the patricians yielded power, and the plebeians gained representation in the Senate.

THE EXPANSION OF THE REPUBLIC

6.2 How did Rome build its empire on military expansion?

Rome was a military state from its beginning, and as it expanded across Italy, it became a society geared for war. Roman armies excelled in organization. They developed armies of small, flexible units, armed with swords and javelins, and went to battle with the least experienced soldiers in the front, the veterans reinforcing them from the rear. Rome also developed sophisticated siege warfare, and catapults to besiege walls and batter them down. As the Romans expanded their possessions steadily outward, by land and sea, their policy of brute force, called their "New Wisdom," served as a warning to all potential foes. In addition, many captives were forced into slavery.

CHAPTER REVIEW (continued)

THE POLITICS OF IMPERIAL RULE

6.3 How did the Romans win support from the people they conquered?

Rome was a republic at home, but an empire outside its borders. Rome often won support even from the people it conquered through political, cultural, economic, and ideological policies that often appeared beneficial, and especially through the granting of citizenship. Full Roman citizenship included voting rights, legal rights over property, legal enforcement of contracts, the right to marry Roman citizens, freedom from property taxes, and protection against arbitrary arrest and imprisonment. The further away from Rome, the fewer the conquered people who were granted citizenship; but they were the elites and they helped Rome to govern.

THE END OF THE REPUBLIC

6.4 How did the generals' power struggles lead to the end of the Republic?

Generals were naturally powerful in a militaristic empire such as Rome. They raised and funded their own armies, so the soldiers were dependent on them, rather than on the state. Sometimes generals fought one another in civil war, as did Lucius Sulla and Gaius Marius, 83–82 B.C.E. Ultimately, Sulla won and had himself declared "dictator." Later Julius Caeser also took power mostly on the basis of his military prowess and organization.

THE ROMAN PRINCIPATE, 30 B.C.E.–333 C.E.

6.5 What were the achievements of Augustus and the Principate?

With Augustus, and for two centuries after his death, Rome became an imperial monarchy, a territorial, political, and economic empire ruled by a single military commander. Augustus stabilized the borders of the empire, ensuring peace and facilitating trade, commerce, and economic growth. He established the *Pax Romana*, an era of peace in an empire under Roman rule, although some critics saw this is simply as suppression of any revolt. Similarly, some critics saw the domestic policies of the empire as overly patriarchal. The public projects Augustus inaugurated beautified Rome and kept its workers employed. Continuing the policy of "bread and circuses," he kept the masses pacified. He built roads and cities, stadiums and baths and aqueducts, throughout the empire. A new "golden age" of arts and literature flourished under his patronage.

THE DISMEMBERMENT OF THE ROMAN EMPIRE

6.6 Why did the Roman Empire decline and fall?

Continual warfare drained the treasury and led to the fragmentation of authority, as power shifted from civilian control by the Roman Senate to rival generals in the battlefields. German troops were inducted into Roman armies; some ultimately declared their independence from Rome. Invasions originated from Asia and pushed against the peoples bordering the empire, who, in turn, invaded Rome. They fragmented the empire into independent states that refused to live under Rome's rule. The new ethic of Christianity, sympathetic to the poor and the suppressed, may have undermined the desire of some Romans to devote themselves to further conquest. Recent scholars have suggested that climate change reduced the agricultural productivity of the Roman Empire, others that epidemic diseases left it more vulnerable to attack, still others that lead in the pipes carrying water reduced intellectual capacity.

THE EASTERN EMPIRE, 330–1453 C.E.

6.7 What allowed the eastern empire to survive after the end of the Roman Empire?

To govern the Roman Empire more efficiently, the Emperor Constantine established a new, second capital in the east. After Rome was sacked, the eastern segment of the empire survived for almost a thousand years as the Byzantine Empire. It was less overextended geographically than the Roman Empire. Its sources of wealth and military manpower were located near the center of political power, which allowed the empire to defend its heartland. The government was very well organized, with a hierarchical civil service, regular tax collection, and a well-ordered military. The western system of law was codified in the Byzantine Empire in the Justinian Code, which helped the government function and eventually became the basis of much of modern European law.

Suggested Readings

PRINCIPAL SOURCES

Boardman, John, Jasper Griffin, and Oswyn Murray, eds. *The Oxford History of the Classical World* (New York: Oxford University Press, 1993). Very useful array of expert articles on Greece and the Roman Empire.

Cornell, Tim, and John Matthews. *Atlas of the Roman World* (New York: Facts on File, 1983). The series of atlases in the Facts on File series are encyclopedic in their coverage, and extremely accessible as well.

Goldsworthy, Adrian. *How Rome Fell: Death of a Superpower* (New Haven, CT: Yale University Press, 2010). Looks at both weakening from within and the challenge of outsiders who ultimately dismembered the empire.

Grafton, Anthony, Glenn W. Most, and Salvatore Settis, eds. *The Classical Tradition* (Cambridge, MA: Harvard University Press, 2012). A reference work of 500 articles in more than 1000 pages. Remarkably comprehensive and useful.

Herrin, Judith. *Byzantium: The Surprising Life of a Medieval Empire* (Princeton, NJ: Princeton University Press, 2007). A consummate scholar presents a readable overview of 11 centuries of history.

Lewis, Naphtali, and Meyer Reinhold, eds. *Roman Civilization: Selected Readings:* Vol I *The Republic and the Augustan Age;* Vol II *The Empire* (New York: Columbia University Press, 1990). This documentary collection is indispensable.

MacCulloch, Diarmaid. *Christianity: The First Three Thousand Years* (New York: Penguin, 2009). Clear and readable on all the aspects of early Christianity in the Roman Empire—and much more.

MacMullen, Ramsay. *Romanization in the Time of Augustus* (New Haven, CT: Yale University Press, 2000). Argues that Roman ways of life were eagerly sought by conquered peoples, especially their leaders, and spread through imitation more than by force. Several of MacMullen's other very readable books illuminate class and religious relationships in imperial and post-imperial Rome. See especially *Roman Social Relations, 50 B.C. to A.D. 284* (New Haven, CT: Yale University Press, 1981).

Time-Life Books. *Time Frame 400 B.C.–200 A.D.: Empires Ascendant* (Alexandria, VA: Time-Life Books, 1988) and *Time Frame A.D. 200–600: Empires Besieged* (Alexandria, VA: Time-Life Books, 1988). These books are more at the advanced high-school level than college, but all volumes in this series are backed by excellent scholarship, clear and effective prose, and lavish, superb illustrations. These two volumes contain important chapters on Rome.

Woolf, Greg ed. *The Cambridge Illustrated History of the Roman World* (New York: Cambridge University Press, 2003). Excellent and lavishly illustrated collection of essays by outstanding scholars.

Woolf, Greg. *Rome: An Empire's Story* (New York: Oxford University Press, 2012). Lucid history of the empire, plus an evaluation of its influence on imperial thinking in the western world to the present.

ADDITIONAL SOURCES

Antoninus, Marcus Aurelius. *Meditations*, trans. H.G. Long, in Whitney J. Oates, ed., *The Stoic and Epicurean Philosophers* (New York: Modern Library, 1940). The classic statement of Stoicism by an emperor of Rome known also for his ruthless military conquests.

Aries, Philippe, and Georges Duby, eds. *A History of Private Life*: Vol. I *From Pagan Rome to Byzantium* (Cambridge, MA: Harvard University Press, 1987). Life cycle, marriage, family, slavery, the household, architecture, the private attitudes of public officials, work and leisure, wealth, public opinion, pleasure, religion, and community are the subjects of three of the fascinating, lengthy essays in this book.

Bradley, K.R. *Slavery and Society at Rome* (Cambridge: Cambridge University Press, 1994). A comprehensive, accessible review.

Brown, Peter. *The World of Late Antiquity, A.D. 150–750* (New York: Harcourt Brace Jovanovich, 1971) and *The Rise of Western Christendom* (Malden, MA: Blackwell, 1996). Brown's scholarship and clarity of presentation on the world of the late Roman Empire and the rise of Christianity make these excellent introductions.

Clark, Gillian. *Women in Late Antiquity: Pagan and Christian Life Styles* (Oxford: Oxford University Press, 1993). Looks at daily life, legal status, family relations, and identity at a time when Christianity and Pagan viewpoints are both prevalent.

Fantham, Elaine, *et al. Women in the Classical World* (New York: Oxford University Press, 1994). A collection of essays on gender relations through texts and artwork.

Finley, M.I., ed. *The Portable Greek Historians* (New York: Viking Press, 1959). An excellent anthology, with perceptive comments.

Frank, Andre Gunder, and Barry K. Gillis, eds. *The World System: Five Hundred Years or Five Thousand* (New York: Routledge, 1993). Many new explorations of trade in the ancient world, and new ways of understanding trade as the context of political as well as economic system-building, make this a fascinating interpretive study.

Garland, Lynda. *Byzantine Empresses: Women and Power in Byzantium, AD 527–1204* (London: Routledge, 1999). Accounts of Theodora—among many others—are useful in assessing her much-debated position as feminist, religious partisan, and savior of Justinian's throne.

Geanakoplos, Deno John. *Byzantium: Church, Society, and Civilization Seen Through Contemporary Eyes* (Chicago, IL: University of Chicago Press, 1984). An excellent analysis of the strengths of the Byzantine Empire, stressing its bureaucratic organization.

Gibbon, Edward. *The History of the Decline and Fall of the Roman Empire*, 3 vols. (New York: Modern Library, 1932). Available in several abridgements. This classic, two-centuries-old study includes important analyses of the Germanic nations, the Huns, the confrontation with early Islam, and the origins of early modern Europe as well as the fall of Rome. Fascinating for its perspective from the age of the European Enlightenment.

Goldsworthy, Adrian. *Caesar: Life of a Colossus* (New Haven: Yale University Press, 2006). Fast-paced, engaging biography, first from a military point of view, by a military historian, but comprehensive on private as well as public life.

Grant, Michael. *Julius Caesar* (New York: McGraw-Hill, 1969). Older biography, but still valuable for its attempt to present the man in terms of the development of Rome into an empire. Attempts to reconstruct the thinking of the politician/general.

Johns, Catherine. *Sex or Symbol? Erotic Images of Greece and Rome* (London: British Museum Press, 1989). An outstanding presentation of selections from the special collections of the British Museum on Greece and Rome, introducing an analysis of the function of sexual art in religious rituals, drama, and erotic titillation.

Jones, A.H.M. *Augustus* (New York: W.W. Norton & Co., 1970). The basic introduction to this pivotal emperor and his accomplishments. Jones is another classical master scholar-writer. Among his many other books, note *The Later Roman Empire, 284–602: A Social, Economic, and Administrative Survey*, 2 vols. (Oxford: Basil Blackwell, 1990).

Luttwak, Edward N. *The Grand Strategy of the Roman Empire* (Baltimore, MD: Johns Hopkins University Press, 1976). A fascinating analysis of Rome's military strategy, stressing "The New Wisdom" of application of overwhelming strength.

Mumford, Lewis. *The City in History* (New York: Harcourt, Brace, and World, 1961). Mumford's classic, moralistic analysis of historic urbanization sees Rome, both city and empire, as a catastrophe of the exploitation of the poor and vulnerable by the rich and powerful.

Procopius. *Secret History*, trans. Richard Atwater (Chicago, IL: P. Covici, 1927; New York: Covici Friede, 1927; reprinted Ann Arbor, MI: University of Michigan Press, 1961). Available online: http://www.fordham.edu/halsall/basis/procop-anec.asp. The most comprehensive ancient source on Justinian and Theodora. A controversial account.

Runciman, Steven. *Byzantine Civilization* (Cleveland, OH: World Publishing Co., 1933). Even after 75 years, this is still a fascinating and readable introduction.

Virgil. *Aeneid*, trans. Rolphe Humphries (New York: Charles Scribner's Sons, 1951). Writing in the age of Augustus, Virgil gives the classic, idealized statement of Rome's mission.

Wells, Peter. *The Barbarians Speak: How the Conquered Peoples Shaped Roman Europe* (Princeton, NJ: Princeton University Press, 1999). Reviews and extends studies of the relationships between Romans and "Barbarians" based on recent archaeological findings.

FILMS

Spartacus (1960; 3 hours and 17 minutes). This Hollywood blockbuster celebrates the slave revolt of Spartacus in 73–71 B.C.E. Directed by Stanley Kubrick and written by Dalton Trumbo, based on a novel by Howard Fast, this film sees the life and politics of Rome from the viewpoint of the slave.

Roman City (2000; 1 hour). Traces the evolution of Rome and cities throughout the Roman Empire. Based on the book *City* by David Macaulay, and narrated by him. Combines narration and animation in a fascinating presentation.

Time-Life. *Lost Civilizations: Rome: The Ultimate Empire* (2002; 50 minutes). Emphasizes the violence underlying the creation and perpetuation of empire, and the violence of the gladiatorial contests in the Colosseum. Includes comments by major scholars along with vivid images and quotations.

When Rome Ruled: Ancient Superpower (2010–11:8 hours). A National Geographic Special with all the strengths – visual beauty; interesting, up-to-date expert commentary – and some of the drawbacks – over-dramatization – of the genre. Originally 8 hours on TV, later available commercially in 6 parts on 3 DVDs.

Crash Course in World History: Rome (2012; 12 minutes). One in a series of 42 frenetic introductions to major subjects in world history. Pitched more at the high-school level. Fun. Informational. Take a look.

7 China

Fracture and Unification: The Qin, Han, Sui, and Tang Dynasties

221 B.C.E.–900 C.E.

By the fifth century B.C.E. the Zhou (Chou) dynasty (1100–256 B.C.E.) was in decline. As the dynasty began to weaken, the powerful, independent states of the region fought among themselves so constantly that China's historians have named the years between about 481 and 221 B.C.E. the Warring States period. After hundreds of years of warfare, in 221 B.C.E. the Qin (Ch'in) dynasty defeated the others, unifying north China and creating the first unified Chinese Empire.

LEARNING OBJECTIVES

7.1 ((	7.2 ((	7.3 ((	7.4 ((
Describe the philosophies of rule in the Chinese empire.	Understand the influence of Confucianism on the Chinese bureaucracy.	Explain the elements of China's underlying unity.	Define "empire" in relation to China.

((Listen on MyHistoryLab

The Great Wall of China. Begun 214 B.C.E., rebuilt repeatedly. "The seven wonders of the world are not comparable to this work," wrote one awestruck seventeenth-century European observer of this most imposing relic of China's past. Faced with brick and stone and averaging 25 feet high and wide, the 1,500-mile-long wall is studded with towers that serve as signaling stations, warning of the approach of mobile enemies.

This chapter will consider the Chinese Empire during its first 1,100 years, from 221 B.C.E. to 907 C.E. During this time China created political and cultural forms that would last for another 1,000 years, and perhaps even to the present.

We examine the key accomplishments under China's imperial rulers—the conquest, consolidation, and confirmation of the empire—and the expansion of China to include "outer China," the distant, conquered provinces inhabited by people not ethnically Chinese. In addition, we outline relationships with peoples to the south and southwest, who were ultimately incorporated into China, and with Korea and Japan, whose cultures were profoundly influenced by China. We close by comparing and contrasting the Chinese Empire with that of Rome.

What were the philosophies of rule in the Chinese empire?

7.1

7.2

7.3

7.4

The Qin Dynasty

7.1 What were the philosophies of rule in the Chinese empire?

The Qin dynasty expanded from a geopolitical base around the confluence of the Yellow and Wei rivers to control the whole of north China and a segment of the south. The Qin conquest ended centuries of fighting among the dynasties of north China that began with the decline of the Zhou dynasty and lasted through the period of the Warring States. The Qin defeated other regional states over the course of perhaps a century, until by 221 B.C.E. it could rightfully claim to have established a unified empire, the first in China's history. Although the dynasty itself lasted only a few years after it succeeded in establishing the empire, the empire persisted with few interruptions to the present.

Military Power and Mobilization

Armed force was fundamental in the Qin's conquest. The *Book of Songs*, dating from the early years of the Zhou dynasty, suggests the constant nature of warfare in early China:

> Which plant is not yellow?
> Which day don't we march?
> Which man does not go
> To bring peace to the four quarters?
>
> Which plant is not brown?
> Which man is not sad?
> Have pity on us soldiers,
> Treated as though we were not men!
>
> … We are neither rhinos nor tigers
> Yet are led through the wilds,
> Have pity on us soldiers,
> Never resting morn or night.   (trans. Waley)

The Qin not only conquered north China but also defeated the Xiongnu (Hsiung-na), border tribes (probably related to the groups that the Romans called the Huns) to the north and west of China proper. They gained authority over northern Korea, and defeated some of the Yue tribes in the south. The first Qin ruler to govern a unified China was Qin Shi Huangdi (r. 221–210 B.C.E.), "the first august emperor of the Qin," not unlike the title "Caesar Augustus of Rome" that Octavian bestowed upon himself.

In addition to their military efforts, the Qin also mobilized tens of thousands of men for enormous public works projects. After conquering the other states of northern China, they fortified and linked the defensive walls that had been

Terra-cotta army from the tomb of Qin Shi Huangdi, Qin dynasty, 210 B.C.E. The vastness of the terra-cotta army—it comprised thousands of soldiers, still being uncovered—buried near the tomb of the First Emperor of Qin, and the care with which each life-size figure was molded, suggest at once the enormous power of the Qin army and the emperor's concern with the afterlife.

7.1 What were the philosophies of rule in the Chinese empire?

7.2

7.3

7.4

KEY TERM

barbarians The Greeks first used the term "barbarous" to designate foreign and uncivilized peoples, those whose languages sounded to Greek ears like the sound *barbar*, rather than like Greek. Today, "barbarian" continues to refer to persons who are considered foreign and uncivilized, and may, in the extreme, also refer to people who are violent, uncontrolled, and, perhaps, uncontrollable.

constructed by local rulers into the 1,500-mile Great Wall of China over a seven-year period with a workforce of one million laborers. This wall was to keep the northern Xiongnu "**barbarians**" out of China proper and, with its 40-foot-high watchtowers constructed every few hundred yards, to serve as a first warning in case of attempted invasion.

The first emperor also conscripted 700,000 laborers to construct his palace, a complex large enough to hold 40,000 people. But perhaps even more impressive was Qin Shi Huangdi's tomb. In 1974 archaeologists digging near his mausoleum discovered a ceramic army of some 7,000 life-size soldiers and horses, arranged in military formation and armed with bronze weapons, spears, longbows, and crossbows (a Chinese invention). In 1976, a second excavation uncovered an additional 1,400 chariots and cavalrymen in four military units. The next year archaeologists discovered a much smaller pit, holding what appeared to be a terra-cotta officer corps. These thousands of figures were not mass-produced. Craftsmen modeled and painted each figure separately, even down to its elaborate hairstyle, which symbolized its specific military office. The figures apparently represented the elite of the imperial troops and were fashioned to accompany the emperor to his tomb and afterlife.

EARLY ADVANCES IN WEAPONRY	
3000 (B.C.E.)	War chariot invented. In Mesopotamia and southeastern Europe first metal swords and shields made (bronze).
2000	First armor made, from bronze scales, in Mesopotamia.
c. 700	The Phoenicians and Egyptians invent galleys—warships powered by oars.
500	Giant crossbows and catapults used by the Greeks and Carthaginians.
200	Hand-held crossbow now being used in China.
300 (C.E.)	Stirrups used in China.
950	Gunpowder used by Chinese for signaling devices and fireworks.
1250–1300	Bronze and iron cannon probably used by the Chinese; in Europe, first recorded use of cannon is 1326.

What were the philosophies of rule in the Chinese empire?

7.1
7.2
7.3
7.4

Economic Power

The Qin undertook enormous public works projects to increase the economic productivity of the empire. During the centuries of their rise to power, they built canals and river transport systems in both the Wei River system in the north and the Min River system in Sichuan in west-central China. In Sichuan they irrigated the region around Chengdu, turning it into a granary for the nation. The transportation and irrigation systems they built in the northern state of Shanxi transformed it into an area so rich in agricultural productivity and the means of transporting it that they could control all of north China from this base. As ironworking became increasingly important in Chinese military and economic development, the Qin also captured the richest sources of iron ore and two of China's best ironworking facilities, crucial resources for fashioning both tools and weapons.

Administrative Power

Administratively, Qin Shi Huangdi ruled through a bureaucracy. He did away with the system of personal allegiance by which officials were appointed on the basis of their personal, often family, ties to the court and therefore owed allegiance to the emperor himself rather than to the empire as an institution. Instead, the emperor chose people for office on the basis of ability; their tasks were fixed and governed by systematic, formalized, written rules, and their work was rewarded or punished according to the degree of their efficiency and fidelity. The Qin divided the empire into some 40 administrative units called "commanderies." Each commandery was staffed with three leading officials: a civil authority, a military authority, and an inspector representing the emperor. The three officials served as checks and balances on one another: no one individual could assert too much power and threaten the control of the emperor at the center.

The Qin standardized as they centralized. They fixed weights and measures, values of coinage, and the size of cart axles and of the roads they traveled. They standardized the legal code. Perhaps most significant of all, the Qin standardized the written form of the Chinese language, possibly the most important single act of political and cultural unification in China's history. To this day, despite great variation in the local forms of spoken Chinese, written Chinese is uniform throughout the country, just as the Qin established it.

Competing Ideologies of Empire

In their public proclamations, Chinese emperors stressed the importance of their philosophy to the actual process of building, sustaining, and guiding their empire. In

AT A GLANCE: CHINA 500 B.C.E.–900 C.E.

DATE	POLITICS	RELIGION AND CULTURE	SOCIAL DEVELOPMENT
500 B.C.E.	• Warring States period (481–221)	• Confucius (551–479)	
250 B.C.E.	• Zhou dynasty ends (256) • Qin Shi Huangdi initiates Qin dynasty (221–206) • Revolts against Qin (207)	• Han Fei Tzu (d. 233) • Daoism • Legalism • Great Wall	
200 B.C.E.	• Liu Bang (206–195) first emperor of Han dynasty		
150 B.C.E.	• Han Wu (141–87)	• Confucian Academy established (124)	• Travels of Zhang Qian
100 B.C.E.	• Reign of usurper Wang Mang (9–23 C.E.)	• Sima Qian (145–85) • Invention of paper	
50 C.E.		• First mention of Buddhism in China	
200 C.E.	• Han dynasty ends (220) • Age of Disunity (221–331) • Three Kingdoms (220–80)		
300 C.E.	• Jin dynasty (265–316) • Northern Wei dynasty (386–534)	• Buddhism expands • Gu Kaizhi (334–406)	
600 C.E.	• Sui dynasty (581–618) • Tang dynasty (618–907)	• Invention of block printing • Grand Canal completed (610) • Buddhist cave art	• Boundaries of empire extended to Mongolia, Turkestan, Afghanistan, Pakistan, and Iran • Tang briefly held northern Korea and Vietnam
650 C.E.	• Empress Wu (625–705)		• First pharmacopoeia
700 C.E.	• Battle of Talas River (751) • An Lushan rebellion (755–63)	• Wang Wei (701–62) • Li Bai (701–61) • Du Fu (712–70) • Porcelain produced	
800 C.E.		• Repression of Buddhism	
900 C.E.	• Collapse of Tang, leading to disunity (907–60) • Song dynasty (960–1279)		

7.1 What were the philosophies of rule in the Chinese empire?

7.2

7.3

7.4

addition, the official historians who compiled China's records were an elite trained in philosophy. As a result, China's history includes a profound concern with the conflicts over the philosophy and ideology of empire. These philosophies and ideologies emerged during the late Zhou dynasty and the period of the Warring States (c. 481–221 B.C.E.). The chaos of the times induced some individuals to engage actively in a search for solutions to Chinese political and social problems; others to disengage and find tranquility apart from society and politics. The three schools of thought that emerged in this period—Confucianism, Daoism (Taoism), and Legalism—deeply influenced every dynasty that ruled China after the Qin.

Confucianism. Kong Fuzi (551–479 B.C.E.), known in Latin as Confucius, a philosopher and political adviser from the small state of Lu in modern Shandong, sought to reform China by redefining Chinese political and ethical thought. Confucius began his career as a scholar. He mastered the six arts of ritual, music, archery, chariot driving, calligraphy, and arithmetic, and then began his career as a teacher. At a time when China was divided into many states, often in conflict, he formulated principles that he thought would bring peace, contentment, dignity, and personal cultural development at least to the elite of his time. Although Confucius was unsuccessful in finding employment as an adviser in any single state, his disciples kept his vision alive, and it has permeated Chinese thought and, often, government policy.

Confucius felt that good government depended on good officials, men of *jen*, or humanity, benevolence, virtue, and culture. Although he was not much concerned with the supernatural, he did believe that a moral order pervaded the universe and that it could be understood. In contrast to the tumult of his own day, Confucius believed that the early days of the Zhou dynasty had been a golden age of peace and order, wisdom and virtue. In those days, political leaders had understood the importance of social hierarchy, ritual, music, and art. The neglect of these elements of humanism and rationalism, and the absence of schools that taught them to new leaders, had reduced China to chaos.

Confucius and his disciples canonized five of China's earliest historical texts as especially fine examples of the philosopher's own thought and his concern for history, music, the arts, and rituals:

- the *Book of Documents*, a collection of various statements of early kings and their ministers;
- the *Book of Changes*, the *I Ching*, which details methods of predicting the future through casting sticks;
- the *Book of Songs*, which contains 305 poems, about half of which relate to the everyday lives of ordinary people, half to issues of court politics and rituals;
- the *Spring and Autumn Annals*, which contains brief chronologies from Lu, Confucius' home state;
- *Rites and Rituals* (three texts, grouped as one), which combines both philosophies and rituals of the court.

In addition, Confucius' disciples recorded his own teachings in *The Analects* (see box overleaf). A large body of interpretation and commentary grew up around each of these texts.

Confucius believed in the essential goodness and educability of each individual, and believed that the virtues of the past could be regained. He believed in the centrality of the "gentleman" (*junzi*), the moral leader who had the vision to move the society toward peace and virtue. Such a gentleman would and should be concerned about political leadership and the proper ordering of the state. For Confucius, however, gentlemen were not born but made, fashioned through proper education. Believing that character, not birth, was important, he taught whoever would come to him, but Confucius' own era was too violent for his teachings to find immediate acceptance.

The Qin dynasty did not welcome his teachings either, but the next dynasty, the Han, did. Under the Han, Confucius' ethical and political values came to dominate the culture and thought of China's scholars and intellectuals, and they continued powerful for most of the following 2,000 years, also influencing the political thought of Korea, Japan, and Southeast Asia.

Moreover, because Confucius expressed his ideas in such general terms, subsequent disciples could adapt them to particular problems. Thus, Confucianism evolved and often transformed into new forms that sometimes maintained its core values and sometimes changed them. For example, Mencius (Mengzi) (*c.* 371–*c.* 289 B.C.E.) had an optimistic view of human nature and believed that education would function to bring out the best in people. He encouraged government leaders to rule in the best interests of the people and society by encouraging harmony according to Confucian principles. Another disciple, Xunzi (Hsün-Tzu) (312–235 B.C.E.), took a more negative view of human nature. Having many years of experience in government, he emphasized different aspects of Confucian thought. Most important, he believed that human nature was inherently selfish and that only through education and participation in rituals would people learn to put the needs of society ahead of their own. Unlike Mencius, Xunzi proposed an education that would emphasize restraints on human behavior.

SOURCE

Confucius and *The Analects*

We have no record that Confucius wrote down his own teachings. *The Analects*, a collection of thoughtful perceptions attributed to him, was apparently recorded and compiled by disciples of his disciples. Because these aphorisms—497 verses in 20 chapters—are brief, unelaborated, unorganized, and written in ideographic form, their exact meaning is not always clear, but these same qualities promote the reader's engagement with and interpretation of the text. *The Analects* have been part of the education of every Chinese school student for centuries, at least until the communist revolution in 1949. The selections here represent typical subjects for Confucius: the importance of formal, humanistic education in forming proper character; teaching and learning by example; focus on the present; and respect for others, especially parents and elders.

A young man is to be filial within his family and respectful outside it. He is to be earnest and faithful, overflowing in his love for living beings and intimate with those who are humane. If after such practice he has strength to spare, he may use it in the study of culture.

Lead them by means of regulations and keep order among them through punishments, and the people will evade them and will lack any sense of shame.

Lead them through moral force (*de*) and keep order among them through rites (*li*), and they will have a sense of shame and will also correct themselves.

In education there should be no class distinctions.

Shall I teach you what knowledge is? When you know something, to know that you know it. When you do not know, to know that you do not know it. That is knowledge.

The noble person is concerned with rightness; the small person is concerned with profit.

I am not one who was born with knowledge; I am one who loves the past and is diligent in seeking it.

The Three Armies can be deprived of their commander, but even a common person cannot be deprived of his will.

The wise have no doubts; the humane have no sorrows; the courageous have no fears.

Before you have learned to serve human beings, how can you serve spirits …?

When you do not yet know life, how can you know about death?

Look at nothing contrary to ritual; listen to nothing contrary to ritual; say nothing contrary to ritual; do nothing contrary to ritual.

What you would not want for yourself, do not do to others.

Zigong asked about government. The Master said, "Sufficient food, sufficient military force, the confidence of the people." Zigong said, "If one had, unavoidably, to dispense with one of these three, which of them should go first?" The Master said, "Get rid of the military." Zigong said, "If one had, unavoidably, to dispense with one of the remaining two, which should go first?" The Master said, "Dispense with the food. Since ancient times there has always been death, but without confidence a people cannot stand." (de Bary and Bloom, pp. 45–60)

Throughout Chinese history, some groups rebelled against Confucius' ethical principles. Peasant rebels, a frequent presence throughout the centuries, condemned Confucius' emphasis on order and harmony. In the late nineteenth and twentieth centuries, as China saw itself fall behind the technological and military achievements of the Western world, Confucian traditions were challenged with renewed vigor (see the chapters entitled "Nationalism, Imperialism, and Resistance," and "Cold War, New Nations, and Revolt against Authority"). Critics argued that Confucianism was incompatible with equality, scientific education, rebellious youth movements, dignity of physical labor, peasant equity, and equal rights for women. The communist government that has ruled China since 1949 attacked Confucius especially bitterly in 1973 and 1974 during the Cultural Revolution, asserting that in his own day Confucius had served as a representative of the slave-owning aristocracy. As communism has more recently been transformed in contemporary China, the study of Confucianism is returning to China's schools.

KEY TERM

Legalism A school of Chinese philosophy that came into prominence during the Period of the Warring States and had great influence on the policies of the Qin dynasty. Legalists took a pessimistic view of human nature and believed that social harmony could be attained only through strong government control and the imposition of strict laws, enforced absolutely.

Legalism. Rejecting Confucianism, the Qin favored a philosophy of government known as **Legalism**, which was characterized by strict laws and strict enforcement, with rewards for those who observed the laws and swift and appropriate punishment for those who broke them. During his reign, Qin Shi Huangdi set up inscriptions on stone in various parts of his empire proclaiming his values and policies. For example, after he put down a rebellion in the far northeast, he inscribed on the city walls:

Then he mobilized armies, and punished the unprincipled, and those who perpetrated rebellion were wiped out.

Armed force exterminates the violent and rebellious, but civil power relieves the guiltless of their labors, and the masses all submit in their hearts.

Achievements and toil are generously assessed, and the rewards even extend to cattle and horses, and his bounty enriches the land.

The August Emperor gave a vigorous display of his authority, and his virtue brought together all the states, and for the first time brought unity and supreme peace.

City walls were demolished [suggesting that peace had been established so that walls were no longer necessary for defense], waterways were opened up, and obstacles were flattened.

When the physical features of the land had been determined, there was no conscript labor for the masses, and all under heaven was pacified.

Men take pleasure in their farmland, and women cultivate their tasks, and all matters have their proper arrangement.

His kindness protects all production, and for long they have been coming together in the fields, and everyone is content with his place. (Sima Qian, trans. Dawson p. 74)

In another inscription he wrote:

When the sage of Qin took charge of his state, he first determined punishments and names, and clearly set forth the ancient regulations.

He was the first to standardize the system of laws, examine and demarcate duties and responsibilities, so as to establish unchanging practices. (p. 82)

He proclaimed a code of sexual conduct:

If a man commits adultery, to kill him is no crime, so men hang on to the standards of righteousness.

If a wife elopes to remarry, then the son will not have a mother, and so everyone is converted into chastity and purity. (p. 83)

In his rulings, Qin Shi Huangdi followed many of the policies of the political philosopher Han Fei Tzu (d. 233 B.C.E.), a student of the Confucian scholar Xunzi. Han Fei Tzu called himself a Legalist because he believed that strict laws, strictly enforced, were the best assurance of good and stable government. Han Fei Tzu summed up the power of the law:

To govern the state by law is to praise the right and blame the wrong … To correct the faults of the high, to rebuke the vices of the low, to suppress disorders, to decide against mistakes, to subdue the arrogant, to straighten the crooked, and to unify the folkways of the masses, nothing could match the law.

The means whereby the intelligent ruler controls his ministers are two handles only. The two handles are chastisement and commendation. (Han Fei Tzu, I:45–7)

📖 Read the Document: **Legalism: The Way of the State (475–221 BCE)** on **MyHistoryLab**

Daoism. Daoism (Taoism) was a philosophy of spontaneity in the face of nature and the cosmos. It was a mystical philosophy, not usually directly applicable to government, but often a solace to public men in their private lives, especially after retirement. Daoism is often seen as an inspiration to artists, and, because it advocates a high regard for nature, it is often seen as an inspiration to natural scientists as well.

The legendary founder of Daoism and the author of its key text, the *Daodejing* ("The Way and its Power") is Laozi (*c.* 604–*c.* 517 B.C.E.), but the school and the book more likely date to the third or fourth centuries B.C.E. Laozi's teachings are cloaked in paradox and mystery:

The Way that can be spoken of is not the constant Way;
The name that can be named is not the constant name.

7.1

7.2

7.3

7.4

What were the
philosophies
of rule in the
Chinese empire?

Rejecting the emphasis on sophisticated learning and education that characterized Confucian thought, Daoists believed that untutored simplicity was powerful:

> Do away with sageliness, discard knowledge,
> And the people will benefit a hundredfold.
> Do away with humaneness, discard righteousness,
> And the people will once more be filial and loving,
> Dispense with cleverness, discard profit,
> And there will be no more bandits and thieves.
> These three, to be regarded as ornaments, are insufficient.
> Therefore let the people have something to cling to:
> Manifest plainness,
> Embrace uncarved wood,
> Diminish selfishness,
> Reduce desires.
>
> What is softest in the world
> Overcomes what is hardest in the world.
> No-thing penetrates where there is no space.
> Thus I know that in doing nothing there is advantage.
> The wordless teaching and the advantage of doing nothing—there are few in the
> world who understand them.

Those who followed Daoism believed in a natural order or path (Dao). They taught that government should leave people alone:

> The more prohibitions there are in the world,
> The poorer are the people.
> The more sharp weapons people have,
> The more disorder is fomented in the family and the state.
> The more adroit and clever men are,
> The more deceptive things are brought forth.
> The more laws and ordnances are promulgated,
> The more thieves and robbers there are.
> Therefore the sage says:
> I do nothing (*wuwei*),
> And the people are transformed by themselves.

(de Bary and Bloom, pp. 79–90)

This Daoist view of simplicity diminishes the need for government: "Let the state be small and the people be few" (de Bary and Bloom, p. 94). Nor is there need to travel. Beauty, peace, and joy are to be found at home:

> Though neighboring states are within sight of one another,
> And the sound of cocks and dogs is audible from one to the other,
> People will reach old age and yet not visit one another. (p. 94)

Daoism can be viewed as a rejection of Confucian principles, but over time many Chinese embraced both Confucianism and Daoism, allowing the former to shape their public lives, while gaining solace from the latter in their private lives. Because Daoism allowed the individual to find his or her own path, over time it began to embrace a variety of popular beliefs, alchemy, mysticism, and magic, all reinforced through a variety of rituals. Finally, Daoism may have facilitated the acceptance of Mahayana Buddhism (see the chapter entitled "Hinduism and Buddhism") in China, since both stressed the idea of transcending the material world.

**Read the Document: Daoism: The Classic of the Way and Virtue (500s–400s BCE)
on MyHistoryLab**

The Struggle between Legalism and Confucianism. The philosophies of Legalism and Confucianism collided during the Qin dynasty. In direct contrast to the Confucianists' reverence for the past, the prime minister Li Si (Li Ssu) (c. 280–208 B.C.E.) argued that the administration of the Qin was far superior to the government of any earlier time. The Qin success was the result of its decision to replace personal, *ad hoc* administration with an orderly system of laws and appointment to office on the basis of efficiency in accordance with Legalist principles.

Li Si recommended that the Confucian classics be collected and burned so that the past could no longer be held up as an alternative to present policies. In 213 B.C.E. the Qin burned the books. Subsequently, as Confucian scholars continued to oppose Qin Shi Huangdi, the emperor had 460 scholars buried alive. Sima Qian, the official, Confucian historian of the Han government, recorded these acts of anti-intellectualism

What were the philosophies of rule in the Chinese empire?

7.1

7.2

7.3

7.4

HOW DO WE KNOW?

The Grand Historians

The Chinese valued recording the past both for itself and for the moral principles it was believed to teach. China therefore prepared and transmitted the most fully and continuously documented history of any ancient empire. Building on this legacy of historical literature, the Han emperor Wu (r. 141–87 B.C.E.) created a new official position, Grand Historian of the Han court, with the responsibility of preparing a comprehensive history of the entire Chinese past.

The first person to hold the post was Sima Tan (d. 110 B.C.E.). He was succeeded by his son Sima Qian (145–85 B.C.E.), one of the greatest of all historians. Father and son transformed their task from one of writing dynastic chronologies to one of evaluating the quality of governments and rulers. They created the art of Chinese history as a commentary on politics and ethics.

At the very end of his great work *Shi Qi*, 130 chapters recounting the history of China from mythological times almost to his own, Sima Qian includes an autobiographical sketch:

Qian was born at Longmen. He ploughed and kept flocks on the sunny slopes of the mountains near the Yellow River. By the age of ten he was reading aloud the ancient writings. At twenty he journeyed south to the Yangtze and Huai rivers, ascended Kuaiji to search for the cave of Yu, espied Jiuyi, went by water down to Yun and Xiang, journeyed north and crossed the Wen and Si to investigate the traditions in the cities of Qi and Lu, and observed the customs handed down by Master Kong [Confucius], and took part in the archery competition held at Mount Yi in Cou. He suffered distress in Po, Xie, and Pengcheng, and returned home via Liang and Chu. Afterwards Qian served as a palace gentleman, and received orders to be sent on the western expedition to the south of Ba and Shu. Having gone south and captured Qiong, Ze, and Kunming, they returned and made their report on the mission. (trans. Dawson, p. xix)

So Sima Qian's training included farming, literature, travel, adventure, anthropological research, archery, court service, and warfare. If historians improve with their own experience of life, since it enables them to understand more fully the lives of the people they study, then Sima Qian was off to a good start.

The highlight of Sima Qian's historical writing is its emphasis on biography, a traditional Chinese literary form that he developed into a vehicle for commenting on the political and ethical policies of the state not only in the past but also in his own time. His judgments could be fierce, and they sometimes got him into trouble. His support for his friend General Li Ling at a time when the general was in great disfavor in court led to Sima Qian's castration. Later, the Han emperor Wu was so angered by Sima Qian's account of his father, Emperor Jingdi, that he had that chapter removed. Eventually, however, imperial feelings mellowed, and Sima Qian won his reputation as the greatest master of the early Chinese historical tradition.

Sima Qian completed his accounts up to about 100 B.C.E. A later historian, Ban Biao (3–54 C.E.), added tens of chapters of "Supplementary Chronicles," and his son Ban Gu (32–92 C.E.) wrote the *Han Shu* ("History of the Han Dynasty") to 22 C.E. Ban Gu established the tradition of compiling a history of each dynasty, a form that continued in the *Hou-Han Shu* ("History of the Later Han") and endured into the twentieth century.

Because the official histories carry their own Confucian, conservative biases, and focus almost entirely on the central government and its court, unofficial material from the provinces is especially useful in giving additional viewpoints. Grave sites and tombs yield documents, inscriptions, and engravings, and these often include relief sculptures of the activities of the deceased during his or her life. The burial goods represent in miniature the deceased's house, tools, carriages, boats, farms, and equipment. They often included terra-cotta figures or painted frescoes of entertainers, musicians, servants, and maids, who had enriched the life of the deceased.

- What were the reasons for recording an official court history of each dynasty?
- What were the reasons for the rise, fall, and return to prominence of Sima Qian?
- How would you evaluate the training of Sima Qian as an historian?

Classical China. In 221 B.C.E., two centuries of internecine rivalry—the "Warring States" period—ended with the rise to centralized power of the Qin dynasty, but internal revolt and external pressure on the borders precipitated further civil war. The Han dynasty emerged as the new rulers in 202 B.C.E. They refortified the northern walls and extended imperial control far to the south and west. In the northwest, they penetrated the Gansu corridor as far as Dunhuang and the central Asian silk routes.

7.1

What were the
philosophies
of rule in the
Chinese empire?

7.2

7.3

7.4

and brutality, which leave the Legalist Qin with a dismal reputation. The cruel intrigues and struggles for succession that helped to end the Qin dynasty confirm that view.

The Mandate of Heaven. One of the enduring philosophical concepts of Chinese imperial politics was the Mandate of Heaven (see the chapter entitled "A Polycentric World"). Heaven—not a personal god but the cosmic forces of the universe—underpinned rulers of high moral stature and undercut those who lacked it. An omnipotent heaven conferred its mandate, or authority to rule, on the moral and revoked it from

7.1

How did
Confucianism
influence
the Chinese
bureaucracy?

7.2

7.3

7.4

the immoral. Dynasties were thus held accountable for their actions, and they could not expect to rule forever. Their loss of cosmic connection would be made manifest, not only in the usual political and economic strife of a weak administration, but also through nature itself going awry in the form of floods, droughts, or other natural disasters. Throughout Chinese history, rebels against an emperor would claim evidence of his having lost the "Mandate," while those supporting new rulers would proclaim their possession of it.

The Fall of the Qin Dynasty

Qin Shi Huangdi died in 210 B.C.E. and was buried in the enormous mausoleum he had created, accompanied by the vast ceramic army he had ordered. Within four years his apparently powerful, centralized, productive, well-organized dynasty had collapsed. Despite the apparent strengths, the Qin had oppressed to their breaking point the nation and its peasantry, the 90 percent of the population who paid the taxes, served in the armies, built the public works projects, and the women who supported all these projects through their work at home. The final crisis began when the emperor sent several hundred thousands of these peasants to fight the Xiongnu in the far north and northwest on both sides of the Great Wall. As the *Han History* later reported,

> For more than ten years they were exposed to the rigors of military life, and countless numbers died … Although the men toiled at farming, there was not enough grain for rations; and the women could not spin enough yarn for the tents. The common people were ruined. (cited in Elvin, p. 27)

In addition to these systemic problems, the fight over the succession to Qin Shi Huangdi's throne destroyed the dynasty. A contest for power broke out among the late emperor's son, the minister Li Si, and another court official, the eunuch Zhao Gao. (Eunuchs were men who had been castrated so that they could be trusted around the women of the court; without families of their own, they could usually be relied upon for their loyalty to the emperor.) In the struggle, the emperor's son murdered many of his father's supporters on the advice of his minister. Fear and disloyalty flourished. Each contestant seemed concerned only for his own survival and aggrandizement. Qin Shi Huangdi had instituted bureaucracy in place of personal rule throughout the empire, but personal politics still dominated the imperial court. Finally, Zhao forced the emperor's son to commit suicide, but then he himself was assassinated. While the court was convulsed in these internal struggles, rebels broke into the capital at Xianyang and captured power. Warfare continued until, in 206 B.C.E., the rebel leader Liu Bang emerged victorious and established the Han dynasty.

Han historians proclaimed their belief that the Qin dynasty had lost the Mandate of Heaven. Nevertheless, the Qin had brought China to a new stage of political development: the empire had been founded; an effective bureaucratic administration had been established; and careers had been opened to new men of talent. All these innovations were to last, in changing measure, for 2,000 years.

The Han Dynasty

7.2   How did Confucianism influence the Chinese bureaucracy?

When Liu Bang (r. 206–195 B.C.E.) prevailed in the warfare that ended the Qin dynasty, the empire remained intact. One ruling family fell and another took its place and asserted its own control, but the empire itself continued united under a single emperor. The principal Legalist ministers who had guided the Qin were replaced, but the administrative bureaucracy continued to function.

7.1
7.2   How did
      Confucianism
7.3   influence
      the Chinese
7.4   bureaucracy?

A Confucian Bureaucracy

Change came in the leadership style of the new dynasty. Liu Bang was himself a commoner and a soldier, perhaps illiterate, with many years of warfare still ahead of him—he died in battle in 195 B.C.E.—but as his ministers he chose educated men with Confucian principles. Slowly, a new social and political hierarchy emerged, with scholars at the top, followed by farmers, artisans, and merchants. Legalism still influenced the administrative systems, and Daoism's emphasis on nature and emotion continued to be attractive, but Confucius' ethical teachings captured the imagination of the court.

The influence of Confucianism appeared in four other areas. First, history became more important than ever. The appointment of Sima Tan and then his son Sima Qian as court historians established the tradition of imperial record-keeping (see box above). The Confucian notion of the importance of tradition and continuity prevailed over the Legalist idea of discounting the past.

Second, in 124 B.C.E. the most powerful and longest-lived of the Han rulers, Wudi or Emperor Wu (r. 141–87 B.C.E.), the Martial Emperor, established an elite imperial academy to teach specially selected scholar-bureaucrats the wisdom of Confucius and its applicability to problems of governance. The emperor also declared that knowledge of the Confucian classics would be a basis for promotion in the imperial civil service. Although the academy could at first educate only 50 men, it multiplied in size until, in the later Han period, it could accommodate 30,000 men. In Han times, the landed aristocracy still gained most of the places in the bureaucracy, but the principle of appointment and promotion based not on birth but on success in an examination in the Confucian classics was finally established during the Tang dynasty (618–907 C.E.).

Third, an imperial conference of Confucian legal scholars was convened in the imperial palace in 51 B.C.E. to codify the principles for applying case law. This established and consolidated the Chinese legal system for centuries to come.

Finally, Confucian scholars, both male and female, began to establish principles of conduct for women. Confucius had spoken of the importance of five relationships in human society: ruler–subject; father–son; husband–wife; older brother–younger brother; and friend–friend. The first four were hierarchical relationships of superior–inferior. Little, however, had been written about the role of women. During the Han dynasty several Confucian scholars addressed the topic. They urged women to be self-sacrificing, serving others, especially the males in their lives: father, brother(s), husband, and son(s). The Source box (opposite) includes examples of such advice by Ban Zhao, sister of one of the Han court historians, and Liu Xiang, who wrote *Biographies of Heroic Women*.

📖 **Read** the **Document: Sima Qian on Qin Shihuang (145–86 BCE)** on **MyHistoryLab**

Jade burial suit of Princess Tou Wan, Western Han dynasty, late second century B.C.E. As a very hard stone, jade was believed to be an effective preservative. When Princess Tou Wan, daughter-in-law of Emperor Jingdi, died, a burial suit was created for her using 2,160 pieces of jade tied together with gold wire. (National Museum of China, Beijing)

SOURCE

Treatises about Women in Han Society

During the Han dynasty, several authors decided to address the subject of women's role in society. Unfortunately, we have far more records on aristocratic women than we do on the peasantry. Ban Zhao (45–116 C.E.), sister of the famous court historian Ban Gu, wrote *Admonitions for Women*, a text of advice on the virtues appropriate for aristocratic women, divided into seven sections on humility, resignation, subservience, self-abasement, obedience, cleanliness, and industry. Ban Zhao explained:

In ancient times, on the third day after a girl was born, people placed her at the base of the bed, gave her a pot shard to play with, and made a sacrifice to announce her birth. She was put below the bed to show that she was lowly and weak and should concentrate on humbling herself before others. Playing with a shard showed that she should get accustomed to hard work and concentrate on being diligent. Announcing her birth to the ancestors showed that she should focus on continuing the sacrifices. These three customs convey the unchanging path for women and the ritual traditions.

Humility means yielding and acting respectful, putting others first and oneself last, never mentioning one's own good deeds or denying one's own faults, enduring insults and bearing with mistreatment, all with due trepidation.

Industriousness means going to bed late, getting up early, never shirking work morning or night, never refusing to take on domestic work, and completing everything that needs to be done neatly and carefully. Continuing the sacrifices means serving one's husband-master with appropriate demeanor, keeping oneself clean and pure, never joking or laughing, and preparing pure wine and food to offer to the ancestors. (Ebrey, p. 75)

Placing a similar stress on the virtues of self-sacrificing service, Liu Xiang (79–8 B.C.E.) wrote the *Biographies of Heroic Women*, which recounted the virtues of 125 women. He especially praised the mother of the philosopher Mencius, the greatest of the Confucian scholars. Liu Xiang quotes Mencius' mother telling her son of her concept of women's obligations:

A woman's duties are to cook the five grains, heat the wine, look after her parents-in-law, make clothes, and that is all! Therefore she cultivates the skills required in the women's quarters and has no ambition to manage affairs outside the house. The *Book of Changes* says, "In her central place, she attends to the preparation of the food." The *Book of Songs* says, "It will be theirs neither to do wrong nor to do good,/ Only about the spirits and the food will they have to think." This means that a woman's duty is not to control or to take charge. Instead she must follow the "three submissions." When she is young, she must submit to her parents. After her marriage, she must submit to her husband. When she is widowed, she must submit to her son. These are the rules of propriety.

The pervasive Confucian stress on hierarchy and deference permeates these prescriptions for women's conduct. However, throughout Han times—but not after—women could inherit property, divorce, and remarry after divorce or widowhood. And even the most highly placed women sometimes rebelled against Confucian ideals.

The greatest exception to the general rule of subordination of women, at least in public, came during the Tang Dynasty, when Wu Zetian clawed her way to power to rule as "Emperor", 690–705 C.E. She had already held effective power for decades through her control over previous emperors who were her husbands, consorts, and sons. Condemned by later Confucian historians for her extraordinary treachery and violence in eliminating rivals and opponents, she was nevertheless also praised for her effective administration of the civil service, her patronage of literature and the arts, her support of Buddhist temples and monks, and her military successes, including the conquest of Korea to the east and large parts of central Asia to the west. A colorful and commanding presence, Wu Zetian has been the subject not only of historians' evaluations but also of numerous works of historical fiction, films, and television productions.

Military Power and Diplomacy

The Han emperors were no less militaristic than the Qin. Confucian principles of moral rectitude held sway among the educated elite, but the government did not dispense with formal legal systems, nor did it forsake offensive or defensive warfare. The standing army numbered between 300,000 and one million, and all able-bodied men between the ages of about 20 and 56 were conscripted, serving for one year of training and one year of duty in the capital or in battle on the frontiers. They could be recalled in case of warfare.

Throughout the Han dynasty, China was engaged in incessant battles with the Xiongnu and other tribes around the Great Wall. Indeed, as we shall see shortly, the Han forced open a corridor through Gansu in the direction of Xinjiang (Turkestan). One reason for this expansion was to open markets for silk in the west. Parthian

7.1
7.2
7.3
7.4

How did Confucianism influence the Chinese bureaucracy?

7.1

7.2 How did
Confucianism
7.3 influence
the Chinese
7.4 bureaucracy?

Chinese expansion. A substantial shift in Chinese population distribution began during the first two centuries C.E., a fact that can be traced from Han census records. As land-hunger and pressure from the Xiongnu and the Tibetans on the northern border forced migration from the densely populated northeast, and as techniques for rice cultivation in the humid basin of the Yangzi improved, the lands to the south were mastered, and population clusters developed along the river valleys. Nevertheless, because of warfare and extreme flooding, the total population actually declined from 58 million to about 48 million.

traders carried goods on this trade route as far as Rome. China also wanted to secure a supply of horses from distant Bactria for the military. As the Chinese Empire expanded, emperors sought new ways of regulating foreign affairs with neighboring peoples, including nomadic groups, such as the Xiongnu. They created a "tributary system," in which the neighboring tributary group would acknowledge Chinese dominance and offer gifts (tribute) to the emperor. In exchange the emperor would send gifts to the ruler of the tributary group. On the northern and western borders, where Chinese, Mongol, Tibetan, and barbarian forces fought, each learned the strengths and weaknesses of the others. A Chinese strength was the crossbow. An important Mongol and Tibetan strength was cavalry, mounted on strong, fast horses. To achieve military parity, the Han emperors sought and found a supply of equivalent horses in central Asia. The Gansu corridor served as an access route, and Emperor Wu garrisoned it with 700,000 soldiers. Administrative records written on wooden strips have survived to tell of the lives of these immigrant soldier-colonizers in some detail.

Population and Migration

In both the south and the northern border regions, the Han established military–agricultural colonies to provide defense and economic development. The Chinese attempted to win the local populations over to Chinese culture. Often they succeeded, but not always. On the borders and in the southeast they met opposition, and rebellions against the Chinese settlers erupted in 86, 83, and 28–25 B.C.E.

During the later Han dynasty the population of northern China declined dramatically, even as the population of the south was expanding, perhaps from immigration from the north as well as from natural growth. The earliest preserved census in the world, taken in China in the year 2 C.E., shows the Chinese heartland clearly to be in the north; the southern population was sparse, mostly settled along the rivers. The second preserved census, taken 138 years later in 140 C.E., showed a sharp overall decline of 10 million people, from about 58 million to about 48 million. The regional distribution had shifted from 76 percent in the north and 24 percent in the south, to 54 and 46 percent respectively. In absolute terms the population of the south actually went up by more than 50 percent, from 14 million to 22 million, while the entire north declined from 44 million to 26 million.

Xiongnu and Tibetan massacres along the northern and western borders contributed to population losses, as did the floods caused when the Yellow River broke its banks and twice changed course, in about 4 C.E. and again in 11 C.E. The military and natural turbulence also impoverished China's civilian population. Meanwhile, the imperial government allocated more and more resources to support the army, expansionism, and the court in the capital city, Chang'an.

In the south, in general, there was little indigenous population and little hostility or resistance to the increase in Han Chinese. The regional Yue or Viet tribes were more often involved in fighting one another, although in 40 C.E. there was a revolt, and violence broke out on at least seven occasions between 100 and 184 C.E. Perhaps the increased resistance in the later years was evoked by the vast increase in the flow of population from the north to the south.

🔍 **View** the **Image: Han Chinese House** on **MyHistoryLab**

Economic Power

Han rulers also encouraged the expansion of China's iron industry. They developed the technique of liquefying iron and pouring it into molds to produce cast iron and later steel. In spite of the demographic decline in the north, the economy of Han China grew with the exploitation of new sources of wealth from along the Yangzi River, Sichuan, and the south. New inventions in mining (including salt mining), paper production, the compass, the breast-strap harness for horses, a redesigned plowshare, hydraulic engineering, and the tapping of natural gas increased wealth and productivity.

The road through the Gansu corridor to Xinjiang brought increased knowledge of distant lands and new trade possibilities. In 138 B.C.E. Emperor Wu dispatched Zhang Qian to inner Asia to seek enemies of the Xiongnu who might serve as allies of the Chinese. Zhang returned 12 years later without new alliances but with precious new information on lands as far west as Bactria, in modern northern Afghanistan. New trade possibilities opened in the import of horses and the export of silk. Parthian traders served as intermediaries between the Chinese and Roman empires. By 57 B.C.E., Chinese silk had reached Rome. The first silk route had been opened. Geography and cartography flourished, and gazetteers began to be published.

Inventory written on bamboo, 95 B.C.E. Government bureaucracy expanded with military and economic power under the Han dynasty, producing an enormous number of documents on wooden and bamboo strips. This inventory lists the equipment of two infantry units. (British Library, London)

Stone relief of harnessed cattle found at Mizhi, Shaanxi province, c. 25–220 C.E. Technological advancements, such as the development of the animal-drawn plow, went hand in hand with the increase in the area of cultivated land under the Han dynasty.

The cost of military expeditions and garrisons and the expenses of the self-aggrandizing court ate up the gains, however. Having dramatically lowered the land revenues when they first took office, the Han emperors began to raise them again. They also began to nationalize private enterprise by bringing it under state control, not in order to promote efficiency or honesty but to gain the profits for the state. Although commerce and business were theoretically held in low regard by Confucianists, businessmen flourished under the Han, and Sima Qian praised their enterprise:

> A family with a thousand catties of gold may stand side by side with the lord of a city; the man with a hundred million cash may enjoy the pleasures of a king. Rich men such as these deserve to be called the "untitled nobility," do they not? (Sima Qian, trans. Watson, p. 356)

Emperor Wu sought to expropriate some of this wealth to pay for his military ventures and his imperial court. He altered coinage, confiscated the land of the nobility, sold offices and titles, and increased taxes. He established government monopolies in the production of iron, salt, and liquor, and he took over part of the grain trade, arguing that this was a means of stabilizing prices, but actually intending to secure profits for his government and its border wars. On his death, his successor, Emperor Zhao, arranged a debate between his chief minister, who advocated continuing the state monopolies on salt and iron, and a number of Confucian scholars, who opposed them. The minister defended and explained the emperor's policy:

> He established the salt, iron, and liquor monopolies and the system of equitable marketing in order to raise more funds for expenditures at the borders. … [O]ur critics … would have the men who are defending our passes and patrolling our walls suffer hunger and cold. … Abolition of these measures is not expedient! (de Bary and Bloom, p. 361)

The Confucianists opposed the policy of costly military expansion and the government plan to take over businesses in order to finance it:

> Never should material profit appear as a motive of government. Only then can moral instruction succeed and the customs of the people be reformed. But now in the provinces the salt, iron, and liquor monopolies, and the system of equitable marketing, have been established to compete with the people for profit, dispelling rustic generosity and teaching the people greed. (pp. 360–61)

The Confucianists also distrusted businessmen as self-serving and corrupt, and they feared that government-run businesses would increase that corruption. The new emperor came to accept the Confucian argument and relinquished at least some government-run monopolies temporarily.

Fluctuations in Administrative Power

The bureaucracy of the early Han seemed to run well, and the adoption of Confucian principles tempered some of the harshness of the Legalist codes. In addition, the wars that the Qin had pursued to establish China's borders made fighting somewhat

7.1

7.2 How did Confucianism influence the Chinese bureaucracy?

7.3

7.4

less necessary for the Han. For 200 years even the problems of succession, problems that had ultimately helped to destroy the Qin dynasty, were negotiated effectively, if sometimes quite cruelly. Nevertheless, the absence of clear principles of imperial succession continued, and in 9 C.E. the Han temporarily fell from power because there was no clear successor.

An Interregnum. In 1 B.C.E., the eight-year-old Emperor Ping inherited the throne. A regent, Wang Mang, was appointed to run the government during the boy's minority, and when Ping died in 9 C.E., Wang Mang became the *de facto* ruler, declaring himself founder of a new dynasty. His policies, however, alienated virtually everyone. These policies—fighting against the Xiongnu, breaking up large estates, reinstating the prohibition on the sale of land, fixing the prices of commodities, terminating the status of the Han nobility and reducing them to commoners, cutting bureaucratic salaries, confiscating villagers' gold in exchange for bronze—inflamed rich and poor, nobility and commoners, and urban and rural folk.

To add to his problems, just at the beginning of Wang Mang's regency, the shallow, silt-laden Yellow River again broke its banks and changed course twice in five years, wreaking immense devastation to property, and loss of life. In 23 C.E., a combination of Xiongnu invasions in the north, the rebellion of Han nobles near the capital, and the revolt of the Red Turbans—a mass movement beginning in 18 C.E. centered in the Shandong peninsula, which had been most devastated by the Yellow River's flooding—brought down Wang Mang and led to the reinstatement of the Han dynasty.

A Weakened Han Dynasty. The later Han dynasty, 23–220 C.E., did not have the same strength as the former Han. To cope with continuing incursions, the later Han made alliances with the barbarians, inviting them to settle within the Great Wall, to provide soldiers for Chinese armies, and even to intermarry with the Chinese, policies that were similar to Rome's actions in its border regions. Although this pattern demonstrated the weakness of the Chinese central government, it also contributed to the **sinicization** of the tribal barbarians, who learned the language, culture, and administrative patterns of the Chinese. Reversing the pattern of tribute of the years of strong government, the later Han gave silk cloth to the border tribes so that they would not invade. Later Han emperors also moved the capital from Chang'an eastward to the less exposed city of Luoyang.

The movement of population to the south increased the wealth of the empire generally, but the increase went largely to merchants and landlords. Peasants continued to be exploited and oppressed by the exactions of both their landlords and the imperial government. As government taxes increased, peasants sold off their private holdings and went to live and farm under the jurisdiction of local landlords, where they sought to evade government taxes and military conscription.

The landlords themselves faced a dilemma. As members of the governing elite, they were obliged to collect and remit taxes to the central government and to turn over their tenants for conscription, but as landlords and local potentates, it was to their advantage to retain the taxes and the tenants' labor for themselves. Strong central governments

KEY TERM

sinicization The adoption and absorption by foreign peoples of Chinese language, customs, and culture.

Two concubines in front of a mirror, *Admonitions ...*, Gu Kaizhi, fourth century C.E. As the Han dynasty collapsed, artists lamented the neglect of the Confucian codes of behavior. Here the court painter Gu Kaizhi (334–406 C.E.) illustrates the text of the poet Zhang Hua (c. 232–300 C.E.): "Men and women know how to adorn their faces, but there is none who knows how to adorn his character ..." (British Museum, London)

7.1

7.2

7.3 What were
the elements
of China's
underlying unity?

7.4

were capable of demanding loyalty and collection; the later Han, however, frequently failed. Peasants absconded, the government's tax and labor bases diminished, and provincial notables developed independent power bases. Peasant revolts, which would become endemic in most of China, broke out with increasing frequency.

Peasant Revolt and the Fall of the Han. The beginning of the end of the Han is usually dated to 184 C.E., when a revolt of hundreds of thousands of peasants broke out. Zhang Jue, a Daoist healer who proclaimed that a new era would begin with the fall of the Han, launched the rebellion, called the Yellow Turban revolt for the headgear worn by the rebels. It broke out simultaneously in 16 commanderies throughout the south, east, and northeast of China. Although this specific revolt was suppressed, it triggered a continuous string of additional outbreaks.

At least four factions struggled for power within the palace: the emperor, who, after the death of Emperor Ling in 189, was a child; the bureaucrats, advisers, palace guards, and regent to the young emperor; the approximately 2,000 eunuchs in the court; and the women of the court and their families. Since each emperor had several wives and consorts, competition among them was fierce, both for their own recognition and for recognition of their sons at court, especially in the selection of the heir to the emperor. After the death of an emperor, his widows and his mother often remained embroiled in court politics to defend their own positions and those of their family.

In the last decades of Han rule, 189–220 C.E., the court was buffeted from the outside and divided on the inside. For example, on September 25, 189 C.E., generals in the court murdered hundreds of eunuchs to remove their influence. By the year 220, when the last Han emperor, Xian, abdicated, the court had no center and the lands of the empire had already been divided among numerous competing warlords.

Disintegration and Reunification

7.3 What were the elements of China's underlying unity?

The fall of the Han brought the disintegration of China into three separate states, but the ideal of a united Chinese empire was not lost. The empire was restored for 50 years, 265–316 C.E., then divided again for 273 years until 589 C.E., when a new dynasty introduced a unification that would last for more than three centuries. Even during periods of disintegration, elements of an underlying unity endured, for China has deep and pervasive common cultural traditions, just as, during periods of powerful imperial rule, elements of divisive regionalism persisted, since China is a huge and diverse country.

Ecology and Culture

On the fall of the Han dynasty, China divided into three states: the Wei in the north, ruling over some 29 million people; the Wu in the south, ruling over 11 million; and the Shu in the west, ruling over 7 million. From 265 to 316 C.E. a single dynasty, the Jin (Chin), reunited China briefly. Then, from 316–589 C.E., China was divided north from south, more or less by the Huai River basin, halfway between the Yellow River to the north and the Yangzi River to the south.

This division was characterized by a number of geographical features. To the north, the top soil is a fine yellow dust, called loess. Borne by winds from the west, it is 250 feet deep to the north of Chang'an, a region with little irrigation. The agriculture in this region has been dry-field farming not dependent on massive irrigation projects and mostly carried on by owner-operators. Its principal crops are wheat, millet, beans, and turnips. The region is intensely cold in winter. The south,

7.1

7.2

7.3

7.4

What were
the elements
of China's
underlying unity?

by contrast, has many waterways, which are useful for both irrigation and navigation. The warmer weather, even subtropical in the far south, makes it possible to grow rice and tea, which were introduced from Southeast Asia probably toward the end of the Han dynasty. The area is typically organized into landlord–tenant estates.

During the centuries of imperial division, six successive dynasties governed the south, while a series of non-Chinese barbarian dynasties ruled the north. Warfare and ecological disaster in the north steadily reduced the population, while people moved south, shifting the balance of population to a southern majority. It appeared that the Chinese Empire, like that of Rome, had lost control of its original homeland and divided forever.

While China was divided politically, however, its culture and ethical ideology persisted, keeping alive its traditions of unity. In the south, especially, the arts, painting, calligraphy, and poetry flourished, frequently with the themes of spiritual survival amid political disarray. The Chinese language, too, continued to unite all literate Chinese as their means of communication.

In the north, China was more open to new social and ethnic syntheses. The Chinese absorbed the barbarians into their continuing cultural life, and, through intermarriage, into China's genetic pool as well. When scholars today note the homogeneity of China's population as "95 percent Han," they are referring to cultural rather than ethnic homogeneity and recognizing the openness of China toward accepting and assimilating neighboring peoples who accept the culture of the "Han." The Chinese themselves echo the importance of this common culture, referring to all who have accepted it as "people of the Han." The nomadic peoples living on the northern borders and settling within the Great Wall at the invitation of the later Han emperors had already begun to absorb Chinese culture. When they became powerful enough to conquer north China, they found that they needed to enlist Chinese bureaucrats to administer their gains. In many regions, the administrators appointed by the new rulers were descended from families whom the Han had employed. Thus, below the surface of foreign rule, a powerful stratum of Chinese elites remained in place.

The most powerful and longest ruling of the nomadic conquerors became the most assimilated. This was the Northern Wei dynasty (r. 386–534 C.E.), also named the Toba Wei after the tribal group that founded it. The longer it ruled, the more assimilated its people became. In 493–94 C.E. they moved their capital from the far west to one of the former Han capitals, Luoyang, in order to consolidate their control of the northeast. But in Luoyang they wore Chinese dress and adopted Chinese names, and many intermarried. The Toba also made their own contributions to China's administrative practices, instituting a new pattern of urban organization by wards in Luoyang. Subsequent dynasties used this system when laying out the restored capital at Chang'an. Still later, Japanese imperial planners copied it in Nara. Similarly, in their attempts to keep agricultural populations from fleeing from northern China, the Toba took over all land ownership for the state and continued to redistribute it in "equal fields" as each generation of cultivators died and new ones inherited the land. According to the "equal fields" system, all families received some land in return for paying a tribute in goods or labor.

The developing, new aristocracy of mixed Chinese–Toba blood alienated the unassimilated Toba troops who

Chinese technology. Classical Chinese cultures were administratively and technologically sophisticated. They mastered diplomacy, bureaucracy, navigation, architecture, chemistry, mechanics, astronomy, printing, and, most dramatically, hydrology. Terraced farming, intensive irrigation systems, and the construction of thousands of miles of navigable canals harnessed the often unpredictable rivers of eastern China, and opened up the inland cities to commerce.

7.1

7.2

7.3   What were
       the elements
7.4   of China's
       underlying unity?

garrisoned the frontiers. They finally revolted and defeated the Northern Wei government in 534 C.E., opening the way for the Sui dynasty, a family of mixed Chinese and foreign parentage, which reunited China.

Buddhism Reaches China

While China was beset by this dynastic turmoil, a new religion was spreading through the country. During the Han dynasty, Buddhism had entered China from its birthplace in India. It is first noted in Chinese historical records in the first century C.E.

Siddhartha Gautama, the Buddha, "the enlightened one" (c. 563–483 B.C.E.), introduced a religion of compassion in the face of a world of pain. Buddhism is discussed at length in the chapter entitled "Hinduism and Buddhism." Here, however, we ask why and how this religion, which later died out in its own native soil in India, was able to take root in far-off China, even in the face of early opposition by Confucian scholars and bureaucrats and an institutionalized Daoist establishment.

Over time, Buddhism's very foreignness may have contributed to its success. The nomadic conquerors who succeeded the Han may have felt comfortable accepting, and even sponsoring, a religion that, like themselves, came from outside China.

Second, Buddhism arose in India, to a large degree, as an antipriestly religion favored by the merchant classes. These merchants sponsored Buddhist monasteries, convents, and cave temples along the silk routes between India and China, some of

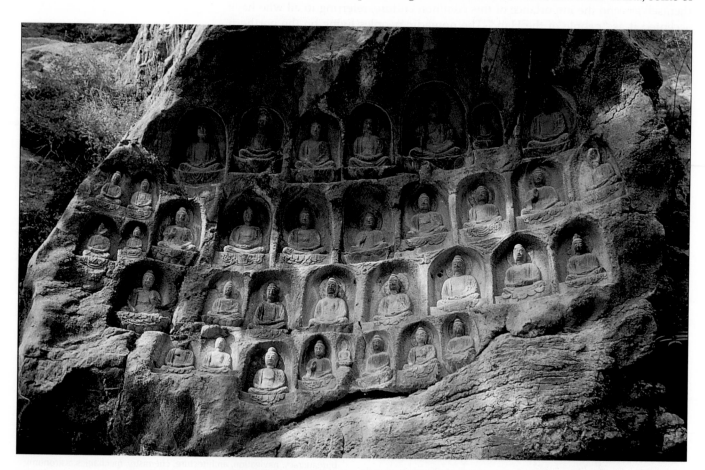

Hill of the Thousand Buddhas, Jinan, Tang dynasty. The increased power of the Buddhist religious establishment in Tang times is reflected in the growth of cave paintings and sculptures. The merchants and missionaries who brought Buddhism to China along the silk route also brought ideas about the iconography of temples and the depiction of the Buddha.

which remain impressive even today. When Buddhism arrived in China with the silk-route merchants, Chinese merchants were already familiar with it, and the new religion appeared cosmopolitan rather than exclusively Indian.

Buddhism persevered in China, securing patronage in several regional courts, capturing the hearts of millions of followers, and ultimately becoming one of the unifying elements in Chinese culture. Eventually it mixed with Confucianism and Daoism, bringing popular new spiritual, intellectual, cultural, and ritual innovations.

Reunification under the Sui and Tang Dynasties

Despite almost 400 years of imperial fragmentation, many elements of Chinese unity were potentially at hand: language, ideology, culture, administration at the local level, aristocratic families with deep roots, and sufficient imperial prestige

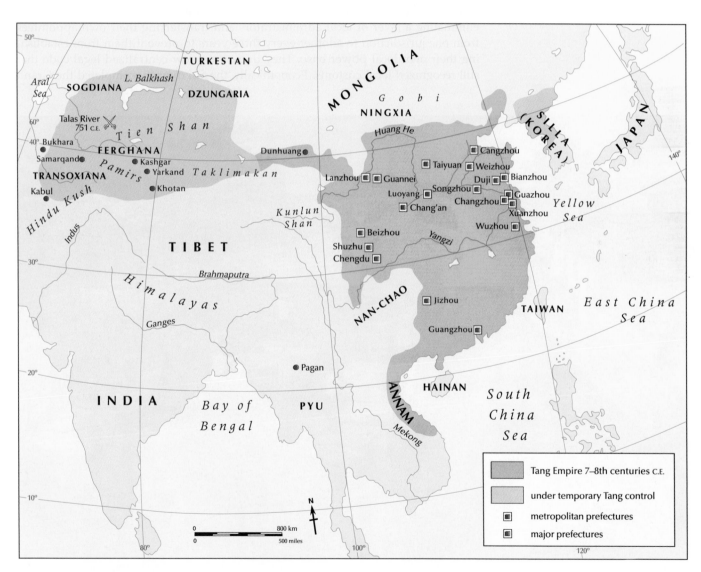

The Tang revival. The Sui dynasty (581–618 C.E.) and its successor, the politically organized Tang, restored the Chinese imperial impulse four centuries after the decline of the Han, extending control along the silk route as far as the Tien Shan mountain range and the arid Ferghana basin. Trade flourished. China finally reached its western limits when its forces were defeated by the imperial armies of the Muslim Abbasid empire at the Talas River in 751 C.E.

7.1

7.2

7.3   What were
the elements
of China's
7.4   underlying unity?

and administrative expertise that even China's conquerors were assimilated to it. To reunite the empire required the restoration of military power, economic productivity, and administrative integration. The Sui dynasty (581–618 C.E.) provided all three.

The Short-lived Sui Dynasty. The Sui dynasty was founded by the emperor Wen (Yang Chien) (r. 581–604 C.E.), a general from one of the northern Chinese states, who usurped power in his own state and then succeeded in conquering and unifying all of inner China. Militarily, Wen raised the status of his militia, settled them on their own lands, and gave them property rights. He thus created an effective, committed, and loyal standing army of peasant-farmers. A powerful crossbow, protective body armor, and constant drills to achieve precision in maneuvers and battle made these troops a formidable fighting force.

Ideologically, the first Sui emperor and his son Yang (Yang Kuang) (r. 604–15), who succeeded him, employed a combination of Confucian, Daoist, and Buddhist symbolism and practice to win popular loyalty. Administratively, they centralized authority, eliminating a layer of local administrators and transferring their own appointees from one jurisdiction to another every three years to prevent them from establishing their own local power base. They drew up a new centralized legal code that still recognized local customs. Economically, the Sui dynasty completed the Grand

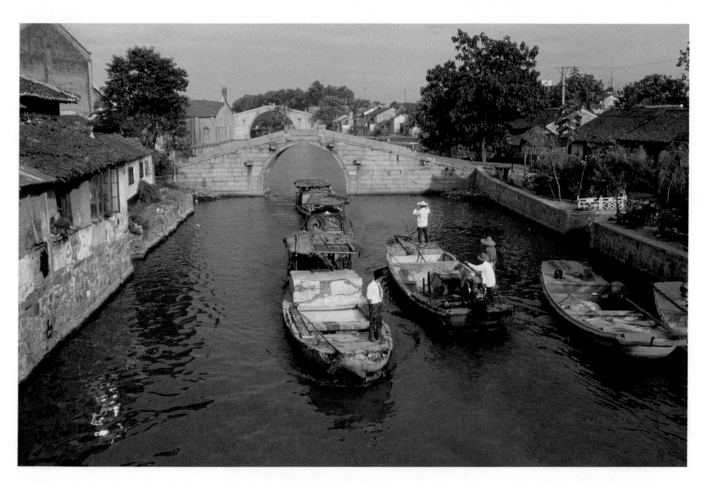

Canal at Suzhou. From about the fifth century B.C.E., the Chinese built canals, partly to tame their rivers, mostly to facilitate trade. The Sui dynasty (581–618 C.E.) connected the major sections of the existing north–south canals to the Grand Canal of China, the longest canal in the world, stretching from Hangzhou in the south to Beijing in the north. As the Grand Canal passed through cities, such as Suzhou, it also connected to canals within the city for local trade.

7.1

7.2

7.3

7.4

What were
the elements
of China's
underlying unity?

Canal from Hangzhou in the south to Luoyang in the center. The canal linked the Yangzi and Yellow river systems, and extensions connected it to the rebuilt capital in Chang'an and, later, to Beijing. The canal allowed the transportation of the agricultural produce of the rapidly developing south to the political-military centers of the north.

The expense of mobilizing and dispatching imperial troops and administrators on their far-flung missions depleted the treasury of the Sui dynasty. The Grand Canal produced many economic benefits, but it cost dearly in manpower. Built in seven years, the canal required the labor of 5.5 million people, and to complete some sections, all commoners between the ages of 15 and 55 were pressed into service. As many as 50,000 police supervised the construction, flogging and chaining those who could not or would not work, and ordering every fifth family to provide one person to supply and prepare food. In addition to these public works, three costly and disastrous military campaigns in Korea and central Asia wasted lives and treasure and sapped the loyalty of the troops. Finally, the leading general of the Sui seized control of the state and, under the imperial name Gaozu, established the new Tang dynasty in 618.

When the Sui fell, after overextending itself militarily and economically, the Tang dynasty (618–907) continued and even strengthened these attributes of empire. Moreover, the Sui and Tang extended China's reign to truly imperial dimensions—that is, beyond China proper to "outer China," Mongolia, Turkestan, and central Asia, as far as the frontiers of modern Afghanistan, Pakistan, and Iran. China also held strong cultural sway over Tibet, although without achieving direct political control. These lands were larger than all of "inner China" in area, although they held perhaps only 5 percent of its population. In addition, Tang China held northern Vietnam and, briefly, northern Korea. China's cultural influence at this time was extremely strong in Japan as well (see below).

Arts and Technology under the Tang Dynasty. Tang policies built on those of the Sui, consolidating and improving them where possible. The Tang dynasty relied more than ever on the imperial examination system to provide its administrators, and in 754 the emperor founded a new Imperial Academy, the Han-Lin Yuan (the Forest of Pens).

The arts and technology, often reinforcing each other, flourished under the Tang as never before. The world's first block printing was invented, partly in response to the needs of Buddhists to disseminate their doctrines, for under the Tang the Buddhist religious establishment became increasingly powerful. Buddhist religious art found expression also in further cave sculptures and paintings. New ceramic manufacturing methods led to the production of the first true porcelain, a product of great beauty and durability. For centuries, China alone knew the secret of its manufacture. Millers developed machinery and gears for converting linear and

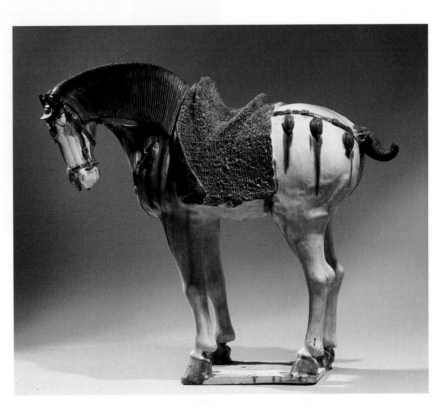

Pottery figure of a Ferghana horse, excavated from a tomb, Tang dynasty (618–907 C.E.). The Tang dynasty opened the Grand Canal, stimulated growth in trade, and expanded the boundaries of the empire. For much of this they were dependent on the mobility of the army, which in turn was dependent for covering great distances on the famed Ferghana horses, immortalized in literature as "the horses that sweated blood." (Idemitsu Museum of Arts, Tokyo)

7.1

7.2

7.3 What were
the elements
of China's
7.4 underlying unity?

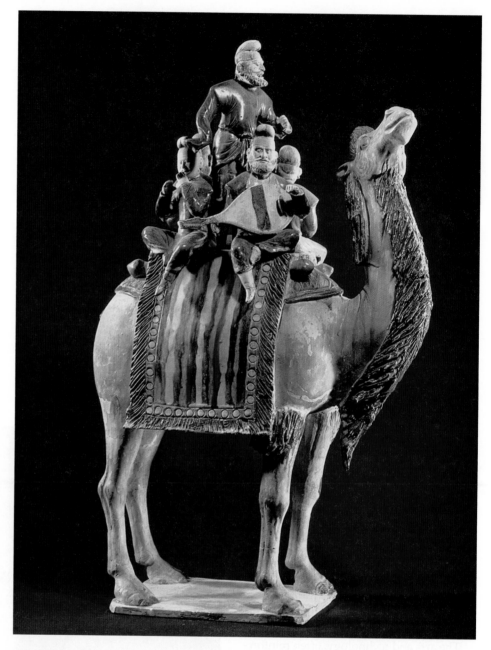

Ceramic model of a group of musicians seated on a camel, Tang dynasty (618–907 C.E.), excavated from a tomb in a suburb of Xi'an. The beards, facial features, and costumes of some of the musicians in this group suggest that they are from central Asia. Such models, commonly found in the tombs of the Tang elite, are evidence of a taste for the goods that came along the silk route from the west, and for the central Asian music that accompanied them.

rotary motion, encouraging further development of both water- and windmills. In 659, China produced the world's first pharmacopoeia, which listed the contents and uses of all known medicines.

Finally, Tang-era poetry of meditation, nature, politics, fate, suffering, and individual identity transmitted its living legacy even to today's readers in China and beyond. Each of the three most famous Tang poets has been seen as linked to a different cultural tradition: Wang Wei (701–62) to Buddhism; Li Bai (Li Bo) (701–61) to Daoism; and Du Fu (Tu Fu) (712–70) to Confucianism, although each was influenced

CHAPTER SEVEN: CHINA 221 B.C.E.–900 C.E.

7.1

7.2

7.3

What were
the elements
of China's
underlying unity?

7.4

by all three traditions. Du Fu's "Autumn Meditation" expresses the tension between the high-stakes hustle-bustle of the imperial court under stress and his own desire for a life of peace within nature:

I've heard them say Chang'an's like a chessboard;
sad beyond bearing, the happenings of these hundred years!
Mansions of peers and princes, all with new owners now;
in civil or martial cap and garb, not the same as before.
Over mountain passes, due north, gongs and drums resound;
wagons and horses pressing west speed the feather-decked dispatches.
Fish and dragons sunk in sleep, autumn rivers cold;
old homeland, those peaceful times, forever in my thoughts!

(trans. Watson, p. 134)

The three centuries of Sui and Tang rule consolidated the theory and practice of Chinese imperial rule even to the present (although today there is no emperor). Since 581, China has been divided into two administrations only once, in 1127–75, and fragmented into several regions only twice, in 907–59 and 1916–49. Apart from these three periods, totalling 133 years, China has stood united for a continuous period of more than 14 centuries.

Caravanserai, Kirghizstan, Tang dynasty (618–907 C.E.). The silk route led traders through hundreds of miles of inhospitable terrain, such as this barren and mountainous region of Kirghizstan in central Asia. This Tang dynasty-era *caravanserai*, the oldest complete example in existence, would have protected traders from the elements and from preying bandits.

7.1
7.2
7.3
7.4

What is the meaning of "empire" in relation to China?

Imperial China

7.4 What is the meaning of "empire" in relation to China?

We opened this unit on empires by noting that the word "empire" signifies rule by one people over another. Let us examine this definition in relation to China. First, within the borders of China, empire frequently meant the **assimilation** of others. In the north, many of the tribal groups against which China fought and against which its rulers constructed the Great Wall nevertheless came to enlist in China's armies, settle its land, assimilate its culture, adopt its language and calligraphy, and intermarry with its peoples.

The ethnic Chinese and the "barbarians" regarded this process as mutually beneficial. Both also understood the dangers: the barbarians might lose their culture and even find themselves in civil war with others of their ethnic group who rejected assimilation; the Chinese might be conquered by their new allies. Indeed, both of these results did occur frequently, and the interchanges transformed the cultures of both the barbarians and the Chinese.

The West and Northwest

The most geographically far-reaching of China's expansions beyond the borders of inner China were to the northwest and west. Emperor Wu's expansion into Gansu and beyond did not survive the early Han dynasty; similarly, the expansion of the Sui and Tang even deeper into central Asia did not survive the Battle of the Talas River and the An Lushan revolt. Nevertheless, China's cultural and symbolic influence over these regions persisted, even after its political, military, and direct economic power was gone. (In the seventeenth century, under the Qing dynasty, China returned to dominate these areas, and it rules them today.)

The South and Southwest

Processes of assimilation also took place in southern China, but they have made much less of a mark in the records. China as an ethnic, cultural, and political entity developed first in the north, around the Yellow River, but as Chinese peoples moved south of the Yangzi they met people of other ethnic groups. As the Chinese encroached, some southern peoples retreated still further south to preserve and develop their own separate national identities. The Vietnamese are the clearest example of this pattern. Other groups of southerners remained as distinct, separate tribal groups, usually in remote areas somewhat difficult to access. Occasionally, these peoples revolted against the Chinese invasion and takeover of their land. The Miao gave the clearest example of this response. Most of the rest assimilated, including some Vietnamese and Miao, without making a lasting impression on the historical records.

Vietnam

For a thousand years China held Annam (northern Vietnam) as a colony. The Han dynasty conquered Annam and incorporated the area as a province of China in 111 B.C.E. It remained part of China until 939 C.E., when, not long after the collapse of the Tang, the Vietnamese rebel Ngo Quyen declared himself king of the independent state of Dai Viet.

During and after Chinese colonization, the Vietnamese were locked in a love–hate relationship with Chinese culture and politics. Chinese scholars and officials, many of them fleeing imperial policies in China, brought to Vietnam their own ideographic script, Confucian ethical principles, and the Confucian literary classics. The Vietnamese adopted them all.

KEY TERM

assimilation The process by which different ethnic groups lose their distinctive cultural identity through contact with the dominant culture of a society, and gradually become absorbed and integrated into it.

CHAPTER SEVEN: CHINA 221 B.C.E.–900 C.E.

7.1

7.2

7.3

7.4

What is the
meaning of
"empire" in
relation to China?

Buddhism also arrived in Vietnam by way of China. The rest of Southeast Asia absorbed Buddhism in its Theravada form from India; Vietnam adopted Mahayana Buddhism as it had developed in China, after about the fifth century C.E. These cultural innovations appealed primarily to the Vietnamese aristocracy. At the level of practical technology, the Chinese also introduced a number of valuable agricultural innovations: the construction of a huge network of dams and waterworks that protect against monsoon flooding every year; the use of human excrement as fertilizer; market gardening; and intensive pig farming.

Although they adopted many Chinese customs, the Vietnamese resented foreign hegemony by the colossus to its north. For example, the two Trung sisters led a military revolt in 39 C.E., succeeded in evicting the Chinese, ruled jointly over Vietnam for

HOW DO WE KNOW?

Poetry as a Source for History

Du Fu's "Ballad of the Army Carts" repeats the heartbreaking pain of war as the troops describe the seemingly endless fighting and dying:

Carts rattle and squeak,
Horses snort and neigh—
Bows and arrows at their waists, the conscripts march away.
Fathers, mothers, children, wives run to say goodbye.
The Xianyang Bridge in clouds of dust is hidden from the eye.
They tug at them and stamp their feet, weep, and obstruct their way.
The weeping rises to the sky.
Along a road a passer-by
Questions the conscripts. They reply:
They mobilize us constantly. Sent northwards at fifteen
To guard the River, we were forced once more to volunteer,
Though we are forty now, to man the western front this year.
The headman tied our headcloths for us when we first left here.
We came back white-haired—to be sent again to the frontier.
Those frontier posts could fill the sea with the blood of those
    who've died,
But still the Martial Emperor's aims remain unsatisfied.
In county after county to the east, Sir, don't you know,
In village after village only thorns and brambles grow,
Even if there's a sturdy wife to wield the plough and hoe,
The borders of the fields have merged, you can't tell east from
    west.
It's worse still for the men from Qin, as fighters they're the
    best—
And so, like chickens or like dogs, they're driven to and fro.
Though you are kind enough to ask,
Dare we complain about our task?
Take, Sir, this winter. In Guanxi
The troops have not yet been set free.
The district officers come to press
The land tax from us nonetheless.
But, Sir, how can we possibly pay?
Having a son's a curse today.
Far better to have daughters, get them married—
A son will lie lost in the grass, unburied.
Why, Sir, on distant Qinhhai shore

The bleached ungathered bones lie year on year.
New ghosts complain, and those who died before
Weep in the wet grey sky and haunt the ear.

(Seth, pp. 48–49)

Du Fu probably wrote this poem of exhaustion and discontent after two decisive and disastrous military operations. In the first, the Battle of the Talas River, on one of the most distant of China's western frontiers, 2,000 miles from Chang'an, Arab armies defeated China in 751. China lost control of its central Asian holdings, and the silk route was opened to the cultural influence of Islam, which displaced Buddhism and Confucianism. Four years later, An Lushan, one of China's frontier generals of Turkish extraction, revolted. Although the Chinese put down the revolt in 763, the cost of the warfare, and the vulnerability it revealed, weakened the Tang dynasty for the entire century and a half leading up to its fall.

The Tang dynasty had extended China's border farther than any other except the Qing (Manchu), which ruled 1,000 years later (1644–1912). Tang holdings in central Asia had flanked and protected the silk route and brought new opportunities for wealth. Ultimately, however, these lands cost more than they brought in economically and militarily. The border groups—Turks, Uighurs, Khitans, and other ethnic groups—no longer accepted Chinese domination, but continually probed the Tang border fortifications. Finally, China ceded control of central Asia to them. In China proper, agricultural and commercial wealth continued to grow, but the central, imperial government could no longer control it. Regional rulers grew in authority and power. In 907 the Tang dynasty finally disappeared, as China splintered into ten separate states. Yet the imperial idea and pattern held. In 960 the Song dynasty arose, ruling all of China until 1127, and the south until 1279.

- What elements of the poem might suggest that Du Fu was influenced by Confucianism?
- Who is the poem's main speaker? What are his feelings about the war?
- How does the poem help us to understand the feelings of the Chinese after the battle's defeat and subsequent developments?

7.1
7.2
7.3
7.4 What is the
meaning of
"empire" in
relation to China?

two years, but committed suicide when their revolt was crushed. They are revered in Vietnam to this day. Leaders of numerous less dramatic revolts against China are also viewed as national heroes, yet, paradoxically, the most profound adoption of Chinese administrative reforms occurred in the fifteenth century, when Vietnam was independent. As a result of Chinese direct rule in the earlier period and Chinese power and proximity during later periods of Vietnamese independence, the country became a Confucian state, with an examination system, an intellectually elitist administration somewhat aloof from the masses, and an intense desire for independence from China.

Korea

Korea came under direct Chinese rule only briefly, but Chinese cultural hegemony profoundly influenced the peninsula. The Han Emperor Wu first conquered northern Korea in 109–108 B.C.E., along with Manchuria. Military garrisons established Chinese control and influence.

Korea, like Vietnam, had borrowed heavily from prehistoric China, including much of Shang technology and, later, iron technology, paper production, printing, lacquerwork, porcelain (although Korean double-fired, pale-green celadon ware had a distinct beauty all its own), wheat and rice agriculture, and the ideographs of written language. In 1446 C.E., at the initiative of their king, Koreans created a written system called *han'gul*, based on phonetics, which they proudly describe as the most scientifically formulated of all the world's scripts. Until after World War II, however, Korean elites suppressed the use of the simple *han'gul*, preferring the more prestigious, more elitist, and more difficult Chinese ideographs.

After the collapse of the Han in 220 C.E., Korea broke free of direct control, although it remained a **vassal** of the Chinese. Some of China's colonies remained in place, but without military capacity. The Sui dynasty sent three expeditions to conquer Korea, but all ended in disaster. The expansive Tang dynasty also tried to retake Korea in the seventh century and succeeded in occupying much of the peninsula in 668–76 C.E. Ultimately, however, Korea regained and maintained its independence, although it was often forced to accept **tributary status**, acknowledging China's regional dominance.

China's power over Korea can be seen far more in terms of cultural hegemony than in terms of political-military rule. Confucianism, law codes, bureaucratic administration, literature, art, and Mahayana Buddhism entered Korean life from China, independent of government pressure. In 935 C.E., after the fall of the Tang, Korea's Silla dynasty also fell. The Koryo dynasty, which took its place, built a new capital at Kaesong, just north of today's South Korean capital, Seoul, and modeled it on Chang'an, the Tang capital in China. Both China and Korea spoke of a "younger brother/older brother" relationship between the two countries.

Japan

China never conquered Japan, but Japan did accept China's cultural hegemony. Indeed, through the seventh and eighth centuries C.E. Japan actively and enthusiastically attempted to model its state, religion, technology, art, and language on those of China. As the Korean peninsula stands between the Chinese mainland and the four major islands of Japan, much of the importation of Chinese forms came to Japan through Korea.

Immigration and Cultural Influences. Although archaeological records show that Japan was populated by the Jomon people of the coastal regions at least as early as 10,000 B.C.E., rice agriculture seems to have begun only about 300 B.C.E., when it was introduced from southern China. Bronze tools and weapons arrived about the first century B.C.E., and the technology for making iron tools about 200 years later.

Waves of immigrants from Korea and China arrived in Japan between about 200 B.C.E. and about 500 C.E. By 500 C.E., approximately one-third of Japan's nobility claimed Korean or Chinese descent, and many artisans and metalworkers in Japan had come from Korea. All was not peaceful between Japan and Korea, however, and invasions and raids were launched from both sides. In this period, the Chinese represented the Japanese by an ideograph that signifies "dwarf," presumably suggesting an inferior status.

In 405 C.E., a Korean scribe named Wani traveled to Japan to teach the Chinese script. This became Japan's earliest written language, and Japan's recorded history begins only in the eighth century C.E. Most of our knowledge of these earlier years comes either from archaeological records or from references in the literature of China and Korea. These archaeological and literary materials tell of the formation of an embryonic Japanese state about the third century C.E., when a clan of people worshiping the sun goddess established their rule over the Yamato Plain in central Honshu Island. Ultimately, the imperial line of Japan claimed descent from this group. They used Chinese written characters and accepted elements of both Confucianism and Buddhism to enrich the polytheistic practices of the indigenous religion, Shinto, and its deification of the Japanese emperor.

After China succeeded in reestablishing its own powerful empire under the Sui and Tang dynasties, Japanese rulers dispatched numerous delegations of hundreds of members each to China to learn and adopt Chinese models. The Chinese calendar and many methods of government were introduced. In 604 C.E. a new 17-point "constitution" was introduced, a guide that was modeled on Chinese practice. The document included reverence for Confucianism and Buddhism, and for the sovereign of Japan, and, on a more mundane level, asserted the government's monopoly over the collection of taxes.

Officially, the Japanese elite recognized the emperor as the head of Japan, but, in fact, he was little more than a figurehead; real power belonged to those behind the throne. Bloody struggles for control of the court in Japan brought Nakatomi no Kamatari to power in 645 C.E. He took the surname Fujiwara, and under this name his family dominated the politics of Japan for centuries to come. (One descendant, Prince Konoe Fumimaro, served as prime minister in 1937–39 and again in 1940–41.) Fujiwara adopted Chinese culture, religion, and government as the way to centralize and unify Japan and to assert his own control. He proclaimed the Taika ("great change") reforms in 646 C.E., consolidating provincial administration and constructing an extensive road system. The reforms also abolished private ownership of land and redistributed it at each generational change.

In 710 C.E. two acts further consolidated centralized rule. First, a new capital, modeled on Chang'an, was built at Nara. Second, the Japanese ruler now claimed to rule through divine mandate, although, unlike the Chinese Mandate of Heaven, it could never be revoked. (To this day, the same family occupies the imperial throne, although after World War II, its divinity

Asian imperial capitals. The Tang capital of Chang'an was gridplanned as a massive rectangle more than five miles square, focusing on the imperial quarters and housing about a million people within its walls. The newly centralized Japanese Yamato state built Nara in imitation of Chang'an: a grid plan incorporated the Todaiji Temple complexes.

233

CHINA'S IMPERIAL DYNASTIES

Listed below are all the imperial dynasties, starting with the Qin, and the two major preimperial ruling houses. Gaps in the date sequences mark those periods when the country was divided between two or more rulers.

Shang	c. 1600–1100 B.C.E.
Zhou	c. 1100–256
Qin	221–206
Han	202 B.C.E.–220 C.E.
Three Kingdoms: Kingdom of Shu Han, Kingdom of Wei, Kingdom of Wu	220–65
Northern and Southern Dynasties	265–589
Western Jin	265–317
Eastern Jin	317–419
Northern Wei	386–534
Sui	581–618
Tang	618–907
Song	960–1279
Yuan (Mongol)	1279–1368
Ming	1368–1644
Manchu (Qing)	1644–1912

was officially repudiated.) At about the same time, again following Chinese models, the Japanese began to record their history for the first time, in the *Nihongi* (in Chinese), and their legends in the *Kojiki*, which was written in a mixture of Chinese and Japanese forms.

The emperor served as the chief priest of Japan's Shinto faith, but as Shinto is a religion that worships the gods of nature—streams, trees, rocks—it can be practiced anywhere. Buddhism, by contrast, provides a more centralized form of organization, through monasteries and temples. Many new Buddhist temples were, therefore, constructed in Chinese form at Nara to centralize worship in Japan. From that time onward Buddhism and Shinto have coexisted in Japan, with millions of Japanese declaring themselves devotees of both faiths.

As centuries passed and Japan became more secure in its own political organization and cultural identity, the reliance on Chinese models declined. But in the centuries when its basic cultural and political identity was formed, Japan had followed carefully and devotedly the hegemonic examples of China, without compulsion or force of any sort.

Read the **Document**: Selection from Nihongi, "The Age of the Gods" on **MyHistoryLab**

Imperial Legacies for the Future:
What Difference Do They Make?

The Roman and Chinese empires are among the greatest in history in terms of longevity, population, geographical extent, and lasting influence. A comparison between them will help to clarify the characteristics and significance of each and to establish guidelines for thinking about other empires of other times, and our own.

Differences

Not surprisingly, there are important differences between these two huge empires, separated by such great distances.

Geopolitical. China's heartland was far larger and more cohesive, geographically and culturally, than Rome's. Rome had as its heartland only central Italy, and even after conquering Italy, it held just that single peninsula bounded by the Alps and the Mediterranean Sea. In the time of Augustus in Rome and the Han dynasty in China, the Roman and Chinese empires each held about 60 million people, but in Rome only a few of those millions lived in Italy. In China virtually all inhabited "inner China." Ninety percent of them were in the north China plain.

Ideological. Although Confucian China spoke of a mythological golden age of equality among people living in harmony with one another and with nature, realistically the Confucianists believed that the best possible government was a well-ordered empire. Many philosophers and writers in imperial Rome, on the other hand, believed in an actual, historical republican past (albeit an idealized past), and always looked back to it as a golden age. Roman imperial expansion and stratification were often regarded as violations of the earlier republican ideals.

Longevity and Persistence. Rome's empire rose, fell, and disappeared, although it lived on as a concept. China's empire has lasted for the past 2,000 years. Dynasties have come and gone, sometimes the empire has broken into fragments, and sometimes it has been ruled by conquering "barbarians," but finally the empire endured as a single political entity. Today, although there is no emperor, China's geopolitical unity continues.

Policy and Powers of Assimilation. As China moved both north and south, it assimilated a great number of the peoples it invaded and conquered. Nonethnic Chinese were absorbed culturally and biologically. Many of the 95 percent of today's Chinese population who are called "Han" are descended from ancestors who were not. Confucian and Buddhist ideology held the empire together, supported by the power of the emperor and his armies. Rome's empire was held together by law and backed by military power. Selected non-Romans could gain citizenship under law, but ethnically and culturally the conquered peoples remained "other." Intermarriage with noncitizens was usually forbidden. Romans maintained the cultural distinctions between themselves and those they conquered far more than did the Chinese.

Language Policy. The Chinese language unified the Chinese Empire across space and through time—even today—far more than Latin did the Roman Empire. Chinese was never subordinated to another language and culture, as Latin was to Greek for many years and in many regions. Nor did Chinese compete with regional languages as Latin ultimately did. Indeed, Chinese helped to bring even neighboring countries—Vietnam, Korea, and Japan—together into a single general cultural unit.

Ideology and Cultural Cohesion. China's Confucian bureaucracy provided a core cultural identity throughout the empire and beyond. Even the alternative political-cultural philosophies of China—such as Daoism, Legalism, and, later, Buddhism—usually (but not always) served to broaden and augment the attraction of Confucianism. Rome's emperor worship did reinforce its cohesion, but its principal philosophies of polytheism, Stoicism, and, later, Christianity did not significantly buttress or augment its imperial rule. The last two may even have diminished popular loyalty to the empire, except in its later continuation in the east as the Byzantine Empire.

Influence on Neighbors. The Roman Empire influenced the lands it conquered, but had less influence on those outside its boundaries. China exercised lasting hegemonic influence even on neighbors it did not conquer, such as Japan, or conquered only briefly, such as Korea. A considerable part of this legacy was religious and cultural as well as political, economic, and administrative.

Similarities

The many points of similarity between China and Rome reveal some basic truths about the nature of empire.

Relations with Barbarians. Both empires faced nomadic groups from central Asia who threatened and penetrated their boundaries. Indeed, the Huns, who invaded Europe, and the Xiongnu, who invaded China, may have belonged to the same ethnic group. Both empires settled the "barbarians" near their borders and enlisted them in their imperial armies. In both cases, the barbarians came to hold great power. Ultimately, however, they dismembered the Roman Empire, while they were absorbed by the Chinese.

Religious Policies. Both empires incubated foreign religions, especially in times of imperial disorder. In China, Buddhism was absorbed into Confucianism and Daoism and helped to sustain the national culture in times of political trouble. In Rome, however, Christianity did not save the empire. In fact, by challenging the significance of earthly power it may even have contributed to the empire's weakness. On the other hand, the political organization of the Roman Empire provided a model for the Roman Catholic Church.

The Role of the Emperor. Both empires ascribed divine attributes to the emperor, and both frequently had difficulty in establishing rules for imperial succession. The Romans often attempted to choose their best general, while the Chinese selected a man who could control the imperial family and court. Neither empire believed that a single imperial family should rule forever. The Chinese believed that eventually the Mandate of Heaven would pass from one dynasty to another.

Gender Relationships and the Family. The family was extremely important for both empires, and both empires subordinated women to men at all stages of life. Both drew analogies between hierarchy and loyalty in a well-run family and those in a well-run empire. Both empires used marriage as a means of confirming political alliances with foreign powers. Both periodically felt that excessive concern with sexual

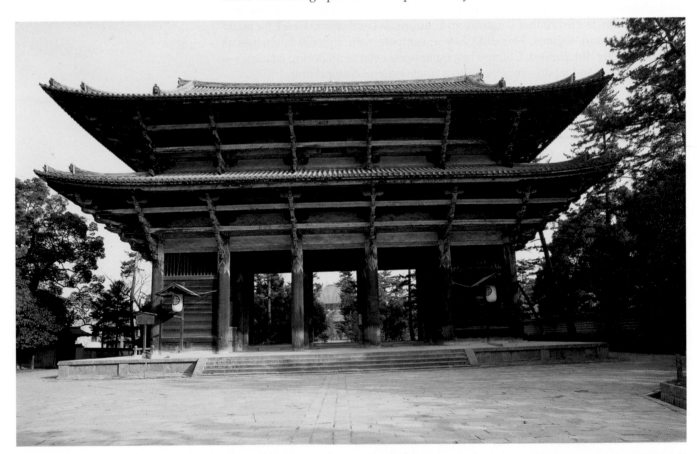

The Nandaimon, or "Great South Gate," of the Todaiji Buddhist temple, 745–52 C.E. The first Japanese Buddhist temples—modeled on the Buddhist temples of China—are among the oldest surviving timber buildings in the world. So faithful and enduring are they that they have become our best examples of Chinese architecture for the period.

relationships distracted energy from the demands of sustaining the empire, and both proclaimed strict codes of sexual morality.

The Significance of Imperial Armies. In both empires the army was crucial in creating and sustaining the political structure in the face of domestic and foreign enemies. The Roman Empire was established and ruled by generals, as were the Qin, Han, Sui, and Tang dynasties in China. Both empires were periodically threatened and usurped by rebel generals asserting their own authority. The cost of the armies, especially on distant, unprofitable expeditions, often drained the finances of the government and encouraged its subjects to evade taxes and military service and even to rise in revolt. Both empires established colonies of soldier-colonizers to garrison and develop remote areas while simultaneously providing compensation and retirement benefits for the troops.

Overextension. Both empires suffered their greatest challenges in confronting simultaneously the strains of overexpansion and the subsequent internal revolts that were triggered by the costs incurred. In Rome these dual problems, along with the barbarian invasions, finally precipitated the end of the empire in the west. In China they led to the loss of the Mandate of Heaven and the downfall of dynasties. The external battles against Qin-Jurchen border tribes, for example, combined with the revolt of the Yellow Turbans, brought down the later Han; the loss of the distant Battle of the Talas River, combined with the internal revolt of An Lushan, sapped Tang power.

Public Works Projects. Throughout their empire the Romans built roads, aqueducts, public monumental structures, administrative/military towns, and the great capital cities of Rome and Constantinople. The Chinese built the Great Wall, the Grand Canal, systems of transportation by road and water, public monumental structures, administrative/military towns throughout the empire, and several successive capitals, notably Chang'an and Luoyang.

The Concentration of Wealth. In both empires, the benefits of imperial wealth tended to flow toward the center and to the elite in the capital cities. The capitals grew to unprecedented size. Both Chang'an and Rome housed more than one million people.

Policies for and against Individual Mobility. To maintain power and stability in the face of demands for change, both empires periodically bound their peasantry to the soil and demanded that the sons of soldiers follow their fathers' occupation. Both found these policies difficult to enforce. Both offered some individual mobility through service in their armies. In addition, the Chinese examination system allowed advancement within the imperial bureaucracy.

Revolts. Both empires experienced frequent revolts against the emperor and his policies. In Rome, which housed a much larger slave population, slaves led some of the revolts. In China they were more typically initiated by peasants. Rome attempted to forestall mass revolts in the capital and other large cities through the provision of "bread and circuses." Both empires faced constant challenges from those living on their peripheries.

Peasant Flight. In both empires during times of upheaval, peasants sought to evade taxes and conscription by finding refuge as tenants on large, landed estates. Whenever imperial government was weak, the largest of these estates challenged the power of the central government.

The influence of the early Chinese Empire continues today, not only in China itself, but also in East Asia, Southeast Asia, and central Asia. Consistent patterns in language, culture, geopolitical organization, and international relations are there to be discovered through the ages. The same is true of Rome throughout the areas it ruled directly in Western and southern Europe, the Mediterranean, and North Africa. To a lesser degree, its influence extends to eastern Europe and to the European settler colonies in the Americas, Australia, and New Zealand. The imperial ideals of China and Rome have entranced many who have studied them, and repelled many as well. As we turn to study the empires of ancient India, these models help to guide our thinking.

CHAPTER REVIEW

THE QIN DYNASTY

7.1 What were the philosophies of rule in the Chinese empire?

Confucianism, Daoism, and Legalism emerged as the leading philosophies of government and of life in China. The Qin dynasty favored Legalism, implementing strict laws and strict enforcement, with rewards for people who followed the laws and swift punishment for those who broke them. Confucianism, adopted by the Han, and generally dominant thereafter, held that good government depended on good officials, moral men of humanity and virtue, wisdom and order. Confucius thought such men could be fashioned through proper education. The Qin burned the books of the Confucianists and apparently killed many Confucian scholars; the Han, Confucian scholars in turn, vilified the Legalists. Daoism was a mystical philosophy, not directly applicable to government. It believed in simplicity and the power of a natural order or path (Dao). Alongside all of these philosophies, Chinese imperial authorities also recognized the importance of a large, powerful imperial army to carry out its will, and it recognized the importance of a productive, accommodative peasantry.

THE HAN DYNASTY

7.2 How did Confucianism influence the Chinese bureaucracy?

Following Confucian principles, a social and political hierarchy emerged in Han China, with scholars at the top, followed by farmers, artisans, and merchants. The Confucian value of the importance of tradition and continuity prevailed, and an elite academy was established to teach scholar-bureaucrats Confucianism's applicability to governing. The Chinese legal system was codified according to Confucian principles. The emperor declared that knowledge of the Confucian classics should be a basis for promotion in the imperial civil service, a principle that was finally established in the examination system of the Tang dynasty.

DISINTEGRATION AND REUNIFICATION

7.3 What were the elements of China's underlying unity?

Even during periods of disintegration, between imperial dynasties, an underlying unity has endured in China. Its cultural and ethical ideologies kept its traditions of unity alive: the arts, painting, calligraphy, poetry; its language, ideology, administration, and theory and practice of imperial rule. China's Confucian bureaucracy provided a core cultural identity throughout space and time.

IMPERIAL CHINA

7.4 What is the meaning of "empire" in relation to China?

The extension of the Chinese empire frequently meant the assimilation of others. Most of the tribal peoples that China conquered gradually came to enlist in China's armies, assimilate its culture, adopt its language and calligraphy, and marry its people. The ethnic Chinese, too, considered this process mutually beneficial. China also exercised lasting hegemonic influence on people it did not conquer, such as the Japanese, who, unforced, adopted many Chinese patterns of life and culture, architecture and politics as they formed their own identity.

Suggested Readings

PRINCIPAL SOURCES

Blunden, Caroline, and Mark Elvin. *Cultural Atlas of China* (New York: Facts on File, 1983). Excellent introductory coverage to history and culture, lavishly illustrated with maps and pictures. Excellent as both narrative and reference.

de Bary, William Theodore, ed., *Sources of East Asian Tradition*, Vol. 1: *Premodern Asia* (New York: Columbia University Press, 2008). Selections from Columbia's outstanding series on China, Japan, and Korea.

de Bary, William Theodore, and Irene Bloom, eds. *Sources of Chinese Tradition*, Vol. I: *From Earliest Times to 1600* (New York: Columbia University Press, 2nd ed., 1999). The premier primary source reference to the thought of the elite of ancient China.

Ebrey, Patricia Buckley, ed. *Chinese Civilization: A Sourcebook* (New York: The Free Press, 2nd ed., 1993). This primary sourcebook covers social and economic materials of everyday life of common people.

Ebrey, Patricia Buckley, Anne Walthall, and James Palais. *East Asia: A Cultural, Social, and Political History*, Vol. 1: *To 1800* (Florence, KY: Wadsworth Publishing Co., 3rd ed., 2013).

Elvin, Mark. *The Pattern of the Chinese Past* (Stanford, CA: Stanford University Press, 1973). Most Chinese history has been written dynasty by dynasty. Elvin seeks to identify deeper patterns of change in the economy and social life. Introduces new approaches.

Twitchett, Denis, ed. *The Cambridge History of China*, Vol. III: *Sui and T'ang China, 589–906*, Part I (Cambridge: Cambridge University Press, 1979). Comprehensive, standard compendium of analysis and narrative.

Twitchett, Denis, and Michael Lowe, eds. *The Cambridge History of China*, Vol. I: *The Ch'in and Han Empires, 221 B.C.–A.D. 220* (Cambridge: Cambridge University Press, 1986). Comprehensive, standard compendium of analysis and narrative.

Waley, Arthur, trans. *The Book of Songs* (New York: Grove Press, 1996). Classic text from a master translator.

Watson, Burton, trans. *The Selected Poems of Du Fu* (New York: Columbia University Press, 2002). An excellent selection and translation.

ADDITIONAL SOURCES

Andrea, Alfred, and James H. Overfield, eds. *The Human Record*, Vol. I (Florence, KY: Wadsworth Publishing Co., 7th ed., 2011). Excellent array of primary sources, arranged and cross-referenced to provide its comprehensive course of study.

Creel, H.G. *Confucius: The Man and the Myth* (Westport, CT: Greenwood Press, reprinted 1972 from 1949 ed.). Little is known about Confucius the man. This classic study tells us what is known and how it has been represented and interpreted.

Friedman, Edward. "Reconstructing China's National Identity: A Southern Alternative to Mao-Era Anti-Imperialist Nationalism," *Journal of Asian Studies* LIII, No. 1 (February 1994), pp. 67–91. An analysis of continuing differences between China's southern, coastal, commercial regions, and its more bureaucratic and politically oriented interior and north.

Han Fei Tzu. *The Complete Works of Han Fei Tzu*, 2 vols., trans. W.K. Liao (London: Arthur Probsthain, 1959). The basis of the Legalist tradition.

Hughes, Sarah Shaver, and Brady Hughes, eds. *Women in World History*, Vol. I (Armonk, NY: M.E. Sharpe, 1995). A reader with materials drawn from all over the world.

Lattimore, Owen. *Inner Asian Frontiers of China* (London: Oxford University Press, 1940). Classic statement of the relationship between China proper and the areas north and west of the Great Wall.

Lockard, Craig A. "Integrating Southeast Asia into the Framework of World History: The Period Before 1500," *The History Teacher* XXIX, No. 1 (November 1995), pp. 7–35. Establishes a point of view for understanding Southeast Asia as a part of the world. Designed for teaching, but widely useful for its range of subjects and their context.

Murphey, Rhoads. *East Asia: A New History* (Boston, MA: Addison-Wesley, 2nd ed., 2000). Standard textbook history.

Needham, Joseph. *The Shorter Science and Civilization in China*, Vol. I, abridged by Colin A. Ronan (Cambridge: Cambridge University Press, 1978). First volume in Needham's monumental work opening up the empire's scientific accomplishments to an English-reading audience.

Past Worlds: The (London) Times Atlas of Archaeology (Maplewood, NJ: Hammond, 1988). Excellent introduction to the entire subject, including archaeology of ancient China. Lavishly illustrated with maps, pictures, and charts.

SarDesai, D.R. *Southeast Asia: Past and Present* (Boulder, CO: Westview Press, 7th ed., 2012). Standard introductory text.

——. *Southeast Asian History: Essential Readings* (Boulder, CO: Westview Press, 2006). Primary documents.

Schirokauer, Conrad, et al. *A Brief History of Chinese and Japanese Civilizations* (Florence, KY: Wadsworth Publishing Co., 4th ed., 2012). A standard text, now updated.

Schwartz, Benjamin I. *The World of Thought in Ancient China* (Cambridge, MA: Harvard University Press, 1985). Fine analysis of philosophies and policies in ancient Chinese thought and politics.

Seth, Vikram. *Three Chinese Poets: Translations of Poems by Wang Wei, Li Bai, and Du Fu* (New York: HarperCollins, 1993). Translations of classical poetry of classical poets. The insistence on rhyme is sometimes monotonous.

Sima Qian. *Historical Records*, trans. Raymond Dawson (New York: Oxford University Press, 1994). Translation from the works of China's preeminent dynastic historian. Clear and readable, with introduction to and evaluation of the historian's life and work.

——. *Records of the Historian: Chapters from the Shih Chi of Ssu-ma Ch'ien*, trans. Burton Watson (New York: Columbia University Press, 1969). Translation from the works of China's preeminent dynastic historian. Places the work in the context of Chinese history and literature.

Sullivan, Michael. *The Arts of China* (Berkeley, CA: University of California Press, 4th rev. ed., 2000). Well-illustrated introduction to classical Chinese painting, sculpture, and fine arts.

Sun Tzu [Sunzi]. *The Art of War*, trans. Thomas Cleary (Boston, MA: Shambhala, 1988). Accessible translation of the classic treatise on fighting a war, often through not fighting. A Zen approach. Consulted by Chinese strategists, including Mao.

Waley, Arthur, trans. *Chinese Poems* (New York: Dover, 2000). Marvelous collection.

FILMS

Hero [Yingxiong] (2002: 99 minutes) Set at the beginning of the Qin dynasty, depicts the battles and assassinations required to establish the new emperor. A blockbuster in China, directed by award-winning Zhang Yimou. Many reviewers saw it as a justification for China's dictatorial Communist government.

Red Cliff [Chi Bi] (2009: 148 minutes) As the Han dynasty declines, four generals connive and fight it out for the succession. Based on a classical story, frequently retold. This version compresses an original two-film sequence, emphasizing the battles, but the political intrigue remains.

Legacy: The Origins of Civilization—China (1992; 1 hour). Michael Wood takes us on a journey into China's past, showing highlights visually, including oracle bones. Beautifully produced. Brief interviews with a few experts. More idiosyncratic than the Time-Life documentary.

Time-Life. *Lost Civilizations: China: Dynasties of Power* (2002; 1 hour). Beautiful visual representation. Brief interviews with a few experts. More of an overview than Wood's reflections.

8 Indian Empires

Cultural Cohesion in a Divided Subcontinent

1500 B.C.E.–1100 C.E.

W hat do we mean by "India"? In this chapter we include the entire subcontinent of south Asia, which includes not only the present-day country of India, but also its neighbors: Pakistan, Bangladesh, Nepal, and Bhutan. Geographers call the entire region a subcontinent because it is so large and so clearly bounded by powerful natural borders. Along its entire southern perimeter it is a peninsula surrounded by oceanic waters: the Arabian Sea to the west and the Bay of Bengal to the east. To the north, the Himalaya Mountains, the highest in the world, form an almost impenetrable barrier. At the eastern and western ends of the Himalayas, rugged spurs of the great range complete the ring of demarcation, but these mountains are lower and more negotiable. Passes, such as the Khyber Pass, make entrance accessible through the northwest mountains, as does a route through the desert along the western Makran coast.

Prince Gautama, Ajanta Cave 1, Maharashtra, India, c. 450–500 C.E. The rock-cut sanctuaries of Ajanta in the northwest Deccan were abandoned for centuries until they were rediscovered in 1817 by British soldiers hunting tigers. The 29 cave temples contain some of the earliest surviving Indian painting and mark the last true flowering of Buddhist art in the subcontinent prior to the ascendancy of Hinduism. Here Prince Gautama, an earlier incarnation of the Buddha, is seated in an ornamental pavilion. Servants are pouring holy water over him.

LEARNING OBJECTIVES

8.1 ((	8.2 ((	8.3 ((	8.4 ((
Describe the important literature of the Aryan immigrants.	Understand the philosophy of the Maurya and Gupta empires.	Describe the consequences of the Hunas' invasion of India.	Compare India's empires with those of China and Rome.

((Listen on MyHistoryLab

The peoples who came to India before 3000 B.C.E., for whom we have no historical record, seem to have arrived from a variety of approaches, probably including some by sea from Africa, Southeast Asia, and the islands of the Pacific. Since 3000 B.C.E., all the major immigrations have come from the northwest. In modern times British traders and rulers also came by sea. They had an important impact on the subcontinent, but they did not stay.

The geographical area of the subcontinent is equal to about one-fourth the size of Europe. The entire region has been unified into a single empire only once, under British rule in the nineteenth and early twentieth centuries. Asoka Maurya (r. *c.* 265–238 B.C.E.) was the first person to come close to achieving that goal, but he never captured the far south. Usually, as today, a number of rulers controlled different regions of the subcontinent. It is not surprising, then, that Indian empires did not last more than a few hundred years. Yet, unlike Rome, and much more like China, India has maintained a persistent cultural unity over several thousand years. In this chapter we will begin to consider why India dissolved politically into many separate states; in the chapter entitled "Hinduism and Buddhism" we will consider the religious and cultural institutions that nevertheless served to bring a loose unity to the subcontinent. We will consider India as an empire based as much on cultural cohesion as on political and military unity.

What was the most important literature of the Aryan immigrants?

8.1
8.2
8.3
8.4

New Arrivals in South Asia

8.1 What was the most important literature of the Aryan immigrants?

The first cities in south Asia appeared in the Indus valley about 2500 B.C.E. That civilization—the Harappan—began to fade about 1500 B.C.E. for reasons that are not fully understood. Perhaps simultaneously, perhaps somewhat later, new waves of "Aryan" immigrants arrived. These new arrivals are named not for their race, but for Sanskrit and the other related **Indo–Aryan** languages they spoke. Archaeologists

KEY TERM

Indo–Aryan A subgroup of the Indo-Iranian branch of the Indo-European group of languages, also called Indic, and spoken in India, Sri Lanka, Bangladesh, and Pakistan. The Indo–Aryan languages are descended from Sanskrit, the sacred language of Hinduism.

HOW DO WE KNOW?

Pottery and Philology

Archaeology can tell us comparatively little about the Aryan way of life in the Ganges River valley. The valley is a humid, subtropical region, where heavy monsoon rains have washed away ancient settlements. It is also densely inhabited, making archaeological excavation difficult if not impossible. As a result, we know less about the Aryan settlements along the Ganges than we do about the earlier Indus valley, where the sparsely populated desert sites allowed relatively easy excavation.

Nevertheless, the distribution of pottery—painted grayware dating primarily from before 500 B.C.E., and northern black polished ware from after that date—helps us to identify and follow the waves of Aryan immigration into the Ganges valley. The more recently discovered ocher-colored pottery in the western Ganges valley and the presence of black and red ware further east suggest that by the time the Aryans arrived indigenous peoples had already settled on the land. Since the late 1970s, archaeological digs have uncovered small settlement sites dating from 1000–600 B.C.E. throughout the Ganges valley. However, it is difficult to trace in any detail the spread and nature of early Aryan civilization without additional excavations of many other cities and small towns.

Philology, the study of the origin and evolution of language as an indication of general cultural evolution, helps to establish the dispersion of Indo–Aryan peoples by tracking the spread of their languages. The first known surviving specimens of writing in the Ganges valley are Asoka's rock and pillar inscriptions in Brahmi script, which date to the third century B.C.E. To track the oral transmission patterns of earlier centuries, anthropologists study texts that recorded them in written form at a much later time, and compare them with the distribution and evolution of today's spoken languages.

- Why is there more archaeological evidence about the Indus valley than about the Ganges valley?
- What is the evidence that indigenous peoples preceded the Aryans in the Ganges valley?
- How do the study of pottery and philology complement each other in an analysis of early settlements in the Ganges valley?

8.1 What was the most important literature of the Aryan immigrants?

8.2

8.3

8.4

are not certain of the geographical origins of the new arrivals; some claim they came from central Asia, others from the Iranian plateau, while a few suggest Europe. In successive waves of immigration, the nomadic and pastoral Aryans, riding the horses of central Asia and light, spoke-wheeled chariots, mixed with indigenous peoples, migrated slowly eastward, and reached the Ganges valley about the year 1000 B.C.E.

Chronicles of the Aryan Immigrants

The greatest sources of information for the Aryan immigrations, settlements, and empires are written materials that preserve earlier oral traditions. Bards and chroniclers collected and composed these materials, although they did not attempt to establish a chronological, interpretive record of the sort found in Greece or Rome or China.

The Vedas. The earliest existing source is one of the four Vedas, the *Rigveda*, 1,028 hymns composed in Sanskrit, about 1500–1200 B.C.E., at the time the Aryans were moving into the subcontinent. The Vedas are religious reflections rather than historical records, but to the extent that they refer to the life of the Aryan peoples who wrote them, their accounts are probably reliable. They do refer to conquests made by the Aryans in the course of their migrations southward and eastward. Three other Vedas, the *Samaveda*, *Yajurveda*, and *Atharva Veda*, were composed some centuries later. Other religious literature of the Vedic millennium (1500–500 B.C.E.) include the *Brahmanas*, which give instructions on rituals and sacrifices, and the *Upanishads*, which are mystical speculations. These were composed about 700 B.C.E. and afterward.

The *Puranas*, or legends and folk tales from earliest times, were finally collected and written down between about 500 B.C.E. and 500 C.E. They contain genealogical lists of rulers from before the first humans were born until historic times, mixing fact and fable, human and divine, and making no attempt to distinguish between them. The tales of the *Puranas* bring the gods of the Aryans into the popular imagination.

The *Mahabharata* and the *Ramayana*. India's two great epics, the Mahabharata and the Ramayana, recount events that took place between 1000 and 700 B.C.E., although the texts themselves place the action in earlier mythic times. Neither is a historical account, but both provide valuable information on the social structures, the ways of life, and the values of the time in which they were written.

Some ten times longer than the Bible, the *Mahabharata* is the longest single poem in the world. Its central story is of a great civil war fought between two branches of the same family. Into its tales, subplots, and asides are woven myth, speculation, folklore, moral teaching, and political reflection, which are central to India's living culture. The intermingling of the great themes of life, death, family, warfare, duty, and power give the *Mahabharata* continuing universal appeal. The most famous single segment of the *Mahabharata* is the profound religious meditation and instruction called the *Bhagavad-Gita*, or "Song of God." The *Gita* takes the form of advice given to a warrior facing battle, but it expands into divine advice on life, death, and rebirth.

The *Ramayana*, which is much shorter, refers to somewhat later times, and there are many versions. The first known written version in Sanskrit was composed by Valmiki about 700 B.C.E. Its core story tells of the victory of the mythical god-king Rama over Ravana, the demon ruler of Sri Lanka, who had kidnapped Rama's wife, Sita. The diverse versions of the *Ramayana* indicate its great popularity and the variety of its uses. Some focus on the battles between north and south, perhaps a reference to the first Aryan invasions of the south about 800 B.C.E. Some southern versions, however, tend to justify Ravana as defending the south against Rama's invasions from the north. The role of Sita is also told in different ways. Men more frequently praise Sita for her adoration of Rama and her willingness to renounce even her life so that his reputation might remain intact. Women, however, are often critical of Rama for inadequately defending Sita in the first place, then for doubting her fidelity to him

Scenes from the *Ramayana*, Indian School, 1713 C.E. After Ravana, the many-headed king of Lanka, abducts his wife, Sita, the god-king Rama sets off to retrieve her with his brother Laxman (with bow and arrow) and an army of monkeys. This rich gouache illustration presents several chapters from the story. (British Library, London)

📖 Read the Document: Excerpt from the *Ramayana* on MyHistoryLab

What was the most important literature of the Aryan immigrants?

8.1

8.2

8.3

8.4

during her captivity in Sri Lanka, and, finally, for bowing to public skepticism of her loyalty by exiling her from his royal court.

Indian sailors, merchants, and priests carried their culture to Southeast Asia, and the *Ramayana* has become a national epic in several of the countries of that region, especially Thailand and Indonesia, where it is often dramatized by live actors and through puppetry. In India, the story is retold each year on the holiday of Dussehra, which celebrates the victory of good over evil with great color and pageantry. Broadcast on Indian national television in serialized form for about a year each in the mid-1980s, the *Mahabharata* and the *Ramayana* drew audiences of hundreds of millions for each weekly episode. Ever popular, these programs are rebroadcast frequently. In the 1980s, the British theater producer Peter Brook staged nine-hour versions of the *Mahabharata*—one in English and one in French—and then restructured the English version as a five-hour film and DVD.

Despite these literary sources and their implicit evidence of major political and social change, there are no purely historical written records for these crucial centuries in Indian history. Gradually, however, other records do begin to appear and to cast light on the changes that were taking place. Codes of law and statecraft, such as the *Artha-sastra* from around 300 B.C.E. and Asoka's rock inscriptions about half a century later, illuminate politics and imperial ideology. Many more such codes appeared in later times, together with Buddhist and Jain texts that usually include chronologies and some interpretation.

AT A GLANCE: INDIA 600–100 B.C.E.

DATE	POLITICS	RELIGION AND CULTURE	SOCIAL DEVELOPMENT
600 B.C.E.	• *Janapadas* established		
500 B.C.E.	• Gandhara and Sind held by Persian Empire (*c.* 518) • *Maha-janapadas* established (500–400)	• Buddha, Siddhartha Gautama (*c.* 563–483) • Puranas written (*c.* 500 B.C.E.–500 C.E.) • Vedic period ends (1500–500)	
400 B.C.E.	• Nanda dynasty in Magadha (*c.* 364–324)		
300 B.C.E.	• Alexander the Great in south Asia (327–325) • Chandragupta Maurya (r. *c.* 321–*c.* 297) founds Mauryan dynasty (324–185) in Magadha • Kautilya writes *Artha-sastra* (*c.* 300)	• *Mahabharata* and *Ramayana* (*c.* 300 B.C.E.–300 C.E.)	
250 B.C.E.	• Bindusara Maurya (r. *c.* 297–*c.* 272) • Asoka Maurya (r. *c.* 265–238)	• Rock inscriptions of Asoka • Asoka enhances spread of Buddhism • Asokan lion column	• Mauryan empire extended from Afghanistan to Bay of Bengal to Deccan
200 B.C.E.	• Sunga dynasty (185–173) • Mauryan Empire fractures, along with unity of India (185)	• Jain influence increases	
150 B.C.E.	• Menander (Milanda) king of Indo-Greek Empire (*fl.* 160–135)	• Sanchi stupa	• Trade contacts with Southeast Asia
100 B.C.E.	• First Shaka king in western India (*c.* 94)	• Sangam poetry from Tamil culture	

8.1

8.2

8.3

8.4

What was the most important literature of the Aryan immigrants?

Visitors from outside have also given periodic "snapshot" accounts of India. These include the observations by Megasthenes (*c.* 350–*c.* 290 B.C.E.), a Greek ambassador and historian sent to the court of Chandragupta Maurya about 300 B.C.E., and Menander (Milinda; *fl.* 160–135 B.C.E.), a Greek king of northwest India who became a Buddhist. Later, about 400–700 C.E., Faxian (Fa-hsien; *fl.* 399–414 C.E.) and Xuanzang (Hsuan-tsang; 602–64 C.E.), Buddhist pilgrims from China, recorded further observations. The travelers' reflections echo their own positions and interests, but in general depict a prosperous country. The earliest of the four visitors, Megasthenes describes India's geography and history, combining many myths with the actual campaigns of Alexander the Great and Indian military forces. He was also fascinated with India's caste system, which he believed to have included seven castes. Like all the travelers, he was impressed by government's respect for foreigners. Faxian, who came much later, traveled as a pilgrim to places associated with the Buddha's life. He described India as a country of rich and prosperous cities, where peace and order prevailed and the wealthy provided for the poor and the disadvantaged.

📖 **Read** the **Document**: **Excerpt from** *Mahabharata* **on MyHistoryLab**

The Establishment of States

Both archaeological and written sources reveal that, as they settled in India, the Aryans began to build a new urban civilization and to form new states. By 700–600 B.C.E., numerous political groupings, called ***janapadas*** (populated territories), began to emerge. Leadership of the territories was centered in specific family lineage groups, and as these lineages grew larger and cleared more forest land to expand their territorial control, the *janapadas* began to take on the political form of states with urban capitals and political administrations. Some constituted themselves as republics, others as monarchies. By 500–400 B.C.E., about the time the Persian armies of Darius reached the Indus, 16 large *maha-janapadas* had emerged in northern India.

KEY TERM

janapada A large political district in India, beginning about 700 B.C.E.

AT A GLANCE: INDIA 50–1100 C.E.

DATE	POLITICS	RELIGION AND CULTURE	SOCIAL DEVELOPMENT
50 C.E.	• Height of Kushana power under Emperor Kanishka (r. c. 78–c. 103)	• *Bhagavad-Gita*	
100 C.E.		• Gandhara Buddha • Rise of Mahayana Buddhism	• Trade flourishes between India and the central Asian trade routes
200 C.E.		• Increasing Hindu–Buddhist influence on Southeast Asia	
300 C.E.	• Gupta Empire (c. 320–540) established by Chandra Gupta I (r. 320–c. 330)	• Sanskrit used for official business • Hindu ascendancy over Buddhism	• Indian trade contacts with Oc Eo, Funan (300–600)
350 C.E.	• Samudra Gupta (r. c. 330–c. 380) expands dynasty throughout north and into south		
400 C.E.	• Chandra Gupta II (r. c. 380–c. 415) expands empire to maximum • Kumara Gupta (r. c. 415–55)	• Cultural "golden age" • Panini, Sanskrit grammarian (*fl. c.* 400) • Faxian, Buddhist pilgrim (*fl.* 399–414) • Ajanta caves (c. fifth to eighth century)	
450 C.E.	• Skanda Gupta (r. 455–67) repulses Huna invasion from central Asia (c. 460) • Budha Gupta (r. 467–97)	• Kalidasa composes "Meghaduta" and *Shakuntala*	• Sanskrit in Southeast Asia; Indian gods; Buddhism
500 C.E.	• Hunas gain control of north	• Classical urban culture declines	
600 C.E.	• Pallavas rise to power at Kanchipuram, south India, under Mahendravarman I (r. c. 600–c. 611) • Harsha-vardhana (r. 606–47) rules north India from Kanauj • Chalukyas rule central India under Pulakeshin II at Badami (608–42)	• Xuanzang, Buddhist pilgrim (602–64)	
700 C.E.	• Arabs conquer Sind (712)	• Ellora temple complex (757–90) (see chapter "Hinduism and Buddhism") • Borobudur, Java (778–824) • Khajuraho temple complex (1025–50) (see chapter "Hinduism and Buddhism") • Vedantic philosophy flourishes • Angkor Wat, Cambodia	
1100 C.E.	• Cholas defeat Srivijaya Empire, Sumatra		

By about 300 B.C.E. four of these large states dominated the rest, and one, Magadha, was beginning to emerge as an imperial power over all. As we saw in the chapter entitled "Dawn of the Empires," Alexander had reached the Indus in 326 B.C.E. and had wanted to continue his sweep all the way across the subcontinent to the ocean that he believed to be at the end of the world. His troops, however, mutinied, refused to proceed further, and forced Alexander to withdraw. Soon thereafter Chandragupta Maurya, the ruler of Magadha, marched his troops into northwest India to fill the power vacuum. With this triumph the Maurya dynasty began to carve out India's first empire.

8.1

What were the philosophies of the Maurya and Gupta empires? 8.2

8.3

8.4

The Empires of India

8.2   What were the philosophies of the Maurya and Gupta empires?

For the following 15 centuries, comparatively brief but influential empires alternated with long periods of decentralized and often weak rule. India nevertheless retained a strong sense of cultural unity, based in large part on its familial, social, economic, and

8.1

8.2   What were the
       philosophies of
8.3   the Maurya and
       Gupta empires?
8.4

religious institutions, along with its widely shared heritage of literary epics. In the following pages, therefore, we analyze not only the two major imperial dynasties of ancient India, the Mauryas and the Guptas, but also the more permanent institutions that mediated between the individual and the state. The religious philosophies and social practices of Hinduism that inspire much of the statecraft of these dynasties are discussed briefly here, and are treated much more fully in the chapter "Hinduism and Buddhism." Hinduism, as we shall see, is not a specific set of dogmas and rituals, but rather the variety of religious beliefs and practices of the peoples of India—excluding only those who explicitly reject them in favor of a different religion. This separation in the discussion of political and religious practices is somewhat artificial, but it allows us to recognize the importance of each system separately and to see them interacting in support of each other.

The Maurya Empire

The Maurya family dynasty succeeded to the throne of Magadha in 324 B.C.E. Its founder, Chandragupta Maurya (r. *c.* 321–*c.* 297 B.C.E.), may have first imagined an India-wide empire from a possible meeting with Alexander the Great, and he conquered much of northern India between 321 and 297 B.C.E. His son Bindusara (r. *c.* 297–*c.* 272 B.C.E.) expanded still further the empire that his father had created, and Bindusara's son Asoka brought the empire of the Mauryas to its greatest extent, ruling from modern Afghanistan in the northwest to the Bay of Bengal in the east and well into the Deccan peninsula in the south. By this time India may have held as many as 100 million people.

Government under the Maurya Dynasty. The Maurya dynasty created an imperial government that ruled over or displaced earlier political structures based only on family lineage. Hereditary family lineage did not cease to be important—after all, the imperial ruling dynasty was itself a lineage—but a new state apparatus stood above it in authority and power. The Mahabharata told of a large family of cousins disintegrating into two hostile armies fighting over the inheritance of power. By the time of the Mauryas, however, this kind of civil war was over. The state stood above such individual families and lineages.

The new empire expressed its theory of politics in the *Artha-sastra*, or manual of politics and economics, which has been attributed to Kautilya, a minister of Chandragupta Maurya. (The date of composition is not certain, and the text may actually have been written down later, but its ideas were current under the Mauryas. The *Artha-sastra* text was lost to historians and was rediscovered only in 1909.) The text spoke of *danda niti*, translated into English alternatively and provocatively as the "policy of the scepter" or the "policy of the big stick." It had a cutthroat view of interstate competition. Even in the earlier age of the *janapadas*, Indian political thought had already expressed itself in terms of the "justice of the fish"—that is, larger states swallowed smaller ones. The *Artha-sastra* postulated that every state must be on constant guard against its neighbors, for all were potential enemies. It counseled that strong states be hedged in through mutual treaties among their neighbors, providing a balance of power, while weak states

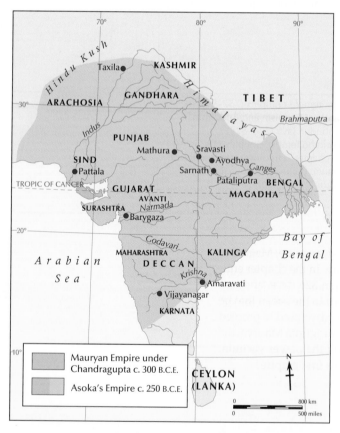

Mauryan India. A younger contemporary of Alexander the Great, Chandragupta Maurya seized control of the kingdom of Magadha and annexed lands to the west, eventually controlling by 300 B.C.E. the strategic trade routes of the Ganges and Indus basins. His grandson Asoka extended the empire west into Seleucid Persia, and south via the wealthy kingdom of Kalinga to gain control of the Deccan by 250.

CHAPTER EIGHT: INDIAN EMPIRES 1500 B.C.E.–1100 C.E.

8.1

8.2

8.3

8.4

What were the
philosophies of
the Maurya and
Gupta empires?

Indo-Greek coins (obverse and reverse), central Asia. The Indian subcontinent was linked to the silk route by trade routes that passed through Afghanistan and the Kushan Empire and continued westward. These economic connections account for the large quantity of Indo-Greek coinage, such as this example showing the Macedonian king Demetrius I (c. 337–283 B.C.E.). (British Museum, London)

should be attacked and conquered. The *Artha-sastra* regarded the immediate circle of neighbors as potential enemies but the next circle beyond them as potential allies, in keeping with the doctrine that "the enemy of my enemy is my friend." Kautilya's advice included suggestions for collecting taxes and encouraging trade. He was also obsessed with using spies. In this competitive world of constant warfare, the state had come into its own.

Regulating Domestic Life. The state had many internal regulatory functions, as well. First among these was the requirement to provide a stable setting in which people had the opportunity to seek the four major goals of life in accordance with Hindu philosophy: *artha* (wealth), *kama* (sensual pleasure), *dharma* (the fulfillment of social and religious duties), and *moksha* (the release from earthly existence and union with the infinite power of the universe, achieved, if at all, at the time of death).

The state helped to enforce rules of behavior between males and females. As in most parts of the world, this relationship charged men with power over women and the responsibility for protecting them, while women were expected to run the household in accordance with the wishes of men and to be available for the pleasure of men. As the *Kama Sutra* explained, "By a girl, by a young woman, or even by an aged one, nothing must be done independently, even in her own house." Women's property rights were always very limited, and in some periods they had none. On the other hand, some professions, notably weaving, were open to women. Hindu views of women's proper role and behavior are discussed briefly in the chapter entitled "Hinduism and Buddhism."

The state also regulated the behavior of its subjects in terms of the rules of caste. In Hindu belief, each person has a social, economic, and ritual position, which is inherited at birth directly from his or her parents. Although this status may, in practice, be changed with difficulty, in theory it remains for life and influences one's status in reincarnation. Caste not only governs private behavior, but also gives people different, unequal status under law. (The origins, rationale, and functions of the caste system as part of Hindu religious belief are discussed in detail below.) It was the task of the state to enforce these caste distinctions, especially their differential rankings, liabilities, and rights in legal proceedings.

📖 **Read** the **Document: Cast(e)aways? Women in Classical India** (200 CE, 6th c. CE) on **MyHistoryLab**

8.1

8.2 What were the philosophies of the Maurya and Gupta empires?

8.3

8.4

Regulating Institutional Life. The state also regulated religious establishments. The larger Hindu temples and Buddhist monasteries developed considerable economic and political power based on the land and resources donated to them by devout followers, especially wealthy landlords, businessmen, and kings. The religious institutions exercised influence over a wide range of public and private decisions made by their devotees; meanwhile, the state attempted to regulate their wealth and power.

The state also enforced rules developed by India's **guilds**, associations of businessmen and producers. Closely associated with the *jati*, or subcastes, these mostly urban groups convened to set work rules, prices, and weights and measures, and to enforce quality control. Independent of the state, the guilds could nevertheless call on it to enforce the regulations on which they had agreed.

Some students of Indian social structures have asked why the business guilds seem never to have attempted to gain direct control of the government in India, as they did in medieval Europe. The answer is not entirely clear, but caste distinctions designated some people for government and military careers, and others for business. Caste regulations separated those who were permitted to take up the bow and the sword and use force to gain control of government from those who could wield influence only through wealth. In Europe, businessmen armed themselves and hired troops; in India, it seems, they did neither. They sought to use their wealth to influence the warrior classes, but not by taking up arms against them.

Recognizing their responsibilities for regulating the interests of conflicting groups internally and the need to remain constantly vigilant against powerful neighbors, Chandragupta Maurya and his son Bindusara attempted to build a highly centralized administration. They appointed well-paid central ministers and bureaucrats, recruited a powerful military, and deployed an efficient system of spies dispersed throughout the empire.

KEY TERM

guild A sworn association of people who gather for some common purpose, usually economic. Guilds of craftsmen or merchants were formed in order to protect and further the members' professional interests and for mutual aid. Compare guilds in Europe, in the chapter entitled "The Opening of the Atlantic and the Pacific."

"The Bimaran reliquary," Gandhara, first century c.e. The central figure of the Buddha is flanked by the Hindu gods Indra and Brahma. This mixed grouping reflects the crossroads nature of the Gandhara region, the border between today's Pakistan and Afghanistan. (British Museum, London)

Asoka, India's Buddhist Emperor. At first Asoka followed the policies of his father and grandfather, and he was especially effective at enlarging the empire through military force. Nine years into his administration, however, he abruptly changed course. In 260 b.c.e. Asoka defeated Kalinga (today's Odisha, formerly Orissa), incorporating this eastern kingdom into his empire. Recoiling from the mass killing required for the military conquest, he determined to become a different person and a different ruler. He converted to Buddhism, a religion firmly committed to nonviolence, and dispatched missionaries throughout his realm and beyond, to parts of south India, Syria, Greece, Egypt, and, probably, Southeast Asia. He sent his own son on a mission to Sri Lanka, and as a result the island kingdom permanently converted to Buddhism.

For 30 years after the Battle of Kalinga, Asoka's reign brought general peace to India. The accompanying, universalistic ethic of Buddhism appealed to a people who were increasingly settling down from nomadism into stable agricultural and urban life. In diminishing the importance of the priestly *brahmin* castes, Buddhism proved especially attractive to merchant castes and guilds, groups that supported Asoka's rule.

Successor States Divide the Empire. Following Asoka's death in 238 b.c.e., no emperor was strong enough to maintain centralized power, and the Mauryan Empire went into a half-century of decline. The Mauryan dynasty came to

SOURCE

Asoka, India's Buddhist Emperor

Until just over 100 years ago, little was known about Asoka, the Mauryan emperor who held sway over the bulk of the Indian subcontinent from 265 to 238 B.C.E. In the nineteenth century, however, edicts that Asoka had inscribed on pillars and rocks to spread his name and ideals were deciphered, and for the first time in modern history Asoka's identity and teachings were understood.

Asoka had constructed at least seven pillar edicts and had inscribed at least 14 major and numerous minor rock edicts that have been discovered and excavated in many regions of India. Most are written in Brahmi script and are the oldest existing writing in India. The script, although an early variant of Sanskrit, had been lost for centuries until a British official, James Prinsep, redeciphered it in 1837. Prinsep analyzed the collective significance of the rock and pillar edicts discovered up to his time along with materials on Asoka found in early chronicles in Sri Lanka.

Asoka's famed conversion to Buddhism, a dramatic turning-point in his life, is described in the Thirteenth Major Rock Edict. The carnage he had created in his military victory at Kalinga and the suffering of his victims had left Asoka with a terrible sense of remorse. As reparation for his actions, he proclaimed his renunciation of violence and acceptance of *Dhamma*, the teachings of the Buddha that promote compassion, tolerance, and honesty.

> A hundred and fifty thousand people were deported, a hundred thousand were killed and many times that number perished. Afterwards, now that Kalinga was annexed, the Beloved of the Gods [Asoka] very earnestly practiced *Dhamma*, desired *Dhamma*, and taught *Dhamma*. (Thapar, *Asoka*, p. 255)

He did not, however, renounce the conquest and annexation of Kalinga, and while he disavowed violence as a general principle, he seemed to retain it as an option of state policy, especially in dealing with the tribal people of the forests:

> The Beloved of the Gods conciliates the forest tribes of his empire, but he warns them that he has power even in his remorse, and he asks them to repent, lest they be killed. (p. 256)

To spread his message and promote a universal faith, Asoka dispatched missionaries throughout his empire and beyond. He also made his own journeys to practice *Dhamma* and help to alleviate suffering, especially in rural areas. The Sixth Major Rock Edict proclaims Asoka's dedication to public welfare:

> I consider that I must promote the welfare of the whole world, and hard work and the dispatch of business are the means of doing so. Indeed there is no better work than promoting the welfare of the whole world. And whatever may be my great deeds, I have done them in order to discharge my debt to all beings. (p. 253)

Asoka's projects for improving the welfare of his people included the founding of hospitals, the planting of medicinal plants and trees, and the building of some 84,000 stupas (Buddhist burial mounds) and monasteries. In his bid to create a more tolerant, compassionate society, Asoka granted religious groups outside Buddhism the freedom to worship, but at the same time encouraged them to respect the beliefs and practices of other sects. He banned animal sacrifice.

Asoka's active contribution to the spread of Buddhism had a lasting impact. His inscriptions offer us tangible evidence of the great influence Buddhism had not only on his own life but also on Indian life and thought as a whole.

📖 **Read** the **Document**: Emperor Asoka, from *The Edicts of Asoka* on **MyHistoryLab**

Lion capital of the pillar erected by Asoka at Sarnath, Mauryan, *c.* 250 B.C.E. The polished sandstone columns erected by the emperor Asoka at places associated with events in the Buddha's life, or marking pilgrim routes to holy places, are of special interest for their 7-foot-high capitals. These provide us with the best remaining examples of Mauryan imperial art and are rich in symbolism. For instance, the Buddha was spoken of as a "lion" among spiritual preachers, whose sermon penetrated to all four corners of the world, just as the lion's roar established his authority in the forest.

Buddha of the "great wonders." Gandhara, third to fourth century C.E. The Hellenistic draping style of the Buddha's clothing illustrates another example of the crossroads nature of the Gandhara region. The Buddha's right hand is raised in the *abhaya mudra*, or hand position expressing reassurance. His palm is marked with the Wheel of the Buddha's Doctrine of Enlightenment. (Musée Guimet, Paris)

an end, and with it the unity of India, when a military commander assassinated the last Maurya king in 185 B.C.E. India dissolved again into a variety of contesting states.

The Sunga dynasty (185–173 B.C.E.) came to rule the core region that remained from Magadha. Indo-Greeks, the inheritors of Alexander's empire stationed in Afghanistan and Bactria, invaded in 182 B.C.E. and captured the northwest all the way through to the coastal cities of Gujarat. They produced a hybrid culture with the Indians they conquered. King Menander, an Indo-Greek, carried on a profound conversation with the Buddhist monk Nagasena, who introduced the king to his religion. Their dialogue is still studied today as the *Questions of King Milinda*. Gandharan art, synthesizing Greek and Indian contributions, flourished in this period, as did the city of Taxila, the great center of trade, culture, and education in the northwest. Finally, large caches of Indo-Greek coinage reflect the importance of trade routes running through the northwest and linking India to the great silk routes of central Asia.

New invaders conquered and displaced the old. In the chapter on China we read of tribal wars in East Asia, on the borders of China, which pushed Mongol groups westward to Rome. One of these tribal groups, the Shakas, invaded and ruled parts of northwest and western India for about a century, from about 94 B.C.E. to about 20 C.E. They, in turn, were displaced by yet another, larger nomadic tribal group from East Asia, known in India as the Kushanas. The geographical extent of Kushana rule is not entirely known, but it seems to have included today's Afghanistan, Pakistan, Kashmir, and India as far south as Gujarat and its ports. The legendary Kushana king, Kanishka (r. *c.* 78–*c.* 103 C.E.), seems also to have promoted Buddhism, and may have adopted it himself. With a single government controlling all these lands, trade between the subcontinent and the central Asian silk routes flourished.

The Gupta Empire

In 320 C.E. a new dynasty began its rise to power in the Ganges valley, apparently through a fortunate marriage. The founder came from a dynasty of no historical fame, but he married a princess of the powerful Licchavi lineage. Reflecting a deep sense of history and a desire to gain legitimacy, he deliberately named himself after the founder of the Mauryan Empire and became Chandra Gupta I (r. 320–*c.* 330 C.E.). His son Samudra Gupta (r. *c.* 330–*c.* 380 C.E.) earned a reputation as one of India's greatest military conquerors. The record of his battles, inscribed on an existing Asoka pillar at Allahabad, touches all regions of India: the far south, the east to Bengal and even Assam, the north to Nepal, and the mountain kingdoms of central India, which had often remained independent because of their inaccessibility.

8.1

8.2 What were the philosophies of the Maurya and Gupta empires?

8.3

8.4

Samudra's son and successor, Chandra Gupta II (r. *c.* 380–*c.* 415 C.E.), conquered the remaining Shakas and annexed western India, including prosperous Gujarat and its ports on the Arabian Sea, for the first time in three centuries. By marrying his daughter to the head of the Vakataka lineage, he cemented an alliance with the Vataka kingdom in central India. Other Gupta alliances were established through marriages with other powerful lineages in the Deccan. The fourth Gupta emperor, Kumara Gupta (r. *c.* 415–55 C.E.), presided over a great empire now at peace.

Gupta rule was often indirect. Following many of their distant military victories, the Gupta emperors abdicated the tasks of administration and withdrew, demanding only tribute payments. Nor did their alliances with other kingdoms and lineages call for direct rule. In the Ganges valley heartland of the empire, the Gupta emperor himself appointed governors at the provincial level, and sometimes even at the district level. At the most local level of the village and the city, however, the Guptas allowed considerable independence to local administrators. The area they administered directly was much smaller than the Mauryan Empire; the two centuries of Gupta rule and influence are considered India's "golden age" more for their cultural brilliance than for their political power.

Gupta India. In the fourth century C.E. the indigenous Gupta dynasty gained control of the middle Ganges and rapidly built an empire straddling the subcontinent from Sind to the Ganges delta, augmented by a web of treaty and tributary arrangements with neighboring powers. This classical age of Indian empires was destroyed by invasions of central Asian peoples in the late fifth century C.E.

Plaque of musician with lyre, central India, fifth century C.E. During the Gupta period, terra-cotta plaques, such as this cross-legged lyre player, were used to adorn the exterior of temples. This one comes from one of the few surviving examples of free-standing brick temples decorated in this way at Bhitargaon in the Gupta heartland. (British Museum, London)

8.1

8.2

What were the philosophies of the Maurya and Gupta empires?

8.3

8.4

8.1

8.2   What were the
       philosophies of
8.3   the Maurya and
       Gupta empires?
8.4

A Golden Age of Learning. The Guptas presided over a resurgence of Sanskrit literature and Hindu philosophy. The great playwright Kalidasa (fifth century C.E.) composed two epic poems: a lyrical poem, "Meghaduta," and the great drama Shakuntala, the first Sanskrit drama translated into a Western language in modern times. Much of the important literature that had been transmitted orally was now transcribed into writing, including the Purana stories of legend and myth. Further emendations were made to the great epics, the *Mahabharata* and *Ramayana*.

The Gupta Empire began to use formal, standardized Sanskrit for its official correspondence. Panini (*fl. c.* 400 B.C.E.) had fixed the essentials of Sanskrit grammar in his *Astadhyayi* (perhaps the most systematic grammar ever produced in any language), but the Mauryas and most other earlier rulers had used Prakrit, a variant of Sanskrit that was closer to the common language of the people. Now Sanskrit law codes, such as the *Laws of Manu*, and manuals of statecraft, such as Kautilya's *Artha-sastra*, were studied, revised, and further codified. Many locally powerful officials patronized scholars, humanists, and artists. Important academic centers for Buddhist learning flourished at Taxila in the northwest and Nalanda in the Ganges valley. Chinese

Wall-painting illustrating the *Vishvantara Jataka*, Cave 17, Ajanta. Gupta period, fifth century C.E. Prince Vishvantara, was, in Buddhist legend, a prior incarnation of the Buddha. The prince was so generous that people jealous of him had him and his family exiled from his father's kingdom. Here the prince informs his wife of the edict.

Buddhist scholars visited and described these academies; by contrast, their descriptions of Hindu academies have not been preserved to the present.

The Resurgence of Hinduism. The Guptas, however, were more dedicated to promoting Hindu religious authority and learning. Major systems of Hindu philosophy returned to favor. The most influential, *Vedanta* (the culmination, or end, of the Vedas), expanded on the teachings of the Upanishads. Vedanta philosophy posed a powerful, attractive, alternative vision to Buddhism, and Hinduism began to regain ascendancy over Buddhism in India.

The caste system was elaborated and enforced in more detail. Rulers, high-level administrators, and wealthy landlords gave patronage to *brahmins* in the form of land grants and court positions. *Brahmin* priests also asserted their role in ritual performance. Buddhism, which had flourished through the patronage of earlier empires and the support of business classes, ceded the performance of many of its own rituals to *brahmin* priests, and began to decline.

Despite its military and cultural achievements, the Gupta dynasty's power began to wane in the late fifth century C.E. The subcontinent was once again politically divided and subject to one wave of invader-rulers after another. These internal divisions and conquests by outsiders—notably the Mughals in the sixteenth century and British in the eighteenth—continued until the modern independence of India and Pakistan in 1947 and of Bangladesh in 1971.

Classical south Asia. After the decline of the Gupta empire, India had no centralized empire for almost 1,000 years. Local powers grew up, often based on different languages and ethnicities. More powerful groups occupied the richest lands, while the weaker were forced into the hills. The roots of today's separate states of India lie in some of these early ethnic kingdoms.

Huna Invasions End the Age of Empires

8.3 What were the consequences of the Hunas' invasion of India?

In the fifth century, new conquerors came through the passes of the northwest, overthrowing the Gupta Empire and establishing their own headquarters in Bamiyan, Afghanistan. These invaders were the Hunas, a branch of the Xiongnu, the nomadic Mongol tribes that roamed the regions north of the Great Wall of China and sometimes invaded. In previous expansions, they had driven other groups west, even into the Roman Empire, as we saw in the chapter "Rome and the Barbarians." Domino-fashion, these groups pushed one another westward. The Shakas had invaded India as a result of this sequence in about 94 B.C.E. The Kushanas followed about a century later. Now the Hunas themselves arrived in force. These same ethnic peoples were called Huns in the Roman Empire, which they invaded under Attila in 454 C.E.

 View the **Image**: Elephanta Water Cave, India on **MyHistoryLab**

The Hunas and their Legacy

Skanda Gupta (r. 455–67 C.E.) repulsed the first Huna invasions, which occurred about 460 C.E. But the continuing Huna presence across India's northwest border

8.1

8.2

What were the consequences of the Hunas' invasion of India?

8.3

8.4

8.1
8.2
8.3
8.4

What were the
consequences
of the Hunas'
invasion of India?

seems to have disrupted international trade and reduced Gupta wealth. Skanda's successor apparently could not hold the empire together, and regional strongmen began to assert their independence. With central control thus weakened, Huna armies invaded again, about 500 C.E., and for the next half-century they fought in, and controlled much of, northern and central India.

From their capital in Bamiyan, Afghanistan, the Hunas ruled parts of India as their own imperial provinces. As in Rome, they earned a reputation for great cruelty, reported not only by Indians but also by Chinese and Greek travelers who visited the region. Huna rule proved brief, however. In 528 C.E. Indian regional princes drove them northwest as far as Kashmir. About a generation later, Turkic and Persian armies defeated the main Huna concentrations in Bactria, removing them as a force in India.

Although it was short-lived, the Hunas' impact on India was considerable. Their invasion weakened the Gupta Empire, enabling regional powers to dismember it and to declare their own independence. Except for a brief reign by Harsha-vardhana or Harsa (r. 606–47 C.E.), king of the north Indian region of Kanauj, no further unification of India was ever seriously attempted from inside the subcontinent until the twentieth century. (The Mughal and British Empires, discussed in the chapters entitled

---

SOURCE

Tamil Culture in Southeast India

The dominant language of the southeast was Tamil, and it developed an especially expressive literature. The poetry of the southern Tamilian academies, called *sangam* poetry and written between 100 B.C.E. and 250 C.E., set in counterpoint the private, bittersweet play of love against a public atmosphere of warfare and strife. This poetry was lost until scholars rediscovered it in the later decades of the nineteenth century. It has been brought to the attention of the English-speaking world especially through the efforts of the late A.K. Ramanujan.

A King's Double Nature
His armies love massacre,
he loves war,

yet gifts
flow from him ceaselessly.

Come, dear singers,
let's go and see him in Naravu

where, on trees
no axe can fell,
fruits ripen, unharmed
by swarms of bees,
egg-shaped, ready
for the weary traveller
in the fields of steady, unfailing harvests;
where warriors with bows
that never tire of arrows
shiver
but stand austere
in the sea winds
mixed with the lit cloud
and the spray of seafoam.

There he is,
in the town of Naravu,
tender among tender women.

Harvest of War
Great king,

you shield your men from ruin,
so your victories, your greatness
are bywords.

Loose chariot wheels
lie about the battleground
with the long white tusks
of bull-elephants.

Flocks of male eagles
eat carrion
with their mates.

Headless bodies
dance about
before they fall
to the ground.

Blood glows,
like the sky before nightfall,
in the red center
of the battlefield.

Demons dance there.
And your kingdom
is an unfailing harvest
of victorious wars.

(trans. Ramanujan, pp. 131, 115)

CHAPTER EIGHT: INDIAN EMPIRES 1500 B.C.E.–1100 C.E.

8.1

8.2

What were the
consequences
of the Hunas'
invasion of India?

8.3

8.4

Bronze figure of Nataraja, Tamil Nadu, southern India, Chola Dynasty, c. 1100 C.E. For their mastery
on conveying grace in motion through the solidity of bronze, Chola sculptures are considered among the
finest artistic works of ancient India. (British Museum, London)

"The Unification of World Trade" and "Nationalism, Imperialism, and Resistance,"
were created by invasions from outside, although the Mughals later settled within
the subcontinent.)

The urban culture of north India dimmed. The Buddhist monasteries, which the
Hunas attacked with especial force, never recovered. On the other hand, by opening
up their invasion routes the Hunas indirectly enriched India's population pool. Gur-
jaras and Rajputs entered western India more or less along with the Hunas, and
settled permanently. The modern Indian states of Gujarat and Rajasthan are named
for them and their descendants.

The legacies of the Hunas in India—the destruction and dismemberment of the
Gupta Empire, the reduction in interregional trade, the decline of culture, and the
introduction of new nomadic groups into already settled imperial lands—quite
closely mirror those of their Hun brothers in the Roman Empire. Even the timings
were similar, products of the same emigration from central Asia. Of the great empires
of the ancient world, only China was capable of defeating or assimilating these invaders without losing its own coherence and identity.

8.1

8.2

8.3

8.4

What were the
consequences
of the Hunas'
invasion of India?

Earthenware sculpture, Nilgiri Hills, south India, early centuries C.E. *Adivasis*, or tribals,
produced distinctive artwork. A buffalo cult among the Todas, the largest of the Nilgiri
Hills tribal groups, led to the creation of this characterful figurine, made to decorate the
lid of an urn containing ashes. (British Museum, London)

Regional Diversity and Power

The history of the Indian subcontinent tends to be written from the perspective of the
Ganges valley as the center of political power and influence. (The settlements of the
central Indus valley discussed in the chapter entitled "River Valley Civilizations" did
not endure, and the region is now a desert.) The Aryans established their centers in
the Ganges region; the Mauryas continued the pattern; so did the Guptas; the later
Mughals established their capitals there; the British ultimately followed Mughal patterns by also placing their capital at Delhi; and today's government of independent
India has followed suit. But other regions of India have always been important, too.
Even at times when India has been unified, regional powers have regularly challenged the supremacy of the Ganges heartland. In periods such as the millennium
from 500 to 1500 C.E., when India had no central empire, the outlying regions asserted
their status as independent states.

The major regions of India speak different languages from one another, although
imperial rulers have usually introduced a unifying link language for interregional
communication: Prakrit under Asoka; Sanskrit under the Guptas; Persian under the
Mughals; and English under the British. Today, India uses two official languages,
Hindi and English. Pakistan uses Urdu and English, and Bangladesh uses Bengali.

The peoples of different regions have immigrated into the subcontinent from
different places and at different times, some preceding the Aryans, others following them. In regions dominated by Aryans, many of these non-Aryans (people who
spoke other languages) found a place within the social system of the Aryans. The
highly stratified Aryan society—marked by caste and *jati*—could make room for the
absorption of various groups by creating new categories for them within the existing
hierarchies. When not consolidated into larger empires, these diverse groups have
created their own political-cultural administrations. The peoples of Gujarat in the
west and Bengal and Orissa in the east have all seen themselves as distinct ethnic

groups, even when they were ruled from the north, and as independent when that rule was broken. Regional dynasties came and went.

The indigenous tribal peoples—referred to today as *adivasis* ("original inhabitants"), because their immigration predates any historical records—generally inhabit less accessible areas, frequently hilly tracts that are not easy to farm. They have attempted to protect their independence from outside exploitation by maintaining their inaccessibility.

The most distinct and separate region was the far south. Here, several lineage and ethnic groups fought to maintain their independence: the Pandyas in the extreme southeast; the Pallavas just north of them along the coast; and then the Cholas and the Chalukyas. Along the southwest coast, the Perumal and Cera lineages dominated. The place of their origin and the time of their immigration are not clearly known, but their languages form a linguistic family called Dravidian, not related to the Sanskritic family of languages of the north. In the Source box above, two poems provide a taste of the literary richness of Tamil, one of the four principal Dravidian languages.

Sea Trade and Cultural Influence: From Rome to Southeast Asia

Imperial governments based inland in the Ganges valley and the northwest based their economic power on their control of land and overland trade through the mountain passes connecting to the silk routes. Many of the regional, coastal powers, on the other hand, profited more from trade by sea. They maintained wide-ranging external connections, from the Roman Empire in the west to Southeast Asia in the east.

Under the Roman emperor Caesar Augustus (r. 27 B.C.E.–14 C.E.), Rome annexed Egypt, thereby opening up a trade route to the east by way of the Red Sea. Rome's great wealth generated a powerful economic demand for goods from Asia. Roman traders learned from the Arabs to sail with the southwest monsoon winds from the Red Sea to the west coast of India. About six months later they could sail back with the northeast monsoon, completing the round trip within a year.

KEY TERM

Adivasis "Original inhabitants." The aboriginal peoples of the Indian subcontinent, who are outside the caste system and live somewhat separately from the rest of society, generally in remote places. Previously referred to as "tribals," they are today sometimes referred to as *vanvasis*, or forest dwellers.

HOW DO WE KNOW?

Coins and Excavations

In his great compendium of trade in the Indian Ocean, *The Periplus of the Erythrean Sea* (c. 50 C.E.), a Greek merchant wrote of the Roman trade with Malabar, the southwest coast of India,

> They send large ships to the market-towns on account of the great quantity and bulk of pepper and [cinnamon]. There are imported here, in the first place, a great quantity of coin; topaz, thin clothing, not much; figured linens, antimony, coral, crude glass, copper, tin, lead, wine, not much, but as much as at Barygaza [the flourishing port of Gujarat, further north] … There is exported pepper, which is produced in quantity in only one region near these markets … Besides this there are exported great quantities of fine pearls, ivory, silk cloth, spikenard from the Ganges, [cinnamon] from the places in the interior, transparent stones of all kinds, diamonds and sapphires, and tortoise shell. (cited in Kulke and Rothermund, p. 106)

Numerous hoards of Roman gold coins throughout south India provide archaeological evidence of trade between Rome and India. In 1945, the British archaeologist Sir Mortimer Wheeler discovered the remnants of a Roman trading post at Arikamedu, a fishing village adjacent to Chennai (formerly Madras). He excavated the brick foundations of large halls and terraces, cisterns, fortifications, and ceramics that had been produced in Italy between 30 B.C.E. and 35 C.E. This outpost suggests that the traders actually carrying the goods across the Arabian Sea were foreign rather than Indian: Arabs, Jews, and Romans. The Roman historian Pliny complained that Rome was sending around 50 million sesterces a year to India to buy its luxuries, although he also noted that they sold in Rome for 100 times that amount.

- What seems to have been the main item exported from Europe to pay for Indian goods?
- Why was this pattern of exports disturbing to the Roman Pliny?
- Is it surprising to you that India's import–export trade with Rome was apparently not carried by Indians, but by Arabs, Jews, and Romans? Why or why not?

8.1

8.2

8.3

8.4

What were the
consequences
of the Hunas'
invasion of India?

Southeast Asia: "Greater India"

Some of the luxury goods shipped to Rome originated in Southeast Asia and were transshipped via India. Indian sailors traveled to all the coastal countries of modern Southeast Asia: Myanmar (formerly Burma), Thailand, Cambodia, Vietnam, Malaysia, and Indonesia. To anchor this trade, they established settlements in port cities such as Oc Eo in Funan, in the southernmost part of modern Vietnam. When they arrived, the sailors and settlers found *brahmin* priests and Buddhist monks already there. Long before any of these trade ventures, in the third century B.C.E., King Asoka had dispatched missionaries to Sri Lanka and to Myanmar to begin the process of converting these lands to Buddhism. Local mythology and Chinese historical records tell (quite different) stories of the arrival of a *brahmin* priest named Kaundinya. As a result of his activities, Funan adopted Sanskrit as the language of the court and encouraged Hinduism.

Funan remained an independent state, not an Indian province. Indeed, in the third century C.E. Funan extended its own rule to southern Vietnam, Cambodia, central Thailand, northern Malaya, and southern Myanmar from its capital at Vyadhapura, near present-day Phnom Penh. Wherever Funan expanded, it encouraged the adoption of Indian culture.

Ironically, Funan later infused Indian culture even among those who conquered it. When Champa expanded southward into Funan lands, the kings of Champa began

Borobudur, Java, late eighth century C.E. This monument, the supreme example of Buddhist art in Southeast Asia and Indonesia, is a fantastic microcosm, reproducing the universe as it was imagined in the Mahayana school of Buddhist theology. The relief sculptures, of which there are some 10 miles, represent the doctrine of *karma*, the cycle of birth and rebirth, of striving, and release from the Wheel of Life.

Angkor Wat, Angkor, Cambodia, early twelfth century C.E. Dedicated to the Hindu god Vishnu, this huge jungle-bound temple complex once served as the centerpiece of the Khmer Empire, originally founded in 880 C.E. Decorated with extensive relief sculpture, the temples of Angkor Wat were intended to emulate mountains in dressed stone.

8.1

8.2

What were the consequences of the Hunas' invasion of India?

8.3

8.4

to adopt the cultural, linguistic, and architectural styles of the Pallavas of south India that were then current in Funan. Bhadravarman, a Champa king, built the first Champa temple to the Hindu god Shiva.

Two additional areas under Funan hegemony later established independent states with strong Hindu and Buddhist cultural elements: Java and the kingdom of Srivijaya in Sumatra. In Java, the ruling Sailendra dynasty built an extraordinary Buddhist temple at Borobudur in 778–824 C.E. When the Sailendras attacked the Khmer peoples of present-day Cambodia, the Khmers unified their defenses under King Jayavarman II (r. 790–850 C.E.). He established a new capital and introduced Hindu temples and philosophies into the whole region around it at Angkor, which later became the location of one of Hinduism's greatest temples, constructed by Jayavarman VII (r. 1181–1219 C.E.).

8.1

8.2

8.3

8.4   How do India's
empires compare
with those of
China and Rome?

The diffusion of Indian religious and cultural forms continued for centuries throughout Southeast Asia. It proceeded almost entirely peacefully, spread by priests and traders. A few exceptions, however, stand out. Two south Indian kings did send military expeditions to Southeast Asia. The Pallava king Nandivarman III (r. *c.* 844–66 C.E.) supported a military camp on the Isthmus of Siam to protect a group of southern Indian merchants who were living and working there. The Chola king Rajendra I (r. 1014–47 C.E.) dispatched a fleet to Sumatra and Malaya and defeated the Srivijaya Empire. It appears that his goal was to keep the trade routes open and to support India's sailors on the competitive sea lanes; he claimed no territory. In 1068–69 C.E., the Cholas apparently intervened in a dispute among rival claimants to rule in Malaya, conquered a large part of the region, but then turned it over to their local client.

India, China, and Rome: Empires and Intermediate Institutions

8.4   How do India's empires compare with those of China and Rome?

A comparison of the long-lived Roman, Indian, and Chinese empires alerts us to the need to analyze empires not only from the top-down perspective of the central administration but also from the bottom up—from their foundations in local regions and institutions.

Comparing India, China, and Rome is not straightforward. To begin with, India lacks the detailed political, military, economic, administrative, and personal records that would facilitate comparison in any detail. Rome and China compiled official histories, and a wide variety of personal accounts have also survived to the present. For India, on the other hand, we must often rely on the observations of foreign visitors for our best accounts. Even the life, writings, and policies of Asoka, now regarded as ancient India's greatest emperor, were lost from historical consciousness for centuries until his rock and pillar edicts were deciphered in the nineteenth century.

Administration

Both Rome and China built institutionalized bureaucracies and systems of administration, lasting for centuries in Rome and millennia in China. By contrast, India's states and empires generally seemed to be extensions of family lineages. Even the most powerful of ancient India's empires, the Mauryan and Gupta, were family holdings. Despite the administrative rigor suggested by Kautilya's *Artha-sastra*, even Chandragupta Maurya's dynasty began to weaken after the death of his grandson Asoka. In India, power remained more personal than institutional.

International Relations

The *Artha-sastra* characterized interstate relations by the law of the fish, the large swallow the small: "When one king is weaker than the other, he should make peace with him. When he is stronger than the other, he should make war with him." Despite Asoka's renunciation of the excessive use of force, the constant rise and fall of kingdoms and small empires throughout India suggest that Kautilya's view generally prevailed. We do not have records of internal revolts against states and empires in India. Instead, dissidents would abscond to a neighboring state where they felt they could live more freely and where they might join the official military to fight against their former ruler.

Invasion of the Hunas

Indian empires did not expand politically or militarily beyond the borders of the subcontinent. Later trade missions in Southeast Asia exported cultural and religious innovations along with their material cargo, but they made little attempt to establish political rule there. On the other hand, outsiders frequently invaded the subcontinent.

Remarkably, the one political experience that the empires of India, Rome, and China shared was invasion and at least partial conquest by the Hunas (Huns, Xiongnu) and by the peoples they displaced. Indeed, the Hunas/Huns play an important role in world history, especially from the third through the sixth centuries C.E. History records not only the builders and sustainers of sedentary empire, but also their nomadic challengers.

Local Institutions and the State

In Rome and China, government touched much of the population directly, through taxes, military conscription, imperial service, and aggressive bureaucracy. The state was fundamental to all areas of life. In India, on the other hand, the state seemed to preside over a set of social institutions that were already deeply rooted and were more persistent through time. These institutions included family lineages, aware and proud of their histories; caste groups, each presiding over its own occupational, ritual, and ethnic niche; guild associations, overseeing the conditions of economic production and distribution; local councils, providing government at the village and town level; and religious sects, which gave their members a sense of belonging, identity, and purpose. The state was important in overseeing the activities of all these groups, but it existed only in the context of their existence. States and empires came and went, but these varied, pervasive institutions carried on in their own rhythms. In India political authority was intimately connected, and sometimes subordinated, to familial, cultural, and religious power.

Indian Empires:
What Difference Do They Make?

Ancient Indian empires shed light both on the later history of India and on the structure of empires generally. Modern India is a direct descendant of its ancient empires and shares their diversity, their many languages and ethnic groups incorporated into the whole, their "unity in diversity." The ancient texts—philosophical, political, and epic—continue to provide a common cultural imagery to the majority of Indians today, and their influence extends to large parts of Southeast Asia. Questions concerning the ethics of rule—answered quite differently by such practitioners of politics as Emperor Asoka and such political advisers as Kautilya, author of the *Artha-sastra*—continue to be debated. Most of all, the power of the subdivisions of empire—regions, castes, guilds, village organizations—retain their importance in modern India and in its south Asian neighbors as well.

The tension between center and periphery, between centralized bureaucracy and regional interest groups, which marks all empires to some degree was—and is—especially prominent in India. While China and Rome draw most attention for their ability to build the central institutions of empire and impose them on their subjects, Indian imperial structures integrated and balanced existing local forms of organization. This is a matter more of degree than of complete difference in philosophy of government: Asoka was willing to use brute force to conquer and subdue enemies of his empire even after his adoption of Buddhism; Rome and China were willing to accommodate local interests if they did not threaten imperial control. Nevertheless, more than Rome or China, India gives us an example of empire built up by integrating its constituent parts rather than by defeating or completely assimilating them.

Because these patterns continue to reappear in empires throughout history and around the globe, these early explorations of Rome, China, and India give us some of the tools we need to analyze the successes—and the failures—of imperial structures down to our own times.

CHAPTER REVIEW

NEW ARRIVALS IN SOUTH ASIA

8.1 What was the most important literature of the Aryan immigrants?

India's two great epics, the *Mahabharata* and the *Ramayana*, recount events from 1000 and 700 B.C.E. Although neither is a historical account, both have given us valuable information on the social structures, ways of life, and values of the time in which they were written. The *Mahabharata* is the longest single poem in the world – ten times longer than the Bible. It includes the *Bhagavad-Gita*, or "Song of God," a profound religious meditation and instruction. There are many versions of the *Ramayana*. Its core story tells of the mythical god-king Rama's victory over the demon-king Ravana, who had kidnapped his wife, Sita. Some versions of the story focus on the battles between north and south; some versions tell the story of Sita in different ways.

Even before these epics, the Aryans brought with them religious literature that formed the basis of Hinduism: the four *Vedas*, the sacrificial rituals of the *Brahmanas*, and the mystical philosophy of the *Upanishads*.

THE EMPIRES OF INDIA

8.2 What were the philosophies of the Maurya and Gupta empires?

The Mauryas and the Guptas were the two major imperial dynasties of ancient India, several centuries apart. They contributed the permanent governing institutions that mediated between the individual and the state. Much of the statecraft of each empire was inspired by religious philosophies and social practices: the Mauryas, after Asoka, by Buddhism; the Guptas by Hinduism. Hinduism is not a specific set of dogmas and rituals, but rather encompasses the variety of religious beliefs and practices of the peoples of India. As new ethnic groups were absorbed by Hinduism, their gods were added to the Hindu pantheon.

HUNA INVASIONS END THE AGE OF EMPIRES

8.3 What were the consequences of the Hunas' invasion of India?

The Hunas (the same ethnic peoples called Huns in the Roman Empire) came through the mountain passes of northwest India in the fifth century C.E. Their legacies include the destruction and dismemberment of the Gupta Empire, a reduction in interregional trade, the decline of culture, and the introduction of new nomadic groups. These consequences closely mirror those of the Huns in the Roman Empire of about the same time period.

INDIA, CHINA, AND ROME: EMPIRES AND INTERMEDIATE INSTITUTIONS

8.4 How do India's empires compare with those of China and Rome?

Comparing India, China, and Rome is not an easy task. Rome and China compiled extensive histories and personal accounts, which have survived to the present day. India does not have the detailed military, economic, administrative, and so on, records that would allow straightforward comparisons. Rome expanded its empire mostly through military conquest, while both China and India also absorbed many of their neighbors through more peaceful cultural assimilation. The political empires of Rome and China persisted far longer than those of India, although the cultural legacies of all of them persisted in various forms till today.

Suggested Readings

PRINCIPAL SOURCES

Embree, Ainslee, ed. and rev. *Sources of Indian Tradition*, Vol. I: *From the Beginning to 1800* (New York: Columbia University Press, 2nd ed., 1988). The principal source for materials on ancient India, especially on high culture, philosophy, and politics.

Kulke, Hersmann, and Dietmar Rothermund. *A History of India* (New York: Routledge, 5th ed., 2010). Brief, accessible, excellent introductory history. Kulke brings his considerable expertise on ancient India to the section on empires.

Thapar, Romila. *Ancient Indian Social History* (New Delhi: Orient Longman, 1978). Principal introduction to the institutions of ancient India.

——. *Asoka and the Decline of the Mauryas* (Delhi: Oxford University Press, 1998). Principal introduction to the empire of the Mauryas.

——. *Early India: From the Origins to A.D. 1300* (Berkeley, CA: University of California Press, 2003). Updates Thapar's classic *History of India* (1966). Definitive, if lengthy, introduction.

——. *Interpreting Early India* (New York: Oxford University Press, 1992). Philosophy of studying ancient India, opposing the use of history to advance political programs.

ADDITIONAL SOURCES

Allchin, F.R., *et al. The Archaeology of Early Historic South Asia: The Emergence of Cities and States* (Cambridge: Cambridge University Press, 1995). Somewhat dated, but very accessible, wide-ranging introduction for a nonspecialist.

Bryant, Edwin. *The Quest for the Origins of Vedic Culture: The Indo–Aryan Migration Debate* (New York: Oxford University Press, 2001). A painstakingly scholarly assessment of claims that the Aryans may have originated within the same regions and peoples as Mohenjo-Daro. Evidence for this interpretation is scanty, however.

Craven, Roy C. *Indian Art* (London: Thames and Hudson, 1997). Concise but lavishly illustrated and well-explained introduction.

Green, Peter. *Alexander of Macedon, 356–323 B.C.* (Berkeley, CA: University of California Press, 1991). For Alexander at the threshold of India.

Hammond Atlas of World History (Maplewood, NJ: Hammond, 5th ed., 1999). Indispensable atlas of world history.

Hughes, Sarah Shaver, and Brady Hughes, eds. *Women in World History*, Vol. I: *Readings from Prehistory to 1500* (Armonk, NY: M.E. Sharpe, 1995). Good readings on India.

Huntington, Susan, and John Huntington. *Art of Ancient India* (Boston, MA: Weatherhill, 1985). Introduction to Indian art. Black-and-white illustrations, perceptive discussion.

Lockhard, Craig A. "Integrating Southeast Asia into the Framework of World History: The Period Before 1500," *The History Teacher* XXIX, No. 1 (November 1995), pp. 7–35. Designed for preparing syllabi, with good conceptual scheme for understanding Southeast Asia.

Past Worlds: The (London) Times Atlas of Archaeology (Maplewood, NJ: Hammond, 1988). Fascinating introduction to history through archaeological finds. Lavishly illustrated with maps, pictures, and charts.

Ramanujan, A.K., ed. and trans. *Poems of Love and War: From the Eight Anthologies and the Ten Long Poems of Classical Tamil* (New York: Columbia University Press, 1985). An outstanding poet and scholar translating classical Tamil poetry.

Richman, Paula, ed. *Many Ramayanas: The Diversity of a Narrative Tradition in South Asia* (Berkeley, CA: University of California Press, 1991). The *Ramayana* has many interpretations and uses. Richman provides an astonishing, scholarly array of them.

Rowland, Benjamin. *The Art and Architecture of India: Buddhist/Hindu/Jain* (New York: Penguin Books, 1977). Still a useful introduction.

SarDesai, D.R. *Southeast Asia: Past and Present* (Boulder, CO: Westview Press, 7th ed., 2012). Standard introductory text.

Schwartzberg, Joseph E., ed. *A Historical Atlas of South Asia* (Chicago, IL: University of Chicago Press, 1978). Scholarly, encyclopedic coverage of history through geography. A superb research tool.

Spodek, Howard, and Doris Srinivasan, eds. *Urban Form and Meaning in South Asia: The Shaping of Cities from Prehistoric to Precolonial Times* (Washington, DC: National Gallery of Art, 1993). Papers from an outstanding international scholarly seminar.

Thapar, Romila. *Cultural Pasts: Essays in Early Indian History* (New Delhi: Oxford University Press, 2000). Principal introduction to the institutions of ancient India.

Tharu, Susie, and K. Lalita, eds. *Women Writing in India 600 B.C. to the Present*, Vol. I (New York: The Feminist Press, 1991). Beginning of the movement to include women's materials in the history of ancient India. Wide-ranging subjects.

Trautmann, Thomas, ed. *The Aryan Debate* (New York: Oxford University Press, 2008). Many perspectives on the view that the Aryans were indigenous to northwest India, and perhaps related to the people of Mohenjo-Daro.

FILMS

Legacy: The Origins of Civilization: India (1992; 58 minutes). Written and presented by Michael Wood. Especially strong on the religious life of India (weaker on other aspects).

Peter Brook's Mahabharata (1990; 5 hours and 25 minutes). A modern, highly acclaimed representation of the classical work, based on his nine-hour stage production, with an international cast.

Mahabharata (1988–1990; 94 episodes, 45 minutes each). Produced and directed by B.R. Chopra and Ravi Chopra. Most popular weekly serial broadcast on Indian TV. Work stopped each Sunday morning as much of the country paused to watch.

Ramayana: The Complete Series (1987–1988; 78 episodes, 45 minutes each). Indian TV blockbuster serial based on the classic story and directed by Ramanand Sagar. Credited with increasing devotion to Hindu mythology in north India. Inspired the production of Chopra and Chopra's *Mahabharata*.

PART FOUR

TURNING POINT: CREATING WORLD RELIGIONS

2500 B.C.E.–1500 C.E.

Religion: Ancient Roots

From earliest times people have felt the need to establish relationships with powers that they believed could protect and support them in life, provide a sense of meaning and purpose, and promise some form of existence after death. (Eliade, *Ordeal by Labyrinth*, p. 154.) Some people have imagined these forces as abstract and remote; others have regarded them as having personalities, as gods, sometimes even in human form. (Some people, of course, do not believe in such powers at all, or are skeptical.)

Early burial rituals reveal evidence of religious beliefs. Archaeologists discovered Neanderthal burials with flint tools, food, and cooked meat at Teshik-Tash in Siberia; the burial of a Neanderthal male with a crippled right arm at the Shanidar cave in the Zagros Mountains of Iraq; and graves covered with red ocher powder, including some group burials, in France and central Europe. As modern humans evolved, they introduced far more elaborate burials. Perhaps the most extraordinary yet uncovered are at Sungir about 100 miles east of Moscow, in Russia. Dating back 32,000 years, the five skeletons uncovered there include one—apparently an adolescent boy—buried with about 5,000 beads, 250 canine teeth of foxes, and carved ivory statues and pendants, and another—apparently an adolescent girl—with 5,274 beads in addition to other objects. These burial rituals suggest that the earliest humans believed life might continue in some form, even after death.

We have already seen that many early cities and states were dedicated to particular gods or goddesses, and

Stonehenge, Wiltshire, England. A ring of massive stone pillars, some with lintels across them, is set in a field of numerous graves and was apparently a shrine for worship. Construction began about 3000 B.C.E. Various theories of its early uses cannot be verified since there are no written records. It remains one of the most popular, and mysterious, sites in England, mostly for tourism, but some also come to worship.

sometimes even carried their names. Gilgamesh, builder of the city of Uruk in Mesopotamia, was two-thirds a god and sought eternal life. In Babylon, Hammurabi transmitted his legal code in the name of the god Shamash. Egyptian hymns proclaimed the divinity of the pharaohs. Chinese of the Shang dynasty used oracle bones to augur the will of transcendent powers. Athens was named for the goddess Athena. When city-states went to war in the names of their gods, the fighting was especially bloody.

The empires we discussed in Part Three sought the validation provided by religious leaders and, in exchange, gave financial and political backing to their religious institutions. These links between political and religious powers were deep and abiding. The caste system of Hinduism established a reciprocal relationship between priests and rulers that provided India with a sense of unity and continuity through the millennia. The emperor Asoka promoted Buddhism. In several states of South and Southeast Asia, Buddhist priests were called upon to validate the

Moses, Tomb of Pope Julius II, Michelangelo Buonarroti, Rome, 1513. Marble. Moses carries the tablets of the law under his right arm. The statue references the Biblical account of Moses receiving the tablets directly from God. Compare the image of Moses in the mosaic in San Vitale, Ravenna, in the chapter "Judaism and Christianity." (San Pietro in Vincoli, Rome)

authority of rulers. (Confucianism, one of the pillars of the Chinese imperial system, presents a profound theory of ethical human relationships, but, unlike the religions just mentioned, Confucianism has little otherworldly focus.) In the western world, rabbis interpreted Jewish law; Roman emperors doubled as high priests; Constantine, emperor of Rome, safeguarded early Christianity; the prophet Muhammed served as political as well as religious head of the Muslim community.

Part Four focuses in greater depth on the role of religion throughout human history, but especially from about 300 C.E. to about 1200 C.E. In this period Hinduism became more fully defined and systematized throughout India; Buddhism rose to great importance in China, Japan, and Southeast Asia; Judaism, exiled from its original home in Israel, spread with the exiles throughout much of western Asia, the Mediterranean basin, and northern Europe; Christianity grew into the great cultural system of Europe; and Islam radiated outward from Arabia, across North Africa westward to the Atlantic and to the far corners of the eastern hemisphere, as far as Indonesia. These five religions often confronted one another, sometimes leading to syncretism, the borrowing and adaptation of ideas and practices; sometimes to competition; and sometimes to direct conflict.

Miracles, Manifestations, and the Historian

Organized religious groups usually build on the religious experiences reported by their founders and early teachers. All five of the religions we study in this part grew from such experiences, and many of these experiences were called miraculous—that is, they are contrary to everyday experience, and they can be neither proved nor disproved. For example, most Hindus believe that gods have regularly intervened in human life, as Krishna is said to have done at the Battle of Kurukshetra. They also believe in the reincarnation of all living creatures, including gods. Buddhists believe in the revelation of the Four Noble Truths and the Eightfold Path to Siddhartha Gautama (the Buddha) under the bo tree at Bodh Gaya in northern India; most also believe that Siddhartha was a reborn soul of an earlier Buddha and would himself be born again. Most Jews have believed in special divine intervention in the lives of Abraham and his descendants, a special divine covenant with the Jewish people, and a revelation of divine law at Mount Sinai. Most Christians have believed in the miracle of Jesus' incarnation as the Son of God and his resurrection after death. Most Muslims believe that God revealed his teachings to Muhammad through the angel Gabriel.

Historians, however, cannot study miracles or judge their authenticity. Historical study seeks proof of events, and such proof is not usually available for miracles. Almost

Krishna instructs Arjuna, India, tenth century c.e. One of the most beloved of the gods of Hinduism, Krishna is often painted in dark blue or black, suggesting his origins as a god of one of India's pre-Hindu tribal groups. He is most famous as the spiritual guide and the chariot driver of Arjuna in the *Bhagavad Gita* religious treatise, and, separately as a great lover, sporting with the milkmaids who often surround him as he plays his seductive flute.

identity combined with political power, group boundaries became even more important, marking in-group from outside-group, separating "us" from "them," sometimes even leading to violent conflict. Historians study these manifestations and effects of religious beliefs:

- **The sanctification of time.** Each religion creates its own sacred calendar, commemorating each year the key dates in the history of the religion and in the life of its community. It marks dates for the performance of special rituals, celebrations, fasts, and community assemblies. In addition to the community calendar, members of religious organizations create their own individual and family calendars to mark the rites of passage—the great life-cycle events of birth, puberty, marriage, maturity, and death. Religions especially formulate rules of marriage in an attempt to channel the raw, powerful, mysterious, and often indiscriminate forces of youthful sexuality into conformity with the norms of the group.

MAJOR RELIGIONS OF THE WORLD, 2011

Religion	Number of followers	Percentage of world population
Christians	2,298,093,000	32.8
Roman Catholics	1,184,358 000	16.9
Protestants	426,065,000	6.0
Orthodox	275,808,000	3.9
Anglicans	87,925,000	1.2
Independents	348,511,000	5.0
Unaffiliated Christians	116,082,000	1.7
Muslims	1,560,391,300	22.3
Hindus	959,941,000	13.7
Nonreligious/agnostics	665,069,410	9.9
Chinese folk religionists	568,451,000	8.0
Buddhists	467,546,000	6.7
Ethnic religionists	269,252,000	4.0
Atheists	136,991,000	2.0
New-religionists	63,201,000	0.9
Sikhs	24,285,000	0.4
Jews	14,875,000	0.2
Baha'is	7,417,000	0.1
Confucianists	6,470,490	0.1
Jains	5,383,400	0.1
Shintoists	2,763,900	0.0
Zoroastrians	198,500	0.0

(Numerical data from *Encyclopedia Britannica Book of the Year 2012*)

by definition, a belief in miracles is a matter of faith, not of proof. Moreover, history is the study of the regular processes of change over time, while miracles, again by definition, are one-time-only events, which stand outside and defy the normal processes of change.

What can be studied are the manifestations and effects of religious beliefs on people's behavior. Sincere believers in religious miracles restructure their lives accordingly, creating and joining religious organizations to spread the word about these miracles and about their own experiences with them. These new organizations formulate rules of membership, and they infuse their beliefs into everyday life by establishing sacred time, sacred space, sacred liturgy, and sacred literature and culture. Historically, when religious

- **The sanctification of space.** Each religion creates its own sacred geography by establishing shrines where miraculous acts are said to have occurred; where saints were born, flourished, or met their deaths; and where relics from the lives of holy people are preserved and venerated. The most sacred of these sites become centers of pilgrimage. Whole cities, and especially their sacred quarters, have been dedicated to gods and goddesses, and thought to be under their special protection.
- **The sanctification of language and literature.** Each religion shapes its own use of language, literature, and artistic imagery. The Sanskrit Vedas and epics, the Pali Buddhist Tripitaka, the Hebrew Bible, the Greek New Testament, and the Arabic Quran have provided linguistic and literary canons across the millennia. Subsequent chapters of this book quote religious scriptures extensively because of their centrality to the world's languages, literatures, and imagery.
- **The sanctification of artistic and cultural creativity.** Religious sensibilities often inspire specific creative efforts, and religious groups often encourage the creation of art, music, and drama to express and enhance their message.
- **The sanctification of family and ancestors.** Many religions link living generations to those that have gone before. Through prayers and periodic ritual performances such as visits to graves and shrines, current generations are informed that even ancestors who are no longer living still deserve, and require, respect and reverence. Ancestor remembrance and worship situate current life in a deeper historical context, and may promote a more conservative outlook on life.
- **The creation of religious organization.** If a powerful leadership emerges, individual religious experience may find expression in institutional structure and more complex organization. At one extreme this may be a hierarchical structure with a single leader at the apex and an array of administrative and spiritual orders down to the most local level, the form of the Roman Catholic Church. At another extreme there may be no formal overall organization, and no formal set of rules and regulations, but instead a loose association of local communities related to one another through common beliefs and social structures, the usual form of Hinduism.

Turning Point Questions

1. How do religions convey ethical messages?
2. In what ways do religions contribute to the arts and the humanities?
3. How have religions affected political and economic institutions?

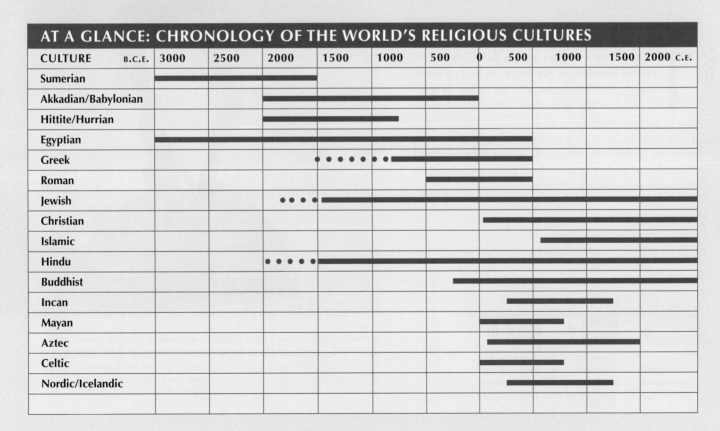

AT A GLANCE: CHRONOLOGY OF THE WORLD'S RELIGIOUS CULTURES

CULTURE B.C.E.	3000	2500	2000	1500	1000	500	0	500	1000	1500	2000 C.E.
Sumerian											
Akkadian/Babylonian											
Hittite/Hurrian											
Egyptian											
Greek											
Roman											
Jewish											
Christian											
Islamic											
Hindu											
Buddhist											
Incan											
Mayan											
Aztec											
Celtic											
Nordic/Icelandic											

9 Hinduism and Buddhism

The Sacred Subcontinent: The Spread of Religion in India and Beyond

1500 B.C.E.–1200 C.E.

This chapter begins with a brief history of early Hinduism, the most ancient of existing major religions, and analyzes its evolution as the principal cultural system of the Indian subcontinent. Buddhism emerged out of Hinduism in India and spread throughout central, eastern, and southeastern Asia, defining much of the cultural and religious life of this vast region. Its history concludes this chapter.

Shiva with the corpse of the goddess Sati, southern India, seventeenth century. Bronze. Lord Shiva, one of the most revered of all the gods of Hinduism, is usually portrayed in awe-inspiring forms because he is the god of destruction, but that destruction sets the stage for later rebirth and reconstruction. (Government Museum, Trivandrum, India)

LEARNING OBJECTIVES

9.1 ((	9.2 ((	9.3 ((
Explain the unique elements in Hinduism.	Explain the reasons for the emergence and spread of Buddhism.	Compare the two religions of the Indian subcontinent.

((Listen on MyHistoryLab

AT A GLANCE: HINDUISM AND BUDDHISM

DATE	POLITICAL/SOCIAL EVENTS	LITERARY/PHILOSOPHICAL EVENTS
1500 B.C.E.	• Caste system	• *Rigveda* (1500–1200)
900 B.C.E.		• *Brahmanas* (900–500)
800 B.C.E.		• *Upanishads* (800–500)
500 B.C.E.	• Siddhartha Gautama (Buddha) (*c.* 563–483) • Mahavir (b. 540), Jain teacher	• Buddha delivers sermon on the Four Noble Truths and the Noble Eightfold Path
300 B.C.E.		• *Mahabharata* (*c.* 300 B.C.E.–300 C.E.) • *Ramayana* (*c.* 300 B.C.E.–300 C.E.)
200 B.C.E.	• Buddhism more widespread than Hinduism in India (until 200 C.E.); spreading in Sri Lanka • Mahayana Buddhism growing in popularity	
10 C.E.	• Fourth general council of Buddhism codified Theravada doctrines • Buddhist missionaries in China (65 C.E.)	• Nagarjuna (*fl. c.* 50–150 C.E.), philosopher of Mahayana Buddhism
300 C.E.	• Spread of Hinduism to Southeast Asia	
400 C.E.	• Hindu pantheon established • Buddhism declining in India	• Puranas written (400–1000) • Faxian's pilgrimage to India • Sanskrit; Hindu gods, temples, and priests in Southeast Asia; Buddhism in Southeast Asia
500 C.E.	• Bhakti begun in south India • Buddhist monks to Japan	
600 C.E.	• Buddhist monks to Southeast Asia • Buddhism flourishes under Tang dynasty (618–907)	• Xuanzang's pilgrimage to India
700 C.E.	• Hindu temples and shrines begin to appear in India • Buddhism begins to decline in China • Buddhism becoming established in Japan	• Hindu philosopher Shankaracharya (788–820) • Saicho (767–822), Japanese Buddhist priest • Kukai (774–835), Japanese Buddhist priest
800 C.E.	• Hindu priests in Southeast Asia • Emperor Wuzong attacks Buddhism in China	• Earliest printed book, *The Diamond Sutra* (868) • Hindu philosopher Ramanuja (*c.* 1017–1137)
1000 C.E.	• Muslim invasion of India (1000–1200) • Buddhist institutions close in India	

Hinduism

9.1   What is unique in the history of Hinduism?

Hinduism began before recorded time. The other major religions of the world claim the inspiration of a specific person or event—Abraham's covenant; the Buddha's enlightenment; Jesus' birth; Muhammad's revelation—but Hinduism emerged through the weaving together of many diverse, ancient religious traditions of India, some of which precede written records. Hinduism evolved from the experience of the peoples of India.

View the **Image: Nine Hindu Planets** on **MyHistoryLab**

The Origins of Hinduism

Because Hinduism preserves a rich body of religious literature written in Sanskrit, the language of the Aryan immigrants of 1700–1200 B.C.E., scholars believed until recently that Hinduism was a product of that migration. Even the excavations at Mohenjo-Daro and Harappa, which uncovered a pre-Aryan civilization, did not at first alter these beliefs. But as excavation and analysis have continued, many scholars

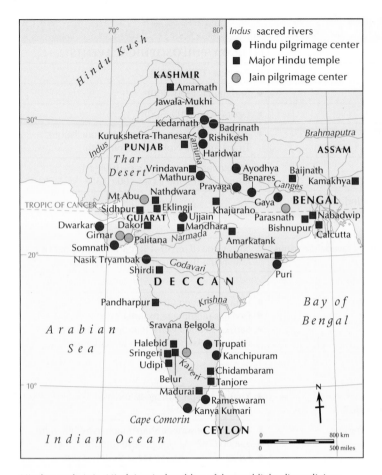

Hindu south Asia. Hinduism is the oldest of the world's leading religions, although its geographic range has been mostly confined to the peoples of south Asia, where its impact has been profound, exemplified by the sacred geography of the subcontinent. Rivers, mountains, and regions associated with divine mythology are important, and networks of pilgrimage centers and temples provide cultural unity.

9.1 What is unique in the history of Hinduism?

9.2

9.3

have come to believe that the Indus valley civilization may have contributed many of Hinduism's principal gods and ceremonies. Excavated statues seem to represent the god Shiva, the sacred bull Nandi on which he rides, a man practicing yogic meditation, a sacred tree, and a mother goddess. Archaeologists increasingly argue that the Aryans absorbed religious beliefs and practices, along with secular culture, from the Indus valley and from other groups already living in India when they arrived.

Contemporary anthropological accounts support this idea that Hinduism is an amalgam of beliefs and practices. These accounts emphasize Hinduism's remarkable ability to absorb and assimilate tribal peoples and their gods. Today, 100 million people, about ten percent of India's population, are officially regarded as *adivasis*, original inhabitants (previously referred to as "tribals"). These peoples were living in India before the arrival of the Aryans, and they have largely attempted to escape Aryan domination by retreating into remote hilly and forested regions, where they could preserve their own social systems. Hindus have, however, pursued them and their lands, building temples in and around tribal areas. These temples recognize tribal gods and incorporate them with the mainstream deities in an attempt to persuade the *adivasis* to accept Hindu religious patterns. Indeed, one of Hinduism's most important gods, Krishna, the blue/black god, was apparently a tribal god who gained national recognition.

As India's peoples have been diverse, so its evolving religious system is diverse. The concept of "Hinduism" as a unified religion comes from outsiders. Greeks and Persians first encountering India spoke of India's belief systems and practices collectively as "Hinduism," that is, the ways of the peoples on the far side of the Indus River. When Muslims began to arrive in India, beginning in the eighth century C.E., they adopted the same terminology.

Sacred Geography and Pilgrimage

Hinduism is closely associated with a specific territory, India. Almost all Hindus live in India or are of Indian descent. Within India itself a sacred geography has developed. Places visited by gods and by saints, as well as places of great natural sanctity, have become shrines and pilgrim destinations. Pilgrims traveling these routes have created a geography of religious/national integration, and modern transportation in the form of trains, buses, and airplanes has increased the pilgrim traffic throughout India. Some of the most important shrines are at the far corners of India, such as Dwarka on the far west coast, Badrinath in the far north, Puri on the east coast, and Rameshwaram near the southern tip. Travel to all these shrines would thus provide the pilgrim with a "Bharat Darshan," a view of the entire geography of India. Such pilgrimage routes have helped to unify both Hinduism and India.

Each locality in city and village is also knit together by religious shrines, ranging from the simple prayer niche, containing pictures and statues of the gods of the

Modern *puja* shrine, India. In this contemporary, crowded, one-room urban apartment the *puja* corner, with its images and pictures of various gods, and its oil lamps, finds its place alongside a television set and the cooking utensils of the household.

What is unique in the history of Hinduism?

9.1

9.2

9.3

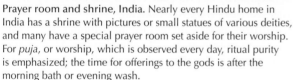

Prayer room and shrine, India. Nearly every Hindu home in India has a shrine with pictures or small statues of various deities, and many have a special prayer room set aside for their worship. For *puja*, or worship, which is observed every day, ritual purity is emphasized; the time for offerings to the gods is after the morning bath or evening wash.

kind found in even the most humble home; through neighborhood shrines, nestled perhaps in the trunk of an especially sacred tree; to local and regional temples.

The Central Beliefs of Hinduism

Hinduism has none of the fixed dogmas of most otherworldly religions, and great flexibility and variety of beliefs exist under the general term "Hindu." Nevertheless, sacred texts do provide a set of beliefs and orientations toward life that are very widely shared. Over time, the introduction of new texts to the Hindu legacy marked the evolution of Hinduism as a living, changing system of beliefs and practices.

The *Rigveda*. Between about 1500 and 1200 B.C.E. *brahmin* priests of the nomadic pastoralist Aryan peoples entering India composed the *Rigveda*, a collection of 1028 verses of Sanskrit poetry, the oldest and most venerated of the four books called, collectively, Vedas. These verses invoke many early gods, including Agni, the god of various kinds of fire; Indra, a phallic god of rain and fertility; Surya, god of the sun; and Varuna, the sovereign of the world who assures that the cosmic law is maintained. They include references to music, dance, and acting as modes of worship.

9.1

9.2

9.3

What is unique
in the history of
Hinduism?

Vedic worship also takes the form of animal sacrifice offered on sacred altars. The *Rigveda* speculates on the creation of the world and on the significance of life in this world, but it does not pretend to offer conclusive answers:

> Who really knows? Who shall here proclaim it? whence things came to be, whence this creation. … This creation, whence it came to be, whether it was made or not—he who is its overseer in the highest heaven, he surely knows. Or if he does not know …? (X:129; Embree, p. 21)

Caste. The Rigveda also introduces the mythic origin and rationale of the caste system, one of the most distinctive features of Hindu life. Caste began, the Rigveda suggests, in a primeval sacrifice of a mythical creature, Purusha. He was carved into four sections, each symbolizing one of the principal divisions of the caste system:

> When they divided Purusha, in how many different portions did they arrange him? What became of his mouth, what of his two arms? What were his two thighs and his two feet called? His mouth became the *brahman* [priest]; his two arms were made into the *rajanya* [or *kshatriya*, warrior]; his two thighs the *vaishyas* [business people and farmers/landlords]; from his two feet the *shudra* [person of the lower working class] was born. (X:90; Embree, pp. 18–19)

Apparently, the Aryans were even then thinking of a social system that separated people by occupation and sanctioned that separation through religion. The caste system that developed in India was probably the most rigidly unequal and hierarchical of any in the world. Caste status was hereditary, passing from parent to child at birth. Each caste was subject to different local legal rules, with upper castes being rewarded more generously and punished less severely than lower. Only upper castes were permitted to receive formal education, and the separate castes were not to intermarry nor even to dine with one another. Their vital fluids were distinct and different, and the blood and semen of one group were not to mingle with those of another. The food fit for one group was not necessarily appropriate for others: *brahmin* priests were to be vegetarians, but *kshatriya* warriors were to eat meat.

Commentators throughout the centuries have searched for additional roots of the caste system, more grounded in social, economic, and political rationales. Many have seen India's caste system as a means of ordering relationships among the multitude of immigrant groups in India's multiethnic population, consolidating some at the top and relegating others to the bottom. Others have seen caste as the result of a frozen economic system, with parents doing all they could to make sure that their children maintained at least the family's current occupational status. They sacrificed the possibility of upward mobility in exchange for the security that they would not fall lower on the social scale.

Many suggested that the system was imposed on the rest of the population by an extremely powerful coalition of *brahmin* priests and *kshatriya* warrior-rulers. Such dominant coalitions are common in world history, and the Indian situation was simply more entrenched than most.

Historians employ the insights of anthropologists as they attempt to understand the historical origins and basis of the caste system. Anthropological observation shows that the four generalized castes of the Vedas are not the actual groupings that function in practice today. Instead, India has tens of thousands of localized castes, called *jatis*—indeed, there are thousands of different *brahmin* groups alone. In practice, caste is lived in accordance with the accepted practices of these local groupings, in the 750,000 villages, towns, and cities of India. From customary law to dining patterns to marriage arrangements, caste relationships are determined locally, and there is no national overarching religious system to formulate and enforce rules. Residents of any given village, for example, may represent some 20 to 30 castes, including all the various craftworkers and artisans. There may be more than one caste claiming

Gouache illustration from Bhanudatta's *Rasamanjari*, 1685. Krishna, the eighth *avatar* (incarnation) of Vishnu, is always depicted with blue or black skin, perhaps because he was originally a god of tribal groups, later assimilated into mainstream Hinduism, along with the peoples who worshiped him. He is renowned for his prowess as a warrior and a lover. In this scene from one of his amorous adventures, a woman stops a forester from felling the tree under which she has arranged to meet Krishna for a romantic tryst.

What is unique in the history of Hinduism?

9.1

9.2

9.3

brahmin status, or *kshatriya*, *vaishya*, or *shudra* status. Anthropologists therefore differentiate between the mythological four *varna* groups of the Vedic caste system and the thousands of *jati* groups through which caste is actually lived in India. Both historians and anthropologists are convinced that the same multitude of castes that they find "on the ground" today existed also in the past. Eventually "outcastes," or "untouchables," emerged, people who were outside the caste system because of the "polluting" work they performed, which might include dealing with dead animals or handling those who died.

Throughout Indian history there have been revolts against the hierarchy of the caste system. In the twentieth century and into the present century the government of India has acted assertively to eliminate the historic discrimination of the caste system, as we shall see in the chapter entitled "China and India." Nevertheless, through the millennia, caste has usually been more important than government in determining the conditions of life of most people. Personal identity and group loyalty were formed far more by caste locally than by government, which tended to be remote.

The *Brahmanas* and *Upanishads*. A second collection of Sanskrit religious literature, dating from about 900–500 B.C.E., sets out rules for *brahmins*, including procedures for sacrifice and worship. These scriptures, the *Brahmanas*, include discussions of the origins of various rituals and myths of the immortal gods.

The *Upanishads*, composed 800–500 B.C.E., are devoted primarily to mystical speculation and proclaim the oneness of the individual and the universe. The universal

9.1

9.2

9.3

What is unique
in the history of
Hinduism?

spirit, *Brahman*, and the soul of each individual, *atman*, are ultimately the same substance, just as individual sparks are the same substance as a large fire. In time, each *atman* will be united with the universal *Brahman*. To reach this unity, each soul will experience reincarnation (*samsara*) in a series of bodies, until it is purged of its attachments to the physical world—which in any case is *maya*, or illusion—and achieves pure spirituality. Then, at the death of this final body, the *atman* is released to its union with the *Brahman*.

The *Upanishads* introduce several concepts fundamental to almost all strands of Hinduism. **Dharma** is the set of religious and ethical duties to which each living creature in the universe is subject. These duties are not the same, however, for each creature; they differ according to ritual status. **Karma** is the set of activities of each creature and the effects that these activities have on its *atman*. Each action has an effect on the *atman*; activities in accord with one's *dharma* purify the *atman*; activities in opposition to one's *dharma* pollute it. "Good *karma*," the good effects brought about by actions in accord with *dharma*, will finally enable the *atman* to win its release from *maya*, the illusions of life on earth; escape *samsara*, or reincarnation; and reach *moksha*, the ultimate union with the *Brahman*. Thus Hinduism sees reward and punishment in the universe as a natural consequence. Good, *dharmic* actions carry their own reward for the *atman*; activities opposed to *dharma* carry their own negative consequences. Activities in this life earn good or bad *karma*.

The *Upanishads* also introduce the concept of the life cycle, with its different duties at each stage. The first stage, *brahmacharya*, is the youthful time of studies and celibacy; the second, *gruhasta*, the householder stage, is for raising a family; the third, *vanaprastha*, literally forest-wandering, is for reflection outside the demands of everyday life; and the last, *sannyasin*, is for immersion in meditation in preparation for death and, ideally, for *moksha*.

These early scriptures established a set of principles that constitute the core of Hindu belief: caste, *dharma*, *karma*, life stages, *samsara*, and, ultimately, *moksha*, the union of the individual *atman* with the universal *Brahman*. They represent a rational system of order in the universe and in individual life. They teach the importance of *dharmic* activities in this world in order to reach *moksha* in the deeper reality beyond. They are transmitted from *guru*, or teacher, to *shishya*, or student. The codification of many of these specific behavioral norms for each caste in *The Law of Manu* attempted to institutionalize the position of the priests and to elaborate on core Hindu beliefs. Written in the first or second century B.C.E., the treatise almost certainly reflected earlier practices, spelling out the appropriate relationships between social classes and between men and women.

Although it reveres the *brahmin* priest (not to be confused with the *Brahman* spirit of the universe), Hinduism is ultimately accessible to each individual, even to those of low caste. Despite the hierarchy of the caste system, Hinduism allows enormous spiritual scope to each individual. It has no core dogma that each must affirm. Each individual Hindu may claim his or her own unique sense of spirituality. This universal accessibility of Hinduism is most clear in three later forms of literature that have become a kind of folk treasury (in contrast to the Vedas, *Brahmanas*, and *Upanishads*, which are the province of the *brahmin* priests).

KEY TERMS

atman The soul of each individual person, identical in its substance to *Brahman*, the universal power. Thus each individual soul is part of the great soul of the universe.

samsara The process and cycle of living, dying, and being reborn.

maya Illusion. The manifest world in which we appear to live is only illusion; there is a reality beyond what we experience here on earth.

dharma The duty of each person, determined in large part by his or her caste.

karma The doctrine that actions have their own appropriate consequences. A person's actions carry their own rewards (or punishments) because they set the directions of his or her life.

MAJOR HINDU GODS AND GODDESSES

A shrine with images of one or more of the thousands of gods in the pantheon can be found in every devout Hindu home. The most widely worshiped gods are probably Shiva with his consort Parvati, and Vishnu with his consorts Lakshmi and Saraswati. But most Hindus offer at least some form of devotion to more than one god.

Brahma	The creator god, whose four heads and arms represent the four Vedas (scriptures), castes, and *yugas* (ages of the world).
Ganesh	The elephant-headed god, bringer of good luck.
Kali	Shiva's fierce consort—the goddess of death—is shown as a fearsome, blood-drinking, four-armed black woman.
Krishna	The eighth *avatar* (incarnation) of Vishnu, depicted with blue or black skin. He is honored for his skills as a lover and a warrior; with his consort Radha.
Rama	The personification of virtue, reason, and chivalry; with his consort Sita, revered for her loyalty.
Shiva	God of destruction, whose dancing in a circle of fire symbolizes the eternal cycle of creation and destruction.
Sitala	Mothers traditionally pray to this goddess to protect their children from disease, especially smallpox.
Vishnu	The preserver, a kindly god, who protects those who worship him, banishes bad luck, and restores good health; with his consorts Lakshmi, the goddess of wealth, and Saraswati, the goddess of wisdom and the arts.

View the **Image: Hindu Gods** on **MyHistoryLab**

The Great Epics. In the chapter entitled "Indian Empires" we discussed India's two great epic poems, the *Ramayana* and the *Mahabharata*. The latter's central story revolves around the civil war between two branches of the family of the Bharatas (from whom India derives its current Hindi name, Bharat). The *Mahabharata* presents moral conflicts, the dilemma of taking sides, and the necessity of acting decisively. At its center stands the *Bhagavad-Gita* ("Song of God"), a philosophical discourse on the duties and the meaning of life and death.

The *Bhagavad-Gita* opens on the field of Kurukshetra before the final battle between the two branches of the Bharata family. Arjuna, leader of one branch, despairs of his options: if he fights, he kills his cousins; if he does not fight, he dies. He turns to his chariot driver, the Lord Krishna, for advice. Krishna's reply incorporates many fundamental principles of Hindu thought. First, Krishna speaks of the duty of Arjuna, a *kshatriya* by caste, to fight: "For a *kshatriya* there does not exist another greater good than war enjoined by *dharma*" (II:31). Each person has a unique *dharma*, largely determined by caste. In this philosophy, changing one's vocational duty is no virtue:

> Better is one's own *dharma* that one may be able to fulfill but imperfectly, than the *dharma* of others that is more easily accomplished. Better is death in the fulfillment of one's own *dharma*. To adopt the *dharma* of others is perilous. (III:35)

The *Bhagavad-Gita* summarizes many of the key doctrines of Hinduism. Lord Krishna promises to help people who do their duty, and points the way toward spiritual fulfillment. The text demonstrates considerable assimilation within Hinduism, for the lord Krishna is dark-skinned, usually represented as blue or black in color. He appears to be originally a non-Vedic, non-Aryan tribal god, perhaps from the south. His centrality in this most revered Sanskrit text suggests the continuing accommodation between the Aryans and the indigenous peoples of India. The *Gita* provided the basis for the continuing emphasis in Hinduism on **bhakti**, mystical devotion to god. "No one devoted to me is lost ... Keep me in your mind and devotion, sacrifice to me, bow to me, discipline your self toward me, and you will reach me" (IX:31,34) is one of many statements in the *Gita* that called for this devotion. *Bhakti* was a revolt within Hinduism against formality in religion, against hierarchy, and against the power of the *brahmin* priesthood. *Bhakti* continues today in the hymns and poetry of the common people and in the multitudes of devotional prayer meetings in every corner of India.

The two epics generally also reflect greater prestige for women than did earlier Sanskrit texts. In the *Ramayana*, Sita appears as a traditionally subordinate wife to Rama, but her commitment to honor and duty surpasses even his; she defends Rama's honor even when he fails to defend hers. She is more heroic than he, although her heroism is defined by her role as dutiful wife. Rama is implicitly criticized for his inability to defend her both from Ravana and from the gossip of his own subjects. In some versions, the criticism is made explicit. In the *Mahabharata* Draupadi is the

Burning the effigy of the evil Ravana. Each year, at the time of the festival of Dusshera, acting troupes throughout India retell the story of the *Ramayana*, climaxing with the victory of Rama over Ravana, the evil king who abducted Rama's wife, Sita. In Ahmedabad, huge effigies of Ravana and his allies are burned, to the delight of the crowds who come to witness this celebration of the triumph of good over evil.

What is unique in the history of Hinduism?

9.1
9.2
9.3

KEY TERM

Bhakti Devotion to god; a personal dedication to and worship of god, often through meditation, music, chanting, dance—different from more formal rituals.

SACRED WRITINGS OF HINDUISM

Vedas	The most sacred of the Hindu scriptures, meaning "divine knowledge." They consist of collections of writings compiled by the Aryans: *Rigveda* (hymns and praises), *Yajurveda* (prayers and sacrificial formulas), *Samaveda* (tunes and chants), and *Atharva-Veda* (Veda of the Atharvans, the priests who officiate at sacrifices).
Upanishads	Philosophical treatises, centering on the doctrine of Brahma.
Brahmanas	Instructions on ritual and sacrifice.
Ramayana	An epic poem, telling how Rama (an incarnation of the god Vishnu) and his devotee Hanuman, the monkey god, recover Rama's wife, Sita, who has been abducted by the demon king Ravana.
Mahabharata	"Great Poem of the Bharatas." Includes the *Bhagavad-Gita* ("Song of God") and consists of 18 books and 90,000 stanzas. The central narrative of civil war, and the innumerable sidebars, emphasize the struggle to do one's duty faithfully.

9.1
9.2
9.3

What is unique in the history of Hinduism?

wife of five noble brothers, and she protects, defends, and inspires them in their struggles, going far beyond the subservient role that women play in the majority of Aryan literature. In the epics, the female force, *shakti*, has gained recognition.

The *Puranas*. The most popular of the gods of Hinduism, Vishnu and Shiva, appear in the *Puranas*, a collection of ancient stories. Here, too, female goddesses appear, often as consorts of the principal gods, such as the goddesses Lakshmi and Saraswati with the lord Vishnu; and the goddesses Parvati, Durga, and Kali with the lord Shiva. These goddesses also help to balance the rather suppressed position of females evident in the earlier Aryan literature.

Temples and Shrines

By the seventh century C.E., fundamental changes had taken place in the form of Hindu worship. Personal prayer, often addressed to representations of the gods in statues and pictures, displaced sacrifice. Hindus built temples of great beauty. The caves at Ellora in western India were fashioned into temples in the eighth century, reflecting the early importance of caves in Hindu worship. Within the cave-temples, sculpture and painting demonstrate the artistic development in religious worship.

SOURCE

The *Bhagavad-Gita* from the *Mahabharata*

Lord Krishna counsels Arjuna to do his duty in leading the fighting of a civil war, even though the warrior has no desire to shed the blood of his relatives. Krishna continues with additional advice—on the importance of proper action for its own sake regardless of praise or condemnation, on reincarnation, and on Lord Krishna's grace upon those who seek him—much of which has been accepted by many Hindus then and now as key principles of life.

Krishna advises Arjuna to act. He notes three kinds of yoga, or discipline, which bring people to spiritual liberation: the yoga of knowledge; the yoga of devotion; and the yoga of action. (The yoga of physical discipline and meditation, known widely today in the West, is yet another form.) In this case, Krishna tells Arjuna, the yoga of action is required:

Do your allotted work, for action is superior to nonaction. Even the normal functioning of your body cannot be accomplished through actionlessness. (III:8)

The key, however, is performing the action because it is right, without concern for its results or rewards.

Action alone is your concern, never at all its fruits. Let not the fruits of action be your motive, nor let yourself be attached to inaction … Seek refuge in the right mental attitude. Wretched are those who are motivated by the fruits of action. (II:49)

Nonattachment is the ideal:

He who feels no attachment toward anything; who, having encountered the various good or evil things, neither rejoices nor loathes—his wisdom is steadfast. (II:59)

… He who behaves alike to foe and friend; who likewise is even-poised in honor or dishonor; who is even-tempered in cold and heat, happiness and sorrow; who is free from attachment; who regards praise and censure with equanimity; who is silent, content with anything whatever; who has no fixed abode, who is steadfast in mind, who is full of devotion—that man is dear to me. (XII:18–19)

In reply to Arjuna's specific anxiety about killing his cousins, Krishna reminds him of the doctrine of reincarnation:

As a man discards worn-out clothes to put on new and different ones, so the disembodied self discards its worn-out bodies to take on other new ones.

… Death is certain for anyone born, and birth is certain for the dead; since the cycle is inevitable, you have no cause to grieve! (II:22, 27)

Krishna also assures Arjuna of his abiding concern for him, and of the god's power to help him: "If I am in your thought, by my grace you will transcend all dangers" (XVIII:58). Arjuna does fight, and wins, and in the end all the warriors who die are reborn.

CHAPTER NINE: HINDUISM AND BUDDHISM 1500 B.C.E.–1200 C.E.

What is unique
in the history of
Hinduism?

9.1

9.2

9.3

Kandariya Mahadeo Temple at Khajuraho, Chandela, c. 1025–50 C.E. The 20 surviving temples
at Khajuraho, although ravaged by time, are still among the greatest examples of medieval Hindu
architecture and sculpture in north India. Beneath the soaring towers, layered bands of sculptures writhe
in a pulsating tableau of human and divine activity. The depictions of athletic lovemaking, which so
scandalized nineteenth-century European travelers, can be linked to *tantric* sects of Hinduism, then
prevalent in the Chandela region.

The bas-reliefs and artwork in the temples at Kanchi and Mahabalipuram in the
south, also built in the eighth century, continue to dazzle viewers today. Magnificent
temples flourished everywhere in India, but especially in the south of the subcontinent. Sexual passion and the union of male and female entered into forms of worship,
symbolically representing passion for, and union with, god, as the temple sculptures
at Khajuraho in north India about 1000 C.E. illustrate.

9.1
9.2
9.3

What is unique
in the history of
Hinduism?

Religion and Rule

Wealthy landowners and rulers, who sought validation of their power and rule through the prestige of *brahmin* priests, often patronized temples. As in many religions, rulers supported priests, while priests affirmed the authority of the rulers. This was especially true in the south. At least as early as the eighth century, new rulers who seized lands occupied by indigenous tribal peoples often imported *brahmin* priests to overawe the *adivasis* with their learning, piety, and rituals, and to persuade them of the proper authority of the king. To pacify the *adivasis*, their gods might be incorporated into the array of gods worshiped in the temple by the priests, just as the *adivasis* would begin to worship the major gods of Hinduism. Anthropologists describe this process as an interplay between the "great" national tradition and the "little" local tradition. As new lands were opened, and *adivasis* were persuaded to accept the new ruling coalition, the temples grew larger and more wealthy.

In exchange for their support, kings rewarded priests with land grants, court subsidies, and temple bequests. *Brahmin* priests and Tamil rulers in southern India prospered together as temples took on important economic functions in banking and money-lending for the villages in their region. Hindu colleges, rest-houses for pilgrims, centers of administration, and even cities grew up around some of these temples.

Bronze sculpture of Vishnu, early Chola period, first half of tenth century C.E. Vishnu is beloved as the tender, merciful deity—the Preserver—and, as the second member of the Hindu trinity, he complements Brahma the Creator and Shiva the Destroyer. He is said to come to earth periodically as an *avatar*, an incarnation in various forms, to help humankind in times of crisis. (Government Museum and National Art Gallery, Madras)

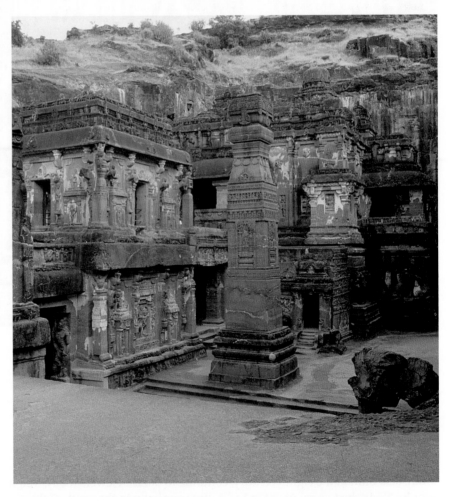

Kailasanatha Temple at Ellora, Rashtrakuta, *c.* 757–90 C.E. Carved into an escarpment of volcanic stone, the 33 shrines of Ellora have for centuries been a pilgrimage center for Hindus, Buddhists, and Jains. The monolithic stone shaft in the foreground, 60 feet high, would have originally supported a trident symbol of Shiva, to whom this temple is dedicated.

HOW DO WE KNOW?

Hinduism in Southeast Asia

Evidence for the influence of Hinduism in Southeast Asia comes from a variety of sources. Even today, the historical stamp of Hinduism endures in Southeast Asia in the names of cities, including Ayuthia in Thailand, derived from Ayodhya in northern India; in the influence of Sanskrit on several Southeast Asian languages; in the popularity of the *Ramayana* and other Hindu literature in the folklore and theater of the region. Moreover, Hindu temples still stand, most spectacularly the Angkor Wat temple complex in Cambodia (see the chapter "Indian Empires,").

Evidence of Hindu influence in Southeast Asia appears also in early reports of Chinese visitors, archaeological remains, and epigraphy (inscriptions on metal and rock). These records are, nevertheless, sparse. *Brahmin* priests appear in the Southeast Asian records only after 800 C.E. It is, therefore, difficult to answer the question "What brought Indian power and prestige into Southeast Asia from about the third century to about the fourteenth century?"

Three theories explaining the appearance of Indian influence in Southeast Asia have been suggested. One argued that Indians initiated contact and attempted to introduce their religion and culture into Southeast Asia. This theory, which stressed the use of military might, is no longer accepted. As noted in the chapter "Indian Empires," there is very little record of Indian military action in the area, and none suggesting a desire for conquest. A second theory—that Indian traders brought their culture with them—has wider acceptance, but it also encounters serious opposition. Trade connections between India and Southeast Asia were numerous, long-standing, and intense. Some cultural and religious influence must have accompanied them, but these contacts were by sea, while much of the Hindu influence was found inland.

A third theory argued that local rulers invited *brahmin* priests to come from India to southeast Asia to build temples, to promote agricultural development on land specially granted to them, to invoke the Hindu gods to validate their authority, and to convince the local population of this divine validation. In the words of one historian, these priests were to serve as "development planners." They brought with them from India principles of government, religious law, administration, art, and architecture. In promoting these religious/political practices through the priests, Southeast Asian rulers were emulating the policies of the Pallava and Chola kings of southern India. But Hinduism did not survive in Southeast Asia. It was superseded by Buddhism and, later, by Islam.

Local kings and Southeast Asian rulers also invited Buddhist monks as well as Hindu priests to Southeast Asia to help to establish and consolidate their power, and they found the Buddhist monks to be as useful as the Hindu *brahmins*, for they served similar political and administrative functions, but in the name of Buddhism. For example, the ruler of the Srivijaya Empire in the East Indies welcomed 1,000 Buddhist monks to his kingdom in the late seventh century C.E. Jayavarman VII, the Buddhist ruler of the Khmer kingdom at the end of the twelfth century, added Buddhist images to the great temple of Angkor Wat, which had been built earlier in the century to honor the Hindu god Vishnu.

By about the fourteenth century, Hinduism had died out in Southeast Asia, while Buddhism continued to thrive. In fact, Buddhism became an enormously successful proselytizing religion throughout Asia. In India, on the other hand, Buddhism withered away, while Hinduism flourished.

- Of the theories explaining the spread of Hinduism in Southeast Asia, why does the theory of the priest as "development planner" seem the most convincing?
- What is the evidence for the coexistence of Hinduism and Buddhism, for a time, in Southeast Asia?
- What was the functional relationship between priests and rulers in Southeast Asia?

Hinduism in Southeast Asia

Hinduism did not generally attract, nor did it seek, converts outside India, but Southeast Asia was an exception. Here, the initiative for conversion grew out of politics, as it had in southern India. The powers of the Hindu temple and the *brahmin* priesthood were imported to validate royal authority in Southeast Asia from as early as the third century C.E. to as late as the fourteenth century.

Trade contacts between India and Southeast Asia date back to at least 150 B.C.E. Indian sailors carried cargoes to and from Burma (Myanmar), the Straits of Malacca, the Kingdom of Funan in modern Cambodia and Vietnam, and Java in modern Indonesia. By the third century C.E., Funan had accepted many elements of Indian culture, religion, and political practice. Chinese envoys reported a prosperous state with walled cities, palaces, and houses. Sanskrit was in use, as was some Indian technology for irrigation and farming. By the fifth century it appears that Sanskrit had spread, Indian calendars marked the dates, and Indian gods, including Shiva and Vishnu, were worshiped, as were representations of the Buddha (see below). Hindu temples began to appear with *brahmin* priests to staff them.

What is unique in the history of Hinduism?

9.1

9.2

9.3

Buddhism

9.2   How did Buddhism emerge and spread?

Buddhism was born in India, within the culture of Hinduism, and then charted its own path. Like Hinduism, it questioned the reality of the earthly world and speculated on the existence of other worlds. Unlike Hinduism, however, Buddhism had a founder, a set of originating scriptures, and an order of monks. In opposition to Hinduism, it renounced hereditary caste organization and the supremacy of the *brahmin* priests. Buddhism spread to Southeast Asia, gaining acceptance as the principal religion of Myanmar, Thailand, Cambodia, Laos, and Vietnam until today. It won multitudes of adherents throughout the rest of Asia as well, in Sri Lanka, Tibet, China, Korea, and Japan. Yet in India itself, Buddhism lost out in competition with Hinduism and its priesthood, virtually vanishing from the subcontinent by about the twelfth century C.E.

The Origins of Buddhism

All we know of the Buddha's life and teaching comes from much later accounts, embellished by his followers. While there is much doubt about almost every aspect of the Buddha's life and teachings, the accounts that exist tell the following story.

The Life of the Buddha. Siddhartha Gautama was born about 563 B.C.E. in the foothills of the Himalaya Mountains of what is now Nepal. His father, a warrior chief of the *kshatriya* caste, received a prophecy that Siddhartha would become either a great emperor or a great religious teacher. Hoping that his son would follow the former vocation, the chief sheltered him as best he could so that he would experience neither pain nor disillusionment.

When he was 29 years old, Siddhartha started to grow curious about what lay beyond the confines of his father's palace. Leaving his wife, Yasadhara, and their son, Rahula, he instructed his charioteer to take him to the city, where he came across a frail, elderly man. Never having encountered old age, Siddhartha was confused. His companion explained that aging was an inevitable and painful part of human experience. As Siddhartha took further excursions outside the palace, he soon came

SOURCE

The "Address to Sigala": Buddhism in Everyday Life

Much of the Buddha's moral and ethical instruction is directed to the monks of the Sangha. In the "Address to Sigala," however, the Buddha speaks to laypeople about their relationships and responsibilities toward one another. The address includes practical advice to husbands and wives, friends, employers, and employees. The lengthy address is translated and summarized here by A.L. Basham.

Husbands should respect their wives, and comply as far as possible with their requests. They should not commit adultery. They should give their wives full charge of the home, and supply them with fine clothes and jewelry as far as their means permit. Wives should be thorough in their duties, gentle and kind to the whole household, chaste, and careful in housekeeping, and should carry out their work with skill and enthusiasm.

A man should be generous to his friends, speak kindly of them, act in their interest in every way possible, treat them as his equals, and keep his word to them. They in turn should watch over his interests and property, take care of him when he is "off his guard" [i.e. intoxicated, infatuated, or otherwise liable to commit rash and careless actions], stand by him and help him in time of trouble, and respect other members of his family.

Employers should treat their servants and workpeople decently. They should not be given tasks beyond their strength. They should receive adequate food and wages, be cared for in time of sickness and infirmity, and be given regular holidays and bonuses in times of prosperity. They should rise early and go to bed late in the service of their master, be content with their just wages, work thoroughly, and maintain their master's reputation. (*Digha Nikaya*, iii:161; cited in Basham, p. 286) to see that pain was an integral part of life, experienced in illness, aging, death, and birth. The search for a remedy for this pervasive sorrow became his quest.

On his fourth and final trip he met a wandering holy man who had shunned the trappings of wealth and material gain. Siddhartha decided to do likewise. Bidding farewell to his family for the last time, he set out on horseback in search of an antidote to sorrow and a means of teaching it to others.

For six years Siddhartha wandered as an ascetic. Nearing starvation, however, he gave up the path of asceticism. Determined to achieve enlightenment, he began to meditate, sitting under a tree at Bodh Gaya near modern Patna, in India. Mara, the spirit of this world, who tempted him to give up his meditation with threats of punishment and promises of rewards, tested his concentration and fortitude. Touching the ground with his hand in a gesture, or *mudra*, repeated often in sculptures of the Buddha, Siddhartha revealed these temptations to be illusions. On the forty-ninth day of meditation he reached enlightenment, becoming the Buddha, "He Who Has Awakened." He had found an antidote to pain and suffering. He proceeded to the Deer Park at Sarnath, near Banaras, where he delivered his first sermon, beginning by setting forth the Four Noble Truths of suffering. The source of suffering, he taught, was personal desire and passion:

> This is the [first] Noble Truth of Sorrow. Birth is sorrow, age is sorrow, disease is sorrow, death is sorrow, contact with the unpleasant is sorrow, separation from the pleasant is sorrow, every wish unfulfilled is sorrow—in short all the five components of individuality are sorrow. This is the [second] Noble Truth of the Arising of Sorrow. [It arises from] thirst, which leads to rebirth, which brings delight and passion, and seeks pleasure now here, now there—the thirst for sensual pleasure, the thirst for continued life, the thirst for power. (Basham, p. 269)

Its antidote followed from this analysis:

> This is the [third] Noble Truth of the Stopping of Sorrow. It is the complete stopping of that thirst, so that no passion remains, leaving it, being emancipated from it, being released from it, giving no place to it. And this is the [fourth] Noble Truth of the Way which Leads to the Stopping of Sorrow. It is the Noble Eightfold Path—Right Views, Right Resolve, Right Speech, Right Conduct, Right Livelihood, Right Effort, Right Recollection and Right Meditation. (p. 269)

A new consciousness could be achieved by a combination of disciplining the mind and observing ethical precepts in human relationships. In the face of continuing rebirths into the pain of life, the Buddha taught that right living could bring release from the cycle of mortality and pain, and entry into *nirvana*, a kind of blissful nothingness. On the metaphysical plane, the Buddha taught that everything in the universe is transient; there is no "being." There exists neither an immortal soul nor a god, neither *atman* nor *Brahman*. The Buddha's teachings about the illusion of life and about rebirth and release were consistent with Hindu concepts of *maya*, *samsara*, and *moksha*, but the Buddha's denial of god put him on the fringes of Hindu thought. His rejection of caste as an organizing hierarchy and of the Hindu priests as connoisseurs of religious truth won him powerful allies—and powerful opponents.

Although much of the Hindu priesthood opposed the Buddha's teachings, the kings of Magadha and Koshala, whose territories included most of the lower Gangetic plain, befriended and supported him and the small band of followers gathered around him. The Buddha taught peacefully and calmly until about 483 B.C.E., when, at the age of 80, he died, surrounded by a cadre of dedicated monks and believers, the original Buddhist *Sangha* (order of monks). See the illustrations from Dunhuang China and from Japan later in this chapter. The threefold motto of all devout Buddhists became "I seek refuge in the Buddha; I seek refuge in the Doctrine; I seek refuge in the *Sangha*."

Mudras. Indian classical sculpture and dance use gestures of the hand and fingers—*mudras*—to convey moods and meanings. The Buddha's *mudras* typically show him in meditation with the right hand straight down pointing towards the earth (A); in protection of others, and counseling a lack of fear with the right hand at shoulder height, facing outward (B); in knowing, with the tips of the thumb and the index together, forming a circle, and the hand held with the palm inward toward the heart (C). Keep these *mudras* in mind as you observe classical Indian forms in this textbook.

9.1

9.2

How did Buddhism emerge and spread?

9.3

KEY TERM

mudra A hand gesture with specific meaning or significance in Indian classical sculpture and dance. One specific *mudra*, for example, indicates teaching, another fearlessness, another revelation, etc. (for example, see illustration of statue of Buddha, below).

The *Sangha*. The *Sangha* was open to all men regardless of caste, and thus drew the antagonism of *brahmins*, although some did join. For a time, women were permitted to form their own convents, but only under special restrictions. Today, Buddhist nuns exist only in Tibet.

The monks wore saffron robes and shaved their heads. They practiced celibacy and renounced alcohol, but did not have to take a vow of obedience to the order and were intellectually and spiritually free. Decisions were made through group discussion, perpetuating the pattern of the early republics of the north Indian hills. Monks studied, disciplined their spirits, meditated, and did the physical work of their monasteries. At first they wandered, begging for their living, except during the rainy months of the monsoon. But as monasteries became richer, through donations of money and land, the monks tended to settle down. They also tended to give up begging, which diminished their contact with the common people.

👁 Watch the **Video**: **Siddhartha Gautama** on **MyHistoryLab**

🔍 View the **Closer Look**: **The Buddha's Footprints** on **MyHistoryLab**

The Emergence of Mahayana Buddhism

A series of general councils began to codify the principles, doctrines, and texts of the emerging community. The first council, convened shortly after the Buddha's death, began the continuing process of collecting his teachings. The second, about a century later, began to dispute the essential meaning of Buddhism. The third, convened at Pataliputra, Asoka's capital, revealed more of the differences that would soon lead to a split over the question of whether the Buddha was a human or a god.

By this time an array of Buddhist *caityas*, or shrines, was growing. In addition to monasteries, great stupas, or monuments filled with Buddhist relics, were built at Barhut, Sanchi, and Amaravati (see map, below). Between 200 B.C.E. and 200 C.E. there were more Buddhist than Hindu shrines in India. Theological discussion flourished, with a heavy emphasis on *metta*, or benevolence; nonviolence; *dharma*, or proper behavior (although not related to caste, since Buddhism rejected hereditary caste); and tolerance for all religions.

The fourth general council, convened in the first century C.E. in Kashmir, codified the key doctrines of Buddhism as they had developed from earliest times. These were the principles of the Theravada ("Doctrine of the Elders") branch of Buddhism, which we have been examining and which is today the prevailing form in Sri Lanka and Southeast Asia, except for Vietnam.

By now, however, a newer school of Mahayana Buddhism had been growing for perhaps two centuries and had become a serious challenge to Theravada. *Mahayana* means "the Greater Vehicle," and its advocates claimed that their practices could carry more Buddhists to **nirvana** because they had **bodhisattvas** to help. A *bodhisattva* was a "being of wisdom" on the verge of achieving *nirvana* but so concerned about the welfare of fellow humans that he postponed his entrance into *nirvana* to remain on earth, or to be reborn, in order to help others.

In addition, Mahayana Buddhism taught that religious merit, achieved through performing good deeds, could be transferred from one person to another. It embellished the concept of *nirvana* with the vision of a Mahayana heaven, presided over by Amitabha Buddha, a Buddha who had lived on earth and had now become a kind of father in heaven. Subsequently, Mahayanists developed the concept of numerous heavens with numerous forms of the Buddha presiding over them. They also developed the concept of the Maitreya Buddha, a suffering servant who will come to redeem humanity.

Some theologians note the similarity of the concept of this Maitreya Buddha to the Christian Messiah, and some suggest that the Buddhists may have borrowed it. They also suggest that Christians may have borrowed the narratives of the virgin birth of

KEY TERMS

nirvana In Theravada Buddhism, the blissful nothingness into which a soul that had lived properly entered after death, and from which there would be no further rebirth. (Compare *nirvana* among Jains, below.) In Mahayana Buddhism, *nirvana* became an abode of more active bliss, a kind of heaven, filled with heavenly activities.

bodhisattva A "being of wisdom" worthy of entering *nirvana*, but who chooses to stay on earth, or be reborn, in order to help others. In Mahayana Buddhism, the Buddha himself is considered also to be one of the *bodhisattvas*.

Great Stupa, Sanchi, third century B.C.E. to first century C.E. With its four gloriously carved gates and majestic central hemisphere, the Great Stupa of Sanchi is the most remarkable surviving example of the 84,000 such Buddhist shrines reputedly erected by the emperor Asoka during the Mauryan Empire. This "world mountain," oriented to the four corners of the universe, contained a holy relic, the object of pilgrims' devotion, and is topped by a three-tiered umbrella representing the Three Jewels of Buddhism: the Buddha, the Law, and the community of monks.

9.1

9.2

How did
Buddhism
emerge and
spread?

9.3

the Buddha and of his temptation in his search for enlightenment, and applied them to Jesus. There are significant similarities in the stories of these two men/gods and their biographies. Further, Mahayanists spoke of three aspects of the Buddha: Amitabha, the Buddha in heaven; Gautama, the historical Buddha on earth; and the most revered of all the *bodhisattvas*, the freely moving Avalokiteshvara. Theologians ask: To what degree do these three Buddhist forms correspond to the Father, Son, and Holy Spirit of Christianity as it was developing at the same time? How much borrowing took place between India and the Mediterranean coast, and in which direction?

Within India, Mahayana Buddhism began to challenge Hinduism more boldly than Theravada had. Wishing to compete for upper-caste and upper-class audiences, Mahayanists began to record their theology in Sanskrit, the language of the elite, rather than the more colloquial Pali language, which Theravada had preferred. Mahayana theologians, most notably Nagarjuna (*fl. c.* 50–150 C.E.), elaborated Buddhist philosophy and debated directly with *brahmin* priests. Buddhist monasteries established major educational programs, especially at Nalanda in Bihar, where the Buddha had spent much of his life, and at Taxila, on the international trade routes in the northern Punjab.

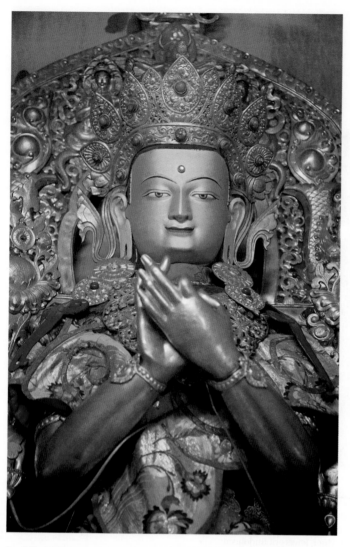

Buddha in Prayer Hall of Drepung Monastery 2, near Lhasa, Tibet. This statue reflects the importance of Indian traditions, but the facial features are more central Asian and even Chinese, while the elaborate headdress, frame, and gilt surfaces suggest an appreciation of wealth that was not part of earlier, Theravada Buddhism. Drepung Monastery, established in 1416, was closely associated with the Dalai Lama and his branch of Buddhism. It became the largest and one of the richest in Tibet.

The Decline of Buddhism in India

From its beginnings in India, Buddhism's strongest appeal had been to *kshatriya* rulers and *vaishya* businessmen, who felt that *brahmin* priests did not respect them. The Buddha himself came from a *kshatriya* family, and his early friendship with the *kshatriya* kings of Magadha and Koshala had ensured their support for his movement. Later kings and merchants also donated huge sums of money to support Buddhist monks, temples, and monasteries. Many people of the lower castes, who felt the weight and the arrogance of all the other castes pressing down on them, also joined the newly forming religion. They were especially attracted by the use of the vernacular Pali and Magadhi languages in place of Sanskrit, and the absence of the financial demands of the *brahmins*.

However, Buddhism began to lose strength in India around the time of the decline of the Gupta Empire (*c.* 320–550 C.E.). Regional rulers began to choose Hinduism over Buddhism, and alliances with priests rather than with monks. At the popular level, lower castes—who had found the anticaste philosophy of Buddhism attractive—apparently also began to shift their allegiance back toward more orthodox Hinduism as an anchor in a time of political change. Also, without imperial assistance, merchants' incomes may have decreased within India, reducing their contributions to Buddhist temples. By the fifth century C.E., the Chinese Buddhist pilgrim Faxian noted weaknesses in Indian Buddhism.

Mahayana Buddhism, with its many godlike Buddhas and *bodhisattvas* inhabiting a multitude of heavens, seemed so close to Hinduism that many Buddhists must have seen little purpose in maintaining a distinction. Finally, Buddhists throughout their history in India had relied on Hindu *brahmin* priests to officiate at their life-cycle ceremonies of birth, marriage, and death, so Hindu priests could argue that they always had a significant claim on Buddhist allegiance.

Readers who are accustomed to the monotheistic pattern of religions claiming the undivided loyalty of

9.1
9.2
9.3

How did
Buddhism
emerge and
spread?

SACRED WRITINGS OF BUDDHISM	
Tripitaka	"The Three Baskets": *Vinaya*, on the proper conduct of Buddhist monks and nuns; *Sutta*, discourses attributed to the Buddha; and *Abhidhamma*, supplementary doctrines. Written in Pali.
The *Mahayanas*	(*Mahayana* is Sanskrit for "Greater Vehicle.") The body of writings associated with the school of Buddhism dominant in Tibet, Mongolia, China, Korea, and Japan. Includes the famous allegory the Lotus Sutra, the Buddhist "Parable of the Prodigal Son."
Milindapanha	Dialogue between the Greek king Milinda and the Buddhist monk Nagasena on the philosophy of Buddhism.
Buddha's Four Noble Truths	Suffering is always present in life; desire is the cause of suffering; freedom from suffering can be achieved by overcoming desires; the Eightfold Path provides the means to accomplish this.

Buddhist Asia. Radiating from the site of Buddha's enlightenment at Bodh Gaya in northeast India, Buddhism spread through Asia in three directions following established trade routes: north across the Hindu Kush and along the silk route to Xinjiang, China, and Korea, eventually reaching Japan; south to Sri Lanka; and east through Burma (then Myanmar) to the kingdoms and islands of Southeast Asia.

9.1

9.2

How did Buddhism emerge and spread?

9.3

9.1

9.2

9.3

How did
Buddhism
emerge and
spread?

their followers will recognize here a very different pattern. Many religions, especially polytheistic religions, expect that individuals will incorporate diverse elements of different religions into their personal philosophy and ritual. We will see more examples of this personal **syncretism** and loyalty to multiple religions as we examine Buddhism's relationship with Confucianism in China and with both Confucianism and Shinto in Japan.

As Hinduism evolved, it became more attractive to Buddhists. Theologians such as Shankaracharya (788–820 C.E.) and Ramanuja (c. 1017–1137 C.E.) advanced philosophies based on the Vedic literature known to the common people, and built many temples and schools to spread their thought. At the same time, Hinduism, following its tradition of syncretism, incorporated the Buddha himself into its own polytheistic universe as an incarnation of Vishnu. A devotee could revere the Buddha within the overarching framework of Hinduism. Finally, neither Buddhism nor Hinduism gave much scope to women within their official institutions of temples, schools, and monasteries. For Hinduism, however, the home was much more central than the public institution, and here women did have a central role in worship and ritual. Buddhism was much more centered on its monasteries and monks. The comparative lack of a role for women, and the comparative lack of interest in domestic life generally, may have impeded its spread.

Buddhism in India declined still further when Muslim traders gained control of the silk routes through central Asia. The final blow came with the arrival of Muslims during the first two centuries of their major invasions of India, between 1000 and 1200 C.E. Muslims saw Buddhism as a competitive, proselytizing religion, unlike Hinduism, and did not wish to coexist with it. Because Buddhism was, by this time, relatively weak and relatively centralized within its monasteries and schools, Muslims were able to destroy the remnants of the religion by attacking these institutions. Buddhist monks were killed or forced to flee from India to centers in Southeast Asia, Nepal, and Tibet. Hinduism survived the challenge because it was much more broadly based as the religion of home and community and far more deeply rooted in Indian culture.

In the 1950s, almost 1,000 years after Buddhism's demise in India, about five million "outcastes" revived Buddhism in India in protest at the inequalities of the caste system, and declared their allegiance to the old/new religion. These "neo-Buddhists" are almost the only Buddhists to be found in India today.

Jainism

Jainism is another religion of India, with many similarities to early Buddhism. At about the time of the Buddha, the teacher Mahavir (b. 540 B.C.E.), the twenty-fourth in a long lineage of Jain religious leaders, guided the religion into its modern form. The religion takes its name from Mahavir's designation *jina*, or conqueror. Like Theravada Buddhists, Jains reject the caste system and the supremacy of *brahmin* priests, postulating instead that there is no god, but that humans do have souls that they can purify by careful attention to their actions, and especially by practicing nonviolence. If they follow the eternal law of ethical treatment of others and devotion to the rather austere rituals of the faith, Jains believe they will reach *nirvana*, which is an end to the cycle of rebirth rather than a rewarding afterlife.

Jainism's emphasis on nonviolence is so powerful that Jains typically do not become farmers lest they kill living creatures in the soil. In a country that is overwhelmingly agricultural, Jains are usually urban and often businessmen. Jainism did not spread outside India, and its four million adherents today live almost entirely in India. Because Jains, like earlier Buddhists, employ *brahmin* priests to officiate at their life-cycle events, and because they intermarry freely with several Hindu *vaishya* (business) subcastes, some consider them a branch of Hinduism, although they do not usually regard themselves as Hindus. One of the regions of Jain strength in India

KEY TERM

syncretism refers to the merging of different traditions from different origins into a single unified practice.

9.1

How did
Buddhism
emerge and
spread?

9.2

9.3

Jain nuns on their way to worship. Although most Jains are laypersons, important monasteries house priests and nuns. These nuns wear mouth-cloths to prevent injury to insects that might otherwise be inhaled.

is western Gujarat, the region where Mahatma Gandhi grew up (see the chapter "China and India"). The Mahatma attributed his adherence to nonviolence in large part to the influence of Jainism.

Buddhism in China

Because of its decentralization and vast geographical diffusion, Buddhism has taken on different forms from place to place, time to time, and state to state. It arrived in new locations in foreign form, but over time each regional culture put its own stamp on Buddhism. We must, therefore, examine the faith and practice of Buddhism in each region separately, by studying the works of the monks, missionaries, poets, architects, and sculptors who spread the faith.

Arrival in China: The Silk Route. The long, thin line of communication over which pilgrims and missionaries carried the message of the Buddha from India to China and beyond was the silk route, the same route that carried luxury products between China and India and then on to the west. The first Buddhist missionaries are mentioned in Chinese records about 65 C.E. They established their first monastery at Luoyang. Over the centuries, many more were built within China and along the silk route.

Chinese pilgrims traveled the silk route in the opposite direction to visit and study in the land of the Buddha, and some, most notably Faxian, who visited in 399–414 C.E., left lasting records of their observations. Thousands came to study at Taxila and Nalanda.

Several of the pilgrims who traveled these routes, especially Faxian, in the early years of the fifth century C.E., and Xuanzang, in the early years of the seventh, brought back both Buddhist texts and important firsthand information from India and the lands along the silk routes. Turning north from India through Kashgar, and then east to Khotan, Turfan, Dunhuang, and on to Chang'an in the heart of China, Buddhist pilgrims provisioned these trade routes with rest-houses, temples, and monasteries, some of them built into caves.

Relations with Daoism and Confucianism. Although Buddhism first appeared in China in the first century C.E., at the height of the Han dynasty, it took firmer root after the dynasty eventually fell. Confucianism, China's dominant philosophy, was

SOURCE

The Transience of Life: A Woman's Perspective from the Tang Dynasty

This anonymous poem of the Tang dynasty, discovered in the Dunhuang cave and translated by Patricia Ebrey and Lily Hwa, illuminates the Buddhist sense of the transience of life as experienced by a woman of high status.

A Woman's Hundred Years

At ten, like a flowering branch in the rain,
She is slender, delicate, and full of grace.
Her parents are themselves as young as the rising moon
And do not allow her past the red curtain without a reason.

At twenty, receiving the hairpin, she is a spring bud.
Her parents arrange her betrothal; the matter's well done.
A fragrant carriage comes at evening to carry her to her lord.
Like Xioshi and his wife, at dawn they depart with the clouds.

At thirty, perfect as a pearl, full of the beauty of youth,
At her window, by the gauze curtain, she makes up in front of the mirror.
With her singing companions, in the waterlily season,
She rows a boat and plucks the blue flowers.

At forty, she is mistress of a prosperous house and makes plans.
Three sons and five daughters give her some trouble.
With her lute not far away, she toils always at her loom.
Her only fear that the sun will set too soon.

At fifty, afraid of her husband's dislike,
She strains to please him with every charm.
Trying to remember the many tricks she had learned since the age of sixteen.
No longer is she afraid of mothers- and sisters-in-law.

At sixty, face wrinkled and hair like silk thread,
She walks unsteadily and speaks little.
Distressed that her sons can find no brides,
Grieved that her daughters have departed for their husbands' homes.

At seventy, frail and thin, but not knowing what to do about it,
She is no longer able to learn the Buddhist Law even if she tries.
In the morning a light breeze
Makes her joints crack like clanging gongs.

At eighty, eyes blinded and ears half-deaf,
When she goes out she cannot tell north from east.
Dreaming always of departed loves,
Who persuade her to chase the dying breeze.

At ninety, the glow fades like spent lightning.
Human affairs are no longer her concern.
Lying on a pillow, solitary on her high bed,
She resembles the dying leaves that fall in autumn.

At a hundred, like a cliff crumbling in the wind,
For her body it is the moment to become dust.
Children and grandchildren will perform sacrifices to her spirit.
And clear moonlight will forever illumine her patch of earth.

(Ebrey, p. 104)

9.1
9.2
9.3
How did Buddhism emerge and spread?

intimately tied to the fate of the imperial government, and only after this central political structure collapsed could Mahayana Buddhism find a place. The mystical character of Mahayana Buddhism especially attracted Daoists. To some degree, the two beliefs competed, but some of the competition eventually led to each validating the other. For example, some Daoists claimed that the Buddha was actually Laozi as he appeared in his travels in India. Many Buddhists, in turn, accorded to Laozi and Confucius the status of *bodhisattva*. In this way, competition sometimes turned into mutual recognition.

As a foreign religion, Buddhism also had special appeal for some of the rulers of northern China in the third through the sixth centuries C.E., since they, too, were outsiders. The Toba rulers of the Northern Wei dynasty (386–534 C.E.) occasionally persecuted Buddhists as a threat to the state, but mostly they felt some kinship to this religion of outsiders. They patronized Buddhist shrines and monks, but they also regulated them.

In the south, with its abundance of émigrés from the northern court, Confucianism was crippled by the severance of its connection with the government. In contrast, newly arriving Buddhists won followers by proposing an organized, aesthetic philosophy for coping with the hazards of life in semi-exile. In southern China, Buddhist arts of poetry, painting, and calligraphy flourished, and monasteries in the south offered refuge to the men who might have been part of the governing Confucian aristocracy in other times. In the southern state of Liang, the emperor Wu (r. 502–49

9.1

9.2

How did
Buddhism
emerge and
spread?

9.3

C.E.) declared Buddhism the official state religion, built temples, sponsored Buddhist assemblies, and wrote Buddhist commentaries.

Doctrinally, Buddhism had important differences from Confucianism, but the two world perspectives seem to have reached some mutual accommodation. For example, Confucianism encouraged family cohesion and the veneration of ancestors, while Buddhist monks followed lives of celibacy; but Buddhist laypeople also valued family, and the monks themselves venerated the Buddha and *bodhisattvas* as their spiritual ancestors. Nevertheless, tension between the two belief systems and organizations never completely dissipated. Confucians thought in terms of government order and control, while Buddhists tended toward decentralized congregational worship within a loose doctrinal framework. In many areas of China, as Buddhist monasteries became wealthy from the donations of local magnates and landlords, Confucian governments moved to regulate their power.

Buddhism's network of pilgrims and monks crisscrossed China, helping to integrate the nation. Through almost four centuries of division in China, from the fall of the Han (220 C.E.) to the rise of the Sui (581), Buddhism continued to grow in both north and south. Indeed, the founder of the Sui dynasty, a Buddhist himself, also patronized Confucianism and Daoism, seeing all these belief systems as vital to earning legitimacy for his government. The Tang dynasty extended this veneration.

Buddhism under the Tang Dynasty. For most of the Tang dynasty (618–907), the intellectual, spiritual, and artistic life of Buddhism flourished. Eight major sects developed, each with a different interpretation of the original message of the Buddha, the importance of rules and regulations, rituals, meditation, scholarship, disciplinary exercises, and devotion. Among the larger and more significant schools was the Pure Land Sect. Its devotees believed that anyone could reach the Pure Land of paradise after death through faith in the Buddha Amitabha, the presiding authority in that realm. Members of the sect demonstrated their faith by continuously repeating the name Amitabha. Devotees also meditated on Guanyin, the *bodhisattva* of mercy (see How Do We Know box, below).

Another sect, Chan Buddhism, taught the importance of meditation. Some followers believed in lengthy disciplines of meditation, which would gradually lead to enlightenment; others in spontaneous flashes of insight, which would lead to the same goal. Both Pure Land and Chan were adopted in Japan as well, where the meditative exercises of Chan became known as Zen.

Buddhists are credited with inventing woodblock printing as a means of reproducing their sacred texts. The earliest woodblock print known is an illustrated copy of the *Diamond Sutra* from 868 C.E., discovered in the Dunhuang Caves. Most of the Buddhist art and architecture of Tang China was destroyed in later persecution, confiscation, and warfare. Its leading representations are now seen in Japan, which, at just about this time, adopted much of Chinese Buddhism as its own and then modified it (see below).

The only woman ever to rule China in her own name, "Emperor" Wu (r. 690–705 C.E.) was a great patron of Buddhism. First ruling indirectly through Emperor Gaozong (d. 683), whose concubine she was, and then, after his death, through two of their sons, in 690 she proclaimed herself the emperor of a new dynasty, which she named the Zhou (not to be confused with the earlier Zhou dynasty discussed early in the chapter entitled "A Polycentric World"). She patronized Buddhism as a means of legitimizing her rule, declaring herself a reincarnation of Maitreya, the Buddha of future salvation. The empress built temples in every province of China. Before she was deposed in 705, she had overseen the warfare that expanded the Tang to its greatest geographical extent, including Xinjiang and Tibet.

Buddhism's Decline in China. Political and military defeats started Buddhism on its decline during the late Tang period in China. In far-off central Asia, Muslim forces

Diamond Sutra, 868 C.E. This superb frontispiece, showing the Buddha preaching to an elderly disciple, comes from the *Diamond Sutra*, a Sanskrit tale transmitted along the silk routes and translated into Chinese in the fifth century. Produced by woodblock to a high standard of technical and artistic achievement, the 17-foot-long sutra is the world's earliest printed book. (British Library, London)

9.1

9.2

9.3

How did Buddhism emerge and spread?

defeated Chinese forces in the decisive Battle of the Talas River in 751. Four years later, the revolt of General An Lushan in northeast China occupied the imperial armies for eight years. China's power in central Asia was broken, and with it the power of Buddhism in these regions. Islam would become the world religion of most of central Asia. Only in Tibet did Buddhism remain powerful, supported by state power. It was carried there from eastern India about the eighth century in a newly emerging form called *vajrayana* Buddhism, "the vehicle of the thunderbolt," or tantric Buddhism, for its *tantras*, or scriptures advocating magic rituals. Tantric Buddhism venerated not only buddhas, *bodhisattvas*, and other divinities, but also their wives or feminine counterparts, new additions to the growing array of sacred personalities. Tantric rituals were secret, esoteric, sometimes sexual, and only for the initiated.

Almost a century later, the Tang emperor Wuzong (r. 840–46) attacked Buddhism and its monasteries. Wuzong was a Daoist, personally opposed to Buddhism. He feared the power of the Buddhist establishment, and the wealth and influence of its various monasteries, especially when the Tang had been weakened by external defeats and internal revolts. Wuzong confiscated the lands and wealth of the Buddhist monasteries. He forced monks and nuns to leave the monasteries, claiming that he personally had defrocked 260,500 monks and nuns. He destroyed sacred texts, statues, and shrines, leaving only 49 monasteries and 800 monks in all of China. Later rulers alternated between reversing and reimposing Wuzong's policies. Although

9.1

How did
Buddhism
emerge and
spread?

9.2

9.3

Dying Buddha, Cave 428, Dunhuang, China, early sixth century C.E. The monastery at Dunhuang was one of the most important of those along the silk route, and the paintings in its 460 caves are spectacular. Here, *bodhisattvas* attend the Buddha at his death, appearing rather ascetic, abstract, and enchanted. Compare the scene from Japan, illustrated in How Do We Know box, below.

Buddhism has remained a presence in China, even to today, it has never recovered its numbers, vitality, or influence.

Buddhism in Japan

Shintoism. Long before Buddhism arrived in Japan, the people of Japan followed "The Way of the Kami," later called Shinto. *Kami* were the powers and spirits inherent in nature. Found everywhere, they could be called upon to help in time of human need. Shrines to the *kami* were built throughout the land, always including a mirror in tribute to the sun goddess, a sword, and a jewel.

Accounts of the *kami* appear in the earliest Japanese records, the *Kojiki* (712 C.E.) and *Nihon shoki* (720 C.E.). These semi-mythological records give a basic history of early Japan, but they—and all accounts of Buddhist saints—must be read with some caution, because they blend myth with factual record. According to the *Kojiki* and *Nihon shoki*, the highest of the *kami* were Amaterasu, the sun goddess, and her obstreperous brother Susa-no-o. Amaterasu's grandson Niniqi descended to earth and set out to conquer Japan. He established himself as Japan's first emperor in 660 B.C.E., and all subsequent emperors trace their lineage directly back to this mythological founder.

With the later arrival of Buddhism, the *kami* continued to have a distinguished and venerated position, often as minor buddhas or *bodhisattvas*. Conversely, the buddhas and *bodhisattvas* were accepted as especially powerful and exalted *kami*, capable of helping those in need. The royal family in Japan knew that the emperor Asoka in India had adopted Buddhism, and they emulated his decision.

Buddhism's Arrival in Japan. Buddhism first came to Japan from China in 552 C.E., via the Paekche kingdom of southwest Korea. The *Nihon shoki* tells of the Paekche

KEY TERM

kami In Japanese thought, the powers and spirits inherent in nature.

king sending Buddhist texts and statues and asking for help in a war against another Korean kingdom, the Silla.

From the beginning, Buddhism had political as well as religious implications. Clans close to the Japanese emperor were divided in their reception of the foreign religion. Those who accepted it regarded Buddhism as a force for performing miracles, especially healing the sick, and many Buddhist monks were especially skilled in medicine. A minority of the clans, however, thought the new religion ought to be banned.

Buddhism found acceptance at a political level in Japan a half-century later under Prince Shotoku Taishi (573–621). The prince effectively ruled the country as the regent to the ruler of the Yamato Plain, the western region of Japan. An enthusiastic Buddhist, Shotoku built many temples, including the Horyuji Temple in the capital city of Nara. A scholar of Buddhist theology, he invited Buddhist clergy from Korea, and he dispatched four Japanese missions to Sui China to learn more about Buddhism,

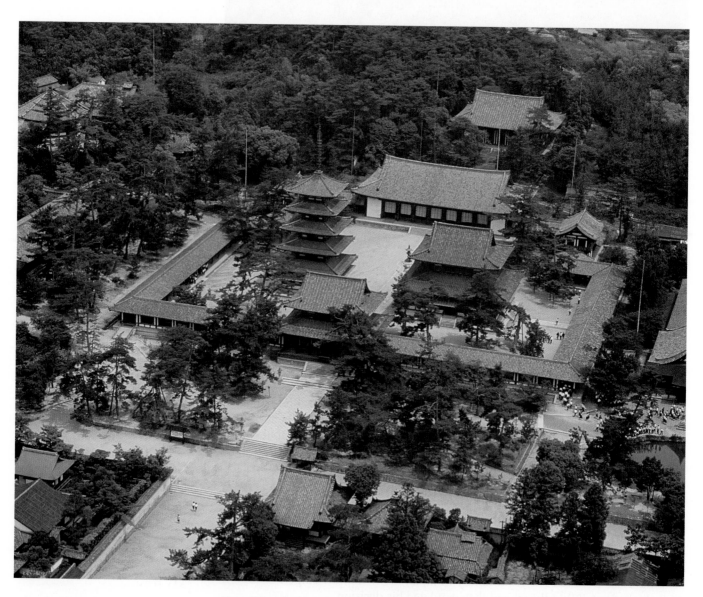

Horyuji Temple, Nara, Japan, 670 c.e. Through the seventh and eighth centuries the Japanese court enthusiastically welcomed Chinese political and artistic forms (see the chapter "China"). This is Japan's earliest surviving example of Buddhist architecture, which was adopted along with Chinese writing, painting, and sculpture. It became a central shrine for all of Japan.

9.1

9.2

9.3

How did
Buddhism
emerge and
spread?

both as a religious system and as a model for centralizing his political rule. At this time China was the premier state of eastern Asia, and Buddhism was seen as one of the principal constituents of its power. In 604, Prince Shotoku introduced a kind of constitution to centralize and strengthen the Japanese government. Among its 17 articles, the first promoted Confucian principles of social organization and the second declared that the Japanese people should "sincerely reverence the three treasures … the Buddha, the Law, and the Monastic orders" (Embree, p. 50).

Buddhism's Role in Unifying Japan. A century later, in 710, the ruling clans of Japan moved their capital to Nara, then called Heijo. Continuing to regard China as the model state of their day, the Japanese rulers copied much of the Chinese structure of authority and administration. They used Chinese ideographs as their written language and adopted Chinese patterns of bureaucracy, taxation, architecture, and land reforms. They modeled their new capital on the city plan of Chang'an, building a smaller version of that Chinese capital at Nara.

Within Nara, Japan's rulers built numerous Buddhist temples, including several of national significance. They encouraged the creation of a system of monasteries and convents throughout the provinces, with the Todaiji monastery, built by the emperor Shomu (r. 715–49), at the apex. That great temple contains one of the world's great repositories of art, holding several thousand treasures from the eighth century, including painting, sculpture, calligraphy, textiles, ceramics, jade, metal- and lacquer-work, masks for drama, and musical instruments.

Buddhism became a pillar in the structure of Japanese national unity and administration. It did not replace Shinto, the indigenous worship of spirits, especially spirits of nature. Rather, it complemented the indigenous system. The emperor performed the official rituals of both Shinto and Buddhist worship.

Buddhism introduced a measure of centralization. Shinto, a less formal system of belief and worship, had spread throughout Japan with no need of a central shrine for its worship of nature. By contrast, the Horyuji Temple near Nara became a central shrine for the nation. In 741 the emperor ordered that a Buddhist temple and pagoda be established in each province. Buddhism and Shinto coexisted in Japan in a pattern that continues today.

As in China, the power and wealth of Buddhist monasteries and temples in Japan, and especially in Nara, alarmed some members of the court. To reduce the power of the Buddhist clergy and to increase the power of his own lineage, Emperor Kammu (r. 781–806) moved the capital again, from Nara to Heian (modern Kyoto) in 794. This move initiated the Heian period in Japanese history and coincided with the decline of the Tang Empire in China. The Japanese government dispatched its last official mission to China in 838. With Japan on the ascendant and China in decline, Japan's Buddhism developed along its own paths, helped by substantial imperial patronage. The emperor himself patronized two young Japanese monks who founded the Tendai and Shingon schools of Buddhism, the two most powerful and enduring Buddhist movements in Japan.

Japanese Buddhism Develops New Forms. The Buddhist priesthood itself became increasingly Japanese, no longer reliant on priests from the Chinese mainland. It also entered more profoundly into politics. The priest Saicho (767–822) studied Tiantai (Tendai in Japanese) Buddhism in China and introduced it into Japan. Based on the Lotus Sutra, Tendai taught that each person could achieve enlightenment through sincere religious devotion. On Mount Hiei, northeast of Kyoto, Saicho built the Enryakuji monastery, which grew rapidly and steadily into one of the most important temple communities in Japan.

Saicho had intended his monastery to remain aloof from politics, and he therefore built it far from the national capital in Nara. Ironically, however, when the capital was moved to Kyoto, the monastery again found itself geographically close to the

The Buddha Imagined in Art

As Buddhism spread through India, and then by land across the silk routes to China and on to Korea and Japan, and by sea to Sri Lanka, Southeast Asia, and Indonesia, the image of the Buddha was transformed. Even his message was transformed, most notably from the simple, ascetic Theravada Buddhism of the early centuries in India to the more complex and colorful Mahayana Buddhism of China and East Asia. Naturally enough, each era and each region had its own context for understanding the Buddha and his message. Each created its own form of worship and evolved its own forms of temple architecture to house that form. We can gain a clearer understanding of the art from a knowledge of the philosophy. Similarly, we can gain a clearer understanding of the philosophy from the art.

All the illustrations in this chapter and the previous one concerning the evolution of Buddhism should be examined

Teaching Buddha, from Sarnath, India, Gupta dynasty, fifth century C.E. Siddhartha Gautama sought to understand the causes of and the remedy for human suffering. After many trials, he finally found his answer on the forty-ninth day of intense meditation. As the Buddha, the Enlightened One, he began to teach his new message. The *mudra*, the hand gesture, here represents the Buddha teaching. (Archaeological Musem, Sarnath)

Guanyin, Buddhist deity, Northern Song dynasty, China, *c.* 1200 C.E. Guanyin, a *bodhisattva*, or enlightened being who remains in this world to relieve human suffering, was a very popular subject in Chinese art: this example in painted wood is particularly sensuous and refined. Buddhist deities are considered to have the spiritual qualities of both genders, and by this date the feminine qualities were accentuated. (Nelson-Atkins Museum of Art, Kansas City, Missouri) carefully for what they reveal about the changing manifestations of Buddhism. For example, compare an early (fifth-century) representation of the Buddha from Sarnath, north India, with a representation of a *bodhisattva* from northern China, some seven centuries later, and a seventeenth/eighteenth-century Japanese illustration of the Buddha's death.

The first illustration, far left, suggests the simplicity of the early Theravada form, presenting the Buddha as teacher, with a number of disciples attending to his discourse. The Buddha found enlightenment through meditation, and the cross-legged lotus position of this sculpture recalls that moment. The Buddha's facial features are characteristic of the people around Sarnath, the place, not far from the Buddha's home, where he reached enlightenment, and where the sculpture was created. The hand gestures, or *mudras*, of Buddhist and Hindu iconography are symbolic. The hand gesture here represents the act of teaching.

The second illustration, center, presents one of the most famous *bodhisattvas* ("enlightened beings"), from China, about 1200. This *bodhisattva* appears androgynous (both male and female) and also Chinese, adapted to Buddhism's new geographic setting. Often, even representations of the Buddha himself take on the appearance of the people who revere him. *Bodhisattvas*, since they can appear anywhere, always take on the form of the local people from among whom they emerge. Note the sensuousness of this representation, quite different from the asceticism of Siddhartha Gautama.

The final representation, on this page, has brought the entire cosmos into the picture. As the Buddha lies dying, he is surrounded by family, followers, and even a wide array of animals. His mother looks down from heaven. The Buddhist universe has expanded a long way in time and space from the early Buddhist image of a single man meditating alone under a bo tree until he reached enlightenment.

Dying Buddha, Japanese scroll, seventeenth to eighteenth century C.E. Here the dying Buddha is attended by human disciples, *bodhisattvas*, grieving animals, and representatives of other worlds. From across the river, another disciple leads the Buddha's mother and her retinue down from heaven to attend his last teaching. Compare the scene as represented at Dunhuang, China, above. (University of Pennsylvania Museum)

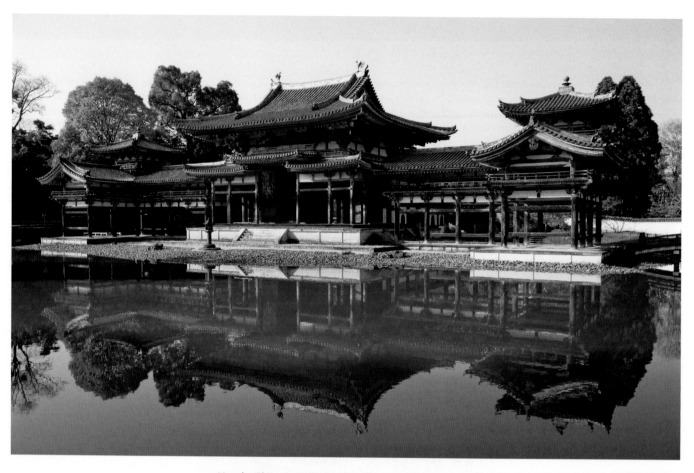

Hoodo (Phoenix Hall), Byodoin Temple, Uji, Japan, eleventh century c.e. The Phoenix Hall of the Byodoin Temple, with its jauntily uplifted roof-corners, indicates how over time the Buddhist style took on a distinctively Japanese flavor and shed its Chinese influence. Contrast with the Horyuji Temple, illustrated above.

9.1

9.2 How did Buddhism emerge and spread?

9.3

national political center. Saicho encouraged the monks to add teaching, administration, and social work in the service of the nation to their religious duties, merging Confucian and Buddhist value systems. His monastery grew to house tens of thousands of monks in some 3,000 buildings. By the eleventh century, an era of deep and violent political fissures in Japanese political life, many Shinto and Buddhist temples supported standing armies to protect themselves and their extensive land holdings and branch temples. Troops from the Mount Hiei monastery began to enter the capital, demanding additional lands and thus completely reversing Saicho's original wishes. The Buddhist clergy thereafter became increasingly intertwined with Japanese politics.

Kukai (774–835), another Japanese Buddhist priest who had studied in China, also returned home to preach a new form of Buddhism. He became abbot of the monastery of the great Toji temple at Kyoto, where he introduced Shingon ("True Word") Buddhism. This emphasizes the repetition of mystic incantations or *mantras*; meditation on colorful, sometimes stunning, geometrically ordered religious paintings, called *mandalas*, of buddhas and *bodhisattvas* in their heavens; complicated rituals; music; and ecstatic dancing. Because the transmission of these forms was closely guarded among believers, Shingon Buddhism was also called Esoteric Buddhism. Creating more accessible forms as well, Kukai introduced rituals, such as the austere and beautiful tea ceremony, in which a formal ritual surrounding the serving and drinking of tea invites deep meditation. Kukai is also credited with inventing the

KEY TERMS

mantra A formula of words and sounds that are believed to possess spiritual power, a practice of both Hinduism and Buddhism.

mandala A symbolic circular diagram of complex geometric design used as an instrument of meditation or in the performance of sacred rites in Hinduism and Buddhism.

kana **syllabary**, a Japanese script in phonetic letters rather than **ideograms**. These innovations, in addition to mysterious, secret rituals, use of herbal medicines, and the elegant pageantry of Shingon, gave Kukai's monastery great popularity and power.

Another Chinese form of Buddhism that deeply influenced Japan was dedicated to Amida or, in Sanskrit, Amitabha, the Buddha of the Infinite Light. In the tenth century, two priests, Kuya (903–72) and Genshin (942–1017), popularized this sect, which taught the importance of chanting the *mantra nembutsu*, "Praise to Amida Buddha." Amidism grew in subsequent generations through the organizational abilities of a series of monks, including Ryonin (1072–1132), who taught the counting of rosary beads to accompany the repetition of the *nembutsu*, a practice that spread to most sects of Japanese Buddhism. By the late twelfth century, Amidism established its independence from other Buddhist sects. Its message of uncomplicated, universal access to salvation had great appeal to the masses.

Chan Buddhism (Zen in Japanese) appeared in Japan during the seventh century, but began to flourish only after the twelfth century. Much of Zen's popularity was a result of the teachings of Eisai, a Buddhist monk who believed that in addition to meditation, Zen should defend the state. Its emphasis on martial arts made Zen Buddhism particularly attractive to the increasingly powerful warrior class. Since then it has deeply influenced Japanese culture, and it remains important in Japan today.

Lasting Buddhist Elements in Japanese Society. Three other elements gave Buddhism a prominence and significance in Japanese life that have continued till today. First, Japanese Buddhism cultivated an especially pure aesthetic dimension, which we have seen here in the representations of the Buddha and *bodhisattvas* and of the architecture and art of the Japanese Buddhist temples. This appreciation of artistic creativity is apparent throughout Japan in formal gardens, in painting and calligraphy, and in the art of presentation of everything from self, to gifts, to tea, to food. Second, Buddhism's emphasis on the transience of all life has inspired much of the greatest Japanese literature, from the *Tale of Genji*, written by Lady Murasaki (c. 978–c. 1015) at the Japanese court 1,000 years ago, to the novels of Mishima Yukio (1925–70), who committed *seppuku*, ritual suicide, immediately after completing his last novel. Third, Buddhism has coexisted and even merged to some degree with indigenous Shinto worship and belief.

📖 **Read** the **Document**: **Excerpt from Lady Murasaki Shibuku's Diary (11th c.)** on **MyHistoryLab**

By the twelfth century Japan had entered its Buddhist Age. Despite occasionally being attacked as a foreign religion and as an excessively wealthy and powerful organization, Buddhism has remained one of the two national religions of Japan. Most Japanese continue to mingle Buddhism and Shinto in their aesthetic and spiritual lives as well as in their ritual practices.

Comparing Hinduism and Buddhism

9.3 How do the two religions of the Indian subcontinent compare?

Hinduism and Buddhism have undergone enormous transformation through their thousands of years of history. Geographically, Hinduism spread across the Indian subcontinent from its roots in the encounter between Aryan immigrants and the indigenous peoples of the Indus valley and northern India. It extended briefly even to Southeast Asia (where a single Hindu outpost still remains on the Indonesian island of Bali). Buddhism spread from the Buddha's home region in the Himalayan foothills throughout India, where it subsequently died out, and most of East and

KEY TERMS

syllabary A writing system in which each symbol represents the syllable of a word, in contrast to **ideogram**.

ideogram (alternative: ideograph) A character or figure in a writing system in which the idea of a thing is represented rather than its name. Languages such as Chinese use ideograms.

Southeast Asia, where it flourishes. Buddhism's array of monasteries and temples, and its veneration of the homeland of the Buddha himself, mark its sacred geography.

Both religions established their own sacred calendars and their control over life-cycle events. In this, Hindu priests took a commanding position since even Buddhists (and Jains) employed them to officiate. Within India this continuing role of the *brahmin* priests ultimately helped Hinduism to absorb Buddhism. Outside India, where no other major religion was already in place, Buddhist priests performed their own rituals and came to predominate.

Both groups developed sacred languages. Buddhists felt that Sanskrit was narrowly limited to Hindu priests and so used Pali, a language closer to the vernacular. Over time, as the common people expressed their own religious feelings in their own languages, the leaders of both religions responded by also using the vernacular. Both religions inspired extensive literature, including philosophy, mystical poetry, drama, and folk tales. Both generated their own artistic traditions in painting, sculpture, and temple architecture.

Organizationally, Buddhism, especially in its early Theravada form, was seen as a religion of its monks. Many common people found comfort and meaning in their philosophy and supported them, but ultimately they turned to *brahmin* priests for their ritual needs. Within Hinduism the caste system structured all classes and occupations into a single framework of relationships, with *brahmins*, *kshatriyas*, and sometimes *vaishyas* predominating. Buddhism's later Mahayana form, with its multitudes of gods, *bodhisattvas*, and heavens, reached out to more people ritually as well as emotionally.

The evolution of Hinduism and Buddhism demonstrates the flexibility of great world religions. A small sect may define itself narrowly, proclaiming a core set of principles and practices and adhering to them rigidly. For its small membership, these restrictions may be the very attraction of the sect. But for a religion to grow in numbers, it must be open organizationally, doctrinally, and ritually to the varied spiritual, psychological, and social needs of diverse peoples. Like the empires we studied earlier, a world religion must be able to accommodate, satisfy, and absorb people of various languages, regions, classes, and previous spiritual beliefs and practices. World religions expand their theologies and practices to incorporate ever more members, until they reach the limits of their flexibility.

Finally, religions and governments have been historically interdependent. Buddhism flourished thanks to the early support of the Buddha's royal allies and later through the backing of the emperor Asoka. It spread to Southeast Asia and to Japan as kings offered their support in exchange for Buddhist legitimation. In China, Buddhism found its opening after Confucian dynasties fell and people searched for new belief systems and new leaders. Hinduism flourished as kings in India struck their own agreements with *brahmin* priests. Conversely, when governments turned against particular religious groups, they could devastate them. And when sizable religious groups shifted their support away from a ruler, they undermined his authority. We shall find more examples of this mutual antagonism in later chapters.

Hinduism and Buddhism:
What Difference Do They Make?

Hinduism keeps alive a major religion of active polytheism. Although many Hindus would argue that behind all the gods a single reality pervades the world, others would argue, more literally, that there are indeed many different gods with influence over the world and its creatures. These advocates of polytheism find a consistency between the diversity of life forms and experiences and the multitude of gods of existence.

Hinduism has given a general cultural unity and depth to much of south Asia, in its arts and literature, its complex and sophisticated philosophical systems, and its hierarchical social, economic, and political order, which is based on caste forms. Today, the government and people of India cope with these legacies in a world that generally proclaims publicly the equality of all people. As a result, contemporary India confronts many conflicts between the historic claims of caste hierarchy and the contemporary demands for equality. Political and religious leaders clash over the most appropriate direction for future development.

Buddhism also continues as the basis of the culture and religion of hundreds of millions of people, most of them in East and Southeast Asia. The religion takes many different forms, from the relative austerity of the Theravada Buddhism of Sri Lanka, to the more elaborated and otherworldly Mahayana forms of Southeast Asia, and the more mystical and isolated forms of Tibetan tantric Buddhism. In many lands Buddhism is practiced freely, often in conjunction with other religions, as in Japan. In China, however, especially in Tibet, Buddhism struggles for survival against a hostile government. To understand religions in history, we must see them in the context of the political, social, and economic systems in which they are embedded.

We turn in the next chapters to three religions—Judaism, Christianity, and Islam—that have been militantly monotheistic. Although Judaism has remained relatively limited in its numbers, Christianity and Islam have been aggressive in their desire to win converts and are now the largest of the world's religions, with over two billion and 1.5 billion followers respectively. Their relationships with the governments alongside which they exist have been checkered. Their impact on spiritual, cultural, social, and aesthetic life has been immense.

CHAPTER REVIEW

HINDUISM

9.1 What is unique in the history of Hinduism?

The roots of Hinduism (like those of Judaism) are the most ancient of the existing major religions. Unlike the world's other major religions, which claim the inspiration of a specific person or event, Hinduism emerged out of the many diverse, ancient traditions of India, including those of immigrants, like the Aryans, who contributed their writings, philosophies, and social system based on family, caste, and locality. Hinduism evolved as the principal cultural system of the Indian subcontinent.

BUDDHISM

9.2 How did Buddhism emerge and spread?

Buddhism emerged out of Hinduism in India and spread throughout central, eastern, and southeastern Asia. Like Hinduism, it questioned the reality of the earthly world and speculated on the existence of other worlds. But Buddhism had a founder—Siddhartha Gautama, the Buddha (the Enlightened One)—a set of scriptures, and an order of priests. Buddhists believed that life was filled with suffering, but the ascetic teachings of the Buddha provided a means of coping. Buddhism was carried by missionaries throughout Sri Lanka, East and Southeast Asia and came to define much of the cultural and religious life of the region, although it virtually died out in India. Later forms of Buddhism were less ascetic, more mystical, and frequently supported by political rulers.

COMPARING HINDUISM AND BUDDHISM

9.3 How do the two religions of the Indian subcontinent compare?

Hinduism and Buddhism differ in key areas, including their principal beliefs and their ideas about the role of the clergy, the role of the home, social hierarchy, and relationship to the government. Buddhism did not accept the caste system, which made it more acceptable to people contesting the power of Brahmans, but, in India, Brahman power ultimately won out. In most other locations, however, Buddhism endured while Hinduism did not.

Suggested Readings

PRINCIPAL SOURCES

Basham, A.L. *The Wonder that Was India* (New York: Grove Press, 1954). Graceful, comprehensive, standard introduction to early Indian history. Dated on the Indus valley, but still valid on imperial India.

Bhagavad Gita, trans. Barbara Stoler Miller (New York: Bantam Books, 1986). A fine, readable, clear translation of one of the greatest classics of Hinduism.

de Bary, William Theodore, *et al.*, comps. *Sources of Japanese Tradition*, Vol. I: *From Earliest Times to 1600* (New York: Columbia University Press, 2nd ed., 2002). Best available repository of primary sources from the literature.

deBary, William Theodore, and Irene Bloom, eds. *Sources of Chinese Tradition*, Vol. I: *From Earliest Times to 1600* (New York: Columbia University Press, 2nd ed., 1999). Best available repository of primary sources from the literature.

Doniger, Wendy. *The Hindus: An Alternative History* (New York: Penguin, 2009). A brilliant work emphasizing changes throughout the history of Hinduism, and the contributions of marginalized groups: women, *adivasis*, outcastes.

Ebrey, Patricia Buckley, ed. *Chinese Civilization: A Sourcebook* (New York: The Free Press, 2nd ed., 1993). An excellent sourcebook, drawn much more from the lives of common people.

Embree, Ainslee, ed. and rev. *Sources of Indian Tradition*, Vol. I: *From the Beginning to 1800* (New York: Columbia University Press, 2nd ed., 1988). Best available repository of primary sources from the literature.

ADDITIONAL SOURCES

Allchin, F.R., *et al. The Archaeology of Early Historic South Asia: The Emergence of Cities and States* (Cambridge: Cambridge University Press, 1995). Accessible, wide-ranging introduction, for nonspecialists.

Andrea, Alfred, and James Overfield, eds. *The Human Record*, Vol. 1 (Florence, KY: Wadsworth Publishing Co., 7th ed., 2012). Excellent collection of primary sources on world history.

Appadurai, Arjun. *Worship and Conflict under Colonial Rule* (Cambridge: Cambridge University Press, 1981). Demonstrates the interweaving of the major temples with the politics, economics, and social structures of their region.

Berger, Peter L. *The Sacred Canopy* (New York: Anchor Books, 1967). A classic introduction to the importance of religion and religious organizations in society.

Blunden, Caroline, and Mark Elvin. *Cultural Atlas of China* (New York: Facts on File, 1983). Superb introduction to China, with fine interpretive essays, maps, and pictures. Especially strong on geography and its implications.

Bodde, Derk. *Essays on Chinese Civilization*, ed. Charles Le Blanc and Dorothy Borei (Princeton, NJ: Princeton University Press, 1981). A classic set of essays on the significance of Chinese civilization.

Conze, Edward. *Buddhist Scriptures* (New York: Penguin Books, 1959). Basic source readings.

Craven, Roy C. *Indian Art* (London: Thames and Hudson, 1997). Excellent introduction to Indian art, especially of the classical period.

The Dhammapada, trans. Juan Mascaro (New York: Penguin Books, 1973). Fine translation and introduction to this Buddhist literary and religious classic.

Dimmitt, Cornelia, and J.A.B. van Buitenen, ed. and trans. *Classical Hindu Mythology* (Philadelphia, PA: Temple University Press, 1978). An exposition of Indian mythology and texts by masters in the field.

Eberhard, Wolfram. *China's Minorities: Yesterday and Today* (Belmont, CA: Wadsworth Publishing, 1982). Fills in the picture for non-Han Chinese, a subject often overlooked.

Eliade, Mircea. *Ordeal by Labyrinth* (Chicago, IL: University of Chicago Press, 1982). Elegant exposition of the role of religion in society.

——. *The Sacred and the Profane* (New York: Harper Torchbooks, 1959). Thought-provoking introduction to the way in which religion moves people and encourages them to create institutions.

——. *Yoga: Immortality and Freedom* (Princeton, NJ: Princeton University Press, 1969). The philosophy of yoga presented clearly and profoundly.

Elvin, Mark. *The Pattern of the Chinese Past* (Stanford, CA: Stanford University Press, 1973). Elvin explores especially the economy of China, its highs and lows.

Elwin, Verrier. *The Aboriginals* (New York: Oxford University Press, 1944). Brief pamphlet introducing *adivasis* and their problems in twentieth-century India.

Hall, Kenneth R. *Maritime Trade and State Development in Early Southeast Asia* (Honolulu, HI: University of Hawaii, 1985). Especially good on the relationships between India and Southeast Asia in trade and in political evolution.

Hall, Kenneth R., and John K. Whitmore, eds. *Explorations in Early Southeast Asian History: The Origins of Southeast Asian Statecraft* (Ann Arbor, MI: Center for South and Southeast Asian Studies, University of Michigan, 1976). Set of outstanding seminar papers.

Hammond Atlas of World History (Maplewood, NJ: Hammond, 5th ed., 1999). Indispensable world-history atlas.

Hughes, Sarah Shaver, and Brady Hughes, eds. *Women in World History*, Vol. I: *Readings from Prehistory to 1500* (Armonk, NY: M.E. Sharpe, 1995). Includes short but interesting sections on husbands and wives, Sita and Rama, and Buddhist nuns.

Kulke, Hermann, and Dietmar Rothermund. *A History of India* (New York: Routledge, 5th ed., 2010). Brief, accessible, excellent introductory history.

Lewis-Williams, David. *The Mind in the Cave: Consciousness in the Origins of Art* (London: Thames and Hudson, 2002). Exploration of meaning in earliest art; includes religious speculations.

Lockard, Craig A. "Integrating Southeast Asia into the Framework of World History: The Period Before 1500," *The History Teacher* XXIX, No. 1 (November 1995), pp. 7–35. Concern with pedagogy leads also to a good conceptual scheme for understanding Southeast Asia.

Martin, Rafe. *The Hungry Tigress: Buddhist Legends and Jataka Tales* (Berkeley, CA: Parallax Press, 1990). Classic legends and tales as a means of transmitting the essential moral lessons of Buddhism.

Murphey, Rhoads. *History of Asia* (Upper Saddle River, NJ: Pearson, 6th ed., 2008). Useful especially for its crossregional explorations.

Needham, Joseph. *The Shorter Science and Civilization in China*, Vol. I, abridged by Colin A. Ronan (Cambridge: Cambridge University Press, 1978). The classic study of Chinese science, demonstrating its methods, findings, and significance.

Nelson, Lynn, and Patrick Peebles, eds. *Classics of Eastern Thought* (San Diego, CA: Harcourt Brace Jovanovich, 1991). Fine collection of basic texts.

Ramanujan, A.K., ed. and trans. *Poems of Love and War: From the Eight Anthologies and the Ten Long Poems of Classical Tamil* (New York: Columbia University Press, 1985). An outstanding modern poet and scholar translating classical Tamil poetry.

——, trans. *Speaking of Śiva* (Harmondsworth, Middlesex: Penguin Books, 1973). Further translations specifically on the Lord Shiva in the imagination of India.

Richman, Paula, ed. *Many Ramayanas: The Diversity of a Narrative Tradition in South Asia* (Berkeley, CA: University of California Press, 1991). The *Ramayana* has many interpretations and uses. Richman provides an astonishing, scholarly array of them.

Rowland, Benjamin. *The Art and Architecture of India: Buddhist/Hindu/Jain* (New York: Penguin Books, 1977). Indian religion can be understood only with reference to its art and architecture. A fine introduction.

SarDesai, D.R. *Southeast Asia: Past and Present* (Boulder, CO: Westview Press, 7th ed., 2013). Good on the context of the spread of Buddhism.

Schwartzberg, Joseph E., ed. *A Historical Atlas of South Asia* (Chicago, IL: University of Chicago Press, 1978). Scholarly, encyclopedic coverage of history through geography. A superb research tool.

Smart, Ninian. *The World's Religions* (Cambridge: Cambridge University Press, 1989). Fine, comprehensive introduction to the major religions.

Thapar, Romila. *Ancient Indian Social History* (New Delhi: Orient Longman, 1978). Thapar's works offer the most accessible, clear, comprehensive introduction to ancient India, its politics, institutions, leaders, economy, social groups, and religions.

——. *Asoka and the Decline of the Mauryas* (New Delhi: Oxford University Press, 1998). Principal introduction to the empire of the Mauryas.

——. *Early India: From the Origins to AD 300* (Berkeley, CA: University of California Press, 2003). Updates her classic *History of India* of 1966. Definitive, if lengthy, introduction.

——. *Interpreting Early India* (New York: Oxford University Press, 1992). Philosophy of studying ancient India, opposing the use of history to advance political programs.

Tharu, Susie, and K. Lalita, eds. *Women Writing in India 600 B.C. to the Present*, Vol. I (New York: The Feminist Press, 1991).

Includes writings from various regions of India, and puts them into context.

Twitchett, Denis, ed. *The Cambridge History of China*, Vol. III: *Sui and T'ang China, 589–906*, Part 1 (Cambridge: Cambridge University Press, 1979). Comprehensive, scholarly, follows Buddhism through its flourishing in China.

Twitchett, Denis, and Michael Lowe, eds. *The Cambridge History of China*, Vol. I: *The Ch'in and Han Empires, 221 B.C.–A.D. 220* (Cambridge: Cambridge University Press, 1986). Comprehensive, scholarly, helps to understand early Buddhism in China.

Zimmer, Heinrich. *Philosophies of India* (New York: Meridian Books, 1956). Classic introduction to the texts and concepts.

FILMS

Legacy: The Origins of Civilization. Disc 1: *India* (1992; 52 minutes). Presented by Michael Wood. (Over)emphasizes the religious nature of Indian civilization. Beautiful images.

An Indian Pilgrimage: Ramdevra (1974; 30 minutes). Follows several contemporary Hindu pilgrims as they travel from their homes to a pilgrim shrine in Rajasthan. Worship is only part of the lengthy, colorful process. New York: Ambrose Video Pub., c2002, c1992.

The Buddha—PBS Documentary – Part 1 (2012) (56 minutes) The man, his message, its spread around the world, and many comments by people today who value and follow his teachings.

10 Judaism and Christianity

Peoples of the Bible: God's Evolution in West Asia and Europe

1700 B.C.E.–1000 C.E.

Into a world that believed in many gods who often fought with one another and interfered capriciously in human life, the Hebrews introduced and perpetuated the concept of a single god whose rule was both orderly and just. In contrast with the many gods of polytheism, each with his or her own temperament and judgment, the new monotheism provided a more definitive statement of right and wrong. At the same time, it demanded much greater conformity in both faith and action, calling for adherence to a strict code of ethics within a community governed by laws proclaimed by a single god. The Hebrews' belief in one god was not simply a reduction in the number of gods from many to one. Their god represented a new religious category of a god above nature and free from compulsion and fate. Their belief in only one god, however, also confronted them with a fundamental theological dilemma, a dilemma for all monotheistic religions: If there is only one god, and if that god is both all-powerful and caring, then why does human life on earth often appear so difficult and unjust?

The four evangelists, from the Gospel Book of Charlemagne, early ninth century. With the exception of the cross, the best-known symbols in early Christianity were associated with the four gospels. Based on a text in the Book of Revelation (4:7), Matthew was represented by a man, Mark by a lion, Luke by a winged ox, and John by an eagle. (Cathedral Treasury, Aachen, Germany)

LEARNING OBJECTIVES

10.1 ((	10.2 ((	10.3 ((
Tell the story of Judaism, its rise and its evolving beliefs.	Trace the evolution of Christianity.	Understand the role of Christianity in the Roman Empire.

((Listen on MyHistoryLab

The Hebrews' early home was in the Middle East, and other peoples in that region sometimes expressed similar ideas. In Egypt, for example, Akhenaten also proclaimed a belief in one god. His declaration of faith, however, came several centuries after that of the Hebrews. More importantly, his new faith did not survive his death and had no lasting effects on his country. Later pharaohs rejected Akhenaten's beliefs and his style of worship. In Mesopotamia, Hammurabi of Babylon issued a law code in the name of his god Shamash, by the year 1750 B.C.E., some 500 years before Hebrew sacred texts record a similar gift of a legal system from their god YHWH, through their leader Moses. Over time, however, the code of Hammurabi was forgotten in Mesopotamia while the Hebrew people kept their legal codes alive as they evolved into the Jewish people.

In their early years the "Hebrews" were known as the people whose legendary founder, Abraham, came from *eber*, meaning "the other side" of the Euphrates River. Later they took on the name of Jews, in honor of one of their tribes, Judah, and of the new territory that they claimed in Judea, in the modern land of Israel and Palestine.

Today there are only about 15 million Jews worldwide, but their role in history has been disproportionate to their numbers. Many of their core beliefs were incorporated into Christianity and Islam, the two great monotheistic faiths that have come to include half the world's population today. Meanwhile Judaism itself adapted to changing conditions over time and space, maintaining its own core beliefs, traditions, and identity as an independent religious community. We begin this chapter with a study of Judaism and then proceed to Christianity, which emerged from it, and challenged it. In the next chapter we explore Islam and the interactions among all three of these closely related, but often bitterly antagonistic, monotheistic religions.

Judaism

10.1 How did Judaism arise and what are its evolving beliefs?

The story of Judaism, as recorded in Hebrew scriptures, begins some 3,800 years ago with one man's vision of a single, unique God of all creation. They tell us that God and Abraham sealed a covenant stating that Abraham's descendants would forever revere and worship that God, and God, in return, would forever watch over and protect them. From then until now Judaism has remained a relatively small, family-based religion, with branches throughout the world, but focused in part in Israel, the land that Jews believe God promised to Abraham.

The Sacred Scriptures

Our knowledge of early Jewish history comes from the scriptures known collectively as the **TaNaKh**: Torah (the Five Books of Moses), Nevi'im (the Books of the Prophets), and Ketuvim (additional historical, poetic, and philosophic writings). Christians have incorporated the entire TaNaKh into their Bible, referring to these scriptures collectively as the "Old Testament." Because the New Testament is written in Greek and the Old Testament in Hebrew, the TaNaKh is often referred to as the "Hebrew Bible."

The narratives of the five books of the Torah abound with miracles, as God intervenes continuously in the history of the Jews. The Torah begins with God's creating the world and contracting his covenant with Abraham. Over the next several generations, the Torah continues, famine struck Israel (then called Canaan), the land God promised to Abraham. Abraham's grandson and his family traveled to the Nile valley of Egypt in search of food. At first invited by the pharaoh to remain as permanent residents, they were later enslaved. About 1200 B.C.E., after 400 years of slavery, the Jews won their freedom and escaped from Egypt under the leadership of Moses through

KEY TERM

TaNaKh A Hebrew term for the books of the Bible that are written in Hebrew. The word is composed of the initial letters of the words Torah (first five books of the Bible, traditionally attributed to Moses), Nevi'im (the books of the Prophets), and Ketuvim (additional historical, poetic, and philosophic writings). These are the three sections of the Hebrew Bible.

AT A GLANCE: JUDAISM AND CHRISTIANITY 1700 B.C.E.–900 C.E.

DATE	POLITICAL/SOCIAL EVENTS	LITERARY/PHILOSOPHICAL EVENTS
1700 B.C.E.	• Abraham travels from Mesopotamia to Israel (c. 1750)	
1600 B.C.E.	• Hebrew slavery in Egypt	
1200 B.C.E.	• Moses (?1300–?1200) • Exodus from Egypt; legal codes formulated; return to Palestine; tribal government under Judges	
1000 B.C.E.	• Period of Kings begins with Saul, David, and Solomon • First temple in Jerusalem	
900 B.C.E.	• Jewish kingdom divides into Israel and Judea	
800 B.C.E.	• Prophets exhort Jewish nation (800–500) • Assyrians conquer Israel and exile Jews (721)	• Numbers (850–650) • Genesis (mid-fifth to eighth century) • Prophets Isaiah, Amos, Micah
700 B.C.E.		• Josiah begins to write down Torah (640) • Deuteronomy (mid-seventh century) • Leviticus (mid-seventh century) • Jeremiah
600 B.C.E.	• Babylonians conquer Judea, exile the people, and destroy the first temple (586) • Jews permitted to return to Judea and rebuild the temple (538)	• Book of Job (600)
300 B.C.E.		• Books of TaNaKh (the Jewish Bible) edited and canonized
100 B.C.E.	• Birth and death of Jesus (c. 4 B.C.E.–c. 30 C.E.)	
10 C.E.	• Rome captures Jerusalem (63) • Christianity emerges from Judaism • St. Paul, Saul of Tarsus, organizes early Christianity (d. c. 67) • Rome destroys second temple (70)	• Gospels (70–100) • Acts (70–80) • Epistles of Paul (50–67)
100 C.E.	• Rome exiles Jews from Judea; Jewish diaspora throughout Mediterranean basin and west Asia (135) • Rabbinical tradition developed (first to fourth century)	
200 C.E.	• Christians persecuted under Severus, Decius, and Diocletian	• Babylonian and Jerusalem Talmuds edited and published (200–500)
300 C.E.	• Christianity legalized (313); declared the official religion of the Roman Empire (392) • Council of Nicaea (325) • Georgia and Armenia convert to Christianity (c. 330)	
400 C.E.	• Council of Chalcedon (451)	• Augustine's *The City of God* and *Confessions*
500 C.E.	• Monasticism in Europe • Clovis converted to Christianity • St. Benedict founds monastery of Monte Cassino	
600 C.E.	• England converted to Christianity	• Venerable Bede, *Ecclesiastical History of the English People*
700 C.E.	• Iconoclastic controversy	
800 C.E.	• Coronation of Charlemagne (800) • St. Cyril and St. Methodius convert Russia, translate the Bible, and create the Cyrillic alphabet	• Einhard, *Life of Charlemagne*
900 C.E.	• Missionaries proliferate among the Vikings	

the miraculous intervention of God. During their journey back to Israel through the wilderness of the Sinai Desert, the contentious group of ex-slaves was forged into a small but militant nation. The Torah records a dramatic miracle at Mount Sinai in which God revealed a set of religious and civil laws for them to follow.

AT A GLANCE: JUDAISM AND CHRISTIANITY 1000 C.E.–1400 C.E.

DATE	POLITICAL/SOCIAL EVENTS	LITERARY/PHILOSOPHICAL EVENTS
1000 C.E.	• Christians capture Toledo from Muslim control and begin *reconquista* (1085) • Split of Western and Eastern Christianity (1054) • First Crusade (1095–99)	
1100 C.E.	• Second Crusade (1147–49) • Third Crusade (1189–92)	• Rabbi Benjamin of Tudela (d. 1173) travels widely in Europe and the Middle East
1200 C.E.	• Fourth Crusade (1202–04) • Children's Crusade (1212) • Crusaders capture Constantinople (1204–61) • Fifth to Eighth Crusades (1218–91)	
1300 C.E.	• Monastic orders	
1400 C.E.	• Christians capture Granada, Spain, complete the *reconquista* (1492), expel Jews and Muslims	

For centuries, Jews and Christians believed that these earliest books of the Bible, which describe the creation of the world and the earliest history of the Jewish people, were the literal word of God. During the past two centuries, scholarship has given us a new sense of the historical place of these books. Today historians ask: When and where were the books of the Hebrew Bible composed and how valid are they as historical documents?

Modern scholarly analysis of the TaNaKh texts became a prominent academic enterprise in Germany during the early nineteenth century. The founders of "Biblical criticism" noted certain inconsistencies in the Biblical texts. For example, the first chapter of Genesis reports that God created man and woman simultaneously, "male and female he created them," while the second chapter reports that God first created man and then removed one of his ribs and created woman from it. The critics noted also that different names are used for God in the Hebrew text—most notably YHWH and Elohim—and they suggested that the different names represent the stylistic preferences of different authors. They noted similarities between the stories and laws of the Bible and those in the literature of other peoples of the region, and they suggested that some of the external stories had found their way into the Biblical accounts. Through rigorous analysis, the Biblical scholars argued persuasively that Josiah (r. 640–609 B.C.E.), the king of the Jewish state of Judea, first made the decision to begin to edit and write down the definitive edition of oral texts that had been passed from generation to generation.

The story of Josiah's reign is told in the Biblical book of 2 Kings, chapters 20–21. Struggling to survive in the face of the powerful Assyrian Empire, Josiah was anxious to promote allegiance to the state and its religion. He centralized Jewish worship in the national

The kingdom of Israel. The first unified Jewish state in Palestine emerged around 980 B.C.E. under King David. He united the tribes of Israel during a period of decline among their more powerful neighbors—Egypt and the Hittites. After the death of his son Solomon (926 B.C.E.), tribal rivalries divided the empire into the kingdoms of Judah and Israel, but the sense of cultural unity survived.

305

Dead Sea Scrolls, Isaiah scroll 1Q Is. 9 verses 58.6–63.4. The 500 or so documents that make up the Dead Sea Scrolls—which date between about 250 B.C.E. and 70 C.E., and were rediscovered in 1947—appear at one time to have formed the library of a Jewish community. As well as providing evidence of the accuracy of Hebrew biblical texts, they give information about the life of the community itself. (Israel Museum, Jerusalem)

10.1 How did Judaism arise and what
10.2 are its evolving beliefs?
10.3

temple in Jerusalem, and collected and transcribed the most important texts of his people. Josiah regarded adherence to the laws laid down in these scriptures as fundamental to the maintenance of the Jewish religion, the Jewish people, and his own Jewish kingdom. From existing literary fragments, folk wisdom, and oral history he had the Book of Deuteronomy, the fifth book of the TaNaKh, written down. Soon, additional literary materials from at least three other major interpretive traditions were also woven together to create the books of Genesis, Exodus, Leviticus, and Numbers. Together with Deuteronomy, these books formed the Torah, or "Five Books of Moses."

With the ravages of time, older copies of the Torah, written in Hebrew on parchment scrolls, began to perish and new ones were copied. The oldest existing Hebrew manuscripts of the entire Torah date only to the ninth to the eleventh centuries C.E., but fragments dating to as early as the second century B.C.E. have been discovered. Stored in caves near the Dead Sea in Israel, these Dead Sea Scrolls have been rediscovered only since 1947. Another very early edition of the Torah is a Greek translation from the Hebrew, the Septuagint. It was prepared for the Greek-speaking Jews of Egypt in the third and second centuries B.C.E. It still exists and is consistent with the Hebrew texts of our own time. In short, the written text of the Torah appears to have been preserved with great fidelity for about 2,600 years, although the oral texts on which the written scriptures were based date back much farther.

The Torah remains one of the greatest examples of myth-history. Although its stories should not necessarily be read as literal, historical records, their version of events gave birth to the Jewish people's concept of itself and helped to define its character and principal beliefs. The stories of the Torah tell us what the Jewish people, and especially their literate leadership, have thought important about their own origins and mission. They also define images of God that have profoundly influenced the imagination and action of Jews, Christians, and Muslims for millennia.

Essential Beliefs of Judaism in Early Scriptures

The Torah fixes many of the essential beliefs and principles of Judaism:

- A single caring God, demanding obedience, who administers rewards and punishments fairly and in accordance with his fixed laws:

  Hear, O Israel, the Lord is our God, the Lord alone. You shall love the Lord your God with all your heart, and with all your soul, and with all your might. (Deuteronomy 6:4–5)

  Know therefore that the Lord your God is God, the faithful God who maintains covenant loyalty with those who love him and keep his commandments, to a thousand generations, and who repays in their own person those who reject him. (Deuteronomy 7:9–10)

- A God of history, whose power affects the destiny of individuals and nations:
  I am the Lord your God who brought you out of Egypt, out of the land of slavery. (Exodus 20:2–3)
- A community rooted in a divinely chosen family and ethnic group:
  Now the Lord said to Abraham, "Go from your country and your kindred and your father's house to the land that I will show you. I will make of you a great nation, and I will bless you, and make your name great, so that you will be a blessing." (Genesis 12:1–2)
- A specific, "promised," geographical homeland:
  When Abraham reached Canaan, God said to him: "Raise your eyes now, and look from the place where you are, northward and southward and eastward and westward; for all the land that you see I will give to you and to your offspring forever." (Genesis 13:14–15)
- A legal system to guide proper behavior: religious, familial, sexual, commercial, civic, ethical, and ritual. The introduction to this code was the Ten Commandments, revered as the heart of the revelation to Moses at Mount Sinai.
- A sacred calendar: Jewish religious leaders reconstituted earlier polytheistic celebrations of nature into a calendar of national religious celebration. A spring festival of renewal was incorporated into Passover, the commemoration of the exodus from Egypt; an early summer festival of first harvest was subsumed into Shavuot, a rejoicing in the revelation of the Ten Commandments at Sinai; and an early fall harvest festival became part of Sukkot (Succoth), a remembrance of the years of wandering in the desert. All these festivals were to be celebrated, if possible, by pilgrimage to the central, national temple in Jerusalem. Celebrations of nature, history, and national identity were fused together.

SOURCE

The Ten Commandments

The Torah contains legal codes governing many aspects of life, including family rules concerning marriage, divorce, and inheritance; civil laws regulating business practices and responsibilities; criminal law mandating rules of evidence and of punishment; rules commanding ethical and charitable behavior, especially toward the weak and helpless, strangers, orphans, and widows; and extensive rules concerning ritual practices of prayer, sacrifice, food, and priestly behavior. At the center of the codes are the Ten Commandments, given, according to the Torah account, directly by God to Moses atop Mount Sinai amidst terrifying thunder, lightning, clouds, and trumpet blasts. These commandments dictate behavior toward God, parents, and fellow humans. They also proclaim the importance of observing a Sabbath day once a week.

I am the Lord your God who brought you out of Egypt, out of the house of slavery.

You shall have no other gods before me. You shall not make for yourself an idol, whether in the form of anything that is in heaven above, or that is on the earth beneath, or that is in the water under the earth.

You shall not bow down to them or worship them; for I the Lord your God am a jealous god, punishing children for the iniquity of parents, to the third and fourth generation of those who reject me, but showing steadfast love to the thousandth generation of those who love me and keep my commandments.

You shall not make wrongful use of the name of the Lord your God, for the Lord will not acquit anyone who misuses his name.

Remember the Sabbath day, and keep it holy. Six days you shall labor and do all your work. But the seventh day is a Sabbath to the Lord your God; you shall not do any work—you, your son or your daughter, your male or female slave, your livestock, or the alien resident in your towns. For in six days the Lord made heaven and earth, the sea, and all that is in them, but rested the seventh day; therefore the Lord blessed the Sabbath day and consecrated it.

Honor your father and your mother, so that your days may be long in the land that the Lord your God is giving you.

You shall not murder.

You shall not commit adultery.

You shall not steal.

You shall not bear false witness against your neighbor.

You shall not covet your neighbor's house; you shall not covet your neighbor's wife, or male or female slave, or ox, or donkey, or anything that belongs to your neighbor.

(Exodus 20:2–17; see also Deuteronomy 5)

10.1 How did Judaism arise and what are its evolving beliefs?

10.2

10.3

To ground the mystical beliefs and forge the Jewish people into a "kingdom of priests and a sacred nation," rules issued in the name of God forbade intermarriage with outsiders; prohibited eating animals which do not have cloven hooves and chew their cud, and fish that do not have scales and fins (Deuteronomy 14 and Leviticus 11) (included in the rules of kashrut, "keeping kosher"); and centralized worship in the hands of a priestly aristocracy. Animal sacrifices were to be offered, but only by the hereditary priests and only in a single national temple in Jerusalem.

The Later Books of Jewish Scripture

The later volumes of the TaNaKh, the books of Nevi'im and Ketuvim, carry an account of the history of the Jewish people from about 1200 B.C.E. to about the fifth century B.C.E. God continues as a constant presence in these narratives, but he intervenes less openly and less frequently. These later records can generally be cross-checked against the archaeology of the region and the history of neighboring peoples, and they seem generally consistent.

The Book of Joshua begins the story about the year 1200 B.C.E., as the Jews returned to Canaan, or Israel, the land promised to them, and made it their home. This Biblical account tells of continuous, violent, political and religious warfare between the invading Jews and the resident Canaanite peoples. Modern scholarship suggests, however, that the number of Jews who had been enslaved in Egypt was not nearly so great as the Torah states (Egyptian records do not mention Jewish slaves at all) and that reentry into the land of Israel was a gradual process, with fewer, more localized battles and considerably more cultural borrowing among all the groups in the region.

Rule by Judges and by Kings. Arriving in Canaan, the Jews first organized themselves in a loose tribal confederacy led by a series of "Judges," *ad hoc* leaders who took command at critical periods, especially at times of war. Despite warnings that a monarchy would lead to increased warfare, profligate leaders, extortionate taxes, and the impressment of young men and women into royal service, the Jews later anointed a king. For three generations (c. 1020–950 B.C.E.), strong kings, Saul, David, and Solomon, are said to have ruled and expanded the geographic base of the people. They established a national center in Jerusalem, where they united political and religious power by building both palace and temple, exalting both king and priest. The earlier warnings against royal excesses, however, proved prescient. Unable to sustain Solomon's legendary extravagances in expenditure and in his relationships with 700 wives, many of them foreign princesses, and 300 concubines, the kingdom split in two, the kingdom of Judea and the kingdom of Israel.

Moses, mosaic in San Vitale, Ravenna, Italy, sixth century C.E. After he had led the Israelite slaves out of Egypt by the miracle of parting the Red Sea, Moses ascended Mount Sinai. There he received from God the Torah, or sacred teachings, beginning with the two tablets of the Ten Commandments. He led his quarrelsome people across the Sinai Desert but died at the border of the promised land.

The Teachings of the Prophets: Criticism, Morality, and Hope. Continuing despotism by their kings and greed on the part of their wealthier citizens ripped apart the social fabric of the two splinter kingdoms. A group of prophets emerged, demanding reform. In powerful

CHAPTER TEN: JUDAISM AND CHRISTIANITY 1700 B.C.E.–1000 C.E.

How did Judaism
arise and what
are its evolving
beliefs?

10.1

10.2

10.3

and sublime language, these men called for a reinstitution of justice, compassion, and ethics. Speaking in the name of God and of the people, they cried out against the hypocritical misuse of religious and political power.

The prophet Isaiah, in the eighth century B.C.E., led the charge:

> When you stretch out your hands, I will hide my eyes from you; even though you make many prayers, I will not listen; your hands are full of blood.
> Wash yourselves; make yourselves clean; remove the evil of your doings from before my eyes; cease to do evil,
> Learn to do good; seek justice, rescue the oppressed, defend the orphan, plead for the widow. (Isaiah 1:15–17)

A century later, Jeremiah continued in the same spirit of moral outrage, rebuking the rulers and people of Judea, the southern kingdom:

> You keep saying, "This place is the temple of the Lord, the temple of the Lord, the temple of the Lord!" This catchword of yours is a lie; put no trust in it. Mend your ways and your doings, deal fairly with one another, do not oppress the alien, the orphan, and the widow, shed no innocent blood in this place, do not run after other gods to your own ruin. (Jeremiah 7:4–6)

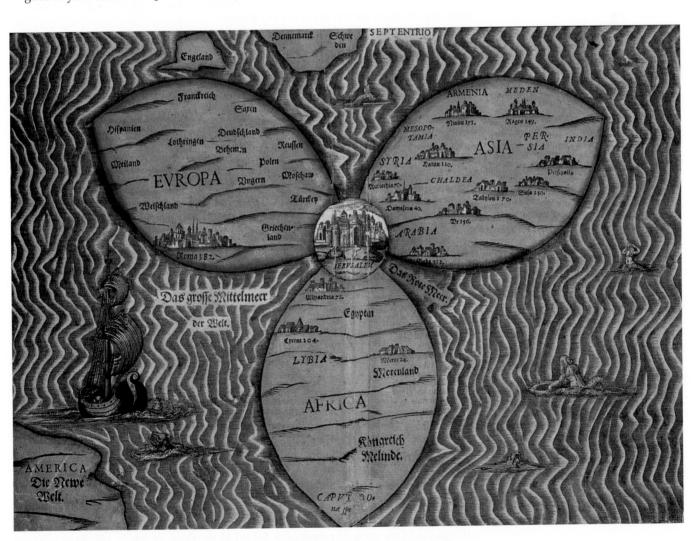

Map of the world by Heinrich Bunting, 1585. Many peoples believed that their capital city was the cosmo-magical axis of the universe. This map, shaped like a clover leaf, places Jerusalem at the center, at the crossroads of Africa, Asia, and Europe.

10.1

How did Judaism
arise and what
are its evolving
beliefs?

10.2

10.3

So even at the time that Israel and Judea developed into powerful kingdoms, the prophets remembered that the beginnings of the Jewish people were in slavery and that a significant part of its mission was to identify with and help the downtrodden. When destruction came, the prophets interpreted it as punishment not of their God, as earlier peoples had often done, but *by* their God. Destruction of a corrupt nation indicated not the weakness of its God, but God's ethical consistency.

Finally, the prophets not only harangued, blamed, and condemned, they also held up visions of a future to inspire their listeners. They saw God transforming human history. He offered rewards as well as punishments. He offered hope. Micah's prophecy in the eighth century B.C.E. is one of the most exalted, and perhaps utopian:

> He shall judge between many peoples, and shall arbitrate between strong nations far away; they shall beat their swords into plowshares, and their spears into pruning hooks; nation shall not lift up sword against nation, neither shall they learn war any more; but they shall all sit under their own vines and under their own fig trees, and no one shall make them afraid; for the mouth of the Lord of hosts has spoken. (Micah 4:1–4)

Micah closed with a vision of great Jewish religious commitment, balanced by equally great appreciation for the diversity of others:

> For all the peoples walk each in the name of its god, but we will walk in the name of the Lord our God for ever and ever. (Micah 4:5)

The Evolution of the Image of God

The Torah portrays God as an evolving moral force in dialogue with humans. In God's early interactions with humans, his nature is still malleable. Disgusted at human disobedience, he destroys almost all humankind through a flood, but he then pledges never to be so destructive again, creating a rainbow as a kind of treaty of peace with humanity (Genesis 6–8). Still fearful of the collective power of humanity, God confounds their intercommunication by dividing them into separate language groups at the Tower of Babel (Genesis 11). While deciding the fate of the sinful cities of Sodom and Gomorrah, God listens to Abraham's plea for the defense: "Far be it from thee to do this—to kill good and bad together; for then the good would suffer with the bad. Far be it from thee. Shall not the judge of all the earth do what is just?" (Genesis 18–19). God apparently bans child sacrifice when he stops Abraham from killing his son Isaac. (The Muslim Quran reports this to be Abraham's son Ishmael.)

When asked by Moses to identify himself by name, God replies enigmatically and powerfully, "I am who I am" (Exodus 3:14). The Hebrew designation for God's name is YHWH, "Being." English-speaking readers have usually rendered it either Jehovah or Yahweh.

In Jewish theology, God is almighty but still directly accessible to every human being through prayer and even through dialogue. Indeed, humans and God come to understand each other by arguing with one another in a process that the contemporary rabbi Arthur Waskow has called "Godwrestling." If Jews are to be God's people and to follow his will, he, in turn, is expected to be a compassionate and attentive ruler.

This view challenged the polytheistic beliefs in self-willed gods, but it left Judaism with no strong answer to the eternal problem of evil in the universe: If there is a single God, and if he is good, why do the wicked often prosper and the righteous often suffer? One Biblical response is found in the Book of Job (c. 600 B.C.E.). To the questions of the innocent, suffering Job, God finally responds with overwhelming power:

Crossing the Red Sea, *c.* 245 C.E. Fresco, synagogue at Dura Europos, Syria. The fresco depicts the Biblical story of the exodus of the Hebrew people from slavery in Egypt. Here, the Red Sea parts, allowing the Hebrews, led by Moses, to escape on dry land, and then returns to its place, drowning the Egyptians who attempt to pursue them. The Dura Europos synagogue is one of the oldest in the world. Its frescoes demonstrate that, despite the Bible's apparent prohibition of visual images, painting flourished, even in synagogues. (National Archaeological Museum, Damascus, Syria)

How did Judaism arise and what are its evolving beliefs?

10.1

10.2

10.3

Who is this whose ignorant words cloud my design in darkness?
Brace yourself and stand up like a man; I will ask the questions, and you shall
   answer.
Where were you when I laid the earth's foundations? Tell me, if you know and
   understand.
Who settled its dimensions? Surely you should know …
Is it for a man who disputes with the Almighty to be stubborn?
Should he that argues with God answer back? (Job 38:2–5; 40:2)

But while God lectures Job for his brashness in questioning his authority and power, he understands Job's anguish at the apparent injustice in the world and ultimately rewards Job with health, a restored family, and abundance for his honesty in raising his questions.

📖 **Read** the **Document**: **Book of Job and Jewish Literature** on **MyHistoryLab**

Patriarchy and Gender Relations

The Torah grants women fewer civil and religious rights (and obligations) than men. By conventional interpretation, women were expected to be responsible for nursing and child-care, tasks that know no time constraints, and they were therefore freed

10.1 How did Judaism arise and what are its evolving beliefs?

10.2

10.3

JEWISH FESTIVALS AND FAST DAYS

Hebrew date	Gregorian date	Name of festival
1–2 Tishre	Sept–Oct	Rosh Hashana (New Year)
10 Tishre	Sept–Oct	Yom Kippur (Day of Atonement)
15–21 Tishre	Sept–Oct	Sukkot (Feast of the Tabernacles)
22 Tishre	Sept–Oct	Shemini Atzeret (Eighth Day of the Solemn Assembly)
23 Tishre	Sept–Oct	Simchat Torah (Rejoicing of the Law)
25 Kislev–2–3 Tevet	Nov–Dec	Hannukah (Feast of Dedication)
14–15 Adar	Feb–Mar	Purim (Feast of Lots)
14–20 Nisan	Mar–Apr	Pesach (Passover)
5 Iyar	Apr–May	Israel Independence Day
6–7 Sivan	May–Jun	Shavuot (Feast of Weeks)
9 Av	Jul–Aug	Tisha be-Av (Fast of Ninth Av)

from all ritual obligations that had to be performed at specific times, for instance prayers at certain times of day.

The regulation of sexuality is fundamental in Biblical Jewish law, as it is in most religions. Women are regarded as ritually unclean each month at times of menstruation, and in childbirth. Men may be ritually unclean as a result of wet dreams or sexual diseases (Leviticus 15), but these occurred with less regularity. Marriage is regarded as the norm, with a strong emphasis on bearing children. Homosexual behavior is strongly rejected. (Today, however, many branches of Judaism have revised gender rules and discarded prohibitions on homosexuality.)

Jewish scriptures credit a few women with heroic roles. Sarah, Abraham's wife, forced him to choose her son as his proper successor, and she gained God's approval (Genesis 16). Jewish midwives in Egypt continued to deliver healthy male babies despite the Pharaoh's decree and death sentence against these children. Deborah led Israel in peace and war during the period of conquering the land of Israel (Judges 4–5). Ruth, a convert, taught the importance of openness to the outside world; she became an ancestor of King David and, therefore, in Christian belief, of Jesus (Book of Ruth). Esther was married to the Persian king and used her position to block the attempts of a court minister to kill the Jews of the Persian Empire (Book of Esther). Although none of these stories can be authenticated externally nor dated exactly, they speak to the significance of individual, exceptional women at turning points in Jewish history, and in the collective mind of the Jewish people.

Defeat, Exile, and Redefinition

Jews represent both an ethnic community and a universal religion. This dual identity became especially clear when foreign conquerors exiled part of the Jewish population from Israel as part of a plan to encourage their assimilation and to open the land to foreign immigration. This dispersion of Jews to various lands ruled by other peoples is known as the **diaspora**.

First, Sennacherib of Assyria dispersed the Jews of the northern kingdom of Israel in 721 B.C.E. These exiles drifted into assimilation and were subsequently referred to as the "**Lost Ten Tribes** of Israel." In 586 B.C.E., Babylonian conquerors destroyed the temple in Jerusalem and exiled thousands of Jews from the southern kingdom of Judea to Babylon, but these Jews remained loyal to their unique identity as a separate community, remembering their homeland:

KEY TERMS

diaspora A dispersion of peoples. Most commonly used to refer to the dispersion of Jews among the gentiles, which began with the Babylonian captivity of the sixth century B.C.E.

Lost Ten Tribes Ten tribes of Israel were exiled from their homeland in 721 B.C.E. They totally assimilated into their new surroundings, lost their Jewish identity, and were lost to history. Periodically, groups in remote areas today claim that they are the Lost Ten Tribes.

By the rivers of Babylon—there we sat down and wept when we remembered
  Zion …
Our captors asked us for songs: "Sing us one of the songs of Zion!"
How could we sing the Lord's song in a foreign land?
If I forget you, O Jerusalem, let my right hand wither!
Let my tongue cling to the roof of my mouth if I do not remember you, if I do not
  set Jerusalem above my highest joy. (Psalm 137)

The Jewish diaspora. Following the Jewish Revolt in 66 C.E., the Roman destruction of the temple in Jerusalem in 70, and the defeat of the Bar-Cochba revolt in 135, the Roman government expelled the Jews from Judea. Their subsequent migrations spread Judaism north into Mesopotamia and Anatolia, followed trade routes throughout the Mediterranean and the Red Sea, and eventually resulted in the establishment of Jewish communities as far afield as northwest Europe and Ethiopia.

10.1

10.2

10.3

How did Judaism
arise and what
are its evolving
beliefs?

When the emperor Cyrus permitted the Jews to return to Judea some 60 years later, many Jews left Babylonia, returned to Judea, rebuilt their temple, and reconstructed national life. But many did not. Those who remained did not assimilate into Babylonian culture, however. Instead, they reconstituted their religion, replacing the sacrificial services of the temple with meditation and prayers offered privately or in synagogues. They replaced the hereditary priesthood with teachers and rabbis, positions earned through study and piety. In academies at Sura and Pumbeditha, towns adjacent to Babylon, rabbis continued the study of the Torah. They interpreted and edited Jewish law, and elaborated Jewish stories and myths, which often conveyed moral principles. The multivolumed record of their proceedings, the Babylonian Talmud, was completed about 500 C.E. So distinguished was the Jewish scholarship of Babylonia that this Talmud was considered superior in coverage and scholarship to the Jerusalem Talmud, which was produced about the same time in academies in Israel.

Jews lived in substantial numbers both in Israel and in the diaspora. Many had chosen to remain in Babylonia even after they were permitted to return to Judea. Many others traveled by free choice throughout the trade and cultural networks that were established by the Persians in the sixth century B.C.E., enhanced by Alexander the Great in the fourth century B.C.E., and eventually extended by the Roman Empire.

A census of the Roman Empire undertaken by the emperor Claudius in 48 C.E. showed 5,984,072 Jews. This figure suggests a total global Jewish population of about 8 million. At the time, the population of the Roman Empire was perhaps 60 million, while that of the Afro-Eurasian world was about 170 million. Most Jews outside Israel continued to look to Jerusalem as a spiritual center, and they sent funds to support the temple.

Judea itself passed from one conqueror to another, from the Persians to Alexander the Great and his successors, and then to the Roman Empire in 63 B.C.E. Struggles simmered continuously under Roman rule, not only between Jews and Romans, but

Menorah procession, Arch of Titus, Rome, c. 81 C.E. The Romans put down the Jewish revolt of 70 C.E. by recapturing Jerusalem, destroying the temple, and looting its sacred objects. This relief from Emperor Titus' triumphal arch shows Roman soldiers carrying off the temple menorah, a seven-branched candelabrum, which today serves as an official emblem of the state of Israel.

How did Judaism
arise and what
are its evolving
beliefs?

10.1

10.2

10.3

also among Jewish political and religious factions. Three major revolts broke out and Roman authorities responded with overwhelming force in suppressing them. In 70 C.E. they destroyed the Jewish temple in Jerusalem, exiled all Jews from the city, and turned it into their regional capital. In 135 C.E. they dismantled the political structure of the Jewish state and exiled almost all Jews from Judea.

Unlike earlier exiles, this Roman dispersion fundamentally and permanently altered Jewish existence, removing all but a few Jews from the region of Israel until the twentieth century. This final exile established the principal contours of Jewish diaspora existence from then on: life as a minority group; dispersed among various peoples around the world; with distinct religious and social practices; united in reverence for sacred texts and their teachings, as interpreted by rabbi-scholars; usually dependent on the widely varying policies of the peoples among whom they lived; and sometimes forced to choose between religious conversion, emigration, or death. Jews preserved their cohesion through their acceptance of the authority of the TaNaKh and the importance of studying it, and their persistence in seeing themselves as a special kind of family even in dispersion.

Minority–Majority Relations in the Diaspora

In general, Jews remained socially and religiously distinct wherever they traveled. This identification was imposed partially from the outside by others, partially by internal discipline and loyalty to the group, its traditions, and its laws. Jewish history

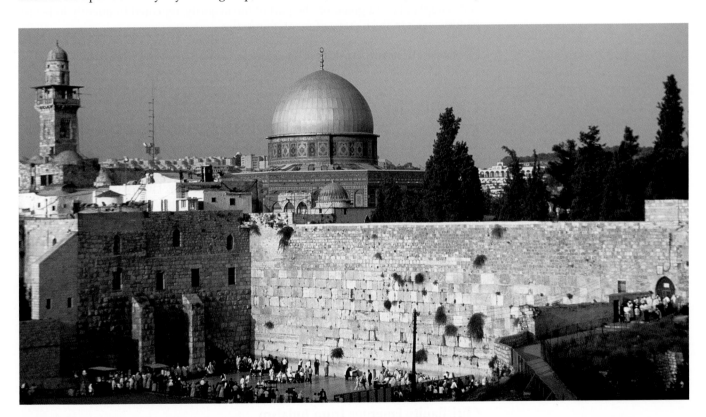

Western Wall, Jerusalem. The wall is the last remaining segment of the Second Temple of the Jewish people. All the rest was destroyed following their exile by the Romans in 135 C.E. It is the holiest shrine in Judaism. Just beyond the wall, on the hill on which the Second Temple once stood, and the First Temple before it, rises the Dome of the Rock, the third most sacred shrine in the Muslim world. The proximity of the shrines, and their claims over the same spaces, has often been a source of tension between the two religious groups.

👁 **Watch** the **Video**: **Old City of Jerusalem** on **MyHistoryLab**

10.1

10.2 How did
Christianity
emerge and
evolve?

10.3

becomes a case study also of tolerance and intolerance of minorities by majority peoples around the world.

In some civilizations, Jewish life in the diaspora survived and even flourished. For example, Rabbi Benjamin of Tudela, Spain, visited Muslim Baghdad in 1160–70 C.E. and reported: "In Baghdad there are about 40,000 Jews, and they dwell in security, prosperity, and honor under the great Caliph, and amongst them are great sages, the heads of Academies engaged in the study of the law. In this city there are ten Academies …" (Andrea and Overfield, Vol. I, p. 245).

There were contrary examples, however. The Book of Esther, written about (and probably during) the Persian diaspora, 638–333 B.C.E., captures the vulnerability of minority existence. A royal minister sees his chance to advance his career and profit, and argues to the king:

> There is a certain people, dispersed among the many peoples in all the provinces of your kingdom, who keep themselves apart. Their laws are different from those of every other people; they do not keep your majesty's laws. It does not befit your majesty to tolerate them. If it please your majesty, let an order be made in writing for their destruction; and I will pay ten thousand talents of silver to your majesty's officials, to be deposited in the royal treasury. (Esther 3:8–9)

The king agrees: "The money and the people are yours; deal with them as you wish" (Esther 3:11). On this occasion, according to Jewish traditions, the actions of Esther saved these Jews from destruction. But the Biblical account captures a pattern of official xenophobia and greed on the part of the majority, repeated frequently in Jewish history—and in the history of many minorities.

📖 **Read** the **Document**: **Expulsion of the Jews from France** (12th Century) on **MyHistoryLab**

Christianity

10.2   How did Christianity emerge and evolve?

While Judaism remained a religion of a relatively small group of people, it gave birth to the most populous religion in the world, Christianity. Here we trace the steps of Christianity's evolution: from the teachings of Jesus, a Jewish preacher and miracle worker who his followers believed to be the son of God, literally; to his disciples who began to spread the word of his teachings, and to transcribe them into writing; to Paul of Tarsus, who took Jesus' message to the broader world of the Mediterranean; to Emperor Constantine, who reversed centuries of persecution of Christians and began the process of making the Roman Empire Christian; to the division of the Catholic Church into Eastern and Western (Roman) branches; to the widespread institution of monasteries and convents throughout the remnants of the Roman Empire, the conversion of the barbarians, and the attempt to construct a new Christian Empire, the Holy Roman Empire.

📖 **Read** the **Document**: **Excerpt from the Gospel According to Luke** on **MyHistoryLab**

Christianity Emerges from Judaism

At the height of Roman rule over Judea, a splinter group within the Jewish people was forming around the person and teachings of Jesus of Nazareth. The times were turbulent and difficult. As a colony of the Roman Empire, Judea was taxed heavily and suppressed economically and politically. The Romans also demanded emperor worship from a people who were devoted to monotheism. Religious and political antagonisms were closely intertwined in an explosive mixture. The Jewish prophets of the Old Testament had promised a final end to such anguish, and many of Jesus' followers believed that he was the "servant" who had been promised to lead them into a brighter future.

In the face of Roman colonialism, the Jews were divided into at least four conflicting groups. The largest of these, the Pharisees, identified with the masses of the population in resenting the Roman occupation, but, seeing no realistic alternative to it, found some comfort in keeping alive and reinterpreting Jewish religious traditions. The more elite Sadducees, the temple priests and their allies, had become servants of the Roman state and preached accommodation to it. A much smaller, militant group of Zealots sought, quixotically, to drive out the Romans through violence. A fourth, still smaller group, the Essenes, lived a prayerful existence by the shores of the Dead Sea, stayed aloof from politics, and preached the imminent end of the world as they knew it.

Into this volatile and complex society, Jesus was born to Joseph, a carpenter, and Mary, his betrothed, about the year 4 B.C.E., in the town of Bethlehem, about 10 miles southwest of Jerusalem. (The year of Jesus' birth is not recorded. The Christian calendar places it at the beginning of the year 1, but it must have taken place no later than 4 B.C.E., for Herod, king at the time of Jesus' birth, died that year.) Biblical accounts report little about his early life, except that his parents took him to Jerusalem to celebrate the Passover holiday when he was 12 years old, and he entered there into probing discussions of religion with teachers sitting in the temple, astonishing onlookers and his parents. Jesus next emerges, at about the age of 30, as a powerful preacher, attracting multitudes to his sermons, which are filled with allegories and parables concerning ethical life, moral teachings, and predictions of the future.

In his calls for rapid and radical religious reform, Jesus found himself in opposition to the more conservative Pharisees, whom he frequently referred to as hypocrites. Like the Essenes, he spoke often of an imminent day of divine judgment of the whole world. He promised eternal life and happiness to the poor and downtrodden people of colonial Judea if only they would keep their faith in God. Similar predictions had also been common among the Jewish prophets centuries before, and Jesus' emphasis on the coming of the kingdom of God resonated strongly with the earlier voices as well as with the Essenes. Jesus' message, however, stressed a future not on earth during people's lifetimes, but in heaven after their deaths. In this he differed from most Jewish beliefs of his time. In addition to his preaching, according to Biblical accounts Jesus also performed exorcisms and miracles, fed multitudes of people, cured the blind and lame among his followers, and even brought the dead back to life. He pursued his unorthodox search for truth in the Galilee, the beautiful and lush northern region of Judea, only recently converted to Judaism. There he continued his preaching, angering both the Roman imperial government, which feared the revolutionary potential of his rabble-rousing, and the Jewish religious establishment, which viewed him as a heretic. Jesus said that he had come "not to abolish the Jewish law but to fulfill it," and his followers accepted much of the moral code of Jewish teachings. But they

Palestine at the time of Jesus. Christianity first emerged as a sect within Judaism when Roman control of Palestine was increasing. Shortly before Jesus' birth, Rome had granted Herod the Great the Kingdom of Judea as a client ruler. Upon his death in 4 B.C.E. the kingdom was divided among his sons, and Judea itself came under direct Roman military rule.

10.1

10.2 How did Christianity emerge and evolve?

10.3

10.1

10.2 How did Christianity emerge and evolve?

10.3

rejected most parts of its legal and separatist covenant. Beginning in a few towns at the eastern end of the Mediterranean Sea, Jesus' followers built an entirely new organizational structure for sustaining and spreading their new faith.

Jesus' followers—mostly common people—revered him as one specially chosen and anointed by God (*Messiah* in Hebrew, *Christos* in Greek). They proclaimed Jesus to be the source of eternal life and accepted him as a miracle worker and the son of God. They believed, according to the Biblical accounts, that his birth had been a miracle, that he had been conceived by the Holy Spirit of God and born to Mary, who was a virgin.

As Jesus' fame spread, the fears of the Jewish religious authorities and the Roman colonial administrators increased. To prevent any potential rebellion, the Roman government seized him when he once again returned to Jerusalem to preach and to celebrate the Passover, and executed him by crucifixion when he was 33 years old.

But death did not stop Jesus' message. His followers believed that he arose from the grave in a miraculous resurrection and triumph over death, and ascended to heaven to join God the Father. Their belief contained equal measures of admiration for his message of compassion and salvation and for his ability to perform miracles. Jesus' disciples took his message of compassion, salvation, and eternal life to Rome. The proud upper classes of Rome scoffed at first, but more and more of the simple people believed. Despite early persecution under several Roman emperors, Christianity increased in influence, until, in the fourth century, it became the official religion of the empire.

Spread through the networks of the empire, the Christian Church ultimately became the most important organizing force in post-Roman Europe. The message of Christianity and the organization of the Church expanded throughout the world. Today more than two billion people, one-third of the world's population, distributed among numerous different churches and denominations, declare themselves followers of Jesus, the simple preacher from Judea.

Jesus' Life, Teachings, and Disciples

Whatever the reality of the miracles associated with Jesus, clearly a new religion, Christianity, emerged from earlier Jewish roots, and, in this process, a number of adaptations and innovations took place.

Adapting Rituals to New Purposes. As we have seen, newly forming religions often adapt rituals and philosophies from existing religions, as, for example, Buddhism adapted the concept of *dharma* from Hinduism. This borrowing and adaptation can be attractive to members of the existing religion who wish to join the new one, for it assures them that their spiritual customs will be maintained. At the same time, a new interpretation gives the ritual a new meaning for the new faith. Jesus' form of prayer and much of his preaching were fully in accord with Jewish tradition. When he accepted baptism from the desert preacher John the Baptist,

Silver crucifix from Birka, Sweden, c. 900 C.E. The cross—signifying Christ's crucifixion—was adopted by Christians as a symbol of their faith as early as the second century. Making "the sign of the cross" was believed to be powerful in warding off evil, and, in later centuries, crusaders were said to "take the cross" when they set off on crusade (a word itself derived from the Latin for cross, *crux*). (Historiska Museet, Stockholm)

HOW DO WE KNOW?

The Search for the Historical Jesus

The only records of Jesus' life are the four Gospels, "the good news accounts," the first four books of the New Testament, which is the second section of the Christian Bible. Named for their authors—Matthew, Mark, Luke, and John—the Gospels are neither unbiased nor contemporary. Mark, probably the oldest of the four, dates to 70 C.E., some 40 years after Jesus' death. As with the early literature of Hinduism, Buddhism, and Judaism, the Gospels represent written recordings of oral traditions. They bring together traditions surrounding Jesus' life as they were transmitted among his followers. Although individual names are associated with them, the actual authors of the Gospels are unknown. Mark, for example, was the most common name in the Roman Empire at the time. Moreover, it appears that they were written for different audiences and therefore tell their stories somewhat differently. Mark, for example, addressed his beliefs in a future life to Christians who were being persecuted in Rome.

Fifty-two additional texts, called by scholars the Gnostic gospels, were discovered near the town of Nag Hammadi in upper Egypt in 1945, and have been subject to intense study ever since. Scholars believe that these texts were transcribed at about the same time as the four Gospels of the Christian Bible, but that they contain accounts of Jesus' teachings that were inconsistent with them and that they were therefore banned by Church leaders and hidden away.

According to the most important of the Gnostic gospels, the Secret Gospel of Thomas, Jesus taught that each individual could find the light of God within himself, or herself, without the necessity of belief in Jesus. "The kingdom is inside of you, and it is outside of you. When you come to know yourselves, then you will become known, and you will realize that it is you who are the sons of the living father". The search for meaning is most important: "Jesus said, 'Let him who seeks continue seeking until he finds. When he finds, he will become troubled. When he becomes troubled he will be astonished, and he will rule over all.'"

The Gnostic gospels also give a greater place to women in the search for religious truth, and they suggest that Jesus had some measure of physical relationship with Mary Magdalene, a prostitute whom he brought back to respectable society. These somewhat mystical gospels, with their message of a greater sexuality for Jesus, were suppressed as heresy in the wake of theological struggles within the Church in the late second century C.E.

The four Biblical Gospels themselves also present additional problems for historical analysis. They begin with the story of the birth of Jesus told as a miracle. According to the Gospels, Jesus was the son of God, born miraculously through Mary, a virgin betrothed to Joseph, a carpenter from Nazareth in the region of the Galilee. Believers certainly accept such an account, but it is not subject to historical verification. Moreover, despite the Gospels' accounts of Jesus' multitudes of followers, and his political and religious influence, neither Roman nor Jewish records of the time take note of his life or his teachings. Tacitus, although scornful of the early Christians, does take note of Jesus' death.

Modern scholars who have attempted to reconstruct the life of Jesus have reached very different conclusions about his essential character, depicting Jesus as political revolutionary, magician, Galilean charismatic, Galilean rabbi, proto-Pharisee, Essene, prophet of the end of days, exorcist, miracle worker, and marginal Jew. All the research, however, no matter how scholarly and how inventive, remains inconclusive. The four Biblical Gospels, despite their richness as religious teachings, have serious shortcomings as religious texts, and the historical validity of the Gnostic gospels is clouded by their official suppression.

- What are the shortcomings of the Gospels as historical texts for understanding the life of Jesus? What are their strengths?
- Historians attempting to characterize the life of Jesus have reached very different conclusions. What kinds of sources do you think they used?
- If the Gnostic gospels had not been suppressed by powerful theologians, do you think the Church might have developed differently? If so, how? If not, why not?

---

however, Jesus prepared the way for adapting an existing practice and giving it new meaning for his followers. A minor practice within Judaism, baptism would later become in Christianity a central **sacrament** of purification enjoined on all members.

Another example of adaptation is Jesus' "last supper," a Passover ritual meal. Jesus ate unleavened, flat bread as a symbol of slavery in Egypt, and he drank the wine that accompanies all Jewish festivals as a symbol of joy. Then he offered the bread and wine also to his disciples with the words, "This is my body ... this is my blood." Thus he transformed the foods of the Passover meal into the **Eucharist**, or Holy Communion, another central sacrament, a mystery through which Christians believe the invisible Christ grants communion to them.

Overturning the Old Order. In his teachings, Jesus also addressed political and social issues, staking out his own often ambiguous positions in relationship to the different and competing philosophies of the day. When Jesus, following John the Baptist, taught, "Repent; for the kingdom of heaven has come near" (Matthew 4:17), he was

KEY TERMS

sacrament In Christian theology, a rite or ritual that is an outward sign of a spiritual grace conveyed on the believer by Christ through the ministry of the Church.

Eucharist From the Greek *eucharistia*, "thanksgiving." The central sacrament and act of worship of the Catholic Church, culminating in Holy Communion, the eating of a sanctified wafer and drinking of sanctified wine as a reminder of Jesus' life, and, in Roman Catholicism, representing the actual act of partaking in his body and blood.

SOURCE

The Beatitudes from the Sermon on the Mount

Jesus' teaching—powerful in direct address, in parable, and in allegory—established his identification with the poor and oppressed, his disdain for the Roman authorities, and his scorn for the Jewish religious leadership of his time. He sounded much like a latter-day Jewish prophet calling his people to reform. The Beatitudes, a list of promises of God's rewards for the simple, righteous people, the first of Jesus' great sermons recorded in the New Testament, was delivered from the top of a hill in Galilee, northern Israel:

Blessed are the poor in spirit, for theirs is the kingdom of heaven.
Blessed are those who mourn, for they will be comforted.
Blessed are the meek, for they will inherit the earth.
Blessed are those who hunger and thirst for righteousness, for they will be filled.
Blessed are the merciful, for they will receive mercy.
Blessed are the poor in heart, for they will see God.
Blessed are the peacemakers, for they will be called children of God.
Blessed are those who are persecuted for righteousness' sake, for theirs is the kingdom of heaven. (Matthew 5:3–10)

10.1

10.2 How did Christianity

10.3 emerge and evolve?

not explicit in describing that kingdom or its date of arrival. But in metaphor and parable he preached that life as we know it on earth would soon change dramatically, or even come to an end.

Jesus' words must have been especially welcome to the poor, as he spoke repeatedly of the "Kingdom of Heaven" in which the tables would be turned:

> It will be hard for a rich person to enter the kingdom of heaven. Again I tell you, it is easier for a camel to go through the eye of a needle than for someone who is rich to enter the kingdom of God. (Matthew 19:23–24)

Jesus declared that the most important commandment was to "Love the Lord your God with all your heart, and with all your soul, and with all your mind," and the second was "Love your neighbor as yourself," both directly cited from the TaNaKh (Deuteronomy 6:7 and Leviticus 19:18). Indeed, he projected these principles into new dimensions, declaring "Love your enemies and pray for your persecutors" (Matthew 5:44). But he also warned that the coming apocalypse would be violent:

> Do not think that I have come to bring peace to earth; I have not come to bring peace, but a sword. (Matthew 10:34)

Jesus and the Jewish Establishment. The gospels depict Jesus' attitude toward Jewish law as ambivalent but often condescending, and his relationship toward the Jewish religious leadership as confrontational. He scoffed at Jewish dietary laws: "It is not what goes into the mouth that defiles a person, but it is what comes out of the mouth that defiles" (Matthew 15:11). He constantly tested the limits of Sabbath restrictions, declaring that: "The Sabbath is made for man, not man for the Sabbath" (Mark 2:27). He restricted divorce, announcing that: "If a man divorces his wife for any cause other than unchastity he involves her in adultery; and anyone who marries a divorced woman commits adultery" (Matthew 5:32). Many of his teachings may have reflected his desire to return to earlier beliefs in faith and spirituality and his belief that the future lay in heaven, not on earth.

Miracles and Resurrection. The gospels describe Jesus' ministry as filled with miracles—healing the sick, restoring sight to the blind, feeding multitudes of followers from just a few loaves and fishes, walking on water, calming storms, and even raising the dead. Reports of these miracles, perhaps even more than his ethical teachings, brought followers flocking to him. The gospel narrative of Jesus' suffering on the cross, presenting him at the final moment of his life as both human and divine in one personage, and, finally, his miraculous resurrection from the grave, his appearances

How did
Christianity
emerge and
evolve?

to his disciples, and his ascent to heaven, complete the miracle and the majesty of his life and embody his promise of eternal life for those who believe in his power.

The stories of Jesus' life and death, message and miracles, form the basis for Christianity, at first a new sect located within Judaism. Although different followers attributed more or less divinity and greater or lesser miracles to him, apparently all accepted Jesus as a new, reforming teacher. Many saw him as the long-awaited "Messiah," a messenger and savior specially anointed by God. His apostles, especially Paul of Tarsus (d. 67 C.E.), now refocused Jesus' message and built the Christian sect into a new, powerful religion. The apostles' preaching, organizational work, and letters to fledgling Christian communities fill most of the rest of the New Testament.

The Growth of the Early Church

At first, the followers of Jesus functioned as a sect within Judaism, continuing to meet in synagogues and to identify themselves as Jews. Peter, described in the Gospels as Jesus' chosen organizational leader, first took the Christian message outside the Jewish community (Acts 10). Declaring circumcision unnecessary for membership, he welcomed gentiles (people who were not Jewish) into the new Church. James, Jesus' brother and leader of the Christian community of Jerusalem, abrogated most of the Jewish dietary laws for the new community (Acts 15). These apostles believed that the rigorous ritual laws of Judaism inhibited the spread of its ethical message. Instead, they chose to emphasize the miraculous powers of Jesus and his followers. They spoke little of their master's views on the coming apocalypse but stressed his statements on the importance of love and redemption.

Paul Organizes the Early Church. Tensions continued to simmer between mainstream Jewish leaders and the early Christians. One of the fiercest opponents of the new sect was Saul from the Anatolian town of Tarsus. Saul was traveling to confront the Christian community in Damascus when he experienced an overpowering mystical vision of Jesus that literally knocked him to the ground. Reversing his previous position, Saul now affirmed his belief in the authenticity of Jesus as the divine Son of God. In speaking within the Jewish community, he had preferred his Hebrew name, Saul. Now, as he took his new message to gentiles, he preferred his Roman name, Paul. Jewish by ethnicity and early religious choice, Roman by citizenship, and Greek by culture, Paul was ideally placed to refine and explicate Jesus' message. He became the second founder of Christianity and dedicated himself to establishing it as an independent, organized religion.

To link the flourishing, but separate, Christian communities, Paul undertook three missionary voyages in the eastern Mediterranean, and he kept in continuous communication through a series of letters, Paul's "Epistles" of the New Testament. He advised the leadership emerging within each local church organization: the *presbyters*, or elders; the deacons above them; and, at the head, the bishop. He promised eternal life to those who believed in Jesus' power. He declared Jewish ritual laws an obstacle to spiritual progress (Galatians 5:2–6). Neither membership in a chosen family nor observance of laws or rituals was necessary in the new religion. Paul proclaimed a new equality in Christianity:

> There is no longer Jew or Greek, there is no longer slave or free, there is no longer male or female; for all of you are one in Christ Jesus. (Galatians 3:28)

Paul formulated a new concept of "**original sin**" and redemption from it. Jews had accepted the story told in Genesis of Adam and Eve's disobedience in the Garden of Eden as a mythical explanation of some of life's harsh realities: the pain of childbirth, the struggle to earn a living, the dangers of wild beasts, and, most of all, human mortality. Paul now proclaimed that Adam and Eve's "original sin" could be forgiven. Humanity could, in a sense, return to paradise and eternal life. Jesus' death on the

KEY TERMS

presbyter In early Christian usage, a member of the governing body of a church.

original sin First understood as the disobedience of Adam and Eve in the Garden of Eden as they ate the forbidden fruit of the Tree of Knowledge. Later understood as the sexual relations between Adam and Eve. In Christian belief, Jesus' death atoned for these sins—for those who believed in him.

cross atoned for original sin. According to Paul, those who believed in Jesus and accepted membership in the new Christian community would be forgiven by God and "saved." Although they would still be mortal, at the end of their earthly lives they would inherit a life in heaven, and, much later, would even be reborn on earth (Romans 5–6).

The Christian Calendar. Like other religions, Christianity established a sacred calendar. People had long celebrated the winter solstice; in the fourth century Christians fixed the observance of Jesus' birth, Christmas, at that time of year, although no one knew the actual date of his birth. Good Friday, at about the time of Passover, mourned Jesus' crucifixion and death; three days later his resurrection was celebrated in the joyous festival of Easter. Corresponding to the Jewish holiday of Pentecost, the anniversary of receiving the Ten Commandments 50 days after the Passover, Christianity introduced its own holiday of Pentecost. It commemorates the date when, according to Acts 2, the "Holy Spirit," the third element of the Trinity along with God the Father and Jesus the Son, filled Jesus' disciples and they "began to talk in other tongues, as the Spirit gave them power of utterance," enabling them to preach to the various peoples of the world. (Modern-day Christian Pentecostals "**speak in tongues**," praying and uttering praises ecstatically, healing through prayer and laying on of hands, and speaking of experiencing spiritual miracles.)

KEY TERM

speaking in tongues A mode of praying and preaching emphasizing ecstasy and even an entering into trances, such that the words of prayer and preaching may not be understood, but are meaningful nonetheless.

Paul's missionary journeys. Following Jesus' trial and crucifixion, about 29 C.E., his disciples, notably the Roman convert Paul, set out to convert non-Jews, or gentiles. Paul's journeys took him throughout the Greco-Roman east Mediterranean, and beyond. These journeys and the epistles Paul wrote began to weave struggling Christian groups into a new religious organization, the Christian Church. Paul died in Rome, apparently a martyr to the emperor Nero.

Over time, special saints' days were designated to mark the lives and deaths of people who helped to spread the new religion. The new Christian calendar, which has become the most widely used in the world, fixed its first year at the approximate date of Jesus' birth. The Jewish Sabbath, a weekly day of rest and reflection, was transferred from Saturday to Sunday.

Gender Relations. Jesus attracted many women as followers, and women led in the organization of several of the early churches. Paul welcomed them warmly and treated them respectfully at first, but women gradually lost their influence as Jesus' disciples institutionalized the Church. Although they taught spiritual equality, early Christians allowed gender and social inequalities to remain. Paul had proclaimed that in Jesus "There is no longer male or female," but he seemed to distrust sexual energies. Like Jesus, he was unmarried. He recommended celibacy and, for those unable to meet that standard, monogamous marriage as a means of sexual restraint:

MAJOR CHRISTIAN FESTIVALS	
January 6	Epiphany
February–March	Shrove Tuesday, or Mardi Gras (day before Ash Wednesday)
February–March	Ash Wednesday (first day of Lent)
February–April	Lent
February 2	Candlemas Day
March–April	Easter
March 25	Feast of Annunciation
April–June	Ascension (40 days after Easter)
May–June	Pentecost/Whit Sunday (50 days after Easter)
May–June	Trinity Sunday (Sunday after Pentecost)
November–December	Advent
December 24	Christmas Eve
December 25	Christmas Day

It is well for a man not to touch a woman. But because of cases of sexual immorality, each man should have his own wife and each woman her own husband. The husband should give to his wife her conjugal rights, and likewise the wife to her husband. (1 Corinthians 7:1–3)

Paul's discomfort with sexuality continued to haunt Christianity. One result was the decision, by about the sixth century, to proclaim marriage as one of the Church's seven sacraments. Marriage would no longer be a contract that a man and woman could enter—or leave—on their own, but a ritual performed by a priest, in the name of Jesus, binding the man and woman forever in an unbreakable bond. For people seeking greater sanctity through celibacy, Church leaders established hundreds of monasteries and convents throughout the Christian world hosting thousands of unmarried, celibate men and women dedicated to the mission of the Church (see below). Many clergy who were not monks, however, continued to marry. In 1139, the second Lateran Council (named for the Pope's Lateran Palace in Rome, where it convened) declared all clerical marriages not only unlawful but also invalid (MacCulloch, p. 373). Despite the protests of many priests, especially those who had married, and despite breaches in practice, the Council's decision prevailed as the law of the Church.

Paul moved to subordinate women, first at home:

I want you to understand that Christ is the head of every man, and the husband is the head of the wife … he is the image and reflection of God; but woman is the reflection of man. Indeed, man was not made from woman, but woman from man. Neither was man created for the sake of woman, but woman for the sake of man. (1 Corinthians 11:3–9)

Then in church:

Women should be silent in the churches. For they are not permitted to speak, but should be subordinate, as the law also says. If there is anything they desire to know, let them ask their husbands at home. (1 Corinthians 14:34–35)

Paul had also declared that spiritually "There is no longer slave or free," but in practice he accepted slavery, saying, "Slaves, obey your earthly masters with fear and

10.1

10.2

10.3

How did Christianity emerge and evolve?

10.1

10.2

10.3

How did
Christianity
emerge and
evolve?

trembling." He did urge masters to be kind to slaves and to "stop threatening them for you know that both of you have the same Master in heaven, and with him there is no partiality" (Ephesians 6:5–9). These contrasting statements would later be invoked to justify both Christian approval and disapproval for the institution of slavery (see the chapter entitled "Political Revolutions in Europe and the Americas").

From Persecution to Triumph

Having established the central doctrines of the new religion and stabilized its core communities, both Peter and Paul moved to expand its geographical scope. They saw Rome as the capital of empire and the center of the international communication network of the time, and they traveled there to preach and teach. Tradition holds that both were martyred there in the persecutions of the emperor Nero, about 67 C.E., and that both are entombed and enshrined there.

In this capital of empire, Christianity appeared as one of several mystery religions, all of which were based on beliefs in supernatural beings. They included the religion of Mithra, a Persian sun god; Demeter, a Greek goddess; YHWH, the god of the Jews; and an eclectic mixture of beliefs called Gnosticism. Romans seemed to be in search of a more inspiring, otherworldly faith than paganism provided, but at the time of the deaths of Peter and Paul, Christianity was still a relatively weak force.

The first Christians, Jews by nationality, were scorned as provincial foreigners. Some Roman authorities thought that Christian beliefs in resurrection and an afterlife undermined pride in citizenship and willingness to serve in the army. About the year 100, the historian Tacitus wrote of:

> a class of persons hated for their vices whom the crowd called Christians. Christus, after whom they were named, had undergone the death penalty in the reign of Tiberius, by sentence of the procurator Pontius Pilate, and the pernicious superstition was checked for a moment only to break out once more, not only in Judaea, the home of the disease, but in the Capital itself, where everything horrible or shameful in the world gathers and becomes fashionable. (Tacitus, *Annals* XV:44)

Paradoxically, because they refused to worship the emperor or to take oaths in his name, official Rome viewed Christians as atheists. Their emphasis on otherworldly salvation and their strong internal organization were seen as threats to the state's authority. Roman leaders also mocked the sacrament of the Eucharist, in which Christians consumed consecrated wafers and wine as the body and blood of Christ, as a sign of cannibalism. Official treatment of Christianity was erratic but often marked by severe persecution. Nero (r. 54–68) scapegoated the Christians, blaming them for the great fire in 64, apparently executing both Peter and Paul among his victims, and sending hundreds of Christians to die in public gladiatorial contests and by burning. Edicts of persecution were issued by emperors Antoninus Pius (r. 138–61), Marcus Aurelius (r. 161–80), Septimius Severus (r. 193–211), Decius (r. 249–51), and Diocletian (r. 284–305). In 257 Emperor Valerian (r. 253–60) was prepared to launch a major persecution of Christians, but he was captured in battle by Persians. In these early years of persecution, thousands of Christians suffered martyrdom.

Despite the scorn and the persecution, Christianity continued to grow. Its key doctrines and texts were written, edited, and approved by leaders in the network of Christian churches. After years of debate, Christian leaders and scholars agreed on the contents of the New Testament by about the year 200, and by 250 the city of Rome alone held about 50,000 Christians among its million inhabitants. Most were of the lower classes, attracted by Jesus' message to the poor, but middle- and upper-class Romans had also joined. In particular, Christianity proved attractive to the wives of Roman leaders, who often contributed to their husbands' conversions. By the reign of Constantine, estimates reported that one out of ten inhabitants of the Roman Empire was Christian.

HOW DO WE KNOW?

Explanations for the Spread of Christianity

Many historians of our own time accept the thrust of Gibbon's explanations (see below), but tend to emphasize more the importance of community within the Church.

"From the outset, the major goal of the Jesus movement was to call into existence a new kind of inclusive community that might arch over all the ordinary human distinctions of race and religion," writes Howard Clark Kee (1991, p. 2). Kee analyzes five different kinds of community that were active in the Roman world during the first two centuries of the Christian era, and suggests that Christianity developed an appeal to each of them: The community of the wise, seeking special knowledge of the future; the community of the law-abiding, seeking appropriate rules of guidance in the present; the community where God dwells among his people, seeking assurance that it was specially selected and cared for; the community of mystical participation, influenced by the mystery religions of the time; and the ethnically and culturally inclusive community, outsiders seeking a place of belonging. Different aspects of the Christian message, developed by different Church leaders, spoke to each of these communities and succeeded in drawing them in.

The historical sociologist Michael Mann cites the psychological and practical rewards of the growing Christian "ecumene," the worldwide community of the Church, with its comprehensive philosophy for living and organizing. Although much of Christianity's message targeted the poor, Mann notes that the religion also drew a large following of urban artisans, whom the aristocratic Roman Empire devalued. Excluded from political power, these working-class people were in search of a comprehensive and welcoming community. They wanted to recreate an earlier, simpler, more participatory era, and they became Christians. As imperial power became increasingly centralized, remote, insensitive, and, later, unstable, "In many ways Christianity represented how Rome liked to idealize its republican past" (Mann, p. 325).

- Jesus and St. Paul promised life after death to Christians. Do Kee and Mann cite this as a reason for Christianity's success in winning new adherents? If so, what terms do they use to indicate this promise? If not, why do you think they omit it?
- Gibbon suggests that a large part of early Christianity's appeal was the miracles that Christ and his disciples were said to have performed. Kee and Mann do not emphasize miracles. Why?
- Both Kee and Mann suggest that different groups were attracted to Christianity for different reasons. Based on what you know of people's motivations for joining religious groups, with which of their reasons would you agree? Disagree?

The Conversion of Constantine. In 313, Emperor Constantine (r. 306–37) had a vision in which a cross and the words *in hoc signo vinces*, "in this sign you will be victorious," appeared to him the night before he won the critical battle that made him sole emperor in the Western Empire. He immediately declared Christianity legal. He funded Christian leaders and their construction of churches, while withdrawing official support from the pagan churches, making Christianity the *de facto* official religion of the Roman Empire. On a personal level, Constantine encouraged his mother, Helena, to embrace Christianity, which she did enthusiastically. Helena had churches built in Asia Minor and the Holy Land, and traveled to Jerusalem seeking the cross on which Jesus died. After her death, she was canonized as a saint in the Catholic Church.

As emperor, Constantine took a leading part in Church affairs. He sponsored the Council of Nicaea in 325, the largest assembly of bishops of local Christian churches up to that time. He convened the council primarily to establish the central theological doctrines of Christianity, but it also established a Church organization for the Roman Empire, a network of urban bishoprics grouped into provinces, with each province headed by the chief bishop of its largest city. In 337, on his deathbed, Constantine accepted baptism.

In 392, Emperor Theodosius I (r. 379–95) declared Christianity to be the official religion of the Roman Empire. He outlawed the worship of the traditional Roman gods and severely restricted Judaism, initiating centuries of bitter Christian persecution of both traditions.

How Had Christianity Succeeded? How had Christianity, once scorned and persecuted, achieved such power? Christian believers attributed the success to divine

10.1

10.2

How did Christianity emerge and evolve?

10.3

10.1

10.2

10.3

How did
Christianity
emerge and
evolve?

assistance. Historians seek more earthly explanations. Let us consider one of the major historians to tackle the topic, Edward Gibbon (1737–94).

In 1776, Gibbon began the publication of his six-volume masterpiece, *The History of the Decline and Fall of the Roman Empire*. A child of the Enlightenment philosophy of his time, which rejected supernatural explanations (see the chapter "Migration"), Gibbon rather sarcastically presented five reasons for Christianity's victories. But beneath his sarcasm Gibbon revealed the profound strengths of the new religion:

- Its "inflexible and intolerant" zeal, derived from its Jewish roots.
- Its promise of resurrection and a future life for believers, soon augmented by the threat of eternal damnation for nonbelievers.
- Its assertion of miraculous accomplishments.
- The austere morals of the first Christians. The Christian search for spiritual perfection, a monogamous sexual code, the rejection of worldly honor, and a general emphasis on equality attracted many converts. In the extreme case, martyrdom won admiration, sympathy, and followers. Later commentators noted that the simplicity and self-sacrifice of the early Christians reminded some Romans of the ideals of the early Republic.
- The Church gradually generated a state within a state through the decentralized leadership of its local bishops and *presbyters*, the structure Paul had begun to knit together. As imperial structures weakened, Christianity provided an alternative community. This Christian community distributed philanthropy to needy people, Christian and non-Christian alike. It also publicized its message effectively—in Greek, the language of the eastern part of the empire.

Many later commentators noted that the Christian community included a local church in which to share the joys and sorrows of everyday life, celebrate life-cycle events, and commemorate major events in the history of the group. At the same time it provided membership in a universal Church that extended to the entire known world, and suggested participation in a life that transcended earthly concerns altogether.

Doctrine: Definition and Dispute

As it grew after receiving official recognition, institutional Christianity refined its theology. The most influential theologian of the period, St. Augustine (354–430), bishop of Hippo in North Africa, wrote *The City of God* to explain Christianity's relationship to competing religions and philosophies, and to the Roman government with which it was increasingly intertwined.

Despite Christianity's designation as the official religion of the empire, Augustine declared its message to be spiritual rather than political. Christianity, he argued, should be concerned with the mystical, heavenly City of Jerusalem rather than with earthly politics. Although Augustine encouraged the Roman emperors to suppress certain religious groups, some elements of his theology supported the separation of Church and state.

Augustine built philosophical bridges to Platonic philosophy, the dominant system of the Hellenistic world of his time and place. Christianity envisioned Jesus, God's son, walking the earth and suffering for his people. He was, literally, very down-to-earth. God, the Father, had more transcendent characteristics, but they were less emphasized in Christian theology at the time. Plato (*c.* 428–348 B.C.E.) and later **Neoplatonic** philosophers, however, provided the model of a more exalted, more remote god, a god that was more accepted among the leading thinkers of Augustine's time. According to Augustine, Plato's god was:

the maker of all created things, the light by which things are known, and the good in reference to which things are to be done; … we have in him the first principle of nature, the truth of doctrines, and the happiness of life. (Augustine, p. 253)

KEY TERMS

Neoplatonic A philosophical system founded by Plotinus (205–70 C.E.) and influenced by Plato's theory of ideas. It emphasizes the transcendent, impersonal, and indefinable "One" as the ground of all existence and the source of an eternal world of goodness, beauty, and order, of which material existence is but a feeble copy.

heresy A belief that is not in agreement with, or that even conflicts with, the official orthodoxy of its time and place. Heretics, those who espoused heresy, were often persecuted.

In addition, Plato's god existed in the soul of every person, perhaps a borrowing from Hinduism (see chapter "Hinduism and Buddhism").

Augustine married these Platonic and Neoplatonic views to the transcendent characteristics of God in Christian theology. This provided Christianity with a new intellectual respectability, which attracted new audiences in the vast Hellenistic world. He also encouraged contemplation and meditation within Christianity, an important element in the monastic life that was beginning to emerge among Christians (as it had among Buddhists). Augustine himself organized a community of monks in Tegaste (now Souk-Ahras), the city of his birth.

In his earlier *Confessions* (c. 400), Augustine had written of his personal life of relatively mild sin before his conversion to Christianity. Now he warned Christians that Adam and Eve's willfulness had led to original sin; sin had unlocked the forces of lust, turning the flesh against the spirit; and lust had called forth a death sentence on all humans in place of the immortality originally intended for them:

> As soon as our first parents had transgressed the commandment, divine grace forsook them, and they were confounded at their own wickedness ... They experienced a new motion of their flesh which had become disobedient to them, in strict retribution of their own disobedience to God ... Then began the flesh to lust against the Spirit ... And thus, from the bad use of free will, there originated the whole train of evil ... on to the destruction of the second death, which has no end, those only being excepted who are freed by the grace of God. (Augustine *City of God*, pp. 422–23)

For Augustine as for Paul, and thus for early Christianity, sexuality was perilous and woman suspect. In early Christian theology, profane flesh and divine spirit confronted each other uneasily.

Augustine also believed that Christians should subordinate their will and reason to the teachings and authority of the Church. Although it is usually associated with the development of Protestant religions much later, the idea of predestination—that is, that individuals could do nothing through their own actions to obtain salvation and entrance to heaven—dominated Augustine's theology. Some Christian theologians, such as Pelagius (c. 354–after 418), rejected Augustine's argument about original sin and taught that human beings could choose between good and evil to determine their own fate. They feared that the growing acceptance of Augustine's beliefs would devalue both public service for the poor and private initiative by less disciplined Christians. Ultimately, Augustine's views prevailed, and popes at the time labeled those of Pelagius **heresy**.

Battles over Dogma. Some theological disputes led to violence, especially as the Church attempted to suppress doctrinal disagreement. The most divisive dispute concerned the nature of the divinity of Jesus. The theologian Arius (c. 250–336) taught that Christ's humanity limited his divinity, and that God the Father, wholly transcendent, was more sacred than the son who had walked the earth. The Council of Nicaea, which Constantine convened in 325 to resolve this dispute, issued an official statement of creed affirming Jesus' complete divinity and his indivisibility from God. The Arian controversy continued, however, especially on the fringes of empire, where Arian missionaries converted many of the Gothic tribes to their own beliefs. Wars between the new Arian converts and the Roman Church ensued, until finally Arianism was defeated in armed battle. Of these struggles,

St. Augustine, Piero della Francesca, 1454–69. Augustine emphasized spiritual rather than worldly issues, encouraged contemplation and meditation, and incorporated Platonic and Neoplatonic concepts of a transcendent god into Christianity. Piero della Francesca's painting captures the austerity and dedication of the saint himself along with the sumptuous and colorful robes he wears, in his capacity as Bishop of Hippo, depicting scenes relating to the life of Jesus. (National Museum of Ancient Art, Lisbon)

10.1

10.2

10.3

How did Christianity emerge and evolve?

How did
Christianity
emerge and
evolve?

the historian Ammianus Marcellinus (*c.* 330– 95) wrote: "No wild beasts are such enemies to mankind as are most of the Christians in the deadly hatred they feel for one another."

In the eastern Mediterranean, too, bitter and violent conflicts broke out among rival Christian theological factions, again over the precise balance between Jesus' divinity and his humanity. Persecution of dissidents by the Orthodox Church in Carthage, Syria, and Egypt was so severe that the arrival in the seventh century of

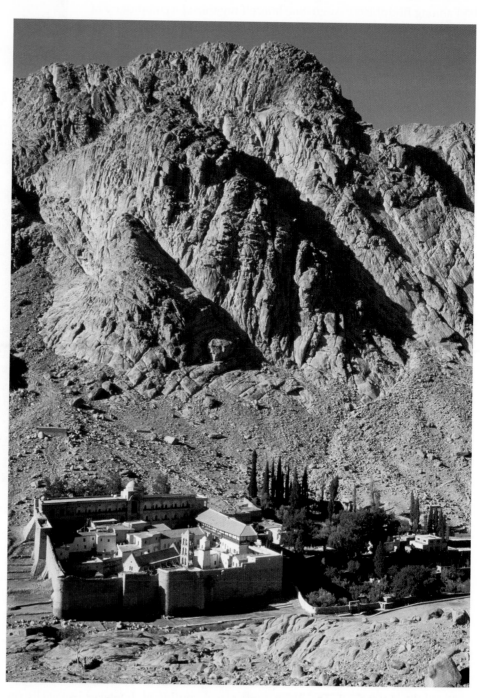

Monastery of St. Catherine, Mount Sinai, 557 c.e. According to the Torah, Moses received the tablets of the law from God on Mount Sinai. For this reason the Byzantine emperor Justinian I (r. 527–65) chose to found the monastery of St. Catherine in the place believed to be the Biblical Mount Sinai. The remote beauty of the place also made it ideal for spiritual meditation.

Muslim rule, which treated all the Christian sects equally, was often welcomed as a respite from the struggles.

By the sixth century, Christians far surpassed Jews in numbers, geographical spread, power, and influence. Christian missionaries continued their attempts to convert Jews, often by coercion. In 576, for example, a Gallic bishop gave the Jews of his city the choice between baptism and expulsion, a pattern that was repeated periodically, although Jews had not yet immigrated into Western Europe in large numbers.

Christianity in the Wake of Empire

10.3   What was the role of Christianity in the Roman Empire?

Christianity spread to Western and northern Europe along the communication and transportation networks of the Roman Empire. Born in Judea under Roman occupation, Christianity now spread throughout the empire, spoke its languages of Greek and Latin, preached the gospel along its trade routes, and constructed church communities in its cities. Thanks to official recognition and patronage, the Church grew steadily. As the Roman imperial government weakened, it enlisted the now official Church as a kind of department of state. While the empire weakened and dissolved, Christianity emerged and flourished.

📖 **Read** the **Document**: Perpetua, *The Autobiography of a Christian Martyr* on **MyHistoryLab**

The Conversion of the Barbarians

During the first millennium C.E., bishops in the Western Church came "from the ranks of the senatorial governing class ... they stood for continuity of the old Roman values ... The eventual conversion of the barbarian leaders was due to their influence" (Matthew, p. 21). "None of the major Germanic peoples who entered the Roman provinces in the fourth and fifth centuries remained pagan for more than a generation after they crossed the frontier" (Mann, p. 335). About 496, Clovis, chief of the Merovingian Franks, rejected Arianism and converted to Roman Christianity, the first barbarian to accept the religion of the empire. He established his capital in Paris and had thousands of his tribesmen converted, for, in general, followers accepted the religion of their leader. Clovis' acceptance of Christianity brought him the support of the Roman ecclesiastical hierarchy, including the pope, and insured the triumph of this version of Christianity in Gaul.

Decentralized Power and Monastic Life

In Western Europe, Christianity developed a multitude of local institutions. Churches, monasteries, and convents were established, and leadership was decentralized. In regions that lacked organized government and administration, local Church leaders and institutions provided whatever existed of order, administration, and a sense of larger community. For several centuries, "Christendom was dominated by thousands of dedicated unmarried men and women" (McManners, p. 89), living in monasteries throughout the Christian world. Missionary activity continued enthusiastically, but now turned northward toward the Vikings and the Slavs, as other geographical doors had been forcibly shut by the victorious Muslim armies emerging from Arabia.

Pope Gregory I (r. 590–604) saw the usefulness of the monasteries and monks in converting and disciplining the barbarians, and he began to encourage the monastic movement. By the year 600 there were about 200 monasteries in Gaul alone, and the

Icon of Mary, Jesus, and SS. Theodore and George, St. Catherine's Monastery, Mount Sinai, sixth to seventh century C.E. The dispute over the use of icons in worship divided the Eastern Orthodox Church for more than a century, 726–843, between iconoclasts who wanted them banned and iconodules who continued to venerate them.

10.1

10.2

10.3 What was the role of Christianity in the Roman Empire?

first missionaries dispatched by Rome arrived in England *c.* 597. By 700 much of England had been converted. In the ninth, tenth, and eleventh centuries, missionary activity was directed toward the "Northmen," the Vikings from Scandinavia, who raided and traded for goods and slaves from North America and Greenland, through the North Sea and the Baltic, down the Volga River, across the Caspian Sea, and on as far as Baghdad. The Vikings came into the Christian fold with only a tenuous link to Rome and a strong admixture of pagan ritual.

Although the pope in Rome had nominal authority over Christian affairs in the West, the Church's power was, in fact, fragmented and decentralized between 500 and 1000. Christianity spread in urban areas through its bishops in their large churches. In rural and remote areas, monks, acting as missionaries, carried the message.

Monasteries, which were small, isolated communities, each under the local control of a single abbot, modeled the spirituality and simplicity of the earliest Christian communities. Because sexual activity was ruled out, monasticism became as accessible to women in convents as to men in monasteries, and was equally valued by both. Many monasteries contained both men and women, each living in celibacy.

The most famous of the early monastics, St. Benedict (*c.* 480–547), founded a monastery at Monte Cassino, about 100 miles southeast of Rome. The writings of Pope Gregory I give us the most detailed information on the life, regulations, and discipline of that exemplary institution, although each monastery had its own variations in administration and practice.

Through a variety of educational institutions, the churches, monasteries, convents, and bishops kept Rome's culture alive in northern and Western Europe. In much of rural Western Europe, local authorities valued the monks not just as the only literate people in the region but also as the most capable in administering land and agriculture. These authorities also sought an alliance with the prestige and power of the Church. They granted land and administrative powers to nearby monasteries, transforming them into important local economic forces. (Compare the administrative roles of Hindu priests and Buddhist monks in south and Southeast Asia in the chapter entitled "Hinduism and Buddhism.") Monks became courtiers and bishops as well as missionaries as they expanded the geographic, social, and economic dimensions of the Church. Until the Fourth Lateran Council (1216) under Pope Innocent III (r. 1198–1216), monasteries could form and dissolve at local initiatives, so we have no record of their exact numbers in the early centuries.

A history of the very decentralized Church of this time would have to be written from the bottom up. The Church in the West was decentralized partly because the Roman Empire was decentralized, having lost its administrative power. There was no longer an emperor in Rome. The Church and what was left of the government in Western Europe groped toward a new mutual relationship.

Read the **Document: Rule of St. Benedict (6th c.) by St. Benedict of Nursia** on **MyHistoryLab**

The Church Divides into East and West

In the far more literate and sophisticated Byzantine Empire, political leaders did not relinquish their power to Church authorities. Indeed, the emperor at Constantinople served as administrative head of the Church, a pattern that had been set by Constantine when he presided over the Council of Nicaea, outside Constantinople.

Today, Eastern Orthodoxy and Roman Catholicism share the same fundamental faith and scripture and maintain official communication with each other, but they developed many historic differences over Church organization, authority, and language. Doctrinally, at the Council of Chalcedon (451) both Eastern Orthodoxy and the Roman Church accepted the belief that Jesus was simultaneously an historical person and one with God. Organizationally, however, the Eastern Church remained far more urban. The West had so few roads and so little trade that it was held together

10.1
10.2
10.3

What was
the role of
Christianity in the
Roman Empire?

Icon of the "Triumph of Orthodoxy," Constantinople, late fourteenth/early fifteenth century C.E. In 843 the Empress Theodora restored the use of icons, an event that is still celebrated in the Eastern Church on the first Sunday in Lent. (British Museum, London)

KEY TERM

see The geographical home of a Church authority: the Vatican in Roman Catholicism, four separate locations for the Eastern Christian churches.

organizationally by its military and ecclesiastical strongholds. The Council of Chalcedon recognized four centers of Church organization, or *sees*, in the East—Antioch, Jerusalem, Alexandria, and Constantinople—with Constantinople predominating and having the same leadership role in the East as Rome had in the West. Rome, once one of

The spread of Christianity. The disciples and early missionaries established Christian communities in southwestern Asia, Greece, Italy, North Africa, and India. On the other hand, Roman persecution, the decline of western Rome, and the rise of Islam hindered its dissemination. The Orthodox Church of Constantinople converted eastern Europe, penetrating Russia; Rome became reestablished as a powerful center; and Celtic missionaries traveled throughout northwest Europe.

What was the role of Christianity in the Roman Empire?

the patriarchates, and the only one in the West, was now deemed an entirely separate administrative center, still under its own emperor and with its own bishop.

The Split Between Rome and Constantinople. Rome and Byzantium have remained divided over the authority of the bishop of Rome to the present. From the sixth century, he has claimed to be pope, *papa*, father of the (Roman) Catholic Church and the direct organizational successor of the apostle Peter. Eastern Orthodox Christianity, however, has never recognized the pope's claim to preeminent authority, accepting as their principal authority the patriarch or bishop of Constantinople. Also, unlike the Roman practice, all but the highest clergy in Eastern Orthodoxy are permitted to marry, so here again the two clergies have not accepted each other's authority. The language of Rome is Latin, while the East uses Greek and the various Slavic languages of eastern Europe.

When Leo IX became pope in 1048, he aimed to expand his influence over all of Europe and sponsored the writing of a treatise that emphasized the pope's power. He sent one of his more zealous reformers to Constantinople to argue against the patriarch of Constantinople's claims to be independent of Rome's control. After failed negotiations, the reformer excommunicated the patriarch; in response, the patriarch excommunicated the reformer. Through this mutual rejection, called the Great Schism of 1054, the two Churches divided definitively into the Latin (later Roman Catholic) Church, which is predominant in Western Europe, and the Greek Orthodox Church, which prevails in the East. Friction between the two groups has waxed and waned over time, with the most direct confrontation coming in 1204, when crusaders dispatched by Rome to fight against Muslims in Jerusalem turned northward and sacked Constantinople instead.

New Areas Adopt Orthodox Christianity. As in the West, monastic life flourished in the Byzantine Empire, with exemplary institutions at remote, starkly beautiful sites such as Mount Sinai and Mount Athos. The greatest missionary activity of the Orthodox monks came later than in the West. Hemmed in by the Roman Church to the west and by the growing power of Islam to the east after about 650, Byzantium turned its missionary efforts northward, toward Russia. The brothers St. Cyril (*c.* 827–69) and St. Methodius (*c.* 825–84) translated the Bible into Slavonic, creating the Cyrillic alphabet in which to transcribe and publish it. When Russia embraced Orthodox Christianity in the tenth century, it also adopted this alphabet. In the late fifteenth century, after the fall of Constantinople to the Turks (1453), Moscow began to refer to itself as the "Third Rome," the spiritual and political heir to the Caesars and the Byzantine Empire.

In other regions of east-central Europe, Rome and Byzantium competed in spreading their religious and cultural messages and organizations. Rome won in Poland, Bohemia, Lithuania, and Ukraine; the Orthodox Church in Bulgaria, Romania, and Serbia. Other

Christ triumphing over evil, Frankish terra-cotta plaque, c. 500–750 C.E. It was not unusual for Western Europeans to represent Christ in contemporary local costume. Here, dressed as a member of the German warrior nobility, he treads the serpent, an emblem of the devil, underfoot. (Musée des Antiquités, St-Germain-en-Laye, France)

333

10.1

10.2

10.3 What was
the role of
Christianity in the
Roman Empire?

national Churches also grew up beyond Rome's jurisdiction, including the Coptic in Egypt, the Armenian, and the Ethiopian. They also asserted their independence from Constantinople, creating a pattern of distinct national Churches that the Protestant Reformation would later adopt.

Christianity in Western Europe

The abrupt, dramatic rise of Islam throughout the Middle East and into the Mediterranean, which we will examine in the next chapter, had an immediate and profound influence on Christianity. By the year 700, Muslim armies had conquered the eastern Mediterranean and the north coast of Africa, key regions of both Christianity and the former Roman Empire. The Muslim Umayyad dynasty pushed on into Spain and crossed the Pyrenees. Stopped in southern France by the Frankish ruler Charles Martel (c. 688–741) at the Battle of Tours in 732, the Umayyad forces withdrew to Spain. Muslim troops captured segments of the southern Italian peninsula, Sicily, and other Mediterranean islands. These Muslim conquests cut Christianity off geographically from the lands of its birth and early vigor. As a result, Christianity became primarily a religion of Europe, where many of its members were recently converted "barbarian" warrior nobles.

📖 Read the Document: **Social Conditions in the Ninth Century** on **MyHistoryLab**

The Pope Allies with the Franks. In Rome, the pope felt surrounded by the hostile powers of Constantinople and Islam to the east and south, and several Gothic kings to the north and west. Seeking alliances with strong men, he turned to a Frank, Charles (Carolus) Martel, who gave his name to the Carolingian family. As we have seen, Martel had repulsed the Muslims at Tours in 732. In 754 his son Pepin III (r. 751–68) answered the call of Pope Stephen II (r. 752–57) for help in fighting the Lombards, who were invading Italy and threatening the papal possessions. Pepin secured a swath of lands from Rome to Ravenna and turned them over to papal rule. In exchange, the pope anointed Pepin and his two sons, confirming the succession of the Carolingian family as the royal house ruling the Franks.

Charlemagne Revives the Idea of Empire. Pepin's son Charles ruled between 768 and 814, achieving the greatest recognition of his power when Pope Leo III (r. 795–816) crowned him Roman Emperor on Christmas Day, 800. In spite of this seeming unity of interests, Charles, who became known as Charles the Great or Charlemagne, rejected the title throughout most of his life and was often at odds with the various popes as he sought to expand an empire of his own. To achieve his goal, Charlemagne spent all his adult life in warfare, continuing the military expeditions of his father and grandfather. He reconquered the northeastern corner of Spain from its Muslim rulers, defeated the Lombard rulers of Italy and relieved their pressure on the pope, seized Bavaria and Bohemia, killed and looted the entire nobility of the Avars in Pannonia (modern Austria and Hungary), and subdued the German Saxon populations along the Elbe River after 33 years of warfare. Himself a German Frank, Charlemagne offered the German Saxons a choice of conversion to Christianity or death.

With Charlemagne's victories, the borders of his kingdom came to match the borders of the dominance of the Church of Rome, except for the British Isles, which he did not enter. The political capital of Western Europe passed from Rome to Charlemagne's

THE CAROLINGIAN DYNASTY

751	Pepin III "the Short" becomes King of the Franks
755	Franks drive Lombards out of central Italy; creation of Papal States
768–814	Charlemagne rules as King of the Franks
774	Charlemagne defeats Lombards in northern Italy
800	Pope Leo III crowns Charlemagne
814–40	Louis the Pious succeeds Charlemagne as "emperor"
843	Treaty of Verdun partitions the Carolingian Empire
870	Treaty of Mersen further divides Carolingian Empire
875–950	New invasions of Vikings, Muslims, and Magyars

SOURCE

Charlemagne and Harun-al-Rashid

Charlemagne spent his life fighting in the name of the pope and on behalf of Christianity. In 777 he invaded Muslim Spain, and by 801 he had captured Barcelona. (His campaigns in Spain gave rise to the epic poem *The Song of Roland* about the defeat of his rearguard in the pass of Roncesvalles. This became the most celebrated poem of medieval French chivalry.)

Yet Charlemagne carried on a valued diplomatic friendship with the most powerful Muslim ruler of his day, Harun-al-Rashid, Caliph of Baghdad (r. 786–809). Charlemagne's adviser, friend, and biographer Einhard (c. 770–840) describes the friendship:

> With Harun-al-Rachid [sic], King of the Persians, who held almost the whole of the East in fee, always excepting India, Charlemagne was on such friendly terms that Harun valued his goodwill more than the approval of all the other kings and princes in the entire world, and considered that he alone was worthy of being honoured and propitiated with gifts. When Charlemagne's messengers, whom he had sent with offerings to the most Holy Sepulchre of our Lord and Saviour and to the place of His resurrection, came to Harun and told him of their master's intention, he not only granted all that was asked but even went so far as to agree that this sacred scene of our redemption should be placed under Charlemagne's own jurisdiction. When the time came for these messengers to turn homewards, Harun sent some of his own men to accompany them and dispatched to Charlemagne costly gifts, which included robes, spices and other marvels of the lands of the Orient. A few years earlier Harun had sent Charlemagne the only elephant he possessed, simply because the Frankish King asked for it. (Einhard, p. 70)

Einhard does not note what gifts Charlemagne might have sent to Baghdad in return, nor does he comment on the political benefits of this interfaith diplomacy between the two great empires—empires that flanked, and confronted, the Byzantine Empire lying between them.

own palace in Aachen (Aix-la-Chapelle) in modern Germany. Although Charlemagne was barely literate, he established within this palace a center of learning that attracted Church scholars from throughout Europe, initiating what historians call the Carolingian Renaissance.

Charles persuaded the noted scholar Alcuin of York, England (*c.* 730–804), to come to Aachen as head of the palace school and as his own personal adviser. The goals of the school were Christian and basic: reading and writing of Biblical texts in Latin, chanting of prayers, knowledge of grammar and arithmetic. This training would prepare missionaries for their work among the peoples of northern Europe. Scribes at the school prepared copies of prayers and Biblical texts for the liturgical and scholarly needs of churches and scholars. In the process they created a new form of Latin script that forms the basis of the lower-case (small) letters we use today. Charlemagne also fostered the arts by bringing to his capital sculpture from Italy and by patronizing local artisans and craftspeople. Alcuin himself had the ear of the emperor, criticizing him for using force in converting the Saxons and convincing him not to repeat the practice by invading England.

Charlemagne's coronation challenged the authority of the Eastern emperor in Constantinople, but during the next years Charlemagne managed, through negotiation and warfare, to gain Constantinople's recognition of his title. There were once again two emperors, East and West.

The Attempt at Empire Fails. The Carolingian family remained powerful until about the end of the ninth century. But then they could no longer fight off the new invasions of the Western Christian world by Magyars (Hungarians), Norsemen, and Arabs. Regional administrators, emboldened by the weakness of the Carolingian emperor, began to act independently of his authority. Only after yet another century would militarily powerful leaders begin once again to cobble together loosely structured kingdoms in northwestern Europe. Meanwhile, political leadership in Europe was generally decentralized in rural manor estates controlled by local lords.

10.1

10.2

10.3

What was the role of Christianity in the Roman Empire?

Bronze and gilt statuette of Charlemagne, c. 860–70 C.E. Charlemagne's ceaseless warfare spread Christianity and Frankish rule across Western Europe, while repelling barbarian intruders and enemies of Rome. In 800 C.E. Pope Leo III showed his gratitude by crowning Charlemagne Roman Emperor. (Louvre, Paris)

Religious leadership in the cathedrals, churches, monasteries, and convents filled the gap, providing a greater sense of overall community and order. In this era, 600–1100 C.E., the Church gave Europe its fundamental character and order. The Magyar and Norse invaders, like the Germans before them, converted to Christianity. By the end of the eleventh century, the Roman Church, as well as the political authorities of Western Europe, were preparing to confront Islam.

Judaism and Early Christianity: *What Difference Do They Make?*

A small group of people, represented in the Bible in the stories of Abraham and his family, brought to the world the concept of monotheism, that one God created and cared for the entire world. As this group of people grew, and became known as the Jewish people, it told the melancholy story of its descent into slavery followed by the sequel of its escape from slavery through the intervention of its God, a story that has inspired oppressed peoples for thousands of years. Then, for about 1,200 years the Jews lived as a politically independent people, although often divided into tribes, with their own governments, on land that they claimed as sacred to them, given to them by their God. During those years, their prophets taught that ethics and morality could prevail in human relations, but only through dedication and hard work, and that unjust rulers should be confronted, whether they were their own rulers or foreign rulers.

Living at a geographical crossroads of people and ideas, the Jews were frequently conquered by other peoples and sometimes exiled from the land they claimed. Nevertheless, in their diaspora in Babylonia, they demonstrated that they could remain cohesive and culturally creative, even far from home. After the Romans exiled the Jews almost completely from their land, they dispersed throughout the world, especially the Roman world. They drew on their earlier experiences to create institutions based on the leadership of their rabbis and allegiance to their law codes and religious customs that enabled them to endure despite the lack of a common home and a cohesive political structure. Even so, life in exile took its toll through oppression and assimilation. At the height of the Roman Empire, there were an estimated eight million Jews in the world. Two thousand years later, there are not quite double that number, 15 million, while Christianity, which grew from Jewish roots, today has more than two billion members.

Christianity originated in Judea and spread throughout Europe. It began with a single Jewish teacher whose message was preached by a handful of disciples and institutionalized through the zeal of a single missionary. It began with a membership of downtrodden Jews, added middling-level gentiles, attracted some of the elites of Rome, and finally converted multitudes of Europe's invading barbarians. It had expanded its own organizational establishment via the network of transportation, communication, and trade put in place by the Roman Empire. Within that empire, it flowered into two separate, far-flung Church hierarchies and several localized structures. When that empire dissolved and contracted, the Church maintained and consolidated its position within the remains of those old Roman administrative and market centers.

As European society became more rural, Christian monasteries and convents were founded in the countryside and often took on administrative and developmental roles alongside their spiritual missions. In short, the Church, like the empire, was much transformed. By the year 1000 it had become the most important organizational and cultural force in Western Europe.

The transformations of both the Christian religious world and the European political world continued after 1000 with extraordinary developments in crusading vigor, trade and commerce, urbanization, intellectual and artistic creativity, and religious reform. We will explore these transformations in the chapter entitled "Establishing World Trade Routes." First, however, we turn to equally startling and revolutionary developments that had created another world religion, originating in the Arabian peninsula only a few hundred miles from the birthplace of both Judaism and Christianity. By the year 1000 it had spread across North Africa, northward into Spain,

Laon Cathedral, west front, c. 1190–95. Gothic architecture, first fully expressed in several cathedrals in northern France, including this one in Laon, was the dominant style in Europe after the twelfth century. Gothic churches were built to communicate, proclaiming the glories of heaven through their confident mastery of space and light and, at the same time, heralding the wealth and power of the Church. Laon's wide façade, monumental doorways, pointed arches, and numerous windows, some with gorgeous rose-hued stained glass, topped by two huge towers, is one of the earliest and best examples of this upward-reaching style.

throughout the Middle East, and on through Iran and Afghanistan into India. Our study of Islam in the chapter called "Islam" will complete our introduction to the origins and early life of the three major monotheistic religions.

CHAPTER REVIEW

JUDAISM

10.1 How did Judaism arise and what are its evolving beliefs?

To a world in which people believed in many gods, who sometimes fought with each other and interfered capriciously in human life, the Hebrews introduced the idea of a single God whose rule was just and orderly. This was a new kind of God, above nature, all-powerful, all-caring, and actively intervening in human history to reward righteous behavior and punish wrong-doing. From its beginnings, Judaism has claimed its origins in a single, select family that suffered centuries of slavery followed by centuries of political independence in a geographical location assigned to it by God. Earlier emphasis on priestly rituals was replaced with prophetic concerns for universal moral issues.

CHRISTIANITY

10.2 How did Christianity emerge and evolve?

Christianity emerged as a sect within Judaism. It began with a Jewish preacher named Jesus, whose followers believed him to be the son of God. He preached a message of compassion, salvation, and eternal life in a world dominated by Jewish ritual and Roman imperialism, and the Romans crucified him. Jesus' disciples, believing in his resurrection, transcribed and spread his message, first to the wider Mediterranean world and eventually across the Roman Empire. Later missionaries carried it around the world. It is today the most populous religion in the world.

CHRISTIANITY IN THE WAKE OF EMPIRE

10.3 What was the role of Christianity in the Roman Empire?

Christianity spread across Europe along the networks of the Roman Empire. Christianity spoke the empire's languages (Greek and Latin), preached its gospel along the empire's trade routes, and constructed church communities in the empire's cities. Christianity emerged and flourished even as the empire weakened and dissolved. In light of its origins and structures, the central Christian organization referred to itself as the Roman Catholic Church.

Suggested Readings

PRINCIPAL SOURCES

Brown, Peter. *The Rise of Western Christendom* (Malden, MA: Blackwell Publishers, 1996). Brown brings to bear expertise on the Roman Empire at the time of Christ to provide context for early Christianity.

Carroll, James. *Constantine's Sword: The Church and the Jews* (Boston, MA: Houghton Mifflin, 2001). Movingly written, often tragic story of the 2,000-year relationship between Christianity and Judaism.

Crossan, John Dominic. *The Historical Jesus: The Life of a Mediterranean Jewish Peasant* (San Francisco, CA: HarperCollins, 1991). One of the clearest interpretations of Jesus in his time.

Kee, Howard Clark, *et al. Christianity: A Social and Cultural History* (New York: Macmillan, 1991). Excellent, scholarly analysis and narrative of early Christianity.

MacCulloch, Diarmaid. *A History of Christianity: The First Three Thousand Years* (New York: Viking Penguin, 2010). A world history of Christianity, beautifully written, comprehensive, insightful, challenging.

The New English Bible with the Apocrypha, Oxford Study Edition (New York: Oxford University Press, 1970). Clear, readable, authentic text produced by an interfaith team of scholars.

Pagels, Elaine. *The Gnostic Gospels* (New York: Random House, 1979). Clear, concise explanation of the significance to our understanding of early Christianity of the Gnostic manuscripts discovered at Nag Hammadi in 1945.

Smart, Ninian. *The World's Religions* (Cambridge: Cambridge University Press, 1989). Useful general survey, clearly written.

Smeltzer, Robert M. *Jewish People, Jewish Thought* (New York: Macmillan, 1980). Excellent general history.

ADDITIONAL SOURCES

Andrea, Alfred, and James Overfield, eds. *The Human Record*, Vol. I (Boston: Wadsworth Cengage Learning, 7th ed., 2012). Superbly chosen selections.

Armstrong, Karen. *A History of God* (New York: Knopf, 1993). Concise history of the evolution of the three major monotheistic religions.

Augustine. *The City of God*, trans. Marcus Dods (New York: Modern Library, 1950). A central work of Christian theology from the late Roman Empire.

Baron, Salo Wittmayer. *A Social and Religious History of the Jews*, Vol. I (New York: Columbia University Press, 1952). First in a multivolume series by one of the leading Jewish historians of his time.

de Lange, Nicholas. *Atlas of the Jewish World* (New York: Facts on File, 1984). Excellent text, helpful maps, beautiful illustrations.

Einhard and Notker the Stammerer. *Two Lives of Charlemagne*, trans. Lewis Thorpe (Harmondsworth, Middlesex: Penguin Books, 1969). The standard primary source on Charlemagne.

Gibbon, Edward. *The History of the Decline and Fall of the Roman Empire*, 3 vols., abridged by D.M. Low (New York: Washington Square Books, 1962). The classic from the age of the Enlightenment. Follows and projects the story through the fall of Constantinople to the Turks.

Grant, Michael. *History of Rome* (New York: Charles Scribner's Sons, 1978). Readable, basic text.

——. *Jesus: An Historian's Review of the Gospels* (New York: Touchstone, 1995). Does the best he can to reconstruct Jesus' life and teachings based on the Gospels.

Halpern, Baruch. *The First Historians: The Hebrew Bible and History* (San Francisco, CA: Harper and Row, 1988). Attempts to demonstrate the extent to which Hebrew stories from the Bible can be authenticated.

Holy Bible. New Revised Standard Version (Grand Rapids, MI: Zondervan Publishing House, 1989). Another excellent, standard translation.

Honour, Hugh, and John Fleming. *The Visual Arts: A History* (Englewood Cliffs, NJ: Prentice Hall, 4th ed., 1995). Excellent textbook approach to the history of art.

Kaufmann, Yehezkel. *The Religion of Israel* (Chicago, IL: University of Chicago Press, 1960). Fascinating analysis of Biblical Judaism, stressing the inability of the early Jews even to comprehend the significance of images in worship.

Kee, Howard Clark. *Who Are the People of God? Early Christian Models of Community* (New Haven, CT: Yale University Press, 1995). Kee stresses the importance of the community of believers in the success of the early Christian Church.

Mann, Michael. *A History of Power from the Beginning to A.D. 1760* (Cambridge: Cambridge University Press, 1986). Mann searches for the success of early Christianity in its sociological composition and appeal.

Matthew, Donald. *Atlas of Medieval Europe* (New York: Facts on File, 1983). Excellent text, useful maps, beautiful illustrations.

McManners, John, ed. *The Oxford Illustrated History of Christianity* (New York: Oxford University Press, 1990). Outstanding set of basic introductory articles by major scholars, highly illustrated.

Meier, John P. *A Marginal Jew: Rethinking the Historical Jesus*, 2 vols. (New York: Doubleday, 1991, 1994). Meier emphasizes Jesus' abilities as a magician and exorcist in attracting followers.

Momigliano, Arnaldo. *On Pagans, Jews, and Christians* (Hanover, NH: University Press of New England for Wesleyan University Press, 1987). Compares the attractions of each of these perspectives, and their confrontations with one another in the early years of Christianity.

Pagels, Elaine. *Beyond Belief: The Secret Gospel of Thomas* (New York: Random House, 2003). Pagels' analysis of the most significant of the Gnostic gospels, and its meaning for her.

Pritchard, James B., ed. *Ancient Near Eastern Texts Relating to the Old Testament* (Princeton, NJ: Princeton University Press, 3rd ed., 1969). Basic compendium of the most important documents. Indispensable for the subject.

Rosenberg, David, and Harold Bloom. *The Book of J* (New York: Grove Weidenfeld, 1990). Analyzes the four major editorial strands in the composition of the Torah, stressing the one that refers to God by his Hebrew name of JHWH.

Rubenstein, Richard L. *When Jesus Became God* (New York: Harcourt Brace, 1999). An account of the armed battle and victory of the Roman Church over the theologian Arius, who declared that Christ's human nature diminished his divine nature.

Sand, Shlomo. *The Invention of the Jewish People* (London: Verso, 2010). Highly controversial book on the origins and evolution of the Jewish people. Early section on Biblical criticism is especially useful here.

Smart, Ninian, and Richard D. Hecht, eds. *Sacred Texts of the World: A Universal Anthology* (New York: Crossroad Publishing, 1982). Useful selection of religious texts.

FILMS

National Geographic. *When Rome Ruled the World: Rise of Christianity* (2011; 50 minutes). From scorned and persecuted mystery religion to a new religious empire arising out of Rome. Includes new research.

BBC. *History of Jerusalem: Making of a Holy City* (2013; 59 minutes). Narrated and presented by Simon Sebag Montefiore, based on his recent, highly acclaimed book. Archaeological and urban perspective on religious history. Part of a trilogy that continues through Muslim and crusader invasions up to the present.

Heritage: Civilization and the Jews (1984; eight parts of one hour each). History of the Jews and their place in the world from earliest times to the present. Narrated by Abba Eban, former foreign minister of the State of Israel.

Documentaries on early Judaism and Christianity abound, many from such excellent producers as the BBC, National Geographic, PBS, and the History Channel. New ones continue to be produced. To review and watch them, check YouTube.

See also "Crash Course in World History" (2012), also available on YouTube. These forty-two 10–12-minute frenetic "lessons" are set more at the high-school than the college level, but can be fun and useful. Episode 11 is "Christianity from Judaism to Constantine."

11 Islam

Submission to Allah: Muslim Civilization Bridges the World

570 C.E.–1500 C.E.

I slam, in Arabic, means "submission." Islam teaches submission to the word of God, called "Allah" in Arabic. Muslims, "those who submit," know God's word primarily through the Quran, the Arabic book that records the teachings of God as they were transmitted to the Prophet Muhammad (570–632). Stories of Muhammad's life, words, and deeds, carefully collected, sifted, and transmitted over many generations, provide Muslims with models of the righteous life and how to live it. According to the Quran, Muhammad was the most recent, and final, prophet of God's message of ethical monotheism. Devout Muslims declare this belief in prayers, which are recited five times each day: "There is no God but God, and Muhammad is his Prophet."

Niche (*mihrab*) with Arabic calligraphy. Muslims pray in the direction of Mecca, and every mosque is marked by a *mihrab*, a niche in the wall, which indicates that direction. This *mihrab* is elegantly ornamented with floral designs and Arabic calligraphy of verses from the Quran, which frame it and mark its center. The color green is traditional and favored in Islam, perhaps referring to the lush vegetation of paradise in the world to come. (Metropolitan Museum, New York)

LEARNING OBJECTIVES

11.1 ((	11.2 ((	11.3 ((	11.4 ((
Tell the history of Islam, its origins and beliefs.	Understand the history of Islam after Muhammad's death.	Describe the flowering of Islam outside the Arab world.	Discuss Muslims' relationship with non-Muslims.

((Listen on **MyHistoryLab**

For Muslims, the teachings of the Quran and of Muhammad's life can be fulfilled only with the creation of a community of believers, the *umma*, and its proper regulation through political structures. Through its early centuries, Islam established administrative and legal systems in the areas to which it spread: Arabia, western Asia, northern Africa, and Spain. As Islam spread later to eastern Europe, central Asia, south Asia, and sub-Saharan Africa, it arrived sometimes with government backing, sometimes without. After the twelfth century, Islam won converts in China and Southeast Asia as a religious and cultural system without government support.

Islam is considered here as a world religion. Because it often unified government and religion into a single system, it may also be compared with the materials in

KEY TERM

umma The community of believers in Islam, which transcends ethnic and political boundaries.

AT A GLANCE: ISLAM

DATE	POLITICAL/SOCIAL EVENTS	LITERARY/PHILOSOPHICAL EVENTS
500 C.E.	● Muhammad (570–632)	
600 C.E.	● Hijra (622), flight to Medina ● Muslim conquest of Mecca ● Orthodox or Rightly Guided Caliphs (632–61) ● Muslim conquest of Iraq, Syria, Palestine, Egypt, western Iran (632–42), Cyprus (649), and Persian Empire (650s) ● Umayyad caliphate (661–750); capital in Damascus ● Muslim conquest of Carthage (698) and central Asia (650–712) ● Husayn killed at Karbala (680); Sunni–Shi'a split	● Revelation of the Quran to Muhammad (610) ● Persian becomes second language of Islam
700 C.E.	● Muslim conquest of Tunis (700), Spain (711–16), Sind, and lower Indus valley ● Muslim defeat at Battle of Tours (732) ● Muslims defeat Chinese at Battle of Talas River (751) ● Abbasid caliphate (750–1258) ● Baghdad founded (762)	● Biography of Muhammad by Ibn Ishaq (d. 767) ● Formulation of major systems of Islamic law
800 C.E.	● Divisions in Muslim Empire (833–945) ● Fez founded (808)	● al-Tabari, *History of Prophets and Kings* ● al-Khwarazmi develops algebra ● Abbasid caliphate establishes "House of Wisdom" translation bureau in Baghdad ● Sufi *tariqa*
900 C.E.	● Persians seize Baghdad (945) ● Cairo founded (969)	● Ferdowsi, *Shah Nama* ● al-Razi, *Encyclopedia of Medicine* ● Turkish becomes third language of Islam ● Mutazilites challenge Islamic orthodoxy
1000 C.E.	● Seljuk Turks dominate Abbasid caliphate (1038) ● Almoravid dynasty in North Africa and Spain (1061–1145) ● Battle of Manzikert (1071) ● First Crusade (1095–99)	● Ibn Sina (Avicenna), philosopher, produces "Canon of Medicine" ● al-Biruni (d. 1046) writes on mathematics and astronomy
1100 C.E.	● Almohad dynasty rules North Africa and Spain (1145–1269) ● Second Crusade (1147–49) ● Salah al-Din (Saladin) recaptures Jerusalem (1187) ● Third Crusade (1189–92)	● al-Ghazali (d. 1111), Muslim philosopher and theologian ● Ibn Rushd (Averroes; 1126–98) ● Maimonides (1135–1204), Jewish physician, philosopher, and theologian
1200 C.E.	● Fourth Crusade (1202–04) ● Sultanate of Delhi (1211–1526) ● Children's Crusade (1212) ● Fifth to Eighth Crusades (1218–91) ● Crusaders driven from west Asia (1291) ● Fall of Baghdad to Mongols (1258); end of Abbasid Caliphate	● Jalal-al-Din Rumi, *Mathnawi* ● al-Juvaini, *History of the World Conquerors* ● Rashid al-Din, *World History*
1300 C.E.	● Mansa Musa's pilgrimage to Mecca (1324) ● Conversion of Malayans and Indonesians to Islam	● Ibn Battuta (1304–c. 1368), traveler ● Ibn Khaldun, *Universal History*
1400 C.E.	● Ottoman Turks conquer Constantinople (1453) ● Christians capture Granada, complete *reconquista* (1492)	

11.1
11.2
11.3
11.4

What is the
history of Islam,
its origins and
beliefs?

"Turning Point: From City-states to Empires" on the expansion of world empires. In this chapter, we trace the growth and spread of Islam as a religious, governmental, and cultural system. We shall also examine its encounters with other religions and empires.

The Origins of Islam

11.1 What is the history of Islam, its origins and beliefs?

Islam emerged in the Arabian peninsula, an area largely inhabited by nomadic Bedouin tribes. The Bedouins organized themselves in clans. Inhabiting the desert, they lacked the sources of water so crucial for the emergence of cities and civilizations in the ancient world; nevertheless, a few cities, such as Mecca, grew up alongside major oases. Mecca flourished as a trading center in the seventh century, but the region in general lacked the governmental institutions and the powerful emperors that supported the emergence of major religions elsewhere. Religiously, the region was polytheistic, worshiping many gods. Mecca held a prominent role in this worship. It held the Ka'aba, a rectangular building that housed a cubical black stone structure, and the sacred tokens of all the clans of Mecca and of many of the surrounding tribes as well. Serving as a center of pilgrimage and trade, Mecca brought enormous economic benefits to the traders of the Quraysh tribes who controlled the city and its shrine.

The Prophet: His Life and Teaching

Born in 570 to parents eminent in the Quraysh tribe, Muhammad was orphaned at an early age, and he was raised by his grandfather and later his uncle. He became a merchant, employed by a wealthy widow named Khadija. When he was 25 years old, he married her and they had four children together.

Muhammad was a deeply meditative person, retreating regularly to a nearby hill to pray and reflect. In 610, when he was 40 years old, his reflections were interrupted, according to Islamic teachings, by the voice of the angel Gabriel, who instructed him: "Recite: In the name of the Lord who created Man of a blood-clot." Over the next two decades, according to Islamic theology, God continued to reveal his messages to Muhammad through Gabriel. Muhammad transmitted these revelations to professionals whose task it was to commit them to memory. The verses were also transcribed on palm leaves, stone, and other material. Soon after Muhammad's death, scribes and editors compiled the entire collection of written and oral recitations into the Quran, which in Arabic means recitations. An officially authorized edition of the Quran was issued by Uthman (r. 644–56), the third ruler of the Islamic community.

Approximately the length of the Christian New Testament, the Quran is considered by Muslims to be the absolute, uncorrupted word of God. Composed in

Trumpet call of the angel Gabriel. Muhammad's religious meditations were interrupted by the angel Gabriel, who commanded him to recite what became the first *surah* (section from the Quran) revealed to humanity. Here the encounter is symbolized by Gabriel's blowing on a trumpet. (British Library, London)

CHAPTER ELEVEN: ISLAM 570 C.E.–1500 C.E.

11.1

11.2

11.3

11.4

What is the
history of Islam,
its origins and
beliefs?

poetic form, the Quran helped to define the literary standards of the Arabic language. Muslims chant and study its text in Arabic, considering each syllable sacred. Even today many Muslims reject translations of the Quran into other languages as inadequate.

In the next century, new technologies led to broader dispersion of the Quran. During the mid-eighth century, as Arab armies defeated Chinese forces in central Asia, the Muslim victors learned from their prisoners-of-war the technology of papermaking. By the end of the eighth century Baghdad had a paper mill; Egypt had one by 900; Morocco and Spain by 1100. Turks brought the art of papermaking to northern India in the twelfth century. One use of paper was, of course, in the administration of the government bureaucracy. Another, perhaps even more important, was in the copying and diffusion of the Quran.

🔍 View the Closer Look: The Quran on MyHistoryLab

The Five Pillars of Islam

The Quran reveals the "five pillars" of Islam, the five ritual expressions that define orthodox Muslim religious belief and practice:

- Declaring the creed, "There is no god but God, and Muhammad is his Prophet."
- Praying five times daily while facing Mecca (2:144), and, if possible, praying also in public assembly at midday each Friday.
- Giving alms to the poor in the community, especially to widows and orphans (2:212 ff.), later recommended at approximately 2½ percent of wealth.
- Fasting each day during the month of Ramadan, the ninth month of the lunar year, although eating is permitted at night, with a major feast marking the month's end (2:179–84).
- Making the *hajj*, a pilgrimage to Mecca, at least once in a lifetime, if possible (2:185 ff.).

Jihad, or sacred struggle, is sometimes called a "sixth pillar" of Islam. It was less stringently required and has been interpreted in different ways. Some scholars interpret *jihad* as a call to physical warfare to preserve and extend the **dar al-Islam**, the "abode of Islam," the lands under Muslim rule, or, later, the lands in which Islam could be practiced freely, even if not under Muslim political rule. Even in this interpretation, however, *jihad* should be practiced only in self-defense, for "God loves not the aggressors" (2:187). Other scholars understand *jihad* as a personal call to the individual, internal, spiritual struggle to live Islam as fully as possible. The Quran gives a capsule description of this proper life:

> True piety is this: to believe in God, and the Last Day, the angels, the Book, and the Prophets, to give of one's substance, however cherished, to kinsmen, and orphans, the needy, the traveller, beggars, and to ransom the slave, to perform the prayer, to pay the alms. And they who fulfil their covenant, and endure with fortitude misfortune, hardship and peril, these are they who are true in their faith, these are the truly godfearing. (2:172–3)

Finally, the Quran promises repeatedly that those who observe Islam faithfully will find their reward in paradise, described as "gardens underneath which rivers flow ... a shelter of plenteous shade" (4:60). On the other hand, those who reject the opportunity to fulfill the teachings of Islam will burn in a fiery Hell forever. Humans must choose between doing good and evil, but the Quran asserts that ultimately free will is limited: "God has power over everything" (4:87).

The Quran emphasized many of the same principles as Judaism and Christianity, including the importance of worshiping a single God and the obligation of the rich to help the poor. As in Christianity, the Quran taught that there would be a final

KEY TERM

dar al-Islam The literal meaning of the Arabic words is "the abode of Islam." The term refers to the land of Islam, that is, territories in which Islam and its religious laws (*shari'a*) may be freely practiced. Some interpreters argue that the rulers themselves must be Muslims and that they must institute *shari'a* law, others argue that freedom for Muslims to follow Islamic practice is the only requirement. Also, sometimes, *dar as-Salam*, "the abode of peace."

The Ka'aba in Mecca, with pilgrims. For Muslims the most sacred space on earth, the very center of the center of holiness, is the black stone, the Ka'aba in Mecca. This is the physical destination of the *hajj* pilgrimage, which every Muslim is called upon to undertake, if possible. Tens of millions of *hajjis* from all parts of the world make the pilgrimage each year.

Judgment Day. Many of the Quran's practices, too, were consistent with the existing rituals of Christians, Jews, and Zoroastrians living in Arabia at the time, and this made acceptance of the new religion easier. For example, regular prayer times and recitals of creed were also central to Judaism and Christianity, as was institutionalized charity. Animal sacrifice was a part of pagan and Zoroastrian religions, and had once been central to Judaism as it was now to Islam. Ritual slaughter of animals for food mirrored Jewish practice, as did male circumcision. Ritual washing before public prayers was also practiced by Zoroastrians.

Responses to Muhammad

In Mecca, Muhammad created the nucleus of the *umma* as people accepted his message. Some were successful businesspeople, some slaves, some tribeless people, some were family members. His wife Khadija became his first disciple; his cousin Ali seems to have been the second.

Most Meccans, however, found Muhammad's moral teachings too demanding, and, when he told them of the physical state—resembling an epileptic fit—in which he received some of the revelations from the angel Gabriel, many questioned his stability. On more practical grounds, they feared that his teachings threatened their own beliefs, especially the idol worship in their homes and in the Ka'aba. Some

HOW DO WE KNOW?

Sources on Early Islam

Much of the historical writing on Islam is based on orthodox Islamic sources or, conversely, on the writings of their opponents. Such sources are not unbiased. In addition, several key documents were written down long after the events they describe, allowing possible alterations in the text. The Quran itself, for example, was compiled some 50 years after Muhammad received his first revelation. Muhammad Ibn Ishaq (c. 704–67) wrote the first Arabic biography of the Prophet more than a century after his death.

Moreover, Islam suffered three civil wars in its first 120 years and considerable internal fighting thereafter; many of the "official" histories were prepared in support of one position or another. Finally, as Islam confronted other religious civilizations, the accounts of its history were frequently tendentious, again supporting one side or another.

In their search for unbiased information, recent historians have made use of sources that were not recorded as historical narratives but that provide data from which history can be written:

The new generation of historians thus uncovered an impressive variety of sources: commercial documents, tax registers, official land grants, administrative seals, census records, coins, gravestones, magical incantations written on bowls, memoirs of pilgrims, archeological and architectural data, biographical dictionaries, inscriptional evidence, and, more recently, oral history. (Eaton in Adas, p. 4)

From these records has emerged a deeper understanding of the culture of Muhammad's homeland in Arabia and of the adjacent Byzantine and Sassanid Persian empires. These records suggest that Islam did not develop within a national vacuum. It incorporated religious, cultural, and social structures that were already present among its neighbors. As it grew and expanded, it incorporated aspects of Arab, Greek, Roman, and Persian civilizations.

- What are some issues in the early history of Islam that have led to the creation of primary source documents with conflicting interpretations?
- What use are tax registers, official land grant documents, and census records in interpreting the early history of Islam?
- If you were to study the degree to which Islam adopted practices from either the Greco-Roman or Persian civilizations, what primary sources would you seek?

Meccans were already monotheists, especially the Jews and Christians who lived in the city, but most of them also rejected his message for they did not believe that their own religions needed the purification that Muhammad proposed. Despite this intense opposition, including apparent threats on Muhammad's life, his family and his branch of the Quraysh tribe stood by him, including some who did not accept his message but trusted his integrity.

After Khadija and some others of his early supporters died, however, Muhammad's position in Mecca became more precarious. Some members of the Muslim community began to leave Mecca in search of a home more accepting of the new teachings.

The *Hijra* and the Islamic Calendar. Largely rejected by his own tribe and the inhabitants of Mecca, Muhammad, too, sought a place that would be more receptive. He welcomed an invitation from the elders of the city of Medina to come with his followers to their oasis city some 200 miles to the north to adjudicate bitter disputes that had arisen among local tribes and to take the reins of government. Muhammad may also have been attracted because Medina had a large Jewish population. As monotheists, they shared the central principle of his faith, and he may have thought that he could ultimately convert them.

Known as the *hijra*, Muhammad's flight under pressure to Medina became a central moment in Islamic history. As Christians begin the year 1 of their calendar with an event in the life of Jesus—his birth—so Muslims begin theirs with the *hijra* and Muhammad's assertion of governmental leadership in Medina, a year that corresponds to the year 622 on the Christian calendar.

Although he failed to convert many Jews, Muhammad found many other inhabitants of Medina who did accept his religious message. This allowed him to consolidate a unified religious community of Muslims. He believed that for Islam to survive, he needed to create a *dar al-Islam*, a government under which Islam could be practiced freely, legally, and securely. In Medina he promulgated codes of business

What is the history of Islam, its origins and beliefs?

11.1
11.2
11.3
11.4

KEY TERM

hijra The "migration" or flight of Muhammad from Mecca, where his life was in danger, to Medina (then called Yathrib), where he was welcomed as a potential leader in 622 C.E. The Islamic era (A.H.: After Hijra) is calculated from this date.

Gender Relations in Islam

Although many readers might consider the relationships between men and women a private matter, in fact in each religion—and empire—that we have studied some official doctrines attempted to regulate gender relationships. In general, they placed women under the authority of men and granted men more legal rights than they accorded to women. Although they often gave women greater importance than men in the private realm of house and hearth, they vested more public power and responsibility with men. Islam also follows this general pattern. The Quran states:

Men have authority over women because God has made the one superior to the other, and because they spend their wealth to maintain them. Good women are obedient. They guard their unseen parts because God has guarded them. As for those from whom you fear disobedience, admonish them and send them to beds apart and beat them. Then if they obey you, take no further action against them. God is high, supreme. (4:34)

According to the Quran, women are to satisfy men's sexual desires and to bear children:

Women are your fields: go, then, into your fields when you please. (2:223)

As in Judaism and Hinduism, sexual intercourse is forbidden during a woman's menstrual period:

Keep aloof from women during their menstrual periods and do not touch them until they are clean again. (2:222)

It might appear that men are the initiators of sexual relations, but women are considered sexually seductive, and the Quran therefore urges the Prophet to:

Enjoin believing women to turn their eyes away from temptation and to preserve their chastity; to cover their adornments (except such as are normally displayed); to draw

Divorce proceedings. A scribe records the accusations of a husband and wife as they petition for a divorce in front of a *qadi*, or judge. A woman had limited rights to divorce her husband, but a man could divorce his wife without stipulating a reason, although in practice matters were rarely that simple. A *qadi* would bring to bear the combined wisdom of scriptural knowledge, local custom, and his own judgment in making an adjudication. (Bibliothèque Nationale, Paris)

their veils over their bosoms and not to reveal their finery except to their husbands, close relatives, and the very old and very young. (24:31)

As witnesses in legal matters, the testimony of two women equals that of one man (2:282). Similarly, in matters of inheritance, "A male shall inherit twice as much as a female" (4:11). Despite these regulations that apparently limit the status of women, some modern scholars assert that Islam actually introduced "a positive social revolution" (Tucker, p. 42) in gender relations. Compared to what came before, Islam introduced new rights for women and gave them greater security in marriage. Islamic law, *shari'a*, safeguarded the rights of both partners in marriage through contractual responsibilities: it insisted on the consent of the bride; it specified that dowry, or bridal gift, go to the bride herself and not to her family; and it spelled out the husband's obligations to support his wives and children, even wives that he might divorce. Although men were allowed to take up to four wives, the Quran added, "But if you fear that you cannot maintain equality among them, marry one only or any slave-girls you may own. This will make it easier for you to avoid injustice" (4:3); so, in practice, only one wife was normally permitted.

These scholars note also that in the life of Muhammad, three women played exemplary roles: his first wife, Khadija, who supported him economically and emotionally when the revelations he received brought him scorn from others; Aisha, the most beloved of the wives he took after Khadija's death; and Fatima, the daughter of the Prophet and wife of the fourth caliph, Ali. Nevertheless, these women drew their importance from their service to prominent men, and were criticized when they attempted more independent roles.

Other scholars, by contrast, have argued that Islam made the plight of women worse than it had been. These scholars argue that in pre-Islamic Arabia, women could initiate marriage, they could have more than one husband, they could divorce their husbands, they could remain in their parents' home area and have their husbands come to live with them, and they could keep custody of their children in case of divorce. In pre-Islamic Arabia, some women, such as Allat, al-Uzza, and Manat were worshiped with great honor, suggesting that there was considerable respect for females.

Of those scholars who feel that the position of women declined under Islam, some put the blame on Islam itself, but others suggest that the teachings of Islam were actually comparatively liberal. These scholars argue that it was contact with the Byzantine and Sassanid empires that reduced women's status. They argue that tribal, nomadic Arabia had treated women with relative equality, but the neighboring empires, with their settled, urban civilizations, veiled women and kept them mostly at home under male domination. The Arabs adopted these practices. In effect, this group of scholars is also saying that the more liberal Quranic rules regarding women were reinterpreted after contact with societies outside Arabia. Whatever the rules of the Quran, in practice gender relations varied widely in different parts of the world of Islam.

Ibn Battuta (1304–c. 1368), a famous Berber (North African) traveler whose adventures took him to much of the known world of Africa and Asia, learned his concepts of gender relations in the Arab heartland of Islam. As he traveled, he was often astonished, and sometimes shocked, by the status of women in other Islamic countries. In the Turkish and Mongol regions between the Black and Caspian seas, wives of local, ruling khans (sultans) owned property. When the senior wife appeared at the khan's residence, Ibn Battuta observes, the khan

advances to the entrance to the pavilion to meet her, salutes her, takes her by the hand, and only after she has mounted to the couch and taken her seat does the sultan himself sit down.

All this is done in full view of those present, and without any use of veils. (Dunn, p. 168)

In the Maldive Islands, in the Indian Ocean, Ibn Battuta was even more scandalized:

Their womenfolk do not cover their heads, not even their queen does so, and they comb their hair and gather it at one side. Most of them wear only an apron from their waists to the ground, the rest of their bodies being uncovered. When I held the qadiship [position of judge] there, I tried to put an end to this practice and ordered them to wear clothes, but I met with no success. No woman was admitted to my presence in a lawsuit unless her body was covered, but apart from that I was unable to effect anything. (McNeill and Waldman, p. 276)

In Mali, West Africa, female slaves and servants went publicly into the ruler's court completely naked. When Ibn Battuta found a scholar's wife chatting with another man, he complained to the scholar. But the scholar quickly put Ibn Battuta in his place:

The association of women with men is agreeable to us and a part of good conduct, to which no suspicion attaches. They are not like the women of your country. (Dunn, p. 300)

Ibn Battuta left immediately and never returned to the man's home.

- In terms of gender relationships, to what degree is Islam concerned with regulating sexual relations and the offspring that may result? Family relationships? Social and legal relationships outside the family? How do regulations in Islam compare with those in other religions?
- What is the evidence that Islam in its early years was more egalitarian toward women than were either the other groups in Arabia or the Byzantine and Sassanid empires outside Arabia? What is the evidence that it was less egalitarian?
- Ibn Battuta was surprised that the treatment of women varied quite widely in the various lands of Islam. Are you surprised? Why or why not?

11.1
11.2
11.3
11.4

What is the
history of Islam,
its origins and
beliefs?

ethics as well as family laws of marriage, divorce, and inheritance, all based on the teachings of the Quran.

Muhammad Extends his Authority. After establishing his authority in Medina, Muhammad sought to gain converts in Mecca and ended up in skirmishes with the Quraysh tribes that opposed him. In 624 he and his followers successfully raided a large Meccan caravan train in the Battle of Badr, reducing Mecca's prosperity by cutting important trade routes and winning local fame for themselves. In 625 the Meccans fought back, defeating Muhammad and his forces at Uhud. In 627 the two sides fought to a draw at the Battle of the Ditch, but Muhammad's reputation grew as he stood up to the powerful Meccans. In 630, following a dispute between the tribes of the two cities, Mecca surrendered to Medina. Muslims gained control of the Ka'aba, destroyed the Meccan idols, and turned the building with its sacred black rock into an Islamic shrine. By the time he died in 632, Muhammad was well on his way to creating from the warring tribes an Arabia-wide federation dedicated to the faith and the political structure of Islam.

Connections to Other Monotheistic Faiths. According to the Quran, Muhammad was only a messenger of God, not the originator of a new doctrine. Indeed, he was not even the founder of Islam: several prophets, including Adam, Noah, Abraham, Ishmael, Moses, and Jesus had prepared the way:

> Say (O Muslims): We believe in Allah and that which is revealed unto us and that which was revealed unto Abraham, and Ishmael, and Isaac, and Jacob, and the tribes, and that which Moses and Jesus received, and that which the prophets received from their Lord. We make no distinction between any of them, and unto Him we have surrendered. (Quran [Pickthall] 2:136)

Muslims claim the Hebrew Abraham, whom Jews see as the father of Jewish monotheism, as the first Muslim: "Abraham in truth was not a Jew, neither a Christian; but he was a Muslim and one of pure faith" (3:60). For this reason, Muslims often refer to Jews, Christians, and Muslims collectively as "children of Abraham."

The teachings of each of the earlier prophets, Muslims believe, were corrupted over time by their followers. Muslims challenge the Christian belief in Jesus as the son of God, and maintain that the Christian doctrine of Jesus' divinity conflicts with the fundamental concept of pure monotheism. The Quran deplores this heresy, declaring: "It is not for God to take a son unto Him" (19:36). The Jews' error was in refusing to accept the Quran as a revised and updated version of the truth already given to them:

> And when it is said unto them: Believe in that which Allah hath revealed, they say: We believe in that which was revealed unto us. And they disbelieve in that which cometh after it, though it is the truth confirming that which they possess. (2:91)

Muhammad and his followers came to believe that the revelations he received were final, uncorrupted, and true. Muhammad did not formulate this message; he only transmitted it as received. For Muslims, in the chain of prophets, Muhammad is the last and final link.

Christian Arabs remained largely aloof from Muhammad's alliances, while some Jews actively opposed his political goals and rejected his claims to religious prophecy. Disappointed in his wish to unite the members of the two monotheistic religions of the region under his leadership, and especially infuriated that some Jewish families had joined his Meccan enemies in war, Muhammad had the Jewish men of the Banu Qurayza clan executed, and the women and children enslaved. Elsewhere in Arabia, however, Jews and Christians, though subject to a special tax, were free to practice their religion.

Successors to the Prophet

11.2   What happened to Islam after Muhammad's death?

When the Prophet died leaving no male heir, the Muslim community feared that the *umma* and its political organization would break up. To preserve them, the Muslim leadership elected Abu Bakr (r. 632–34), one of Muhammad's closest associates and the father of his wife Aisha, as **caliph**—that is, successor to the Prophet and head of the Muslim community. The next three caliphs were similarly elected from among Muhammad's relatives and companions, but amidst much more dissension.

Abu Bakr mobilized to prevent Muslims from deserting their new religion and the authority of its government, attacking those who tried. Arabia was convulsed in tribal warfare. The contending tribes fought for power and looted one another, as they had traditionally. Their battles spilled over the borders of the Arabian peninsula, as did their search for allies. The Byzantine and Sassanid empires saw the Arab troops encroaching on their territories and fought back, but at the Battle of Ajnadayn (634) in southern Palestine, the Arab clans combined to form a unified army and defeated the Byzantine army. With this victory, the Arab warriors were no longer simple raiders in search of plunder. They were now at war for the control of settled empires.

Conquest followed conquest—Damascus in 636, Jerusalem in 638—but the northward march stopped as Byzantine troops held fast at the borders of the Anatolian peninsula. The Byzantine Empire defended its Anatolian borders for another four centuries, and its Balkan territories for eight. But the Sassanid Empire collapsed almost immediately. In 637 Arab armies defeated the Persians in battle, seized their capital, Ctesiphon, and forced the last emperor to flee. Meeting little opposition, Arab armies swept across Iraq, Iran, Afghanistan, and central Asia. Other Arab armies now turned toward northern Africa, taking Egypt in 641–43 and Tripoli in 643.

The second caliph, Umar I (r. 634–44), established the early principles of political administration, as a "rightly guided" caliph, in the conquered territories. The troops were not to interfere with the way of life of the conquered populations. The early caliphs did not encourage conversion to Islam, lest the political and social status of conqueror and conquered become confused. Also, since Muslims were exempted from land taxes and poll taxes, the conversion of conquered peoples would cause considerable loss of tax revenue to Umar's government.

To prevent the armies and administrators from interfering with the economy and the social traditions of the newly conquered territories, Umar ordered the occupiers to live somewhat apart from the conquered populations. Muslim armies built new garrison cities, such as Basra, Kufa, Fustat, and Merv, and added new neighborhoods to existing cities for their troops and administrators. They largely left local systems of taxation and administration in place, and incumbent personnel often kept their jobs, but the new government confiscated lands that had been owned by the state and its officials and claimed them for itself.

These new arrangements proved unstable. In the new garrison cities, conqueror and conquered lived side by side, and they could not effectively be segregated socially and culturally. In addition, the troops soon argued that their pay was not adequate. Their incomes lagged, even as the new conquests enriched the top-level administrators. What had become of Islam's call for a more egalitarian society? In essence, the imperial aims of the ruling class and the religious goals of Islam were pulling in opposite directions.

Civil War: Religious Conflict and the Sunni–Shi'a Division

The jockeying for power among various political, economic, tribal, and religious interest groups precipitated a series of civil wars. A contingent of Arab troops from Egypt assassinated the third caliph, Uthman (r. 644–56), complaining that under his

KEY TERM

caliph The spiritual head and temporal ruler of the Muslim community.

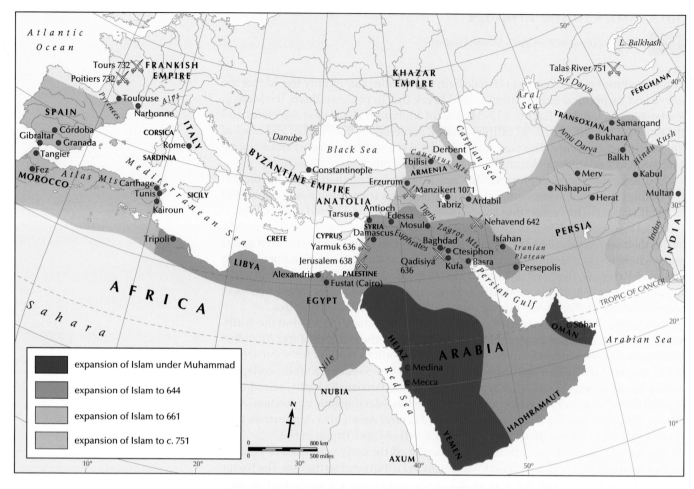

The expansion of Islam. The Muslim faith spread with astonishing speed from its center at Mecca, exploiting the weakness of the Byzantine and Sassanid empires. Within a century of the death of the Prophet Muhammad in 632, Arab armies had reached the Atlantic coast in the west, and the borders of India and China in the east.

KEY TERMS

Shi'a Short form for *shiat Ali*, "follower of Ali." In choosing a successor to Muhammad, the shi'a argued for Ali, his cousin/son-in-law, his closest male relative. From that time on, they remained a separate sect within Islam, representing about 20 percent of all Muslims worldwide, and a majority in countries such as Iran and Iraq.

Sunni From the Arabic *sunna*, the words and acts of Muhammad, as recorded in **hadiths**. The Sunni are the majority group in Islam, representing just over 80 percent of the total. They differed from the Shi'a in choosing Uthman as the first successor of Muhammad, and argued that they were following the wish and example of the Prophet.

administration their local governors were cruel, their pay was inadequate, and class divisions were destroying Arab unity.

Uthman's successor, Ali (r. 656–61), was elected despite considerable opposition. Supporting his election most strongly was the *shiat Ali*, "the party of Ali," usually referred to simply as the **Shi'a** or Shi'ites. This group felt that the caliph should be chosen from the family of the Prophet. They had opposed the election of the first three caliphs. Ali, as the cousin and also the son-in-law of Muhammad, having married his daughter Fatima, was the first caliph to fit their requirement. In opposition, members of Uthman's family, the Ummayad clan, preferred one of their own. They argued for acceptance of the first three caliphs as legitimate since they were chosen by the *umma* and reflected the *sunna*, or example, of the Prophet. They and their followers called themselves **Sunnis**. Finally, a third group, who had long opposed the Umayyad for their own reasons, feared that Ali might reach an accommodation with their rivals, and assassinated him.

After Ali's assassination, the Umayyad leader, Mu'awiya (r. 661–80), declared himself caliph. Moving the capital out of Arabia to Damascus in Syria, Mu'awiya distanced himself from the original Muslim elite of the Arabian peninsula. He opened Islam to more cosmopolitan influences and a more professional style of imperial administration.

11.1

11.2

What happened
to Islam after
Muhammad's
death?

11.3

11.4

Tension remained high among the various religious and tribal factions, however, and civil war broke out again on Mu'awiya's death in 680. His son Yazid I (r. 680–83) claimed the caliphate, but Husayn, son of the assassinated Ali, took the field against him. When Husayn was killed in battle at Karbala, Iraq, in the year 680, he joined his father as the second martyr of the Shi'a branch of Islam.

The Shi'as stressed the importance of religious purity, and they wanted the caliph to represent Islam's religious principles rather than its imperial aspirations. They felt that Ali, in addition to his heritage as a member of the family of the Prophet, represented that purer orientation, and they would recognize only descendants of Ali as **imams**, religious leaders who were also rightful caliphs. From 680 onward, Shi'as went into battle for the appointment of their imams to fill the position of caliph.

One after another, all of the first 11 Shi'a imams are believed to have died as martyrs, either in battle or through assassination. After the death of the eleventh, in 874, and the disappearance of his son, the hereditary line ended. From that time onward, "twelver" Shi'as have looked forward to the reappearance of the "hidden" twelfth imam, referred to as the *mahdi*, or "rightly guided one," a messiah, to usher in a new age of Islam, truth, and justice. Meanwhile, they have usually been willing to accept the authority of the current government, while stressing matters of the spiritual rather than the temporal world.

The great majority of Muslims, however, regarded the caliph as primarily a political official, administering the empire of Islam. They accepted the rule of the Umayyads, based on Sunni teachings and the importance of the *umma* in making political decisions.

The division between Sunni and Shi'a, which began over the proper succession to the caliphate, has continued to the present—long after the caliphate ceased to exist—as the principal sectarian division within Islam. Some 83 percent of the world's Muslims today are Sunnis, 16 percent are Shi'as. The split is largely geographical, with Shi'as forming 95 percent of the population of Iran and about 60 percent of that of Iraq.

The Sunni–Shi'a division is the most significant in Islam, but it is not the only one. At the death of the sixth imam, in 765, there was another conflict over acceptance of the seventh. The majority chose the imam's younger son, but a minority followed the elder son, Ismail. The Ismailis, a branch of Shi'as, proselytized actively and led frequent rebellions against the caliphate. Later the Ismailis also divided. One branch lives on today, mostly in Pakistan and India, revering the Aga Khan as its leader.

The Umayyad Caliphs Build an Empire

After the succession struggle on Mu'awiya's death, the Umayyads consolidated their rule and embarked on wars of imperial conquest. To symbolize their imperial power, the Umayyad caliphs constructed elegant, monumental mosques in Jerusalem in 691 (the Dome of the Rock); in Medina, 706–10; Damascus, 706–14; and, again, Jerusalem (the al-Aqsa Mosque), 709–15. They also began to create an imperial bureaucracy that owed its allegiance to the state rather than to the current ruler personally.

Life in the cities eroded the solidarity of tribal society. A new social structure was developing that was dividing the Arab upper and lower classes while mixing the Arab and non-Arab elites. The Umayyad caliphs looked to Islam as the glue that could hold the splintered society together. They sought actively to convert the conquered peoples and assimilate them into a single Muslim *umma*. By the middle of the eighth century, conversions to Islam were increasing among the urban populations, as was the use of Arabic as the language of administration, literature, and everyday speech.

The Umayyads quickly expanded their empire through a series of enormously successful imperial conquests. Arab armies conquered the entire northern coast of Africa by 711. In North Africa, after initial resistance, most of the conquered Berber

KEY TERMS

imam In Islam, a title for a person whose religious leadership or example is to be followed.

mahdi According to Islamic tradition, this messianic leader will appear to restore justice, truth, and religion for a brief period before the universal Day of Judgment.

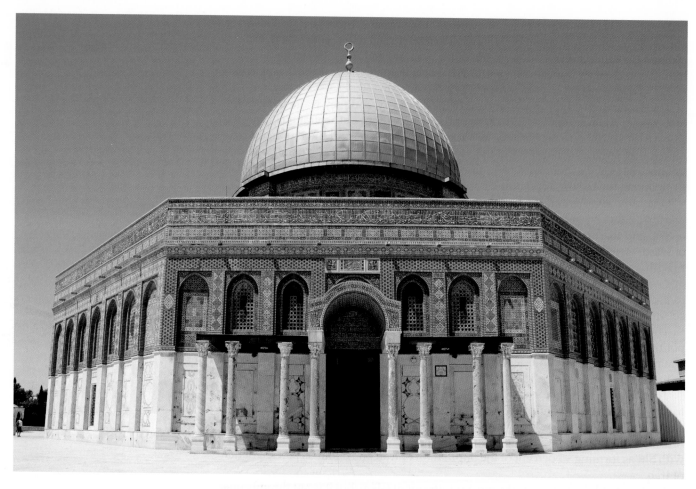

The exterior of the Dome of the Rock, Jerusalem, first constructed in 692. The first Umayyad caliph, Abd al-Malik (r. 685–705), built this shrine as the first major monument in Islamic history. It celebrates the triumphal conquests of the Umayyad dynasty as it emerged from Arabia and defeated both the Byzantine and Persian empires to carve out a new empire of its own.

11.1
11.2
11.3
11.4

What happened
to Islam after
Muhammad's
death?

tribes converted to Islam. At one extreme, conversion was accompanied by intermarriage, and some of the Arab conquerors and Berber peoples intermingled to the point where it was no longer possible to distinguish among them ethnically. In other cases, whole tribes converted. They became part of the Islamic world but remained in their tribal groupings. Often they conducted their own internal administration as if they were a small state. Other Muslim armies marched eastward, capturing large parts of central Asia, and raiding repeatedly in the Indus valley region of Sind.

Between 711 and 756, Arab and Berber forces crossed the Straits of Gibraltar and completed the conquest of Spain. Muslim raiders also moved into France, but Charles Martel and Frankish armies pushed them back south of the Pyrenees in 732 after the Battle of Tours.

Muslim governments continued to rule at least parts of Spain for seven and a half centuries, until 1492. During those years the relationship between Muslims, Christians, and Jews was sometimes strained. Sometimes, however, they were very fruitful.

The Umayyads copied the imperial structures of the Byzantine and Persian empires: wars of imperial conquest, bureaucracy in administration, monumentality in architecture, and regal opulence at court. They used Arabic as their language of administration, and encouraged conversion to Islam.

However, Umar's successors were not as committed to the program of equality under Islam as earlier caliphs had been. Their implementation was inconsistent, and various interest groups were frustrated by the vagaries of their changing fortunes. Many Sunni religious leaders, although pleased with the new emphasis on Islam, were offended by the imperial pomp of the Umayyads and their use of religion for blatantly political purposes. Many Shi'as continued to nourish the hope that one of their imams would displace the Umayyads and take his rightful place as caliph. In Kufa, Iraq, Shi'as revolted in 740, but the revolt was suppressed, and its leaders were executed.

The Ummayads had raised conflicting expectations. Non-Arab Muslims, whose taxes were not lowered or were lowered only temporarily, railed against the government for not delivering on its promises. Arabs were unhappy that their own taxes were being raised to compensate for the reductions offered to others.

The Umayyad armies, which were overextended and exhausted, began to lose major battles. The Turks drove them from Transoxiania in central Asia; the Khazars stopped them in Armenia in 730; Charles Martel halted the Umayyad advance in France in 732; the Greeks destroyed a major Muslim army in Anatolia in 740; in North Africa Berber rebels, although defeated in 742, destroyed an Umayyad army of 27,000 in the process. Umayyad forces did win the critical Battle of the Talas River in 751, halting the advance of Chinese forces westward and opening central Asia and its silk routes to Islamic religious and cultural missions, but they did not push forward. Military advances stopped. Pulled in many conflicting directions, without the strength to reply, the caliphate was drawn into a third civil war.

The Third Civil War and the Abbasid Caliphs

The Abbasid clan in northern Iran—descended from an uncle of Muhammad named Abbas and also claiming support from descendants of the line of Ali—revolted against the Umayyads. Supported by Arab settlers in Iran who were protesting against high taxes, by Shi'as who were seeking their own rule, and also by a faction from Yemen, the Abbasid clan overthrew the Umayyad caliphate. In 750, Abu al-Abbas al-Saffah initiated the new Abbasid caliphate, which ruled in reality for a century and a half but held power in name until 1258. Signaling new policy directions, the Abbasid caliph built a new capital at Baghdad, 500 miles east of Damascus, along the banks of the Tigris River, in the heart of the historic Fertile Crescent.

The Abbasid caliphs continued the tasks of the Umayyads in trying to bring order and unity to an empire of heterogeneous peoples, and they followed many of the principles set forth by Umar II. They used Arabic as a unifying language of official communication and administration, and continued to urge non-Muslims to convert. They recruited widely among all the peoples of the empire to fill administrative and military positions, and as the bureaucracy expanded, Nestorian Christians, Jews, Shi'as, and numerous ethnic groups became prominent in the Abbasid administration.

For a century the Abbasids succeeded—to a surprising degree—in solving the problems of administering large empires. They kept their administration cosmopolitan and centralized, yet at the same time in touch with local communities. They rotated their officers so that none could become entrenched and semi-independent in a distant posting. They regularized taxes. They employed spies as well as troops of soldiers and armed police. They also attempted to maintain good relations with local notables, such as village headmen, large landowners, *qadis* (judges), officials of local mosques, religious teachers, money-lenders, accountants, merchants, and family patriarchs, who were the critical sources of information and power in the villages and towns.

The Weakening of the Caliphate

Inevitably, however, the Abbasid caliphate, too, encountered difficulties. The process of choosing a successor to the caliph remained unresolved. At the death of Caliph

Clay figurine of a female slave from Khirbat al-Mafjar, Syria, *c.* eighth century. Female slaves had their place in the world of the Umayyad dynasty and beyond. Often the objects of passionate love, many were accomplished singers and highly educated.

11.1

11.2

What happened to Islam after Muhammad's death?

11.3

11.4

KEY TERM

qadi A judge in Islamic legal practice.

Portrait of Mahmud of Ghazni, from Rashid al-Din's *World History*, 1306–07. Mahmud (998–1030), a Sunni Muslim prince, is shown putting on the traditional diplomatic gift of a robe of honor, bestowed by the Abbasid caliph. Regional rulers sometimes declared their independence from central control, but Mahmud of Ghazni was careful to include the caliph's name on his coinage, thereby presenting himself as a loyal subject. The variety of headdresses, clothing, and facial types gives evidence of the immense geographical extent of the Abbasid caliphate. (Edinburgh University Library)

Harun-al-Rashid (r. 786–809), his two sons fought for the throne, provoking a fourth civil war. Recruiting troops proved an even bigger problem. Throughout the empire, local strongmen were invited to ally their troops to the caliph's armies, but these military contingents naturally owed their allegiance not to Baghdad but to the local potentate.

The caliphs expanded sharply the use of slave troops in their armies. Slave troops, mostly from central Asia, were often poorly disciplined, and sometimes various contingents turned on one another. At the same time the civilian bureaucracy became more corrupt and more distant from the general population, and tax collection was increasingly turned over to exploitative, semi-independent **tax farmers**. Corruption and reliance on slaves isolated the caliphs from their own civilian populations—the more imperial the caliphate, the more distant it became from the original Islamic ideals of equality and simplicity.

The Emergence of Quasi-independent States. As a consequence, revolts struck the caliphate. In 868 a Turkish commander established a virtually independent dynasty that included Egypt and Syria, until the caliph regained them in 905. The slaves in the salt mines of southern Iraq waged a successful revolt for 15 years, from 868 to 883. In 867, frontier troops in central Iran revolted and won control of southern and western Iran. Ismaili and Shi'a religious leaders organized revolts throughout the empire. Denying the legitimacy of Abbasid claims to rule and highlighting the exploitation of the village and tribal masses by the distant and corrupt administration in Baghdad, they won many victories in the name of their own views of Islam. Inspired by the Ismailis, peasant and Bedouin raiders attacked Mecca, briefly carrying away the sacred Ka'aba stone, the most venerated shrine in the holy city.

The Fatimid clan, claiming to be the rightful successors of the Prophet, conquered Egypt and much of northern Africa. They broke openly with Baghdad, declaring themselves the legitimate caliphs. In Iraq, other rebels took control first of the regions around Baghdad and then, in 945, of Baghdad itself. The caliph was permitted to continue to rule in name, but in effect the empire as a unified, centralized administration

KEY TERM

tax farmer An official entrusted with collecting taxes. The total amount to be collected was fixed by the government, and any collection exceeding that amount belonged to the tax farmer. The system encouraged exploitation of the taxpayer.

was finished. The unity of the Abbasid state dissolved, although the nominal authority of the caliph was still accepted everywhere.

Turkic-speaking Peoples and their Conquests. Meanwhile, in the seventh and eighth centuries, the consolidation of the Tang dynasty in China had revived the pressure on the pastoral, nomadic peoples of inner Asia, pushing them westward, just as the Han had done centuries before. This time the pastoral nomads encountered peoples who had converted to Islam. As a result of contacts with Muslim scholars and mystics, many of the nomadic peoples converted as well.

One of these groups, the **Turkic**-speaking Qarluq peoples, gained control of Bukhara (992) and Samarqand (999) in modern Uzbekistan. They propagated Islam and began to sponsor the development of the Turkish language and a Turkish–Islamic civilization.

Another Turkic-speaking group, led by the Seljuk (or Saljuq) family, entered central Asia, conquered Afghanistan and Iran, and seized Baghdad in 1055. In Baghdad, the Seljuk Turks kept the Abbasid caliph on his throne and ruled in his name. They titled themselves sultans, claiming authority over the secular side of government, while leaving the administration of religious affairs to the caliph.

The Mongols and the Destruction of the Caliphate. In the twelfth century, a new threat destabilized empires from China to Europe, including the areas under Muslim rule. In Karakorum, Mongolia, Temujin (c. 1162–1227), later called Chinggis (Genghis) Khan ("Universal Ruler"), forged a confederation of Mongol and Turkish peoples, who rode outward, east and west, creating the largest land-based empire in history. The story of the Mongol expansion is told in "Establishing World Trade Routes."

KEY TERM

Turkic/Turkish Turkic languages are a family of related languages spoken by peoples of central Asia and their descendants. The most widely spoken of these languages is Turkish.

Byzantium and Islam. The Byzantine Empire remained the bastion of Christian political power in Asia Minor for 1,000 years after the fall of Rome in the West. A powerful new force for Islam, the Seljuk Turks, appeared out of central Asia in the eleventh century. After invading Persia and Syria, they defeated a Byzantine army at Manzikert in 1071 and began to infiltrate the Byzantine heartland.

The empire of Timur, c. 1360–1405. The final stage of Mongol power was inspired by Timur's ambitions. Originating in Samarqand, his armies struck southeast to India, north to the Khanate of the Golden Horde, and west against the Ottoman and Egyptian Mameluke empires. The empire fragmented after Timur's death, but his descendants patronized Islamic culture in the capital cities of Samarqand and Bukhara.

11.1

11.2

11.3 How did Islam flower outside the Arab world?

11.4

KEY TERM

Sufi In Islam, a member of one of the orders practicing mystical forms of worship that first arose in the eighth and ninth centuries C.E.

Muslims whose lands the Mongols conquered felt devastated. An eyewitness observer, Ibn al-Athir, records his despair in the face of the early waves of invasions in 1220–21:

> For some years I continued averse from mentioning this event, deeming it so horrible that I shrank from recording it … To whom, indeed, can it be easy to write the announcement of the death-blow of Islam and the Muslims, or who is he on whom the remembrance thereof can weigh lightly? O would that my mother had not borne me, or that I had died and become a forgotten thing ere this befell … These [Mongols] spared none, slaying women and men and children, ripping open pregnant women and killing unborn babes. (McNeill and Waldman, pp. 249–51)

In 1258, Chinggis's grandson Hülegü (c. 1217–65) conquered Baghdad and executed the caliph, ending the Abbasid Empire. The Mongols might have continued further on their conquests in western Asia, but the death of Hülegü's brother in China diverted their attention. Meanwhile, the sultan in Cairo defeated the Mongol troops at the Battle of Ain Jalut, near Nazareth (1260), ending their threat of further advance. Mongol rule in west Asia continued, however, until 1336. Significantly, even after it lost its political power to the Mongols, Islam continued to expand and gain converts.

View the **Closer Look**: **A Mongol Passport** on **MyHistoryLab**

Spiritual, Religious, and Cultural Flowering

11.3 How did Islam flower outside the Arab world?

When the caliphate fell, the *umma* seemed to fall with it. Its political focus was destroyed. Earlier historians have therefore characterized 1258 as a downward turning point, ushering in a protracted decline. More recent writers, however, emphasize the continuing growth of Islam outside the Arab world. The descendants of the Mongols themselves converted to Islam within a century of their arrival in Islamic lands. Muslim scholars, mystics, and merchants carried Islam throughout the entire region of the Indian Ocean by sea, and along the length of the silk routes by land.

When Timur the Lame (Tamerlane or Tamburlane; 1336–1405) led his Turkish invaders along many of the same routes and in many of the same kinds of campaign as Chinggis Khan had done, sacking or capturing Delhi (1398), Aleppo (1400), Damascus (1401), Ankara (1402), and Bukhara (1402), he had the support of Islamic scholars and mystics, the **Sufis**. Timur's descendants patronized Islamic scholarship, and within a century Samarqand and Bukhara had become major capitals of Islamic culture. They also patronized Turkish as a literary language, encouraging its development as the third language of Islam along with Arabic and Persian.

Today, approximately 17 percent of the world's Muslim population lives in Southeast Asia, an area never subject to the rule of the caliphate; 30 percent lives in south Asia, where conversion took place almost entirely after its fall; 12 percent lives in sub-Saharan Africa, again virtually untouched by the caliphate. In short, some 60 percent of today's Muslims are descended from peoples who had no connection to the Abbasid caliphate in Baghdad. In the following pages we consider the factors

CHAPTER ELEVEN: ISLAM 570 C.E.–1500 C.E.

11.1

11.2

How did Islam
flower outside
the Arab world?

11.3

11.4

that enabled Islam to flourish and spread as a religion and a civilization even after
its historic political center collapsed.

Read the **Document: A Contemporary Describes Timur** on **MyHistoryLab**

Islam Reaches New Peoples

The end of the caliphate did not mean the end of the spread of Islam; quite the contrary. Regional rulers, finding themselves more independent, pursued policies of
political and military expansion while proclaiming the religion and culture of Islam
as their own.

India. A Muslim government run by slave soldiers who had earned their freedom
established itself in Ghazni, Afghanistan, as early as 962. From that base, Muslims
launched raids into India and established their rule over the Punjab. In 1211, the
Muslim general who conquered Delhi declared himself an independent sultan, initiating a series of five dynasties, which are known collectively as the Sultanate of
Delhi (1211–1526). By 1236 they controlled northern India; by 1335, almost the entire
subcontinent.

Delivering a lecture. A traditional saying—"Kings are the rulers of the people, but scholars are the
rulers of kings"—indicates the esteem in which learning is traditionally held by Muslims. Moreover,
the transmission of knowledge was deemed a major act of piety. A well-stocked library serves as the
backdrop for a lecture, in which a teacher would first dictate a text, then discourse upon it. (Bibliothèque
Nationale, Paris)

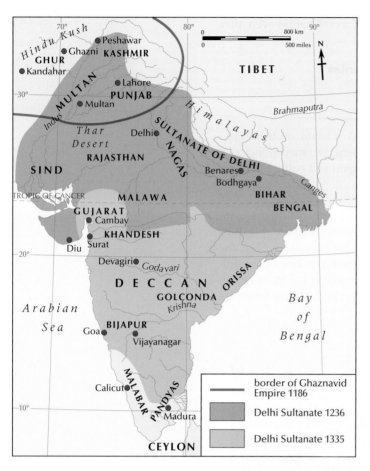

The rise of the Delhi Sultanate. The Muslim Afghan Ghaznavid Empire was the first of a number of Afghan and Turkic powers who, exploiting divisions among local Hindu rulers, established their hegemony in northern India. Based at Delhi, six successive Muslim dynasties commanded varying territorial extents, but only briefly, in the mid-fourteenth century, did they completely control the Deccan.

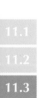

11.1

11.2

11.3   How did Islam flower outside the Arab world?

11.4

When Delhi's power dimmed, numerous Muslim rulers controlled other regions of India. These regional governments, in particular, stayed close to their subjects, encouraged the development of regional languages, and provided new opportunities to Sufis (Muslim mystics and teachers) to introduce and practice Islam in new areas. In 1526, temporarily, and in 1556, more permanently, a mixture of Mongol and Turkish Muslim invaders conquered India, heralding the start of a new era, the Mughal (from Mongol) Empire.

Most, but not all, of the Muslim rulers recognized the importance of a respectful religious accommodation with the overwhelming Hindu majority. The first Muslim invaders in Sind in the eighth century extended a protected status to Hindus usually granted only to monotheists. They argued that behind the many forms of god in Hinduism there was just one reality. They also recognized that warfare against so large a majority of Hindus was impossible. They allowed Hindus to practice their own religion as long as they accepted Islamic rule. Usually they protected Hindu temples, although in some instances they defaced shrines as a means of asserting their own supremacy. For example, they destroyed the famous Shaivite temple at Somnath, western India, in 1024. The Turkish forces occupying Bengal and Bihar also destroyed the last remaining libraries and monasteries of Buddhism in that region, delivering the final death blow to a religion that had already seen most of its following in India disappear.

The Muslim conquest of India opened the subcontinent to Persians, Afghans, Turks, and Mongols seeking jobs with the new governments. This immigration brought a variety of Islamic practices to India, where no single orthodoxy prevailed. Diverse Muslims coexisted with diverse Hindus, venerating some saints and sharing some devotions in common. India's population became 20–25 percent Muslim. Many were descendants of Muslim immigrants near the top of the social hierarchy; others were converts, escaping untouchability at the bottom of the caste system. The vast majority of India's population, however, remained Hindu.

Southeast Asia. The beginning of mass conversions of Southeast Asians to Islam came in the fourteenth and fifteenth centuries, and today, Malaysia and Indonesia are overwhelmingly Muslim. Ocean traders and Sufis from India seem to have accomplished most of the missionary work. The traders offered increased economic opportunities to those local people who would adopt Islam, while the Sufis and the regional kings of Southeast Asia exchanged support for one another in a familiar pattern of interdependence between religious and political leaders.

Sub-Saharan Africa. As in Southeast Asia, Islam was first carried to sub-Saharan Africa by traders and Sufis. They came from three directions: from Mediterranean North Africa across the Sahara to West Africa; from Egypt up the Nile to East Africa; and from India and Arabia across the Indian Ocean to the coast of East Africa.

The Arab conquest of North Africa in the seventh and early eighth centuries set the scene for increasing contact between Arab and Black Africans. As traders, and

Islam in south and Southeast Asia. The disruption of centralized political power in the Muslim world did not stop the expansion of Islam in Africa and southern Asia. Arab maritime traders carried their faith to the shores of India and onward throughout maritime Southeast Asia. The Indian heartland was conquered by successive waves of Muslim invaders, who, by 1400, secured the key Indo-Gangetic plain.

11.1

11.2

11.3

11.4

How did Islam flower outside the Arab world?

sometimes as warriors, the Arabs began to cross the Sahara. When they reached the southern "shore" of the Sahara [the sahel], they found flourishing kingdoms in place, their power derived from control of the desert trade routes and the taxes they imposed on this trade. Founded (according to legend) in about 300 C.E., Ghana was the largest of these sub-Saharan kingdoms. (This Ghana is located approximately in the area of modern Mali, and is not to be confused with modern Ghana, to the southeast.) By the ninth century Ghana was both a partner and a rival of the northern Berbers for control of Saharan trade. Along these routes, gold, slaves, hides, and ivory were transported northward in exchange for copper, silver, metal goods, horses, dried fruit, cloth, and salt transported southward.

By the eleventh century, a network of Islamic traders extended from the Atlantic Ocean in the west to modern-day Nigeria in the east, from the Sahara in the north to the fringes of the forested areas in the south. The traders included people of the Mandingo, Jakhande, and Dyula ethnic groups. Traders from the north invited their southern counterparts to adopt their religion, and Sufis came to establish new communities of faith and good works. Although the common people were not much affected until the nineteenth century, leading traders and rulers began to convert to Islam.

Trade connections were not the only source of converts. A wave of conversions also followed the domination of Ghana in the eleventh century by the Almoravid dynasty of Morocco. The Almoravids and their Berber allies waged a holy war to convert the Ghanaians, although many of the new converts continued to participate in indigenous religious practices even while officially accepting Islam. The Almoravids fought among themselves, as well as against the Ghanaians, and their cattle degraded the ecology of the region. Groups that had been ruled by, or allied with, the kingdom of Ghana began to assert their autonomy, until in about 1235 the Keita kings of Mali, with greater access to the Niger River, surpassed Ghana in importance. Mali's founding king, Sundiata, is commemorated in the national epic of his nation, the *Sundiata*, as a great hunter and warrior possessed of magical powers. Although he himself observed African religious practices along with Islam, he encouraged his people to accept Islam.

About a century later, a more orthodox Muslim came to rule Mali. Mansa Musa (r. 1307–32) made the *hajj* to Mecca in 1324, disbursing legendary amounts of gold along the way. He and subsequent rulers of Mali sought prestige through public affiliation with, and support for, Islamic institutions. They made improvements in Timbuktu, the most important trading city on the Niger River, at its northern bend near the Sahara, transforming the city into a major center of Arabic and Islamic studies. In the late fifteenth century, however, Sonni Ali (r. 1464–92), king of the Songhay people, slightly to the east, destroyed the empire of Mali and diminished its connection to the Islamic world of North Africa. Mali's rulers and people resumed the kind of halfway position between Islam and traditional African religions that Sundiata had held. Islam continued to be important in the private life but not the governance of the country. Mosques, for example, were treated as sanctuaries, so long as they were not used for political meetings.

Ironically, at the death of Sonni Ali, one of his former generals, al-Hajj (the informal title often given to a person who has completed the *hajj* pilgrimage) Muhammad Askia (r. 1493–1528) helped to restore connections with major Islamic centers in North Africa. Timbuktu resumed its growth. By the mid-sixteenth century, when it was under the rule of Songhay, Timbuktu held between 150 and 180 Quranic elementary schools, which, in turn, laid the foundations for more advanced education. Timbuktu's scholarship matched that of Morocco, and leading scholars of Morocco came to learn from Timbuktu's leading scholar, Ahmad Baba (1556–1627). In 1591, however, the power of the city and its trading networks was undercut by the conquest of the region by Moroccan forces. Although the Moroccans were also Muslims, they acted as conquerors rather than as members of the same religious community, and the status of Muslims actually declined.

From Ghana, Mali, and Songhay, Islam was spreading eastward across Africa. For example, at the beginning of the twelfth century, the king of Kanem converted to Islam, made a pilgrimage to Mecca, and constructed a religious school in Cairo for students from Kanem. His subjects followed him in converting to Islam. When his Saifawa ruling dynasty was forced militarily to leave Kanem in the mid-fourteenth century, it reestablished its Muslim state in nearby Bornu. Islamic influences from Kanem and Bornu, in turn, reinforced the religious message brought by the scholars accompanying traders from Mali to the neighboring Hausa people in Kano in modern northern Nigeria. In these lands, too, Islamic practices and local religious practices often blended, with the people choosing whichever seemed most efficacious in their personal lives. Kings often responded similarly, following the practices that seemed most associated with their military victories, and abandoning those that seemed to accompany defeats.

Still farther east, the upper Nile valley had been mostly Christianized by the time Muslim traders, gold miners, and slave traders arrived. As Muslim governments in Egypt began to push southward, however, they defeated the Nubian Christian kingdom and Islam began to take root, with the first Islamic states in Nubia dating to around 1500. The state of Sinnar, ruled by the Funj dynasty, became the most important of these states, in part because its subjects were expected to accept the Islamic religion of its rulers, and it gave special privileges to Islamic holy men and scholars.

By the eighth century, Islam arrived on Africa's east coast. As it crossed from Arabia and Yemen into East Africa, it met fierce resistance in Ethiopia, which had become staunchly Christian. Nevertheless, about 1630, a Portuguese missionary estimated that Muslims made up one-third of Ethiopia's population. A mosque at Shanga, off the east coast of Kenya, dates to about the beginning of the ninth century. At about the same time, al-Masudi, an Arab historian and sailor, reported Muslim settlers on the east coast of Africa. Much larger growth appeared in the thirteenth century, and by the fourteenth century more than 30 communities had built their mosques along the East African coast. Kilwa, in southeastern Tanzania, was the most important settlement and port, and modern archaeologists have been busy excavating its medieval remains along with those of other coastal towns. Philologists also study the interaction between the Arabic language of the overseas traders and the Swahili language of the African coast as trading necessities brought the two languages—and the two peoples—together.

Islam in Africa. Islam entered sub-Saharan Africa as a result of trade. Trans-Saharan caravans from Egypt, Libya, and Morocco gradually introduced the faith overland among the trading kingdoms of West Africa, while the Arab traders of the Indian Ocean carried the message south by sea along the east coast of the continent.

Law Provides an Institutional Foundation

One of the central features of Islamic society that survived the fall of the caliphate was the law. The legal systems of Islam, *shari'a*, lived on and flourished. For Muslims, as for other populations, law expresses in formal terms the standards of proper conduct. Law supports the fundamental Islamic duty of *hisba*, "to promote what is right and to prevent what is wrong" (Musallam in Robinson, p. 175). Muslims encounter their legal system in the regulation of public life; in family matters of marriage, divorce, parental responsibilities, and inheritance; and in the *shari'a*'s advice on such daily activities as eating, dressing, and housekeeping.

As the early caliphs and the Abbasids began to confront legal questions, they appointed to resolve them. The *qadis* searched the classical texts of the Quran, the *hadith* (quotations from Muhammad), and biographies of the Prophet for their core teachings, and then relied on a combination of local custom and their own deliberation and judgment (*ijtihad*) in rendering final decisions.

Seeking to overcome wide differences in local practices, four great legal scholars of the eighth and ninth centuries formulated the major systems of Islamic law that

How did Islam flower outside the Arab world?

11.1
11.2
11.3
11.4

KEY TERMS

hadith Traditional records of the deeds and utterances of the prophet Muhammad, and the basis, after the Quran, for Islamic theology and law.

ijtihad A method of Quranic interpretation based on text, local custom, and the personal judgment of the *qadi*, or judge.

endure today: the system of Abu Hanifah (699–767), in use mostly in the Arab Middle East and south Asia; of Malik ibn Anas (*c.* 715–95) in North, central, and West Africa; of Muhammad al-Shafii (767–820) in East Africa, southern Arabia, and Southeast Asia; and of Ahmad ibn Hanbal (780–855) in Saudi Arabia. Although most localities have followed one or another of these systems since about the tenth century, the existence of multiple systems has allowed flexibility in interpretation. Under certain circumstances, local legal experts have the option of drawing on any of the four texts. Because Shi'ites maintain different traditions of authority, encompassing the teachings of Ali and the early imams, they have also developed different schools of law. The most widespread is that of Jafar al-Sadiq (d. 765).

The personnel of the legal system are the ***ulama*** (singular *alim*), the religiously trained scholars of Islam who interpret and implement the law. The *ulama* constitute a class that includes *qadis* and their assistants, Quran reciters, prayer leaders, and preachers. The *ulama* are sometimes trained in formal theological schools or, more frequently, are simply apprenticed to senior *ulama*. Islam has no formal hierarchical, bureaucratic institution of *ulama*—indeed, it has no official Church. Informal networks of respected *ulama* have provided cohesion, stability, and flexibility within Islam, regardless of the changing forms of government.

Ideally, *ulama* and ruler worked together to decide and implement religious policy, but when Caliph al-Mamun (r. 813–33) proclaimed that he had the right to give authoritative interpretations of the Quran, the *ulama* mobilized the population of Baghdad against him. He responded with an inquisition to root out these opponents. The only major leader who stood up to him was Ahmad ibn Hanbal, the greatest *hadith* scholar of his generation, who argued that only the scholars had the authority to interpret Quranic text. The people supported him, and to escape the continuing popular protest, Caliph al-Mutasim (r. 833–42) moved his capital from densely populated Baghdad to Samarra, 60 miles away.

In 848–49, Caliph al-Mutawakkil (d. 861) withdrew the claim of caliphal authority in religious matters. The *ulama* had won, but the battle had so embittered relations between caliph and *ulama* that their spheres of influence were forever separated: the caliph had authority over matters of state; the *ulama* over matters of religion. The caliphs came to represent the imperial aspirations of the state, while the *ulama* represented the everyday needs and wishes of the people. Over time, such departures from popular accountability cost them the caliphate. But the *ulama* endured, in touch with the people, serving as their religious guides and frequently providing welfare services as well.

Sufis Provide Religious Mysticism

Law brings order to life. It makes concrete the responsibilities of one individual to another and to society in general. In Islam it also fixes the formal obligations due to God. The *ulama* conveyed and interpreted this message, carrying it to people in vastly different societies. Sufis also spread Islam to many parts of the world, but they were much less interested than the *ulama* in strict religious doctrine and emphasized devotion to Allah instead.

📖 **Read** the **Document: Sufi Poetry: Hafez, from the Diwan** on **MyHistoryLab**

The Role of Mysticism. As the Umayyad Empire weakened, many people inhabiting it began to reject the materialism of its leaders and turned to a pious asceticism. For these spiritual seekers, Sufis revealed Islam's inner, mystical path to God. Early Sufis found and transmitted the inner discipline of mind and body and the purification of the heart that enabled their followers to feel that they experienced God directly as the ultimate reality. They usually disdained worldly pleasures. One of the earliest of the Sufis, Hasan al-Basri (643–728), concluded: "This world has neither worth nor weight

KEY TERM

ulama The theologians and legal experts of Islam.

CHAPTER ELEVEN: ISLAM 570 C.E.–1500 C.E.

11.1

11.2

11.3

11.4

How did Islam
flower outside
the Arab world?

with God, so slight it is" (Esposito, 1991, p. 102). Although most Sufis were men, some, like Rabi'a al-Adawiyya (d. 801), were women. Rabi'a, the Hindu Mirabai, rejected marriage in order to devote herself to God: "Love of God hath so absorbed me that neither love nor hate of any other thing remain in my heart" (Embree, p. 448).

As we have seen throughout this part, every theistic religion has an aspect of devotional love of God, expressed through spontaneous prayer, private meditation, fasting, and asceticism, and, often, through physical disciplines, music, dance, and poetry. In Islam these aspects were adopted by the Sufis, who also absorbed influences from the mystics of other religions, especially monasticism from Christianity and Buddhism, and ecstasy in prayer from Hinduism.

Through their lives of exemplary devotion to God and people, the Sufis enhanced the message of Islam. They attracted people through the simplicity of their piety, their personal love of God, and their dedication to the needs of others. Some developed a reputation for magical powers. The mosques where they lived and prayed, and the mausolea in which they were buried, were revered as sacred shrines. A sixteenth-century folk ballad of eastern Bengal tells of one such Sufi saint:

> At that time there came a Mahomedan pir [Sufi] to that village. He built a mosque in its outskirts, and for the whole day sat under a fig tree … His fame soon spread far and wide. Everybody talked of the occult powers that he possessed. If a sick man called on him he would cure him at once by dust or some trifle touched by him. He read and spoke the innermost thoughts of a man before he opened his mouth … Hundreds of men and women came every day to pay him their respects. Whatever they wanted they miraculously got from this saint. Presents of rice, fruits, and other delicious food, goats, chickens, and fowls came in large quantities to his doors. Of these offerings the pir did not touch a bit but freely distributed all among the poor. (Eaton in Adas, pp. 21–22)

Individual mystics appeared in Islam from its earliest days, drawing their inspiration directly from the Quran. Centuries later, they began to form **tariqas**, or mystical

Whirling dervishes. Sufism represents the mystical, contemplative strand of Islam—a strand that is captured vividly by this example of "whirling dervishes," the Mawlawi religious order closely linked to the teachings of the thirteenth-century Persian poet Jalal-al-Din Rumi. Their slow, revolving dance helps to create higher states of consciousness, while being a ceremonial ritual in its own right.

KEY TERM

tariqa In Islam, a generic term meaning "path," referring to the doctrines and methods of mysticism and esoterism. The word also refers to schools or brotherhoods of mystics, which were often situated at a mosque or the tomb of a Muslim saint.

SOURCE

Al-Ghazali, the "Renewer of Islam"

The more solemn *ulama* and the more emotional Sufis were often suspicious of one another. Deeply disturbed by the tension between the two perspectives, the revered scholar Abu Hamid Muhammad al-Ghazali (1058–1111) finally formulated a synthesis of the intellectual and mystical sides of Islam that has proved satisfying to Muslims ever since.

Born and educated in Iran, al-Ghazali was appointed at the age of 33 to teach philosophy at the leading *madrasa*, or theological institute, in Baghdad. During four years there, Ghazali began to doubt the importance of rationality in life, and searched for more holistic ways of experiencing the world. Torn between holding his prestigious tenure at the *madrasa* and giving it up to pursue new roads toward truth, Ghazali was on the verge of breakdown:

> For nearly six months … I was continuously tossed about between the attractions of worldly desires and the impulses towards eternal life. In that month the matter ceased to be one of choice and became one of compulsion. God caused my tongue to dry up so that I was prevented from lecturing. One particular day I would make an effort to lecture in order to gratify the hearts of my following, but my tongue would not utter a single word nor could I accomplish anything at all. This impediment in my speech produced grief in my heart, and at the same time my power to digest and assimilate food and drink was impaired; I could hardly swallow or digest a single mouthful of food. (al-Ghazali, p. 57)

In 1095 Ghazali resigned his post. He traveled to Damascus, Jerusalem, and Mecca, and then returned to his home town, where he lived the monastic life of a Sufi mystic for ten years:

> I learnt with certainty that it is above all the mystics who walk on the road of God; their life is the best life, their method the soundest method, their character the purest character. (p. 60)

During his time of contemplation, Ghazali wrote a great number of philosophical and theological works, including the influential *Revival of the Religious Sciences*, exploring the relationship between religion and reason. He asserted the importance of mystical experience and a direct, personal understanding of God, while at the same time defending the doctrine and authority of the Islamic faith.

In 1106 Ghazali was persuaded to return to teaching, now proclaiming the complementarity of Sufism and rationality:

> Just as intellect is one of the stages of human development in which there is an "eye" which sees the various types of intelligible objects, which are beyond the ken of the senses, so prophecy also is the description of a state in which there is an eye endowed with light such that in that light the unseen and other supra-intellectual objects become visible. (p. 65)

By the end of his life, Ghazali's reconciliation of Sufism and rationality within Islam had earned him the title "Renewer of Islam."

11.1

11.2

11.3

11.4

How did Islam flower outside the Arab world?

brotherhoods, often located at the mosque or mausoleum of an especially revered saint. Some *tariqas* emphasized ecstatic practices; others were more sober and meditative. The *tariqa mawlawiya* was founded by Jalal-al-Din Rumi (1207–73) in Konya, Turkey. Rumi is most famous for his expression of ecstatic worship through the dance of the "whirling dervishes." Rumi's Persian language text, the *Mathnawi*, expressed in rich and evocative lyrics his love of God: "The result of religion is nothing but rapture" (Rumi, *Mathnawi* 1:312, Vitray-Meyerovitch, p. 83).

Intellectual Achievements

As the *ulama* provided order to the social structures of Islam, and the Sufis spread its spiritual powers, other intellectuals further enriched its cultural depth.

History. The historian and theologian al-Tabari (*c.* 839–923) introduced formal historical writings with his *History of Prophets and Kings*. The segment on prophecy recorded the contributions from Abraham through Muhammad; the record of kings covered rulers from Biblical times to his own and included eyewitness reports of relatively recent events.

With the conquest of Iran in the mid-seventh century, Persian became the second language of Islam. (The arrival of the Turks in 923 introduced Turkish as the third.) The Persian poet Ferdowsi (940–1020) wrote an epic poem on the mythical origins of the Persian peoples, in which one of his central themes is the tragedy that befalls "a good man whose king is a fool."

The Mongols also supported historical writing, including al-Juvaini's (1226–83) *History of the World Conquerors*, which told of Chinggis Khan's conquests, especially in Iran. Rashid al-Din (1247–1318) wrote *World History*, which many regard as the first attempt at a history of humanity, as it integrates Chinese, Indian, European, Muslim, and Mongol history into a single cosmopolitan perspective.

Although others, notably Rashid al-Din, had attempted to write comprehensive, narrative histories, Ibn Khaldun (1332–1406) of Tunis is often viewed as the first to apply social science theory to the study of history. His *Universal History* stressed a cyclical theory of history, in which vigorous nomadic peoples regularly conquered urban peoples who were settled, cultured, and contented, took over their cities, settled into lives of luxury, and then themselves fell prey to the next round

Mihrab in the Great Mosque, Córdoba, Spain, *c.* 961–76. Under the Umayyads, Córdoba grew to be by far the most prosperous city in Western Europe, second only to Baghdad in the Islamic world. At its height, the city is said to have contained some 300 public baths and 3,000 mosques within its walls. Shown here is the most important surviving mosque. Great attention was lavished on the decoration of the Great Mosque, and the *mihrab*, a small domed chamber indicating the direction of Mecca, is considered unique for its horseshoe-shaped doorway, a stylistic innovation of the Muslims in Spain.

of invasion from more robust nomads. The theory seemed to fit the comings and goings of nomadic invaders from Arabia, Mongolia, and central Asia that characterized his times. Among Ibn Khaldun's other interpretive themes that still seem insightful today are: "The differences between Easterners and Westerners are cultural [not innate]" (p. 51); "The differences between peoples arise principally from the differences in their occupations" (p. 80); and, perhaps, "Scholars are of all men those least fitted for politics and its ways" (p. 64).

Philosophy. Theology and philosophy had been regarded as inferior to revelation in early Islam, but as Muslims came into contact with the philosophies of the Hellenistic and Indian worlds, they were drawn to concepts of Platonism and Neoplatonism in particular. The caliphate established in Baghdad a "house of wisdom," a translation bureau under Hunayn ibn Ishaq (803–73). In the next 200 years some 80 Greek authors were translated, including Aristotle, Plato, Galen, and Euclid. So, too, were writings from Syriac, Sanskrit, and Persian.

A group of Islamic philosophers, called Mutazilites, "those who keep themselves apart," began to challenge orthodox Islamic belief, arguing that the attributes of God in the Quran were not literal but metaphorical, that human actions and life were not predetermined, and that the Quran had not existed eternally. Al-Farabi (c. 870–950) argued that philosophical knowledge gained through study and thought was of higher value than revelation from God. Similar notions of the supremacy of philosophy were expressed by al-Kindi (d. 870), Ibn Sina (Avicenna; d. 1037), and Ibn Rushd (Averroes; 1126–98). Such philosophical speculation was marginal to mainstream Islamic thought, and actually found more resonance among Christian and Jewish philosophers of the time.

Christian thinkers in Europe were indebted to the Muslims for keeping alive the Hellenistic traditions, for with the fall of the Roman Empire in the West the intellectual traditions and resources of the European Classical world had been neglected and forgotten. Now, thanks to Arabic translations and Islamic thought, Christian and Jewish philosophers grappled both with the original texts from Greece and India, and with the newer concepts introduced by Muslim thinkers.

Mathematics, Astronomy, and Medicine. The intersection of intellectual traditions also enriched mathematics, astronomy, and medicine. Indian scholars brought their texts on astronomy to Baghdad as early as 770. The caliph had them translated into Arabic, which was becoming the common language of scholarship throughout the empire. Arabs adopted and transmitted Hindi numerals and the decimal system, including the zero, throughout the empire and into Europe, where they were (mis) named "Arabic" numerals. A few decades later, al-Khwarazmi (d. c. 846) used Indian texts in conjunction with scholarship from Greece and Iran to develop algebra (from the Arabic al-jabr, "restoration"). (The word algorithm comes from al-Khwarazmi's name.) Al-Biruni (d. 1046) wrote extensively on number theory and computation, and later scholars developed the trigonometry we study today.

Al-Biruni also wrote al-Qanun al-Mas'udi, a compendium of Islamic astronomy, which incorporated findings from throughout the empire. Arabic mathematical and astronomical theories apparently informed Copernicus' sixteenth-century theories of a **heliocentric** universe.

Medical wisdom and herbal remedies were transmitted from one end of the empire to the other. Al-Razi (Rhazes; c. 865–c. 935) compiled an encyclopedia of medicine giving the views of Greek, Syrian, Indian, Iranian, and Arab writers on each disease, and including his own clinical observations and opinions. Ibn Sina, noted above for his contributions to philosophy, produced the even more encyclopedic Qanun fi'l-tibb ("Canon of Medicine"), which included volumes on the pharmacology of herbs, the functioning of organs, fevers, and surgery. The Qanun was translated into Latin and dominated medical thinking for 300 years.

KEY TERM

heliocentric A system in which the sun is assumed to be at the center of the solar system—or of the universe—while Earth and the other planets move around it.

The Extension of Technology

11.1
11.2
How did Islam
flower outside
the Arab world? 11.3
11.4

By 751, at the end of the Umayyad dynasty, Islam served as a network of communication that linked all the major civilizations of Eurasia. For example, as we noted above, Muslims learned papermaking from the Chinese and transmitted the technology throughout their domain. European Christians learned the art from Muslims in Spain.

Exchanges of information on agriculture and crops also enriched the world of Islam. Between the eighth and tenth centuries, Arabs brought from India hard wheat, rice, varieties of sorghum, sugar cane, bananas, sour oranges, lemons, limes, mangoes, watermelon, coconut palm, spinach, artichokes, eggplants, and the key industrial crop, cotton. All these crops were introduced throughout the empire, wherever climatic conditions were favorable. This may well have been the largest agricultural exchange in world history up to that time. Because most of these crops from India were warm-weather crops, many of them facilitated summer cropping in areas that had previously lain fallow in that season. To replicate the monsoon climate of India, Muslim officials improved existing forms of irrigation (underground water canals and water-lifting mechanisms) and invented new ones (certain kinds of cistern). Agricultural productivity diversified and increased, encouraging population increase in general and urban growth in particular.

City Design and Architecture

Muslim governments built great cities and adorned their public spaces lavishly and often exquisitely. The largest of the cities were the political capitals. Baghdad was built on the west bank of the Tigris River in 762 to serve as the capital of the Abbasid dynasty, and it served that purpose for almost 500 years. In the ninth century, with between 300,000 and 500,000 people in 25 square miles, Baghdad became the largest city in the world outside China.

As the caliphate declined, and Baghdad with it, regional capitals grew in importance: Bukhara, Nishapur, and Isfahan in the east, and Cairo, Fez, and Córdoba in the west. The Fatimid rulers of Egypt began their administration in Fustat and expanded that existing city into al-Qahira (Cairo) in 969. In Morocco, King Idris II (r. 791–828) built Fez in 808 as the capital of the Idrisid dynasty, which had been founded by his father. A later dynasty, the Almoravids, built their capital Marrakesh in 1070. In Andalusia, southern Spain, the Umayyads developed Córdoba into one of the most cosmopolitan cities of the Islamic world. It achieved its greatest splendor in the mid-tenth century, but was sacked by Berbers in 1013 and never fully recovered. The architecture of these cities proclaimed the splendor of Islam and the power of the Muslim rulers.

Although the daily prayers in Islam may be performed privately, Friday noon prayers require collective assembly, so all cities and most neighborhoods within cities also constructed mosques for public services. Wealthy rulers proclaimed their power and piety by building monumental central mosques, as they did early on in Jerusalem, Medina, and Damascus. The Abbasids constructed an enormous central mosque in Baghdad, and during the years that Samarra served as their capital (848–52) a huge mosque was constructed there, too. Great mosques were also built at Qayrawan in Tunisia, Fez in Morocco, and Córdoba in Spain.

As the Seljuk Turks conquered and then joined the world of Islam, they built an especially monumental mosque at Isfahan in the late eleventh century, and then rebuilt it 50 years later after Ismaili Shi'as burned it down. Ottoman architects, most notably Hoja Sinan (1490–1578), constructed magnificent mosques, such as the Selimiye at Edirne and the Sulaymaniye in Istanbul, and other public buildings that incorporated Byzantine and Islamic forms. When Islam crossed the Sahara Desert, a new architectural form developed: the Sahelian mosque (see the chapter entitled

The Great Mosque and minaret of al-Mutawakkil, Samarra, Iraq, 848–52. Although now only a shadow of its former glory, this 1,150-year-old mosque remains the largest of its kind in the world. Essential elements of simple mosque architecture emerge clearly through the ruins: a central courtyard or atrium, and a minaret, or tower, from which the *muezzin* (crier) summons the community to worship.

11.1

11.2

11.3   How did Islam
flower outside
11.4   the Arab world?

"Establishing World Trade Routes"). When Mansa Musa returned from his trip to Mecca in 1325, he brought with him an Arab architect to supervise the construction of mosques and *madrasas* (theological schools), especially in Timbuktu.

Because Islam teaches that all the dead should be honored, and some believe that the saintly among them could confer blessings, mausolea have a special significance and sanctity. The followers of Timur (Tamerlane), for example, built an enormous tomb for him at Samarqand in 1405. Some burial shrines reveal extraordinary personal love and devotion. In 1632–49 Emperor Shah Jahan built perhaps the best known of all Islamic buildings, the Taj Mahal in Agra, India, as a mausoleum for his wife Mumtaz Mahal, who died giving birth to their fifteenth child. At a more humble level, simple tombs of local holy men are found throughout the Islamic world, attracting followers, especially women, who pour out their hearts in prayer, trusting that the sanctity of the saint will carry it to God.

The public architecture of mosques, mausolea, and, to a lesser extent, the royal and governmental buildings that frequently adjoin them anchored the formal religious and political institutions of the Islamic city. The bazaar, or market area, was home to business activities. Business in Islam was an honored profession. Muhammad himself

11.1
11.2
11.3
11.4

How did Islam
flower outside
the Arab world?

had been a caravan operator, and his first wife had been a businesswoman. Even today, mosques often control the land immediately adjacent to them and lease it to businesses so that the rents can support the mosque.

Islamic cities were, in effect, nodes on international trade routes linking the Islamic world to Europe and China. These trade routes enabled the movement not only of goods but also of people and ideas from one end of Eurasia to the other. The *hajj* to Mecca was also instrumental in creating a communication network among the regions and peoples of Islam.

The *Rihla*, or travelogues, of Ibn Battuta demonstrate the opportunities for travel open to a person of culture. In 30 years of traveling from his home in Tangier, he traversed approximately 73,000 miles of territories that today belong to some 50 different countries. Thanks to his mastery of Arabic and his knowledge of *shari'a*, Ibn Battuta found a welcome reception, and frequently temporary employment and gifts of wives and wealth in the lands he traversed. Muhammad Tughluq, sultan of Delhi, appointed him a *qadi* and, later, his envoy to China.

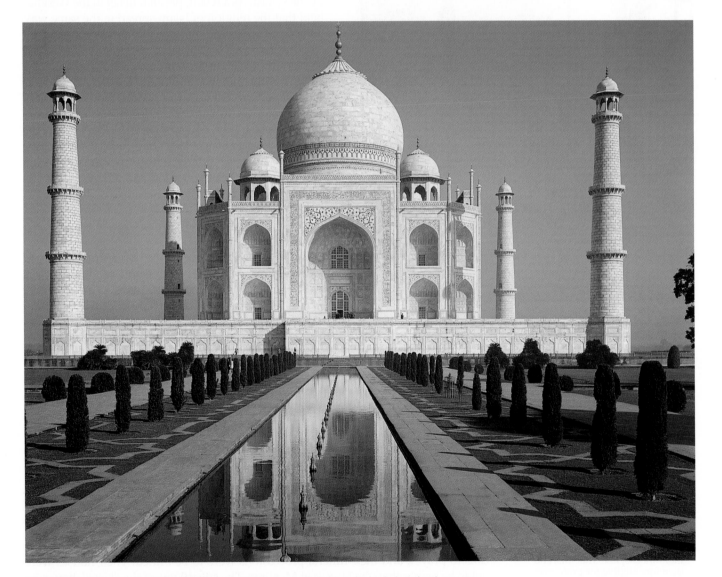

The Taj Mahal, Agra, India, 1632–48. Built by India's emperor Shah Jahan for his beloved wife Mumtaz Mahal, who died in childbirth, this mausoleum complex is considered the finest example of Mughal architecture, blending Indian, Persian, and Islamic styles. One of the most beautiful buildings in the world, the Taj was designated a UNESCO World Heritage site in 1983.

Bronzesmith, Isfahan bazaar, Iran. In Islam, religion and business are integrally linked, in that the land adjoining mosques is often leased to market traders whose rents support the buildings and their activities. Closest to the mosque are the "noble trades," such as books, perfumes, and religious objects. Here, a bronzesmith works outside his shop in the bazaar at Isfahan, which has been thriving since the third century.

Ibn Battuta's tales of adventure reflect the unity of the Islamic world. Despite its diversity, this world was held together by reverence for the Quran, the *shari'a*, the Arabic language (supplemented by Persian and Turkish), the political officials who ruled in its cities, and the scholars and merchants who traveled through them.

Relations with Non-Muslims

11.4 How did Muslims interact with non-Muslims?

Early Islamic governments spread their worldly power by the sword. As a result, popular belief in the West has held that the religion of Islam spread in the same way. Although conversion by force was practiced occasionally (just as it was by Christianity), by and large forced conversion to Islam was unusual. For example, the early "rightly guided" caliphs and the early Umayyads did not seek to convert the people they conquered. They preferred to rule as Arab Muslim conquerors over non-Arab, non-Muslim subjects. Only when the later Umayyads feared that they could not continue minority rule over so large a majority did they decide actively to seek conversion of, and alliance with, the conquered peoples.

Dhimmi Status

From the earliest days of Muslim conquest, non-Muslims were offered three options. The first was to convert to Islam. The second was to accept "protected," *dhimmi*, status as worshipers of one God who accepted Muslim rule. All the monotheistic "peoples of the book"—Christians, Jews, and Zoroastrians—were eligible for this status. Later, Islamic governments in India also extended *dhimmi* status to Hindus. The *dhimmi* were often required to pay a special tax, but they could follow their own religion and their own personal law regarding marriage, divorce, and inheritance, and they were to be protected by the Muslim government. The third option was to fight against the Muslim state, an option that few chose.

The status of the *dhimmi* was spelled out in "The Pact of Umar," a document ascribed to Umar I, the second caliph. It prescribed second-class status for the *dhimmi*. They were not to build new houses of worship nor to reconstruct old ones. They were not to convert anyone to their religion. They were not to wear the same clothing as Muslims, but to wear distinguishing garments. The sounds of their prayers, their calls to prayer, and their funeral processions were to be muted. Their houses were not to be higher than the houses of Muslims. The special tax on the *dhimmi*, however, was not mentioned in this document. Perhaps designed to encourage non-Muslims to gain first-class citizenship by converting, these rules were nevertheless not crippling to life, and, indeed, they were often unenforced. Travelers throughout the Muslim

KEY TERM

dhimmi Translates as "protected." A term applied to Jews, Christians, Zoroastrians, and others who were accepted as monotheists, like Muslims, and therefore eligible for protection that allowed them to practice their faith, but required them to pay a special tax.

world noted that Jews and Christians often held some of the highest positions in public and private life, and were self-governing in their religious life.

A principal goal of conquest, however, remained the creation of a *dar al-Islam*, a land with a government under which Islam could be practiced freely. This did not mean that the people of the land were forced to become Muslims, only that the Muslims among them must have the freedom to practice their religion and sustain their culture.

Later, when many Muslims lived under non-Muslim governments, the *ulama* declared that any government that permitted freedom of religion to Muslims could be a *dar al-Islam*. The alternative was a *dar al-Harb*, an "abode of war," which had to be opposed because it restricted the practice of Islam.

The Crusades

At opposite ends of the Mediterranean, Muslims and Christians fought each other in war for centuries. The goals, for both combatants, were victory in the name of god and religion, but also political control and economic profit. For the Church, the centerpiece of this warfare was a series of campaigns, usually numbered as eight, fought between 1095 and 1291, in the name of recovering for Christians and Christianity lands in the Middle East that had fallen under Muslim control, especially the "Holy Land" where Jesus had lived and died. The participants, mostly men, but many women, too—mostly non-combatants, but also fighters; wives and sisters of male crusaders; and prostitutes accompanying the armies of the faithful—were called "crusaders" because they wore the emblem of the cross on their clothing. The Church promised them indulgences, formal promises of speedy forgiveness of sins, and swift entry into heaven after death.

After Arab armies captured Jerusalem in 638, they built new, glorious mosques to proclaim their own dominance, but they allowed Christians to continue their religious practices without hindrance and permitted Jews to return to Jerusalem officially for the first time since their exile by the Romans in 135. Centuries later, after Muslim Turkish armies won the Battle of Manzikert in 1071 and opened Anatolia to conquest, the Byzantine emperor Alexius I called on Pope Urban II to help roll back the Muslim advance and recapture Jerusalem and the Holy Land. The pope seized this opportunity to unite Western Europe and its various rulers under his own banner in the name of religion. He promoted the crusades and promised indulgences to those who fought. On a more earthly level, the pope promised that the property and assets of the crusaders back home would be protected in their absence. Many pious Christians responded to his call: rich and poor, men and women, old people and children. Christian rulers, knights, and merchants joined in, driven by religious inspiration as well as political and military ambition, and by the promise of trade opportunities that might accompany the establishment of a Latin kingdom in the Middle East. In the course of the first four crusades—the major crusades—more than 100,000 people participated.

At first, the European Christian crusaders were successful—and brutal. In 1099 they captured Jerusalem, killing about 3,000 of its Muslim residents, men, women, and children, and many Jews as well. They turned the Dome of the Rock into a church and the adjacent al-Aqsa Mosque into an official residence. The savagery of the crusaders—reported in both Christian and Muslim sources—ushered in centuries of confrontation far more bitter than ever before. At the time, however, Muslim leadership in the region was divided, and did not respond. Then Salah al-Din (Saladin; *c.* 1137–93), who had established a new dynasty in Egypt, organized his armies and recaptured Jerusalem in 1187. In the key battle on the way to Jerusalem, the Battle of Hattin, Saladin killed thousands of Christian soldiers and then beheaded the members of the Knights Templar and Knights Hospitaler who had survived. More crusades followed. When Richard I of England, called the Lion-Heart (r. 1189–99),

THE CRUSADES

First Crusade (1095–99)	Proclaimed by Pope Urban II, the crusade was motivated by the occupation of Anatolia and Jerusalem by the Seljuk Turks. The crusaders recaptured Jerusalem and established several Latin kingdoms on the Syrian coast.
Second Crusade (1147–49)	Led by Louis VII of France and the Holy Roman Emperor, Conrad III, this was a disaster from the crusaders' point of view.
Third Crusade (1189–92)	Mounted to recapture Jerusalem, which had been retaken by Salah al-Din (Saladin) in 1187. Personal rivalry between the leaders, Philip II Augustus of France and Richard I of England, undermined the crusaders' unity.
Fourth Crusade (1202–04)	This crusade against Egypt was diverted, at the instigation of the Venetians, to sack and divide Constantinople, which led to half a century of Western rule over Byzantium.
Children's Crusade (1212)	Thousands of children crossed Europe on their way to Palestine. Untold numbers were sold into slavery in Marseilles, France, or died of disease and malnutrition.
Fifth Crusade (1218–21)	King Andrew of Hungary, Cardinal Pelagius, King John of Jerusalem, and King Hugh of Cyprus captured, then lost, Damietta, Egypt.
Sixth Crusade (1228–29)	The Holy Roman Emperor, Frederick II (r. 1212–50), led the crusade that, through negotiation with the sultan of Egypt, recovered Jerusalem. The city was finally lost in 1244.
Seventh Crusade (1249–54), Eighth Crusade (1270–91)	Both led by the French king Louis IX (r. 1226–70), who was inspired by religious motives, but both were personal disasters. Louis died during the Eighth Crusade. He was later canonized.

captured Acre on the Mediterranean coast in the Third Crusade (1189–92), he massacred thousands of its men, women, and children. By 1291, however, Muslim forces had reconquered Acre—in an equally bloody victory—and all other crusader outposts. Although four additional crusades followed, none succeeded in capturing and holding any outposts in the Holy Land.

The crusader soldiers themselves were inspired by religion, but they also attacked many in their path for their own profit. As early as 1096, *en route* overland to Jerusalem on the First Crusade, crusaders paused to slaughter and plunder Jews, who were now seen as a threat to Christianity even closer to home than the Muslims of the Middle East. In 1204, during the Fourth Crusade, Roman Catholic armies, acting against the direct orders of the pope, attacked the city of Zara in Croatia, and Constantinople, the capital of the Byzantine Empire (their presumed ally). Instead of uniting Christianity and defeating the Muslims, these crusaders further divided an already splintered Christianity, and ultimately lost out to Muslims. Older research often terminated its study of the crusades at the end of the Eighth Crusade, in 1291, but more recent scholars see rivalry and battles between Christians and Muslims preceding the crusades for the Holy Land, and continuing for centuries after them. Many include under the term "crusades" additional battles in the name of the Roman Catholic Church against nonbelievers and non-Catholics throughout Europe. Sometimes they include campaigns of colonization in the name of the Church, such as the military conquest of South America. On the other hand, in 2000, Pope John Paul II publicly apologized for "violence in the service of truth" that sometimes characterized the Church's

Illustration of the Second Crusade (1147–49). Lance-bearing Christian forces face a Muslim army in this scene from the Second Crusade. The fleur-de-lys emblem, here sported on his shield by the French king Louis VII, was adopted at almost the same time by his opponent, the ruler of Aleppo. (British Library, London)

relations with others—especially Muslims and Jews—throughout the centuries. The very word "crusade" continues to carry powerful connotations of religious missions backed by armed force.

A Golden Age in Spain

At the other end of the Mediterranean, in Spain, Islam flourished and coexisted with the Christian and Jewish communities of the peninsula. Through a century of immigration, conquest, administration, and intermarriage, beginning in 711, Umayyad and Berber invaders brought Islam to a central position in Spain. They also revitalized trade by breaking the Byzantine monopoly over the western Mediterranean, and they introduced new crops and new irrigation techniques from western Asia. Abd al-Rahman III (r. 912–61) asserted his independence from the Abbasids by declaring himself a caliph rather than just a sultan. A series of rulers expanded the ornate mosque at Córdoba, making it one of the architectural showcases of Islam.

Eastern scholars of law and philosophy immigrated to the flourishing court. Poets developed new styles, based in Arabic but also influenced by local Spanish and Latin forms. Greek philosophical and medical treatises were translated into Latin as well as Arabic, thus opening intellectual communication with the educated classes in Christendom. Although some Christians revolted against Islamic and Arabic inroads, and were killed in battle (850–59), many more adopted Arabic lifestyles.

By 1030, the caliphate in Spain had disintegrated. Various armed struggles had broken out between the provinces and the capital, between townsmen and rural Berber immigrants, and between converts and Arabs. The conflicts did not, however, impede the spread of Islam. As in the eastern Mediterranean, provincial administrations replaced the central caliphate and brought the culture of their courts closer to the general population. Sufis spread their ascetic and devotional teachings.

The vacuum in the central government did, however, provide an opening for various Christian forces to begin the *reconquista*, the Christian reconquest of Spain. In 1085 Alfonso VI (r. 1065–1109), king of León—then king of León and Castile—captured Toledo. By the mid-thirteenth century all of Spain, with the exception of Granada, was in Christian hands.

During the years of the *reconquista*, culture continued to flourish. Until the mid-thirteenth century, Christian rulers in Spain patronized the rich, hybrid culture. They translated the Bible, the Talmud, and the Quran into Castilian. Arabic texts on astrology and astronomy, and the philosophical works of Muslim thinkers, including al-Kindi, al-Farabi, and Ibn Sina, were translated into Castilian and Latin, as was the philosophy of the Jewish thinker Moses Maimonides and his codification of Jewish religious law. Spain was the entryway into Western Europe for classical writings and their reworking through the prism of Islamic civilization.

With the fall of Seville to the Christian *reconquista* in 1248, Granada remained as the only Islamic kingdom in Spain. Nestled on a spur of the Sierra Nevada mountains in the south, the city flourished thanks to an influx of talented Muslims fleeing the advancing Christian armies, and the enterprise and vigor of its rulers. Two of the kings of the Nasrid dynasty, Yusuf I (r. 1333–54) and Muhammad V (r. 1354–59, 1362–91), built a complex of buildings called in Arabic *Qalat al-hamra*, or the Alhambra. This red citadel served as their home, a city within a city. Their legacy is today the best-preserved palace of medieval Spain. (See illustration, overleaf.)

By the fourteenth century, Christianity had become triumphal and intolerant. Jews and Muslims were forced to accept baptism and convert to Christianity, although many of them continued to practice their original religions in secret. In 1478, at the request of the Spanish rulers, the Roman Catholic Church established the Spanish Inquisition to hunt down those suspected of being insincere converts, whether Jews (called Marranos) or Muslims (called Moriscos). The first Grand Inquisitor, Tomás de Torquemada, began his work in 1483, and brought people to trial not only for

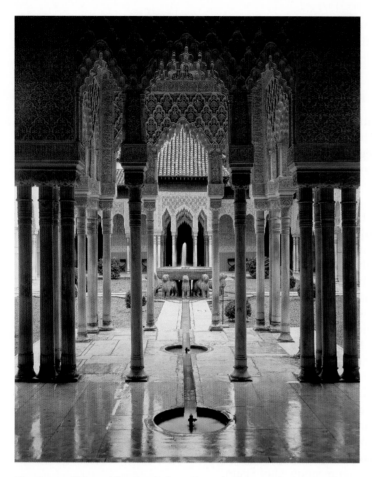

The Court of Lions, Alhambra Palace, Granada, fourteenth century. The elegance of this courtyard, with its central fountain and a dozen stone lions whose mouths are waterspouts, testifies to the power and aesthetic taste of the last Islamic kingdom left in Spain, until the Christian *reconquista* was completed in 1492.

apostasy and heresy, but also for sorcery, sodomy, polygamy, blasphemy, and usury. Under Torquemada's direction, about 2,000 people were burned at the stake, making his name a watchword for the fanatical misuse of religious authority.

Granada fell in 1492 to the Catholic rulers Ferdinand and Isabella. Muslim rule in Spain was broken. In 1492 Ferdinand and Isabella expelled the Jewish population from Spain. After the unsuccessful revolt of 1499–1500, Muslims, too, had to choose between exile and conversion to Christianity. In 1566 use of the Arabic language was banned in Spain. The golden age of religious tolerance and cultural exchange was over.

View the **Closer Look**: **A Cordovan Ivory Jar** on **MyHistoryLab**

Judaism, Christianity, and Islam: *What Difference Do They Make?*

Judaism, Christianity, and Islam share many common ancestors. They are all monotheistic religions and believe in divinely given written scriptures. They observe many similar rituals and practices. These include encouraging regular prayer, providing charity for the poor, and valuing pilgrimage to sacred places. Each also promises that behavior will receive its proper rewards and punishments in the future, on earth and in an afterlife. Finally, all three balance and integrate strands of mysticism, legalism, and pious devotion. Given these commonalities, the three religions would appear to be naturally suited to coexistence and even to mutual reinforcement. And, indeed, at times, notably in Spain for many years, the three faiths have coexisted and gladly learned from one another. But such warm, reciprocally beneficial coexistence has been the exception rather than the rule.

Perhaps two factors can explain the friction that has often characterized the relationships among these religions. First, all three have been proselytizing religions—although Judaism abandoned this practice early in the Christian era—and their very closeness has made them bitterly competitive. Each has had some feeling that it has come the closest to the essential truths of God and the world, and that the others have failed to recognize this. Both Christianity and Islam, for example, accuse Judaism of stubbornly refusing to accept later revelations that modify and update its original truths. Both Judaism and Islam accuse Christianity of a kind of idolatry in claiming that God begat a son who was actually a form of God and who walked the earth in human form. Both Judaism and Christianity reject the idea that God gave a special, final revelation to Muhammad. In each case these religions have looked at one another and said that, despite elements of deep commonality, there exist also fundamental differences. Indeed, within each of these religions, at various times, internal divisions have turned one group against another amid cries of heresy and calls to armed opposition. Truth was to be maintained, asserted, and defended through the force of arms. (Religions with less insistence on doctrinal correctness, such as Hinduism and Buddhism, have had fewer, and less violent, religious wars.)

Conversion and Assimilation

Only in the last two decades has serious research been done on conversion to Islam, asking exactly how the process worked. For example, Nehemia Levtzion edited a set of studies, *Conversion to Islam*, in 1979, examining the motives of converts. Levtzion argued that "assimilation" was a better term than "conversion" for describing the process of becoming a Muslim. People in conquered areas, especially, were not so much overwhelmed by political conquest as they were impressed with the richness of the culture that Islam brought to them. They found that their lives were enriched by the rituals, philosophy, art, and sense of belonging to a world system that came with joining the *umma*, the Islamic community.

Richard Bulliet's *Conversion to Islam in the Medieval Period: An Essay in Quantitative History* (1979) demonstrates that conversion took place at different rates in each of the six societies he examines: Arabia, Egypt, Iraq, Syria, Iran, and Spain. He notes the problems of finding data to understand the process, since "medieval Islam produced no missionaries, bishops, baptismal rites, or other indicators of conversion that could be conveniently recorded by the Muslim chronicler" (p. 4). For data, Bulliet examines the speed of adoption of Muslim names in each of the six societies. He concludes that rapid acceptance of Islam went hand in hand with a breakdown in central political rule. As centralized Islamic rule fragmented, paradoxically, Sufis carried the word of Islam more freely and with more backing from local governments.

We also know of the very large-scale assimilation to Islam by the Mongol successors of Chinggis (Genghis) Khan and of the followers of Timur the Lame (Tamerlane or Tamburlane). These ruling groups were assimilated by Islam because the new civilization they encountered offered them cultural, political, social, economic, and spiritual rewards that were not available in the religions and cultures of their birth.

Finally, the great assimilation that took place outside the heartlands of Islamic conquest, in sub-Saharan Africa and Southeast Asia, was carried by traders and later supported by Sufis and *ulama*. In both these huge areas, the trade networks by land and sea were so densely worked by Muslims that indigenous traders began to assimilate Islam into their lives, either from religious conviction or from the promise of trade advantage. They stayed to join one of the world's richest and most widespread civilizations, the *umma* of Islam.

- Nehemia Levtzion prefers the term "assimilation" rather than "conversion" to describe the process by which people adopted Islam. What does he mean by each term? Do you agree with his argument? Why or why not?
- Besides political rulers, what other groups successfully encouraged large numbers of people to accept Islam? In what geographical regions of the world were they most effective?
- What was the problem faced by Richard Bulliet in determining how many people accepted Islam? How did he attempt to solve this problem? Do you think his solution appropriate? Why or why not?

Second, as each religion developed, it sought the support of government. It often sought to *be* the government. Truth was to be reinforced by power. Basic competition over spiritual and philosophical truths spilled over into competition also for tax monies, office, land, the public acceptance of specific ritual and architectural symbols, and suppression of opposition. When they could, these religions marched through the world armed. Until recently, in the lands where they predominated, the state and religion were usually intimately bound up with each other, and in many places the leader of the state expected that his subjects would accept his religion as their own, or at least give it preferential treatment.

Historically, Christianity came to dominate the European lands formerly held by the Roman Empire and traveled with its European faithful to the New World. Islam dominated North Africa and the Asian lands formerly held by the Persian and Alexandrine empires, and it traveled with armies, saints, and traders to India and Southeast Asia. This identification of different religions with particular geographical parts of the world was typical also of Hinduism, identified with India and, to a much lesser extent, with Southeast Asia; and of Buddhism, identified with the Indian sub-continent, East and Southeast Asia, and the routes connecting them. Judaism, which lost out to its younger successors both in numbers and in gaining the support of governments, remained everywhere a minority religion, dependent on the tolerance of others, preserving the memory of its ancient homeland in Israel.

Nevertheless, amid the carving up of the world into zones of religious dominance backed by supportive governments and frequent warfare among religious groups, there were also times of mutually beneficial coexistence, sharing of cultures, and recognition of the commonalities of these religions and of the common humanity of their faithful. In many regions, such as the Middle East, and in cities along the various trade routes all over the world, members of different religions lived side by side, often developing mutual understanding, respect, and trust. And always the voice of the mystic, like that of Jalal-al-Din Rumi, called out for recognition of the oneness of God and the unity of God's universe:

> What is to be done, O Moslems? for I do not recognize myself.
> I am neither Christian, nor Jew, nor Gabr [Zoroastrian], nor Moslem.
> I am not of the East, nor of the West, nor of the land, nor of the sea;
> I am not of Nature's mint, nor of the circling heavens.
> I am not of earth, nor of water, nor of air, nor of fire;
> I am not of the empyrian, nor of the dust, nor of existence, nor of entity.
> I am not of India, nor of China, nor of Bulgaria, nor of Saqsin;
> I am not of the kingdom of Iraqain, nor of the country of Khorasan.
> I am not of this world, nor of the next, nor of Paradise, nor of Hell;
> I am not of Adam, nor of Eve, nor of Eden and [the angel] Rizwan.
> My place is the Placeless, my trace is the Traceless;
> 'Tis neither body nor soul, for I belong to the soul of the Beloved.
> I have put duality away, I have seen that the two worlds are one;
> One I seek, One I know, One I see, One I call.

> (McNeill and Waldman, p. 242)

CHAPTER REVIEW

THE ORIGINS OF ISLAM

11.1 What is the history of Islam, its origins and beliefs?

Islam, arising in Arabia, especially in the cities of Mecca and Medina, teaches submission to the word of God, which Muslims know primarily through the Quran, the book that records the teachings of God as they were transmitted to the Prophet Muhammad. Along with the Quran, stories of Muhammad's life, words, and deeds provide Muslims with models of the righteous life and how to live it. According to the Quran, Muhammad (570–632) was the most recent, and final, prophet of God.

SUCCESSORS TO THE PROPHET

11.2 What happened to Islam after Muhammad's death?

When Muhammad died, Muslims feared that the *umma*, the community of believers in Islam, would break up. Muhammad had been both the religious and political leader of the new Islamic community, and to preserve that organization, the leadership appointed one of Muhammad's close associates as his successor. The succession was disputed, however, and a series of civil wars was fought between rival factions.

SPIRITUAL, RELIGIOUS, AND CULTURAL FLOWERING

11.3 How did Islam flower outside the Arab world?

Even after the consolidated political leadership of Islam—the caliphate—fell to Mongol invaders, Islam continued to grow and spread. Descendants of the Mongols converted to Islam, as did many of the peoples of south and Southeast Asia. Muslim scholars, mystics, and merchants carried Islam throughout the Indian Ocean and the length of the silk road; trade caravans introduced Islam to sub-Saharan Africa. Today, virtually 60 percent of Muslims are descended from peoples who had no connection to the caliphate.

RELATIONS WITH NON-MUSLIMS

11.4 How did Muslims interact with non-Muslims?

From the earliest days of Muslim conquest, non-Muslims had three choices: convert to Islam; accept "protected," or *dhimmi*, status as worshipers of one God (Christians, Jews, Zoroastrians, and later Hindus); or fight against the Muslim state (few chose this option). A principal goal of conquest, however, remained the creation of a land with a government under which Islam could be practiced freely. This did not mean that the people of the land were forced to become Muslims, only that the Muslims among them must have the freedom to practice their religion and sustain their culture. Periods of fighting among the monotheistic religions alternated with periods of peace and mutual support.

Suggested Readings

PRINCIPAL SOURCES

Donner, Fred. *Muhammad and the Believers: At the Origins of Islam* (Cambridge: Harvard University Press, 2010). Discusses the innovations Islam introduced against the background of existing local practice.

Esposito, John. *Islam: The Straight Path* (New York: Oxford University Press, 1991). Clear, basic exposition of the development and significance of Islam by a lifelong, non-Muslim scholar.

——, ed. *The Oxford History of Islam* (New York: Oxford University Press, 1999). Brings together an array of clear, well-illustrated essays by outstanding scholars on the origin and evolution of Islam, including materials on law, society, science, medicine, technology, philosophy, and Islam and Christianity.

Hodgson, Marshall G.S. *The Venture of Islam*, 3 vols. (Chicago, IL: University of Chicago Press, 1974). Hodgson's classic reinterpretation of Islam, seeing it not only in alliance with political power, but also as an attractive global culture.

Keddie, Nikki R., and Beth Baron, eds. *Women in Middle Eastern History* (New Haven, CT: Yale University Press, 1991). Presents a wide variety of feminist perspectives on women in Islamic cultures.

Lapidus, Ira M. *A History of Islamic Societies* (Cambridge: Cambridge University Press, 2nd ed., 2002). A comprehensive, even encyclopedic account by a single scholar.

Lewis, Bernard, ed. and trans. *Islam from the Prophet Muhammad to the Capture of Constantinople*, 2 vols. (New York: Oxford University Press, 1987). Outstanding anthology of primary sources, grouped as politics, war, religion, and society.

McNeill, William H., and Marilyn Robinson Waldman, eds. *The Islamic World* (Chicago, IL: University of Chicago Press, 1983). Outstanding anthology of primary sources.

Watson, Andrew. *Agricultural Innovation in the Early Islamic World* (Cambridge: Cambridge University Press, 1983). An account of the major crops of India transplanted westward to the very ends of the Islamic world. A kind of precursor to the later Columbian Exchange.

ADDITIONAL SOURCES

Adas, Michael. *Islamic and European Expansion* (Philadelphia, PA: Temple University Press, 1993). Contains excellent interpretive historiographic articles on Islam in world history.

Ahmed, Leila. *Women and Gender in Islam* (New Haven, CT: Yale University Press, 1992). Demonstrates the variety of practices chronologically around the world.

Andrea, Alfred J. *Encyclopedia of the Crusades* (Westport, CT: Greenwood Press, 2003). A single volume brings together a brief, cogent introduction with entries on people, places, battles, concepts, and activities of the crusades, including the *reconquista* in Spain.

Bulliet, Richard W. *Conversion to Islam in the Medieval Period: An Essay in Quantitative History* (Cambridge, MA: Harvard University Press, 1979). An innovative assessment of the rate of conversion through a study of name change.

Costello, E.J., trans. (from Gabrieli Francesco, trans. from Arabic). *Arab Historians of the Crusades* (Berkeley, CA: University of California Press, 1969). Through the eyes of Arab historians, the crusades appear less religious, more brutal and cruel, and much more concerned with money, than in most Western accounts.

Dunn, Ross E. *The Adventures of Ibn Battuta* (Berkeley, CA: University of California Press, 1986). An interpretive study of the great Muslim traveler as an introduction to the culture and lands of his travels.

Eaton, Richard M. "Islamic History as Global History," in Adas, *op. cit.*, pp. 1–36. Brings new social-science sources to bear in interpreting the rise and significance of Islam.

——. *Essays on Islam and Indian History* (New York: Oxford University Press, 2000). Important revisionist views of Muslim–Hindu interaction, usually emphasizing the achievement of accommodation.

Embree, Ainslee T., ed. *Sources of Indian Tradition, Volume I: From the Beginning to 1800* (New York: Columbia University Press, 2nd ed., 1988). The outstanding anthology of primary sources.

Ferdowsi. *The Legend of Seyavash* (London: Penguin Books, 1992). Classic tales of the early rulers of Persia.

al-Ghazali. *The Faith and Practice of al-Ghazali*, trans. W. Montgomery Watt (London: Allen and Unwin, 1953). Tells of the tribulations of the master as he painfully sought a synthesis between legalism and mysticism in Islam.

Grabar, Oleg. *The Alhambra* (Cambridge, MA: Harvard University Press, 1978). A beautiful, scholarly account of the architectural marvel.

Hodgson, Marshall G.S. *Rethinking World History: Essays on Europe, Islam, and World History*, ed. Edmund Burke III (Cambridge: Cambridge University Press, 1993). A reassessment of Hodgson's classic scholarship on Islam to demonstrate its relevance to world history.

Ibn Khaldun. *An Arab Philosophy of History*, ed. Charles Issawi (London: John Murray, 1950). An abridgment of Khaldun's *Universal History*, the fourteenth-century classic of contemporary social science.

The Koran, trans. N.J. Dawood (London: Penguin Books, 1990). Probably the most readable translation.

The Koran, trans. M. Pickthall (New York: Alfred A. Knopf, 1930). An early translation into contemporary English created by a convert to Islam.

The Koran Interpreted, trans. A.J. Arberry (New York: Macmillan, 1955). The translation most acceptable to Muslim scholars.

Levtzion, Nehemia, ed. *Conversion to Islam* (New York: Holmes and Meier, 1979). Argues that conversion to Islam was

at least as much a cultural process of assimilation as a sudden change in belief.

——. "Islam in Africa to 1800s: Merchants, Chiefs, and Saints," in Esposito (1999), pp. 475–507. Very useful overview of many of the states and regions of sub-Saharan Africa.

Lewis, Bernard. *Islam and the West* (New York: Oxford University Press, 1993). Basic but controversial interpretive account of cultural and political interaction, by a master.

Maalouf, Amin. *The Crusades through Arab Eyes* (London: Al Saqi Books, 1984). Brings together accounts written by Arab historians and contemporary observers from 1096 to 1291.

Morony, Michael. *Iraq after the Muslim Conquest* (Princeton, NJ: Princeton University Press, 1984). Account of the conquests of Chinggis (Genghis) Khan, his successors, and their legacies.

Niane, D.T. *Sundiata: An Epic of Old Mali* (Harlow, Essex: Longman, 1965). The classic epic of the founder-ruler of Mali.

Riley-Smith, Jonathan., ed. *The Atlas of the Crusades* (New York: Facts on File, 1991). Some 80 maps, each prepared by an expert, chart the campaigns in Europe as well as in the Mediterranean and the Middle East, to 1571.

Robinson, Francis, ed. *The Cambridge Illustrated History of the Islamic World* (Cambridge: Cambridge University Press, 1996). Beautifully produced, one-volume scholarly introduction to the Islamic world, lavishly illustrated.

Trimingham, John S. *Sufi Orders in Islam* (Oxford: Oxford University Press, 1971). An account of several different Sufi *tariqas*, their leadership, history, and commitments.

Tucker, Judith. "Gender and Islamic History," in Adas, *op. cit.*, pp. 37–74. A succinct, provocative historiographical assessment of various interpretations of the status of Muslim women through the ages and around the world.

Vitray-Meyerovitch, Eva de. *Rumi and Sufism* (Sausalito, CA: Post-Apollo Press, 1987). Basic introduction to Rumi, his poetry, and his place in the Sufi movement.

FILMS

The Alhambra and the Reign of Queen Isabella of Spain (2006; 53 minutes). Slow-moving, but remarkable in showing the power of Isabella, her choice to be buried in the Islamic Alhambra, and good views of Islamic architecture and art.

Cities of Light: The Rise and Fall of Islamic Spain (2007; 2 hours). Explores the relationships among Muslims, Christians, and Jews, revealing a golden age, followed by ages not so golden. Tracks the development and transfer of knowledge and philosophy. Fascinating and comprehensive.

PART FIVE

TURNING POINT: TRADE

1300–1700

Trade Routes Connect the Continents

Many westerners, and especially Americans, begin the study of modern history with the voyages of Christopher Columbus. Historians often refer to this story, beginning with Columbus, as the "master narrative" because it has dominated the study of world history for many years and because it has been perpetuated by the "masters," the heirs of Columbus' voyages and conquests, the people who have benefited from them.

There are good reasons for identifying Columbus' four expeditions, between 1492 and 1504, as the turning point that ushers in the modern age in world history. They transformed the Atlantic from a moat that separated the eastern and western hemispheres into a bridge that joined them. They inspired Ferdinand Magellan (c. 1480–1521) to explore the Atlantic and the Pacific, bringing the entire globe into touch. The consequences were immense, and immensely different for different peoples. No sooner did Europeans "discover" the New World than they conquered much of the land and many of its peoples. European kings, merchants, and priests grew rich, powerful, and proud on the basis of the gold and silver they brought from the New World, the land they seized and cultivated there, the laborers they forced into servitude, and the souls they claimed for Christianity. Columbus opened the door.

The *Santa Maria* (front) versus a Chinese junk (behind). This illustration of the difference in size between the Santa Maria, Christopher Columbus' flagship in his voyage across the Atlantic in 1492, and a Chinese junk of the same time period, suggests the difference in commercial power between the Chinese and the Europeans. It was the desire to enter more fully into the vast Asian trade that led the Europeans, and Columbus, to attempt to find new routes to China and India.

Despite these dramatic and powerful changes introduced by Columbus' discoveries, more recent narratives frame the story differently. They start out with Columbus' goals; he landed in the Americas, but he had set sail in search of new sea routes to China and India. The lucrative Indian Ocean trade, from which Spain felt excluded, was his intended target. So the newer narratives begin with an account of the trade networks of this earlier period, usually from about 1300. By that date the sea routes were fully operational. Even the land routes, the silk routes across Asia, were functional once again, protected by their Mongol conquerors.

Newer narratives also underline the continuing independence of the great Asian nations, in particular India and China. Like Latin America, Asia succumbed to significant European control, but only centuries later, and with much more limited consequences for their cultures. The British conquest of India dates only to 1757. China's loss of some of its sovereignty to Europeans came later still, after the Opium War of 1839–42. From this Asian perspective, 1492 appears less compelling as a turning point. The newer narratives do not question the significance of

Columbus' voyages in creating a new world geography, magnifying the power of the Spanish throne, and transforming South America into Latin America through the introduction of Christianity and the cultures and languages of Spain and Portugal. They do, however, consider these transformations in the larger context of the history of the entire world.

Our account of trade in world history follows these more recent interpretations. We begin in the period around 1300, when trade in the Indian Ocean was flourishing but Spain and Portugal were blocked from participating by the restrictions imposed by the pope, the power of the Ottoman Empire, and the economic dominance of the ships and traders of Venice. Sailing for Spain, Columbus attempted to outflank all these blockages and to enter that lucrative trade network through the back door, by way of the Atlantic. (Simultaneously, the Portuguese, facing the same obstacles, were also attempting to find an alternate route—by sailing around Africa.)

In the chapter "Establishing World Trade Routes," we study the geography of the principal pre-Columbian trade

King Edward I Returns from Gascony, anon., 1470. Miniature. This is an example of a ship with triangular lateen sails. Europeans adapted these sails from Arab models because they enabled ships to tack against the wind as well as run with it. (British Library, London)

routes by land and sea. They were not yet unified, or global, but they were capable of linking Western Europe, most of Africa, and Eastern Asia. We explore the role of traders and their relationship with political rulers from 1300 to 1500. Long-distance merchants coordinated delivery of goods from one end of Afro-Eurasia to the other. Through the thirteenth and fourteenth centuries Mongol descendants of Chinggis Khan provided security along central Asia's silk routes, opening them after hundreds of years of abandonment. Traders and travelers including Marco Polo and Ibn Battuta explored these routes; we read about a few of their adventures.

"The Opening of the Atlantic and the Pacific" chapter turns to the Atlantic and Mediterranean coasts of Europe, remote from the world's main trade routes, but developing on their own. As Viking sailors forsook their raiding expeditions and began to settle down in their northern lands, commercial shipping began to ply the waters between ocean and sea in greater safety. Shipping increased as Europe grew wealthier from improvements in agriculture and renewed urban growth. Epidemics sometimes accompanied trade missions. The devastating "Black Death" wiped out more than one-third of the population in many places from China to Western Europe, with relationships of wealth and power dramatically restructured in its wake. The businessmen and artisans of newly prospering European cities developed new institutions, such as guilds; supported new inventions, such as the printing press; and accepted new philosophies of business, such as early capitalism, based on free markets, risk-taking, and the principles of

Siege of Vienna by Turks on July 14, 1683, Frans Geffels, 17th century. Oil on canvas. The Ottoman Empire began in central Asia and extended most of the way across North Africa and well into Europe. In 1529, led by Suleiman the Magnificent, and again in 1683, Ottoman armies set siege to Vienna, Austria, but this was as far as they were able to reach. Subsequently, forces led by the Habsburg empire pushed them eastward. (Wien Museum)

supply-and-demand economics. Religious philosophy, too, was evolving to accommodate more earthly desires for personal profit.

Christian Europe was changing, in part, because it was learning from its Muslim Arab neighbors in Spain and on the Mediterranean's southern shores. Europeans incorporated into their fleets the caravel ships and triangular lateen sails used by Arab sailors. Christian scholars and artists began to reclaim the cultural heritage of the ancient Greeks and Romans, which they had forgotten, relearning them from the Muslims and Jews who had kept them alive. They called the culture that emerged a *renaissance*, a rebirth of humanistic creativity that had been lost for more than 1,000 years. Both the Church and prosperous businessmen supported the new forms of cultural expression.

Western Europe's economic growth was blocked, however, by Arab, Ottoman, and Venetian control over trade routes in the eastern Mediterranean and beyond. Portugal, situated on the Atlantic, set out to circumvent these obstacles by circumnavigating Africa; in 1488 Bartolomeu Dias rounded the Cape of Good Hope and showed that the venture was feasible. In 1492, when Columbus promised the new rulers of Spain that he could find yet another, competitive, new route to the riches of the East by crossing the Atlantic, and win new converts to Christianity into the bargain, they agreed to finance his risky venture.

Columbus' voyages did initiate new chapters in world history, as we see in the chapter "The Unification of World Trade." They opened vast new resources of wealth—in land, gold, silver, and captive labor—for Europe to exploit (or develop, depending on the point of view). They heralded the destruction of powerful Native American empires and the deaths of millions of Native Americans, through warfare and disease. They made South America into Latin America, by introducing and imposing the languages, culture, and religion of Spain and Portugal. The "Columbian Exchange" of crops enriched diets and nutrition throughout the world, but the exchange of microbes, especially smallpox, killed millions, especially Native Americans.

The Portuguese pushed on with their voyages around the coast of Africa; Vasco da Gama reached the west coast of India in 1498. They attempted to assert control over Indian Ocean shipping, and to tax it; local peoples viewed these impositions as a form of piracy. The Portuguese also sought to convert souls to Christianity, sometimes threatening death as the alternative.

In the longer run, northern Europeans in the Netherlands, England, and France, more devoted to commerce than were the Iberians, reaped still greater profit from the new, global opportunities. At about the same time, many of the northern Europeans accepted the Protestant Reformation, rejecting Catholicism in favor of new denominations. This conversion provoked a lasting historical debate over the relationship between commercial success and religious affiliation.

Other world empires responded to these developments in varied ways. Alarmed by the new power of the Western Europeans, Russia tried to catch up militarily and commercially, although the Russian monarchy jealously preserved its political powers. The Ottoman Empire was strong enough militarily to lay siege to Vienna in 1529 and to battle again to take the city in 1683—both times unsuccessfully—but its commerce slipped into the hands of foreigners, especially the French, and the empire began its long descent. The Mughals ruled India effectively from 1556 until the early 1700s, but then, as Mughal power faltered, Europeans began to expand from their small trading fortresses along the coasts deep into the interior of the country. The Chinese and the Japanese excluded most European commerce throughout this period, although Jesuit priests won hundreds of thousands of converts. India and China would ultimately succumb to European control, but only after centuries of internal decay that left them vulnerable.

The expansion of world trade and transportation also brought vast migrations. Millions left Europe in search of economic, and sometimes religious, opportunity. They founded "New Europes" in the Americas, South Africa, Australia, and New Zealand, as well as colonial outposts around the world. Millions of Asians migrated from one region of that immense continent to another. The armies of the Ottomans conquered and occupied Turkey; the Mughals conquered and occupied India; and the Safavids conquered and occupied Persia. Millions of Chinese migrated northward as they drove the Mongols out of China's walls and as hardy crops from the Columbian Exchange opened these new territories to fruitful cultivation. Urban concentrations increased as new dynasties and rulers constructed new capitals. Two of the most devastating changes in history also marked this period: the death of tens of millions of Native Americans, the victims of warfare and disease; and the forced transportation of some ten million people taken as slaves from Africa, mostly to work the sugar plantations of the New World. The chapter "Migration" introduces demography as a means of following the lives of these migrants, mostly common people, mostly illiterate, who left no written records. The individual stories of the migrants are lost, but the statistical methods of the demographers help us to recover their collective experience.

Turning Point Questions

1. Why have the expeditions of Christopher Columbus been identified as a turning point?
2. Where were the existing trade networks in Columbus' time, and who participated in them?
3. How important were the demographic changes of this period? Describe them.

12 Establishing World Trade Routes

The Geography and Philosophies of Early Economic Systems

1300–1500

Today, long-distance, international trade forms a substantial part of the world's commerce and includes even the most basic products of everyday food and clothing. In earlier times, however, long-distance trade represented only a small fraction of overall trade, mostly supplying such luxuries as silks, gold, and spices for the wealthy. Because these goods were extremely valuable relative to their weight, merchants could carry them over thousands of miles and still sell them for handsome profits. Some commercial goods, such as raw wool and cotton, were traded over intermediate distances of a few hundred miles. The transportation costs of such raw materials were justified by the **value added** during further processing into finished goods after importation.

Trade in the Gulf of Cambay, Boucicaut Master, India, 1410. Vellum. As the main port of northwestern India, Cambay excited the wonder of painters and artists in far-off Europe. This illustration from the *Livre des Merveilles* (*The Book of Wonders*) of 1410 represents Cambay's ships and traders in European guise—not surprisingly, because the artist had never been to the city. (Bibliothèque Nationale, Paris)

LEARNING OBJECTIVES

12.1 ((	12.2 ((	12.3 ((	12.4 ((	12.5 ((	12.6 ((
Understand the ways in which societies regulate trade.	Describe Asia's extensive trading networks.	Understand how the Chinese focus on internal trade affected its culture.	Understand the legacy of the Mongol Empire.	Know the goods that were traded across the Sahara.	Describe trade in the Americas before Europeans invaded.

((Listen on **MyHistoryLab**

By far the largest share of trade before 1500 was local: food crops traded for local hand manufactures or raw materials. These goods were necessities, but they had little value in relationship to their weight. Often, they were bartered in exchange for other local goods rather than sold for money in more distant markets. This local exchange of goods is a fundamental part of local and regional history, but the study of world history focuses on long-distance trade and its importance in knitting together distant regions of the world.

	12.1
How do societies regulate and control trade?	
	12.2
	12.3
	12.4
	12.5
	12.6

World Trade: A Historical Analysis

12.1 How do societies regulate and control trade?

Historians studying world trade seek to understand its social as well as its economic consequences. What social benefits have been achieved by international trade? Who has benefitted? Who has been harmed? To answer these questions we must examine the rules and regulations of the various systems of trade. For example, was trade mostly open and free, allowing anyone to enter and take his or her place among the buyers and sellers, or was access restricted? Were prices negotiated directly between buyers and sellers, or did government or trade organizations or religious institutions fix prices and conditions of trade? What have been the trade-offs between benefit and harm under each system? These questions, of course, are not only historical. The present-day debate over the "globalization" of trade—the transformation of the world into a single marketplace—demonstrates their enduring relevance. Recurrent protests against the 159-member-nation World Trade Organization, as it seeks to expand and regulate international trade, vent the intense passions that continue to surround these questions today.

To what degree should governments regulate or control economic markets? In a completely **free-market economy**, conditions of trade would not be regulated; prices would vary only in terms of the relationship between the **supply** of goods and the **demand** for them, and people would be free to conduct business as they chose. Societies, however, do regulate trade. For example, governments that wish to ensure that everyone has food may declare that agricultural production should be expanded and industrial production limited. In wartime, governments may ration food and essential commodities to ensure that everyone has access to at least minimum quantities. By taxing some items at high rates and others at low rates, governments can selectively promote or limit production and trade. Business may be more or less regulated, but government never leaves it completely unregulated.

Even in the earliest societies, such as those of Egypt, Mesopotamia, and China, government officials, often in alliance with priests, had the power to regulate trade. Nevertheless, market economies based on private profit existed there as well. This trade for private profit was embedded in deeper political, social, religious, and moral structures of society. For example, governments intervened in civilian economies to ensure adequate supplies of war materials for their armies. Concern for the general welfare, or fear of civic unrest, encouraged other interventions to ensure adequate food and basic necessities for the poor; such scholars as Karl Polanyi and James Scott sometimes contrast this **moral economy** with the free-market economy. Governments, especially those not subject to democratic controls, can, of course, also be predatory, taxing their populations for the benefit of government projects and officials, without regard to the welfare of the people.

The Traders

To understand world trade, we must look not only at the systems of trade, their rules and regulations, but also at the traders themselves. Long-distance private trade

KEY TERMS

value added An economist's term for the increase in value from the cost of raw materials to the cost of finished products. It is the value added to the raw material by processing, manufacture, and marketing.

free-market economy An economic system in which the means of production are largely privately owned and there is little or no government control over the markets.

supply and demand In economics, the relationship between the amount of a commodity that producers are able and willing to sell (supply) and the quantity that consumers can afford and wish to buy (demand).

moral economy An economy whose goal is providing basic necessities for all members of a society before allowing any particular members to take profits; in contrast to a free-market economy.

trade diaspora A diaspora is a dispersion over far-flung territories of a group of people who have a common bond. Usually this is an ancestral bond, such as in the Jewish diaspora and the African diaspora. A trade diaspora refers to the network of international traders who relate to one another through the bonds of their trade.

silk route The set of rough roads or transportation links across central Asia carrying trade and cultural exchange as far as China, India, and the eastern Mediterranean.

flourished most profitably in major port cities around the world. The merchants who carried on this port-city trade were often foreigners, with some independence from local political and social structures. Although they might occupy marginal positions in their host societies, they held central positions in the international trade networks. These long-distance merchants encouraged and brokered trade between the society in which they were living and the far-flung networks of international merchants. They formed **trade diasporas**, networks of interconnected commercial communities living and working in major trade cities throughout Africa, Europe, and Asia. Trade diasporas appear in the archaeological record as early as 3500 B.C.E., and some endured for millennia.

During the height of the Roman Empire, for example, traders from Rome sailed the waters of the Mediterranean Sea and the Indian Ocean, on rare occasions all the way to China. Most of these traders were not ethnically Roman. Usually they were descendants of the major trading communities of the eastern Mediterranean: Jews, Greek-speaking Egyptians, and Arabs. Long after the sack of Rome, small religious communities of Jews, Christians, and Muslim Arabs persisted along the southwest coast of India, a legacy of these ancient diaspora traders. Typically, the merchants

AT A GLANCE: WORLD TRADE, GLOBAL (compare box in Chapter 13)

DATE	POLITICAL/SOCIAL EVENTS	TRADE DEVELOPMENTS	EXPLORATION
1050	• Almoravids destroy Kingdom of Ghana (1067)		
1100		• Age of Great Zimbabwe in southern Africa	
1150		• Papermaking spreads from Muslim world to Europe	
1200	• Foundation of first Muslim empire in India • Chinggis Khan establishes Mongol Empire (1206–1405) • Decline of Mayan civilization in Central America; rise of Incas in Peru • Rise of Mali, West Africa		
1250	• Osman I founds Ottoman dynasty in Turkey (1290–1326) • Emergence of Empire of Benin • Mongols fail to conquer Japan (1281)		• Marco Polo arrives in China (1275)
1300	• Height of Mali (Mandingo) Empire under Sultan Mansa Musa (r. 1307–32)		• Ibn Battuta's travels in East Asia and Africa (c. 1330–60)
1350	• Ming dynasty in China succeeds Mongol (Yuan) Dynasty (1368)		
1400	• Ottoman Turks establish foothold in Europe at Gallipoli • Aztecs form alliances controlling Central Mexico (1428)	• China reconstructs and extends Grand Canal • Zheng He's seven voyages (1405–33)	
1450		• Decline of Kilwa and Great Zimbabwe in southeast Africa (c. 1450)	• Bartolomeu Dias sails around the Cape of Good Hope (1488) • Columbus reaches the Americas (1492) • Vasco da Gama reaches India (1498)
1500	• Zenith of Songay Empire of the middle Niger region (1492–1529) • Hernán Cortés and Spanish conquistadores defeat Aztecs and seize Mexico (1519–21) • Francisco Pizarro and Spanish conquistadores defeat Incas and seize Peru		

who conducted trade were marginal to their host societies rather than citizens within them. They were not unregulated by the hosts, nor were they totally subordinated, but they were allowed to make profits in return for the economic benefits they brought to the port city.

In a world that had no international courts or legal systems, shared religion and ethnicity often formed the basis for conducting long-distance trade. For example, Jews were able to carry on international trade across the entire eastern hemisphere. Their religious diaspora in numerous distant points of settlement supported their trade diaspora. They were dispersed in small communities from China to Western Europe and Africa, and their common faith formed a bond of trust that enabled them to establish highly efficient trade networks. During the period of Tang–Abbasid control over the **silk route**—the eighth and early ninth centuries C.E.—Jews were a preeminent trading community along the trade routes linking Europe and China. Charlemagne's ninth-century European empire employed them to carry trade in southern Europe. Baghdad, astride many of the key trade routes in western Asia, held the most prominent Jewish community in the world at the time, and there were also notable Jewish communities in Calicut and Cochin in southern India and in Kaifeng, China. When the Portuguese explorer Vasco da Gama reached Calicut in 1498, a local Jewish merchant was able to serve as interpreter. Cairo, Egypt, one of the world's great trade centers, also sheltered a significant Jewish community, including many long-distance traders.

How do societies regulate and control trade?

12.1
12.2
12.3
12.4
12.5
12.6

World trade routes. Between 1100 and 1500 a relay system of trade by land and sea connected almost all populous regions of Eurasia, as well as North and East Africa. Long-distance traders carried goods along their own segments of these routes, and then turned them over to traders in the next sector. The western hemisphere was still separate, and had two major trade networks of its own.

12.1

12.2 What were the main Asian trade networks?

12.3

12.4

12.5

12.6

Other groups of global traders also formed commercial networks on the basis of shared religion and ethnicity, although they were generally less extensive geographically, for example Christian Armenians, Jain and Hindu Gujaratis from western India, and Fukienese from the southeast coast of China. Like the Jews, these trading communities operated within their own social and religious networks, enjoying trade relations with local people, but not encouraging their religious conversion. On the other hand, overseas Muslim trade communities often sought to attract converts to Islam, as happened especially in Indonesia and Southeast Asia.

Asia's Complex Trade Patterns

12.2 What were the main Asian trade networks?

As the largest continent, with the largest population and the oldest civilizations, Asia contains trade networks that date back thousands of years. By 1250, a set of interlinked trade networks connected the main population and production centers of Asia, Africa, and Europe. The map "Trading ports and cities, Indian Ocean, 1200–1500 C.E.," opposite, illustrates the comprehensive geographic coverage of these networks. From east to west, Japan and China were linked by land routes to central Asia and by sea lanes to the Indian Ocean. Both land and sea routes continued westward to Arabia, western Asia, and on to the Mediterranean and Europe. Well-developed sea traffic linked also to the East African coast, where land routes extended into the African continent. North–south routes ran through China, central and western Asia, and Europe, and from the Mediterranean across the Sahara by camel. Centralized transportation companies that could carry goods all the way from East Asia to Western Europe did not yet exist, but arrangements could be made for even this long voyage to be completed stage by stage.

📖 **Read** the **Document: The English in South Asia and the Indian Ocean (early 1600s)** on **MyHistoryLab**

HOW DO WE KNOW?

The Records in the Cairo Genizah

Information on Mediterranean cultures and their trade connections into the Indian Ocean, from the tenth through the thirteenth centuries, has come to historians from the Cairo Genizah (Hebrew for a repository of old papers), studied by Solomon Goitein from the 1950s through the 1980s. Jewish law requires that the written name of "God" not be destroyed but be stored for later burial; the Genizah was the storage point in Cairo for such documents for several centuries. Because paper was scarce and often reused, the manuscripts in the Genizah include massive bundles of notes and manuscripts on secular as well as sacred aspects of life: on trade and commerce, on social organization in general, and on the Jewish community in particular. Marriage contracts "state in detail and with great variety the conditions regulating the future relations of the newly married, and thus constitute a precious source for our knowledge of family life" (I:10). Wills and inventories of estates are "veritable mines of information" (I:10). Letters of correspondence, both personal and business, "form the largest and most important group [of manuscripts]. They are our main source not only for our knowledge of commerce and industry, but also for various other subjects, such as travel and seafaring" (I:11). "There are hundreds of letters addressed to various authorities containing reports,

petitions, requests for help, demands for redress of injustice, applications for appointments, and a great variety of other matters" (I:12). Religious responses are frequent, questions and answers between commoners and sages concerning religious philosophy, doctrine, and practice. Most women were illiterate, but they dictated many letters to scribes: "We hear the female voice guiding the male pen" (I:12). For the most part the writing is in Arabic, but transcribed in Hebrew letters.

Because the Jewish community was interwoven with all the others, these centuries-old manuscripts have proven to be a gold mine for historians studying the life of Cairo, its citizens, and their external connections throughout the Mediterranean Sea and the Indian Ocean.

- Given the nature of the Genizah repository, what kinds of record do you think would be most fully represented? Least well represented?
- How might records of family life and those dictated by women help to fill out the records of business transactions?
- How important was Cairo as a trade center at this time?

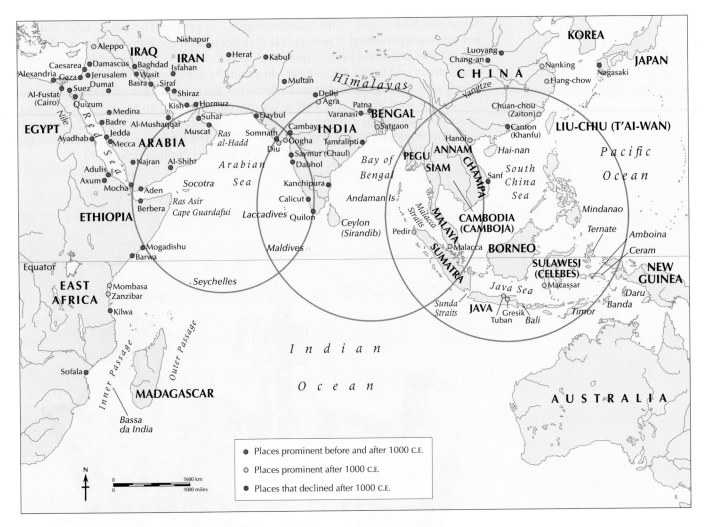

Trading ports and cities, Indian Ocean, 1200–1500 C.E. The Indian Ocean was the pivot of long-distance sea-borne trade from the Mediterranean to the South China Sea. Each of its port cities housed a rich diversity of merchants of many ethnicities and cultures. Trade goods did not travel on a single ship the whole length of this region. Rather, they would be loaded at a port in one of the three regions, offloaded and reloaded in the next for shipment to the third.

12.1

12.2

What were the main Asian trade networks?

12.3

12.4

12.5

12.6

The Indian Ocean

The great crossroads of the world's shipping lanes in the period 1300–1500 was the Indian Ocean. Its waters encompass three distinct geographical sectors, each with its own cultural orientation. The western sector—the Arabian Sea—extends from the East African coast across the ports of Arabia and continues to the west coast of India. From the time of Alexander the Great and the Roman Empire, Greek sailors plied these lanes. By the first century B.C.E. they had learned to use the monsoon winds to navigate these waters swiftly and efficiently. From the fourth to the eighth century, following the decline and fall of the Roman Empire, two new groups dominated this western region of the Indian Ocean: sailors from Axum (modern Ethiopia and Eritrea) and its Red Sea port of Adulis, and sailors from Sassanid Persia, a west Asian empire on the ascendant at the time.

Arab Traders. From the eighth to the sixteenth century, Arab Muslim traders and sailors became masters of the Arabian Sea, named for them, and the Indian Ocean sea lanes. This was the area made famous by the legendary exploits of Sinbad the

12.1
12.2   What were the
12.3   main Asian trade
       networks?
12.4
12.5
12.6

Sailor (see Source box, "The Arabian Nights," opposite). The rise of Arab Muslim sea traders represented a remarkable transformation for this ethnic and religious group. The Arabs had been accustomed to land trade—Muhammad himself was a camel driver and leader of caravans—but trade by sea was different. They took to this new way of life eagerly and came to dominate the sea lanes from the Mediterranean coast in the west all the way east to Guangzhou (Canton) and Hangzhou in China, frequently displacing existing communities of sailors. (For the commercial and cultural importance of Hindu and Buddhist sailors and traders in these areas from the seventh to the tenth century, see the chapter entitled "Indian Empires.")

Arab trader, illustration from the *Maqamat* of al-Hariri, twelfth century. Regional shipping routes linked into the oceanic, intercontinental routes. This ship, with Arab passengers and Indian, and perhaps African, crew, sailed the Persian Gulf connecting Mesopotamia and the Indian Ocean. (Bibliothèque Nationale, Paris)

SOURCE

The Arabian Nights

Arab Muslim traders of the Indian Ocean fill the pages of some of the best-loved tales of world literature. *The Thousand Nights and One Night* (also called *The Arabian Nights*), fables originally written in Persian during the years of the Abbasid Empire (750–1258), include the tales of the seven voyages of Sinbad (Sindbad) the Sailor, who won a fortune through a series of hazardous (if unbelievable) adventures at sea. The adventures—supposedly told night after night by Scheherazade to the emperor, Harun al-Rashid (r. 786–809), as a ploy to postpone her scheduled execution—are fanciful, but Sinbad's description of his departures on each of his voyages is based on the reality of Indian Ocean shipping. This translation from the beginning of the third voyage is by Richard F. Burton, who brought the complete tales to the English-speaking world in the late nineteenth century.

> I returned from my second voyage overjoyed at my safety and with great increase of wealth, Allah having requited me all that I had wasted and lost, and I abode awhile in Baghdad-city savouring the utmost ease and prosperity and comfort and happiness, till the carnal man was once more seized with longing for travel and diversion and adventure, and yearned after traffic and lucre and emolument, for that the human heart is naturally prone to evil. So making up my mind I laid in great plenty of goods suitable for a sea voyage and repairing to Bassorah [Basra], went down to the shore and found there a fine ship ready to sail, with a full crew and a numerous company of merchants, men of worth and substance; Faith, piety and consideration. I embarked with them and we set sail on the blessing of Allah Almighty and on His aidance and His favour to bring our voyage to a safe and prosperous issue and already we congratulated one another on our good fortune and bon voyage. We fared on from sea to sea and from island to island and city to city, in all delight and contentment, buying and selling wherever we touched, and taking our solace and our pleasure, till one day … [and here begin the fabulous adventures of the third voyage]. (*The Thousand Nights and One Night*, vol. 4, pp. 2031–32)

Islam encouraged trade. The *hajj* (pilgrimage to Mecca), required of every Muslim who could manage it at least once during his or her lifetime, necessitated travel, and international trade connections flourished as a result. A Muslim trade colony had operated in Sri Lanka as early as about 700 C.E. Arab traders sailed first to India, then to Southeast Asia, and some even on to the southeast coast of China. Muslim Arab traders also played critical roles in the development of African trade networks, by sea linking the East African coast to various ports along the shores of the Indian Ocean, and by land connecting north and south across the Sahara.

Lacking wood in Arabia, Arab sailors depended on others to build their ships, or obtained teak from southern India to build their own. For reasons that remain unclear, they did not use metal nails in the construction of their ships, but "stitched" the wooden planks together with coir—the fiber of coconut husks—or other fibers. Like the Greek sailors before them (and Malay sailors even earlier), they learned to sail with the monsoon winds. Catching the proper seasonal winds in each direction and using their **lateen sails** to maximum effect, sailors could complete a round trip from Mesopotamia to China in less than two years. The Arab Muslim Ahmad Ibn Majid included extensive recommendations on travel dates appropriate to the monsoon winds in his comprehensive fifteenth-century guide to navigation in the Indian Ocean.

Islam Spreads. Along with their trade goods, Muslims also conveyed their religious philosophies and practices. Distant merchants, who encountered Muslims in order to trade, often absorbed elements of Islam. In the thirteenth century, as the Muslim sultanate of Delhi came to rule northern India, many of the Hindu oceangoing traders, especially those along the west coast in Gujarat, converted to Islam. As they traded, they carried their new religion with them. In regions as distant as Malaysia and Indonesia, locals began to assimilate to the religion. Carried not by military power but by traders, Islam came to be the dominant religion in Indonesia (the most populous Muslim country in the world today), and to attract tens of millions of Chinese adherents. When the ruler of Malacca converted to Islam, about 1400, the trading circuit of Muslim merchants was complete. The entire length of the Indian Ocean littoral,

12.1

12.2

What were the main Asian trade networks?

12.3

12.4

12.5

12.6

KEY TERM

lateen sail A triangular sail affixed to a long yard or crossbar at an angle of about 45 degrees to the mast, with the other free corner secured near the stern. The sail was capable of tacking against the wind on either side. Lateen sails were so named when they appeared in the Mediterranean, where they were associated with Latin culture, although their origin was actually far away.

12.1
12.2
12.3
12.4
12.5
12.6

How did China's focus on internal trade affect its cultural growth?

from East Africa through India and on to Indonesia, housed a Muslim, largely Arab, trading diaspora.

Arabs did not sail into the Atlantic or Pacific oceans; they had no need. They sailed at will throughout the most lucrative seas of the world they knew. They had no problem of access. When Europeans explored new routes to reach the wealth of India and China in the fifteenth century, the Arabs were already there.

China: A Magnet for Traders

12.3 How did China's focus on internal trade affect its cultural growth?

By 1200 China was the world's most economically advanced region, a magnet for world trade. China is so huge, however, that its internal trade far outweighed its external trade. Others came to China to obtain its rich and varied products far more regularly than the Chinese traveled abroad in search of the products of others. China's policy towards trade varied during the centuries we are considering here, partly as a result of changes in imperial policy, partly in response to external pressure. Even though it possessed a highly integrated system of internal markets and reached extraordinary levels of agricultural and industrial productivity, the Song dynasty (960–1279) was overrun by Mongol invaders and had to abandon territory, relocate to the south, and reconstruct its economy. The Ming dynasty (1368–1644) overthrew the Mongols and undertook a series of spectacular ocean voyages. Then, in a reversal of policy, later Ming emperors forbade the Chinese to trade overseas. Nevertheless, merchants from abroad continued to pour in, eager to do business with the Middle Kingdom.

Internal Trade

When Marco Polo arrived in China from Venice in 1275, the splendor and wealth of the country overwhelmed him. He described its Mongol ruler, Kubilai Khan, as "the mightiest man, whether in respect of subjects or of territory or of treasure, who is in the world today or who ever has been, from Adam our first parent down to the present moment." Polo correctly reported that China in the late 1200s was the richest, most technologically progressive, and largest country in the world.

The foundations of China's wealth had been in place for centuries, its population, territory, power, and wealth growing through successive dynasties from Qin to Tang. Under the Song, China underwent an economic revolution. A revolution in agriculture underpinned the advance: better soil preparation and conservation; improved seeds that often allowed more than one crop per season; better water control and irrigation; and more local specialization of crops. The new techniques were implemented most intensively in the lower Yangzi valley, as the Song moved south from China's historic northern base around the Yellow River. Indeed, they maintained regional capitals, two of which also served as national capitals: Kaifeng in the north and Hangzhou in the south, near the mouth of the Yangzi. Thanks to the invention of woodblock printing in the ninth century under the Tang dynasty, ideas could spread rapidly. One of the first uses of print had been to conserve and spread religious concepts; the oldest printed book extant in the world is a copy of the Buddhist *Diamond Sutra* from 868. Now the new method of printing was put into the service of disseminating the new farming methods.

Agricultural improvements—plus China's traditional excellence in textile production and remarkable innovations in the most advanced coal and iron industry in the world—inspired a trade revolution. Common people became involved in the mass production of goods for sale. Domestically, this included the production of military goods for an army of over a million men. Trade became monetized, with copper

Going on the River at the Qingming Festival, Kaifeng, Zhang Zeduan, Song dynasty scroll. The multitude of Chinese junks on the Yellow River suggest the well-developed channels of trade in northern China. (National Palace Museum, Taiwan)

12.1
12.2
12.3
12.4
12.5
12.6

How did China's focus on internal trade affect its cultural growth?

as the principal currency. Chinese currency was so popular in Japan at this time that it became the most important medium of trade. In 1024, in Sichuan province, paper money was printed for the first time in the world. (Sometimes the government printed an excess of paper money, giving rise to inflation.) Merchants invented new credit mechanisms to facilitate trade. Government control of trade—quite marked under the Tang—was sharply reduced in favor of greater market freedom, and trade made up an increasing share of government revenue. Customs offices in the nine official ports, especially the largest, Canton and Zaitun (Quanzhou), collected import taxes of 10 to 15 percent of the value of goods. In 1128, maritime trade brought in 20 percent of China's total cash revenue. Merchants were valued for the taxes the state could collect from them. Those who paid the most were rewarded with official rank.

The international merchants were enjoying the peak of a highly integrated national system of trade and commerce, a system built on domestic as well as international water transport. To integrate the system of waterways, portage of goods was arranged at points of dangerous rapids and cataracts. To ensure smooth passage, double locks were installed on the man-made Grand Canal; this system helped to link the agricultural wealth of the south with the administrative cities of the north. Tugboats with human-powered paddle-wheels serviced the main ports. Chinese oceangoing ships, equipped with axial rudders, watertight bulkheads, and magnetic compasses, gained a reputation as the best in the world.

International Trade

As early as the fourth century C.E., the Chinese traded in the South China Sea and the Indian Ocean, although probably only as far west as present-day Sri Lanka (Ceylon). With the decline of the Tang dynasty in the ninth century, they largely withdrew from this oceanic trade and concentrated instead on inland issues, reflecting their geographical location in the Yellow River valley and the north. After 1127, however, they returned to oceanic enterprise, when the Song dynasty was driven from northern China by the invasions of the Tatars and other northern peoples. With various

12.1
12.2
12.3
12.4
12.5
12.6

How did China's
focus on internal
trade affect its
cultural growth?

outside groups in control of the old overland silk routes, sea-borne trade was an obvious alternative. Thanks to their industrial innovations, the Song could supplement the traditional exports of silk and porcelain with products of iron and steel. To carry their expanding trade, the Chinese mastered the craft of building large ships, and Chinese merchants established new patterns of commercial exchange, including sophisticated credit systems. In addition to a merchant marine, China constructed a powerful navy.

The great luxury products of China—silk, porcelain, and tea—continued to attract thousands of foreign merchants. Many were Muslim Arabs; a few Lombards, Germans, and French also came to trade. They were treated as welcome guests, and special quarters in the port cities were set aside for them. In issues that involved no Chinese but only these foreigners, they could apply their own laws. Shops with foreign goods and foreign schools catered to their interests. Nevertheless, these merchants followed Chinese commercial rules, and many became quite Sinicized in their manners. When they ended their sojourn in China, they were often feted with large farewell feasts.

The Voyages of Zheng He. In the early years of the Ming dynasty, China's emperors adopted policies of expansionism by land and self-assertion at sea. The Ming emperor Yung-lo (r. 1402–24) dispatched a series of seven oceangoing expeditions under the Muslim eunuch Zheng He. The first voyage set out in 1405 with 62 large junks, 100 smaller ships, and 30,000 crew. The largest ships were 450 feet long, displaced 1,600 tons, and held a crew of about 500; they were the largest ships built anywhere up to that time. They carried silks, porcelain, and pepper. The first expedition sailed as far as Calicut, near the southwest tip of India. In six further missions between 1407 and 1433, Zheng He sailed to ports all along the shores of the Indian Ocean, at least twice reaching the East African ports of Mogadishu, Brava, Malindi, and Kilwa. Interested in exotic treasures that could not be found in China, Emperor Yung-lo seemed most pleased with exotic animals brought from distant lands, especially a giraffe sent to him by the sultan of Malindi on the fourth voyage, in 1416–19. These colossal expeditions demonstrated both the skill of Admiral Zheng He and the vision of Emperor Yung-lo. On the basis of these voyages, many historians believe that the Chinese would have been able to cross either the Atlantic or the Pacific Ocean—had they wished. But they did not push their expeditions any further and, in 1433, the Ming emperor terminated his sponsorship of the Indian Ocean voyages.

Why did the emperor end these voyages? Why did China not dispatch missions to Europe, and even to the western hemisphere? Why did the Chinese choose instead only to receive European shipping, beginning with the Portuguese in 1514?

Many answers seem plausible. The Ming turned their energy inward, toward consolidation and internal development. They pushed the Mongols out of China and beyond the Great Wall fortification along the northern border, but an invasion of Mongolia failed in 1449. Thereafter, the Ming limited their military goals. They rebuilt the Great Wall and restricted their forces to the defense of their land-based empire.

In 1411 the Ming reconstructed and extended the Grand Canal from Hangzhou in the south to Beijing in the north. The canal was a cheap, efficient means of shipping the grain and produce required by the northern capital. The man-made inland waterway also reduced the importance of coastal shipping, further enabling the Ming emperors to turn their backs on the sea. The faction of eunuchs, dedicated court servants such as Zheng He, who urged the government to continue its sponsorship of foreign trade, lost out to other factions that promoted internal development. International private shipping was also curtailed.

The Ming government limited contact with foreigners and prohibited private overseas trade by Chinese merchants. In 1371, coastal residents were forbidden to

12.1
12.2
12.3
12.4
12.5
12.6

How did China's focus on internal trade affect its cultural growth?

A Chinese Junk, from *Jan Huyghen van Linschoten: His Discourse of Voyages into the East and West Indies*, Johannes Baptista van Doetechum, 1579–92. Engraving. Apparently first an invention of the Malay sailors of the South China Sea, and adapted by the Chinese, these ships could carry more than 1,000 tons of cargo and hundreds of sailors. (Private collection)

SOURCE

Chinese Ships in South Indian Harbors: An Account by Ibn Battuta

The fourteenth-century traveler Ibn Battuta (1304–c. 1368) did not usually comment on ships and sailors. He was far more interested in his encounters with people on land. In the south Indian port of Calicut, however, he was so impressed with the capacity and design of the Chinese ships that he gave a remarkable description. He notes that, while the Chinese allowed only Chinese ships to dock in their ports, the pilots and crew were not necessarily Chinese:

> We traveled to the city of Calicut, which is one of the chief ports in Malabar [the southwest coast of India], and one of the largest harbors in the world. It is visited by men from China, Sumatra, Ceylon, the Maldives, Yemen, and Fars [Persia], and in it gather merchants from all quarters … there were at the time thirteen Chinese vessels, and we disembarked. Every one of us was lodged in a house and we stayed there three months as the guests of the infidel [Zamorin ruler of Calicut], awaiting the season of the voyage to China. On the Sea of China traveling is done in Chinese ships only, so we shall describe their arrangements.
>
> The Chinese vessels are of three kinds; large ships called *chunks* [junks], middle-sized ones called *zaws* [dhows], and small ones called *kakams*. The large ships have anything from twelve down to three sails, which are made of bamboo rods

> plaited like mats. They are never lowered, but turned according to the direction of the wind; at anchor they are left floating in the wind. A ship carries a complement of a thousand men, six hundred of whom are sailors and four hundred men-at-arms, including archers, men with shields and arbalests, who throw naphtha. Each large vessel is accompanied by three smaller ones, the "half," the "third," and the "quarter." These vessels are built only in the towns of Zaytun [Quanzhou] and Canton [Guangzhou]. The vessel has four decks and contains rooms, cabins, and saloons for merchants; a cabin has chambers and a lavatory, and can be locked by its occupant, who takes along with him slave girls and wives. Often a man will live in his cabin unknown to any of the others on board until they meet on reaching some town. The sailors have their children living on board ship, and they cultivate green stuffs, vegetables and ginger in wooden tanks. The owner's factor [representative] on board ship is like a great *amir* [nobleman]. When he goes on shore he is preceded by archers and Abyssinians with javelins, swords, drums, trumpets, and bugles. On reaching the house where he stays they stand their lances on both sides of the door, and continue thus during his stay. Some of the Chinese own large numbers of ships on which their factors are sent to foreign countries. There is no people in the world wealthier than the Chinese. (Ibn Battuta, pp. 234–36)

SOURCE

River Trade in China

China is such a huge country that most of its trade is internal; only a small fraction of local productivity makes its way to foreign markets. The vast and profitable trade in silk, both domestic and export, depended ultimately on the hard work of millions of spinners and weavers and their families. Similarly, river trade—some of which would ultimately be transshipped overseas—depended, at least partially, on the investments of common people. The four sources below support that assertion. The first is from Marco Polo, attesting to the abundance of river trade in China. The second is from Pao Hui, writing in the thirteenth century about the financing of overseas river trade. The third is a Song dynasty scroll illustrating the multitude of Chinese junks sailing on the Yellow River at Kaifeng. The fourth, a prose poem, describes the contribution of the women who produced and marketed the silk for which China was famous.

First, Marco Polo writes of the Yangzi River:

> I assure you that this river runs for such a distance and through so many regions and there are so many cities on its banks that truth to tell, in the amount of shipping it carries and the total volume and value of its traffic, it exceeds all the rivers of the Christians put together and their seas into the bargain. I give you my word that I have seen in this city [I-ching] fully five thousand ships at once, all afloat on this river. Then you may reflect since this city, which is not very big, has so many ships, how many there must be in the others. (cited in Elvin, pp. 144–45)

Then compare Pao Hui on the financing of river trade in Southern Song China:

> All the people along the coast are on intimate terms with the merchants who engage in overseas trade, either because they are fellow countrymen or personal acquaintances. Leakage [of copper currency] through entrusting occurs when the former give the latter money to take with them on their ships for the purchase and return conveyance of foreign goods. They invest from ten to a hundred strings of cash, and regularly make profits of several hundred per cent. (Shiba Yoshinobu, p. 33)

Third, examine Zhang Zeduan's twelfth-century scroll painting, *Going on the River at the Qingming Festival* (above). At this time, the city of Kaifeng, situated on the Yellow River and at the crossroads of some of China's most important canals, was the hub of water-borne traffic for all of northern China. Inland Kaifeng and Hangzhou, on the coast, were China's most important regional capitals. They formed the apex of a regional system of urbanization that unified the whole country.

Market towns sprang up throughout China, enabling almost every rural family to sell its products for cash and to buy city goods. In turn, the small market towns were linked to larger cities, which provided more specialized products and access to government administrators. Here, families could buy and sell, arrange a marriage, determine the latest government rulings, hear about new farming possibilities, and learn the dates and the results of academic examinations. These towns were so widespread that nearly every farm family lived within reach of one.

At the base were the rural families, struggling to survive by producing commodities demanded by the traders. Hand manufacture, especially of cotton and silk cloth, often supplemented farm production in rural areas. Invention made the process more productive. In particular, a reeling machine, invented around the eleventh century, drew several silk filaments at once from silkworm cocoons immersed in boiling water. It then drew the filaments through eyelets and hooks and finally banded them into silk thread.

The rural producers were integrated into the market system either through direct, personal access or through brokers who supplied raw materials and bought the finished product. Women were the chief producers in this supplemental rural industry. They also carried the finished product to market. Conditions of production and of marketing could be savage. Xu Xianzhong's "Prose Poem on Cotton Cloth," our fourth source, presents the harshness of both aspects. It is not clear whether the women in the marketplace are selling their cloth, or themselves, or both:

> Why do you ignore their toil? Why are you touched
> Only by the loveliness that is born from toil?
>
> Shall I tell you how their work exhausts them?
> By hand and treadle they turn the rollers of wood and iron,
> Feeling their fibre in between their fingers;
> The cotton comes out fluffy and the seeds fall away.
> The string of the cotton bow is stretched so taut
> It twangs with a sob from its pillar.
> They draw out slivers, spin them on their wheels
> To the accompaniment of a medley of creakings.
> Working through the darkness by candlelight,
> Forgetful of bed. When energy ebbs, they sing.
> The quilts are cold. Unheard, the waterclock flows over.
>
> When a woman leaves for market
> She does not look at her hungry husband.
> Afraid her cloth's not good enough,
> She adorns her face with cream and powder,
> Touches men's shoulders to arouse their lust,
> And sells herself with pleasant words.
> Money she thinks of as a beast its prey;
> Merchants she coaxes as she would her father.
> Nor is her burden lifted till one buys.
>
> (cited in Elvin, pp. 273–74)

CHAPTER TWELVE: ESTABLISHING WORLD TRADE ROUTES 1300–1500

12.1
12.2
12.3
12.4
12.5
12.6

練絲

連邨煮繭香
事誰家娘盈盈
意媚窑頰拍拍手
探湯上盆頰色長
好轉軸頭緒
晚来得少休女
伴語隔墙

Ink and watercolor print showing silk manufacture, Chinese, early seventeenth century. During the Song dynasty (960–1279), long-distance trade across central Asia dwindled. Maritime trade, with its very much safer and cheaper routes, now offered a viable alternative, and silk, along with porcelain and tea, continued to attract the merchants of the world. Unwinding filaments from silkworm cocoons in order to make yarn was considered women's work, as this Ming dynasty print suggests. (Victoria and Albert Museum, London)

travel overseas. In response to the smuggling that resulted, the government issued further prohibitions in 1390, 1394, 1397, 1433, 1449, and 1452. The repetition of this legislation reveals that smuggling did continue. Nevertheless, for the most part, private Chinese sailors were cut off from foreign trade. The government regarded the expeditions of Zheng He as political missions to exact tribute from outlying countries. Although products were exchanged on these voyages, trade was not their official purpose. So, while both private and government trade flourished in the interior of China, and while thousands of Chinese emigrated to carry on private businesses throughout Southeast Asia, China's official overseas trade came to a standstill. Zheng He's expeditions stand out as spectacular exceptions to the generally complacent and inward-looking character of the Chinese Empire.

The decision to limit China's international trade proved costly. Chinese society became introverted and, although economic growth continued, Chinese culture stagnated. Under the Song dynasty, Chinese technology had been the most innovative in the world. Creativity continued even under the Mongols, but by the beginning of the Ming dynasty, China was less imaginative. Military technology improved but

Statuette of silk-route trader, Chinese, tenth century. Statuettes, found in tombs in China from the time of the Tang dynasty, record the presence of traders from Mediterranean regions who traversed the thousands of miles of the silk routes. From their features, scholars believe that they were Semitic peoples: Jews from the Fertile Crescent, Egyptians, and other Levantines. Some of them eventually settled along the trans-Asian routes. (Seattle Art Museum)

then it, too, stagnated. China had invented gunpowder before 1000 C.E., but used it only sporadically. In the early fifteenth century, Ming cannons were at least equal to those anywhere in the world, but metal was in short supply, and further development was limited. The Ming laid siege to few fortress cities, so they had little need for heavy artillery. In fighting against invasion from the north, the crossbow was the weapon of choice. At first, when China was much more advanced than its adversaries, decisions to limit further military innovation seemed inconsequential. Later, however, they would render the country vulnerable to distant, newly rising powers.

Central Asia: The Mongols and the Silk Routes

12.4 What is the legacy of the Mongol Empire?

The Song dynasty developed the waterways of China, but the great central Asian overland silk routes had declined after the ninth century along with the Tang dynasty that had protected and encouraged them. Under the Mongol Empire (1206–1405), the largest land empire ever known, traffic on the silk routes revived.

The two million Mongols who inhabited the plateau region of central Asia were divided into several warring tribes, each led by a *khan*, or ruler. The land was poor and the climate harsh. The Mongols shepherded their cattle, sheep, and goats in a circular pattern of migration called **transhumance**: in the brief summers they moved their herds northward to pasture; in winter they turned back south. They spent most of their waking hours on horseback and mastered the art of warfare from the stirrups, with bow and arrow as well as sword by their side.

Intercontinental Trade Flourishes

Cultural historians credit the Mongols with little permanent contribution because they were absorbed into other, more settled and sophisticated cultures. But they did establish, for about a century, the *Pax Mongolica*, the Mongolian Peace, over a vast region, in which intercontinental trade could flourish across the reopened silk routes. Reports from two world travelers, Ibn Battuta (1304–*c.* 1368) of Morocco and Marco Polo (1254–1324) of Venice, give vivid insights into that exotic trade route.

Ibn Battuta. During his 30 years and 73,000 miles of travel, Ibn Battuta commented extensively on conditions of travel and trade. For example, in central Asia he encountered a military expedition of Oz Beg Khan (d. 1341), the ruler of the *khanate*, or sub-empire, of the Golden Horde: "We saw a vast city on the move with its inhabitants, with mosques and bazaars in it, the smoke of the kitchens rising in the air (for they cook while on the march), and horse-drawn wagons transporting the people" (cited in Dunn, p. 167). The tents of this camp/city were Mongol **yurts**. Made of wooden poles covered with leather pelts, and with rugs on the floor, they could be readily disassembled for travel.

Later, Ibn Battuta was granted his request to travel with one of Oz Beg Khan's wives along the trade route as she returned to her father's home in Constantinople to give birth to her child. Ibn Battuta reported that the princess traveled with 5,000 horsemen under military command, 500 of her own troops and servants, 200 female slave girls, 20 Greek and Indian pages, 400 wagons, 2,000 horses, and 500 oxen and camels. They crossed from Islamic Mongol territory to Christian Byzantium.

HOW DO WE KNOW?

The Mongol Empire

Because it was the largest contiguous land empire in history, understanding the entire Mongol Empire requires competence in the Mongolian, Chinese, Persian, Arabic, Turkish, Japanese, Russian, Armenian, Georgian, and Latin languages. No scholar can be expected to master all these, but serious scholars are expected to know at least one or two of them and to use others in translation. Surprisingly, Mongolian may not be the most important. Before Chinggis Khan, the language was not written and there are no archives of the Mongol Empire, at least none that have survived. The only major historical text in Mongolian is *The Secret History of the Mongols*, and, although some scholars think it inauthentic, it is our principal source for the biography of Chinggis Khan. Another text from his time, the *Altan Debter*, or *Golden Book*, is lost, but Persian and Chinese historians mention it, and their references show the book to be consistent with, although not the same as, *The Secret History*.

Chinese and Persian texts are the next most important, discussing Mongol rule over the two empires flanking, and captured by, the Mongol Empire. In China, the major text is the official dynastic history of the Yuan, or Mongol, dynasty. In Persia, several authors are important, most notably Rashid al-Din. Until his time, the Mongol conquest posed a problem for Muslim historians: the conquest of the Abbasid Empire was not supposed to happen. Muslims were to conquer others, as they had done with great consistency; they were not supposed to be conquered themselves. During Rashid al-Din's time, however, the Mongols converted to Islam. Rashid al-Din must have understood this well, since he himself had converted from Judaism. He wrote the history of the Mongol Empire, which, he said, marked a new era in world history. Later, he wrote *Jami' al-tawarikh* (*Collection of Histories*), recording the history of all the peoples touched by the Mongols from the Chinese in the east to the Franks in the west. It was the first example of the form of a world history. For the last 20 years of his life, until he was assassinated as the result of a court intrigue in 1318, Rashid al-Din served as principal adviser to the Il-Khan ruler of Persia.

In 1240 the Mongols captured and sacked Kiev, the most important city in Eastern Europe, and moved on into Poland and Hungary; a number of European sources discuss their conquests. These included such men as Giovanni de Piano Carpini, who was sent by Pope Innocent IV to visit the Khans, and William of Rubruck, who visited the Mongols at the behest of the king of France, Louis IX. The most comprehensive account is by Matthew Paris, who chronicled European reactions to the Mongol advances from his post at St. Albans, England. The most popular came from travelers, of whom the most famous was Marco Polo.

Reflecting on this array of European visitors, plus the Tunisian Muslim scholar Ibn Battuta, the Nestorian Christian Rabban Sauma, the Armenian king He'tun, the Chinese Confucian Zhou Daguan, and all the multitude of travelers who "journeyed along the traditional land-based Silk Roads … as well as the sea routes from West, South, and Southeast Asia to southern Chinese ports" (Rossabi, pp. 60–61), the historian Morris Rossabi concludes that "the Mongol period was the onset of global history" (p. 60).

- The most important biography of Chinggis Khan is in Mongolian, but Mongolian is not the most important language for the study of the Mongolian empire. How do you explain this paradox?
- Why are Chinese and Persian important languages for studying the Mongol Empire?
- Would you consider Rashid al-Din's *Collection of Histories* a history of the world? Why or why not?

Marco Polo. Marco Polo was a merchant in a family of merchants, and his account of his travels to and in China was particularly attuned to patterns of trade. His numerous descriptions of urban markets support the idea of an urban-centered trade diaspora. For example, consider his description of Tabriz in northwest Persia:

> The people of Tabriz live by trade and industry; for cloth of gold and silk is woven here in great quantity and of great value. The city is so favourably situated that it is a market for merchandise from India and Baghdad, from Mosul and Hormuz, and from many other places; and many Latin merchants come here to buy the merchandise imported from foreign lands. It is also a market for precious stones, which are found here in great abundance. It is a city where good profits are made by travelling merchants. The inhabitants are a mixed lot and good for very little. There are Armenians and Nestorians, Jacobites and Georgians and Persians; and there are also worshippers of Mahomet, who are the natives of the city and are called Tabrizis. (Polo, p. 57)

Central Asian routes challenged travelers and their animals. Despite the *Pax Mongolica*, merchants still had to be prepared to defend themselves from attack. As Marco Polo recounts,

12.1
12.2
12.3
12.4
12.5
12.6

What is the legacy of the Mongol Empire?

Among the people of these kingdoms there are many who are brutal and blood-thirsty. They are forever slaughtering one another; and, were it not for fear of the government … they would do great mischief to travelling merchants. The government imposes severe penalties upon them and has ordered that along all dangerous routes the inhabitants at the request of the merchants shall supply good and efficient escorts from district to district for their safe conduct on payment of two or three groats for each loaded beast according to the length of the journey. Yet, for all that the government can do, these brigands are not to be deterred from frequent depredations. Unless the merchants are well armed and equipped with bows, they slay and harry them unsparingly. (p. 61)

For those merchants and statesmen who did reach Beijing, the *khan* maintained a massive service industry to provide hospitality. Polo noted, in particular, an army of prostitutes:

I assure you that there are fully 20,000 of them, all serving the needs of men for money. They have a captain general, and there are chiefs of hundreds and of thousands responsible to the captain. This is because, whenever ambassadors come to the Great Khan on his business and are maintained at his expense, which is done on a lavish scale, the captain is called upon to provide one of these women every night for the ambassador and one for each of his attendants. They are changed each night and receive no payment; for this is the tax they pay to the Great Khan. (p. 129)

Almost everything we know about Marco Polo's life is based on the colorful account he left us of his travels through Asia. Little is known of his childhood years in Venice or his education. Polo's father and uncle, both Venetian merchants, traveled from their home in 1260 on a trade mission as far as the northern end of the Caspian Sea. Then war broke out, and their route home was blocked. But the route eastward was open, so the brothers traveled on to Beijing, where Chinggis Khan's grandson Kubilai Khan (1215–94) ruled.

The Great Khan invited the men to return with more information on Christianity and a delegation from the pope. The information and delegation never materialized, but in 1271 the two brothers, bringing along the 17-year-old Marco, set out for China again. They arrived in 1275 and remained there for 17 years. How exactly they occupied themselves during this time is unclear from Marco's account, but it was not uncommon for foreigners to find employment in the Mongol state. Kubilai Khan, it appears, was so enchanted by Marco's tales of foreign lands that he sent him on repeated reconnaissance trips throughout the empire. The Polos eventually set off for home in about 1292, reaching Venice in 1295 and reuniting with relatives and friends who had believed them long-since dead.

Soon after his homecoming, Marco was captured in battle by Genoese sailors and imprisoned. He dictated the tales of his travels to his fellow prisoner Rustichello, a writer of romances. Europe now had its most complete and consistent account up to that date of the silk route and of the fabulous Chinese empire of Kubilai Khan. Marco's *Travels* was soon translated into several European languages, introducing to Christian Europe a new understanding of the world.

For seven centuries scholars have hotly debated the authenticity of Marco Polo's account. No original copy of *The Travels* exists, and scholars have been faced with some 140 manuscript versions that were copied in various languages and dialects from scribe to scribe before the invention of printing. In a book titled *Did Marco Polo Go to China?*, Frances Wood emphasizes the arguments against. Polo did not mention any of the phenomena that should have caught his attention during his reported time in China: Chinese writing, tea, chopsticks, footbinding, the Great Wall. Despite his claims to frequent meetings with Kubilai Khan, Marco Polo is not mentioned in any

Marco Polo, from *Li Livres du Graunt Caam, c.* 1400. The great world traveler is shown setting sail for China from Venice in 1271. Europe was eager for news of the Mongol Empire—potential allies against the Muslim enemy—and a steady stream of intrepid merchants and missionaries brought back amazing reports of the Khan's court. The exotic reminiscences of Marco Polo are by far the most famous. (Bodleian Library, Oxford)

12.1
12.2
12.3
12.4
12.5
12.6

What is the
legacy of the
Mongol Empire?

Chinese records of the time. Wood concludes that Polo's work is actually based on materials gathered from others and that he himself never traveled beyond the Black Sea. As a travel narrative, Wood asserts, the book must be a fabrication, but as an account of what was known of China at the time, it is a rich and influential source of information. However, many commentators are equally adamant that Polo did complete all the travels that he claimed; the debate over the extent of his journeys continues.

📖 **Read** the **Document: Marco Polo on Chinese Society under the Mongol Rule (1270s)** on **MyHistoryLab**

Chinggis Khan and the Mongol Empire

The reopening and protection of the silk routes in the time of Marco Polo was the work of the Mongols, who emerged from Mongolia on a career of world conquest, led by Chinggis Khan. Temujin, later called Chinggis (Genghis) Khan, was born in about 1162 into one of the more powerful and more militant Mongol tribes. His father, chief of his tribe, was poisoned by a rival tribe. About three generations before Temujin's birth, one of his ancestors, Kabul Khan, had briefly united the Mongols, and Temujin made it his own mission to unify them once again. He conquered the surrounding tribes, one by one, and united them at Karakorum, his capital. Although skilled at negotiation, Temujin was also infamous for his brutality. Historian Rashid al-Din (1247–1318), writing almost a century after Temujin's conquests, reports his declaration of purpose, emphasizing women as the spoils of warfare: "Man's greatest good fortune is to chase and defeat his enemy, seize all his possessions, leave his married women weeping and wailing, ride his gelding, and use the bodies of his women as a nightshirt and support, gazing upon and kissing their rosy breasts, sucking their lips which are as sweet as the berries of their breasts" (cited in Ratchnevsky, p. 153).

Temujin defeated the Tartars and killed all surviving males taller than a cart axle. He defeated the rival Mongol clans and boiled alive all their chiefs. In 1206, an assembly of all the chiefs of the steppe regions proclaimed him Chinggis Khan—"Universal Ruler." He organized them for further battle under a pyramid of officers leading units of 100, 1,000, and 10,000 mounted warriors, commanded, as they grew older, by his four sons. Promotion within the fighting machine was by merit. Internal feuding among the Mongols ended and a new legal code, based on written and recorded case law, called for high moral standards from all Mongols.

Chinggis turned east toward China. On the way he captured the Tangut kingdom of Xixia, and from Chinese engineers he mastered the weapons of siege warfare: the mangonel and trebuchet, which could catapult great rocks; giant crossbows mounted on stands; and gunpowder, which could be launched from longbows in bamboo-tube rockets. In 1211, Chinggis pierced the Great Wall of China, and in 1215 he conquered the capital, Zhongdu (modern Beijing), killing thousands.

Chinggis departed from China to conquer other kingdoms. His officials and successors continued moving south, however, until they captured all of China, establishing the Yuan dynasty (1276–1368). They conquered Korea and large parts of Southeast Asia as far as Java, and attempted, but failed, to take Japan as well. The planned assault on Japan in 1281 was stopped by *kamikaze*, "divine winds," which prevented the Mongol fleet from sailing.

Chinggis himself turned west, conquering the Kara-Khitai Empire, which included the major cities of Tashkent and Samarqand. He turned southward toward India, reaching the Indus River and stationing troops in the Punjab, but he was unable to penetrate further. Turning northwest, he proceeded to conquer Khwarizm. In the great cities of Bukhara, Nishapur, Merv, Herat, Balkh, and Gurgan, millions were reported killed, surely an exaggeration, but still an indication of great slaughter. Chinggis went on to capture Tabriz and Tbilisi.

After Chinggis' death in 1227, his four sons continued the expansion relentlessly. In the northwest they defeated the Bulgars along the Volga and the Cumans of the southern steppes and then entered Russia. They took Moscow, destroyed Kiev, overran Moravia and Silesia, and set their sights on the conquest of Hungary. To the terrified peoples in their path, it looked as if nothing could stop the Mongols' relentless expansion. But in 1241, internal quarrels did what opposing armies could not: they brought the Mongol advance in Europe to a halt. During the dispute over succession that followed the death of Chinggis' son Ögedei (1185–1241), the Mongols withdrew east of Kiev. They never resumed their westward movement, and central and Western Europe remained untouched.

12.1
12.2
12.3
12.4
12.5
12.6

What is the
legacy of the
Mongol Empire?

Chinggis Khan in a book by Rashid al-Din, fourteenth-century. Ink and gouache on vellum. Most of the information we have on Chinggis Khan comes from the peoples he defeated, and they portray him as a brutal, bloodthirsty savage, but information from the Mongol perspective credits him with consolidating an array of local tribes into a unified nation, and introducing discipline, order, law, and careers open to talent. His conquests re-opened and protected silk routes that had been largely abandoned for almost a thousand years. (Bibliotheque Nationale, Paris)

In the southwest, under Chinggis' grandson Hülegü (c. 1217–65), the Mongols captured and destroyed Baghdad in 1258, ending the five-century-old Abbasid dynasty by killing the caliph. But in the next year, Möngke, Chinggis' grandson and the fourth and last successor to his title as "Great Khan," died while campaigning in China, and many of the Mongol forces withdrew to attend a general conclave in Karakorum to choose his successor. In 1260, Mongol forces were defeated by a Mamluk army at the

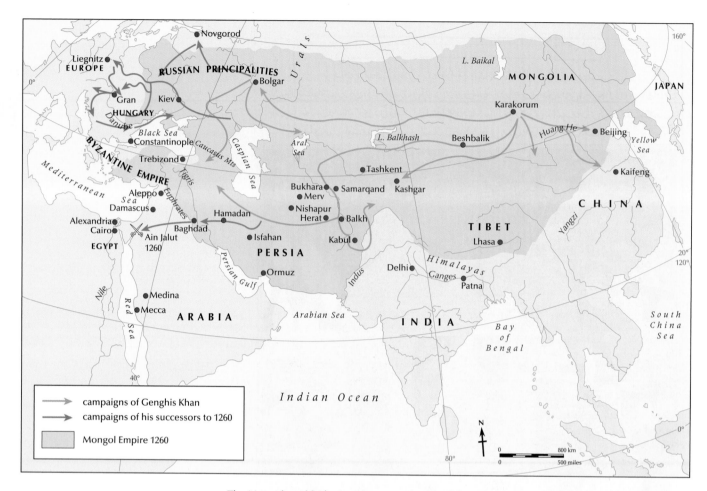

The Mongol world. The irruption across Eurasia of the Mongols, an aggressive steppe nomad people, remains one of the most successful military undertakings of all time. Within 30 years the campaigns of Chinggis Khan took the Mongol cavalry east to the Chinese heartland and west to Kievan Russia, the Caucasus, and Persia. His immediate successors consolidated China, entered Europe, and went on to establish a network of trans-Asian empires.

12.1

12.2

12.3

12.4 What is the legacy of the Mongol Empire?

12.5

12.6

battle of Ain Jalut, in modern Jordan, ending forever their drive to the southwest (see map "The Mongol world," above).

📖 **Read** the **Document: The Mongols: An Excerpt from the Novgorod Chronicle, 1315** on **MyHistoryLab**

The End of the Mongol Empire

Mongol rule was extensive but brief. At their apogee, 1279–1350, the Mongols had ruled all of China, almost all of Russia, Iran, Iraq, and central Asia. The huge empire was administered through four separate geographical *khanates*, each under the authority of a branch of Chinggis Khan's family. Over time, central authority declined and the four *khanates* separated, each becoming an independent empire. Often they fought with one another.

The Mongols could not govern their empire from horseback, and they were soon absorbed by the peoples they had conquered. They intermarried freely with the Turks, who had joined them as allies in conquest. In Russia, Mongols and Turks merged with Slavs and Finns in a new Turkish-speaking ethnic group, the Tartars. In Persia and China they assimilated into local culture, converting to various

12.1

12.2

12.3

12.4

12.5

12.6

What is the
legacy of the
Mongol Empire?

beliefs, including Christianity, Buddhism, and Confucianism. In most of the areas inhabited by Muslims, the Mongols and their Turkish allies typically converted to Islam.

As the four segments of Chinggis Khan's empire went their own separate ways, slowly they were driven from their conquests. By 1335, the male line of Chinggis and his grandson Hülegü died out in the Il-Khan Empire in Persia. The Ming dynasty defeated and evicted the Mongol rulers in 1368, ending the Yuan dynasty. The Chagatai *khanate* was destroyed after 1369 by Timur the Lame (Tamerlane, 1336–1405), a powerful Turkic leader who sought to recreate the empire of Chinggis Khan. In 1480, Russia's Ivan III defeated the Golden Horde (named not, as one might think, for their numbers, but for their tents, *ordu* in Turkish) and pushed them out of his territories, although the last Mongol state in the Crimea was conquered only in the eighteenth century.

The Mongol Legacy

The accounts of the merciless brutality of Chinggis Khan and the Mongols, recorded above, and earlier in "The Mongols and the Destruction of the Caliphate" in the chapter entitled "Islam," along with the claims of hundreds of thousands murdered and raped by their troops in war and revenge, present a picture of unchecked military sadism. But other accounts praise the Mongols for ultimately creating peace and stability in the lands they conquered, allowing the emergence of new economic institutions, technological innovations, and the flourishing of cultural, literary, and artistic creativity. The Mongols' tolerance also permitted various religious traditions to coexist. Even the historians, such as Rashid al-Din and Ata al-Mulk Juvaini, who write of the Mongols' merciless military devastations, credit them with allowing and encouraging humane administration, which took account of local traditions. This accommodation to local patterns of culture and governance became even more true in China under Kubilai Khan. While conquered women were treated savagely, Mongol women were highly valued as custodians of the homes and the herds of these nomadic warriors. Some, like Sorghaghtani Beki, Chinggis' war captive, daughter-in-law, and mother and teacher of four of the most powerful Mongol rulers—Möngke, Kubilai, Hülegü, and Arigh Böke—earned fame for their wisdom, power, and discretion.

Excavations in the Mongol capital of Karakorum, Shangdu (Xanadu), the summer capital of Kubilai Khan, and numerous Mongol sites in Russia have revealed exquisite artworks in gold, jade, silk, and porcelain, as well as frescoes. The Mongols may not have created these works, but they recognized their beauty and patronized their creators. Chinggis himself had a Uighur Turk scholar adapt the Turkic script for use as the first written language for Mongolian, although it was not widely accepted.

In terms of reopening the silk routes,

Unprecedented contact between East and West was one of the most important Mongol contributions. The Pax Mongolica, or Mongolian peace, facilitated the exchanges of people, ideas, and technologies. The various Eastern and Western civilizations, which were exposed to foreign techniques and views, chose and modified whatever they borrowed from others to suit their own needs. Iranians introduced chickpeas, carrots, eggplants, and pasta to China; they translated Iranian medical texts into Chinese while a Chinese agricultural text was translated into Iranian, and Chinese motifs and techniques in porcelain influenced Iranian pottery. (Rossabi, p. 71)

The most famous travelers from the west to Mongol China are doubtless the Polo family, but their expeditions for trade followed earlier ones dispatched for religious reasons. After the Mongol victory at the Battle of Legnica in 1241, European leaders feared further invasion of Europe. Pope Innocent IV dispatched Giovanni de Piano

12.1

12.2

12.3

12.4

12.5   What goods were
traded in sub-
12.6   Saharan Africa?

Carpini to the Mongol Khans in 1245, to bring back more information and perhaps to negotiate some agreements. The mission ultimately led him to the Great Khan at Karakorum, but without any diplomatic or religious result. The king of France, Louis IX, sent William of Rubruck on a mission to Karakorum to convert the Great Khans to Christianity in 1253, again with no diplomatic or religious success. Nevertheless, links were created between Karakorum and Western Europe.

The Mongols were brutal, in the mold of empire-builders throughout history, but they were also creative, and they facilitated creativity in others. They valued trade and cultural exchange and they facilitated them as well, effectively reopening the silk routes that had lain unused for about three centuries.

From Mongol to Ming: Dynastic Transition

During the 90 years of Mongol rule, 1279–1368, China's population plummeted from a high of 100 million to just over 50 million. Despite the splendor of Kubilai Khan in his capital at Beijing, the Chinese economy did not serve everyone equally well. Marco Polo told of especially bitter poverty and class division in southern China, where the Han Chinese of the Southern Song dynasty experienced Mongol rule as cruel and exploitative: "In the province of Manzi almost all the poor and needy sell some of their sons and daughters to the rich and noble, so that they may support themselves on the price paid for them and the children may be better fed in their new homes" (Polo, p. 227). Revolution simmered until 1368, when the Ming dynasty overthrew the Mongols and ruled for almost three centuries, until 1644.

Under the Ming dynasty, the population increased sharply. By 1450 it had reached 100 million again, and by 1580 the population was at least 130 million. Plagues and rebellions caused the population to fall back to 100 million by 1650, but from that trough it rose consistently into present times. The population settled new territories as it grew. The origins of the Chinese Empire had been in the Yellow River valley in the north. At the time of the Han dynasty, more than 80 percent of the population of China lived north of the Yangzi valley. Under the late Tang dynasty, the population was divided about equally between north and south. Warfare with the Mongols in the north drove more migrants south, and at the height of the Mongol Yuan dynasty up to 90 percent of the population lived in the south. Economically, the south produced rice, cotton, and tea, three of China's most valuable products, not available in the northern climate. Closer to the sea lanes of Southeast Asia and the Indian Ocean, the south also developed China's principal ports for international commerce. The Song built a powerful navy and Chinese merchants carried on regular trade with Southeast Asia, India, and the Persian Gulf. After the Mongols were defeated, however, migration began to reverse. By about 1500, 25 percent lived in the north and movement back in that direction was increasing.

Trade in Sub-Saharan Africa

> 12.5   What goods were traded in sub-Saharan Africa?

Africa south of the Sahara was well integrated into extensive webs of trade relationships. In East Africa, traders along the coast procured gold and ivory from the interior of the continent and sold them to the seafaring merchants of the Indian Ocean. In far-off West Africa, traders dispatched caravans of goods on camelback across the Sahara, linking the merchants and rulers of the Mediterranean coast with the forest cultivators and miners in the south.

📖 **Read** the **Document**: Strabo on Africa (1st c. CE) on **MyHistoryLab**

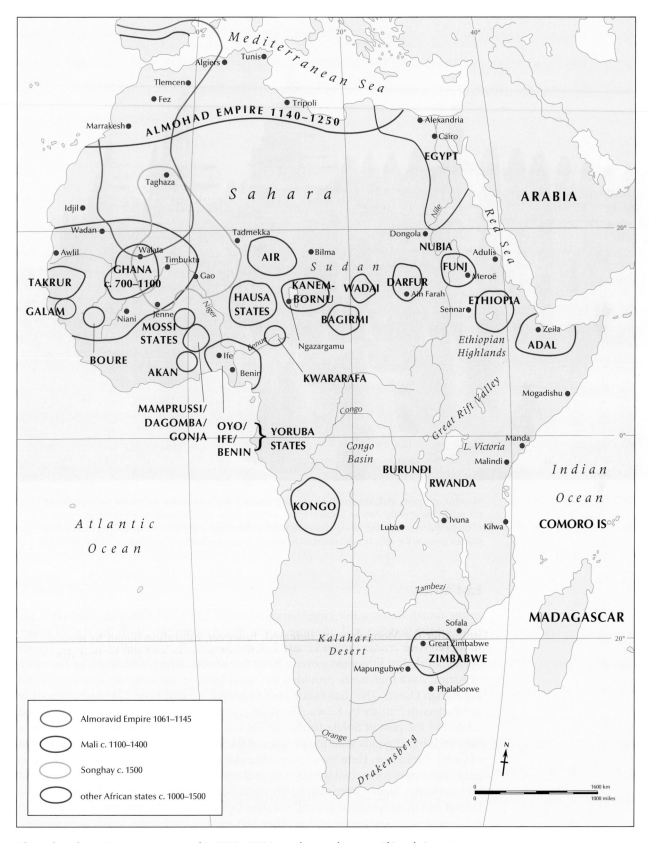

African kingdoms. Many states appeared in 1000–1500 in northern and western Africa, their power based on control over long-distance trade—gold, ivory, and slaves moving north; metalware, textiles, and salt carried south. Ghana, Mali, and Songhay are discussed in the text. These states, protected from marauders by the Sahara, could usually maintain their independence.

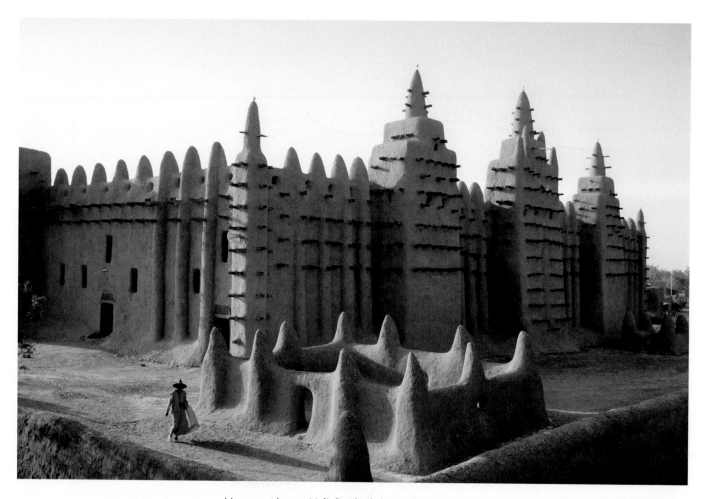

Mosque at Jenne, Mali, first built fourteenth century. The spectacular mud-brick mosques found in the major towns of the African savanna states, such as Jenne and Timbuktu, point to the acceptance of Islam by the merchant and ruling classes in the thirteenth and fourteenth centuries. The mud, which washes away in the rain, needs continual renewal—hence the built-in "scaffolding" of the structure.

12.1
12.2
12.3
12.4
12.5   What goods were
traded in sub-
12.6   Saharan Africa?

East Africa

In the fourth century, the kingdom of Axum in Christian Ethiopia dominated the trade of the Red Sea and, to some extent, the Arabian Sea. With the rise of Islam, however, Arab traders gained control of the flow of merchandise, and Arab armies began restricting Ethiopian power. After the ninth century, and south of the Horn of Africa, Arab merchants provided the main trading link between East Africa and the Indian Ocean. The first major port to spring up had been Manda, followed in the thirteenth century by Kilwa. The ruling Arab dynasty along the coast also seized control of the port of Sofala further to the south. Through local African merchants they exchanged goods with the peoples of the interior, especially at the trading post of Great Zimbabwe. Here they found abundant supplies of such valuable metals as gold and copper (often cast into ingots) and animal products: ivory, horns, skins, and tortoise shells. Slaves were also an important commodity. Great Zimbabwe was the largest and most remarkable of all the developing towns. Architecturally, it featured a 100-acre stone enclosure and another 100 smaller enclosures in the surrounding region.

From these inland sources, goods were transported to the coastal ports and shipped onward to Arabia and India in exchange for spices, pottery, glass beads, and cloth. In the port cities of Africa's east coast, the Swahili language of the nearby

12.1

12.2

12.3

12.4

What goods were
traded in sub-
Saharan Africa?   12.5

12.6

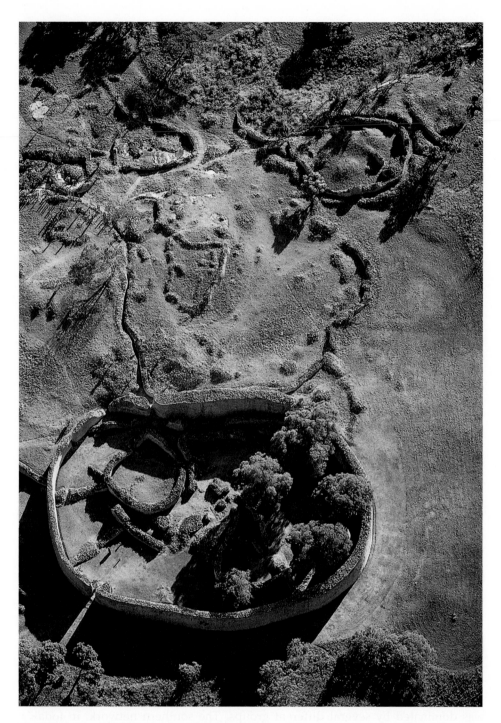

Great Zimbabwe. The biggest and most celebrated of several stone enclosures in East Africa dating from the tenth to the fifteenth century, Great Zimbabwe provided raw materials for trade at the coastal settlements, especially gold, copper, tin, and iron, and was also a trading post for luxury goods—Islamic pottery and cowrie shells were dug up at the site.

African peoples received from these Indian Ocean traders a strong admixture of Arabic vocabulary, enriching Swahili and ensuring its place as the dominant language of the coastal trade.

📖 **Read** the **Document: Descriptions of the Cities of Zanj** on **MyHistoryLab**

12.1

12.2

12.3

12.4

12.5

12.6 How did Americans trade before 1500?

West Africa

The domestication of the camel in the second to fifth century c.e. opened the possibility of regular trans-Saharan trade. Oases provided the necessary watering points for caravans, as well as producing dates, a major commodity of trade. The first written records since Roman times of this trans-Saharan trade begin with the arrival of Muslim traders in the eighth century.

For the most part, African political units were local, but three large empires arose in succession around the northern bend in the Niger, near Timbuktu, where the sahel, the arid fringe of the desert, meets the vast Sahara itself. These three empires—Ghana (*c.* 700–*c.* 1100), Mali (*c.* 1100–*c.* 1400), and Songhay (*c.* 1300–*c.* 1600)—kept the trade routes open and secure. In contrast with most governments in other parts of the world, which amassed wealth and power by controlling land and agriculture, these empires of arid lands drew their power from control over trade, traders, and trade routes.

Gold, slaves, cloth, ivory, ebony, pepper, and kola nuts (stimulants) moved north across the Sahara; salt, dates, horses, brass, copper, glassware, beads, leather, textiles, clothing, and foodstuffs moved south. Gold was the central attraction. In the fourteenth century, the gold mines of West Africa provided about two-thirds of the gold used in trade in the eastern hemisphere. In 1324, when the Muslim emperor of Mali, Mansa Musa (r. 1307–32), passed through Cairo on his way to Mecca, he dispensed so much gold in gifts to court officials and in purchases in the bazaar that commodity prices in Cairo were inflated for years to come. A European map of 1375 showing a seated Mansa Musa as ruler of Mali is annotated as follows: "So abundant is the gold found in his country that he is the richest and most noble king in all the land."

There were many natural break-points for the north–south trade. From the Mediterranean coast to the northern fringe of the desert, trade was borne by packhorse; across the desert, via oases, by camel; across the arid sahel and the grassy savannah lands south of the Sahara again by pack animal; and, finally, through the tropical forest, impenetrable to larger animals and afflicted with the lethal tsetse fly, it was borne by human porters. For the most part, locally dominant trade groups carried the trade from one market center to the next in short relays. A few trading communities, however, notably the Soninke and, especially, their Mande-speaking Dyula branch, established trade diasporas that negotiated with the rulers.

📖 Read the **Document: Leo Africanus' Description of West Africa (1500)** on **MyHistoryLab**

Trade in the Americas Before Columbus

12.6 How did Americans trade before 1500?

The western hemisphere spawned two major trade networks. The northern network served primarily the area that is Mexico today, although in those years this region was dominated by several different groups. The southern network, in today's Ecuador, Peru, and northern Chile, ran north–south in two parallel routes, one along the Pacific Coast, the other inland along the spine of the Andes Mountains. East–west routes, linking the coastal settlements with those of the mountains, rose to altitudes of 15,000 feet. In both North and South America, goods were carried by pack animals and by humans; the American Indians had not invented the wheel. Boats were used on streams and rivers. Along the South American coast, near the equator, the Incas sailed boats constructed of balsa wood, while the Mayans of the Yucatán paddled canoes through their river systems. There was little traffic between North and South America and virtually none between the eastern and western hemispheres, except for rare voyages, such as that by Leif Eriksson, the Viking explorer who reached Newfoundland about the year 1000.

The Inca Empire

In the Andes Mountains of South America, a significant and long-lasting hub of civilization grew up after 600 C.E. A series of different peoples dominated the region, and by the time the Incas consolidated their empire in the early fifteenth century, these mountain peoples had built an extensive network of trade roads, connecting settlements over hundreds of miles north to south and linking some 32 million people (see map "Classic cultures of the Americas" in the chapter "A Polycentric World").

Inca trade was conducted up and down the mountainsides. With peaks as high as 20,000 feet, the Andes hosted several different ecological zones, encouraging product differentiation and trade. The valleys below produced sweet potatoes, maize, manioc, squash, beans, chile peppers, peanuts, and cotton. The hills above provided white potatoes, quinoa, coca, medicines, feathers, and animal skins. The highland people specialized in manufacture and crafts, including gold working.

The state controlled this trade between the ecological zones. Under Inca rulers, from the early 1400s until the Spanish conquest in 1535, many of the best of the 15,000 miles of roads through the Andes were open only to government officials.

Central America and Mexico

In the Yucatán peninsula of Mesoamerica the Mayan peoples had flourished from 200 B.C.E. to 900 C.E. Initially Mayan traders operated without interference, amassing a disproportionate share of wealth. Archaeologists suggest that the increasing wealth of the traders created social tension, and that ultimately the traders were brought under the control of the state, creating a new set of unequal relations dominated by kings rather than merchants.

By the time the Spanish arrived, in the 1520s, the Maya were in decline and the Aztecs dominated the valley of Mexico. The Spanish soldiers wrote vivid accounts of the great marketplace of the Aztec capital, Tenochtitlán, including this summary in a letter by the Spanish leader Hernán Cortés:

> This city has many squares where trading is done and markets are held continuously. There is also one square twice as big as that of Salamanca, with arcades all around … There are streets of herbalists where all the medicinal herbs and roots found in the land are sold. There are shops like apothecaries', where they sell ready-made medicines as well as liquid ointments and plasters. There are shops like barbers', where they have their hair washed and shaved, and shops where they sell food and drink. (Cortés, pp. 103–04)

The market met every fifth day, with perhaps 40,000 to 50,000 merchants swarming in, rowing their canoes across the lake to the island on which Tenochtitlán was built. In many ways, the market was like the great fairs of medieval Europe, drawing merchants from distant corners of the kingdom and beyond.

But how independent were these Tenochtitlán merchants? The Spanish described the city's market as being under tight government control. In addition to officers who kept the peace, collected taxes, and checked the accuracy of weights and measures, a court of 12 judges sat to decide cases immediately.

A guild of traders, called *pochteca*, carried on long-distance trade, which expanded steadily through the fifteenth century. They led trade expeditions for hundreds of

Photograph of a *quipu*. In the Inca empire, which extended from Ecuador to central Chile, trading was facilitated by an extensive road network. This *quipu*, a device of knotted string used to record dates and accounts, would have been a handy aid to the traveling South American businessman in the early 1400s. (Musée du quai Branly)

12.1

12.2

12.3

12.4

12.5

12.6

How did Americans trade before 1500?

La Gran Tenochtitlán, Diego Rivera. 1945. The great Mexican muralist Diego Rivera told the story of his people on the walls of several of Mexico City's most prominent civic buildings with a boldness that attracted casual passersby as well as art connoisseurs. His depiction of the Aztec capital, Tenochtitlán, before the arrival of Europeans, suggests the majesty of the city, but does not overlook the harshness of the life of many of its inhabitants. (Palacio Nacional, Mexico City)

12.1

12.2

12.3

12.4

12.5

12.6 How did Americans trade before 1500?

miles, exchanging city-crafted obsidian knives, fur blankets, clothes, herbs, and dyes for such raw materials as jade, seashells, jaguar skins, feathers from forest birds, and, in the greatest volume, cotton from the Gulf coast. The traders gathered both goods and military intelligence for the ruling Aztec families. Royal troops protected them and sometimes used attacks on traveling *pochteca* as a justification for punitive reprisals and the confiscation of land. The *pochteca* lived in their own wards in the towns, had their own magistrates, and supervised the markets on their own. They were to marry only within the guild and, although they remained commoners, they could send their sons to temple schools. Their main god, Yiacatecutli, resembles the Toltec god Quetzalcoatl, and this, too, suggests that they were to some degree foreigners living in a trade diaspora, with a high degree of independence from the state and temple.

The civilizational hubs in Mexico and in the Andes functioned independently of one another and both flourished, of course, prior to Columbus, and almost entirely isolated from the rest of the world. When Europeans arrived in the sixteenth century brandishing new weapons, commanding new military organizations, and transmitting new diseases, the Americans were unprepared for the challenges.

📖 **Read** the **Document: Tlaltecatzin of Cuauhchinanco: "Song of Tlaltecatzin" (14th c.)** on **MyHistoryLab**

World Trade Routes Before Columbus: *What Difference Do They Make?*

The years around 1500 marked a turning point in world trade patterns. Before 1500, trading routes crisscrossed Africa, Europe, and Asia. These routes connected with one another, although they were not unified into a single system of trade. Long-distance trade goods would travel in stages, carried first by one set of traders and then transferred to another, as goods were transported to their final destination. The most important long-distance traders were the Muslim Arab sailors and merchants of the Indian Ocean routes and beyond to the ports of China. Chinese traders dominated the East Asian waterways and only occasionally sailed into the Indian Ocean. In the thirteenth and fourteenth centuries, Mongol rulers provided protection along the old silk routes, reopening these land passages through central Asia. At this time, however, few European traders ventured into eastern Asia.

Africa's west coast was fully integrated into these systems through Arabian Sea trade with Arabia and the west coast of India. The western regions of Africa were united among themselves, and with the Mediterranean coast, by caravan trade, especially after the domestication of the camel. The *hajj* pilgrimage assured that Muslim Africans, even from the western regions, would travel across that vast continent to reach Mecca; some would continue even beyond.

The western hemisphere had two sets of regional routes—mostly unconnected with each other—one centering on Mesoamerica, the other on the Andes Mountains of South America. The Americas remained separated from the rest of the world by the vast expanses of the Atlantic and Pacific oceans.

As European traders grew more active after 1500, they attempted to subordinate preexisting regional systems to their own centralized control from European headquarters. Within a single generation they seized control of the Americas. Asian countries, however, were much more powerful and tended to pay little attention to the newly arriving Europeans. Following early, problematic encounters, China and Japan mostly kept the visitors out. European control over global trade increased as northwestern Europe industrialized after 1750, after which the European traders and their governments, supported by new productivity at home as well as by new ships and new guns, began to assert themselves. They challenged the legacies of Arab and Chinese supremacy in the east, and Native American isolation in the west, and began to introduce new regimes of trade and domination into world history.

CHAPTER REVIEW

WORLD TRADE: A HISTORICAL ANALYSIS

12.1 How do societies regulate and control trade?

Networks of trade have flourished since at least 3500 B.C.E. Societies regulate trade in different ways, for instance by expanding or limiting production, or by taxing items at different rates. In wartime, governments may ration food and other commodities to ensure that everyone has access to minimum quantities. Sometimes governments trade through their own agents; sometimes they allow and encourage private trade; often they do both. They may allow anyone to trade, or they may restrict trading to only certain individuals or groups.

ASIA'S COMPLEX TRADE PATTERNS

12.2 What were the main Asian trade networks?

The main population centers of Asia, Africa, and Europe were connected by a set of interlinked trade networks that were thousands of years old. Japan and China were joined by land routes—the silk routes—to central and southern Asia and by sea routes to the Indian Ocean. Both land and sea routes continued westward to Arabia, western Asia, and the Mediterranean and Europe. Well-developed sea traffic linked to the East African coast, and land routes then extended into the African continent. The Mediterranean and sub-Saharan Africa were connected after about the second century C.E. by camel caravan routes across the Sahara Desert.

CHAPTER REVIEW (continued)

CHINA: A MAGNET FOR TRADERS

12.3 How did China's focus on internal trade affect its cultural growth?

Despite early years of oceanic exploration, later the Ming dynasty became inward-looking, and despite some policies of expansionism both across the Great Wall to the north and by ship across the Indian Ocean, by the sixteenth century the government limited its contact with foreigners and prohibited its merchants from trading overseas. Although economic growth continued, cultural growth stagnated. Where once Chinese technology had been the most innovative in the world—the Chinese invented gunpowder, woodblock printing, and many improvements in agriculture—it became less imaginative. Development of cannon work was limited, and Chinese soldiers even returned to the use of the crossbow.

CENTRAL ASIA: THE MONGOLS AND THE SILK ROUTES

12.4 What is the legacy of the Mongol Empire?

Although the Mongols are infamous for the stories of the brutality of their disciplined, horse-mounted armies, over time they created stability in the lands they conquered. This allowed for new economic institutions and technological innovations to emerge, and for cultural, literary, and artistic creativity to flourish. The Mongols tolerated different religious traditions; and they generally accommodated local patterns of culture and governance. Intercontinental trade expanded across the vast silk routes, which the Mongols reopened and protected. This unprecedented contact between east and west was one of the Mongols' most essential contributions.

TRADE IN SUB-SAHARAN AFRICA

12.5 What goods were traded in sub-Saharan Africa?

South of the Sahara Desert, African societies were well integrated into an extensive trade network. In East Africa, traders on the coast collected gold, copper, ivory, and slaves from the interior and sold the goods to merchants who carried them across the Indian Ocean. West African traders sent caravans of gold, slaves, cloth, ivory, ebony, pepper, and kola nuts north across the Sahara, and procured salt, dates, horses, brass, copper, glassware, leather, beads, foodstuffs, and textiles in return.

TRADE IN THE AMERICAS BEFORE COLUMBUS

12.6 How did Americans trade before 1500?

There were two major trading networks in the Americas: a northern network, which served the areas now known as Central America and Mexico; and a southern network, with two sectors, one that ran along the Pacific coast in the countries now known as Ecuador, Peru, and Chile, and another, parallel one, that ran along the spine of the Andes Mountains. Goods were carried by pack animals, by humans, and by boats on rivers. There was very little trade between north and south, but within each region trade, and trading cities, prospered.

Suggested Readings

PRINCIPAL SOURCES

Abu-Lughod, Janet L. *Before European Hegemony: The World System A.D. 1250–1350* (New York: Oxford University Press, 1989). A résumé of the principal trade routes around 1250. Unfortunately omits African routes.

Adas, Michael, ed. *Islamic and European Expansion* (Philadelphia, PA: Temple University Press, 1993). Key collection of historiographical essays on major topics in world history, 1200–1900. Articles by Richard Eaton and Judith Tucker on Islam and William McNeill on "gunpowder empires" are especially helpful for this unit.

Chaudhuri, K.N. *Trade and Civilization in the Indian Ocean: An Economic History from the Rise of Islam to 1750* (Cambridge: Cambridge University Press, 1985). A survey of goods, traders, ships, regulations, and competition among those who sailed and claimed to control the Indian Ocean.

Cortés, Hernán. *Letters from Mexico*, trans. from the Spanish and ed. Anthony Pagden (New Haven, CT: Yale University Press, 1986). Newest edition of Cortés' letters.

Curtin, Philip. *Cross-Cultural Trade in World History* (Cambridge: Cambridge University Press, 1984). Classical statement of the significance and ubiquity of trade diasporas.

Dunn, Ross. *The Adventures of Ibn Battuta* (Berkeley, CA: University of California Press, 1986). Dunn uses Ibn Battuta and his travels as the center-point of an analysis of Islamic life throughout the Islamic ecumene in the fourteenth century.

Elvin, Mark. *The Pattern of the Chinese Past* (Stanford, CA: Stanford University Press, 1973). Primarily economic history, focused heavily on the central questions of why China did so well economically until about 1700, and so badly after that time.

Mann, Charles O. *1491: New Revelations of the Americas before Columbus* (New York: Vintage Books, 2006). A popularly written survey, comprehensive and up to date. Also seeks comparisons between the past and the present.

Rossabi, Morris. *The Mongols: A Very Short Introduction* (New York: Oxford University Press, 2012). Immensely accessible, brief account by one of the leading scholars.

ADDITIONAL SOURCES

Bentley, Jerry H. *Old World Encounters* (New York: Oxford University Press, 1993). Survey of the range of crosscultural, long-distance encounters—especially through trade, religion, and culture—throughout Afro-Eurasia from earliest times to about 1500. Engaging.

Chaudhuri, K.N. *Asia Before Europe* (Cambridge: Cambridge University Press, 1990). Survey of the economic and political systems of Asia before the impact of colonialism and the Industrial Revolution. Comprehensive, comparative, and thoughtful.

Columbia University. *Introduction to Contemporary Civilization in the West*, vol. I (New York: Columbia University Press, 2nd ed., 1954). Very well-chosen, long source readings from leading thinkers of the time and place. Vol. I covers about 1000 to 1800.

Crosby, Alfred W. *Ecological Imperialism: The Biological Expansion of Europe, 900–1900*

(Cambridge: Cambridge University Press, 1986). The biological—mostly destructive—impact of European settlement around the world, a tragedy for native peoples from the Americas to Oceania.

Frank, Andre Gunder, and Barry K. Gills, eds. *The World System: Five Hundred Years or Five Thousand?* (London: Routledge, 1993). In this somewhat tendentious, but well-argued, account, globalization is nothing new.

Ghosh, Amitav. *In An Antique Land* (New York: Knopf, 1993). A novel, travelogue, historical fiction of Indian Ocean exchanges in the twelfth century and today. Captivating. Much of the tale is based on the research in Goitein's study, below.

Goitein, Shelomo Dov. *A Mediterranean Society: The Jewish Communities of the Arab World as Portrayed in the Documents of the Cairo Genizah,* 6 vols. (Berkeley, CA: University of California Press, 1967–83). Extraordinary research resulting from the examination of a discovered treasury of about 10,000 documents from about 1000 to 1300. Despite the title, gives insight into a variety of communities of the time.

Hanbury-Tenison, Robin. *The Oxford Book of Exploration* (New York: Oxford University Press, 1994). An excellent collection of primary sources on exploration.

Hourani, George Fadlo. *Arab Seafaring in the Indian Ocean in Ancient and Early Medieval Times* (Princeton, NJ: Princeton University Press, 1951, reprinted 1995). The standard introduction. Examines the trade routes and the ships before and after the coming of Islam.

Ibn Battuta. *Travels in Asia and Africa 1325–1354,* trans. from the Arabic and selected by H.A.R. Gibb (New Delhi: Saeed International, 1990). Selections from the writings of one of the greatest travelers in history.

Ibn Majid, Ahmad. *Arab Navigation in the Indian Ocean Before the Coming of the Portuguese,* trans., introduced, and annotated by G.R. Tibbetts (London: Royal Asiatic Society of Great Britain and Ireland, 1971). Translation of Ibn Majid's classic fifteenth-century guide for navigators, along with very extensive discussion by Tibbetts placing the author and work in context and discussing contemporary theories of navigation.

Komaroff, Linda, and Stefano Carboni, eds. *The Legacy of Genghis Khan: Courtly Art and Culture in Western Asia, 1256–1353* (New York: Metropolitan Museum of Art; New Haven, CT: Yale University Press, 2002). Lavishly illustrated catalogue of

blockbuster art exhibit, with numerous interpretive essays as well.

Levathes, Louise. *When China Ruled the Seas: The Treasure Fleet of the Dragon Throne, 1405–33* (New York: Oxford University Press, 1996). Scholarly study of the expeditions of Zheng He.

Menzies, Gavin. *1421: The Year China Discovered America* (New York: William Morrow, 2003). Menzies brings together many scraps of evidence in concocting the argument that Zheng He actually did sail to America. The evidence does not hold.

Polanyi, Karl, Conrad M. Arensberg, and Harry W. Pearson, eds. *Trade and Market in the Early Empires* (Chicago, IL: The Free Press, 1957). Fundamental argument by historical anthropologists that early trade was mostly regulated by rulers and priests.

Polo, Marco. *The Travels,* trans. from the French by Ronald Latham (London: Penguin Books, 1958). One of the most fascinating and influential travelogues ever written.

Ratchnevsky, Paul. *Genghis Khan: His Life and Legacy,* trans. and ed. Thomas Nivison Haining (Oxford: Blackwell, 1991). The current standard biography of the personally elusive Chinggis Khan.

Raychaudhuri, Tapan, and Irfan Habib, eds. *The Cambridge Economic History of India. Volume 1:* c. 122–c. 1750 (Cambridge: Cambridge University Press, 1982). Collection of articles of fundamental significance.

Risso, Patricia. *Merchants and Faith: Muslim Commerce and Culture in the Indian Ocean* (Boulder, CO: Westview Press, 1995). Among the questions explored is "What difference did it make to be a Muslim?"

Schele, Linda, and David Freidel. *A Forest of Kings: The Untold Story of the Ancient Maya* (New York: William Morrow and Co., 1990). The story of the deciphering of the Mayan ideographs and the histories of warfare that they reveal, by two of the leading researchers.

Scott, James C. *Weapons of the Weak: Everyday Forms of Peasant Resistance* (New Haven, CT: Yale University Press, 1987). Peasants and the poor also have ways of resisting oppression. This eye-opening book shows how they work.

Shiba, Yoshinobu. *Commerce and Society in Sung China,* trans. Mark Elvin (Ann Arbor: University of Michigan, Center for Chinese Studies, 1970). Detailed, scholarly inquiry into the functioning of the Sung economy.

Shaffer, Lynda Norene. *Maritime Southeast Asia to 1500* (Armonk, NY: M.E. Sharpe, 1996). Useful survey on the voyages, trade goods, markets, towns, and government of the region—from earliest times.

Skinner, G. William. "Marketing and Social Structure in Rural China," *Journal of Asian Studies* XXIV, no. 1 (November 1964), pp. 3–43. Classic account of the interlocking structure of urban development in China from local market towns through national capitals of trade.

The Thousand Nights and One Night: A Plain and Literal Translation of the Arabian Nights Entertainment, 6 vols. in 3, trans. Richard F. Burton (New York: Heritage Press, 1946). These charming tales are set in a world of Arab sea trade.

Toussaint, Auguste. *History of the Indian Ocean,* trans. June Guicharnaud (Chicago, IL: University of Chicago Press, 1966). Broad historical sweep of exploration, trade, cultural exchange, fighting, and rule in and of the Indian Ocean from earliest times to the 1960s. Very useful survey.

Watt, James C.Y., and Anne E. Wardwell. *When Silk Was Gold: Central Asian and Chinese Textiles* (New York: Metropolitan Museum of Art in cooperation with the Cleveland Museum of Art; distributed by Harry N. Abrams, 1997). The catalogue of a blockbuster exhibit. See this and understand why silk was valued so highly. Available in pdf form on the museum website: metmuseum.org/research/metpublications/When_Silk_Was_Gold_Central_Asian_and_Chinese_Textiles.

Wood, Frances. *Did Marco Polo Go to China?* (Boulder, CO: Westview Press, 1996). One of the more recent, and lucid, statements of the controversy, by the head of the China Department at the British Library, London.

FILMS

Diego Rivera: Art and Revolution (1999; 11 minutes). A video news report from a Rivera exhibit in Los Angeles. Rivera's revolutionary proclivities appear in all his work, including his representation of pre-Spanish Mexico.

Secrets of the Silk Road exhibit, University of Pennsylvania Museum of Archaeology and Anthropology, 2010–11. Much of this remarkable exhibition is online, including a series of nine hour-long lectures by experts in the field. Begin at http://penn.museum/silkroad/events_lectures.php. The lectures, occasionally under different names, are also available on YouTube, but begin your access here.

The Vikings (2000; reissued 2011; 110 minutes). Demonstrates that the Vikings were much more than a nation of marauders and raiders. Impact on Europe, all the way to Russia and Byzantium. Up-to-date archaeological research.

13 The Opening of the Atlantic and the Pacific

Economic Growth, Religion and Renaissance, Global Connections

1300–1500

Until 1492, no continuous links connected the eastern and western hemispheres, although there had certainly been some voyages between them. The expeditions of Leif Eriksson and other Vikings from Scandinavia around the year 1000 are well documented and authenticated by the artifacts they left behind in their temporary settlements on the northeast coast of North America. Some of the foods of Polynesia—sweet potatoes and manioc—apparently came from South America, presenting evidence of contacts, even more fleeting, across the Pacific. However, permanent contact between the two major continental landmasses of the world was established only with Christopher Columbus' conquest of the Atlantic Ocean in 1492. The consequences for the people of both hemispheres were enormous.

French caravel, 1555. Watercolor on paper. The sturdy caravel, with its three masts and its array of both square and lateen (triangular) sails, was adapted by Europeans from the Arab ships of the Indian Ocean and became the ship of choice for oceanic exploration. Christopher Columbus and Vasco da Gama both sailed in caravels. By arming his caravel with cannons, Gama transformed it into a weapon of war.

LEARNING OBJECTIVES

13.1 ((	13.2 ((	13.3 ((
Understand the changes that made the Atlantic voyages possible.	Describe the European economic and cultural rebirth, the Renaissance.	Describe the early world explorations of the Europeans.

((Listen on MyHistoryLab

Oseberg Viking ship. The Vikings built magnificent ships that enabled them to sail the coasts of Western Europe, penetrate the Mediterranean Sea, trade on the rivers of northern Russia, and even cross the Atlantic, reaching North America. The Oseberg ship, named for the place in which it was excavated in 1904–05, was buried about 834, and remains one of the finest Viking ships still in existence. (Vikingskiphuset Museum, Bygdøy, Oslo)

We have seen that Arab traders and Chinese admirals (and Polynesian sailors) also had the capacity to cross the oceans before Columbus' expedition, but chose not to. Europeans, with the exception of the Vikings, also did not venture out into the oceans, so long as the ports of the Middle East provided access to the great markets of Asia. Only when that access was reduced and profits were curtailed, while their own economics and technologies grew stronger, in the fifteenth century, did they launch their voyages across the Atlantic. Even then, they were not exploring for new lands, but only for new routes to well-known markets. In a surprise that altered the history of the world forever, the attractions of Asian trade led, by accident, to the European discovery and conquest of entire continents, with their own civilizations, of which the Europeans had known nothing.

In order to comprehend the enormity of this turn of events, we briefly look backward in time to the economic and cultural transformations in Europe that made the Atlantic voyages possible, and then forward to the European economic and cultural **Renaissance**, or "rebirth," that accompanied and resulted from them. Developments in trade and commerce never take place in a vacuum, as these cultural changes make abundantly clear.

KEY TERM

Renaissance From the French for "rebirth," a period of cultural and intellectual creativity in Western Europe between 1300 and 1570. The artists and intellectuals who created the movement saw themselves reconnecting with the traditions of ancient Greece and Rome, thus giving a "rebirth" to European culture. The cultural rebirth was accompanied by an expanding urban economy, another rebirth.

Scandinavian and Arab Muslim invasions, ninth to tenth centuries. Europe was subjected to repeated invasions that temporarily disturbed the continent but then increased its power. The Vikings, north Germanic peoples, settled and developed Scandinavia, and their interaction with the Slavs gave shape to Russia. The Muslims brought with them an understanding of the culture of ancient Greece and Rome that Europeans had forgotten. (Adapted from *The Times Atlas of World History*, 5th ed., London: Times Books.)

13.1

13.2

13.3

What changes in Western Europe made Atlantic explorations possible?

Economic and Social Changes in Europe

13.1 What changes in Western Europe made Atlantic explorations possible?

By the mid-1200s, Western Europeans were beginning to emerge from agrarian, manorial economies and from the localized political systems of administration and order that had marked the Middle Ages. As forests were cut down and additional lands were brought under metal-tipped plows pulled by horses with more efficient harnesses, agricultural productivity increased. Crop surpluses became available for sale to feed the craftsmen and merchants who began to migrate from the countryside into towns. Cities, which for centuries centered primarily on their churches, now increased the size of their marketplaces. Giovanni Villani describes the patterns of consumption in Florence, Italy, in 1338. Its population of about 100,000 made it the

416

HOW DO WE KNOW?

"Eurocentric" History?

As the study of world history moves toward modern times, a central question arises: How much attention, and what kind of attention, should we allot to the role of Europe? To what degree should world history be "Eurocentric"? The question has two dimensions: How significant were Europe's innovations, spread throughout the world by industrialization and imperialism? On balance, was Europe's influence beneficial or detrimental?

Europe usually gets more space than other regions in the modern world, because many innovations that have made the modern world what it is—capitalism, the nation-state, the Industrial Revolution, global imperialism—found first and deepest expression in the West. Some historians, such as David Landes, who is renowned for his studies in the history of economics and technology, therefore embraced a Eurocentric approach enthusiastically. "As the historical record shows, for the last thousand years, Europe (the West) has been the prime mover of development and modernity" (Landes, p. xxi). And, Landes argues, development and modernity have been for the best: "Some would say that Eurocentrism is bad for us, indeed bad for the world, hence to be avoided. Those people should avoid it. As for me, I prefer truth to goodthink. I feel surer of my ground" (p. xxi).

William McNeill, author of the influential world history *The Rise of the West* (1963), responded more cautiously. When his classic book was republished in 1991, he wrote a retrospective introduction, in which he regretted some elements of his earlier excessive "Eurocentrism": "I gave undue attention to Latin Christendom," he wrote (p. xviii); "My failure to understand China's primacy between A.D. 1000 and 1500 is particularly regrettable" (p. xix).

How had McNeill made these two interrelated errors? First, he explains, "*The Rise of the West* tends to march with big battalions, looking at history from the point of view of the winners—that is, of the skilled and privileged managers of society—and shows scant concern for the sufferings of the victims of historical change." Second, "in the years 1954 to 1963, when the book was being written, the United States was, of course, passing through the apex of its postwar capacity to influence others thanks to its superior skills and wealth." Looking for "winners," McNeill read the emerging American power—based on earlier European power—of his own day backward into the past. Nevertheless, McNeill presents not an abject apology for his earlier writing,

but an explanation: Winners do have disproportionate influence compared to victims; America's rise to power was a part of world history. Eurocentricity (including its American offspring) seemed a natural approach.

From his revised perspective, however, McNeill suggests an alternative to Eurocentrism:

"I should have made room for the ecumenical process. How this might be done remains to be seen. Somehow an appreciation of the autonomy of separate civilizations (and of all the other less massive and less skilled cultures of the earth) across the past two thousand years needs to be combined with the portrait of an emerging world system, connecting greater and greater numbers of persons across civilized boundaries" (p. xxii).

Many scholars have come to a similar conclusion and have chosen to emphasize the interconnections among peoples. In *Europe and the People without History* (1982), Eric Wolf, a historical anthropologist, writes:

"Following the global effects of European expansion leads to a consideration of the search for American silver, the fur trade, the slave trade, and the quest for new sources of wealth in Asia … I then trace the transition to capitalism in the course of the industrial revolution, examine its impact on areas of the world supplying resources to the industrial centers, and sketch out the formation of working classes and their migrations within and between the continents" (p. 23).

Europeans may have initiated many of these changes, but each of the world's peoples responded in its own way.

The Indian-born, Western-educated historian and anthropologist Dipesh Chakrabarty takes Wolf's position a step further. He acknowledges the enormous contribution of the West to the modern world:

Concepts such as citizenship, the state, civil society, public sphere, human rights, equality before the law, the individual, distinctions between public and private, the idea of the subject, democracy, popular sovereignty, social justice, scientific rationality, and so on all bear the burden of European thought and history. One simply cannot think of political modernity

continued p. 418

---

fifth largest city in Europe, and every day its residents consumed "over 2,300 bushels of grain and drank in excess of 70,000 quarts of wine. Some 4,000 cattle and 100,000 sheep, goats, and swine were slaughtered each year to provide the city with meat" (cited in Brucker, pp. 51–52). The basis of Florence's wealth, like that of many cities in northern Italy and Flanders, in particular, was the manufacture of cloth. Villani reports that its textile industry employed 30,000 workers. As their manufacture and trade increased, Western Europeans felt increasingly aggrieved by the difficulty of doing business in the Middle East and the eastern Mediterranean.

View the **Closer Look: The Joys and Pains of the Medieval Joust** on **MyHistoryLab**

What changes in Western Europe made Atlantic explorations possible?

13.1

13.2

13.3

HOW DO WE KNOW? (continued)

"Eurocentric" History?

without these and other related concepts that found a climactic form in the course of the European Enlightenment and the nineteenth century. (Chakrabarty, p. 4)

But Chakrabarty cautions against the Eurocentric argument that European innovations would later be adopted wholesale by the rest of the world, "first in Europe, then elsewhere". Instead, like Wolf, he argues that peoples of other regions have adapted these innovations, each in their own way. One of his first examples is universal suffrage. Introduced first in the West, where literacy rates were relatively high, it was subsequently introduced more widely, including in countries, such as India, with very low levels of literacy. But India is not simply in the preliminary stages of developing European democracy. It is generating a new form of democracy, with different kinds of interest group, different methods of communication, and different kinds of relationship with the spirit world and ancestors, than those evolved in Europe. This is all right. Europe had its way of doing things; India and other countries have theirs. Europe is not the decisive guide and mentor to others; its way is not the only way. Chakrabarty titles his book *Provincializing Europe*.

The debate over the place of Europe in world history continues. It is difficult to envision a history of the modern world that does not give Europe an important place, because of its own cultural innovations and because of its globe-spanning industries and empires. But Europe is not itself unified; and, despite Landes' claims, not all its effects were positive. Each people created its own response to the Europeans, expressing its own unique character, which deserves its own separate study.

- Landes specializes in the history of technology; McNeill is a generalist; and both Wolf and Chakrabarty are trained in anthropology as well as history. To what extent do you think their specializations influence their attitudes toward Eurocentrism?
- With which of the four scholars do you most agree? Disagree? Why?
- Compare and contrast the accounts of Columbus' arrival in the New World as they might be written by a Eurocentric scholar and by one of the Taino people of the Caribbean who met him.

13.1
13.2
13.3

What changes in Western Europe made Atlantic explorations possible?

KEY TERM

guild A sworn association of people who gather for some common purpose. In the towns of medieval Europe, guilds of craftsmen or merchants were formed to protect and further their business interests and for mutual aid. Compare guilds in India, in the chapter "Indian Empires."

Workers and the Landed Gentry

As business increased, local traders and manufacturers formed trade organizations called **guilds**. These guilds regulated prices, wages, the quality and quantity of production and trade, and the recruitment, training, and certification of apprentices, journeymen, and masters. The guilds also represented their members in town governments and thus helped to keep industrial and commercial interests at the forefront of the civic agenda. Guilds were the principal means through which the commercial classes—merchants, artisans, and learned professionals—could counter the entrenched prerogatives of the landed aristocrats and win legal privileges for themselves, their businesses, and their cities. Guild members were mostly males, but widowed female heads of households and workshops were also included among the voting members.

Most guilds were organized within a single locality, but international traders organized international guilds corresponding to their commercial interests. The most famous and powerful of them was the Hanseatic League. More geographically dispersed and ethnically diverse, and therefore less closely knit, than a true guild, it was founded in the mid-thirteenth century to represent the interests of leading shippers of the cities of Germany and the Baltic and North Sea. From its headquarters in the city of Lübeck, the League established its own commercial trading posts as far west as London and Bruges (in modern Belgium), and as far east as Novgorod in Russia. Throughout the region, it lobbied for legal systems that favored its members. Sturdy cargo ships belonging to the League carried grain, timber, furs, tar, honey, and flax westward from Russia and Poland, and woolen goods eastward from England. From Sweden they carried copper and iron ore. In the fourteenth century about 100 towns were affiliated with the League. Nevertheless, as states such as the Netherlands (United Provinces), England, and Sweden grew powerful and asserted their control of the Baltic, the League began to die a natural death, after dominating the commerce of its region for almost two centuries.

Textiles and Social Conflict

What changes in Western Europe made Atlantic explorations possible?

13.1

13.2

13.3

In two regions of Western Europe, northern Italy and Flanders, the manufacture of textiles came to dominate the urban economies. In these regions early modern European capitalism was born. Capitalist entrepreneurs organized production, employed large numbers of laborers, and created markets for buying and selling, taking economic risks in hope of making profits. In Florence, between 200 and 300 workshops provided a livelihood for almost a third of the city's population, producing a total of 100,000 pieces of woolen cloth each year. Other cities of northern Italy, although smaller, had similar workshops.

The new organization of textile production created a complex class structure. Among the manual workers in the chain of production, guild masters and the aspiring journeymen and apprentices within the guilds held the best positions: shearing the sheep; fulling the cloth (that is, shrinking and thickening it by moistening, heating, and pressing it); and dyeing the wool. Weavers, carders, and combers were lower on the pay and social scales. The weavers, more skilled than the others, were better positioned to organize themselves into a guild.

Capitalist traders, in search of private profit, organized the manufacture in a **putting-out system**. They estimated the market demand for production and supplied workers with the raw materials and equipment necessary to meet it. Laborers then produced the finished products, sometimes in workshops but more typically in their own homes. Usually they were paid by the piece. An army of poor people washed, warped, and spun the wool. The additional income of female and child laborers, employed at even lower pay and in worse conditions than the men, enabled working families to survive.

Sheep in pen being milked, Luttrell Psalter, fourteenth century. Woolen-cloth merchants had congregated in Flanders from an early stage. By the twelfth century the industry needed English wool to function to capacity. Before the fourteenth century, overland transport was so expensive that only small and valuable objects could be traded profitably over long distances; the emergence of sea routes lowered the transport costs of bulk goods, such as wool and grain. They could now be traded internationally, and profitably. (British Library, London)

KEY TERM

putting-out system In this system, employers provide employees with raw materials and the orders for turning them into finished products, which they then buy on completion. The employees carry out the work at home, thus reducing the production cost for the employer.

419

AT A GLANCE: WORLD TRADE, MOSTLY EUROPEAN (compare box in Chapter 12)

DATE	POLITICAL/SOCIAL EVENTS	TRADE DEVELOPMENTS	EXPLORATION
1150	• Salah al-Din (Saladin), sultan of Turkish Syria and Egypt, retakes Jerusalem (1187) • St. Francis of Assisi (1182–1226) • St. Dominic (1170–1221) • St. Clare of Assisi (1194–1253)	• Market fairs in Champagne region, France	
1200		• Rise of craft guilds in towns of Western Europe • Foundation of Hanseatic League (1241)	
1250		• Increasing Venetian links with central Asia and China (1255–95) • Revolt of craftworkers in Flanders	
1300	• Hundred Years War between England and France (1337–1453) • Black Death in Europe (1346–50)	• West Africa provides two-thirds of the gold of the eastern hemisphere	
1350	• Ghettoization of Jews in Western Europe • Ashigawa Shoguns dominate Japan (1338–1573)	• Revolts of urban workers in Italy and Flanders	
1400	• Ottoman Turks establish foothold in Europe at Gallipoli	• Great Chinese naval expeditions reach east coast of Africa and India under Zheng He	• Portugal's Prince Henry the Navigator sponsors expeditions to West Africa
1450	• Turks capture Constantinople (1453) • Printing of Gutenberg Bible (1455) • Wars of the Roses in England (1453–85) • Jews driven from Spain (1492) • Treaty of Tordesillas (1494)	• Medici family in Florence: Giovanni, Cosimo, Lorenzo	• Bartolomeu Dias sails round Cape of Good Hope (1488) • Christopher Columbus reaches the Americas (1492) • Vasco da Gama reaches the Malabar coast, India (1498)
1500	• Machiavelli, *The Prince* (1513) • Muslims in Spain forced to convert or leave	• Portugal sets up trading port of Goa, in India (1502); Portuguese ships armed with cannons	• Ferdinand Magellan's voyage around globe (1519–22)

13.1
13.2
13.3

What changes in Western Europe made Atlantic explorations possible?

KEY TERM

ghetto The part of a city to which a particular group is confined for its living space. Named originally for an area adjacent to an iron foundry (in Italian, *ghetto*) in sixteenth-century Venice where Jews were segregated by government order, the term has been used most often to designate segregated Jewish living areas in European cities. It is also used, more broadly, to indicate any area where specific groups are segregated whether by law, by force, or by choice.

Occasionally class antagonisms between employer and employee grew into open conflict. Revolts broke out in the Flemish cities of Douai, Tournai, Ypres, and Bruges at the end of the thirteenth century. The leaders were mostly craftsmen, and they usually demanded that guild members be allowed to participate in city government and thus have a voice in regulating the conditions of trade and manufacture. Workers outside the guild organizations could only hope that increased wages, shorter hours, and better conditions of work might trickle down to their level as well.

In the fourteenth century, such class antagonisms multiplied. Increasingly impoverished workers, suffering also from plagues, wars, and bad harvests, confronted increasingly wealthy traders and industrialists. Workers were forbidden to strike and, in some towns, even to assemble. Nevertheless, class unrest continued to grow, especially in Florence, the greatest industrial center of Western Europe. In 1345, ten wool-carders were hanged for organizing workers.

Business and the Church

In its efforts to establish its independent power, the urban business community confronted not only landed aristocrats and organizations of urban workers, but also an often hostile clergy. From earliest times, the Roman Catholic Church had taken a dim view of the quest for private profit and wealth. St. Augustine (354–430) perpetuated

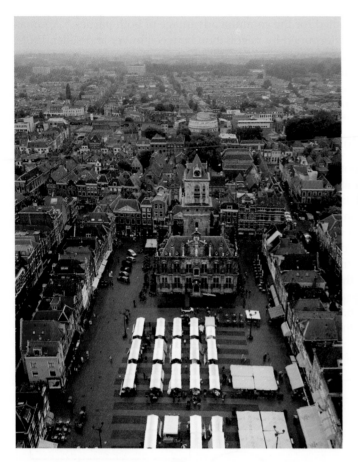

Aerial view of present-day Delft, western Netherlands. Here, gabled medieval townhouses are seen surrounding the bustling market square in Delft. Since the late 1500s the town has been famous for its pottery and porcelain known as delftware. Dutch products began to compete in European markets with porcelain imports from China.

Painting of Hertogenbosch, Netherlands, 1530. Compare today's photograph of a medieval square on market day (left) with this view of a cloth market in another Dutch town, painted in 1530. The layout, construction, and function of the stalls are virtually identical.

the disdain. In the High Middle Ages (c. 1000–c. 1400) theologians seriously debated whether it was possible for a merchant to attain salvation.

Because the Church forbade Christians to take and give interest on loans, Jews carried out much of the business of money-lending. In fact, Jews were so much a part of the merchant classes in early medieval northern Europe that a traditional administrative phrase referred to "Jews and other merchants." Church laws forbidding Jews to own land also pushed them into urban life and commerce. By the end of the thirteenth century, Christian rulers forced Jews to live in **ghettos**, specific areas of the cities to which they were confined each night. In European society, Jews were stigmatized four times over: alien by religion, foreign by ancestry, money-lenders by occupation, and segregated by residence. Nevertheless, Jews were tolerated as an economically vital trade diaspora until local people mastered the intricacies of business. After that, Jews were often persecuted, sometimes murdered, and repeatedly exiled—from England in 1290, from France in 1394, from Spain in 1492, and from many German cities.

As commerce increased, the Roman Catholic Church began to revise its opposition to business and businessmen. St. Thomas Aquinas (1225–74) addressed the issue directly in his *Summa Theologiae*. Justifying commerce, he wrote: "Buying and

What changes in Western Europe made Atlantic explorations possible?

13.1

13.2

13.3

13.1
13.2
13.3

What changes in
Western Europe
made Atlantic
explorations
possible?

selling seem to be established for the common advantage of both parties." Aquinas wrote of a "just" price, determined by negotiation between buyer and seller. Profit was allowed if its uses were deemed appropriate: "Nothing prevents gain from being directed to some necessary or even virtuous end, and thus trading becomes lawful." Traders were allowed compensation for their labor, and businessmen were allowed to charge interest on commercial loans.

Plague and Social Unrest

Europe's growing economy was undermined in the fourteenth century by extraordinary disasters: famine, civil upheavals, and, worst of all, a plague that killed one-third of the population. Until recently, the plague, called the Black Death, was believed to be the bubonic plague, but research in the twenty-first century suggests that it may have been a different, undetermined, form of plague. Whatever it was, the disease apparently followed the Mongols from central Asia into China in 1331. China's population, estimated at 123 million in 1200, dropped to 65 million in the census of 1393. (Part of the decrease was caused by warfare between the Chinese and the Mongols, but a large part must also have been caused by the plague.) The plague reached Crimea in 1346. There, plague-infested rats boarded ships, disembarking with the disease at all the ports of Europe and the Near East. Within the next five

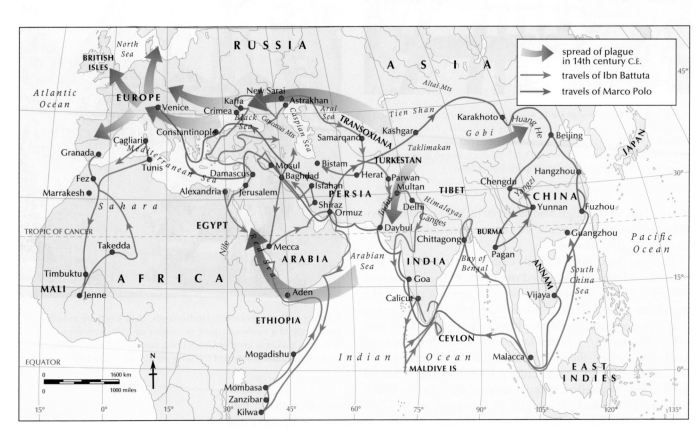

The routes of the plague. The central and eastern Asian stability imposed by Mongol rule—the "Mongol Peace"—brought mixed benefits. Trade flourished, and travelers, such as Ibn Battuta and Marco Polo, were able to write remarkable accounts of the lands they visited. At the same time, however, vectors for other travelers, such as the rats that carried plague, also opened up. The Black Death, which originated in central Asia, was one of a succession of plagues that followed the trade routes by land and sea, decimating parts of Europe and China.

View the Map: The Spread of the Black Death and Peasant Revolts on MyHistoryLab

SOURCE

Giovanni Boccaccio Describes the Black Death

Giovanni Boccaccio (1313–75) captured the horror of the Black Death in the introduction to his otherwise droll and humanistic classic of the era, *The Decameron*:

> In the year of Our Lord 1348 the deadly plague broke out in the great city of Florence … At the onset of the disease both men and women were afflicted by a sort of swelling in the groin or under the armpits which sometimes attained the size of a common apple or egg. Some of these swellings were larger and some smaller, and all were commonly called boils. From these two starting points the boils began in a little while to spread and appear generally all over the body. Afterwards,

the manifestation of the disease changed into black or livid spots on the arms, thighs, and the whole person … Neither the advice of physicians nor the virtue of any medicine seemed to help … almost everyone died within three days of the appearance of the signs—some sooner, some later …

> The calamity had instilled such horror into the hearts of men and women that brother abandoned brother, uncles, sisters, and wives left their dear ones to perish and, what is more serious and almost incredible, parents avoided visiting or nursing their very children, as though these were not their own flesh. (xxiii–xxiv)

years the plague killed one in three people, reducing Europe's population from 70 million in 1300 to only 45 million in 1400.

The catastrophe reshuffled the social classes. Peasants who survived benefited from the labor shortages that followed, gaining higher wages and access to more land, freedom from labor services, and geographical mobility. They began to form a new class of property-owning farmers. Together with urban industrial workers and guild members, they rioted more frequently and boldly against kings and nobles who attempted to raise taxes to fund their wars.

In urban areas, too, workers became scarce, and those who survived demanded higher wages, better working conditions, and more civic rights. In Florence, for example, the Ciompi (the lowest class of workers, named for the neighborhood in which they lived) revolted, supported by lower-level artisans. In 1378 they presented their demands to city officials: open access to the guilds, the right to unionize, a reduction of worker fines and punishments, and the right "to participate in the government of the City." They gained some of their goals, but Florence's powerful business leaders ultimately triumphed. By 1382 the major guilds were back in control, and soon a more dictatorial government was in power. Similar revolts occurred in Flanders, but on a smaller scale and with no more success.

In the aftermath of the Black Death the dissolution of the norms of everyday life, and of the certainties of the class structure, inspired Europeans to reassess their fundamental values and institutions. People's belief in God and their own future were shaken to their foundations. Some kind of new culture, some kind of renaissance, was waiting to be born.

 Read the **Document**: **Black Death** on **MyHistoryLab**

The Triumph of Death, French, 1503. This sixteenth-century work recalls the enormous loss of life caused by the plague of 1348. Brought back from East Asia by Genoese merchants, the disease is estimated to have killed between 20 and 50 percent of Europe's inhabitants. Contemporary medicine was impotent in the face of the disease, the onset of which meant almost certain death. (Bibliothèque Nationale, Paris)

13.1

13.2   What was
the European
13.3   Renaissance?

The Renaissance

13.2   What was the European Renaissance?

The new economy underpinned the European Renaissance—a rebirth of Classical ideals in European thought, literature, art, manners, and sensibilities. Many of the wealthier merchants became patrons of the arts, encouraging an outpouring of painting, sculpture, architecture, poetry, and prose. They identified with their cities, sponsoring creative town planning to increase their efficiency as markets and their beauty as artistic designs, and hiring superb architects to enhance their visual splendor. Both patrons and artists were usually devout members of the Church, and an increasingly

The Renaissance in Italy, 1300–1570. From 1300 to 1570 in Italy, artists and intellectuals worked to fuse the Christian tradition (originating in antiquity but developed during the Middle Ages) with the Greco-Roman tradition in a movement fundamental for the later evolution of the modern civilization of the West: the Renaissance. This map shows the principal places that are associated with the names of important figures.

wealthy Church became one of the greatest patrons of the arts. Nevertheless, the creativity of the Renaissance gave a new orientation to religious expression, more earthy, more fleshy, more this-worldly than it had been throughout **medieval**—"middle period"—European times. Scholars of the fifteenth century already drew this three-part division of time into the ancient, medieval, and Renaissance worlds. They saw the Renaissance as a reconnection with the culture of the ancient world of Greece and Rome, across a thousand years of medieval time, and they praised themselves and their colleagues for making the great leap backward in time.

The Roots of the Renaissance

When so great a transformation as the Renaissance takes place, however, affecting economics, technology, religion, culture, aesthetics, and social and political structures, it is not usually possible to determine exactly what is cause and what is effect, nor to specify an exact date of its initiation. Some historians do attempt to show that a single cause predominates—some, for example, stressing economics, others political or social influences—but most see the various transformations as intertwined. For example, even when historians emphasize one aspect or another of the Renaissance, as we have done with trade, they identify its roots in other aspects of life as well. They detect glimmerings of the Renaissance in a shift in religious as well as secular values toward a more worldly and rational, less ascetic, less spiritual outlook. They date the beginnings of this shift, as we have seen in the chapter entitled "Islam," at least as early as the mid-eleventh century. At that time, contact with Arab Muslim civilization reacquainted European scholars with ancient Greek philosophy, which Arab scholars had kept alive. These changes in philosophic values supported the opening to trade, just as trade later gave support to new directions in philosophy.

Christian Scholars. Christian scholars, especially in Spain (where Christians, Muslims, and Jews lived side by side), began the systematic translation of Arabic texts into Latin. They sought to reestablish the link with the ancient Roman and Greek texts that the Arabs had preserved and developed, and that the Christian world had lost. The works of the Muslim philosophers Avicenna (Ibn Sina) (980–1037) and Averroes (Ibn Rushd) (1126–98) and the Jewish philosopher Maimonides (1135–1204) helped to restore the emphasis on logic and philosophy that Aristotle had taught. In the eleventh century, Church leaders began to suggest that pure faith was not enough to attain salvation. St. Anselm (1033–1109) stressed the need for an intellectual basis for faith while Peter Abelard (1079–1142), emphasized the need for a rational approach to the interpretation of texts.

Meanwhile, the new wealth and power of their Church offended some Roman Catholics, and they challenged the Church to live up to its early ideals of compassion for the poor and simplicity in everyday living. New orders of priests and nuns began to form as a way of returning to these early ideals: Franciscans followed the teachings of St. Francis of Assisi

13.1
13.2
13.3

What was
the European
Renaissance?

KEY TERM

medieval The "middle period." Europeans of the Renaissance period, who felt that they were, at last, reconnecting with the glories of ancient Greece and Rome, called the ten centuries between the end of the Western Roman Empire and the beginning of the Renaissance "the medieval period." They used the term pejoratively. More recent scholars see that very long period as far more complicated and diverse, and analyze it by specific geographical regions and into much smaller periods of time.

Avicenna, French School, eighteenth century. Oil on canvas. Ibn Sina, called Avicenna by Christian Europeans, was one of the foremost Islamic students of Aristotle's work. He influenced Church scholars, who relearned Greek scholarship through him. (Bibliothèque de la Faculté de Médecine, Paris)

13.1

13.2

13.3

What was
the European
Renaissance?

St. Francis, Simone Martini, *c.* 1320. Fresco. St. Francis of Assisi gave away all his possessions to the poor. When his father disowned him, he stripped naked and, cloaked in a robe given him by the bishop of Assisi, went from place to place begging for food, offering service, and preaching. The religious order that he founded became the largest in Europe. (S. Francesco, Assisi, Italy)

(1182–1226), Dominicans followed St. Dominic (1170–1221), and the "Poor Clares," an order of nuns, followed St. Clare of Assisi (1194–1253).

Universities. Universities were founded to preserve, enhance, and transmit knowledge. Most emphasized practical disciplines: medical studies at Salerno, legal studies at Bologna, theological studies at Paris—all founded before 1200. Later, students and professors from Paris crossed the English Channel and founded the University of Oxford about 1200, with Cambridge University following shortly afterward. By 1300 there were about a dozen universities in Western Europe; by 1500, nearly a hundred.

Curricula centered on theology, but also included grammar, dialectic, rhetoric, arithmetic, music, geometry, and astronomy. The theology curriculum, in particular, required the approval of the Church. This could be problematic, as is illustrated by the career of St. Thomas Aquinas, the greatest Christian theologian of his age, who paved the way for the new ideas of the Renaissance. Contentiously, he also welcomed the systematic rationality of Aristotle. While many Church leaders rejected Aristotelian logic as contradicting the teachings of the Church, Aquinas declared that logic and reason, as taught by Aristotle, and faith, as taught by the Church, were

Theological lecture at the Sorbonne, Paris, fifteenth century. Manuscript illumination. Sponsored by the Church, universities were founded primarily for the study of theology, but some included specializations in medicine and law. All the students were male and most were quite serious-minded. (Bibliothèque de Troyes, France)

13.1

What was
the European
Renaissance?

13.2

13.3

complementary. In places where they did appear to conflict, he conceded that divine truths must take precedence: "Some divine truths are attainable by human reason, while others altogether surpass the power of human reason." Although Aquinas gave divine revelation precedence over human reason, on the eve of the Renaissance he opened the door of the Church to the importance of reason in all human endeavors.

Aquinas was ahead of his time. For more than 50 years, the Franciscan order of priests banned the reading of his works, and the universities of Paris and Oxford condemned many of his doctrines. But within a century, his synthesis of logic and faith, of Aristotle and the Church, became the new standard orthodoxy of Roman Catholicism.

In addition to modifications in official theology, the coming together of dozens of exuberant young male students in the universities (no matter how rigorous the rules and regulations) led to quests for individual expression and challenges to authority. The "Golliard Poets" took their name from the Biblical Goliath, a kind of early antichrist. These poets reveled in the pleasures of youth and ridiculed the conventions of sobriety, solemnity, and sanctity. They wrote parodies that were usually irreverent and sometimes obscene, for example, a *Drunkard's Mass*, a *Glutton's Mass*, and an *Office of Ribalds*. They mocked the most sacred beliefs of their time, declaring, "I believe in dice … and love the tavern more than Jesus." They declared their blessings for one another: "Fraud be with you."

Such turmoil in religious and philosophical attitudes, both official and unofficial, helped to pave the way for the transformations of the Renaissance.

427

HOW DO WE KNOW?

Islamic Influences on the European Renaissance

Arab thinkers, their translations of Classical Greek works, and their comments on them helped to inspire the European Renaissance. Averroes' Arabic translations of and commentaries on Aristotle revealed that philosopher's works to Western Europeans who had lost contact with the originals. In addition to his philosophy, Avicenna's *Qanun* (Canon) of medicine remained central to European medical thought for centuries. Al-Khwarazmi's work in mathematics remained influential for centuries, and lives on in our lexicon today in the word *algorithm*, which is based on his name. From the tenth to the twelfth century, Arabs, Christians, and Jews lived in such proximity, and even harmony, in parts of Spain—the home of these three scholars—that linguistic borrowing back and forth became common. Poetic and prose forms were also borrowed, especially from Arabic literature to Latin and the Romance languages. European scholars, such as Gerard of Cremona, sought out the best in Arabic thought in order to translate it. We have also seen that Europeans adapted Arab technology, such as the caravel, which gave them access to the oceans of the world.

Despite this rich harvest of culture and technology from the Arab world, we have the harsh, even hysterical judgment of Petrarch (1304–74), one of the greatest Italian poets of the Renaissance, often called "the father of humanism":

> I implore you to keep these Arabs from giving me advice about my personal condition. Let them stay in exile. I hate the whole lot … You know what kind of physicians the Arabs are. I know what kind of poets they are. Nobody has such winning ways; nobody, also, is more tender and more lacking in vigor, and, to use the right words, meaner and more perverted. The minds of men are inclined to act differently; but, as you used to say, every man radiates his own peculiar mental disposition. To sum up: I will not be persuaded that any good can come from Arabia. (Cassirer *et al.*, p. 142)

What has happened between the early welcome given to Arabic learning and its bitter, summary rejection by Petrarch? Several interpretations are possible. First, Arabic influence was always greatest in Spain, where Muslims ruled much of the country for centuries, in some regions for almost eight centuries. Other European countries, such as Petrarch's Italy, were influenced less. Even in Spain, as Christians began to reconquer the country, they

began to focus on Muslims as political and religious enemies rather than as cultural colleagues. A similar change occurred over time throughout the Christian world as the launching of the crusades, after 1095, crystallized a new political antagonism between the two religious communities. The passing of time also brought new cultural currents to Europe, as the development of new vernaculars, especially in the Romance languages (such as Spanish, Italian, and French), broadened and deepened the base of culture, making it more nationalistic. The Western Europeans also developed their own intellectual competences and institutions, reducing their reliance on others. The European Renaissance took Western Europeans in new directions. Meanwhile, Islam, which suffered severe political and military defeats in Spain and in Baghdad (1258), became less open to new intellectual currents.

Scholars sometimes designate three different periods as "renaissances" in Western Europe. The first was the Carolingian Renaissance, initiated by Charlemagne about 800; the second was the Renaissance of the High Middle Ages, about the middle of the eleventh to the middle of the thirteenth century, significantly influenced by Muslim scholarship and learning; the third was the best known, and most influential, the Renaissance of the mid-fourteenth to the mid-sixteenth century. Each of the later renaissances built on the earlier ones, but also discarded some of their qualities. In Petrarch's dismissal of Arabic poetry and of Arabs generally we see a dramatic transformation in the attitudes of Christian thinkers, as their own religious and philosophical traditions became less open, and more hostile, to the influences of other cultures.

- The fourteenth-century Renaissance took place primarily in Italy and in northwestern Europe. Why do you think it did not take place in Spain, where so much earlier cultural development took place?
- Petrarch turned against Arabic learning, but not against the early Greek philosophers. Would such a division have been possible in twelfth-century Spain? Why or why not?
- Arabic learning could be seen as more successful because it continued to adhere to traditional paths, whereas Western Christian scholarship could be seen as a failure for turning in new directions. Would you accept such a characterization?

Humanism

The Renaissance began in the cities of Italy, where thriving economies provided an economic foundation, the Church provided an intellectual foundation, and both the Church and the commercial elite provided patronage to artists and intellectuals. Italy was also the heartland of the Roman Empire, a natural place in which to forge a reconnection to that ancient world. The central motivating philosophy of the Renaissance was **humanism**, the belief that the proper study of man is man. Asserting the importance of the individual, humanism challenged the monopoly of the Church over the interpretation of cultural life. Renaissance humanism held strongly to a belief in God, but assigned him a less overwhelming, less intimidating role in human

CHAPTER THIRTEEN: THE OPENING OF THE ATLANTIC AND THE PACIFIC 1300–1500

13.1

What was
the European
Renaissance?

13.2

13.3

life and action. In his *Oration on the Dignity of Man*, Giovanni Pico della Mirandola (1463–94) places in the mouth of God himself the most succinct statement of this humanistic perspective of the Renaissance:

> I have given you, Adam, neither a predetermined place nor a particular aspect nor any special prerogatives in order that you may take and possess these through your own decision and choice. The limitations on the nature of other creatures are contained within my prescribed laws. You shall determine your own nature without constraint from any barrier, by means of the freedom to whose power I have entrusted you … I have made you neither heavenly nor earthly, neither mortal nor immortal so that, like a free and sovereign artificer, you might mold and fashion yourself into that form you yourself shall have chosen.

According to this typical Renaissance perspective, God gives humankind the power to shape its own destiny.

New Artistic Styles

Renaissance art continued to emphasize religious themes, but it also began to reflect the influence of humanist and commercial values. Masaccio's painting *Trinity with the Virgin, St. John, and Donors* (1427) demonstrates the evolution of geometric perspective in painting, revealing not only a new artistic technique but also a new, objective interrelationship of individuals with the world.

Vitruvian Man, Leonardo da Vinci, c. 1492. Pen and ink on paper. Renaissance artists studied the proportions of the human body carefully and represented it accurately. Leonardo's drawing suggests the geometric perfection of the body, relating it both to the circle and to the square, and thus to a perfect and harmonious cosmos. (Galleria dell'Accademia, Venice)

View the **Closer Look: Leonardo Plots the Perfect Man** on **MyHistoryLab**

Trinity with the Virgin, St. John, and Donors, Masaccio, 1427. Fresco. During the Renaissance, people began to rethink their relationship with God and the world around them; at the same time, artists were developing a new means of depicting reality. According to some art-history scholars, Masaccio's monumental fresco is the first painting created in correct geometric perspective (the single vanishing point lies at the foot of the cross). (S. Maria Novella, Florence, Italy)

13.1

13.2

13.3

What was
the European
Renaissance?

By the fifteenth century, religious, commercial, and artistic sensibilities appear joined together. Portraiture flourished as major artists depicted their patrons, frequently the elites of the Church and of commerce. *The Arnolfini Wedding Portrait*, painted in 1434 in Flanders by Jan van Eyck, presents the marriage of an international businessman, probably an Italian stationed in Flanders. Simultaneously, Van Eyck signaled the economic success of his subject through the elegance of the physical setting of the marriage and his religious concerns through the symbolism of the dog (Fido?), representing fidelity; the removed clogs indicating that the ground is sacred; and the mirror suggesting the all-seeing eye of God.

The richest fruits of Renaissance creativity matured in Florence, where the illustrious Medici family provided lavish patronage. The family's fortune had been built by the merchant banker Giovanni de' Medici (1360–1429), and was enhanced by his son Cosimo (1389–1464) and great-grandson Lorenzo (1449–92). In this supportive environment, creative artists developed and expressed their genius. They included Filippo Brunelleschi (1377–1446), who designed and completed the dome of the Cathedral of Florence, the greatest architectural and engineering triumph of his time; Michelangelo Buonarroti (1475–1564), the sculptor of such masterpieces as the *David*, which is in Florence, and the painter of the Sistine Chapel ceiling in Vatican City; Leonardo da Vinci (1452–1519), scientific inventor, anatomist who drew *Vitruvian Man* (see above), and painter of the *Mona Lisa* (also known as *La Gioconda*); and Niccolò Machiavelli (1469–1527), author of *The Prince*, a harsh and hard-nosed philosophy of government. At the same time, the general population of the city of Florence enjoyed high standards of literacy and expressiveness. Michelangelo's subsequent move to Rome, where he sculpted the statues of *Moses* and the *Pietà*, and painted the Sistine Chapel, reminds us that the Church, too, remained a great patron of the arts.

Read the **Document**: **Renaissance Artists (1568) Vasari** on **MyHistoryLab**

Developments in Technology

Creativity flourished in the practical arts as well as the fine arts, and contributed substantially to the rise of merchant power. Local techniques were enhanced by innovations encountered in the course of trade, especially with the Arab world. Improvements in sailing technology included a new design for the ships themselves. In the thirteenth century the caravel of the Mediterranean, with its lateen sails, used mostly by Arab sailors, was blended with the straight sternpost and stern rudder of northern Europe. The caravel could also be rerigged with a square sail for greater speed in a tailwind. The astrolabe, again an Arab invention,

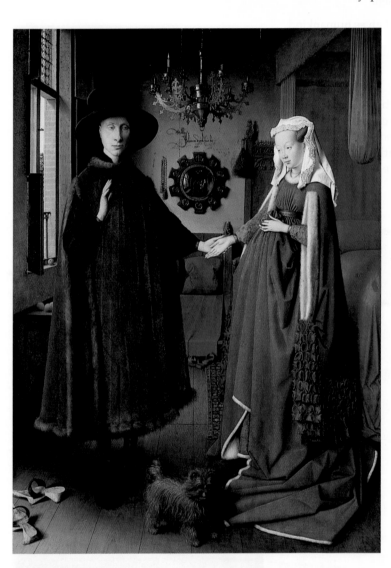

The Arnolfini Wedding Portrait, Jan van Eyck, 1434. Oil on oak. Giovanni Arnolfini, an Italian merchant living in Flanders, commissioned this pictorial record of his marriage. On the far wall, Van Eyck has written in Latin "Jan van Eyck was here," much as a notary would sign a document. Art historians assure us that although the wife may look pregnant on her marriage day, in fact this is simply what women looked like in the large-hooped skirts of the day. (National Gallery, London)

Read the **Document**: **The Office and Dutie of an Husband (1529) Juan Luis Vives** on **MyHistoryLab**

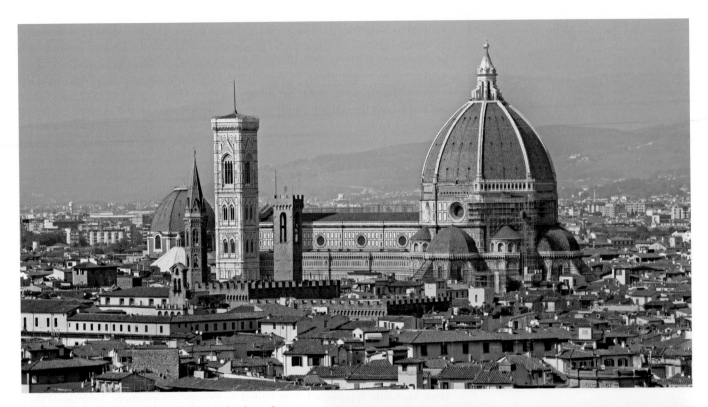

Basilica di Santa Maria del Fiore, Florence. The dome that sits atop the Cathedral (Duomo) of Florence, and dominates the skyline of the city, was built by Filippo Brunelleschi and completed in 1436, 142 years after the design of the cathedral was approved. The dome was and remains the largest masonry dome in the world, built of 37,000 tons of materials, including 4 million bricks. Brunelleschi's unparalleled structural innovations were matched by his creation of hoisting machinery to put it all into place.

Sistine Chapel ceiling (post-restoration), Michelangelo Buonarroti, 1508–12. Fresco. Renaissance humanism praised the ability of human beings to be creative and original, yet it continued to be anchored in religious imagery. Pope Sixtus IV commissioned Michelangelo to use his imagination in painting the ceiling of the Sistine Chapel in the Vatican, Rome, with Biblical scenes. (Musei Vaticani, Rome)

The cannon. From the 1450s, innovations in weapons changed the nature of warfare. The most dramatic changes affected the cannon, as shown here in *Four Books of Knighthood*, 1528.

13.1

13.2 What was the European Renaissance?

13.3

helped sailors to determine their longitude at sea. The rediscovery in the early fifteenth century of Ptolemy's *Geography*, written in the second century C.E. and preserved in the Arab world, helped to spark interest in proper mapping. (An error in longitude in Ptolemy's map led Columbus to underestimate the circumference of the globe by about one-third. This error emboldened him to set out across the Atlantic and, later, to believe mistakenly that he had reached East Asia.)

Cannons, especially when mounted on ships, gave European merchants firepower not available to others. Although the Chinese had invented gunpowder centuries before, the Europeans put it to use in warfare in the fourteenth century and became the masters of gun making. By the early 1400s they were firing cannonballs. The Ottoman Turks employed Western European Christians to build and operate the cannons they used in 1453 to besiege and conquer Constantinople. The Turkish rulers of Persia also employed European gunners and gun manufacturers, and copied their works. By the late 1400s European warring powers were energetically competing in an "arms race" to develop the most powerful and effective cannons and guns. Leonardo and others worked on the mathematics of the projectiles. When Portuguese ships began to sail into the waters of the Indian Ocean after 1498, claiming the right to regulate commerce, their guns and cannons sank all opposition. Some historians have called this era the Age of Gunpowder Empires.

The Chinese had also invented the principle of movable type and the printing press, but, again, the Europeans surpassed them in implementation. Movable type was better suited to Europe's alphabetic languages than to Chinese ideographs. By 1455, in Mainz, Germany, Johannes Gutenberg (*c.* 1390–1486) had printed the first major book set in movable type, the Bible. By the end of the century at least 10 million individual books in some 30,000 different editions had been produced and distributed.

The Chinese also created clocks centuries before the Europeans, as early as the eleventh century, although they were apparently turned by waterwheels and regulated by an elaborate escapement mechanism. European cities recognized the need to announce the passage of time, but at first did it simply by ringing bells in public, imprecisely. Around 1300, Europeans invented their first mechanical clocks, about the same time as they invented cannons and spectacles. No one knows exactly who did it or where. A church in Milan installed a clock made of iron in 1309. The Milanese were also the first to erect a public clock to strike the hours, in 1335. It had no hands, only a bell that rang once for one o'clock, twice for two o'clock, and so on. Perhaps the inspiration for the new invention came from China, but in any case, as the historian Alfred Crosby points out in his study of the importance of quantification for the economic development of urban Europe, "Hours were of central significance to city dwellers, whom buying and selling had already initiated into the vogue of quantification" (Crosby, 1997, p. 76).

In fourteenth-century Italy, two centuries after the decimal system had been absorbed from India via the Arab world, businesspeople began to develop double-entry bookkeeping. This facilitated the accurate accounting of transactions and the efficient tracking of business profits and losses. In 1494 Luca Pacioli (*c.* 1445–*c.* 1514), a Franciscan friar and mathematician, published the method in systematic form.

By the end of the fifteenth century, some people in Western Europe were ready for new adventures. The Renaissance brought new energy not only through its humanist philosophy and art, but also through its technological inventions. Newly emerging political rulers and urban businessmen in Western Europe were also inspired. One of their more practical goals was very specific: to gain direct access to the wealth of the Indies and China. They did that. In the process they also discovered a new world.

A New World

13.3 Where did the early European explorers go?

During the centuries after the demise of the Roman Empire, the Mediterranean Sea and its coastline had gradually devolved into three cultural and political spheres: Muslim, Byzantine, and Roman Catholic. By about 950, Muslims had established their dominion by land along the eastern and southern coasts of the Mediterranean and held parts of southern Italy as well as major islands in the Mediterranean: Cyprus, Crete, and Sicily. The southern and southeastern Mediterranean had become a "Muslim lake." Even so, the Byzantine Empire continued to control the northeastern shores, while various Frankish and Germanic Christian powers held the north-central coast. (See map "Byzantium and Islam" in the chapter entitled "Islam.")

These divisions had three results. First, the Mediterranean became a war zone. Warfare between the Christians of southern Europe and the Muslims of the Middle East and North Africa persisted from the eighth century until 1571, when the naval Battle of Lepanto, in Greek waters, fixed generally accepted zones of control between them. Second, trade stability oscillated in response to Europe's internal economy and warfare in the Mediterranean. Third, and most important to our story here, the European merchants felt hemmed in. The valuable merchandise and profitable trade coming from the Indian Ocean basin—the spices of India and Indonesia; the silk and porcelain of China; and the gold, ivory, and slaves of East Africa—were controlled by Middle Eastern Muslim traders.

This last, the eastern Mediterranean trade blockage, is often seen as a religious confrontation, but in fact trade opportunities often trumped religious rivalries. The crusades, beginning in 1096, which brought Christians and Muslims into armed conflict, simultaneously brought new opportunities for commerce across the Mediterranean to Middle Eastern ports and increased demand for the merchandise that arrived there from Asia. Although on several occasions popes forbade Catholics to trade with

The Conquest of Granada on January 2, 1492, Rodrigo Aleman, Toledo Cathedral, late fifteenth century. The conquest of Granada by the Catholic king Ferdinand II and Queen Isabella I of Spain marked the final victory of the *reconquista*, the Christian recovery of all of Spain from Muslim rule. Here, the Moorish king Boabdil is handing over the keys to the town.

Where did the
early European
explorers go?

Muslims, these prohibitions were generally disregarded. Religious and ethnic differences may have compounded the tensions, but the main contest was the competition for profits among the very diverse groups of traders.

European merchants and princes began to seek alternative routes to the lucrative products of the Indian Ocean. This search took on special intensity in Western Europe, which was geographically farther from the Middle East and closer to the Atlantic. Beginning in 1277, a maritime route between Italy and Spain in the Mediterranean and England and Flanders in northwestern Europe brought regular trade to Europe's north Atlantic coast. By the early fifteenth century, European trade generally was picking up, as the continent recovered from the devastation of the Black Death. Increasingly prosperous, and bold, Western Europeans were prepared to attempt two new routes to Asia: one south around the coast of Africa and then east to India; the other west across the Atlantic.

Most of the dynamism of Western European trade through the fifteenth century emanated from the relatively secular city-states of Flanders and Italy, but in the Iberian peninsula Portugal and Spain created a powerful new merger of the missionary desire to spread Catholicism with the economic desire for wealth. The Portuguese crown dispatched sailing expeditions along the African coast that ultimately reached the Cape of Good Hope, turned north into the Indian Ocean and onward to India, and were poised to continue to China. The newly unified government of Spain commissioned Christopher Columbus to sail westward in search of a new route to the Indies. Instead Columbus discovered a "New World."

The Early Explorers, 800–1000

There had been some excursions onto the waters of the Atlantic Ocean before Christopher Columbus made his famous voyage in 1492. From the eighth until the twelfth century, the European North Atlantic was primarily the province of marauding raiders from the north. These Vikings, the ancestors of today's Norwegians, Swedes, and Danes, were colonizers, fishermen, and traders. One group from Norway began to settle Iceland around 870 and Greenland about 982. Under Leif Eriksson they reached Newfoundland in North America about 1000 and established a settlement there as well, but it did not endure. Danes and Norwegians plundered along the entire Atlantic coast of Europe. In 859 they sailed through the Strait of Gibraltar and attacked ports along the Mediterranean. Arabs from North Africa and Spain were launching similar attacks in the Mediterranean at about the same time.

The Vikings were also traders and colonizers who often fostered urban development in the places they conquered. (See map "Scandinavian and Arab Muslim invasions," above.) They founded the town of Dublin, in Ireland, in 841, and they conquered much of northern England, establishing the kingdom of York in the 870s. Vikings also conquered the French territory of Normandy in the late eighth century, from where in 1066 their leader, William of Normandy (William the Conqueror), conquered England. The Normans, as these "Northmen" came to be known, also founded a kingdom in southern Italy and Sicily and established a principality in Antioch.

👁 Watch the **Video: Who Were the Vikings?** on **MyHistoryLab**

The Swedes turned eastward across the Baltic Sea and founded trading cities along the river systems of Russia, establishing their capital first at Novgorod in the early ninth century and then in Kiev in 882. They proceeded all the way south to the Black Sea, where they traded with the Byzantine Empire. Swedish settlements became catalysts for the formation of the political and economic organization of the Slavic people in whose midst they were established. Kiev became the capital of the first Russian state; its people were called the "Rus." By about 1000 the Vikings became

CHAPTER THIRTEEN: THE OPENING OF THE ATLANTIC AND THE PACIFIC 1300–1500

13.1

13.2

13.3

Where did the
early European
explorers go?

more peaceful, and their raids ceased as their home regions in Scandinavia developed
into organized states and accepted Christianity. They lost interest, as well, in further
exploration westward across the ocean.

Earlier voyages across the North Atlantic other than those of the Vikings are not
recorded historically, and are unlikely to have occurred. There is no known crossing
of the South Atlantic. Africans carried on only limited coastal shipping, and Europeans were leery of the hazards of the West African coast, especially south of Cape
Bojador. In addition, they recognized that the prevailing winds on the African coast
blew from north to south, and they feared that, while they might be able to sail south,
they might not be able to return north.

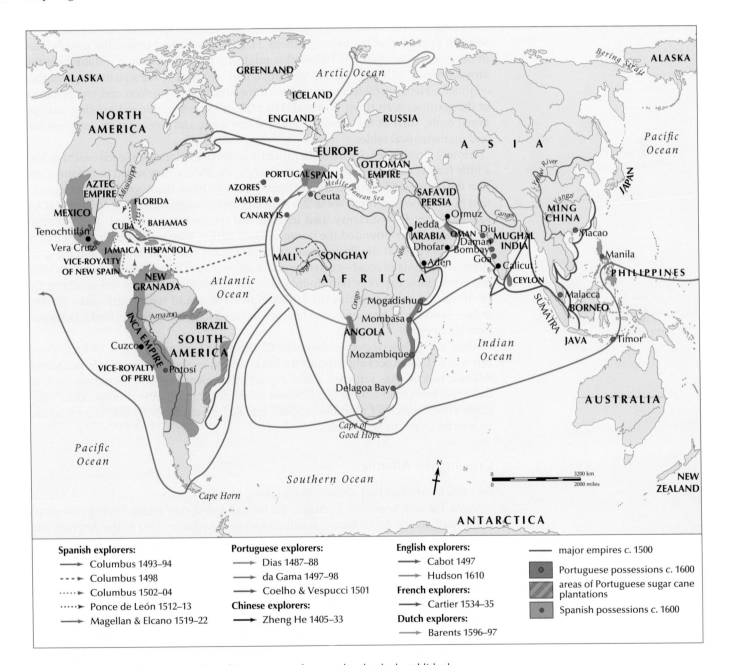

World exploration, 1450–1600. Spanish and Portuguese explorers and traders had established
settlements in South America and the Caribbean by 1600, and commercial depots on the coasts
of Africa, India, the Pacific islands, China, and Japan—at a time when English, Dutch, and French
explorations of North America had just begun.

Down Africa's Atlantic Coast

Portugal was particularly well situated geographically to explore the Atlantic coast of Africa as the opening step in finding an alternative route to India, despite the fears of the unknown. In 1415 Portugal captured Ceuta on the Moroccan coast of North Africa, one of the major points of the trans-Saharan trade in gold and slaves and under the control of Muslims. Then, to get closer to the sources of supply, Portuguese ships, under the direction of Prince Henry (1394–1460), later called the Navigator, sailed down the coast of West Africa.

Henry had two goals. He wanted to defeat Muslim power over African trade routes. Inspired by legend, he sought to establish contact and a military alliance with the mythical Christian king Prester John, sometimes said to rule in Mesopotamia, sometimes in Africa. He imagined that together the two kingdoms could defeat the Muslim powers that lay between them. Henry also wished to test the possibilities of oceanic exploration. He believed it might be possible to reach India by sailing around Africa, although no one in Europe had any idea of the size or shape of that continent. Henry established a center for the study of navigation and shipbuilding at the southwestern tip of Portugal. His staff of experts employed existing navigational tools, such as the astrolabe and the compass, and created new geographical and mathematical tables.

Slowly, Prince Henry's men attempted a series of explorations, each reaching just a little further down the African coast. Fearing the shoals, they sailed out to the west, into the ocean, and allowed the northern winds to blow them south. On an expedition in 1444 they captured some 200 Africans and brought them back to Portugal for sale as slaves. Prince Henry died in 1460, but the project continued. As the Portuguese expeditions rounded the hump of West Africa, they proved their profitability. They reached what the Portuguese called the grain coast, the ivory coast, the gold coast, and the slave coast—each named for its principal exports to Portugal. In 1488, the Portuguese explorer Bartolomeu Dias (*c.* 1450–1500) reached the southern tip of Africa and turned northward for 300 miles. He would have continued—toward India—with his two caravels, but his crew refused to go further. The route, however, now lay open.

Dias' career intersected with that of Christopher Columbus (1451–1506). Columbus was in Lisbon seeking support for his intended exploration westward across the Atlantic just as Dias returned. Dias' report made clear that an alternative route to India had been found; there was no need to risk the transatlantic attempt. The Portuguese crown rejected Columbus' appeal, and so he went to the Spanish court, where he was received more favorably.

Crossing the Atlantic

By 1488, Columbus had already been trying for three years to gain backing for his venture. He was known in Portugal, for he had sailed on various Portuguese ships as far north as the Arctic Circle, south almost to the equator, east to the Aegean, and west to the Azores. Finally, in Spain he received the backing he needed from the newly merged thrones of Ferdinand of Aragon and Isabella of Castile. In his voyage in 1492, Columbus depended on two geographical estimates, and he got both wrong. He underestimated the total circumference of the earth and he overestimated the total east–west span of the Eurasian continent. The globe was bigger than he thought, and so was the oceanic distance that he had to traverse. Nowhere in his figures was there the space for two continents of which he and the people of Europe knew nothing, despite Leif Eriksson's earlier voyages. When Columbus arrived in the Bahamas, he thought he had reached islands off the eastern coast of Asia. Although he found only a little gold, he believed—and promised his patrons—that an abundance of it yet awaited him. He promised also a virtually limitless supply of cotton, spices and

SOURCE

The Journal of Columbus' First Voyage to the Americas

Columbus kept a day-by-day journal of his first voyage. The original has been lost, but fortunately the priest Bartolomé de Las Casas (1474–1566) prepared an abstract, which he used in writing his own *Historia de Las Indias* (1875). Columbus' leading biographer in English, Samuel Eliot Morison, calls the abstract "The most important document in the entire history of American discovery." This account of what Columbus saw and how he related to it is written sometimes in the first person of Columbus, and sometimes in the third person, as the voice of Las Casas. Note especially the overwhelming importance given to religion:

Prologue: Your Highnesses, as Catholic Christians and Princes devoted to the Holy Christian Faith and the propagators thereof, and enemies of the sect of Mahomet and of all idolatries and heresies, resolved to send me, Christopher Columbus, to the said regions of India, to see the said princes and peoples and lands and the disposition of them and of all, and the manner in which may be undertaken their conversion to our Holy Faith, and ordained that I should not go by land (the usual way) to the Orient, but by the route of the Occident, by which no one to this day knows for sure that anyone has gone …

12 October 1492: At two hours after midnight appeared the land, at a distance of two leagues … Presently they saw naked people, and the Admiral went ashore in his barge, and [others] followed. The Admiral broke out the royal standard, and the captains [displayed] two banners of the Green Cross, which the Admiral flew on all the vessels as a signal, with an F and a Y, one at one arm of the cross and the other on the other, and over each letter his or her crown … and said that they should bear faith and witness how he before them all was taking, as in fact he took, possession of the said island for the King and Queen …

15 October: It was my wish to bypass no island without taking possession, although having taken one you can claim all …

22 October: All this night and today I was here, waiting to see if the king here or other people would bring gold or anything substantial, and many of this people came, like the others of the other islands, as naked and as painted, some of them white, others red, others black, and [painted] in many ways … any little thing I gave them, and also our coming, they considered a great wonder, and believed that we had come from the sky …

1 November: It is certain that this is the mainland and that I am before Zayto [Zaytun] and Quisay [Hangzhou] [two great port cities of China], 100 leagues more or less distant the one from the other …

6 November: If they had access to devout religious persons knowing the language, they would all turn Christian, and so I hope in Our Lord that Your Highnesses will do something about it with much care … And after your days (for we are all mortal) … you will be well received before the eternal Creator …

12 November: Yesterday came aboard the ship a dugout with six young men, and five came on board; these I ordered to be detained and I am bringing them. Afterwards I sent to a house which is on the western bank of the river, and they brought seven women, small and large, and three boys. I did this because the [Indian] men would behave better in Spain with women of their country than without them …

27 November: Your Highnesses ought not to consent that any foreigner does business or sets foot here, except Christian Catholics, since this was the end and the beginning of the enterprise …

22 December: The Indians were so free, and the Spaniards so covetous and overreaching, that it was not enough that for a lace-tip or a little piece of glass and crockery or other things of no value, the Indians should give them what they asked; even without giving anything they [the Spaniards] wanted to get and take all, which the Admiral had always forbidden …

23 December: In that hour … more than 1000 persons had come to the ship, and that all brought something that they owned, and that before they come within half a crossbow shot of the ship, they stand up in their canoes with what they brought in their hands, saying "Take! Take!" (cited in Morison, pp. 41–179)

aromatics, timber, and slaves. He characterized the people of the lands he had come upon as ready for conversion to Christianity. He reported all these observations in a letter to Ferdinand and Isabella (see "Source" box, above).

Six months later, Columbus embarked on a much larger expedition with 17 ships, 1,200 men (including six priests to carry on the work of conversion), and enough supplies to establish a permanent settlement. The expedition, however, yielded no serious commercial gains, and it took Columbus two years to gain support for a third expedition, in 1498, with only six ships. For the first time, he landed on the

13.1

13.2

13.3

Where did the early European explorers go?

Vasco da Gama, Portuguese School, *c.* 1524. Gama's expedition in 1497–99 on behalf of the Portuguese crown completed the sea link from Europe around Africa to India. On his next voyage, in 1502–03, he established the policy of using military force to create Portuguese power in the Indian Ocean. (National Museum of Ancient Art, Lisbon)

13.1

13.2

13.3 Where did the early European explorers go?

continental landmass, in what is today Venezuela. Even at the end of his life, after yet another, fourth, voyage that brought him to Central America, Columbus recognized neither the enormity of his mistake nor the enormity of his discovery. He never realized that he had not found China, Japan, India, or islands off the coast of Asia. Nor did he realize that he had discovered a "New World."

Amerigo Vespucci (1454–1512) of Florence was the first person to recognize Columbus' error and his success. In 1499, sailing with a Spanish fleet after Columbus' third expedition, Vespucci traveled some 1,200 miles along the coast of South America. He recognized clearly that this was a continental landmass, but he did not yet realize which one. In a second voyage, 1501–02, this one under the flag of Portugal, he traveled some 2,400 miles down the coast of South America. He reported carefully on all that he saw: humans and their customs and tools, animals, plants, and hints of great treasures. Unlike Columbus, however, Vespucci was cautious: "The natives told us of gold and other metals and many miracle-working drugs, but I am one of those followers of Saint Thomas, who are slow to believe. Time will reveal everything" (cited in Boorstin, p. 250). On his return to Spain, Vespucci was asked by Queen Isabella to establish a school for pilots and a clearinghouse for information brought back from the New World. In 1507 the clergyman and mapmaker Martin Waldseemüller published a new map of the world as known at the time, and on it he named the new western areas "America." In 1538, Gerardus Mercator published his large and influential map of the world, designating the two new continents as North America and South America. Vespucci himself died in 1512 of malaria, contracted on his voyages.

Crossing the Pacific

Only the eastern coast of the Americas was known to Europeans when the Spaniard Vasco Nuñez de Balboa (1474–1517) followed the guidance of one of his Native American allies, crossed the Isthmus of Panama, climbed a peak, and, in 1513, became the first European to see the Pacific Ocean from the east. Four years later, Balboa was falsely accused of treason against the king of Spain, and was beheaded. With the recognition that the Americas were continental in size, and that another ocean lay between them and Asia, Charles V of Spain commissioned Ferdinand Magellan (*c.* 1480–1521) to sail west, find a passage around the southern tip of South America, proceed across the Pacific—no matter how long the voyage—and reach the Spice Islands of East Asia. Magellan set out in 1519 with five ships and about 250 sailors from several different European countries. The voyage became the first circumnavigation of the globe, yielding the first accurate picture of the full magnitude of the planet and completing the picture of most of its main contours. It took just 12 days less than three years. Only 18 men completed the trip. Magellan himself was killed in a skirmish with Mactan tribal warriors on the Philippine island of Cebu. Europeans became aware of Australia and its peoples in the 1500s, but did not map it carefully until the late 1700s.

Legacies to the Future:
What Difference Do They Make?

Voyages of exploration, trade, conquest, and settlement evoke a sense of wonder at the skill and daring of the captains and sailors who embarked for the unknown with so few and such small ships and such limited equipment, and the foresight of the governments and businesspeople who organized and financed them. Each participant was called by a different set of values: the desire to chart the unknown; the pressure to find a new home; the quest for profit; the urge to proselytize; the lust for conquest; the competition for national superiority. Often, many of these motives were mixed together. The legacy of these people is the achievement of a geographically known and integrated globe. It is not, however, a single, simple legacy, but a variegated set of mixed legacies that includes competition, greed, self-righteousness, and violence. Few participants prepared for oceanic voyages with the greater good of the entire world at heart. Most, instead, sought benefits for themselves, their region or nation, or their religious group. They looked out on a huge and diverse world from relatively narrow and often self-interested perspectives.

By 1521 European traders had established a permanent connection between the eastern and western hemispheres for the first time, following Columbus' voyages across the Atlantic and Magellan's circumnavigation of the world. Meanwhile, inspired by the early explorations of Henry the Navigator along the west coast of Africa, Portuguese sailors rounded the Cape of Good Hope and opened new routes into the Indian Ocean. These explorations followed centuries of Western European economic expansion, national consolidation, and intellectual renaissance. Explorers were motivated by their mixed desire for knowledge, profit, national aggrandizement, and Christian proselytizing.

CHAPTER REVIEW

ECONOMIC AND SOCIAL CHANGES IN EUROPE

13.1 What changes in Western Europe made Atlantic explorations possible?

In the 1200s, Western Europeans were emerging from agrarian, manorial economies. Productivity increased as new lands were opened and new innovations introduced. Crop surpluses were available to feed the merchants and craftspeople who established themselves in greater numbers in the cities. Cities, formerly centered on their churches, now increased the size of their marketplaces. As their own economies and technologies grew stronger, Western Europeans began to look for new routes to the great markets of Asia.

THE RENAISSANCE

13.2 What was the European Renaissance?

The Renaissance was a nearly 300-year period of cultural and intellectual creativity in Western Europe, beginning about 1300. The artists and writers who created the movement saw themselves as reconnecting to the traditions of the ancient Greeks and Romans, and thus producing a renaissance, or "rebirth," of Classical ideals in thought, literature, art, and sensibilities. With their increasing success in trade and manufacture, urban businessmen became patrons of the arts, and creativity flourished.

A NEW WORLD

13.3 Where did the early European explorers go?

Seeking routes to the lucrative Asian markets, Western Europeans tried two new directions: the Portuguese headed south along the western coast of Africa until they could turn east toward India; the Spanish headed west across the Atlantic Ocean. By 1600, Portuguese and Spanish explorers and traders had established commercial depots along the coasts of Africa, India, China, Japan, and the Pacific Islands. Westward, they had established settlements in South America and the Caribbean. The English, Dutch, and French had begun also to explore North America.

Suggested Readings

PRINCIPAL SOURCES

Adas, Michael, ed. *Islamic and European Expansion* (Philadelphia, PA: Temple University Press, 1993). Key collection of historiographical essays on major topics in world history, 1200–1900. Articles by Richard Eaton and Judith Tucker on Islam and William McNeill on "gunpowder empires" are especially helpful for this section.

Boorstin, Daniel J. *The Discoverers* (New York: Random House, 1983). Extremely well-written, engaging history of four kinds of invention and discovery. One is maritime, mostly European explorers and cartographers 1400–1800.

Chakrabarty, Dipesh. *Provincializing Europe: Postcolonial Thought and Historical Difference* (Princeton, NJ: Princeton University Press, 2000).

Chaudhuri, K.N. *Trade and Civilization in the Indian Ocean: An Economic History from the Rise of Islam to 1750* (Cambridge: Cambridge University Press, 1985). A survey of goods, traders, ships, regulations, and competition among those who sailed and claimed to control the Indian Ocean.

Crosby, Alfred W. *Ecological Imperialism: The Biological Expansion of Europe, 900–1900* (Cambridge: Cambridge University Press, 1986). The biological—mostly destructive—impact of European settlement around the world: a tragedy for native peoples from the Americas to Oceania.

Curtin, Philip. *Cross-Cultural Trade in World History* (Cambridge: Cambridge University Press, 1984). Classical statement of the significance and ubiquity of trade diasporas.

Landes, David S. *The Wealth and Poverty of Nations: Why Some Are so Rich and Some so Poor* (New York: W.W. Norton, 1999). Credits the Western European world with creating the institutions that made its economic growth flourish.

McNeill, William H. *The Rise of the West: A History of the Human Community, with a Retrospective Essay* (Chicago, IL: University of Chicago Press, 1991). Reopened the professional field of modern history. Analyzes the basis of power, and those who created it, in global perspective, in each time period.

Wolf, Eric R. *Europe and the People without History* (Berkeley, CA: University of California Press, 1982). Laments history's emphasis on the powerful, and attempts to correct the imbalance by bringing into the historical record peoples who have been left out.

SECONDARY SOURCES

Aquinas, St. Thomas. *Summa contra Gentiles* and *Governance of Rulers* (excerpts) in Columbia University, *Introduction to Contemporary Civilization in the West,* cited below. Aquinas defined the field

of thirteenth-century Roman Catholic theology—and beyond.

Bloch, Marc. *Feudal Society*, 2 vols. (Chicago, IL: University of Chicago Press, 1961). Classic, if dated, comprehensive view of the workings of feudalism in Western Europe.

Boccaccio, Giovanni. *The Decameron*, trans. Frances Winwar (New York: Modern Library, 1955). Delightful tales, set against the background of the Black Death, which raged through Western Europe in the 1340s.

Braudel, Fernand. *Capitalism and Material Life, 1400–1800*, trans. Miriam Kochan (New York: Harper and Row, 1973). Comprehensive survey of the beginnings of the modern capitalist system in Europe.

——. *The Mediterranean and the Mediterranean World in the Age of Philip II*, trans. Sian Reynolds (New York: Harper and Row, 2 vols, 1973). Magisterial work that introduces Braudel's concept of three complementary time frames in the study of history: short range, middle range, and *longue durée.*

Brotton, Jerry. *The Renaissance: A Very Short Introduction* (New York: Oxford University Press, 2006). Excellent, concise survey. Credits Islamic learning with helping to inspire the Renaissance.

Brucker, Gene. *Renaissance Florence* (Berkeley, CA: University of California Press, 1969). Older, but still classic account.

Cassirer, Ernst, Paul Oskar Kristeller, and John Herman Randall, Jr. trans. and eds. *Philosophy of the Enlightenment* (Chicago: University of Chicago Press, 1956).

Chaudhuri, K.N. *Asia Before Europe* (Cambridge: Cambridge University Press, 1990). Survey of the economic and political systems of Asia before the impact of colonialism and the Industrial Revolution. Comprehensive, comparative, and thoughtful.

Cipolla, Carlo. *Clocks and Culture, 1300–1700* (New York: W.W. Norton, 2003). Presents the technology of early clocks, and then credits them with increasing people's sensitivity to the importance of time, especially in the world of work.

Cohn, Samuel K., Jr. *The Black Death Transformed: Disease and Culture in Early Renaissance Europe* (London: Arnold, 2002). Studies and summarizes the research on the nature of the Black Death and its longer-term effects.

Columbia College, Columbia University. *Introduction to Contemporary Civilization in the West*, vol. 1 (New York: Columbia University Press, 2nd ed., 1954). Very well-chosen, long source readings from leading thinkers of the time and place. Vol. I covers about 1000–1800.

Crosby, Alfred. *The Measure of Reality: Quantification in Western Europe, 1250–1600* (Cambridge: Cambridge University Press, 1997). By quantifying the processes of work and productivity, people gained greater understanding and control of them, and increased their efficiency.

Fernandez-Armesto, Felipe. *Columbus* (New York: Oxford University Press, 1991). Careful, sensitive biography of the man and his times.

Frank, Andre Gunder, and Barry K. Gills, eds. *The World System: Five Hundred Years or Five Thousand?* (London: Routledge, 1993). In this somewhat tendentious, but well-argued, account, globalization is nothing new.

Gabrieli, F. "The Transmission of Learning and Literary Influences to Western Europe,' in Holt, P.M., Ann K.S. Lambton, and Bernard Lewis, eds., *The Cambridge History of Islam*, vol. 2B: *Islamic Society and Civilization* (Cambridge: Cambridge University Press, 1970), pp. 851–89. Comprehensive summary of the influence of Islamic learning on Europe. Especially good on contrasting different time periods.

The Hammond Atlas of World History, ed. Richard Overy (Maplewood, NJ: Hammond, 1999). Excellent, standard historical atlas.

Havighurst, Alfred F., ed. *The Pirenne Thesis: Analysis, Criticism, and Revision* (Lexington, MA: D.C. Heath, rev. ed. 1969). Well-selected pieces from Pirenne, his critics, and supporters. Well introduced, supported, and summarized, although mostly European in orientation.

Hohenberg, Paul M., and Lynn Hollen Lees. *The Making of Urban Europe*, 1000–1950 (Cambridge, MA: Harvard University Press, 1985). Brief but comprehensive text on the significance of cities to the history of Europe. Special attention to the social development of cities and their residents.

Huff, Toby. *The Rise of Early Modern Science* (New York: Cambridge University Press, 2nd ed., 2003). Controversial analysis of how Western European Christians developed early science, and why Arabs and the Chinese did not.

Levenson, Jay A. *Circa 1492: Art in the Age of Exploration* (Washington, DC: National Gallery of Art, 1991). Catalogue of an astounding art exhibit, covering the arts in all the major regions of the world at the time of Columbus' voyages.

MacCulloch, Diarmaid. *Christianity: The First Thousand Years* (New York: Penguin, 2009). Thoughtful, incisive, lucid.

Morison, Samuel Eliot, trans. and ed. *Journals and Other Documents on the Life and Voyages of Christopher Columbus* (New York: The Heritage Press, 1963). The crucial documents.

Pirenne, Henri. *Medieval Cities: Their Origins and the Revival of Trade*, trans. Frank D. Halsey (Princeton, NJ: Princeton University Press, 1925). Classic statement of the importance of free merchants to the rise of commercial cities and the development of the modern world. Dated, and more limited than claimed, but pathbreaking and enormously influential.

——. *Mohammed and Charlemagne*, trans. Bernard Miall (New York: W.W. Norton, 1939). Key revisionist text citing the Islamic victories in the Mediterranean as the end of Roman Europe and the beginning of rebirth in the north under Charlemagne.

Polanyi, Karl, Conrad M. Arensberg, and Harry W. Pearson, eds. *Trade and Market in the Early Empires* (Chicago, IL: The Free Press, 1957). Fundamental argument by historical anthropologists that early trade was mostly regulated by rulers and priests.

Reynolds, Susan. *Fiefs and Vassals* (Oxford: Clarendon Press, 1994). Scholarly, influential examination of "feudalism," arguing that the word is used to cover too wide a variety of regional and temporal patterns.

Subrahmanyam, Sanjay. *The Career and Legend of Vasco da Gama* (Cambridge: Cambridge University Press, 1997). The most thorough available account of the man, his contributions, and the historical puzzles surrounding them, presented in overwhelming scholarly detail.

Tuchman, Barbara. *A Distant Mirror: The Calamitous Fourteenth Century* (New York: Knopf, 1978). Engaging history of a century filled with war and plague.

Wills, John E., Jr. "Maritime Asia, 1500–1800: The Interactive Emergence of European Domination," *American Historical Review* XCVIII, no. 1 (February 1993), pp. 83–105. Survey of European entrance into and domination of Indian Ocean and Chinese sea lanes.

FILMS

The Battle of Lepanto (2012; 30 minutes). Reveals not only the diverse forces arrayed on each side, but also the technology of naval warfare and the treatment of the sailors.

Forgetting the Arabs: Europe on the Cusp of the Renaissance (1999; 27 minutes). Argues that after the fall of Baghdad in 1258, the Muslim world rejected new ideas and thinking, while European Christians expanded their personal intellectual freedom.

Italy, Age of Architects (2007; 1 hour 25 minutes). Uses Leonardo as a touchstone to examine many aspects of the Italian Renaissance, especially engineering, architecture, and city planning.

The Medici: Godfathers of the Renaissance, 4 parts (2003; 2 hours). Comprehensive, engaging account of 300 years of European history seen through the experiences of a single family.

14 The Unification of World Trade

New Philosophies for New Trade Patterns

1500–1776

By 1500, ocean voyages of exploration and trade had bridged the eastern and western hemispheres, initiating a new phase of world history. Most regions of the world began to enter into a single system of trade and exchange.

Persian forces under Imam Quli Khan fight to capture the port of Hormuz from the Portuguese. Miniature, seventeenth century. Since 1507, the Portuguese had controlled the port of Hormuz and, with it, the Persian Gulf, effectively blocking other countries from trading with Persia and the Mesopotamian region by sea. In 1622, British and Persian forces combined to remove the Portuguese garrison from Hormuz, opening trade in the Gulf and shifting the balance of power. (British Library, London)

LEARNING OBJECTIVES

14.1 ((	14.2 ((	14.3 ((	14.4 ((	14.5 ((
Define capitalism.	Describe Spain and Portugal's early overseas exploration and exploitation.	Describe the background to the rise of the Dutch, French, and British empires.	Define "nation-state".	Describe the goals of Peter the Great.

((Listen on MyHistoryLab

What is
capitalism?

14.1

14.2

14.3

14.4

14.5

In Western Europe, these overseas trade opportunities were restructuring public life, increasing the power of private businessmen. In other parts of the world, however, government continued to be a more formidable force, more important than private business. The largest city in Europe, for example, was not an Atlantic Ocean port but Constantinople (modern-day Istanbul), the capital of the Ottoman Empire. It, too, was an important commercial city, serving the eastern Mediterranean and the Middle East, but it owed its importance and size—700,000 residents—more to its political role than to its trade (which was, in any case, falling into the hands of foreigners). In India, China, and Japan, government authorities generally dominated business interests. There were exceptions, but government control was the usual pattern.

Each major region of the world also had a very different experience in confronting the new international world system of trade being fashioned by the Europeans. The Americas, for example, succumbed almost immediately. The Chinese, on the other hand, remained somewhat independent of the system until the mid-nineteenth century, and in some ways China at first actually dominated the system. Even though the Chinese and Indians were not the shippers carrying the goods overseas, it was their products and their economies that evoked a very large proportion of international trade. Chinese products—especially silks and porcelain—were the objects of a great deal of the trade. The Europeans sailed in order to get them, as well as the spices and textiles of India and Indonesia; and to get gold and, later, some ten million slaves from Africa. Almost half the silver of the New World mines went to China to pay for exports to Europe. Asians and Africans may not have sailed as widely and aggressively as Europeans did after 1500, but it was the goods of Asia and Africa that motivated the European voyages.

The Birth of Capitalism

14.1 What is capitalism?

In Western Europe, a system of trade and exchange emerged, dedicated to the pursuit of private economic profit through the private ownership of wealth and the means of its production. The system took root in the textile workshops of Italy in the south and Flanders in the north, and soon extended to banking and international trade. Through the power of their wealth—that is, their capital—and of their collective organization, the owners of these workshops, the bankers, and the traders began to develop the economic system that we now call capitalism.

Capitalism claimed to allow individuals to exchange their products and labor in free, unregulated markets. It fought off the restrictive rules of Church and government. It argued instead that in a free-market exchange the prices of goods and of labor would result from the balance between supply and demand. These market prices would serve as a message to producers and consumers, alerting them to what the market did and did not want at the moment. The lure of the market would encourage people to risk investing their accumulated wealth in economic activities that might earn profits (although they might also suffer losses).

Despite these free-market claims, and their desire to be free of regulation, capitalists frequently persuaded governments to support and assist them in their money-making projects. In exchange, capitalists lent their financial support to government. In the city of Venice, for example, in the thirteenth century, capitalists gained control of the economy, as the city grew to a population of nearly 200,000. By the 1300s, through banking and trade, they gained control of the government of the city of Florence, with its 100,000 residents. Capitalist philosophies began to overcome more restrictive economic philosophies.

Major Western European governments had been following principles of **mercantilism**, the belief that government should regulate trade—especially by restricting the outflow

KEY TERM

mercantilism An economic policy pursued by many European nations between the sixteenth and eighteenth centuries. It aimed to strengthen an individual nation's economic power at the expense of its rivals by stockpiling reserves of bullion, which involved government regulations of trade.

of gold and silver—for the greater strength of the state. Slowly these governments were persuaded that allowing businessmen more freedom of trade would in fact benefit the state even more by generating more taxable wealth. Capitalists and governments worked together to achieve the goals of both: protection and encouragement for the businessmen; taxes for the state.

SOURCE

Adam Smith on Capitalism

By the late eighteenth century, as European economies were expanding, they became the subject of discussion and debate among businesspeople, political leaders, and philosophers. Adam Smith (1723–90) had already established a reputation as a moral philosopher before he turned to writing what became his most famous work. In 1776 Smith published *An Inquiry into the Nature and Causes of the Wealth of Nations* (generally referred to simply as *The Wealth of Nations*) a book of 1,000 pages, the first systematic explanation of a newly emerging philosophy of economics, later called capitalism.

In contrast to the mercantilist views of his day, Smith argued that national wealth was not to be measured by treasuries of precious metals, but rather by levels of productivity and of trade. He opened his great work with an illustration from a pin factory where a division of labor into specialized tasks of production increased output dramatically. Smith further argued that when workers specialize in what they do best, and then exchange their products in the market, productivity increases. The competitive free market guides production: goods that consumers want to buy attract higher prices, and producers supply them in order to earn good profits; unwanted goods earn no profits, and producers stop producing them. This law of supply and demand in the market, argues Smith, leads to the production of the amounts and kinds of goods that suit the wishes of consumers and the capacity of producers. According to Smith's Law of Accumulation, profits are reinvested in further production.

Smith reached a new and surprising conclusion: wealth comes not from the command of a ruler, nor the regulations of the clergy, nor the altruism of members of the community, but as a result of people pursuing their own economic self-interest and exchanging the fruits of their labor in the market. "It is not from the benevolence of the butcher, the brewer, or the baker that we expect our dinner, but from their regard to their self-interest. We address ourselves, not to their humanity, but to their self-love, and never talk to them of our necessities, but of their advantages" (Smith, p. 14).

Although Smith did not use the term, today we call the system he analyzed capitalism—that is, most wealth, or capital, rests in private, nongovernmental hands, and economic decisions on price, supply, and demand are made through the free market rather than by government. Critics of this capitalist market system, in which buyer and seller negotiate freely over prices, equated capitalism's self-interest with greed, but Smith explained how competition transformed self-interest into community benefit: if a greedy producer charges too much for his goods, someone will undercut him and lower prices will result; if he pays his employees too little, they will abandon him

and seek work elsewhere. Out of the conflicting self-interests of individual members of the society, paradoxically, social harmony will emerge. Smith, who was a professor of moral philosophy at the University of Edinburgh, disagreed with those who said that rulers or priests must regulate the economy to achieve equity. Like an "invisible hand," the impersonal market would do the job.

Believing that the free, unregulated market would correct most economic imbalances, Smith opposed government intervention. He argued for a hands-off government policy of *laissez-faire* toward the market—that is, let people do as they choose. But he did recognize that some necessities for economic growth were beyond the powers of any single, small producer: "The erection and maintenance of the public works which facilitate the commerce of any country, such as good roads, bridges, navigable canals, harbors, et cetera, must require very different degrees of expense" (vol. 5, p. 1), and therefore Smith urged government to promote these public works. He believed that education was fundamental to economic productivity. Private education was more effective than public education, but government-supported public education was better than none.

Smith recognized, of course, that the market did not always succeed in balancing supply and demand. Huge businesses that formed virtual monopolies could control whole industries and manipulate market forces. Their size gave them unfair leverage and Smith wanted them broken up. *The Wealth of Nations* attacked the British East India Company, the joint stock company that virtually monopolized Britain's trade in Asia and had even become the acting government of Bengal in India. Smith argued that its monopoly should be broken. His plea, however, did not bring about a change.

Capitalism was the prevailing economic philosophy in Britain in the years of its economic supremacy in the nineteenth century, and the new system spread to many other countries as well. As we shall see in the following chapters, many critics blamed free-market, *laissez-faire* capitalism for the inhumanity and cruelty of the slave trade, the seizure of colonies overseas, and the vulnerability of workers at home. Smith understood these problems, but argued that they were corruptions of the market system rather than natural products of it. He condemned slavery as a form of kidnapping and theft of human beings, rather than a free-market exchange. Similarly, he deplored the European destruction of the Native American states and populations as a violation of human ethics: "The savage injustice of the Europeans rendered an event which ought to have been beneficial to all ruinous and destructive to several of those unfortunate countries" (Smith, p. 416).

AT A GLANCE: THE INTERCONNECTING WORLD

DATE	EUROPE	THE AMERICAS	ASIA AND AFRICA
1500	• Communero revolt in Spain (1520–21) • Luther excommunicated (1521)	• Four voyages of Christopher Columbus (1492–1504) • Hernán Cortés conquers Tenochtitlán (1521)	• Portuguese establish trading posts in East Africa (1505) • Portugal captures Goa, India (1510) • Portuguese missionaries arrive in China (1514)
1525	• Henry VIII becomes head of new Anglican church (1534) • First stock exchange in Antwerp (1538) • Calvin establishes Presbyterian theocracy in Geneva (1541)	• Francisco Pizarro captures Inca emperor Atahualpa (1532) • Potosí silver mine discovered (1545)	• Mughals invade India (1526) • St. Francis Xavier arrives in Japan (1549)
1550	• Council of Trent (1545–63) • End of Hundred Years War (1558) • Tobacco introduced into Europe (1559); potato (c. 1565)	• Portuguese begin sugar cultivation in Brazil (c. 1560)	• Akbar consolidates Mughal Empire (1556–1605) • Spanish capture Manila, Philippines (1571) • Portuguese establish colony in Angola (1571)
1575	• Spanish Armada defeated by England (1588) • Henry IV of France issues Edict of Nantes (1598)		• Matteo Ricci arrives in China (1582) • Japan invades Korea (1592)
1600	• Dutch, English, and French East India Companies founded • The Netherlands win independence from Spain; Bank of Amsterdam established (1609)		• Tokugawa shoguns begin consolidation of Japan (1603) • Christianity outlawed in Japan (1606) • Dutch found Batavia (Jakarta), Indonesia (1619)
1625	• Portugal declares independence from Spain (1640) • Peace of Westphalia (1648) • Russia captures Siberia (1649)		• Manchus conquer China and form Qing dynasty (1644)
1650	• English Navigation Act (1651) • Louis XIV of France, the "Sun King" (r. 1643–1715)		• Dutch capture Cape of Good Hope (1652)
1675	• War of the League of Augsburg (1688–97) • Bank of England created (1694)		• Qing dynasty establishes "Canton system" (1683)
1700	• Peter the Great founds St. Petersburg (1704) • War of the Spanish Succession (1702–13) • Act of Union creates Great Britain (1707)		• Edo, Japan, has one million people
1725	• War of Austrian Succession (1740–48)		
1750	• Seven Years War (1756–63) • Adam Smith, *The Wealth of Nations* (1776)	• War of American Independence (1775–81)	• After English victory at Plassey, English gain Bengal (1757)

Western European businessmen led in sponsoring new international trade initiatives that emphasized private profit and national aggrandizement. As a result, the trading centers of northwestern Europe grew ever larger. By 1700, London had a population of 550,000; Paris, 530,000; Lisbon, 188,000; and Amsterdam, 172,000. Each of these cities was both a national capital and a major trading center. Economic and political interests reinforced one another.

14.2 What regions of the world did Spain and Portugal explore?

The Empires of Spain and Portugal

14.2   What regions of the world did Spain and Portugal explore?

The first European nations to dominate the new overseas trade and colonization, however, were Spain and Portugal, countries in which business communities were relatively weak. There, political rulers made the principal economic decisions. Both countries directly faced the Atlantic Ocean. Portugal's rulers saw the Atlantic as their front door; Spain's rulers, just consolidating their country in 1492, saw it as a route to riches, power, and proselytizing.

Spain's New World Conquests

KEY TERM

conquistadores The Spanish soldiers who invaded and conquered the kingdoms of the New World, especially in Mexico and Peru.

The four voyages of Christopher Columbus between 1492 and 1504 revealed to the Spanish crown some of the opportunities for agricultural development, religious conversion, and exploitation of resources in gold and silver to be found in the Americas. Spanish settlers began first to colonize the islands of the Caribbean and the north coast of South America. Spanish **conquistadores**, in response to tales of great riches, marched inland to conquer what they could. In 1519, Hernán Cortés began his expedition into Mexico from Veracruz with 600 Spaniards, a few guns, and 16 horses. Because the Aztecs under Moctezuma II dominated and plundered the various tribes living in the surrounding region, Cortés was joined by thousands of Native Americans who wished to overthrow the powerful Aztec empire at Tenochtitlán, modern-day Mexico City. Cortés' small force entered the city without a struggle, possibly helped by a woman, La Malinche or Marina, who became his translator, his informer, his mistress, and the mother of his son. The peace did not last, however, and after the Spaniards massacred several Aztec leaders during a festival, the population revolted. They killed Moctezuma, believing that he had collaborated with Cortés, and they forced the conquistadores out of the city. Cortés suffered heavy losses, perhaps as many as two-thirds of his men and several horses. The Spaniards retreated to Tlaxcala, where their new Native American allies nursed them back to health and helped them to retake Tenochtitlán. The Spaniards conquered the capital city again in 1521 after a bitter four-month siege; and so the empire was theirs. In the next 20 years they captured the Yucatán and most of Central America, although revolts continued in the region. Cortés became ruler of the Kingdom of New Spain, reorganized in 1535 as the Vice-Royalty of New Spain.

Emperor Atahualpa arrested by Francisco Pizarro in 1532. When Pizarro landed on the northern coast of Peru on May 13, 1532, he brought with him a force of 200 men with horses, guns, and swords. The Inca emperor Atahualpa, backed up by thousands of troops, felt he had little to fear from the Spanish and, as this contemporary Peruvian drawing shows, accepted Pizarro's seemingly friendly invitation to meet, accompanied by only his bodyguards. It was a trap, and Pizarro arrested and later executed him. (Compare this picture to that in the Introduction to this book of Cortés and the Aztecs in Mexico.)

View the **Closer Look: The Meeting of Cortés and Moctezuma** on **MyHistoryLab**

Read the **Document: Excerpt from The Broken Spears, an Indian account of the conquest of Mexico** on **MyHistoryLab**

Read the **Document: Anonymous (Aztec): The Midwife Addresses the Woman Who Has Died in Childbirth** on **MyHistoryLab**

In South America, Vasco Nuñez de Balboa found a portage across the Isthmus of Panama in 1513. Now the Spanish could transport their ships from the Atlantic coast overland across the Isthmus and sail south along the Pacific Coast to Peru. Rumors of great stores of gold encouraged these voyages to the Inca Empire. Like the Aztecs, the Inca were divided. In 1525,

14.1

14.2

14.3

14.4

14.5

What regions
of the world
did Spain and
Portugal explore?

after the death of their king Huayna Capec (possibly from smallpox), a civil war broke out between two of his sons—Huáscar and Atahualpa—over who should rule the empire. Fighting was fierce and ended only in 1532, when Atahualpa captured Huáscar and executed him. In the same year, Francisco Pizarro, leading a force of some 200 men, captured Atahualpa. Although given a room full of gold as ransom for the emperor's life, Pizarro feared a revolt and killed him. In 1533 he captured the Inca capital, Cuzco. The Spanish conquistadores fought among themselves for years until Spain established the Vice-Royalty of Peru in the mid-sixteenth century as the South American counterpart to the Vice-Royalty of New Spain in the north. Revolts against the Spaniards continued until they captured and beheaded the last Inca emperor, Tupac Amarú, in 1572.

Why the Inca and Aztec Empires Fell. How had a few hundred Spanish soldiers and their Native American allies succeeded in overthrowing the two largest empires in the Americas? The answer has four parts. First, as we have seen, the conquered Native Americans were not a single united people, but many different, competitive, and even warring peoples. In conquering the dominant groups—Moctezuma's Aztecs in Mexico and Atahualpa's Inca in Peru—the Spanish found many allies among the enemies of these groups. In addition, the Inca were weakened by their own civil war. Second, unlike the Native Americans, the Spanish possessed firearms, steel armor and weapons, and horses—animals never before seen in the Americas. The Spaniards also fought differently from the indigenous populations, shooting their guns from a distance rather than engaging in the hand-to-hand warfare practiced by the Aztecs. Third, the Aztecs and Inca were demoralized when their commanders-in-chief were captured. The two Indian empires were highly centralized, and the removal of their leaders left them disorganized. (Less centralized and more remote groups, like the Araucanians of central Chile, held out far longer, winning a revered place as patriots and heroes in Latin American history and poetry.) And, finally, Native Americans had no immunity to European diseases, such as smallpox, that were new to the Americas. The diseases proved far more deadly than the warfare.

Legend once had it that the Indians viewed the invading Spanish as gods. In this telling, the Spanish gods were returning to their homelands and were therefore deserving of obedience, rather than resistance. Recent scholarship has dispelled this as a fiction created by the Spanish.

📖 Read the **Document: Bernal Diaz del Castillo, from the True History of the Conquest of New Spain** on **MyHistoryLab**

Making the Conquests Pay. After the conquests, the Spanish began to reorganize the economies of the Americas. They established the *encomienda* system, assigning the taxes and labor of local Indian populations to Spanish colonists who were also to convert them to Christianity, if possible. The Native Americans were enslaved in conditions of great cruelty. The *encomienda* system was first established on the island of Hispaniola, where in 20 years the native population fell from several million to 29,000. Humane voices, especially of such priests as Bartolomé de Las Casas, opposed the *encomienda* system, but it continued until so many Indians had died that it could no longer function. In most of Mexico and Peru the system had ended by the late 1500s, but it operated for another century in Venezuela; for another two centuries, until 1791, in Chile; and until the early 1800s in Paraguay.

The systems that replaced it were not much more humane. The *repartimiento* system in central Mexico and the similar *mit'a* system in Peru forced the local population into low-paid or unpaid labor for a portion of each year on Spanish-owned farms, in mines and workshops, and on public works projects. These systems, too, were forms of unofficial slavery. Not all labor was coerced, however. Spanish-owned plantations or *haciendas*, agricultural estates producing commercial crops and

KEY TERMS

encomienda A concession from the Spanish crown to a colonist, giving the colonist permission to exact tribute from a specified number of Native Americans living in a particular area. Conditions were harsh and the Spanish attempted to convert the Indians to Christianity.

repartimiento A system by which the Spanish crown allowed colonists to employ Indians for forced labor, in conditions of virtual slavery.

mit'a A system of forced labor in Peru, begun under Inca rule, by which indigenous communities were required to contribute a set number of laborers for public works for a given period. Conditions were virtually those of slavery.

hacienda A large rural estate in Spanish America, originating with Spanish colonization in the sixteenth century.

14.1

14.2 What regions of the world did Spain and Portugal explore?

14.3

14.4

14.5

Inca–Spanish wooden drinking vessel, Peru, c. 1650. This painted Inca ritual drinking vessel made of wood, known as a *kero*, represents people of three different cultures: to the left, an Inca dignitary; in the center, a Spaniard playing a trumpet; and on the right, one of the earliest depictions of a black African in South America, a man playing a drum.

livestock, employed both free and indentured labor. The *haciendas* often produced commercially the newly imported products of the eastern hemisphere—wheat, cattle, pigs, sheep, chickens, horses, and mules—in addition to the indigenous local crops of maize, potatoes, and manioc (cassava).

Perhaps the worst conditions existed in silver mines, which also used paid labor at very low wages. The immense Potosí mine in Upper Peru (today's Bolivia) employed 40,000 Native American miners in the seventeenth century. Tunnels destroyed the landscape, and working conditions were inhuman. Children were put to work, forced to crawl through cracks into the mines and to labor without breaks.

From the Spanish perspective, the most valuable products of the Americas throughout the sixteenth century were gold and silver. The mine at Potosí, discovered in 1545, was the largest silver mine in the world. Smaller mines were opened in Mexico in 1545 and 1558. In 1556 a new method of separating silver from ore by using mercury, available from Almadén in Spain, was discovered. (The toxic qualities of mercury were not known at the time.) Between 1550 and 1800 Mexico and South America produced more than 80 percent of the world's silver and more than 70 percent of its gold.

The precious metals were exported each year from Latin America eastward to Europe and westward to the Philippines for transshipment to China. In Europe, the enormous influx of precious metals helped to generate a centuries-long wave of inflation, since the infusion of silver was not matched by an increase in the production of commercial goods. By 1600, prices were three or four times higher than in 1500, with the rise being highest in port cities most exposed to the influx of the silver, and lowest in remote inland areas. The gap between rich and poor widened, as wages did not keep pace with the increase in prices, while entrepreneurs gained more money for investment. Some benefits did accrue to borrowers, since they could repay their loans in currency or silver of diminished value.

Meanwhile, the Spanish captured Manila in 1571 and established it as their chief trade center in East Asia. They used silver from the New World to pay for purchases of silks, textiles, spices, and, later, tea from India and China. Between one-third and half of all American silver produced between 1527 and 1821 found its way to China, and the Mexican peso became a legal currency in China. Asian traders demanded payment in silver because Europe itself produced very little of interest to them. The Chinese preferred silver to gold, and even used gold to buy silver. This Chinese demand for silver was the driving force in the transpacific trade. For some years in the early seventeenth century, Chinese demand also drove an equal importation of silver from the countries of East Asia itself, funneled through Japan and its traders.

Merchant Profits. The gold and silver mines of the Americas, which brought enslavement and poverty to the Native Americans, benefited the Spaniards themselves less than they did the merchants of Antwerp, Genoa, Amsterdam, London, and Paris. The Spanish did not have the commercial infrastructure necessary to absorb their newly captured resources and invest them profitably. They also lacked the ships to carry the trade generated by the new finds of gold and silver. The experienced merchants of the trade cities of Europe organized the necessary commercial services. They exchanged the raw metals for cash and bills of exchange, provided loans to cover the period from the arrival of one shipment of silver to the next, arranged the purchase of goods needed by the Spanish, and supplied the necessary shipping. In the sixteenth century, the most important of these commercial centers was Antwerp (Belgium), with its skilled and wealthy merchants from Antwerp, England, France, Portugal, Italy, Spain, and Germany. The one major exception to this pattern was the trade with China, across the Pacific, in which Spain remained the major European participant.

Warfare and Bankruptcy. Many regions of Europe at this time were "owned" by particular families, who had the responsibility for protecting them and the rights to tax them and bequeath them to others. These families often intermarried, in which case sometimes whole countries changed rulers. Spain's Charles V (r. 1515–56) inherited Spain and the Spanish colonies in Africa, the Americas, Naples, and Sicily from his mother's parents, Ferdinand and Isabella. From his father's family, the House of Burgundy, he inherited the Netherlands and the German lands owned by the Habsburg family. He became the most powerful ruler in Europe.

Plan of Potosí and the Cerro Rico (Rich Hill), Upper Peru. This seventeenth-century painting shows Potosí and the hills in which the lucrative silver mines were located. The mines at Potosí employed some 40,000 poorly paid Indian laborers and tens of thousands of horses—shown in this painting ascending and descending the hills—to transport the material and drive the machinery.

14.1
14.2
14.3
14.4
14.5

What regions of the world did Spain and Portugal explore?

14.1
14.2   What regions
14.3   of the world
       did Spain and
14.4   Portugal explore?
14.5

Raised in Flanders, Charles V spoke no Spanish, and his pride and foreignness alienated the Spanish. He appointed courtiers from Flanders to offices in Spain, and he used Spanish wealth to fund his political programs in central European territories. The Spaniards revolted. The nobles wanted to stop the drain of money to central Europe and the assignment of offices to foreigners. They wanted Charles to return to Spain. As civil order broke down, artisans and business classes in Castile revolted against the great landholders in the Communero revolt of 1520–21. The revolutionaries had conflicting goals, however, and as they fought one another to exhaustion Charles easily retained his hold on government.

But when Charles entered into wars against the Ottoman Turkish Empire in eastern Europe and on the Mediterranean, and into Christian religious wars in northern and central Europe (see below), he bankrupted even the silver-rich treasury of Spain. After his abdication in 1556, his son Philip II (r. 1556–98) continued the politics of warfare and suffered much the same fate. Even Philip's military victories were financial defeats.

Portugal's Empire

Isabella and Ferdinand united their thrones, creating modern Spain, in 1492, but the western third of the Iberian peninsula, Portugal, remained a separate state. (For 60 years, from 1580 to 1640, it was incorporated into Spain, but otherwise it has remained separate until today.) In terms of worldwide exploration and trade, Portugal, under the leadership of Prince Henry the Navigator, who sponsored many voyages along the coast of Africa, had entered the field earlier and more vigorously than Spain (see the section entitled "Down Africa's Atlantic Coast" in "The Opening of the Atlantic and the Pacific" chapter).

The Portuguese in Africa. Portugal sought souls for Christianity, gold for its national treasury, grain and fish for its domestic food supply, and slaves for its new sugar plantations. Portuguese entrepreneurs, having seen sugar plantations in the eastern Mediterranean, planted their own on Madeira and other islands in the Atlantic Ocean off the coast of Africa. (Spanish landlords and businessmen did the same in the Canary Islands.) These new plantations needed laborers, and Portugal went to Africa to obtain them.

As the Portuguese explored Africa, they also built fortresses—such as El Mina in modern Ghana—as assembly and shipping points for their purchases of slaves and gold. For the most part, the Portuguese remained in their coastal enclaves of fortresses, trading posts, and Christian missionary outposts. At some points, however, they did venture inland to explore, trade, evangelize, and attempt to conquer. From El Mina on the Gold Coast, for example, they went inland to trade directly with Mane and Soninke merchants. In the Kingdom of Kongo, they converted King Nzinga Mbembe (r. 1507–43) and many of his people to Christianity, although the Portuguese slave trade in the Kongo ultimately alienated the people from their king. King Mbembe wrote to the king of Portugal that the slave trade was destroying the Kingdom of Kongo as its people turned predatory toward one another. He wanted the trade stopped on humanitarian grounds. His plea was ignored. The Portuguese, and the Kongolese themselves, desired the profits of the trade.

In Angola, on the west coast, the Portuguese went directly inland to bring slaves to the coast, and claimed the region as their colony in 1484. By 1500, Lisbon was receiving some 1,500 pounds of gold and 10,000 slaves each year from West Africa. On the east coast of Africa, the Portuguese sacked the Swahili trading city of Kilwa to gain control of the Indian Ocean trade, and claimed Mozambique for its rich gold supplies. Although the Portuguese mostly stayed in coastal enclaves such as Sofala, and established an outpost on Mozambique Island, they also traveled inland along the Zambezi River.

14.1

What regions
of the world
did Spain and
Portugal explore?

14.2

14.3

14.4

14.5

The fortress of São Jorge da Mina (later called El Mina), African Gold Coast, 1482. Built at the order of King John II of Portugal in 1482, this fortress—like many others—provided a fortified trading post designed both to protect Portuguese trade from rival Europeans and to serve as a supply base. At the beginning of the sixteenth century, trade was in gold and kola nuts with imports of American crops such as maize and cassava, and transshipment of slaves. It was not until the late seventeenth century that the export of slaves became the main trade on the Gold Coast. The European traders remained mostly in such fortresses along the coast, and relied on African traders to bring goods from the interior to them.

The Portuguese in Brazil. In 1500, a Portuguese expedition to India was blown off course in the Atlantic and landed in Brazil. The Portuguese claimed the land but did little to develop it until pressed by competition from other European powers. By the mid-sixteenth century, they had established some coastal towns (including a colonial capital at Salvador), introduced Jesuit missionaries, and planted the first of the plantations that would make Brazil the first of the huge plantation colonies in the Americas. By 1700 Brazil had 150,000 slaves—half its total population—working its sugar plantations.

By this time, other nations, such as Spain, had developed sugar plantations in the Caribbean, contesting Brazil's leadership and undercutting prices and profits. In 1695, however, gold and diamonds were discovered in the interior mountains of Brazil (in the state later named Minas Gerais, or General Mines), and by the mid-eighteenth century Brazil was mining some 3,000 tons of gold each year, mostly through slave labor. Unfortunately, as often happens with windfall profits from the discovery of raw materials, Portugal and Brazil spent the profits on goods from other countries, especially Britain, without developing new economic enterprises of their own. When the gold began to run out in the mid-eighteenth century, Brazil and Portugal found themselves in debt to Britain, and hooked on British imports, but without further means of paying.

The Portuguese in the Indian Ocean. Throughout the sixteenth century, even taking into account the emerging sugar profits from Brazil, Portugal's main overseas interests lay in Asia. In 1498 Vasco da Gama had extended Portugal's voyages of exploration eastward. Departing from the east coast of Africa, with the assistance of a local pilot who knew the route, he sailed into one of the world's liveliest arenas of trade, the Indian Ocean and the west coast of India. Almost immediately, the Portuguese introduced armed violence into trade relations that had been peaceful. In 1500 an armed Portuguese expedition sailed under Pedro Alvarez Cabral (*c.* 1468–1520) with instructions from the government to establish a fort and trading post at Cochin, India, to promote relations with other "Christian kingdoms" in India, and to impede Muslim shipping to the Red Sea. Cabral had numerous armed engagements with ships in the Indian Ocean and in ports on India's southwest coast. In fighting at Calicut, 54 of his men were killed and substantial goods were lost. In response, Cabral bombarded Cochin, killing between 400 and 500 people and destroying considerable goods and property.

When da Gama returned on his second voyage, in 1502, he came with 21 armed ships to assert Portuguese power. At the height of its Indian Ocean power, Portugal held some 50 ports, with Goa serving as its capital in the Indian Ocean. To the extent that they could enforce it, the Portuguese forced ocean traders to pay them a tax of passage—previously unheard of—and demanded that they put into port at Portuguese centers, especially Goa. The Portuguese were making money as much from their own kind of piracy as from trade. Their reputation for violence spread.

By 1600, however, it became clear that the Portuguese could not maintain their coercive system. Many of their own merchants operated as private traders despite the official state monopoly; Portuguese officers were often corrupt; their military was not well disciplined; and they lacked the manpower to actually enforce the controls they asserted over Indian Ocean traders. Most of all, the much larger oceangoing nations of England and France, and the Netherlands as well, entered the Indian Ocean waters in substantial force, and tiny Portugal was no match for them. Portugal remained in the east, but only as a minor power.

The Spanish and the Portuguese Empires: An Evaluation

Those who claim that Europe's wealth was built on the exploitation of people overseas certainly have some justification, but the experiences of Spain and Portugal demonstrate that exploitation alone was not enough. To build and sustain wealth, countries must be able to use wealth effectively. They must conceive and implement policies of economic growth. They require banks and instruments of exchange to store and transmit money. They need commercial intelligence to create and evaluate strategies for investing capital sensibly and profitably. They must develop efficient means of transporting goods and people. They must not allow their commercial aims to be excessively deflected by warfare. Both Spain and Portugal lacked these facilities. Furthermore, both were hierarchical societies where prestige belonged to those in the aristocracy. It was common in both Spain and Portugal to use mercantile wealth to buy into the nobility and purchase land, and then cease to engage in trade and commerce. Thus, both countries built enormous global empires based on their ocean explorations, but by the end of the sixteenth century both these empires were on the wane, first challenged and then surpassed by countries that established successful commercial communities.

Culturally, Spain and Portugal were far more successful. The influence of their languages and cultures remains dominant in Latin America today, and they continue to have an effect on areas as far-flung as the Philippines (for Spain) and Angola, Mozambique, Goa, and tiny Macao (for Portugal). But as economic and political powers, Spain and Portugal, despite their early, extraordinary successes, were soon eclipsed by the commercially astute nations of northwestern Europe.

Trade and Religion in Western Europe

14.3 What were the background conditions for the rise of the Dutch, French, and British empires?

14.1

14.2

14.3 What were the background conditions for the rise of the Dutch, French, and British empires?

14.4

14.5

Spain's King Charles V and his son Philip II fought wars explicitly devoted to matters of religion. These wars siphoned off the vast treasures that Spain brought from the Americas and diverted her from economic and commercial growth. To understand the choice Spain made for religious warfare, we must analyze the competing claims between Catholics and Protestants that divided Western Europe in the sixteenth and seventeenth centuries. We will also consider scholarly arguments over the extent to which religious philosophy has a direct impact on national economic development. (See "How Do We Know" box, below.)

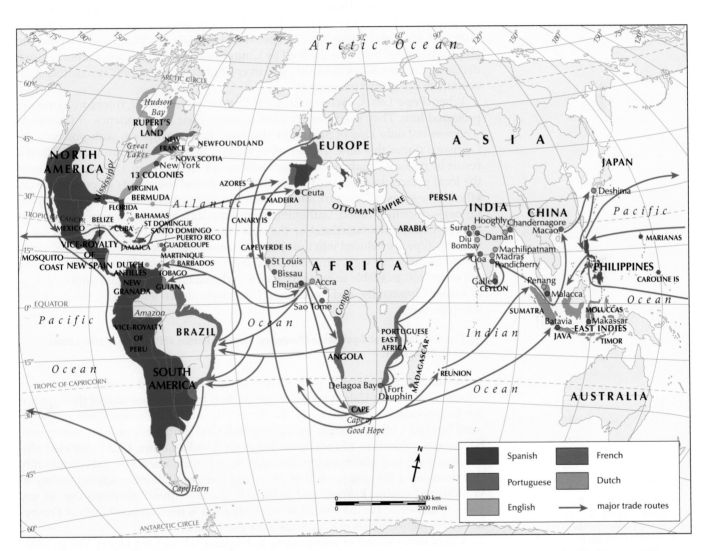

The first European trading empires, about 1750. European sea-borne intercontinental trade was dominated by Spain and Portugal in the sixteenth century. The Spanish rapidly colonized Central America, the Andes Mountain regions, and the Philippines. The Portuguese concentrated on the coast of Brazil, East and West Africa, and the Arabian Sea ports of India. A century later the Dutch, English, and French followed, establishing settler colonies in North America and South Africa and fortified trading posts along the coasts elsewhere. Compare with the maps in the chapter entitled "Nationalism, Imperialism, and Resistance" to see the expansion of European empires.

The Protestant Reformation

Catholicism had won the hearts, spirits, and tithes of the overwhelming majority of the population of Western and central Europe. By 1500 the Roman Catholic Church had become so wealthy and powerful that several reformers charged it with straying from Jesus' early simplicity and his message of compassion for the poor.

Martin Luther (1483–1546), a pious German monk who lived in a monastery in Wittenberg and taught in the university there, shared this criticism of the Church's wealth and further asserted that the Church claimed too much power over individual conscience. Luther doubted the importance of most of the sacraments and the authority of the Church. He kept his doubts private, however, until in 1517 a friar came to Wittenberg selling **indulgences**. These were pardons, marketed by the Church, offering individuals exemption from punishment for their sins in exchange for donations to the Church. Outraged by the idea that pardons were available for purchase and that the Church was the vendor, Luther posted on the door of the castle church his Ninety-five Theses, statements of his belief, asserting that faith alone justifies the believer in the eyes of God. Individuals can and do have direct relationships with God, he wrote; priests were not needed to mediate. Only God had the power to absolve people of their sins. Pressed by Church authorities to recant, Luther refused, declaring the primacy of the individual over Church organization: "It is neither right nor safe to act against conscience."

When Pope Leo X excommunicated Luther, several local rulers in Germany protected him. They used the occasion to assert their independence of Charles V, who was not only king of Spain but also Holy Roman emperor, with powers over Germany. (From this time, Luther often aligned himself with local rulers. When a revolt of peasants against their landlords swept Germany in 1524, Luther urged the local princes to suppress the revolt by force, and thousands of peasants were killed.) The kings of Denmark and Sweden and many of Germany's princes adopted Luther's doctrine (called Lutheranism in America), and this region of northern Europe became the heartland of the new denomination. Printing presses using movable type, introduced into Europe by Johannes Gutenberg about 1450, helped to spread the new message, while Luther's new German translation of the Bible made the sacred text available to ordinary readers who could not read Latin, the language of earlier Christianity, and freed them from dependence on priestly readings and interpretations.

📖 **Read** the **Document: Against the Murdering, Thieving Hordes of Peasants, Martin Luther** on **MyHistoryLab**

In Geneva, Switzerland, John Calvin (1509–64) preached another doctrine of reform. Like Luther, Calvin spoke of justification by faith alone and of the supremacy of individual conscience, and he denied the authority of the Church. Calvin went beyond Luther, though, in arguing that God grants his grace to whomever he chooses, regardless of individual behavior. Unlike Luther, Calvin rejected alliances with existing governments, although he did create a new religious community that dominated the government of the city of Geneva. Calvinism spread widely in Western and central Europe, and in New England, without the patronage of any political authority. (In the United States, Calvinism is the dominant faith of Presbyterianism, named for its elected leaders, or presbyters.)

A third major strand of reform arose in England, where King Henry VIII (r. 1509–47) broke from the Church, not for reasons of doctrine, but to claim authority over the entire Catholic establishment within England—churches, monasteries, and clergy—and to gain for himself a divorce, which the Church had forbidden, from the first of his six wives. Henry had no doctrinal quarrel with Rome. He simply wanted to be head of the English Church himself, and in 1534 Parliament named him "Protector and Only Supreme Head of the Church and Clergy of England," a title that

KEY TERM

indulgences In the Roman Catholic Church, the remission from the punishments of sin, obtainable through good works or special prayers and granted by the Church through the merits of Christ and the saints. In the sixteenth century, the Church began to sell indulgences, precipitating the reforms of Martin Luther.

What were the background conditions for the rise of the Dutch, French, and British empires?

John Calvin weighing the Bible against popish pomp. Woodcut. Calvin had studied the writings of the first generation of reformers, including Martin Luther, and accepted without question the idea of justification by faith alone and the Biblical foundation of religious authority. This contemporary woodcut shows him weighing what he saw as the extraneous ceremonial trappings and overweening bishops of the Catholic Church against the simple truth of the Bible.

was passed on in slightly modified form to later English sovereigns. In England, Henry's new church was called Anglican. (Its members in the United States are called Episcopalians.)

Each of the three reform movements rejected the authority of the pope, stressed the freedom of individual conscience in matters of faith, and permitted their clergy to marry. Collectively, these various protests against the power and doctrine of the Catholic Church were called Protestantism, or the **Protestant Reformation**.

The Counter-Reformation. Its religious monopoly challenged, the Catholic Church countered with the Council of Trent, a gathering of Church authorities who met irregularly for 18 years, from 1545 to 1563, to address questions of Church doctrine and internal reform. The Council reaffirmed the basic doctrines of Catholicism. It reasserted the necessity of the celibacy of the clergy and encouraged greater religious devotion among them. And it created new religious orders to purify the Church and transmit its teachings. The Society of Jesus, founded in 1534 by Ignatius Loyola (1491–1556), was especially dedicated to education, secular as well as religious, and to carrying the message of the Church around the world. From 1540 Francis Xavier (1506–52) introduced the Jesuit vision to India, Indonesia, and Japan, baptizing thousands of new Christians. In Paris in 1625, Vincent de Paul (1581–1660) began his work among the wretched of the slums, a humanitarian mission that continues around the world today.

The Catholic Church was fighting for an international, universal vision of the world under its own leadership, while the various Protestant movements encouraged separate national states, each free to choose its own religion.

KEY TERM

Protestant Reformation The movement, in sixteenth-century Europe, in which Luther, Calvin, Henry VIII, and others broke away from the Catholic Church.

The Reformation in Europe. The tide of religious reform was felt throughout Europe and changed its political map. The early commitment of most of northern Europe to Calvinism, Lutheranism, or Anglicanism was counterbalanced by the recovery of Catholicism of France and Poland. Counter-Reformation zeal, combined with political confrontation and dynastic rivalry, culminated in the Thirty Years War (1618–48), fought across Europe's heartland at enormous cost.

Spanish Defeats

Inspired by Protestant doctrines and chafing under Spanish rule, the Netherlands, including today's Holland and Belgium, rose in revolt against control by the Habsburg family. Although geographically small, the Netherlands was among the wealthiest of Philip's possessions. Netherlanders were offended by the excessive quantity and deficient quality of the Spanish administrators sent to govern them. They also feared that Philip would extend to the Netherlands and all non-Catholics the **Spanish Inquisition**, a royal tribunal originally established in 1481 to monitor and enforce proper Catholic observance, especially among Muslims and Jews who were converting under pressure of the *reconquista*.

Many of the peoples of the Netherlands had abandoned Catholicism for new Protestant movements, and many Protestants from other countries had come seeking asylum. In the Netherlands, Protestants and Catholics had reached an

KEY TERM

Spanish Inquisition A court established with the consent of the Vatican to search out and punish Jews who claimed to have converted to Christianity but were still secretly practicing the Jewish religion, which had been outlawed in Spain in 1492. Subsequently the Inquisition, which was not bound by civil law and which employed torture, also turned against Christians who were not properly observant.

CHAPTER FOURTEEN: THE UNIFICATION OF WORLD TRADE 1500–1776

14.1

14.2

14.3

What were the
background
conditions for the
rise of the Dutch,
French, and
British empires?

14.4

14.5

accommodation, and neither community wished to see that harmony destroyed by the Inquisition. Philip's government refused to pay attention, and the Netherlands erupted in fury. A civil war ensued in which thousands were killed, property was destroyed, and churches were desecrated. By 1576, however, the Netherlands had suffered enough, and representatives of all the Netherlands united across religious lines to expel the Spanish. In the same year, Queen Elizabeth I of England (r. 1558–1603), the daughter of Henry VIII, publicly aligned her country with the rebels in the Netherlands and began to pursue a policy of alliance with Protestant forces throughout

HOW DO WE KNOW?

Weber and Tawney on Religion and Capitalism

In *The Protestant Ethic and the Spirit of Capitalism*, the social scientist Max Weber (1864–1920) argued that Protestantism's emphasis on individual achievement and divine grace tended to promote economic enterprise and capitalism. Weber claimed that Protestant ministers urged their followers to demonstrate their virtue through devotion to thrift, discipline, industriousness, and business.

> Striving for wealth is objectionable only when it has the aim of a carefree and merry existence. But as exercise of duty in a calling it is not only morally permitted but actually commanded … Worldly Protestant asceticism acted effectively against the spontaneous enjoyment of wealth; it limited consumption, especially that of luxuries. On the other hand, it eliminated traditional inhibitions against the acquisition of property; it burst the bonds of the profit motive by not only legalizing it, but even viewing it as directly willed by God … He desired rational and utilitarian use of wealth for the purposes of the individual and the community. (cited in Columbia University, *Man* Vol 2 pp. 84, 89)

According to Weber, Protestantism encouraged entrepreneurs to dedicate themselves to making money and laborers to finding satisfaction in hard work.

> The bourgeois entrepreneur could, and felt that he ought to, follow his economic self-interest in the certainty of being in God's good grace, and of being visibly blessed by Him. This remained true as long as he observed the formal rules of the game, kept his morals spotless, and did not make objectionable use of his wealth. In addition, the power of religious asceticism made available to him sober, conscientious, eminently capable workers who regarded their labor as their divinely ordained purpose in life. Even more, it gave him the comforting assurance that the unequal distribution of the goods of this world was the direct consequence of God's Providence which followed out His unknown aims by these distinctions as well as by this selective show of grace. (cited in ibid., p. 93)

Weber extended these arguments to assert that, ultimately, Protestant religious leaders had made the pursuit of profit through hard work into the essence of religion.

Subsequent authors, however, notably the British social historian R.H. Tawney, rejected Weber's arguments. Capitalist thought and practice had preceded Protestantism, and some Catholic areas, such as northern Italy and parts of France, were strongly capitalistic, while some Protestant areas, notably in north Germany, were not. "There was plenty of the 'capitalist spirit' in fifteenth-century Venice and Florence, or in south Germany and Flanders, for the simple reason that these areas were the greatest commercial and financial centers of the age, though all were, at least nominally, Catholic" (Tawney, p. 262, n. 32). It was difficult to show any historically consistent correlation between religious doctrine and economic policy.

Tawney's most significant quarrel with Weber, however, was over Weber's argument that religion had ceded the central place in life to the pursuit of economic gain, at least temporarily. Weber was not pleased with this transformation, but he claimed to observe it. Tawney, on the contrary, argued that moral issues concerning the welfare of the entire society always underpin economic ones. They never become secondary:

> A reasonable estimate of economic organization must allow for the fact that, unless industry is to be paralyzed by recurrent revolts on the part of outraged human nature, it must satisfy criteria which are not purely economic … natural appetites may be purified or restrained, as, in fact, in some considerable measure they already have been, by being submitted to the control of some larger body of interests. (ibid., p. 233)

Debates over the relationship between religious doctrine and business practice continue unabated and unresolved today in relation to religion in general and to all major religions in particular. These debates continue also outside the Western world. For example, today, when East Asian economies are flourishing, Confucian traditions are praised for encouraging development. A century ago, when those economies were lagging, the same Confucian traditions, interpreted differently, were blamed for the lack of development.

- Can you cite examples of religious sentiments influencing economic actions?
- Can you cite examples of economic actions having no relation to religious, moral, or social concerns?
- Do you side with Weber's argument that to a large degree the pursuit of economic growth has taken precedence over religious, moral, and social concerns? Or would you agree with Tawney that, in the long run, economic issues must always be subordinated to larger issues?

Europe. In reply, Philip II prepared to invade England. In 1588 the Spanish Armada set sail for England with 130 ships, 30,000 men, and 2,400 pieces of artillery. In an astonishing reversal, the Armada was destroyed by the English and by a fierce storm, which was quickly named "the Protestant wind." The northern Netherlands won its independence in 1609, although Spain did not acknowledge it until 1648, after years of intermittent warfare.

The Thirty Years War. The year 1648 brought the Peace of Westphalia, which ended a century of religious warfare in Europe, in general, and a destructive Thirty Years War in particular. Most of the fighting involved the Habsburg rulers, and mostly they suffered losses. In 1555 the Peace of Augsburg had decided that in the Holy Roman Empire (the political structure that dominated central Europe), each constituent political region would have its own religion—*cuius regio, eius religio*, "whose realm, his religion." Each region—there were at least 300 of them—would follow the religion of its local ruler. But over the years, as older rulers died, competition arose in choosing their successors, and thus the religion of the region. In addition, new strands of Protestantism, such as Calvinism, sought to expand the range of options beyond Lutheranism and Catholicism.

In 1608 the Protestant states formed a Protestant League to defend their interests; in 1609, the Catholics followed suit. The Thirty Years War was taking shape. It involved not only religious warfare, but also warfare of local states against one another for purely political gain, and also warfare of local states against the authority of the Holy Roman emperor. Outside powers, including the Dutch Republic, the Swedish Empire, and the Kingdom of France, as well as the Spanish Habsburg Empire, took sides, more for reasons of national power and pride than for religion; the mostly Catholic French, for example, backed the Protestants against the Spanish, the Catholic Habsburgs. The Peace of Westphalia, which attempted to bring order from the chaos of the varying warring factions and goals, largely brought an end to the religious warfare, and also confirmed the significance of political authority. Even the small states within the Holy Roman Empire were validated as independent entities. As the Holy Roman Empire itself was revealed as a shell, the concept of the nation-state emerged more powerful.

Habsburg Spain came out a loser once again. It had backed its Habsburg relatives, the discredited Holy Roman emperors. It had to recognize formally the loss of the Dutch Republic. It had paid a heavy price for its continuous warfare against the Islamic Ottoman Empire in southeastern Europe, especially in contributing one segment of the navy that had successfully opposed the Ottoman fleets at Lepanto in 1571. In 1640, Portugal, which had been united with Spain since 1580, declared its independence once again, and other constituent units of Spain, especially Catalonia in the northeast, fought costly, if unsuccessful, wars for independence. Finally, about mid-century, the stream of silver from the Americas—which had financed much of the warfare—dried up, dwindling from 135 million pesos in the decade 1591–1600 to 19 million in 1651–60. Spain had squandered a fabulous windfall of silver and gold. Its preeminent position in Europe following its discovery and conquest of the Americas was now broken. England, France, and the Netherlands emerged as the rising powers of Europe; their self-confidence and their economies flourished; and their merchant classes organized to travel the world. They were increasingly powerful nation-states.

The Dutch Republic: Seaborne Merchant Enterprise

In the early seventeenth century, the Dutch had the most efficient economic system in Europe. The Dutch Republic bordered the North Sea and lived from its largesse. Fishing was its great national industry. One of every four Dutch people was reliant on the herring industry—catching, salting, smoking, pickling, and selling. Others depended on cod fishing and whaling. Using windmills to pump water from low lands enclosed in dikes, the Dutch reclaimed land from the sea—364,565 acres between 1540 and 1715—and from inland lakes—another 84,638 acres. With such an investment of capital and effort the Dutch worked their land carefully and efficiently. They developed new methods of crop rotation, planting turnips in the fall to provide winter food for humans and sheep. At other times of year they raised peas, beans, and clover to restore nitrogen to the soil. With these cropping patterns, the Dutch no longer had to leave one-third of their land fallow each year. They farmed it all, increasing productivity by 50 percent. In addition, the Dutch established one of the largest textile industries in Europe, based on wool from their own sheep and on huge quantities imported from England.

On the seas and in the rivers, the Dutch were sailing 10,000 ships as early as 1600, and for the next century they dominated the shipping of northern Europe. From the Baltic they brought timber and grain to Amsterdam and Western Europe. In exchange, from the ports of Portugal, Spain, and France they carried salt, oil, wool, wine, and, most of all, the silver and gold of the New World. Often they warehoused in Amsterdam the trade goods en route to other ports, earning additional profits on the storage. They used substantial amounts of the timber themselves to build the most seaworthy, yet economical, ships of the day.

14.1
14.2
14.3
14.4
14.5

What were the background conditions for the rise of the Dutch, French, and British empires?

The Return to Amsterdam of the Dutch East India Fleet, Andries van Eertvelt, 1599. In 1602 the Dutch East India Company was granted a monopoly over Dutch trade and authorized to seize control of the Portuguese trade routes in the Indian Ocean. The company owned a fleet of ships, armed with cannon, which carried pepper, indigo, raw silk, saltpeter, and textiles from India to Western Europe. In the later 1600s, large-scale exports of textiles were also carried from India to Africa in payment for slaves going to the Caribbean. (Johnny Van Haeften Gallery, London)

SOURCE

National Joint Stock Companies: Instruments of Trade and Colonization

National joint stock companies were one of the key commercial innovations of Dutch, French, and British financiers in the seventeenth century, giving them an enormous advantage in overseas trade. Forerunners of the modern business corporation, the companies sold stock publicly, sometimes for a single expedition, but more commonly for all the expeditions and activities of the company. Financiers invested in expectation of the great profits that might come from successful shipping ventures. Their potential losses and liabilities were limited to the value of their investment; the rest of their personal property was protected. Individual states gave legal charters to these companies in expectation of the benefits of trade for the country. These national companies were chartered for expeditions throughout the world. Those to the Americas were designated "West India Companies," and those toward Asia were "East India Companies." The companies of each state usually saw themselves in competition with one another, sometimes leading to armed struggle. And their missions included colonization, and sometimes proselytizing, as well as trade.

The government-issued "Edict Providing for the Establishment of a Company of the West Indies" of 1664, establishing the French West India Company, is representative of the aspirations of the state and of the merchants looking to the Americas for both settlement and trade:

> We have recognized that colonial trade and navigation are the only and true means of raising commerce to the brilliant position it holds in foreign lands; to achieve this and to stimulate our subjects to form powerful companies we have promised them such great advantages that there is reason to hope that all those who take interests in the glory of the State, and who wish to profit by honorable and legitimate means will willingly participate ... but as it is not sufficient for these companies to take possession of the lands which we grant them, and have them cleared and cultivated by the people they send there at great expense, if they do not equip themselves to carry on ... commerce ... it is also absolutely necessary, in order to carry on this trade, to provide numerous ships to carry each day the goods which are to be sold in the said countries, and bring back to France those which they export. (cited in Columbia University, *Contemporary* vol. 1, pp. 815–20)

Investment in the Company was open to foreigners as well as to native-born French.

The Company was "obliged to introduce into the lands granted above, the number of clergy necessary for preaching the Holy Gospel, and instructing these peoples in the faith of the Catholic, Apostolic and Roman religion; and also to build churches." It also had many of the attributes of a sovereign state:

> The said Company may build forts in all places it shall judge necessary for the defense of the said country ... may arm and equip for war such number of vessels as it shall deem fitting for the defense of the said countries and the security of the said commerce ... may negotiate peace and alliances in our name, with the Kings and Princes of the countries where it wishes to establish its settlements and trade ... and, in case of insult, declare war on them, attack them, and defend itself by force of arms. (Ibid.)

In the Indian Ocean, trade in spices was a large part of the Companies' business. Between them, the British and Dutch East India Companies carried 13.5 million pounds of pepper to Europe in the peak year of 1670, the British share mostly from India, the Dutch share from Indonesia. Other goods included indigo, raw silk, saltpeter, and, increasingly, Indian textiles. There were also large-scale exports of textiles carried by Europeans from India to Africa in payment for slaves going to the Caribbean.

The Companies' ships were armed. Their representatives established fortresses and trading centers on the coasts of Asia and of the Americas, and the Companies became, in effect, miniature governments. Malachy Postlethwayt, in his *Universal Dictionary* of 1751, wrote that the Dutch East India Company

> makes peace and war at pleasure, and by its own authority; administers justice to all ... settles colonies, builds fortifications, levies troops, maintains numerous armies and garrisons, fits out fleets, and coins money. (cited in Tracy, *The Political Economy of Merchant Empires*, p. 196)

In India, in the seventeenth century, the British, French, and Dutch East India Companies set up trading posts within towns. Until the end of the century, the Mughal emperors and local governments generally welcomed the foreign traders as the means of stimulating the Indian economy through trade and enriching the government through taxes. Following its victories at Plassey in 1757 and Buxar in 1765, however, the British East India Company became the *de facto* government of the province of Bengal in India—with the right to collect taxes and the responsibility for providing order and administration. The Company's holdings continued to expand over the next century, until it was effectively the ruler of almost all of India. The British government regulated the East India Company from its founding in 1600, and finally disbanded it and took over direct rule of India after the Indian revolt of 1857.

KEY TERM

bourse Another name for stock exchange, especially in Europe.

The Dutch also developed commercial institutions to underpin their dominance in trade. The **bourse**, or stock exchange, was opened in Amsterdam in the mid-sixteenth century as the Dutch were gaining control of the Baltic trade, and it was reopened in 1592 as they captured a dominant role in supplying grain to Mediterranean countries. In 1598 they initiated a Chamber of Insurance; in 1609 the Bank of Amsterdam was established. This bank accepted coins from all over the world, assessed their gold and silver content, and exchanged them for gold florin coins that were fixed in weight and value and became the standard everywhere. The Dutch government guaranteed the safety of deposits in the national bank, thereby attracting capital from throughout Europe. Depositors were able to draw checks on their accounts. For two centuries, until the French Revolution in 1789, Amsterdam was the financial center of Europe.

In 1602 Dutch businessmen founded the Dutch East India Company, a joint stock company dedicated to trade in Asia. The Company captured several Portuguese ports, but concentrated on the most lucrative of all the East Asian centers, Java and the Moluccas, the Spice Islands of today's Indonesia. In 1619 the Dutch East India Company founded Jakarta, which served as its regional headquarters until 1950, when Indonesia won its independence. In 1623 they seized Amboina in the Moluccas, killing a group of Englishmen they found there, and forcing the English back to India. The profits from these possessions reinforced Dutch economic precedence in Europe.

In 1600 a group of Dutch traders reached Japan. By 1641, all other foreigners had been expelled, but, because they did not engage in missionary activity, the Dutch were permitted a small settlement on Deshima Island, off Nagasaki, and for two centuries they were the only European traders allowed in Japan. In 1652, the Dutch captured from the Portuguese the Cape of Good Hope at the southernmost tip of Africa, and established there the first settlement of Afrikaners, South Africans of Dutch descent.

In the Americas, the Dutch West India Company raided the shipping of the Spanish and the Portuguese, and then founded their own rich sugar plantations in Caracas, Curaçao, and Guiana. For a few decades they held Bahia in Brazil, but the Portuguese drove them out in 1654. In North America, they established New Amsterdam on Manhattan Island.

Despite their commercial skill and success, the Dutch could not ultimately retain their supremacy. The English Navigation Act of 1651 permitted imports to England and its dependencies only in English ships or in those of the exporting country, and this effectively restricted Dutch shipping. Three indecisive, draining wars followed, from 1652 to 1674. Additional years of warfare on land against France further exhausted Dutch resources. In 1700 the Dutch Republic had a population of 2 million people; at that time the population of the British Isles was 9 million, and that of France 19 million. An aggressive, skilled, small country simply could not continue to compete with two aggressive, skilled, large countries.

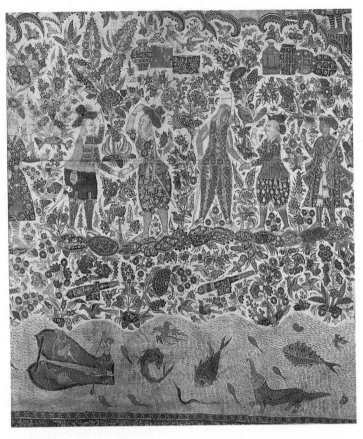

Indian cotton cloth, late seventeenth century. This detailed portrayal of Dutch traders suggests that they have come far across the seas to trade in a rich array of goods. The Indian gentleman on the far right may find the Dutch doffing of caps and handshakes a strange form of greeting, quite different from the form used in India of joining one's hands in the "namaste" salutation.

14.1

14.2

14.3

What were the background conditions for the rise of the Dutch, French, and British empires?

14.4

14.5

France: A Nation Consolidated

Between 1562 and 1598, France endured nearly four decades of civil warfare because the crown was unable to control the various factions, religious groups, and regions of the country. Struggles between Catholics and Protestants, called Huguenots in France, helped to fuel the warfare. The worst moment came in 1572 as the queen of France, Catherine de' Medici, unleashed the "St. Bartholomew's Day massacre" in

14.1

14.2

14.3 What were the background conditions for the rise of the Dutch, French, and British empires?

14.4

14.5

which thousands of Huguenots were murdered. In 1589 Henry of Navarre, a Huguenot, who had escaped the massacre only by temporarily renouncing his faith in favor of Catholicism, came to the throne as Henry IV (r. 1589–1610). As king, he recognized the importance of Catholicism to the majority of the French people and to the stability of his rule, so he once more abandoned his Protestant faith and joined the Catholic Church, making the apocryphal comment, "Paris is worth a Mass." In 1598, hoping to heal the schism between the religious communities, and perhaps remaining emotionally committed to the Protestant community, he issued the Edict of Nantes, which gave Protestants equal civil rights with Catholics. Twelve years later, he was assassinated by a Catholic militant.

Louis XIII (r. 1610–43), his successor, chose as his chief minister Cardinal Richelieu. Although a cardinal in the Roman Catholic Church, Richelieu was more nationalist than clerical. Following his advice, the king amended the Edict of Nantes, restricting some of the civil rights of Protestants, and some of their rights to control private militias, but reaffirming their rights to practice their religion. He joined with Protestant rulers in Sweden, the Netherlands, and parts of Germany to defeat the Catholic Habsburg Empire in order to increase the stature of France. He built up France's armies, cultivated allies among France's neighbors, and encouraged the French nobility to invest in trade by land and sea.

His successor, Louis XIV, in an extraordinarily long and forceful reign (r. 1643–1715), made France the most powerful country in Europe. Under the Sun King, as Louis was known, France set the standard throughout Europe for administration, war, diplomacy, language, thought, literature, music, architecture, fashion, cooking, and etiquette. Although they had been slower than other European countries to enter transoceanic trade, the French now began to assert a global presence, trading in India, Madagascar, the American Great Lakes, and the Mississippi River; establishing colonies in the West Indies; and staking a claim to Canada. By 1690 Louis XIV had raised an army of 400,000 men, equal to the combined armies of England, the Habsburg Empire, Prussia, Russia, and the Dutch Republic. At this time, the French navy was also larger than that of the English, with 120 ships of the line (warships) compared to the English navy's 100. Also, as we have seen, in 1700, France had a population of 19 million, more than double that of the British Isles.

Louis XIV boasted "L'état, c'est moi" ("I am the state"), by which he meant that the powers of the state rested in him alone. His leading religious adviser, Bishop Jacques-Bénigne Bossuet (1627–1704), linked the king's power to divine right, asserting that "Royalty has its origin in the divinity itself." Louis continued to assert the right of the king to appoint the Catholic clergy in France, and in 1685 he revoked the Edict of Nantes in the belief that a single, dominant religion was more important than the toleration of minorities within his kingdom. This act cost France the services of many of its Huguenot artisans, who fled to the Netherlands, Britain, and Brandenburg (Germany).

Louis XIV's chief economic adviser, Jean-Baptiste Colbert (1625–96), pursued a policy of mercantilism—fostering the economic welfare of his own state against all others—by strengthening state control over the national economy even more aggressively than had Richelieu. To facilitate trade, he abolished local taxes on trade throughout central France (a region as large as England), although his government was not powerful enough to do away with these internal tariffs throughout the entire country. Colbert established a Commercial Code to unify business practice throughout the country. To improve communication and transportation, he built roads and canals, including a link between the Bay of Biscay and the Mediterranean. He set quality standards for hand manufacturers and gave financial incentives to the French manufacturers of such luxury goods as silks, tapestries, glass, and woolens. Meanwhile, the needs of the army created huge national markets for uniforms, equipment, and provisions. All these policies benefited private business as well as the state. Nevertheless, many businesspeople, who sought greater freedom of trade, rejected the mercantilist assertion that the export of gold and silver weakened the national economy and that state monopolies should dominate certain economic fields, including much of foreign trade.

The growth of French military and economic strength disturbed the **balance of power** among the leading states of Europe and precipitated a series of wars. The War of the League of Augsburg, 1688–97, and the War of the Spanish Succession, 1702–13, reduced France's power when she was forced to cede to Britain the North American colonies of Newfoundland and Nova Scotia and all French claims to the Hudson Bay territory. Britain began to pull ahead in overseas possessions.

🔍 View the **Closer Look**: Versailles on **MyHistoryLab**

Britain: Establishing Commercial Supremacy

In the same wars, Britain won from Spain the *asiento*, the right to carry all the slave cargoes from Africa to Spanish America, plus one shipload of more conventional goods each year to Panama. These officially recognized trading rights also provided cover for British ships to engage in the business of piracy and smuggling, which flourished in the Caribbean, where buccaneers preyed on Spanish commerce.

In the eighteenth century the most valued properties in the Americas were the sugar-producing islands of the Caribbean. In the Atlantic the most valuable trade was in human cargo—the slaves who worked the sugar plantations. In Asia, control of sea lanes and of the outposts established by the various East India companies was the prize.

Competition for dominance in all three regions continued between the French and the British through three more wars in the eighteenth century: the War of Austrian Succession, 1740–48; the Seven Years War, 1756–63; and the War of American Independence (the American Revolution), 1775–81. These wars demonstrated the importance of sea power, and here Britain triumphed. Around 1790, the French population outnumbered the British 28 million to 16 million, and French armies outnumbered the British by an even greater ratio, 180,000 to 40,000. But the British navy had 195 ships of the line, compared with France's 81.

Suffering defeats at sea, the French retreated from their colonial positions. In the Peace Settlement at Paris in 1763, at the end of the Seven Years War, they turned over their immense, but thinly populated, holdings in North America east of the Mississippi to the British, and those west of the Mississippi to Spain. They kept their rich, sugar-producing islands in the Caribbean: Saint-Domingue (Haiti), Guadeloupe, and Martinique. In India, although they lost out in other locations, they kept Pondicherry on the southeast coast and a few additional commercial locations. The French navy was deployed against the British in America during the American Revolution, but it was completely crushed during the Napoleonic Wars. The British, although they lost the 13 colonies of the United States in 1783, triumphed everywhere else because of the great strength of their navy. They held Canada. They held their islands in the Caribbean. They increased their holdings in India, and they dominated the sea lanes both across the Atlantic Ocean and through the Indian Ocean.

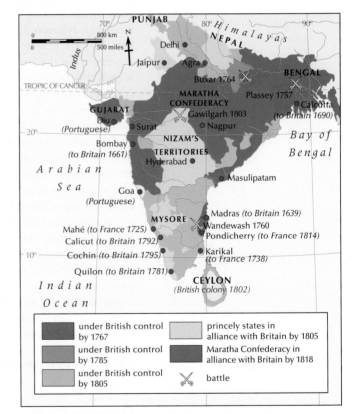

British power in India to 1818. The weakening of the Mughal Empire created a situation that was exploited by the British and French East India Companies. They created strategic alliances with local independent princes and competed for power on land and sea. With Robert Clive's victory at Plassey (1757), the English gained Bengal, a power base that allowed them to expand steadily. Their control over India was not secure, however, until their final defeat of the Maratha confederation in 1818.

14.1

14.2

14.3

14.4   What is a
"nation-state"?

14.5

Institutionally, Britain surpassed all other European countries, even the Netherlands, in supporting sophisticated economic enterprise. Recognizing the importance of a stable currency, England had fixed the value of the pound sterling in 1560–61 at 4 ounces of silver, and maintained that valuation for two and a half centuries. The Bank of England, created in 1694, could transact its business with a currency of fixed value. Moreover, Britain never defaulted on her debts and so earned the trust of the international financial community. In times of war as well as peace, Britain could borrow whatever sums she needed. Politically, Britain developed a new system of constitutional monarchy after 1688 that gave strong support to private commercial interests, as we shall see in more detail in the chapter entitled "Migration." The French later ridiculed Britain as "a nation of shopkeepers," but geographically, militarily, institutionally, politically, and agriculturally, the British were building the capacity to become the most effective businessmen in the world. They were building a nation-state and a capitalist economy.

The Nation-state

14.4   What is a "nation-state"?

The term "nation-state" is generally used to describe a politically sovereign state with a socially cohesive population. The *state* occupies a geographic territory, is administered by its own independent government, and controls adequate size and force not to be swallowed up by another. The *nation* is based on some combination of shared language, religion, history, ethnicity, and aspiration. Usually the nation also defines itself, in part, in terms of its relationships with other nation-states. Nation-states may emerge from the break-up of larger empires—which may contain several nations within themselves—or from the coalescence of small units into larger ones through conquest or merger. Both these processes had been continuing in Western Europe for centuries. Small units, such as the region around Paris under Hugh Capet, were expanding into states, while large units, like Charlemagne's empire, were dissolving.

The nation-states of Europe developed relatively efficient central governments that were capable of collecting taxes, keeping the peace, and raising and deploying armies and navies effectively to wage war. Their authority was generally recognized and accepted—even welcomed—by most of the people within their borders. That authority was different in different nation-states: England, France, and Portugal were monarchies; the Netherlands was ruled by a coalition of businessmen; and Spain was part of the larger Habsburg Empire.

Nation-states took an interest in the economic welfare of their people, although there, too, different states adopted different policies at different times, some capitalist, some mercantilist but with independent merchants, some state-controlled. They engaged in external, overseas trade and commerce and, in this period of time, colonization. The development of overseas trade and colonization was a large part of their transformation from small, locally governed units into nation-states.

Q View the **Closer Look: The Encampment of the Imperial Army** on **MyHistoryLab**

Diverse Cultures, Diverse Trade Systems

14.5   What were the goals of Peter the Great?

In their competition for trade routes and colonies around the world, the nation-states of Europe came to define themselves in relation to one another and in relation to the other civilizations with which they were engaging. Conversely, other peoples around

14.1

14.2

14.3

14.4

14.5

What were the goals of Peter the Great?

the world began to redefine themselves politically and culturally in terms of European experiences. This self-definition in terms of "**the other**" is certainly not the only element in the definition of the nation-state, but it is important.

By the mid-1700s, the nation-states of Western Europe had become the object of both fear and emulation. They were feared because of their economic and military powers. They could, and did, fight wars, conquer territories, create colonies, and dominate trade networks. Two of the most ancient societies of East Asia, China and Japan, kept the Europeans at arm's length for centuries, keeping their ports mostly closed against the new arrivals. Other governments emulated the Europeans, in order to develop the strength to resist them even while becoming more like them. This was the response of Russia under Peter the Great.

Western European nation-states had become an exception in the prominence and independence they afforded to their merchant communities. In most other parts of Eurasia, huge polyglot empires, composed of diverse peoples speaking diverse languages, were more typical than small nation-states. Their emperors usually allowed trade and traders to flourish, but only under imperial supervision or outright control. The empires of Russia, the Ottomans, the Mughals, China (under the Ming and Qing dynasties), Japan, and Southeast Asia provide case studies of various styles of political rule and relationships between rulers and merchants. As Europeans arrived, these empires had to design policies to deal with them. Some of the empires were losing control of their own administrations as European traders gained increasing power in Asia. Others saw the threat of overwhelming European economic invasion and took precautions to avoid that fate. Russia introduced Western-style education and manners for its upper class, prepared new ports to take advantage of new possibilities in commerce, built up its armaments to ensure that it would not be left behind militarily, and brutalized and taxed its serfs to pay for the innovations. China and Japan chose instead to shut the European traders out.

Russia's Empire under Peter the Great

At the end of the seventeenth century Russia had little direct contact with the market economies of northwestern Europe. The country was geographically remote by land, and by sea its principal ocean port was Archangel (Arkhangelsk) at the extreme north, on the White Sea, ice-bound for most of the year. The foreign trade that did exist was carried by foreign ships traveling Russia's great rivers, especially the Volga. Russia belonged to the Greek Orthodox branch of Christianity, so communication with the Church of Rome and its Western European networks was also limited. Mongol rule had oriented Russia's ties more toward central Asia than toward Western Europe. Finally, to the west, Russia was surrounded by generally hostile neighbors: Swedes, Poles, Germans, and Lithuanians.

Russia began to take its modern form only after Ivan III (r. 1462–1505) overthrew Mongol domination in 1480. Muscovy, the territory around Moscow, became the core of an expanding independent state. At first, Russia expanded southeastward, defeating the khanate of Astrakhan in 1556 and capturing the Volga River basin south to the Caspian Sea with its access to the silk trade of Persia. It also expanded eastward all the way to the Pacific (1649), capturing Siberia and its rich population of fur-bearing animals; their pelts became one of Russia's principal exports.

Because of its isolation and foreign rule, Russia had only a tiny urban trading class and very few big city markets. As late as 1811, only 4 percent of its population was urban. The overwhelming majority of its people lived as **serfs**, bound not directly to specific owners, but to specific land and its landlords, with little possibility for economic, social, or geographic mobility. After 1675 landlords gained the right to sell serfs off the land, even to urban owners. Occasional serf uprisings, such as that led by Stepan Razin (Stenka Razin; d. 1671) in 1667, were brutally suppressed, and the gulf between free people and serfs increased.

KEY TERMS

the other Using the term "the other" establishes a relationship between two individuals or groups that define themselves in terms of contrast with each other. Normally the definition implies that one has most of the virtues, and "the other" has most of the vices. Occasionally the word is used in verb form, "othering," meaning the process of defining "the other" in negative terms, and oneself in terms of positive virtues.

serf An agricultural worker or peasant bound to the land and legally dependent on the lord. Serfs had their own homes, plots, and livestock, but they owed the lord labor, dues, and services. These services could be commuted to rent, but serfs remained chattels of the lord unless they were emancipated, or escaped. Serfdom declined in Western Europe in the late medieval period, but persisted in parts of eastern Europe until the nineteenth century.

14.1

14.2

14.3

14.4

14.5

What were the
goals of Peter the
Great?

When Peter I, the Great (r. 1682–96 as co-emperor, or tsar, with his half-brother; 1696–1725 as sole emperor), became sole emperor, he saw Sweden, the most powerful country in north-central Europe, as his principal external enemy. Sweden already held Finland and the entire eastern shore of the Baltic, bottling up Russia without any Baltic port. Worse, in a crushing blow, 8,000 Swedish troops survived a siege and defeated 40,000 Russian attackers at the Battle of Narva in 1700. In 1695 he failed to capture the Ottoman fortress on the Sea of Azov, the gateway to the Black Sea, although he returned in the next year by land and sea, with about ten times the number of troops as the Ottomans, and triumphed.

Recognizing the general weaknesses of his nation, Peter set out to construct in Russia a powerful state based on a powerful army and navy. In 1697, traveling under an assumed name in order to evade royal protocol, Peter embarked on a "Grand Embassy of Western Europe," especially England and the Netherlands, but also Baltic ports and the Holy Roman Empire. He searched for allies for the wars he expected against the Turks, as Russia pushed further toward the Black Sea; he gathered information on the economic, cultural, and military-industrial practices of the Western European powers; and for several months he even worked as a ship's carpenter in Amsterdam.

Impressed by the strength of the Western European countries, Peter invited military experts from the West to Russia to train and lead his troops. He bought Western European artillery and copied it. He established naval forces and reorganized the army along Western lines, in uniformed regiments, armed with muskets. He promoted metallurgy, mining, and the manufacture of textiles, largely as means of supplying his troops. By 1703–04 Peter had started to build a new capital, an all-weather port and "window on the West," in St. Petersburg, on land that he conquered from Sweden. Commercially, geographically, and architecturally, he designed St. Petersburg as a Western city. In the construction of the city 30,000 people died from disease, drowning, or lack of food.

In 1709, when Sweden again invaded Russia, Peter was prepared. He retreated until the Swedes fell from the exhaustion of pursuing him through the severe Russian winter. Then, holding his ground at Poltava in south Russia, he defeated the remaining Swedish troops. The Swedish army was finished as an imperial force, and Russia began to seize additional Baltic possessions.

Peter's goals for Westernization were not exclusively military. He wanted Russia to be counted among the powers of Europe, and this would require cultural and economic ties as well. Peter required Western-style education for all male nobles. He established schools for their children, and sent many to study in Western Europe. He demanded that aristocrats acquire the morals and tastes of the European elites. He made them abandon their Russian dress in favor of the clothing of Western Europe, and he forced the men to shave or trim their beards in the Western style. He introduced "cipher schools" for teaching basic reading and arithmetic, established a printing press, established and edited Russia's first newspaper, and funded the Academy of Sciences, which opened in 1724, a year before his death. Collectively, these reforms drove a wedge between the nobility and the mass of Russians.

Economically, Peter pushed for the creation of new enterprises. He built a fleet on the Baltic and encouraged exports. He organized new companies headed by groups of Russians and foreigners, and supplied them with working capital and serf laborers. He accepted the mercantilist concept of an economically strong state and saw no role for a free market in achieving it. To finance these state-organized initiatives, Peter introduced heavy taxes, which fell especially severely on the peasantry.

No democrat, Peter demanded loyalty and obedience to himself. He created a new system of administration with himself as head. He brought the Eastern Orthodox Church under state control and subordinated its clergy to his authority. He streamlined local and central government. He created a new "state service," including both civil and military officials, and made appointments to it based on merit, completely without regard to family status, birth, or seniority. Foreigners could serve within this service, serfs could be elevated, and nobles could be demoted; all depended on performance. In 1722 he introduced a new Table of Ranks, which automatically gave noble status to officials who reached the eighth position out of 14. The newly elevated nobles were the chief administrators of his new policies of Westernization. These revolutionary moves did not survive long after Peter's death.

Peter strengthened the economic and political position of the ruling classes, the landowners, and the rising urban professional and business classes, while exploiting the peasantry ruthlessly. He allotted to the nobility some 175,000 serfs and 100,000 acres of land in the first half of his reign alone. Conscription, programs of forced labor, a poll tax, and indirect taxes on everything from beekeeping to salt provoked two major uprisings in the Russian interior between 1705 and 1708. Peter suppressed them brutally. An iron-willed autocrat, Peter brought his nation into Europe and made it an important military and economic power, but millions of Russians paid a terrible price.

Peter achieved many of his goals, establishing a strong central administration, a powerful military, some commercial enterprise, international trade connections, and diplomatic contact with the nations of Western Europe. He did not, however, free Russia's merchants to carry on the kind of independent economic activity

14.1
14.2
14.3
14.4
14.5

What were the goals of Peter the Great?

	The Principality of Moscow c. 1300		Vasily III (1505–33)		Alexis (1645–76)		Elizabeth (1741–62)		Nicholas I (1825–55)
	The Grand Principality of Moscow 1462		Ivan IV the Terrible (1533–84)		Peter I the Great (1682–1725)		Catherine II the Great (1762–96)		Alexander II (1855–81)
	Ivan III the Great (1462–1505)		Michael Romanov (1613–45)		Anna (1730–40)		Alexander I (1801–25)		acquired (1533–1689)

The expansion of Russia, 1462–1881. By the end of the fifteenth century, Mongol forces in Russia had been destroyed and Russia began an expansion that took it all the way from its center in Moscow westward to the Baltic Sea, and eastward across Siberia to the Pacific Ocean. The territories gained by Peter the Great were especially important not because of their size, but because they included the strategic warm-water port that became St. Petersburg. Catherine the Great's conquests took Russia further into Europe in the west, and to the Black Sea in the south.

Peter the Great. Alarmed by the growing power of his Western European neighbors, and by Russia's relative weakness, Peter the Great undertook to modernize his country, especially its military, economic, and cultural life. He built his program, however, on the backs of Russia's serfs.

14.1

14.2

14.3

14.4

14.5 What were the goals of Peter the Great?

KEY TERM

enlightened despotism A benevolent form of absolutism, a system of government in which the ruler has absolute rights over his or her subjects. The term implies that the ruler acts for the good of the people, not in self-interest.

characteristic of Western European commerce. He kept the largest enterprises, such as weapons manufacture and shipping, in the hands of the state. Considered an **enlightened despot**—a ruler who advanced new concepts of intellectual inquiry and legal rights, at least for the nobility, but held on to power for himself—Peter died in 1725. Since he had had his own son jailed and killed rather than permit him to sidetrack reforms, Peter was succeeded for two years by his wife and then by other family members.

In 1762 Catherine II, the Great, assumed the throne by overthrowing the widely disliked and feared Tsar Peter III, her husband. She ruled for 34 years, presiding over a "golden age." Catherine won especially important military victories over the Ottoman Empire in Turkey, expanding the borders of Russia through the Crimea and into the Black Sea, extending Peter the Great's earlier invasions. She combined with Austria and Prussia to partition Poland out of existence, with Russia carving out the largest sector for itself. She dispatched colonizers across the Bering Straits to begin to develop Russian America. She added about 200,000 square miles of territory to the Russian Empire (see map, above). She invited to Russia several leaders of the Enlightenment in France, and continued the adoption of French language, manners, and cultural styles in literature and architecture at the court and in the capital. She declared herself in favor of important educational and social reforms,

The Founding of St. Petersburg, Bartolomeo Carlo Rastrelli, Russia, 1723. This bronze relief commemorates the founding of St. Petersburg in 1704. Peter the Great intended his capital to be an all-weather port and a "window on the West." As part of his drive for Westernization, he decreed that the aristocracy must abandon their Russian dress in favor of European clothes. The garb of the men depicted here indicates clearly that his edict was already being implemented. (The State Hermitage Museum, St. Petersburg)

14.1
14.2
14.3
14.4
14.5

What were the
goals of Peter the
Great?

including the founding of the first state-financed institution of higher education that admitted women, the Smolny Institute, but she proved at least as despotic as Peter the Great. The reforms she introduced to bring the standards of Western Europe to Russia were for the emerging middle classes and the nobility, not for the serfs; the serfs were taxed to pay for the innovations. After brutally suppressing a revolt by hundreds of thousands of serfs led by Yemelyan Pugachev (1726–75), Catherine reduced the already low status of Russia's own serfs and expanded the burden of serfdom onto the peoples of the newly conquered lands as well. Catherine wished to be seen as an enlightened despot, and, like Peter the Great, she earned both halves of that designation.

📖 **Read** the **Document**: **Adan Olearius: A Foreign Traveler in Russia (early 17th c.)** on **MyHistoryLab**

Ottomans and Mughals

Two powerful empires, the Ottoman and the Mughal, were rising in Asia at about the same time as Spain and Portugal were advancing in Europe and overseas. Indeed, there was some connection. In 1600 all four empires were approaching the height of their powers. By 1700 all were declining sharply because of overextension, draining warfare, weak state systems, and lack of attention to technological improvements, especially in the military. All four also allowed control of their economic affairs to fall into the hands of foreigners. By the end of our period, all were subordinated to a greater or lesser degree to the newly risen French and British.

The Ottomans did not control their own trade or its profits. At first, because of political alliances with France, only French ships were allowed to trade with the Ottomans. After 1580, trade opened more widely and the English and Dutch entered the arena, along with Jews, Armenians, Venetians, and Genoese. The situation came to resemble that of Spain, whereby the empire's new riches went into the hands of foreign merchants. A shift in the balance of trade also weakened the central government. To pay for increasing amounts of imported manufactured goods, the Ottomans exported more agricultural raw materials. This increasing reliance on agriculture strengthened the position of landed estate holders and enabled them to break free of central control. In addition, the Ottomans could no longer defend their borders. We have seen that Peter the Great and Catherine the Great succeeded in seizing Ottoman territories adjacent to the Black Sea as well as others leading to the Caspian.

In governing their empire, the Ottomans allowed a great deal of self-rule to the various religious communities. Leaders in each religious community (*millet*) established and adjudicated family and personal law, and also oversaw tax collection. The *millet* system opened a breach for other countries to involve themselves in the internal affairs of the Ottoman Empire. They intervened in support of minority groups with which they identified. The French intervened on behalf of the Roman Catholic minority, the Russians on behalf of the Eastern Orthodox, and the British on behalf of the Protestants. The Ottomans were losing control over their internal administration and over their land.

📖 **Read** the **Document**: **Venetian Observations on the Ottoman Empire (late 16th c.)** on **MyHistoryLab**

📖 **Read** the **Document**: **The Decline of the Ottomans (1592)** on **MyHistoryLab**

In India, between 1556 and 1605, the Mughal emperor Akbar established one of the most powerful and enlightened empires of the time. Ruling as head of a mostly Muslim invading force, Akbar wisely incorporated many members of the Hindu majority, and of non-Muslim minority groups, into his administration, army, court, and harem. Akbar's administrative reforms also brought changes in trade

Idris Giving Instruction to Mankind on the Art of Weaving, Mughal period, *c.* 1590. In the Islamic tradition, the mythical Idris gives instruction and protection to pious and skilled weavers. Here weavers wash, dry, spin, skein, and weave their wool, while courtiers present rolls of cloth for inspection. Most production was localized, as suggested here, although a few examples of large, well-organized workshops with wage labor and centralized management also existed, mostly under the control of Mughal courts. When pressured, weavers organized in boycotts and strikes to resist the exactions of rulers and merchants, and to defend the honor of their pious artisanry. (British Library, London)

patterns. City markets encouraged the production of luxury goods for the court and everyday goods for the common people. Even parts of village India—90 percent of India's population—were drawn into the city-based cash economy.

The markets contained a wide array of craftsmen, shopkeepers, and sophisticated specialists. Money-lenders and money-changers were active throughout the urban system, enabling the smooth transfer of funds across the empire. Their *hundis* (bills of exchange) were accepted throughout the empire, and these financial instruments facilitated the work of government officials in collecting and transmitting in cash the taxes and rents on land. Indian cities boasted wealthy financiers and important guild organizations. The guilds, much like those in Europe, regulated and supervised the major trades. Business flourished and prospered. Among the multitude of India's castes, some were charged specifically with carrying on business.

Indian traders were highly mobile and therefore had some independence from the political fortunes of the rulers of the time. If particular rulers could not defend their territory against foreign invasion or maintain law and order, or if they tried to extort excessive taxes, the merchant communities could leave for other cities more amenable to their pursuits. Conversely, rulers who wanted to improve their commercial prospects lured these footloose merchants with offers of free land and low taxes. Thus, even in the event of political decline or catastrophe in one region, India's business might shift location and continue to flourish.

Indian businessmen continued to carry on coastal and oceangoing trade, but, because India had no navy, the imperial government could not support or protect these ventures very effectively. In 1686, for example, the British blocked Indian trade between Bengal and Southeast Asia and even seized ships belonging to the officers and family members of the Mughal rulers. Emperor Aurangzeb replied by land, forcing the British out of their settlement at Hoogly. But the British relocated, built a new town, Calcutta, and continued their maritime commerce and armed competition. Furthermore, although Indian businessmen created sophisticated economic institutions within family-held firms, they did not usually develop impersonal business firms like the European joint stock companies. When the European joint stock companies arrived on the subcontinent, they opened a new scale of overseas operations. Finally, although they might flee oppressive rulers, Indian merchants did not normally arm themselves or contract for armed forces, as did many European merchants, especially the joint stock companies. Rather than following the pattern slowly beginning to develop in Western Europe, Indian merchants remained generally subordinate to political and military rulers.

Ming and Qing Dynasties in China

The Ming dynasty in China had largely closed the country to foreign trade in favor of developing the internal economy and defending its borders by land and by sea. The Ming repaired the Great Wall to keep out Mongols and Manchus, and extended it by 600 miles. Having reduced the size and power of their navy, the Ming were harassed by Japanese and Chinese pirates on their coasts. The Ming responded meekly by avoiding the sea and reviving the system of inland transportation by canal. The pirate attacks escalated into minor invasions of the mainland, penetrating even into the Yangzi River basin. Following national unification at the end of the sixteenth century, the new Japanese government brought their pirates under control, but in 1592 Japan invaded Korea, with plans for an ultimate assault on China. Warfare continued for years, mostly within the Korean peninsula, until Japan finally withdrew in 1598.

14.1
14.2
14.3
14.4
14.5
What were the goals of Peter the Great?

Portuguese ships and sailors, lacquer screen, Chinese, seventeenth century. The ship itself and the faces of the sailors are not depicted as hostile, although at the beginning of the previous century the Portuguese had been expelled from China for aggressive actions, and by mid-century they were restricted to coastal enclaves.

HOW DO WE KNOW?

How Europe Surpassed China Economically and Militarily

During the period covered in this chapter, the balance of power between Europe and Asia was changing. The most remarkable shift was the slow, steady economic progress of Western European nations compared to China, still the most powerful and wealthy nation of the time. We have examined advances in European shipping and armaments, and the consolidation of their commercial classes and their nation-states. Why did China not keep pace?

Mark Elvin, an economic historian, tackled this question in a classic study, *The Pattern of the Chinese Past* (1973), a sketch of Chinese economic and social history from earliest times. Elvin praises the creativity of the Tang and Song dynasties, crediting the period from the eighth to the twelfth centuries with "revolutions" in farming, water transport, money and credit, market structure and urbanization, science, and technology. But "the dynamic quality of the medieval Chinese economy disappeared … some time around the middle of the fourteenth century" (p. 203). Elvin gives three reasons for this disappearance: the Chinese frontier began to fill up with people and resources; commerce with the outside world decreased sharply; and philosophy became introspective, less concerned with practical problems. The result was "quantitative growth, qualitative standstill," or what Elvin calls a "high-level equilibrium trap." That is, economic growth continued and new natural resources were tapped, but most of the gains were eaten up by the population growth.

For example, Elvin writes, from the sixteenth through the nineteenth centuries, New World crops were introduced, agricultural techniques were improved, market networks were extended, the legal status of the peasantry was improved, and entrepreneurship and invention flourished. But the population doubled from about 200 million people in 1580 to about 400 million in 1850. "Agricultural productivity per acre had nearly reached the limits of what was possible without industrial-scientific inputs" (p. 312), and these inputs were simply unavailable. Technological innovation occurred, but resources for implementing them were scarce. Wood, clothing fibers, land, draft animals, and metals were in short supply. In this "high-level equilibrium trap," the Chinese economy worked well enough in its traditional forms but there were few incentives for making changes. More important, the changes that might have increased productivity would have required more capital and human resources than were available. China was stuck.

Had the West faced such a trap, and, if so, how had it avoided it? Kenneth Pomeranz, another economic historian, gives his answers in *The Great Divergence: China, Europe, and the Making of the Modern World Economy* (2000). Yes, he says, "Europe, too, could have wound up on an 'east Asian,' labor-intensive path" (p. 13) in which there were few incentives and even fewer resources available to create innovations to improve productivity. Its escape was "the result of important and sharp discontinuities, based on both fossil fuels [coal] and access to New World resources" (p. 13). The fossil fuels became important only later, during the Industrial Revolution, but the New World resources became important almost immediately after their discovery by Europeans. The New World "relieved the strain on Europe's supply of what was truly scarce: land and energy … crucial factors leading out of a world of **Malthusian constraints**" (p. 23). The New World provided a place for some of Europe's "excess" population. It also provided richly productive land, an abundance of gold and silver, the lucrative slave trade, and millions of slaves who created a new market for European products. (Here Pomeranz is not considering the fate of the slaves.)

Was the lucky discovery of the New World the major differentiation between the European economic experience and the Chinese? Pomeranz also credits "war, armed long-distance trade and colonization" (p. 166). The joint stock company organized for overseas trade and colonization represented a significant breakthrough for the "unified management of trading voyages and cargoes too big for a single investor" (p. 171). The backing of the state for these ventures—without excessive, crippling interference—was probably another (p. 173). The use of "force to create monopolies or near-monopolies (mostly in spices)" was a third (p. 182). The competition among the European powers for trading and colonizing supremacy was a fourth element in driving their economic success (p. 194).

Between Elvin and Pomeranz we get a comprehensive, comparative survey of the factors at work in China and in Europe—ecological, demographic, and institutional—that led to China's relative economic stagnation during the Ming and Qing dynasties and Western Europe's dynamism in the same time frame, during an era of innovation, overseas exploration, trade, and early colonization.

- When did the economic productivity and wealth of Western Europe surpass that of China?
- To what degree did the stagnation in China's economy result from a lack of planning and hard work?
- To what degree did the success of Western Europe's economy result from planning and hard work?

KEY TERM

Malthusian constraints The British scholar Thomas Malthus believed that population would always grow faster than food supply, leading to famine that would limit excess population.

The Western presence was limited at this stage. The few Portuguese who arrived in China after 1514 were mostly Jesuit missionaries. Their influence was felt far more in the culture of the court than in the commerce of the marketplace. Matteo Ricci (1552–1610), one of the most prominent of the Jesuit missionaries to China, shared with government officials in Beijing his knowledge of mathematics, cartography, astronomy, mechanics, and clocks, while he mastered the Chinese language and many of the Confucian classics. The Jesuits concentrated their efforts on winning over the elites of China, and by 1700 some 300,000 Chinese had converted to Christianity.

Despite the shutdown of most international trade, China's economy expanded, at least until about 1600. With one-fifth of the world's population within its borders, China generated an immense internal economy; its canal system encouraged north–south trade. Using kaolin clay, Chinese artisans created porcelain stronger and more beautiful than ever. The weaving and dyeing of silk expanded near Suzhou; cotton textiles flourished at Nanjing; and Hebei specialized in iron manufacture.

In the late Ming period, private seagoing trade with Southeast Asia began to flourish again, often carried by families who had sent emigrants to the region and thus had local contacts. Within China, however, local authorities on the south coast regulated these merchants and limited this trade. Modern scholarship suggests that had the Chinese government supported its own traders at home, instead of restricting them, they too might have been effective in building overseas merchant empires. The Chinese merchants

> could, in terms of entrepreneurship and daring, do everything that the various Europeans could do. But they were helpless to produce the necessary institutional change in China to match European or even Japanese power. They were never the instruments of any effort by Ming or Qing authorities to build merchant empires; nor could they hope to get mandarin or ideological support for any innovative efforts of their own. (Gungwu, cited in Tracy, *The Rise of Merchant Empires*, p. 401)

When Europeans came to trade, the Chinese government restricted them to coastal enclaves. The Portuguese, for example, were confined to Macao, where they remained until 1999. Nevertheless, the trade was enormous. As we have seen, between one-third and one-half of all the silver of the New World ultimately went to China, much of it shipped across the Pacific and through Manila, which the Spanish established as their port in the Philippines in 1571. Much of the silver paid for silk, porcelain, tea, and other products, but the Chinese also purchased silver for its own sake, paying for it with gold. Despite this new wealth, by the time the Dutch and British arrived in the 1600s the quality of the Ming administration had weakened.

The Qing dynasty, ruled by Manchus from north of the Great Wall, captured the government of China from the Ming in 1644 and secured the southeast coast in 1683. They established the "Canton system," restricting European traders to the area around Canton (Guangzhou), and entrusting their supervision and control to a monopoly of Chinese firms called the Cohong. Because of these restrictions, and because of the vast size of China, European merchants had little direct effect on the Chinese interior. Also, like the Mughals in India, the Manchu rulers of China were an inland people, far more concerned with control of land than with trade by sea. While they limited overseas trade, they pushed their political military control aggressively into central Asia, doubling the size of the empire (see map in "Migration," below).

Although most historians emphasized the role of Europe in enlarging the world economy through overseas voyages, more recent scholarship notes that it was the vast internal markets of China, the wealth of its luxury goods, and its hunger for New World silver—along with the spices of India and the Spice Islands—that attracted the Europeans. From this perspective, the dominant economic force in the world economy between 1500 and 1776 was not the vigor of European exploration and trade but the richness of the Asian markets that attracted them in the first place. The "pull" of the Chinese market attracted the "push" of the European merchants.

Tokugawa Japan

As in China, the early European influences on Japan were religious as well as economic. Roman Catholicism appeared with the arrival of the Jesuit priest Francis Xavier (1506–52) in 1549. In common with the Jesuits in China, Xavier adapted to

14.1

14.2

14.3

14.4

14.5

What were the goals of Peter the Great?

14.1
14.2
14.3
14.4
14.5

What were the goals of Peter the Great?

local cultural practices in dress, food, residence, and, of course, language. In response, the Japanese warmly welcomed the Jesuits. Japan's **shogun**, or chief military administrator, Oda Nobunaga (1534–82), encouraged the Jesuits in their missionary work, and even after his assassination, Christianity expanded its foothold in Japan. As in China, converts numbered in the hundreds of thousands, and they were mostly from among the Japanese elites. (Among the European contributions to Japanese everyday life were tobacco, bread, playing cards, and deep-fat frying, which inspired the Japanese specialty of tempura.)

The Japanese government became apprehensive about so large a group of elite converts. There had been early signs of this change in policy. In 1597, after a Spanish ship captain boasted of the power of his king, and after Spain founded Manila, the shogun Toyotomi Hideyoshi crucified 6 Franciscan missionaries and 18 Japanese converts. In 1606 Christianity was outlawed, and in 1614 Shogun Tokugawa Ieyasu began to expel all Christian missionaries. Some 3,000 Japanese Christians were murdered. In 1623 the British left Japan; in 1624 the Spanish were expelled; in 1630 Japanese were forbidden to travel overseas. In 1637–38, in reaction to a revolt, which was more a rural economic protest than a religious uprising, 37,000 Christians were killed. The Portuguese were expelled. Only a small contingent of Dutch traders was permitted to remain, confined, as we have seen, to Deshima Island off Nagasaki. A limited number of Chinese ships continued to visit Japan each year and some diplomatic contact with Korea continued, but Japan chose to live largely in isolation.

As in China, the suppression of contact with outsiders did not cripple Japan. Its process of political consolidation continued, from the Battle of Sekigahara (1600), which marked the ascension of Tokugawa Ieyasu as shogun, until 1651. The country was unified and peaceful. Privately owned guns were virtually banned. Agriculture prospered as the area of land under cultivation doubled, and the production of cash crops, such as indigo, tobacco (transplanted from the New World), sugar cane, and mulberry leaves as food for silkworms, increased. The population almost doubled, from 18 million in 1600 to 30 million by the mid-1700s, at which point it stabilized temporarily.

The new government was in the hands of the *samurai* warrior classes, who made up about 7 percent of the population. They benefited most from the improved conditions, and there were some violent protests against increasing disparities in income, but standards of living and of education generally improved. City merchants, *chonin*, emerged as a newly wealthy and powerful class, dealing in the new cash commodities of agriculture and hand manufacture. They supplied banking, shipping, loans, and other commercial services, and founded family businesses, some of which endure even today. The Tokugawa capital Edo (modern Tokyo) grew to a million people by 1700, among the largest cities in the world at the time. In a reversal of the contemporary European pattern, Japan was doing well despite cutting off almost all international trade.

📖 Read the Document: Japan Encounters the West on MyHistoryLab

Southeast Asia

Southeast Asia was one of the great prizes of international commercial competition throughout our period, and foreign merchants from China, Japan, India, Arabia, and Europe were active in its markets. Yet the indigenous merchants of the region did not themselves become major factors in the international side of the trade. Foreign traders began their activities on the coast and then moved inland, taking control of local markets. They also fought among themselves. By 1640, for example, the Dutch East India Company expelled from the Indonesian archipelago not only the local merchants but also European competitors. By this time, the spice trade was

KEY TERMS

shogun The military dictator of Japan, a hereditary title held by three families between 1192 and 1867. Although they were legally subservient to the emperor, their military power gave them effective control of the country.

samurai The hereditary warrior-aristocrats of Japanese society, known for their codes of honor and loyalty. Only *samurai* were permitted to wear swords in their everyday dress.

beginning to level off and the Dutch were in the process of restructuring the economies of Southeast Asia, especially Indonesia, to produce commercial crops valued in Europe, such as sugar, coffee, and tobacco. In the Philippines, the Spanish asserted similar power.

Local rulers entered into commercial agreements with the foreign traders that enriched themselves and the foreigners, but not their own local merchant communities. Commercial profits were repatriated from Southeast Asia to Europe, creating ever more serious divisions between rich and poor, powerful and powerless. The Dutch East India Company, backed by the government of the Netherlands and its military power, had brought Southeast Asia into this new world system, as participant and as victim.

The Influence of World Trade: *What Difference Does It Make?*

We close this exploration of world trade in the year 1776. We have witnessed enormous changes from 1300, when we began, in the chapter "Establishing World Trade Routes," and even from 1500, when European explorers began their oceanic voyages. During these centuries, an entirely new set of trade networks opened, crisscrossing the Atlantic Ocean. Major elements in these new trade relationships included the export from the western hemisphere of enormous quantities of gold and silver to Europe and onward to Asia, and the export of millions of people in slavery from Africa to the plantations of the Americas. A vast exchange of commodities plants, animals, and diseases also opened across the Atlantic; we discuss this "Columbian Exchange" in the chapter entitled "Migration." Another completely new transoceanic trade route opened across the Pacific. There, Spanish galleons carried other streams of silver from the west coast of the Americas, especially from the mines of Potosí, to China to purchase its silks and porcelains and, later, its tea, and, for a while, its gold.

The earlier center of ocean trade, the Indian Ocean, continued to be important, but now European traders—Portuguese, followed by Dutch, British, and French—gained control of the intercontinental segments of that trade. Its coastal port cities hosted increasingly diverse communities of international traders, and the newly arriving European traders fortified both their ships and their overseas trading posts. In East Asia, on the other hand, China and Japan sharply restricted European territorial access, although they continued to trade with the foreigners.

Within Europe, nation-states and private traders increased their political and military power on the basis of the profits of international trade and an accepted policy of supporting it with oceangoing fleets and navies. The new philosophy of capitalism extolled and promoted the rising power of private business at home and abroad. New religious denominations also appeared, with philosophies that rationalized economic acquisitiveness. Competition increased among individuals, companies, and nations in the technology of shipping, the sophistication of commercial strategy, the manufacture of armaments, and the training and disciplining of armed forces at home and overseas. In general, the Spanish and Portuguese lost out to the Dutch, French, and British.

Throughout this era, the most powerful and wealthy of the world's empires were still Asian, but by the end of it, Europeans, hungry for profit and often eager to spread the gospel of Christianity, were fashioning the frameworks for their own overseas empires of unprecedented size.

CHAPTER REVIEW

THE BIRTH OF CAPITALISM

14.1   What is capitalism?

Capitalism is an economic system in which most wealth, or capital, is held by private individuals who make their economic decisions to buy and sell based on supply and demand, free choice, and the information available to them. Although the system was formally explained only in the late eighteenth century, by Adam Smith, and the word was first used only in the mid-1800s, a system of trade and exchange had already developed among the owners of textile workshops in Italy and Flanders in the 1500s, and it soon extended to bankers and international traders. These wealthy and powerful businessmen dedicated themselves to the pursuit of private profit through the private ownership of wealth and the means of its production. As opposed to mercantilists, who believed that government should regulate trade in order to stockpile precious metals for the benefit of the state, the new capitalists argued for allowing the free market to determine the prices of goods and labor, and that what was good for the individual was good for the state.

THE EMPIRES OF SPAIN AND PORTUGAL

14.2   What regions of the world did Spain and Portugal explore?

European intercontinental trade was dominated at first by Spain and Portugal. Both countries faced directly on the Atlantic Ocean, and both nations' rulers saw the ocean as their route to riches, power, and religious proselytizing. While the Portuguese focused on the coasts of Brazil, Africa, and India's Arabian Sea ports, the Spanish colonized Central America, the west coast of South America, and the Philippines. To defuse tension between them, Pope Alexander VI issued the Treaty of Tordesillas, establishing the general boundaries of their separate New World possessions.

TRADE AND RELIGION IN WESTERN EUROPE

14.3   What were the background conditions for the rise of the Dutch, French, and British empires?

The Dutch, British, and French had greater experience in seafaring and in international business than the Spanish and Portuguese. Instead of developing their own fleets and commercial capacities, the Spanish and Portuguese relied on their northern neighbors, so that the Dutch, the British, and the French profited not only from their own voyages and outposts, but they also gained from the services they provided to the Spanish and Portuguese. The defeat of the Spanish Armada in 1588, by storms and by the British, further consolidated British supremacy.

THE NATION-STATE

14.4   What is a "nation-state"?

"Nation-state" is the name used to describe a sovereign state with a cohesive population. The "nation" enjoys some combination of shared language, religion, ethnicity, history, and so on. The "state" occupies a territory that it can control and protect, and it is administered by an independent government. A nation-state may emerge from the dissolution of a larger empire, or it may grow as smaller units coalesce into larger units, either through conquest or merger.

DIVERSE CULTURES, DIVERSE TRADE SYSTEMS

14.5   What were the goals of Peter the Great?

Peter the Great (1672–1725), alarmed by the growing power of the Western European nations (and wishing to see Russia among them), set out ruthlessly to modernize Russia. He required Russia's elites to adopt Western-style morals, education, dress, and style, even down to insisting the men wear their beards in the Western style. He invited Western military experts to train and lead his troops, and he promoted metallurgy, mining, and textile manufacture. He gave opportunity for government service to people of talent, but he did not permit democratic participation in government. Peter the Great achieved many of his goals, establishing a strong central administration, a powerful military, commercial enterprises, and diplomatic and trading contacts with the West, under a highly centralized, dictatorial regime with continued serfdom for most people.

Suggested Readings

PRINCIPAL SOURCES

Braudel, Fernand. *Capitalism and Material Life 1400–1800*, trans. Miriam Kochan (New York: Harper and Row, 1973). Highly influential overview of the beginning of capitalism as the guiding economic force in modern Europe.

Brockey, Liam Matthew. *Journey to the East: The Jesuit Mission to China, 1579–1724.* (Cambridge, MA: Harvard University Press, 2007). Discusses the life and work of Jesuit missionaries more typical than Matteo Ricci, who was larger than life.

Chaudhuri, K.N. *Trade and Civilization in the Indian Ocean* (Cambridge: Cambridge University Press, 1985). Comprehensive survey of the ecology, politics, traders, and trade of the Indian Ocean.

Elvin, Mark. *The Pattern of the Chinese Past* (Stanford, CA: Stanford University Press, 1973). An interpretive economic history from pre-Han to Qing China. Thoughtful analyses of successes and failures.

Kennedy, Paul. *The Rise and Fall of the Great Powers* (New York: Vintage Books, 1987). Examines histories of great power rivalries, including the Western European rivalries in the age of exploration and trade. Seeks balance between military power and economic health.

McNeill, William H. "The Age of Gunpowder Empires, 1450–1800," in Michael Adas, ed., *Islamic and European Expansion* (Philadelphia, PA: Temple University Press, 1993), pp. 103–09. Brief survey of the effects of gunpowder on warfare and on the nations that used it in warfare.

Mintz, Sidney W. *Sweetness and Power: The Place of Sugar in Modern History* (New York: Penguin Books, 1985). Anthropological focus on the Caribbean sugar plantation, but places it also in the context of world trade patterns, advertising, and changing food choices.

Perdue, Peter. *China Marches West: The Qing Conquest of Central Eurasia* (Cambridge, MA: Harvard University Press, 2005). Brilliant study of the statecraft, military actions, and ethnic and ecological significance of Qing China's enormous territorial conquests.

Thornton, John. *Africa and Africans in the Making of the Atlantic World, 1400–1680* (Cambridge: Cambridge University Press, 1992). Sees Africans as active participants in the slave trade and other trading activities, not simply as passive in the affairs of others.

Tracy, James D., ed. *The Political Economy of Merchant Empires* (Cambridge: Cambridge University Press, 1991). An excellent account of the merchant empires that emerged in the Early Modern period.

——, ed. *The Rise of Merchant Empires* (Cambridge: Cambridge University Press, 1990). Tracy brings together the papers of an exciting academic conference on the merchant empires of the age of exploration and early colonization. Specialized, but very important coverage. "The Rise" discusses primarily the merchant activity, and "Political Economy" primarily the imperial effects.

ADDITIONAL SOURCES

Bayly, C.A. *Indian Society and the Making of the British Empire* (Cambridge: Cambridge University Press, 1988). Sees the effects of British colonization in the early years through the eyes and activities of Indians.

Braudel, Fernand. *Civilization and Capitalism 15th–18th Century*. Vol. 2: *The Wheels of Commerce*, trans. Sian Reynolds (New York: Harper and Row, 1986). Remarkable synthesis of the transformation of early modern Europe through its economy, social life, and culture. Volume 1 is published as *Capitalism and Material Life 1400–1800*; see above.

——. *Civilization and Capitalism 15th–18th Century*. Vol. 3: *The Perspective of the World*, trans. Sian Reynolds (New York: Harper and Row, 1986). Third volume in the series. Looks more at the importance of international relations.

——. *The Mediterranean and the Mediterranean World in the Age of Philip II*, 2 vols., trans. Sian Reynolds (New York: Harper Torchbooks, vol. 1: 1972; vol. 2: 1973). This study of the Mediterranean demonstrated Braudel's style of history, including the consideration of geological influences, long-standing institutional influences, and short-term political and personal influences. Highly influential for its style of history as well as its subject matter.

Columbia University. *Introduction to Contemporary Society in the West*, 2 vols. (New York: Columbia University Press, 2nd ed. 1954). A superb reader of some of the most influential thinkers from medieval times to the mid-twentieth century, presented in long, rich excerpts.

Columbia University. *Man in Contemporary Society*, 2 vols. (New York: Columbia University Press, 1955). A superb reader of

some of the most influential thinkers, from mid-nineteenth to mid-twentieth century, presented in long, rich excerpts.

Das Gupta, Ashin, and M.N. Pearson, eds. *India and the Indian Ocean 1500–1800* (Calcutta: Oxford University Press, 1987). Articles on the vital trade and politics of the major actors in the Indian Ocean.

Duara, Prasenjit. *Rescuing History from the Nation* (Chicago, IL: University of Chicago Press, 1995). A critical challenge to the idea that the nation-state is a creation of the modern West and that it has a fixed meaning.

Ebrey, Patricia Buckley. *Cambridge Illustrated History of China* (Cambridge: Cambridge University Press, 2nd ed., 2010). Excellent basic survey. Pictures help to tell the story. Some emphasis on women in Chinese history.

Flynn, Dennis, and Arturo Giráldez. "'Born with a Silver Spoon': The Origin of World Trade in 1571," *Journal of World History* VI:2 (October, 1995), 201–21. In the year in which Spain established its Asian base in Manila, world trade over the Pacific came of age, with silver as the leading commodity.

Gungwu, Wang. "Merchants without Empire: The Hokkien Sojourning Communities," in Tracy, ed., *The Rise of Merchant Empires*, pp. 400–21. Traces the overseas activities of merchants of the south China coast, whose opportunities in China were blocked by government.

Kamen, Henry. *Empire: How Spain Became a World Power, 1492–1763* (New York: HarperCollins, 2003). Analyzes the empire globally, accounting for the many non-Spanish groups that participated in constructing and administering it.

Lapidus, Ira. *A History of Islamic Societies* (Cambridge: Cambridge University Press, 2nd ed., 2002). A 1,000-plus-page comprehensive, well-written history.

Mann, Charles C. *1493: Uncovering the New World Columbus Created* (New York: Alfred Knopf, 2011). Comprehensive survey of the effects of bringing the hemispheres into permanent trade relationships. Up-to-date scholarship. A pleasure to read.

Palmer, R.R., and Joel Colton. *A History of the Modern World* (New York: Knopf, 9th ed., 2002). Once *the* major text; now considered too Eurocentric, and very Francophile, but still excellent.

Pomeranz, Kenneth. *The Great Divergence: China, Europe, and the Making of the Modern World Economy* (Princeton, NJ: Princeton University Press, 2000). How did Europe surpass China? An economic historian explores various explanations, including the exploitation of New World resources; coal in Britain; and armed merchant exploration and trade.

Reid, Anthony. *Southeast Asia in the Age of Commerce 1450–1680*. Vol 1: *The Land Below the Winds*; Vol 2: *Expansion and Crisis* (New Haven, CT: Yale University Press, vol. 1: 1988; vol. 2: 1993). Excellent collection of conference papers on the impact of foreign merchants on Southeast Asia.

Schama, Simon. *The Embarrassment of Riches* (New York: Knopf, 1987). Study of the early modern Netherlands, especially its artistic wealth.

Smith, Adam. *An Inquiry into the Nature and Causes of the Wealth of Nations* (New York: Modern Library, 1937). The classic philosophical rationale for capitalism.

Spence, Jonathan D. *The Memory Palace of Matteo Ricci* (New York: Penguin Books, 1985). An account of the work and significance of Matteo Ricci in China, filled with cultural information. Spence is especially interested in ways different peoples trained their powers of memory.

Steensgaard, Niels. *The Asian Trade Revolution of the Seventeenth Century* (Chicago, IL: University of Chicago Press, 1973). Argues that most Asian traders were small-scale and not well organized.

Tawney, R.H. *Religion and the Rise of Capitalism* (New York: Harcourt, Brace, & Co., 1926). Argues, against Max Weber, that Catholicism also showed substantial economic entrepreneurship and that religious and moral principles will always be included in economic considerations.

Thomas, Hugh. *Rivers of Gold: The Rise of the Spanish Empire, from Columbus to Magellan* (New York: Random House, 2004). The first 30 years of conquest seen largely through the eyes of the men who carried it out.

Weber, Max. *The Protestant Ethic and the Spirit of Capitalism*, trans. Talcott Parsons (London, 1930). Argues that religious beliefs do have considerable impact on economic performance, and that, in the modern world, religious enthusiasm had been supplanted by economic aspirations.

Wolf, Eric. *Europe and the People without History* (Berkeley, CA: University of California Press, 1982). Historical anthropologist demonstrates that non-European societies are not unchanging. Their recent history has been heavily influenced by the capitalist West.

FILMS

Adam Smith: The Wealth of Nations (2004; 19 minutes). Point-by-point explication and analysis of the major ideas of Smith's major book. Also places it in historic context of economic thinking.

Catherine the Great (2005; 120 minutes). Excellent PBS documentary. Emily Bruni as Catherine captures the intrigue of the woman and of the time, place, and situation. With scholarly evaluations.

No Rest for the Wicked: Protestantism and Economics (2006; 59 minutes). Parts are directly related to the economy of the 1500s through the Industrial Revolution and up to the present. Accepts the connection between Protestantism and the quest for economic growth and profit.

Peter the Great (1999; 32 minutes). Examines family dynamics as well as the military, industrial, cultural, and religious transformations that Peter introduced in bringing Russia into modern Europe.

15 Migration

Demographic Changes in a New Global World

1300–1750

Conventionally, historians write about particular individuals and particular events. In the twentieth century, however, and especially in its second half, historians began to examine **demographics**—that is, human populations viewed collectively, in quantitative terms. Demographers use "vital statistics" such as life expectancy, birth rates, death rates, and marriage rates in order to address such questions as: When and why do populations grow and decline? What are the impacts of disease, war, and famine? What are the effects of improvements in agriculture and living standards? What is the distribution of population by age, gender, class, and household size? Through large-scale analyses, demographers seek to identify and interpret patterns of change. Although the statistics may at first seem dry, they can tell fascinating stories.

Portrait of a Black Man, Albrecht Dürer, 1508. Charcoal on paper. In the late 1400s, several delegations of Africans from the Atlantic Coast came to Europe, especially to Portugal, in Portuguese ships, mostly for commercial exchange, Christian religious pursuits, and new weapons technology. The largest number of Africans in Europe at this time, however, were brought as slaves. This portrait by the great German painter Albrecht Dürer is exceptional, portraying his subject as intelligent, clear-eyed, thoughtful, and independent of spirit. (Graphische Sammlung Albertina, Vienna)

LEARNING OBJECTIVES

15.1 ((	15.2 ((	15.3 ((	15.4 ((	15.5 ((	15.6 ((
Define the "New Europes."	Describe Russia's expansion in the seventeenth century.	Explain the rise of slavery in the Atlantic Ocean basin.	Describe the Asian migrations of 1300 to 1750.	Describe why the population of some continents grew faster than others between 1000 and 1800.	Describe migration to the very large cities before 1800.

Demographic aggregate studies are often the closest we can come to understanding the lives of average people. Historically, most people could neither read nor write, and so they have left us no written record. Although we are not able to know their individual biographies, through demographic studies of aggregate groups we may be able to gain a better understanding of the societies in which they lived and died. We know that migration led to the mixing of peoples, commodities, and cultures in the marketplace. It also led to mixing in homes and families as immigrants and host groups met, mated, and married. We may find occasional, individual stories of this mixing, but demographic data gives us a more comprehensive—although not individual—perspective.

Today, governments gather statistical information as a matter of course. However, to find information on earlier periods that lack such systematic official data collection, historians must search other sources. Church registers of births and deaths, travelers' accounts, and ships' records of passengers and cargo, for example, can all provide demographic data. In this chapter we will examine demographic data specifically concerned with migration, the movement of populations across geographical space, from one region to another, and between countryside and city.

New topics in the study of the past are often inspired by new experiences in the present. In our own time, demographic shifts are dramatically altering our world, both in the population explosion that has doubled the earth's population in the last 30 years and in the migrations of hundreds of millions of people from region to region and from rural areas to cities. The United States, in particular, stresses its identity as a nation of immigrants. In recent decades its population has also shifted internally, from north to south, from east to west, from countryside to city, and from city to suburb. European countries, which have not usually considered themselves homes for new immigrants, are experiencing the inflow of millions of immigrants from poorer countries seeking economic opportunities in the wealthier regions of the European Union. China, having relaxed its restrictions on internal immigration, is experiencing the migration of millions of its citizens from poorer villages in the interior to wealthier cities along its coast. Such demographic transformations evoke comparisons with earlier eras, especially the period 1500–1750, when the populations of whole continents were restructured, and when cities, some of them newly founded, experienced enormous population growth.

Sometimes research is motivated by the availability of new tools. Population history requires quantitative information and the statistical tools to work with it. Within the last generation, demographers have made great strides in developing new methodology, some of it as a result of new data-processing capabilities. Demographic computer modeling provides additional, new replies to the question: "How do we know?"

Here we will explore four major subjects: first, the formation of "New Europes" around the globe as settlers from Europe set out in all directions, often with catastrophic consequences for native populations. Second, the trade in slaves that brought some ten million people from Africa to the Americas—against a background of the long-standing historic trade in slaves in many parts of the globe. Third, the overland migrations of Mongols and Turks, who emerged from central Asia to invade China in the east, Russia and the Balkans in the west, and India in the south. Finally, we will analyze migrations from rural areas to cities in several different parts of the world, and compare and contrast peoples' reasons for moving.

KEY TERM

demographics The study of human populations in quantitative terms, usually considered a sub-field of sociology. Demographers consider such data as birth and death rates, fertility and morbidity, and immigration and emigration, among many others.

15.1 What were the "New Europes"?

15.2

15.3

15.4

15.5

15.6

The "New Europes"

15.1 What were the "New Europes"?

From 1500 to 1750 developments within Europe increased the continent's influence in the world and expedited the emigration of millions of Europeans to establish "New Europes" around the globe. These developments included:

- the increasing powers of traders in the diaspora cities of trade around the globe;
- the increasing power of European nation-states and their support for overseas trade;
- the shifting of trade to the Atlantic (from the Indian) Ocean;
- the increasing pace of technological invention in Europe, especially in guns and ships;
- the increasing discipline and order within European armies;
- the importation of immense quantities of gold and silver from the New World, much of which was sent to China and India to pay for imports to Europe;
- the exploitation of the labor of millions of slaves taken from Africa to work the plantations of the New World; and
- the spreading of the message of aggressive Christianity.

As we have seen, in the sixteenth century both Spain and Portugal built enormous global empires. The voyages of Columbus revealed undreamed-of gold and silver reserves in the Americas, and many Europeans who came after him were prepared to kill Native Americans and to seize their lands. Hernán Cortés conquered the Aztec nation of Mexico in 1519 and Francisco Pizarro conquered the Incas in 1533. The death and destruction that followed were monumental, but warfare was not the greatest killer.

Aztec smallpox victims, sixteenth century. The Spanish conquest of the Americas owed more to the diseases they brought with them than to their armed forces. The Native Americans had never encountered these diseases, especially smallpox, and had no immunity. They died in horrific numbers—up to 90 percent in many regions. (Biblioteca Nazionale Centrale di Firenze)

📖 Read the Document: Smallpox Epidemic in Mexico, 1520, from Bernardino de Sahagún, *Florentine Codex: General History of the Things of New Spain*, 1585 on MyHistoryLab

The Columbian Exchange

The peoples of the eastern and western hemispheres had had no sustained contact. Columbus' voyages ushered in a new era of interaction. This "Columbian Exchange" brought both new opportunities and catastrophe. The new opportunities came with the intercontinental exchange of plants and animals. The catastrophe devastated the Amerindians, who had no resistance to the diseases carried by the Europeans.

The Devastation of the Amerindian Population. Historian Alfred Crosby, a pioneer in the study of the exchange of microbes, cites the lowest currently accepted estimate of the Amerindian population in 1492 as 33 million, and the highest as perhaps 50 million. By comparison, Europe at the time had a population of 80 million. The death of millions of Amerindians followed almost immediately after Europeans began to arrive. At its lowest point after the coming of Europeans, the population of the western hemisphere dropped to 4.5 million. The biggest killers in this demographic catastrophe were not guns, but diseases: smallpox, measles, whooping cough, chickenpox,

What were the "New Europes"? 15.1

15.2

15.3

15.4

15.5

15.6

bubonic plague, malaria, diphtheria, amoebic dysentery, and influenza. The populations of the New World, separated by thousands of years and thousands of miles from those of the Old, had little resistance to its diseases. Up to 90 percent of the population died.

View the **Interactive Map**: Native American Population Loss 1500–1700 on **MyHistoryLab**

Benefits of the Columbian Exchange. More happily, links between the hemispheres also brought an exchange of food resources. From South America, the cassava spread to Africa and Asia and the white potato to northern Europe. Sweet potatoes traveled to China, as did maize (corn); China is today the second largest producer of corn, after the United States. Today, Russia produces ten times more potatoes by weight than does South America, while Africa produces almost twice as much cassava as does South America.

Flora and fauna migrated from east to west as well. Wheat was the leading Old World crop to come to the New World, but perhaps an even greater contribution came in domesticated animals: cattle, sheep, pigs, and goats. Domesticated horses, too, were imported from the Old World to the New. In the long run, these exchanges of food sources did much to increase the population of the world fourteen times, from about 500 million in 1492 to 7 billion today. But not everyone participated in this growth; there were demographic winners and losers. Peoples of the European continent in 1492 were the biggest winners; Asians generally did well; Amerindians and other indigenous populations in all the "New Europes" were among the biggest losers. Millions of Africans were forcibly transported overseas into chattel slavery, initiating new diaspora communities under abysmal conditions.

North America

After nearly a century of Spanish and Portuguese supremacy in the New World, the Dutch Republic, England, and France mounted formidable challenges. All three had developed expertise in the construction of high-quality ships, and all three fostered business groups skilled in trade and motivated by profit, with strong ties to political leadership. At first, all three concentrated on the Caribbean and its potential for profits from plantations. They seized and settled outposts: England most notably in the Bahamas and Jamaica, France in Saint-Domingue (modern Haiti), and the Dutch along the Brazilian coast and in Curaçao. Later they turned to the North American mainland.

Some of the earliest European immigrants to North America were pushed out of Europe by the "**price revolution**" created by the availability of New World silver. The influx of the precious metal into Europe, and into the European trade networks in Asia, inflated prices; wages did not keep pace. Pressured by this decline in their economic condition, people living at the margins of European society sought the opportunity of new frontiers in North America. Through the seventeenth and early eighteenth centuries, these European immigrants—farmers, artisans, laborers, and agricultural workers—came in waves and appropriated different regions for their purposes. In Virginia they came at first looking for gold, beaver furs, deer skin, and a northwest passage to Asia. They failed in all these goals, and at first they failed even to survive. Of the first 900 colonists arriving in 1607–09, in Jamestown, only 60 were alive at the end of the two years; most died from famine and disease. Some 9,000 came between 1610 and 1622; at the later date, only 2,000 were alive.

After 1618 the Crown-appointed administrators of the colony offered 50 acres to anyone who would come to settle; by this date Virginia's tobacco crop became the staple product of its economy. Settlers continued to come, but the life was difficult, attractive mostly to people of the lower social classes. Many signed on as **indentured laborers**, contracting to work for a fixed period of years, usually about seven,

KEY TERMS

price revolution The massive inflation in Europe from the late 1400s to the early 1600s, caused in large part by the influx of silver and gold from the New World, but also by increased mining of precious metals in Europe, general population increase, and, in particular, increases in urban populations. The inflation tended to help urban entrepreneurs but to harm farmers and landholders.

indentured labor Labor performed under signed indenture, or contract, which binds the laborer to work for a specific employer, for a specified time (usually years), often in a distant place, in exchange for transportation and maintenance.

15.1

15.2

15.3

15.4

15.5

15.6

What were the
"New Europes"?

in exchange for ocean passage and fixed labor with a specific employer in the New World. About 75 percent of these laborers were male, most between 15 and 24 years of age. Since their masters cared little for them, they were bought and sold, sometimes worked to death, and treated not much differently from slaves. With their own lives so cheap and precarious, at the whim of both man and nature, the further massacre of Native Americans, who were seen as alien, savage, non-Christian, and an obstacle to European invasion and expansion, became a way of life for the land-hungry settlers.

Maryland also grew tobacco, but its goals included more than mere economic profit. In 1632 the English Crown had given the land to George Calvert, Lord Baltimore, and he established there a religious refuge for Catholics, who were at that time an oppressed minority in England. Catholics formed a minority of the population of the colony, but they were legally protected. Their relationships with the Native Americans, however, were also murderous.

In New England, the first collective settlement of Europeans was the Pilgrim colony founded in 1620. Dissenters from the official doctrines of the Church of England, the Pilgrims also sought a religious haven in the New World. Their community was

European settlement in eastern North America. Along the Atlantic coast of North America and Canada, Britain established an array of colonies. Thirteen of them revolted in 1776 to form the United States, but the northern areas remained loyal. The British restricted settlement across the Appalachian Mountains so that land was held by indigenous nations and, still further west, claimed by the French. Florida was held by the British from 1763 to 1783, but otherwise was a Spanish possession until it was invaded and conquered by the United States in 1818.

What were the
"New Europes"?

15.1

15.2

15.3

15.4

15.5

15.6

bound together by the Mayflower Compact, an agreement they drafted on board ship to the New World, establishing a governing body "for the general good of the colony; unto which, we promise all due submission and obedience." Of the 102 Pilgrims who landed at Plymouth, fewer than half survived the first year, but, with the help of Native Americans who befriended the settlers, the colony took root.

In 1630 another group of settlers, the Puritans, arrived in New England. The Pilgrims wished to separate from the Church of England; the Puritans wished only to purify it. They were richer and better educated than the Pilgrims. Many had some college education. The English king Charles I (whom many suspected of secret Catholicism and who clashed with Protestant hardliners at home), eager to get them out of England, gave them a charter to establish the Company of the Massachusetts Bay. By the end of the year, 1,000 had settled; within a decade, 20,000. Many more chose to settle in the sugar plantations of the Caribbean islands.

The Puritans had left England to seek their own religious freedom, but in New England, they denied it to others. People like Roger Williams, a minister who endorsed the separation of Church and state, were forced to flee. The Puritans were narrow in their outlook, but fiercely devoted to community, discipline, work, education, and spreading their view of religion. They scorned Native Americans, fought them, and confiscated their land with little compunction.

The Dutch began to explore and develop the land at the mouth of the Hudson River in 1609, and claimed it in the name of the Dutch Republic in 1624. The next year they purchased an island from the Manhatta Indians and established on it the town of New Amsterdam. The British captured this settlement from the Dutch in 1664 and, the next year, renamed it New York. The area developed its own polyglot, pragmatic, tolerant business ethic under the successive administrations of these two European colonizing countries.

Perhaps the most inspiring settlement was the Quaker colony of Pennsylvania, founded by William Penn, a British aristocrat who had joined the Society of Friends, as Quakers are called formally, inspired by a lecture on the Society's principles of freedom of conscience, nonviolence, and pacifism. Pennsylvania and its first capital, Philadelphia (whose name means "brotherly love") (and which is the home town of this book's author), became known throughout Western Europe for religious toleration, and people of many countries and faiths immigrated there: "English, Highland Scots, French, Germans, Irish, Welsh, Swedes, Finns, and Swiss … Mennonites, Lutherans, Dutch Reformed, Baptists, Anglicans, Presbyterians, Catholics, Jews," and a few hermits and mystics. Indeed, even Native Americans immigrated to flee the violence against them that was endemic elsewhere. Unfortunately, the non-Quaker immigrant-invaders did not share Penn's early commitment to tolerant, peaceful interracial relationships with the Native Americans, regulated by legal contracts and personal contacts. After Penn's death, they too pushed the native peoples off the land, although with less violence than elsewhere.

While the English were establishing numerous diverse, thriving colonies along the Atlantic Coast, from Newfoundland to South Carolina, and inland on Hudson's Bay, the French were

Puritans arrive in New England. Religious freedom and economic opportunity were the two great attractions for European immigrants to the New World. Many of the immigrants from England were dissenters from the established official Church. Their independence was a background factor that later helped to inspire the American Revolution in 1776. Some of the dissenters, however, like the Puritans, were themselves intolerant toward others who settled in their communities, forcing them to conform or leave.

Read the Document: William Bradford, excerpt from Of Plymouth Plantation on MyHistoryLab

15.1 What were the "New Europes"?

15.2

15.3

15.4

15.5

15.6

settling, lightly, the inland waterways of the St. Lawrence River, the Great Lakes, and the Mississippi River, as well as Gulf Coast Louisiana. During the global warfare between Britain and France, the Seven Years War of 1756–63, British military forces conquered the North American mainland from the Atlantic to the Mississippi. Their victory ensured that North America would be English-speaking. French cultural influences and migration, however, continued to be felt in the region of Quebec, and it continues as a French-speaking province today. Far across the continent, a few hundred Russians were arriving in Alaska from across Siberia and the Bering Straits (see below). By 1750, about four million people of European origin inhabited North America.

The Antipodes: Australia and New Zealand, 1600–1900

Crossing the Atlantic became relatively quick and easy, but reaching Australia and New Zealand, on the opposite side of the globe, was quite a different matter. Even their neighbors had established only minimal contact with them. There had been some landings in the sixteenth century by Asians who came to the north coast of Australia in search of a species of sea slug that looked like a withered penis when smoked and dried. The slugs became Indonesia's largest export to the Chinese, who valued them as aphrodisiacs.

Historians and cartographers reading information inscribed in later French maps debate whether or not Portuguese sailors reached Australia in the 1520s; in any case, there is no evidence of any continuing contact. In the early 1600s, a few Dutch sailors reached parts of the coast, several wrecking their ships in the process. Between 1642 and 1644, under commission from the Dutch East India Company, the Dutch commander Abel Tasman (c. 1605–59) began the systematic exploration of New Zealand; the sea—later named for him—that separates Australia from New Zealand; the island that was later named Tasmania; and the north coast of Australia. He reported "naked beach-roving wretches, destitute even of rice … miserably poor, and in many places of a very bad disposition" (cited in Hughes, p. 48). With such unpromising descriptions reaching England, and the general decline of Spanish, Dutch, and Portuguese power, Australia remained almost untouched by Europeans for a century and a half, and the pattern of immigration from Europe lags behind the pattern going to the western hemisphere by a similar amount of time. Then the English conquered and sent migrants to the Pacific Islands.

In 1768, the English captain James Cook (1728–79) set out on a three-year voyage that took him to Tahiti to record astronomical observations; to Australia to determine the nature of the "Southern Continent" reported by Tasman; to map New Zealand; and, thanks to the zeal of a young amateur botanist, Joseph Banks (1743–1820), to report on the natural resources of all these distant lands. The success of Cook's three-year voyage was made possible by new navigational instruments that could chart longitude and thus establish location at sea, and by discoveries of proper food supplements containing vitamin C to prevent scurvy among the sailors. (Vasco da Gama had lost two-thirds of his crew to scurvy on his round-trip journey to India; Ferdinand Magellan had lost 80 percent of his on his trip across the Pacific.) Cook's descriptions of the people he encountered in Australia differed sharply from those of Tasman. He found them peaceful—unlike the Maori of New Zealand. This sealed the fate of Australia.

On the basis of Cook's report, the British government decided that Australia could serve as the "dumping ground" it had been seeking for the prisoners who were overcrowding the jails at home. (Until the Revolutionary War, the American colonies had served this purpose.) British settlement in Australia thus began in the form of penal colonies. From 1788, when the first shipload of convicts arrived, until the 1850s, "transportation" to Australia was the only alternative for British prisoners sentenced to death. Under the "assignment system," convicts were assigned for the

SOURCE

Captain Cook Encounters the Aboriginals of Australia

Abel Tasman's description of the fierce Maori of New Zealand discouraged Europeans from further exploration of those islands. A similarly dismal, and racist, report on Australia was written by the only European to have visited it, William Dampier, who had come to the north coast from New Holland (Indonesia) in 1688:

> The inhabitants of this country are the miserablest people in the World … They have great Heads, round Foreheads, and great Brows. Their Eye-lids are always half closed, to keep the Flies out of their Eyes … therefore they cannot see far.
>
> They are long-visaged, and of a very unpleasing aspect; having no one graceful feature in their faces.
>
> They have no houses, but lye in the open Air, without any covering; the Earth being their Bed, and the Heaven their Canopy …
>
> I did not perceive that they did worship anything. (cited in Hughes, p. 48)

Captain Cook's view was the absolute contrary:

> They may appear to some to be the most wretched people upon Earth, but in reality they are far happier than we Europeans; being wholy unacquainted not only with the superfluous, but the necessary Conveniencies so much sought after in Europe, they are happy in not knowing the use of them. They live in Tranquility which is not disturb'd by the Inequality of Condition: The Earth and sea of their own accord furnishes them with all things necessary for life, they covet not Magnificent Houses, Houshold-stuff, etc., they live in a warm and fine Climate and enjoy a very wholesome Air, so that they have very little need of Clothing and this they seem to be fully sencible of, for many to whome we gave Cloth etc. to, left it carlessly upon the Sea beach and in the woods as a thing they had no manner of use for. In short they seem'd to set no Value upon any thing we gave them, nor would they ever part with any thing of their own for any one article we could offer them; this in my opinion argues that they think themselves provided with all the necessarys of Life and that they have no superfluities. (Cook, Vol. I, p. 399)

Cook took with him on the voyage a young botanist, Joseph Banks. Banks' descriptions of the Aboriginals presented them as timid, without property, and few in number. Although Banks was not proposing colonization, those who wished it could find encouragement in his comments. Banks and his associate Daniel Solander brought back from the three-year trip some 30,000 specimens representing 3,000 species, of which 1,600 had never before been seen by European scientists. Not all of these were from Australia, but in honor of the work of Banks and Solander, Cook named his principal harbor in Australia "Botany Bay."

Australia was distant from Europe, but based on Cook's discoveries, it seemed to hold rich promise for future encounters.

---

duration of their sentences to particular masters, about 90 percent of them private individuals and about 10 percent government officials superintending public works projects. Conditions among the prisoners were extremely harsh, and sexual relationships in particular reflected both the demography and the harshness. Men outnumbered women among the prisoners by a ratio of 6 to 1; in the cities, 4 to 1; in the countryside, 20 to 1. Both prostitution and rape were common among the women; homosexuality flourished among the men. Beginning in 1835, new prison acts in Britain began to provide for prisons at home, and the use of Australia as a prison colony quickly declined. By 1868, the last convict ship unloaded its cargo of Irish prisoners in Western Australia.

The early British colonization of Australia began at Botany Bay, adjacent to Sydney, and then at other points along the southeast coast, the best watered and most fertile part of the country. Because mountains pressed close against the coast and fresh water was scarce, progress inland was problematic, and settlement by Europeans was slow, based on commercial agriculture in wool, dairy cattle, and the cultivation of sugar.

The coming of Europeans, even in small numbers, destroyed the fragile ecology of the indigenous civilization, which survived only in the center and far north of the continent. As in other "New Europes," European diseases killed off the overwhelming majority of the Aborigines, the indigenous Australians. In addition, their hunting grounds were displaced by the sheep and cattle, fences and pasturage of the British settlers. Finally, the savagery and the explicit policies of the British, both official and unofficial, overwhelmed them. A large proprietor of sheep and cattle "narrated as a good thing, that he had been one of a party who had pursued the

What were the "New Europes"?

15.1

15.2

15.3

15.4

15.5

15.6

A government jail gang, Sydney, New South Wales, eighteenth century. After they lost their colonies in the American Revolution and their prison colonies among them, the British were searching for a new pen for their convicts. Australia met their needs. The first shipload of convicts arrived in 1788, the last in 1868. (Private collection)

blacks, in consequence of cattle having been rushed by them, and he was sure they shot upwards of a hundred … [H]e maintained that there was nothing wrong in it, that it was preposterous to suppose they had souls" (Hughes, p. 277).

At first, the Australian Aborigines, who lived nomadically by hunting and gathering, retreated in the face of white advances, but later they began to resist, defending their ancestral territories as best they could with bows and arrows and spears against British weaponry. They resisted in some places for up to ten years, stealing British

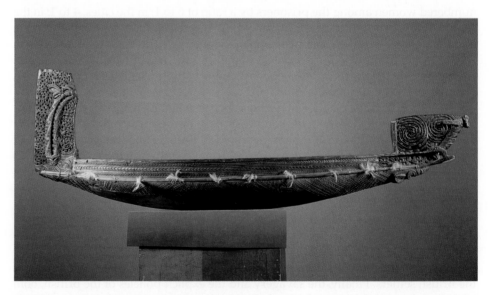

A model war canoe, Gisborne, New Zealand, eighteenth century. Until the end of the eighteenth century, a Maori war canoe was the most prized and decorated clan possession.

British colonies in 1830

British territory 1806

British expansion by 1830

British expansion by 1854

Great Trek from 1835

Transvaal
(South African Republic 1852)

Orange Free State 1854

Limpopo

Johannesburg
Pretoria

Kalahari

Witwatersrand
Vaal

BECHUANA

Delagoa
Bay

Orange
Kimberley
Bloemfontein

SWAZI

GRIQUA

BASUTO
ZULU

NATAL
PONDO
Durban

Atlantic
Ocean

Graff-Reinet

CAPE COLONY
XOSA

Drakensberg

Indian
Ocean

Cape
Town
Cape of
Good Hope

Port
Elizabeth

QUEENSLAND
1859

Great Dividing Range

SOUTH
AUSTRALIA
1836

NEW
SOUTH
WALES
1855

Moreton
Bay

Brisbane

Port Augusta

Darling

Murray
Murrumbidgee

Adelaide

Bathurst
Port
Macquarie

Botany
Bay
Newcastle

Sydney

VICTORIA
1855

Melbourne

Tasman

Sea

Bass Strait

Port Dalrymple
Macquarie Harbour

Launceston

Hobart
TASMANIA
Port Arthur

Southern
Ocean

area settled by 1830

area settled by 1850

1855 date of creation
of state

▲ penal colonies

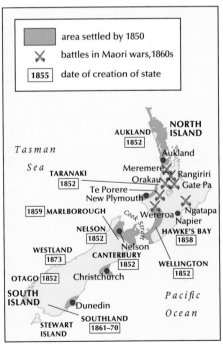

area settled by 1850

battles in Maori wars,1860s

1855 date of creation of state

NORTH
ISLAND

AUKLAND
1852

Tasman

Sea

Aukland

TARANAKI
1852

Meremere
Orakau

Rangiriri
Gate Pa

Te Porere
New Plymouth

Ngatapa
Wereroa
Napier

1859 MARLBOROUGH

Cook Strait

HAWKE'S
BAY
1858

NELSON
1852

WESTLAND
1873

Nelson

CANTERBURY
1852

WELLINGTON
1852

OTAGO 1852

Christchurch

SOUTH
ISLAND

Dunedin

STEWART
ISLAND

SOUTHLAND
1861–70

Pacific

Ocean

British settlement in India, Australia, New Zealand, and South Africa. From India, the British sought the profits of trade and, later, the glory of conquest and the extortion of taxes and cheap labor. Elsewhere they sought to establish settler colonies. British colonists ousted the Dutch from Cape Colony, grasped the habitable littoral of southeast Australia (initially colonizing it with prisoners and other social outcasts), and claimed the world's most southerly inhabitable territory, New Zealand, as a promised land for its swelling early nineteenth-century population.

15.1   What were the
"New Europes"?

15.2

15.3

15.4

15.5

15.6

Captain Hobson signing the Treaty of Waitanga with Maori chiefs, 1840. The treaty was intended to secure the annexation of New Zealand to the British government, while guaranteeing the constitutional rights of the Maoris. But language difficulties and cultural differences caused misinterpretation of the fine print, and the settlers' sense of racial superiority over the "natives" eventually precipitated wars and the conquest of Maori lands.

guns and learning to use them, attacking sheep, cattle, horses, and homes. The British response to the resistance was intensified by the belief that the Aborigines could neither be attracted nor compelled into productive work for the settlers. In 1788, when Europeans first arrived to settle Australia, there had been perhaps 300,000 Aborigines. By 2000, the 19 million inhabitants of Australia were 92 percent European, 7 percent Asian, and 1 percent Aboriginal. Today, most of Australia's 50,000 full-blooded Aborigines, and many of its 150,000 part-Aborigines, live on reservations in arid inland regions.

The devastation caused by the arrival of British settlers was repeated in New Zealand. The Maori, an east Polynesian people, had arrived and settled there about 750 C.E. They had lived there for almost a thousand years, probably in isolation, until Tasman reached New Zealand's west coast in 1642. The Maori killed four members of his party and prevented his landing. More than a century later, Cook explored New Zealand for four months and found the Maori brave, warlike, and cannibalistic. Banks, who was on the voyage, wrote: "I suppose they live intirely [sic] on fish, dogs, and enemies."

The people may have been fierce, but the seals and whales in the coastal waters, and the flax and timber on the land, attracted hunters and traders from Australia, America, and Britain. The first missionaries came in 1814 to convert the Maori. Warfare against and among the Maori was made more deadly by weapons introduced by Europeans. Diseases accompanying the European arrival, especially tuberculosis, venereal diseases, and measles, cut the Maori population from about 200,000 when Cook arrived to perhaps 100,000 in 1840 and to 42,000 by the end of the century. In 1840, British settlers signed a treaty with a group of Maori chiefs that gave sovereignty to the British Crown. Although they declared equal rights under law for Maoris and Europeans, in practice they enforced racial inequality. The British confiscated Maori lands on North Island and precipitated wars that drove the Maori from some of New Zealand's richest lands.

South Africa, 1652–1820

15.1

15.2

How did Russia expand in the seventeenth century?

15.3

15.4

15.5

15.6

The Dutch East India Company sent the first European settlers to South Africa in 1652. They established Cape Town to facilitate shipping between Europe and Asia. The Company soon invited Dutch, French, and German settlers to move inland and to create ranches in Cape Colony. By 1700, the Europeans held most of the good farmland in the region; by 1795, they had spread 300 miles north and 500 miles east of Cape Town. The colony then had a total population of 60,000, of which one-third were whites. The African peoples consisted of two main ethnic groups—the Khoikhoi herdsmen and the San hunters—with some from other African groups and some peoples of mixed ancestry.

In 1795, Britain took control of the Cape Colony from its Dutch settlers to prevent it from falling to France, which had conquered the Netherlands during the Wars of the French Revolution. In 1814, the Dutch formally ceded the Cape to the British, and the first British colonists arrived in 1820. The continuing struggle for land and power among the British, Dutch, and Africans is discussed in the chapter entitled "Political Revolutions in Europe and the Americas."

Russian Expansion

15.2 How did Russia expand in the seventeenth century?

Russian penetration of Siberia began in the late sixteenth and early seventeenth centuries. Trappers, traders, and explorers moved in as Russian troops and Cossacks continued to reclaim land from the Mongol conquerors. They built trading forts and declared Russian sovereignty all the way to the Bering Sea, and, in the eighteenth century, even on to Alaska. Later they were joined by Russian farmers seeking to establish farms to provide food for the settlers in this bleak region. Many of the local Siberian inhabitants—living nomadic lives with their reindeer, or persisting as hunter-gatherers—succumbed to new diseases carried by the invaders, the universal consequence. Many survivors, however, saw new opportunities offered by the traders and began to alter their way of life, settling into villages. Most adopted Christianity.

In the eighteenth century the fur trade declined; mining, especially of silver, remained as the most important local industry. Meanwhile, the Russian government used Siberia to incarcerate its political prisoners as well as common criminals. Larger-scale settlement in this remote region came only much later, aboard the trans-Siberian railway, which first reached this region in 1891.

The first Europeans known to have arrived in Alaska came from across the Bering Straits in 1741, and claimed the land for Russia. A handful of Russians, fewer than one thousand, including Siberians, came to inhabit Russian America, with most of their settlements in what is today Alaska, and one—Fort Ross (1812–41), named apparently for Russia—in what is today northern California. The explorers sent back word of fur-bearing otters, seals, and beavers. Traders followed and established trading posts. The first permanent Russian settlement was established on Kodiak Island; the second on Unalaska Island, for which all of "Russian America" was named; the third at present-day Sitka, which became the capital of Russian America. In 1799 Tsar Paul I granted to the founder of the Russian-American Company a monopoly over the fur trade and a mandate to colonize Alaska.

The Russian record of dealing with indigenous inhabitants, Aleuts and others, was as dismal as that of Europeans on the east coast. The Russian fur traders forced the natives into working for them in conditions that often resembled slavery. When the Aleuts revolted, the Russians killed many of them; and European diseases killed far more.

15.1
15.2
15.3 Why did slavery rise in the Atlantic Ocean basin?
15.4
15.5
15.6

The small Russian settlement at Fort Ross closed in 1841 as the fur-bearing animals in the area had been hunted to exhaustion and agreements were reached with Americans and British settlers to supply food needed by the Russians in Alaska.

🔍 View the **Closer Look**: **The Remezov Chronicle** on **MyHistoryLab**

Slavery: Enforced Migration, 1500–1750

15.3 Why did slavery rise in the Atlantic Ocean basin?

Most European emigrants were free people who moved by choice. But throughout the seventeenth and eighteenth centuries, Africa contributed more immigrants to the New World than did Europe. These Africans came as slaves, taken as captives and transported against their will. Trading in African slaves was not new. The Romans had included Africans among their slaves and, as we have seen in the chapter entitled "Establishing World Trade Routes," since about the seventh century C.E. Arab camel caravans had carried gold and slaves northward across the Sahara to the Mediterranean in exchange for European cotton and woolen textiles, copper, and brass. On its east coast, Africa had long been integrated into the Indian Ocean trade by Muslim and Arab traders. They exported from Africa gold, slaves, ivory, and amber, and imported cotton and silk cloth.

Portuguese and, later, other European merchants and sailors reoriented the trade routes of Africa to the Atlantic coast. Caravans continued to cross the desert, but far more trade now came to the new coastal town fortresses constructed at such places as St. Louis, Cape Coast, Elmina, Bonny, Luanda, Benguela, and on São Tomé Island. Here, Africans brought gold and slaves to trade to the European shippers. The number of slaves sold rose from under 1,000 a year in 1451–75, when Portugal began to trade in slaves from the West African coast, to about 7,500 a year in the first half of the seventeenth century, to about 50,000 a year throughout the eighteenth and the first half of the nineteenth centuries. In all, the transatlantic slave trade carried some ten million people from Africa to the western hemisphere to work as slaves, generally on sugar, tobacco, and cotton plantations.

📖 Read the **Document**: **William Bosman, from A New and Accurate Description of the Coast of Guinea Divided into the Gold, the Slave, and the Ivory Coasts** on **MyHistoryLab**

The Plantation Economy

The slaves took on economic importance in direct proportion to the expansion of the sugar-plantation economy of the Caribbean after 1650. In the 1700s, the plantations reached their maximum productivity and profitability. Between 1713 and 1792 Britain alone imported £162 million of goods from the Caribbean, almost all of it sugar. This was half again as much as all British imports from Asia during the same period. France held the richest single sugar colony in the Caribbean, Saint-Domingue.

Historian Philip Curtin analyzed the structure of the plantation economy that produced the sugar, and stressed six key points:

- It relied on slave labor.
- It was organized as an early, large-scale capitalist enterprise with gangs of laborers.
- Its owners held legal rights over the lives of the workers.
- It supplied a crop for export to distant European markets but often did not grow its own food; it was completely reliant on international trade for profits and for necessities.

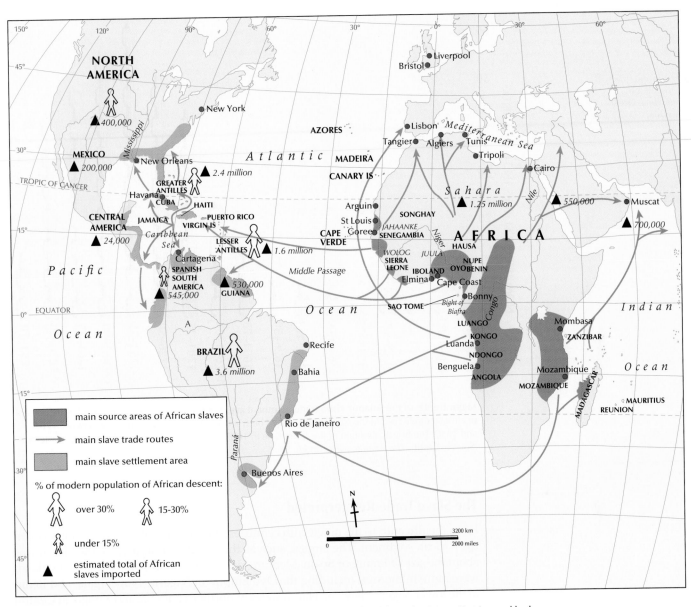

The African slave trade, c. 1550–1800. A trade in sub-Saharan African slaves dated from the Roman Empire, and had been lucratively developed by Arab merchants since the eighth century. Similarly, trade in African slaves to Arabia and India also went back centuries. The impact of Western European entrepreneurs seeking cheap labor for the Americas was, however, unparalleled. About ten million Africans survived the Middle Passage by boat from Africa to the Americas between about 1550 and the late nineteenth century; they formed a new African diaspora in the New World.

📖 Read the **Document**: **A Defense of the Slave Trade, July 1740** on **MyHistoryLab**

15.1
15.2
15.3
15.4
15.5
15.6

Why did slavery rise in the Atlantic Ocean basin?

- Its "political control over the system lay on another continent and in another kind of society."
- In its organization, the sugar plantation was a forerunner of factory labor.

Slaves died young on the sugar plantations of the Caribbean and Brazil, where many owners believed it was cheaper to work them to death and buy replacements from among those coming from Africa than to feed, clothe, and house them adequately to sustain life. In North America, which concentrated on producing other crops and where planters encouraged their slaves to reproduce, they fared somewhat better.

🔍 View the **Closer Look**: **A Sugar Plantation in the West Indies** on **MyHistoryLab**

15.1

15.2

15.3 Why did slavery
rise in the
15.4 Atlantic Ocean
basin?

15.5

15.6

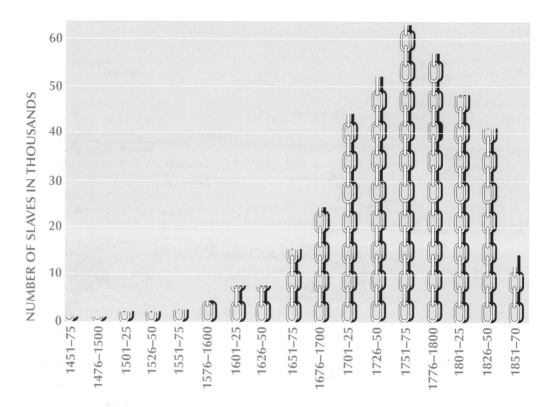

Major trends of the Atlantic slave trade in annual average number of slaves imported. Sixty percent of all slaves delivered to the New World arrived between 1721 and 1820; 80 percent between 1701 and 1850. The British abolition of the slave trade in 1807 had some effect, but it did not stop the trade. (Source: Curtin, *The Atlantic Slave Trade*)

The Slave Trade Reinterpreted

From the fifteenth to the nineteenth centuries, individual states were taking form on the African continent. The largest, such as the Songhay Empire of West Africa, was about the size of France or Spain. Medium-size states, the size of Portugal or England, were more numerous, including the Oyo Empire in Nigeria, Nupe, Igala, and Benin in the lower Niger valley; the Hausa states of northern Nigeria; and Kongo, in Central Africa. Slavery and the slave trade were important to the rise and decline of these states. In a region where land was not privately owned, slaves represented the main form of wealth. A rich state held many slaves. Slaves were a source of labor, a means for their owners to increase wealth. According to historian Paul Lovejoy, "there were at least as many enslaved people in Africa as there were in the Americas, at any time in the past … At the outbreak of the U.S. Civil War, there were probably more slaves in the Muslim states of West Africa than in the Confederacy, or indeed in Cuba and Brazil" (Lovejoy, p. xxiv).

The trade in slaves was a means of further increasing wealth. Long before Europeans arrived on the Atlantic coast, slavery was big business in these African states, much of it transacted by Arab Muslim traders. Systematic data on the slave trade to the New World comes from ship logs (see How Do We Know? box, opposite). Data on slaves carried northward across the Sahara and eastward across the Indian Ocean from Red Sea and East African ports are less systematic. Lovejoy presents recent estimates of total traffic in black slaves transported and sold in these three regions, 650–1600 c.e.: across the Sahara 4,820,0000; from Red Sea ports 1,600,000; and from East African ports 800,000. He looks at the estimated total of 7,220,000 and calls it a rough approximation of a realistic figure that could be anywhere between 3.5 million

HOW DO WE KNOW?

How Many Slaves?

Philip Curtin's *The Atlantic Slave Trade: A Census*, published in 1969, presented a landmark study on the demographics of the slave trade. Concluding that the existing estimate of 15 million slaves carried from Africa to the New World had been accepted with little basis in research, Curtin investigated the numbers. He limited his research to data already published rather than undertaking original archival searches of his own. From the import records of specific African and American ports, shipping records, and projections based on historical slave populations in the Americas, Curtin produced the first systematic analysis of the quantity of slaves delivered to the Americas. (Other researchers at the time had been reviewing data on the slave trade primarily for individual countries, or even individual ports, either exporting or importing.)

In the early 1990s, a group of historians began seriously discussing, then planning, then finding funding for, and finally (in 1993) initiating "a single multisource dataset of trans-Atlantic slave trade voyages," integrating data on the British, Dutch, French, and Portuguese trade. As they analyzed and standardized available data, they also began collecting more. By 1999, they realized that materials on the Spanish and Portuguese trade were underrepresented, but were available. With increased funding, they were able to launch an expanded project, "Voyages: The Trans-Atlantic Slave Trade Database," with "information on more than 35,000 slave voyages that forcibly embarked over 12 million Africans for transport to the Americas between the sixteenth and nineteenth centuries." The data are available on line (http://www.slavevoyages.org) by aggregate data, by voyage, and in some cases by individual slave. The "database identifies 91,491 Africans taken from captured slave ships or from African trading sites. It displays the African name, age, gender, origin, country, and places of embarkation and disembarkation of each individual." The best available estimates today tell us that 12.5 million Africans were forced to undertake the Middle Passage and around 10.7 million completed it, the largest forced migration in modern history.

The largest importers of slaves were Brazil, with almost 6 million, and the Caribbean, with about 3.3 million. The United States imported only about 3.4 percent of all the slaves brought to the Americas, about 305,000 out of 12.5 million. Curtin had discussed this earlier: "Contrary to the parochial view of history that most North Americans pick up in school, the United States was only a marginal recipient of slaves from Africa. The real center of the trade was tropical America, with almost 90 percent going to the Atlantic fringe from Brazil through the Guianas to the Caribbean coast and islands" (p. 74).

Curtin also explored the effects on reproduction of the slave trade. Only about 40 percent of the slaves sold overseas were women, and so in Africa population losses to the next generation

were proportionately limited; but in the Americas, with fewer females, the slaves did not reproduce their own numbers. These rates of reproduction, however, varied in different areas. North America imported relatively few slaves because those who were imported reproduced more abundantly than slaves elsewhere, for reasons yet unknown: "Rather than sustaining the regular excess of deaths over births typical of tropical America, the North American colonies developed a pattern of natural growth among the slaves … By the end of the eighteenth century, North American slave populations were growing at nearly the same rate as that of the settler populations from Europe" (p. 73). Various hypotheses have been put forward to explain the higher rates of reproduction in North America. The first, and perhaps most obvious, holds that slaves in North America were better treated than elsewhere. The second argues that slaves in North America apparently breast-fed their children for only one year, in contrast to the two years more typical in the Caribbean. Breast-feeding has a contraceptive effect that would have reduced birth rates more in the Caribbean than in the U.S.

Curtin analyzed slavery as a business. For example, he pointed out that the location of the most active slave-trading varied over time, according to the law of supply and demand. Where slaves were plentiful, often because of warfare and the seizing of captives who could be sold into slavery, prices fell; then more European slavers arrived to take advantage of the low prices, increasing demand, raising prices, and encouraging European slavers to look elsewhere. The marketplace shifted as prices oscillated. The result seems to be that no area was constantly a supplier, but that each had time to recover some of its population losses. On the other hand, no area remained immune to the economic attractions of the market. The sale and purchase of slaves infected the entire coastline. The findings of "Voyages" bear out this supply–demand relationship in the geographical and cost basis of transatlantic slavery. The "Voyages" website makes available to the public vast quantities of raw data, as well as analysis, and will allow further research by students as well as professional historians.

View the **Closer Look**: **A West African View of the Portuguese** on **MyHistoryLab**

- Philip Curtin's studies of the slave trade say very little about moral aspects. What is the importance of information about the systems and statistics of plantation slavery, separate from the consideration of morals?
- Please give examples of ways in which the slave trade was subject to the economic laws of supply and demand.
- What regions of the Americas imported the most slaves?

and 10 million. He estimates another 900,000 total across all these regions in the seventeenth century, and another 1,300,000 in the eighteenth (Lovejoy, pp. 56–57). The total of these numbers, although accumulated over a much longer period of time, is comparable to the totals for the transatlantic slave trade.

15.1

15.2

15.3 Why did slavery
rise in the
Atlantic Ocean
basin?

15.4

15.5

15.6

A slave market, from *Al Magamat* (*The Meetings*), fourteenth century. Muslims owned and traded slaves from the earliest days of the Islamic religion. Their trade in slaves included Africa, southeastern Europe, Arabia, and the lands surrounding the Indian Ocean. Islamic law governing the treatment of slaves made the practice relatively humane; slaves were used more frequently for domestic service than for gang labor. In principle, Muslims were not permitted to enslave other Muslims. Practice often differed, but granting freedom to Muslim slaves was considered virtuous. (Bibliothèque Nationale, Paris)

If the numbers were so large, asks researcher Ronald Segal, why are more blacks not in evidence in Muslim North Africa, Arab countries, and India? His answer: the absence of racial prejudice led to high rates of intermarriage and absorption of the slaves into the general population.

Although slavery in Islamic countries was usually quite different from the plantation slavery of the New World, plantations in southern Morocco in the fifteenth century, cotton plantations in Egypt, grain producers in East Africa, and clove plantations in Zanzibar and Pemba all in the nineteenth enslaved gangs of slave laborers. Segal also notes that black Africans were often used as soldiers and even generals and admirals in the armed forces of countries from Spain to Bengal. Sometimes they rose to these positions despite their legal status as slaves.

This prevalence of slavery in Africa, and of international commerce in African slaves, helps to explain a turnabout in the interpretation of the slave trade. In this interpretation, Africans are active participants who helped to build up this important trade. When European traders offered new opportunities, African businessmen, who were already active in the internal slave trade, joined in, continuing to control the trade up to the water's edge. European demand drove the vast increase in the slave trade, but Europeans lacked the military strength, the immunity to disease, and the knowledge of the terrain to enter the interior of the continent. They stayed in coastal enclaves, while Africans captured the slaves and brought them to be purchased. Occasionally, African rulers attempted to limit the trade, but both African and European traders seemed beyond their control.

15.1

15.2

15.3

15.4

15.5

15.6

What were the
Asian migrations?

Some of the trading communities of Africa—ethnic groups that traditionally facilitated and controlled trade—probably profited, including the Jahaanke of the Gambia–Niger River region; the Juula of northern Ghana, Ivory Coast, and the Upper Niger River; the Wolof of Senegal; and the Awka and Aro of Iboland in Nigeria. A new community of African–Portuguese traders was also born as Portuguese and Africans along the coast bonded and had children.

Scholars differ in evaluating the effects of the slave trade on the total economy of Africa. Some, following the pioneering work of Walter Rodney in his *How Europe Underdeveloped Africa* (1972), cite dire economic consequences. The slave trade abducted from Africa millions of its strongest and most resilient men and women; no one can estimate the opportunities lost for their native lands. The slave trade also encouraged warfare among African nations for the purpose of capturing prisoners who could then be sold as slaves. Similarly, it encouraged kidnappers. Some more recent historians, however, suggest that the slave trade, despite its enormous absolute size, was small relative to the total size of Africa's population and internal economy, and therefore had little effect. In addition, Crosby points out that Africa received new crops such as maize and manioc (cassava) as part of the Columbian Exchange. These became staple foods and, ironically, may actually have increased the population more than the export of slaves depleted it. And, of course, slavery established a new population of African origin—a new African diaspora—throughout the western hemisphere. This debate over the size and significance of the slave trade continues.

Asian Migrations, 1300–1750

15.4   What were the Asian migrations?

Just as Europeans were transforming the Americas and other parts of the world through their migrations, Asians were conquering and moving into their own new territories. Vast, successive waves of immigrant conquerors swept out of central Asia between 1300 and 1750, creating three new empires and several new ruling dynasties within the existing empire of China. Turkic-speaking invaders founded the Ottoman Empire, which sprawled across western Asia, southeastern Europe, and North Africa; the Safavid Empire in Persia; and the Mughal Empire in south Asia. In China, the Mongol descendants of Chinggis Khan and, later, the Manchus created new dynasties that ruled over the existing empire.

The conquests of the Western Europeans and the central Asians show remarkable similarities. The time frame for these invasions and conquests is roughly parallel because they are related to one another. The Ottoman conquests blocked access to the eastern Mediterranean and the Middle East, providing the inspiration for the Europeans to launch their overseas explorations. The distances each group traveled, thousands of miles, were equally vast. Both were ultimately motivated by a desire to conquer and subdue that frequently led to ruthless cruelty. Both imposed new cultures on the peoples they conquered—but the degree of this imposition was starkly different.

The contrasts are equally remarkable. The Asians traveled overland. Although they could be very violent, they did not so utterly destroy the peoples they conquered, perhaps because the peoples the Asians conquered had immunity to each other's diseases thanks to their long contact. Since the Asian conquerors were mostly nomadic horsemen with little experience of sedentary society, they were limited in the degree to which they could influence their subjects. Instead, over time they tended to adopt the ideas and institutions of the peoples they conquered, rather than displacing existing societies with new ones of their own design. In large measure they were assimilated by the peoples they defeated. By the early eighteenth century, as Western Europe was increasing in power and wealth, all four of the Asian empires were in decline.

Eurasian empires, 1650. Eurasia on the eve of European expansion was dominated by a complex of huge, interlocking, land-based empires, linked by overland trade routes, and by the Arab trading ecumene of the Indian Ocean. The four empires highlighted here were land-based, inward-looking, and ill-prepared for the challenge of European imperialism that would arrive by sea and, over the next 400 years, effectively undermine them.

15.1

15.2

15.3

15.4 What were the Asian migrations?

15.5

15.6

The Ottoman Empire, 1300–1700

The Ottoman Empire was named for Osman, a Turkish leader whose military victory in 1301 established its foundation in northwest Anatolia. As the Ottomans expanded from this local base they confronted the Byzantine Empire to the west and the Seljuq Turks—another Turkic-speaking group—to the east. Through the thirteenth and fourteenth centuries they expanded their holdings, capturing much of Anatolia and crossing into Europe to take Gallipoli in 1354. The Ottoman Empire rose to prominence at the same time as Spain and Portugal did in Western Europe and was at its height in 1600. By 1700, however, it had begun to decline.

Three groups led and sustained the Turkish invasions. The *gazis* were Turkish warriors inspired by Islam to conquer territories and bring them under the *dar al-Islam*, a government hospitable to Islam. **Sufis** were members of religious orders, often practicing mystical and ecstatic rituals, who accompanied the troops and introduced Islam within the conquered regions. Each of the Sufi orders established its own centers, which served to unite the groups and often acted as recruiting grounds for more Sufis. Finally, the *janissaries* were slaves captured or bought as young boys from among the conquered populations, usually from among the Christians of the Balkans, to be converted to Islam and trained rigorously to serve as the elite of the Turkish armies. Removed from their families and usually not permitted to marry, the *janissaries* owed full allegiance to the Ottoman sultan, although they periodically revolted in protest at lack of pay or proper recognition. The system began in the late 1300s, at a point when the Ottomans needed to strengthen their armies for warfare on two fronts, Anatolia and the Balkans. Although the Janissary corps continued into the nineteenth century, it began to decline in importance by the early 1600s as the Janissary troops, and their special vigor and dedication, were

KEY TERMS

Sufi In Islam, a member of one of the orders practicing mystical forms of worship that first arose in the eighth and ninth centuries C.E. Some Muslims see Sufis as fulfilling the mission of Islam; others criticize them as not adhering strictly enough to the formal laws and practices of Islam.

janissaries The elite corps of the Ottoman armies. Captured or bought as children from Christian families, usually in the Balkans, these soldiers were converted to Islam and trained.

CHAPTER FIFTEEN: MIGRATION 1300–1750

15.1
15.2
15.3
15.4
15.5
15.6

What were the
Asian migrations?

diluted through more conventional recruitment of more conventional troops. At its greatest strength, in the mid-sixteenth century, this slave infantry numbered about 35,000.

After establishing a foothold in Europe, the Ottomans invited Turkish warriors into the Balkans and occupied northern Greece, Macedonia, and Bulgaria. At the Battle of Kosovo in 1389 they secured Serbia and took control of the western Balkans. Demographically, however, the invaders were not so numerous in this region, nor did they force widespread conversion. A census of 1520–30 showed that about one-fifth of the Balkan population was Muslim, about four-fifths was Christian, and there was a small Jewish minority, many of whom moved to the empire after they were expelled from Spain in 1492. In conquering Anatolia, the Turks had displaced local agricultural communities and became the majority population. In the Balkans, they settled among the local population rather than displacing it.

Under Mehmed II, "The Conqueror" (r. 1451–81), the Ottomans moved on to conquer Constantinople in 1453 and then the remainder of Anatolia, the Crimea on the north of the Black Sea, and substantial areas of Venice's empire in Greece and the Aegean. They saw themselves not only as builders of a new empire, but also as conquerors and inheritors of the Byzantine Empire and of the great Roman Empire that had preceded it. They began the process of rebuilding Constantinople into a great capital city, and by 1600 it had become the largest city in Europe, with 700,000 inhabitants. The capital attracted a great influx of immigrant scholars to its *madrasas*, religious schools, and to its bureaucratic jobs, which required Islamic learning and knowledge of the law.

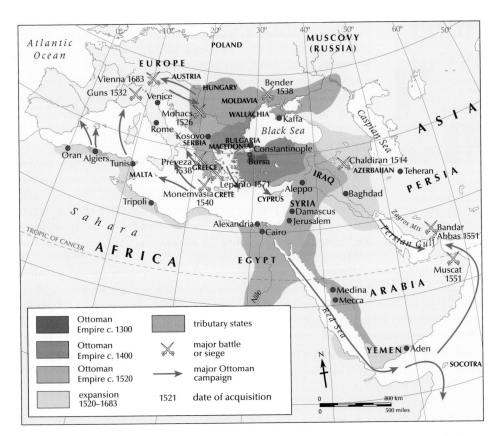

Ottoman empires, 1300–1700. As the Mongols ceased their advance, some of the peoples who had traveled with them began to assert independent power. The Ottoman Turks began to establish their new empire, which conquered Constantinople in 1453 and thrust far into southeastern Europe as well as the Mediterranean coast. Babur, a Mughal, began the conquest of India in 1526, and his grandson Akbar proceeded to construct one of the largest, most powerful, and most cultured empires of his day.

Siege of Beograd (Belgrade) by Mehmed II, sixteenth-century Persian manuscript. The Ottoman sultan Mehmed II conquered Constantinople (Istanbul) in 1453, and pushed on into and beyond the Balkans. In 1456 he besieged the city of Belgrade, the gateway to Hungary—unsuccessfully. In 1521, however, the Ottomans did successfully capture the city, solidifying their hold on southeastern Europe. (Topkapi Palace, Istanbul)

Selim I (r. 1512–20) decisively defeated the Shi'a Safavid Empire in Persia at the Battle of Chaldiran in 1514. He turned next against the Mamluk Empire of Egypt, conquering its key cities of Aleppo and Damascus, and its capital, Cairo. These victories also gave the Ottomans control of the holy cities of Jerusalem, Mecca, and Medina, and of both coasts of the Red Sea.

Suleiman (Süleyman) I, "the Magnificent" (r. 1520–66), returned to battle in Europe, adding Hungary to his empire and pushing to the gates of Vienna. As they entered central Europe, the Ottomans confronted the Habsburg Empire. Alliances here crossed religious lines, with Catholic France sometimes joining with the Muslim Ottomans against the Catholic Habsburgs. In a series of battles, which collectively formed a kind of world war, the Ottomans were defeated at sea in 1571 at Lepanto, off the coast of Greece, by a coalition of the papacy, Venice, and the Habsburgs. Finally, in 1580, a peace treaty confirmed the informal boundaries that still endure in the Mediterranean today between predominantly Christian Europe to the north and west, and predominantly Muslim North Africa and western Asia to the south and east.

Battles on land continued until 1606, when the peace treaty of Zsitva Torok confirmed Ottoman rule over Romania, Hungary, and Transylvania, but recognized the Habsburgs as their equals. Financially and militarily drained by two centuries of warfare with the Habsburgs in the Balkans and southeastern Europe, the Ottomans halted their expansion into these areas in 1606. In 1683, a last attempt to seize Vienna failed. North of the Black Sea, where Russia, Poland, and the Ottomans fought, the empire had greater success, taking control of substantial parts of the Ukraine in 1676. These victories, however, marked the maximum extent of Ottoman dominance in the region. Russia had built up its military power under Peter I, the Great (r. 1682–1725), and consolidated it under Catherine II, the Great (r. 1762–96), and now, in the mid-1700s, pushed the Ottomans back. Attempting to regain lost territory, throughout the late 1700s the Ottomans once again brought in Western European experts to retrain their military, as they had in capturing Constantinople, but this effort was too little, too late. The Ottoman Empire had fallen too far behind the Western Europeans and the Russians both economically and militarily. It could no longer catch up.

Through both immigration and natural increase, the population of the Ottoman Empire seems to have more than doubled, from 12–13 million in 1520–30, in the early years of the rule of Suleiman I (at a time when Spain may have had 5 million inhabitants; England 2.5 million; and Portugal 1 million), to 17–18 million in 1580, to possibly 30–35 million by 1600. This doubling, or even tripling, of the Empire's population was consistent with the general population increase of the Mediterranean basin, which rose from 30–35 million in 1500 to 60–70 million in 1600.

Safavid Persia, 1400–1700

In the thirteenth century the Mongols and Turks first devastated and then repopulated Persia. The invaders systematically exterminated the populations of the first cities they confronted; those in others, hearing of the massacres, fled. The invading Mongols and Turks then settled on the land, reducing to serfdom those who remained behind, and

15.1

15.2

15.3

15.4 What were the Asian migrations?

15.5

15.6

taxing them into poverty. By the end of the century, however, the invaders began to assimilate Persian ways, rebuilding the cities; redeveloping the irrigation works; supporting agriculture and trade, including the silk routes to China; and adopting both the religion of Islam and the culture of Persia, with its monarchical traditions.

In 1370 the successor to the Chagatai branch of the Mongols, Timur the Lame (*c.* 1336–1405), came to power, ruling Iran and much of northern India, Anatolia, and northern Syria from his capital in Samarqand. With this further set of invasions, Turkish peoples came to constitute about 25 percent of Iran's population, which is still the ratio today. The Mongol/Turkish invaders were pastoral peoples, and under their rule substantial agricultural land once again reverted to pasturage and villagers turned to nomadic existences, farming in valley bottoms and herding sheep in nearby mountain highlands.

Culturally, some of the Turks, as well as other ethnic groups in Iran, later came to accept the militantly religious teachings of Shaykh Safi al-Din (1252–1334). His followers, called Safavids, claimed political as well as religious authority. In 1501, a disciple of the teachings of Safi, Shah Isma'il (1487–1524), declared himself the hidden imam, the long-awaited political/religious messiah of Shi'ite Muslims. He occupied Tabriz and proclaimed himself the Shah of Iran.

The Safavids found it difficult to bring together the diverse peoples and interests of Iran. The greatest achievement was by Shah Abbas (r. 1588–1629), who built up the military capacity of the country. He did this, in part, by importing European weapons, equipment, technicians, and advisers. He acquired and built muskets and artillery that were capable of matching those of the Ottomans. Like other Safavid rulers, he brought slaves from Georgia, Armenia, and Turkish lands to form the core of his armies. Abbas also built a great capital city at Isfahan. He encouraged trade and commerce there by inviting Armenian merchants as well as many artisans, including ceramicists who could produce "Chinese" porcelains. He invited Chinese potters to teach Iranians their trade, and some of them remained and settled in Isfahan. Abbas, however, murdered competing religious leaders and groups, including other Shi'a groups as well as Sunnis and Sufis. His successors in the middle of the century gave official sanction to efforts to convert both Jews and Zoroastrians to Islam by force. But they did not succeed in bringing all the powers of his decentralized realm into a centralized monarchy.

By the end of the seventeenth century, the Safavid army was unraveling, its central administration was failing, regional powers were reasserting themselves, and Iran was in anarchy. Despite the occasional brilliant military conqueror, such as Nadir Shah (1688–1747), another Turkish/Mongol immigrant, who took the throne in 1736, Iran was already moving toward partition, first internally, and later at the hands of Europeans and Russians.

The defeat of Pir Padishah by Shah Rukh in 1403, Persian, 1420–30. Shah Rukh, son of Timur the Lame, was a direct ancestor of the Safavid Persians. During his reign, he had to deal with several rebellions, including one by the Sarbadars, a brigand community in Khurasan. Leading the decisive charge, Shah Rukh's army commander beheads one of the rebel cavalrymen. (Victoria and Albert Museum, London)

View the **Closer Look: A Safavid Battle Tunic** on **MyHistoryLab**

15.1
15.2
15.3
15.4 What were the Asian migrations?
15.5
15.6

India: The Mughal Empire, 1526–1707

The Mughals, a mixture of Mongol and Turkish peoples from central Asia, rose to power a little later than the Ottomans. In 1526 Babur (Zahir-ud-Din Mohammad, 1483–1530), a descendant of Timur the Lame on his father's side and of Chinggis Khan on his mother's side, invaded India and conquered Delhi and Agra, establishing himself as sultan. His son Humayun was defeated in battles with Afghans and driven out of India, but he fought his way back through Afghanistan and into north India before his death. The task of continuing the conquest and consolidating its administration fell to Humayun's son Akbar (1542–1605), perhaps India's greatest ruler.

Akbar, Emperor of India. Akbar was reared in exile, with his father, in the rugged terrain of Afghanistan. His childhood was dominated by physical pursuits, and he grew up without learning to read and write, although he loved to have others read to him. Akbar's father, Humayun, succeeded in returning to India and reestablishing his authority in Delhi, but when he died (after falling down a staircase), the fourteen-year-old Akbar acceded to the throne.

Four years later, Akbar began to govern as absolute monarch. Raised on stories of his ancestors Timur the Lame and Chinggis Khan and of his grandfather Babur, Akbar now set about creating an empire of his own. He showed no mercy to those who would not submit to his rule. In 1568, protracted fighting in the Mewar district culminated in a siege of the historic fortress of Chitor and ultimately the massacre of its entire population of 30,000 inhabitants. In 1572–73 Akbar conquered Gujarat, gaining control of its extensive commercial networks and its rich resources of cotton and indigo. Then came Bengal to the east, with its rice, silk, and saltpeter, Kashmir to the north, Orissa to the south, and Sind to the west. Each new conquest brought greater riches.

A great conqueror, Akbar spent years on the move with his troops, but he also built new capitals for himself, first at Agra (where his grandson would build the Taj Mahal), later at nearby Fatehpur Sikri. With his chief revenue officer, Todar Mal, he established an administrative bureaucracy modeled on a military hierarchy. He surveyed each region of India down to village level, evaluated its fertility, and established the land revenue each was to pay. His administrators collected the payment in cash. These reforms brought village India into a cash economy, while city markets encouraged the production of luxury goods for the court and everyday goods for the common people. Mughal officials, aware that their wealth would revert to the emperor at their death, lived a life of lavish consumption.

Akbar understood immediately that as a foreigner and a Muslim in an overwhelmingly Hindu country, he would have to temper conquest with conciliation. He allowed the fiercely independent Hindu Rajputs, who controlled the hilly territory of Rajasthan, to keep their ancestral lands, and he offered them roles in his government and armies. In return they paid tribute to him, supplied him with troops, and gave him their daughters in marriage alliances, since Muslims could practice polygamy. He appointed Hindus to one-third of the posts in his centralized administration. Two-thirds went to Muslims who immigrated in large numbers from Iran, Afghanistan, and central Asia to the expanding Mughal court. In 1562 Akbar discontinued the practice of enslaving prisoners-of-war and forcing them to convert to Islam. In 1563 he abolished a tax on Hindu pilgrims traveling to sacred shrines. The next year, most importantly, he revoked

Abul-Fazl presenting his book of the Akbarnama to Akbar, c. 1600. Surrounded by his courtiers, the emperor Akbar receives from his principal administrator, Abul-Fazl, the Akbarnama, an array of Mughal miniature paintings that illustrate the military, diplomatic, economic, and administrative life of Akbar's empire and government. Note the diversity in appearance and dress of the courtiers. Abul-Fazl himself was an Indian Muslim educated in Persian fashion, while Akbar was a soldier of Turkish and Mongol descent. At its best, such diversity was a mark of strength in the Mughal court. (Chester Beatty Library, Dublin)

15.1
15.2
15.3
15.4
15.5
15.6

What were the
Asian migrations?

the *jizya*, the head tax levied on non-Muslims. Between 20 and 25 percent of India's population became Muslim, most through conversion, the rest the result of immigration.

Akbar encouraged and participated personally in religious discussions among Muslims, Hindus, **Parsis** (Indians who followed Zoroaster; their name means "Persians," from the area in which Zoroaster had greatest influence), and Christians. (Jesuits visiting the court mistook Akbar's inquiries into Catholic doctrine as a willingness to convert.) Muslim Sufis spread their message in Hindi, a modern derivative of Sanskrit, the sacred language of Hindus. At the same time they inspired the creation of the Urdu (camp) language, the language of common exchange between the invaders and the resident population. Urdu used the syntactical structure of Hindi, the alphabet of Arabic and Persian, and a vocabulary of words drawn from Sanskrit, Persian, and Arabic. Akbar, in particular, encouraged these kinds of cultural **syncretism** and the mixing of groups. His tolerant practices and encouragement of integration resulted in still more individuals migrating to India.

In 1582 Akbar declared a new personal religion, the *Din-i-Ilahi*, or Divine Faith, an amalgam of Islamic, Hindu, and Parsi perspectives. He also incorporated some concepts of divine right, declaring himself the vice-regent of God and appointing himself ultimate arbiter on disputes concerning Islamic law. Elaborate ceremonials at court emphasized the emperor's supremacy, and he was careful to encourage reverence among the common people as well. Orthodox Muslims, however, saw Akbar's pronouncements as heresy and went into opposition. Several were jailed.

In 1600, at the height of Akbar's rule, the population of India reached 140–150 million, with about 110 million contained within the Mughal Empire, about the same population as China and twice that of the Ottoman Empire at its largest. The population increase that occurred all over Afro-Eurasia at this time affected India as well, and the population of the subcontinent in 1800 probably reached about 200 million.

During a reign that spanned half a century, Akbar presided over a glittering court, in which the fine arts, literature, and architecture flourished. He transformed himself from conquering despot of a foreign religious minority to respected emperor of all Hindustan. In a half-century of rule, 1556–1605, Akbar had established one of the great empires of the world.

Akbar's great-grandson and third successor, Aurangzeb (Alamgir, r. 1658–1707), continued the Mughal conquest almost to the southern tip of the country. But Aurangzeb forsook Akbar's tolerance. He imposed a poll tax on Hindus and desecrated their shrines and statues, antagonizing them and fomenting resentment. Aurangzeb's military adventures in the south overextended his armies and overtaxed the peasantry to the point of revolt. Hindu Marathas in western India and **Sikhs** in the north, as well as the Afghan Nadir Shah, who invaded from Iran in 1739, rose against the Mughal Empire. By the middle of the eighteenth century, the empire lay weak and open to new invaders from Western Europe—the British and the French.

China: The Ming and Manchu Dynasties, 1368–1750

In 1211 Chinggis Khan invaded and conquered China, destroying the Song dynasty in the process. His descendants established the Yuan dynasty, which ruled for a century (1271–1368) until the Ming dynasty drove it out and established its own long and successful rule (1368–1644).

By 1600 China's economy was flourishing and the country contained about one-fifth of the world's population, some 150 million people. Fearing another invasion from the north, like the Mongols', the Ming emperor rebuilt the Great Wall and stationed large numbers of troops nearby. Such anxiety was well founded. Invaders from the north, the Jurchen (or Manchus) of Manchuria, challenged China's power and sophistication, and contributed—along with natural disasters, virulent

KEY TERMS

Parsis ("from Persia") Those followers of the teachings of Zoroaster who fled Persia around the tenth century in the face of persecution by Muslim invaders.

syncretism The mixing of different cultural traditions into new forms. The term is also used to refer to hybridity in other areas, such as art, music, philosophy, and religion.

Sikh Member of a religious community founded in the Punjab region of northern India by Guru Nanak in the sixteenth century. Sikhism combines *bhakti*, devotional Hinduism, with Islamic Sufism. In the face of the militant opposition of their neighbors, Sikhs also became a militant armed people.

Attacks on the borders by land and sea. Chinese picture scroll, early seventeenth century. Through the fifteenth and sixteenth centuries, the Ming dynasty was bedeviled by raids and attacks from the barbarian peoples on China's northern frontiers. The Great Wall underwent major reconstruction during this period. Meanwhile coastal residents were forced to take to their boats to battle the pirates who attacked their settlements. (Historiographical Institute, University of Tokyo)

epidemics, and the failure of irrigation systems—to a catastrophic fall in China's population. The Mandate of Heaven passed from the Ming as the Manchus established a new dynasty, the Qing (1644–1911).

The Qing expanded the borders of China, more than doubling the geographical size of the country. They conquered and controlled Tibet, Xinjiang, Outer Mongolia, and the Tarim Basin, the heartland of the old silk routes. One of their most important European contacts was with Russia, and disputes between the two empires were negotiated in the Treaty of Nerchinsk (1689), the first Chinese–European treaty negotiated on terms of equality. The treaty facilitated trade between China and Russia and delimited their border along the Amur River, although the border between Mongolia and Siberia was not fixed.

The country's population began to grow again in the eighteenth century, fed by new crops introduced into China from the New World. Sweet potatoes, for example, were widespread in coastal China by the mid-eighteenth century, while maize and the Irish potato became common in the north and in the southwest. Peanuts had spread rapidly in southern and southwestern China in the late Ming, and were also becoming an important crop in northern China by the end of Qianlong's reign (r. 1736–95). All these crops, which grew well even on poor and hilly land, helped to improve the health of China's rural workers and enabled the population to increase rapidly.

Global Population Growth and Movement

15.5 Why did the population of some continents grow faster than others between 1000 and 1800?

Population size is both the result and the cause of larger changes in society. The numbers are important markers.

Demographers estimate that Europe's population more than tripled between 1000 and 1700, with the greatest growth coming after the Black Death epidemic

15.1
15.2
15.3
15.4
15.5 Why did the population of some continents grow faster than others between 1000 and 1800?
15.6

15.1
15.2
15.3
15.4
15.5
15.6

Which groups of people migrated to the very large cities before 1800?

of 1348–51. The plague killed off perhaps one-third of Europe's population, but it soon increased again to its former level and then continued to multiply. The New World across the Atlantic provided a new home for some of the increased millions.

In the tropical and subtropical regions of the New World, European settlers introduced plantations, which created an immense demand for labor. Beginning in the early 1500s, as we have seen, Africans were seized as slaves to satisfy that demand. By the time the Atlantic slave trade was successfully abolished, three and a half centuries later, Africa had lost some ten million people. The native populations of the Americas were even more devastated, with up to 90 percent of their people lost, in some areas, although the total population in the Americas was slowly augmented by immigration from Europe.

Asia more than held its own, with about two-thirds of the world's population. Between 1000 and 1800 the proportion actually grew from 63 percent to 69 percent of the total. Although there were massive population movements of Mongols and Turks, these migrations do not affect these counts since almost all of the movement was within Asia.

Europeans increased fastest of all. They not only multiplied within Europe but also, in the words of Alfred Crosby, "leapfrogged around the globe [to found] Neo-Europes, lands thousands of kilometers from Europe and from each other" (Crosby, p. 2). In 1800 North America contained almost five million whites, South America about 500,000, Australia 10,000, and New Zealand a few thousand.

Then came the deluge. According to Crosby, "between 1820 and 1930, well over fifty million Europeans migrated to the Neo-European lands overseas … approximately one-fifth of the entire population of Europe at the beginning of that period" (p. 5). The number of peoples of European ancestry who were settled outside Europe grew from 5.7 million in 1810 to 200 million in 1910. These nineteenth-century figures take us into the times of the Industrial Revolution and its massive transformations, which are covered in the next part of this book; but the demographic diffusion across the world had already begun by 1800.

The expansion of Europe was not unique in world history, yet it was probably the most numerically sizable and geographically widespread mass migration ever seen: a migration across vast expanses of water, creating permanent links between continents of the world that had been almost entirely separate, and bringing European dominion over three new continents.

Cities and Demographics

15.6   Which groups of people migrated to the very large cities before 1800?

Studies of population movement analyze not only migration across global regions, but also the movement from rural to urban areas, and from one urban area to another. Because cities serve as centers for government, administration, economic production, trade, art, and culture, migrations into (and out of) cities also tell us something about the transformation of society. The evolution from nomadic to urban society is one of the most striking examples.

As we know from Part Two, "Settlement Patterns," we expect urban occupations, diversity of population, and rates of innovation to be very different from those of the countryside. What then was happening in terms of rural–urban movement in the various regions of the world—and in the capital cities of the empires—that we have been studying? Although an examination of capital cities is not decisive, it is suggestive. We expect that capitals of strong states will attract large and vibrant populations. Here we compare four capital cities that were especially important in attracting migrants in the various empires we have examined.

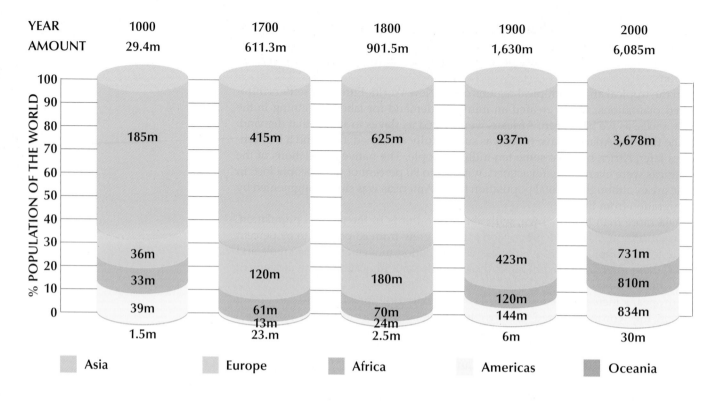

YEAR	1000	1700	1800	1900	2000
AMOUNT	29.4m	611.3m	901.5m	1,630m	6,085m

% POPULATION OF THE WORLD

1000: 185m, 36m, 33m, 39m, 1.5m

1700: 415m, 120m, 61m, 13m, 23.m

1800: 625m, 180m, 70m, 24m, 2.5m

1900: 937m, 423m, 120m, 144m, 6m

2000: 3,678m, 731m, 810m, 834m, 30m

Asia   Europe   Africa   Americas   Oceania

World population totals and distribution. In the 1,000 years to the year 2000, the world's population multiplied 20 times from less than 300 million to 6,000 million (the United Nations estimate as of October 1999). In 2013, it was slightly more than 7,000 million. Moreover, the distribution of that population by geographical origin has shifted. For most of the millennium, the proportion of people in Europe grew fastest, but in the last century, that trend reversed. Since 1900, the percentage of people in Africa, the Americas, and Oceania has grown fastest. The decline in population in the Americas between 1000 and 1700 represents the death of Native Americans; the rise after 1700 represents, in large part, immigration from Europe and Africa. In all time periods Asia has contained by far the largest proportion of the world's population.

15.1

15.2

15.3

15.4

15.5

15.6 Which groups of people migrated to the very large cities before 1800?

Isfahan

In Iran, Shah Abbas (1537–1629) made Isfahan his capital in 1598. One of the largest and most beautiful cities of its time, it contained perhaps half a million people in its 25-mile circumference. Its two most monumental features were an elegant 2½-mile-long promenade, the Chahar Bagh, lined by gardens and court residences encouraged by Shah Abbas, and, in the center of the city, the *maidan*, a large public square one-third of a mile long and one-tenth of a mile wide. The *maidan* was lined on one side by two tiers of shops, and on the other sides by the royal palace, the royal mosque, and the smaller Lutfullah mosque. The *maidan* served as marketplace, meeting-place, and even as a sports field where polo was played.

Shah Abbas fostered artisanal production and trade, and Isfahan welcomed merchants and craftsmen from around the world. In the extended bazaar, which stretched for 1½ miles from the *maidan* to the main mosque, were located shops, factories, and warehouses, as well as smaller mosques, *madrasas*, baths, and *caravanserais* (travelers' hostels, resting places for caravans). Up to 25,000 people worked in the textile industry alone. Chinese ceramicists were imported to train workers in porcelain manufacture, and carpets and metalwork were also anchors of Isfahan's craft production.

Despite their differences in religion, Shah Abbas and the European powers shared a political and military opposition to the Ottoman Empire, which lay between them. In the early 1600s Shah Abbas allowed both the English and the Dutch to open trade offices in Isfahan. He also practiced religious tolerance towards foreigners, perhaps

15.1
15.2
15.3
15.4
15.5
15.6

for reasons of practical statecraft. Various Roman Catholic missions were established. Christian Armenians, forced by Shah Abbas to immigrate from their earlier home in Julfa to expand Isfahan's commerce, built their own suburb, New Julfa, appropriate to their status as prosperous merchants. A Jewish quarter also grew up in the north-western part of the city, but later in Shah Abbas' reign Jews were persecuted and forced to convert to Islam or to leave.

Shah Abbas maintained absolute command and imported soldiers who were totally loyal to him. He also kept his forces supplied with up-to-date weapons, for he understood that Iran's status and survival depended on them, surrounded as it was by the hostile Ottoman Empire to the west, continuing threats from nomads to the north, and a powerful, if friendly, Mughal Empire to the east. In a report of 1605 to Pope Paul V, the friar Paul Simon described the Shah as ruthless, dictatorial, and militarily prepared with forces recruited from far and near:

> His militia is divided into three kinds of troops: one of Georgians, who will be about 25,000 and are mounted; the second force … is made up of slaves of various races, many of them Christian renegades: their number will be as many again … The third body consists of soldiers whom the great governors of Persia are obliged to maintain and pay the whole year; they will be about 50,000. (Andrea and Overfield, pp. 91–92)

Which groups of people migrated to the very large cities before 1800?

Delhi/Shahjahanabad

Each Mughal emperor built his own capital. Akbar ruled primarily from Agra, about 100 miles south of Delhi, but in 1569 he built a new capital at Fatehpur Sikri, about 20 miles from Agra, to honor a Sufi saint who had prayed there for a male heir for the emperor. By the end of the century, however, a shortage of water forced Akbar to abandon his beautiful, architecturally eclectic capital city and return to Agra. His son Jahangir preferred to rule from Lahore, and he built up that Punjabi city as his capital. Akbar's grandson Shah Jahan (r. 1628–58) rebuilt Delhi as his own capital and gave it his own name.

Built in a semicircular shape, with a radius of 10–12 miles, Shahjahanabad (City of Shah Jahan) had a population apparently reaching two million by the mid-seventeenth century. As it was a newly rebuilt city, almost all its residents were immigrants. The merchant and artisan population, in particular, was composed of foreigners, including Armenians, Persians, central Asians, and Kashmiris.

In his study *Shahjahanabad* (1990), historian Stephen Blake describes the Delhi of Shah Jahan as recapturing the spirit of imperial authority vested in it over centuries, most recently by the Delhi sultanate. It served also as a religious center, a place of pilgrimage revered throughout India for its tombs and graves of saints and holy men. The inner city was encircled by a massive stone wall, 3.8 miles long, 27 feet high, and 12 feet thick. At the convergence of the main streets stood the palace-fort, the home of the emperor and the administrative center of the Mughal Empire. The city had its splendors. The poet Amir Khusrau inscribed on the walls of the private audience hall of the emperor: "If there is a paradise on earth, it is here, it is here, it is here." Opposite it, set on a small hill 1,000 yards to the west, rose the *masjid-i-jami*, the Friday mosque, or chief public mosque of the city. In keeping with Islamic architectural principles, gardens with streams

Shah Jahan leaving the Great Mosque at Delhi by elephant, seventeenth century. Akbar's grandson Shah Jahan restored and rebuilt Delhi in the 1600s to serve as the capital of the Mughal Empire. In 1739 the Persian emperor Nadir Shah conquered the city and looted its treasures, including the famous Peacock Throne. Today, with neighboring New Delhi, it is India's capital and second largest city.

15.1
15.2
15.3
15.4
15.5
15.6

Which groups of
people migrated
to the very large
cities before
1800?

of water running through them to delight the eye and the ear were included in the landscaping.

The larger city housed an assembly of military camps, each under the leadership of one of the emperor's leading generals. M. Gentile, a Frenchman visiting in the mid-eighteenth century, wrote: "There are many mansions of the nobles, which one can compare to small towns and in which reside the women, equipment, and bazaars (or public markets) of the nobles" (Blake, p. 179). The twentieth-century historian Percival Spear referred to Shahjahanabad's "nomadic court and its tents of stone" (Toynbee, p. 237), the architecture reminding him that the Mughals "had started as nomads in the central Asian steppes, and until their last days they never forgot their origin" (p. 238). Each nobleman also built his own mosque. But the main function of the city was as the center of administrative and military power. Visitors to India observed that in reality the largest city in India was the military camp commanded by the emperor in the field. When he went to war, as Shah Jahan's son Aurangzeb did for years at a time, hundreds of thousands of soldiers and camp followers accompanied him; Shahjahanabad itself was deserted.

Constantinople (Istanbul)

Constantinople (Istanbul, the Turkish name, has been most often used since 1453, but the name was introduced officially only in 1930) had been the capital of the much-reduced Byzantine Empire when Sultan Mehmed II captured it and made it his own capital in 1453. In 1478 Constantinople had about 80,000 inhabitants; between 1520 and 1535, there were 400,000; and some Western observers estimated a

SOURCE

Ibn Khaldun on Urban Life in the Fourteenth Century

The great social philosopher Ibn Khaldun of Tunis (1332–1406) described the transition from nomadic to sedentary and urban forms, and the "softening" of the invaders that occurred in the process of urbanization. His analysis presents a very early philosophy of the flowering and decline of civilization, an analysis that other historians would later repeat. This analysis also presents Arab peoples as nomadic and rough, at first, but urbane and sophisticated after two or three generations of urban life.

It is rare that the age of the state should exceed three generations, a generation being the average age of an individual, that is forty years or the time necessary for full growth and development.

We said that the age of the state rarely exceeds three generations because the first generation still retains its nomadic roughness and savagery, and such nomadic characteristics as a hard life, courage, predatoriness, and the desire to share glory. All this means that the strength of the solidarity uniting the people is still firm, which makes that people feared and powerful and able to dominate others.

The second generation, however, have already passed from the nomadic to the sedentary way of life, owing to the power they wield and the luxury they enjoy. They have abandoned their rough life for an easy and luxurious one ...

As for the third generation, they have completely forgotten the nomadic and rough stage, as though it had never existed.

They have also lost their love of power and their social solidarity through having been accustomed to being ruled. Luxury corrupts them, because of the pleasant and easy way of living in which they have been brought up. As a result, they become a liability on the state, like women and children who need to be protected ...

... the rulers of a state, once they have become sedentary, always imitate in their ways of living those of the state to which they have succeeded and whose condition they have seen and generally adopted.

This is what happened to the Arabs, when they conquered and ruled over the Persian and Byzantine empires ... Up until then they had known nothing of civilization. (Ibn Khaldun, pp. 117–19)

Ibn Khaldun's depiction of nomadic conquerors being ultimately absorbed and assimilated into the civilizations they conquer presents a process that is frequently repeated in world history. We have seen it in the barbarian conquests described in the chapters entitled "Rome and the Barbarians" and "China." His portrait of the decadence and decay of civilizations does not, however, fit all cases. In India, for example, Aurangzeb provoked fatal rebellions when he tried to rule too strictly over too many people, from too remote a location. Aurangzeb's fatal flaw was not decadence but excessive zeal.

15.1

15.2

15.3

15.4

15.5

15.6

population of 700,000 by 1600. Istanbul had become a city of Turks—58 percent of the population in the sixteenth and seventeenth centuries—but there were also Greeks, Jews, Armenians, and Tziganes, or gypsies.

The vast **conurbation** was composed of three major segments plus numerous suburbs. Central Constantinople housed the government center, with trees, gardens, fountains, promenades, and 400 mosques; sprawling, uneven bazaars where luxuries as well as day-to-day necessities could be purchased; and the Serai, near the tip of the peninsula, where the government officials lived in their palaces and gardens. Across the small waterway, called the Golden Horn, were the ports and major commercial establishments of Galata. Here the Western ships came; here were the Jewish businessmen, shops and warehouses, cabarets, the French ambassador, and Latin and Greek merchants dressing in the Turkish style and living in grand houses. On Galata, too, were the two major arsenals—that of Kasim Pasha and the Topkhana—marking the Ottoman commitment to military power. On the Asian side of the Straits of the Bosphorus was the third part of Istanbul, Üsküdar, a more Turkish city, and the terminus of the great land routes through Asia.

Historian Fernand Braudel sees in Constantinople the prototype of the great modern European capitals that would arise a century later. Economically, these cities

Which groups of people migrated to the very large cities before 1800?

Constantinople, late fifteenth century. Constantinople (Istanbul), spanning the straits that separate Europe and Asia, has been a pivotal location from the time Constantine established it as the eastern capital of the Roman Empire. The segments of the city reflect the rule and civilization of Rome, the Byzantine Empire, and, after 1453, the Ottoman Empire. In addition, as a great trading city, it houses communities of businessmen from around the world.

KEY TERM

conurbation An enormous, complex city, made up of many parts, each of which may be a small town or city by itself—a megalopolis.

15.1

15.2

15.3

15.4

15.5

15.6

Which groups of
people migrated
to the very large
cities before
1800?

produced little, but they processed goods passing through, and were the "hothouses of every civilization" (Braudel, 1973, I:351), where new ideas and innovations arose and created a new order. Braudel remarks that cities that were only political capitals would not fare well in the next century; those that were economically productive would. Beginning in the late sixteenth century, the economy of Istanbul was undercut by changes in the world economy. As trade shifted to the Atlantic and to European powers that sailed around the African continent instead of through the Middle East, the Ottoman Empire and its capital were left as a comparative backwater.

London

By comparison with the Asian and east European capitals, London had a very different pattern of immigration and employment. While Delhi, Isfahan, and Constantinople declined during the late seventeenth and early eighteenth centuries in response to negative political and economic factors, London grew, primarily for economic reasons.

E.A. Wrigley, one of the founding members of the Cambridge Group for the History of Population and Social Structure, has examined the changing demography of London between 1650 and 1750 to analyze the city's relationship with British society and economy. Wrigley begins with London's extraordinary population growth, from 200,000 in 1600, to 400,000 in 1650, to 575,000 by 1700 (when it became the largest city in Western Europe), to 675,000 in 1750, and 900,000 in 1800. London dominated the development of all of England. In 1650 London held 7 percent of England's total population; in 1750, 11 percent.

Before the twentieth century, as a rule, large cities everywhere in the world were so unsanitary that death rates exceeded birth rates, so London's population growth reflects not only births within the city, but also large-scale immigration to compensate for high death rates. Wrigley estimates that by the end of the 1600s, some 8,000 people a year were migrating into London. Since the entire population of England at this time was only five million, and growing at the rate of about 16,000 each year, London was siphoning half of England's population growth into itself.

With so high a proportion of England's population living in London, or at least visiting the city for a substantial part of their lives, the capital must have had significant influence on the country as a whole. Wrigley suggests that the high levels of population growth in London in the seventeenth century may have been a significant factor in the birth of industrialization in the eighteenth.

Wrigley suggests several relevant causal relationships. The first group concerns economics: London's growth promoted the creation of a national market, including transportation and communication facilities; it evoked increasing agricultural productivity to feed the urban population; it developed new sources of raw materials, especially coal, to provide for them; it led to the development of new commercial instruments; and it had the effect of increasing productivity and purchasing power. Demographically, London's high death and immigration rates kept England's rate of population growth relatively low. Sociologically, London's growth disseminated new ways of thinking about economics and its importance. Londoners placed increasing value on production and consumption for the common person, encouraging higher levels of entrepreneurship throughout the country.

London's growth could have led simply to the urban ruling elites commandeering the production of the countryside for their own benefit. Such parasitism was common in imperial capitals elsewhere, as we have just seen in the Asian capital cities. In London, however, a government increasingly dominated by commercial classes reinforced the values of production and increased consumption for the common person.

📖 **Read** the **Document: How They Died: Coroner's Rolls from the 14th Century, 1322–1337** on **MyHistoryLab**

Migration and Demography:
What Difference Do They Make?

Numbers count. Demography helps us to discover patterns in history and to formulate questions about issues that need further study. In this chapter, we have employed the methods and insights of demography to examine four great migrations in world history between 1500 and 1750. We have explored the formation of "New Europes" around the globe, the numbers and motivations of the new immigrants, and the (often catastrophic) fate of the original inhabitants. Second, we have analyzed the size, geography, and economic consequences of the slave trade both in Africa, where people were seized, sold, and exported, and in the plantation economies that absorbed most of them. Third, we have tracked the migrations and conquests of Turkic-speaking and Mongol peoples from central Asia to new empires in India, Persia, and the Middle East, and a new dynasty in China. Finally, we have discussed the move from rural areas to cities—the spread of urbanization—and contrasted the motives for this move in more traditional political capitals of empire with those in younger, more trade-oriented capitals.

These migrations have attracted the continuing interest of demographic historians. Their research has helped us to assess the connections between these great migrations of the past and events in our own world. They have also helped to alert us to related demographic processes continuing in our own world today: rapid population growth and its consequences for global ecology; global migrations for economic opportunity—both of highly skilled technical workers seeking highly paid jobs and of unskilled day laborers seeking subsistence work; the migration of jobs from richer, higher-wage areas of the world to poorer, lower-wage areas (labor remaining stationary but jobs moving from one location to another); migration from rural areas to cities and from cities to suburbs; migration of refugees fleeing warfare and oppressive governments; the global diffusion of diseases, such as AIDS, that seem to originate in one location and spread rapidly around the world.

These migration issues also alert us to related policy issues that persist in our own times: for example, language policies in areas of the United States with large Hispanic populations, and cultural policies in areas of Europe with large-scale Muslim immigration. Another issue is the encouraging of migration as a policy to change the ethnic composition of a region. The Chinese government today, for example, encourages people of Han Chinese ancestry to immigrate into Tibet and Xinjiang in order to make these two provinces more Chinese and less Tibetan and Uighur. Even worse, some governments have undertaken programs of mass murder—genocide—to rid their territories of unwanted peoples. The government of Serbia, for example, implemented "ethnic cleansing" in 1999 against Albanian Muslims as part of the battle for control of Kosovo province (with constant, conscious references on both sides to the conquest of Kosovo by the Ottoman Turks in 1389); the Ottoman Turkish government murdered more than 1.5 million Armenians in 1915. In the most extreme case, German national policy in the 1930s and 1940s sought to exterminate the Jews. These and other issues of demography continue to arise around the globe and alter human history. We will return to them repeatedly in our study.

CHAPTER REVIEW

THE "NEW EUROPES"

15.1   What were the "New Europes"?

The "New Europes" is the name given to the places all around the globe settled by Europeans between 1500 and 1750. Leaving Europe by the millions, they established their way of life in the New World, Australia and New Zealand, and South Africa, increasing the power of European nation-states and shifting the center of trade from the Indian Ocean especially to the Atlantic Ocean. The migrations often had devastating consequences for the people who were already living in these "new Europes." These people the Europeans pushed aside.

RUSSIAN EXPANSION

15.2   How did Russia expand in the seventeenth century?

Russia began to expand into Siberia in the late sixteenth and early seventeenth centuries, reclaiming land the Mongol conquerors had seized. Building trading outposts, and eventually joined by farmers, Russian troops declared the land Russian all the way to the Bering Sea.

SLAVERY: ENFORCED MIGRATION, 1500–1750

15.3   Why did slavery rise in the Atlantic Ocean basin?

Trade in African slaves had existed long before Europeans began to take Africans to the New World. We have encountered it in the Code of Hammurabi (c. 1750 B.C.E.), in ancient Greece, and in the Roman Empire. Arab traders had carried African slaves across the Sahara Desert to the Mediterranean and across the Indian Ocean to Arabia and India. But as West Europeans began to develop the Americas in the sixteenth century, they sought cheap labor especially for their plantations, mostly for sugar but also for tobacco and cotton. The African trading routes were reoriented. New coastal fortresses were built on Africa's western coast, and slaves were brought to the European shippers. The movement of African slaves across the Atlantic Ocean was unparalleled. In all, some ten million people were taken from Africa to the western hemisphere. The plantation economy depended on them.

ASIAN MIGRATIONS, 1300–1750

15.4   What were the Asian migrations?

As immigrant conquerors swept out of central Asia, they created new empires—the Ottoman, the Safavid, and the Mughal—and new ruling dynasties inside of China's existing empire. These Asian conquests were similar in many ways to the conquests of the Americas by Western Europeans, but the contrasts are even more remarkable. Notably, although both conquerors imposed new cultures on the peoples they defeated, the Asians did not overwhelm them, as the Western Europeans did. In fact, over time, the Asian conquerors were assimilated by the people they subdued; they adopted many of their ideas and institutions.

GLOBAL POPULATION GROWTH AND MOVEMENT

15.5   Why did the population of some continents grow faster than others between 1000 and 1800?

Europe's population tripled in these years, and many of those millions then migrated to the New World. The overwhelming majority of the indigenous population of the Americas was killed by warfare and, much more, by European diseases. About ten million Africans were taken to the Americas, increasing the population of the New World while reducing that of the African continent. The Asian population grew in this period, but the population of the continent as a whole did not change much, as almost all of the population movement was within Asia. Europeans meanwhile multiplied not only within Europe, but also within the "New Europes."

CITIES AND DEMOGRAPHICS

15.6   Which groups of people migrated to the very large cities before 1800?

Cities attracted migrants before the nineteenth century. Four examples suggest that political and military administration were the most important attractions, but trade and commerce also had their pull. Delhi/Shahjahanabad was a center of India's administrative and military power, with a population of nearly two million. Newly rebuilt, most of its residents were immigrants, and it especially attracted foreign merchants and artisans. The city of Isfahan, capital of Iran under Shah Abbas, held half a million people. Its large public bazaar attracted merchants and craftsmen from around the world. Isfahan fostered artisans and trade, and porcelain manufacture, metalwork, and carpets anchored the city's craft production. Constantinople, capital of the Byzantine Empire and then of the Ottoman Empire, was an enormous megalopolis, with three major parts and vast suburbs. Located at the terminus of the silk route, it held communities of businessmen from around the world. London's population exploded, and as more people came to England's capital city, a national market of transportation and communication facilities developed. To feed the urban population, agricultural productivity was increased; new sources of raw materials, such as coal, were developed. London's government was increasingly dominated by the commercial, more than military-political elites.

Suggested Readings

PRINCIPAL SOURCES

Braudel, Fernand. *Capitalism and Material Life 1400–1800*, trans. Miriam Kochan (New York: Harper and Row, 1973). Introduction to a whole new way of thinking about the rise of capitalism in Europe, emphasizing both institutions and natural ecology.

———. *The Mediterranean and the Mediterranean World in the Age of Philip II*, 2 vols., trans. Sian Reynolds (New York: Harper and Row, 1973). Braudel looks at long-run ecological issues, medium-run institutional configurations, and short-run political decisions in this landmark study.

Crosby, Alfred W. *Ecological Imperialism: The Biological Expansion of Europe, 900–1900* (Cambridge: Cambridge University Press, 1986). Extremely well-written and well-argued discussion of the biological consequences of the encounters of distant civilizations with one another.

Curtin, Philip D. *The Atlantic Slave Trade: A Census* (Madison, WI: University of Wisconsin Press, 1969). The pioneering work in quantifying the Atlantic slave trade.

——. *The Rise and Fall of the Plantation Complex: Essays in Atlantic History* (Cambridge: Cambridge University Press, 1990). Comprehensive account of the plantation organization, economy, and significance.

Hughes, Robert. *The Fatal Shore. The Epic of Australia's Founding* (New York: Knopf, 1986). Engagingly written, exciting, thoughtful presentation of Australian history from the first arrival of Europeans to about 1870, when the system of penal transportation ended.

Manning, Patrick. *Migration in World History* (New York: Routledge, 2nd ed., 2013). Study of migration from earliest times till today with a theoretical framework as well as concrete examples. Sophisticated in its methods.

Mintz, Sidney W. *Sweetness and Power: The Place of Sugar in Modern History* (New York: Penguin Books, 1985). Fascinating anthropological study that begins with the Caribbean sugar plantation, extends to the uses of sugar by the wealthy, the sugared cup of tea of the British industrial worker, the Chinese tea crop, and the advertising industry that brought much of this together.

Northrup, David, ed. *The Atlantic Slave Trade* (Lexington, MA: D.C. Heath, 1994; 2nd ed., 2001). Excellent selection of articles on causes, effects, demography, and economics of the slave trade and of abolition.

——. *Indentured Labor in the Age of Imperialism, 1834–1922* (Cambridge: Cambridge University Press, 1995). Comprehensive survey of the system of indentured labor that followed the abolition of the slave trade and slavery, and its demographics.

ADDITIONAL SOURCES

Andrea, Alfred J., and James H. Overfield, eds. *The Human Record: Sources of Global History*, vol. 2 (Florence, KY: Wadsworth Publishing Co., 6th ed., 2008). The excerpts are extremely well chosen for global and topical coverage.

Blake, Stephen P. *Shahjahanabad* (Cambridge: Cambridge University Press, 1990). Scholarly study of the capital city of Shah Jahan, demonstrating the influence of military-camp architecture and design.

Chevigny, Hector. *Russian America. The Great Alaskan Adventure* (New York: Viking Press, 1965). The story of the migration, the economy, and the international politics.

Cook, James. *The Journals of Captain James Cook on His Voyages of Discovery*, ed. J.C. Beaglehole, 2 vols. (Cambridge: Cambridge University Press [for the Hakluyt Society],

1955 and 1961). Read Cook's own accounts in his own words.

Dale, Stephen F. *The Muslim Empires of the Ottomans, Safavids, and Mughals* (New York: Cambridge University Press, 2010). A comparative perspective. Good attention to culture as well as politics.

Frykenberg, R.E., ed. *Delhi through the Ages: Essays in Urban History, Culture and Society* (Delhi: Oxford University Press, 1986). Wide-ranging collection of scholarly articles from an important conference, covering Delhi from earliest times almost to the present.

Gates, Henry Louis, Jr. *Wonders of the African World* (New York: Knopf, 1999). Introduction to Africa for a general audience by a leading Harvard scholar.

Goodwin, Godfrey. *The Janissaries* (London: Saqi Books, 1994). Difficult to access, because the author moves between idiosyncratic situations and general movements—but the information is there.

Ibn Khaldun. *An Arab Philosophy of History*, trans. Charles Issawi (London: John Murray, 1950). In the fourteenth century, Ibn Khaldun of Tunis, an early social scientist, proposed a reading of history consistent with the experiences of both the nomadic and the sedentary peoples of North Africa and the Middle East.

Inalcik, Halil. *The Ottoman Empire: The Classical Age, 1300–1600*, trans. Norman Itzkowitz and Colin Imber (New York: Praeger Publishers, 1973). A standard, accessible history by an eminent scholar.

Klein, Herbert S. "Economic Aspects of the Eighteenth-century Atlantic Slave Trade," in James D. Tracy, ed., *The Rise of Merchant Empires* (Cambridge: Cambridge University Press, 1990), pp. 287–310. Important analyses of the slave trade, including slaves' birth and survival rates.

Lamb, Jonathan, "Captain Cook and the Scourge of Scurvy," 2011, BBC online; http://www.bbc.co.uk/history/british/empire_seapower/captaincook_scurvy_01.shtml (accessed August 2013).

Lapidus, Ira M. *A History of Islamic Societies* (New York: Cambridge University Press, 2nd ed., 2002). Comprehensive, global presentation..

Lovejoy, Paul. *Transformations in Slavery: A History of Slavery in Africa* (New York; Cambridge University Press, 3rd ed., 2012). The most up-to-date information on kinds of slave labor and demographic numbers.

Northrup, David. *Africa's Discovery of Europe, 1450–1850* (New York: Oxford University Press, 2nd ed., 2009). First contacts both in Africa and Europe, seen through African eyes. Innovative scholarly contribution.

Robinson, Francis. *Atlas of the Islamic World since 1500* (New York: Facts on File, 1982). Excellent reference by an outstanding British scholar. Well written and beautifully illustrated.

Rodney, Walter. *How Europe Underdeveloped Africa* (Washington, DC: Howard University Press, 1972). Classic statement of the exploitation of Africa by the European slave trade and imperialism.

Segal, Ronald. *Islam's Black Slaves: The Other Black Diaspora* (New York: Farrar, Straus, and Giroux, 2001). A survey of the history of the Arab slave trade in Africa and the Indian Ocean region.

Spence, Jonathan D. *The Search for Modern China* (New York: W.W. Norton and Co., 1990). A standard history, engagingly written, thorough, good on narrative and analysis.

Thornton, John. *Africa and Africans in the Making of the Atlantic World, 1400–1640* (Cambridge: Cambridge University Press, 1992). Sees Africans as active in creating their own world, including as businessmen conducting the slave trade.

The [London] Times Atlas of World History, ed. Geoffrey Parker (London: Times Books, 5th ed., 1999). Invaluable reference. Well-balanced treatment of all world areas.

Toynbee, Arnold. *Cities of Destiny* (New York: Weathervane Books, 1967). Colorful introduction to some of the most famous and influential cities. Illustrations and maps are lavish in this coffee-table book.

Voyages: The Trans-Atlantic Slave Trade Database. A massive international research project has created this single multisource dataset of transatlantic slave voyages. Indispensable quantitative information. http://www.slavevoyages.org.

Wrigley, E.A. *Population and History* (New York: McGraw-Hill Book Company, 1969). Explains the uses of demographic study in history.

——. "A Simple Model of London's Importance in Changing English Society and Economy 1650–1750," *Past and Present* XXXVII (1967), pp. 44–70. Demographic analysis suggests the importance of London in preparing the way for the industrialization of England.

FILMS

Islam: Empire of Faith—The Ottomans (2001; 53 minutes). Looks at the empire politically, but also as a religiously based empire, with considerable attention to art and architecture.

The Ottoman Empire (1996; 47 minutes). Looks at the empire primarily through a political–military–administrative lens. Some attention to religion, especially in conflict with Safavids of Persia; less attention to art and architecture.

PART SIX

TURNING POINT: REVOLUTION

1640–1914

Coping with Western Revolutions

Explosive events, "revolutions," punctuated the years 1640–1914. One cluster of revolutions—in England, North America, France, Haiti, and Latin America—advocated for new political philosophies and introduced new political structures. Many historians refer to them collectively as constituting the "Age of Democratic Revolution." Some of the revolutions built on one another; for example, Americans revolted against England in order to gain the same rights that English people had won in their own internal revolution. Recently freed slaves in Haiti revolted against France when the French failed to implement the promise of the French Revolution to abolish slavery. Latin American generals revolted against Spain while the Spanish were preoccupied with fighting against France and its revolutionary doctrines.

Execution of the Defenders of Madrid, 3rd May, 1808, Francisco de Goya, 1814. Oil on canvas. Goya, a Spaniard, saw the French Revolution and the Napoleonic Wars that followed through the prism of the violence inflicted on his homeland. The bitter warfare at the French invasion of Spain, and the Spanish resistance, inspired this agonized painting. (Prado, Madrid)

King George V and Queen Mary of England in Delhi during a state visit (*darbar*) to India, 1911. The *darbar* ceremony was the traditional form in which a ruler demonstrated publicly his ascendancy as those under him payed homage. When the king and queen of England visited India for the first time in 1911, an appropriately regal *darbar* was arranged in Delhi attended by the local rulers and elites of British India, as well as the highest levels of British officialdom. There was an underlying irony: at the time, the British capital in India was Calcutta, but that city was in revolt against recent government policies, so the *darbar* was staged instead in Delhi, the capital of the former Mughal Empire.

Beginning about the same time, a series of innovations in economic organization and the uses of machinery dramatically increased the quantity and quality of economic productivity. Most historians name this transformation the "Industrial Revolution." These revolutions in politics and economics inspired equally dramatic social revolutions, which affected the individual, the family, the neighborhood, and the community.

All three of these revolutions originated in Western Europe, but ultimately they touched people all over the world, who then formulated their own varied responses, adaptations, and, sometimes, rejections. For purposes of analysis, this part of the book will consider these three revolutions sequentially: political in the chapter entitled "Political Revolutions in Europe and the Americas," industrial in "The Industrial Revolution," and social in "Nationalism, Imperialism, and Resistance."

The triple revolution unfolded rather quickly, but the groundwork had been laid over centuries. We have already seen unprecedented expansion in global exploration, commerce, and migration from the thirteenth century. By the seventeenth century, this continuing expansion brought long-standing European political, economic, and social

Cheyle Singh, Rajah of Benares, Flatters Warren Hastings, anon., 1784. Engraving. The British East India Company began its transformation into the *de facto* government of a significant part of India in 1757, with the conquest of Bengal. By 1775 its rule had extended far up the Ganges River and encompassed Benaras, one of the most sacred cities of Hinduism. Now the local Rajah paid homage to the chief British official, the Governor General of the East India Company. Compare this early, local ceremony with the Darbar extravaganza in 1911.

philosophies and institutions under fierce attack. The battles inside Europe, however, did not cripple the continent; quite the contrary. During this period of struggle at home, Europeans were establishing political colonialism, economic imperialism, Christian evangelism, and technological innovation first in the Americas and then, more slowly, around the globe. The new forms percolated, sometimes swiftly, sometimes drop by drop, into everyday life and consciousness everywhere. Each society adapted in its own way and in its own time, however, so the results were diverse and often unexpected. Revolutions did not follow linear trajectories.

Historians of revolution argue over the relative importance of new ways of thinking and of new interest groups, new ideas, and new people. Both are important. Over the past few chapters we have given greater attention to the interest groups, especially merchants and international traders. Their increasing wealth and political assertiveness fuelled demands for new rights and new representation in government.

We open this section, however, by looking at new ways of thinking about the universe, for this period saw the growing importance of science and mathematics. Attempts to understand the universe by applying new instruments (such as the telescope) and advanced mathematics (such as calculus) to the observation of the natural world brought a new understanding of the place of earth and humankind in the solar system. They culminated in Sir Isaac Newton's theory of universal gravitation. Social philosophers—called *philosophes* in France—began to apply systematic, rational, scientific thinking to worldly institutions. They challenged such long-standing institutions as the "divine right of kings" and hereditary aristocracies. We therefore open our study of political, industrial, and social revolutions with an analysis of some of the revolutionary scientific ideas that helped to inspire them.

The Slave Trade (Slaves on the West Coast of Africa), François Auguste Biard, c. 1833. Oil on canvas. Biard has painted an unequivocal condemnation of the commercial traffic in people as they are inspected and purchased. A white man brands one female slave, while a black man whips another. To the rear right of the market, rows of shackled slaves await their turn on the block. (Wilberforce House Museum, Hull, England)

Strawbridge and Clothier Department Store, Philadelphia, c. 1907. This photograph presents the commercial successes of the industrial revolution at the turn of the nineteenth century, with its department stores, horse-drawn street cars carrying commuters from all corners of the city and suburbs, crowds of shoppers and business people, and exuberant advertising. Many of the residents would have been recent immigrants from Europe, and some African-Americans, from the deep, post-civil-war South.

Turning Point Questions

1. This part of the book argues that the most important revolutions of the period 1640–1914 began in Europe and were then carried to other parts of the world. What were the major components of these revolutions?
2. What new developments in European life set the stage for these revolutions?
3. Several countries in Europe were fighting through revolutions at home while expanding their influence overseas. In fact, they were encouraging new revolutions that would ultimately turn against themselves. Please give examples.
4. Which do you think is more important in inspiring revolution, new revolutionary classes or new revolutionary ideas? To what degree do they go together?

16 Political Revolutions in Europe and the Americas

The Birth of Political Rights in the Age of Enlightenment

1649–1830

A revolution is a fundamental and often rapid change in the way a system operates—whether political, economic, intellectual, or social. A political revolution, for example, not only removes some people from office and replaces them with others; it also changes the fundamental basis on which the new leaders come to power, the authority they claim, and their mission in office. Leaders of revolutions usually state their goals in terms of lofty, non-negotiable principles. As revolutionary struggles unfold and as different groups rise and fall, however, they may lurch in unexpected ways from one political position to another, relatively swiftly and often violently.

The Sleep of Reason Produces Monsters, Francisco de Goya, 1797. Engraving. Goya (1746–1828) creates a terrifying scene challenging a key tenet of the Enlightenment: that human reason will produce progress. It suggests that when the mind's defenses are down, as in sleep, we are prey to internal monsters. Reason has its limits. Around 1900, the first psychoanalyst, Sigmund Freud, explored the limits of reason more thoroughly, but arrived at a similar point of view.

LEARNING OBJECTIVES

16.1 ((	16.2 ((	16.3 ((	16.4 ((	16.5 ((	16.6 ((	16.7 ((	16.8 ((
Understand the advancements of the Scientific Revolution.	Understand the political theories of Locke and Hobbes.	Describe England's civil war and revolution.	Understand the central beliefs of the Enlightenment thinkers.	Discuss the goals and achievements of the American Revolution.	Describe the differences between the American and French revolutions.	Discuss the importance of the Haitian Revolution.	Understand the disillusionment of the Latin American revolutionaries.

((Listen on **MyHistoryLab**

In a major revolution several groups may participate and cooperate in the struggle to replace an existing government. Nevertheless, each group may have its own goals, and these goals may be in conflict. Once it becomes likely that a new government will replace the old, the conflicts among the revolutionary partners begin to surface. Each group seeks to privilege its own programs and personnel and to have them incorporated into the new government. This struggle to control the new government may be even more brutal, violent, chaotic, and unpredictable than the battle to overthrow the old. The stakes are high. Major revolutions have long-term effects, not only for participants in that place and time, but also for people of later generations and far-flung locations.

The three political revolutions we consider here all share these characteristics of major revolutions. The "Glorious Revolution" of 1688 in England, the revolt of the American colonies against British rule in 1776, and the French Revolution of 1789 all removed one set of rulers and replaced them with another, changed the basis of authority of the state and its relationship to its citizens, and proposed new missions for the state. (By "state" we mean the entire mechanism of government, its officers, its institutions, and its organization.) All these revolutions were fought in the name of principle. The revolution in England was considered "bloodless," although it was the culmination of half a century of intermittent civil warfare. The American and French revolutions precipitated lengthy wars.

All three of these revolutions have been characterized as "democratic" because they increased the participation of more (but not all) of the people in government. All of them at some time tried to balance two additional, competing goals: they sought to protect the rights of propertied people while increasing the power of the government (although not of the king). These goals were not, and to this day are not, fully compatible. Individual rights to private property and the rights of the state often conflict. So we must be careful in our understanding of the "democracy" that emerged from these revolutions.

Collectively, for Europeans and Americans, the revolutions that occurred in the years between 1688 and 1789:

- situated the authority of government on earth rather than in heaven and thus increased the influence of the secular over the otherworldly;
- separated the function and power of organized religion from the function and power of the state.
- rejected the theory that governments were based on a **divine right of kings** in favor of the theory that governments derive their just powers from the consent of the governed;
- encouraged the creation of an effective bureaucracy to administer the affairs of government;
- emphasized the principle of individual merit, of "a career open to talent," rather than promoting people on the basis of personal and hereditary connections;
- helped to solidify the nation-state as the principal unit of government;
- extended effective power over the state to classes of people hitherto excluded, especially to men of the professions and business;
- encouraged the growth of business and industry for private profit;
- inspired the revolutionary leaders to export their new ideologies and methods to new geographical areas, sometimes by force; and
- precipitated wars of heretofore unknown degrees of military mobilization, geographical extent, and human destructiveness.

"Liberty," "equality," "fraternity," "natural rights," "the pursuit of happiness," "property," and "no taxation without representation" were the battle cries of these various revolutions. As frequently happens, the results were often unintended, unanticipated, and ironic. The political forms that actually resulted did increase human

KEY TERM

divine right of kings A political doctrine influential in the sixteenth and seventeenth centuries which held that the monarch derived his authority from God and was therefore not accountable to earthly authority. James I of England (r. 1603–25) was a foremost exponent.

517

freedom for many people in many countries, but they often coexisted with slavery, patriarchy, colonialism, and warfare.

These ironies revealed themselves starkly in two further revolutions that were inspired in part by these first three. In 1791, the slaves of Haiti, a French colony, revolted and abolished slavery. The French ultimately refused to sanction the revolution against slavery—despite their own revolution for human rights. Then, in the first three decades of the nineteenth century, many of the colonies of Spain and Portugal in Latin America fought for and won their independence. But the triumphant generals of the revolution fought among themselves and their dreams of vast, unified, powerful nations dissolved into the reality of smaller, weaker states. The triumphant elite—the descendants of the European settlers in these colonies—suppressed indigenous peoples, people of mixed Spanish–Amerindian ancestry, and people of African descent, thereby spreading disillusionment throughout the continent.

AT A GLANCE: THE AGE OF REVOLUTIONS

DATE	EUROPE	NORTH AMERICA	LATIN AMERICA
1640	• Galileo dies; Newton is born (1642) • Civil wars in England (1642–46; 1647–49; 1649–51) • Execution of King Charles I of England (1649) • Hobbes' *Leviathan* (1651) • Restoration of English monarchy (1660) • Royal Society of London founded (1662)		• Portugal takes Brazil from the Dutch (1654)
1670	• The "Glorious Revolution" in England (1688) • The English Bill of Rights (1689) • John Locke's *Second Treatise on Government* (1689) • *Philosophes*: Diderot (1713–84); Voltaire (1694–1778); Rousseau (1712–78); Montesquieu (1689–1755)		
1760	• Tennis Court Oath (June 20, 1789) • French Revolution (1789–99) • "March of the Women" (1789) • "Great Fear" (1789)	• British levy taxes on Americans in the Stamp Act (1765) • American Declaration of Independence (1776); War of Independence (1775–81) • Constitution (1789)	• Revolts against European rule in Peru, Colombia, and Brazil (1780–98) • Tupac Amarú revolt, Peru (1780)
1790	• "Second French Revolution" (1791–99) • "Reign of Terror" (1793–95) • Napoleon seizes power (1799); Emperor (1804) • *Concordat* between Napoleon and Pope Pius VII (1801) • Napoleon issues Civil Code (1804) • Napoleon invades Russia; finally defeated (1812)	• Bill of Rights ratified (1791) • Louisiana Purchase from France (1803)	• Toussaint L'Ouverture leads slave revolt against French in Saint-Domingue (Haiti) (1791) • Haiti proclaims independence (1804) • Joseph Bonaparte, king of Spain (1808) • Bolívar and San Martín lead revolts against Spain (1808–28) • Paraguay declares independence (1810–11)
1820	• Congress of Vienna (1814–15) • Reform Act extends voting franchise in Britain (1832) • Britain abolishes slavery in its empire (1833)	• President Andrew Jackson evicts Cherokee Indian Nation: "Trail of Tears" (1838) • Warfare with Mexico ends in victory for America (1848) • United States abolishes slavery (1863, 1865)	• Mexico wins independence (1821) • Prince Pedro declares Brazil independent (1822)

The Scientific Revolution

Before the political revolutions came revolutions in thought. People changed their ideas about government before they actually changed the government. And even before they changed their ideas about the political universe, they changed their ideas about the natural universe.

Advancements in Science

In his book *Revolution in Science* of 1985, I. Bernard Cohen writes that the study of the history of science is a surprisingly new field. Although some of the scientists we shall consider here spoke of their findings as revolutionary, the first academic historian to write of a scientific revolution seems to have been a Ph.D. candidate at Columbia University, Martha (Bronfenbrenner) Ornstein. In her dissertation of 1913 she summarized the importance of the array of scientific discoveries and inventions that included the telescope, which "utterly revolutionized the science of astronomy," "revolutionary changes in optics," "Linnaeus's revolutionary work" in the classification of plants and animals, "the revolution in the universities" toward systematic, empirical research, and the role of scientific societies as carriers of culture. There had been, she wrote, "a revolution in the established habits of thought and inquiry, compared to which most revolutions registered in history seem insignificant."

In 1948, in a series of lectures, one of the most distinguished of professional historians, Herbert Butterfield, wrote that the scientific revolution of the seventeenth century "overturned the authority in science not only of the Middle Ages but of the ancient world ... [It] outshines everything since the rise of Christianity and reduces the Renaissance and Reformation to the rank of mere episodes, mere internal displacements, within the system of medieval Christendom." This was not a one-time revolution. Butterfield saw it as a kind of "continuing historical, or history making force acting right up to the present time." Beginning in the 1950s, especially in *The Copernican Revolution* (1957) and *The Structure of Scientific Revolutions* (1962; 3rd ed. 1996), Thomas Kuhn turned his attention to the process of scientific investigation as a method of thought and research that constantly challenges conventional thinking and stands ready to overthrow it. Kuhn argued that most scientific research is based on small, incremental advances in human knowledge. He called this "normal science." "Revolutionary science" occurs when scientists break completely with existing explanations of their field, finding them inadequate, and create new theories that are better able to account for all the data available. Galileo and Newton created revolutionary science.

A Community of Scientists

What made seventeenth-century science revolutionary? First, the seventeenth century marked the move from the individual scientist working alone to the creation of a community of scientists, in touch with one another, sharing knowledge and ideas, and building a collective structure of thought and method. It would still be possible for a scientific genius such as Leonardo da Vinci (1452–1519) to die with his work unrecognized, and even unknown, but that was becoming less likely. Leonardo, most famous for his paintings *The Last Supper* and the *Mona Lisa*, also carried out research in human anatomy through the dissection of cadavers; he wrote of the circulation of the blood through the body and of the path of the earth around the sun; he drew sketches for such inventions as submarines and airplanes. But he did not circulate these scientific and technological ideas. At the time of his death they remained confined to his own notebooks, and they were not discovered and publicized until the

16.1

16.2

16.3

16.4

16.5

16.6

16.7

16.8

How did the
Scientific
Revolution
challenge
previous
concepts of the
natural world?

twentieth century. The creation of scientific academies in the seventeenth century made it much less likely that such genius would remain hidden.

Second, science added four new qualities to its methods: mathematical formulations, quantifying and expressing relationships in nature in mathematical forms; **empiricism**, accepting the evidence of direct observation over theoretical and philosophical explanations; technological innovations in equipment, such as the telescope and the microscope; and a belief in the freedom of inquiry, encouraging scientists to follow their findings and their imagination regardless of received opinion and official doctrine. All these qualities are found in the great revolution in astronomy and physics from Copernicus through Kepler and Galileo, and on to Newton.

View the **Closer Look**: The Sciences and the Arts on **MyHistoryLab**

Nicholas Copernicus. Nicholas Copernicus (1473–1543), an outstanding Polish astronomer, was commissioned by Pope Paul III to devise a new calendar that would correct the errors of the Julian calendar. The Julian calendar was based on a 365¼-day year, while the actual time it takes the earth to circle the sun is 11 minutes and 14 seconds less. The calendar year was therefore continuously losing time: just a few minutes each year, but by the sixteenth century this amounted to about ten days. Holidays, such as Christmas and Easter, began to slip backward into different seasons. The pope commissioned Copernicus to analyze the astronomy underlying the calendar.

In the sixteenth century, people accepted the model of the second-century Greek astronomer Ptolemy, which shows the earth at the center of the universe. The sun, the moon, the planets, and the stars went around it. As a mathematician, Copernicus began tracking the movements of all these bodies. He was able to fashion a mathematical system that showed the earth at the center of the universe, as accepted belief had it, but he also found a much simpler, though still complicated, formula that showed the sun, not the earth, at the center of the solar system. His new formulation also showed the earth turning on its axis every 24 hours, rather than having the entire cosmos revolve around the earth.

As a rule, scientists faced with more than one workable explanation choose the simpler one, and with his new, simpler model of a solar system Copernicus could explain the calendrical difficulties that had been his principal assignment. But this new explanation would land him in serious trouble with the Church, and he knew it.

The concept of the earth at the center of the universe as taught by Ptolemy had been adopted as the official doctrine of the Catholic Church because it was consistent with Biblical passages (Joshua 10:13; Ecclesiastes 1:4–5) that spoke of the sun's circle around the earth. The consequences of challenging that belief frightened Copernicus, as he wrote to the pope in his letter of transmission introducing his findings:

> I may well presume, most Holy Father, that certain people, as soon as they hear that in this book about the Revolutions of the Spheres of the Universe I ascribe movement to the earthly globe, will cry out that … I should at once be hissed off the stage … Thinking therefore within myself that to ascribe movement to the Earth must indeed seem an absurd performance on my part to those who know that many centuries have consented to the establishment of the contrary judgment, namely that the Earth is placed immovably as the central point in the middle of the Universe, I hesitated long whether, on the one hand, I should give to the light these my Commentaries written to prove the Earth's motion … These misgivings and actual protests have been overcome by my friends … [one of whom] often urged and even importuned me to publish this work which I had kept in store not for nine years only, but to a fourth period of nine years … They urged that I should not, on account of my fears, refuse any longer to contribute the fruits of my labors to the common advantage of those interested in mathematics … Yielding then to their persuasion

KEY TERM

empiricism The theory that all knowledge originates in experience; the practice of relying on direct observation of events and experience to determine reality.

I at last permitted my friends to publish that work which they have so long demanded. (cited in Kuhn, 1957, pp. 137–38)

In the end, Copernicus stuck to the principles of his mathematical commitments and his conscience. He presented the truth as he understood it, but he published his complete findings only on his deathbed. They created much less of a stir than might have been expected, since they were published as a mathematical study, *De Revolutionibus*, comprehensible only to the most learned astronomers and mathematicians of his day. They became the object more of technical study than of theological debate.

Johannes Kepler. Copernicus' model, although a huge step forward, was not entirely satisfactory, because it still represented the planets' orbits as circular. They are not. The breakthrough that enshrined the sun-centered universe was made by Johannes Kepler (1571–1630). For ten years Kepler worked through the rich observational data he inherited from Copernicus and from the greatest astronomer of the next generation, Tycho Brahe (1546–1601), and finally reached a new understanding. The sun was at the center of the solar system, and the planets, including the earth, moved around it. Their orbits, however, were not circles but ellipses, and they moved not at a fixed speed, but at varying speeds depending on their position on the ellipse. With this new insight, Kepler designed a model of the solar system that was simple, comprehensive, and mathematically consistent with the data available. He published his results in 1609 in *On the Motion of Mars*.

Map of the heavens according to Nicholas Copernicus, *c.* 1543. Copernicus placed the sun in the middle of his solar system with the earth circling it. He also demonstrated the tilt and rotation of the earth's axis as it traveled in its yearly orbit. In these findings he differed from Ptolemy, the second-century Greek astronomer, but he did continue to see the solar system as bounded, with an array of fixed stars and constellations marking its outer limits. (British Library, London)

The theological argument was now clearly drawn. The earth was no longer the center of God's creation. Thomas Kuhn writes: "Copernicanism required a transformation in man's view of his relation to God and of the bases of his morality."(Kuhn, 1957, p. 193) There was no longer a fixed, heavenly location for God's throne. The perfection of the universe—with the earth at the center of a series of fixed, concentric, crystalline circles in which the planets traveled—was contaminated. Protestant leaders, believing in the literal word of the Bible, and led by Martin Luther himself, attacked the heliocentric universe of Copernicus as early as 1539. The Catholic Church, at first allowing much more latitude to individual belief in this matter, was slower to condemn, but in 1610 it officially designated the Copernican model a heresy, and in 1616, *De Revolutionibus* and all other writings that affirmed the earth's motion were put on the Index, an official list of texts that were forbidden to be taught or even read.

Galileo Galilei. For many years the split between the mathematical astronomers and the Church continued rather quietly, with the mathematicians generally winning out among educated audiences. Then, in 1609, the Italian astronomer Galileo Galilei (1564–1642) turned the newly invented telescope skyward and changed forever what we know about the heavens, how we know it, and its significance in the eyes of the nonspecialist, general public. Galileo added new empirical evidence and new technology to the toolkit of astronomy, opening new avenues of knowledge and popularizing them. The telescope had been created in the Netherlands. Galileo was the first to turn it toward the skies, and he made one discovery after another: the Milky Way is not just a dull glow in the sky but a gigantic collection of stars; the moon's surface is

How did the Scientific Revolution challenge previous concepts of the natural world?

16.1
16.2
16.3
16.4
16.5
16.6
16.7
16.8

16.1
16.2
16.3
16.4
16.5
16.6
16.7
16.8

How did the
Scientific
Revolution
challenge
previous
concepts of the
natural world?

irregular, covered with craters and hills; the moon's radiant light is a reflection from the sun; the sun has "imperfections," dark spots that appear and disappear across its surface; the earth is not the only planet with moons—Galileo observed at least four satellites circling Jupiter.

Galileo wrote: "We shall prove the earth to be a wandering body [in orbit around the sun] … This we shall support by an infinitude of arguments drawn from nature" (Galilei, p. 45). Over and over Galileo stressed the validity of his own empirical observations. "With the aid of the telescope this has been scrutinized so directly and with such ocular certainty that all the disputes which have vexed the philosophers through so many ages have been resolved, and we are at last freed from wordy debates about it." "One may learn with all the certainty of sense evidence"; "All these facts were discovered and observed by me not many days ago with the aid of a spyglass which I devised, after first being illuminated by divine grace"; "our own eyes show us." Galileo appealed to sense evidence, to direct observation, to empirical information, and demonstrated its complete accessibility to anyone who looks through a telescope. He wrote for a general audience, not for university scholars; he wrote in Italian, not in Latin. The publication of Galileo's discoveries increased public interest in astronomy, and that public interest gradually turned into public acceptance.

The Catholic Church, deeply enmeshed in its cold war with Protestantism, finally turned against him. In 1633 Galileo was tried by the Roman Inquisition and found guilty of having taught his doctrines against the orders of the Church. Under threat of torture, the 69-year-old scientist publicly recanted his beliefs and was sentenced to house arrest for the rest of his life. (In 1992, on the 350th anniversary of Galileo's death, Pope John Paul II called the Church's error the result of "a tragic mutual incomprehension." There is no "incompatibility between the spirit of science and its

Galileo demonstrating his telescopic discovery of Jupiter's satellites to the councilors of Venice in 1610. Wood engraving, French, nineteenth century. Galileo opened entire new vistas in astronomy by improving the telescope and turning it towards the heavens. He trusted his direct observations even when they brought him into confrontation with Church authorities who preferred to believe Biblical and ancient Greek perspectives.

Read the Document: Galileo Galilei, "Letter to Madame Christine of Lorraine, Grand Duchesse of Tuscany" on MyHistoryLab rules of research on the one hand and the Christian faith on the other." On the contrary, he asserted, "It is a duty for theologians to keep themselves regularly informed of scientific advances." *L'Osservatore Romano*, November 4, 1992.)

Isaac Newton. In the same year as Galileo's death in Italy, Isaac Newton (1642–1727) was born in England, on Christmas Day. He studied at Cambridge University and became a professor of mathematics there at age 26. In the course of his research, he discovered the calculus, a discovery he shared, separately, with the German mathematician Gottfried Wilhelm Leibnitz (1646–1716). A mathematical system especially useful in calculating motion along curved lines, the calculus was immediately valuable in predicting the celestial course of planets and the earthly trajectory of artillery shells. Another area of Newton's early research was in optics, focusing on the spectrum of light as it passed through a prism. Then he turned his attention to the new problems raised by Copernicus, Kepler, and Galileo: Why do heavy bodies always fall toward earth even as the earth is moving through space? What moves the earth? What moves the planets and what keeps them in their orbits? Before Copernicus, Ptolemy's view of the fixed spheres of the universe answered those questions. But without those fixed spheres, how should we understand the movements of the heavens?

In finding the universal law of gravity, Newton showed that the laws of planetary motion formulated by Kepler, the laws of earthly movement discovered by Galileo, and the principles of inertia of motion identified by the French mathematician and philosopher René Descartes (1596–1650), were all consistent. The universal principle of gravitation, coupled with the principle of inertia—that a body once set in motion tends to continue moving at the same speed in the same direction—explains the means by which the universe holds together. Moreover, these forces of inertia and gravity are universal, operating in the same way on earth as in the wider universe. Discovering the universal law of gravity required a leap of the imagination; working out its mathematics was the toil of genius. Newton worked out the formula for the pull of gravity: all matter moves as if every particle attracts every other particle with a force proportional to the product of the two masses, and inversely proportional to the square of the distance between them. This force is universal gravitation. In 1687 Newton published the results in his *Mathematical Principles of Natural Philosophy*.

In common with all later scientists, Newton did not try to explain why this force worked, only how it worked. This new law had enormous philosophical implications, for it explained the "glue" in the Copernican system of the universe. It also had very practical consequences in understanding and predicting the tides. The great advances in mathematics underpinned not only theoretical research, but also practical invention in the form of time-keeping, mapping, and processes that required accuracy, such as the aiming of artillery and the construction of steam engines.

In recognition of his revolutionary contributions, in 1703 Newton was named President of the Royal Society,

How did the Scientific Revolution challenge previous concepts of the natural world?

16.1
16.2
16.3
16.4
16.5
16.6
16.7
16.8

Newton experiments with light. Newton's first published papers were in optics. Here he worked as an experimental scientist rather than as a theoretical mathematician. By passing the rays of the sun through a prism he demonstrated that white light was an amalgam of colored rays. Using this information he built a reflecting telescope, using a mirror to focus light, thus avoiding the chromatic aberration that appeared in a refracting telescope.

📖 **Read** the **Document: Isaac Newton, from Opticks** on **MyHistoryLab**

16.1
16.2 How did the ideas of Locke and Hobbes influence political and social science?
16.3
16.4
16.5
16.6
16.7
16.8

England's national academy of science. The Society stressed its commitment to resisting arbitrary authority, including the authority of ancient, received wisdom. It chose as its motto *"Nullius in verba,"* meaning "Nothing in words": scientific facts should be found and verified through experimentation. The king of England had given a royal charter to the Royal Society of London in 1662, creating what continues today as the world's oldest surviving national academy of science. The Society marked the transformation of science from the work of individual, somewhat isolated scholars to an institutionalized, recognized set of disciplines of national importance.

William Harvey, Anthony van Leeuwenhoek, Carolus Linnaeus. The discoveries in astronomy, physics, and mathematics were the leading sectors in the scientific revolution of the seventeenth century, but they were not alone. In England, William Harvey (1578–1657) published *On the Movement of the Heart and Blood* (1628), based on years of laboratory research and vivisection of animals, demonstrating the circulation of blood through the body. In the Netherlands, Anthony van Leeuwenhoek (1632–1723) improved the newly invented microscope, the other great advance in optics along with the telescope, to see and then create drawings of blood corpuscles, spermatozoa, and bacteria. His observations enabled him to argue that reproduction even among tiny creatures occurred through sexual mating, not spontaneous generation. Leeuwenhoek was a businessman in the cloth trade, not specially educated in the sciences, and his election as a Fellow of the Royal Society of London in 1680 demonstrated that amateurs were welcome in this new research.

Leeuwenhoek's research expanded the knowledge of the number and variety of microscopic creatures. Carolus Linnaeus (1707–78) developed a system of classification for these and all other known creatures in nature, *Systema Naturae* (1735), including an analysis of sexual reproduction in plants. The further evolution of eighteenth-century science was well under way.

The new science expanded human powers and self-understanding. Some scholars, frightened by the new discoveries, agreed with Blaise Pascal, a devout Christian French mathematician: "I am terrified by the eternal silence of these infinite spaces." But more took heart, along with poet Alexander Pope, that a brave, new world of rationality was dawning:

Nature and nature's law lay hid in night;
God said, "Let Newton be," and all was light.

The new world of science swept away much superstition, at least for the time, and suggested that rationality and science could create a new world in which people could trust their senses to gather empirical information and to act on it, a world in which the laws of nature could be discovered and calculated, a world in which science would inspire technological invention in the practical arts of making human life more productive and more comfortable. Throughout the eighteenth century, this vision of natural law and the power of human reason to improve the world spilled over from science and technology to philosophy and political theory. Not everyone agreed, however, on what constituted an improvement.

Human Rights: Philosophical Rationales

16.2 How did the ideas of Locke and Hobbes influence political and social science?

The political and social "sciences" are not as precise as the natural sciences. The processes of human life in society do not lend themselves to laboratory experiments and mathematical formulas. Nevertheless, the study of society and the creation of institutions for governing it do rest on philosophy that can be examined and revised in light of practical experience. In the seventeenth and eighteenth centuries, theoretical

16.1

How did the
ideas of Locke
and Hobbes
influence
political and
social science?

16.2

16.3

16.4

16.5

16.6

16.7

16.8

speculation about society and politics translated into revolutionary practice. The role of the monarch, of hereditary power, of property, of citizenship, of the power of the state—all were undergoing intense review, in theory and in practice. For example, the political theories of two Englishmen, Thomas Hobbes (1588–1679) and John Locke (1632–1704), laid the foundations for their country's Glorious Revolution.

Hobbes and Limits on Power

The philosophy justifying England's Glorious Revolution of 1688 had developed over many years. Thomas Hobbes at first seemed to justify the enormous, existing power of the king over the citizens. In his most influential work, *Leviathan* (1651), he declared: "Nothing the sovereign representative can do to a subject, on what pretence soever, can properly be called injustice, or injury." This appears to be a justification for the absolute power of the king, but Hobbes was actually providing a rationale for limiting that power. He declared that the king could claim authority not by virtue of special, personal rights, nor by virtue of representing God on earth, but because "every subject is author of every act the sovereign doth." In other words, the king has authority to the extent that he represents the will of the people.

📖 Read the **Document**: **Thomas Hobbes, The Leviathan** on **MyHistoryLab**

The "State of Nature." Hobbes, like others of his time, was trying to understand the English monarchy in terms of its origins. He postulated the myth of a prehistoric, individualistic, unruly, **state of nature**, which people had rejected in order to create a society that would protect them individually and collectively. Uncontrolled by law and a king, Hobbes famously wrote, "the life of man [is] solitary, poor, nasty, brutish, and short … During the time men live without a common power to keep them all in awe, they are in that condition which is called war; and such a war, as is of every man against every man." To escape such lawlessness, men had exchanged their individual liberties for social and political order. Their (mythical) **social contract**, not divine appointment, had created monarchy in order to serve the people.

Locke and the Right of Revolution

The political accomplishments of the Glorious Revolution are even more closely associated with the writings of John Locke, who had fled England for the Netherlands in 1683, returning only after the revolution was complete. While he was in the Netherlands, Locke wrote his most important essay on political philosophy, *The Second Treatise on Government*, although it was not published until 1689, after the Glorious Revolution had been implemented and Locke felt safe to return to England. Since Locke's philosophy parallels not only the English revolution but also many subsequent ones, his arguments deserve careful attention.

As Hobbes had done, Locke argued that government is a secular compact entered into voluntarily and freely by individuals. If there are to be kings, they too must live under the constitution. Locke, like Hobbes, based his argument on a mythical, prehistoric "state of nature," which people forsook in order to provide for their common defense and needs. He, however, stressed the importance of common consent in the earlier mythical contract. The contract continues to be legitimate only so long as the consent continues. If they no longer consent to the contract, the people have the right to terminate it. Going beyond Hobbes, Locke explicitly proclaimed the right of revolution in his *Second Treatise*:

> There remains still in the people a supreme power to remove or alter the legislative, when they find the legislative act contrary to the trust reposed in them. For all power given with trust for the attaining of an end, being limited by that end, whenever

KEY TERMS

state of nature The mythical situation in which people lived without any legal codes or contracts, each free to do exactly as he or she pleased, without the restrictions of law and society, but also without the protection of law and society.

social contract A mythical, unwritten agreement among early people in a "state of nature" to establish some form of government. This "contract" generally defines the rights and obligations of the individuals and of the government.

16.1

16.2

16.3

16.4

16.5

16.6

16.7

16.8

How did the
ideas of Locke
and Hobbes
influence
political and
social science?

that end is manifestly neglected, or opposed, the trust must necessarily be forfeited, and the power devolves into the hands of those that gave it, who may place it anew where they shall think best for their safety and security. (p. 92)

Locke postulated the "equal right that every man hath to his natural freedom, without being subjected to the will or authority of any other man ... Absolute monarchy, which by some men is counted the only government in the world, is indeed inconsistent with civil society." Majority rule is Locke's basis of government: "The act of the majority passes for the act of the whole, and of course determines as having by the law of nature and reason, the power of the whole."

📖 Read the Document: John Locke, *Essay Concerning Human Understanding* on **MyHistoryLab**

Locke, Hobbes, and Property

Locke was not proposing radical democracy; he was not advocating one person, one vote. For Locke, government existed to serve the interests of property owners: "Government has no other end but the preservation of property ... The great and chief end therefore, of men's uniting into commonwealths, and putting themselves under government, is the preservation of their property." Indeed, after the initial, mythical social contract had established the government's authority, succeeding generations had signalled their continuing acceptance of that contract by allowing their property to be protected by the government. "The supreme power cannot take from any man any part of his property without his own consent. For the preservation of property being the end of government, and that for which men enter into society, it necessarily supposes and requires, that the people should have property." Taxes, therefore, cannot be levied unilaterally or arbitrarily. "If anyone shall claim a power to lay and levy taxes on the people, by his own authority, and without such consent of the people, he thereby invades the fundamental law of property, and subverts the end of government."

Hobbes had already indicated the growing importance of property and industry to seventeenth-century England. Without peace and stability, he wrote, "there is no place for industry; because the fruit thereof is uncertain; and consequently no culture of the earth; no navigation, nor use of the commodities that may be imported by sea; no commodious building; no instruments of moving, and removing, such things as require much force; no knowledge of the face of the earth; no account of time; no arts; no letters; no society" (p. 895).

Hobbes wanted an economically productive society that promoted agriculture, industry, commerce, and invention. Locke saw private ownership of property and private profit as the means to achieving that end. He considered the property-owning classes of England to be the nation's proper leaders and administrators. He asserted the importance of the **enclosure acts** by which England was dividing up the common lands of each village, turning them into private property, and selling them. These enclosure acts were creating a new, wealthier landlord class, which turned its energies to increasing agricultural productivity. At the same time the acts forced those rural people who had owned no land of their own, but who had been grazing their animals on common land, to give up their independence. Most found work with more prosperous landlords, and some moved to the cities in search of new jobs.

Neither Hobbes nor Locke showed concern for the nonpropertied classes. In their mythical state of nature, land had been abundant—available for the taking—and anyone could become a property owner. But in the time in which they actually lived and wrote, as in our own time, access to unclaimed, unowned property was not so easy. Indeed, when Locke notes that "the turfs my servant has cut ... become my property," he assigns the labor of the landless servant to his landed master. In practice, Locke's theory justified the government of England by Parliament under

KEY TERM

enclosure acts Laws passed in England between 1450 and 1640, and culminating in 1750–1860, which converted public lands held in common into parcels of land to be sold to private owners.

SOURCE

Universal Suffrage vs. Property Rights

E.P. Thompson, the twentieth-century British historian, emphasized the contributions of common people to history. In his groundbreaking *The Making of the English Working Class* of 1963 (pp. 22–23), Thompson cites statements made in 1647 at an army council meeting. Participants were attempting to determine the role of the common people in electing Parliament.

Oliver Cromwell's son-in-law General Ireton proposed extending the franchise, but only to men of property, fearing that private property might otherwise be abolished: "No person hath a right to an interest or share in the disposing of the affairs of the kingdom ... that hath not a permanent fixed interest in this kingdom ... If you admit any man that hath a breath and being, why may not those men vote against all property?"

The common soldiers replied more democratically and more bitterly. One asserted: "There are many thousands of us soldiers that have ventured our lives; we have had little property in the kingdom as to our estates, yet we have had a birthright. But it seems now, except a man hath a fixed estate in this kingdom, he hath no right ... I wonder we were so much deceived." In short, if we are asked to fight on behalf of the government, we should have a voice in electing it.

---

constitutional law, which limited the power of the king and transferred it to the hands of the propertied classes—the system that was evolving in his time. Locke's is the voice of the improving landlords and the rising commercial classes who made the Glorious Revolution.

Civil War and Revolution in England, 1642–51

16.3   What were the causes and outcomes of the Glorious Revolution?

16.1
16.2
16.3 What were the causes and outcomes of the Glorious Revolution?
16.4
16.5
16.6
16.7
16.8

At about the time Hobbes was writing, England was in continuing revolt against its sovereigns. Religion was the burning issue, and it seemed that no sovereign could satisfy the conflicting wishes of dissenters—Roman Catholics, Presbyterians, Puritans, and Quakers—and the official Anglican Church. Frustrations simmered but had no focus until both James I (r. 1603–25) and his son Charles I (r. 1625–49) ran out of money to administer their governments and convened Parliament to request additional funds. They did not expect that Parliament would question their right to levy taxes as they chose; Parliament did not expect that the kings would reject its restrictions on royal power. Both sides were wrong. The struggle between kings and Parliament ultimately resulted in civil war and the beheading of Charles I.

Civil War, 1642–51

Many members of Parliament—landowners, increasingly wealthy city merchants, lawyers, Puritans and other religious dissenters, as well as Anglican clergy—refused to give the kings the money they requested. They challenged royal authority, and proposed increased power for an elected legislature, promotion by merit in government jobs, and, most of all, religious tolerance in private and public life. Rejecting these proposals, Charles I attempted to levy taxes without the sanction of Parliament. Civil war ensued, from 1642 to 1651, and the Parliament that Charles had convened in 1640 ultimately executed him. Oliver Cromwell, an ardent Calvinist and military genius, ruled as Lord Protector of England from 1653 until his death in 1658. He defeated those who rebelled against his new government in both Ireland and Scotland, and joined those two kingdoms to England to form the British Commonwealth. In spite of his victories, neither Cromwell nor Parliament was able to achieve a new form of effective government, and the monarchy was restored in 1660. (The new government dug up Cromwell's body from Westminster Abbey, hung it in chains, beheaded it, and left the head impaled on a pole outside the Abbey for several

An Eyewitness Representation of the Execution of Charles I, by John Weesop, 1649. Charles' belief in the divine right of kings and the authority of the Church of England led eventually to a civil war with Parliament—which he and his supporters lost. At his subsequent trial, the king was sentenced to death as a tyrant, murderer, and enemy of the nation and beheaded at Whitehall, London, on January 30, 1649. On the left is William Juxon, bishop of London; on the right is the unidentified executioner. (Private collection)

16.1
16.2
16.3
16.4
16.5
16.6
16.7
16.8

What were the causes and outcomes of the Glorious Revolution?

years.) Nevertheless, the Civil War established the principle that the monarchy could be abolished. A critical question still remained: What would be England's religion? That issue was resolved—in favor of Protestantism—in the Glorious Revolution of 1688.

The Glorious Revolution, 1688

Charles II (r. 1660–85) and his brother James II (r. 1685–90) continued to claim more powers than Parliament wished to sanction. James, a Catholic, favored Catholics in many of his official appointments. When a son was born to him, leading nobles feared that James and his successors might reinstitute Catholicism as England's official religion a century and a half after Henry VIII had disestablished it in favor of the Church of England. They invited James II's daughter Mary and her husband, William of Orange, ruler of the United Provinces of the Netherlands—both resolute Protestants—to come to England to rule as king and queen. Responding to Parliament's invitation, William and Mary arrived in England in 1688, marking the Glorious Revolution. They confirmed their new rule by defeating the troops still loyal to James II at the Battle of the Boyne in Ireland in 1690.

The Bill of Rights. Although the new monarchs had been invited primarily to resolve religious conflicts, their ascension to the throne also resolved the power conflict between monarch and Parliament. The Bill of Rights enacted by Parliament in 1689 stated principles that had been evolving for decades in the relationship between the monarchy and the people of England. It stipulated, among other clauses, that no

16.1
16.2
16.3
16.4
16.5
16.6
16.7
16.8

taxes could be raised nor armies recruited without prior parliamentary approval; no subject could be arrested and detained without legal process; and no law could be suspended by the king unilaterally. The Glorious Revolution thus not only displaced one monarch in favor of another but also limited the powers of the monarchy under constitutional law. Parliament had asserted its power over the king. After all, the new king and queen had been selected by noblemen and confirmed by Parliament. In addition, as William continued his wars against France, he had to defer to Parliament for funds.

The Glorious Revolution also brought some resolution to the issues of religion in politics that had beset England for so long, although rebellion against the religious provisions continued in Scotland and especially Ireland. The Anglican Church remained the established Church of England, but the Toleration Act of 1689 granted Puritan Dissenters—but not Roman Catholics—the right of free public worship. Parliament did not yet revoke the Test Act, which reserved military and civil offices for Anglicans only. Cromwell had already permitted Jews to return to England, almost 400 years after their expulsion in 1290.

📖 **Read** the **Document: The English Bill of Rights (1689)** on **MyHistoryLab**

The Enlightenment

16.4   What were the central beliefs of the Enlightenment thinkers?

In the century between the Glorious Revolution in England and the American and French revolutions, a movement in philosophic thought emerged called the Enlightenment. Its intellectual center was in France, although key participants lived in America, Scotland, England, Prussia, Russia, and elsewhere. (Locke, for example, is usually considered an early Enlightenment thinker.) The French leaders of the Enlightenment were called *philosophes* ("philosophers") and they built on the scientific revolution of the sixteenth and seventeenth centuries. In contrast to such Roman Catholic doctrines as original sin and the authority of the Church over human reason, the *philosophes* argued that human progress was possible through the steady and unrestricted expansion of knowledge, or "enlightenment." Their challenge to authority that was not based on rationality and their belief that human institutions should be administered by the most competent people and serve the welfare of the general population, rather than an elite, hereditary minority, helped to inspire the American and French revolutions.

The *Philosophes*

The *philosophes* believed in a world of rationality, in which collected human knowledge and systematic thought could serve as powerful tools for finding order in the universe and for solving key problems in political and economic life. "The perfectibility of humanity is indefinite," proclaimed the philosopher and scientist the Marquis de Condorcet (1743–94). Their concern for clarity of thought, combined with the desire to solve practical problems in public life, gave them considerable influence over the restructuring of new political institutions in their age of revolution. The authors of the American Declaration of Independence and of the French Declaration of the Rights of Man and the Citizen drew much of their inspiration from the *philosophes*. The *philosophes* believed in order, but also in freedom of thought and expression. For them, public discussion and debate were the means of finding better ideas and solutions. Indeed, the *philosophes* were in constant dialogue and debate with one another. They often met in salons, comfortable settings for dinner and conversation often hosted by talented, educated, aristocratic women.

KEY TERM

philosophes A group of eighteenth-century writers and philosophers, mostly French, who emphasized human reason as the key to progress. They advocated freedom of expression and social, economic, and political reform.

16.1
16.2
16.3
16.4
16.5
16.6
16.7
16.8

What were
the central
beliefs of the
Enlightenment
thinkers?

In terms of spiritual and religious beliefs, most *philosophes* were deists: they allowed that the world may have required an original creator, like Aristotle's prime mover, but that once the processes of life had begun, he had withdrawn. Their metaphor was that of a watchmaker who built the mechanism, started it moving, and then departed. Humanity's fate thereafter was in its own hands.

Charles de Secondat, Baron de Montesquieu. Travel influenced the *philosophes'* thought, opening their minds to a wider range of ideas. Charles de Secondat, baron de Montesquieu (1689–1755), traveled widely and wrote the *Persian Letters*, satirical criticism of French institutions including the monarchy and the Catholic Church, in the form of dispatches supposedly sent by two visitors to France to readers at home. Twenty-seven years later, in 1748, Montesquieu wrote his most influential work, *The Spirit of Laws*, in which he recognized that different countries need different kinds of government, and advocated a separation of powers based on his (mis)understanding of the British system of government. The authors of the United States Constitution later acknowledged their debt to Montesquieu's thought.

Denis Diderot's *Encyclopedia*. The most famous academic product of the *philosophes* and the Enlightenment was the *Encyclopedia, or Rational Dictionary of the Arts, Sciences, and Crafts*, compiled by Denis Diderot (1713–84) and containing articles by leading scholars and *philosophes*. The *Encyclopedia* reaffirmed faith in human progress based on education:

> The aim of an *Encyclopedia* is to collect all the knowledge that now lies scattered over the face of the earth, to make known its general structure to the men among whom we live, and to transmit it to those who will come after us, in order that the labors of past ages may be useful to the ages that will follow, that our grandsons, as they become better educated, may become at the same time more virtuous and more happy, and that we may not die without having deserved well of the human race. (Columbia University, pp. 988–89)

Diderot called for further social and political revolution: "We are beginning to shake off the yoke of authority and tradition in order to hold fast to the laws of reason." (p. 992). Challenging authority meant being open to multiple perspectives rather than holding a single truth, and Diderot built this concept into the structure of his volumes:

> By giving cross-references to articles where solid principles serve as foundation for the diametrically opposed truths we shall be able to throw down the whole edifice of mud and scatter the idle heap of dust. … If these cross-references, which now confirm and now refute, are carried out artistically according to a plan carefully conceived in advance, they will give to the *Encyclopedia* the … ability to change men's common way of thinking. (p. 996)

The *Encyclopedia* ultimately filled 17 volumes of text and 11 of illustrations.

Voltaire. Another *philosophe*, François-Marie Arouet, better known as Voltaire (1694–1778), declared: "*Ecrasez l'infame!*" ("Crush the infamy!") of superstition, intolerance, organized religion, and the power of the clergy. Voltaire wrote extensively: *Elements of the Philosophy of Newton* (1738) explicated new scientific evidence of the rational order and the human ability to comprehend the universe; *Philosophical Letters on the English* (1734) argued for freedom of religion, inquiry, and the press; *Essai sur les moeurs* (1756), translated as *Universal History*, gave a humanistic context to historical development and placed the responsibility for human fate in human hands. The most famous of Voltaire's writings, the novel *Candide* (1759), satirized the false comforts promised by the Church and by governments. In his travels, the young man Candide experiences the bitter reality of natural and man-made catastrophes, earthquakes and wars, and pervasive human deceitfulness. This was not "the best of all possible worlds," as his mentor Pangloss proclaimed. Nevertheless, Candide, and Voltaire, conclude, life could yield real, if limited, contentment to those who surrendered false beliefs, concentrated on the practicalities of their own lives, and "cultivated their own gardens."

Read the **Document**: **Voltaire, on Social Conditions in Eighteenth-century France** on **MyHistoryLab**

The Philosophers at Supper, Jean Huber, 1750. Voltaire (1), Condorcet (5), and Diderot (6) are among the figures depicted in this engraving, a visual checklist of important Enlightenment thinkers. Seeing the Western world as emerging from centuries of darkness and ignorance, these French intellectuals promoted reason, science, and a respect for humanity—ideas that would underpin the intellectual case for the French Revolution of 1789. (Bibliothèque Nationale, Paris)

"Enlightened Despotism"

The *philosophes* were not, however, committed to popular democracy. Voltaire, for example, preferred benevolent and **enlightened despotism** to badly administered self-rule. In the best of all possible worlds, there would be an enlightened ruler such as Frederick II, the Great, of Prussia (r. 1740–86), at whose court Voltaire lived for several years; or Catherine II, the Great, empress of Russia (r. 1762–96), of whom he was a close friend; or their contemporary, Joseph II, emperor of Austria (r. 1765–90). All three ruled countries in which the administration was efficient, taxes were reasonable, agricultural and handicraft production was encouraged, freedom of expression and religion was allowed, the military was strengthened, and powerful empires resulted. The enlightened despot acted in disciplined ways, subject in his or her mind to the law of nature. But the population at large had no say or vote in the administration. In other words, for these rulers, and for Voltaire, good government did not necessarily require self-government.

Proclaiming the concept of enlightened despotism, colonial governments often claimed the mantle of the Enlightenment to justify their rule, arguing that they were using knowledge and reason, and softening the use of brute force, as the foundation of their administration. In 1784 Warren Hastings, Governor General of the British holdings in India, explained:

> Every accumulation of knowledge and especially such as is obtained by social communication with people over whom we exercise dominion founded on the right of conquest, is useful to the state ... it attracts and conciliates distant affections; it lessens the weight of the chain by which the natives are held in subjection; and it imprints on the hearts of our countrymen the sense of obligation and benevolence. (cited in Metcalf and Metcalf, p. 61)

Implementing this Enlightenment philosophy, Hastings founded, for example, the Asiatic Society of Bengal, dedicated primarily to the translation and analysis of ancient Indian texts.

Jean-Jacques Rousseau. Skepticism regarding democratic government was carried further in the works of Jean-Jacques Rousseau (1712–78), perhaps the most enigmatic and ambiguous of all the eighteenth-century French thinkers. Rousseau questioned the primacy of intellect and human ingenuity. In common with Hobbes and Locke, he wrote of the "state of nature," but, unlike them, he seemed, in some ways, to wish to return to it. His *Social Contract* (1762) opened with the lament "Man is

16.1
16.2
16.3
16.4

What were the central beliefs of the Enlightenment thinkers?

16.5
16.6
16.7
16.8

KEY TERM

enlightened despotism A benevolent form of absolutism, a system of government in which the ruler has absolute rights over his or her subject. The term implies that the ruler acts for the good of the people, not in self-interest.

16.1
16.2
16.3
16.4
16.5
16.6
16.7
16.8

16.4 What were the central beliefs of the Enlightenment thinkers?

born free; and everywhere he is in chains." In his *Discourse on the Origin of Inequality* (1755), Rousseau wrote: "There is hardly any inequality in the state of nature; all the inequality which now prevails owes its strength and growth to the development of our faculties and the advance of the human mind, and becomes at last permanent and legitimate by the establishment of property and laws" (Columbia University, p. 1147).

Rousseau proposed a democracy far more radical than that put forward by the other *philosophes*, yet he also seemed to justify a repressive tyranny of the majority. Like Locke and Hobbes, he mythologized an original social contract that transformed the state of nature into a community, and he attributed great power to that community: "Each of us puts his person and all his power in common under the supreme direction of the general will … Whoever refuses to obey the general will shall be compelled to do so by the whole body. This means nothing less than that he will be forced to be free" (p. 1153).

Political philosophers have argued for more than two centuries over the paradox of Rousseau's "general will." How is the citizen "forced to be free"? Is this a proclamation of freedom, justification for suppressing minorities, or a proposal for creating a totalitarian state?

Adam Smith. Adam Smith, whose advocacy of the free market we have already examined (see the chapter entitled "The Unification of World Trade"), is sometimes grouped with the *philosophes*, with whom he carried on extensive discussion and correspondence. Like Locke, Smith believed that it was normal for people to want to "better their condition" materially. He saw that this attempt was not always successful, but suggested:

> It is well that nature imposes upon us in this manner. It is this deception which rouses and keeps in continual motion the industry of mankind. It is this which first prompted them to cultivate the ground, to build houses, to found cities and commonwealths, and to invent and improve all the sciences and arts, which ennoble and embellish human life. (*Moral Sentiments*, IV.1.10)

Smith sanctioned personal consumption. He argued that the desire for consumer goods was natural and beneficial, not selfish, as many religious leaders warned. In his view, economies were driven by consumer demand, which stimulated producers to meet it. Especially after 1492, as the public became aware of new products from "new worlds," the desire to consume increased. Suppliers responded accordingly. Writing in 2008, the economic historian Jan de Vries argued further that those families in northwestern Europe that were smaller, married later, and had larger incomes were the source of much of the demand; they sought new products for their homes and dinner tables. These families restructured their use of time so that all adults, women as well as men, were increasingly likely to develop skills and produce products with market value. Families spent more time both producing and consuming. They were creating what de Vries called an "Industrious Revolution," a forerunner of the Industrial Revolution.

Much less optimistically, Smith recognized that private consumption would engender jealousy and envy. Private property, therefore, needed to be protected, and this, he agreed with Locke, was the task of government: "Civil government, so far as it is instituted for the security of property, is in reality instituted for the defense of the rich against the poor, or of those who have some property against those who have none at all" (*The Wealth of Nations*, p. 674).

At the time of the American and French revolutions, these arguments for enlightenment, rationality, experimental science, secularism, private profit and ownership, "fellow feeling," and limitations on the power of government all clamored for changes in politics, economics, and social life. But what would be the substance and direction of those changes? How would they be implemented, and by whom?

Revolution in North America, 1776

16.1
16.2
16.3
16.4
16.5 What were the goals and achievements of the American Revolution?
16.6
16.7
16.8

16.5 What were the goals and achievements of the American Revolution?

As British settlers began to colonize North America, Australia, and South Africa in the seventeenth and eighteenth centuries, they assumed that they shared in the political and legal rights of all Britons. By the 1760s, however, North American settlers were beginning to resent British control over their political and economic life. Control over American trade, restrictions on the development of American shipping, and the resulting limits on the development of certain kinds of manufacture, were as galling as the issue of taxation. The British victory of 1763 over the French in the Seven Years War in North America, concluding a global cluster of wars between the two powers, ended the threat of attack by French or Native Americans, and freed the American colonists from further need of British troops. However, the British continued to maintain a large army in North America and to tax the colonies directly to pay for it. The Stamp Act of 1765 levied taxes on a long list of commercial and legal documents. The colonists protested with riots, destruction of government property, and a boycott of British goods until Parliament repealed the Act.

📖 **Read** the **Document: Benjamin Franklin and the British Parliament, "Proceedings Regarding the Stamp Act"** on **MyHistoryLab**

Further imperious decrees of King George III stoked increasing anger until, finally, the Americans revolted, declaring themselves an independent country in 1776 and fighting a war to end British rule over them. The American Declaration of Independence set out their list of "injuries and usurpations." It reflected the American resolve to secure the same legal rights as Britons had won at home almost a century earlier. It charged the king with "taking away our Charters, abolishing our most valuable Laws, and altering fundamentally the Forms of our Governments." It blamed the king for abrogating the social contract that bound the colonies to Britain. It declared, ultimately, the right of revolution.

The Boston Tea Party, 1773. Protesting against the British tax on tea. American colonists cheer as radicals dressed as Native Americans throw tea from British ships into Boston harbor. (Yale University Art Gallery, New Haven, Connecticut)

16.1

16.2

16.3

16.4

16.5

16.6

16.7

16.8

What were
the goals and
achievements
of the American
Revolution?

The American Revolution went further in establishing political democracy than had the Glorious Revolution in Britain. It abolished the monarchy entirely, replacing it with an elected government. Having declared that "all men are created equal," with unalienable rights not only to life and liberty, but also to the vague but seductive "pursuit of happiness," the revolutionaries now set out to consolidate their commitments in a new legal structure. Their leaders, such men as George Washington, Benjamin Franklin, Thomas Jefferson, and James Madison, were soldiers, entrepreneurs, and statesmen of considerable erudition, common sense, restraint, and balance.

The Constitution and the Bill of Rights, 1789

After the Americans won their war for independence, 1775–81, and achieved a peace treaty with Britain in 1783, political leaders of the 13 colonies met in Philadelphia to establish a framework for their new nation. They drafted a new Constitution, which took effect in 1789, and a Bill of Rights, which was ratified in 1791. The American Bill of Rights, the first ten amendments to the Constitution, guaranteed to Americans not only the basic rights enjoyed by the British at the time, but more: freedom of religion (and the separation of Church and state), press, assembly, and petition; the right to bear arms; protection against unreasonable searches and against cruel and unusual punishment; and the right to a speedy and proper trial by a jury of peers. The Americans established a federal system of government. The states individually set the rules for voting, and many, but not all, removed the property requirements. By 1800, Vermont had instituted universal manhood suffrage, and South Carolina, Pennsylvania, New Hampshire, and Delaware extended the vote to almost every adult white male taxpayer.

Historians of the early United States situate the more radical American approach to political liberty in at least four factors: religious, geographic, social, and philosophical. First, a disproportionate number of the settlers coming to America from

Signing of the Declaration of Independence, July 4, 1776, John Trumbull, 1786–97. What began as a protest against colonial trade restrictions and the limiting of political liberty grew into a revolutionary struggle and the birth of a nation. The Declaration of Independence enshrined the principles underlying the new United States and later influenced freedom fighters all over the world. (Capitol Collection, Washington, DC)

Britain and Europe were religious dissenters, seeking spiritual independence outside the established churches of their countries. Their widespread, popular beliefs in the importance of individual liberties carried over from religion into politics. Second, the availability of apparently open land presented abundant individual opportunity to the new Americans (as they dispossessed Native Americans). Later, the historian Frederick Jackson Turner would formulate his "frontier thesis," arguing that the relative freedom and openness of American life were based, psychologically as well as materially, on the presence of seemingly endless open frontier land. Third, landed and aristocratic privilege was absent, and the artisan classes were strong in the urban population. Finally, eighteenth-century political thought had generally grown more radical, especially among the *philosophes* in France. By the time the Americans wrote their Bill of Rights, the French Revolution was well under way.

16.1
16.2
16.3
16.4
16.5
16.6
16.7
16.8

What were the goals and achievements of the American Revolution?

The First Anti-imperial Revolution

The American Revolution, in addition to securing British rights for Americans, was also, and perhaps more importantly, the first modern anticolonial revolution. The trade and taxation policies imposed by Britain had pushed businessmen and artisans into opposition to British rule. Other nations, notably France, eager to embarrass Britain and to detach its most promising colonies, provided financial and military support, which helped the Americans to win their independence. One of the goals of the revolution was to open to settlement the North American continent west of the Appalachian Mountains. The British prohibition on this westward movement stood in their way, quite different from Spanish and Portuguese settlement policy in Latin America.

As the newly independent Americans migrated westward, annexing land as they went, they began to develop imperial interests of their own, expressed in the mystique of "manifest destiny." This popular belief in America's natural growth across the continent inspired the European Americans in their constant warfare against Native American Indians. It led Thomas Jefferson to acquire the huge Louisiana Purchase from France in 1803. Texans were encouraged to assert their independence from Mexico in 1836 and were then absorbed into the American Union in 1845. Warfare with Mexico in 1846–48 ended in victory for the United States and the annexation of the southwest. Other annexations of land in North America took place more peacefully, with negotiations with Britain for the Oregon country in 1844–46 and with Russia for the purchase of Alaska—"Russian America"—in 1867.

Nevertheless, over the centuries America served as an inspiration to anticolonial forces. Jawaharlal Nehru, leading India's struggle for independence from Britain in the twentieth century, cited the American Revolution as a model for his own country: "This political change in America was important and destined to bear great results. The American colonies which became free then have grown today [1932] into the most powerful, the richest, and industrially the most advanced country in the world." (Nehru, p. 355).

The "Other"

The American Revolution, however, did not bring democracy to everyone. The greatest shortcoming was slavery. The system was finally ended only by the American Civil War (1861–65), the bloodiest in the history of the nation. Even afterward, racial discrimination characterized American law until the 1960s, and continues to mark American practice up to the present. The status of the Native American population actually worsened after the revolution, as settlers of European extraction headed west, first by wagon train and later by railroad. They slaughtered American Indians, pushed them out of the way, confined them to remote, semi-barren reservations, destroyed the buffalo herds on which their nomadic existence depended,

16.1
16.2
16.3
16.4
16.5
16.6
16.7
16.8

What were
the goals and
achievements
of the American
Revolution?

and discouraged the preservation of their separate cultures and languages. For the indigenous peoples the effects of the revolution were exactly opposite to those of the settler-invaders: expansion became contraction, democracy became tyranny, prosperity became poverty, and liberty became confinement.

The hypocrisy of democratic statements on the one hand and atrocities against American Indians on the other peaked in the presidency of Andrew Jackson (1829–37). Jackson fought against economic and political privilege and to extend opportunity to the common man, yet he ordered the United States Army to evict the Cherokee Nation from their lands in Georgia and to drive them to the "Great American Desert" in the west, in direct defiance of the Supreme Court of the United States. About 25 percent of the 15,000 Indians forced onto this "Trail of Tears" died *en route*.

How did America reconcile its ideals of equality and liberty with the enslavement of blacks and the confinement of American Indians? It did so by considering

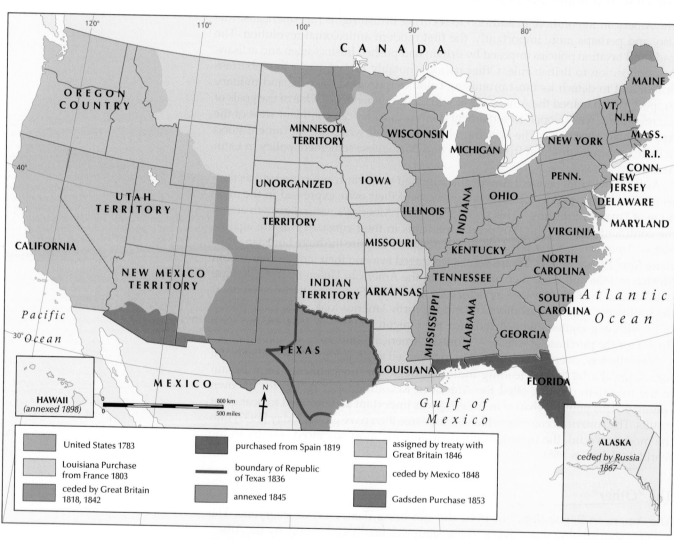

The growth of the United States. The westward expansion of the United States was effected by territorial cession, acquisition, and conquest. Following independence in 1783, the Louisiana Purchase from France (1803) and the annexations of west and east Florida from Spain doubled the nation's size. Another doubling occurred with the annexation of Texas (1845); the acquisition of Oregon Territory (1846); military victory over Mexico (1848), which brought the southwest; the purchase of Alaska from Russia (1867); and the annexation of Hawaii in 1898. In less than a century the United States had become one of the world's largest nations. In all cases, European immigrants and their descendants displaced Native Americans.

non-whites and non-Europeans as "other"—that is, as biologically inferior. The concept of race was often used as a definition, usually made by a quick, if approximate and sometimes inaccurate, visual measure, and often as a legal standard. The physician and natural scientist Samuel George Morton (1799–1851), for example, helped to found the "American School" of ethnography, which claimed that there were races among humans, that they had been created separately and unequally, and that they could be identified by skull capacity. He based his findings on his own collection of hundreds of skulls, some from ancient Egypt. The fixing of legal identity by race, based on identification primarily by color, became especially common in the southern United States in dealing with slaves, ex-slaves, and free blacks. For many years, racial definition was also used as a legal standard in excluding Asians from immigrating. If nonwhites were considered not quite equal biologically to whites, the unalienable right to liberty could be abridged. Once the revolutionary principle of equality was accepted in America and elsewhere, the battle lines were drawn between those who wished to narrow its application to an "in-group" while excluding "others," and those who wished to apply it to all peoples. That battle continues today, in law and in practice, in the United States and around the globe.

16.1
16.2
16.3
16.4
16.5
16.6
How did
the French
Revolution
differ from the
American?
16.7
16.8

The French Revolution and Napoleon, 1789–1812

16.6 How did the French Revolution differ from the American?

The American Revolution, with its combined messages of colonial revolt, constitutional government, individual freedom, and equality under law, inspired many peoples at the time and over the centuries. But in comparison with European countries and their experiences, America and its revolution were unique. At the end of the eighteenth century, America was a country of four million people on the fringes of a continental wilderness, without traditions of class and clerical privilege, and founded in large measure by dissidents. Building on existing British freedoms and fighting a war (with the support of several international allies) against a distant colonial government, the leaders of the revolution were an educated, comfortable elite. The French Revolution, on the other hand, was an internal revolt against entrenched feudal, clerical, and monarchical privilege within the most populous (24 million people) and most powerful European state of its time. It unleashed powerful, combative internal factions, none of which could control the direction or the velocity of revolutionary events inside or outside France. The French Revolution immediately affected all of Europe, most of the western hemisphere, and indeed the whole world. Some would argue that the battles over its central principles continue even today. The twentieth-century Chinese leader Zhou Enlai, when asked to assess the effects of the French Revolution, famously replied: "It's too soon to tell."

From Protests to Revolution, 1789–91

The French Revolution, like the English civil wars of the 1640s, was triggered by the king's need for funds. Much like Charles I, King Louis XVI (r. 1774–92) decided to solicit these funds by convening leaders of the French people through the Estates-General in 1789.

From this point on, political, social, and ideological change proceeded very rapidly as political institutions, social classes, and philosophical beliefs challenged one another in a continuous unfolding of critical events. France was divided, hierarchically, into three Estates: first the clergy, numbering about 100,000 and controlling perhaps 10 percent of the land of France; second the nobility, perhaps 300,000 men, who owned approximately 25 percent of the land; and third everyone else. The Third Estate included a rising and prosperous group of urban merchants and professionals

16.1
16.2
16.3
16.4
16.5
16.6 How did the French Revolution differ from the American?
16.7
16.8

(estimated at 8 percent of the total population), as well as working-class artisans and the 80 percent of the French population who were farmers. The wealth that the king wished to tap was concentrated in the first two estates and in the **bourgeoisie**, the leading urban professional and commercial classes, of the Third Estate.

The Estates-General had not been convened since 1614, and the procedures for its meeting were disputed, revealing grievances not only against the king but also among the representatives. The nobles wished to seize the moment to make the Estates-General into the constitutional government of France, with the king subordinate to it. They wanted guarantees of personal liberty, freedom of the press and speech, and freedom from arbitrary arrest. They also wanted minimal taxation, but they might have conceded that point in exchange for greater political power. Under their proposed constitution, the Estates-General would meet in three separate chambers: one for the clergy; one for the nobility; and a third for everyone else.

Leaders within the Third Estate, which had long regarded the nobility as parasitic and resented their multitude of special privileges, rejected the new proposals. They drew their inspiration for a more democratic, representative, inclusive, and accountable government from the writings of the *philosophes*, and the experience of the revolutions in England and, especially, America. Their local spokesman and leading pamphleteer was actually a clergyman, the Abbé Emmanuel-Joseph Sieyès (1748–1836), who wrote *What Is the Third Estate?* (1789). The tract opened with a catechism of three political questions and answers: "(1) What is the Third Estate? Everything. (2) What has it been in the political order up to the present? Nothing. (3) What does it demand? To Become Something." The leaders of the Third Estate asked for an end to the privileges that had enriched and empowered the clergy and the nobility while reducing the opportunities available to everyone else and impoverishing the French crown. Many saw the king as an ally in the struggle against the nobility. They proposed that the entire Estates-General meet in a single body, since the king had granted them as many representatives as both of the other two estates combined.

KEY TERM

bourgeoisie From the French word for town, *bourg*. Originally applied to the inhabitants of walled towns, who occupied a socio-economic position between the rural peasantry and the feudal aristocracy. With the development of industry, the bourgeoisie became identified more with employers, as well as with other members of the "middle class": professionals, artisans, and shopkeepers.

The Oath of the Tennis Court, Jacques-Louis David, 1790. In this dramatic composition, David captures the moment when the Third Estate asserted their sovereignty as the elected representatives of France. The merchants, professionals, and artisans who attended the hastily convened meeting swore to remain in session until they had drawn up a new constitution—one that would end the vested interests of the nobility and clergy. (Musée Carnavalet, Paris)

When the Parlement of Paris ruled that the three estates should meet separately, as the nobility had wished, the Third Estate was enraged. For six weeks its members boycotted the Estates-General when it was convened in May 1789. On June 13 a few priests joined them, and four days later the Third Estate, with its allies, declared itself the "National Assembly." The king locked them out of their meeting hall. On June 20 they met on a nearby indoor tennis court and swore the "Oath of the Tennis Court," claiming legal power, and declaring that they would not disband until a new constitution was drafted. Louis XVI, frightened by these events and unwilling or unable to assert his own leadership, called up some 18,000 troops to defend him from possible attack at his palace in Versailles where all these events were taking place.

The Revolt of the Poor. Meanwhile, in Paris, 12 miles away, and throughout France, mobs were rising against organized authority. The harvest had been poor, and the price of bread in 1789 was near record heights. Some farmers refused to pay their

16.1
16.2
16.3
16.4
16.5
16.6
16.7
16.8

How did the French Revolution differ from the American?

SOURCE

Jean-Jacques Rousseau's *Emile* and Olympe de Gouges' *The Rights of Woman*

Wealthy, cultured Parisian women hosted the salons in which *philosophes* crafted the intellectual and moral foundations of the Enlightenment. As the French Revolution took shape, the refinement of the salon gave way to battles in the street, and a new group of women began to play a new, and equally central, role. Housewives, unable to afford to feed their families in a time of high prices, assembled in the "March of the Women" from Paris to Versailles in October 1789, forcing King Louis XVI to return to Paris under a kind of house arrest. Their militancy paved the way for the execution of the King two years later and the escalation of the revolution into its next, most violent stage. When Charles Dickens wrote *A Tale of Two Cities*, his novelistic account of the French Revolution, he created Madame Defarge as the central symbol of revolutionary zeal, literally knitting plots of revenge against the aristocracy.

Nevertheless, several of the most prominent *philosophes* and revolutionaries depicted women as significantly different from, and less capable than, men. The Huguenot medical doctor Louis de Jaucourt wrote this in his entry on women in Diderot's *Encyclopédie*: "The laws and customs of Europe unanimously and decisively give authority to the male because he is the one with the greatest strength of mind and body" (cited in Schiebinger, p. 216). Jean-Jacques Rousseau, in *Emile*, his classic treatise on education, advocated a bold and assertive husband, Emile, as the teacher of his self-reliant but uneducated and highly accommodating wife, Sophie:

> Her education is neither showy nor neglected; she has taste without deep study, talent without art, judgment without learning. Her mind knows little, but it is trained to learn; it is well-tilled soil ready for the sower … What charming ignorance! Happy is he who is destined to be her tutor. She will not be her husband's teacher but his scholar; far from seeking to control his tastes, she will share them. She will suit him far better than a blue-stocking and he will have the pleasure of teaching her everything. (http://www.gutenberg.org/catalog/world/readfile?fk_files=3275614&pageno=334)

Emile epitomized the widespread belief in "sexual complementarity," the theory that men and women have different, complementary roles.

Not everyone agreed, however; even in the late 1700s, many saw this point of view as demeaning to women. The Marquis de Condorcet argued for more egalitarian education for women and for their full participation in civic affairs and democratic processes, including voting. He argued that if women had been less well educated than men, it owed not to their lack of capacity, but to a poorly designed educational system. Mary Wollstonecraft denounced Rousseau's theories of education and sexuality in issuing her classic argument for full equality, *A Vindication of the Rights of Woman* (1792).

Writing under the pen name Olympe de Gouges, the playwright Marie Gouze (1748–93) entered directly into the political arena of the revolution. She appropriated the language of the revolution's *Declaration of the Rights of Man and the Citizen* (1789) to expose its lack of concern for the rights of women; Gouze issued her demand for full equality as a *Declaration of the Rights of Woman and the Citizen*:

> Article I. Woman is born free and remains equal in rights to man. Social distinctions can be founded only on general utility …
> Article XVII. The right of property is inviolable and sacred to both sexes, jointly or separately. (Bell and Offen, pp. 105–06)

Gouges addressed her document to the French queen, Marie-Antoinette, urging her to adopt this feminist program as her own and thus win over France to the royalist cause. In 1793 the radical Jacobins in the Assembly, condemning Gouges for both royalism and feminism, had her guillotined.

📖 Read the **Document: Jean-Jacques Rousseau, Emile** on **MyHistoryLab**

📖 Read the **Document: Olympe de Gouges, Declaration of the Rights of Women and the Female Citizen** on **MyHistoryLab**

16.1
16.2
16.3
16.4
16.5
16.6 How did the French Revolution differ from the American?
16.7
16.8

taxes and their manorial dues, and many city people were hungry. Beggars and brigands began to roam the countryside and move toward Paris.

In the capital, mobs stormed the Bastille, which was a combination of jail and armory. Meeting violent resistance, they murdered the governor of the Bastille, the mayor of Paris, and a number of soldiers. Encouraged by the events in Paris, peasants in the countryside organized against France's remaining feudal institutions. They seized and destroyed documents that demanded feudal dues and taxes. The peasants felt an (unfounded) "Great Fear," as it was called, that landlords were attempting to block reform by hiring thugs to burn the harvest. In response, peasants attacked the estates of the nobility and the clergy, and their managers, although they launched few violent attacks on individual persons.

In an attempt to contain these revolutionary disorders, the king, in Versailles, now recognized the National Assembly, the new group formed by the Third Estate and its allies, as representatives of the people. He authorized it to draft a new constitution.

The National Assembly abolished what was left of feudalism and serfdom, the tithe for the Church, and the special privileges of the nobility. It issued the "Declaration of the Rights of Man and the Citizen" with 17 articles, including:

- Men are born and remain free and equal in rights; social distinctions may be based only upon general usefulness.
- The aim of every political association is the preservation of the natural and unalienable rights of man; these rights are liberty, property, security, and resistance to oppression.
- The source of all sovereignty resides essentially in the nation …
- Law is the expression of the general will … All citizens, being equal before it, are equally admissible to all public offices, positions, and employments, according to their capacity, and without other distinction than that of virtues and talents …
- For the maintenance of the public force and for the expenses of administration a common tax is indispensable; it must be assessed equally on all citizens in proportion to their means …
- Society has the right to require of every public agent an accounting of his administration.

Women marching to Versailles on October 5, 1789. Engraving. Angered by reports of a luxurious banquet staged by the king while they themselves lacked adequate food, a large crowd of Parisians, mostly women, stormed Versailles and laid siege to the royal palace. Louis XVI and his family were saved by the intervention of the French general the Marquis de Lafayette.

The Declaration further affirmed freedom of thought, religion, petition, and due process under law. It represented a triumph for the doctrines of the *philosophes*.

Meanwhile, hungry mobs in Paris continued to edge toward insurrection. In October, led by housewives, market women, and revolutionary militants protesting the high price of bread, 20,000 Parisians marched to the royal palace in Versailles. This "March of the Women" broke into the palace, overwhelmed the National Guard, and forced the royal family to return to Paris where they could be kept under surveillance.

Over the next two years, the National Assembly drew up a constitution, which called for a constitutional monarchy; did away with the titles and perquisites of nobility and clergy; introduced uniform government across the country;

The women of Les Halles taking Louis XVI from Versailles, 1789. Engraving. The previous illustration shows the women setting out for Versailles, angry, determined, and struggling. Here, they return in triumph with their quarry. Contemporary cartoons and engravings told the story of the revolution as it unfolded. (Bibliothèque Nationale, Paris)

disestablished the Roman Catholic clergy and confiscated the property of the Church; and convened a new Legislative Assembly, for which about half the adult Frenchmen were entitled to vote, essentially by a property qualification. Protestants, Jews, and agnostics were admitted to full citizenship and could vote and run for office if they met the property qualifications. Citizenship would be based not on religious affiliation but on residence in the country and allegiance to its government. Except for the radical—and polarizing—anticlerical position, the actions of the French Revolution thus far seemed quite similar to those of England and America. They were consistent with the optimistic and activist worldview of the *philosophes*. The new constitution was finally promulgated in September 1791, following a wave of strikes and an official ban on labor organizations.

International War, the "Second" Revolution, and the Terror, 1791–99

In June 1791, Louis XVI and his queen, Marie-Antoinette, attempted to flee France but were apprehended and held as virtual prisoners in the royal palace. Shocked and frightened, thousands of aristocrats emigrated to neighboring countries that were more respectful of monarchy and aristocracy. News of the abolition of feudal privilege and of the Civil Constitution of the Clergy filled the nobility and clergy across Europe with dread. Leopold II, the Habsburg emperor (r. 1790–92) and brother of Marie-Antoinette, entered into discussions with other rulers to consider war against the new French government. The French National Assembly, meeting under the new constitution, began to mobilize both in response to this threat and in anticipation of extending the revolution. In April 1792, it declared war on the Austrian monarchy; for the next 23 years, France would be at war with several of the major countries of Europe.

Events careened onward at a great pace. The war went poorly for France, and mobs stormed the royal palace, attempting to kill the king and beginning the Second French Revolution. Louis sought protection in the National Assembly and was imprisoned; all his official powers were terminated. The Assembly disbanded and called for a new National Convention—to be elected by universal male suffrage—to draw up a new constitution. Amid mob violence, the new Convention met in September 1792. Its leaders were **Jacobins**, members of a nationwide network of political clubs named (ironically) for a former convent in Paris where they had first met. They divided into the more moderate **Girondins**, named for a region of France and in general representing the provinces, and the **Montagnards**, representatives mostly from Paris, who drew their name from the benches they occupied on the uppermost

16.1
16.2
16.3
16.4
16.5
16.6
16.7
16.8

How did the French Revolution differ from the American?

KEY TERMS

Jacobins A French revolutionary party founded in 1789. It later became the most radical party of the revolution, responsible for implementing the Reign of Terror and executing the king (1793).

Girondins French revolutionary group formed largely from the middle classes, many of them originally from the Gironde region. Relatively moderate.

Montagnards Members of a radical French revolutionary party, closely associated with the Jacobins and supported by the artisans, shopkeepers, and sansculottes. They opposed the more moderate Girondins.

left side of the assembly hall. By 361 to 359 votes, the Convention voted to execute the king in January 1793. The "Second Revolution" was well under way.

Outside the Assembly, the Paris Commune, the government of Paris, represented the workers, merchants, and artisans of the city, who were generally more radical than the Convention. They were called the **sansculottes**, "without breeches," because the men wore long trousers rather than the knee breeches of the middle and aristocratic classes. In June 1793, the Commune invaded the National Convention and forced the arrest of 31 Girondins on charges of treason, leaving the more radical Montagnards in control.

To govern in the midst of the combined international and civil warfare, the Convention created a Committee of Public Safety, which launched a Reign of Terror against "counterrevolutionaries." It executed about 40,000 people between mid-1793 and mid-1794. At Nantes, in the Vendée region of western France, the center of the royalist counterrevolution, the Committee intentionally drowned 2,000 people. To wage war abroad it instituted a *levée en masse*, or national military draft, which raised an unprecedented army of 800,000 men, and mobilized the economic resources of France to support it.

The Committee intensified the campaign against feudal privilege, rejecting the payment of compensation to the manor lords, who lost their special rights over their tenants. It promoted instruction in practical farming and craft production, spoke of introducing universal elementary education, and abolished slavery throughout France's colonies. It introduced a new calendar, counting Year 1 from the founding of the French Republic in 1792, giving new names to the 12 months, and dividing each month into three weeks of ten days each. In 1794 the most important leader of the Committee, Maximilien Robespierre (1758–94), introduced the Worship of the Supreme Being, a kind of generalized civic religious ritual that alienated the Catholic majority in France.

By July 1794, French armies were winning wars against the other European powers, and the domestic economy seemed to be recovering. The members of the Convention, partly out of fear for their own lives, managed to end both the mob-inspired violence and the official Terror. The Convention outlawed and guillotined Robespierre. It relaxed price controls and, when working-class mobs threatened the Convention, called in the troops and suppressed the revolt. In 1795 it instituted yet another constitution, this time calling for a three-stage election of a representative government. Almost all adult males could vote for electors who, in turn, chose a national legislative assembly composed of men who did have to meet property qualifications and who, in turn, chose an executive of five Directors. When the elections of 1795 were threatened by insurrection, the Convention called upon General Napoleon Bonaparte (1769–1821) to protect the process.

The Directory, as the executive body was called, governed from 1795 to 1799. With the execution of the monarch, the manorial system and the privileges of the nobility and clergy had come to an end, and the Directory ratified the new peasant and commercial landowners in the possession of their new property.

KEY TERMS

sansculottes From the French, "without breeches." Members of the militant, generally poorer classes of Paris, so called because they wore trousers rather than the knee breeches of affluent society.

Napoleon Crossing the Alps, Jacques-Louis David, *c.* 1800. Having chronicled the revolution with his brush, David became Napoleon's official painter. The heroic style of the portrait projects the emperor's enormous confidence as he heads for military glory in the Italian campaigns of 1796–97. The truth of the journey was rather different: Napoleon crossed the Alps on a docile but sure-footed mule, not a fiery stallion. (Palace of Versailles, near Paris)

HOW DO WE KNOW?

The Historiography of the French Revolution

The study of the French Revolution remains the preeminent subject of French historiography, producing a seemingly endless variety of interpretations. Three approaches, however, have predominated. The first emphasizes the importance of ideas, stressing the *philosophes* as the precursors of revolution. This interpretation tends to focus on the first three months of the revolution and the significance of the *Declaration of the Rights of Man and the Citizen*. R.R. Palmer's *The Age of the Democratic Revolution* (vol. I, 1959), for example, favors this reading. Palmer sees the French Revolution, and a number of other revolutions in Europe and the United States at about the same time, as conflicts between "Proponents of 'aristocratic' and 'democratic' forms of community" (Vol. I, p. 22). At least in its origins, the French Revolution begins in the competition of philosophies and ideologies. A second interpretation gives less importance to bourgeois philosophy and stresses instead the significance of class interests in the revolution. It tends to highlight the next chronological stage, as urban workers and rural peasantry increased their protests and demonstrations. It emphasizes the economic difficulties of France between 1770 and 1789, which led the peasants to attack landlords, urban workers to take to the streets, and Parisian women to march to Versailles. Georges Lefebvre's *The Coming of the French Revolution* (1939) represents this position. A more recent interpretation (influenced by literary theory) speaks of the revolution as "discourse," an interplay of ideas and interest groups that constantly shifts, or "skids," as events unfold. This interpretation begins also with the weakness of the French king and government. This weakness forced Louis XVI to convene the Estates-General as his means of raising taxes. In contrast to earlier interpretations, which stressed the antagonism between the classes, here we see the three estates as willing to work together against their common antagonist, the king and his administration. The newly convened representatives were, however, in turmoil over the most effective way of organizing under these new conditions. (They were more like members of the salons of the *philosophes* than members of organized political parties, for that was their experience.) As different groups and different individuals contested for attention and prominence, the direction of the revolution changed. With each new event—for example, the execution of Louis XVI—ideas were reassessed and groups reshuffled themselves into new alignments. François Furet's *Interpreting the French Revolution* (1978) is the leading statement of this point of view. The narrative presented in our text incorporates elements of all three interpretive perspectives.

There is a broader issue, too. Historians sometimes envision events as part of a long sweep of related trends. They look for these trends, and even for general theories of revolution. Sometimes they see them occurring because of circumstances that are unique and unpredictable. The French Revolution presents both aspects. On the one hand, it was an outgrowth of larger trends: the ideals of the *philosophes*, the legacy of the revolutions in England and America; a faltering economy. On the other hand, specific events unfolded day by day in quite unpredictable ways; had they turned out differently—as an extreme example, had the one-vote majority to guillotine the king been reversed—the outcome of the revolution might have been quite different. To understand the French Revolution, both these perspectives—the grand sweep and the contingency—are necessary.

- In your own understanding of historical change, which do you think counts for more, the ideas or interests? Why?
- In the French Revolution, what is the evidence for the importance of ideas? For the importance of interests?
- In your own understanding of historical change, which do you think counts for more, the grand sweep or the contingency? Give an example from one of the revolutions, other than the French Revolution, that illustrates your point of view.

However, the Directory itself was unpopular and unstable, and the greater freedom benefited its opponents while at the same time enabling the Catholic Church to make a strong comeback. The elections of Directors in 1797, 1798, and 1799 were disputed, and on each occasion army officers were called in to dismiss the Directors, until, in 1799 Napoleon, acting with the Abbé Sieyès, staged a *coup d'état* and had himself appointed First Consul. His position was upgraded in 1802 to consul for life and, in 1804, to emperor. Losing the right of free elections, France itself became a (benevolent) despotism. The process that historians usually call the French Revolution was over.

Napoleon in Power, 1799–1812

As head of government, Napoleon Bonaparte consolidated and even expanded many of the innovations of the revolution. To maintain the equality of classes and to systematize the administration of justice, he codified the laws of France. The Code Napoléon or Civil Code, which was issued in 1804, pressed for equality before the law and the principle of a career open to talent, that is, the idea that all people should have access to professional advancement according to their ability, rather than to their birth or social status. Uniform codes of criminal, commercial, and penal law

16.1
16.2
16.3
16.4
16.5
16.6
16.7
16.8

How did the French Revolution differ from the American?

16.1

16.2

16.3

16.4

16.5

16.6 How did the French Revolution differ from the American?

16.7

16.8

were also introduced. The administration was organized into a smoothly functioning service throughout France.

Fearing a counterrevolution led by the Church, Napoleon reached a *concordat* or agreement with the pope. The French government continued to hold the former Church lands, but agreed in exchange to pay the salaries of the clergy (including Protestants and others) and to allow the pope to regain authority over the appointment and discipline of Roman Catholic clergy. Protestants, dissenters, Jews, and others were reaffirmed in full citizenship, with all the rights and obligations that such status entailed, as long as they swore their allegiance to the state. In many conquered cities, including Rome and Frankfurt, French armies pulled down the ghetto walls that for centuries had segregated Jews from other citizens. The government hired a large bureaucracy to administer the state. It selected personnel mostly on the revolutionary principle of a "career open to talent."

This openness of opportunity suited Napoleon very well. He had come from the island of Corsica, of a modest family, and made his mark as a military officer. He had no respect for unearned authority. Nor was he formally religious. He earned his power through his military, administrative, and leadership skills. In a striking exception to the principle of advancement by merit, however, Napoleon appointed his brothers kings of Spain, Holland, and Westphalia, his brother-in-law king of Naples, and his stepson viceroy of the kingdom of Italy. He himself continued to lead the forces of France in military victories over the powers of Europe.

The Napoleonic Wars and the Spread of Revolution, 1799–1812

As a son of the revolution, Napoleon sought to spread its principles by force of arms. By 1810 he had conquered or entered into alliances with all the major powers and regions of Europe except Portugal, the Ottoman-held Balkans, and Britain. In each conquered state, Napoleon introduced the principal legal and administrative reforms of the French Revolution: equality of rights, religious toleration, codified law, free trade, an end to feudal privilege, and efficient and systematic administration, including statistical accounting, registration of documents, and the use of the metric system. In many areas of Europe, Napoleon was welcomed for the reforms he brought.

There were, however, flaws in Napoleon's policies, and they finally destroyed him. First, he attempted to conquer Britain, and ultimately the naval power of that island nation and the land forces of its allies, especially those of Russia, proved too strong. Napoleon could not break the British hold on continental shipping, and he was defeated at sea by Lord Nelson at the Battle of Trafalgar, off the southwest coast of Spain, in 1805. When the Russian emperor supported Britain, Napoleon invaded Russia in 1812 and mired his army irretrievably in the vastness of that country during the bitterness of its winter. During that campaign, 400,000 of Napoleon's troops died from battle, starvation, and exposure; another 100,000 were captured.

Finally, the nations Napoleon conquered began to experience the stirrings of nationalism and the desire for self-rule. Haiti, which had achieved virtual independence in the 1790s, resisted Napoleon's attempt to reimpose French rule and reinstitute slavery in the island. Some 50,000 French troops perished there, most by such diseases as yellow fever, but many at the hands of revolutionary slaves. European peoples, too, did not want their countries to be colonies of France. By 1813 Napoleon had been defeated by his disastrous losses in Russia and by a coalition of European armies; the French were driven back to their borders. In 1814 Napoleon abdicated and Louis XVIII (r. 1814–15; 1815–24) assumed the throne of France. Napoleon escaped from exile on the Mediterranean island of Elba only to be defeated and exiled again in 1815, this time to St. Helena in the South Atlantic. The Napoleonic era was over. The **Congress of Vienna**, an assembly of representatives of all the powers of Europe, led by the most influential states, concluded diplomatic agreements that established a balance of power (see Key Term in the chapter entitled "The Unification of World

KEY TERMS

concordat Agreement reached between the pope and Napoleon on the powers of the Church and the state in postrevolutionary France, 1801.

Congress of Vienna In 1815 the Congress brought together diplomats from the leading countries of Europe to resolve problems raised by the Napoleonic Wars and their aftermath. It redrew national borders, established a balance of power, and enshrined conservative government in Europe for about 30 years.

The empire of Napoleon. Napoleon, fired by revolutionary zeal, fought brilliantly to bring much of Europe under his dominion, often installing his relatives as rulers. Napoleonic institutions were introduced to Italy, the Low Countries, Germany, and Poland by force of arms. By 1812 he seemed invincible, but Britain's strength at sea and Napoleon's disastrous losses on land in his invasion of Russia (1812) led to his downfall.

Trade") between them and redrew the postwar map of Europe. Political conservatism enveloped France and Europe for a generation.

📖 **Read** the **Document**: **Sir Harry Smith on Napoleon's Army in Spain** on **MyHistoryLab**

Haiti: Slave Revolution and the Overthrow of Colonialism, 1791–1804

16.7 What was the importance of the Haitian Revolution?

The formal philosophy and rhetoric of enlightenment and revolution proclaimed the natural desire of all humans to be free, and in the slave plantations of the Caribbean local slave revolts were common, feared, and ruthlessly suppressed. In the western sector of the island of Hispaniola in the colony of Saint-Domingue (modern Haiti),

16.1
16.2
16.3
16.4
16.5
16.6
16.7
16.8

What was the importance of the Haitian Revolution?

545

French planters had established one of the most brutal of the slave plantation systems. By 1791, some 500,000 black slaves formed the overwhelming majority of the population, with 40,000 whites, many of them owners of plantations and slaves, and 30,000 free people of color, both mulatto and black. For decades, the slaves had escaped psychologically and culturally through the practice of *vodoun* (**voodoo**), a religion that blended the Catholicism of their masters with religious practices brought from Africa. Physically, they had escaped through **maroonage**, flight from the plantations to the surrounding hills. Sometimes the escaped slaves, **maroons**, established their own colonies. In the 1750s one of the maroons, François Makandal, built among the maroon colonies a network of resistance to slavery. Inspired to independence by *vodoun* beliefs, and using poison to attack individual plantation owners, Makandal apparently planned to poison the water supply of Le Cap, the main town of northern Saint-Domingue. He was captured and burned at the stake in 1758.

The Slave Revolt

In 1791, slave revolts broke out across Saint-Domingue. The inspiration seems to have been the natural desire for freedom, perhaps abetted by news of the American and French Revolutions. One of the earliest rallying cries, delivered by the poet Boukman Dutty in Haitian-French patois, *"Coute la liberté li pale nan coeur nous tous"* ("Listen to the voice of liberty which speaks in the hearts of all of us"), implied no knowledge of those revolutions.

The revolt spread. From guerrilla warfare by maroon bands, it grew to general armed struggle and civil warfare. In the western part of Saint-Domingue, white planters welcomed the support of British troops who came as allies to suppress the slave revolt and also to drive out the French. The **mulattoes**—those of mixed-race parentage—were free people, and some of them owned slaves. They now sought their own rights of representation and were divided over the issue of slavery. In the eastern part of Saint-Domingue, a new leader, Pierre Dominique Toussaint L'Ouverture (c. 1743–1803), a freed black, established an alliance with the Spanish rulers against both the slave system in Saint-Domingue (but not in the Spanish part of the island) and the French. Toussaint incorporated the rhetoric of the French Revolution into his own. In 1794, under Robespierre, the French National Assembly abolished slavery in all French colonies. In response, Toussaint linked himself to France as he continued his war against slaveowners, who were now aligned with the British and who resisted the new French decree. By May 1800, Toussaint had become the effective ruler of Saint-Domingue.

📖 **Read** the **Document: Slave Narrative, "The History of Mary Prince, A West Indian Slave," Related by Herself, London (1831)** on **MyHistoryLab**

The Anti-imperial Revolt, 1804

When Napoleon came to power in 1799 he reversed French policy on slavery. He dispatched 20,000 French troops to recapture the island of Saint-Domingue and to reinstitute slavery, as he did in Guadeloupe in 1802. Napoleon's representative deceived Toussaint into suspending his revolution. Toussaint was imprisoned in 1802 and exiled to France, where he died the next year. Nevertheless, unified black and mulatto armies, now under many different cooperating leaders, continued the struggle against France, drove out its forces, and, once again, abolished slavery. As many as 50,000

Pierre Dominique Toussaint L'Ouverture, French lithograph, early nineteenth century. The colony of Saint-Domingue (present-day Haiti) in the West Indies had made a fortune for the French through sugar plantations worked by African slaves. In the 1790s, under the leadership of Toussaint L'Ouverture, it became the site of a slave revolution that eventually led to independence. The former slave acquired his surname because of the ferocity with which he made an opening (*"ouverture"*) in the enemy ranks.

The revolution in Haiti. One of the most dramatic revolutions occurred on the Caribbean island of Hispaniola. A slave revolt in 1791 in the French region, Saint-Domingue, spread rapidly, briefly penetrating and uniting with the Spanish sector, Santo Domingo. Despite interventions by French and British forces, and the incarceration and exile of its leader, Toussaint L'Ouverture, in 1802, Haiti gained its independence from France in 1804. It was the first successful slave revolt in history.

French troops died of yellow fever, and thousands more became military casualties. On January 1, 1804, Saint-Domingue at last proclaimed its independence and its new name of Haiti, the Carib name for "mountain." This completed the only known successful slave revolution in history.

Britain Abolishes the Slave Trade, 1807

Initially, the British tried to assist in putting down the slave rebellion in Haiti. When they failed, their subsequent decision to limit the spread of slavery by abolishing the slave trade in 1807 reflected, in part, their fear of further revolts. In 1833 Britain abolished slavery throughout its Empire, although "freed" slaves were required to work for their former masters for a period of time to compensate them for their loss of "property." The United States, a slave-holding country, feared that the Haitian slave revolt might spread northward, and prohibited all trade with Haiti in 1806. In 1808, following Britain's lead, America outlawed participation in the international slave trade, although it abolished internal slavery only with the Civil War (1861–65). Elsewhere, however, the Atlantic slave trade continued at about three-quarters of its highest volume. That trade did not end effectively until slavery was abolished in 1876 in Puerto Rico, in 1886 in Cuba, and in 1888 in Brazil.

Independence and Disillusionment in Latin America, 1810–30

16.8 Why did the leaders of the Latin American revolutions feel disillusioned, despite their accomplishments?

In the period 1810 to 1826, virtually all the countries of Latin America expelled their European colonial rulers and established their independence. Latin Americans drew inspiration from the intellectual and political legacies of the American, French, and Haitian revolutions, although few wanted to move so far toward democratic rights as the Europeans had done, and many were frightened by the events in Haiti.

All of Latin America—except for Portuguese Brazil—was wrested from Spain by the sword. The greatest of the revolutionary leaders—Simón Bolívar of Venezuela

16.1
16.2
16.3
16.4
16.5
16.6
16.7
16.8

Why did the leaders of the Latin American revolutions feel disillusioned, despite their accomplishments?

547

HOW DO WE KNOW?

Abolition: Historians Debate the Causes

Why were the slave trade, and then slavery itself, abolished in the Atlantic countries? To what extent was the spread of democratic revolution responsible? Analyses differ. Historians who emphasize the significance of the Haitian Revolution, as C.L.R. James and David Nicholls do, stress the fear that the uprising of the slaves engendered among slaveowners. In the lands of the Caribbean, including northeastern Brazil, black slaves working the high-mortality plantations formed up to 90 percent of the population. Local rebellions already occurred frequently, and large-scale revolution now appeared a real possibility. The abolition of the slave trade provided some limit on the size of the slave population, although total abolition—a much more expensive act for the slaveowners—would come only later.

A second school of thought, shared by such historians as David Brion Davis and Orlando Patterson, stresses the importance of compassion as a motive. Davis emphasizes the increasing influence of humanitarian sentiment in European Christian thought from the seventeenth century:

> The philosophy of benevolence was a product of the seventeenth century, when certain British Protestants, shaken by theological controversy and the implications of modern science, looked increasingly to human nature and conduct as a basis for faith. In their impatience with theological dogma, their distaste for the doctrine of original sin, their appreciation for human feeling and sentiment, and their confidence in man's capacity for moral improvement, these Latitudinarians, as they were called, anticipated the main concerns of the Enlightenment, and laid an indispensable foundation for social reform. (Davis, 1975, pp. 348–49)

The emphasis on compassion increased in reaction against the growing scale and unprecedented cruelty of slavery in the New World. Among Christian groups opposing slavery, Quakers and Methodists stood out. The birth and growth of both these denominations—Quakerism under the leadership of George Fox (1624–91) and Methodism under John Wesley (1703–91)—were contemporary with the development of mass slavery in the Americas. Other branches of Christianity had long since made peace with the institution of slavery, contenting themselves with promising a gentler existence in life after death. Quakers and Methodists, however, had to confront the reality of slavery for the first time in one of its cruelest New World forms. In Britain, William Wilberforce (1759–1833), a philanthropist and member of the Clapham Sect (a group of well-to-do Evangelicals) played a major part in the antislavery movement. As a member of Parliament, he led the campaign to abolish the slave trade and to emancipate existing slaves.

The *philosophes* argued a third, similar but more intellectual, position against slavery. They argued that slavery violated the law of nature; it was inconsistent with the nature of humankind. Montesquieu (1689–1755), in his assessments of the nature of laws and government, argued that "the call for slavery was the call of the wealthy and the decadent, not for the general welfare of mankind."

Finally, an economic critique began to develop in the eighteenth century. Slavery was not profitable to society, certainly not to the slave, and not to the development of a more productive economy in the long run. In *The Wealth of Nations*, Adam Smith argued that slavery, in common with all examples of monopoly and special privilege, inhibited economic growth. Lacking the opportunity to acquire wealth and property for himself, the slave would find it in his interest to work as little as possible. Slaveowners advocated their system not so much for its economic benefits as for the power it gave them over others, despite economic losses. The leading exponents of this rationale for abolition in recent times have been Marxists, led by Eric Williams in his classic *Capitalism and Slavery* (1944). Many economic historians disagreed with this analysis, most notably Robert Fogel and Stanley Engerman, who published *Time on the Cross* in 1974, an elaborate two-volume statistical study linking economics with statistics (econometrics) to show the profitability of slavery. The historian Seymour Drescher argued bluntly (1977) that abolition was "econocide"—economic disaster—for Britain. Drescher sided with the humanitarian assessment: abolition was implemented despite its economic costs.

What to do without slaves? The successor system to slavery was not free labor. Indentured labor, supplied in large part by vast contract immigration from India and China, filled the labor needs of the postslavery Caribbean as well as those of new plantation economies in the Indian Ocean in Fiji, Mauritius, and Réunion, and in South and East Africa. Although not quite slaves, indentured servants traded many of their basic economic and political rights for a number of years in exchange for their livelihood.

Finally, with the export of slave labor from Africa banned, European entrepreneurs began in the later nineteenth century to explore the possibility of shifting the production of primary products to Africa itself and to employ on-site personnel to perform the necessary work. Although this system sounded like free labor, in fact the wages were so low and conditions so abysmal that many observers saw these economic initiatives as a newer form of slavery transplanted back to Africa.

- What evidence have we seen in this chapter that the Haitian revolution played an important part in the abolition of slavery?
- What evidence do you have from this chapter, and from other studies, that would support the importance of humanitarianism in the abolition of slavery? What evidence do you have for the importance of economics?
- What is the difference between slavery and indentured labor?

16.1
16.2
16.3
16.4
16.5
16.6
16.7
16.8

in the north, José de San Martín of Argentina in the south, Antonio José de Sucre of Ecuador, and Bernardo O'Higgins of Chile—combined military skill with intellectual, administrative, and diplomatic accomplishments.

Independence Movements

Amerindians and *mestizos* led the first series of revolts, in the late 1700s. In 1780, in Cuzco, Peru, Tupac Amarú, a *mestizo* with Inca ancestors, led 70,000 rebels against Spanish rule. **Creoles** did not join with him in the revolt, and Tupac Amarú was captured and executed in 1783. The entire revolt was brutally crushed. The Comunero Revolt in Colombia in 1781 drove the viceroy from Bogotá but ended with few concessions by the Spanish and internal fighting among the rebels. Mulattoes led a revolt in Bahia, Brazil, in 1798. At the time of all these revolts, Spain and Portugal were still independent, powerful countries and, with the aid of Creoles and *mazombos*, they suppressed the revolts. In general, the Creoles and *mazombos* saw their fate linked more to the Spanish and Portuguese rulers than to the Amerindians or to those of mixed parentage.

The Napoleonic Wars in Spain, however, gave the colonies the opportunity to declare their independence, with the Creoles now leading the way. The revolts were bloody and successful. In virtually every Latin American revolt, leadership was provided by a Creole elite, most of whom feared the potential power of the Amerindian, *mestizo*, mulatto, and African majority. Such men as Father Miguel Hidalgo (1753–1811) in Mexico, Simón Bolívar (1783–1830) in northern South America, and José de San Martín (1778–1850) in southern South America were all Creoles, as were their leading generals, administrators, and supporters. They were familiar with European traditions and events, and many of them had studied in Europe. Indeed, the revolutions benefited the Creoles most, although they formed less than 5 percent of the total population. They were determined to preserve the old system, with its low-paid and slave labor. The new Creole elite simply drove out the Spanish and Portuguese rulers and took their places. Other Latin Americans—*mestizos* and Amerindians—gained little. On the Caribbean islands of Cuba and Puerto Rico there were no rebellions. The elites there, frightened lest the slave revolt of Haiti be repeated on their own islands, remained loyal to Spain.

Simón Bolívar. As soldier, diplomat, general, administrator, visionary, newspaper publisher, law giver, national president, dictator, lover, and disillusioned revolutionary, Simón Bolívar dominated public life in Latin America for most of two decades, from 1810 until his death in 1830. The son of a Venezuelan Creole aristocrat, Bolívar studied in Europe from age 16 to 19, primarily in Spain. He married in 1802 and returned to Caracas with his bride, but within a year she died of yellow fever. Devastated, Bolívar vowed to devote his life to politics. He returned to Europe for travel and continued study of the *philosophes*. Returning to Venezuela in 1807, he joined in the movements for independence that swept the region, especially after Napoleon's troops invaded Spain, undercutting Spanish authority and power in the Americas.

He failed in many of his early efforts. Assigned to diplomatic duty in England, he was unable to gain recognition and material support for the Venezuelan revolution. In 1811 he was serving as an army officer when Venezuela lost its independence within a year of declaring it. In 1813 he captured Caracas and reasserted Venezuelan independence, but he was defeated and exiled in 1814. Despite the military defeats, he wrote visionary documents. His *Manifesto of Cartagena* (1812) was a rallying cry for revolutionary forces to continue the struggle against Spain. His *Letter from Jamaica*, written in exile in September 1815, vowed to end not only Latin America's political suppression, but also its economic servitude.

Bolívar renewed his military expeditions and began to earn fabulous success, especially after he received monetary and military support from Haiti and Britain in

Why did the leaders of the Latin American revolutions feel disillusioned, despite their accomplishments?

KEY TERMS

mestizo A person of mixed race. In Central and South America it usually denotes a person of combined Indian and European descent.

Creole In the sixteenth to eighteenth centuries, a white person born in Spanish America of Spanish parents.

mazombo An American-born direct descendant of Portuguese settlers.

16.1
16.2
16.3
16.4
16.5
16.6
16.7
16.8

Why did the leaders of the Latin American revolutions feel disillusioned, despite their accomplishments?

Liberation movements in Latin America. The collapse of Iberian rule in Latin America was virtually complete by 1826. Sustained campaigns by Simón Bolívar and Antonio José de Sucre demolished Spanish control of Venezuela, Colombia, Peru, and Ecuador while, from the south, José de San Martín led the Argentine and Chilean Army of the Andes north to Lima. In 1822, the Portuguese crown prince Pedro declared Brazil's independence from Portugal, without the need for an armed struggle. Liberation brought many internal power struggles and divisions, leaving the present-day South American map with an array of some 20 republics.

return for freeing South American slaves. In 1819 his forces defeated the Spanish and established the Republic of Colombia with himself as president and military dictator. Within two more years they liberated Venezuela and Ecuador, filling out the borders of the federation. In Quito, Ecuador, he met Manuela Saenz, who left her husband to join him. She remained with Bolívar for the rest of his life, despite his numerous affairs and the public scandal of their own relationship.

As Bolívar made conquests from the north, various movements began their struggles for independence from the region of Rio de la Plata, now Argentina. José de San Martín emerged as one of the great military strategists of history. He put together an Army of the Andes and promised freedom to slaves who joined his forces. He later claimed they were his best soldiers. Bringing together former slaves and soldiers, he crossed the high Andes Mountains with mules and llamas, successfully defeating the Spaniards in Chile and mounting attacks on Peru. He refused to rule over Chile in favor of Bernardo O'Higgins, the Creole leader there, but he could not effectively take Peru. Ultimately, he met with Bolívar in Guayaquil, Ecuador, in 1822. No one really knows what they discussed, but after the meeting, San Martín retired to France, leaving the conquest of South America to Bolívar.

By 1825, through brilliant military action, Bolívar captured Peru and Upper Peru, later named Bolivia in his honor, and became president of both. Just as his dreams of a single united region seemed to reach fruition, however, they dissolved in warfare among his generals, who now fought for the independence of each of the constituent units. Bolívar tried to hold the federation together through dictatorial rulings, but his high-handedness further alienated his former supporters and he narrowly escaped an assassination attempt in 1828 as Manuela Saenz covered his exit. Bolívar withdrew from political leadership in 1830. A few months later he died in the agony of tuberculosis, indebted and disillusioned.

Bolívar's dream of "Gran Colombia" dissolved into Colombia, Venezuela, and Ecuador. Further south, the Spanish Vice-Royalty of La Plata dissolved into Argentina, Paraguay, Uruguay, and Bolivia. For a decade, 1829–39, under General Andrés Santa Cruz, a *mestizo*, Peru and Bolivia were united, but then broke apart, to the relief of some of their neighbors. Chile, isolated by the Andes to its east, and open to the outside world via the Pacific Ocean to its west, also became a separate, independent nation. In total, 18 nations emerged from Spanish America.

Warfare among many of the new states and the violent repression of the Indian and African-American populations (25 percent of Brazil's population in 1850 were slaves) gave prominence and power both to national armies and to private military forces throughout Latin America. The military strongmen, or *caudillos*, came to control local areas and even national governments. Personal rule, restrained only minimally by official codes of law and formal election procedures, prevailed in many countries up to the late twentieth century. (See Source box on Pablo Neruda's epic history of Latin America in verse, *Canto General*, below.)

Mexico. The early Mexican independence movement differed from that in South America because of its attack on Creole elites. The priests Father Miguel Hidalgo and Father José Maria Morelos (1765–1815) understood that peasant poverty was a product of Spanish and Creole rule. Hidalgo led the first wave of Mexico's revolt; when he was executed, in 1811, Morelos took command. He sought to displace the Spanish and Creole elites, to abolish slavery, and, unlike Hidalgo, to revoke the special privileges and landholdings of the Church. He was captured and executed by the Spanish in 1815. By the time Mexico won its independence, in 1821, its revolution was controlled by its most conservative Creole elite. For two years it was ruled as a monarchy, but in 1823 it was proclaimed a republic. Military leaders, businessmen, and foreign powers all struggled for control, and Mexico remained unstable for decades, although one of Morelos' goals, the abolition of slavery, was achieved in 1829.

Mexico's size was reduced by half. Following years of rebellions, Central American regions broke away from Mexico and formed a union, although that dissolved in internal regional antagonism in 1838. With waves of immigrants entering from the United States, and encouraged by the United States government, Texas declared its independence from Mexico in 1836. Nine years later the United States annexed Texas, precipitating the Mexican–American war. In the peace settlement, America gained the territories of its current southwestern states.

KEY TERM

caudillo A military leader who takes political power.

Simón Bolívar, Antonio Salas (attrib.), 1825. Bolívar was the most important military leader of the Latin American revolution. Despite a life of extraordinary adventure and accomplishment, he failed to bring about the unification of South America that he so passionately desired.

📖 Read the Document: Simon de Bolívar, "Address to Second National Congress" (Venezuela), 1819 on **MyHistoryLab**

📖 Read the Document: Jose Morelos, Sentiments of the Nation (Mexico), 1813 on **MyHistoryLab**

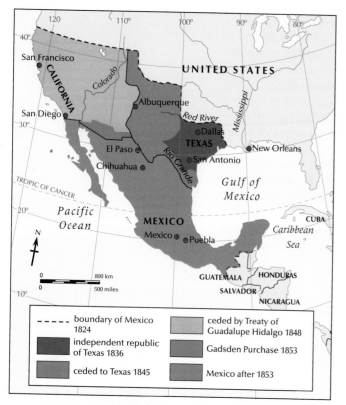

Mexico, 1824–53. In 1821 the Vice-Royalty of New Spain, with its capital in Mexico City, won its independence from Spain. By 1823, the Central American countries seceded, leaving Mexico with its current southern border. Then, piece by piece, the northern areas were lost to the United States: Texas through secession from Mexico (1836) and annexation by the United States (1845); some territories through warfare (1846–48); and some through purchase (1853).

Brazil. Brazil, the largest country in Latin America in terms of both geography and population, followed a different pathway to independence, and this helps to explain why it did not break apart after independence. When Napoleon invaded Portugal in 1807, the Portuguese royal family, assisted by Britain, fled to Rio de Janeiro and ruled the Portuguese Empire from the Brazilian capital for 13 years. King Dom João (John) VI (r. 1816–26) raised Brazil's legal status to equal that of Portugal and expanded Rio into a center of trade, administration, education, and cultural institutions.

In 1821 João returned with his court to Lisbon, but left his son and heir, Prince Pedro, in Rio. When the Parliament, or Cortes, in Lisbon attempted to cut Brazil and Rio back to size, the American-born Brazilian elite, the *mazombos*, counseled defiance. In 1822 Pedro declared Brazil independent, and Portugal did little to stop the move. Pedro was soon crowned "Constitutional Emperor and Perpetual Defender of Brazil," but the effective rulers of Brazil were its *mazombo* elite. Brazil was thus spared the warfare and disintegration characteristic of Spanish Latin America, but it was ruled by similar American-born descendants of Iberian families. While the former Spanish colonies became republics, Brazil became a monarchy under a member of the Portuguese royal family.

View the **Closer Look**: *Imagining Brazilian Independence* on **MyHistoryLab**

After Independence: Religious, Economic, and Cultural Issues

Many of the new nations of Latin America sought to increase their own power by breaking the authority and wealth of the Catholic Church. Many confiscated Church lands, refused to collect tithes to fund the Church, demanded a voice in the selection of clergy, and limited Church control over educational facilities. Many Native American Indians also wanted to reduce the power of the Church in favor of a greater appreciation of indigenous cultures, both outside Christianity and in syncretic movements that joined existing indigenous beliefs and rituals with Christian practices. Mexico, which had a large Indian and *mestizo* population, was most eager to limit Church power, and its continuing struggles were the bloodiest. Over time, in each country, individual accommodations were made between Church and state, and to this day they continue to renegotiate their positions.

Economically, until at least 1870, Latin America remained overwhelmingly agrarian, with the *hacienda*, a kind of feudal estate, continuing as the principal institution for organizing production and labor. The vast majority of the *hacendados* were Creole, while the workers were overwhelmingly Indian and *mestizo*. Many Indians remained in villages, where their participation in any larger, external, national economy was marginal. Since ancestry counted so profoundly for each group, the ethnic and racial composition of its population, whether native- or foreign-born, whether Indian, African, *mestizo*, or Caucasian, in large measure determined the fate and the culture of each colony.

As production for foreign markets increased, a new form of foreign domination, **neocolonialism**, arose. The principal new power was Britain, and its method was economic investment and control. By 1824, there were 100 British commercial firms,

SOURCE

An Epic Verse History of Latin America

In many parts of the world, historical traditions are kept alive not only in formal historical writing, but also in art, music, and poetry. Some of Latin America's most distinguished authors work in this tradition. The Chilean writer Pablo Neruda (1904–73), a recipient of the Nobel Prize for Literature in 1971, advanced a critical and disillusioned vision of Latin America in its first century of independence. In *Canto General* (1950), Neruda's epic poem of Latin American history, he paints the Spanish settlement of the land as a harsh and tawdry process:

> The land passed between the entailed estates,
> doubloon to doubloon, dispossessed,
> paste of apparitions and convents,
> until the entire blue geography was
> divided into haciendas and encomiendas.
> The mestizo's ulcer, the overseer's
> and slaver's whip
> moved through the lifeless space.
> The Creole was an impoverished specter
> who picked up the crumbs,
> until he saved enough
> to acquire a little title
> painted with gilt letters.
> And in the dark carnival
> he masqueraded as a count,
> a proud man among beggars,
> with his little silver cane.

The *conquistadores* of the sixteenth century had been expelled by the **libertadors** of the early nineteenth century, but the infrastructure of shopkeepers, clergy, administrators, and hangers-on that had become established in Latin America remained in place as the real inheritors of the revolution. Neruda scowled:

> Soon, undershirt by undershirt,
> they expelled the conquistador
> and established the conquest
> of the grocery store.
> Then they acquired pride
> bought on the black market.
> They were adjudged
> haciendas, whips, slaves,
> catechisms, commissaries,
> alms boxes, tenements, brothels,
> and all this they called
> holy western culture.

Neruda singles out the petty businessmen as the new, but unworthy, elite of Latin America. In more enterprising regions, bigger businessmen and investors occupied the leadership positions. These men of practical affairs combined with craftsmen on the one hand, and with government policymakers on the other, to introduce limited industrial development in the twentieth century.

Early Evening Refreshment in the Praca do Palaccio, Rio de Janeiro, Jean-Baptiste Debret, 1835. Lithograph. The port and capital city of Rio has long been famous for its fun-loving life and for a modicum of racial integration. But Brazil did not abolish slavery until 1888. All three elements are suggested in this lithograph. (Bibliothèque Nationale, Paris)

16.1
16.2
16.3
16.4
16.5
16.6
16.7
16.8

Why did the leaders of the Latin American revolutions feel disillusioned, despite their accomplishments?

staffed by 3,000 British citizens, functioning in Latin America. Shipping to and from Latin America was carried primarily by British ships. Britain's economic domination of Latin American economies increased with the growing productivity and profitability of its Industrial Revolution at home.

In the mid-nineteenth century, Latin America was home to an amalgam of philosophies and practices. From the United States and France, it inherited a legacy of revolution in the name of representative democracy and individual freedom. From Spain and Portugal it inherited a loyalty to more conservative, religious, hierarchical traditions. From Africa it inherited rich traditions of religion, food, music, and dance. From its own history of settlement it received a diverse mix of peoples from three continents, often in uneasy relationship with one another. From the international economy Latin America inherited a subordinate position, dependent on outside supply, demand, and control.

Political Revolutions:
What Difference Do They Make?

Charles Dickens opened *A Tale of Two Cities*, his novel set against the background of the French Revolution, with the famous passage: "It was the best of times. It was the worst of times … it was the season of Light, it was the season of Darkness, it was the spring of hope, it was the winter of despair." Having examined the unfolding of this period of political revolution, we can better understand Dickens' paradoxical characterization. All the revolutionary movements were filled with ironies. The English revolutions succeeded in establishing constitutional government that slowly expanded to include ever larger segments of the population, and to include freedom of religion among its guarantees. But, less than a century later, the government that emerged from those revolutions refused to grant to its American subjects the rights enjoyed by Britons, provoking the American War for Independence. It did abolish the slave trade and slavery, but only in the early nineteenth century, and by that time, as we shall see in the chapter entitled "The Industrial Revolution," Britain had captured extensive, non-settler colonies overseas.

The *philosophes* spoke of human perfectibility and advocated human reason. They provided rationales that inspired revolutions in America, France, and Latin America, yet many preferred benevolent despotism, which they considered more efficient than democracy. One of the greatest *philosophes*, Rousseau, has been interpreted from many perspectives, as espousing government alternatives from radical democracy to totalitarian dictatorship. Later experience throughout the world, to our own day, continues to test the limits of the power of rationality in governing human affairs.

The War for Independence in North America freed Britain's 13 colonies there and created the United States. The new nation introduced a limited democracy that nonetheless sanctioned attacks on Native Americans and permitted slavery. The most profound of all the revolutions of its time, the French Revolution, ended in class antagonism, with the monarchy restored, after much of Europe had been convulsed in more extensive warfare than it had ever seen before. In the course of his conquests, Napoleon abolished feudal privileges throughout Europe and introduced new codes of law and bureaucracies recruited on the basis of merit, but he established imperial governments, often in the hands of his own blood relatives, which provoked new anti-French nationalism among the peoples he conquered. In Haiti, in response to the slave revolt, Napoleon reversed France's stated opposition to slavery, and lost tens of thousands of soldiers to battle and disease. Haiti's successful slave revolt became a successful war for independence, but foreign opposition to the island's new government, and an internal lack of competent economic leadership, left it impoverished. Wars for independence in Latin America freed that continent from direct political control from overseas, but power was seized by Creole and *mazombo* elites who lorded it over the Native American multitudes. In addition, the new nations soon fell into economic dependence on their former colonizers.

Of all these revolutions, the French Revolution's legacy is the most ambiguous. Many scholars have looked to the radical Terror as a precursor to twentieth-century totalitarianism. Others, however, have examined the revolution in terms of what it accomplished rather than what it failed to do. The French Revolution ended religious discrimination, and France went much further than England in allowing worshipers of all faiths, including Jews, to become full citizens. Although Napoleon reversed the decision, the National Convention abolished slavery, making it clear that distinctions of color and race should not matter in civic life. Still other scholars have recognized that, while class antagonism remained, the French Revolution established legal equality for most males, including freed slaves, who inhabited the country. Finally, the French Revolution in many ways legitimized the notion of revolution as a means of achieving political and social change. It inspired the Russian Revolution of 1917 and the later Chinese student movement, which staged a revolutionary parade at Tiananmen Square, Beijing, in support of French revolutionary ideals on the bicentenary of the revolution of 1789. In short, the ideas of the French Revolution remain a powerful inspirational force today.

CHAPTER REVIEW

THE SCIENTIFIC REVOLUTION

 16.1 How did the Scientific Revolution challenge previous concepts of the natural world?

The discoveries of the Scientific Revolution suggested a new world dawning, one in which natural law and the power of human reason would come to the fore. This vision of a new world of rationality and science grew out of a community of scientists, sharing knowledge and building a structure of knowledge. They rejected traditional sources of knowledge, often based on supposed divine revelation, and sought empirical evidence and proofs for what they knew. Their ways of thinking then inspired challenges to traditional theories of politics and society based on rule by hereditary aristocrats.

HUMAN RIGHTS: PHILOSOPHICAL RATIONALES

16.2 How did the ideas of Locke and Hobbes influence political and social science?

Thomas Hobbes's theories on the limits of power and on the social contract between individuals and governments, and John Locke's assertion of the importance of common consent in that social contract, laid the foundations for the claim to the right of revolution. Ultimately that concept, that rulers are responsible to their people, inspired civil war and revolution in England (1642–51 and 1688), and, later, the American Revolution of 1776, the French Revolution of 1789, and many subsequent political and social revolutions.

CIVIL WAR AND REVOLUTION IN ENGLAND, 1642–51

16.3 What were the causes and outcomes of the Glorious Revolution?

The struggle between the ruler and the ruled, the king and the citizens' representatives in Parliament, began as a challenge to the king's attempt to levy taxes without the consent of Parliament; struggle between Catholics and Protestants for religious recognition and political power added an important additional dimension. The civil war culminated in the Glorious Revolution of 1688. The king was overthrown in the civil war, and although the monarchy was subsequently restored, a Bill of Rights enacted after the Glorious Revolution established constitutional powers of Parliament over the king. As well, some of the religious issues that had burned for many years were resolved with the Anglican Church continuing as the established Church of England and a Toleration Act granting some non-Anglicans the right to free public worship.

THE ENLIGHTENMENT

16.4 What were the central beliefs of the Enlightenment thinkers?

The intellectuals associated with the Enlightenment built on the ideas of the Scientific Revolution to argue for rationality, freedom of thought and expression, and social, economic, and political reform. These thinkers believed in human progress based on education, secularism, and limitations on the power of government. They generally preferred democracy, but many were quite content with "benevolent despotism," non-democratic governments that nevertheless attended to the welfare of their people.

REVOLUTION IN NORTH AMERICA, 1776

16.5 What were the goals and achievements of the American Revolution?

The American Revolution went even further on the road to democracy than England's Glorious Revolution. Declaring "all men are created equal," the American revolutionaries abolished the monarchy and established an elected government "of, by, and for the people," with basic rights that included freedom of religion, press, assembly, and petition; protection against cruel and unusual punishment; and the right to a speedy trial by a jury of one's peers. The new nation's Declaration of Independence inspired freedom-fighters all over the world. It did not, however, provide equal rights for women, and it left slavery in place—two issues that would continue to engage the Americans for decades, if not centuries.

THE FRENCH REVOLUTION AND NAPOLEON, 1789–1812

16.6   How did the French Revolution differ from the American?

The American Revolution was launched from a lightly populated region of the world, far distant from Europe, by a relatively small group of educated elites fighting, with the help of allies that opposed Britain, against a distant colonial government. The French Revolution, by contrast, was an internal revolt—a kind of civil war—led by merchants, artisans, professionals, and the poor—the Third Estate—against entrenched feudal, monarchical, and clerical powers in the most powerful, and most populous, state of its time. The revolutionaries sought to end the vested interests of the nobility and the clergy once and for all. Following the Americans' lead, they declared a constitution establishing freedom of thought, religion, petition, and due process under the law.

HAITI: SLAVE REVOLUTION AND THE OVERTHROW OF COLONIALISM, 1791–1804

16.7   What was the importance of the Haitian Revolution?

Probably inspired by the revolutions in France and America, and certainly by the natural human desire for freedom, the revolution in Haiti was the first successful slave revolt in history. It unfolded in two stages: first a revolution of slaves against their owners, then a revolution against the French colonizers who attempted to reinstate slavery. Fear of further slave revolts was one of the factors leading Britain to abolish its slave trade, in 1807. The next year, America too outlawed participation in the international slave trade (internal slavery continued until the Civil War ended it).

INDEPENDENCE AND DISILLUSIONMENT IN LATIN AMERICA, 1810–30

16.8   Why did the leaders of the Latin American revolutions feel disillusioned, despite their accomplishments?

Inspired by revolutions in America, France, and Haiti—and seizing the opportunity created by the Napoleonic wars that occupied the attention and troops of their European colonizers—almost all the Latin American countries expelled their colonial rulers and established their independence in the years 1810–26. The leaders of these revolts were almost entirely drawn from the European-born population and their descendents; they took power for themselves, not for the indigenous populations. The new nations were politically independent, but they remained largely economically dependent on their former colonizers. Finally, despite the wishes of revolutionaries like Simón Bolívar, the new nations were unable to join together into a single unified political entity.

Suggested Readings

PRINCIPAL SOURCES

Burns, E. Bradford, and Julie Charlip. *Latin America: A Concise Interpretive History* (Englewood Cliffs, NJ: Prentice Hall, 9th ed., 2010). The most recent edition of a standard work, especially strong on Brazil.

Craveri, Benedetta. *The Age of Conversation* (New York: New York Review Books, 2006). From the seventeenth century, aristocratic women hosted the salons that led into the French Enlightenment of the eighteenth century.

Englund, Steven. *Napoleon: A Political Life* (Cambridge, MA: Harvard University Press, 2004). Adds to the literature on Napoleon in the mind of the French.

Furet, François. *Interpreting the French Revolution*, trans. Elborg Foster (Cambridge: Cambridge University Press, 1978). A masterful summary by one of the leading experts. Stresses the constant changes in direction of the revolution as it unfolded.

Galilei, Galileo. *Discoveries and Opinions of Galileo*, trans. Stillman Drake (New York: Anchor Books, 1957). Galileo's own observations and statements, fresh and clear, with helpful commentary.

Hobsbawm, Eric. *The Age of Revolution 1789–1848* (New York: New American Library, 1962). A personal, magisterial interpretation from a Marxist, class-oriented perspective. Although the interpretation is now challenged, this remains an important introduction to the period and issues.

Hochschild, Adam. *Bury the Chains: Prophets and Rebels in the Fight to Free an Empire's Slaves* (New York: Houghton Mifflin, 2005). Traces the activities of the men who established the British abolition movement. Very well written. Inspirational.

James, C.L.R. *The Black Jacobins* (New York: Random House, 1963). A stirring account of the activities and significance of the Haitian revolution.

Knight, Franklin W. "The Haitian Revolution," *American Historical Review* 105:1 (February 2000), pp. 103–15. A review of the most recent scholarship on the revolution.

Kuhn, Thomas S. *The Copernican Revolution* (Cambridge, MA: Harvard University Press, 1957). A case study of the methods of science in working through received interpretations and developing new ones through the experiences of Copernicus.

———. *The Structure of Scientific Revolutions* (Chicago, IL: University of Chicago Press, 3rd ed., 1996). A generalized assessment of the methods through which scientists revise and sometimes discard older theories and develop new ones.

Lefebvre, Georges. *The Coming of the French Revolution*, trans. R.R. Palmer (Princeton, NJ: Princeton University Press, 1947). A classic Marxist interpretation of the revolution.

Nash, Gary B., *et al. The American People: Creating a Nation and a Society* (White Plains, NY: Longman, 7th ed., 2006). Leading textbook account.

Palmer, R.R. *The Age of the Democratic Revolution* (Princeton, NJ: Princeton University Press, vol. 1, 1959; vol. 2, 1964). A lucid, comprehensive interpretive account of the revolutions covered in this chapter. Stresses the philosophy behind each revolution.

Thompson, E.P. *The Making of the English Working Class* (New York: Vintage Books, 1966). Cultural as well as economic factors that inspired working people to see themselves as a class and to struggle for rights.

Williams, Eric. *Capitalism and Slavery* (Chapel Hill, NC: University of North Carolina Press, 1944). Williams portrays capitalism as promoting slavery when it is in the economic interests of slaveowners, and as working for abolition when these interests change.

ADDITIONAL SOURCES

Abernethy, David B. *The Dynamics of Global Dominance: European Overseas Empires, 1415–1980* (New Haven, CT: Yale University Press, 2000). Traces and analyzes the expansion and contraction of empire, and evaluates its legacy. Thoughtful, lucid, and engaging.

Andrea, Alfred, and James Overfield, eds. *The Human Record*, 2 vols. (Florence, KY: Wadsworth Publishing Co., 6th ed., 2008). Excellent selection of documents and visuals.

Bell, Susan Groag and Karen M. Offen, eds. *Women, the Family, and Freedom: The Debate in Documents*, vol. 1, 1750-1880 (Stanford, CA: Stanford University Press, 1985). Excellent selection of documents on the feminist movement, with insightful commentary.

Boorstin, Daniel. *The Discoverers* (New York: Random House, 1983). Lucid, engaging account of the work of specific scientists and explorers and their impact on history.

Chevigny, Hector. *Russian America: The Great Alaskan Venture, 1741–1867* (Portland, OR: Binford and Mort, 1965). Told as a gripping story of adventure.

Cohen, I. Bernard. *Revolution in Science* (Cambridge, MA: Harvard University Press, 1985). Analyzes 450 years of major scientific revolutions and their interaction with the larger society. Magisterial yet lucid.

Columbia University. *Contemporary Civilization in the West*, vol. 1 (New York: Columbia University Press, 2nd ed., 1954). Outstanding sourcebook with lengthy excerpts from highly influential thinkers and actors.

Curtin, Philip. *The Rise and Fall of the Plantation Complex* (New York: Cambridge University Press, 1989). Excellent analysis of the plantation itself and its significance to world trade and politics.

Davis, David Brion. *The Problem of Slavery in the Age of Revolution, 1770–1823* (Ithaca, NY: Cornell University Press, 1975). Analyzes the tensions between the idea of freedom and the practice of slavery.

——. "Looking at Slavery from Broader Perspectives," *American Historical Review* 105:2 (April, 2000), pp. 452–66. Global, comprehensive review of the literature.

De Vries, Jan. *The Industrious Revolution: Consumer Behavior and Household Economy, 1650 to the Present* (New York: Cambridge University Press, 2008). Argues that family-centered economic demand for consumer goods preceded and evoked market supply.

Drescher, Seymour. *Econocide* (Pittsburgh, PA: University of Pittsburgh Press, 1977). Argues that the abolition of slavery was an economically costly decision, taken, primarily, for moral reasons.

——. *The Problem of Slavery in Western Culture* (New York: Oxford University Press, 1966). Explores the tension between slavery and the ideals of individual freedom and democracy.

Fick, Carolyn E. *The Making of Haiti* (Knoxville, TN: University of Tennessee Press, 1990). A comprehensive, cogent account.

Fogel, Robert William, and Stanley L. Engerman. *Time on the Cross*, 2 vols. (Boston, MA: Little, Brown, 1974). A controversial, influential assessment of the economics of slavery.

Genovese, Eugene. *From Rebellion to Revolution* (Baton Rouge, LA: Louisiana University Press, 1979). A study of slave revolts and their significance to abolition.

Halévy, Élie. *England in 1815* (New York: Barnes & Noble, 1961). A classic account of a society successfully avoiding revolution.

Hammond Atlas of World History, ed. Geoffrey Parker (Maplewood, NJ: Hammond, 5th ed., 1999).

Hanke, Lewis, and Jane M. Rausch, eds. *People and Issues in Latin American History* (New York: Markus Weiner, 3rd ed., 2006). A useful reader.

Hobbes, Thomas. *Selections*, ed. Frederick J.E. Woodbridge (New York: Charles Scribner's Sons, 1958). Primary sources.

Hobsbawm, Eric. *The Age of Empire 1875–1914* (New York: Vintage Books, 1987). Excellent, comprehensive account.

Hughes, Robert. *Goya* (New York: Knopf, 2003). Thoughtful, thorough, provocative, well-illustrated interpretation of the man and his art in their time.

Kolchin, Peter. *American Slavery 1619–1877* (New York: Hill & Wang, 1993). Comprehensive treatment, even of the period after 1865, with comparisons to slavery in other societies.

Locke, John. *The Second Treatise on Government* (Arlington Heights, IL: Crofts Classics, 1982). Primary source.

McClellan III, James F., and Harold Dorn. *Science and Technology in World History* (Baltimore, MD: Johns Hopkins University Press, 1999). Outstanding coverage of science and technology from various parts of the world.

Márquez, Gabriel García. *The General in His Labyrinth*. trans. Edith Grossman (New York: Knopf, 1990). Fictionalized account of the end of the life of General Simón Bolívar.

Metcalf, Barbara D., and Thomas R. Metcalf. *A Concise History of India* (Cambridge: Cambridge University Press, 2002). Especially strong on issues of identity and the importance of Muslims and of women.

Nehru, Jawaharlal. *Glimpses of World History* (New Delhi: Jawaharlal Nehru Memorial Fund and Oxford University Press, 1982). Nehru wrote this socialistic account of world history from jail as a series of letters to his daughter.

Neruda, Pablo. *Canto General*, trans. Jack Schmitt (Berkeley, CA: University of California Press, 1991). A personal, critical assessment of Latin American history in verse by a master poet.

Nicholls, David. "Haiti: Race, Slavery and Independence (1804–1825)," in Léonie J. Archer, ed., *Slavery and Other Forms of Unfree Labour* (London: Routledge, 1988), pp. 225–38. On the relationship of slavery to race in Haiti.

Patterson, Orlando. *Freedom in the Making of Western Culture* (New York: Basic Books, 1991). Discusses how slavery and racism conflict with the promise of freedom and democracy.

Rousseau, Jean-Jacques. *The Social Contract*, trans. Maurice Cranston (New York: Viking Penguin, 1968). Primary source.

Schiebinger, Londa. *The Mind Has No Sex? Women in the Origins of Modern Science* (Cambridge, MA: Harvard University Press, 1989). Examines (mostly patriarchal) attitudes toward women among scientists and philosophers in the era of the Enlightenment and early modern science.

Smith, Adam. *The Theory of Moral Sentiments* (Charlottesville, VA: Lincoln-Rembrandt Publishers, 6th ed., 1986). Primary source.

——. *The Wealth of Nations*, books I–III (New York: Viking Penguin Classics, 1986). Primary source.

Thompson, Vincent Bakpetu. *The Making of the African Diaspora in the Americas 1441–1900* (New York: Longman, 1987). A view that transcends the experience of individual countries to see the comprehensive picture.

Tocqueville, Alexis de. *The Old Regime and the French Revolution*, trans. Gilbert Stuart (Garden City, NY: Doubleday Anchor Books, 1955). Classic analysis that locates precipitating factors in the revolution, and indicates that many endured long afterward.

Turner, Frederick Jackson. *The Frontier in American History* (New York: Henry Holt, 1920). Classic interpretation of the significance to America of huge frontier spaces in the west.

Wilentz, Sean. *Chants Democratic: New York and the Rise of the American Working Class, 1788–1850* (New York: Oxford University Press, 1984). Important contribution to working-class history.

MUSEUM DISPLAY

"Year of Proof: Making and Unmaking Race," Penn Museum, Philadelphia, PA: Display of hundreds of skulls from the collection of the nineteenth-century physician Samuel Morton, accompanied by evaluation of his racially charged interpretations. On display, 2013. See http://www.penn.museum/current-changing-exhibits/year-of-proof (accessed June 12, 2013).

FILMS

Égalité for All: Toussaint Louverture and the Haitian Revolution (2009; 1 hour). Broadcast on PBS. Gives a full account of the Haitian Revolution.

The English Civil War: Series of films produced by the Open University, United Kingdom. Even the introductions to each of the films, and thus each of the units of the course, are very useful. Begin with http://www.open.edu/openlearn/history-the-arts/history/tremors/the-english-civil-war-tremors-introduction.

The French Revolution (2005; 100 minutes). A History Channel production, with expert historians and dramatic reenactments. http://www.youtube.com/watch?v=CUrEJBsWLfA

Simón Bolívar: Liberator (2000; 30 minutes). Straightforward narrative presentation. Sees the international context and connections of Bolívar's career.

17 The Industrial Revolution

A Global Process

1700–1914

One of the key indicators of human progress has always been improvement in the tools that we use and the ways in which we organize production. Today we usually associate advanced industry with the Western world, but the most advanced civilization of premodern times was China of the Song dynasty (960–1279). China earned its reputation not only for its neo-Confucian high culture—its painting, poetry, and classical education—but also for its agricultural progress with new crops and more efficient harvesting. It produced armaments on a massive scale, including gunpowder and siege machines. The Song imperial government issued paper money and constructed extensive river and canal networks, which commercial ships navigated profitably. Under the Song, China was technically innovative, inventing the compass, improving the technology of silk production, ceramics, and lacquer, and vastly expanding printing and book production. China's advances in iron manufacture were so extensive that deforestation became a problem in parts of the north. (Until coal took its place, wood was used to smelt the iron ore.) The iron improved the strength and durability of tools, weapons, and the construction of major building projects, especially bridges. Other parts of the world lagged behind China's innovations in trade, commerce, and industry.

International Exhibition, World's Fair, South Kensington, London, 1862. At its core, the Industrial Revolution substituted inanimate power for human and animal energy. Before the Industrial Revolution, Western Europe had lagged economically behind China and India. New machinery dramatically altered that balance.

LEARNING OBJECTIVES

17.1 Describe the first stage of the Industrial Revolution.

17.2 Discuss the Industrial Revolution's effects on global society and power balances among nations.

17.3 Identify the key social changes of the Industrial Revolution in Europe and beyond.

17.4 Describe the labor movements emerging from the Industrial Revolution.

17.5 Discuss new patterns of life in the cities.

Beginning in the eighteenth century, however, Western Europe, and especially Britain, caught up with and surpassed China, and the rest of the world, in economic power and productivity. In the Turning Point entitled "Trade," we surveyed some of the changes that enabled regions of Western Europe to emerge from their singular concentration on agriculture as the basis of their economy: to increased concern with commerce, trade, and exploration; increased family demand for products for the household and the dining table; new technology; and commitment to financial success and the pursuit of profit. Slowly these new economic interests led to the creation of new tools: better ships; new and improved commercial instruments and organizations, such as the joint stock company; and even the adoption and adaptation of some of China's earlier inventions, including the compass, gunpowder, and movable type for printing. Businesspeople in Western Europe pursued new economic possibilities with a vigor and flexibility that were sometimes admirable, as in the search for new technologies, and sometimes morally reprehensible, as in the use of millions of slaves in the creation of vast sugar plantations in the Caribbean basin and in the extraction of gold and silver from New World mines through coerced labor for

AT A GLANCE: INDUSTRIALIZATION IN THE WEST

DATE	BRITAIN	REST OF EUROPE	NORTH AMERICA
1760	• James Watt improves Newcomen's steam engine (1763) • James Hargreaves introduces spinning jenny (1764)		
1780	• Combination Act forbids workers to unionize (1799); repealed 1824		• Eli Whitney invents cotton gin (1793)
1800	• Luddite riots (1810–20) • Peterloo Massacre, Manchester (1819)		
1820	• George Stephenson's locomotive *Rocket* (1829) • Factory Act forbids employment of children (1833) • Chartist movement calls for universal male suffrage (1838)	• Invention of photography in France by Louis Jacques Mandé Daguerre (1839) • Worker revolts in Paris, Prague, Vienna, and Russia (1830)	• First transatlantic steamship lines in operation (1838) • Revolver invented by Samuel Colt (1836)
1840	• Sir Edwin Chadwick issues report on the Poor Laws (1842) • Friedrich Engels, *The Condition of the Working Class in England* (1845) • Repeal of the Corn Laws (1846) • Bessemer steel converter (1856) • Samuel Smiles, *Self Help* (1859)	• Year of Revolutions—in France, Austria, and Prussia (1848) • Marx and Engels, *The Communist Manifesto* (1848)	• Invention of the sewing machine (1846)
1860	• Under Prime Minister Gladstone, Liberal government begins to provide universal state-supported education (1870) • Liberals under Gladstone and Tories under Disraeli compete for workers' votes • Trade Union Act guarantees right to strike (1871)	• Siemens-Martin open-hearth steel production, Germany (1864) • Growth of chemical industries (after 1870) • Massacre of the Paris Commune (1871) • Bismarck unifies Germany (1871) • Germany's SPD is first working-class political party (1875)	• American Civil War (1861–65) • Richard Gatling invents the machine gun (1861) • Thomas Edison invents early form of telegraph (1864) • Invention of the typewriter (1867) • Canada becomes unified dominion (1867) • Edison establishes private industrial development lab (1876)
1880	• London Dock strike (1889)	• Labor unions legalized in France (1884) • May 1 recognized in France as annual "Labor Day" (1890)	• American Federation of Labor founded (1886) • Kodak camera (1888) • Homestead Steel strike (1892)

17.1 What events gave birth to the Industrial Revolution?

17.2

17.3

17.4

17.5

the benefit of European businessmen. All these economic initiatives—innovation at home and exploitation overseas—paved the way for the Industrial Revolution, which began in the eighteenth century.

This modern **Industrial Revolution** began with simple new machinery and minor changes in the organization of the workplace, but these were only the first steps. Ultimately, the Industrial Revolution multiplied the profits of the business classes and increased their power in government and public life. It broadened and deepened in its scope until it affected humanity globally, transforming the locations of our workplaces and homes, the size and composition of our families and the quality and quantity of the time we spend with them, the educational systems we create, the wars we fight, and the relationships among nations. As a global process the Industrial Revolution restructured the procurement of raw materials in the fields and mines of the world, the location of manufacture, and the range of international marketplaces in which new products might be sold. As the masters of the new industrial productivity adopted this global view of their own economic activities, their ventures became imperial in scope. They marshalled the powers of their governments to support their global economic capacities. Reciprocally, the governments relied on the power of industrialists and businesspeople to increase their own international strength politically, diplomatically, and militarily. The balance of wealth and power in the world shifted, for the first time, toward Europe, and especially toward Britain, the first home of the Industrial Revolution.

KEY TERM

Industrial Revolution Once defined primarily in terms of new technology in Britain and Europe, now recognized also as a global phenomenon of unprecedented transformation in social organization and political/military power.

The Industrial Revolution in Britain, 1700–1860

17.1 What events gave birth to the Industrial Revolution?

The Industrial Revolution began in Britain around 1700, and although it is called a "revolution," it took more than 150 years to be fully realized. During this period, Britain created and mechanized a cotton textile industry, which soon became the world's most productive; created a railway network, which transformed the island's transportation and communication systems; and launched a new fleet of steam-powered ships, which enabled Britain to project its new productivity and power around the globe. Economic historians agree, however, that the industrial changes were possible because agriculture in Britain—the basis of its preindustrial economy—was already undergoing a process of continuing improvement. The transformation was so fundamental that it is called an agricultural revolution. (This agricultural revolution in the use of new tools and implements in producing new crops for market profit was actually a second agricultural revolution. As we saw in the chapters entitled "The Dry Bones Speak" and "From Village Community to City-state," the first occurred about 15,000 years ago, when nomadic peoples began to domesticate crops and animals and settle into villages.)

A Revolution in Agriculture

Britain (along with the Dutch Republic, as the Netherlands was known until 1648) had the most productive and efficient commercial agriculture in Europe. Inventors created new farm equipment and farmers were quick to adopt it. Jethro Tull (1674–1741), as an outstanding example, invented the seed drill (which replaced the old method of

Seed drill, 1701. Jethro Tull (1674–1741) is a key figure of the eighteenth-century agricultural revolution, which saw new technology harnessed to farming techniques. Tull's machine drill employed a rotary mechanism that sowed seeds in rows, permitting cultivation between the rows and thus reducing the need for weeding.

What events
gave birth to
the Industrial
Revolution?

17.1
17.2
17.3
17.4
17.5

scattering seeds by hand on the surface of the soil with a new method of planting systematically in regular rows at fixed depths); a horse-drawn hoe; and an iron plow that could be set at an angle that would pull up grasses and roots and leave them to fertilize the land. New crops, such as turnips and potatoes from the New World, were introduced. Farmers and large landlords initiated huge irrigation and drainage projects, increasing the productivity of land already under cultivation and opening up new land. The word "**agronomy**," the systematic concern with field crop production and soil management, entered the English language in 1814.

As noted in the chapter entitled "Political Revolutions in Europe and the Americas," governments revised dramatically the laws regarding land ownership in order to stimulate productivity. In Britain and the Netherlands, peasants began to pay landowners commercial rents that fluctuated with market conditions, rather than paying fixed, customary rents and performing compulsory labor services. Moreover, lands that had been held in common by the village community and used for grazing sheep and cattle by shepherds and livestock owners who had no lands of their own were now parceled out for private ownership through a series of enclosure acts.

Enclosures had begun in England in a limited way in the late 1400s. In the eighteenth century the process resumed and the pace increased. In the period 1714–1801, about 25 percent of the land in Britain was converted from community property to private property through enclosures. The results were favorable to landowners, and urban businessmen began to buy land as agricultural investment property. Agricultural productivity shot up; landowners prospered. But hundreds of thousands of farmers with small plots and cottagers who had subsisted through the use of the common lands for grazing their animals were now turned into tenant farmers and wage laborers. The results were revolutionary and profoundly disturbing to society. Peasant riots broke out as early as the middle of the sixteenth century. In one uprising, 3,500 people were killed.

The process continued throughout the period of the early Industrial Revolution as many of the dispossessed farmers turned to rural or domestic industry to supplement their meager incomes. Later, rural workers left the land altogether for new industrial jobs in Britain's growing cities. The capitalist market system transformed British agriculture and emptied the countryside, providing capital and workers for the Industrial Revolution. The economist Joseph Schumpeter (1883–1950) called capitalism a process of "creative destruction." In the agricultural revolution and the Industrial Revolution we see evidence of both: the often painful destruction of older ways of life and the creation of new, uncharted ways.

A Revolution in Textile Manufacture

The first important commercial product of the Industrial Revolution in England was cotton textiles. Until the mid-eighteenth century, the staple British textile had been woolens, woven from the wool of locally raised sheep. By then, however, European traders in India realized that the cotton cloth of India was far more comfortable and far easier to clean. As they began to import these light, colorful, durable cotton textiles, the Indian fabrics began to displace woolens in the British market. The British government responded by manipulating tariffs and import regulations to restrict Indian cotton textiles, while British inventors began to produce new machinery that enabled Britain to surpass Indian production in both quantity and quality. The raw cotton would still have to be imported from subtropical India (and later from the southern United States and Egypt), but the British could create at home their own manufacturing processes that turned it into cloth, increasing British jobs and profits, and cutting back on the purchase of finished cloth in India, thus undercutting jobs and profits there.

Merchants organized much of the early industrial production through the putting-out system (see Key Term in the chapter entitled "The Opening of the

KEY TERM

agronomy The systematic concern with field crop production and soil management. The term was first used in 1814.

Spinning and Weaving Wool, Isaac Claesz Swanenburgh, c. 1600. Oil on wood. This image shows the steps involved in spinning wool for the textile industry in the Dutch Republic. (Stedelijk Museum, Leiden)

17.1 What events gave birth to the Industrial Revolution?

17.2

17.3

17.4

17.5

Atlantic and the Pacific"). They would drop off raw cotton at workers' homes where women would spin it into yarn, which men would then weave into cloth, which merchants would later pick up. The spinning wheel, which had been in existence for centuries, allowed women to produce fairly uniform yarn. Men wove the yarn on looms that required two men sitting across from each other, passing the shuttle of the loom from left to right and back again. In 1733, John Kay invented the "flying shuttle," which allowed a single weaver to send the shuttle forth and back across the loom automatically, without the need for a second operator to push it. The spinners could not keep up with the increased demand of the weavers until, in 1764, James Hargreaves introduced the "spinning jenny," a machine that allowed the operator to spin several threads at once. The earliest jennies could run eight spindles at once; by 1770, it was 16; and by the end of the century, 120. Machines to card and comb the cotton to prepare it for spinning were also developed.

Thus far, the machinery was new, but the power source was still human labor, and production was still concentrated in rural homes and small workshops. Then a series of inventions led to the mechanization of the cotton industry. In 1769, Richard Arkwright patented the "water frame," a machine that could spin several cotton strands simultaneously. Powered by water, it could run continuously. In 1779, Samuel Crompton developed a "spinning mule," a hybrid that joined the principles of the spinning jenny and the water frame to produce a better quality and higher quantity of cotton thread. Unfortunately, Crompton was too poor to patent it, but he sold designs for it to others. Now British cloth could rival that of India. Fascinated by Arkwright's water frame, Edmund Cartwright believed he could make a fortune by applying the principles of the technology to weaving. After some experiments, he patented the power loom in 1785, with water power harnessed to drive the shuttle.

Meanwhile, in the coalfields of Britain, mine owners were seeking more efficient means of pumping water out of mine shafts. The key development was the steam engine. By 1712, Thomas Newcomen had mastered the use of steam power to drive the water pumps. In 1763, James Watt a technician at the University of Glasgow, was experimenting with improvements to Newcomen's steam engine, when Matthew Boulton a small manufacturer, provided him with the capital necessary to develop larger and more costly steam engines. By 1785 the firm of Boulton and Watt was manufacturing new steam engines for use in Britain and for export. In the 1780s, Arkwright used a new Boulton and Watt steam engine instead of water power. From this point, equipment grew more sophisticated and more expensive. Spinning and weaving moved from the producer's home or small workshop by a stream of water to new steam-powered cotton textile mills, which increased continuously in size and productivity. Power looms, such as Cartwright's, invented to cope with increased spinning capacity, became commercially profitable by about 1800. Increasingly, in the 1800s, power looms became one of the most important technologies of the Industrial Revolution.

The new productivity of the machines transformed Britain's economy. It took hand spinners in India 50,000 hours to produce 100 pounds of cotton yarn. Crompton's mule could do the same task in 2,000 hours. Arkwright's steam-powered frame, available by 1795, took 300 hours; and automatic mules, available by 1825, took just 135 hours. Moreover, the quality of the finished product steadily increased in terms of strength, durability, and texture. Cotton textiles became the most important product of British industry by 1820, making up almost half of Britain's exports.

Prior to this mechanization, most families had spun and woven their own clothing by hand; thus the availability of machine-made yarn and cloth affected millions of spinners and weavers throughout Great Britain. As late as 1815 owners of new weaving mills continued the putting-out system. When cutbacks in production were necessary, the home workers could be cut. Thus the burden of recession could be shifted onto the shoulders of the home producer, leaving the mill owners relatively unscathed. In 1791, home-based workers in the north of England burned down one of the new power-loom factories in Manchester. Machine-wrecking riots followed for several decades, culminating in the Luddite riots of 1810–20. Named for their mythical leader, Ned Ludd, the rioters wanted the new machines banned. Soldiers were called in to suppress the riots.

The textile revolution had an impact on economies around the world, devastating some, energizing others. India's industrial position was reversed. Its markets for hand-manufactured textile were undercut by Britain's new industrial production, and India, ironically, became the textbook example of a colonial economy, supplying raw cotton to Britain and importing machine-manufactured cotton textiles from Britain.

James Hargreaves' spinning jenny. Named for his daughter, Hargreaves' invention was a spinning machine that prepared natural fibers for weaving. It thus made possible the expanded production of cotton cloth. The Industrial Revolution was built on such relatively simple innovations as this jenny and the even earlier "flying shuttle" of John Kay, 1733. Compare the picture opposite to see how much more machine-intensive/labor-free is the production process of the spinning jenny.

What events gave birth to the Industrial Revolution?

17.1
17.2
17.3
17.4
17.5

The Industrial Revolution. In the early nineteenth century, the Industrial Revolution spread throughout the trading nations of Western Europe (and enmeshed their colonies, which provided both raw materials and markets). The early use of water power gave way to steam engines; coal became the power source. Canal transportation was superseded by railways, driven by steam. The density of the rail network and of the coal and iron fields in England reflects that country's lead in early industrialization.

🔍 View the **Interactive Map: European Industrialization** on **MyHistoryLab**

17.1
17.2
17.3
17.4
17.5

What events gave birth to the Industrial Revolution?

The United States, on the other hand, prospered, but its prosperity gave a new impetus to slavery. Britain's new machine-operated mills required unprecedented quantities of good-quality cotton. Raw cotton was oily and full of seeds, and it was impossible to process it into yarn without first cleaning it or removing the seeds. In the United States, the invention of the cotton gin by Eli Whitney in 1793 enabled workers to clean 50 pounds of cotton in the time it had previously taken to clean 1 pound. This solved part of the supply problem. The plantation economy of the United States revived and expanded, providing the necessary raw cotton, but, unfortunately, it also gave slavery a new lease on life. American cotton production rose from 3,000 bales in 1790 to 178,000 bales in 1810, to 732,000 bales in 1830, and 4,500,000 bales in 1860. Almost all the cotton was produced by slave labor. The industrialization that had begun in Britain was reshaping the world economy.

Interior of Crystal Palace, designed by Joseph Paxton for the Great Exhibition of 1851 in London. This glass-and-iron exhibition hall, a landmark of early modern architecture, was a celebration of the powerful Victorian economy and an expression of British technological accomplishment and imperial might.

Read the **Document**: **Chadwick's Report on Sanitary Conditions (1842)** on **MyHistoryLab**

The Iron Industry

Developments in the textile industry began with a consumer product that everyone used and that already employed a substantial handicraft labor force; they mechanized and reorganized the process of production and relocated it from homes and small workshops to large factories. Other industrial innovations created new products. Britain's iron industry, which had been established since the mid-1500s, at first burned wood to heat iron ore and extract molten iron, but by about 1750 new mining processes provided coal, a more efficient fuel, more abundantly and more cheaply. About 1775, the iron industry relocated to the coal and iron fields of the English Midlands. A process of stirring the molten iron ore at high temperatures was introduced by Henry Cort in the 1780s. This "puddling" process encouraged the use of larger ovens and integrated the processes of melting, hammering, and rolling the iron into high-quality bars. Productivity increased dramatically. As the price of production dropped and the quality increased, iron was introduced into building construction. The greatest demand for the metal came, however, with new inventions. The steam engine, railroad track and locomotives, steamships, and new urban systems of gas supply and solid and liquid waste disposal all depended on iron for their construction. Britain's world market share of iron multiplied from 19 percent in 1800 to 52 percent in 1840—that is, Britain produced as much manufactured iron as the rest of the world put together.

With the new steam engine and the increased availability and quality of iron, the railroad industry was born. The first reliable locomotive, George Stephenson's *Rocket*, was produced in 1829. It serviced the Manchester–Liverpool route, reaching a speed of 16 miles per hour. By the 1840s, a railroad boom swept through Britain and Europe, and crossed the Atlantic to the United States, where it facilitated the westward expansion of that rapidly expanding country. By the 1850s, most of the

MAJOR DISCOVERIES AND INVENTIONS 1640–1830	
1640	Theories of numbers: Pierre de Fermat
1642	Calculating machine: Blaise Pascal
1650	Air pump: Otto von Guericke
1656	Pendulum clock: Otto von Guericke
1665–75	Calculus: Isaac Newton and Gottfried Wilhelm Leibnitz (independently)
1698	Steam pump: Thomas Savory
c. 1701	Seed drill: Jethro Tull
1712	Steam engine: Thomas Newcomen
1714	Mercury thermometer: Gabriel Fahrenheit
1733	Flying shuttle: John Kay
1752	Lightning conductor: Benjamin Franklin
1764	Spinning jenny: James Hargreaves
1765	Condensing steam engine: James Watt
1768	Hydrometer: Antoine Baumé
1783	Hot air balloon: Joseph and Étienne Montgolfier
1783	Parachute: Louis Lenormand
1785	Power loom: Edmund Cartwright
1789	Hydrogen, oxygen, nitrogen in air: Antoine Lavoisier
1793	Cotton gin: Eli Whitney
1800	Electric battery: Alessandro Volta
1807	Steamboat: Robert Fulton
1815	Miner's safety lamp: Humphry Davy
1818	Bicycle: Karl von Sauerbrun
1823	Digital calculating machine: Charles Babbage
1824	Portland cement: Joseph Aspdin
1825	Electromagnet: William Sturgeon
1826	Heliography (pre-photography): Joseph Niépce
1828	Blast furnace: James Neilson
1829	Steam locomotive: George Stephenson

What events gave birth to the Industrial Revolution?

17.1

17.2

17.3

17.4

17.5

HOW DO WE KNOW?

Why Did the Industrial Revolution Begin in Britain?

Historians have long debated the origins of the Industrial Revolution. The term itself was used at least as early as 1845, in the opening of Friedrich Engels' *The Condition of the Working Class in England*: "The history of the English working classes begins in the second half of the eighteenth century with the invention of the steam engine and of machines for spinning and weaving cotton. It is well known that these inventions gave the impetus to the genesis of an industrial revolution. This revolution had a social as well as an economic aspect since it changed the entire structure of middle-class society" (p. 9).

Arnold Toynbee (the uncle of a twentieth-century historian with the same name) was apparently the first professional historian to use the term. In a set of lectures delivered in 1880–81, Toynbee identified 1760 as the beginning of the process. He chose this date in recognition of the inventions discussed in this chapter. In 1934, John Nef, economic historian at the University of Chicago, argued that because the iron industry was in place by the mid-sixteenth century, that date was a more appropriate choice. More recent historians, such as Fernand Braudel, have also seen the roots of industrialization stretching back for centuries. They have stressed the underlying economic, political, social, intellectual, and scientific transformations that we have discussed in the last few chapters. All these processes coalesced in the British economy in the late eighteenth century to create the Industrial Revolution:

- increasing productivity in agriculture;
- new merchant classes in power, and the evolution of a capitalist philosophy of economics that justified their power;
- a powerful state that supported economic development, despite the capitalist doctrine of laissez-faire, which called for the state to stay out of business;
- the rise of science, with its new, empirical view of the world, and of technology, with its determination to find practical solutions to practical problems;
- a social structure that allowed and even encouraged people of different classes to work together, especially artisans, who worked with their hands, and financiers, who provided capital;
- more intense patterns of global trading for buying raw materials and for selling manufactured products;

- an expanding population that increased both the labor supply and the demand for production;
- slave labor in plantation economies, which brought more than a century of exceptional capital accumulation;
- the discovery of enormous deposits of gold and silver in the New World, which also increased capital accumulation; and
- "proto-industrialization"—that is, early forms of industrial organization that introduced new skills to both management and labor, paving the way for large-scale factory production.

This question of the origins of the Industrial Revolution is not purely academic. The debate carries serious implications for planning industrial development in today's world. As many newly independent nations with little industry seek to industrialize, they ask: Does industrialization mean simply the acquisition of machinery and the adaptation of advanced technology? Or must a nation also experience a much wider range of agricultural, economic, philosophical, scientific, political, and social changes? How, and under what terms, can it raise the capital necessary to begin? What are the tasks confronting a government wishing to promote industrialization? We shall examine these twentieth-century questions in the final chapters of this book. Those countries that have achieved high levels of industrialization—mostly the countries of Europe and their daughter civilizations overseas; Japan; and now some of the countries of East Asia (see the chapter entitled "China and India")—have experienced a wide range of fundamental changes, akin to many of those experienced by Britain.

- Among the characteristics that made the Industrial Revolution possible, do some seem to you more important than others? Which ones? Why?
- Which processes that we usually include in the "Industrial Revolution" are changes in machinery and equipment? Which are changes in the social structure of society?
- Which of these processes seem to be continuing to the present and continuing to influence contemporary economics?

17.1
17.2
17.3
17.4
17.5

What events gave birth to the Industrial Revolution?

George Stephenson's locomotive *Rocket*, 1829, from a chromolithographic cigarette card of 1901. On October 14, 1829, the *Rocket* won a competition for an engine to haul freight and passengers on the Manchester–Liverpool Railway. The success of Stephenson's invention stimulated a boom in locomotive construction and track laying around the world.

SOURCE

Conflicting Images of Early Industrial Life: The English Romantic Poets

In the century 1750–1850, Britain was transformed by industrialization. Factories, cities, and the working class all multiplied. One response to the turmoil created by these changes was Romanticism, a new international movement in literature and the arts, which opposed the rationalism of the Enlightenment and glorified emotion. Romantic poets in Britain, such as William Wordsworth (1770–1850) and Samuel Taylor Coleridge (1772–1834), turned away from the belief in modern progress through science and rational knowledge toward nature, history, and their own inner feelings. They saw a great vision of a new aesthetic beauty emerging. Wordsworth's view of London's natural glories represents this Romantic perspective.

Upon Westminster Bridge, September 3, 1802

Earth has not anything to show more fair:
Dull would he be of soul who could pass by
A sight so touching in its majesty;
This City now doth, like a garment, wear
The beauty of the morning; silent, bare,
Ships, towers, domes, theatres, and temples lie
Open unto the fields, and to the sky;
All bright and glittering in the smokeless air.
Never did sun more beautifully steep
In his first splendour, valley, rock, or hill;
Ne'er saw I, never felt, a calm so deep!
The river glideth at his own sweet will:
Dear God! the very houses seem asleep;
And all that mighty heart is lying still!

William Wordsworth

Others, such as the poet William Blake (1757–1827), who were closer to the lives of working-class people, saw the great suffering caused by industrialization. Devoutly religious and nationalistic, Blake nevertheless condemned the British people, the government, and the Church of England for tolerating "a land of poverty" in the very midst of "a rich and fruitful land." While Wordsworth looks over London from the vantage point of a bridge, Blake walks its streets and looks into the faces of its inhabitants:

London

I wander thro' each charter'd* street,
Near where the charter'd Thames does flow,
And mark in every face I meet
Marks of weakness, marks of woe.

In every cry of every Man,
In every Infant's cry of fear,
In every voice, in every ban,
The mind-forg'd manacles I hear.

How the Chimney-sweeper's cry
Every blackning Church appalls;
And the hapless Soldier's sigh
Runs in blood down Palace walls.

But most thro' midnight streets I hear
How the youthful Harlot's curse
Blasts the new-born Infant's tear,**
And blights with plagues the Marriage hearse.

William Blake (1792)

*charter'd = licensed by the government, controlled, owned
**the infant is blind at birth, from venereal disease transmitted by the parent

No matter how upsetting Blake's view of London may be, the even more lacerated heart of the Industrial Revolution was actually in the Midlands and north of England, around the cities of Manchester, Birmingham, and Liverpool.

23,500 miles of today's railway network in Britain were already in place, and entrepreneurs found new foreign markets for their locomotives and tracks in India and Latin America.

The new locomotives quickly superseded the canal systems of Britain and the United States, which had been built mostly since the 1750s, as the favored means of transporting raw materials and bulk goods between industrial cities. Until the coming of the steam-powered train, canals had been considered the transportation means of the future. (The speed with which the newer technology displaced the older is one reason historians resist predicting the future. Events do not necessarily proceed in a straight-line process of development, and new, unanticipated developments frequently displace older patterns quite unexpectedly.)

Steamships, using much the same technology as steam locomotives, were introduced at about the same time. The first transatlantic steamship lines began operating in 1838. World steamship tonnage multiplied more than 100 times, from 32,000 tons in 1831 to 3,300,000 tons in 1876. With its new textile mills, iron factories, and steam-driven transportation networks, Britain soon became the "workshop of the world."

What events gave birth to the Industrial Revolution?

17.1
17.2
17.3
17.4
17.5

Industrialization—Stage Two, 1860–1914

17.2 How did the Industrial Revolution transform societies and politics around the world?

Between 1860 and the outbreak of World War I in 1914, a "second Industrial Revolution" further transformed world productivity, the ways in which humans lived their lives, and the power balances among the major nations and regions of the world. The principal technological advances came in steel, chemicals, and electricity.

The Steel and Chemical Industries

New technology soon allowed iron ore to be converted to steel cheaply and abundantly. Iron is produced in blast furnaces and can be of high quality, but the final product contains some impurities. Steel production involves removing the impurities first and then adding carbon to the iron ore to create a much stronger and more versatile product, which can be shaped into bars, plates, and other structural components, such as girders.

The obvious benefits of industrialization led to competition among nations. Germany, united as a country in 1871 under Otto von Bismarck, quickly forged ahead. By 1900 it was producing more steel than Britain, 6.3 million tons to Britain's 5 million tons; in 1913, on the eve of World War I, Germany's lead had grown to 17.6 million tons against 7.7 million tons. Germany also led with a number of additional technological inventions, especially the internal combustion engine, the diesel engine, and the automobile.

Chemical industries grew, especially after 1870, as synthetic substances—notably derivatives of coal—began to augment and replace the earlier reliance on natural substances from vegetables, such as alkalis and dyes. Synthetic aniline dyes were made from coal tar. Both fertilizers and explosives could be made from synthetic nitrogen and phosphates. Artificial fertilizers added to a revolution in agricultural productivity, while explosives helped in the construction of engineering feats, such as the new tunnels through the Alps in Europe, the Suez Canal in North Africa, and the Panama Canal in Central America. Soda, made from the coal by-product ammonia, was used in manufacturing both soap and glass. New drugs and insecticides enhanced the quality of human life, while perfumes and cosmetics made their way to the marketplace, as many middle-class and some working-class women, such as department store clerks, sought luxury goods to add a touch of romance to their lives. Plastics, produced from coal tar acids, became available in the late nineteenth century.

Electrical Inventions

Electrical inventions sparked one another throughout Europe and across the Atlantic in the United States, as well. In Britain in 1831 Michael Faraday first demonstrated the principle of electromagnetic induction by moving a metal conductor through a magnetic field to generate electricity, a process repeated regularly today in high-school classrooms. By 1850, several companies were producing simple electric generators. In the 1860s,

A canal connects two oceans. The construction of the Panama Canal in 1905, linking the Atlantic and Pacific oceans, ranks as one of the greatest engineering feats of all time. The task involved removing about 175 million cubic yards of earth as well as sanitizing the entire area, which was infested by mosquitoes that spread yellow fever and malaria.

in Germany, Ernest Werner von Siemens developed a practical dynamo. In the United States in the 1880s, Nikola Tesla invented methods to transmit power effectively over long distances, patenting the alternating current generator in 1892.

The best-known inventor of the age was the American Thomas Alva Edison, who acquired more than 1,000 patents for his innovations, 225 of them between 1879 and 1882, for incandescent light bulbs, fuses, sockets, switches, circuit breakers, and meters. More important than any single invention, however, was Edison's establishment in 1876 of probably the world's first private industrial development laboratory, in Menlo Park, New Jersey, a rural area halfway between New York and Philadelphia. Until this time, invention had been largely an individual achievement, based on the skill and luck of the individual inventor. Edison's new research facility institutionalized the process of invention, and encouraged research and development and the commercialization of such products as the phonograph.

New Products and New Producers

The second Industrial Revolution corresponded to the era of big business. In Germany, the rising power in Europe, large **cartels** or collaborative business associations were formed to produce electronic equipment and chemicals. For steel production, each major producing country had its own giants: Krupp in Germany, Schneider-Creusot in France, Vickers-Armstrong in Britain, and, largest of all, the United States Steel Corporation. These huge corporations integrated the entire process of production from raw material to finished product. They owned their own coal mines and iron

Machine shop, West Lynn works, United States, c. 1898. The United States led the way in the mass production of household goods. In the nineteenth century, people immigrated to the big cities from rural America and from overseas to work in factories—often for low pay, with long hours, and in hot, noisy conditions. The factory system expanded hugely after 1913 when Henry Ford introduced assembly-line technology to the production of motor cars. Compare with a factory in India, illustrated in the chapter entitled "Methods of Mass Production and Destruction."

17.1

17.2 How did the Industrial Revolution transform societies and politics around the world?

17.3

17.4

17.5

KEY TERM

cartel An association of independent producers or businessmen whose aim is to control the supply of a particular commodity or group of commodities in order to regulate or push up prices.

works, produced steel, and manufactured such final products as ships, railway equipment, and armaments.

Industrial concentration displaced the artisan in favor of mass production and mass consumption. In these mass-market innovations, the United States was frequently the leader, producing the sewing machine (invented by Elias Howe in 1846); the typewriter (1867); clocks and watches, the everyday time-keepers of the new office and factory routines; the telephone, phonograph, and cinema; and small arms, such as the revolver, invented by Samuel Colt in 1836, and the repeating rifle, designed by Christopher Spencer in 1860. The machine gun, invented by Richard Gatling in 1862, was improved several times. In 1883 it took on the name of the Maxim gun, for the American Hiram Maxim, who created a gun that had a range of almost 1½ miles and could shoot 11 rounds per second.

Warfare and industrialization went hand in hand. In the United States, for example, the Civil War (1861–65) not only restored a political union but also marked the victory of the industrializing, urban, free-labor north over the rural, plantation-economy, slave-holding south. Wars of white immigrants against Native Americans accompanied the construction of new crosscontinental railroads. Wars against Mexico completed the borders of the contiguous United States, and wars against Spain brought the United States its first overseas colonies.

MAJOR DISCOVERIES AND INVENTIONS 1830–1914	
1831	Dynamo: Michael Faraday
1834	Reaping machine: Cyrus McCormick
1836	Revolver: Samuel Colt
1837	Telegraph: Samuel Morse
1839	Vulcanized rubber: Charles Goodyear Photography: Louis Jacques Mandé Daguerre
1852	Gyroscope: Léon Foucault
1853	Passenger elevator: Elisha Otis
1856	Celluloid: Alexander Parkes Bessemer converter: Henry Bessemer Bunsen burner: Robert Bunsen
1858	Refrigerator: Ferdinand Carré Washing machine: Hamilton Smith
1859	Internal combustion engine: Etienne Lenoir
1862	Rapid-fire gun: Richard Gatling
1866	Dynamite: Alfred Nobel
1867	Typewriter (no single inventor)
1876	Telephone: Alexander Graham Bell
1877	Phonograph: Thomas Alva Edison
1879	Incandescent lamp: Thomas Alva Edison
1885	Motorcycle: Edward Butler Electric transformer: William Stanley Vacuum flask: James Dewar
1887	Motorcar engine: Gottlieb Daimler/Karl Benz
1888	Pneumatic tire: John Boyd Dunlop Kodak camera: George Eastman
1895	Wireless: Nikola Tesla X-rays: Wilhelm Roentgen
1896	Radioactivity: Antoine Becquerel
1897	Diesel engine: Rudolf Diesel
1898	Submarine: John P. Holland Radium and polonium: Pierre and Marie Curie
1902	Radio-telephone: Reginald Fessenden
1903	Airplane: Wilbur and Orville Wright
1905	Theory of relativity: Albert Einstein
1911	Combine harvester: Benjamin Holt
1914	Tank: Ernest Swinton

Worldwide Effects of the Second Stage

Profits from all these businesses, civilian and military, spilled over into finance capital, the purposeful reinvestment of capital into new business to reap extra profits. Financiers sought new opportunities in far-flung regions of the world. The industrial development of the Americas offered huge opportunities, and Britain became the largest investor. From the 1840s, for example, the railway networks of both North and South America were in large part financed by British investors. The availability of such investment capital made the task of industrial and urban development easier in the Americas, because the necessary sums could be borrowed and repaid later.

These borrowings, and the industrialization and urbanization that came from them, encouraged the immigration that helped to increase the population of North America from 39 million in 1850 to 106 million in 1900, and that of South America from 20 million to 38 million in the same period. The United States absorbed these investments without losing political control of its own internal development, and became the most industrialized of all countries. South America, however, became an early example of **neocolonialism**, in which foreign economic control leads to indirect foreign political control.

Canada enjoyed internal self-government within the British Empire from 1840 and, in 1867, became a unified dominion that included Ontario, Quebec, Nova Scotia, and New Brunswick. It attracted increasing immigration and investment, especially after the United States' frontier filled in with its own immigrants. Nova Scotia and New Brunswick had joined the original provinces of Quebec and Ontario on condition that a railroad be built to link them with Quebec. More dramatically, the Canadian Pacific Railway was completed in 1885, spanning Canada from east to west. Between 1900 and 1916, some 73 million acres of land were planted with wheat and other commercial crops. Four hundred million dollars per year were invested in this sector and in the mining of coal, gold, lead, zinc, nickel, and copper.

In Russia and the Ottoman Empire, the largest investments came from France. In the six decades leading up to World War I, Russia's industrial output grew at a rate of 5 percent per year. It produced more steel than France, Italy, or Japan; by 1914 it had 46,000 miles of railroad track and was the world's fourth largest industrial power. It could not, however, keep up with the industrial advances of the United States and Germany. Similarly, Russia's railway mileage seems less adequate when the immense expanse of the country, by far the largest in the world, is considered. The proportion of Russian industrial production remained at about 8 percent of the world total from 1880 to 1914, and most of its heavy industry was owned by foreigners.

Overall global investments were immense, with Britain far in the lead. By 1914 Britain had invested some $20 billion, France about $8.7 billion, and Germany about $6 billion. The global age of **finance capital** was in full swing.

📖 **Read** the **Document**: **Working Conditions of Women in the Factories (early 20th c.)**
M.I. Pokrovskaia on **MyHistoryLab**

17.1
17.2
17.3
17.4
17.5

What were the key social changes of the Industrial Revolution in Europe and beyond?

Industrial Society

17.3   What were the key social changes of the Industrial Revolution in Europe and beyond?

So far we have concentrated on the immense new productivity of industrialization, and on the abundance and the wonders of new products. But how did the workers fare? What were the conditions of life for those who worked the machines that produced this new wealth? Reports from the early years in Britain, the birthplace of the Industrial Revolution, relate with horrifying regularity the wretched conditions of the working class. Popular literature, including the novels of Charles Dickens (1812–70); official government reports; political tracts; and the cries of labor organizers all echo the same theme: in the midst of increasing national wealth, workers suffered wracking poverty and degradation. However, by the end of our period (1914), the condition of working-class people in Western Europe and the United States, at least, was becoming comfortable. What had changed? How? What was the significance of the change? These questions remain important today as increasingly sophisticated machines continue to produce more abundant and more sophisticated products—and more anxiety in the lives of workers.

Population Growth and the Industrial Revolution

Many demographic studies suggest that levels of population and industrialization increased together. The population of Europe almost doubled between 1750 and 1850, from 140 to 265 million, and then jumped to 400 million by 1900. At the same time, emigration carried an additional 50 million people outward from Europe, especially to the Americas, Australia, and South Africa. At first demographers attributed most of the gains to industrialization, but much of this population increase occurred before the introduction of machinery, and the increase seems to have been worldwide: China's population multiplied four times between 1650 and 1850. Historians now believe the main cause of the overall population growth was the availability of new foods, such as maize, provided by the Columbian Exchange, but the Industrial Revolution had important effects on the specific patterns of growth and migration.

KEY TERMS

neocolonialism The control of one country by another through economic rather than political-military domination, a method frequently employed after the end of formal, political colonization.

finance capital The capital necessary to finance the creation of new industry. The importance of finance capital marked the transition to an age of larger businesses than ever before and gave finance capitalists, who provided the investments, unprecedented power.

Demographers note two waves of change that followed the Industrial Revolution. First, death rates fell as people ate better and kept cleaner, and as public health measures increased the safety of the water supply, improved the sanitation of cities, combated epidemics, and taught new standards of personal hygiene. Second, parents began to realize that improved health increased the likelihood that their children would live to adulthood, and that it was not necessary to produce numerous children to ensure that two or three or four would survive. Urban birth rates went down as parents began to practice family planning. The old "iron law of wages" had argued that as income increased people would simply use the surplus to have more children; this did not happen. After years of rapid growth, by about 1900 the populations of industrial areas began to stabilize.

Winners and Losers in the Industrial Revolution

New entrepreneurs, men creating successful new industrial enterprises, often profited handsomely in this era. Their literary representative was Samuel Smiles (1812–1904), whose book *Self Help*, published in 1859, advocated self-reliance as the key to "a harvest of wealth and prosperity." Smiles described the careers of many of these self-made new men—the "industrial heroes of the civilized world"—for example, Josiah Wedgwood, a potter, the son and grandson of potters, who created a new form of pottery that still bears his name. Wedgwood transformed the British pottery industry, earning great profits for himself and providing employment in his factories for 20,000 workers. As industries of all sorts expanded, each nation had its own examples of "captains of industry": in Germany, four generations of the Friedrich Krupp family, manufacturers of steel and weapons; in the United States, Andrew Carnegie, also in steel manufacture, and J. Pierpont Morgan, in investment banking.

The lives of the entrepreneurial elites provided inspiration to some, but they were obviously not representative of the majority. In Britain, the economic and political power of the inherited nobility declined. Their wealth, based on land ownership, diminished as that of the new industrial class grew. More to the point, handicraft workers were displaced by the new mechanization. In 1820 there were 240,000 handloom weavers in Britain; in 1840, 123,000; and by 1856, only 23,000. Some of these workers found jobs running the new power looms, but many could not make the transition and fell into poverty. While attending his father's cotton mill in Manchester, Friedrich Engels (1820–95) compiled devastating accounts of *The Condition of the Working Class in England* (1845). His description of the St. Giles slum in London demonstrates his moral outrage:

> Heaps of garbage and ashes lie in all directions, and the foul liquids emptied before the doors gather in stinking pools. Here live the poorest of the poor, the worst paid workers with thieves and the victims of prostitution indiscriminately huddled together … [T]hey who have some kind of shelter are fortunate in comparison with the utterly homeless. In London fifty thousand human beings get up every morning, not knowing where they are to lay their heads at night. (pp. 34–38)

Government reports, although more restrained in tone, sustained these horrific views. Official committees studied conditions in the factories and neighborhoods of Britain's growing industrial cities and in its mines. In 1831, an investigation into the conditions of child labor in cotton and linen factories found children beginning work at the age of six, usually for 12- and 13-hour days. They were often given food so wretched that, despite their hunger, they left it for pigs to eat. Workplaces were cramped and dirty all year long, and were especially damaging to health during the long nights of winter, when gas, candles, and oil lamps added their soot and smoke to the air of the factory. Still worse conditions were revealed by the Committee on the Conditions in Mines in 1842. Children worked underground for 14 hours each

KEY TERM

iron law of wages The belief that as incomes increased people would choose to have more children. By 1900, this "iron law" reversed: as incomes increased, people chose to have fewer children.

What were the key social changes of the Industrial Revolution in Europe and beyond?

Putters or trolley boys, from *Mines and Miners* by L. Simonin, early nineteenth century. Until the reforms of the 1870s, owners of factories and mines were able to force children as young as five and six to work up to 16 hours a day—often in hazardous conditions. Orphans and pauper children were especially vulnerable, since employers merely had to keep them fed and sheltered in return for their services. The resulting disease, industrial injury, and illiteracy tended to make poor families even poorer.

day. Legally, they could work from the age of nine, but parents needing extra income frequently brought even younger children to work.

Investigations led to remedial legislation. The Factory Act of 1833 prohibited the employment of children under the age of nine in textile mills and provided for paid inspectors to enforce the legislation. Parliament passed a new Poor Law in 1834, which provided assistance just adequate to sustain life. The Poor Law required that recipients live in government workhouses and participate in government-created work projects, but these provisions were not usually enforced. A law of 1842 prohibited the employment of women, and children under the age of ten, in coal mines. The Ten Hour Act of 1847 extended this ruling to cover factories and limited women's work hours. In practice, men's hours were also soon reduced.

Sir Edwin Chadwick (1800–90), an investigator for the Royal Commission on the Poor Laws, issued his Inquiry into the Condition of the Poor in 1842 after taking abundant testimony from workers in factories and mines, homes and workplaces. Chadwick noted that the British government had already begun legislating the conditions of child labor and of tenement construction. He now urged further legislation to provide for sewerage, drainage, sanitation, and a clean water supply. His report suggested that not only the poor workers but also their employers, the community, and the government would benefit. Chadwick's report helped to inspire broad support for the Public Health Act of 1848 and the creation of a Board of Health.

📖 Read the **Document**: **Industrial Society and Factory Conditions (early 1800s)** on **MyHistoryLab**

Redefining Gender

By creating factories, the Industrial Revolution drove a wedge between the home and the workplace that dramatically affected both. Wives who had been accustomed to working alongside, or at least in proximity to, their husbands on the farm or in the shop now found that the major source of employment was away from home. The Industrial Revolution forced redefinitions of identities. What should the woman's role and place be now? How should motherhood and work be balanced? In a world that expected most females to be under the protection of males, how were single women to define, and fend for, themselves? In what voice should the feminist movement address these complex issues?

17.1

17.2

17.3 What were the key social changes of the Industrial Revolution in Europe and beyond?

17.4

17.5

As the Industrial Revolution began in semi-rural locations, its labor force was drawn primarily from young, (as yet) unmarried women, frequently daughters of local farmers. Some of the early factory owners built boarding houses for the women and treated them protectively, as young wards. Francis Cabot Lowell (1775–1817) built mills at Waltham, Massachusetts, on this principle. He promised the women hard work, with pay adequate to help their families and to save toward marriage. After his death, his partners extended his example by establishing a new town, Lowell, with the largest cotton mill built to that date. By the 1840s, about half the mills in New England followed this model. Factory work had its demands of order, discipline, and the clock, and the dormitory-boarding houses were somewhat crowded, but the labor historian Alice Kessler-Harris quotes approvingly the very warm assessment of the Lowell experience from one of its workers in the 1830s: it was "the first field that had ever been open to her outside of her own restricted home … the first money they earned! When they felt the jingle of silver in their pocket, there for the first time, their heads became erect and they walked as if on air."

As new machinery became heavier, as factory work became more prevalent, and as a five-year-long economic depression beginning in 1837 pressed down on both the American and British economies, the workforce shifted. Men, often farmers and immigrants, moved into the factories, displacing the women. The men demanded higher pay, which factory owners had previously hoped to avoid by hiring women. The culture of the industrializing world of that time, primarily in Britain, called for men to support their families. A young, unmarried woman might earn just enough for herself, and that would be considered adequate, but a man required a "**family wage**." The rising productivity of constantly improving machinery made this family wage possible, and it became the baseline standard for industry, although workers had to struggle for it for decades. Women were thus displaced from factory work and brought back to the home.

By the second half of the nineteenth century, "**domesticity**" became the desired norm for middle- and even working-class women and their families. Most middle-class women spent a great deal of time caring for their families and homes, and the new urban domesticity increased their level of security and comfort. Life expectancy, a basic index of well-being, rose rapidly for women in Britain, slightly more than for men. It increased from 44 years in 1890, to 52 in 1910, to 60 in 1920. Living standards began to rise and generally continued to rise into the twentieth century. New systems of ventilation, heating, lighting, indoor plumbing, and running hot and cold water contributed to domestic comfort and made life easier for those who could afford these services, although they often did not reach working-class neighborhoods.

Urban conditions made children less of an economic benefit, as they had been on family farms, and more of an economic burden. Family planning increased. Child-bearing became less frequent, freer from infection thanks to antisepsis, less painful with the use of anesthesia, and safer with the professionalization of the practice of medicine. The presence of children in the home also decreased as free, compulsory education, beginning as early as the 1830s and 1840s, began to take them to school for several hours each day.

With more time freed from traditional domestic responsibilities, some women began to enter into the array of **white-collar jobs** that were opening. The most respectable jobs provided satisfying work that also fit the culturally approved role of women as caregivers and nurturers: teaching in the new school systems and nursing in the new hospitals. Other women worked as sales personnel in the new department stores (where they also shopped), and as secretaries and clerks in the new offices, although these were primarily male occupations in the nineteenth century. A very few went into the professions: medicine, law, journalism, and business.

While domestic concerns and new technological wonders engaged the middle classes, and were desired by the working classes, for a great number of people they

KEY TERMS

family wage A wage, usually earned by a male head of household, adequate to support a family. The concept suggested that a woman's place was in the home and that the male husband–father was the family breadwinner.

domesticity An ideal that valued the woman who stayed at home, raising children, keeping the home as comfortable as possible, and making it a safe haven to which her husband could return after his daily work earning a family wage.

white-collar jobs Professional and clerical jobs; office work; clean work. This kind of occupation became more prevalent as the Industrial Revolution also created these kinds of urban, service job.

What were
the key social
changes of
the Industrial
Revolution in
Europe and
beyond?

"The New Machine for Winding up the Ladies," anon., English cartoon, c. 1840. Upper-class English women wore corsets, devices made of whalebone that constricted the waist painfully, making it appear as tiny as possible and, by contrast, accentuating the hips, buttocks, and breasts. The corsets were often so tight that they interfered with women's ability to breathe properly and encouraged "swooning." The cartoonist mocks these practices.

📖 Read the Document: John Stuart Mill on Enfranchisement of Women (1869) on MyHistoryLab

were out of reach. The 15–20 percent of adult females who had to work as principal breadwinners for themselves and their families confronted more basic problems of earning a living. The value placed on domesticity as the proper role for females, and the concomitant view that men should earn a family wage but that women needed only supplementary income, made the plight of the working woman doubly difficult. These women, often immigrants, desperately poor, and without male support, were seen no longer as proud and independent, as the first industrial women workers had been, but as unfortunate objects of sympathy and pity.

They found jobs where they could. Domestic service was most common, employing two to three times as many women as industry, even in industrialized countries. On the margins of society, other women earned a living through prostitution. In the second half of the nineteenth century, censuses in the largest cities, London and Paris, routinely reported tens of thousands of prostitutes walking the streets, serving in brothels, or, occasionally, employed in more comfortable settings by more prosperous clients. These women were condemned by conventional society, but they often found this job the only one that paid enough to enable them to support their families. Most worked only until about the age of 25, by which time they usually found other work or were married—a rosy picture painted by the middle classes, but often contradicted by working-class experience.

Economic and Political Reform

Britain's growing urban, industrial population demanded political and economic change. The government, recognizing that industrialization was transforming Britain away from its aristocratic and agrarian traditions and fearful of the consequences, responded initially by trying to repress the movement for reform. The Peterloo Massacre at St. Peter's Fields in Manchester in 1819 demonstrated the government's

What were the key social changes of the Industrial Revolution in Europe and beyond?

The Peterloo Massacre, published October 1, 1819 by Richard Carlile. Colored etching. By the early 1800s, Britain was becoming more urban and more industrial. New constituencies demonstrated for new laws, such as universal male suffrage, and cheaper imported food (corn). On August 16, 1819, the government dispatched mounted soldiers to St. Peter's Fields, Manchester, to break up a protest of 80,000 people, killing 11 and wounding 400. The etching suggests that the protestors were not a rabble, but respectable urbanites. Lines were now drawn between old, rural aristocrats and these newly rising urban interest groups.

position. A huge but peaceful demonstration by some 80,000 people called for universal male suffrage, the annual election of the House of Commons in Parliament, and the abolition of the **Corn Laws**. The Corn Laws had raised the tariff on grain to levels that effectively banned importation, thus keeping the price of basic foodstuffs high, favoring landowners and farmers at the expense of the growing urban, industrial population. Mounted soldiers, brandishing their swords, charged into the crowd of demonstrators, killing 11 and wounding some 400. The government applauded the soldiers and passed further legislation to restrict free expression.

By 1832, however, partly because of revolutions on the European continent, and partly because of riots in Britain, the mood in Parliament had changed. The Reform Act of 1832 expanded Parliamentary seats for urban constituencies and increased the number of voters by about 60 percent, although voters still totaled only about 800,000 in all of Britain. (England, Scotland, and Wales took their first official census in 1801—an important mark of an industrializing society—and registered a total population of about 10.5 million. Ireland was not included.) A far greater proportion of the new voters, however, were professionals rather than industrial workers. In 1835 Parliament enacted a Municipal Corporations Act, which reformed elections and administrations in large cities, enabling them to cope more successfully with the problems of growth and industrialization.

On some fundamental issues Parliament moved slowly, and sometimes it refused to move at all. It rejected, overwhelmingly, the petitions submitted between 1838 and 1848 by the Chartists, a national working-class organization calling for universal male suffrage, an end to property qualifications for members of Parliament, and equal electoral districts. Parliament feared that universal suffrage would bring an end to the sanctity of property and the capitalist economic system.

KEY TERM

Corn Laws Laws that restricted the import of food into England. These laws favored rural agricultural producers at the expense of urban consumers. Repealed in 1846.

In 1846, however, Parliament did repeal the Corn Laws. With this victory of the urban constituencies and the triumph of free trade, Britain gave up its policy of self-sufficiency in food and entered fully into the international trade system to purchase its food and sell its manufactured goods. A second Reform Act, in 1867, doubled the electorate to about two million, about one-third of all adult males. The Act enfranchised many urban working men, although it continued to exclude most of those agricultural and industrial workers who lived in the countryside.

The two major political parties competed for the votes of the working classes. The Liberals, under William Gladstone, began to provide universal, state-supported education (1870), and legalized labor unions (1871). The Tories, under Benjamin Disraeli, extended the acts regulating public sanitation, conditions of labor in factories and mines, and housing for the poor (1876–80). In 1884, under Gladstone, a third Reform Act doubled the electorate again. (Britain adopted universal male suffrage for men aged 21 and older in 1918.)

Women's Suffrage. While women finally gained the right to vote in both Britain and the United States after World War I, it was not without a long and often violent struggle. The Chartists had peacefully demanded that women obtain the right to vote, without success. Women's suffrage committees were formed, but legislators in Parliament rejected most of their demands. The failure to win suffrage through peaceful means led Emmeline Pankhurst and her daughter Christabel to form suffragette organizations, which became increasingly violent. Although many people abhorred the violence, many more grew sympathetic to giving women the right to vote. The participation of women in the national effort in World War I softened opposition, and in 1918 the vote was extended to British women aged 30 and over, provided they were married to householders, or met other

WOMEN'S EMANCIPATION 1790–1928	
c. 1790	Olympe de Gouges writes the polemical *Declaration of the Rights of Woman and the Citizen*
1792	Mary Wollstonecraft writes *A Vindication of the Rights of Woman*, regarded as the first manifesto of the women's movement in Britain
1794	Condorcet writes of the desirability of establishing equality of civil and political rights for men and women in *Progrès de l'esprit*
1829	*Sati* (ritual suicide by Hindu widows) is banned in India
1848	Elizabeth Cady Stanton and Lucretia Mott organize the first women's rights convention, at Seneca Falls, New York
1850	Beginnings in Britain of national agitation for women's suffrage
1857–72	Married Women's Property Acts allow British women to keep their own possessions on marriage
1866	Mott founds American Equal Rights Association
1868	First public meeting of women's suffrage movement held, in Manchester, England
1869	In Britain women ratepayers may vote in municipal elections; Cady Stanton is first president of U.S. National Woman Suffrage Association
1890	Footbinding beginning to die out in China
1903	Emmeline Pankhurst founds Women's Social and Political Union
1906	Pankhurst and her daughters launch militant campaign in Britain
1913	Suffragettes protest in Washington, DC; International Women's Peace Conference held in the Netherlands
1914–18	Women assume workplace responsibilities outside the home during World War I
1918	British women householders over 30 years granted the vote
1919	Constance de Markiewicz is the first woman elected to Parliament in Britain
1920	19th amendment to the Constitution gives U.S. women the vote
1928	British women over 21 years granted the vote

Emmeline Pankhurst with her daughter Christabel, 1908. This mother-and-daughter team founded the Women's Social and Political Union (1903), the most renowned of Britain's suffrage movements. Their campaigns were militant and disruptive. They set fire to public buildings, smashed windows, sabotaged mailboxes, slashed paintings in London's National Gallery, and pelted government officials with eggs. Emmeline was jailed repeatedly, and force-fed when she went on hunger strikes.

📖 **Read** the **Document**: "Freedom or Death" (1913) Emmeline Pankhurst on MyHistoryLab

17.1

17.2

17.3

17.4   How did workers organize during the Industrial Revolution?

17.5

The Great Procession, June 18, 1910. Not only women campaigned for their right to vote: in this procession of the Women's Social and Political Union, a hunger strikers' banner is hoisted aloft by male supporters.

qualifications of income and education. In 1928 the Representation of the People Act gave British women voting rights equal to those of men.

In the United States, women turned to conventions and voluntary associations to promote suffrage. One of the most important conventions was held in Seneca Falls, New York, in 1848. This convention called not only for the right to vote but also for increased educational and employment opportunities for women. Other conventions followed. Women first gained the right to vote in local and school board elections in some western states, and finally gained national voting rights with the ratification of the Nineteenth Amendment to the U.S. Constitution in August 1920.

📖 Read the Document: An Indian Nationalist on Hindu Women and Education (early 19th c.) on MyHistoryLab

📖 Read the Document: The Seneca Falls Convention (1848) on MyHistoryLab

Labor Movements and Socialism

17.4   How did workers organize during the Industrial Revolution?

Like women, who organized to obtain political rights, the working class organized to improve labor conditions. Social historian E.P. Thompson identifies the London Corresponding Society, founded in 1792, as perhaps "the first definitely working-class political organization formed in Britain." Workers were forbidden to unionize under the Combination Act of 1799, but in 1824 this law was repealed. Small trade unions took root, usually finding their greatest success among the better-off "aristocracy of labor"—the machinists, carpenters, printers, and spinners. Sometimes they would go on strike; politically they organized for suffrage campaigns; and some helped to organize cooperative enterprises. The right to strike was recognized officially with the Trade Union Act of 1871. Unskilled workers began increasingly to join unions, with miners and transport workers usually in the lead. By 1914, four million Britons held membership in trade unions.

17.1
17.2
17.3
17.4
17.5

How did workers organize during the Industrial Revolution?

Karl Marx and the Workers' Revolution

In Britain, workers first created their own organizations, which then gained the support of political party leaders. Elsewhere, political leaders and theorists took the lead in organizing small groups of workers. Foremost among the theoreticians was the German Karl Marx (1818–83). A well-educated journalist of Jewish ancestry, Marx called for a worker-led revolution. He organized revolutionary **socialists** through active campaigning, wrote polemical tracts calling for revolution, such as *The Communist Manifesto* (1848; with Friedrich Engels), and produced three volumes of scholarly analysis and critique of the capitalist system, *Das Kapital* (1867).

Marx began his studies in Berlin at a time when Western and Central Europe were alive with revolutionary sentiments—both of workers seeking new rights and of nationalists seeking greater political representation. Marx moved to London, where he spent the rest of his life, much of it in active scholarship in the British Museum.

He believed that wealth is produced not so much by capitalists, who control the wealth, but by the **proletariat**—the laborers—who do the actual physical work of production. Because employers do not generally accept this point of view, workers do not receive proper compensation for their contribution. Violent revolution is the only recourse "to raise the proletariat to the position of ruling class, to establish democracy." In a stirring call to this revolution, Marx and Engels created the Communist Party and prepared its manifesto, concluding: "Let the ruling classes tremble at a Communist revolution. The proletarians have nothing to lose but their chains. They have a world to win. Workingmen of all countries, unite!" (*The Communist Manifesto*, p. 44). Until the revolution would take place, Marx and Engels called for many shorter-term legislative goals, including "a heavy progressive or graduated income tax … free education for all children in public schools … and … abolition of child factory labor in its present form." Many other labor groups shared these goals, and they were subsequently adopted in almost all industrialized countries.

Marx and Engels called for the establishment of a powerful, worker-led government to assume control of the economy, and they looked forward to a still later time when the state would be unnecessary and would "wither away." They identified the state as "the organized power of one class for oppressing another," so when workers ruled the state there would be no need for further oppression and the state would vanish. Marx and Engels gave no further description of this utopia, but it would be based on their central and most radical tenet: "The theory of the Communists may be summed up in the single sentence: Abolition of private property" (p. 23). Their theory included a view of history that saw class struggle as perpetual: "The history of all hitherto existing society is the history of class struggles." The current form of the struggle was **bourgeoisie** vs. proletariat. The bourgeoisie themselves had created the proletariat by organizing the new factories that employed and exploited them. Marx condemned the sexual ethics of the bourgeoisie. Despite their official reverence for the family, Marx accused them of sexual abuse of their workers, economic perpetuation of prostitution, and wife-swapping among themselves: "Our bourgeois, not content with having the wives and daughters of their proletarians at their disposal, not to speak of common prostitutes, take the greatest pleasure in seducing each other's wives." Marx heaped scorn on religion, charging the bourgeoisie with using it as an "opiate" to divert the proletariat from its fundamental economic concerns. Marx was a materialist, arguing that economics is the basis of life; ideas and intellectual life are based on economic status: "Man's consciousness changes with every

KEY TERMS

socialist Socialists believed that too much wealth was going into the hands of the owners of property and industry, and too little to the workers who actually produced the wealth. They were divided sharply, however, about the precise definition of the problem and the appropriate paths of struggle for change.

proletariat A collective noun designating the working class that produces wealth. The singular is "proletarian."

bourgeoisie A collective noun designating the class that owns and directs the means of production. In Marxist thought, the bourgeoisie and the proletariat need each other, but are also always in conflict over the distribution of wealth.

Statue of Marx (left) and Engels, Statue Park, Budapest, Hungary. During the Cold War, when the USSR dominated the politics of Hungary, this statue sat in the capital city, Budapest. After the Cold War and the end of Russian domination, the government of Budapest collected most of the statues of communist and Russian heroes from within the city and reassembled them in Statue Park, on the suburban fringe, as a museum of a time that had, thankfully, passed.

change in the conditions of his material existence, in his social relations and in his social life … The ruling ideas of each age have ever been the ideas of its ruling class."

Marx wrote of the conflict between the roles of mother and of worker. With Engels, Marx condemned the "double oppression" of women by both capitalism and the family, but he praised capitalism for freeing women from being regarded as property. He encouraged women in their struggle for citizens' rights and economic independence. In *The Origins of the Family, Private Property, and the State* (1884), Engels argued that the form of the family was not fixed. It had evolved substantially in the past, and he proposed further, revolutionary change:

> The peculiar character of the supremacy of the husband over the wife in the modern family, the necessity of creating real social equality between them and the way to do it, will only be seen in the clear light of day when both possess legally complete equality of rights. Then it will be plain that the first condition for the liberation of the wife is to bring the whole female sex back into public industry, and that this in turn demands that the characteristic of the monogamous family as the economic unit of society be abolished. (pp. 137–38)

In retrospect, some of the most enduring criticisms made by Marx and Engels have been cultural rather than economic. They identified five critical areas of social-cultural tension during the height of the Industrial Revolution. Many of them still exist:

- the problem of coping with rapid change. *The Communist Manifesto* observed: "All that is solid melts into air";
- the alienation of factory workers from their work, as they became insignificant cogs in great systems of production;
- the alienation of workers from nature, as farmers left the countryside to find jobs in urban industries;
- the dominance of the husband over the wife in the modern family and the ending of earlier conditions of equality; and
- the economic competition that drove workers as well as owners to subordinate their own humanitarian and personal goals to the unceasing economic demands of the capitalist system.

📖 **Read** the **Document: Capitalism Challenged: The Communist Manifesto (1848) Karl Marx and Friedrich Engels** on **MyHistoryLab**

Labor Organizations

The year 1848, when *The Communist Manifesto* was published, saw political and economic rioting across much of Europe. In part, people were reacting against the three decades of political conservatism that had reigned over Europe since the end of the Napoleonic wars. In part, the working classes were beginning a long, sustained revolt against the hardships of the new industrial system. In the United States, too, workers

17.1

17.2

17.3

17.4 How did workers organize during the Industrial Revolution?

17.5

580

17.1

17.2

17.3

17.4

How did workers
organize during
the Industrial
Revolution?

17.5

protested and organized. 1848 was not so much the turning point here; 1865, the end of the Civil War in the United States, was more significant. The struggles in Europe, and especially France, were far more violent, but America, too, saw blood in the streets.

Austria and Germany. In central Europe, protesting students and workers briefly took control of Prague and Vienna in 1848 and then were suppressed in both cities by regular forces of the Austrian army at the cost of thousands of casualties. In Prussia, in the same year, worker demands for more democracy and more worker rights joined with demands for a new constitution that would lead toward the creation of a new nation of Germany from the merger of Prussia with the many small German-speaking states of the former Holy Roman Empire. At first it appeared that the Prussian king, Frederick William IV (r. 1840–61), would grant these demands. A Constituent Assembly was convened in Frankfurt to write a new German constitution. In the end, however, the king reasserted his divine right to rule and rejected the constitution. Under these circumstances, the smaller states refused to join in a unified government. Conservative forces remained in control of central Europe.

A new wave of labor unrest and strikes swept across the region in the late 1860s and early 1870s, signaling the growing strength of labor. In the newly created Germany, chief minister Otto von Bismarck (1815–98) pursued diverse and sometimes conflicting strategies to keep working people allied to his government. He extended universal male suffrage to the North German Confederation in 1867 and then to all of Germany when he unified the country in 1871. But he limited the power of the legislature and diluted the power of the vote so that government ministers remained responsible to the king, not to Parliament. When Germany's opposition Social Democratic Party (SPD) became Europe's first political party based on the working classes, in 1875, Bismarck sharply restricted its organizational activities.

On the other hand, declaring, "I too am a socialist," Bismarck passed legislation providing workers' disability and accident insurance and, in the 1880s, the first compulsory social security system in Europe. This legislation, however, covered only male industrial workers, not women or children. The SPD created a separate organizational structure for women, which had enlisted 174,751 women members by 1914, the largest movement of women in Europe. However, the number includes not only women seeking independent expression, but also those who sought to ally themselves with their husbands as members of the party. Working women's organizations were undercut by the opposition of male unionized workers, who feared that the women would take away their jobs or, at least, increase the labor pool and thus drive down wages. Even so, thanks to government policies, worker militancy, and the example of Britain's painful experiences, Germany did not repeat the worst conditions of child and female labor, and of the excessive hours and brutal conditions of industrial work.

📖 **Read** the **Document**: **Socialism: The Gotha Program (1875)** on **MyHistoryLab**

France. Worker revolts broke out repeatedly in France, many of them inspired by the French revolutionary tradition and others by the low wages and poor working conditions that characterized French industry. Skilled artisans, displaced by new industries, often organized these revolts. Even before the Industrial Revolution took root, worker and artisan revolts played a leading role in the French Revolution—and were crushed along with it. They boiled over again in 1848, first in a revolt against the monarchy of Louis Philippe (r. 1830–48). In response, a provisional republic was proclaimed, followed by the establishment of government-sponsored workshops to provide employment for the poor. A new, far more conservative government was elected, however, and it closed the workshops in Paris. The poor people of the city barricaded city streets, and the army was called out. More than 10,000 people were killed or injured in the ensuing street riots.

17.1
17.2
17.3
17.4
17.5

How did workers organize during the Industrial Revolution?

Massacre of the Paris Radicals, Edouard Manet. The slaughter meted out to the Paris Commune of 1871 is graphically depicted by the post-Impressionist painter Manet. Left-wing urban leaders tried to set up their own state-within-a-state, but the communards were put down brutally by the national government. At least 20,000 were summarily executed and over 40,000 were taken prisoner. (Museum Folkwang, Essen)

Later in the century, the revolts were increasingly dominated by industrial workers. In 1871, much of the potential leadership of a workers' movement was once again wiped out. The French national government killed at least 20,000 people and exiled another 10,000 in the Paris Commune, an uprising of urban leaders in Paris.

After the revolt of 1848, Napoleon III commissioned Baron Haussmann (1809–91) to redesign the city of Paris to break down older, smaller neighborhoods, in which revolt had incubated, and to replace them with the large, glorious, easily policed boulevards of the modern French capital. After 1871, that project expanded. Ironically, the revolts resulted in the deaths of tens of thousands of the poor and oppressed and the stunning urban redesign of one of the most beautiful cities in the world.

A decade later, some of the exiles from the Paris Commune returned and organization began again, this time with greater success. In 1884 *syndicats*, or labor unions, were legalized. Two competing federations were formed, one calling primarily for mutual help, the other for political action. Together, they numbered 140,000 members in 1890, a figure that more than quadrupled to 580,000 by the end of the century. By 1909, an umbrella group, the Confédération Génerale de Travail, numbered nearly a million. In 1890, May 1 was recognized as an annual "Labor Day." French politics, however, was dominated by the wealthier business leaders. Industrial workers organized, but they commanded less influence than farmers, shopkeepers, and small businessmen.

The United States. In the United States, labor began to organize especially with the industrialization that began after the Civil War (1861–65). A number of craft unions joined together to form the National Labor Union in 1866, which claimed 300,000 members by the early 1870s. The Noble Order of the Knights of Labor, founded as a secret society in 1869, grew into a mass union, open to all workers, with 700,000 members in 1886. America's most successful labor organization was the American Federation of Labor, a union of skilled craftworkers, founded in 1886 by Samuel Gompers (1850–1924). Its membership grew to a million by 1900 and two million by 1914. Women were not allowed to join, but in 1900 the International Ladies Garment Workers Union, which organized male and female workers who made women's clothing, was formed—with men dominating its leadership.

A series of strikes in America throughout the 1890s led to violence, sometimes in response to falling wages, often in response to poor working conditions or to the excessive control of workers' lives by managers and owners. Hired detectives, local police, and even soldiers attacked strikers and were attacked in return. Steel workers near Pittsburgh lost the Homestead Steel strike in 1892, when the governor of Pennsylvania sent in 8,000 troops. A strike at the Pullman Palace Car Company in Chicago ended when a court injunction forced the workers back to their jobs. In the ensuing violence, scores of workers were killed. In resolving a strike of hat makers in 1908, the United States Supreme Court ruled that trade union members were personally liable for business losses suffered during strikes. Until this ruling was reversed in the 1930s, militant unionism was virtually dead.

The United States did develop powerful labor organizations, mostly in the twentieth century, but, in contrast with Britain and other European nations, it never produced a significant political party based primarily on labor. Historians cite several reasons: labor organization in the United States was fragmented into craft-specific unions; in this nation of immigrants, workers also held multiple identities, and their ethnic identities frequently inhibited them from building union solidarity with those of other ethnic groups; many immigrants came to America to earn money and return home, and so did not commonly develop a commitment to active unionization; pay scales and working conditions in the United States were significantly better than in Europe, further muting worker grievances; and, finally, the capitalist ideology of the country discouraged class divisions, and the government restricted labor organization.

Workers in the Nonindustrialized World

Wherever they reached, the new industrial products displaced old handicraft industries and workers. The craftsmen could not compete with the speed, consistent quality, and low price of the machine-made products. Many of them were ruined. The Indian cotton textile industry provided the most striking example. In 1834–35, the highest-ranking British official in India lamented: "The bones of the cotton weavers are bleaching the plains of India." Lord Bentinck's remark was especially true in Bengal, eastern India, a region that had participated heavily in the export trade, but to some degree it rang true throughout India. And as a general observation on the fate of handicraft workers, the comment correctly captured the problem globally. Many of the displaced workers were pushed into agricultural work, especially as their countries could no longer compete as exporters of (hand-) manufactured goods and were transformed into exporters of raw materials and importers of finished manufactures. Some could find jobs in other crafts, not yet overtaken by the new industries. Some could continue their old crafts by cutting back farther and farther on their meager profits and incomes in order to try to compete with the machines. A few could produce fine handicrafts for the specialized luxury market. In the industrializing world, too, artisans were also displaced, but the rapidly expanding industries could absorb many of them. The craftspeople mourned the devaluation of their handicraft skills. The cold, standardized rhythms of the machines wore down their spirits. But they had jobs and, as industrialization increased productivity, their incomes rose. Countries without much industrialization fared much worse.

SOURCE

Tariffs, Wealth, and Poverty: Reflections on America and India by Pandita Ramabai

Pandita Ramabai (1858–1922) traveled in the United States for three years, 1886–89, and on her return home published a travelogue in Marathi. Translated literally as *The Peoples of the United States*, it has been published in English as *Pandita Ramabai's American Encounter*. In India, Ramabai was a pioneering reformer for women's education. American women impressed her for their public accomplishments individually and in the groups they often organized. Indeed, the whole country impressed her. One of the areas in which America compared most favorably with India was in its control of its own tariff policy. American industry did so well, Ramabai argues, because it closed its markets to imports that might be competitive. She criticizes the Indian people for not similarly excluding foreign competitive goods, but she does not give any indication of recognizing that America was free to set its own exclusionary tariffs; India, under British colonial rule, had no such freedom. Her audience, however, would surely have understood that. Or was Ramabai urging her fellow Indians simply to boycott foreign goods voluntarily—to say no—even without formal tariffs? Some Indian nationalists of her time were beginning to argue for that, and by the early twentieth century, this would be the official position of the Indian National Congress, as we shall see in the chapter entitled "China and India." Ramabai contrasted the prosperity of the United States with that of India:

The goods which come into this country from foreign countries are charged a heavy customs duty … The people here take great precautions to prevent the domination of foreign countries in trade and in other matters, and to prevent their becoming slaves of others … This is worth remembering by the people of our country who look to England for everything, who rely entirely on England, and who use English goods to the detriment of native industries and trade. The American said that drinking the tea and wearing the clothes imported from England harms the industries of his country; therefore he would never drink such tea or wear English clothes, but would content himself with whatever good or bad clothes were available in his own country. And he also acted accordingly. That is why this country has reached such prosperity today. And what have we achieved? We have given our gold and bought pots of pewter in return; we have shut down our handlooms and started wearing cheap English clothes. Like the Indians of North America, we have succumbed to the lure of shiny, colored glass beads; and we have sold our precious gem-studded land to foreigners in return for glass beads and glass bottles filled with wine. Now we are screaming because the wine has started to claim our lives, and the fragments of broken glass have made gaping wounds in our feet. This is why our country is in such a wretched state! This clearly shows that the United States and India are on opposite sides of the globe! (Ramabai, p. 227)

17.1
17.2
17.3
17.4 How did workers organize during the Industrial Revolution?
17.5

Indentured Labor. In some of the poorest countries—most notably India and China—indentured labor away from home (see the chapter entitled "Migration") became an alternative to unemployment for a wide range of peoples. Between 1831 and 1921, about two million people made their way from India and China and, to a lesser extent, from Africa, the Pacific Islands, and Japan, as indentured laborers to work primarily in sugar plantations around the world. Four factors encouraged this mass migration. First, the end of slavery forced a search for alternative sources of labor. Slavery did not end all at once, with the British ban on the slave trade in 1807, nor with Britain's outlawing slavery in its colonies in 1833. It continued in the United States until 1863, in Cuba until 1886, and in Brazil until 1888. (Illegally, slavery continues today in many locations and in many different forms.) After the formal end of slavery, many slaves continued to labor in conditions of semi-slavery. Nevertheless, the system was finished and a new source of labor was needed to supplement the quasi-slave population that continued. Second, the production of sugar increased globally, and dramatically, throughout the nineteenth century, from 300,000 tons in 1790 to ten million tons in 1914. Laborers were required even beyond the number of slaves previously employed in its cultivation and harvest.

Third, imperial reach connected far-flung regions of the world, making possible this international flow of labor. Indian indentured laborers traveling to the West Indies, Mauritius, or Fiji remained within a single imperial system, with relatively similar laws, a single language of rule, and established systems of transportation and communication. Some 1.3 million of them made the move. Similarly, indentured laborers from France's West African colonies migrating to the French Caribbean, or to Réunion in the Indian Ocean, moved within a single system. The 387,000 Chinese who emigrated under terms of indenture—the majority of them to Cuba and Peru—were less tied into a single empire, but they were part of the global economic system that the Europeans had developed. This was also true for the 65,000 Japanese who migrated to Hawaii. The fourth element in the indentured traffic was the technological capacity to move so many people around the globe, forth and back, because the indentures of the servants were for limited periods (usually five to seven years), after which they might go "back home." Sometimes they were encouraged to return, sometimes not.

The indentured laborers were not displaced persons in the industrial system as the craftsmen were. Most were farm laborers to begin with, but it was the industrial system that created the mechanisms of the indenture system. Many observers compared the conditions of gang labor on sugar plantations to the rigors and routinization of the factory floor. The overwhelming majority of the servants were male, although the absence of females was probably tempered by the knowledge that after five or seven years the men might return home to establish family life. Many observers thought the women who did sign on as indentured laborers were mostly prostitutes. Some were, but most, like the men, recognized that even the low pay of the overseas indentured laborer was at least double that of the Indian or Chinese agricultural worker. They signed on in order to try to improve their situation. Although indentured servitude had some of the attributes of slavery, it was for a limited time, and thus offered the prospect of freedom at the end of years of indenture. For many it was a trap, but for some it was an escape.

17.1
17.2
17.3
17.4
17.5

How did workers organize during the Industrial Revolution?

Chinese Cheap Labor, published in *Every Saturday*, July 29, 1871. Wood engraving. The engraving depicts workers on the Milloudon Sugar Plantation, Louisiana. As slavery was abolished, region by region, around the world, plantation owners often attempted to replace the now-freed slaves with cheap laborers, especially from India and China. By 1870, some 2,000 Chinese were working in the cotton fields of Mississippi and Arkansas, and on plantations and shrimp farms in Louisiana. Although hundreds of thousands of indentured laborers came to such areas as the Caribbean, altering the balance of local population significantly, in the United States the experiment failed as workers and employers clashed over rights and pay. Indenture was illegal in the United States after 1867, and the Chinese Exclusion Act kept out cheap Chinese labor after 1882.

📖 **Read** the **Document**: **Lee Chew, "Life of a Chinese Immigrant" (1903)** on **MyHistoryLab**

New Patterns of Urban Life

17.5 How did patterns of urban life change?

The core habitat of industrialization was the city. During the eighteenth century, cities began a period of growth that has continued without break until today. In the largest cities, by the late 1800s this process began to include middle-class suburbanization, which was made possible by the new railroad transportation systems for goods and passengers. In the early twentieth century, automobiles, buses, and trucks enlarged the system to ever-greater dimensions.

Much of the urban growth in the nineteenth century was a direct result of industrialization. The steam engine, which could be constructed anywhere, made the location of industries more flexible. Factories sprang up near ports, at inland transportation hubs, in the heart of locations rich in raw materials (such as the Midlands of England, Silesia in central Europe, Hubei Province in China, and Bihar in India), and near large concentrations of consumers, such as the great cities of Paris, London, Buenos Aires, and São Paulo. New industrial metropolises dotted the map.

Immigrants streamed into the new cities for jobs, as the balance between urban and rural populations tilted continuously cityward. Farmers became factory workers and so did the children of artisans. All found the new industrial city shocking. As they exchanged the lifestyles of farm and workshop for regimes of routinization, standardization, and regulation, they discovered that the skills they had previously mastered were of little use. At the same time, opportunities beckoned: cultural, educational, recreational, social, and, most important, economic. In the early years of the Industrial Revolution, conditions of labor and of public health were abysmal; later, as

SOURCE

Diverse Perspectives

Like the proverbial elephant that appeared different to each person who approached it from a different perspective, the industrial city signified something different to each observer. Wordsworth and Blake (see Source box, above) saw early nineteenth-century London very differently. From the middle of the century, poets from other cities provide still different views.

Charles Baudelaire (1821–67) presents the hardworking people of Paris—indeed the city itself—as just struggling to get by at the break of a new day:

Parisian Scenes: Daybreak

The crow of a rooster, far off, cuts through the hazy air.
A sea of fog bathes the buildings.
Men in agony in the workhouses
Heave their dying breath in undignified gasps.
The debauched return home, broken by their work.
The shivering dawn robed in pink and green
Advances slowly along the deserted Seine,
And somber, aging, Paris, rubbing its eyes,
Picks up its tools, and goes back to work.

Charles Baudelaire

While Baudelaire was anguished with his city's lonely despair, in the United States Walt Whitman (1819–92) sang rapturously of the dynamism of his own Manhattan, New York:

Mannahatta

… The down-town streets, the jobbers' houses of business, the
  houses of business of the
ship-merchants and money-brokers, the river-streets,
Immigrants arriving, fifteen or twenty thousand in a week,
The carts hauling goods, the manly race of drivers of horses, the
  brown-faced sailors,
The summer air, the bright sun shining, and the sailing clouds
  aloft,
The winter snows, the sleigh-bells, the broken ice in the river,
  passing along up or down
with the flood-tide or ebb-tide,
The mechanics of the city, the masters, well-form'd, beautiful
  faced, looking you straight in the eyes,
Trottoirs throng'd, vehicles, Broadway, the women, the shops
  and shows,
A million people—manners free and superb—open voices—
  hospitality—the most
courageous and friendly young men,
City of hurried and sparkling waters! City of spires and masts!
City nested in bays! My city! …

Walt Whitman

Back Queen Street, Deansgate, Manchester, *Illustrated London News*, 1862. As this drawing of the housing conditions of the Manchester cotton operatives shows, accommodation in this city could be spartan. Manchester, in particular, with its high mortality rate, desperately needed the attentions of voluntary agencies that were attempting to better the living conditions of those who had been drawn to work in the new industries. Despite the fact that many workers emigrated to the United States or to British colonies overseas, the population continued to grow at a great rate, with adverse consequences for public health and housing.

productivity increased, workers organized, employers and governments paid heed, and conditions started to improve. "City lights" began to be more attractive. The nineteenth century began the age of global urbanization.

The Nature of the City

Philosophical and sociological speculations on the nature of the city flourished. In Germany, Max Weber (1864–1920) analyzed the modern industrial city as a new creation. He contrasted, negatively, its freewheeling life and amorphous institutions against the close-knit guilds and political and religious associations of earlier self-governing European cities, especially medieval cities (see the chapter entitled "The Opening of the Atlantic and the Pacific"). Weber concluded that the sprawling industrial city—open to any immigrant who wished to come and embedded within a nation-state that controlled its life and politics—was quite different from, and less humane than, the self-contained city of earlier times. Europe, at least, was living in a new era.

Many observers agreed, apprehensively. To them the openness of the new industrial city and the lack of institutional ties among its citizens seemed to be leading to breakdowns of both the social fabric and the individual personality. The division of labor was turning the individual into a specialist concerned only with narrow interests; the sense of personal or community wholeness was lost. And the sheer multitude of people and experiences in the city was also forcing the individual to retreat even further into a small, private niche. The urban dweller, they felt, was evolving into a person swift of intellect to achieve his own needs, but lacking concern for and integration with the larger community.

Some observers claimed to see the negative effects of urban individualism as part of an historical process that would ultimately lead to disaster. Oswald Spengler (1880–1936), a German philosopher of history, declared that the enormous "world-cities" of his day were inevitably destroying the spirit of the folk peoples that had built them. Such attacks on urban life perpetuated the centuries-old cultural struggle between the cosmopolitan city of businessmen and the (perhaps imagined) homogeneous countryside of the common folk.

Many scholars believed that quantitative statistical studies would enable both residents of the industrial city and their observers to understand most clearly the

17.1
17.2
17.3
17.4
17.5

How did patterns of urban life change?

587

How did patterns
of urban life
change?

processes through which they were living and to make plans for future directions. Just as accurate measurement and assessment had helped to bring in the industrial era, so they helped in its evaluation. Two men—Adna Ferrin Weber, an academic researcher, and Charles Booth, a businessman who wanted to understand the problems of urban poverty in order to combat them—launched quite different, exemplary, quantitative studies of the city that inspired public action as well as further research (see How Do We Know? box, opposite). With such studies as these, the new academic discipline of sociology—the formal study of humans in society—grew in importance.

📖 **Read** the **Document**: **Advice on Keeping Children on the Farm (1881)** on **MyHistoryLab**

Living in the City

In the United States, with millions of immigrants streaming into cities in search of industrial jobs, urban diversity was accepted, even valued, and certainly studied. Scholars at the University of Chicago examined their own city, the world's fastest-growing industrial metropolis of the day, studying neighborhoods as well as the metropolis as a whole.

The "Chicago School of urban ecology" argued that urbanites did not live their lives downtown, as so many previous scholars had implied, but in local neighborhoods, each of which had its own characteristics. Within these neighborhoods, people's lives were not so disconnected, isolated, or alienated as they might appear superficially. At the end of the day, most people went back to their own homes in their own neighborhoods, places where they had a strong sense of self and community. The variety of social and economic lifestyles multiplied with the size of the city and the diversity of its functions. Neighborhoods reflected this diversity.

Paris, a Rainy Day, Gustave Caillebotte, 1876–77. An Impressionist's-eye-view of life in an urban setting. Although a number of studies suggest that the burgeoning urban development of the turn of the century ground down the poor, for the bourgeoisie, with leisure time on their hands, cities provided a backdrop for pleasure. (Art Institute, Chicago)

HOW DO WE KNOW?

Quantifying the Conditions of Industrial Urbanization

"The most remarkable social phenomenon of the present century is the concentration of population in cities." These words open *The Growth of Cities in the Nineteenth Century* by Adna Ferrin Weber (no relation to Max Weber), published in 1899, the first comprehensive quantitative study of the subject. More than a century later, it remains an invaluable introduction to the central topics. In the rivalry between city and countryside, Weber generally paid tribute to the role of the city:

> In the last half-century [1848–98], all the agencies of modern civilization have worked together to abolish this rural isolation; the cities have torn down their fortifications, which separated them from the open country; while the railways, the newspaper press, freedom of migration and settlement, etc., cause the spread of the ideas originating in the cities and lift the people of the rural districts out of their state of mental stagnation. Industry is also carried on outside of the cities, so that the medieval distinction between town and country has lost its meaning in the advanced countries. (pp. 7–8)

Apart from their cultural contributions, cities and industry were needed to absorb the surplus growth of rural population. In most of Europe, except France, Weber writes, "the rural populations, by reason of their continuous increase, produce a surplus which must migrate either to the cities or foreign lands" (p. 67). Without cities and industrial jobs, what would happen to this surplus population? This implied rhetorical question continues to be relevant in our own day.

Weber began with a statistical summary and an analysis of levels of urbanization in his own time, and traced it back through the nineteenth century. As part of his research, he attempted global coverage, and he gathered his data from official government publications as well as unofficial population estimates from around the world. In general, he found industrialization the main reason for city growth. England and Wales, 62 percent urban, were by far the most industrialized and the most urbanized regions on earth. The next closest were Australia, at 42 percent, and various parts of Germany, at about 30 percent. In general, the largest cities were growing fastest. London, the world's largest city in 1890, held 4.2 million people; New York, the second largest, 2.7 million. The least industrialized countries were the least urbanized—below ten percent—but most of these countries did not maintain statistical records.

In contrast to the gloom of poverty and oppression pictured by Marx and Engels a half-century earlier, Weber radiated optimism about the direction of urban life, including increasing levels of longevity and personal comfort. Describing conditions that only the wealthiest could enjoy, he wrote:

> Consider the conveniences at the disposal of the *fin de siècle* [end of the century] housewife: a house with a good part of

the old-fashioned portable furniture built into it, e.g., china cabinets, refrigerators, wardrobes, sideboards, cheval glasses [full-length, swivel mirrors], bath tubs, etc.; electric lights, telephones and electric buttons in every room, automatic burglar alarms, etc. … [Weber then quotes another urban advocate:] Thus has vanished the necessity for drawing water, hewing wood, keeping a cow, churning, laundering clothes, cleaning house, beating carpets, and very much of the rest of the onerous duties of housekeeping, as our mothers knew it. (pp. 218–20)

A judicious scholar, Weber did not omit the many negative aspects of city life at the end of the nineteenth century. Although death rates in the city had been declining steadily, urban death rates in 1899 remained higher than rural ones in most countries. In one of the worst examples, during the decade 1880–90, when the expected length of life at birth for all of England and Wales was 47 years, in Manchester, one of the greatest centers of the early Industrial Revolution, it was 29. Industrialization exacted its costs. Nevertheless, Weber reviewed the public health measures, such as water and sewerage systems and the provision of clinics, that had already been effective in other places, strongly advocated more of them, and remained optimistic about the urban future—if urbanites could cooperate for the common good.

Weber's pioneering statistical work gives us one flavor of industrial urbanization at the end of the nineteenth century. Charles Booth (1840–1916) gives quite another. Booth led a team of researchers in London, which produced the 17 volumes of *Life and Labour of the People in London*. Between 1886 and 1903, Booth and his colleagues systematically visited thousands of homes throughout London, interviewing workers to discover how the working people of the metropolis labored and lived. They concentrated their efforts in East London, the most industrialized, and most distressed, area of the city. The researchers asked questions about such critical issues as occupations, levels of income and consumption, housing size and quality, quantity and quality of amenities. They began with these statistical questions and proceeded to qualitative discussion of the neighborhoods and their character. They concluded by asking what was being done, and what could be done, to improve conditions, especially through religious institutions.

- For Weber and for Booth, what was the relationship between formal, quantitative study of the city, and action to deal with its problems?
- How might Weber's global research be integrated with Booth's local, community research? How might the research of one influence the research of the other?
- Based on other readings from this chapter, what, if anything, is surprising about the findings of Weber and Booth?

A comprehensive perspective on the city would have to take account of neighborhoods as well as business districts. These commercial areas were themselves quickly increasing in size, complexity, and facilities. By the 1870s, department stores,

Guaranty Building in Buffalo, New York, designed by Louis Henry Sullivan, 1894–96. Sullivan's designs for steel-frame construction of large buildings—made possible because steel was now readily available and the elevator had been invented—were the forerunners of today's skyscrapers. Sullivan's working principle that "form follows function" applied to the tall buildings (up to ten stories in the late nineteenth century) he designed. It was important to maximize the limited space in city centers, and the idea of carrying buildings upward instead of outward met the need.

17.1

17.2

17.3

17.4

17.5 How did patterns of urban life change?

KEY TERM

garden city self-contained planned town combining work, residential, agricultural, and recreational facilities, and surrounded by a rural belt.

coffeehouses, pubs, and restaurants had added urbanity to the central business district, attracting retail shoppers, window shoppers, and people with some leisure time. Theaters, concert houses, museums, the press and publishing houses, libraries, clubs, and a multitude of new voluntary associations provided culture and entertainment. They also created a "public sphere"—a setting in which citizens form and circulate their most influential civic ideas, goals, and aspirations. Here was the modern analogue of the ancient Greek *agora*.

A new transportation system made possible this specialization of commercial, cultural, industrial, and residential neighborhoods within the city. London opened its first underground railway system in 1863, the first major subway system in the world, and others followed. From the 1870s, commuter railways began to service new suburbs, and electric trolleys came into service after 1885. The availability of steel at commercial prices made possible the construction of skyscrapers, and the invention of elevators made them accessible. The first skyscrapers rose in the 1880s, beginning with ten-story buildings in Chicago.

📖 **Read** the **Document**: George Waring, "Sanitary Conditions in New York" (1897) on **MyHistoryLab**

Urban Planning

Out of the many examinations of urban living, town planning as a profession was born. One of the central problems of the industrializing city of the early nineteenth century was overcrowding. Poor ventilation, inadequate sanitation, polluted water, alienation from nature, and poor health—especially tuberculosis—resulted as densities in urban cores reached, and even surpassed, 100,000 people per square mile. By the last decades of the century the electric trolley cars and commuter railways offered the means to reduce population densities through suburbanization, and the city expanded in area as never before. At first the density in the center did not appear to diminish, for the stream of new immigrants to the city matched and even exceeded those who were suburbanizing.

By the late 1800s, town planners began seeking comprehensive solutions to the new problem: How to provide space for population increase, allow for geographical expansion, yet continue to provide green space, while fostering participation in both the local community and the metropolis as a whole? The British reformer Ebenezer Howard (1850–1928) proposed a "Group of Slumless Smokeless Cities": a provocative concept of a region of 250,000 people on 66,000 acres (about 13 square miles). This would have been far too miniature to cope with the problems of a London or a New York. Its intense control over the planning process also demanded political decisions that might not be possible within a participatory democracy. Nevertheless, the **garden city** concept of a core city ringed by separate suburbs, each set in a green belt, linked to one another by rapid transit, provided provocative, creative, somewhat utopian thinking for the new urban problems dawning with the new century.

The Industrial Revolution:
What Difference Does It Make?

By the beginning of the twentieth century, the Industrial Revolution had brought unprecedented wealth and power to those who had mastered its technology—especially the rulers and elites of the nations of Western Europe and the United States. Applying inanimate power, where previously there had been only humans and animals, brought new productivity. Agriculture changed first, through enclosures and new agricultural practices, becoming both more intensive and more extensive, so that fewer farmers could feed more people, freeing—and forcing—many of their fellow workers to leave their farms for urban, industrial jobs. In the cities, steam power and, later, electrical power enabled factories and the new goods they produced to multiply.

Families were restructured in the new urban, industrial settings, with changing relationships between husbands and wives, and more formal schooling for children. Women raised their voices, demanding an equality that they had felt on the family farm and were in danger of losing on the factory floor and in the urban household, with its smaller family groups, greater longevity, and proportionately fewer years spent raising children.

Railway tracks and steamship lines girdled the earth, and the oceans were connected by canals. Electricity lit up the night, provided the bright lights of the city, powered telephones and telegraphs, and supplied energy to factories and homes in remote areas. With a feeling of self-satisfied triumphalism, the masters of this industrializing world conquered much of the land surface of the globe and made it their colonial possession, thus bringing remote areas into the web of the industrial world, whether they wished to be there or not.

In the industrialized countries, the earlier years of poverty, insecurity, filth, and high death rates for industrial workers seemed to be passing as increasing productivity provided more material benefits, unions provided representation, and governments began to legislate in their favor—although the battles for workers' welfare were far from over. Antagonism between captains of industry and their workers continued.

Millions of people were on the move, from village to city, from country to country, and from continent to continent. Most traveled as free immigrants, but almost ten million people from poorer countries traveled as indentured laborers to supply the still-flourishing plantations of the world in the aftermath of the abolition of slavery. New kinds of social relationships formed among industrial workers as they arrived in new urban neighborhoods, with opportunities and constraints quite different from those they left behind in their rural homes. They were living in a world transformed, and now they were transforming themselves by building new kinds of community along with their neighbors, friends, and coworkers. In studying these industrial migrants and workers, the academic discipline of sociology was born and flourished.

The Industrial Revolution restructured the world profoundly, as thoroughly as the agricultural revolution had done some 15,000 years earlier. Today we speak of living in a postindustrial world. Our sources of energy, our means of transportation and communication, our international and intercontinental connectivity, our cities, our political institutions, our levels of technical and professional education, our family and gender relationships are in many respects different from those at the height of the Industrial Revolution, yet they are all built on the transformations of that era. Those of us who live in countries that went through the Industrial Revolution still live with its infrastructure. Those of us who live in countries that did not directly experience the full weight of that revolution—in large parts of Africa and Asia, in particular—are now trying to understand which parts of it we must recreate in order to cope with the modern world, and which parts we may "leapfrog," finding a new way of achieving some of the benefits of that revolution without going directly through it; establishing networks of cell-phone communication, for example, and using that technology, without ever establishing a network of landlines, with all their infrastructure and expense; connecting remote areas by air without ever establishing a network of railway lines. While one group is emerging from the Industrial Revolution, another may be attempting to bypass it.

CHAPTER REVIEW

THE INDUSTRIAL REVOLUTION IN BRITAIN, 1700–1860

17.1 What events gave birth to the Industrial Revolution?

The Industrial Revolution began in Britain, where agriculture had already become productive enough to free up people for non-farming occupations. Inventors crafted simple new machinery and small changes, at first, in the way people worked. The economic potential of their new inventions attracted investment from established businessmen so they could continue to build equipment that improved agricultural productivity; to produce machines, such as the steam engine; to mechanize the cotton textile industry; and to create the railroad industry and a globe-spanning network of steamships. Soon, Britain had become "the workshop of the world."

INDUSTRIALIZATION—STAGE TWO, 1860–1914

17.2 How did the Industrial Revolution transform societies and politics around the world?

The main technological advances of the second industrial revolution were in steel, chemicals, and electricity. World productivity was transformed, and so were the balances of power among nations. As the profits of the business classes multiplied, their power grew, too. Cartels formed to produce electronic equipment and chemicals. Financiers looked for new chances to build businesses around the globe; in the Americas, especially, British investors backed new industrialists. Such backing gave the monied classes more power than ever, and governments relied on the power of industrialists and businesspeople to increase their own strength internationally. The balance of wealth and power in the world shifted, for the first time, toward Europe, and especially toward Britain.

INDUSTRIAL SOCIETY

17.3 What were the key social changes of the Industrial Revolution in Europe and beyond?

There were multiple transformations as a result of the Industrial Revolution, in where people lived and worked; in family size, composition, and daily life; and in the role of women in society. Despite the rise of national wealth, the profits did not trickle down: workers often lived in squalor and poverty; 6-year-old children worked in coalmines for 14 hours a day. By the "second stage," legislation regulated child labor, and free, compulsory education got them into school for several hours a day. New laws concerning public health provided for sewerage, sanitation, and a clean water supply. As more men entered into industrial jobs and organizations, they won the right to vote, a right not yet extended to women.

LABOR MOVEMENTS AND SOCIALISM

17.4 How did workers organize during the Industrial Revolution?

When the law forbidding Britain's workers to unionize was repealed in 1824, small trade unions formed, made up of machinists, carpenters, printers, and spinners. Workers organized suffrage campaigns (for both male and female voting rights); organized cooperative enterprises; and sometimes went on strike. With the Trade Union Act of 1871, the right to strike was made official. Miners and transportation workers began to join unions, and by 1914, four million Britons belonged to trade unions.

The 1848 publication of *The Communist Manifesto*, by Karl Marx and Friedrich Engels, coincided with the beginning of a sustained struggle against the hardships and inequalities of the new industrial system. Worker revolts broke out across Europe and the United States. Meanwhile, workers in the nonindustrialized world suffered as they attempted to compete with machines by cutting their profits, or else were displaced entirely. Millions of poor people in the world's poorer regions, especially India, China, and Africa, signed on as indentured laborers in plantations especially in the Caribbean, but also in the Indian Ocean islands. They took the place of slaves who had been emancipated.

NEW PATTERNS OF URBAN LIFE

17.5 How did patterns of urban life change?

Cities grew enormously during the Industrial Revolution. Millions streamed into the cities to find work, as farmers and artisans turned into workers in the new factories. Department stores, coffeehouses, and pubs sprang up; museums, libraries, and clubs offered a new public sphere in which residents could meet and circulate. Skyscrapers enabled business enterprises to rise upward as well as outward. In these crowded industrializing cities, residents endured inadequate ventilation, inadequate sanitation, and polluted water. Tuberculosis spread. By the end of the nineteenth century, inventions such as the electric trolley car and the commuter railroad were making it possible for populations to spread out a bit, which reduced urban overcrowding, expanding the geography of cities, and leaving a core city surrounded by a ring of suburbs.

Suggested Readings

PRINCIPAL SOURCES

Adas, Michael, ed. *Islamic and European Expansion* (Philadelphia, PA: Temple University Press, 1993). Excellent anthology of historiographical articles that introduce modern world history. Several articles on the period of the Industrial Revolution and its effects on men and women.

Headrick, Daniel R. *The Tools of Empire* (New York: Oxford University Press, 1981). The Industrial Revolution gave to Europeans the tools to create empire: weapons, steamships, and quinine.

Marx, Karl, and Friedrich Engels. *The Communist Manifesto* (New York: International Publishers, 1948). The great critique of the evils of industrial capitalism and a revolutionary agenda to overthrow it.

Stearns, Peter N. *The Industrial Revolution in World History* (Boulder, CO: Westview Press, 1993). Excellent introduction to the background, development, and significance of the Industrial Revolution in global scope and historical time depth.

Thompson, E.P. *The Making of the English Working Class* (New York: Vintage, 1966). Thompson taught us to see the working class not only in Marxist terms but also in cultural terms, to understand their lives as more than just revolutionary fighters.

ADDITIONAL SOURCES

Andrea, Alfred, and James Overfield, eds. *The Human Record*, vol. 2 (Boston, MA: Houghton Mifflin, 6th ed., 2008). Excellent anthology for world history.

Bairoch, Paul. *Cities and Economic Development*, trans. Christopher Braider (Chicago, IL: University of Chicago Press, 1988). Heavily quantitative assessment of cities' role in economic development.

Bell, Susan Groag, and Karen M. Offen, eds. *Women, the Family, and Freedom: The Debate in Documents*, vol. 1, *1750–1880* (Stanford, CA: Stanford University Press, 1985). Excellent selection of documents on the feminist movement, with insightful commentary.

Braudel, Fernand. *Civilization and Capitalism 15th–18th Century: The Perspective of the World*, trans. Sian Reynolds (New York: Harper and Row, 1984). Excellent, sweeping background to the Industrial Revolution.

Davis, Lance E., and Robert A. Huttenback. *Mammon and the Pursuit of Empire* (Cambridge: Cambridge University Press, 1989). Stresses the importance of economic interests, private and public, in the creation of empire.

DeVries, Jan. *The Industrious Revolution: Consumer Behavior and the Household Economy, 1650 to the Present* (New York: Cambridge University Press, 2008). Stresses the importance of the demand side of economics, and the significance of the family unit in making the demand decisions.

Engels, Friedrich. *The Condition of the Working Class in England*, trans. W.O. Henderson and W.H. Chaloner (Stanford, CA: Stanford University Press, 1968). *The* explication of the horrors of early industrialization in England, written by a young businessman who became a communist because of what he saw with his own eyes.

——. *The Origins of the Family, Private Property, and the State*, ed. Eleanor Burke Leacock (New York: International Publishers, 1973). Condemns the contemporary (1884) status of women and urges fundamental restructuring.

Hobsbawm, Eric. *The Age of Capital 1848–1875* (New York: Vintage Books, 1975). This series by Hobsbawm provides an excellent overview of the period of the Industrial Revolution. Global, but strongest on Europe. Critical of capitalism.

——. *The Age of Empire 1875–1914* (New York: Vintage Books, 1987).

Kennedy, Paul. *The Rise and Fall of the Great Powers* (New York: Random House, 1987). Great empires since 1500 have been built and preserved by careful attention to the balance between guns and butter—between military expenditure and a thriving civilian economy.

Landes, David. *The Unbound Prometheus: Technological Change and Industrial Development in Western Europe from 1750 to the Present* (Cambridge: Cambridge University Press, 2nd ed., 2003). Landes has mostly praise for the European initiative, creativity, and hard work that created the Industrial Revolution.

Lenin, V.I. *Imperialism, the Highest Stage of Capitalism* (Beijing: Foreign Languages Press, 1965). The classic view that industrial nations seek empires as marketplaces for buying raw materials and selling finished products because home markets alone are insufficient.

Perrot, Michelle. *Workers on Strike; France, 1871–1890*, trans. Chris Turner with Erica Carter and Claire Laudet (Leamington Spa: Berg, 1987). Useful study of labor organization in industrial France.

Ramabai Sarasvati, Pandita. *Pandita Ramabai's American Encounter: The Peoples of the United States* (1889), trans. and ed. Meera Kosambi (Bloomington, IN: University of Indiana Press, 2003). A rare travelogue by an Indian woman, concerned with economic, social, and political

development in America with special attention to women's progress.

Revel, Jacques, and Lynn Hunt, eds. *Histories: French Constructions of the Past*, trans. Arthur Goldhammer *et al.* (New York: New York Press, 1995). How French historians understand the significance of their nation's history. New interpretations for new times.

Sennett, Richard, ed. *Classic Essays on the Culture of Cities* (Englewood Cliffs, NJ: Prentice Hall, 1969). An excellent selection of classical sociological essays.

Wallerstein, Immanuel. *The Modern World-system 1: Capitalist Agriculture and the Origins of the European World-economy in the Sixteenth Century* (San Diego, CA: Academic Press, 1974). The fullest exposition of the theory of core-periphery exploitative development, with Europe and the United States as the core and Asia, Africa, and Latin America as the periphery.

Weber, Adna Ferrin. *The Growth of Cities in the Nineteenth Century: A Study in Statistics* (Ithaca, NY: Cornell University Press, 1963). A dissertation that became a key to the quantitative understanding of urban growth worldwide.

FILMS

The City (1939; 40 minutes). Lewis Mumford's documentary extolling the virtues of countryside over city, and the new suburban lifestyles as the most practicable alternative.

Global Industrialization (30 minutes). Classroom documentary, number 19 in the series *Bridging World History*. Takes us onto sugar plantations, into older factories, and also into newer ones in today's developing world, providing comparative perspectives. www.learner.org/courses/worldhistory/unit_main_19.html (accessed September 2013).

Metropolis (1927; 2 hours 33 minutes). Fritz Lang's pessimistic view of the future as capitalist productivity, and capitalist masters, determine the patterns of people's lives.

Modern Times (1936; 1 hour 27 minutes). The great classic made by and starring Charlie Chaplin. Although set in the depression of the 1930s, its caricature of life on an assembly line is timeless, touching, and hilarious.

No Rest for the Wicked: Protestantism and Economics (2006; 59 minutes). Parts are directly related to the Industrial Revolution. Accepts the connection between Protestantism and the quest for economic growth and profit.

18 Nationalism, Imperialism, and Resistance

Competition among Industrial Powers

1650–1914

French armies marching across Europe under Napoleon in the early 1800s imposed their imperial governments and their legal systems on the nations they conquered. The new message seemed clear: a nation organized for war and administration could enter regions outside its own borders to fight, conquer, legislate, rule, and tax. Military and political catastrophe awaited those without this power. The Industrial Revolution, beginning in England in the eighteenth century and sweeping across the globe, demonstrated similar capacity in its new forms of economic organization. When a single national government could combine military and industrial power, it wielded the power to build a global empire. Britain's takeover of India, for example, marked not only a political victory but also an economic conquest. The political and industrial revolutions, when fused as they were in France and England, demonstrated that empires could be far more powerful than nation-states. Inspired and frightened, acquisitive and defensive, other regions

OUR VISITORS.

JONATHAN. "Ah! Mister, and, pray, what can I do for you?"
JAPANESE VISITOR. "If you please, I would like to borrow a little of your light."

Cartoon in *Harper's Weekly*, 1860. How do you read this cartoon? Is it a (racist) proclamation of the triumphs of Western technology? Or is it a condemnation of Western arrogance in proclaiming its technological superiority over societies far older and far more culturally sophisticated? Or is it a combination of both?

LEARNING OBJECTIVES

18.1 ((	18.2 ((	18.3 ((	18.4 ((	18.5 ((	18.6 ((	18.7 ((
Define nationalism.	Explain why some nationalist movements fail.	Explain how European nations gained control of most of the globe.	Describe the process of empire-building in Africa in the nineteenth century.	Understand the changes in gender relations in the European colonies.	Describe the reasons for anticolonial resentment and revolt.	Chart Japan's movement from isolation to full participation in the world.

joined in the competition to create unified nations and empires. In this chapter we will look at successful attempts at nation-building and empire-building, and at some unsuccessful attempts as well. We will examine the role of women, who played an important part in the building and administration of empire, usually behind the scenes. Power, gender, and sexuality often went hand in hand. We examine also anticolonial revolts, successful and unsuccessful. We close with a case study of Japan, which faced the threat of colonial conquest and reorganized itself to maintain its independence. This is a textbook case of successful national resistance to foreign colonial domination, which ultimately resulted in Japan conquering its own empire and challenging the empires of Europe.

18.1 What is nationalism?

18.2

18.3

18.4

18.5

18.6

18.7

Nationalism

18.1 What is nationalism?

Nationalism, an appreciation of belonging to one's country and a commitment to serve on its behalf, has two faces. As a positive force, it promises to unite and empower the masses of a nation to work together for a common good. It views other nations as potential allies or as friendly competitors. As a negative force, it threatens to force the masses to serve the state and to turn one nation against another in destructive warfare.

In several of the cases we study here, the first goal of nationalism was to create a modern, independent nation where none existed. Independence movements from within the Ottoman Empire fought to free their regions from imperial control; the American colonies fought to create a new nation, independent from England. In Italy and Germany, national movements took smaller regional fragments and unified them into a larger nation. National movements have also created the reality of a modern nation out of a historical memory, as was the case with Zionism.

Nationalism in the Ottoman Empire

As powerful nations built empires by conquering other peoples, they often met resistance in the form of anti-imperial nationalism. In their fierce competition, rival empires sometimes fanned the flames of anti-imperial nationalism in the conquered territories of their enemies. Throughout the nineteenth and early twentieth centuries, Western European nations encouraged regional revolts within the Ottoman Empire, ultimately detaching huge territories from Ottoman control.

Revolts against the Ottomans broke out in the Balkans from 1815 onward in the name of individual nationalities. With British and French diplomatic and military support, Greece won its independence in 1829. The Western European powers also supported successful movements for greater autonomy and limited self-government in Serbia and in Wallachia and Moldavia (in present-day Romania). The Saud family had already won similar autonomy for parts of Arabia in the early nineteenth century. The French began their occupation of Algeria in 1830. Muhammad (Mehemet) Ali seized the opportunity to make Egypt effectively independent of the Ottomans in 1832. The Ottoman Empire was unable to hold on to its territories.

The Ottoman Empire was especially vulnerable to nationalistic revolts from within that were supported by resistance from without. It had organized its conquered peoples in the *millet* system, which differentiated subjects by religious communities. Each *millet* had a religious leader responsible for enforcing its religious laws and customs and for collecting taxes on behalf of the imperial government. This opened the door to Western, industrializing powers to enter into Ottoman politics. Different religious groups within the empire looked outward to their coreligionists in other countries for protection, if they felt their rights and privileges were under attack. The

KEY TERMS

millet **system** The Ottoman Empire's system of rule through religious communities. Legal issues among members of individual *millets*, or religious groups, were administered by the group itself, and taxes were also collected by the *millets* on behalf of the empire. *Millets* kept in close contact with their coreligionists in other countries, sometimes undermining the power of the Ottoman government.

AT A GLANCE: THE WORLD BEYOND THE INDUSTRIALIZED WEST

DATE	OTTOMAN EMPIRE	INDIA, SOUTHEAST ASIA, CHINA	AFRICA
1800		• Sir Stamford Raffles establishes Singapore for the British (1819)	• British forces drive Napoleon from Egypt (1801); Muhammad Ali assumes rule (1807) • Shaka seizes leadership of Zulu kingdom near Cape Colony (1816)
1820	• Greece wins independence; Serbia, Wallachia, and Moldavia gain autonomy (1829) • France gains control of Algeria from empire (1830) • Muhammad Ali renders Egypt effectively independent (1832)	• Java War, Dutch vs. Indonesians (1825–30) • Dutch introduce cultivation system in Indonesia (1830) • First Opium War (1839–42): China cedes Hong Kong to the British	• Great Trek north by the Boers (Afrikaners) (1834–41) • French invade Algeria (1830); warfare with Abd al-Qadir (1841)
1840	• Crimean War (1853–56) • Westernization encouraged in the Hatt-i Humayun edict (1856)	• Taiping Rebellion begins (1850); suppressed 1864 • "First War for National Independence" in India (1857) • Russians seize Amur River region (1858) • Second Opium War (1856–60): Beijing occupied by French and British	• David Livingstone lands along Angola coast for first African expedition (1841)
1860	• Young Turks forced into exile (1876) • Russian attack through the Balkans reaches Istanbul (1877)	• Russians seize Maritime Provinces (1860) and Ili valley in Turkestan (1871–81)	• Suez Canal opens (1869) • Diamonds and gold discovered in the Cape Colony region • Egyptian *khedive* forced to add Europeans to his cabinet (1878)
1880		• France seizes all of Indochina (1883–93) • Germany annexes eastern New Guinea and the Marshall and Solomon islands (1880s) • Japan defeats China in warfare (1894–95) • Boxer Rebellion (1898–1900)	• Bismarck's Berlin Convention apportions Africa among competing powers (1884) • General Kitchener retakes Sudan in Battle of Omdurman (1898) • Rhodesia (now Zimbabwe and Zambia) named after Cecil John Rhodes (1898) • Boer War (1899–1902) • Ethiopia defeats Italian forces at Adowa (1896)
1900	• Italy takes Libya from weakened empire (1911)	• India's first steel mill at Jamshedpur, Bihar (1911) • Subcontinent has 35,000 miles of railroad track (1914)	• Maji-Maji revolt against German rule in Tanganyika (1905–07) • Belgian Parliament takes over control of the Congo (1908) • British form Union of South Africa (1910) • Natives Land Act closes 87 percent of South African land to African ownership (1913)

Greek Orthodox community, in particular, looked toward Russia; Roman Catholics looked to France; and Protestants looked to Britain. Religious missions from these countries received special privileges within the Ottoman Empire, and often served as bases for trade and intelligence-gathering as well. Foreigners trading within the empire were permitted the right to trial by judges of their own nation.

The Ottoman form of decentralized government, through religious communities, was thus quite different from that of Western Europe, where the unified nation-state was becoming the norm. In addition, the Ottomans had not kept up with the industrial development of the rest of Europe. Because of its weaknesses, Western Europeans began to call the Ottoman Empire "the sick man of Europe." On the one hand, the other European empires welcomed and exploited Ottoman weakness. On the other, such weakness threatened to embroil them in imperial adventurism in competition and conflict with one another.

Between 1839 and 1876, Sultan Abdul Mecid I and his successor enacted the Tanzimat (Restructuring) reforms to bring the Ottoman legal code and its social and educational standards into closer conformity with those of Western European states. The reforms were limited, and ultimately they were reversed; the sultans were reluctant to give up too much power. The reforms did, however, create a new, Western-oriented elite that threatened traditional Ottoman imperial government and its administrative and military officials. After 1876, the Young Turks, as these reformers were called, were forced into exile.

Meanwhile, the Crimean War of 1853–56 revealed the greedy competition of European empires as they assaulted Ottoman weakness. France and Russia claimed mutually conflicting concessions from the Ottomans for control over the Christian Holy Land. France based its claims on its protection of resident Roman Catholics and their interests, Russia on the protection of the Eastern Orthodox. In a further attempt to wrest land from the Ottomans, in 1851 Russia also occupied regions of present-day Romania and Bulgaria, along the Danube River. The Ottomans proved unable to recover their territory, lost their fleet in warfare with Russia in 1853, and

What is
nationalism?

18.1

18.2

18.3

18.4

18.5

18.6

18.7

HOW DO WE KNOW?

What is Nationalism?

For most people in today's world, nationality is an important part of personal identity, and historians find nationalism to be a central concern of the past two centuries. Some stress the significance of particular forms of nationalism, others argue that national identity is, and can be, constantly shaped and reshaped. In this sense historians of national identity are similar to historians of gender identity: they not only wish to understand where we have been, but also want to use these explorations of the past as a means to search for alternative futures.

One of the first historians and philosophers of nationalism, the Frenchman Joseph-Ernest Renan (1823–92), captured the twofold nature of nationalism in his lecture "What is a Nation?," first delivered at the Sorbonne in 1882. It looks both backward and forward in creating a unified vision. Nationalism requires a fundamental shared history in the lives of the citizens, but the past alone is not enough for constructing a nation. That task requires also a vision of what the nation might become and a political commitment to constructing such a future. More dramatically, in considering the nation as a "spiritual principle," Renan asserted his belief that in his time nationalism was displacing religion as a central concern:

A nation is a spiritual principle, the result of profound historical complications; a spiritual family, not a group determined by the configuration of the soil. We have now seen what do not suffice for the creation of such a spiritual principle; race, language, interests, religious affinity, geography, military necessities. What more, then, is necessary? …

A nation is then a great solidarity, constituted by the sentiment of the sacrifices that its citizens have made, and of those that they feel prepared to make once more. It implies a past; but it is summed up in the present by a tangible fact—consent, the clearly expressed desire to live a common life. (pp. 80–81)

More recently, the anthropologist Benedict Anderson has referred to the nation as an "imagined political community," stressing the importance of human imagination, creativity, and persuasion—all expressed through the public media—as the means by which the idea of the nation is created, refined, and disseminated. "It is imagined because the members of even the smallest nation will never know most of their fellow-members, meet them, or even hear of them, yet in the minds of each lives the image of their communion" (Anderson, p. 15). For Anderson, as for Renan, the nation is not so much an entity existing in nature as an institution created by leaders who are successful in gaining acceptance for their idea of the nation.

In addition to Renan's "spiritual principle," modern nationalism comprises two additional elements. First, at least since the French Revolution, the modern nation exists in a world of other nations, frequently competitive with one another. To some degree, each nation defines itself in its relationship with others. Second, at least since the French Revolution and the Industrial Revolution, the nation has been the vehicle for the spread of trade networks and capitalism throughout the world. The significance of the nation in achieving economic goals has given great power to national identity.

- How well does Renan's concept of the nation as a "spiritual family" fit the nationalism expressed in the American Constitution? How well does it fit the nationalism of the various Italian and German spokesmen?
- How might a nation express its desire to continue a common life? How might it reject that desire?
- How does Renan's concept of a "spiritual family" compare with Anderson's idea of an "imagined community"? Are they actually referring to the same relationship but with different words, or are their concepts different?

PART SIX TURNING POINT: REVOLUTION

18.1 What is
nationalism?
18.2
18.3
18.4
18.5
18.6
18.7

The Kanûn-i Esâsî, the first constitution under Ottoman rule, 1876. Turkish postcard, 1895. As the Ottoman Empire grew weaker and came ever more dangerously under attack from foreign powers, a group of advisors prevailed upon Sultan Abdul Hamid II to issue a constitution. Here the sultan (to the woman's right), the grand vizier, and representatives of the *millets*, the parliamentary representatives of the major religious and social groups in the country, grant freedom (represented by a woman without an Islamic veil) to Turkey. Above flies an angel carrying a banner, written in Turkish with the motto "Liberty, Equality, Fraternity." In reality, the sultan kept all significant power. The parliament created by the constitution was dissolved within a year of its establishment, and the empire continued to weaken.

seemed vulnerable to still further losses. Britain and France came to assist them, declaring war on Russia in 1854. The Italian regions of Sardinia-Piedmont, hoping to gain recognition for their attempts to unify Italy, also contributed troops to the British–French alliance. Although Austria remained neutral, its threats of joining the anti-Russian coalition weighed heavily in the Russian decision to abandon its hold not only on Romania and Serbia, but also on the Crimean peninsula, which it had taken from the Ottomans.

A new Russian attack through the Balkans, however, reached Constantinople itself in 1877; Britain threatened to counterattack. An international conference in Berlin resolved the conflict for the moment, but tensions ran high. The mixture of Ottoman weakness, aggressive expansionism on the part of major European countries, assertive nationalism in the Balkans, and increasing militarization with increasingly powerful weapons threatened to precipitate a larger war. It arrived in 1914.

📖 Read the Document: J.A. MacGahan: The Turkish Atrocities in Bulgaria (1876) on MyHistoryLab

American Nationalism

American nationalism and imperial expansion, set apart geographically from the Old World by vast oceans to the east and west, seemed to express a different political philosophy. Foreign observers, like France's Alexis de Tocqueville (1805–59), commented on the newness of America and its lack of history. A substantial proportion of America's institutions, and of its population, was drawn from the British Isles, but immigrants came from all over the world. Some, including Native

American Indians (who had arrived thousands of years before the Europeans), African-American slaves, and women, were excluded from full citizenship. But the pattern for future inclusion was also being set. The United States Constitution declared that a nation is not necessarily composed of people who share a common history, geography, language, race, ethnicity, religion, and language. A nation could be formed on the basis of a new vision of the present and future and adherence to a common law. Many (although not all) new immigrants could join this nation, and, after slaves were freed, so could they, although racism remained a powerful force of exclusion and discrimination. Native Americans remained torn between allegiances to Indian nations and the American nation. Despite these divisions, the American Constitution illustrated the degree to which a nation was constituted by the will of its people, and especially of its leaders, rather than by primordial historical legacies.

In 1861, some 85 years after its establishment, the American nation was faced with a struggle for survival when the 11 Confederate States of America seceded from the Union. The Confederacy claimed greater rights for constituent states, especially the right to sanction slavery, and it favored agrarian over industrial economic policies. Some 500,000 men died in the Civil War that followed. Immediately following the war, the victorious central government instituted generous policies favoring reconciliation (often at the expense of the recently freed slaves), although later these policies became more punitive. After the war, with unity secure and northeastern business leaders asserting great powers, the industrial and economic expansion of the United States set a pace exceeding that of any other nation.

📖 Read the **Document: Albert Beveridge, "The March of the Flag" (1898)** on **MyHistoryLab**

The New Nations of Italy and Germany

In the heart of Europe, nationalism grew in hard soil. The great powers of Austria, Prussia, Russia, France, and Britain suppressed national uprisings by peoples within their empires. When they drafted the peace settlements at the Congress of Vienna in 1814–15, after the Napoleonic Wars, they set limits on national movements in central Europe. A generation later, led by Prince Clemens von Metternich (1773–1859), foreign minister of Austria, conservative leaders of the major European powers successfully quelled powerful nationalistic uprisings in Poland, Prussia, Italy, and Hungary between 1846 and 1849. The revolts of 1848 in Austria, Germany, and France included protests against the economic directions of the growing capitalist economy of the time, and are discussed at greater length in the chapter entitled "The Industrial Revolution." (Belgium did gain national independence, from the Dutch, in 1830.) Only in the 1850s did nationalism win major victories in lands under these empires. Then the several divided nations of Italy and Germany began successfully to unite to form new nations. In each country, cultural nationalism preceded political mobilization.

Before 1870, neither Italy nor Germany existed as the unified nations we know today. Each was divided into many petty states under the control of different rulers. In Italy, the largest single state was the kingdom of Sardinia-Piedmont, but other states were controlled by other rulers. The area around Venice was controlled by Austria, and the region around Rome by the pope. Most of the small states of Germany had been included within Charlemagne's empire, founded in 800 C.E., and then within its successor institution, the Holy Roman Empire. Each of these states had its own ruler and even its own system of government. The largest, Austria, was in itself a significant state. The smallest had only a few thousand inhabitants. In addition, to the east lay Prussia, a powerful state that was beginning to think of itself as the leader of the German-speaking peoples.

What is nationalism?

18.1
18.2
18.3
18.4
18.5
18.6
18.7

The unification of Italy and Germany. The middle years of the nineteenth century saw popular forces drawing together the disparate territories of central Europe into modern nation-states. In Germany the political, military, and economic strength of Prussia had been growing for more than two centuries, and Bismarck's wars with Denmark (1864), Austria (1866), and France (1870) eventually secured the union. In Italy the expansion of Sardinia-Piedmont into Lombardy, Venetia, and Rome, and Garibaldi's march through the south, united the nation.

As nation-states formed in Western Europe and demonstrated the economic, political, military, and cultural power that came from unity, regional leaders in Italy and Germany also sought unification for themselves. A common language and clearly demarcated geographical borders were considered vital elements in national unity, and were helpful to Italy in consolidating its peninsular nation. Germany, however, lacked clear natural geographic boundaries and faced the question as to which German-speaking states would be included within the new country and which would not.

Giuseppe Mazzini (1805–72) provided a prophetic vision for Italy. In 1831 he founded Young Italy, a secret association urging Italian unification and independence from foreign control by the French, Austrians, and Spanish. Mazzini's *On the Duties of Man* expressed his nationalistic, democratic, and humanistic views:

O my brothers, love your Country! Our country is our Home, the House that God has given us, placing therein a numerous family that loves us, and whom we love; a family with whom we sympathize more readily, and whom we understand more quickly, than we do others; and which, from its being centered round a given spot, and from the homogeneous nature of its elements, is adapted to a special branch of activity. (Columbia University, p. 570)

When Mazzini's cultural view was joined to the political organization of Camillo Cavour (1810–61), prime minister of Sardinia-Piedmont in 1852 under King Victor Emmanuel II, the nationalist movement was poised for political victory. Cavour formed a brief alliance with Napoleon III of France against Austria. This enabled the king to annex Lombardy. The adjacent regions of Parma, Modena, and Tuscany joined the kingdom in 1860 following a plebiscite, or popular vote. In the same year, the charismatic military commander Giuseppe Garibaldi (1807–82) led 1,150 followers, wearing red shirts, into the south Italian Kingdom of the Two Sicilies, which collapsed and subsequently joined Piedmont after a plebiscite. Venetia, the region around Venice, was added after a war in which Italy allied with Prussia against Austria. Finally, Rome was annexed in 1870 after French troops, which had protected the papal territories, were withdrawn to fight against Prussia. Through the various contributions of Mazzini, Cavour, Garibaldi, Victor Emmanuel II, Napoleon III, war, and popular votes, Italy had become a unified nation.

At about the same time, Prime Minister Otto von Bismarck of Prussia (1815–98) was unifying the multitude of small German states into a single German nation under William I (king of Prussia 1861–88, emperor of Germany 1871–88). From 1828 a customs union, *zollverein*, had created a free-trade area throughout many of the German states, establishing an economic foundation for unification; increasing industrialization provided the financial and military underpinnings for it. The cultural basis of German unity was also already solidly established. For example, the brothers Jakob and Wilhelm Grimm, founders of the modern science of linguistics, had analyzed the various German dialects and collected fairy tales from all parts of the region, publishing them in 1812 as a unifying folklore for the nation. And just as Mazzini had done in Italy, the German historian and philosopher Heinrich von Treitschke (1834–96) urged Germany to fulfill its natural destiny as a unified, authoritarian, imperial power. Unlike Mazzini, however, Treitschke stressed "The Greatness of War" in creating the nation:

When the State exclaims: My very existence is at stake! then social self-seeking must disappear and all party hatred be silent. The individual must forget his own ego and feel himself a member of the whole, he must recognize how negligible is his life compared with the good of the whole. Therein lies the greatness of war that the little man completely vanishes before the great thought of the State. The sacrifice of nationalities for one another is nowhere invested with such beauty as in war. …

Statue of Giuseppe Garibaldi by Urbano Lucchesi in Lucca, Italy, nineteenth century. Garibaldi led a small army that conquered various independent regions of Italy and brought them under the unified rule of King Victor Emmanuel II. By 1860 virtually all of modern Italy had been brought together, except the Papal States centered on Rome, which were conquered—all except Vatican City—and annexed in 1870. Virtually every city and town in Italy has a statue of Garibaldi on prominent display.

What is nationalism?

18.1

18.2

18.3

18.4

18.5

18.6

18.7

BISMARCK

1870

AMBITIEUX GREDIN

« Je t'ai saisi ; j'ai mis l'écriteau sur ton front ;
et maintenant la foule accourt et te bafoue. »

French cartoon portraying Prince Otto Eduard Leopold von Bismarck, Prime Minister of Prussia, 1870. Political figures have traditionally been treated irreverently by cartoonists, but this caricature is savage. The French were outraged by Bismarck's ambitions to have the Prussian prince Leopold installed on the Spanish throne—a key factor in the war between the two countries in 1870–71.

It is indeed political idealism which fosters war … The heroes of a people are the personalities who fill the youthful souls with delight and enthusiasm, and amongst authors we as boys and youths admire most those whose words sound like a flourish of trumpets. He who cannot take pleasure therein, is too cowardly to take up arms himself for his fatherland.

Now Bismarck instituted a policy of **blood and iron**. Two wars were the key. In 1866, Bismarck defeated Austria and formed the North German Confederation, excluding Austria. In 1871, he defeated France, annexing Alsace and Lorraine. In light of these victories the southern states of Germany—Bavaria, Baden, and Württemberg—also joined the newly formed nation.

The Rise of Zionism in Europe

One of the last of the nationalist movements to arise in nineteenth-century Europe was Zionism, the movement to recreate a Jewish homeland. Jews had been dispersed into Europe even during the time of the Roman Empire. By the beginning of the twentieth century, their principal European locations were in central and eastern Europe, in Poland, Russia, and Ukraine, although Western Europe also held important Jewish communities. Through the centuries Jews had prayed for a return to Zion, their ancestral homeland in modern Israel. In the second half of the nineteenth century, under the influence of various European nationalist movements, some philosophers proposed going beyond prayer. They looked forward to the establishment of a political state.

The move from prayer to political organization took concrete form towards the end of the nineteenth century. Suffering from **pogroms** in the Russian Empire and discrimination in much of the Austro–Hungarian Empire, Jews felt increasingly persecuted. On assignment in Paris to report on the trial of Alfred Dreyfus, a Jewish officer in the French army unjustly accused of treason, the Viennese Jewish journalist Theodor Herzl (1860–1904) encountered fierce anti-Semitism. Shocked to find such ethnic and religious hatred in the capital of the liberal world, where Jews had gained citizenship during the French Revolution, Herzl concluded that Jews could be free, independent, and safe only in a country of their own. In 1897, he founded the Zionist movement. Because Palestine, the goal of most of the early Zionists, was already the home of 600,000 Arabs, Jewish nationalism simultaneously, if unintentionally, took the form of a colonizing movement originating in Europe. Not all Jews embraced Zionism, although as discrimination and persecution increased in the twentieth century, the Zionist dream became an increasingly desirable alternative to remaining in Europe.

602

Failed Nationalisms and Delayed Nationalisms

18.2 Why do some nationalist movements fail?

18.1

Why do some nationalist movements fail?

18.2

18.3

18.4

18.5

18.6

18.7

Historians usually record the accomplishments of successful nationalist movements. These create states whose history demands attention and, sometimes, admiration. But many nationalist movements fail, perhaps most of them. They never generate enough enthusiasm to bring their wishes to fruition, especially as they often face enormous obstacles: smaller regions within larger states, perhaps with their own languages and cultures, reject membership in the larger political structure and undercut its nationalism in favor of their own. These smaller regions may succeed in creating their own, smaller states. On the other hand, if a proposed state is too small or too weak, it will not succeed in winning a place against the opposition of larger states or empires.

Sometimes nationalisms are suppressed and defeated for very long periods of time but then emerge successful, in the form of new, or reborn, political nations. These long-delayed successes serve as inspiration to other nationalist proponents to continue their struggles even when they seem to be defeated. They keep hope alive.

The Disappearance of Poland

Take, for example, Poland. In the mid-eighteenth century, civil war and Russian territorial grabs so weakened the government of Poland that it could not resist partition and the further loss of territory. In 1772 Poland's neighbors, Russia, Prussia, and Austria, divided among themselves about one-third of Poland's land and half of its population. By 1791, Poland was regaining strength, but then confrontation over a new, liberal constitution led the conservatives to seek Russian assistance in national politics. Both Russia and Prussia intervened, dispatching troops, which dismembered the country in a second partition, with the Russians again taking the lion's share. The Poles revolted against these losses in an armed struggle led by Tadeusz Kosciuszko. They were crushed by Russia and Prussia. The victors combined with Austria in a third partition of Poland in 1797. This time nothing was left. The nation of Poland disappeared from the map of Europe, to return only in 1918, recreated by the peace treaties following World War I.

Africa, West and East: The Rise and Fall of States

In Africa, a series of religious movements for the purification of Islam led to the establishment of new, religion-based states, and even empires, in the eighteenth century. By about 1900, however, these states came into confrontation with expanding European colonialism, which defeated and dismembered them.

In the Sahel—the dry, semi-desert area immediately south of the Sahara, stretching from the Atlantic Ocean to the Red Sea—political and religious movements of Islamic revival flourished. Most of them were directed at keeping Muslims loyal to the faith and bringing polytheistic Africans under Muslim rule. They were not aimed at confronting Christianity. Some historians do believe, however, that the movements drew some of their inspiration from the knowledge among the Muslims that the regional balance of political power was shifting from an increasingly weak Muslim Middle East and Africa to an increasingly powerful Christian Europe. The formation of states, and sometimes empires, would help in strengthening religious devotion among African Muslims and in resisting Christian inroads.

In West Africa, three movements stand out for special attention. They began in states founded in the eighteenth century by the Fulani peoples. In Hausaland, modern northern Nigeria, Usman dan Fodio (1754–1817), a prominent Sufi teacher, condemned the rulers for corruption, sacrilege, persecution of true Muslims, and

KEY TERMS

blood and iron Bismarck's policy of using warfare against enemies as a means of unifying his new nation. Subsequently the term has been used to designate the policy of any government committed to foreign warfare as a means of internal unification.

pogrom A murderous attack on a group of people—usually based on their ethnicity or religion—that is sanctioned by the government, either officially or unofficially.

18.1

18.2 Why do some nationalist movements fail?

18.3

18.4

18.5

18.6

18.7

polytheistic practices. For years dan Fodio organized his opposition, gathering supporters from nearby groups. Frustrated by the inconsistent responses he received from the Hausaland rulers, he urged his followers to arm themselves for coming conflict. The outbreak of hostilities began when a new sultan attacked a group of dan Fodio's followers in 1804. More a religious leader than a general, dan Fodio called on his son and his brother to lead the military campaigns that ultimately brought all of Hausaland under his control from the new capital at Sokoto. The Sokoto empire tended to favor Fulani people over Hausa, even though not all the Fulani were Muslims. For the most part, however, it encouraged both Fulani and Hausa to unite in a single Islamic empire. Sokoto carried on commerce with the British, agreeing to a trade treaty in 1853 and conceding further privileges in 1885. In 1903, however, British forces assaulted Sokoto, defeating the kingdom and incorporating it into their own administration. The descendants of dan Fodio continue today, however, primarily in religious roles, as nominal sultans of Sokoto and leaders of the Islamic community of the region.

"Departure of Samori Toure," *Le Petit Parisien*, January 15, 1899. Engraving. Captured by the French on September 29, 1898, Toure had held off the French advance into his territories for four years, but ultimately he could not withstand the superior armed forces of the Europeans.

Other *jihads*, or holy wars, were smaller in geographical and military scale. They were usually concerned with purifying the Islamic faith and practices of rulers and subjects. These included *jihads* in West Africa in the small states of Futa Toro and Futa Jallon, and the somewhat larger Massina. In Massina, al-Hajj Umar (c. 1794–1864), having returned from a pilgrimage to Mecca, and having visited Sokoto, gathered followers and armed them. ("Al-Hajj" or "el-Hajj" is the title earned by someone who has completed the *hajj* pilgrimage to Mecca.) Umar captured the kingdom of Massina and made it the center of his empire. He attempted to gain support from the French on the coast of West Africa, but they were unwilling. When he subsequently attacked French river traders, perhaps seeking to capture their guns, the French-controlled armed forces repulsed his attack.

Another leader who built an empire in the name of Islam, Samori Toure (c. 1830–1900), organized Mandinka and Diola ethnic groups under his military leadership. Although at one point he declared himself *almami*, or leader of the faithful, his devotion to Islam was sometimes compromised by battles against fellow Muslims and his murder of Muslim scholars in his capture of the town of Kong. Toure's empire, just south of the bend of the Niger River, and the empire founded by al-Hajj Umar, were both situated in the path of French imperial conquest eastward from the Atlantic. In 1893–94, both were defeated and brought under French control. Although Toure's record is marred by his raiding for slaves (in order to barter them for guns), by his scorched-earth policy of retreat before the French, and by his destruction of Kong, the town to which he transferred his capital as he retreated, he is nevertheless credited by most historians as a guerrilla leader who held off the French for two years in his original empire and for two more in his second empire. In 1898 the French captured him and exiled him to Gabon, where he died in 1900.

In East Africa, near Khartoum, a religious leader named Muhammad Ahmed declared that he was the Mahdi, a messiah figure who would bring a new age that would restore the true religion. In 1881, he began to build a state in the Sudan. The Mahdi began his movement in opposition to the Egyptian government, but in 1882 the British reentered Egypt, seized Cairo, and claimed the Nile valley as effective rulers of the region. The British and the Mahdi were on a collision course. At first the Mahdi and his military leadership were victorious. In 1885, they defeated an Egyptian force commanded by British General Charles Gordon at Khartoum. Later that year the Mahdi died, leaving his state to a successor who, although Muslim, was far less militant than the founder. For some time Britain did not respond to this new state and its political and military successes. A decade later, however, it sent another force under General Horatio Herbert Kitchener to retake the Sudan for Egypt and to avenge Gordon's defeat and death. At Omdurman, Kitchener's army destroyed the Mahdists, killing 11,000 men and wounding 16,000 in a single battle on September 2, 1898, while losing just 40 of its own soldiers. Such was the power of the Maxim machine gun against an army that believed that their religious faith would make them impervious to bullets. Kitchener proceeded to reclaim Khartoum. The total imbalance of military force and strategy between the British and the Muslim forces could not have been clearer, and neither could the willingness of the African Muslims to fight and die for their cause and their religion.

Mehemet Ali, Louis Charles Auguste Couder, 1840. Oil on canvas. As head of an Albanian cavalry troop called in by the Ottoman sultan to rule Egypt after the French and British left by 1803, Muhammad (Mehemet) Ali built up the army, improved and further commercialized the trade in fine Egyptian cotton, built state-run cotton textile factories, and introduced European-style education and printing presses. But the taste for European fashions that he promoted led Egypt into debt and then into the clutches of powerful European commercial powers. (Château de Versailles)

Egyptian Loss of Independence

Egypt, of course, is part of Africa, but, unlike the Islamic states just discussed, its experience in state-building came far more from its involvement with Europe. It tried to model its nationalism on what it learned from that continent. It failed to carry through its plans for modernizing its economy and politics, however, in large part because of European manipulation. As a result, it lost its independence to European colonialism.

Napoleon's invasion of Egypt in 1798 was influential, but very brief. Egyptian nationalists, backed by Ottoman and British military forces, drove them out by 1801. Two years later, the British also withdrew their troops. To lead the battles against the French, the Ottoman sultan had called in a troop of Albanian cavalry. After the fighting, its commander, Muhammad (Mehemet) Ali (1769–1849), took over the rule of Egypt, although he served nominally as a viceroy of the Ottoman Empire. Ali introduced some new industries and then decided to concentrate on the cultivation of cotton as a cash crop for Europe's booming textile industry. To enable year-round cultivation, he built extensive new irrigation works. He also encouraged the development of Egypt's own textile mills. For the most part, he kept this economic modernization in the hands of the state rather than private entrepreneurs. He streamlined

18.1

Why do some nationalist movements fail?

18.2

18.3

18.4

18.5

18.6

18.7

18.1
18.2
18.3
18.4
18.5
18.6
18.7

How did Europeans gain direct political control of four-fifths of the land surface of the globe?

the administration and built a system of secular state schools to train administrators and officers, especially by training students in Western scholarship. He introduced a government printing press, which in turn encouraged the translation of European books into Arabic.

A professional soldier, Ali modernized the army and marched his newly equipped forces up the Nile, captured the Sudan, and established his capital in the city of Khartoum in 1830. He also gained control of the holy cities of Mecca and Medina in Arabia to counter the power of the militantly Islamic Wahabi movement there. Fundamentally secular in outlook, Ali attempted to reach accommodation with the moderate Islamic forces in Egypt rather than attack them or bring them around to his own perspectives. His son Ibrahim succeeded him and commissioned a French firm to build the Suez Canal, which was opened in 1869. To commemorate this event, Ibrahim's son, Ismail, commissioned the building of a European-style opera house in Cairo. (Giuseppe Verdi's opera *Aïda*, a tale of love, treachery, and warfare set in ancient Egypt, received its world premiere there in 1871.) Ismail also expanded Egyptian territorial holdings both eastward along the coast of the Red Sea and southward, inland, toward the headwaters of the Nile.

Muhammad Ali's modernization program brought mixed results. Egypt entered the international economy based in Europe, but soon the country was spending more on imports, military modernization, and beautification projects in Cairo than it was earning in exports. In addition, Egypt adopted an economic policy of encouraging **monoculture** (specializing in a single crop for export), in this case fine-quality cotton. This decision left the country vulnerable to the instability of international prices on this single crop. As Egyptian debts rose, European creditors pressured their governments to force the *khedive* (the title given to Muhammad Ali and his successors) to appoint European experts as Commissioners of the Debt in 1876. In 1878 the *khedive* was forced to add French and British representatives to his cabinet. In 1881 the European powers went further: they had the Ottoman sultan dismiss the *khedive*, Muhammad Ali's grandson. When an Egyptian military revolt then seized power, Britain sent in its forces, primarily to protect the Suez Canal. They stayed on as the power behind the throne until the 1950s. For Egypt, entanglement with Europe proved a two-edged sword. It spurred economic and political nationalism, but then subverted and crippled it.

The European Quest for Empire

18.3   How did Europeans gain direct political control of four-fifths of the land surface of the globe?

Nationalism triumphed in creating powerful modern nation-states, but at the cost of fierce and violent competition among them. Similarly, the emergence of a global capitalist marketplace was also based on sharp competition, much of it between joint stock companies, backed by their home governments. The Industrial Revolution intensified the competition, first between industrialized and nonindustrialized countries, such as Britain and India, and later among the newly industrializing nations and their industrialists.

The greatest competition for imperial power took place overseas, beyond the borders of Europe. Empires were not new, of course, but advanced technology and new strategies of financial and economic dominance multiplied their power. By 1914, peoples of Europe and of European ancestry had settled and were ruling, directly or indirectly, 85 percent of the earth's land surface: Canada, the United States, most of Latin America, Siberia, Australia, New Zealand, and substantial parts of South Africa by invasion, settlement, and conquest; most of India, Southeast Asia, and Africa by direct rule over indigenous populations; China mostly by indirect rule. The map "European and other empires in 1914," below, indicates the holdings of each major

KEY TERM

monoculture An agricultural economy focused on a single crop, usually a cash crop for export, at the expense of others, including food crops.

imperial power in the eastern hemisphere. British holdings were so widespread—from India, to Australia and New Zealand, to Africa—that it was said that "the sun never sets on the British Empire." The French dominated West Africa, beginning with regions directly across the Mediterranean from France itself, and important parts of Southeast Asia.

Many regions of the world, such as Latin America, were nominally independent, but in fact their economies were controlled by European financial investors and their governments, especially the British. Some states, such as Russia and the Ottoman Empire, were dominated in large part by capital from northwestern Europe, although they also, in turn, held their own colonial areas. An important school of political thought, led by Immanuel Wallerstein, gives the term "**world system**" to these newly emerging relationships that brought together many different areas of the world into a single economic and political framework of inequality. According to this viewpoint, northwestern Europe and the United States had become the core regions, dominating world economic and political power, while most of the rest of the world, excepting Japan, was subordinated into their periphery.

The leading states of Western Europe—especially Britain, France, and the Netherlands—had achieved their power through their "dual revolutions," political and industrial. Politically and socially they had achieved, or seemed to be in the process of achieving:

- consolidated nation-states;
- parliamentary democracies;
- bureaucratic administrations;
- freedom of the press, assembly, and religion;
- freedom from wrongful arrest and torture; and
- increased levels of literacy and general, public education.

Economically and industrially, they had achieved or seemed to be in the process of achieving:

- high levels of productivity;
- competence in new methods of science and technology;
- relatively high levels of health and of medical care;
- an integrated world economy;
- powerful weaponry;
- high levels of trade and international exchange; and
- high levels of economic entrepreneurship and legal protection of property.

Western Europeans began to define themselves as people who had mastered these qualities, in contrast to the peoples whom they were colonizing and dominating, who lacked them. Misinterpreting Charles Darwin, some believed that their power was a phenomenon of nature. Darwin (1809–82) shook much of the Christian world when he published *On the Origin of Species* in 1859. In this work he suggested that the various forms of life on earth had developed over millions of years through the mechanism of natural selection, which allowed some species to survive while others died out. Soon after this work appeared, the philosopher Herbert Spencer (1820–1903) (mis)represented Darwin's concept of "survival of the fittest" as a doctrine that explained and justified the rule by the strong over the weak. Spencer's "**social Darwinism**" argued that those who were strong deserved their superiority, while those who were weak deserved their inferiority. Spencer also believed that Europeans belonged to particular races and that these races were more advanced than those of other regions. He thoroughly approved of the existing social-political order that confirmed wealthy, powerful, white, male Europeans in positions of dominance. Rudyard Kipling's "The **White Man's Burden**," published in 1899, set these beliefs in verse:

18.1
18.2
18.3
18.4
18.5
18.6
18.7

How did Europeans gain direct political control of four-fifths of the land surface of the globe?

KEY TERMS

world system A theory held by some social scientists concerning the political and economic organization of the world in modern times. It posits that a few countries, the "core," dominated most of the others, "the periphery," and exploited them. During the period of imperialism this dominance was both political and economic. Afterward it was mostly economic, taking the form of neocolonialism.

social Darwinism A theory popularized by Herbert Spencer, based on a misreading of Charles Darwin's theory of the survival of the fittest. Darwin argued that those plants and animals best suited to a particular environment survived best in that environment. Spencer took this to mean that whichever creatures were dominant ought to be dominant. For example, among humans the rich and powerful deserved to be rich and powerful; conversely, the poor and powerless deserved their low status.

White Man's Burden A concept, based on the title of a poem by Rudyard Kipling, that white men were superior to people of color, and that it was the duty of the former to rule over, serve, and improve the latter. The concept was often invoked, sometimes self-righteously, sometimes sarcastically, to justify a colonial system that was, in fact, hugely exploitative, a situation not mentioned in the poem.

European imperialism, to 1870. By the middle of the nineteenth century, revolutions had brought independence to most of the Americas. Since Africa was largely impenetrable, European imperialists focused on Asia. Russia had spread across Siberia to the Pacific, and the United States extended from the Atlantic to the Pacific, while Britain controlled India, South Africa, Australia, and New Zealand. In 1867 Canada achieved "dominion" status—virtual political independence.

18.1

18.2

18.3 How did Europeans gain direct political control of four-fifths of the land surface of the globe?

18.4

18.5

18.6

18.7

Take up the White Man's burden—
Send forth the best ye breed—
Go bind your sons to exile
To serve your captives' need;
To wait in heavy harness,
On fluttered folk and wild—
Your new-caught, sullen peoples,
Half-devil and half-child.

Kipling (1865–1936) argued that Europeans had an obligation to bring their civilization to those they conquered, although he saw this civilizing mission as a thankless task. Kipling's poem, perhaps naively, perhaps self-righteously, perhaps sarcastically, cites only the moral burdens of colonization without any reference to its economic and political profits for the colonizer.

📖 Read the Document: Imperialism and the White Man's Burden (1899) Rudyard Kipling on MyHistoryLab

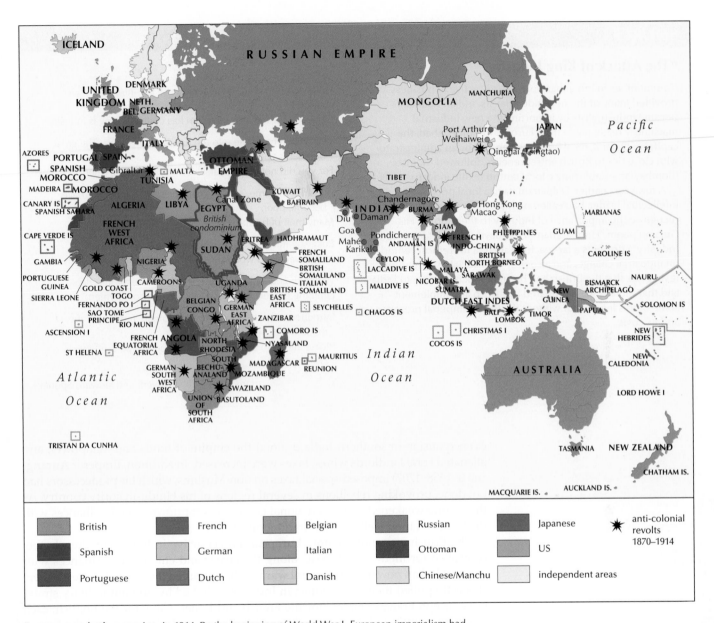

European and other empires in 1914. By the beginning of World War I, European imperialism had reached its zenith, with four-fifths of the land area of the globe under the direct political control of Europeans or people of European ancestry. Only Antarctica remained unclaimed. Although imperial power was sustained by technological, naval, and military superiority, insurrections were widespread and increasingly well organized. Imperial trade established a global economic system and spread European cultural values. Japan consciously pursued the European model of imperial expansion by conquering Korea and Taiwan. China was under the control of the Manchus, who had invaded from the north in 1644 and ruled through the Qing dynasty.

18.1
18.2
18.3
18.4
18.5
18.6
18.7

How did Europeans gain direct political control of four-fifths of the land surface of the globe?

The British in India

The British East India Company had come to India in the seventeenth century to buy spices and hand-made cotton textiles in exchange for bullion, wool, and metals. The Mughal government of India granted the Company permission to trade, and through the seventeenth century it established trading posts, called factories, in crucial port locations, first at Surat on India's west coast, and then at Madras (now Chennai) in 1639, Bombay (now Mumbai) in 1661, and Calcutta (now Kolkata) in 1690. During the eighteenth century, the Mughal imperial government began to weaken. Mughal

SOURCE

"The Attack of King Industry"

Communities in India that were already active in business provided many of the new industrialists. Indian financiers became industrialists by importing the new industrial machinery ready-made from Europe. In Ahmedabad, the capital of Gujarat, local businessmen, led by an administrator with close ties to British entrepreneurs, followed Mumbai (Bombay) in establishing a local cotton textile industry in 1861.

A few years earlier, Dalpatram Kavi, a local poet and intellectual leader, had called on his fellow countrymen to recognize the importance of industry to their future. His Gujarati poem "Hunnarkhan-ni Chadayi" ("The Attack of King Industry") presents a far-reaching agenda for reform centering on industrial change, and also proposes social restructuring. It suggests that the British had brought much of value to India and that Indians were prepared to absorb and implement some of this legacy, but without the British imperial presence and its costs.

Fellow countrymen, let us remove all the miseries of our
   country,
Do work, for the new kingdom has come. Its king is industry.

Our wealth has gone into the hands of foreigners. The great
   blunder is yours
For you did not unite yourselves—fellow countrymen.

Consider the time, see for yourselves. All our people have
   become poor,
Many men of business have fallen—fellow countrymen.

Put away idleness. Fill the treasuries with knowledge.
Now awake and work new wonders—fellow countrymen.

With kith and kin keep harmony. Do not enter into debt.
Limit the dinners for your caste—fellow countrymen.

Introduce industry from countries abroad and master the
   modern machinery.
Please attend to this plea from the Poet Dalpat—fellow
   countrymen.

(trans. Chimanbhai Trivedi and Howard Spodek)

18.1
18.2
18.3
18.4
18.5
18.6
18.7

How did Europeans gain direct political control of four-fifths of the land surface of the globe?

overexpansion in southern India drained the empire of funds and manpower, and alienated rural landlords whose taxes were increased. In addition, Emperor Aurang-zeb (r. 1658–1707) imposed special taxes on non-Muslims, which his predecessors had not done, provoking rebellions in several regions of his Hindu-majority country. As the empire weakened, various regional contestants for power sought alliances with the British in their well-fortified trading outposts.

The British were not the only European power active in India. The French, too, controlled fortified trading posts along the coasts and entered into alliances with regional Indian powers. The general warfare that engulfed the two nations elsewhere (1744–48) pulled them into conflict in India as well. Led by brilliant military strategists, Joseph Francis Dupleix for the French and Robert Clive for the English, each side won significant battles, but ultimately Clive proved victorious and the French decided to cut back their Indian commitments. When warfare resumed in India, as a result of the Seven Years War (1756–63), a global struggle between Britain and France, the British easily defeated the French to emerge as the principal European power in India.

As Mughal central authority weakened, several rebellious leaders in the provinces sought alliances with the British to break free of Mughal control. They offered the British a share in their tax collections and political authority. In several regions the British accepted these invitations to alliance and, beginning in Bengal with the Battle of Plassey (1757), they soon gained control of large areas of the country. The British East India Company itself became the instrument of rule, since it was the institutional representative of the British in India. In London, the British Parliament established a Board of Control to oversee the activities of the Company, but in large measure this joint stock trading company had become the political master of large, and increasing, regions of Indian territory.

The Company in Charge. As a commercial enterprise, the Company's principal motive was the acquisition of profits, and now, as rulers, they adopted two policies to maximize them. First, they increased tax collection, both by raising rates and by increasing the efficiency of collection. Second, they manipulated tariffs, lowering them in India so that British manufactures would have easy access to Indian markets, and lobbying to raise them in Britain in order to block the import of Indian textiles. The beginning of Britain's Industrial Revolution and of the Company's establishment of control over large regions of India occurred at approximately the same time, in the second half of the eighteenth century. Colonial control thus immediately protected and facilitated the development of British industry, while effectively blocking Indian competition. (See Source box on Pandita Ramabai's lament over British control of India's economy, especially its tariff policies, in the chapter entitled "The Industrial Revolution.")

India was transformed into the model colony, importing manufactured goods from Britain's industries and exporting raw materials to its factories and distribution centers: raw cotton, which the British manufactured into cloth; jute for making sacks; leather; and enormous quantities of tea, as India displaced China as the leading provider of tea to Europe. Throughout the second half of the nineteenth century and the first years of the twentieth, two-thirds of India's imports from Britain were machine-manufactured textiles. Iron and steel goods came second. India became a lucrative destination for overseas investment, and about 20 percent of all overseas British investment in the late nineteenth century was in India.

Indian Industry. India's own taxes, however, paid for the building and maintenance of the Indian railway system, one of the most extensive in the world, with some 35,000 miles of track by 1914. It made possible a range of diverse activities: the widespread deployment of colonial troops, increased commerce that benefited both Indians and British businessmen, the relief of famine through the shipping of food from areas of surplus harvests to areas of shortfall, the geographical spread of political dissidence, and pilgrimage visits to religious shrines throughout the country.

Victoria Terminus Railway Station, Bombay. Named in honor of the British queen and empress of India, and opened on the date of her Golden Jubilee, 1887, it is now renamed Chatrapati Shivaji station, Mumbai. Built in Gothic style as the headquarters for the great Indian Peninsular Railway, the station resembles St. Pancras station in London. British architecture in India often copied models from the home country, especially for buildings dedicated to modern industry and transportation.

18.1
18.2
18.3
18.4
18.5
18.6
18.7

How did Europeans gain direct political control of four-fifths of the land surface of the globe?

18.1
18.2
18.3
18.4
18.5
18.6
18.7

How did Europeans gain direct political control of four-fifths of the land surface of the globe?

Demonstrating the power of colonial rule, the British manufactured all the components of the system—engines, cars, tracks—in Britain. Thus, even though the financing was drawn from Indian taxes, the profits of the manufacture, the expertise in engineering, and the industrial plant that built the railway industry went to Britain rather than to India.

Under British colonial rule, India began its own industrial revolution with cotton textiles, primarily in Bombay. This textile industry was started mostly by local Gujaratis, inhabitants of the western Indian region of Gujarat, who had long family histories of involvement in business. The need to found new industries to compete with the British found expression even in local poetry, as "The Attack of King Industry" makes clear (see Source box, above). (In Calcutta, where jute textiles were produced, industry was largely pioneered by British investors.) Mining began in the coal fields of Bengal, Bihar, Orissa, and Assam, and in 1911 the Tata family of Bombay—a Parsi family, descendants of immigrants from Persia who had come to India in the eighth century—built India's first steel mill at Jamshedpur, Bihar. At the start of World War I, factory employment in all of India had reached about a million (out of a total population of about 300 million). While employment in large, mechanized factories was increasing, many hand craftsmen were being displaced, so the actual percentage of people earning their living by manufacturing of all sorts stayed approximately the same, at about ten percent of the workforce (and has continued about the same until today).

British Imperial Rule. In 1857, Indians revolted against rule by the British East India Company. The British called this a "mutiny" of army troops, but later scholars have shown it to be a more geographically widespread and more general opposition to British rule. Some nationalist historians have called it "India's First War for National Independence," but the revolt lacked unified leadership and direction. The British crushed the revolt, and from then on they ruled India directly, imposing their influence throughout the administrative and educational systems of the country. Concepts based on European political revolutions were introduced directly and indirectly through the formal secondary and post-secondary education system, the law courts, the press, and even very limited elections. English replaced Persian as the official language of government. As a result, imperialism confronted its internal contradiction: How could an imperial power preach and teach the values of self-rule and democracy while maintaining its own foreign rule? Conversely, could it maintain imperial control while teaching the virtues of home-rule and democracy?

📖 **Read** the **Document: Arrival of the British in the Punjab (mid-19th c.)** on **MyHistoryLab**

The British in Burma, Malaya, and Singapore

India was the "jewel in the crown" of Britain's colonial possessions, but Burma and Malaya had their importance as well. Neighboring Burma was annexed in a series of wars, in 1826, 1852, and 1885, and administered by the British from its Indian headquarters until 1935. The British turned the colony into a major exporter of rice, timber, teak, and oil, and developed the port of Rangoon (Yangon) to handle the trade. Further east, in Malaya, the British established a settlement at Penang in 1786; took Malacca from the Dutch in 1795; and established Singapore in 1819 as their major port in the region. They developed commercially profitable methods for extracting and exporting Malayan tin and turned Malaya's rubber plantations into the world's largest producers. They built Singapore into one of the largest and most geopolitically important ports in the world. Malaya and Burma, like India, became classic colonies, exporting raw materials to the colonizers and importing finished products from them.

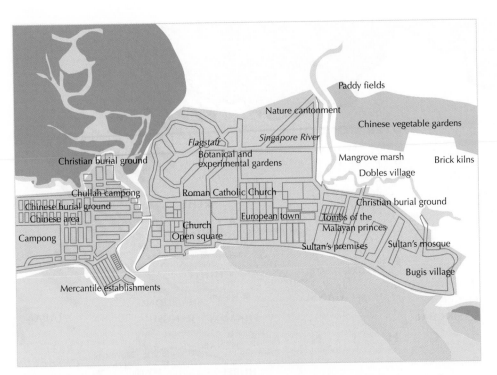

18.1
18.2
18.3 How did Europeans gain direct political control of four-fifths of the land surface of the globe?
18.4
18.5
18.6
18.7

A map of the town and environs of Singapore, from an actual survey by G.D. Coleman, 1839. Singapore was not an indigenous town that gradually grew up around a bustling port; it was purposely founded in 1819 on the site of a fishing village by Sir Stamford Raffles, who saw its potential as a trading center. The British actively encouraged immigration to the new port, and divided the thriving city into separate areas for the different ethnic groups that lived and worked there. The divisions can be seen clearly on the map.

Europeans in China, 1800–1914

Colonialism in China was different. To discuss colonialism in this period in China, we must begin not with the Europeans but with the Manchus, who established the Qing dynasty (1644–1912) and were enthusiastic colonizers. Even before they invaded and ruled China, the Manchus had established a state in their homeland of Manchuria, made Korea a vassal state, and controlled Inner Mongolia as a dependency. After establishing their rule in China, the Qing dynasty expanded westward, annexing new lands equal to the size of China itself (see the chapter entitled "Migration."). They also conquered Taiwan and subordinated the peoples of Southeast Asia into tributary relationships. Revolts broke out against Manchu rule, but until 1800 they occurred mostly at the periphery of the empire and posed no serious threat to the dynasty.

The very size, power, and historical eminence of China created a sense of invulnerability. But China's leaders were not keeping up with changes taking place in the outside world. In 1793, for example, Emperor Qianlong sent a letter to King George III of England, dismissing his request to open trade relations between the two countries: "There is nothing we lack ... nor do we need any more of your country's manufactures" (cited in Teng and Fairbank, p. 19). Although the emperor may have been exaggerating his independence for his own propaganda purposes, as some historians argue, the Chinese willingness to learn from the outside world was limited.

Meanwhile, by the early 1800s China faced a range of internal problems that demanded attention. A continuously rising population put pressure on resources and government administrative capacity. The 100 million people of 1650 had tripled to 300 million by 1800 and reached 420 million by 1850. More land was needed.

The decline of the Qing dynasty. During the course of the nineteenth century, the authority of the Qing (Manchu) dynasty in China was undermined. Beset by the aggressive actions of European colonial powers, the Qing granted extensive trade and territorial concessions. Internally, a series of increasingly violent rebellions, both within the Chinese heartland and in the western (often Muslim) regions, brought the dynasty to the verge of collapse by the end of the century.

Developing Manchuria seemed a suitable reply to the problem, but the Manchus would not permit Chinese settlement in their homeland. Nor did the Manchus increase the size of their bureaucracy to service the rising population, preferring to delegate administrative responsibilities to local authorities, a response that was inadequate.

One strength of the Chinese economy was the sale of tea, silk, and porcelain to the West in exchange for silver and gold. The Europeans trading with China, however, wished to staunch this outflow of bullion. Discovering that China would accept opium in place of precious metals, the British encouraged the growth of opium in their Indian colony and shipped it to China. The centuries of paying for Chinese exports with silver and gold came to an end. By the 1820s China was purchasing so much opium that it began to export silver!

📖 Read the Document: Letter to Queen Victoria (1839) Lin Zexu on MyHistoryLab

The Opium Wars. Fearing for the health of both its people and its treasury, China banned the import of opium in 1839. It was too late. Proclaiming the ideology of "free trade," the British rejected the Chinese demand. When the incorruptible, and inflexible, Imperial Commissioner Lin Zexu tried to confiscate and destroy the British stores of opium, British shipboard cannon shelled Chinese ships and port installations in the harbor at Guangzhou (Canton). This Opium War of 1839–42 was no contest; the Chinese emperors' lack of interest in Western science and technology had left China without modern cannons and steamships. In defeat, China ceded to Britain the island of Hong Kong as a colony, and opened five treaty ports in which foreigners could live and conduct business under their own laws rather than under the laws of China.

The steamer *Nemesis* destroying 11 Chinese junks at Cherpez, Canton, China. E. Duncan, 1843. When the Chinese government tried to prevent British merchants from illegally importing opium, the British bombarded the Chinese coast, triggering the Opium War in 1839–42. These wars continued sporadically through the 1840s and 1850s. (National Maritime Museum, London)

18.1

18.2

18.3

18.4

18.5

18.6

18.7

How did Europeans gain direct political control of four-fifths of the land surface of the globe?

France and the United States soon gained similar concessions. Foreign settlements were established in the new treaty ports and became the centers of new industry, education, and publishing. The focus of international trade began to relocate from Guangzhou to the foreign settlements at Shanghai, at the mouth of the Yangzi River, a more central location along the Chinese coast.

Still China refused to establish the formal diplomatic recognition and exchange that the European powers demanded. A second set of wars, in 1856–60, led to the occupation of Beijing by 17,000 French and British soldiers and the sacking of the imperial Summer Palace. More treaty ports were opened, including inland centers along the Yangzi River, now patrolled by British gunboats. Europeans gained control over the administration of China's foreign trade and tariffs; the opium trade continued to expand; and Christian missionaries were given freedom to travel and proselytize throughout China. The Chinese government was powerless to resist, and some Chinese worked actively with the foreigners as intermediaries in business and administration.

The Taiping Rebellion. Chinese history is filled with peasant revolts. The Taiping Rebellion (1850–64) was one of the largest. It almost toppled the Qing dynasty, and before it was suppressed some 20 million people died. Here, at the end of the revolt, regional, loyal troops are pursuing and defeating the rebels in their last stand at Nanjing. The representation of the Taiping here as a ragtag group of fleeing rabble is a view from the victors' perspective. It does not suggest just how powerful, and dangerous, these rebels had been.

The Taiping Rebellion. As the Manchu government weakened in the last decades of the nineteenth century, revolts broke out, foreign powers continued to seize parts of the country and its tributaries, and there were more calls for internal reform. (The Chinese situation showed similarities with events in the Ottoman Empire at about the same time.) The greatest of the internal revolts, the Taiping Rebellion, began in 1850 and was led by Hong Xiuquan, a frustrated scholar who claimed visions of himself as the younger brother of Jesus Christ. The main demands of the Taiping leaders, however, were concrete: an end to the corrupt and inefficient Manchu imperial rule, an end to extortionate landlord demands, and the alleviation of poverty. Beginning in the southwest, the Taiping rebels came to dominate the Yangzi valley and established their capital in Nanjing in 1853. The imperial government was unable to respond effectively, but regional military leaders, equipped with more modern weapons, finally defeated the revolt with the help of the "Ever Victorious Army," a mercenary force composed of American and European soldiers, winning more power for themselves. By the time the Taiping Rebellion was suppressed in 1864, some 20 million people had been killed. At about the same time, additional rebellions broke out among tribal peoples near Guangzhou, among the Miao tribals in Guizhou, and among Muslims in Yunnan and Gansu. The largest of all the rebel groups, the Nien, arose in the north, in the valley of the Yellow River. That river burst its banks in 1851 and again in 1855, with the loss of thousands of lives and the devastation of vast swathes of agricultural land. When the government failed to provide relief, peasants rose in rebellion. Collectively, these various rebellions cost another ten million lives.

With the central government fully occupied with these internal revolts, foreign imperialists began to expand their territorial claims. Russians seized border areas in the Amur River region (1858), the Maritime Provinces (1860), and, for ten years, the Ili valley in Turkestan (1871–81). France defeated Chinese forces in a local war and seized all of Indochina (1883–93). Most humiliating of all, Japan, having embraced Western technology and imperialist ambitions, defeated China in warfare in 1894–95. China ceded Taiwan to Japan, granted it the right to operate factories in the treaty ports, and paid a huge indemnity. Korea also passed to Japanese control, although formal colonial rule did not follow until 1910. The historic relationship of China as teacher and Japan as disciple, which dated back at least to 600 C.E., had been abruptly reversed. The new industrial age had introduced new values and power relationships.

The Boxer Rebellion. By the last years of the nineteenth century, China was in turmoil. In Beijing, a group of nationalists, called "Boxers" by the Europeans because of their belief that martial arts rendered them invincible in struggle, were enraged by foreign arrogance in China. They burned Christian missions, killed missionaries, and laid siege to the foreign legations for two months. The imperial powers of Europe and the United States put down this revolt and exacted yet another exorbitant indemnity. The Europeans and Americans did not, however, wish to take over the government of China directly. They wanted to have a Chinese government responsible for China. They wanted to preserve China as a quasi-colony, and so they supported the Manchus in the formalities of power, even as they steadily hollowed out the content of that power.

The implementation of colonialism in China was often a joint enterprise. The colonizers cooperated in suppressing the Boxer revolt and in administering the colonial port cities, such as Shanghai. In these cities, the British, French, American, and Japanese governments each governed its own colonial neighborhood-settlement, each with its own cultural and architectural style. These settlements were mostly adjacent to one another, and they coordinated their administrations. A group of Chinese modernizers began to organize new industries, beginning with textiles, later developing Western weapons and steamships. However, the government, now in the hands of the aging dowager empress Cixi, who controlled the heir apparent until she died in 1908, blocked their reforms. Frustrated nationalists called for revolution. Their leading organizer was Sun Yat-sen (Sun Yixian), a Cantonese educated in Honolulu, where he became a Christian, and in Hong Kong, where he became a doctor. Sun called for a twofold anticolonial revolution: first against the Manchus and then against the European, American, and Japanese powers. Only after the first revolution succeeded in overthrowing Manchu rule in 1911 did Sun begin to push against the Western powers and Japan. The story of that struggle is told in the chapter "China and India."

Boxers on the march. The mostly poor peasants who formed the Boxer Rebellion of 1898–1900 blamed hard times on foreign interference and Christian missionaries. Renowned for the ferocity of their attacks, the rebels terrified Western residents as they marched into Tianjin (pictured). A 20,000-strong force, comprising soldiers from different colonial powers, finally crushed the revolt in Beijing.

The French in Algeria and Southeast Asia

We have already seen that weakness in the Ottoman Empire gave foreigners the opportunity to prey on its possessions in the Balkans and in Egypt. In North Africa, the French led the scavengers. By the late seventeenth and early eighteenth century,

18.1
18.2
18.3
18.4
18.5
18.6
18.7

How did Europeans gain direct political control of four-fifths of the land surface of the globe?

18.1

18.2

18.3   How did Europeans gain direct political control of four-fifths of the land surface of the globe?

18.4

18.5

18.6

18.7

both Tunis and Algiers were only nominally under Ottoman rule. Both regions profited from piracy and were finally invaded by seafaring nations, Algeria by the French and Tunis by the Americans. (The phrase "to the shores of Tripoli" in the American Marine Corps hymn comes from this expedition.) The French attack on Algeria in 1830 began as a campaign against piracy, but relations between the ruler of Algiers and the French government spun out of control, and ultimately the French demanded and got his surrender and control over his possessions.

Algiers was politically fragmented, however, and the French found themselves at war with other regional leaders, especially Abd al-Qadir, son of the head of one of the most important Muslim brotherhoods, or religious/political organizations, in the Middle East. Resistance swelled under al-Qadir, and he began to build a small state with its own administration and a modernized army of 10,000 men trained by European advisers. At first, the French avoided confrontation with al-Qadir, who stayed south of their holdings, but in 1841 warfare broke out. Before the French won, they had committed 110,000 troops (a third of their army) to the war and had attacked neighboring Morocco to block reinforcements to their enemy. Revolts continued to simmer. The last and largest was repressed in 1871, with 3,000 French soldiers reported killed. Since the French resorted to a policy of destroying the crops of al-Qadir's army, reliable estimates put Algerian casualties as high as one-third of the total Algerian population. French armies seized rural areas, opening them for military occupation and settlement.

During the years of fighting and thereafter, tens of thousands of Europeans came to settle in Algeria, some in connection with the military, some in search of economic opportunity. About half were French, but all began to adopt French language and culture and to think of themselves as French people living in Algeria. By the 1850s there were 130,000 of them and by 1900 more than half a million, about 13 percent of the population. Christians (and, after 1870, Jews) were deemed to be citizens of France; Muslims were legally subjects of the French empire. After a change of government in France in 1870, Algeria was formally annexed to France, and French citizens—but not subjects—in Algeria received the right to vote for members of the French National Assembly in Paris. Through official land transfers and sales, the best land came into French hands and was developed into commercial agriculture, while Algerian farmers were generally left with small, under-capitalized holdings. Algerians had been deprived of their best lands, and left out of the middle and upper reaches of the administration and of commercial enterprises. Algeria was governed for the French.

Because it was a settler colony and geographically so near to France, Algeria marked the beginning of French colonialism in North Africa—but only the beginning. In the later 1800s, France captured all the vast expanse of French West Africa, which included parts of sub-Saharan Africa (see map, "Africa in 1914," below). France administered French West Africa from Dakar, Senegal, an Atlantic port on the westernmost point of Africa, which had been one of France's earliest points of contact and trade—especially slave trade—going back to the mid-1600s.

French colonialism conquered Southeast Asia much later than North Africa. Invading Vietnam in 1857, the French claimed to be avenging the murder of several French missionaries and Vietnamese Christians some two decades earlier. They were also seeking overseas markets and a French share in the colonization of Asia. In a series of wars and occupations, the French took possession of all of French Indochina (see map, "The decline of the Qing dynasty," above) by 1887. They reserved all but minor positions in their administration for French officials. They built public works—railroads, highways, bridges, canals, ports—all to benefit the French and facilitate the export of raw materials, such as rice, coal, and rubber, and the import of finished products. A few wealthy, landowning Vietnamese who collaborated with the French administration did well, but most of the peasantry saw their standard of living, and the amount of food they had to eat, decline under French colonialism.

18.1
18.2
18.3
18.4
18.5
18.6
18.7

How did Europeans gain direct political control of four-fifths of the land surface of the globe?

Dutch tobacco processing in Java, 1830. The Dutch "cultivation system," introduced in 1830, forced Indonesian farmers to turn over 20 percent of their land to growing commercial crops for Dutch enterprise, even though this often left inadequate land for producing food crops. The profits for the Dutch merchants and government were, however, enormous.

The Dutch in Indonesia

The Dutch in Indonesia are much less well represented in historical literature than are the British and French in their colonies, probably because of the linguistic difficulties of studying the subject. Dutch is not used much outside the Netherlands, and Bahasa Indonesia and other Indonesian languages are not used much outside Indonesia. Nevertheless, the subject is of great interest and importance.

As we saw in the chapter entitled "The Unification of World Trade," the Dutch East Indies Company had been active as a trading company in Indonesia since the beginning of the seventeenth century. It went bankrupt in 1799, however, because of poor management and the (often illegal) competition of private traders. After 15 years of French and then British rule during the Napoleonic Wars, in 1815, the Dutch government took over direct rule of its Indonesian holdings. Prepared to assert their renewed control, the Dutch ruled through especially high levels of violence and cruelty. The Java War of 1825–30 reflected many background economic and political grievances, and it finally erupted when the Dutch built a highway through property housing the tomb of a Muslim saint. In the brutal combat that followed, 15,000 government soldiers were killed, including 8,000 Dutch. On the other side, some 200,000 Javanese died in the war and in the famine and disease that followed.

In 1830 the Dutch introduced a new, particularly exploitative economic policy called *Kulturstelsel*, "**the cultivation system.**" The Indonesian peasants were forced to devote 20 percent of their land to the production of cash crops, especially coffee, sugar, and indigo, to be turned over to the Dutch for export to the Netherlands as a kind of taxation. From 1840 to 1880 the estimated profits sent back to the Netherlands equaled 25 percent of the total budget of that country. By 1870, however, complaints reached Amsterdam from both within and outside Indonesia against this system, which prevented Indonesians from growing the food they needed. The Dutch government implemented a new "Liberal Policy" permitting capitalist investment in Indonesia from the Netherlands and lifting the harsh, restrictive regulations imposed

KEY TERM

the cultivation system A system of Dutch rule over Indonesian agriculture that forced peasants to devote 20 percent of their land to cash crops for export. This policy took away the peasant's right to determine his use of his own fields, and diminished the production of food.

European expansion in Africa. Steamboats, machine guns, and quinine (to combat malaria) all gave Europeans new access to the interior of Africa in the later nineteenth century, and they intensified their nationalistic competition. The British pursued the dream of linking their possessions from Cape Town to Cairo, while France seized much of North and central Africa. Bismarck's Berlin Conference of 1884 tried to apportion the spoils among all the competing powers.

on agriculture, and on cultivators, by the cultivation system. Plantations and industries began to flourish, their profits surpassing those of agriculture. Rubber, copra (dried coconut meat, from which coconut oil is extracted), tin, and oil became even more valuable export products than coffee, sugar, tea, and tobacco. At the same time, the government, determined to control all the outlying islands, also expanded its political administration from its center on the island of Java. These more aggressive and intrusive political and economic policies, often referred to by historians as the "new imperialism," were typical also of the colonial expansion of the British and the French in their colonies at about the same time.

By 1901, reevaluations of the Liberal Policy declared it, too, to be harsh and exploitative. The government declared a new "Ethical Policy," designed to improve the health and education systems of the islands. The results were not pervasive, but they did help to raise up a small, new group of leaders, educated in Western forms, who came to challenge Dutch rule, and ultimately bring it to an end (in 1949).

18.1

18.2

18.3

18.4 What was the process by which Europeans expanded their control into Africa in the nineteenth century?

18.5

18.6

18.7

European Competition and Cooperation: Empire-building in Africa

18.4 What was the process by which Europeans expanded their control into Africa in the nineteenth century?

When European traders arrived in India and China they found huge countries governed by powerful empires. Sub-Saharan Africa was quite different. It was much larger and more diverse, an entire continent, second only to Asia in size, with many states and with even more areas under the control of local families, clans, and ethnicities. Each area had its own history, and the experience of each different European group also varied in each different region.

In sub-Saharan Africa, the early European experience was mostly limited to the shoreline of the west coast, as the Europeans sought a shipping route to Asia. The European traders found that they could buy the slaves they wanted in the port towns they established along the coast, without going inland themselves: African rulers and merchants captured, collected, and brought the slaves to them for sale. The Europeans for the most part accepted this commercial arrangement as economically efficient. It saved them from conflict with local African rulers, and it did not endanger their health by bringing them into contact with diseases against which they had no immunity. Even from their coastal enclaves, the Europeans were able to make a considerable mark on Africa, purchasing and transporting ten million slaves to the New World over a period of four centuries.

In this coastal trade, the European sailors and commercial agents were often competitive, and some coastal enclaves were seized first by one group of Europeans and then by another. The fortress at El Mina, for example, in today's Ghana, was built by the Portuguese in 1482, seized by the Dutch in 1637, and then taken by the British in 1871. But the coast was long, the trade extensive and open, and the sailing expeditions often cooperative with one another. European port towns were always more Afro-European than European, since the Europeans stayed only briefly while their mixed-race descendants remained, along with a much larger number of slaves. Saint Louis, for example, in modern Senegal, was home in 1810 to about 10 Europeans, 500 Afro-Europeans, 500 free Africans who had absorbed European culture, and about 2,200 slaves. The British outlawed the slave trade in 1807, and attempted to end it by forcefully seizing slave ships belonging to all nations. Nevertheless the trade continued for decades, suggesting that the slave ships were cooperating with one another to avoid the British antislavery patrols at sea.

18.1
18.2
18.3
18.4
18.5
18.6
18.7

What was the process by which Europeans expanded their control into Africa in the nineteenth century?

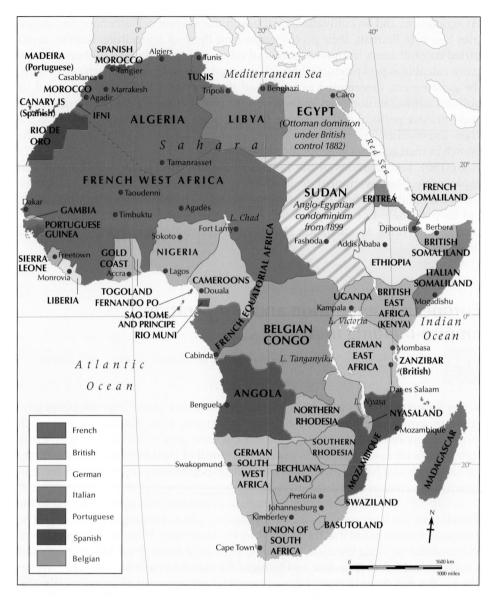

Africa in 1914. By the end of the nineteenth century, Africa presented European imperialists with their last chance to claim a "place in the sun." In a scramble for territory, Belgium, Germany, and Italy joined Spain, Portugal, Britain, and France in carving up the continent, riding roughshod over native concerns with brutal insensitivity. Conflict among the colonists was common, the war between the British and Dutch in South Africa being the most bloody.

The Competition for South Africa

In the settlement of South Africa, cooperation gave way to competition and warfare. The Dutch established the first substantial European colony in sub-Saharan Africa in 1652, at the Cape of Good Hope on the southern tip of the continent. The settlement grew steadily, and immigrants from other European countries—especially Britain—joined it.

European expansion at the Cape had disruptive effects on local populations. As the Dutch and then the British set out to the rural areas to farm, they displaced the Khoikhoi people who had been resident in the area. The Khoikhoi chiefdoms dissolved in the face of warfare, displacement, and catastrophic smallpox epidemics that decimated their numbers. Some of the Khoikhoi, along with other African peoples, were taken as slaves to fill the labor needs of the Europeans. In 1708 the population of the Cape consisted of about 1,700 free citizens, including free blacks, and 1,700 slaves. By 1800 it totaled about 75,000, of whom one-third were free and two-thirds were slaves, mostly African but some of mixed race.

As a result of the Napoleonic Wars, military and legal control of the Cape Colony passed from the Dutch to the British. British laws and social practices were instituted, including the development of limited representative government, the abolition of the slave trade, and, in 1833, the abolition of slavery throughout the British Empire. Nevertheless, Europeans controlled the best land of the region. Their former slaves could aspire only to be wage workers, not landowners or farmers. Property restrictions on voting effectively kept Africans removed from political power, and the Masters and Servants Act of 1856 limited the freedom of black workers, especially their freedom of geographical movement.

For the 8,000 people of Dutch descent, however, these limits on black freedom were not enough. They declared their opposition to the more liberal British customs of the colony, especially the abolition of slavery. They decided to separate themselves from the British and, in search of new land for farming, they departed on a march, or **Great Trek**, northward in the years between 1834 and 1841. These people, usually called Boers (meaning "farmers" in Dutch), or Afrikaners (for the African dialect of Dutch they spoke), ultimately founded two new republics, the Orange Free State and the Transvaal (see map, "European expansion in Africa," above). Meanwhile, the Cape Colony expanded eastward, partly to keep out the Boers. As they migrated, the Boers fought, conquered, displaced, and restricted to reservations the African peoples they encountered. Seeking labor to work the land, they often captured and virtually enslaved Africans living around them.

This geographical expansion of the European Cape Colony further destabilized a region already passing through a *mfecane*, or time of troubles. In 1816, Shaka (*c.* 1787–1828) seized the leadership of his small Zulu kingdom just to the north and east of the Cape Colony. He organized a standing army of 40,000 soldiers, trained them rigorously, housed them in stockades separate from the rest of the population, and armed them with newly designed short stabbing spears, enormously effective in hand-to-hand combat. He instituted new battle formations, similar to those used by the ancient Greeks, with a massed center and flanks that could encircle the enemy and cut off its rear. By 1828, when Shaka was assassinated by two half-brothers, his kingdom had expanded, forcing local peoples to flee their lands. Some moved into the Cape Colony, but the vast majority turned north and east, traveling hundreds of miles into present-day Mozambique, Zimbabwe, Zambia, and Tanzania, and displacing other peoples in turn. All these movements combined—the Boer trek, Shaka's Zulu expansion, and the migration of peoples fleeing before both of these advances—created the *mfecane* in southern and eastern Africa. Cape Colony itself, however, remained relatively tranquil, continuing to serve as a port in transoceanic trade.

When the Suez Canal restructured the shipping routes between Asia and Europe in 1869, ending the need for the long voyage around Africa, South Africa might have become a quiet colonial backwater. But in the 1870s

KEY TERMS

Great Trek Between 1834 and 1841 the Dutch settlers in the British Cape Colony left the British-dominated areas to the south to establish their own control in the north. The Dutch felt the British were too liberal in their treatment of blacks.

mfecane Literally "time of troubles," the period in southern Africa from about 1816, when Shaka took control of the Zulu kingdom, until about 1841, when the Dutch completed their Great Trek. The expansion of the Zulus and the migration of the Dutch dislodged local kingdoms and peoples, increasing political instability throughout the region.

THE RHODES COLOSSUS
STRIDING FROM CAPE TOWN TO CAIRO.

"The Rhodes Colossus." Cecil John Rhodes became one of the main champions of British rule in southern Africa, promoting colonization "from Cape Town to Cairo." The statesman and financier divided his time between diamond mining and annexing territories to British imperial rule. Rhodesia (now Zimbabwe and Zambia) was named for him in 1894.

623

18.1
18.2
18.3
18.4
18.5
18.6
18.7

What was the process by which Europeans expanded their control into Africa in the nineteenth century?

diamonds were discovered at Kimberley, and in the 1880s the world's largest known deposit of gold was found at Witwatersrand. Competition for this new wealth intensified the general hostility between the Boers and the British into full-scale warfare. The British army of 450,000 men finally defeated the Boer army of 88,000 in the three-year South African War, which the British called the Boer War (1899–1902). In 1910, the British consolidated their own two colonies (Cape and Natal) with the two Boer republics into the Union of South Africa, which became a self-governing country. After 1913, whites in South Africa had the same sorts of political institutions and rights as in the British dominions of Australia and Canada. Because of the European domination of the life of the colony, South Africa was considered a white settler colony despite its overwhelming black majority.

Sierra Leone and Liberia: Havens for Former Slaves

The British, Americans, and Africans, working together, responded to the abolition of the slave trade and slavery, in part, by establishing two new colonies, Sierra Leone and Liberia, as refuges for freed slaves, and by founding new businesses, mostly based on tropical agricultural products, to replace slave trading in the export economy.

Freetown, in Sierra Leone, was founded in 1787 to serve as a haven for freed slaves. At first these were mostly black Americans, freed by the British during the American Revolution, and rebels from Jamaican slavery. After the abolition of the British slave trade in 1807, increasing numbers were slaves recaptured at sea by the British navy and set free. Between 1807 and 1864, the British navy brought more than 50,000 recaptured slaves to Sierra Leone and granted them freedom. To cope with these numbers, the British reorganized Sierra Leone in 1808 as a formal British colony and promoted Christianity and Western culture among its residents. Some of the freed slaves, especially the Yoruba, used Sierra Leone as a staging point from which to return inland to the societies from which they had been taken. Most, however, remained in Sierra Leone, which continued to grow. The ex-slaves had come from very different regions of West Africa, and missionaries attempted to unify them into a single Christian nation by providing them with a common education. In 1827 the Anglican Church Mission Society founded Fourah Bay College, an important institution for training African clergy. One of its first graduates, Samuel Crowther, became the first African bishop of the Anglican Church (1864). The overwhelming majority of Sierra Leone's population were Africans who joined the colony on their own.

Following the example of Sierra Leone, the American Colonization Society received a charter from the United States government in 1816 to found a site on the West African coast for the repatriation of freed American slaves. In 1822, the first settlers arrived at the site that later became Monrovia, named for American president James Monroe. In 1847, when Monrovia held about 5,000 settlers, it formally declared its independence from the United States government. Nine years later it joined with its surrounding settlements to form the country of Liberia as an independent state, although it was still heavily reliant on American assistance. Americans supported Liberia for diverse reasons: some saw it as a haven for former slaves, others saw it as a dumping ground in which America could rid itself of ex-slaves. As in Sierra Leone, the population of freed slaves always formed a small minority of the total population. Even today, descendants of repatriated slaves, known as Americo-Liberians, form only 2.5 percent of the total population of about 3.2 million.

Cooperation among Africans and Europeans

Europeans and Africans had cooperated for centuries in the slave trade. As that trade ended in the North Atlantic, both Europeans and Africans sought new export commodities. British schemes to develop cotton plantations on the Niger River failed disastrously as European personnel succumbed to tropical illnesses to which they had no resistance. French schemes for plantations in the Ivory Coast and Gabon similarly failed. Foreigners did establish some economic enterprises inland—and often the same person served as the representative of government and the representative of European business interests. Most of the basic agricultural and animal commodities, however, were produced and transported by Africans. Ivory—much in demand in the West for piano keys and billiard balls—continued to be a staple throughout much of the continent. New market crops included palm nuts and kernels, peanuts, timber, dyes, wax, honey, and redwood. As steamships started to ply Africa's rivers, bulkier crops were added: cotton, coffee, sugar cane, and sugar products. Rubber came in the 1870s. In the area around the Congo River, cassava, citrus fruit, tobacco, and maize were introduced. Despite its abolition in the British Empire, the slave trade flourished for most of the nineteenth century in the South Atlantic and throughout Africa. The increase in commercial cropping, ivory harvesting, and copper and metal mining and production required labor. Often "freed" slaves were forced into labor on the new plantations and in the expanding caravan trade, especially in East Africa. Arab caravan leaders impressed slaves into the ivory trade in great numbers and with high mortality rates.

The transport networks within Africa were for the most part run by Africans themselves. In the east, Arab traders sometimes also conducted caravans from the coast to the Lake District. The Arab traders were backed financially and militarily by the Arab planters of Zanzibar with their rich harvest of cloves. The profit to be made from cloves in Zanzibar and from coordinating caravan transportation in East Africa was so great that the Arab ruler of the Oman Empire, Sayyid Said, moved his capital from Muscat, on the Arabian peninsula (see map, "Ottoman empires, 1300–1700," in the chapter entitled "Migration"), to Zanzibar in 1840.

For most of the nineteenth century, the Afro-Europeans did well in business, education, and local public affairs in a relatively open environment. Commercial profit became more important than political power. Beginning in the 1880s, however, Europeans in larger numbers arrived to take over direct political and economic power and impose increasingly racist policies. Steamboats penetrated more deeply into the continent, upriver from the ports. Many of the African transport workers were displaced from their jobs, and some European commercial and administrative officials took up positions inland. Europeans also owned and managed some of the great plantations and industries in the interior: rubber in the Congo, coffee plantations in East Africa, and diamonds and copper in the Congo and South Africa. Joseph Conrad's great novel *Heart of Darkness* (1899) captures the remote setting and the foreboding mood of that transformation to European overlordship.

Read the **Document: Mary Kingsley and the Bubi of Fernando Po** on **MyHistoryLab**

The Scramble for Africa

Many adventurers were drawn to Africa in the late eighteenth and early nineteenth century, further opening the interior of the continent to outsiders. The best known was David Livingstone (1813–73), a Scottish missionary and able scientist, who began his career in South Africa in 1841, intent on establishing a missionary station and providing medical assistance to Africans. He returned home briefly in 1852, but by 1853 he was back in Africa. For three years he crossed and recrossed the continent. Livingstone was distinguished for learning African languages, treating Africans with respect, and constantly campaigning against the slave trade that was endemic in the African interior. Two subsequent, grueling adventures of exploration in equatorial Africa lasted a total of 13 years. Livingstone died in 1873 in what is today Zambia. In accordance with his wishes, his heart was buried in Africa, under a tree near the place where he died.

18.1
18.2
18.3
18.4
18.5
18.6
18.7

What was the process by which Europeans expanded their control into Africa in the nineteenth century?

What was the process by which Europeans expanded their control into Africa in the nineteenth century?

In 1871, when premature rumors of Livingstone's death reached Europe, the New York *Herald* newspaper dispatched the explorer Henry Morton Stanley (1841–1904) to try to find him. Stanley not only located Livingstone, but also carried out expeditions of his own—traveling with an armed retinue that resembled a military expedition or a slave caravan. On Stanley's return through Europe, Leopold II, King of the Belgians (r. 1865–1909), engaged him to establish trading stations along the Congo River. The colonization of central Africa was beginning. Stanley, representing the king, negotiated treaties with hundreds of local chiefs. The treaties gave Stanley himself the power to establish a Confederation of Free Negro Republics, an estate of some 900,000 square miles, which functioned as a kind of slave plantation within Africa for the personal economic benefit of King Leopold. The brutality of Stanley's treatment of Africans was perhaps the worst in the annals of European colonialism in Africa.

📖 **Read** the **Document**: H. M. Stanley in Uganda (1870s) on **MyHistoryLab**

The Berlin Conference. As European powers explored and colonized central Africa, they came into direct competition with one another. Fearing the consequences of this competition, Germany's chancellor, Bismarck, convened a conference for the European powers and the United States to establish ground rules for fixing borders among European colonies in Africa. The **Berlin Conference** (1884–85) assigned the administration of the Congo—a region named for the Congo River and for the now-defunct, historic Kingdom of Kongo—to Leopold II personally as a kind of fiefdom. The Congo became, in effect, Leopold's private estate, 80 times larger than Belgium itself. Its economic purpose was, first, the harvesting of natural rubber from vines in the jungles and, later, the exploitation of the area's rich mineral reserves, especially copper. Laborers were forced to work as slaves at gunpoint. Workers could be killed or have their hands cut off for failing to make quotas. Company agents killed and maimed workers who resisted. Ten million Congolese died as a result of the king's rule. In 1908, recognizing both the cruelty and the economic losses of the Congo administration, the Belgian parliament took over control of the colony from the king, but the Congo remained one of the most harshly administered of all the African colonies.

The Berlin Conference divided up the lands of Africa on paper, generally apportioning inland areas to the European nations already settled on the adjacent coast. These nations were then charged with establishing settlements in those regions, and they quickly did so, dispatching settlers in a "**scramble for Africa**." Backed by their new weapons, especially machine guns, and their new steamboats, European governments forced one-sided treaties on African chiefs who often did not understand the significance of the documents they signed. The chiefs frequently became, in effect, the agents of Europeans for recruiting labor and collecting taxes. In exchange, the Europeans protected the

KEY TERMS

Berlin Conference Convened by Otto von Bismarck of Germany to settle peacefully European disputes over territory in Africa.

scramble for Africa The rush of European nations to colonize the parts of Africa that were assigned to them in the international negotiations at the Berlin Conference.

Congolese plantation workers. For decades the Congo was administered as a private estate of King Leopold II of Belgium. Its rubber plantations and copper mines brought immense wealth to him and his country, but he treated the Congolese with sadistic brutality. Workers were killed and maimed for failing to reach the production quotas set for them. In 1908, following an investigation of the cruelty of the system, the Belgian government took control of the colony, but treatment of the Congolese people remained harsh.

Why Did Europeans Colonize the World?

The Industrial Revolution in Western Europe and the United States ushered in an era of imperialism that brought most of the world's land under European political control. Why did the industrializing nations assert their power in this way? To some extent, the answer seems obvious: they relished the power, wealth, and prestige that apparently came with imperial possessions. They also claimed to welcome the opportunity to serve others. Further, the industrial system they were building took on a life of its own, requiring ever-increasing sources of raw materials and more markets in which to sell. But why was trade alone not enough? Why did the industrialists feel it was necessary to take political control as well? Were there additional motives behind imperialism? And did the results of imperialism match the aspirations of the imperial rulers?

We cannot answer all these questions fully, but a review article by Patrick Wolfe in *The American Historical Review*, "History and Imperialism: A Century of Theory, from Marx to Postcolonialism," helps us to review and sort out some of the most prominent explanations.

Karl Marx deplored the exploitation of colonialism, but, as a European, he valued some of its contributions. Britain, he emphasized, brought to India a new economic dynamism, with railroads, industrial infrastructure, and communications networks. Ultimately this transformation would lead to capitalism and then socialism. Marx wrote in 1853: "Whatever may have been the crimes of England, she was the unconscious tool of history in bringing about that revolution" (Marx and Engels, p. 21).

J.A. Hobson, a British economist writing in 1902, and V.I. Lenin, the leader of the communist revolution in Russia, writing in 1916 argued that the desire to control raw materials and markets drove imperialism. Hobson pointed out that the profits of the imperial system went mostly to the rich. He believed that if imperialism were ended overseas, a concentration on investment and industry at home would provide greater opportunities to the working classes in Europe. M.N. Roy, a founder of the Communist Party of India, disagreed with Hobson, arguing that the profits of imperialism did provide economic gains to European workers and that they would therefore support the system. The revolt against the imperial, and capitalist, system would have to begin among the workers in the colonies who were more exploited.

Several analysts have tried to grasp the imperial system as a whole, understanding the impact of colonizer and colonized upon each other. Some, like Marx, saw the system introducing valuable modernization into the colonies. Most, like Immanuel Wallerstein and the American economists Paul Baran and Paul Sweezy, argued that the imperial power would always seek to keep the colonies in a position of dependency and underdevelopment. The imperial rulers might introduce some technological innovations, such as railways that were necessary for their trade, but they had no interest in enabling the colonies to become economic and technological rivals. Indeed, one reason for imposing imperial domination was to prevent the colony from taking control of its own economic policies.

Ronald Robinson and John Gallagher, British historians writing in the 1960s, and the French philosopher Louis Althusser, writing in the 1970s and 1980s, stressed the need to evaluate imperialism case by case. British imperialism in Egypt, for example, was quite sophisticated and benign compared with the raw cruelty of Belgian imperialism in the Congo. Even within individual colonies, imperialists treated different regions and groups differently, for example incorporating educated urban groups into the administration while treating plantation workers almost like slave labor. Imperial rule also varied considerably depending on the administration in power in the imperial country and on the local imperial representatives on the scene. All three scholars eschewed generalizations and emphasized the complexity of the imperial enterprise.

Finally, some of the most recent scholarly analyses of imperialism—often referred to as postcolonial analyses—have stressed the cultural impact of imperialism on both colonized and colonizer. Imperial rulers usually drew a sense of pride from their conquest and exalted their own culture for possessing colonies. David Cannadine argues that the British ruled their colonies with considerable pomp and ceremony, attempting to sustain a hierarchy of privilege and heredity, which incorporated the most prominent elites of the colonized people, in an attempt to replicate the conservative society that they imagined still existed in England. The British ruled large parts of India and Africa through local aristocratic rulers. One-third of India, by area, was ruled by these local "princes." (Of course, another reason for indirect rule was to save money on administration.) On the other hand, Cannadine's elites aside, most colonized peoples suffered a sense of inferiority. They had been conquered by foreigners. Their great historic traditions had somehow failed them.

The postcolonial literature that analyzes this cultural confrontation has expanded rapidly, with contributions by such literary critics as Edward Said, Homi Bhabha, and Gayatri Chakravorty Spivak. Indeed, as industrialization has brought peoples of the world into ever closer contact, and political philosophies have collided with one another, questions of personal and group identity have increased everywhere.

- Among the scholars who argue that economics is the main force behind imperialism, there are differences of opinion. What are these differences? Which point of view seems most persuasive to you?
- Some scholars have argued that political gain has been the main force behind imperialism. What evidence do you see to support this viewpoint?
- Many contemporary scholars argue that the colonizing countries have been influenced by colonialism culturally just as much as have the colonized. What examples of this influence can you cite?

African Musician, Aloysius O'Kelly, *c*. 1880. Oil on canvas. As European artists painted African scenes they often portrayed people of striking beauty and strength against exotic backgrounds. This musician may have been a *griot*, a bard whose songs and chants preserved the history of his people. (Taylor Gallery, London)

18.1

18.2

18.3

18.4 What was the process by which Europeans expanded their control into Africa in the nineteenth century?

18.5

18.6

18.7

chiefs from resistance and rebellion. As the chiefs ceded power to the Europeans, they gained power over their own people.

On the occasions when Africans resisted these agreements, Europeans responded with force. The Germans crushed perhaps the greatest of the unsuccessful rebellions, the Maji-Maji revolt of 1905–07 in Tanganyika. Led by Kinjikitile Ngwele, who claimed to have magic water (*maji*) that would make his followers invulnerable to wounds, the rebels refused to perform forced labor on the cotton plantations. The uprising ended with 70,000 rebels dead, including those who succumbed to disease and malnutrition. Other less spectacular revolts were similarly suppressed with violence.

Europeans and Labor Relations in Africa

Throughout Africa, Europeans confronted the problem of recruiting labor for their new farms and enterprises. By confiscating African land and redistributing it among themselves, they took farms away from Africans and produced a new wage-labor force. The 1913 Natives Land Act of South Africa closed 87 percent of South African land to African ownership; the small percentage that remained was the most marginal land. The newly displaced labor force was especially vital for the new coffee plantations in the highlands of East Africa. In the farming areas of Kenya, northern Rhodesia, Nyasaland, and Angola a system of tenancy without wages developed, a kind of share-cropping system. Within their colonies in Angola and Mozambique, the Portuguese used intimidation to coerce labor, but the Africans often fled or otherwise subverted the plans of their colonizers. The British colonies, which used the carrot of (low) wages, seemed more successful in eliciting production. Along the African coast, indentured laborers from India, China, and Southeast Asia were imported by the thousands to work in the sugar plantations.

The greatest problem was finding labor for the South African diamond and gold mines (and later for the great copper mines in the Congo as well). European colonial governments imposed taxation, which had to be paid in cash, forcing all Africans to find some way of raising the money. Jobs in the mines were one alternative. Because the Europeans feared the revolutionary potential of a stable African labor force in the mines, they usually recruited workers on contracts for only one or two years at a time. They split up families, housing the male workers in barrack-like accommodations near the mines while exiling their families to distant reservations, where the women and children carried on limited farming and craft production. Because the mine owners did not pay the workers enough to support their families, the farming and handicrafts of the women in effect subsidized the salaries of the workers in the mines.

Trade unions in the mines organized only the white skilled workers and kept Africans out. In 1906, when the mines employed 18,000 whites, 94,000 Africans, and 51,000 Chinese indentured laborers, the white skilled workers went on strike to protest their being squeezed out by the Chinese and blacks. Owners brought in Afrikaner workers to break the strike, but ultimately the Chinese miners were repatriated and the skilled jobs were reserved for whites. Race thus trumped both the free markets of capitalism and the solidarity of labor unions.

Gender Relationships in Colonization

18.5   How did colonial living affect European concepts of gender, race, and sexuality?

The Europeans who traveled overseas to trade beginning in the sixteenth century were almost invariably males, and they frequently entered into sexual liaisons with local women. As the men stayed longer, these relationships became increasingly important for business and administration as well as for social and sexual pleasure. In the Senegambia (present-day Senegal and Gambia), as the Senegal Company forbade its traders to marry locally, the French men found signares (concubines or mistresses) among the local peoples. These women helped the men to negotiate local languages, customs, and health conditions.

In India, the **nabobs**, successful traders and administrators who often became wealthy, were not forbidden to marry local women. They fathered Anglo-Indian children who came to form a small but important community of their own, especially in the large port cities of Bombay, Madras, and Calcutta.

As Europeans began to establish colonies, and as women began to travel to these colonies, usually with their husbands but sometimes in search of husbands, European women discouraged such relationships. More rigid sexual boundaries were established. In both India and Africa the relationships between colonizing men and colonized women became fewer and more distant. New guidelines for interracial behavior restricted not only sexual but also social relationships. As these relationships between men and women became less free, so, too, did the informality among the men across ethnic lines.

Nautch dancers, Hyderabad, Willoughby Wallace Hooper and George Western, 1860s. Observing and enjoying Nautch dancing (a redundancy, since *nautch* means "dance") was one of the pleasures of Indian princely courts, and Europeans soon developed a taste for the art. Photographers, too, were attracted by the elegance of the dance and the dancers, as this picture suggests. The languid beauty of these dancers hints, correctly, that sometimes the women might have been prized—by Indians and Europeans alike—for other talents in addition to the dance. (British Library, London)

KEY TERM

nabob A corruption of the title "Nawab," for an Indian Muslim ruler, nabob referred to a British trader or administrator who grew rich in India. Often used sarcastically.

18.1

18.2

18.3

18.4

18.5

18.6

18.7

How did colonial living affect European concepts of gender, race, and sexuality?

How did colonial living affect European concepts of gender, race, and sexuality?

Earlier historians attributed this increasing social distance between Europeans and the peoples they colonized to the restrictive attitudes of European women, who blocked their husbands from mixing with the local women. More recent, feminist scholarship has attributed the responsibility for the increased distance to both husband and wife. Both exhibited racism. Whatever may have been the differences of opinion between European men and women concerning the relationships between European men and the colonized women, almost all Europeans wished to restrict local men from having intimate contact with European women. As colonial settlements increased in size and stability, each family tended to view itself, somewhat pompously, as representative of the rulers, a colonial outpost in miniature.

Did the colonizing women form a solidarity with their colonized sisters? Most contemporary historians think not. The colonizers tended to focus on flaws, as they saw them, in the gender relations among the colonized peoples, and then set out to introduce reform. In India the British outlawed *sati*, the practice of widows burning themselves to death on their deceased husbands' funeral pyres; they introduced a minimum age of marriage; and they urged the remarriage of widows despite upper-caste Hindu resistance. In Africa they sought to end polygamy. In each case, the colonial government emphasized the superiority of its own practices and the good fortune of the colonized to have the Europeans there to save them from themselves. The European colonizers pointed to their interventions in gender relations to justify and praise their own colonial rule. The colonizing women did the same.

The colonial presence did introduce new patterns of gender relations into the colonies, based on the European models. At least some of the colonized peoples chose to move toward a more European style of gender relations. They wanted more education for women, greater freedom of choice in marriage, more companionate marriages, and an end to *sati* in India, to polygamy in parts of Africa, and to footbinding in China. People adopted new customs sometimes because they seemed to

Christmas in India, sketch by E.K. Johnson, *The Graphic*, 1881. Just as most European men did not usually socialize or form a solidarity with the men whose country they had colonized, so, too, the women kept themselves apart and their lives centered on their families and their European friends. The wife would oversee the running of the household as she was accustomed to doing at home. Here an *ayah* looks after the youngest child in much the same way that a nanny would have back in England.

be improvements on local practices, and sometimes because the new behavior won favor for the colonized peoples with the colonizing masters.

Later, as nationalism took root, local peoples began to reject at least some of the foreign practices because of their colonial associations. Some women who had welcomed the aspirations of Western feminist freedoms, such as equal educational opportunity, the right to work outside the home, setting limits on family size, owning property, and equal rights under law, began to feel that these "freedoms" contradicted traditional family values in their own society, and they came to reject them. Such local women also looked more critically at the relationships between European men and women, and often found them fraught with tension and anxiety. They caricatured at least some of the colonial intrusions into their family and gender relationships as "white men saving brown women from brown men."

18.1

18.2

18.3

18.4

18.5

Why did colonized peoples revolt? 18.6

18.7

Anticolonial Revolts

18.6 Why did colonized peoples revolt?

Conquest by European colonial powers generally evoked anxiety and resentment among the colonized. Not for everyone, of course. Some of the conquered people found new jobs, education, business opportunities, and professional opportunities. Some praised the imperial powers for imposing peace among otherwise warring factions and imposing a rule of law that limited the arbitrary rule of local officials. New medical and technological systems raised the standard of living.

For the most part, however, the conquered peoples were resentful—or they became resentful. They might see some benefits to early colonial rule, but they also saw the looting of local treasuries and the imposition of confiscatory taxes. They cringed at the insults to indigenous rulers who were rudely displaced. Sometimes, in some places, where colonizers confirmed and protected local leaders in their power, their subjects were infuriated because now those leaders were impervious to local complaints. Later, as new systems of administration were introduced, they saw the "glass ceilings" that kept qualified local people out of higher-level jobs. Even when new colonial businesses offered new opportunities, the bulk of the profits was sent back to the colonizing country. The new educational, legal, and administrative systems undermined local traditions, culture, and religion. The use of a foreign language in public life—the norm in colonial situations—further inhibited the development of indigenous cultures. At least as significant as any of these more tangible frustrations were the racism and disrespect colonized peoples experienced from most of the colonizers, and which they deeply resented. Sooner or later, most colonized people wanted their independence. In region after region they rose in revolt against colonial rule.

Many of the early revolts looked backward, to restoring the institutions that had preceded colonialism. The 1857–58 revolt in India and the Mahdist uprising on the upper Nile in 1881–98 fit this pattern. So did a revolt of an Islamic mystical brotherhood, led by Shamil, "ruler of the righteous and destroyer of the unbeliever," against Russian rule in the Caucasus Mountains, 1834–59; Emilio Aguinaldo's revolt against United States colonial rule in the Philippines, 1898–1902; and continuing peasant revolts against Dutch rule in the islands of Indonesia, 1881–1908.

📖 **Read** the **Document**: **Mark Twain, "Incident in the Philippines" (1924)** on **MyHistoryLab**

Later, armed revolts and nonviolent political movements against colonial rule became more forward-looking. Their leaders sought not a simple return to the past but a newly restructured nation, usually incorporating significant elements of the past with new goals based in part on innovations introduced by colonial powers. In India, the Indian National Congress, founded in 1885, proposed a pattern of parliamentary

18.1

18.2

18.3

18.4

18.5

18.6

18.7

What were the stages in Japan's move from isolation to full participation in the world of nation-states?

democracy for India, often with an admixture of Hindu reformism. In Egypt in 1907, the reformist People's Party, led by Saad Zaghlul (1857–1927), became the core of the nationalist Wafd Party after 1919. The Young Turk party, formed in 1878 in patriotic anger against the Ottoman defeats in the Balkans, grew into a revolutionary party by 1908. Indonesia's first nationalist association was formed in 1908, South Africa's in 1912, and Vietnam's in 1913.

Each of these organizations had a conception of the future nation it was constructing, modeled in part on European military, economic, political, and administrative forms, but also incorporating its own cultural, religious, and social dimensions. Perhaps the most comprehensive of all these responses was that of Japan. By the mid-1850s, that country had witnessed foreigners colonize and humble the ancient and venerable Chinese Empire. When American warships entered Japanese waters in 1853, the Japanese feared that a similar fate awaited them. They took dramatic action to ensure that they would not fall victim to colonial rule.

Japan: From Isolation to Equality

 18.7   What were the stages in Japan's move from isolation to full participation in the world of nation-states?

Japan was unified in its ethnicity, with accepted legends of its national history; a single dynasty of emperors that related back to the founding of the nation in the seventh century B.C.E.; a single national language; an integrated national political structure; and an island-based geography. Japan's insular nature was intensified in the early 1600s when the government closed the country to foreign, especially European, contact. Faced with military attack from Western nations in 1853, however, and aware of recent Western invasions of China, Japan recognized the need to transform its institutions and its society. The history of Japan after 1853 charts its extraordinary move from isolation to full, prominent participation in the world of nation-states.

The End of the Shogunate

By 1639, as we saw in the chapter entitled "The Unification of World Trade," Japan had shut down commerce and contact with the European world. The exception was a Dutch outpost, virtually quarantined on Deshima Island in Nagasaki harbor, which was allowed to receive one ship each year. The Japanese also permitted the Chinese to trade at Nagasaki, but only under severe restrictions. Some trade could also pass to China through the Ryukyu Islands, under the guise of "tribute," and Korea could trade through the islands of Tsushima. Otherwise, Japan was isolated. In the late 1700s and early 1800s, European ships would occasionally attempt to establish contact, but the Japanese turned them away.

In 1853, however, the United States dispatched Commodore Matthew Perry (1794–1858) with a small squadron, including three steam frigates, to force Japan to open to trade, as China had been opened in the Opium War a decade before. Japan lacked the means to resist the Americans and the European powers that soon followed, and over the next few years, under pressure, the country opened more ports, at first on the periphery, but then at Nagasaki, Kobe, and Yokohama. Japan opened Edo (Tokyo) and Osaka to foreign residents, and then granted the foreigners extraterritorial legal rights. Foreigners were permitted to determine Japan's tariff policies. In 1863 and 1864, in the face of firing on their ships, British, French, Dutch, and American naval forces demolished Japanese coastal forts and supplies and forced Japan to pay an indemnity. Like China, Japan seemed headed toward control by foreigners.

Unlike in China, however, young, vigorous leaders seized control of the government of Japan, forcing a dramatic restructuring of the nation's politics, administration, class structure, economy, technology, and culture. These leaders, for the most

KEY TERMS

han In Japan, a territory or feudal estate controlled by a feudal lord, or *daimyo*. *Han* were abolished in 1871.

Eastern Ethics; Western Science The watchword of Sakuma Zozan in Japan, urging acceptance of Western science and technology, but rejecting Western culture and ethics in favor of those of Japan. This position was found in many countries colonized by Europeans.

Revere the Emperor; Expel the Barbarian A much more conservative position than "Eastern Ethics; Western Science," urging rejection of almost everything coming from Western colonization.

Meiji restoration The reforms effected in Japan in the name of the emperor Mutsuhito (r. 1867–1912), who was known as the Meiji emperor. During his reign, constitutional changes restored the emperor to full power, displacing the militarily powerful shogun, and Japan adopted many Western innovations as it became a modern, industrial, militarized state.

SOURCE

Fukuzawa Yukichi: Cultural Interpreter

Born into the lower levels of the feudal aristocracy in Kyushu, Fukuzawa Yukichi (1834–1901) had a thirst for knowledge that took him to Osaka, Nagasaki (for Dutch learning), the United States in 1860 with the very first Japanese official mission (and again in 1867), and Europe in 1862. Fukuzawa rejected government office, the usual alternative, in favor of private life as a journalist and teacher. He earned a reputation as the foremost interpreter of the West to Japan; his books describing the West as he understood it sold in the hundreds of thousands to a nation hungry for such observation and interpretation. He founded a school in Tokyo that later became Keio University, the training ground of many of Japan's business leaders. The following excerpts are from Fukuzawa's *Autobiography*, published in 1899. He states his goal of interpreting the West fairly, even though he knows he will face opposition.

> The final purpose of all my work was to create in Japan a civilized nation, as well equipped in both the arts of war and peace as those of the Western world. I acted as if I had become the sole functioning agent for the introduction of Western culture. It was natural then that I would be disliked by the older

type of Japanese, and suspected of working for the benefit of foreigners … I regard the human being as the most sacred and responsible of all orders, unable in reason to do anything base … In short, my creed is that a man should find his faith in independence and self-respect. (p. 214)

He investigates the style of Western institutions:

> For instance, when I saw a hospital, I wanted to know how it was run—who paid the running expenses; when I visited a bank, I wished to learn how the money was deposited and paid out. By similar first-hand queries, I learned something of the postal system and the military conscription then in force in France but not in England. A perplexing institution was representative government. … For some time it was beyond my comprehension to understand what they [political parties] were "fighting" for, and what was meant, anyway, by "fighting" in peace time. "This man and that man are 'enemies' in the House," they would tell me. But these "enemies" were to be seen at the same table, eating and drinking with each other. (p. 134)

part young samurai warriors in the *han* (feudal estates) of Choshu and Satsuma at the southern extreme of Japan, recognized that the current government was not capable of coping with the European threat. Great diversity of opinion flourished among the approximately 250 different *han* in Japan, but the most powerful regional leaders felt that the shogun, or military governor, who ruled Japan in the name of the emperor, should be removed and the emperor himself should be restored as the direct ruler of Japan. The young samurai, members of Japan's hereditary military elite, would then formulate the policies of the new administration in his name.

The samurai were able to employ some of the technological information introduced by the Dutch from their station in Nagasaki harbor. Indeed, in 1811 the shogunate had established an office for translating Dutch material, and it was expanded into a school for European languages and science in 1857. Some of the *han*, including Satsuma, Choshu, and Mito, did the same. By 1840, some Japanese were already casting Western guns and artillery. Sakuma Zozan (1811–64), one of the advocates of adopting Western military methods, coined the motto "**Eastern Ethics; Western Science.**" Japan could adopt Western technology, he counseled, especially military technology, while still maintaining its own culture.

Sakuma believed that opening the country was both necessary and beneficial. Not everyone agreed, however, and in 1860 a group of samurai from the conservative *han* of Mito argued a contrary position: "**Revere the Emperor; Expel the Barbarian.**" The lines of conflict were sharpening. Political violence increased as exponents of the opposing positions attacked each other. Mito loyalists assassinated Sakuma and another reform leader in 1864 and then committed ritual suicide. Attacks on foreigners taking up residence and conducting business in Japan also increased.

In 1868, the forces of Choshu and Satsuma, joining with those of several more remote *han*, seized control of the emperor's palace in Kyoto and declared the shogunate ended, the lands of the shogun confiscated, and the emperor restored to imperial power. Most of the fighting was over by November, although naval battles continued into early 1869. The **Meiji restoration** ended the power of the shogunate forever and

18.1
18.2
18.3
18.4
18.5
18.6
18.7

What were the stages in Japan's move from isolation to full participation in the world of nation-states?

633

THE MEIJI RESTORATION AND INDUSTRIALIZATION IN JAPAN

1853	Commander Perry sails into Edo Bay, ending 250 years' isolation
1854	Treaty of Kanagawa gives United States trading rights with Japan
1860s	Series of "unequal treaties" gives United States, Britain, France, Russia, and Netherlands commercial and territorial privileges
1868	*Daimyo* force Tokugawa shogun to abdicate. Executive power vested with emperor in Meiji restoration
1871	Administration is overhauled; Western-style changes introduced
1872	National education system introduced, providing teaching for 90 percent of children by 1900
1872	First railway opened
1873	Old order changed by removal of privileges of samurai class
1876	Koreans, under threat, agree to open three of their ports to the Japanese and exchange diplomats
1877	Satsuma rebellion represented last great (unsuccessful) challenge of conservative forces
1879	Representative system of local government introduced
1884	Western-style peerage (upper house) created
1885	Cabinet government introduced
1889	Adoption of constitution based on Bismarck's Germany
1889	Number of cotton mills has risen from three (1877) to 83
1894–95	War with China ends in Japanese victory
1895	Japan annexes Taiwan and Pescadores Islands
1902	Britain and Japan sign military pact
1904–05	War with Russia ends in Japanese victory
1910	Japan annexes Korea
1914	Japan joins World War I on side of Allies

KEY TERM

daimyo The feudal lords of Japan, who, by the sixteenth century, controlled almost the entire country.

brought the ***daimyo*** and their young samurai to power in the name of the emperor Meiji (r. 1867–1912). The emperor assumed the throne at the age of 14 and reigned over a national transformation of astonishing scope and speed.

📖 **Read** the **Document: A Comic Dialogue, 1855** on **MyHistoryLab**

🔍 **View** the **Closer Look: Japanese Views of American Naval Technology** on **MyHistoryLab**

The Meiji Restoration

Japan's new leaders began to search the world for new political, economic, and military models that might be adapted to Japan's needs. A two-year overseas goodwill mission set out in 1871 to deepen relationships with the heads of state of the treaty powers, to discuss future treaty revisions, and to enable Japanese leaders to experience the West at first hand. Fifty-four students accompanied the mission. A ministry of education was established in 1871, and its first budget included funds for sending 250 students abroad to study. Many of these students became leaders in the new Japan. Foreign instructors were also brought to Japan. The late shogun's government had employed some foreigners in industrial enterprises. The Meiji rulers imported far more: American experts to introduce large-scale farming practices; German doctors to teach medicine; Americans to teach natural and social sciences.

Restructuring Government. The emperor was brought from his home in Kyoto to Edo, the former capital of the shogun, which was renamed Tokyo ("Eastern Capital") in 1868. In 1869, the *daimyo* of four of the most important *han* turned over their estates to the emperor, setting the pattern for other *daimyo* to follow and to unify the country. The *daimyo* retained certain rights of tax collection, which kept them financially well off, and stipends were paid to the samurai to avoid outright revolt. For a decade, revolts did simmer until the largest of them— 40,000 troops in Satsuma under the reluctant leadership of Saigo Takamori—was crushed in 1877. Japan's national government held firm.

Following years of discussion, and study of European and American constitutions, in 1889 a constitution was promulgated, creating a bicameral, elected parliament, called the Diet. Democracy, however, was restricted. Only the nobility voted for the House of Peers. Only about one percent of the population, only males, could vote for the House of Representatives. The Diet could vote on important legislation, but only the executive could introduce it. The Constitution was presented not as the victory of a popular movement imposing limits on an autocratic government, but as a gift bequeathed by the emperor to his people. The emperor retained, at least in theory, all executive powers, including the right to make war and peace, and to conclude treaties. Despite all these limitations, Japan's Diet of 1890 was the first parliamentary form of government in Asia.

The core of the central government's new army was established in 1871. Money was invested in modern equipment, much of it manufactured in Japan. An army staff college began to train an officer corps following a German model, while the navy adapted a British model, often purchasing its ships from Britain. Service in the

18.1
18.2
18.3
18.4
18.5
18.6
18.7

What were the stages in Japan's move from isolation to full participation in the world of nation-states?

The Residence of Foreign Merchants from Overseas, Utagawa Sadahide, 1861. Color woodblock print. For decades following the Meiji Restoration in 1868, Japanese elites adopted western fashions not only in military training, agricultural techniques, and industrialization, but also in basic educational strategies, clothing, and etiquette. (Arthur M. Sackler Gallery, Smithsonian Institution)

armed forces introduced Japanese conscripts to new ways of life, some travel, reading and writing, Western-style uniforms and shoes, nationalism, and reverence for the emperor. Japan was becoming the most powerful nation in East Asia.

Restructuring the Economy. Recognizing an economic principle that underlay the Industrial Revolution in Britain, Japan first built up its agriculture. It needed the profits, and it needed the food and manpower that an effective agriculture would make available for urban industry. New seeds, fertilizer, and methods were introduced throughout the islands, and agricultural colleges spread the new techniques and information. In the 1880s, agricultural production went up by about 30 percent, and from 1890 to 1915 by 100 percent. This production included not only food crops but also tea, cotton, and silk, mostly for the export market. The profits did not go to the peasants but to the landlord, who invested them in commerce or industry. Poorer peasants were squeezed off the land by high rents, and all peasants were heavily taxed to fund the large expenses of industrialization and militarization.

In large-scale industrialization, the government was the entrepreneur. It built the first railway line, between Tokyo and Yokohama, in 1872. In two decades about 2,000 miles of track followed. The government financed coal mines, iron mines, a machine-tool factory, cement works, glass and tile factories, wool and cotton textile mills, shipyards, and weapons manufacture. However, the industry that contributed the most, silk, which accounted for more than 40 percent of all Japan's exports, was developed largely by private entrepreneurs.

Cultural and Educational Changes. Under the Tokugawa shogunate, 1603–1867, each *daimyo* had his own capital (see the chapter entitled "The Unification of World Trade"). As a result, Japan had a rich array of administrative towns and cities spread throughout the country. During the Meiji restoration, they provided the network for

18.1
18.2
18.3
18.4
18.5
18.6
18.7

What were the stages in Japan's move from isolation to full participation in the world of nation-states?

Ginza District, Tokyo, about 1930. A general view showing the heart of the "new" Tokyo, sometimes known as Japan's Broadway. As Japan became more Westernized, its cities, especially Tokyo, adopted the architectural and urban design patterns, as well as the transportation patterns, of the West. The Nippon Bridge (pictured) was considered the center of the Japanese empire. All distances were computed from this point.

the diffusion of new cultural patterns. Some cities stood out: Kyoto, the home of the emperor, was the center of traditional culture; Osaka was the most important business center; and Edo (Tokyo) was, by the mid-1800s, the largest and most flourishing of the major cities, with a population of half a million to a million people.

Tokugawa urban culture had mixed strains. At the center of business life were merchants dedicated to making money. Yet they liked entertainment and found it outside their homes. Homes were for wives, children, and household duties. The amusement quarters of the city were for restaurants, theater, artistic culture, the female companionship of geisha entertainers, and prostitutes.

Social networks based on neighborhoods, shrines, guilds, and civic needs, such as firefighting, provided a sense of community, and cities grew relatively slowly in the first generation of the restoration. By 1895 only 12 percent of Japan's population of 42 million lived in cities. Industrialization in large factories had barely begun. In 1897 only 400,000 workers in all of Japan were working in factories employing more than five workers. By the turn of the century, however, the institutional and economic changes of the restoration were taking effect, and urban populations multiplied.

Western cultural styles, both superficial and profound, proliferated in Meiji Japan. The Gregorian calendar and the seven-day week, with Sunday as a holiday, were adopted in 1882, and the metric system in 1886. Samurai men began to prefer Western haircuts to the traditional shaved head and topknot. The military dressed in Western-style uniforms, and in 1872 Western dress became mandatory at all official ceremonies. Meat eating was encouraged, despite Buddhist ethics, and sukiyaki, a

CHAPTER EIGHTEEN: NATIONALISM, IMPERIALISM, AND RESISTANCE 1650–1914

18.1
18.2
18.3
18.4
18.5
18.6
18.7

The expansion and modernization of Japan. Responding to the threats of foreign gunboats, Japanese samurai leaders overthrew the long-established Tokugawa shogunate and restored imperial power under Emperor Meiji in 1868. Within 50 years, industrial development, growing international trade, and territorial expansion made Japan a world power. It initially asserted its control over neighboring islands, and then took advantage of Manchu decline; victories over China (1894–95) and Russia (1904–05) established Japanese control over Taiwan, Korea, and Karafuto (southern Sakhalin), and its dominant influence over Manchuria and even parts of mainland China.

18.1
18.2
18.3
18.4
18.5
18.6
18.7

What were the stages in Japan's move from isolation to full participation in the world of nation-states?

Meiji classroom scene, c. 1900. The Meiji rulers saw education as critical to Japan's modernization. The Charter Oath declared that "Knowledge shall be sought throughout the world." Even before the Meiji, educational standards had been high; under the Meiji they approached 100 percent literacy.

meat and vegetable dish especially cooked at the table, was developed as part of Japanese cuisine.

Japanese readers turned avidly to Western texts. Philosophers of the Enlightenment drew attention to individual rights. Herbert Spencer's emphasis on the survival of the fittest, derived from Darwin's theory, proved attractive as a justification for Japan's assertion of its growing power and coming imperialism. The Scottish author Samuel Smiles' popular text *Self Help* (1859), advocating pulling oneself up by the bootstraps, also found a receptive readership.

Tokugawa Japan had valued formal education. Samurai had attended Confucian-based schools run by the *han*; commoners had studied in schools located in Buddhist temples. At the time of the Meiji restoration, an estimated 45 percent of adult men and 15 percent of adult women could read and write, about the same proportions as in advanced European countries. Building on this, the government introduced a highly centralized system of education and then mandated compulsory attendance. By 1905, over 90 percent of both boys and girls of primary-school age were attending school. The schools were recognized for high quality, for providing public education superior to private schools, and for helping to move the country from the feudal, hierarchical society of Tokugawa Japan to a more egalitarian system than that of most European countries. At the university level, a series of excellent institutions was established throughout Japan, beginning with Tokyo University in 1886.

Gender Relations. The Meiji restoration opened up entirely new arenas of public life and achievement for Japanese men. For a few years before marriage, some Japanese women, too, found new opportunities in education, in factory employment, and in a handful of new cultural venues. For the most part, however, women's public options were restricted. As the emperor's position was restored, so was male dominance in the home reinforced. Women and minors were prohibited from joining political organizations and from holding or attending meetings in which political speeches or lectures were given. (The vote was granted to women in Japan only after World War II.)

The Civil Code of 1898 reinforced patriarchy within the family, granting the male head of the family unquestioned authority. Women had few legal rights. At marriage, control over a woman's property passed to her husband. Fathers held exclusive right to custody over children. Concubinage was abolished in 1880, but society sanctioned prostitution and the discreet keeping of mistresses. As high-school education was extended to women, the Girls' High School Law of 1899 declared its goal to create "**good wives and wise mothers**." Within the home, women held great authority and respect, often controlling the family budget, but they were allowed virtually no place in the public life of Japan.

Equality in the Family of Nations. From the beginning of the Meiji restoration, Japan sought to end the demeaning provisions of **extraterritoriality**, which required that foreigners charged with legal crimes in Japan be tried by foreign courts rather than by Japanese courts. Japan also sought to regain control of its own tariffs. These goals provided the rationale for introducing new legal systems that were more consistent with those of Western countries. If Japan's laws were in accord with those of Europe, there would be no justification for continuing extraterritoriality. The British relinquished extraterritoriality in 1899 when the new legal codes took effect. Other nations followed suit, and Japan reciprocated by allowing foreigners to establish residences outside the treaty ports. Additional treaties returned full control over tariffs to Japan in 1911.

War and colonization also seemed important to full membership in the European community of nations. Japan had forced the establishment of a legation in Korea in 1876. As political leaders in that country divided over policy issues, some sought support from conservative China, others from progressive Japan. When fighting between the groups broke out in 1894, both China and Japan sent in troops, and war began between the two powers. Japan defeated the Chinese fleet and captured Port Arthur (the naval base in southern Manchuria) and the port of Weihaiwei on the Shandong Peninsula. Peace negotiations awarded Taiwan and the Pescadores Islands to Japan, as Japan supplanted China as the dominant nation of East Asia. Korea was formally recognized as independent, but Japan held sway there nonetheless.

In the first years of the twentieth century, two further engagements with the West ratified Japan's arrival among the powers of the world. First, in 1902, Britain and Japan signed an alliance, the first military pact on equal terms between a European and a non-Western country. It brought together the most powerful navies of Europe and of East Asia. The treaty blocked Russian aspirations and further secured Japan's semi-colonial control over China. Second, in response to continuing Russian penetration of Manchuria and increasingly hostile diplomacy, Japan attacked the Russian fleet in Port Arthur in 1904. A Russian fleet dispatched from the Baltic was intercepted and annihilated by the Japanese in 1905 as it crossed the Straits of Tsushima. Fighting far from the center of their country, the Russian army was also defeated.

An Asian power had defeated a European power for the first time since the victories of the Ottomans in eastern Europe in the seventeenth century. In Russia, the defeat precipitated a revolution against the government in 1905. The American President Theodore Roosevelt convened a peace conference—for which he was awarded the Nobel Prize for Peace—which gave Japan a protectorate over Korea, predominant

18.1

18.2

18.3

18.4

18.5

18.6

18.7

What were the stages in Japan's move from isolation to full participation in the world of nation-states?

KEY TERMS

good wives and wise mothers The stated goal of high-school education for girls in Japan. Women were expected to stay in the home (except, perhaps, for a few years before marriage).

extraterritoriality Legal immunities enjoyed by the citizens of a sovereign state or international organization living within a foreign host country.

rights over southern Manchuria, and control of southern Sakhalin Island. In 1910, with no European power protesting, Japan formally annexed Korea. Japan had reached the international status it had desired—less than half a century after embarking on its quest. The values of nationalism, technological innovation, and imperialism had become as supreme in Japan as they were in Europe.

Nationalism and Imperialism: *What Difference Do They Make?*

Nationalism inspired existing nations with pride in their past and aspirations for their future. It gave them a sense of their potential strength and power. It often united people in collective efforts and encouraged a greater sense of equality and common purpose among them. This was part of the message of the British, American, and French revolutions. For regional groupings that were not political nations, such as Italy and Germany, the spirit of nationalism often inspired action toward unifying their divided regions into nations. For groups that felt themselves denied their national identity by a larger power that had colonized them—the Greeks, Romanians, and Bulgarians under the Ottoman Empire, and much of the world under European colonialism—nationalism offered the promise of autonomy and control over their own affairs. At its best, nationalism encouraged nations to learn from one another, as each had something unique to contribute.

Nationalism also inspired competition among nations that sometimes evoked greatness, but has also frequently led to warfare, conquest, and colonialism. It led to disputes among groups claiming national identity and national geographic borders that were difficult, if not impossible, to resolve. It accompanied, and sometimes encouraged, racism and arrogance. It created and perpetuated economic systems of great inequality in which the terms of trade were set by the powerful for their own benefit, often causing great suffering to the weak. All these aspects of nationalism, positive and negative, continued into the twentieth century—in ways that we shall explore later—and remain powerful today.

The political and industrial revolutions of the eighteenth and nineteenth centuries bound nations and peoples together more tightly than ever before. Historically great nations such as China and Japan, which had lived mostly within their own regions, were pulled into greater participation in the global economy, politics, and culture. New political and industrial relationships raised questions about the goals and the proper functions of the international economy: Is its purpose to create business profits or to provide for overall human welfare? Can it do both? How? Can the benefits of international competition be encouraged and its powers of destruction limited?

In this chapter we have seen European nations, and later Japan and the United States, backed by the power of their industrial revolutions, assert their control over most of the globe. Imperialists usually claimed that they were benefiting the peoples they ruled and cited statistics on new transport lines, new health clinics, new schools, and new political institutions. The conquered peoples usually pointed to evidence to the contrary: economies devastated, politics suppressed, cultural traditions undermined, and populations divided and turned against one another. These legacies continued into the twentieth century, and they persist today as former colonizers and former colonies adjust their economies, cultures, and relations to one another. Consciously and unconsciously the world proceeds against a background in which some nations conquered and lorded it over others. The sensitivities of those relationships are still quite raw, as we see today when powerful nations attempt to exert their will politically, economically, and culturally over weaker ones—and the weaker choose to accept these conditions, to modify them, or to resist.

CHAPTER REVIEW

NATIONALISM

18.1 What is nationalism?

Nationalism refers to a people's sense of shared identity, the feeling among citizens that they belong to their country and are committed to working on its behalf. Carving an independent country out of an existing empire was nationalism's first goal in places such as the Ottoman Empire; the revolution of the American colonies against the British Empire was another example. In other locations, the goal was merging smaller territories into a new, larger nation, as in Germany and Italy. On the downside, nationalism may lead a country to suppress internal minorities and to turn nations against each other in warfare.

FAILED NATIONALISMS AND DELAYED NATIONALISMS

18.2 Why do some nationalist movements fail?

Many, perhaps most, nationalist movements do not succeed. It is hard to inspire the enthusiasm required to build a new state, and the enormous obstacles involved include the opposition of bigger, more powerful states. Such was the case with new states that arose in West Africa, East Africa, and Egypt and were then conquered and colonized by European nations. Sometimes, as in the case of Poland, nationalism is overwhelmed by more powerful, conquering nations; at other times the nationalism is successful in creating an independent nation.

THE EUROPEAN QUEST FOR EMPIRE

18.3 How did Europeans gain direct political control of four-fifths of the land surface of the globe?

The Western Europeans saw themselves as superior—politically, socially, economically, industrially, and racially (or genetically)—to the peoples of the world they set out to colonize and conquer. It was not only their destiny to conquer others, it was also their "White Man's Burden" to improve them. From India, to China, to Algeria and Southeast Asia and Indonesia, European imperialist nations competed fiercely among themselves for colonies.

EUROPEAN COMPETITION AND COOPERATION: EMPIRE-BUILDING IN AFRICA

18.4 What was the process by which Europeans expanded their control into Africa in the nineteenth century?

Aided by the invention of steamboats, machine guns, and quinine, European nations moved into sub-Saharan Africa and then "scrambled" to claim territory, fighting each other (British and Dutch colonists fought an especially bloody war over South Africa) and brutalizing the native peoples. Taking control of the best lands, and establishing laws that gave them essentially all the political power, Europeans came into greater and greater competition with each other. They resolved this with the Berlin Conference, at which they fixed new borders and divided up all of Africa among themselves. When Africans resisted, the imperialists responded with force.

GENDER RELATIONSHIPS IN COLONIZATION

18.5 How did colonial living affect European concepts of gender, race, and sexuality?

In the beginning of the colonization period, white European men entered into relationships with native women, forming important business and social partnerships and having children. But the social distance between the colonialists and the native peoples increased with time and the arrival of (jealous) European women and families. Convinced of the superiority of their own practices, colonizers in India outlawed *sati*, the practice of a widow's joining her husband on his funeral pyre (sometimes voluntarily, sometimes not), and introduced a minimum age for marriage. In Africa, colonizers tried to put an end to polygamy. Some of the colonized peoples began to adopt some European styles of gender relations, seeking more education for women, an end to footbinding in China, and more freedom of choice in marriage, for example. Later, under the influence of nationalism, local peoples would come to reject or modify many of these new practices because of their connection to colonization. They also asked why European rulers had paid so much attention to gender issues and so little to basic issues of governance, such as economic development and increasing education.

ANTICOLONIAL REVOLTS

18.6 Why did colonized peoples revolt?

Some of the colonized peoples did see new jobs and new opportunities as a result of their conquest by Europeans. But many, of course, resented the conquerors: the racism and disrespect; the looting of their local treasuries; the imposition of taxes, with much of the revenue being dispatched back to Europe. The Europeans removed local leaders from their posts and put their own people in charge, and they arranged businesses so that the bulk of profits went back to the colonial power. New educational systems undermined local culture and religion, while the use of a foreign language in public life alienated local people from the administration and limited the development of indigenous cultures. In time, colonial people felt that they had learned all there was to be learned from the colonizers and wanted to be independent.

JAPAN: FROM ISOLATION TO EQUALITY

18.7 What were the stages in Japan's move from isolation to full participation in the world of nation-states?

The island nation of Japan had been a self-sufficient, insular country since its founding in the seventh century B.C.E. In the 1600s, Japan had even closed its ports to almost all foreign contact. But in 1853, United States gunboats forced Japan to open its doors to trade, and European powers soon followed. Recognizing that the current government could not cope with or fend off this threat from foreigners, new leaders seized control of Japan's government. They restored the emperor to the throne and set out to restructure the nation's institutions and society. Within 50 years, industrial development, international trade, educational reforms, and territorial expansion had made Japan a world power.

Suggested Readings

PRINCIPAL SOURCES

Abernethy, David. *The Dynamics of Global Dominance: European Overseas Empires, 1415–1980* (New Haven, CT: Yale University Press, 2000). Presents European expansion through a series of phases, notes its extraordinary power in reshaping the world, but sees it as ultimately self-liquidating. Comprehensive.

Bayly, C.A. *The Birth of the Modern World 1780–1914* (Malden, MA: Blackwell, 2004). A masterpiece of synthesis, combining political, economic, social, and cultural history in a global, interactive framework, by a master historian.

Cooper, Frederick, and Ann Laura Stoler, eds. *Tensions of Empire: Colonial Cultures in a Bourgeois World* (Berkeley, CA: University of California Press, 1997). Excellent selections on the effects of colonialism on the identity of colonizer and colonized. Several essays on feminist perspectives.

Curtin, Philip, *et al. African History from Earliest Times to Independence* (New York: Longman, 2nd ed., 1995). Masterly study, especially good on the combination of history and anthropology. Four authors bring specialization across regions, disciplines, and styles of understanding. The narrative sometimes wanders among them.

Davis, Mike. *Late Victorian Holocausts: El Niño Famines and the Making of the Third World* (New York: Verso, 2001). Brings together many classic arguments about imperial exploitation of colonies, and emphasizes the cruelty of this exploitation at a time when major famines were also devastating colonial economies.

de Bary, William Theodore, ed. *Sources of Japanese Tradition,* vol. 2: Parts 1 and 2 (New York: Columbia University Press, 2nd ed., 2006). Outstanding collection of primary sources, especially on the cultural leaders and philosophies of Japan, from earliest to modern times.

—— and Richard Lufrano, eds. *Sources of Chinese Tradition,* vol. 2 (New York: Columbia University Press, 2nd ed., 2000). Outstanding source book, especially on cultural issues, from the Qing dynasty to the present. Vol. 1 carries the earlier history.

Hay, Stephen, ed. *Sources of Indian Tradition,* vol. 2 (New York: Columbia University Press, 2nd ed., 1988). Superb anthology of primary sources, especially strong on the religious and cultural bases of modern India and their influence on its politics, from about 1500 to the present. Vol. 1 carries earlier periods.

Hobsbawm, Eric. *The Age of Capital 1848–1875* (New York: Vintage Books, 1975). This series of Hobsbawm's books provides a well-written narrative sweep of world history through this period, from a leftist perspective. Often uses examples from popular culture, especially music.

——. *The Age of Empire 1875–1914* (New York: Vintage Books, 1987).

——. *The Age of Revolution 1789–1848* (New York: New American Library, 1962).

Hochschild, Adam. *King Leopold's Ghost* (New York: Houghton Mifflin, 1998). Narrates the horrifying story of the king's rule of the Congo, and the shipping agent who discovered and exposed it.

July, Robert J. *A History of the African People* (Prospect Heights, IL: Waveland Press, 5th ed., 1998). Clearly written survey, especially good on political history.

Morris-Suzuki, Tessa. *The Technological Transformation of Japan* (Cambridge: Cambridge University Press, 1994). Follows the technical and managerial decisions that brought Japan to parity and even superiority in economic and technological modernization.

Said, Edward W. *Culture and Imperialism* (New York: Vintage Books, 1993). Said's various books emphasize the ways in which imperial powers used their own interpretation of culture to assert their supremacy over the countries they dominated and, often, to get the colonized people to believe them.

ADDITIONAL SOURCES

Adas, Michael, ed. *Islamic and European Expansion* (Philadelphia, PA: Temple University Press, 1993). Excellent collection of introductory historiographic essays on the period 1000 to 1914 in world history.

Anderson, Benedict. *Imagined Communities* (London: Verso, 1983). Stresses the importance of the vision of nationalists in creating new nations, and the critical role of commercial publishing (print capitalism) in popularizing these visions.

Andrea, Alfred, and James Overfield, eds. *The Human Record,* vol. 2 (Florence, KY: Wadsworth Publishing Co., 7th ed., 2011). Superb collection of primary documents on modern history.

Bayly, C.A. *Origins of Nationality in South Asia* (New York: Oxford University Press, 1998). Seeks to discover how Indians developed the concept of a modern nation from their own cultural materials as well as from new conceptions brought from the West.

Bhabha, Homi K. *The Location of Culture* (New York: Routledge, 2004). Analyzes the relationship between colonized and colonizer, as it appears after the fact, after independence. An extremely difficult, complex, read in postcolonial theory.

Bose, Sugata. *A Hundred Horizons: The Indian Ocean in the Age of Global Empire* (Cambridge, MA: Harvard University Press, 2009). Seeks the unities in the Indian Ocean basin in the nineteenth and twentieth centuries. Densely written.

Braudel, Fernand. *The Identity of France,* trans. Sian Reynolds (New York: Harper and Row, 1988). Fascinating discussion of the process by which the various, disparate regions of France were unified into a single nation.

Briggs, Asa. *A Social History of England* (New York: Viking Press, 1983). Standard, well-written, well-illustrated history, stressing social conditions and change over politics or economics.

Burns, E. Bradford. *Latin America: A Concise Interpretive History* (Englewood Cliffs, NJ: Prentice Hall, 9th ed., 2010). Excellent survey from a slightly leftist and critical perspective.

Burton, Antoinette. *Burdens of History* (Chapel Hill, NC: University of North Carolina Press, 1994). Sees European women adopting positions sympathetic to imperialism as a means of showing that they deserved the same rights as men because they shared the same political perspectives.

Cannadine, David. *Ornamentalism* (New York: Penguin, 2001). The British ruled their empire with full displays of pomp and hierarchy, imitating what they perceived as the structure of their society at home.

Chatterjee, Partha. *The Nation and Its Fragments* (Princeton, NJ: Princeton University Press, 1993). Analyzes some of the movements by which India began to come together as a nation. Thematically notes the importance of religion. Geographically stresses the Bengal region.

Cheng, Pei-kai, and Michael Lestz with Jonathan Spence, eds. *The Search for Modern China: A Documentary Collection* (New York: W.W. Norton, 1999). Excellent selection, very well annotated. Designed to accompany Spence's textbook of the same name, but also stands alone.

Collcutt, Martin, Marius Jansen, and Isao Kumakura. *Cultural Atlas of Japan* (New York: Facts on File, 1988). Superb introduction with fine text, maps, and illustrations that all work well together.

Columbia University. *Introduction to Contemporary Civilization in the West,* vol. 2 (New York: Columbia University Press, 3rd ed., 1960). Outstanding sourcebook with lengthy excerpts from highly influential thinkers and actors.

Conrad, Joseph. *Heart of Darkness* (Mineola, NY: Dover Publications, 1990). A classic, brief novel on the cruelty and corruption of the "ruler" of a European outpost in the Congo interior.

Cooper, Frederick. *Colonialism in Question: Theory, Knowledge, History* (Berkeley, CA: University of California Press, 2005). Excellent review of recent scholarship on "the cultural turn" in the study of imperialism.

Dalpat-Kavya Navnit. *Selections from Dalpat the Poet,* in Gujarati, ed. Deshavram Kashiram Shastri (Ahmedabad: Gujarat Vidyasabha, 1949). Dalpat's poetry expressed his beliefs that Indians in the mid-nineteenth century had much to learn from the British, including the methods of industrialization.

Davis, Lance E., and Robert A. Huttenback. *Mammon and the Pursuit of Empire* (Cambridge: Cambridge University Press, 1989). Argues that imperialism did not pay, at least not financially, at least not after the beginning phases. A careful economic analysis.

Eley, Geoff, and Ronald Grigor Suny, eds. *Becoming National* (New York: Oxford University Press, 1996). Excellent analysis of several major Western theories on the meaning of nationalism.

Engels, Friedrich. *The Origins of the Family, Private Property and the State*, ed. Eleanor Burke Leacock (New York: International Publishers, 1973). Engels saw the exploitation of women as the first kind of economic exploitation that ultimately led to its fullest expression in the capitalist system.

Fujimura-Fanselow, Kumiko, and Atsuko Kameda, eds. *Japanese Women* (New York: Feminist Press, 1995). Twenty-seven essays on many aspects of women in public and private life, their changing status, including men's views of the change.

Gluck, Carol. *Japan's Modern Myths: Ideology in the Late Meiji Period* (Princeton, NJ: Princeton University Press, 1985). Analyzes not only the formal ideologies, but also how they were received and perceived by the Japanese public.

Hanke, Lewis, and Jane M. Rausch, eds. *People and Issues in Latin American History*, vols. 1 and 2 (New York: Markus Wiener Publishing, 3rd ed., 2006). Standard historical survey often presented through biography.

Headrick, Daniel R. *The Tools of Empire* (New York: Oxford University Press, 1981). Steamships, guns, and quinine were among the prerequisites of the European conquest of Africa.

Hertzberg, Arthur, ed. *The Zionist Idea* (Philadelphia, PA: Jewish Publication Society, 1997). Still the best primary-source introduction to early Zionist thought and its evolution, with a 100-page introduction.

Hirschmeier, Johannes. *The Origins of Entrepreneurship in Meiji Japan* (Cambridge, MA: Harvard University Press, 1964). Sees the economic transformation of Japan as the key to its development and demonstrates how it developed under government guidance.

Hutchinson, John, and Anthony D. Smith, eds. *Nationalism* (New York: Oxford University Press, 1994). Survey of source material on the meaning and significance of nationalism by nationalist leaders from around the world.

Kennedy, Paul. *The Rise and Fall of the Great Powers* (New York: Random House, 1987). Kennedy's discussion of what makes empires powerful and what weakens them is engaging and provocative.

Lenin, V.I. *Imperialism, the Highest Stage of Capitalism* (Peking: Foreign Languages Press, 1965). Perhaps the strongest argument ever for the importance of the capitalist competition for markets, both for raw materials and for finished goods, as the basis for imperialism.

Marx, Karl and Friedrich Engels. *The First Indian War of Independence 1857–1859* (Moscow: Foreign Languages Press, n.d., c. 1960). As a journalist covering this war, Marx took a pro-European, imperialist position: British rule in India was a benefit that would bring the colony into the modern world. Surprising?

Metcalf, Barbara, and Thomas R. Metcalf. *A Concise History of Modern India* (Cambridge, MA: Cambridge University Press, 2nd ed., 2006). Fast-paced. Especially interesting on Muslims, women, cultural reinterpretation, film, and architecture.

Moore, Barrington, Jr. *The Social Origins of Dictatorship and Democracy* (Boston, MA: Beacon Press, 1966). A classic of comparative history analyzing especially the role of the peasantry in revolutions from England to China.

Oliver, Roland. *The African Experience: From Olduvai Gorge to the 21st Century* (Boulder, CO: Westview Press, 2nd ed., 2008). Sensitive, thoughtful, brief survey of African history by a master of the field.

Perdue, Peter. *China Marches West: The Qing Conquest of Central Asia* (Cambridge, MA: Harvard University Press, 2005). Brilliant, comprehensive study of Chinese imperialism in central Asia.

Renan, Joseph-Ernest. "What is a Nation?" in Hutchison, William G., trans. *The Poetry of the Celtic Races, and Other Essays by Ernest Renan* (London: The Walter Scott Publishing Co., 1896), pp. 61–83. A classic essay.

SarDesai, D.R. *Southeast Asia Past and Present* (Boulder, CO: Westview Press, 6th ed., 2009). Useful survey text.

Schirokauer, Conrad. *A Brief History of Chinese and Japanese Civilizations* (Fort Worth, TX: Harcourt Brace Jovanovich, 2nd ed., 1989). Useful survey text.

Seagrave, Sterling, with Peggy Seagrave. *Dragon Lady: The Life and Legend of the Last Empress of China* (New York: Knopf, 1992). Biography of the woman who ran China's politics for her young son, and actively opposed modernization.

Spivak, Gayatri Chakravorty. "Subaltern Studies: Deconstructing Historiography," in Ranajit Guha and Gayatri Chakravorty Spivak, eds. *Selected Subaltern Studies* (New York: Oxford University Press, 1988), pp. 3–32. The subaltern scholars set out to reveal the importance of the little guy who had been left out; Spivak notes that the scholars left out women.

Strobel, Margaret. "Gender, Sex, and Empire," in Adas, *op. cit.*, pp. 345–75. Excellent introduction to issues of gender relations in imperial settings.

Teng, Ssu-yu, and John K. Fairbank. *China's Response to the West: A Documentary Survey, 1839–1923* (New York: Atheneum, 1963). A superb, standard source book.

Vickers, Adrian. *A History of Modern Indonesia* (Cambridge, MA: Cambridge University Press, 2005). From the arrival of the Dutch to the present. Lively and engaging.

Waley-Cohen, Joanna. *The Sextants of Beijing: Global Currents in Chinese History* (New York: W.W. Norton, 1999). A somewhat revisionist recounting of China's extensive contact with the outside world, attacking the concept of Chinese isolation.

Wallerstein, Immanuel. *The Modern World-system 1: Capitalist Agriculture and the Origins of the European World-economy in the Sixteenth Century* (San Diego, CA: Academic Press, 1974). Wallerstein's perspective on the core countries' dominance over the periphery is classic, but Eurocentric, problematic, and densely argued.

Wilentz, Sean. *Chants Democratic: New York City and the Rise of the American Working Class, 1788–1850* (New York: Oxford University Press, 1984). What was special about the American working class? Why did it not form a working-class political party? Wilentz's answers are cogent and lucid.

Wolf, Eric R. *Europe and the People without History* (Berkeley, CA: University of California Press, 1982). Wolf, a historical anthropologist, looks at the systems of domination in modern history from the viewpoint of the colonized and the worker.

Wolfe, Patrick. "History and Imperialism: A Century of Theory, from Marx to Postcolonialism," *American Historical Review* CII, no. 2 (April 1997), pp. 388–420. Enormously useful survey.

Yukichi, Fukuzawa. *The Autobiography of Yukichi Fukuzawa*, trans. Eiichi Kiyooka (New York: Columbia University Press, 1966). Fukuzawa's nineteenth-century views of the West are insightful.

FILMS

The Wrong Empire (segment 11 in *A History of Britain*, 2000). BBC Production narrated by eminent historian Simon Schama.

Japan, Memoirs of a Secret Empire (2004; 55 minutes). Tokugawa samurai government confronts Commodore Perry, compromises with him, and comes to an end.

Liberia (2002; 1 hour 30 minutes). Documentary covering from Haitian slave revolts to the recent past. Large sections on the establishment of Liberia as a refuge for American slaves.

Shaka Zulu (1986). Ten-part miniseries produced by the South African Broadcasting Company. More historical fiction than documentary, but a good introduction to this world at the time of the *mfecane*.

Shogun (1980, remastered 2003; 10 hours). TV video drama based on the book, of an English sailor who comes to Japan, wants to become a samurai warrior, and lives through the turmoil of Tokugawa Japan.

White King, Red Rubber, Black Death (2006; 1 hour 30 minutes). BBC documentary on King Leopold's grotesque rule in the Congo.

TURNING POINT: EXPLODING TECHNOLOGIES

1914–1991

For Death and Life

The twentieth century began with great promise. The political and industrial revolutions of the previous two centuries encouraged Western Europeans to believe that they were mastering the secrets of securing a long, productive, comfortable, and meaningful life for the individual and the community.

They believed that they were transmitting these benefits around the globe through their colonial policies, and that their colonial possessions would continue long into the foreseeable future. The Polish poet Wislawa Szymborska (1923–2012) captured this optimism in the opening of her poem "The Century's Decline" of 1986:

American atomic weapons test in the Marshall Islands, northern Pacific, 1950. Soon after World War II other nations besides America undertook to create atomic weapons: Russia, Britain, France, and somewhat later China, India, Pakistan, and North Korea. An international arms race had begun. Many began to believe that the mark of a powerful nation was the possession of nuclear weapons.

Our twentieth century was going to improve on the
others …
A couple of problems weren't going
to come up anymore:
hunger, for example,
and war, and so forth.

But World War I, global economic depression, World War II, the Cold War, and revolts throughout the colonial world shattered many of these European illusions. Later stanzas of Szymborska's poem reflect these shocks:

Anyone who planned to enjoy the world
is now faced
with a hopeless task.

(For the complete text of "The Century's Decline," see Source box later in this chapter.)

What had gone wrong? Technology can produce catastrophe as well as creativity. Optimists at the beginning of the century overemphasized its positive potential and underestimated the problems of deciding its purposes, uses, and controls in a world of competition among nations, religions, ethnic groups, and ideologies.

The first half of the century saw technology put to use more in warfare than in peace, but the second half brought a resurgence of optimism: the United Nations emerged as a potential forum for conflict resolution and international bargaining, and the Cold War was contained as an armed truce, coming to an end almost without bloodshed (although many proxy wars had been fought in its name).

Technology—especially information and communications technology and biotechnology—was once again promising beneficial revolutions globally and in everyday life.

The world had heard such promises before, and once again the voices of caution were loud and clear: prosperity and opportunity were not trickling down to billions of impoverished people, neither in rich nor in poor countries; ethnic and religious violence broke out repeatedly around the globe; problems of gender identity, growing increasingly sensitive throughout the twentieth century, continued to expose tensions in family and public life; and technologies of destruction continued to multiply side by side with technologies of productivity.

The Olympics and International Politics

The world of sports provides its own window into the world of global politics and economics, war and peace. When, where, by whom, in front of what audiences, and for what stakes sports are to be "played" are questions decided through political, economic, and cultural negotiations. In the most famous of all competitions, the modern Olympic Games, these external forces appear clearly and repeatedly. The ups and downs of the Olympics have reflected the ups and downs of the world outside the arena.

The Olympic Games in Athens reopened in 1896 thanks to the enthusiastic promotion of a Frenchman, Baron Pierre

Women racing in the 100 meters, Olympic Games, Amsterdam, 1928. Women competed in the Olympics for the first time in 1900, in lawn tennis and golf. In 1928 they participated in track and field events. This breakthrough in international sports mirrored breakthroughs in social and political life, for around the same time, in the years just after World War I, women were gaining the vote in several European countries and the United States.

Jesse Owens accepting the gold medal in the long jump, and signaling his contempt for Nazi racist ideology and practices with an American salute, at Hitler's Berlin Olympics, 1936. The Germans employ instead the fully outstretched arm salute that had come to characterize Nazi form.

de Coubertin. As a founding member of the International Olympic Committee (IOC), Coubertin had struggled for many years to revive the Olympic Games of ancient Greece, last staged in 393 c.e. Although Coubertin stressed his love of athletics, he succeeded in part because of the rampant nationalism of his age. Nations were eager to compete against one another, and sports provided a welcome, nonviolent format. The competition among athletes became a form of peaceful competition among nations. In 1896, some 13 nations of Western Europe and the United States participated; by 2012 some 193 nations and 11 territories from all over the world took part.

The decision to hold the first revived Olympic Games in Greece was in part meant to reconnect with the home of the original Games, but it was designed also to deliver a political message to the Ottoman Empire, Greece's former colonial ruler and hostile neighbor: Greece had revived herself as an independent nation, and other regions of the Balkans were also seeking independence.

Not only politics, but also gender relations found their expression in the Olympics. Women had not been allowed to compete in the ancient Olympic Games, and they were barred from the first modern Olympics as well. Women competed in the Olympics for the first time in 1900, in lawn tennis and golf, and they participated in track and field events in the Amsterdam Olympics of 1928. This breakthrough in gender relations mirrored more wide-ranging victories for feminism in society at large, most especially the right to vote, which was accorded to women in several

European countries and the United States in the decade just after World War I.

As politics heated up again, and the National Socialist (Nazi) Party rose to power in Germany, Berlin requested and received the right to stage the 1936 Olympics. The head of the German government and Nazi party, Adolf Hitler, used the Games to promote an image of a resurgent Germany and its ideology of Aryan racial supremacy. (Leni Riefenstahl's documentary film *Triumph of the Will*, 1935, produced for the German government, captured the intensely nationalistic spirit evident in the Nazi party parades and demonstrations at Nuremberg that preceded the occasion.) In the end, however, the African-American athlete Jesse Owens delivered a great slap in the face to Hitler's racial theories of Aryan supremacy by winning the gold medal in the 100- and 200-meter races, the long jump, and as part of the 400-meter relay race. Altogether, American track-and-field teams, which included several African-American athletes, won 12 gold medals. The confrontation of the two value systems was played out on the sports field a few years before it reached the battlefield. The Games were cancelled in 1940 and 1944; World War II intervened.

The right to host the Olympics has always been a mark of national accomplishment. The first 13 summer Games were hosted by cities in Western Europe and the United States. The 14th Games, held in Melbourne, Australia, in 1956, were the first departure from that pattern. From that time, hosting of the Games became far more international. By

A member of the International Olympic Committee talks with a masked Palestine Liberation Organization terrorist at the Munich Olympics, 1972. Eight Palestinians invaded the Olympic village and killed eleven Israeli athletes. One West German policeman and five Palestinians also died in the confrontation.

according Japan the right to host the 16th Games, in 1964, the IOC recognized Japan's reentry into the community of nations after its defeat in World War II. In subsequent years, additional nations sought and received the right to host the Olympics as a badge of their growing significance in international affairs: Mexico in 1968, Russia in 1980, Korea in 1988, China in 2012, Brazil is scheduled for 2016.

The dark as well as the bright side of international politics has spilled over into the Olympic Games. During the 1972 Munich Games, eight Palestinian terrorists brought the warfare of the Middle East to the Olympics. They invaded the Olympic Village, where athletes live during the Games, murdered two Israeli athletes, and seized nine more as hostages. Negotiations between Olympics officials and the terrorists failed. All the Israeli hostages, one West German policeman, and five of the Palestinians were killed.

In 1979, after the USSR invaded Afghanistan, United States President Jimmy Carter responded symbolically by refusing to allow America to compete in the 1980 Olympics in Moscow. In retaliation, the USSR refused to participate in the 1984 Olympics in Los Angeles. Despite the high aspirations of Baron Coubertin in 1896, Olympic competition could not be sealed off from international politics; on the contrary, the two have always been tightly intertwined.

Turning Point Questions

1. Can you imagine an Olympic Games in which athletes compete as individuals rather than as part of national teams? How would this be different?
2. Do you agree that sports as public competition mirror world events? Give examples.
3. In 1936, most eligible nations attended Hitler's Munich Olympics. In 1980, the United States boycotted the Moscow Olympics because of the Soviet invasion of Afghanistan. Do you think either of these decisions was appropriate? Why?

19 Methods of Mass Production and Destruction

Technological Systems

1914–1937

From the early years of the Industrial Revolution, people understood that the organization of human life would never again be the same. The neighborhood workplace and factory, the regional cities and towns, and the most intimate relationships among friends and family were transformed. At the global level, relationships between nations were realigned; rapidly industrializing countries challenged each other for supremacy.

Modern Times, 1936. In one of the greatest and most enduring comedic films, Charlie Chaplin takes aim at the capitalist industrial system, blaming it for impoverishing the world in the Great Depression of the time, and for driving the workers insane through the mind-numbing boredom of its production lines. Here, Chaplin satirizes the effects of the system on "The Little Tramp," his trademark character representing Everyman. Contrast this satiric, crazed view with the proud, even triumphal representation of industrialization illustrated at the beginning of the chapter "The Industrial Revolution."

LEARNING OBJECTIVES

19.1 ((•
Explain the changes caused by the period's technological growth.

19.2 ((•
Understand why some areas of the world made rapid technological progress while others did not.

19.3 ((•
Outline the chief causes of World War I.

19.4 ((•
Describe the most important actions of the Soviet Union's leaders in the first decade after the revolution.

19.5 ((•
Describe changes in American life after World War I.

19.6 ((•
Describe the causes of the Great Depression and the responses of the leaders involved.

((• Listen on **MyHistoryLab**

19.1
19.2
19.3
19.4
19.5
19.6

How did new technologies affect people's ways of life in the industrializing world?

As advocates had feared and critics had warned, many of the results were horrific. World War I resulted from a small crisis, a single political assassination, that spun out of control. Ultimately, the crisis goaded the most powerful nations of Europe to attack one another with their new weapons, the most lethal ever: tanks, airplanes, and poison gas. Russia could not keep up with the military technology of its neighbors. Its citizens suffered grievously during a war for which they were not prepared, until communist revolutionary leaders overthrew the government and took Russia out of the Great War. The Soviet Union's new leaders foresaw, correctly, that a new world war would be coming, and they promised to build up an industrial and military capacity second to none, even at the expense of the living standards of the common people. They chose **"guns over butter"**—military expenditure over domestic consumption. This decision to gear the economy towards war preparation, with full employment, spared Russia the global depression that afflicted most of the rest of the world. The depression resulted from economic decisions that seemed to favor the rich over the poor, increasing an imbalance of wealth that ultimately undermined the welfare of both. It came to an end only when the outbreak of World War II forced factories into full production and full employment. When World War II ended, the soldiers returned from the front and prosperity began to return as well. In America, and soon after in Western Europe, new appliances that were at first luxuries soon became necessities in middle-class homes; families became smaller, cities larger, automobiles more numerous, and lives longer. The new technologies of the industrial age served the tasks their masters set for them—for construction as well as destruction.

Technology in the Twentieth Century

19.1 How did new technologies affect people's ways of life in the industrializing world?

"Technology" refers not only to inventions but also to the systems that produce and sustain them. Thomas Hughes, a historian of science and technology, offers this comprehensive definition:

> In popular accounts of technology, inventions of the late nineteenth century, such as the incandescent light, the radio, the airplane, and the gasoline-driven automobile, occupy center stage, but these inventions were embedded within technological systems. Such systems involve far more than the so-called hardware, devices, machines and processes, and the transportation, communication, and information networks that interconnect them. Such systems consist also of people and organizations. An electric light-and-power system, for instance, may involve generators, motors, transmission lines, utility companies, manufacturing enterprises, and banks. Even a regulatory body may be co-opted into the system. (Hughes, 1989, p. 3)

The power and creativity of the technological enterprise became the most pervasive characteristic of the twentieth century. By 1914, when World War I began, many of the most important innovations were already in place, producing, or on the verge of producing, dramatic alterations in the world. Many of these innovations led to increased production of capital goods, such as machinery and steel, and many of them touched directly on the quality and style of life.

Transportation and Communication

By the early twentieth century, transport and communications networks made even the most distant places accessible and provided unprecedented mobility between them. In the cities, subways brought faster travel and shorter waiting times. Commuter trains extended the new mobility further. Many urban workers

KEY TERM

"guns vs butter" This refers to the budget decisions that governments have to make between military spending and domestic, often welfare, spending.

19.1

19.2

19.3

19.4

19.5

19.6

How did new technologies affect people's ways of life in the industrializing world?

The City, Fernand Leger, 1919. Oil on canvas. After World War I, Leger began to paint Paris as a city built by machinery, filled with machinery, and reveling in machinery. Even its people seemed mechanical. Contrast Caillebotte's 1876–77 painting which presents the Paris of bourgeois elegance. Leger and his artist friends with their abstract, often cubist, often surrealist styles captured the new post-War exaltation of machinery in their paintings, sculptures, architectural designs, and advertising, and in the new moving pictures and musical compositions they were creating. (The Philadelphia Museum of Art)

who could afford the costs of commuting began to live in the suburbs. Industry, too, migrated to the suburbs, where it could adopt new, sprawling, single-story factory design.

In 1908, Henry Ford's automobile factory produced 10,607 Model T cars. In 1913, using the moving assembly line he had developed, Ford's factory turned out 300,000 cars—one car every 93 minutes. The Ford Motor Company made the automobile practical and cheap enough to be accessible to a mass market. Trucks were marketed at first in the hundreds and, by 1918, in the hundreds of thousands. Commercial bus operations began in Birmingham, England, in 1904 and in New York, Paris, and London in the next year. As automobiles, trucks, and buses multiplied, pressure mounted for the construction of roads, and vast industries developed around the new vehicles: rubber for tires, glass for windows, steel for bodies and engines, and electrical systems for lights, starters, and, later, luxury equipment. Automobiles provided both workhorses for industry and fantasies for private consumption, opening up new vistas of personal mobility and, for courting couples, new possibilities of privacy.

Airplanes developed swiftly from toys to commercial and military utilities. In 1903, the Wright brothers proved that heavier-than-air flight was possible, and by 1914, airplanes could fly at 60 to 70 miles per hour. Almost as soon as they were invented, planes were drafted for military service. In World War I, both sides used them.

Ships were certainly not new, and even steamships had existed for decades, but their design was improved. In 1907, the *Lusitania* crossed the Atlantic in five days. (In 1915, during World War I, it was torpedoed and sunk, as discussed below.)

Communication, too, took on new speed and reach. Virtually instantaneous radio telegraphy was in place across the Atlantic by 1901 and across the Pacific in 1902. By 1907, there were six million telephone users in the United States alone.

👁 **Watch** the **Video**: **Rural Free Delivery Mail** on **MyHistoryLab**

How did new technologies affect people's ways of life in the industrializing world?

19.1
19.2
19.3
19.4
19.5
19.6

Urban Life

New kinds of metropolises provided homes for massive populations served by trams, cars, buses, trucks, highways, and new systems for water, sewage, lighting, and public health. Cities installed electrical grids to light up the night, replacing gas lighting. In addition to street lighting and domestic lighting, electricity meant that from the early twentieth century workshops and factories could operate in shifts, round the clock. Agricultural time, based on the alternating, natural rhythms of daytime, nighttime, and seasonal changes, gave way to mechanical clocktime and calendartime. Particularly after alternating current (AC) was adopted over direct current (DC), the ability to transmit power over long distances freed entrepreneurs from earlier technical constraints in locating their factories. They no longer required a waterfront location. The human tie to nature, in time and space, was attenuated.

The growth of cities, in number, territory, population, and proportion of total population, continued as one of the most striking features of the ongoing Industrial Revolution in the early twentieth century. They expanded on the basis of technological change and immigration. The mechanization of agriculture drove people off the farms; new jobs in manufacturing, bureaucracy, and service industries drew them to the cities, sometimes from nearby rural areas, sometimes from great distances. Rates of urbanization and of economic development were closely correlated. Countries with high rates of industrial and economic development had high rates of urbanization, and vice versa. Although many of the newcomers found city life disorienting, many others found it exciting and full of attractions, such as the new movie theaters and dance halls. Department stores offered fashionable displays to entice buyers. City streets themselves provided spectacle, where men and women could see and be seen.

📖 **Read** the **Document**: **Richard K. Fox**, from *Coney Island Frolics* (1883) on **MyHistoryLab**

Technology and Gender Relations

Changes in technology precipitated profound changes in gender relationships. The invention of new household appliances facilitated women's domestic work, although some historians have also argued that by making such work easier, they created a culture in which women actually did more of it. For example, instead of one annual "spring cleaning," women began to use their vacuum cleaners to clean the house more frequently.

Automobiles gave adolescents new opportunities for the exploration of their sexuality out of the sight of parents. As further stimulus to exploration, Hollywood films introduced risqué themes and featured the best of American technology as props. Many individuals believed that films sold a culture of sex, which needed to be combated, hence the censorship of the Hays Code of the 1930s. Technology made birth control easier. Family size in England and Wales, for example, declined from 6.16 children in the 1860s to 2.82 children in 1910–14. But not everyone was pleased with the changes. Many people continued to believe that a woman's role was to raise children. Margaret Sanger in the United States, Marie Stopes in Britain, and Theodore van de Velde in the Netherlands published manuals emphasizing the enjoyment of sex by both men and women in marriage and, at the same time, advocating family planning. Sanger was arrested for sending her magazines through the mail, then for opening the first "family planning" clinic in the United States, in New

Marie Curie and Pierre Curie. Nineteenth- and early twentieth-century women increasingly carved out places for themselves at the forefront of intellectual, scientific, and political life. The Polish-born French scientist Marie Curie, seen here in 1895 with her husband and collaborator, Pierre, was awarded two Nobel Prizes (physics, with Pierre, 1903; chemistry, 1911) for her pioneering studies of radiation. Here, the husband-and-wife team appear to be riding bicycles for pleasure, but, toward the end of the nineteenth century, bicycles also gave women more freedom by providing inexpensive personal transportation and encouraging more casual, comfortable styles of dress.

19.1 How did new technologies affect people's ways of life in the industrializing world?

19.2

19.3

19.4

19.5

19.6

York in 1916. Police booked her as a "public nuisance." Only in 1936 did courts in the United States decide that information on birth control was not pornographic and give doctors the right to discuss the subject with their patients.

Scientific Research and Development

Educational facilities multiplied: basic education was provided to prepare workers for new job requirements; research laboratories were set up to incubate creativity and invention; and institutes were established to concentrate on advances in scientific theory.

A revolution in chemistry multiplied productivity in agriculture and industry, changing the food people ate and the clothing they wore. Industrial chemists developed new filaments that made incandescent lighting commercially viable. They created purer and stronger steel. Organic chemists working with coal and coal tar developed a wide array of new synthetic products, beginning with dyes, and including a wide range of consumer products. Most notably, by 1909, Fritz Haber and his colleagues in Germany had invented a process for making ammonia (NH_3) directly from nitrogen and hydrogen found in the air, without the need for mineral products, paving the way for the massive inexpensive production of artificial fertilizers as well as explosives used in construction and poison gas used in war (see below).

In physics, the major discoveries were theoretical and were achieved by individual thinkers, most of whom occupied research positions in universities and were in touch with the informal, but substantial, world society of scientists.

Albert Einstein. The most revolutionary of the theoretical physicists was the German Albert Einstein (1879–1955), whose theory of special relativity was published in 1905, when he was 26 years old. Practical applications implicit in this theory came decades later, but the philosophical significance (for those who could understand it) was immediate and revolutionary.

Einstein changed the way we look at the world. His special theory of relativity started from the postulate that the speed of light is constant and unchanging. If that is so, he argued, neither time nor motion is fixed. Both appear relative to the observer. For example, light from two stars may appear to arrive at the same time on earth, but the light has actually left each star at different times relative to earth because each star is a different distance from earth. In another paper published in 1905, Einstein set forth the principle that mass and energy are interchangeable, a relationship he expressed in the equation $E = mc^2$, energy equals matter times the speed of light squared. (The search for the atomic bomb was later undertaken on the basis of this formula, for the bomb represented the transformation of matter into enormous quantities of energy.)

In 1916, Einstein published his general theory of relativity, which explored the nature of gravity and gave a new explanation for it. Physical masses do not attract other masses; rather, they actually bend space toward themselves, so that objects roll toward them. Einstein thus overturned the basis of Newtonian physics, the intellectual structure on which physics had rested for two centuries. This indeterminacy in physics unsettled centuries of scientific thought and helped to usher in a period of great indeterminacy in world affairs.

The Downside of Progress

Not all scientific and industrial progress was directed toward peaceful uses. The chemical, metallurgical, and electrical marvels of the early twentieth century were devoted to military as well as to civilian goals, and the peaceful competition in invention and production was matched by military competition. The competition between Britain and Germany was especially sharp, as Britain's share of world manufacturing output dropped while Germany's rose. (The greatest gains were actually made by the United States, but America was far away and was perceived by itself and by Europeans as relatively uninvolved in Europe's contests.)

The British–German competition compelled attention. This was evident in the size of their armed forces. In 1914, on the eve of World War I, Germany's lead over Britain in terms of army and navy personnel stood at 891,000 against 532,000. (The United States had only 164,000 in its armed forces.) Both Russia, with 1,352,000, and France, with 910,000, had even more men under arms, but the Russians were not so well equipped, and neither country could keep up with British and German sea power. Here Britain held a commanding lead, with 2,714,000 warship tons to Germany's 1,305,000 tons.

Most observers did not expect the competition to lead to war, however, because of the system of alliances the great powers had created to preserve the peace. The **balance of power** between the Triple Alliance (Germany, Austria–Hungary, and Italy) and the Triple Entente (France, Russia, and Britain) was expected to keep each side aware of the potential costs of war and the benefits of peace. All these nations and empires understood that a miscalculation could embroil them in catastrophic war, but images of rationality and progress led political leaders to discount such fears—to their peril, as we shall discuss below.

Fritz Haber. The life of Fritz Haber (1868–1934) makes painfully clear, on a personal level, the irony—and tragedy—of intertwining technology for humanitarian benefit with the technology of warfare. In 1909, Haber synthesized ammonia from the nitrogen in the air, making possible the nitrogen fertilizers that have dramatically increased food production throughout the world. Haber was awarded the Nobel Prize for chemistry in 1918. In 1915, however, between the time of the invention and the award of the prize, Haber also developed and introduced the use of poison gas in World War I. An ardent German patriot, he developed the gas against the advice of many of his scientific colleagues, and his strenuous arguments for its deployment went against the spirit, although not the wording, of international agreements on the limits of warfare. His wife, Clara Immerwahr, also a brilliant scientist, and one of the first women in Germany to earn a Ph.D. in science, vigorously opposed Haber's obsession with chemical warfare. When the gas was first used on the Western Front, 5,000 Allied soldiers died and 10,000 were injured (see below). Ten days later Haber's wife shot herself dead. Biographers of both husband and wife agree that their quarrel over the gas was not the only factor in her decision, but apparently it did have a role. Nevertheless, and even after Germany's defeat, Haber continued to manufacture poison gas secretly, in violation of international treaties.

International Role Reversals

19.2 Which areas of the world did not keep pace with rapid industrialization? Why not?

Since the Industrial Revolution began, inventions in Europe had challenged, displaced, and even destroyed traditional hand manufacture in the vast areas of the world that did not experience this revolution. As the pace of scientific invention and technological application increased, this displacement intensified, causing immense

19.1

19.2 Which areas of the world did not keep pace with rapid industrialization? Why not?

19.3

19.4

19.5

19.6

KEY TERM

balance of power In international relations, a policy that aims to secure peace by preventing any one state or alignment of states from becoming too dominant. Alliances are formed to build up a force equal or superior to that of the potential enemy.

turmoil. In several cases, foreign colonial rule compounded the economic and technological disparities. Four examples—from India, China, Latin America, and the Ottoman Empire—reveal the process.

Before the Industrial Revolution, India had the largest textile industry in the world, and China manufactured fine silks, porcelain, and iron. When the Spaniards first entered Mexico City, they were awed by its advanced urban structures. The Ottoman Empire preserved much of the knowledge of the ancient world during the late medieval and early modern periods, and transmitted it to those Europeans interested in reclaiming it also for themselves. In many respects, culturally, and even economically, these Asian and American empires were more sophisticated than Europe. The Industrial Revolution reversed many of these relationships as Europe began to lead the world in scientific discovery and technological application. Some regions failed to recognize the new threats posed by European advances and were left behind. Many were intentionally prevented from responding as Europeans intervened with political and military power to sustain their own growing industrial supremacy.

India

In the nineteenth century the hand spinners and weavers of India were superseded and impoverished by the mechanized spindles and looms of Britain. In the late nineteenth and early twentieth centuries, continuing invention in Europe destroyed still more of India's industries. In 1883, the German chemist Adolf von Baeyer determined the chemical structure of indigo, and in 1897 his company made synthetic indigo available commercially. At that time, Indian farmers were producing about 9,000 tons of indigo per year. By 1913, India produced only 1,000 tons and was importing synthetic indigo from Germany. Later developments—in plastics, for example—would

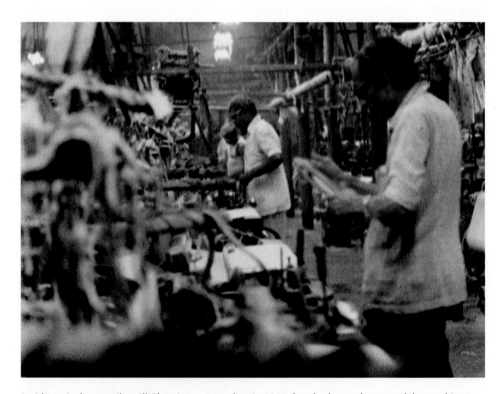

Inside an Indian textile mill. The picture was taken in 1981, but the factory layout and the machinery are older, dating to the 1930s. Compare them with the American machine shop, c. 1898, in the chapter entitled "The Industrial Revolution," and the Japanese factory of the 1930s in the chapter "World War II." Under British colonial rule, most industrial machinery in India had to be imported from England. Only after independence in 1947 did Indians begin to manufacture more of their own machinery.

19.1
19.2
19.3
19.4
19.5
19.6

Which areas of the world did not keep pace with rapid industrialization? Why not?

similarly displace hand-manufactured goods and the jobs that went with them. Technological progress in one region caused economic dislocation and suffering in other regions, a process that continues to this day.

In 1911, Britain asserted its supremacy over India through the majestic symbolism of the *durbar*—a royal convocation—in Delhi, presided over by the king-emperor George V, who traveled to India to make the first ever appearance of a British monarch in the colony. The princes and the elites of India, dressed in their splendor, attended as his vassals. The British proclaimed their power and enumerated their contributions to Indian progress, but in their hubris they willfully overlooked the disruptions their rule was causing and the rising resentment toward them on the part of the masses and of the elites who represented them.

The *durbar* was held in Delhi because Calcutta, the city that had served as the capital of British India for a century and a half, was seething with discontent against British rule. Indians were protesting not only Britain's economic and technological policies but also its political policies of control and its religious policies of **divide and rule**, which emphasized historic examples of antagonism (rather than historic examples of cooperation) between Hindus and Muslims in order to turn them against one another and make it easier for Britons to rule the country. The combined outcry against all of these policies forced the British government to transfer the capital itself. Indian leaders increasingly called for self-rule. Bal Gangadhar Tilak (1856–1920) summed up the Indians' growing demand: "Freedom is my birthright and I shall have it." Their struggle was yet in its early stages. It would take another decade, and new leadership, to consolidate an anticolonial political alliance between leaders and the masses.

China

We have already seen the struggles that occurred in China in the last years of the nineteenth century over the proper policies for confronting Western domination. For the most part, the traditionalists defeated the reformers at the imperial court. China chose to strengthen its industrial capacity and restructure the official civil-service examinations to put greater emphasis on science and technology, but the attempted reforms were too little and too late. In 1911, China had only one million industrial workers out of a population of 400 million. Most industry was on a small scale, much of it in textiles. Faith in the viability of the Confucian traditions, and in the government that implemented them, was dying out. After 70 years of military defeat, colonial subordination, peasant revolt, and intellectual contentiousness, China was ripe for revolution. The Mandate of Heaven was passing from the Manchu dynasty.

Revolution began in China in October 1911 with a bomb explosion in the Wuhan area that triggered a series of army mutinies and civilian revolts. Within a month, the Manchu government promulgated a civil constitution and convened a provisional national assembly. Yuan Shihkai (1859–1916), the most powerful military official in China, was elected premier. In January 1912, the boy emperor Puyi (r. 1908–12) abdicated, ending 2,000 years of China's imperial tradition.

Yuan received full powers to organize a provisional republican government. But he exceeded his mandate. In January 1916, he took the title of emperor, provoking widespread revolt. Under severe military attack and critically ill, Yuan died in June of that year.

With no effective governing center, China entered a decade of rule by warlords, regional strongmen who had their own independent militias. Some of the warlords controlled whole provinces, others only a few towns or segments of railway line. Some had formal military training, others were simply local strongmen. Some sought to play a role in forming a powerful national government, others wanted to continue China's division. Many were rapacious. Old, painful Chinese proverbs took on new reality: "In an age of chaos, don't miss the chance to loot during the fire," and "In

KEY TERMS

durbar A showy convocation of notables paying obeisance to, and receiving gifts from, the most powerful political leaders; a means of demonstrating and ratifying the relative position of each.

divide and rule A policy, usually unstated, by which a ruling power would encourage quarrels among its subjects so that they did not unite to challenge the ruling authority, and it could present itself as indispensable to keeping the peace. The rulers claimed that the divisions were inherent among the populations; anti-imperialists claimed the rulers created them for their own purposes.

Founder of the GMD. Sun Yat-sen (Sun Yixian), photographed here in Western dress according to his custom, is considered the "father of the nation," even though he spent much of his life abroad and never achieved his own political ambitions. He was a revolutionary and helped to found the Guomindang. Although unable to stay in power himself, he influenced China's most important figures of the next generation: Chiang Kai-shek and Mao Zedong.

19.1

19.2 Which areas of the world did not keep pace with rapid industrialization? Why not?

19.3

19.4

19.5

19.6

the official's house, wine and meat are allowed to rot, but on the roads are the bones of those who starved to death."

The leading revolutionaries looked to Sun Yat-sen (1866–1925) as their mentor. Although raised in a peasant household, Sun received his secondary education in a missionary school in Hawaii and his medical training in Hong Kong. He spent most of his adult life in China's port cities or abroad.

In 1895, Sun had attempted a coup, but it failed and he was exiled. He was in the United States organizing for revolution when the uprising of 1911 began. He returned to help found the Guomindang (GMD), China's leading revolutionary party. Sun was elected first president of the United Provinces of China, but a jealous and fearful Yuan exiled him in 1913. Sun returned to Guangzhou in the early 1920s and led his movement from that port city, but he never regained political office.

Sun's "Three People's Principles" included a heavy admixture of Western thought. The first principle, nationalism, called for revolution against foreign political control, beginning with the ousting of the Manchus from China, and against foreign economic control, which had rendered China

> the colony of every nation with which it has concluded treaties; each of them is China's master. China is not just the colony of one country, but the colony of many countries. We are not just the slaves of one country, but the slaves of many countries … Today we are the poorest and weakest nation in the world, and occupy the lowest position in international affairs … other men are the carving knife and serving dish; we are the fish and the meat … we must espouse nationalism and bring this national spirit to the salvation of the country. (de Bary, p. 321)

Sun's second principle, democracy, emphasized a predominantly Western political model: "Since we have had only ideas about popular rights, and no democratic system has evolved, we have to go to Europe and America for a republican form of government" (cited in Andrea and Overfield, p. 350). He did, however, claim the separation of powers as an ancient Chinese tradition. Sun's third principle, under the heading "People's Livelihood," revealed his ambivalence toward Western technology and organization. He proclaimed the need for new technology:

> First we must build means of communication, railroads and waterways, on a large scale. Second we must open up mines. Third we must hasten to develop manufacturing. Although China has a multitude of workers, she has no machinery and so cannot compete with other countries. Goods used throughout China have to be manufactured and imported from other countries, with the result that our rights and interests are simply leaking away. (de Bary, p. 327)

But Western-style industrialization was not his chosen model. Fearing "the expansion of private capital and the emergence of a great wealthy class with the consequent inequalities" in China, Sun called for a different path: state ownership and "state power to build up these enterprises." He thought Marxism irrelevant for China: "In China, where industry is not yet developed, Marx's class war and dictatorship of the proletariat are impracticable." China's economic problem was not unequal distribution but lack of production.

Chinese of all political parties revered Sun, but they lacked the power to implement his plans. They had fallen too far behind the technology and military organization of the Western powers. China's weakness was revealed in the peace treaties ending World War I: The areas of China that had been controlled by Germany were not returned to China, but were transferred to Japanese control. The Chinese protested this decision in the May Fourth Movement at home, but they could not get the decision reversed. Sun did, however, inspire two leaders—Chiang Kai-shek (Jiang Jieshi) and Mao Zedong—who contested for dominance in China for a quarter-century following his death in 1925 and attempted to restore China's precolonial stature in the world. We shall read about their struggles in the chapter entitled "China and India."

19.1
19.2
Which areas of the world did not keep pace with rapid industrialization? Why not?
19.3
19.4
19.5
19.6

Latin America

Through the late nineteenth and early twentieth centuries, Latin America began to industrialize, largely with investments from overseas. At first, Britain was the principal investor, but after World War I the United States assumed that role. For the most part, economic and technological innovations were initiated by foreigners in search of profits. Most of the investments were concentrated in primary production—that is, farming and mining—rather than in industrial manufacturing. At the time of World War I, for example, the United States was buying about one-third of Brazil's exports, mostly coffee, rubber, and cocoa. (Half of Brazil's exports consisted of coffee.) Members of the Creole and *mazombo* elites, mostly descendants of the earlier settlers who had come from Spain and Portugal, saw that they too could share in the new earnings and win some acceptability among Europeans, and they joined in the new commerce. But for the most part the initiatives came from outside.

Most of the elites were content to treat their nations as private estates. Control and patronage mattered—money and profits were means to an end, not ends in themselves. In "Ariel", an essay written in 1898, the Uruguayan philosopher José Enrique Rodó (1872–1917) analyzed Latin America's trend in the direction of an industrial democracy on the United States model and rejected it. He saw that path as crude, even barbaric, and inconsistent with the more leisurely, elitist, cultured world of the Creole rulers of Latin America. In the absence of democratic systems, most governments in Latin America were still in the hands of *caudillos*, military strongmen who governed on their own authority.

Not everyone was content with a system of control by local elites. During the Liberal Era, 1870–1930, businessmen who were participating in the new commerce and industry began to think of new goals: more education, more industrialization, more independence from foreign investors, and more consistent government, with a larger, formal voice in politics for themselves—but not for the new immigrants who were streaming into Latin America, nor for the Native Americans who were pushed off the best lands onto the worst, and into the lowest-paying jobs. Toward the end of the nineteenth century, a huge influx of immigrants from Europe, especially Italy, brought with it ideas of industrial development and union representation, and by the early twentieth century, important labor unions were in place in the larger nations of Latin America. Another group advocating reform and national pride was the army, especially its junior officers. Often drawn from middle-class urban families and aware of modern technology through their knowledge of weaponry, army officers were more attentive to the importance of education, industrialization, business, and stable government.

In some countries these groups worked together and achieved their goals, but even the most progressive states, such as Argentina and Uruguay, failed to undertake what might have been the most influential reform of all. They did not restructure the landholding patterns that left wealthy landlords in charge of impoverished peasants. The reformers were urban people, and they were commonly related to the landlords; they had little practical sympathy for the agricultural laborers and no intention of sharing power or profits with them.

19.1
19.2 Which areas of the world did not keep pace with rapid industrialization? Why not?
19.3
19.4
19.5
19.6

Argentina. Argentina was divided between a landowning elite that turned toward bourgeois elements in Europe as its model, and those who wanted a different, American model to emerge. For fifty years after independence in 1816, these factions fought a civil war. The landholders won. By the 1850s, some 825 of these landholders held an area within Argentina equal to the size of England; at least, that was the claim of their critics. Argentina's rulers through the mid-nineteenth century, men like Juan Manuel de Rosas (dominant 1829–52) and his successors, especially General Julio Argentino Roca (1870s), had appropriated these lands by driving Argentina's natives, Indians, from the country's vast plains—the pampas—and from Patagonia in the south. (They had followed the model of the United States.) Their ranches, surrounded by barbed-wire fences, were miniature states. (In this, they did not follow the United States, where the Homestead Act made land available to masses of settlers.) Their exports of beef, grains, and wool made Argentina wealthy. The wealth attracted millions of immigrants; between 1880 and 1930, Argentina received 2.5 million, the highest ratio of immigrants to total population in the world, about twice the ratio of the United States. The largest single national group came from Italy. The wealth, and potential for wealth, also attracted foreign investment, mostly from Britain, mostly into railroads and facilities to export beef, wool, and grains to Europe. Refrigerated railway cars and industrialized meat-packing plants facilitated this process. For decades, Argentina received more investment from England than India did; in 1889, half of all English overseas investment went to Argentina.

The investments and the wealth, however, created two fundamental imbalances. The first was between the rich landowners, many of whom lived luxuriously in the capital city, Buenos Aires, "the Paris of South America," and the poor. The poor—the other Argentines—included the *gauchos*, cowboys, who worked the ranches; the farmers living in remote areas of the country that were not connected to the international markets; the workers in the meat-packing and other export-based industries; and urban workers in local factories. Most immigrants fell into these categories. The second imbalance was in the economy, which was built fundamentally on the export of agricultural products to Europe and the import of European goods, but had little industry of its own. World War I sharply reduced the overseas investments from Europe, and the worldwide depression sharply reduced the demand for exports. Argentina had staked its fortunes on these foreign investments and export industries. World War I (in which Argentina remained neutral) and the depression suggested that Argentina—in common with much of Latin America—had made some serious mistakes in its long-term economic policy.

The Mexican Revolution, 1910–20. In 1910, urban and rural leaders in Mexico rose up against the dictatorship of Porfirio Díaz (1830–1915), who had been ruling the country since 1876. At the age of 80, Díaz seemed poised to retire from the presidency. Under his leadership, Mexico had seen the development of mining, oil drilling, and railways, in addition to increasing exports of raw agricultural products. The middle-class urban Creole elite had prospered through this industrialization, but the salaries of the urban workers had declined, and rural peasants had fared even worse. Ninety-five percent of the rural peasantry owned no land, while fewer than 200 Mexican families owned 25 percent of all the land of Mexico, and foreign investors owned another 20–25 percent. One single *hacienda* sprawled over 13 million acres and another over 11 million acres. Huge tracts of land lay fallow and unused while peasants went hungry.

Democratic elections were relatively new to Mexico, and when Díaz changed his mind and ran for reelection as president, he imprisoned his principal challenger, Francisco Madero (1873–1913). Díaz won, but rebellions against his continuing rule broke out across the country, and he soon resigned and went into exile in Paris. Regional leaders then asserted their influence as Mexico erupted into civil war. Issues were ethnic, economic, and religious.

19.1

19.2

Which areas
of the world
did not keep
pace with rapid
industrialization?
Why not?

19.3

19.4

19.5

19.6

Mexican revolutionaries. General Francisco "Pancho" Villa (center) and Emiliano Zapata (right, sporting his flamboyant moustache) sit with their Mexican revolutionary army, men who had come from many different occupations and walks of life to join the ranks. The radical leaders hailed from different parts of the country—Zapata from south of Mexico City and Villa from the northern border—but they shared common goals.

Leaders emerged to represent the *mestizos*, people of mixed race and culture, who demanded a dramatic break with the past control by the Creole elite. The two most radical, Francisco "Pancho" Villa (1878–1923) and Emiliano Zapata (1879–1919), advocated land reform, and implemented it in the areas they captured during the civil war. They attracted mixed groups of followers, including farm workers, agricultural colonists, former soldiers, unemployed laborers, cowboys, and delinquents. In November 1911, Zapata called for the return of land to Indian *pueblos* (villages). Tens of thousands of impoverished peasants followed him, heeding his cry of "Tierra y Libertad" ("Land and Liberty") and accepting his view that it was "better to die on one's feet than to live on one's knees." Zapata's supporters seized large sugar estates, *haciendas* with which they had been in conflict for years.

With Díaz in exile, Madero became president, but he was removed by a coup and then assassinated in 1913. General Víctoriano Huerta (1854–1916) attempted to take over and to reestablish a repressive government similar to that of Díaz. Opposed by all the other major leaders, and also by President Woodrow Wilson of the United States, who sent American troops into Veracruz to express his displeasure with Huerta, the general was forced from power in March 1914. Another general, Alvaro Obregón (1880–1928), who made free use of the machine gun, won out militarily, but he agreed to serve under Venustiano Carranza (1859–1920), who had himself installed as provisional president.

The civil war continued, and control of Mexico City changed hands several times, but ultimately the more conservative leaders, Carranza and Obregón, forced out Villa and Zapata. Carranza became president in 1916 and convened a constituent assembly that produced the Mexican Constitution of 1917, promising land reform and imposing restrictions on foreign economic control. The new constitution protected Mexican workers by passing a labor code that included minimum salaries and maximum hours, accident insurance, pensions, social benefits, and the right to unionize and

19.1
19.2
19.3
19.4
19.5
19.6

Which areas
of the world
did not keep
pace with rapid
industrialization?
Why not?

strike. It placed severe restrictions on the Church and clergy, denying them the rights to own property and to provide primary education. (Most of the revolutionaries were anticlerical. Zapata was an exception in this, as the peasantry who followed him were devoted to the Church.) The constitution also decreed that no foreigner could be a minister or priest, vote, hold office, or criticize the government.

Enacting the new laws was easier than implementing them. On the material level not much changed at first. Then in 1920, Obregón deposed Carranza and became president. He distributed three million acres of land to peasants, ten percent of whom benefited. This redistribution helped to establish the principles of the revolution, demonstrating good faith on the part of the state and putting new land into production, although the state did not provide the technical assistance needed to improve productivity. Politically, Obregón began to include new constituencies in his government, including the labor movement, represented by a Labor Party, and the peasants, represented by a National Agrarian Party. The institutionalization of their presence in government promised new stability through wider representation. The representation, everyone recognized, was not only by social class but also by ethnicity and culture. *Mestizos* and even indigenous Indians achieved a place in government. Mexico's struggle against the threefold problems of racial discrimination against Indians, economic discrimination against the poor, and the denial of both problems behind a façade of political rhetoric was an inspiration throughout Latin America. It had come at a high price: one million dead out of a total population of about 15 million.

The Ottoman Empire

Unlike Mexico, which was generally dependent on European powers for its economic investment capital and initiatives, the Ottoman Empire retained its economic autonomy (although French capital was used to construct its major technological achievement, the Suez Canal). Unlike India, the empire did not lose its sovereignty, but like China, it lost many of the attributes of self-rule, while remaining formally independent. The Ottoman Empire fell behind the industrial and political developments in Western Europe and America, and it slowly disintegrated.

The process by which the Ottoman Empire became "the sick man of Europe" took more than a century. We have already reviewed the first stages, in which the Ottomans lost control of Egypt, Greece, and most of their holdings in the Balkans. Despite its attempts at reform and reorganization, the empire was defeated by the Russians in war in 1878. In 1881, European bankers declared that the Ottoman Empire was not properly managing its finances and was defaulting on its debts. The Europeans demanded and obtained official representation in the offices of the Ottoman treasury. European powers also claimed rights to intervene in internal Ottoman affairs in order to defend the rights of Christian communities living in the Islamic Ottoman Empire. They stationed representatives of various Christian denominations in Constantinople to assert and represent those rights. Despite this foreign religious and political surveillance, the Ottoman government supported a series of attacks on the restless community of Armenian Christians in

Young Turks overthrowing the government of Ottoman sultan Abdul Hamid II in 1909. He had ruled since 1876, a period in which the Ottoman Empire had grown steadily weaker and more out of touch with the Westernizing measures favored by the Young Turks. The Islamic scholar on the hill agrees that it is acceptable to dispose of the sultan, although in reality the revolutionaries did not kill him; they merely deposed him.

The end of the Ottoman Empire. The last decades of the nineteenth century saw the Ottoman presence in Europe decline as Austria–Hungary, Russia, and several aspiring new nations challenged its power. Arab revolt and internal dissent, combined with the Turkish defeat in World War I, brought to an end 450 years of Ottoman domination. Turkey was the core residual state, while several other regions were mandated to British and French control.

19.1

19.2

Which areas of the world did not keep pace with rapid industrialization? Why not?

19.3

19.4

19.5

19.6

Anatolia, fearing continuing revolt from them. About 200,000 Armenians were killed in 1895.

In 1908, a group of progressive army officers and liberal professionals—collectively called "Young Turks"—seized control of the government under the sultan. During these years, however, the dismemberment of the empire continued. Almost all its remaining European and North African holdings were stripped away. Bulgaria declared its independence in 1908, the same year that Austria-Hungary annexed Bosnia. In the Italo-Turkish War of 1911–12, Italy seized the North African territories of Libya and the offshore Dodecanese Islands. Bulgaria, Serbia, and Greece aided Albania in gaining its independence in 1912.

19.1
19.2
19.3
19.4
19.5
19.6

What were the
chief causes of
World War I?

A second Balkan war in the next year concerned the appropriate size of Bulgaria and control over Albania. Serbians, Greeks, Austrians, and even Italians were involved. The decision, favored by Austria, to make Albania an independent kingdom infuriated the Serbians, who wanted to control the region for its access to the sea, and agitated the Russians, who had backed the Serbians as brother Slavs. The economic and military competition among the great powers was embedded in these still larger issues of nationalism, a powerful force in early twentieth-century Europe.

People's reverence for their nation-states, and for their shared languages, history, ethnicity, and aspirations within those states, had grown so passionate that they were willing to fight and die for them. Cynics argued that the masses of the population were being manipulated into battle by industrialists in each country who stood to profit from war production, but the national feelings were powerful in themselves. Nationalism evoked just as much emotional commitment among the citizens of smaller, newer states with little economic base in military production—such as the Balkan states—as it did among the great empires.

By 1914, the dismemberment of the Ottoman Empire, the resulting power struggle in the Balkans, and the constant warfare for control of the area created one of the most dangerous geopolitical regions in the world. Having fallen behind the industrial and military advances of its European rivals, the Ottoman Empire could no longer keep the peace in its region. Without effective Ottoman rule, the multitude of rival ethnic and religious groups encouraged strife and invited the intervention of the major powers of Europe. As noted, these powers were already deeply involved in competition for arms, markets, and prestige, and they were committed to mutually antagonistic military alliances, which, for decades, had preserved the peace through a balance of power.

On the one hand, peace and progress appeared to be the hallmarks of the era. On the other hand, international relations were tense and in a state of flux. Peripheral areas had become central. Historically great powers had become colonies and pawns in the hands of relative newcomers. Ethnic tensions and nationalisms of various sorts seemed to appear everywhere, especially in the Balkans. From one point of view, the status of world politics and economics appeared rosy and optimistic; from another, it was tense and potentially explosive.

World War I

19.3 What were the chief causes of World War I?

Background Tinder and Initial Spark

On June 28, 1914, a Serbian nationalist assassinated Archduke Franz Ferdinand, heir to the Austro-Hungarian throne, and his wife. The assassin was outraged because the Austro-Hungarian Empire had seized Balkan territories with heavily Serbian populations. His bullets were the matches that lit the spark of World War I (called the Great War until World War II surpassed it in magnitude). The Balkan region, like much of central Europe, was home to many relatively small ethnic, religious, and linguistic groups. In the intensely nationalistic environment of the times, each asserted its right to at least some level of self-determination within larger states, and often to a state of its own. The disintegration of the Ottoman Empire inspired further hopes for these national claims. So it was not only large industrialized states like Britain and Germany that confronted one another; smaller, more localized regions were also jealous of their status.

📖 **Read** the **Document**: **The Murder of Archduke Franz Ferdinand at Sarajevo 1914 Borijove Jevti** on **MyHistoryLab**

World War I. European rivalries for political and economic superiority, within Europe and throughout its imperial holdings, erupted in 1914. A fragile system of alliances designed to contain the ambitions of Germany and Austria–Hungary (the Central Powers) collapsed, resulting in a conflict of horrific proportions. Turkey joined the Central Powers. In France and Belgium a stalemate war of attrition developed. In the east a war of thrust and counterthrust caused enormous popular dissent and exhaustion, eventually bringing the collapse of the Turkish, Russian, and Austrian empires alike. In all, 20 million people died.

19.1
19.2
19.3
What were the chief causes of World War I?
19.4
19.5
19.6

One month after the murder, Austria–Hungary declared war on Serbia, triggering a domino effect. Under the system of alliances that had been built up over the preceding three decades, countries now came to the aid of one another. Russia mobilized its armies to defend Serbia and to take up positions on the borders of Germany. Fearing attack, Germany declared war on Russia and its ally, France. Intending to strike France quickly and decisively, and envelop its forces in a pincer movement, Germany sent massive forces across Belgium, violating an international treaty guaranteeing Belgian neutrality. In defense of Belgium and support of France, Britain declared war on Germany on August 4, as did Britain's geographically remote ally Japan. The alliance system, which had been expected to prevent war among the highly competitive and nationalistic states of Europe, had instead drawn all the major powers into

Life in the trenches. World War I became notorious for its trench warfare, in which combatants dug themselves into positions but made few territorial gains. The horrifying drudgery, the cold, the wet, the shelling, the machine-gun fire, the nervous tension, the smell of corpses and mustard gas lasted for years. By the end of the conflict in 1918, some 10 million soldiers had lost their lives. (Imperial War Museum, London)

📖 **Read** the **Document: Excerpt from Four Weeks in the Trenches** on **MyHistoryLab**

19.1

19.2

19.3 What were the chief causes of World War I?

19.4

19.5

19.6

what had begun as a regional conflict in the Balkans. The lack of any organized system for preserving international order was clearly exposed. Christopher Clark's book *The Sleepwalkers: How Europe Went to War in 1914* (2013) demonstrates how statesmen in one country after another made decisions based on what they saw as the welfare of their own countries, without understanding that these decisions, taken in succession and collectively, would plunge them into world war. Within one week, all the major powers of Europe were at war. In November, the Ottoman Empire joined Germany and the Austro-Hungarian Empire in an alliance called the Central Powers. On the other side the British, French, and Russians, joined by the Italians in 1915, formed an alliance called the Allied Powers (the Allies).

War: A Stalemate from the Start

Europe had not faced continent-wide warfare since the end of the Napoleonic Wars a century earlier. Despite all their armaments, neither side was prepared militarily or psychologically for the years of devastating trench warfare of the western front. Germany, attacking France through Belgium, expected a quick victory, but the French line held, and meanwhile the Russians opened an eastern front with unexpected speed, forcing the Germans to divide their troop strength. Once the German troops had lost the momentum of their opening offensive, fighting bogged down into a costly stalemate that lasted for years.

The Battle of the Marne River in northeastern France, fought to a draw between September 5 and 12, set the pattern. Each side continuously extended its battle lines outward until the enemies faced each other over a 400-mile front that stretched from the North Sea to Switzerland. Each side hunkered down in trenches for a kind of siege warfare, armed with machine guns and artillery, and protected by barbed wire. Attacks by either side, going "over the top" of the trenches, were met by devastating machine-gun fire. In addition, Germany later introduced poison gas, leading to subsequent international bans against its use (although many nations today continue to store poison gas in their armories). In the first month alone, each side suffered more than a quarter-million casualties and used up quantities of ammunition that they thought would last for any future war. Erich Maria Remarque captured the horrors of this trench warfare in his novel *All Quiet on the Western Front* (1929). Soldiers lived in mud and knew that it could be deadly to leave their trenches. Disease killed many. Altogether millions were killed in battle and millions more were wounded, often with horrendous injuries. A new industry of prosthetics developed to replace absent faces and lost limbs. Generals called for any new weapons they thought might change the course of war, and the use of new technologies—such as aircraft and aerial bombing—generally only brought more loss of life.

Major campaigns to overwhelm the opponent by sheer numbers in direct infantry charges resulted in catastrophic losses. In February 1916, the Germans attacked at Verdun, near the confluence of the borders of France, Belgium, and Germany. The battle ground on for six months, with casualties of about 350,000 on each side, before the Germans gave up their attack. In July 1916, the Allies opened their own attack at

19.1

19.2

19.3

What were the
chief causes of
World War I?

19.4

19.5

19.6

the Somme River, some 50 miles to the north. The French were still bogged down at Verdun, but the British brought in heavy artillery and even some of their new tanks, which could penetrate the barbed wire and the trenches to knock out enemy machine guns. There were, however, few tanks, and the main strategy of the generals on both sides was simply to throw waves of attacking men at one another, directly into the machine-gun fire of the enemy. The cost in lives was almost unbelievable. In four months, the Germans lost a half-million men, the British 400,000, and the French 200,000. On the Western Front the war was essentially a stalemate from this time until the end.

In the east, the Germans defeated the Russians repeatedly, yet the ill-equipped, ill-fed, ill-commanded Russians continued to fight. In 1914, in the first months of the war, 225,000 Russian troops were captured by the Germans at the Battles of Tannenberg and the Masurian Lakes. In 1915, the Germans and Austro-Hungarians launched major offensives against Russia, killing, wounding, or taking captive two million Russians, many of whom fought with their bare hands. To send relief to Russia through the Black Sea, the British, French, Australians, New Zealanders, and Indians (under British command) landed some 450,000 troops on the Gallipoli Peninsula, at the entrance to the Dardanelles and the Black Sea. In the course of almost a year of fighting, 145,000 of these men were killed or wounded, and the operation was terminated.

In June 1916, Russia launched its own counteroffensive, but by 1917 the war had alienated the Russian people almost entirely. On International Women's Day, March 7, 1917, thousands of women joined thousands of industrial workers on the streets of the capital, Petrograd (St. Petersburg), to protest the high prices of food and other basic necessities, largely a result of wartime shortages, and to demand the tsar's abdication. Troops in St. Petersburg mutinied, in part because they refused to attack the women. The tsar abdicated, and although the new provisional Russian government attempted to continue the war, the army collapsed. In November a revolutionary government captured power and sued for peace, withdrawing Russia from the war. (The Russian Revolution, one of the most significant consequences of the war, is discussed in detail below.)

The British opened another front against the Ottoman Empire by siding with the Arabs of Arabia and Palestine in their struggles against Ottoman imperial rule. Colonel T.E. Lawrence, "Lawrence of Arabia," took charge of this insurrection and, with his support, Emir Husayn of Hejaz (the west coast of Arabia, including Mecca) declared himself king of the Arabs. Thanks to this pressure of Arabs against Turks, General Edmund Allenby was able to push through Turkish lines and capture Jerusalem and Damascus in a series of battles remembered for their tactical brilliance and their use of armed cavalry and air support. Faced with this combination of Arab revolt and British military victories, the Ottomans sued for peace in October 1918.

In Africa, British and French forces seized the German colonies of Togo, Cameroon, South West Africa, and Tanganyika (now Tanzania), vowing that the Germans should never come back. Similarly, in East Asia and the Pacific, Japan, an ally of Britain, declared war on Germany in 1914 and quickly took over the German concessions in China and the German-held Marshall and Caroline islands. In 1915 it presented China with a list of "Twenty-one Demands" to which the Chinese had to accede, against their wishes. China felt it was being turned into a colony of Japan.

In the Atlantic, both Britain and Germany disregarded the accepted law of the sea permitting the shipment of cargo unrelated to military equipment and supplies. The British, whose navy was by far the world's most powerful, regularly stopped all ships bound for Germany and other enemy states and confiscated their cargo. The Germans, with a smaller navy, were less able to carry out such a policy. Instead, they directly attacked shipping bound for England and France, torpedoing and sinking ships, especially in the waters surrounding the British Isles. The largest of these ships,

Faisal, son of Hussain of Mecca, with his delegates and advisors at the Versailles peace conference, 1919. Faisal was briefly king of Syria, and later Iraq. His entourage includes Colonel T. E. Lawrence "of Arabia," fourth from the left. Lawrence had become a hero to the Arabs as he organized them to fight against the Ottoman Empire in World War I, promising them self-government. But ultimately, when the peace conference left them under British and French control, the Arabs came to view him as a traitor to their cause.

the *Lusitania*, was torpedoed off the Irish coast in May 1915, and 1,200 passengers, including 118 Americans, drowned as the ship sank.

America had been slow to enter the war, both because it preferred the peace of neutrality and because it saw no overriding virtue in one side over the other in this war of contending imperial powers. The sinking of the *Lusitania* inclined the Americans to the side of the Allies—reaffirming also a basic preference for more democratic Britain and France over more autocratic Germany and Austria–Hungary—but it took another two years and additional provocations for America to join in the conflict.

In January 1917, Arthur Zimmerman, Germany's foreign minister, sent a secret telegram instructing the German ambassador in Mexico City to offer the president of Mexico "an understanding on our part that Mexico is to reconquer her lost territory in Texas, New Mexico, and Arizona," if Mexico joined in an alliance with Germany against the United States. The telegram was intercepted, translated, and published in the United States, astonishing its citizens and inflaming public opinion against Germany. At about the same time, at the end of January 1917, Germany announced to the Americans that it would begin unrestricted submarine warfare, sinking on sight all merchant ships around the British Isles and in the Mediterranean.

The United States, which had remained neutral, declared war against Germany and the other Central Powers in April 1917. This decision sealed the fate of the combatants, all of whom were thoroughly exhausted by three years of relentless, enervating, disastrous warfare. The American contribution was smaller, and much briefer—only about four months of actual combat—than that of the major European countries, but it came at a decisive time. By the end of the war, a year and a half later, the United States had four million soldiers and sailors under arms—two million of them in France and another million on the way—had lent $10 billion in military and civilian assistance, and had set its farms and factories to producing record amounts of food and supplies. Shipping capacity multiplied from one million tons before the war to ten million by the end. Consumer production facilities in the United States were restructured to provide military equipment and supplies. Sugar and other consumer commodities were rationed. (Eight thousand tons of steel were saved in the manufacture of women's corsets.)

View the Image: The Technology of War on MyHistoryLab

Once the United States began providing its abundant supplies and fresh troops, the Allied victory was secure. In the spring and summer of 1918, the German high command made a last attempt at an offensive, but they could not withstand the Allied counterattack. Germany sought an armistice. It took effect at 11 a.m. on November 11—11/11/11. Russia, Austria–Hungary, Turkey, and Bulgaria had already withdrawn from battle. The war was finally over.

The cost in life defied imagining. Some 70 million armed forces were mobilized. Most were European, but there were also 1.4 million from India who served in the Middle East, East Africa, and France; 1.3 million from the "white" dominions; and

19.1

19.2

19.3 What were the chief causes of World War I?

19.4

19.5

19.6

HOW DO WE KNOW?

War Experiences Subvert Colonialism

Colonial powers employed their colonial armies in fighting both world wars, transporting them from one battlefront to another. Military service overseas often transformed the soldiers, making them skeptical of the advantages of European civilization. Some European soldiers came to realize that at least some of the people they colonized did not respect them but rather feared and hated them. A young journalist from India, Indulal Yagnik, serving briefly as a World War I correspondent in Iraq, wrote of his growing realization of the resentment Arabs felt for British colonization. He saw Arab women in particular transmitting their resentment by asserting their religious and cultural conventions. He began to understand more fully the opposition to colonialism shared by Indians and Arabs:

> We understood … that in the entire region Arabs regarded the English as their enemies. Bitter antagonism dripped from their eyes. They moved about like lost undertakers, joking among

themselves but stopping the moment they saw the British. They talked with the foreigners mechanically, speaking only when it was completely unavoidable. They took their few cents in pay, and otherwise behaved like defeated and dependent enemies. Their dignified women hid themselves in burkhas, which covered them from head to foot. The white soldiers must have sensed their independent temper, however, and therefore their military superiors issued strict orders not to talk with the local women. (Yagnik, p. 262)

- How did Yagnik's experiences in Arabia strengthen his anticolonial viewpoint?
- How important was Arab women's behavior in convincing Yagnik and the British that the Arabs were anticolonial?
- Does the evidence suggest that Arab women were more anticolonial than the men?

134,000 from other British colonies. The French recruited 600,000 soldiers from their colonies in Africa and Southeast Asia; 40,000 of the Africans died fighting for the liberation of France. Another 200,000 came to work in factories in France. Almost ten million soldiers had been killed and 20 million wounded. England lost one million; France 1.5 million, Germany almost two million, Russia 1.75 million, the Austro-Hungarian Empire somewhat more than one million, Italy a half-million, the Ottoman Empire 325,000, and the United States 115,000.

View the **Closer Look**: **The Development of the Armored Tank** on **MyHistoryLab**

19.1

19.2

19.3

19.4

19.5

19.6

What were the chief causes of World War I?

Colonial troops in battle, World War I. More than a million soldiers from Europe's African and Asian colonies served in World War I alongside French, British, American, and other troops on the Western Front, in the Middle East, and in Africa. More than 100,000 died in battle. After fighting on behalf of others, the troops returned from war inspired to demand greater freedom from colonial control for their own homelands.

19.1
19.2
19.3   What were the chief causes of World War I?
19.4
19.5
19.6

Postwar Expectations and Results

After the bloodshed, destruction, and chaos of the war, it was clear that the world was in for major changes. Defeat forced the end of four historic empires: the Ottoman, the Austro-Hungarian, the German, and the Russian. Internal revolution had brought the 2,000-year-old Chinese Empire to an end shortly before the war began, and Japanese wartime conquests in China suggested that Chinese sovereignty might also be in danger.

In addition, promises had been made during wartime that raised aspirations around the globe. Perhaps the most utopian and celebrated of all these promises issued from Woodrow Wilson. The American president had declared that the goal of the Allies was to "make the world safe for democracy." Allied war aims, as expressed by Wilson in his Fourteen Points, called for:

> A free, open-minded, and absolutely impartial adjustment of all colonial claims, based upon a strict observance of the principle that in determining all such questions of sovereignty the interests of the population concerned must have equal weight with the equitable claims of the Government whose title is to be determined. (cited in Hofstadter, pp. 224–25)

As leader of the country that had swayed the balance of victory, and as an intellectual in politics, Wilson commanded attention. Colonized peoples, and minority groups within many different nations, responded to his apparent message that all peoples should have a voice in their own government. Millions of people in the colonies had contributed to the war effort of their colonizers. They expected—and sometimes they were explicitly promised—political rewards after the war.

The Arab regions of the Ottoman Empire, for example, understood Wilson's agenda to include independent states for them. They had fought alongside the British against the Ottoman Empire, and they expected that this wartime contribution would be rewarded. Moreover, in 1915, the British high commissioner (ambassador) in Egypt had privately told Mecca's leading official, Sharif Husayn, that Arabs would receive some kind of independence if they fought against the Ottoman Turks. In addition, and just before the Armistice was signed in 1918, Britain and France declared as their goal "the complete and definitive liberation of the peoples so long oppressed by the Turks and the establishment of national governments and administrations drawing their authority from the initiative and free choice of indigenous populations."

Jews also looked forward to important changes. Had not the British government promised them "the establishment in Palestine of a national home for the Jewish people" if the Ottoman Empire was conquered? This declaration, issued by Britain's foreign secretary, Lord Balfour, in 1917, may have been issued primarily to enlist Jewish support for Britain against the Ottoman Empire, which held Palestine at the time. It captured the imagination of Jews around the world, especially those who had already emigrated from eastern Europe to settle in Palestine and those left behind in conditions of discrimination and persecution. The Arabs, however, noted that the same Balfour Declaration promised that "nothing shall be done which may prejudice the civil and religious rights of existing non-Jewish communities in Palestine." They believed these two promises to be incompatible.

India, which had not only contributed 1.4 million men, but also paid £100 million in 1917 and some £20–30 million each year toward Britain's wartime debts, had also received a promise in 1917. The secretary of state for India, Edwin Montagu, declared Britain's goal to be "the increasing association of Indians in every branch of government, and the gradual development of self-governing institutions, with a view to the progressive realization of responsible government in India as an integral part of the Empire."

Many linguistic and ethnic minorities scattered among the nations of eastern and central Europe, in particular Czechs, Slavs, Estonians, Latvians, and Lithuanians, also looked forward to gaining independent states of their own. The Chinese anticipated the return of some colonial territories, at least those of Germany, which had been seized during the war by the Japanese. Africans in Africa, almost entirely under colonial rule, and in the African diaspora, often suffering from crippling discrimination, also took heart. Wilson's pledges appealed, for example, to the brilliant African-American scholar and activist W.E.B. DuBois, and the Pan-African movement he headed. Although they had no official status, a group of 58 delegates from Africa and the African diaspora convened in Paris at the time of the conference, demanding equality for all people and an end to a kind of internal colonization of blacks in the United States, and to the colonization of Africa by European powers.

One issue—women's suffrage—demanded attention at the national level by individual sovereign governments. In several major states the vote was granted. Before the war, only a few nations and regions had granted women the right to vote: Norway, New Zealand, and some of

Pan-African Congress, Brussels, 1921. The first Pan-African Congress convened in Paris at the time of the peace conference, 1919, to press for "the international protection of the natives of Africa," direct supervision of colonies by the League of Nations, a right to education for colonized people, the global abolition of slavery, and an end to capital punishment for plantation workers. In 1921, representatives from the Americas, the Caribbean, Europe, and Africa met again to survey their (lack of) gains and to reaffirm their agenda. Some leaders, such as W.E.B. DuBois of the United States (second from right), stressed the need for joint action among the races.

the states in Australia and in the western United States. The suffrage movements elsewhere had not won their objectives. With the end of the war, however, populations and their legislatures, grateful for the contribution of women to the war effort—in the armed services, in factories, and at home—reconsidered. In 1918, Britain granted the vote to women over the age of 30, and in 1928 it extended that right to women over the age of 21. Germany granted women's suffrage in 1919 and the United States in 1920.

 Read the Document: A Turkish Officer Describes the Armenian Massacres (1915–1916) on MyHistoryLab

19.1
19.2
19.3
What were the chief causes of World War I?
19.4
19.5
19.6

The Paris Peace Settlements

Thirty-two states were invited to the peace conference convened in Paris in 1919, and many unofficial delegations arrived as well. They met amid optimistic hopes and high expectations. In the end, the American, British, and French delegations were the most critical to the negotiations. (Communist Russia, which had just undergone its revolution and was still fighting a civil war, was not invited.) Political borders across Europe and the Middle East were redrawn, punishing the states that had lost the war or, in the case of Russia, had withdrawn from it. Four great empires—Russian, Austro-Hungarian, Ottoman, and German—were destroyed by the war, its attendant revolution in Russia, and its peace settlement in Paris.

From territories of the former Russian empire four new states were carved out: Poland, Estonia, Latvia, and Lithuania. Finland had already claimed its independence in 1917. The Austro-Hungarian Empire was dissolved. Austria–Hungary itself was reduced in territory and population and divided into two separate states.

The new postwar nations. In the wake of World War I, old empires fell and new states and colonies (euphemistically called mandates and protectorates) were created. The Austro-Hungarian and Ottoman empires were eradicated. A belt of nation-states was established throughout central and eastern Europe; some had brief lives and were soon annexed by Russia. The core of the Ottoman Empire became Turkey, while other segments were mandated to Britain and France as quasi-colonies.

Czechoslovakia and Yugoslavia, both of them weak and insecure, were created from its former territories.

The Ottoman Empire also disappeared; its core region in Anatolia and the city of Istanbul became the new nation of Turkey. Turkey itself was marked for further dismemberment into spheres controlled by France, Italy, and, most provocatively, by Greece, the centuries-old Christian enemy of the Muslim Turks. An independent Armenian state was to be established in eastern Turkey on the shores of the Black Sea, and an independent Kurdistan just to the south of it. Only the armed resistance of Turkish forces led by General Mustafa Kemal (1881–1938) prevented those intentions from being carried out. Kemal, later called Atatürk, Father of the Turks, drove out the foreign troops stationed in Turkey and preserved the geographical and political independence of his state until Turkey's full sovereignty was recognized by the Treaty of Lausanne in 1923. From the remainder of the Ottoman Empire's European territories, Romania and Greece were expanded. From its Middle Eastern regions, four new nations, predominantly Arab in population, were created—Syria, Lebanon, Iraq, and Palestine.

Germany, too, lost its status as an empire as Emperor William II fled to the Netherlands in the last days of the war and, in 1919, Germans voted to establish a democratic government. At the peace convention, Germany was severely punished by the

19.1

19.2

19.3

What were the
chief causes of
World War I?

19.4

19.5

19.6

victors. In the west, Alsace-Lorraine was ceded to France; large areas in the east went to Poland; and small areas were portioned out to Lithuania, Belgium, and Denmark. Germany was additionally ordered to pay heavy, seemingly unlimited, reparations for the cost of the war, although in practice not much was actually collected. Most galling for Germany, it was forced officially to accept total responsibility for causing the loss and damage of the war. Germany signed the Treaty of Versailles and left Paris humiliated and resentful, but, despite the loss of land and the financial reparations, potentially still powerful. Many observers, most notably the economist John Maynard Keynes, predicted that the punitive provisions of the Treaty would lead to another war.

All four of these great empires had held vastly diverse ethnic, religious, and cultural minorities within their borders. The Paris negotiators intended that the new states and new borders they carved out would give some of the larger minorities their own states and protect hostile ethnic groups from one another and from external domination. Minority rights and legal safeguards were also legislated into the constitutions of the new states and the remaining cores of the old empires. In accord with the principle of national self-determination, ten new states were born (or reborn), and 14 states were specifically charged with protecting racial, religious, and linguistic minorities within their borders, assuring those minorities of equal rights with all citizens, including the right to primary-school instruction in their mother tongue. These measures were viewed as inherently fair and as removing the kind of nationalistic provocation that had led to the recent war.

The League of Nations

The Paris Peace Conference was supposed not only to resolve issues emerging directly from the war, but also to find a way out of the use of war as a means of solving conflict. It was intended to ensure that "the Great War" would also become known as "the war to end all wars." Thus the conference was also dedicated to creating an international organization to preserve peace. In 1920, inspired primarily by Wilson, the delegates created a League of Nations. However, the League, crippled by three congenital defects, never met its goals. First, its principal sponsor, the United States, refused to join because of Congressional opposition, a humiliating repudiation of Wilson's dream. The world's most powerful technological, industrial, financial, and military power—also the power that had most inspired the League—withdrew into the isolation of its ocean defenses.

Second, despite its rhetoric, the new states it created, and the new protection for minority rights that it advocated, the League failed to resolve the complex issues of national identities within Europe and of colonialism overseas. In central Europe, nationality groups were widely dispersed. Some groups – such as Ukrainians, Croatians, and Jews – were considered too small to form nations; some larger groups did have their own states, but they also had many members dispersed as minorities in neighboring states, such as Germans in Czechoslovakia. The wishes of minority groups for national autonomy—for example, for the official use of their own languages within larger nations and language groups—could not be satisfied in any practical way, and many minorities continued to feel aggrieved.

Colonies Disappointed. Similarly, as colonial governments did not relinquish their powers, the antagonism of colonized peoples toward their rulers intensified. The Arab world, for example, felt itself betrayed by the British and the French. Prince Faisal, who had fought on behalf of the Arabs against the Ottoman Empire, alongside Lawrence of Arabia, represented the Arab peoples at the peace talks and was bitterly disappointed to discover that France and Britain had their own, secret plans for these Arab states. France and Britain had publicly promised self-government to Arab regions of the Middle East that fought with them against the Ottomans,

19.1

19.2

19.3 What were the
chief causes of
19.4 World War I?

19.5

19.6

but secretly, between themselves, they had actually signed an agreement in 1916 to divide these regions among themselves. The four new states were "mandated" to European powers for tutelage until they would be considered ready for independence. Although the term "mandate" was used, the reality was semi-colonial status. Britain received mandatory power over Iraq and Palestine, and France over Syria and Lebanon. Faisal himself was designated king of Syria, briefly, when a group of Syrians declared an independent state in 1920, but he was deposed and exiled by the French four months later. The British, however, believed that Faisal could help them to keep Iraq quiet under their mandatory rule, and so they made him king of Iraq in 1921. He ruled, at least nominally, until his death in 1933.

Halfway around the world, Japan sought and was awarded control over the East Asian possessions of Germany that it had captured during the war. Some of these colonial possessions were in the Shandong Peninsula of north China, and China naturally claimed them for itself. In Paris, Chinese protestors physically blocked the nation's delegates from attending the signing ceremonies that turned these lands over to Japan. China never did sign the peace agreements. Within China, student-led protests against the treaties began on May 4, 1919, initiating a bitter critique of China's international humiliation, of its cultural links to the West, and of the apparent bankruptcy of its own historical traditions. This "May Fourth Movement" also helped to sow the seeds of the Chinese Communist Party, which was founded in 1921.

In India, Britain fell short of its wartime promise to expand the institutions of self-government; on the contrary, it passed the Rowlatt Acts, which restricted freedom of the press and of assembly. At the start of the war, most Indians seem to have trusted that Britain would bring self-government back to India, even if the process seemed very slow. Mohandas Karamchand Gandhi (1869–1948), who was becoming the leader of the Indian national movement, had even attempted to recruit troops, unsuccessfully, for the British war effort. All this changed after the war as the British cracked down and the Indians protested. (We discuss this topic in more detail in the chapter entitled "China and India.")

In Africa, Europeans continued to administer the colonies they had seized in the late nineteenth century. British settlers began to move into new settlements, especially in the highlands of Kenya and in Southern Rhodesia (today's Zimbabwe). Especially in the British colonies, African tribal leaders were incorporated into the ruling structures, following some of the policies of indirect rule first evolved in India.

The existence of the League of Nations and its mandate system did, however, begin to suggest that colonialism might be limited over time. In Egypt, the Wafd Party began demonstrations and riots that persuaded the British to grant Egypt nominal independence while still controlling its foreign policy and defense, and the Suez Canal. In 1921, Britain granted dominion status to a new state in southern Ireland, ending centuries of colonial oppression (but leaving Northern Ireland still a part of Great Britain). It granted Iraq nominal independence in 1932.

The final congenital defect of the League of Nations was that it had no armed forces. This lack limited its willingness to intervene in disputes and made it impossible for it to back up even the decisions it was willing to take. The great powers signed the Kellogg–Briand Pact in 1928, agreeing to settle their disputes without warfare, but the pact proved meaningless. The League effectively died with its failure to mount serious resistance to: Japan's invasion of China in 1931; Italy's invasion of Ethiopia in 1935, which turned one of only two independent countries in Africa (Liberia was the other) into a colony; Germany's rearmament through the 1930s, in violation of the Paris peace treaties; and the outbreak of the Spanish Civil War in 1936.

🔍 **View** the **Closer Look**: **An Ethiopian View of the Battle of Adowa** on **MyHistoryLab**

The Russian Revolution

19.4 What were the most important actions taken by the leaders of the Soviet Union in the first decade after the revolution?

19.1

19.2

19.3

19.4

What were the most important actions taken by the leaders of the Soviet Union in the first decade after the revolution?

19.5

19.6

The Great War ended three centuries of rule by the Romanov dynasty and brought to power in Russia a new form of government that most Western European nations and the United States found dangerous and threatening. Others, including some Americans, found it an interesting alternative to the decadence of the West. They saw it as a dream for a better world. The Russian Revolution of 1917 challenged the capitalist order by instituting communism, which advocates the abolition of private property and the control of a country's economic resources by the state, at least temporarily. Russia's new leadership argued that the Communist Party should spearhead this system, by the use of violence if necessary. Leaders of the party believed that Russia could telescope the development process and catapult itself quickly into the ranks of the wealthy and powerful nations. It proclaimed itself the model for, and leader of, colonized and backward countries in overthrowing foreign control and capitalist economic development. It argued that poor nations had been intentionally "underdeveloped" by, and for, the rich. The new communist system established by the Russian Revolution endured through years of hardship and of war, both civil and international. Its policies and its power frightened many of the more developed, capitalist, and democratic countries of Europe, and the United States.

The Build-up to Revolution

Geographically and politically, Russia has one foot in Europe, the other in Asia. As we have seen, Peter the Great (r. 1682–1725) turned westward, founding St. Petersburg as his capital, port, and window on the west. Catherine II, the Great (r. 1762–96), further nurtured the European Enlightenment at the Russian court. Stunned by his defeat in the Crimean War (1853–56) at the hands of Britain and France in alliance with Turkey, Tsar Alexander II (r. 1855–81) adopted a more liberal policy. He freed Russia's serfs in 1861, instituted the *zemstvo* (rural council) system of local self-government in 1864, reduced censorship of the press, reformed the legal system, encouraged industrialization, and promoted the construction of a nationwide railway system. Tsar Nicholas II (r. 1894–1917) furthered heavy industrialization under two progressive ministers, Count Sergei Witte (1849–1915) and Peter Stolypin (1862–1911), and allowed the birth of some representative political institutions, but he rejected the democratic reforms demanded by intellectuals, workers, and political organizers.

Despite the industrialization introduced under Nicholas II, on the eve of World War I Russia lagged far behind the Western European countries economically and industrially. At 175 million, its population was about 75 percent larger than that of the United States, more than 250 percent larger than that of Germany, and 400 percent larger than that of Britain; but its energy consumption was 10 percent that of the United States, 30 percent that of Germany, and 25 percent that of Britain. Its share of world manufacturing was 8 percent

Poster commemorating "The Internationale," the rallying anthem of the Communist movement. Karl Marx (left) and Friedrich Engels (right), pictured in the banner at the top of the poster, collaborated in developing the theoretical principles underlying "scientific socialism" and in organizing a working-class movement dedicated to revolting against capitalism.

19.1

19.2

19.3

19.4

19.5

19.6

What were the
most important
actions taken
by the leaders
of the Soviet
Union in the first
decade after the
revolution?

compared with the United States' 32 percent, Germany's 15 percent, and Britain's 14 percent.

Nicholas II had made great strides in increasing industrial production. Energy consumption increased from 4.6 million metric tons equivalent in 1890 to 23 million in 1913; railway mileage grew from 22,000 miles in 1890 to 46,000 miles in 1913; and the per capita level of industrialization doubled from 1880 to 1913. But during that same period, the United States' per capita level of industrialization quadrupled, Germany's rose three and a half times, and France's, Italy's, Austria's, and Japan's all slightly more than doubled. In a rapidly industrializing world, Russia had to race much faster just to keep up. To obtain the capital to build its industries Russia invited foreign investment, but this opened the nation to foreign control. In 1917 foreigners held nearly 50 percent of the Russian national debt. Russia was Europe's largest debtor.

Russia's agriculture was unproductive and its technology primitive. The aristocrats held enormous power over the land and the peasants who worked it. An exploited peasantry living in *mirs* (village collectives) had neither the economic incentive nor the technical training to produce more. The small parcels of land they farmed privately were subdivided into tiny plots, as sons in each generation shared equally in the inheritance of their fathers. Finally, the government forbade the sale of village land to outsiders. This prevented exploitation by absentee landlords, but it blocked the investment from outside the village that might have funded agricultural improvement through new technology. Productivity stagnated. The sharp class divisions between the peasants and the gentry persisted, marked by differences not only in wealth and education, but also in dress and manners. Moreover, the cost of industrialization and the repayment of foreign loans had to be squeezed out of the agricultural sector. The result was a mass of peasants impoverished, technologically backward, despised by the wealthy elite, and suffering under the weight of a national program of industrialization for which they were made to pay.

Lenin and the Bolshevik Revolution

Several revolutionary groups protested these conditions, each offering a different plan. The Social Democrats followed George Plekhanov (1857–1918), who saw the need for more capitalist development in Russia to create new urban working and middle classes, which Plekhanov's party would then organize to overthrow the bourgeoisie. Plekhanov was actually an orthodox Marxist thinker who believed that before a communist revolution could emerge, capitalism would first have to lay the foundations of industry and create a proletariat of industrial workers. A lawyer, Vladimir Ilyich Ulyanov (1870–1924), later calling himself Lenin, advocated a far more immediate and abrupt communist revolution, and stressed the need for the Communist Party to provide leadership. In 1902, in a pamphlet entitled *What Is to Be Done?*, Lenin underlined the need for an absolutely dedicated core of leaders to carry out the revolution: "Give us an organization of revolutionaries and we will overturn Russia!"

In January 1905, with revolutionary feelings running high, some 200,000 factory workers and others in St. Petersburg, led by a priest, Father Gapon, assembled peacefully and respectfully to deliver to the tsar a petition for better working conditions, higher pay, and representative government. On that "Bloody Sunday," January 22, the tsar was not actually in the city; but his troops fired on the demonstrators, killing several hundred and wounding perhaps a thousand. The government's lack of moral authority was unmasked. By the end of the month almost 500,000 workers were on strike, joined by peasant revolts, mutinies of soldiers, and protests by the intelligentsia of doctors, lawyers, professors, teachers, and engineers.

Before this domestic turmoil erupted, the tsar had committed Russia to war with Japan, but defeats at sea and on land further revealed Russia's inadequacies in both technology and government organization. The defeat in the Russo-Japanese War, domestic tax revolts in the countryside, and strikes in the industrializing cities forced the tsar to respond. Yielding as little as possible, he established the first *duma*, or parliament, representing peasants and landlords, but allowing workers only scant representation. The tsar limited the powers of the *dumas*, frequently dismissed them, sometimes jailed their members, and chose their class composition selectively to divide the principal revolutionary constituencies, workers and bourgeoisie. The *dumas* endured as a focus for democratic organization and aspiration, but they were unable to work cooperatively, and the tsar was able to stave off revolution for a decade.

Unable to match the new technological warfare of other European countries, Russia suffered about three million dead—soldiers and civilians combined—and perhaps four million wounded in World War I. These losses finally united the many forces of opposition and brought down the monarchy. In the midst of revolutionary ferment, in March, 1917—as we have seen—10,000 women in St. Petersburg marched to protest the rationing of bread and demanded the tsar's abdication. Ordered by the government to fire on the protesters, the army refused.

The army mutiny forced the tsar to abdicate—in the first Russian revolution of 1917—and established a new provisional government, but the war persisted. The turmoil of mutiny and desertion in the army, food shortages, farm revolts, and factory strikes ground on. More radical groups sought to seize control. Lenin, with the assistance of the German government, which wished to sow discord in Russia, returned from exile in Switzerland. With the motto "Peace, Land, Bread," he called for immediate withdrawal from the war, land for the peasants, and a government-run food-distribution system. Lenin organized an armed takeover of the government headquarters, railway stations, power plants, post offices, and telephone exchanges. On November 7 (October 25 on the old, Julian calendar), this revolutionary coup succeeded. The provisional government of Alexander Kerensky (1881–1970) fell and the communists seized power in the second Russian revolution of 1917. Confounding Marxist doctrine, the revolution had occurred not in one of Europe's most capitalist and industrialized countries, but in one of the most industrially backward. In March 1918, by signing the Treaty of Brest–Litovsk with Germany, the new government took Russia out of World War I.

Civil war between revolutionary "Red" and antirevolutionary "White" forces enveloped the country. Contingents of troops from 14 countries (including a small number of Americans in the Baltic and 8,000 at Vladivostok on the Pacific) joined the Whites. The Bolshevik government took over ownership of land, banks, the merchant marine, and all industrial enterprises. It confiscated all holdings of the Church and forbade religious teaching in schools. It established the Cheka, or security police, and instituted a reign of "Red Terror" against its opponents' "White Terror." In Yekaterinburg, the local **soviet** executed the tsar, his wife, and their children. By 1920, the communists, as the Bolsheviks now called themselves, were victorious in the civil war. In 1921, they banned all opposition—even dissenting voices within their party—and made the Central Committee, now under Lenin's control, the binding authority

The Odessa staircase scene from Sergei Eisenstein's silent film *Battleship Potemkin*, 1925. In a film famous for both its artistry and its revolutionary message, Eisenstein presents the ruthlessness of the troops of the Russian tsar in suppressing the revolt of 1905 that began in part with a mutiny on the battleship *Potemkin* in Odessa harbor. The troops move forward, relentlessly shooting and clearing a crowd of thousands of civilians supporting the mutiny. A young mother, shot dead, falls against her baby's pram, sending it careering down hundreds of steps, presumably to the baby's death.

19.1
19.2
19.3
19.4
19.5
19.6

What were the most important actions taken by the leaders of the Soviet Union in the first decade after the revolution?

KEY TERM

soviet A council of workers, the primary unit of government in the Soviet Union at local, regional, and national levels, also adopted by other communist regimes.

675

Vladimir Lenin and Joseph Stalin at Gorki, Russia, 1922. After Lenin's premature death in 1924, Stalin battled to eliminate his rivals, and he emerged as supreme dictator of the Communist Party in 1929. He soon abandoned Lenin's New Economic Policy in favor of a series of brutal five-year plans to enforce the collectivization of agriculture and industry. (See also photographs in the Introduction of Lenin delivering a speech, one picture with Trotsky in attendance, a second with Trotsky airbrushed out.)

in the government. Lenin began the pattern of imprisoning his opponents in labor camps—a policy that was later expanded under his successors into a huge network of camps for political opponents of the government.

World war and civil war, which were followed by even more devastating drought, famine, and economic dislocation, convinced Lenin of the need for economic stability and provided an incentive to increase production. In 1921, he implemented the New Economic Policy (NEP), which allowed peasants to sell their products on the open market and middlemen to buy and sell consumer goods at a profit. The central government, however, controlled the "commanding heights" of the economy: finance, banking, international trade, power generation, and heavy industry.

State Planning in Soviet Russia

Lenin sought Russia's industrial transformation. In 1920, as he established the State Commission for Electrification, he declared: "Communism is Soviet power, plus electrification of the whole country." He invited German and American technicians to Russia to help the country improve productivity, harnessing capitalist means to communist goals. He took special interest in the system of scientific management and time studies in the workplace that had been introduced in America by the engineer Frederick Taylor.

Read the **Document**: **Lenin Calls for Electrification of All Russia (1920)** on **MyHistoryLab**

Lenin's death in 1924 ushered in a bitter power struggle from which Joseph Stalin (1879–1953) emerged triumphant over Leon Trotsky (1879–1940). Trotsky, a brilliant, ruthless man, who had organized the Red Army, had argued that through careful but bold planning a technologically backward country like Russia could leapfrog stages of growth and, through the "law of combined development," quickly catch up to the more advanced nations. Stalin defeated and banished Trotsky, who was eventually assassinated in Mexico (see photos in the Introduction of Lenin delivering a speech: one picture with Trotsky in attendance, a second with Trotsky airbrushed out). Then he implemented Trotsky's program. He declared his driving nationalist passion that Russia must no longer lag behind the more developed nations:

> [T]hose who fall behind get beaten. But we do not want to be beaten. No, we refuse to be beaten! One feature of the history of old Russia was the continual beatings she suffered for falling behind, for her backwardness. She was beaten by the Mongol Khans. She was beaten by the Turkish beys. She was beaten by the Swedish feudal lords. She was beaten by the Polish and Lithuanian gentry. She was beaten by the British and French capitalists. She was beaten by the Japanese barons. All beat her—for her backwardness: for military backwardness, for cultural backwardness, for political backwardness, for industrial backwardness, for agricultural backwardness. She was beaten because to do so was profitable and could be done with impunity. … That is why we must no longer lag behind. (cited in Andrea and Overfield, p. 398)

Stalin's rhetoric appealed not only to his immediate audience in Russia, but also to a more global audience of poorer states and colonies beginning to protest against their subordination and to seek independence and development.

19.1

19.2

19.3

19.4 What were the most important actions taken by the leaders of the Soviet Union in the first decade after the revolution?

19.5

19.6

19.1
19.2
19.3
19.4
19.5
19.6

First, however, Stalin concentrated on building up Russia, emphasizing "socialism in one country." To achieve "combined development," in 1928 he instituted nationwide, state-directed **five-year plans** that covered the basic economic structure of the whole country. In place of capitalism, in which market forces of supply and demand determine production goals, wages, profits, and the flow of capital, labor, and resources, Stalin instituted government planning to make those decisions, from the large-scale national macro level to the small-scale local micro level.

Where could Russia find capital to invest in industrial development, especially with most world capital markets closed to the communist state? Stalin turned to his own agricultural sector and peasantry. By artificially lowering the prices farmers received for their agricultural products and raising the prices for their agricultural tools and materials, Stalin used his planning apparatus to squeeze capital and labor out of agriculture into industry. But he squeezed so hard that agricultural productivity fell and peasants withheld their crops from the artificially deflated market. State planning was off to a rocky start.

Nevertheless, in 1929 Stalin increased the role of the state still further. He collectivized agriculture: more than half of all Soviet farmers were now compelled to give up their individual fields and to live and work instead on newly formed collective farms of 1,000 acres or more. The communist government increased the use of heavy machinery and large-scale farming operations, stipulated the goods to be produced and their sales prices, encouraged millions of peasants to leave the farms for work on the state's new industrial enterprises, and eliminated wealthier peasants and middlemen.

Although some farmers were living more comfortably in 1939 than in 1929, many others were not. Hundreds of thousands of better-off peasants, *kulaks*, who refused collectivization, were apparently murdered (although recently uncovered secret-police records claim that the number was only about 19,000), and millions were transported to labor camps in Siberia and elsewhere. Peasants who owned animals preferred to slaughter them rather than turn them over to collectives. There had been over 60 million head of cattle in the **USSR** in 1928; by 1933, there were fewer than 35 million. Initiative shriveled as the more entrepreneurial farmers were turned into a kind of rural proletariat. The government continued to collect high proportions of the agricultural production to pay for the import of foreign technology and machinery for its industrial programs. Although few developing countries today are willing to reduce private consumption below 80 percent of the national product, Russia reduced it to little over 50 percent. Much of the difference went to industrial development. Again, a government chose guns over butter. The political coercion and chaos introduced by these policies, combined with bad harvests in southeast Russia, led to the tragic deaths of between two and three million peasants by 1932.

While the peasants suffered enormous hardship, industry flourished. At first, Russia hired foreign technology and imported foreign machinery. Despite ideological differences with the United States, Stalin, like Lenin before him, saw the necessity of importing American materials, machinery, and even some organizational programming. In 1924 Stalin declared:

American efficiency is that indomitable force which neither knows nor recognizes obstacles; which continues on a task once started until it is finished, even if it is a minor task; and without which serious constructive work is inconceivable. … The combination of Russian revolutionary sweep with American efficiency is the essence of Leninism. (Hughes, 1989, p. 251)

Meanwhile, the Russian government was training its own personnel and learning to construct its own massive industrial plants. At the falls of the Dnieper River, the communist state constructed the largest hydroelectric power station in the world in 1932. In the early 1920s, the USSR had imported tens of thousands of tractors, most of them Fords and International Harvesters from the United States. By the 1930s, however,

KEY TERM

five-year plan A state-directed plan, frequently prepared by a communist government, to control the economy and to direct its growth. It contrasts with capitalist, laissez-faire, free-market economies, in which the government allows the forces of supply and demand to guide the market.

kulak A prosperous peasant in late tsarist and early Soviet Russia. The leaders of local agricultural communities, *kulaks* owned sizeable farms and could afford to hire labor.

USSR Union of Soviet Socialist Republics. The country formed from the union of Russia and some fifteen other nations under a single communist government, 1917–91.

19.1
19.2
19.3
19.4
19.5
19.6

What were the most important actions taken by the leaders of the Soviet Union in the first decade after the revolution?

Russia constructed a giant plant at Stalingrad to manufacture its own tractors. At Gorki (Nizhny Novgorod) the government built a plant based on the American Ford model at River Rouge, Michigan. At Magnitogorsk, in Siberia, it constructed a steel complex based on US Steel's plant in Gary, Indiana.

From 1928 to 1938, Russia's per capita level of industrialization nearly doubled. From 1928 to 1940, the production of coal increased from 36 to 166 million tons, that of electricity from 5 to 48 billion kilowatt hours, and that of steel from 4 to 18 million tons. The planners began to convert a nation of peasants into a nation of industrial workers, as the urban population of the country increased three and a half times from 10.7 million in 1928 to 36.5 million in 1938, from 7 percent of the country's population to 20 percent. Stalin explained: "The independence of our country cannot be upheld unless we have an adequate industrial basis for defense" (cited in Kochan and Abraham, p. 368).

Most dramatically, the Soviet increases came when Western Europe and North America were reeling under world depression (see below). The communist system won new admirers in the West. The American political comedian Will Rogers commented: "Those rascals in Russia, along with their cuckoo stuff have got some mighty good ideas. ... Just think of everybody in a country going to work." The journalist Lincoln Steffens wrote: "All roads in our day lead to Moscow." The British political critic and historian John Strachey exclaimed: "To travel from the capitalist world into Soviet territory is to pass from death to birth."

Many political leaders of countries under European colonial control saw the Russian example—telescoped development, state planning, rapid industrialization, the transformation of the peasantry into an urban labor force, emphasis on education and health services, national enthusiasm in rebuilding a nation along scientific lines—as just what they needed. As a political prisoner in British India in July 1933, Jawaharlal Nehru, future first prime minister of independent India, wrote to his daughter:

> People often argue about the Five Year Plan. ... It is easy enough to point out where it has failed. ... [but] One thing is clear: that the Five Year Plan has completely changed the face of Russia. From a feudal country it has suddenly become an advanced industrial country. There has been an amazing cultural advance; and the social services, the system of social, health, and accident insurance, are the most inclusive and advanced in the world. In spite of privation and want, the terrible fear of unemployment and starvation which hangs over workers in other countries has gone. There is a new sense of economic security among the people ... further ... this Plan has impressed itself on the imagination of the world. Everybody talks of "planning" now, and of Five-Year and Ten-Year and Three-Year plans. The Soviets have put magic into the word. (Nehru, pp. 856–57)

To spread the word and build a global organization, in 1919 the communists reestablished the Communist International, or Comintern, which recruited communist organizers throughout the capitalist and colonized worlds. They also supported such organizations as the League against Imperialism, founded in 1927, which brought together leaders from colonized countries, and those who supported them from around the world. This League enabled like-minded revolutionaries to meet and share their ideas and plans.

Women in the Soviet Union

For women, too, the soviet system led to great change, although perhaps less than promised. As elsewhere, World War I had

Russian poster for women textile workers, 1930. Despite the government's difficulties in enforcing "equal pay for equal work," women's rights improved markedly under the communist system. This poster appears to idealize full-time employment combined with raising a family. This art style of presenting work and workers in idealized form is called "Socialist realism."

19.1
19.2
19.3
19.4
19.5
19.6

What aspects of American life changed in the yeras after World War I?

brought Russian women into factories, fields, and even the armed forces, and recruitment continued during the civil war. Over 70,000 women served in the Red Army. In 1921, some 65 percent of Petrograd's factory workers were women. In 1917, the first Soviet marriage law constituted marriage as a civil contract and provided for relatively easy divorce and child-maintenance procedures.

The government ordered equal pay for equal work, but the provision was not enforced. To bring law into line with practice, and recognizing the lack of availability of effective birth control, abortion on demand was granted as a right; so was maternity leave with full pay. When the men returned from the war, they wanted their jobs back and their women at home, but Russian women retained most of the benefits they had won. "Legally speaking, Russian women were better off than women anywhere in the world" (Kochan and Abraham, p. 337). Over the next decades, Russian women entered professions so rapidly that they became the majority in medicine and teaching and a substantial minority in engineering, technical occupations, and law.

In practice, however, women bore the **double burden** of shouldering the major responsibility for running their homes and caring for their families while also working full time. With the introduction of state-planned heavy industrialization after 1929, the double burden increased. The factories invited their labor, while food shortages forced them to spend more time and energy in ration lines. Abortion became so common that it was once again outlawed for a time after 1936. The struggle to balance the new legal equality and protection with older social and family traditions continued.

Postwar America

19.5   What aspects of American life changed in the years after World War I?

America left World War I as the technological and financial leader of the world. The factories that had supplied war goods returned to producing domestic consumer products that made the American middle and upper classes the envy of many around the world. Automobile registration rose from about a half-million in 1910 to over eight million in 1920 and 23 million in 1930. In addition, in 1930, American farms employed some 920,000 tractors and 900,000 trucks.

In 1910, there were 82 phones per thousand Americans; in 1930, there were 163. Only in the early twentieth century did wealthier people begin to introduce indoor flush toilets and cast-iron bathtubs; by 1925, America was producing five million enameled bathroom fixtures annually. Thanks to the struggles of labor unions, the work week was being reduced from 60 hours per week to 45. Paid vacations were becoming common, with 40 percent of large companies giving at least one week of paid vacation per year. Diet improved; sales of fresh vegetables increased 45 percent in the decade after World War I. Life expectancy increased by 13 years between 1900 and 1930, from 47 years to 60 years.

All the technological innovations discussed earlier in this chapter were introduced in America early on, if not first. Electricity replaced steam as the major source of power. In 1929, electrical generators produced 80 percent of all industrial power, and two-thirds of America's homes were electrified. Electrical appliances became common. Commercial radio began broadcasting in 1920, and millions of homes soon had receivers, with many people building their own. Movies became the main mass entertainment, with the first "talkie," *The Jazz Singer*, released in 1927. In 1929, some 100 million people attended the movies each week. Watching such stars as Charlie Chaplin, Gloria Swanson, Mae West, Greta Garbo, and Rudolph Valentino gave viewers new ideas—and new fantasies—for their own lives. The films also gave audiences around the world their own peculiar version of American life.

KEY TERM

double burden The burden on working women of combining their paid job with the unpaid tasks of housework and child-raising as well; implies that working men are not sharing the housework and child-care.

New farm technology. The American Burger tractor, invented in 1889, was the first to install an internal- combustion engine. With the introduction of automated farm machinery, huge tracts of land around the world were brought under cultivation and food productivity soared. Here, in 1917, a woman from Vassar College in Poughkeepsie, New York, plows a field as part of the war effort.

Women's lives changed during this decade. Although the sale and prescription of the means of birth control were illegal in most states, Margaret Sanger convened the first birth-control conference in 1921, and traveled across the United States and around the world promoting birth control. The size of American families dropped from 3.6 children in 1900 to 2.5 in 1930. About 25 percent of all women of working age worked outside the home, most of them in office jobs, teaching, and nursing. In 1920, American women were constitutionally granted the right to vote. Images of postwar America include risqué flappers, increased recognition of the sexuality of women as well as men, illegal drinking in speakeasies (after prohibition was introduced by the Eighteenth Amendment to the Constitution in 1919), and a general flamboyance. These images may have been true for an urban, upper middle-class, white population, a small—if conspicuous—minority of the total population, but for most of working-class and rural America, life was still quite difficult.

19.1

19.2

19.3

19.4

19.5 What aspects of American life changed in the years after World War I?

19.6

📖 Read the **Document: Eighteenth Amendment (1919)** on **MyHistoryLab**

📖 Read the **Document: Margaret Sanger, "Happiness in Marriage"** on **MyHistoryLab**

🔍 View the **Image: Clara Bow, the "It" Girl. Film Still, 1927** on **MyHistoryLab**

🔍 View the **Map: Changing Lives of American Women, 1880–1930** on **MyHistoryLab**

In addition, fear permeated some corners of America. The United States, with its great industrial, agricultural, and administrative power, engaged in international commerce. But it refused to join the League of Nations and generally withdrew from participation in international politics outside Latin America, where it had substantial financial investments and repeatedly intervened with military force. It seemed to fear involvement outside its own hemisphere.

Internally, in the years immediately after the war, American industry suffered many worker strikes. One-third of a million workers struck against US Steel in 1919. In the same year, the Boston police force went on strike. The home of the US attorney general, A. Mitchell Palmer, was bombed. Coming as it did just after the Communist Party took over the government of Russia, the industrial and political turbulence triggered a "**Red Scare**," a fear that communists would take over the United States. Palmer began to round up, jail, and deport thousands of people accused of being communists, anarchists, and radicals. Hundreds of aliens were deported. The Ku Klux Klan revived and resumed its terrorism of Catholics, Jews, and African-Americans, especially the black soldiers returning from war who might no longer "know their place." At its height, in the early 1920s, the Klan enrolled several million members. By the end of the decade, the fear and frenzy had abated, but new, perhaps greater, fear was in store, as the stock-market crash of October 29, 1929, following years of economic difficulties on America's farms, ushered in the Great Depression.

KEY TERM

Red Scare The fear that communists would take over the United States, especially powerful in the years just after the Communist Revolution in Russia, 1917.

Worldwide Depression

19.1
19.2
19.3
19.4
19.5
19.6

19.6 What were the causes of the Great Depression and how did the leaders of various nations respond?

Periods of economic depression were considered normal in a free-market economy, as the forces of supply and demand would periodically fall out of step and then come back into line. But the Great Depression, which destabilized domestic and international politics worldwide, but especially in Europe, was extreme in its extent and duration. On October 29, 1929—"Black Tuesday"—the New York Stock Exchange crashed. Investors had bid up the price of stocks far beyond their intrinsic value, and suddenly, recognizing an imbalance between price and value, many withdrew their investments. The decline continued for years. By 1933, stocks were worth 15 percent of their value in 1929.

While the stock-market crash represented the most dramatic moment of the Great Depression, underlying agricultural problems had already created some of the preconditions, while government economic policies magnified the severity of the financial problems. Throughout the 1920s, farmers who had produced at record levels during the war, to help feed embattled allies as well as domestic consumers, had difficulty cutting back production, resulting in huge unsold surpluses and a depression in agriculture. Faced with such economic difficulties, countries closed their borders to imports so that they could sell their own products internally without competition. But as each country raised its barriers, international markets contracted and economic anxiety rose.

Mass unemployment swept Britain, America, and Germany; the unemployment rate among industrial workers in Germany reached 30 percent in 1932. Latin American countries, notably Argentina, that had been approaching a European standard of living, found their economies devastated, turned away from European markets, and sought to salvage what they could through domestic development. The value of world trade in 1938 was 60 percent below what it had been in 1929.

In 1921, two million unemployed in Britain were collecting unemployment insurance, thanks to an act that had been passed a decade earlier. The government also provided an old-age pension system, medical aids, and subsidized housing. But the Great Depression increased this unemployment to almost three million. Unemployment payments multiplied while tax collections dropped. The **welfare state** expanded and government remained stable, but the depression ground on.

America, the country most dedicated to private enterprise and "rugged individualism," and therefore most reluctant to expand government social welfare programs, saw national income drop by half between 1929 and 1932. Almost 14 million people were unemployed. Elected in 1932 in the midst of national despair, President Franklin Delano Roosevelt rallied the nation with charismatic optimism, declaring that "the only thing we have to fear is fear itself." Roosevelt believed that America's private enterprise system was fundamentally sound, but that it needed short-term assistance from the government to weather the depression, and permanent safety nets, also provided by the government, to ensure that weaker individuals would not succumb to the pressure of an intensely competitive economy. In accord with this philosophy, Roosevelt instituted social welfare programs as a means of preserving America's capitalist economic structure. He provided financial relief for the unemployed; public works projects to create construction jobs; subsidies to farmers who would reduce production and eliminate surpluses; and federal support for low-cost housing and slum clearance. A Civilian Conservation Corps was established, ostensibly to promote

KEY TERM

welfare state A government that assumes responsibilities for the welfare of its citizens, including such necessities as education, old-age pensions, health care, and unemployment benefits. A more capitalist state leaves these responsibilities to private initiative.

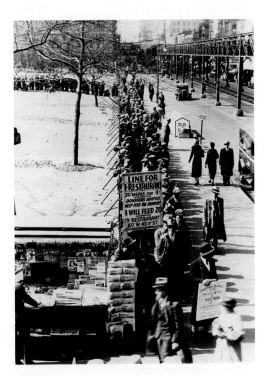

The Great Depression, 1929. One of many breadlines that wove their way through New York City during the Great Depression. This one was at Sixth Avenue and 42nd Street.

19.1
19.2
19.3
19.4
19.5
19.6

What were the causes of the Great Depression and how did the leaders of various nations respond?

conservation and reforestation, but mostly to provide some three million jobs to the young. The Tennessee Valley Authority created an immense hydroelectric program, combining flood control with rural electrification and regional economic development.

Roosevelt increased the regulation of business and promoted unions. The Securities and Exchange Commission, created in 1929, regulated the Stock Exchange. The National Recovery Administration encouraged the regulation of prices and production until it was judged unconstitutional in 1935. The Social Security Act of 1935 introduced unemployment, old-age, and disability insurance—policies already in place in parts of Western Europe well before World War I. Child labor was abolished. Forty hours of work was set as the weekly norm, and minimum hourly wages were fixed. Union organization was encouraged and union membership grew from four million in 1929 to nine million in 1940. The most capitalist of the major powers thus accepted the welfare state.

The economy of communist Russia developed separately from the capitalist economy of the United States and Western Europe. In 1928 Russia introduced centralized national planning, emphasizing heavy industrialization. Although agriculture suffered and levels of private consumption plummeted, factories flourished, industrial employment rose, and Russia avoided the worst effects of the Great Depression.

In Germany, the depression followed on the heels of catastrophic inflation. In the 1920s the government induced hyperinflation to pay the resented war reparations, thus wiping out the savings of the middle classes and amplifying resentment over the punitive Versailles Treaty, including its emphasis on German war guilt and its insistence on German disarmament. By 1924, industrial production had recovered—but then the depression wiped out the gains. Germany depended on loans from several nations, especially the United States, to pay its enormous bill for war reparations. Following the stock-market crash of 1929, however, American financiers, who were suddenly strapped for cash, called in these loans, undercutting first the German economy, which could not afford the repayments, and then the economies of the countries Germany had been paying.

Germany's new government was perceived by many as a weak and precarious experiment in constitutional democracy in a nation accustomed to a military monarchy. Left-wing parties, often communist, and right-wing parties, finally Nazi, confronted one another at the ballot box, in the factories, and in violent street fighting, with thugs on all sides assaulting one another, and often physically attacking prominent citizens as well. Germany's *kulturkampf*, or battle over cultural values, began to be waged in the streets.

During the **Weimar** period, Germany's cultural life achieved extraordinary artistic creativity. In architecture, the **Bauhaus** movement of such innovators as Walter Gropius (1883–1969) and Ludwig Mies van der Rohe (1886–1969) redefined the function of buildings and their architects; in music and drama, Bertolt Brecht (1898–1956) and Kurt Weill (1900–50), the creators of *The Threepenny Opera* and its antihero, Mack the Knife, created new forms in cabaret presentations that challenged social conventions; in "classical" music, atonal composers, such as Alban Berg (1885–1935) and Arnold Schoenberg (1874–1951), rejected the conventions of the traditional seven-note musical scale; in literature, novelists, such as Erich Maria Remarque (1898–1970), with his antiwar novel *All Quiet on the Western Front*, and Hermann Hesse (1877–1962), with his musings on Buddhism, won universal attention and acclaim; filmmakers such as Fritz Lang, in *Metropolis* (1927), pioneered futuristic, philosophical themes; philosophers explored the role of philosophy in a democracy. Weimar culture emerged from one war only to be destroyed, or exiled, by another. Its leading personalities were threatened and ultimately driven out of Germany. Totalitarian force, political ideology, and finally Nazism, backed by thugs on the streets, triumphed, at least temporarily, over aesthetic and cultural creativity.

📖 Read the **Document**: **The Great Depression: An Oral Account (1932)** on **MyHistoryLab**

KEY TERMS

kulturkampf German for "struggle over culture" or "culture war." The struggle among proponents of different views of culture for recognition and for control over state policies. Such struggles are normal in any society, but in Germany between the world wars they became intense. They were waged philosophically and physically, and, ultimately, by banishing from the nation unwelcome cultural ideas, and those who held them.

Weimar The constitution of the new German government after World War I was written in the city of Weimar. That government espoused democracy and cultural creativity, but was attacked from communists on the left and Nazis on the right, and was taken over by Nazis in 1933. Since then, "Weimar" has stood for a government that is democratic and idealistic, but weak and fragile.

Bauhaus A movement in architecture arising in Germany between the world wars. It was characterized by an emphasis on streamlined forms and a rejection of ornamentation. It followed the motto "form follows function." Its work became controversial among political parties. When the Nazis took over Germany they destroyed the Bauhaus school, and most of its masters fled the country.

SOURCE

How Should We Live?

The Polish poet Wislawa Szymborska, winner of the Nobel Prize for Literature in 1996, reflects on the disillusionment of the twentieth century and assumes that life should and must go on nevertheless. "How should we live?" she asks at the close of one of her most poignant poems, "The Century's Decline," written in the 1980s. In this poem, however, she offers no answers:

Our twentieth century was going to improve on the others.
It will never prove it now,
now that its years are numbered,
its gait is shaky,
its breath is short.

Too many things have happened
that weren't supposed to happen,
and what was supposed to come about
has not.

Happiness and spring, among other things,
were supposed to be getting closer.
Fear was expected to leave the mountains and the valleys.
Truth was supposed to hit home
before a lie.

A couple of problems weren't going
to come up anymore:
hunger, for example,
and war, and so forth.

There was going to be respect
for helpless people's helplessness,
trust, that kind of stuff.
Anyone who planned to enjoy the world
is now faced
with a hopeless task.

Stupidity isn't funny.
Wisdom isn't gay.
Hope
isn't that young girl anymore,
et cetera, alas.

God was finally going to believe
in a man both good and strong,
but good and strong
are still two different men.

"How should we live?" someone asked me in a letter.
I had meant to ask him
the same question.
Again, and as ever,
as may be seen above,
the most pressing questions
are naive ones.

Wislawa Szymborska

Methods of Production and Destruction:
What Difference Do They Make?

The early twentieth century taught us skepticism. The greatest triumphs of science and technology could be transformed into instruments of death. Principles of physics that had been accepted as laws for two centuries and more were found to be only fragments of larger principles. Public health measures and medicine extended life spans; world warfare cut them down. Nationalism inspired people to work for the betterment of their country and its people, but at the same time to compete with, and make war against, those in neighboring countries, and often to limit freedoms of minorities, even at home. Revolutions continued for a decade and more, benefiting many people, but not fulfilling their promises to the masses. Great empires, some of them hundreds of years old, one of them 2,000 years old, toppled and dissolved in civil warfare. A world war ended, but because the issues that had caused it remained unresolved, indications were that it would soon resume in some form. Perhaps most frightening of all, totalitarian governments came to power in parts of the world that had been considered among the most civilized, only to challenge and subvert the whole basis of modern civilization, as we shall see in the chapter entitled "World War II." This chapter's stories of warfare, imperialism, economics, science, and technology were clearly unfinished. Many of them are still unfolding.

CHAPTER REVIEW

TECHNOLOGY IN THE TWENTIETH CENTURY

19.1 How did new technologies affect people's ways of life in the industrializing world?

Technology exploded in the early years of the twentieth century. Trains and subways, cars, buses, trucks, and the roads and highways to drive them on, multiplied. Vast rubber, glass, steel, and electrical industries developed to provide for the new vehicles. In the cities, water, sewage, and electrical lighting systems were constructed. With electricity, factories and workshops could operate around the clock, and these factories did not have to be located on waterfronts—power could be transmitted across great distances. With the mechanization of agriculture, people left the farms for the cities and new jobs in manufacture, service industries, and government. Major discoveries in chemistry led to a wide range of new consumer products and changed the food people ate and the clothes they wore. Many technological advances in chemistry, metallurgy, and electricity were devoted to military uses, despite the recent catastrophic experience with world war, which killed at least 20 million people, 1914–18. Poison gas, tank warfare, and the first aerial bombings were among these new technologies.

INTERNATIONAL ROLE REVERSALS

19.2 Which areas of the world did not keep pace with rapid industrialization? Why not?

Before the Industrial Revolution and European conquest, India, China, the Ottoman Empire, and some parts of pre-Columbian America were in many ways more sophisticated than the European nations. India's textile industry was the largest in the world, and China produced silk, porcelain, and iron. Mexico City featured advanced urban structures, and the Ottoman Empire provided Europeans with much of what they knew about the ancient world, for they had preserved it. But the Industrial Revolution reversed these relationships. As Europe began to lead the world in scientific discovery and technological application, India and China were more and more left behind, especially after they lost their sovereignty—control over their own governments—to the European imperialists. The Ottoman Empire remained independent, but it fell to the West's industrial and political superiority, and slowly disintegrated.

WORLD WAR I

19.3 What were the chief causes of World War I?

A system of alliances had been developed among the highly competitive and nationalistic states of Europe in the decades before the war. On June 28, 1914, a Serbian assassin killed the heir to the Austro-Hungarian throne, Archduke Franz Ferdinand, and his wife. A month later, Austria-Hungary declared war on Serbia, and the Great War (as it was called, until World War II came along and was even bigger) erupted by domino effect, as the system of alliances took effect, and nations came to the aid of their allies: Russia mobilized to defend Serbia; Germany declared war on Russia and its ally, France, and sent forces across neutral Belgium; Britain and Japan declared war on Germany. Within one week, all of Europe's major powers were at war. The expectation and hope for this alliance system had been that it would prevent war—that the balance of power would deter aggression. Instead, it drew all the major powers into a regional conflict. The weaponry that had been touted as defensive was turned to the offense.

THE RUSSIAN REVOLUTION

19.4 What were the most important actions taken by the leaders of the Soviet Union in the first decade after the revolution?

They overthrew the Romanov ruling dynasty and murdered many of its leaders. They defeated their opponents, and their foreign allies, in a five-year civil war. The new Bolshevik government took over all ownership of the land, the banks, the churches, and industry. It established a security police and banned all opposition; the leader of the Central Committee, Vladimir Lenin, began to imprison his opponents in labor camps. In an effort to increase the productivity of Russia's backward agriculture, Lenin also implemented a New Economic Policy, which allowed the impoverished peasantry to sell their produce on an open market, and middlemen to buy and sell goods at a profit. Seeking to transform Russia's industry, now under central government control, Lenin invited German and American technicians to Russia to help the new nation improve productivity.

POSTWAR AMERICA

19.5 What aspects of American life changed in the years after World War I?

With European countries, even the victors, devastated by the human and material costs of World War I, America emerged as the world's technological, industrial, agricultural, and financial leader. Cities continued to expand as factories turned from producing war goods to producing domestic consumer products. Car ownership skyrocketed, and the number of phones per person doubled. Thanks to the strength of American labor unions, the work week was reduced, and paid vacations became common. By 1929, two-thirds of American homes were electrified. Soon millions of Americans had radios and electrical appliances. Sales of vegetables increased nearly 50 percent after the war, and life expectancy increased by 13 years. Thanks to better knowledge of birth control (which was still illegal in most states), the size of American families dropped, and more women took jobs outside the home. In 1920, women gained the right to vote.

WORLDWIDE DEPRESSION

19.6 What were the causes of the Great Depression and how did the leaders of the various nations respond?

Agricultural problems set the scene for financial collapse. American farmers could not cut back their wartime levels of production despite decreased demand. Agricultural prices dropped, depressing the economy. Then, in October 1929, investors suddenly sold out of an overpriced stock market, and the New York Stock Exchange crashed. To cover their losses, American bankers called in their loans from European clients, who could not repay them; the depression became global. Newly elected President Roosevelt implemented public works projects, subsidized farmers, increased stock market and banking regulation, and introduced some measures of the welfare state including subsidized low-income housing, and unemployment, old age, and disability insurance. England already had welfare state measures in place and muddled through, but with 3 million people unemployed. Communist Russia, outside the global capitalist economy, continued with its own internal system of state planning and industrial expansion, and was largely unaffected by the depression. Agricultural production suffered, but because of poor internal planning rather than global markets. In Germany, the National Socialist (Nazi) party came to power, partly in reponse to the economic pain of the depression. To increase employment and productivity, the Nazis began public works projects, especially highway building, and massive illegal rearmament and militarization (see the chapter entitled "World War II").

Suggested Readings

Adas, Michael. *Machines as the Measure of Man* (Ithaca, NY: Cornell University Press, 1989). Technologically inventive peoples have often presented themselves as morally superior as well.

Akcam, Taner (trans. Paul Bessemer). *A Shameful Act: The Armenian Genocide and the Question of Turkish Responsibility* (New York: Metropolitan Books, 2006). Comprehensive treatment of a highly sensitive subject.

Andrea, Alfred, and James H. Overfield, eds. *The Human Record*, vol. 2 (Florence, KY: Wadsworth Publishing Co., 6th ed., 2008). Excellent collection of primary sources. New editions have been published about every fourth year.

Bulliet, Richard W., ed. *The Columbia History of the 20th Century* (New York: Columbia University Press, 1998). Excellent collection of essays.

Burns, E. Bradford. *Latin America: A Concise Interpretive History* (Englewood Cliffs, NJ: Prentice Hall, 9th ed., 2010). Excellent survey from a slightly leftist and critical perspective.

Camus, Albert. *The Myth of Sisyphus* (New York: Vintage Books, 1959). *The* existential novel, counseling persistence even in the face of unyielding fate.

de Bary, William Theodore and Richard Lufrano, comps. *Sources of Chinese Tradition*, vol. 2 (New York: Columbia University Press, 2nd ed. 2000) Outstanding selection of primary documents.

Freud, Sigmund. *Civilization and Its Discontents* (New York: W.W. Norton and Co., 1961). Theorizes a constant, universal struggle between the psychological forces of order and disorder, love and destruction.

Fromkin, David. *A Peace to End All Peace: The Fall of the Ottoman Empire and the Creation of the Modern Middle East* (New York: Henry Holt, 2001). Focuses on the dissolution of the Ottoman Empire and the states that emerged from it.

Gandhi, Mohandas Karamchand. *Hind Swaraj* or *Indian Home Rule* (Ahmedabad: Navajivan Press, 1938). A radical critique of the modern, industrial, materialistic world.

Hemingway, Ernest. *For Whom the Bell Tolls* (New York: Scribner, 1940). A classic, semi-autobiographical novel from the Spanish Civil War.

Hofstadter, Richard, ed. *Great Issues in American History*. vol. 2 (New York: Vintage Books, 1959). Excellent selection of primary documents.

Howard, Michael, and William Roger Louis, eds. *The Oxford History of the Twentieth Century* (New York: Oxford University Press, 1998). Excellent collection of 27 essays grouped by time frame, geography, and theme, by distinguished historians.

Hughes, Thomas. *American Genesis* (New York: Viking, 1989). Looks at science and technology as the keys to understanding United States history.

——. *Networks of Power: Electrification in Western Society, 1880–1930* (Baltimore, MD: Johns Hopkins University Press, 1983). Fascinating, innovative history of American technology.

Keegan, John. *A History of Warfare* (New York: Knopf, 1994). The history of warfare through styles of war rather than strict chronology. Themes are stone, flesh, iron, and fire.

Kennedy, Paul. *The Rise and Fall of the Great Powers* (New York: Random House, 1987). Excellent summary of the fates of the leading countries in terms of wealth and power.

Kochan, Lionel, and Richard Abraham. *The Making of Modern Russia* (London: Penguin Books, 1983). Useful, but somewhat dated because new information has come as archives are opening.

Kragh, Helge. *Quantum Generations: A History of Physics in the Twentieth Century* (Princeton, NJ: Princeton University Press, 1999). From X-rays to superstring theory. Covers discoveries, theories, politics, impact.

Landes, David S. *The Wealth and Poverty of Nations* (New York: W.W. Norton, 1999). History of the Industrial Revolution, giving great credit to Western ingenuity.

Lewis, David Levering. *W.E.B. DuBois: Biography of a Race 1868–1919* (New York: Henry Holt, 1993); *W.E.B. DuBois, 1919–1963: The Fight for Equality and the American Century* (New York; Henry Holt, 2000). Pulitzer Prize-winning biography of one of the titans in the global fight against racism.

McClellan, James E., and Harold Dorn. *Science and Technology in World History: An Introduction* (Baltimore, MD: Johns Hopkins University Press, 2nd ed., 2006). Demonstrates the relationship between science and technology across time and space. Impressive.

MacMillan, Margaret, and Richard Holbrooke. *Paris 1919: Six Months that Changed the World* (New York: Random House, 2003). Lucid account of the aspirations, deliberations, and (mostly) failures of the "peacemakers" following World War I.

Mazower, Mark. *Dark Continent: Europe's Twentieth Century* (New York: Knopf, 1999). This was not a century in which Europe could take a lot of pride.

Nehru, Jawaharlal. *Glimpses of World History* (New Delhi: Oxford University Press, 1982). The Indian leader's history, generally Marxist and anti-imperial.

Pacey, Arnold. *Technology in World Civilization* (Cambridge, MA: MIT Press, 1990). Fine summary. One of the earlier attempts to provide such comprehensive coverage.

Remarque, Erich Maria (trans. A.W. Wheen). *All Quiet on the Western Front* (Boston, MA: Little, Brown, 1958). Tragic, classic novel of World War I.

Rosenberg, Rosalind. "The 'Woman' Question," in Bulliet, *op. cit.* pp. 53–80. Excellent discussion of feminism.

Spence, Jonathan. *The Search for Modern China* (New York: W.W. Norton, 1999). Superb introduction to the field.

Stoltzenberg. Dietrich. *Fritz Haber: Chemist, Nobel Laureate, German, Jew: A Biography* (Philadelphia, PA: Chemical Heritage Foundation, 2004). Haber invented the chemical production of fertilizer, which increased human life, and poison gas, which destroyed it.

Szymborska, Wislawa. *View with a Grain of Sand* (San Diego, CA: Harcourt Brace, 1995). Poetry of the Nobel Prize-winning poet. Reflects the harrowing experiences of Poland through the twentieth century.

Vallye, Anna, ed. *Léger: Modern Art and the Metropolis* (Philadelphia: Philadelphia Museum of Art, 2013). Catalogue of a blockbuster exhibit showing the immense influence of new industrial machinery on post-World War I artists.

Winn, Peter. *Americas: The Changing Face of Latin America and the Caribbean* (Berkeley, CA: University of California Press, 1992). Written to enhance a PBS series on Latin America and the Caribbean. Especially good on Argentina, but dated in terms of contemporary Latin America.

Yagnik, Indulal. *Autobiography*, trans. Devavrat N. Pathak, Howard Spodek, and John Wood, 3 vols. (New Delhi: Manohar Publishers, 2011). Fascinating life, from childhood in a small town in western India, to youthful work as Gandhi's editor, to left-wing organizer and critic.

FILMS

All Quiet on the Western Front (1930; 2 hours 16 minutes). Adapted from Erich Maria Remarque's novel of life and love in the horror of World War I.

For Whom the Bell Tolls (1943; 2 hours 46 minutes). From Ernest Hemingway's novel, starring Gary Cooper and Ingrid Bergman.

Lawrence of Arabia (1962; 3 hours 36 minutes). Blockbuster: seven Academy Awards including best picture and best actor. Through T.E. Lawrence's conflicts, captures the struggles among English, Arabs, and Turks in World War I.

Madame Curie (1944; 2 hours 4 minutes). Winner of two Nobel Prizes, Marie Curie is portrayed more for romantic interest than for her career, but that comes through, too.

The Sheikh (1921; 1 hour 20 minutes). With Rudolph Valentino. See the heartthrob of silent films in a classic.

Tango Bar (1935; 58 minutes). See tango singer and dancer Carlos Gardel at his best, a reminder of the importance of this Argentinian dance in world culture.

The Threepenny Opera (1931; 1 hour 50 minutes). Sense the decadence in Germany and Austria between the wars.

Triumph of the Will (1935; 1 hour 50 minutes). Leni Riefenstahl's worshipful propaganda documentary of the Nazi party's 1934 session in Nuremberg. Beautiful and very frightening.

Viva Zapata (1952; 1 hour 53 minutes). Hagiographic biography with Marlon Brando as Zapata.

Dr. Zhivago (1965; 3 hours 11 minutes). Based on the Pulitzer Prize-winning novel by Boris Pasternak, a personal, fictional view of the Russian Revolution.

20 World War II

To Hell and Back

1937–1949

The Great War demonstrated levels of man-made devastation never seen before. Yet hope springs eternal; optimists believed that the League of Nations, created at the end of the war, would insure that this had been "the war to end all wars." Unfortunately, pessimists proved more prescient.

Nazi rally at Nuremberg, 1937. Nazi Party members fill a stadium at a party meeting in Nuremberg, 1937.

LEARNING OBJECTIVES

20.1 ((	20.2 ((	20.3 ((	20.4 ((	20.5 ((	20.6 ((	20.7 ((	20.8 ((
Explain the role of thugs in the rise of fascism in Italy and Germany.	Understand the efforts undertaken for world peace in the 1920s.	Describe the steps that led the world back to war.	Recount the major events of the first years of World War II.	Understand why World War II has been called a "total war."	Discuss the changes in the image of human progress brought about by World War II.	Discuss the founding of the United Nations and post-war resettlement.	Describe the memorials to World War II.

(((Listen on MyHistoryLab

No sooner had the Paris peace treaties been signed than leading economists predicted disaster. In *The Economic Consequences of the Peace*, published in 1920, British economist John Maynard Keynes argued that the treaties would push Germany and Austria into starvation. Like all of Europe, these countries would suffer from the crippling disruption of coal and iron supplies, transport, and imports of food and raw materials. In addition, the treaties stripped Germany of her overseas colonies and investments and her merchant fleet. It imposed on her crushing financial reparations to be paid to the victor nations. Keynes blamed the leaders of Britain, France, Italy, and the United States for their shortsightedness in making these demands, and he warned that starving people "in their distress may overturn the remnants of organization, and submerge civilization itself in their attempts to satisfy desperately the overwhelming needs of the individual."

In the next year, from a very different perspective, the Irish poet William Butler Yeats added his own fears concerning a profound cultural sickness that he saw infecting all of Europe in the wake of the war and the Russian Revolution:

Things fall apart; the centre cannot hold;
Mere anarchy is loosed upon the world,
The blood-dimmed tide is loosed, and everywhere
The ceremony of innocence is drowned;
The best lack all conviction, while the worst
Are full of passionate intensity. ("The Second Coming," 1919, cited in Wilkie and
    Hurt, p. 1655)

Yeats put no faith in rationality or technological progress, although he professed a belief in some mystical religious experience that was yet to come:

Surely some revelation is at hand;
Surely the Second Coming is at hand. (*ibid*.)

A decade later, worldwide depression confirmed the fears and pessimism of Keynes and Yeats. Sigmund Freud, the Austrian psychoanalyst who pioneered profound studies of the human mind and spirit, wrote of even deeper anxieties. He questioned the direction of all civilized, technologically advanced societies and feared that they might all be destroyed: "Men have gained control over the forces of nature to such an extent that with their help they would have no difficulty in exterminating one another to the last man. They know this, and hence comes a large part of their current unrest, their unhappiness and their mood of anxiety" (Freud, pp. 34–35).

The events of the next years, 1930–39, continued to feed the worst fears of the economist, the poet, and the psychoanalyst, and the outbreak of World War II at the end of the decade confirmed their bitter and tragic predictions. The first half of the twentieth century was the most violent period in history. Because of the cause-and-effect relationship between World War I and World War II, many historians see the entire period as a single long war, with a pause of two decades, including a global depression, serving as an uneasy intermission.

Some bright spots brought hope during the interwar period: the birth of the League of Nations; an agreement among major naval powers meeting in Washington to limit the size of their navies; the Kellogg–Briand Pact of 1928, signed in Paris by 65 nations, promising to renounce war as a means of resolving conflict; and the return of some prosperity in the mid-1920s. The optimism proved evanescent. Especially after the Great Depression, uncertainty, insecurity, and fear ruled the hearts of individuals and nations. In response, political leaders arose, in several countries around the globe, who promised that they could return their countries to certainty, security, and potency, if only their people would turn over dictatorial powers to them. Often the people listened and agreed, and often those who did not were beaten, exiled, or murdered. Powerful leaders and powerful governments demanded allegiance and obedience, believing that they could sweep away all barriers, domestic and

20.1 How important were thugs in the rise of fascism in Italy and Germany?

international, that stood in their way. Democratic government, with its trust in the collective wisdom of the people, its suspicion of too-powerful rulers, and its protection of minority rights and of individual rights of expression, was put on the defensive. The three major powers that chose fascist government—Germany, Italy, and Japan—had had almost no experience with democratic forms of government, and for a time in the late 1930s and early 1940s they seemed to be successful in mobilizing their nations into war machines. Ultimately, however, these fascist dictatorships overstretched their power and brought destruction down upon their nations and peoples. But, along the way, they destroyed many others as well. At least 50 million people died in World War II.

By the end of the second stage of this 30 years' war, 1914–45, the image of humanity had been shattered. Yet, once again hope flickered in the ashes of destruction. In a renewed attempt to "save succeeding generations from the scourge of war," the United Nations Organization (UN) replaced the League of Nations. With the passage of time, people around the world also began to ask the historian's questions: What lessons should we draw from this experience? What is important for us to remember and how should we remember it? They argued profoundly over the answers.

The Rise of Fascism

20.1 How important were thugs in the rise of fascism in Italy and Germany?

Desperate times evoke desperate responses. We have already seen in the chapter entitled "Methods of Mass Production and Destruction" one of these desperate responses: the triumph of communism in the Soviet Union. In this chapter we shall continue to follow its development. First, however, we analyze the rise of **fascism** in Italy in the 1920s under Benito Mussolini (1883–1945), in Germany after 1933 under Adolf Hitler (1889–1945), and, to a lesser degree, in Japan, where military leaders took power under the authority of the emperor throughout the 1930s.

The term fascism derived from the Latin word *fasces*, the bundle of sticks carried by officials in ancient Rome as a symbol of power. Mussolini used the word and the symbol in proclaiming the power of the group—individually weak, but collectively strong. Fascism exalted the nation over the individual. It called for centralized autocratic government, often in alliance with major business leaders, with tight control of the economy and social life of the nation. It demanded the suppression of all opposition through unofficial paramilitary organizations of thugs who often took to the streets to attack and eliminate their opponents physically and brutally. If and when fascists succeeded in capturing office, they used the armed forces of the government to suppress opposition. They glorified warfare as a virtue. Fascism vested the power of the nation in a supreme leader. In Italy Mussolini, who had himself referred to as *Duce* (pronounced doo-chay), or supreme leader, filled that function. Why people supported fascism is unclear. Some followers must have been attracted by the promise that violence could solve the nation's problems, and many more by the belief that a dictatorship could deliver a more prosperous economy than could an irresolute, quarrelsome parliamentary government.

Fascism in Italy

Although it had been on the side of the victors after World War I, Italy suffered from wartime losses of people and property, economic depression, and the social unrest that beset much of Europe. Labor strikes and peasant unrest in the form of nonpayment of rent and occasional seizures of land spread throughout the country. Governments elected in 1919 and again in 1921 were not able to deal effectively with the unrest. Mussolini organized groups of men—mostly thugs—from among the

KEY TERM

fascism A political philosophy, movement, or government that exalts the nation over the individual, the antithesis of liberal democracy. It advocates a centralized, autocratic government, often in alliance with major business leaders, led by a disciplined party and headed by a dictatorial, charismatic leader.

war's former soldiers, calling them *fascio di combattimento*, groups of combatants, and dressed them in a uniform of black shirts. These "Black Shirts" were his core supporters. When his attempts to win power through elections in 1921 brought him only about seven percent of the vote, he turned his men loose on the streets to beat up labor organizers, communists, socialists, and local officials belonging to communist and socialist parties. The fascists claimed proudly that they killed 3,000 opponents in Italy from 1920 to 1922.

Announcing that the nation had descended into chaos, Mussolini declared a "March on Rome" in 1922 and threatened to take over the government. King Victor Emmanuel III capitulated and asked Mussolini to govern for a year as prime minister with full emergency powers. In the next elections, in 1924, Mussolini's party—through the use of violence, intimidation, and fraud—took more than 60 percent of the vote. Seizing control of the state, Mussolini abolished all other parties, took away the right to strike, destroyed labor unions, and sharply censored the press. He instituted his own propaganda wing within the government to indoctrinate Italians into endorsing his programs.

He organized the country's economy into 22 major economic categories. For each category he had fascist representatives of labor, employers, and government meet to decide wages, prices, working conditions, and industrial policies. All the representatives were assigned to a government minister and brought into the parliament. In fear of Mussolini's power, organized labor toed the line. Mussolini built roads, drained several hundred thousand acres of swamp for wheat production and malaria control, and "**made the trains run on time**," as the government boasted. While communists, socialists, liberals, and labor-union leaders had little appreciation for either the man or his methods, businessmen and others wanting a society that functioned with little public turmoil gave their approval.

They also took patriotic pride in the new colonial war that he led: in 1935, Mussolini attacked Ethiopia, completing its conquest in 1936. When the League of Nations demanded that Italy withdraw, Mussolini scoffed: great nations should have colonies. The League did nothing of substance to punish him, much less expel him from his conquests. On the contrary, Mussolini withdrew Italy from the League.

📖 Read the **Document: Benito Mussolini, "The Political and Social Doctrine of Fascism"** on **MyHistoryLab**

Hitler Rises in Germany

Mussolini's fascism drew the admiration of the young Adolf Hitler in Germany. Born in neighboring Austria, Hitler dropped out of high school at 16 and went to the national capital, Vienna, at 19, supporting himself with odd jobs, especially painting pictures. Much in prewar Vienna offended him: the wealthy royalty and aristocrats of the court; the prosperous businessmen; the socialist workers; the easy internationalism of the artists and intellectuals; and most of all the Jews, who had assimilated into Austrian society and often held high positions in business and the professions. Like many in Vienna, Hitler became a virulent racist, exalting the "pure" German "race" and disparaging all others in a hierarchy that stretched downward from northern Europeans to southern Europeans, to Africans, and finally to Jews at the very bottom.

Hitler felt more at home in Munich, Germany, where he moved in 1913. When World War I broke out, he volunteered for military service—serving as a dispatch runner—and came to value warfare as a blood-stirring and liberating experience. After the war, he began to work against the communist influences that were spreading among workers. In 1919 he joined the anticommunist German Workers' Party and became its head. He transformed the party into the National Socialist German Workers' Party—abbreviated as "Nazi"—thus launching his political career. Following Mussolini's model, the Nazis built up a group of storm troopers, the SA—a paramilitary

KEY TERM

made the trains run on time The boast of Mussolini—that he made the trains run on time—became the criticism of his democratic opponents. Both he and they saw the force of the police and military as the means of this accomplishment. For Mussolini it evoked pride; for his critics, despair and even ridicule. For the critics, the cure—excessive state police power—was greater than the problem: inefficiency. Nowadays the phrase is normally used to caricature a government eager to achieve efficiency but unconcerned about the effect on individual freedom.

How important were thugs in the rise of fascism in Italy and Germany?

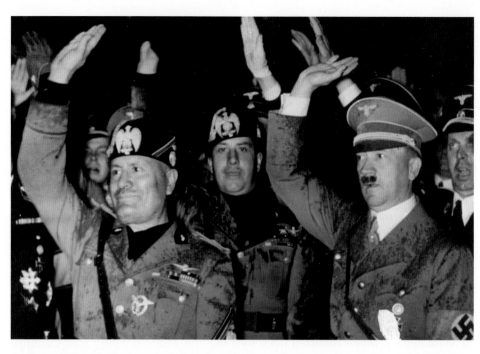

Mussolini and Hitler. The two men constructed the European alliance that, with Japan, formed the Axis Powers of World War II. At first, Italy's Mussolini was the dominant member, having come to power in 1922, but Hitler, although he came to head the German government only in 1933, ultimately set the agenda. Both men believed in strong government, with almost unlimited powers to the head of state (themselves), and minimal individual rights. Both glorified warfare, and Hitler, in particular, promulgated a racial hierarchy that condemned those at the bottom to extermination.

organization that often attacked its opponents violently in the streets—and gave them a uniform of brown shirts. The organization of these thugs was just one sign of Hitler's disdain for the democratic German government of his day, usually called the Weimar Republic for the city in which it had been founded.

As in Italy, many people in Germany preferred the order imposed by these paramilitary groups to what they perceived as the weakness of parliament and to the street demonstrations of communists and socialists. They feared, in particular, the spread of the influence of the communist revolution that had captured Russia, a historic adversary not far away from their eastern border. They perceived a struggle, often expressed in street-gang warfare, between two authoritarian forms of government, fascism and communism, and they preferred fascism as the lesser of the two evils, partly because the Russian communist dictatorship was already clearly visible, while the German fascist dictatorship had not yet appeared in its full force. Also, they saw that Russian communism had suppressed private, big business, while fascist leaders promised to work with the German business community as a means of building up the country. The Weimar democracy seemed tentative and feeble by comparison with either of these two aggressive ideological systems.

The Weimar Republic, an elected government of both working- and middle-class membership, had succeeded the German monarchy, which withdrew from power at the end of World War I. Neither the militant right wing, which wanted a more centralized and powerful government under more autocratic leadership—like the Nazis—nor the militant left wing, which wanted a socialist or even communist government and hoped for a revolution like that in Russia had much respect for Weimar. Both saw the centrist, democratic government as too weak.

The year 1923 was especially difficult. Germany could not keep up with its payments of war reparations. To collect, France seized the highly industrialized Ruhr valley, provoking national outrage in Germany, a good part of it directed against

How important were thugs in the rise of fascism in Italy and Germany?

20.1
20.2
20.3
20.4
20.5
20.6
20.7
20.8

the weakness of the Weimar government itself. In addition, extraordinary inflation completely eroded the value of the German mark, making it hardly worth the paper it was printed on, wiping out the savings of the middle class, impoverishing the lives of workers, and endangering the stability of the government. Among those who further inflamed public opinion against the government, Hitler attempted a *putsch* (revolt) to overthrow it, in Munich in 1923. Some army officers had already failed in an attempted *putsch* in 1920. Hitler also failed, and was imprisoned for nine months. But he gained greater popular attention, and during his months in jail he wrote *Mein Kampf* ("My Struggle"), his political manifesto, filled with his denunciation of the government, strident nationalism, plans for a Germany restored to—and beyond—her former greatness, the subordination of eastern Europe to Germany, and bitter, all-consuming anti-Semitism. He blamed Jews for being allied on the left with the communists and on the right with the capitalists, as too foreign from the German mainstream, and as too assimilated into modern German life. Hitler made Jews into the scapegoat he could blame for all of Germany's woes.

📖 **Read** the **Document**: Adolf Hitler: *Mein Kampf* (1923) on **MyHistoryLab**

Recognizing and frightened by the dangers of an unstable Germany, the French conceded and withdrew from the Ruhr, and the former wartime allies (with the exception of the Soviet Union) rescheduled the reparation debts to make them less onerous. For a few years, prosperity returned to Germany, but then the international depression of 1929 swept the country back into poverty and renewed humiliation. Germany seethed in anguish. Communists on the left and Hitler on the right blamed German democracy and the Weimar government for the nation's troubles. Hitler became the strongest voice in the opposition. In a series of national elections between 1928 and 1932, his Nazi party's proportion of seats in the German parliament, the Reichstag, went from about 2 percent to about 46 percent, although in the next election, later in 1932, it fell to just below 40 percent. He gained support not only from backers who approved his entire program, but also from many conservatives, including army officers and influential businesspeople, who differed on many points from Hitler's crude nationalism and racism, but saw him as their chief defense against communism. In 1933, German political leaders turned to Hitler—the head of the largest single party in the Reichstag—to head a coalition government. Hitler became chancellor of Germany by entirely legal processes.

In order to rule without the constraints of a coalition, Hitler called another election later in the year. In a contest marked by the violence of the SA, suspension of freedoms of speech and press, and a fire in the Reichstag building that Hitler blamed on the communists (although many claimed the Nazis had actually set the fire), the Nazis gained 44 percent of the vote. This was not enough, so Hitler announced a national emergency and, again using his SA thugs to intimidate the opposition, obtained the votes of a majority of the Reichstag to rule as dictator.

Once in power, Hitler moved swiftly to establish the kind of state that is often called **totalitarian**—that is, a state in which the individual is subordinated to a centralized administration that controls the national economy, politics, media, and culture, usually under a single dictator or a small council. As Mussolini had himself called *Duce*, so Hitler had himself called *Führer*, or leader. In 1925, Hitler had created the SS, another paramilitary organization, dressed in black uniforms. Although initially subordinated to the SA, the SS rose in prominence. All political parties apart from the Nazis were abolished. On June 30, 1934, the "night of the long knives," Hitler had the SS murder many leading Nazis whom he viewed as opponents and rivals. He established a secret police force, the Gestapo, in 1936. Opposition leaders were killed or dispatched to concentration camps. Churches were forbidden to criticize the government, and they were encouraged to cut their ties with overseas branches of their denominations. By contrast, the government encouraged the

KEY TERMS

putsch (German) An attempt to seize control of the government, often by the military. A coup d'etat.

totalitarianism A totalitarian state is one that seeks total control of the economy, politics, media, and culture of the state, under a single dictator or party. It does away with individual rights, proclaiming the rights of the state—as defined by its dictator—superior to those of any individual or group.

worship of pre-Christian Teutonic gods. Strikes were forbidden and employers were granted new powers in dealing with workers. Policies were based on bogus "racial science": Hitler declared that "Aryans," especially Germans and Scandinavians, were the most elevated of races, and Jews the lowest. Jews were dismissed from public office, including university service and the civil service. No matter how high their position, or the history of their service to Germany, in 1935 all Jews were stripped of citizenship. By now, seeing the handwriting on the wall, many had begun to flee the country, including two Nobel laureates whom we encountered earlier: the chemist Fritz Haber and the world's most distinguished theoretical physicist, Albert Einstein. On the night of November 9–10, 1938, synagogues and Jewish-owned businesses throughout Germany were attacked by German paramilitary forces and by mobs in the *Kristallnacht* assault, the "night of (broken) glass."

Why did Germans tolerate, and even participate in, this new order? Some, of course, accepted totalitarianism as appropriate. Others, frightened by the prospect of chaos, poverty, and communism, saw it as a severely flawed, but better, alternative. In addition, after 1933, Hitler commanded the use of force in the country, not only through the thugs of the SS, but also through the officially legitimate use of the army, police, and secret police. Citizens could protest only at risk to their safety and even lives. Finally, Hitler's program for rebuilding the country economically and militarily had great appeal. So, too, did his emphasis on the need for *Lebensraum*, space for living, an expansion of Germany's territory first into Austria and Czechoslovakia and then through Poland, the Ukraine, and Russia. The Nazi propaganda machine, orchestrated by Joseph Goebbels, indoctrinated the nation, often spreading "**the big lie**" because, as Hitler wrote in *Mein Kampf*, "in the big lie there is always a certain force of credibility."

Hitler set the nation to work on programs of public works, building housing and superhighways, draining swamps, and reforesting rural areas. In 1936, following the Soviet model, he introduced state planning, although unlike the Russian case, he worked within the framework of private property. He urged Germany to become economically self-sufficient, and its skilled scientists developed many artificial products, such as rubber, plastics, and synthetic fibers, that enabled it to reduce its imports. Germans went back to work, and Germany escaped the severe unemployment suffered in most European countries during the Great Depression. The most remarkable dimension of Hitler's rebuilding program, however, was the most dangerous and most threatening: in violation of the Paris peace accords, he began rebuilding Germany's military, and soon he deployed these forces in missions that precipitated World War II.

Hitler's Germany shared many characteristics with Mussolini's Italy. Both had developed strong governments that brooked no opposition. Both pursued policies of militarism and both glorified war. The leaders in both nations set themselves up as the unchallenged and unchallengeable rulers of their states. In October 1936, the two governments proclaimed an "axis" that bound them together in international affairs. The next month, Germany signed an Anti-Comintern Pact with Japan, pledging mutual support against possible attacks from the USSR. The next few years would bring together Germany, Italy, and Japan, along with their allies, as the Axis Powers in World War II. (The British, French, Soviets, Americans, and their allies would call themselves the Allied Powers.)

Japan Between the Wars

During the Meiji restoration, Japan achieved an astonishingly rapid reorganization of its government, administration, economy, industry, and finances. As we saw in "Nationalism, Imperialism, and Resistance," Japan followed Western examples in seizing colonies for itself and asserting a sphere of influence in China. Reversing its previous student–teacher relationship with China, it defeated China in Korea in 1895

KEY TERMS

Lebensraum In German, "room for living." The claim was that Germany needed to expand and take over the land of its neighbors because its own land was overcrowded. Similar claims on neighbors' lands have been issued by many nations throughout history.

the big lie A propaganda technique, defined by Hitler as a lie so colossal that no one would believe the liar would dare to say it if it were not true.

How important
were thugs in the
rise of fascism
in Italy and
Germany?

20.1
20.2
20.3
20.4
20.5
20.6
20.7
20.8

Workers winding induction regulator coils in a Shibaura Engineering Works plant, Tsurumi, Honshu, Japan, 1930. In the 1920s and 1930s the Japanese often borrowed from Western models by inviting foreign firms to establish Japanese branches; by obtaining licenses to produce foreign technology; and by adapting that technology to Japanese conditions. Their industry consequently "leapfrogged" ahead very rapidly.

and became the dominant nation of East Asia. Japan signed a military alliance with Britain in 1902, subordinated the island of Taiwan (1895) and the Korean peninsula (1910) into colonies, and defeated Russia by land and sea in East Asia, in 1904–05. For the first time in modern history, an Asian nation had defeated a European country.

World War I profoundly affected politics in East Asia. Japan was seated as one of the victorious Five Great Powers at the 1919 peace conference in Paris—the only non-Western nation accepted as an equal at the proceedings. It was assigned control over Germany's Pacific colonies, including the Liaotung peninsula in north China, which Japan had seized in 1914. This led to the May Fourth Movement of Chinese students in China, a student demonstration that metamorphosed into a broader movement for Chinese reforms both at home and in international relations (see the chapter entitled "Methods of Mass Production and Destruction"). In the end, China refused to sign the Versailles Treaty.

World War I presented Japan with an unprecedented economic opportunity. While other industrialized countries were occupied with war in Europe, Japan developed its industries relatively free from competition. Between 1914 and 1918 Japan's gross national income rose by 40 percent, and for the first time the country exported more than it imported. Heavy industry showed particularly impressive growth. Manufacturing increased by 72 percent while the labor force expanded by only 42 percent, indicating the growing use of machinery to increase productivity. Transport increased by 60 percent. Between 1914 and 1919 Japan's merchant marine almost doubled, to 2.8 million tons. The production and export of consumer goods also advanced. In the first decades of the twentieth century, Japan's most important exports were textiles, primarily silk, 80 percent of which was produced by women.

As a latecomer, Japan could take advantage of technology already developed in the West (the "leapfrogging" path that Trotsky preached in Russia). Japanese industries practiced three different patterns in importing that technology. Some signed agreements with foreign firms to establish branches in Japan; some negotiated

Samurai warrior. The ancient and proud warrior class of the samurai worshiped athletic prowess, swordsmanship, and fierce loyalty to the emperor. In 1877 the last 400,000 samurai were pensioned off to become *shizoku*, Japanese gentry, but their virtues lived on in the country's psyche. In times of crisis, the warriors' values turned Japanese nationalism into a potent force.

KEY TERM

dual economy An economy of two largely unconnected tiers: one, usually small, tier of large-scale, modern, highly mechanized, highly capitalized businesses with large workforces in each unit, but since the total number of units is small, this is a relatively small proportion of the total workforce; the other of small-scale workshops with little capital, limited mechanization, and a small workforce in each unit, but since the total number of units is large, this is a relatively large proportion of the total workforce, usually producing traditional goods and services.

licenses to use the new technology; and some practiced "reverse engineering," analyzing and reproducing foreign machinery, with adaptations appropriate to Japanese needs. Adaptation produced innovations—for example, in applying chemical research to agricultural and even ceramics production. Private firms imported most of the foreign technology, but the government also encouraged research by funding state universities, laboratories, and the development of military technology.

Japan bridged the **dual economy**, the separation between large-scale and cottage industries that has inhibited growth in many countries. In a dual economy, one sector consists of large, highly capitalized, technically advanced factories employing thousands of workers producing modern products; the other sector includes small-scale workshops, with relatively low capitalization and less up-to-date equipment, often employing fewer than 30 workers, producing traditional goods. In most countries, the small-scale sector tends to shrivel as larger firms achieve economies of scale and put it out of business. Governments, too, often invest their resources in large industries, neglecting the small sector. But in Japan, the smaller factories adopted appropriate scale and new technology, and began to produce new goods needed by the larger industries. From the early years of the century, Japan evolved systems of subcontracting between the large and small sectors, which made them interdependent and complementary.

Poor harvests in 1918 provoked a sharp rise in the price of rice, Japan's staple food. Massive riots broke out in hundreds of cities and towns, lasting 50 days, involving some 700,000 people, and resulting in 25,000 arrests and 1,000 deaths. The government responded by importing rice and other staples from its colonial territories in Korea and Taiwan. The riots represented the growth of Japan's urban voice as the urban proportion of the population rose from just over 10 percent in 1890 to close to 50 percent in the 1920s (and to 91 percent by 2012). Labor was increasingly organized and the citizenry politicized. In 1925 all male subjects over the age of 25—some 12.5 million people—were given the vote.

The riots also reminded Japan of its increasing dependence on its colonies for daily commodities. In the later 1920s, Taiwan and Korea provided 80 percent of Japan's rice imports and 66 percent of its sugar. For industrial raw materials, such as minerals, metals, petroleum, fertilizers, and lumber, Japan had to look farther afield, and this would lead it into fatal colonial adventures.

In the 1920s, industrial production increased by 66 percent. The *zaibatsu* (huge holding companies or conglomerates) came to control much of the Japanese economy and were very influential in politics. The four largest—Mitsui, Mitsubishi, Sumitomo, and Yasuda—were controlled by individual families, and each operated a bank and numerous enterprises in a variety of industries, ranging from textiles to shipping and machinery. A Mitsubishi mining company, for example, would extract minerals, which would then be made into a product by one of the Mitsubishi manufacturing companies. Next, this product would be marketed abroad by a Mitsubishi trading firm and transported in ships of another Mitsubishi affiliate. The whole process would be financed through the Mitsubishi bank.

The *zaibatsu* combined large size with an ability to shift production to meet demand. The *zaibatsu* families also held considerable influence in government, both

20.1

20.2

20.3

20.4

20.5

20.6

20.7

20.8

What efforts for world peace made people optimistic in the 1920s?

through the capital they controlled and through their close family links with prominent politicians. The Major Industries Control Law of 1931, for example, encouraged large companies in key industries to join in **cartels** to regulate production and prices.

International respect, growing wealth, rising urbanization, increasing industrialization, high rates of literacy, universal male suffrage (1925), and the institutionalization of political parties suggested that Japan was embracing liberal democracy. But the political power of the *zaibatsu* and the military undermined people's faith in democratic practice. Because Japan's traditional Shinto religion emphasized the emperor's divinity and asserted the leading role of Japan's samurai warrior ethic, the military held extraordinary power, both under law and in popular opinion. In contrast to most democratic countries, in which the civilian government controls the military, Japanese law specified that the ministers of war and of the navy had to be active generals or admirals. Conversely, the formal powers of Japan's Diet, or parliament, were restricted. In theory, the Japanese emperor held the ultimate political authority for the country, and the political leaders who dominated public policy at home and abroad spoke in his name. The reality of power was ambiguous, and historians debate how much the emperor actually exercised himself and how much was exercised by others in his name.

Many of the samurai military elite began to claim expanded powers for the armed forces. They wished to protect Japan, a resource-poor island nation that was especially vulnerable to shifts in international trade and its regulation. The world depression of 1929 shocked the Japanese economy as the value of exports dropped 50 percent between 1929 and 1931. Unemployment rose to three million, with rural areas hardest hit. Many civilians seemed to agree with the military: the future would look brighter if Japan could reorganize and control the economy of East Asia for its own benefit. Although the civilian government continued to criticize the military, generals gained increasing control of the state and turned it toward military goals.

Scholars argue over the use of the term "fascism" in relation to Japan. Many prefer to term the Japanese experience "ultranationalism." Unlike Italy and Germany, where nationalism itself was new and the takeover of the state by fascist leaders using violence even newer, Japan had been nationalistic for millennia, with an emperor who was considered to be divine. Nevertheless, as Japan rebuilt itself in the early decades of the twentieth century, two generations after the Meiji restoration, it shared many of the fascist elements of Germany and Italy, which were to become its allies: a powerful military took over the principal tasks of government, using the symbolism of state authority—the emperor—to justify their actions; violent attacks by the military leaders silenced domestic opposition through beatings and murders; and an aggressive and expansionist foreign policy brought Japan's armies into war with its neighbors and annexed them.

Optimism Revives, Temporarily

20.2   What efforts for world peace made people optimistic in the 1920s?

The 1920s had appeared to usher in a time of peace. The League of Nations was founded in 1920. It was not entrusted with peace-keeping missions, but it was expected to be a forum in which international conflicts could be managed through negotiation. It also carried out valuable humanitarian work in fighting epidemic disease in eastern Europe and in resettling political refugees—Russians fleeing the communism of the Soviet Union and Greeks and Armenians expelled from Turkey, for example. The League's Intellectual Cooperation Organization promoted cultural activities to bring together people from around the world. Among the members of its advisory committee were Albert Einstein of Germany, Marie Curie of France, the composer Béla Bartók of Hungary, and the novelist Thomas Mann of Germany. The

KEY TERM

cartel An association of producers or businessmen whose aim is to control the supply of a particular commodity or group of commodities in order to regulate or push up prices.

20.1
20.2
20.3 How did the world end up in another global war so soon after the first one?
20.4
20.5
20.6
20.7
20.8

organization's annual meetings in Geneva, Switzerland, attracted representatives not only from Western European countries and the United States, but also from Mexico, Venezuela, Brazil, Japan, China, Egypt, Poland, Czechoslovakia, Hungary, and India, even though the last was still a colony of Great Britain.

Individual nations also pursued independent paths to preventing war and promoting peace. In 1921, a conference was convened in Washington, DC, to set limits on competition in naval forces. It achieved agreement on a 5:5:3 ratio in the total tonnage of large ships in Britain, the United States, and Japan respectively, with other World War I allies accepting lower limits. In 1925, the major powers, meeting in Locarno, Switzerland, signed a number of agreements designed to relieve some of the burden of guilt that Germany had been forced to accept for the war, and to reintegrate Germany into the European diplomatic world. Germany accepted its western borders with France and Belgium unconditionally and agreed that it would use only diplomacy, and not force, in any attempt to alter its eastern borders with Poland and Czechoslovakia. To reinforce this agreement, France agreed to defend Poland and Czechoslovakia in case of any future attack. (Britain did not sign, arguing that its interests were not involved.) In 1928, a total of 65 nations signed the Pact of Paris (known as the Kellogg–Briand Pact), agreeing to renounce war as a means of settling international conflict. By 1928, optimism—and prosperity—had returned to the European world. By 1925, the index of manufacturing in Western and central Europe had surpassed that of prewar 1913. Russia, the worst hit of all world powers by the war, had returned to 70 percent, from a low of 13 percent in 1920. Lasting peace, too, seemed to have been achieved.

The Descent Toward War

20.3 How did the world end up in another global war so soon after the first one?

Then came the Great Depression and its economic and political pressures. Most remarkably, as the democratic, capitalistic countries of Western Europe, the United States, and Latin America struggled with the world depression of the 1930s, the USSR, Germany, Italy, and Japan were thriving. Each of the four had adopted dictatorship, national planning, and militarization. Indeed, three of them—Germany, Italy, and Japan—launched military campaigns in the 1930s that would ultimately result in World War II, while the fourth, the USSR, built up a massive military force in anticipation of having to fight them off. The build-up of the militaries and the war campaigns fed on one another. The cost of maintaining the armed forces became so exorbitant that only war victories could pay for them, and to achieve war victories ever-increasing militarization was necessary.

The Steps to War

In 1931, strongly influenced by its wealthy business conglomerates, the *zaibatsu*, and by hypernationalist officers in the armed forces, Japan seized Chinese arsenals in Manchuria and began to take over the entire province. Japanese troops had been in place in Manchuria since their victory over the Russians in 1905. As justification for the takeover, they blamed China for the murder of a Japanese officer in Mukden, Manchuria, and for boycotts of Japanese goods. In 1932, Japan declared Manchuria an independent state, which it then ruled, establishing the last Chinese emperor, Puyi, who had been deposed in 1912 as a puppet head of government. China, joined by several small nations, protested to the League of Nations. Japan quit the League, and, in any case, the League took no serious action. None of the other powers felt threatened. They did not want to commit troops, and the Western Europeans did not want to alienate Japan at a time when they felt the need for it as a partner in a quiet alliance against the Soviet Union. As noted, many in Japan opposed Japanese militarism, but, as in Germany, violent attacks stifled the opposition. Between 1930 and 1936, two prime ministers, one finance minister, and one important banker were assassinated. Speaking out against militarism in Japan was dangerous.

In 1935, Italy invaded Ethiopia. Despite the poignant speech of the Ethiopian emperor Haile Selassie before the League of Nations, despite his revelation that the Italians were spraying chemical weapons from airplanes on his defenseless people below, despite his warning that all small nations were in danger of being swallowed up by larger and more powerful ones, despite his charge that some members of the League were supplying Italy with war materials, the League of Nations did nothing of substance to block the Italian annexation of Ethiopia. International faith in the League as a force for peace plummeted.

The Spanish Civil War. In 1936, civil war broke out in Spain. The country had been in turmoil as a relatively bloodless revolution deposed the king of Spain in 1931 and established a democratic Spanish republic. For five years, power oscillated between the conservative rightists, including members of the clergy, the military, and the business elites, and the liberal leftists, including workers, socialists, communists, and anarchists. In elections in 1936, the leftists (republicans) won, and the rightists (nationalists), led by General Francisco Franco (1892–1975), began an insurrection that turned into a civil war. Many observers called this a "dress rehearsal" for World War II because Germany and Italy sent men (Italy sent 50,000 soldiers), money, and weapons to aid Franco and the rightists, while the Soviet Union sent technicians, political advisers, and equipment to bolster the republican government. The major democratic governments of Western Europe—including those of Britain and France—condemned Franco, but sent no support and prohibited the shipment of weapons. The United States declared its neutrality and declared an embargo on the export of arms to Spain. Privately, thousands of volunteers from the democratic nations went to Spain as volunteers to serve with the republican forces. The

THE MARCH TO WAR

1935–36	Italy conquers Ethiopia
1936–39	Spanish Civil War
July 7, 1937	Japanese troops invade China
September 1938	Appeasement in Munich; Germany annexes Sudetenland
September 1939	Nazi–Soviet Pact: Germany invades Poland; Britain and France declare war; Poland partitioned between Germany and Russia
March–April 1940	*Blitzkrieg*: German forces conquer Denmark and Norway
May–June 1940	Italy declares war on Britain and France; German forces conquer France, the Netherlands, and Belgium
June 1940–June 1941	Battle of Britain; Britain holds firm against German bombing attacks
June 21, 1941	German forces invade USSR
December 7, 1941	Japanese bomb US Navy, Pearl Harbor
January–March 1942	Japan conquers Indonesia, Malaya, Singapore, Burma and the Philippines
June 1942	US Navy defeats Japanese at the Battle of Midway
1942–43	End of Axis resistance in North Africa; Soviet victory in Battle of Stalingrad
1943–44	Red Army slowly pushes Wehrmacht (the German armed forces) back to Germany
June 6, 1944	Allies land in Normandy (D-Day)
February 1945	Yalta conference: Churchill, Roosevelt, and Stalin discuss postwar settlement
March 1945	US planes bomb Tokyo
May 7, 1945	Germany surrenders
August 6, 9, 1945	US drops atom bomb on Hiroshima, and then on Nagasaki
August 15, 1945	Japan surrenders

American writer Ernest Hemingway immortalized this International Brigade in his novel *For Whom the Bell Tolls* (1940). Hitler used the war as an opportunity to test the air force he was building. Mostly he used his planes to transport Franco's troops, but on April 28, 1937, German squadrons supporting Franco bombed and destroyed the unprotected civilian town of Guernica, a local cultural center in the Basque region of northern Spain. The raid killed 1,645 civilians and wounded thousands more. Horrified, seething with rage, and transformed politically, the Spanish artist Pablo Picasso immediately painted *Guernica*, perhaps the most famous antiwar painting in history, depicting the anguish, pain, and suffering of men, women, children, and animals. The Spanish Civil War continued for three years; 600,000 people died. Franco's victory established a right-wing dictatorship that lasted four decades until his death in 1975. The League was not able to resolve the conflicting claims peacefully, and it commanded no armed forces of its own. Armed nationalism triumphed over unarmed internationalism.

20.1
20.2
20.3
20.4
20.5
20.6
20.7
20.8

How did the world end up in another global war so soon after the first one?

Guernica, Pablo Picasso, 1937. Oil on canvas. Picasso painted this 20-by-12-foot black, white and grey masterpiece as a protest against the German bombing of the village of Guernica during the Spanish Civil War. It is one of the most famous of all antiwar paintings. Picasso refused to allow it to be moved to Spain until after Franco's death in 1975. It is now on display in a Madrid gallery specially built for it. (Museo Nacional Centro de Arte Reina Sofía, Madrid)

👁 **Watch** the **Video**: **The Art of Pablo Picasso** on **MyHistoryLab**

Japan Invades China. On July 7, 1937, Japan invaded China. The pretext was an assault on Japanese troops near Beijing; the goal was the takeover of China. Within months, Japan gained control of most of the densely populated eastern half of the country, while the Chinese armed forces withdrew ever deeper into the interior and continued to fight until the very end of World War II. The League of Nations condemned Japan, but took no substantive action. The Japanese refer to this war as the "Pacific War." In global terms, the Japanese invasion of China is usually considered the beginning of World War II, although the war in Europe did not begin until September 1939.

Hitler's Early Conquests

After his appointment as chancellor in 1933, Hitler began almost immediately to expand Germany's military position despite the restrictions of the Paris peace treaties. In 1933 he took Germany out of the League of Nations and out of a disarmament conference that was taking place at the time. In 1934, Nazis in neighboring Austria assassinated the prime minister and demanded union with Germany. Hitler's proposed takeover of Austria at this time was prevented only by Mussolini, who declared his opposition to German troops occupying a neighboring country and stationed Italian troops at the Austrian border. In 1935, Nazi intimidation influenced voters in the rich, industrialized Saar region, on the border with France, to vote for annexation to Germany. Most provocatively, in 1935, Hitler began to rearm Germany. In 1936 he sent his new troops into the Rhineland, German territory just west of the Rhine River that had been designated a demilitarized zone. No one acted to oppose him. In March 1938, now with Mussolini's consent, German troops moved into Austria, declaring an *Anschluss*, or union, of Germany and Austria.

Next, Hitler focused on Czechoslovakia, particularly the Sudeten area, where some three million Germans lived as a minority in the larger Slavic state. He threatened to

20.1
20.2
20.3   How did the world end up in another global war so soon after the first one?
20.4
20.5
20.6
20.7
20.8

20.1
20.2
20.3
20.4
20.5
20.6
20.7
20.8

invade the Sudetenland to annex it to Germany. As fears of war spread, the British prime minister, Neville Chamberlain, and the French premier, Edouard Daladier, flew to Munich to negotiate the fate of Czechoslovakia. They persuaded the Czechs to cede the Sudetenland to Germany, which left the rest of the country open to further German unilateral action. They had persuaded Czechoslovakia to sign its own death warrant, and they had bought off Hitler by offering up Czechoslovakia, not allowing themselves to realize that they had only delayed the war that was to come. The image of Chamberlain returning from Munich to London to proclaim that he had won "peace for our time" has, ever since, served as a symbol of the folly of appeasing aggressors. The Germans invaded and took over the remainder of Czechoslovakia in March 1939. In April, Italy took over Albania.

Russia was willing to fight against Germany over the issue of Czechoslovakia only if the French or British would join in, but they would not. Indeed, the British seemed to give more diplomatic attention to Germany, their potential enemy, than to the Soviet Union, their potential ally. On August 23, 1939, the USSR stunned the world by signing a nonaggression pact with Germany, its geopolitical arch-enemy and ideological rival. A secret protocol of the treaty was an agreement to divide up Poland between them if Poland's territory were ever conquered. For Hitler, the way was now clear. On September 1, German forces invaded Poland. On September 3, Britain and France finally declared war on Germany. The European theater of World War II had opened.

World War II Reaches Europe

20.4   What were the key events in the first years of World War II?

The early results were ominous. Implementing its strategy of *Blitzkrieg*, or lightning war, Germany sent one million troops into Poland, with armored forces in the front and air support overhead. Poland was not equipped to defend itself, and within a month organized resistance had ended. Germany incorporated western Poland into its new empire.

Meanwhile the Soviet Union invaded and seized eastern Poland, in accord with its nonaggression pact with Germany. The Soviets also stationed troops in the Baltic countries of Lithuania, Latvia, and Estonia and attacked Finland to seize part of its land. The League of Nations expelled the Soviet Union, but it got all the lands it claimed from the Finns.

Despite their declaration of war, France and Britain took no immediate military action against Germany. The lull through the winter of 1939–40 is often called the "phony war." In April 1940, however, Hitler resumed his strategy of *Blitzkrieg*.

The War in Europe

Germany occupied Denmark and Norway in April. In May, German armies invaded Belgium, Luxembourg, the Netherlands, and France. Nothing could stop them. The French had prepared an elaborate "Maginot Line" of defended trenches, underground bunkers, minefields, and barbed wire that they thought was impregnable. The Germans went around the line to the northwest and penetrated France. German tanks also entered France through Luxembourg and the Ardennes forest, which the French had thought impassable by tanks. Everywhere the Germans scored victories. With Rotterdam under air attack, the Netherlands surrendered. Belgium sued for peace. British, and some French, troops retreated to the French seaport of Dunkirk, and on June 4, leaving their armor behind them, they were hastily evacuated to England. On June 10, Mussolini joined the attack on France, and soon invaded Greece as well. On June 13, the Germans occupied Paris, and on June 22, France surrendered.

20.1
20.2
20.3
20.4 What were the
key events in
the first years of
World War II?
20.5
20.6
20.7
20.8

The country had been conquered in less than two months of fighting. Germany chose to administer the northern two-thirds of France directly. The southern third was administered from the town of Vichy by French officials who collaborated with the Germans. Some French joined General Charles de Gaulle with French forces in exile; some began guerrilla warfare against the Germans. Most acquiesced in the conquest and went about their daily life under German occupation.

Britain now stood alone on the western front against Germany, and Hitler attacked. He launched heavy bombing of London and other strategic cities in Britain throughout the summer and autumn of 1940. Winston Churchill, who had replaced Chamberlain as prime minister in May 1940, confronted the desperation of the situation directly and addressed his nation in rhetoric that stirred the blood and strengthened the backbone. Within a few days of assuming office, Churchill announced in Parliament: "I have nothing to offer but blood, toil, tears, and sweat!" And a month later:

> We shall go on to the end, we shall fight in France, we shall fight on the seas and oceans, we shall fight with growing confidence and growing strength in the air, we shall defend our island, whatever the cost may be, we shall fight on the beaches, we shall fight on the landing grounds, we shall fight in the fields and in the streets, we shall fight in the hills; we shall never surrender.

Despite heavy losses, including 20,000 dead in London alone, the British held firm, thanks to the Royal Air Force, the invention of radar, and success in cracking German secret codes. By the end of 1940, Germany abandoned the Battle of Britain in the air, and gave up plans to invade the island by sea.

To the east, the Soviet Union, operating under cover of the nonaggression pact, had not only seized the eastern half of Poland and parts of Finland, and incorporated the Baltic States into its empire, but had also seized and incorporated parts of Romania that it had lost in World War I, and began to target the Balkan states. Hitler moved first. He brought Romania, Bulgaria, and Hungary into the Axis, and occupied Yugoslavia and Greece. Then, in an unexpected, fierce attack, he turned his forces eastward, broke the nonaggression treaty, and invaded the Soviet Union on June 22, 1941, a date thereafter viewed in the USSR as its Pearl Harbor. A German army of three million men and some 3,500 armored vehicles, covered by the air support of the Luftwaffe (the German air force), invaded a 2,000-mile front in the USSR. The Soviets retreated from the central European lands they had taken, and moved hundreds of miles into the interior of their own country. They transported whole industrial plants deep into the interior as well. Finally, Stalin, who had been taken completely by surprise by the attack despite his years of preparation for warfare, counterattacked. The Soviet army, under General Georgi Zhukov, pushed the Germans back from their positions around the capital, Moscow, relieving the city. The Germans, as Napoleon had done a century and a half earlier, retreated from Moscow in the face of the counteroffensive and the severe winter.

The European war had another front, in North Africa. In September 1940, the Italians, who held Libya, invaded Egypt, heading for the Suez Canal. To protect the canal, Churchill diverted troops and supplies from the Battle of Britain to North Africa. The British forces defeated the Italians in Egypt and Libya and even forced them out of Ethiopia. The Germans, however, under General Erwin Rommel, entered North Africa and battles raged back and forth between them and the British in 1941 and 1942. British lines, however, held at El Alamein, west of Alexandria, and the Suez Canal remained in British hands. Nevertheless, German submarines in the Mediterranean closed down transportation across that sea, and took a heavy toll on shipping across the Atlantic.

Hitler reorganized his Russian campaign in 1942, directing his troops to the south, in the direction of the rich oil fields of the Caucasus Mountains and the Caspian Sea. By the summer of 1942, Germany had taken all the western possessions of the Soviet Union—the Baltic States, Byelorussia, Poland, and the Ukraine—stood at the

World War II in Europe. Fighting began in 1939 with a *Blitzkrieg*, or lightning war, by Germany and her ally Italy. By late 1942 the Axis Powers controlled most of Europe. But Germany's invasion of the Soviet Union in 1941 brought the power of that huge state into opposition and enmeshed Germany in exhausting land war. Britain held out defensively and then began to fight back, especially after the United States entered the war, bringing in air power and material support. By early 1944, the tide had turned.

20.1

20.2

20.3

20.4 What were the key events in the first years of World War II?

20.5

20.6

20.7

20.8

gateway to Leningrad in the north, besieged Stalingrad in the south, and held its lines not far off from Moscow in the center. Historians sometimes compare Hitler's position to that of Napoleon. Each man held approximately the same areas of Western Europe and each launched an assault into Russia that would devastate the country and force it into deep retreat, but would also leave the aggressor itself exhausted. To the west, each faced a determined Britain that responded to attack with unexpected and ultimately victorious tenacity. The presence of the United States in World War II, however, would add a new ingredient.

From the beginning of the war in Europe, in September 1939, President Franklin Delano Roosevelt had supported Britain and the Allies, but his support was limited by the isolationist feelings of many Americans. Roosevelt was able to lift the ban on the sale of arms, and in 1940, he sent a shipment of arms to England; later in the same year he added 50 destroyers in exchange for the right to establish military bases in some British possessions in the west. The United States also began military conscription, increased the size of its armed forces, and secured bases in Greenland and Iceland in order to protect American and Allied shipping. In 1941, the United

20.4 What were the key events in the first years of World War II?

States Congress introduced the Lend–Lease program to provide weapons and supplies to the Allied forces. Still, however, Roosevelt could not commit his country to war—until Japan attacked at Pearl Harbor in December of that year. To understand this attack, we return to the Pacific theater of warfare.

📖 Read the **Document**: Gertrud Scholtz-Klink, **"Speech to the Nazi Women's Organization (Germany), 1935** on **MyHistoryLab**

📖 Read the **Document**: Barbara Woodall and Charles Taylor, **Letters to and from the Front, (1941–44)** on **MyHistoryLab**

The War in the Pacific, 1937–42

In 1937, a clash between Chinese and Japanese troops at the Marco Polo Bridge near Beijing had triggered the beginning of the Pacific War. The Japanese had not expected the fierce resistance of the Chinese. Planning to end the "China problem" with a single quick victory that would terrify the enemy into suing for peace, the Japanese army launched a full-scale attack on Nanjing. Japanese troops murdered, raped, and pillaged in what is now generally known as the Rape of Nanjing. Twelve thousand noncombatant Chinese were killed in the first three days after Nanjing was captured, and 20,000 cases of rape were reported in the first month. In the first six weeks some 200,000 civilians and prisoners-of-war were killed in and around the city. The atrocities set an ugly precedent for later Japanese cruelty toward many of the nations they defeated throughout Asia during the war.

In the face of repeated Japanese advances, the Chinese government retreated to Chongqing, on the upper Yangzi River deep in the interior of the country. The Chinese, like the Russians retreating before the Germans, followed a **scorched-earth** strategy, leaving little in their wake that the enemy could use. The war in China became a stalemate. Even in 1945, when Japan itself was under attack, about a million Japanese soldiers were still fighting in China, and another 750,000 were in Manchuria. China's sheer persistence helped to wear out the Japanese.

KEY TERM

scorched earth A strategy of defensive warfare, in which everything that might be of use to an invading army is destroyed by the defending army as it retreats.

Former Japanese Prime Minister Yukio Hatoyama and his wife Miyuki pay their respects in front of a display of human bones at the Nanjing Massacre Museum during a trip to Nanjing, Jiangsu province, January 17, 2013. Despite this gesture of reconciliation, the Nanjing massacre continues to embitter Chinese views of Japan and the Japanese. Memorials like this one paradoxically attempt to put events into the past, and at the same time to ensure that they are remembered.

In September 1940, Japan signed the Tripartite Pact, formally aligning itself with Germany and Italy. But Axis plans were not well coordinated. Japan could have joined the war against the USSR, opening a second front from Manchuria, as Germany wished. Instead, it signed a neutrality pact with the Soviet Union in April 1941 and turned southward to capture French Indochina, putting it on a collision course with the United States.

Isolationist pressure in America had thus far kept the United States out of armed warfare. However, the American government responded to Japanese aggression in China and Southeast Asia by placing an embargo on trade with Japan and by freezing its assets in July 1941. Resource-poor Japan, fearing for its supplies of oil and other raw materials, now had to choose between pulling back from China and confronting the United States in open warfare. Many Japanese resented American resistance to Japan's growing power as just another example of white man's colonialism. On December 7, 1941, Japan bombed the American Pacific fleet at Pearl Harbor, Hawaii. Attacking with more than 300 planes, the Japanese destroyed several battleships and seriously damaged three cruisers, three destroyers, and other ships. They also destroyed at least 180 airplanes. More than 2,000 people were killed and 1,000 were wounded. The attack severely crippled American seapower in the Pacific, although the navy was able to repair some of the ships. The United States was also extremely fortunate that the three aircraft carriers attached to the Pacific fleet were training elsewhere at the time. America declared war the next day. In Britain, Winston Churchill immediately understood the consequences: "Hitler's fate was sealed. Mussolini's fate was sealed. As for the Japanese, they would be ground to powder. All the rest was merely the proper application of overwhelming force" (cited in Kennedy, p. 347).

The Japanese leaders who advocated the attacks—and many had opposed them— believed they could defeat America if they struck before American industrial power and troop mobilization could move into high gear. So, on the same day as the attack on Pearl Harbor, Japan also attacked the Philippines, Hong Kong, Malaya, and other bases in Southeast Asia and the Pacific. By the middle of 1942, Japan had conquered the Philippines, the Malay peninsula and Singapore, Indonesia, parts of New Guinea, Indochina, Thailand, and Burma. In the Pacific, Japan's attacks reached almost to Australia. Designating the conquests as the "Greater East Asia Co-Prosperity Sphere," Japan attempted to build an imperial system that would provide raw materials for its industries and markets for its finished products and that would willingly adopt Japanese cultural practices as well.

The plan did not work. The colonial economies could not produce and deliver the supplies that Japan wanted, and, more crucially, Japan could not absorb the agricultural products they could produce. Market structures based on the existing integration of world trade systems were not easily reorganized. Instead of implanting its culture, Japan's occupations evoked nationalistic opposition. Its treatment of conquered peoples and prisoners-of-war was notably harsh and earned it a reputation for cruelty. The brutalizing of thousands of Korean, Chinese, and Filipina women to serve as "sex slaves" for Japanese soldiers came to international attention half a century after the war was over.

Turning the Tide

By the end of 1942 the Allied counteroffensive had begun. The alliance of Britain, the Free French (an exile government based in London under the leadership of de Gaulle), the Soviet Union, the United States, and some twenty other countries slowly evolved. Roosevelt already called them the United Nations. Roosevelt and Churchill, establishing a Combined Chiefs of Staff, decided to concentrate on the western and African fronts, leaving the main fighting against Japan for later.

In the Battle of the Atlantic, the British and American navies successfully fought German U-boats (submarines) and protected the ocean's shipping routes. American

20.1
20.2
20.3
20.4
20.5
20.6
20.7
20.8

What were the key events in the first years of World War II?

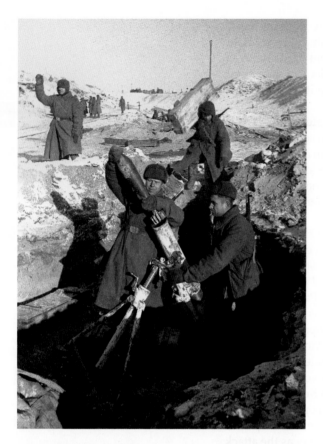

Russian troops defending Stalingrad. In seven months of siege and warfare, July 1942 to February 1943, Russians and Germans suffered a combined two million casualties—killed, captured, and wounded—in the bloodiest battle in modern history. The Soviet victory turned the war around on the eastern front. The German offensive across Russia was halted and Axis troops were pushed onto the defensive, slowly but steadily retreating before Russia's armies.

troops could now be transported to Europe in relative safety. Under General Dwight Eisenhower, Allied forces launched a huge, surprise, amphibious invasion of Algeria and Morocco in November 1942 and pushed eastward. By the spring of 1943, they were met by British forces moving westward from Egypt under General Bernard Montgomery. By May 1943, North Africa was completely recaptured and the sea lanes of the Mediterranean were again safe for shipping.

The Soviets called on their allies to open a massive, land-based western front that would relieve the German pressure on the USSR. The Americans and the British deferred such an attack until they had made more thorough preparations, leaving the Soviets to rely on their own resources, and to doubt the commitment of the British and Americans to their Soviet allies. In the winter of 1942–43, the Soviet Union held out successfully against German troops at the Battle of Stalingrad, but at the cost of the lives of up to half a million Soviet soldiers. More Soviets died in the Battle of Stalingrad, between September 1942 and February 1943, than Americans died in the entire war. The Axis powers lost fewer: about 150,000 killed and 90,000 captured. Stalingrad was the turning point in the eastern front. Once the siege was lifted, General Zhukov—already a hero for lifting the siege of Moscow in 1941—opened a Russian counterattack that began to push the Germans steadily westward. By now, also, food, supplies, and materials were reaching the Soviet troops under the American Lend–Lease program. The millions of Soviet troops deployed in these waves of assault tied down millions of Axis troops, as in Operation Bagration, the USSR's massive offensive in the summer of 1944. In that year, the Soviet Union recaptured the Ukraine, Byelorussia, the Baltic states, eastern Poland, Romania, and Bulgaria. In early 1945 they entered Germany. Their battles on the eastern front also allowed the Allies to open fronts in Western Europe with greater safety.

In contrast to the large-scale warfare of the massed armies of the major belligerents, in many countries, **partisan** underground resistance also developed on both sides—sometimes against the Allies, especially against the Russians in eastern Europe, more frequently against the Axis Powers. Because warfare had become so mechanized and so overwhelming in its size and scope, the importance of the partisans was usually more social and psychological than military. In some cases, however, they were quite significant, even militarily.

Yugoslavia presented the most extreme case. It was captured by the Axis Powers in April 1941 and partitioned among them, with Germany and Italy taking the largest shares. From one part of the country an independent state of Croatia was created and placed in the charge of the Ustasa party, run by fanatical anti-Serbs. Even the Nazis were shocked at their virulence. Ustasa murdered hundreds of thousands—estimates run as high as two million—Serbs and other "undesirables" in 1941. Two groups of Serbian resistance fighters formed, one led by a Serbian officer in the Yugoslav army, the other by a communist named Josip Broz (1892–1980), who took the name Tito. Tito himself was not a Serb—he had a Croat father and a Slovene mother—but he fought on behalf of Yugoslavia as a leader of Serbian troops. The two leaders and their groups could not cooperate, so they fought separately against the Axis armies, and sometimes they fought against each other. Tito proved the more effective, and in 1943, after Italy withdrew from the Axis, Britain and America gave him direct support. By the end of the war, Tito commanded some 250,000 men and women and had emerged as the undisputed leader of Yugoslavia.

20.1

20.2

20.3

20.4 What were the key events in the first years of World War II?

20.5

20.6

20.7

20.8

In the spring of 1943, the American and British air forces, from their bases in Britain, began bombing German cities. Unable to target military positions with accuracy, the air assaults became, in effect, attacks on civilians as well as on military objectives. In July 1943, the German city of Hamburg was mostly destroyed in firebombings, with far more civilian than military casualties. Some officers debated the morality of these attacks, but they continued and even increased. In February 1945, the Allies firebombed the German city of Dresden, leveling most of it and killing some 50,000 civilians. Since the city had no military or strategic value, the raids were widely condemned as purely punitive.

On July 10, 1943, the Allies invaded Sicily to begin their Italian campaign, moving quickly northward through the Italian "boot." On July 23, Mussolini's government fell. In September 1943, Italy surrendered and switched sides, joining the Allies. Fighting continued, however, as German armies invaded and held the capital, Rome, and northern Italy. Rome was liberated by Allied and partisan forces only in June 1944, and the entire country in April 1945. Mussolini himself was captured and executed on April 29, 1945 by communist Italian partisans as he attempted to escape to Switzerland. His body was taken to Milan, where it was suspended upside down at a gas station for public viewing.

The long-awaited land invasion of Western Europe began. **D-Day**, June 6, 1944, brought the largest amphibious military operation in history as Allied forces—American, British, and Canadian troops—invaded Normandy and began the push eastward. More than 4,000 ships transported the men; some 10,000 aircraft provided support. On the first day, 130,000 men landed by ship and parachute; within a month, one million had landed. Although there were some disagreements over strategy among the Allied generals, the American Eisenhower and the British Montgomery, and some setbacks—as in the Battle of the Bulge, in the Ardennes forest of Belgium—the new offensive steadily pushed the Germans back. Paris was liberated in August. Allied troops entered Germany in September.

Bombers on a raid. By World War II aircraft of all kinds were poised for combat. Here an SAAF/BAF Beaufighter fires three-inch RPs (rocket projectiles) during an attack on German positions in the Yugoslavian town of Zuzemberg (modern-day Zuzemberk, Slovenia) in 1945. The astronomical cost of bombs and aircraft contributed to the Allies' wartime expenditure of $1,150,000,000,000. (Imperial War Museum, London)

View the **Image**: Operation Overlord, Normandy, 1944 on **MyHistoryLab**

In the last few months of the war, however, a new technology of destruction was introduced. In September 1944, Germany launched V-2 missiles for the first time against Britain, ushering in an age of missile warfare. Because the guidance systems were not yet well developed, most of the V-2s missed their targets.

As the Allies conquered Germany in bitter combat—Russian troops invading from the east, and American, British, French, and Canadian forces from the west—Hitler retreated to his bunker in Berlin. On April 30, 1945, with the Soviet armies closing in, he killed himself. Germany surrendered a week later, on May 7, and the war in Europe finally ended. The war in the Pacific continued for another three months.

The War in the Pacific, 1942–45

Even though the war in the Pacific received less Allied attention than the war in Europe, once America committed its industrial and technological strength to fighting

KEY TERMS

partisans Partisan fighters, or partisans, are guerrilla warriors fighting in the resistance against occupying armies. The term is used especially for the resistance against the Germans and Italians in World War II, and against Franco in Spain.

D-Day Often used in the military as the day on which an important operation is to begin; more generally, signifies any date targeted for special action. Since the Normandy landing, June 6, 1944, the term "D-Day" has most often referred to that historic invasion.

20.1
20.2
20.3
20.4
20.5
20.6
20.7
20.8

Why is World
War II called a
"total war"?

Summary executions in the Pacific. Japanese soldiers were notoriously brutal in their treatment of prisoners during World War II. British servicemen captured in the Pacific theater were forced to construct the Burma Railway, and many died of starvation and disease in the process. Some were murdered in cold blood, as here, the imminent execution of three Allied fighters before open graves.

Japan, the tide turned. Despite the losses of most of their Pacific fleet, in June 1942 American naval forces won their first battle at Midway Island. Then, from bases in Australia, they moved northwestward, "island hopping," taking Guadalcanal and New Guinea, recapturing the Philippines and the Pacific island chains. During the spring of 1945 they captured Okinawa after three months of brutal fighting. As early as March 1944, the Americans had begun firebombing Japanese cities. Japan had expected Americans to become tired of the war and negotiate a peace, but instead America demanded unconditional surrender.

The firebombing intensified. On a single day—March 9, 1945—83,793 people were killed, 40,918 were injured, and 267,000 buildings were destroyed in Tokyo alone. Burning and starving—caloric intake had dropped from a daily standard of 2,200 to 1,405 by 1944—Japan fought on. Finally, on August 6, 1945, America dropped the atomic bomb on Hiroshima. With the European war won, the USSR invaded Manchuria and Korea on August 8. On August 9, America dropped a second atomic bomb, this time on Nagasaki. On August 15, 1945, Japan offered its unconditional surrender.

Japan lay in ruins. Some two million Japanese had died in the war, a fourth of its national assets were destroyed, industrial production was at barely ten percent of prewar levels, millions of homes had been destroyed, and Japan had lost all its colonial holdings. Mass starvation was prevented only by food imported by the occupation authorities.

Assessing the War

20.5   Why is World War II called a "total war"?

World War II is often called a "total war" because it involved the entire populations and economies of the nations that fought it. The distinction between military and civilian disappeared. Noncombatants were bombed and killed on both sides. It is estimated that 50 million people died, 30 million of them civilians. The heaviest fighting was in the Soviet Union, which lost more people than any other country, about

World War II in the Pacific. Japan mounted combined operations in 1941 in East Asia and Southeast Asia, and across the Pacific, opening a war front from the borders of India to Hawaii. This supremely aggressive move was meant to secure the resources and markets needed to sustain the "Greater East Asia Co-Prosperity Sphere." It proved impossible to defend: Chinese resistance, a daring US island-hopping campaign in the Pacific—culminating in the explosion of atomic bombs over Hiroshima and Nagasaki— and Soviet assaults on Manchuria defeated Japan completely.

20.1
20.2
20.3
20.4
20.5
20.6
20.7
20.8

20.5 Why is World War II called a "total war"?

20 million. (The devastation was so widespread, and so overwhelming, that some have estimated 40 million.) Japan lost two million people and Germany just over four million. Although there are no reliable statistics, well-informed estimates report from ten to 20 million dead in China. Britain and the United States each lost about 400,000. Six million Jews died in Nazi concentration camps along with hundreds of thousands of Poles, **Roma** (gypsies), homosexuals, and handicapped people.

Japan's early victories over European colonizers provided a double shock. Asians were able to defeat the most advanced European countries and the United States, at least for some time. As these victories enhanced the image of Japanese power, they undermined the image of the Europeans in Asia. After the war, when the European colonizers attempted to return—the British to Burma and Malaya, the French to Indochina, the Dutch to Indonesia—local nationalist groups rose in protest, sometimes armed, and eventually achieved independence. The Japanese victories helped to pave the way toward the end of European colonialism in the Pacific region.

War and Technology

World War II witnessed a dramatic increase in the use of technology—tanks, submarines, and aircraft—as well as in the number of troops. The sheer cost was staggering, and the forces that could spend more on armaments won the war. The combatants competed in their capacity to produce weapons, especially aircraft (see the chart below). Tanks, too, were vital weapons. In 1944, Germany produced 17,800; the Soviet Union 29,000; the United States 17,500; and Britain 5,000 (Kennedy, p. 353). No wonder that after the initial shock and advantage of their first attacks, the Axis Powers began steadily to fall behind the Allies. The technological and industrial capacity of the Axis Powers simply could not keep up.

The Mobilization of Women

The military and industrial needs of World War II put new demands on the labor force, deeply affecting women's lives. The demands of keeping factories running at full blast during the war while putting millions of soldiers onto the battlefields required an unprecedented commitment of labor. Already during World War I, millions of women began to work outside the home for pay, and the stereotypes of "men's work" and "women's work" began to erode. This experience contributed to the achievement of women's suffrage in the United States (1920) and in Western

KEY TERM

Roma (gypsies) An itinerant people, probably originally from northern India, now usually resident in south and southwest Asia, Europe, and the Americas. "Gypsy" is today usually considered a derogatory term; "Roma" is more formal and more polite.

ARMAMENTS PRODUCTION OF THE POWERS, 1940–43 (billions of 1944 dollars)

	1940	1943
Allied combatants		
US	(1.5)	37.5
USSR	(5.0)	13.9
Britain	3.5	11.1
Axis combatants		
Germany	6.0	13.8
Japan	(1.0)	4.5
Italy	0.75	—

(bracketed figures denote combatants not yet at war but already preparing war materials)　　(Source: Kennedy, p. 355)

AIRCRAFT PRODUCTION OF THE POWERS, 1939 AND 1944

	1939	1944
Allied combatants		
US	5,856	96,318
USSR	10,382	40,300
Britain	7,940	26,461
Axis combatants		
Germany	8,295	39,807
Japan	4,467	28,180
Italy	1,800	—

(Source: Kennedy, p. 354)

European nations. Although South American countries were not much involved in World War I, many of them—Brazil, Cuba, Ecuador, El Salvador, and Uruguay—also granted female suffrage between 1929 and 1939 (Rosenberg, p. 67). The majority of women had not remained in the workforce after World War I ended, but after World War II unprecedented numbers of women continued to work in industrial and unconventional jobs.

The mobilization of women was, however, culturally specific. Different combatant countries followed differing family and gender policies. The largest of the Allies—the United States, Britain, and the USSR—generally encouraged women to join the wartime workforce. "Rosie the Riveter," a woman working in an American munitions factory, became the recognized symbol of women's contribution to factory work in these Allied countries. The Axis Powers, on the other hand, did their best to keep women at home despite the needs of the war. Hitler offered women "emancipation from emancipation." He offered marriage loans to married women who left their jobs, and then cancelled 25 percent of the repayment of the loan in exchange for the birth of each child. The Nazis banned abortion and closed sexual counseling clinics. Mussolini excluded women from government office, doubled the fees of female students in secondary schools and universities, and tried to prevent rural women from relocating to cities. In China, while the communists encouraged women to join in the struggle directly, the nationalists kept them at home.

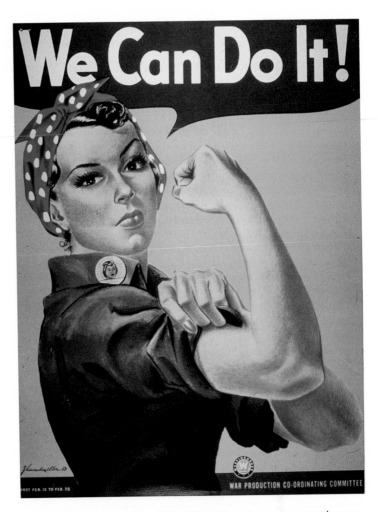

"Rosie the Riveter," symbol of World War II American women workers, on a poster from the War Production Coordinating Committee.

As the troops returned from war to their old jobs, women tended to return from factory and military service to the home, both by choice and because of social pressure. However, gender relations could not remain unaffected by wartime experience. After the war, feminism found new voices. Simone de Beauvoir published *The Second Sex* in France in 1949, advancing the argument that while sex is biological, **gender**—the behavioral traits associated with each sex—is learned. She wrote: "One is not born, but rather becomes, a woman." In the United States, Betty Friedan's *The Feminine Mystique* (1963) challenged women of the postwar generation to ask if life as homemaker in suburbia was fulfilling, to consider working outside the home, and to advocate for equal conditions in that work.

In Europe and the United States the new feminism became a powerful, if controversial, force. In other parts of the world, the concept of new roles for women outside the home and community was more disputed. Often the very fact that new concepts of gender relations came from the West, from colonial powers, influenced their reception, making them more attractive to some, more suspect to others.

The War's Horrors

Two horrors distinguished World War II from all other wars that came before. Massive warfare was not new; military leaders from Alexander the Great to Chingghis Khan to Napoleon had attempted world conquest. But the atomic bombs dropped by the United States on Japan—a weapon capable of destroying all life on earth—changed both the nature of war and peace and humanity's conception of itself. And the policy

KEY TERM

gender The social attributes of being male or female, in contrast to the biological attributes of sex. Thus, bearing children is an attribute of the female sex, but caring for children can be done by males or females. If females are expected to care for children, that is an attribute of gender, not sex, since both males and females are capable of doing it.

SOURCE

Women as Spoils of War: Japan's Comfort Women

From earliest recorded history, stories of warfare include accounts of soldiers abusing women and of victors seizing women as their reward. The story of Japan's "comfort women" during World War II carries this to an unusually cruel extreme. From 1932 to 1945, thousands of women—estimates vary from a few thousand to 200,000—were rounded up and forced into sexual slavery by the Japanese military as "comfort women" serving in "comfort stations"—that is, as captive sexual slaves in brothels administered by the Japanese armed forces. Although the situation was widely known in the military and was the subject of a Japanese novel in 1947 (later made into a movie), the facts were generally swept under the rug. The largest group of women, by nationality, was taken from Korea; these women were especially badly treated since the Japanese historically have looked down on Koreans. In 1990, the Korean Council for the Women Drafted for Military Sexual Slavery by Japan began to collect and publish the stories of many Korean women who had been taken by the Japanese and who were willing to talk publicly, 50 years after the events. In 1992 and again in 1994 Japanese prime ministers apologized publicly for the damage done to the women. In 1998 Japan began to contribute financial compensation to each of the women still living. In 2007, an organization of surviving sex slaves demanded an official apology from the Japanese government. Despite all the evidence, and the preceding apologies and payments, the Japanese prime minister denied that the abuse had taken place. A few days later, the Japanese parliament did issue an official apology.

The testimony of Kim Young-shil, interviewed in North Korea in 1992, tells not only of sexual slavery but also of racial cruelty:

There was a girl next to my cubicle. She was younger than I, and her Japanese name was Tokiko. One day an officer overheard her speaking to me and accused her of speaking Korean [which had been forbidden]. He dragged her out to a field and ordered all of us to come out there. We all obeyed. He said, "This girl spoke Korean. So she must die. You will be killed if you do too. Now, watch how she dies." He drew his sword. Horrified, I closed my eyes and turned my face away. When I opened my eyes, I saw her severed head on the ground.

On Sundays we were made especially busy. Soldiers stood in line in front of our cubicles. They got ready for their turn by undoing their puttees from their legs, rolling them up and holding them in their hands. They shamelessly exhibited their lust like animals in heat. Many of them could not control themselves and shouted, "Madaka? Hayaku! Hayaku!" ["Not finished yet? Hurry! Hurry!"] Some even came into my cubicle even before the act was finished.

I was totally exhausted. I could keep neither my sense of humiliation nor my dignity. I felt like a living corpse. When soldiers came to my room and did it to me one after another, it was done to a lifeless body. Again. And again. And again.

(Schellstede, pp. 50–51)

KEY TERM

genocide The act of murdering an entire people. Originally used for the Nazi attempt to exterminate the Jewish people, it has been used since then to indicate the attempt to murder a substantial segment of a designated population.

of the Nazis to obliterate an entire people—the Jews—from the world, without any ostensible economic or territorial goal, and to mobilize the full resources of the state against this unarmed opponent, constituted a new goal, executed by new technology. It was later given a new name, **genocide**.

The Holocaust. Anti-Semitism was not new in Europe, but the Nazi program was unprecedented. First, it reversed the trend of acceptance and civic equality for Jews advanced a century and a half earlier by the French Revolution. Second, it targeted Jews as an ethnic or racial group rather than as a religious community. This was not a policy for conversion or even for exile. Anyone with a Jewish grandparent was considered Jewish under Nazi laws and marked for death. Third, the Nazi program put the entire power of the nation into the task of wiping a people off the face of the earth, using all the technological and organizational skills at its disposal to carry out the mission, and continuing with it even when it was clear that the larger war was lost.

Hitler had made clear his belief in racial hierarchy—with Jews at the bottom. Once in power, he set out to enslave and later to exterminate these "lesser peoples." He built concentration camps where prisoners were used as slave labor before being gassed and cremated. Millions of Jews were brought to the camps by a railway network specially constructed for the purpose. Even in the closing days of the war, when Germany had clearly been defeated, Hitler ordered the trains and the crematoria to continue operations. By 1945, some six million Jews, accompanied by millions from other "inferior" races, especially Roma and Poles, and also by homosexuals and handicapped people, had been murdered. The Holocaust, as this butchery was

20.1
20.2
20.3
20.4
20.5
20.6
20.7
20.8

Why is World
War II called a
"total war"?

The liberation of Belsen. Shocked British soldiers liberating
Belsen concentration camp in northwestern Germany in 1945
found 60,000 Jews and other victims of the Holocaust dying of
starvation, typhus, and tuberculosis. Some 100,000 had already
died in the camp, half of them Soviet prisoners-of-war. Many
prisoners had been used for medical experiments. Framed by an
open grave, a Dr. Klein is shown speaking to Movietone News.
His experiments included injecting benzine into his victims to
harden their arteries. He was responsible for thousands of deaths.

📖 **Read** the **Document**: **The Holocaust: Memoirs from the
Commandant of Auschwitz (1940s)** on **MyHistoryLab**

HOW DO WE KNOW?

The Milgram Experiment and the "Final Solution"

How could people carry out acts of such inhumanity as the
genocide against the Jews? Perhaps the leaders of Nazi Germany
were insane—unrepresentative of normal people. But what about
the ordinary Germans who said they were simply following orders?
To what extent do people follow orders more or less blindly even
if they know they are inflicting pain? In 1961, the Yale University
psychologist Stanley Milgram set up an experiment to find out.
He solicited volunteers from in and around the university, brought
them to a laboratory and explained that the experiment would test
the effects of punishment on learning. The volunteer, who was to
play the role of "Teacher," was briefly introduced to the "Learner,"
who was to learn pairs of words read aloud by the Teacher. Each
time the Learner failed to learn properly, the experimenter would
instruct the Teacher to inflict punishment by delivering an electric
shock. The first time, the shock was 15 volts, the second 30 volts,
and each successive shock would add 15 volts up to a maximum,
on the thirtieth failed attempt, of 450 volts.

The Teacher was told that the experiment would test the efficacy
of the shocks in promoting learning. In fact, the experiment was
to test how much voltage the Teacher would apply to the Learner.
Teacher and Learner were sent to separate rooms, but the Teacher
could see the Learner through a window. As the Learner made
mistakes the experimenter told the Teacher to apply the voltage
shocks. At the tenth shock, 150 volts, the Learner—who was an
actor playing the role—demanded to be let out of the experiment.
But this was not permitted. At this point only ten of the Teachers
refused to give any more shocks. Seventy continued applying
greater voltage for each wrong answer, in accordance with the

experimenter's orders. The Learner continued moaning, shrieking,
and demanding to be let out of the experiment. By the time the
twentieth shock—300 volts—was administered, the Learner said
that he refused to give any more answers. By this point, 21 of the
volunteers stopped administering shocks despite the commands of
the experimenter. At the twenty-first level, the Learner screamed
out in sheer pain and gave no answer. Five more volunteers
stopped their participation. From the twenty-third shock onward,
the Learner remained silent, perhaps unconscious, perhaps dead.
Nevertheless, most Teachers continued applying the shocks on
command. Of the 80 volunteers, 51 continued to administer
the shocks all the way to the top level—450 volts—long after
the Learner appeared to be unconscious, if not dead. Milgram
concluded that, at least within the confines of this narrowly
bounded experiment, "normal" people follow orders in inflicting
pain, even to the point of murder, so long as they believe the
person in charge has the authority and the expertise to give the
orders.

- Do you think Milgram's experiment is a valid way to research
  the question of why apparently normal people followed orders
  in wartime and the Holocaust? Why or why not?
- If you were the Teacher in the experiment, at what level do you
  think you would quit? Do you think you are different from the
  majority here? Why or why not?
- Were you surprised at the results of Milgram's experiment? Why
  or why not?

20.1
20.2
20.3
20.4
20.5 Why is World
War II called a
"total war"?
20.6
20.7
20.8

named, made World War II into a conflict of good versus evil even in the eyes of many Germans after the war. The moral crisis and the appalling devastation of the Holocaust are impossible to comprehend fully, but the writing of survivors, such as Elie Wiesel (see below), helps us to understand them at least partially.

The A-Bomb. The atomic bomb was tested for the first time on July 16, 1945, just weeks before it was used in Japan. As the fireball rose over the testing grounds at Alamogordo, New Mexico, J. Robert Oppenheimer, the bomb's architect and director of the $2 billion Manhattan Project that produced it, quoted from the Hindu *Bhagavad Gita*: "I am become Death, the destroyer of worlds." Of the 245,000 people living in Hiroshima on August 6, 70,000 died that day and another 70,000 in the next few months, while still others suffered radiation poisoning, cancer, and genetic deformation. Three days later, a second bomb was dropped on Nagasaki, and five days after that, on August 14, Japan surrendered unconditionally. Today, despite years of continuing efforts toward arms control, there are tens of thousands of nuclear bombs and warheads on missiles, submarines, and airplanes capable of destroying human life many times over. Several nations that do not yet possess nuclear weapons are at work trying to develop or buy them. Most recently, fears have increased that terrorist individuals or groups might gain access to small nuclear devices.

Debate has raged over the wisdom and purpose of using the atomic bomb to end the war in the Pacific. Critics see the act as racist, pointing out that this weapon was not used in Europe (in fact the bomb had not yet been prepared when Germany surrendered in May 1945). Cynics suggest that its real purpose had less to do with defeating Japan than with demonstrating United States power to the Soviet Union. Those who justify the use of the bomb suggest that losses of life on both sides would have been higher had the Allies invaded Japan's home islands. The use of the bomb

A-bomb devastation. On August 6, 1945, the *Enola Gay* Super-Fortress aircraft released the first atom bomb ever used in warfare over Hiroshima, an important Japanese military base and seaport. About 70,000 people were killed instantly. By the end of 1950, a total of perhaps 200,000 had died from burns, radiation, and related illnesses. On August 9, a second nuclear bomb was dropped on Nagasaki. On August 15, Japan announced its surrender. Debates continue to rage as to the importance of the nuclear explosions in Japan's decision.

Read the **Document**: An Eyewitness to Hiroshima (1945) on **MyHistoryLab**

20.1

20.2

20.3

20.4

20.5

20.6

20.7

20.8

certainly saved Allied lives, and it may even have saved Japanese lives. The casualties in the battles for Pacific islands had been in the hundreds of thousands, and war in Japan itself might have cost a million Allied troops and even more Japanese. Finally, the advocates argue, in a war of such scope and brutality, combatants inevitably use the weapons that are available. The question of why a second bomb was dropped at Nagasaki, three days after Hiroshima, remains an additional problem.

Some of the war technology, however, had by-products of use to civilians. Nuclear energy itself could be employed under careful supervision for peaceful uses in power generation and medicine. Radar, which Britain developed to protect itself from Germany in the Battle of Britain in 1940, was valuable in commercial aviation. Drugs, such as sulfa and penicillin, entered the civilian pharmacopoeia. But the technology of warfare drew the lion's share of the scientific and technological budgets of many nations, including the largest industrial powers, the United States and the USSR, and of many developing countries as well.

The Tortured Image of Humanity

20.6 How was the image of human progress undermined by World War II?

Until World War I, the Western idea of human progress through rationalism, science, and technological invention had been widely accepted. There had been no war between the great European powers since the conflict of 1870–71 between France and Germany, and even that had been relatively small and contained (although 250,000 people died). Democracy seemed both progressive and ascendant. Life expectancy and quality seemed to be improving steadily.

The colonial dominance of Europe over ancient Asian and African civilizations had the effect of reaffirming Europeans' belief in the supremacy of their technology and political systems. Students from all over the world were coming to Europe's universities to study Western sciences and arts. If machines were "the measure of man," European civilization measured best of all, and was steadily gaining ground.

Some contrary voices, however, were already breaking through the self-congratulation. Mohandas Karamchand Gandhi (1869–1948) of India, writing in 1906 in *Hind Swaraj* or *Indian Home Rule*, caricatured and devalued Western accomplishments, especially technological accomplishments, from a different perspective:

> Formerly when people wanted to fight with one another, they measured between them their bodily strength; now it is possible to take away thousands of lives by one man working behind a gun from a hill. This is civilization. Formerly, men worked in the open air only as much as they liked. Now thousands of workmen meet together and for the sake of maintenance work in factories or mines. Their condition is worse than that of beasts. They are obliged to work, at the risk of their lives, at most dangerous occupations, for the sake of millionaires. Formerly, men were made slaves under physical compulsion. Now they are enslaved by temptations of money and of the luxuries that money can buy. … This civilization takes note neither of morality nor of religion. Its votaries calmly state that their business is not to teach religion. Some even consider it to be a superstitious growth. Others put on the cloak of religion, and prate about morality. … Civilization seeks to increase bodily comforts, and it fails miserably even in doing so. (Gandhi, p. 36)

Gandhi concluded: "This civilization is such that one has only to be patient and it will be self-destroyed."

At about the same time, in Vienna, in the heart of central Europe, Sigmund Freud (1856–1939) developed the new art of psychoanalysis. Freud ascribed humanity's most profound moving force not to rationality, the pride of European science and technology, but to sexuality. He argued that people did not understand their own deepest drives; these were hidden in the unconscious. He, too, questioned the ability of European civilization to survive:

> There are two tenets of psychoanalysis which offend the whole world and excite its resentment. … The first of these displeasing propositions of psychoanalysis is this: that mental processes are essentially unconscious … [the] next proposition consists in the assertion that … sexual impulses have contributed invaluably to the highest cultural, artistic, and social achievements of the human mind. … Society can conceive of no more powerful menace to its culture than would arise from the liberation of the sexual impulses and a return of them to their original goal. (Freud, pp. 25–27)

New, nonrepresentational, or abstract, art also seemed to question the significance of rationality. The most innovative and honored of its creators, Pablo Picasso (1881–1973), drew from African "primitive" art to create new forms of his own. Through these African-inspired innovations, he demonstrated that the West had much to learn from the naturalism and spirituality of cultures that it dominated politically, economically, and militarily.

Voices of despair multiplied. Even the end of war did not bring renewal. T.S. Eliot's "The Waste Land" (1922) depicts, among its many gloomy scenes, the impending reunion of a wife with her husband, a soldier returning from World War I. The anticipation is grating and crude, even foreboding, rather than loving and romantic. The poet warns the wife:

> Now Albert's coming back, make yourself a bit smart.
> He'll want to know what you done with the money he gave you
> To get yourself some teeth. He did, I was there.
> You have them all out, Lil, and get a nice set.
> He said, I swear, I can't bear to look at you.
> And no more can't I, I said, and think of poor Albert,
> He's been in the army four years, he wants a good time,
> And if you don't give it to him, there's others will, I said.

She replies, with some venom:

> Oh is there, she said. Something o' that, I said.
> Then I'll know who to thank, she said, and gave me a straight look.

Eliot (1888–1965), perhaps the most influential English-language poet of his generation, captures an arid, spiteful, loveless individual relationship and suggests that the same empty bitterness pervades the entire society.

With the far greater destruction of World War II and its atomic bombs and genocide, literature reflected humanity at rock bottom, estranged from itself and from the universe. In 1941, at the age of 12, Elie Wiesel had immersed himself in the practices of Hasidic, orthodox, devotional Judaism in Sighet, Hungary. In reply to the question, "Why do you pray?" he had said, "Why did I pray? A strange question. Why did I live? Why did I breathe?" But in 1944, after three years in a Nazi ghetto, he arrived in Birkenau, adjacent to Auschwitz, the hungriest of the concentration camps.

> Not far from us, flames were leaping up from a ditch, gigantic flames. They were burning something. A lorry drew up at the pit and delivered its load—little children. Babies! Yes, I saw it—saw it with my own eyes … those children in the flames. (Is it surprising that I could not sleep after that? Sleep had fled my eyes.)
>
> So this was where we were going. A little farther on was another and larger ditch for adults. I pinched my face. Was I still alive? Was I awake? I could not believe it. How could it be possible for them to burn people, children, and for the world to keep silent? No, none of this could be true. It was a nightmare. (Wiesel, p. 16)

Wiesel soon becomes aware of someone reciting the Kaddish, the Jewish prayer for the dead. "For the first time, I felt revolt rise up in me. Why should I bless His name?

The Eternal, Lord of the Universe, the All-Powerful and Terrible, was silent. What had I to thank Him for?" (Wiesel, p. 22). Long-cherished images of humanity and of the gods it had held sacred perished in the Holocaust. Yet Wiesel found the courage to make of his experiences in the death camps the stuff of literature and the basis of a new morality:

> Never shall I forget that night, the first night in camp, which has turned my life into one long night, seven times cursed and seven times sealed. Never shall I forget that smoke. Never shall I forget the little faces of the children, whose bodies I saw turned into wreaths of smoke beneath a silent blue sky.
>
> Never shall I forget those flames which consumed my faith forever.
>
> Never shall I forget that nocturnal silence which deprived me, for all eternity, of the desire to live. Never shall I forget those moments which murdered my God and my soul and turned my dreams to dust. Never shall I forget these things, even if I am condemned to live as long as God Himself. Never. (Wiesel, pp. 41–43)

To transmit this horrible personal history, to warn humanity of its own destructiveness, and to proclaim the need to preserve life became Wiesel's consuming passion. The award of the Nobel Peace Prize in 1986 recognized his mission.

From Japan, which suffered the world's first and (so far) only nuclear explosions in warfare, came similar meditations of anguish and despair, followed later by a commitment to prevent such catastrophe in the future. A student in Hiroshima Women's Junior College, Atsuko Tsujioka, remembered the atomic attack on her city in which 70,000 people were killed instantly and tens of thousands lingered to die later or to be misshapen and genetically damaged from the persistent radiation:

> It happened instantaneously. I felt as if my back had been struck with a big hammer, and then as if I had been thrown into boiling oil. … That first night ended. … My friends and the other people were no longer able to move. The skin had peeled off of their burned arms, legs and backs. I wanted to move them, but there was no place on their bodies that I could touch. … I still have the scars from that day; on my head, face, arms, legs and chest. There are reddish black scars on my arms and the face that I see in the mirror does not look as if it belongs to me. It always saddens me to think that I will never look the way I used to. I lost all hope at first. I was obsessed with the idea that I had become a freak and did not want to be seen by anyone. I cried constantly for my good friends and kind teachers who had died in such a terrible way.
>
> My way of thinking became warped and pessimistic. Even my beautiful voice, that my friends had envied, had turned weak and hoarse. When I think of the way it was then, I feel as if I were being strangled. But I have been able to take comfort in the thought that physical beauty is not everything, that a beautiful spirit can do away with physical ugliness. This has given me new hope for the future. (cited in Andrea and Overfield, pp. 417–19)

On a national scale, Japan's peace parks at both Hiroshima and Nagasaki record the nuclear destruction as well as subsequent commitments to seeking international peace. Since World War II, Japan has been committed to keeping nuclear arms out of Japan and has been intensely involved in the efforts of the UN to work for peace. Its increased wealth and potential military power in the Pacific, however, put stress on Japan's antimilitaristic patterns in the early twenty-first century.

The French existentialist author Albert Camus (1913–60), perhaps the most influential voice in European literature in his time, wrote in 1942, the year France fell to Germany: "There is but one truly serious philosophical problem, and that is suicide.

The Nobel Peace Prize winner Elie Wiesel at the World Economic Forum, 1998. Wiesel survived the Holocaust and devoted his life to alerting the world to its horrors, so that it might never happen again. Unfortunately, other "smaller" Holocausts continue to occur without effective external intervention.

20.1

20.2

20.3

20.4

20.5

20.6

How was the image of human progress undermined by World War II?

20.7

20.8

715

HOW DO WE KNOW?

The Decision to Drop the Atom Bomb

Because nuclear weapons have so thoroughly changed the nature of war, peace, and diplomacy, and even the way we think about the future of life on earth, attitudes toward them continue to change. Since Hiroshima and Nagasaki remain the only wartime deployment of the bomb, the decision to use it has received intense scrutiny. Even as the Manhattan Project was developing the bomb, at least one of the scientists central to its development counseled against using it. Leo Szilard wrote: "A nation which sets the precedent of using these newly liberated forces of nature for purposes of destruction may have to bear the responsibility of opening the door to an era of devastation on an unimaginable scale" (cited in Rhodes, *The Making of the Atomic Bomb* [1986], p. 749). President Harry S. Truman nevertheless chose to drop the bomb, not once, but twice. In the immediate aftermath of the explosions and Japan's surrender, an overwhelming proportion of Americans approved the decision. Even then, however, "pacifist groups, a number of atomic scientists, some religious leaders and organizations, and a scattering of political commentators, both liberal and conservative, condemned the atomic attacks because of their indiscriminate killing of civilians and/or the failure of the United States to give Japan an explicit warning about the bomb before Hiroshima" (Walker, p. 98).

The United States Strategic Bombing Survey, published in July 1946, concluded that "certainly prior to 31 December 1945, and in all probability prior to 1 November 1945, Japan would have surrendered even if the Atomic bombs had not been dropped" (cited in Walker, p. 100). Such a "counterfactual" judgment, however, cannot be proved or disproved.

In 1961, the former State Department official Herbert Feis, in his book *Japan Subdued*, agreed that the Japanese would have surrendered by the end of the year, even without the bomb and even without an invasion. Nevertheless, he wrote, "the impelling reason for the decision to use [the bomb] was military—to end the war victoriously as soon as possible" (cited in Walker, p. 104). He also noted that had there been an invasion, American casualties would probably have been in the thousands rather than the hundreds of thousands.

Gar Alperovitz, first in his dissertation and then in his book *Atomic Diplomacy*, concluded on the basis of diplomatic sources, and especially the diary of Henry Stimson, Secretary of War, that Truman used the bomb more to impress the Russians and improve his bargaining position with them than to subdue the Japanese. Secretary of State James Byrnes, for example, told the American ambassador to the Soviet Union, Joseph E. Davies, that American possession of the bomb "would have some effect [on the Soviets] and induce them to yield and agree to our position" (cited in Walker, p. 64). Through the 1970s and 1980s, scholarship responding to new documents tended to confirm a composite account: the bomb had been used both to end the war quickly—although the Japanese would have surrendered even without the bomb and without an invasion—and to intimidate the Russians.

J. Samuel Walker, who summarizes these debates in his book *Prompt and Utter Destruction*, adds three more arguments that have been suggested as reasons for the use of the bomb. "Justifying the costs of the Manhattan Project" was one. How could the government spend $2 billion, and employ the efforts of 600,000 workers, and then not use and demonstrate the result? As Stimson put it when he heard that the first test bomb had been successful: "I have been responsible for spending two billions of dollars on this atomic venture. Now that it is successful I shall not be sent to prison in Fort Leavenworth" (cited in Rhodes, p. 686). Also, there was a "lack of incentives not to use the bomb." As Stimson wrote, "I believe that no man, in our position and subject to our responsibilities, holding in his hands a weapon of such possibilities for accomplishing this purpose and saving those lives, could have failed to use it and afterwards looked his countrymen in the face." Finally, Truman believed he was dealing with an enemy that was "a beast." Loathing of Japan as a cruel and bitter enemy enabled Truman to use the bomb with a clear conscience. In questioning charges of racism, Walker adds that Truman might have used the bomb against Germany as well, but Germany had surrendered by the time the bomb was ready.

Questions concerning necessity and morality remain with us. They surround not only the use of the bomb in the past, but also its potential use in the future.

- In light of these assessments, would you have chosen to use the bomb on August 6, 1945? Would you have used it again on August 9? Why or why not?
- Which reasons would you consider appropriate for using the bomb? Which would you consider inappropriate?
- What have been the bases for different scholars arriving at different conclusions about the reasons for the decision to drop the bomb?

Judging whether life is or is not worth living amounts to answering the fundamental question of philosophy" (*The Myth of Sisyphus*, p. 3). Perhaps, however, rock bottom had been reached, or perhaps hope is part of human nature, even in conditions of apparent hopelessness, for Camus answered his own question with an affirmation, which he repeated in 1955 in his preface to the English translation of the work: "This book declares that even within the limits of nihilism it is possible to find the means to proceed beyond nihilism … Although *The Myth of Sisyphus* poses mortal problems, it sums itself up for me as a lucid invitation to live and to create, in the very midst of the desert" (p. 3).

Out of the Rubble: The United Nations and Resettlement

20.7 How did the United Nations come to be created and how were people resettled after the war?

Out of the rubble of the war, both victors and losers had to restructure new relationships. The creation of the United Nations organization represented one of their most hopeful responses.

The United Nations

President Roosevelt first used the term "United Nations" publicly on New Year's Day, 1942, when he issued a joint declaration of war aims with Britain, the USSR, China, and 22 other countries. Planning for a permanent organization began in 1944, culminating in the Charter of the UN, which was signed in San Francisco by 50 countries on June 26, 1945 (and by Poland, also considered a founding member, in October of that year). The main purpose of the organization was "to save succeeding generations from the scourge of war," and its major institutions were designed to respond to threats to the peace. The UN General Assembly, in which every member country was represented and had a vote, provided a forum for the discussion of the major threats to world peace. The Security Council, with five permanent members (the United States, the USSR, Britain, France, and China) and several others elected for fixed terms by the General Assembly, could dispatch peace-keeping forces. An International Court of Justice was created to decide disputes among member states. In 1946, the League of Nations was formally dissolved and the UN took on many of its missions, such as promoting public health through the World Health Organization (WHO), and educational, economic, and cultural activities through the United Nations Educational, Scientific, and Cultural Organization (UNESCO). In its early years, the peace-keeping function of the UN was stymied by the mutual hostility of the United States and the Soviet Union. As permanent members of the Security Council, each had the right to veto major policy decisions of the UN, leaving the organization mostly powerless to resolve key conflicts between these two postwar superpowers. Nevertheless, its service as a forum for discussion and its humanitarian activities ensured the place of the UN in the new, emerging international order. Its role increased in significance through the years.

SOURCE

Preamble to the Charter of the United Nations

We the peoples of the United Nations determined

- to save succeeding generations from the scourge of war ...
- to reaffirm faith in fundamental human rights, in the dignity and worth of the human person, in the equal rights of men and women and of nations large and small, and
- to establish conditions under which justice and respect for the obligations arising from treaties and other sources of international law can be maintained, and
- to promote social progress and better standards of life in larger freedom,

and for these ends

- to practice tolerance and live together in peace with one another as good neighbors, and
- to unite our strength to maintain international peace and security, and
- to ensure, by the acceptance of principles and the institution of methods, that armed force shall not be used, save in the common interest, and
- to employ international machinery for the promotion of the economic and social advancement of all peoples,

have resolved to combine our efforts to accomplish these aims.

📖 Read the **Document: Charter of the United Nations (1945)** on **MyHistoryLab**

How did the
United Nations
come to be
created and how
were people
resettled after the
war?

Postwar Resettlement

Almost 100 million soldiers served under arms during World War II, many of them in foreign lands. Some 20 million of them were killed. Millions more were captured as prisoners-of-war and required repatriation, resettlement to the areas from which they came. Millions of civilians had also been resettled or imprisoned by conquering armies that feared revolt among their newly subject populations. In addition, Germany and Japan had fought, in part, for *Lebensraum*, living space. They had dispatched millions of their civilians to new homes in newly conquered territories. These civilians, too, had to return to their original homes—or, at least, to new homes. Additional millions had been displaced by the warfare, fleeing as best they could from approaching armies. National borders were redrawn as a result of the war, especially in central and eastern Europe, and nationals of various countries often chose, or were forced, to relocate in accord with the new national geographies. Finally, millions also traveled in the hope of finding lost family members and in search of food.

During the war, for example, millions of Germans moved, as soldiers or civilians, into eastern Europe and the Baltic countries. The Soviets exiled about 500,000 of these Germans to Siberia. They also deported some two million Poles and 180,000 Balts to Siberia, and replaced them with about equal numbers of Russians and Ukrainians.

In the years immediately following the war, some 15 million Germans who had been living or fighting in eastern Europe returned to Germany. Four and a half million Poles, most of whom had fled the Nazis or the communists (or both), returned to Poland. The Soviets continued to enforce population exchanges, exiling almost two million Ukrainians and central Asian peoples to Siberia, along with some 300,000 more Balts to eastern Russia and Siberia. Here, too, they replaced them with about equal numbers of Russians and Ukrainians regarded as loyal to the new communist administration. Some 300,000 Balts fled westward to escape their new masters. Hundreds of thousands of other, smaller groups—Hungarians, Slavs, and Finns—also moved. Of the Jews who survived deportation and the Holocaust, some attempted to return to their prewar homes, especially in Poland; some of these were met by hostility and persecution. About 320,000 Jews, survivors of the Holocaust in Europe, emigrated to join the effort to create a new Jewish homeland in Palestine.

Similar migrations occurred in East Asia as some 5.5 million Japanese returned home. Most were demobilized soldiers, but hundreds of thousands were civilians who had established homes in Korea and Taiwan over several decades of Japanese colonization. In Manchuria and North Korea, Soviet troops, who had entered the war in Asia only in its last few days, seized about half a million Japanese soldiers and relocated them to labor camps in Siberia, where they were put to work on construction projects. Thousands of others were murdered by Chinese taking revenge. Of the Japanese prisoners-of-war in Siberia, about ten percent died. Almost all the rest were repatriated to Japan between 1946 and 1949.

All these movements were quite different from the return home by millions of victorious American troops. 400,000 American soldiers had been killed, but the American mainland was essentially untouched, and the troops were repatriated in more or less orderly fashion to their own homes. Moreover, in gratitude for their service and in eagerness to reintegrate the troops peacefully and productively into civilian life, the United States government instituted new programs such as the G.I. Bill of Rights, which enabled millions of veterans to go to college, an aspiration that might otherwise have been beyond their means. The booming wartime and postwar economy of the United States made these veterans' benefits financially possible, and soon the addition of millions of more highly educated veterans increased the productivity of the country's workforce still further. The postwar period in the United States—and elsewhere—brought a baby boom, a rapid rise in the birth rate as the country, and much of the world, recovered from a decade and a half of economic depression and world war.

Remembering the War

20.8 How have different memorials commemorated the events of World War II?

Remembering and representing World War II has proved contentious. The devastation was so painful that many survivors wanted simply to forget and to return to rebuilding their lives. Historian Tony Judt believes that forgetting may have been the best alternative, in the short run. If individuals and nations had turned immediately to reliving their memories and taking revenge, Judt asserts, the world might not have been able to move on. Judt writes only about Europe, but his evaluation may hold for East Asia as well. He argues that there is a time to forget, and that the time to remember comes only later. Here we consider seven different memorials of the war, the messages they were designed to convey, and some of the disputes over those messages.

The Nuremberg Trials and the Tokyo Tribunal

The stated goal of the trials at Nuremberg, Germany, in 1945 and 1946 (convened by the United States, the Soviet Union, Great Britain, and France) and the Tokyo Tribunal of 1946–48 (convened by American General Douglas MacArthur, as head of the American occupational government of Japan) was to demonstrate that crimes against humanity would be punished under international law in trials administered through public, systematic procedures. Individual leaders, not just nations, could be found guilty of war crimes. The trials provided an opportunity for the world to grasp more fully the reality of the war's atrocities. They, nevertheless, had significant differences. Nuremberg was convened by four countries, with equal voice: the US, the USSR, Great Britain, and France. Tokyo had much wider participation, with judges selected from eleven different countries, including China, India, and the Philippines, but the tribunal itself was convened by General MacArthur. MacArthur chose all the judges, and the President of the United States appointed an American to head the prosecution. At Nuremberg, twenty-two of the most powerful surviving Nazi leaders were brought to trial for crimes against humanity, including planning, initiating, and waging of wars of aggression in violation of international treaties; mass murder; and genocide. Twelve were sentenced to death and seven to lengthy prison terms; three were acquitted. In Tokyo, twenty-eight were tried on similar charges; one was found mentally unfit and charges were dropped, two died during the trial, seven were executed, and sixteen were sentenced to life imprisonment. Of those sixteen, three died in prison; all the others were paroled and granted clemency by 1958.

Some critics argued that the trials simply administered "victor's justice," judging people for crimes that had not been classified as crimes at the time they were committed. Cynics further noted that the men who were brought to trial had been on the losing side. Would they have been prosecuted for these crimes had they won? Were not the British and American bombing of Dresden, for example, and the use of the atomic bomb also examples of war crimes? On the one hand, the trials generated enormous cynicism. Nevertheless, the exposure of the evil of the war crimes and the appearance of the accused on trial had a cleansing effect for the war's victims as well as for its witnesses. The trials served, at least in theory, as a warning that might curb the worst excesses of political leaders in the future.

Memorial Museums and Exhibitions

There have been many memorials to World War II in the form of museums and public displays. Here we consider five, two of them created to remember the Holocaust, two to remember Hiroshima, and one to consider the significance of the war as a whole.

20.1
20.2
20.3
20.4
20.5
20.6
20.7
20.8

How have different memorials commemorated the events of World War II?

20.1
20.2
20.3
20.4
20.5
20.6
20.7
20.8

How have different memorials commemorated the events of World War II?

The Terror House. Hungary had been allied with Germany during the first part of the war. In 1944, when Hungary considered withdrawing from the alliance, the Nazis occupied the country. After the war, it was occupied by Soviet troops until 1989. Both Germany and the Soviet Union treated Hungary as captured territory and exploited the land and its people for their own benefits. Each, in turn, used the same mansion in the center of Budapest as the headquarters for its secret police. There the occupying governments held, questioned, tortured, and murdered Hungarian prisoners. In 2002, the now independent government of Hungary opened the house as a museum of the horrors of both occupations, a "Terror House."

The Terror House implicitly compares the German Nazi occupation with that of the Russian communists. It presents the Russian occupation as longer, more pervasive, and perhaps more destructive. Critics of this perspective point out that the Nazis killed far more people. They accuse the museum of playing politics with history, since many currently active political leaders have old ties to these foreign governments. Several walls of the museum display pictures of perpetrators of political crimes, and some of those pictures are of men and women still active in contemporary Hungarian politics. The Terror House museum argues that the past is still living in Hungary and that political criminals—especially from the more recent communist era—are still at large and still powerful.

Memorials to Hiroshima. Two museums, one in Hiroshima itself, the other in Washington, DC, demonstrate the continuing battles over the representation of the atomic bombing of Hiroshima. Japan opened the Peace Memorial Park and Museum at Hiroshima in 1955 "as reminders of the past and contributions to a future of lasting peace." The museum's exhibits of photographs and artifacts from the atomic blast of August 6, 1945, display the devastation of nuclear weapons. The museum projects the message that such weapons of mass destruction should be banned. Critics of this museum note that the exhibit presents the nuclear attack in isolation. While it does not present Japan simply as an innocent victim, neither does it suggest any link between the use of the bomb and the Japanese attack on Pearl Harbor and the subsequent war in the Pacific. The display is about the deadly power of the A-bomb, not about the significance of the war in which it was used or about the Japanese role in that war.

Criticism from a reverse direction forced the reorganization of an American museum display intended to commemorate the heroism of the flight of the *Enola Gay*, the plane that dropped the atomic bomb on Hiroshima. In 1995, the Smithsonian Institution prepared a major display at the National Air and Space Museum in Washington, DC, to commemorate the fiftieth anniversary of the bombing. By this time, many critics had already declared that the bomb had not been necessary to victory over Japan, and that its use had been at best a mistake and at worst a war crime. These critics suggested that victorious nations have the same responsibility as defeated nations to consider questions of morality and proportionality in their decisions regarding war and peace. (See the How Do We Know? box, above.) The Smithsonian had intended to include some of this criticism in its exhibition, but so many groups across the United States protested the very idea of an exhibition dedicated to commemorating the *Enola Gay* that the entire exhibit was scaled back and presented in a different context. The *Enola Gay* protest emphasized the gap that persisted, after half a century, between the critical views of some American scholars and the generally more approving views of the American public as to the necessity and morality of the use of nuclear weapons.

👁 **Watch** the **Video**: **Atomic Bomb at Hiroshima** on **MyHistoryLab**

Remembering the Holocaust. Finally, disputes over Holocaust memorials indicate that different audiences understand this event in various ways. Auschwitz, the concentration camp in Poland where between one and 1.5 million people were killed, has become the name almost synonymous with the Holocaust. The camp, along with Birkenau, about two miles away, was established as a museum in 1947. The Auschwitz–Birkenau State Museum has become a major tourist attraction, with many tour buses arriving daily.

Ninety percent of those killed at Auschwitz were Jews, and the exhibits in the museum now reflect that proportion. But the earliest prisoners under the Nazis were Polish nationalist leaders, mostly Catholic, and a substantial segment of the museum is set in the context of nationalism, memorializing the suffering of the Polish people under Nazism and the bravery of the Polish armed forces, who continued to fight in guerrilla warfare from within Poland, and in other countries as well, even after their defeat by the Nazis. Another segment of the museum is devoted to the thousands of Soviet prisoners-of-war who were also held in the camp, especially in the war's early years. From the end of the war until 1989, the period of Soviet occupation of Poland, the government gave most attention to these segments of the camp. Only after 1989 were the Jewish segments expanded. Still later, other exhibits were added, dedicated to the tens of thousands of Roma who were killed in the two camps. Not only do each group of Nazi victims receive attention in different sections of the museum, but even the signage is different from section to section, depending on the expected audience: always in Polish and English; often in Hebrew; in the memorial to the Roma, in German.

Auschwitz recalls the suffering of many different groups of people, and, in many respects, it considers them separately. Critics of the museum suggest that its

Holocaust Memorial, Berlin, inaugurated 2005, architect Peter Eisenman. Constructed after years of political debate and architectural competition, a field of 2,711 concrete slabs fills about two city blocks in the center of Berlin. (The dome of the Reichstag, Germany's parliament building, is visible a few blocks away.) The slabs rise in height from a few inches at the edges to almost 16 feet in the center. Meanwhile the ground slopes irregularly downward from the edges to the middle, creating an interactive experience designed to be disorienting, representing a supposedly ordered system that has lost touch with human reason. Although its architect, the American Eisenman, purposely did not put names on the slabs so that the field would not feel like a cemetery, it does.

20.1
20.2
20.3
20.4
20.5
20.6
20.7
20.8

How have different memorials commemorated the events of World War II?

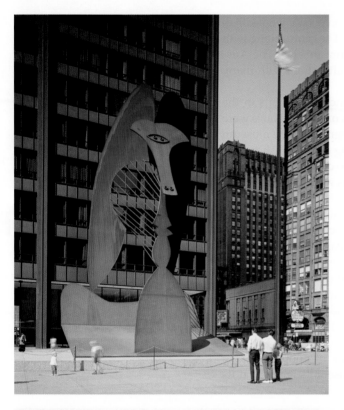

The Chicago Picasso, 1967. On the opposite page, Léopold Senghor's poem calls for a greater Africanization of the world's cultures as an antidote to the world wars of the Western powers and Japan. One of the greatest artists of that time, Pablo Picasso, had already been incorporating African forms into his work since 1907 when he attended an African art exhibition in Paris. In 1967, in response to a commission for a gigantic sculpture for a central civic space in Chicago he created an image with a face clearly reminiscent of the West African Fang masks that he had first seen and adapted 60 years earlier.

organization has encouraged different groups to engage in comparative victimhood, as each points out ways in which it has suffered more than the others.

In 2005, in the very heart of Berlin, a few minutes' walk from the Reichstag building where the parliament meets, Germany opened its Memorial to the Murdered Jews of Europe. Spread over four and a half acres, the memorial is a field of gravestones of uneven height, short and shallow at the edges of the field, higher and dug deeper into the ground toward the center. Visitors who enter the field become participants in the display, walking deeper and deeper into the sunken earth pathways, becoming more and more overwhelmed and disoriented by the unmarked gravestones rising ever further above their heads. Specific information on the Holocaust is available at an underground information point, but the field remains an open enigma for each "participant" to engage with and interpret individually. Critics of this exhibit have claimed that Germany already has enough memorials to the war and the Holocaust, and that the country needs no further reminders of this part of its history. Periodically, swastikas (the Nazi symbol) have desecrated the stones. Nevertheless, the government of Germany has plainly made a commitment to confront its past with this enormous, personal memorial in the very center of its capital city.

Two World Wars:
What Difference Do They Make?

So many lives around the world were so deeply affected by these events that their interpretation continues to be contentious today. Genocide has continued and racial hatred persists, even as Holocaust memorials cry out, "Never again." Nuclear weapons have been reduced, but tens of thousands continue to menace civilization, and more nations and terrorist groups seek them out.

The end of World War II also saw the rise of two "superpowers," the United States and the Soviet Union, which came into their own through their victories in the war and the weakened conditions of Europe's former imperial powers. They then began a new contest for power, a "Cold War," which divided the world into two spheres of influence and struggle.

Nevertheless, the two world wars also inspired enormous change for the good. New technologies that had been developed especially for wartime, such as radar, aeronautics, communications, and antibiotics, found applications in peacetime. The UN proved to be more durable, more flexible, and more effective than the League of Nations. Europe developed new institutions that transformed the continent in mostly peaceful and productive ways. (Yugoslavia later proved to be the great exception; see the chapter "Contemporary History: Evolution, Settlements, Politics, and Religion.")

Colonized countries, arguing that European powers could no longer claim to be models, demanded and received their independence. Many argued that it was time for the formerly colonized countries to help Europe find its way out of its 30 years of hatred and destruction. The Senegalese poet and statesman Léopold Sédar Senghor held out the promise that Africa, finding its freedom and voice anew, could help Europe to return to health and sanity after a generation of destruction:

The Africa of the empires is dying, see, the agony of
   a pitiful princess
And Europe too where we are joined at the navel.
Fix your unchanging eyes upon your children, who
   are given orders
Who give away their lives like the poor their last
   clothes.
Let us report present at the rebirth of the World
Like the yeast which white flour needs.
For who would teach rhythm to a dead world of
   machines and guns?
Who would give the cry of joy to wake the dead and
   the bereaved at dawn?
Say, who would give back the memory of life to the
   man whose hopes are smashed?
They call us men of coffee cotton oil
They call us men of death.
We are the men of the dance, whose feet draw new
   strength pounding the hardened earth.
(cited in Okpewho, p. 134)

After 30 years of the worst warfare and destruction
ever known, who could predict what new vistas lay
ahead?

Léopold Sédar Senghor (1906–2001), poet, professor, philosopher,
statesman. Born in Senegal, Senghor studied, and later taught, at universities
in France. He helped to found the philosophical movement of "Negritude,"
asserting the importance of ways of thinking and feeling that he considered
distinctively African. For several years, under colonialism, Senghor represented
Senegal in the French Assembly, and, after Senegal became independent in
1960, he became the first president of the new nation, 1960–80.

CHAPTER REVIEW

THE RISE OF FASCISM

20.1 How important were thugs in the rise of fascism in Italy and
Germany?

Fascism arose in Italy and Germany in the 1930s. In both countries, ordinary street thugs played an oversized role, as they formed unofficial paramilitary organizations and took to the streets to attack opponents. In Italy,
Benito Mussolini organized men from among the Great War's ex-soldiers,
dressed them in uniforms, and sent these "Black Shirts" out to the streets to
beat and kill his opponents. In Germany, Adolf Hitler's paramilitary thugs
were dressed in brown shirts, and these storm troopers similarly attacked
people in the streets. Some political leaders were assassinated. In both
countries socialism and communism, with assistance from Russian agents,
seemed to be on the rise. Militant combat broke out on the streets and
chaos threatened. Many citizens considered fascism preferable to communism and order preferable to the seeming chaos of street demonstrations.
They were relieved to see the brown shirts and the black shirts winning
the street-gang fights.

OPTIMISM REVIVES, TEMPORARILY

20.2 What efforts for world peace made people optimistic in the
1920s?

The League of Nations, a forum for negotiating international conflicts, was
founded in 1920. The following year, an international conference convened
to set limits on the competition in naval forces among nations. In 1925, the
major world powers met again to sign agreements meant to reintegrate
Germany, which had been held responsible for the war, into the European

diplomatic world. And in 1928, 65 nations signed the Pact of Paris, which
renounced war as a means to settling conflicts among them. World peace
seemed to be at hand.

THE DESCENT TOWARD WAR

20.3 How did the world end up in another global war so soon
after the first one?

The pressures of the world's Great Depression played a role in the steps
to another war. The countries that adopted dictatorship and militarization—Germany, Japan, Italy, and the Soviet Union—were thriving in the
1930s, while the rest of the world struggled with the economic and political pressures of the depression. All these nations launched military campaigns in the 1930s: the Italians invaded Ethiopia; the Germans and Italians
sent military support to the fascists in the Spanish Civil War, while the
Russians supported the democratic forces; the Japanese invaded China; the
Germans annexed Austria, with Italy's consent, and then prepared to
invade Czechoslovakia.

Hitler's focus on Czechoslovakia was an important turning point.
British and French leaders met with the Czechs and with Hitler in 1938 and
persuaded Czech leaders to agree to Germany's annexation of the Sudeten
region, where many Germans lived. They believed this victory would
appease Hitler's appetite. However, a few months later, Hitler invaded
and conquered all of Czechoslovakia. Abruptly and surprisingly, the USSR
signed a secret non-aggression agreement with the Germans, agreeing to
divide Poland between them if Poland were ever conquered. In September
1939, the Germans invaded Poland. Great Britain and France declared war
on Germany.

CHAPTER REVIEW (continued)

WORLD WAR II REACHES EUROPE

20.4 | What were the key events in the first years of World War II?

Fighting began in 1939 with Hitler's strategy of *Blitzkrieg*, lightning war, which sent troops into western Poland. (Russia invaded and took over eastern Poland, following the two countries' secret agreement.) Germany then invaded Belgium, Luxembourg, the Netherlands, and France. Mussolini joined the German attack on France, and in 1940 Hitler turned his *Blitzkrieg* against Great Britain, bombing the country from the skies. Britain withstood the attacks, and Germany eventually gave up the attempt to invade the island nation. When Germany invaded the USSR in June 1941, breaking its nonaggression pack with the Soviets, it brought upon itself all the power and force of the Soviet army. The Germans were soon bogged down in an exhausting land war in the east. Britain meanwhile continued to hold off the Germans, and when the United States entered the war, following the Japanese attack on its Navy at Pearl Harbor in December 1941, the tide began to turn. Even so, by late 1942 Germany and Italy controlled most of Europe while their Japanese ally had gobbled up much of China and Southeast Asia.

ASSESSING THE WAR

20.5 | Why is World War II called a "total war"?

Unlike previous wars, World War II involved the entire populations and economies of the nations that fought the war. By the end of the war, at least 50 million people had been killed in countries all over the world. Noncombatants on both sides were bombed and died by the millions. Jews in particular were targeted for elimination, sent to Nazi concentration camps along with Roma (gypsies), homosexuals, Poles, and handicapped people. New words were coined for the horror: "genocide," the mass killing of targeted groups of people, and "Holocaust," the genocide of the Jews in World War II. Tanks and airplanes strafed the land and submarines attacked from the sea. The new and fearful technology of the atomic bomb served finally to end the war in the Pacific, even as it raised questions about the wisdom and purpose of using such an instrument. On the home front, with tens of millions of soldiers off fighting, civilians were mobilized, especially women, to take over their jobs in factories and elsewhere, at least in the United States, Great Britain, and the USSR.

THE TORTURED IMAGE OF HUMANITY

20.6 | How was the image of human progress undermined by World War II?

With the destruction of World War II, its genocide and atomic bombs, ideas about humankind changed. Literature was filled with despair. The optimism of the period before World War I, which had resurfaced briefly between the wars, was shattered. People could hardly believe the devastation, and writers such as Elie Wiesel, a Holocaust survivor, sought to warn humanity of its own destructive history. Wiesel devoted his life to assuring that such horrors as the Nazi death camps would never happen again. In Japan, which suffered the catastrophe of two atomic bombs, peace parks were built to serve as memorials not only to the nuclear destruction, but also to affirm the nation's commitment to international peace.

OUT OF THE RUBBLE: THE UNITED NATIONS AND RESETTLEMENT

20.7 | How did the United Nations come to be created and how were people resettled after the war?

Planning for a "United Nations" (a phrase coined by FDR in 1942) began while World War II raged. The United Nations was chartered as a permanent organization near the end of the war, in June 1945, to serve as a forum for discussion among nations, and as a place to organize humanitarian assistance in a new world order. Its principal purpose was to prevent war, and its institutions were designed to respond to threats to peace. Its peace-keeping force could be dispatched around the world.

The war left millions of people in need of repatriation: soldiers, prisoners of war, civilian refugees, displaced peoples. Because many national borders had been redrawn, many refugees found that their old homes were now, legally, in new countries. Hundreds of thousands of Jewish survivors emigrated to Palestine, where they planned to create a new homeland. Revenge killings and rapes often contradicted the image of a return to a peaceful Europe. Most prisoners of war were returned to their homes, but some prisoners and some returning soldiers were sent by the Soviets to labor camps. The Chinese seized and murdered many Japanese prisoners. In the US, war veterans were offered new programs, such as the G.I. Bill, that promoted integration into civilian life and enabled them to go to college.

REMEMBERING THE WAR

20.8 | How have different memorials commemorated the events of World War II?

After the war, the Allies convened the Nuremberg Trials, which put some of the most notorious Nazis on trial for crimes against humanity. The trials allowed the world to begin to grasp the reality of the Holocaust, and they served as a warning against other possible Hitlers. Similar trials were convened in Tokyo to identify and punish war criminals. Many memorials to World War II have been built around the world, all meant to remember the war or some element of its atrocities—the death camps, the bombs at Hiroshima and Nagasaki—and to consider the war's significance, and to mobilize future resistance against war and racism.

Suggested Readings

PRINCIPAL SOURCES

Conot, Robert E. *Justice at Nuremberg* (New York: Harper and Row, 1983). A full account of the trial, and of many of the crimes and their perpetrators. The book was the basis for the absorbing film *Judgement at Nuremberg*.

Dower, John. *Embracing Defeat: Japan in the Wake of World War II* (London: Allen Lane, 1999). Superb account of Japan under American occupation, 1945–52.

Freud, Sigmund, *Civilization and Its Discontents* (New York: W.W. Norton and Co., 1961). Freud explains the battle between love and war. He is not sure which will win out.

Judt, Tony. *Postwar* (New York: Penguin Press, 2005). Marvelous, magisterial account of postwar Europe. Elegantly written.

Kennedy, Paul. *The Rise and Fall of the Great Powers* (New York: Vintage Books, 1989). Very good on the human and economic costs of war.

Straus, Ulrich. *The Anguish of Surrender: Japanese POWs of World War II* (Seattle, WA, and London: University of Washington Press, 2003). Rich exploration of the psyche, and impact, of Japanese soldiers who chose to surrender and were imprisoned.

Weinberg, Gerhard. *A World at Arms: A Global History of World War II* (Cambridge: Cambridge University Press, 1994). Massive one-volume history of the war, in all theaters, examining the use of both force and diplomacy.

Wiesel, Elie. *Night* (New York: Bantam Books, 1962). Terrifying personal account of Wiesel's youth in the concentration camps.

Yoshimi, Yoshiaki (trans. Suzanne O'Brien). *Sexual Slavery in the Japanese Military During World War II* (New York: Columbia University Press, 1995). A comprehensive account of the sexual slavery of the "comfort women" and their demands for reparations from the Japanese government.

ADDITIONAL SOURCES

Alperovitz, Gar. *The Decision to Use the Atomic Bomb* (New York: Knopf, 1996). Examines the entire range of debate by both decision-makers and later commentators.

Andrea, Alfred, and James H. Overfield, eds. *The Human Record*, vol. 2 (Boston, MA: Houghton Mifflin, 3rd ed., 1998). Excellent collection of primary documents.

Bosworth, R.J.B. *Mussolini* (London: Oxford University Press, 2002). Biography.

Browning, Christopher. *Ordinary Men: Reserve Police Battalion 101 and the Final Solution in Poland* (New York: HarperCollins, 1992). An excellent analysis of ordinary people involved in the Holocaust.

——. *The Path to Genocide: Essays on Launching the Final Solution* (Cambridge: Cambridge University Press, 1992). An analysis of Nazi policy on Jews.

Bulliet, Richard W., ed. *The Columbia History of the 20th Century* (New York: Columbia University Press, 1998). Excellent selection of academic articles.

Camus, Albert. *The Myth of Sisyphus, and Other Essays*. Trans. from the French by Justin O'Brien. (New York: Knopf, 1955). An early classic in the new wave of philosophical literature of "existentialism."

Cook, Haruko Taya, and Theodore F. Cook. *Japan at War: An Oral History* (New York: New Press, 1992). Japanese civilians and soldiers recall their experiences.

De Grazia, Victoria. *How Fascism Ruled Women: Italy, 1922–1945* (Berkeley, CA: University of California Press, 1992). An examination of the ideas of womanhood under fascism in Italy.

Eliot, T.S. *Collected Poems 1909–1962* (New York: Harcourt Brace Jovanovich, 1936). Includes "The Waste Land." Eliot's poetry, with its startling imagery, irony, and often despairing search for meaning in the midst of a barren culture, defined modernism in literature.

Friedan, Betty. *Feminine Mystique* (New York: Dell, 1963). Argued that American women were living unfulfilling lives at home after their children were grown, and that they should be participating more in public life.

Gandhi, Mohandas Karamchand. *Hind Swaraj* or *Indian Home Rule* (Ahmedabad: Navajivan Press, 1938). The Mahatma's classic denunciation of the materialism of Western civilization.

Hilberg, Raul. *The Destruction of the European Jews*, 3 vols. (New York: Holmes and Meier, 1984). Comprehensive analysis of the Holocaust.

Hitchcock, William. *The Bitter Road to Freedom: A New History of the Liberation of Europe* (New York: Free Press, 2008). Remarkable account of the tribulations of returning to normality after the war.

Keegan, John, ed. *The Times Atlas of the Second World War* (New York: Harper, 1989). Indispensable for following and understanding the unfolding of the war.

Kershaw, Ian. *The "Hitler Myth": Image and Reality in the Third Reich* (London: Oxford University Press, 2001). A collection of essays attempting to explain why people followed Hitler.

Keynes, John Maynard. *The Economic Consequences of the Peace* (New York: Harcourt Brace Jovanovich, 1920). A highly influential critique of the terms of the peace agreements as setting the stage for renewed warfare.

Mailer, Norman. *The Naked and the Dead* (New York: Rinehart, 1948). "Generally regarded as the finest American literary portrayal of the Pacific War"—Dower, *op. cit.*, p. 503.

Morris-Suzuki, Tessa. *The Technological Transformation of Japan* (Cambridge: Cambridge University Press, 1994). The history of technological change in modern Japan, through invention and borrowing.

Okpewho, Isidore, ed. *The Heritage of African Poetry* (Harlow, Essex: Longman Group, 1985). Remarkable anthology with interesting discussions.

Overy, Richard. *Why the Allies Won* (New York: W.W. Norton, 1995). An assessment of the economic, strategic, political, and moral balance between the combatants.

Peukert, Detlev J.K. *The Weimar Republic* (New York: Hill and Wang, 1993). Excellent social and political history of the Weimar Republic and the conditions that led to the rise of Hitler.

Rosenberg, Rosalind. "The 'Woman' Question," in Bulliet, *op. cit.*, pp. 53–80. Superb, brief survey of the major issues.

Schellstede, Sangmie Choi, ed. *Comfort Women Speak: Testimony by Sex Slaves of the Japanese Military* (New York: Holmes and Meier, 2000). The "comfort women" tell their own stories. Includes photographs of the women today, and a United Nations report on the situation.

Slater, Laura. *Opening Skinner's Box: Great Psychological Experiments of the Twentieth Century* (New York: W.W. Norton, 2004). One of the experiments presented and discussed is Stanley Milgram's.

Speer, Albert. *Inside the Third Reich: Memoirs* (New York: Macmillan, 1970). An insider's account of Nazi administration and wartime operations.

Spiegelman, Art. *Maus: A Survivor's Tale*, 2 vols. (New York: Pantheon Books, 1996). Astonishing. A son's deeply affecting account of his father's Holocaust experience told in comic-book (graphic-novel) form with mice for Jews and cats for Nazis. Pulitzer Prize-winning literary breakthrough.

Takeyama, Michio (trans. Howard Hibbett). *Harp of Burma* (Rutland, VT: C.E. Tuttle, 1966). Novel interpreting the Pacific War through the eyes of a Japanese soldier who becomes a Buddhist priest.

Walker, J. Samuel. *Prompt and Utter Destruction: Truman and the Use of Atomic Bombs against Japan* (Chapel Hill, NC: University of North Carolina Press, 1997). Discusses the pros and cons of the decision to bomb, in light of the knowledge policymakers had at the time.

Wilkie, Brian, and James Hurt, eds. *Literature of the Western World*, vol. 2 (New York: Macmillan, 1984). Excellent anthology. Gives complete works.

FILMS

BBC History of World War II (original 1984; reissued 2005; 12 CDs). Massive documentation, mostly on the war in Europe, largely through British eyes.

For Whom the Bell Tolls (1943; 2 hours 46 minutes). Ernest Hemingway's passionate love story set in the middle of the Spanish Civil War adapted for film. A classic for both the love story and the characterization of the war.

Hiroshima Mon Amour (1959; 1 hour 30 minutes). Examines memories of war and their impact on personal relations; love between a Japanese man and a French woman after World War II. An early "new wave" film in France.

Judgement at Nuremberg (1961; 3 hours) Stanley Kramer's film, with its all-star cast, explores the nature of evil, and of national conceptions of honor and duty in one of the pivotal investigations of World War II.

Night and Fog (1954; 32 minutes). Director Alain Resnais takes us into the remnants of the concentration camps to show their cruelty, sadism, and destruction beyond belief. See this film paired with *Triumph of the Will* for a devastating contrast of Nazi pomposity and the death it meted out.

The Power of Art: Picasso (2006; 1 hour). The eminent historian Simon Schama presents the painting of *Guernica* as the crowning creation of Picasso's career. Intermingles art, politics, personal life, and history.

Tokyo Trial (2006; 2 hours). Not easily available commercially, but try YouTube. English translations of Chinese and Japanese dialogue make no sense, but courtroom scenes are in English. Mostly seen through the eyes of the Chinese judge in the trial.

Triumph of the Will (1935; 2 hours). Leni Riefenstahl's homage to Hitler through her spectacular filming of the Nazi party rally in Nuremberg in 1934. One of the greatest propaganda films ever. Horrifying.

21 Cold War, New Nations, and Revolt Against Authority

Remaking the World After the War

1945–1991

Two issues dominated the years following World War II. The first was the Cold War. Two powers, the Soviet Union and the United States, previously at the periphery of Europe's dominance, now surpassed Europe in military and political influence. In competition to establish their own new power in the postwar world, they challenged each other politically and threatened each other militarily, insisting that the peoples of the world choose sides between them. Few political, economic, or cultural events of this period escaped their intense competition.

Zhou Enlai, Bandung Conference, Indonesia, 1955. Zhou Enlai (center) arrives at the Bandung Conference along with many third-world leaders to articulate a postcolonial world order.

LEARNING OBJECTIVES

21.1	21.2	21.3	21.4	21.5	21.6
Explain the reasons for the Cold War between the USSR and the US.	Explain why "1968" has become shorthand for a time of cultural restlessness.	Understand why decolonization happened so quickly, once the initial process had begun.	Explain why many "third-world" nations objected to the pressures imposed on them by the Cold War.	Outline the steps by which the Soviet Union dissolved.	Evaluate the major postwar strategies for achieving peace through negotiation and institution-building.

Listen on MyHistoryLab

The USSR and the US competed to develop the most advanced forms of technology, especially for warfare: nuclear weapons, intercontinental ballistic missiles to deliver them, and the control of space, symbolized in the race to put satellites into orbit and to send astronauts to the moon. One of the great surprises of this period in history, however, is that throughout 45 years of armed-to-the-teeth confrontation, the two nations never attacked each other directly. They did, however, recruit other nations as surrogates and battlegrounds for their competition. Many of these arenas of their conflict were newly independent states.

The achievement of independence by more than 50 European colonies was the second great event of the years following the war. Each of these newly independent nations sought its own road to development. Many sought to cooperate with like-minded, friendly nations for their mutual support, and almost all were solicited by the two new **superpowers** to take sides in their global competition.

The two global transformations intersected. The US and the USSR courted, and infiltrated, the new nations, seeking to win them over as allies politically and to exploit their resources economically. The superpowers sought to sell some of their weaponry to the new nations as a means both of gaining allies and of earning profits. On the other hand, many of the new nations developed their own low-tech military strategies. On battlefields around the world each of the superpowers found itself pinned down by guerrilla warriors seeking to establish their own independence of foreign control. The USSR confronted revolts among its central European satellite states, while the US intervened repeatedly in Latin America.

In the most dramatic examples, guerrilla warfare bled America in Vietnam and the USSR in Afghanistan, ultimately helping to bring down the governments of all four countries. Later military strategists would refer to battles between these unequal, contrasting military technologies and strategies—guerrilla warriors versus conventional national armies—as **asymmetrical warfare**, with outcomes not always easy to predict. Even at the time, however, China laughed at the irony of the superpowers' dilemma, especially America's. American conventional military forces were not strategically powerful enough to defeat the guerrillas, and nuclear weapons were too powerful to use. China mocked the United States as a "**paper tiger**."

While the Cold War and the emergence of new nations took center stage in the first decades after the war, three other developments also merit consideration. First, some nations sought to minimize the risk of the destructive potential of future war. France and Germany, in particular, enemies in both world wars and, earlier, in the Franco-Prussian War of 1870–71, initiated programs of mutual economic cooperation designed to create a different, peaceful future. Japan renounced entirely the use of nuclear weapons. Both Japan and the countries of Europe resolved to seek peaceful conflict resolution rather than further warfare. They rejected the belligerence of the Cold War. Both, however, relied heavily on the American military as a shield to defend them against potential enemies, especially against the Soviet Union in Europe and China in Asia.

Second, nongovernmental organizations (NGOs)—which Americans have more commonly called volunteer organizations—carried out many significant tasks of economic development, ecological sustainability, human rights, and social welfare, often supplementing government programs. NGOs offered private citizens the opportunity to work on vital problems of development that the government did not, or could not, address adequately.

Finally, apart from the political and economic concerns of the postwar period, cultural patterns, too, were shifting, sometimes dramatically. The United States and Europe, in particular, were shocked by the vigor of youth revolts aimed at ending the war in Vietnam, restructuring educational institutions, and opening new freedoms in sexuality, dress, speech, and self-expression. The year 1968 was a time of cultural confrontation; it encouraged revolts against authority everywhere, including the factory workplace and the university campus.

KEY TERMS

superpower The term ascribed to both the US and the USSR in recognition of their power, especially their military power, far greater than that of any other country in the world at the time.

asymmetrical warfare Warfare between groups armed and equipped very differently, and often using different strategies, usually between lightly armed guerrilla warriors and conventionally equipped armies of powerful states. Terror tactics and disinformation are also considered tactics of asymmetrical warfare. The term came into wide use in the 2000s, but it is also applicable to earlier guerrilla warfare.

paper tiger The mocking comment of the Chinese toward the Americans, who had vast arrays of conventional and nuclear weaponry, but could not cope with simply armed warriors, often guerrillas, fighting for their homelands in Korea, Vietnam, and elsewhere.

The Cold War: US vs. USSR

21.1   What were the reasons for the Cold War between the USSR and the US?

From the middle of the nineteenth century, many leaders of the United States believed in its "manifest destiny." They believed that America had a message to spread about proper governance in the world, first by setting an example, and second by actively taking its message to other nations. President Woodrow Wilson had done the latter with his Fourteen Points during World War I, as had Franklin Roosevelt in his Four Freedoms address and the Atlantic Charter (with Winston Churchill) during World War II. These extroverted missions often alternated with introverted periods of isolationism, but after World War II the extrovert United States prevailed. It emerged from the war victorious and by far the richest, most powerful, and most industrially productive country in the world, and it acted with a vigorous sense of optimism, but, at the same time, with a fear that its prominence was threatened by the rising power of the USSR.

Postwar Europe. Western and eastern bloc competition, following their alliance in crushing Nazi Germany, crystallized in the Cold War. The Soviet Union annexed territories in the Baltic states and eastern Poland and set up a string of puppet communist states later known as the Warsaw Pact alliance, from East Germany to Bulgaria. The Western Allies formed the countervailing NATO alliance. The stalemate continued for 45 years.

🔎 **View** the **Interactive Map**: **Shifting Borders: Eastern Europe** on **MyHistoryLab**

In the first years after the war, the United States promoted a **Pax Americana**, a worldwide peace dominated by American power and enforced by American arms and wealth. As one of its first missions, it sought to help to rebuild the economies of war-torn countries, especially in Western Europe and Japan, and to keep communist influences out. Through its $12 billion investment in the **Marshall Plan**, it encouraged the reconstruction of Western Europe along mixed capitalist–socialist and democratic patterns. It paid special attention to Germany, attempting to reestablish its brief experience with democracy and to rebuild its economy. It paid even more attention to Japan, which it occupied militarily and politically for seven years. Although they had been devastated by war, both these defeated nations retained important industrial plants that were still in operation, and their workers and entrepreneurs had not forgotten their skills. Within a decade Germany (with Western Europe in general) and Japan had recovered economically to prewar levels and were beginning to experience an economic "miracle" that would make them still more prosperous. They were once again becoming powerhouses of the global economy.

American assistance provided a margin that helped them to speed this recovery, and, ironically, to institute social welfare measures more comprehensive, and more socialistic, than those of the United States. America also extended financial and political assistance to political parties and NGOs that struggled to establish themselves against communist challenges. America's involvement in the political life of its allies was usually public, but occasionally it was more secretive, as it backed parties it considered friendly and opposed others. America was especially active in France and Italy, where communist political parties regularly attracted upward of 25 percent of the vote, and where communist labor unions were capable of leading millions of workers on strikes against capitalist enterprises and conservative government policies.

The Soviet Union had a similar sense of mission for extending its power territorially and ideologically. In 1919, just two years after the success of their own revolution, Soviet leaders had reestablished the Comintern (Communist International) to encourage communist parties and revolutionaries throughout the world. Under Joseph Stalin, the Comintern continued to dispatch agents around the world to promote communist revolution. To some nations that had been devastated by World War II, and to others just emerging from colonialism and seeking a model for rapid modernization, the Soviet Union's government-sponsored industrial successes were attractive. Its ability to survive ferocious punishment in World War II, fight back, and triumph, despite untold material damage and the deaths of some 20 million people, earned its people and its government great respect in the world community. In the postwar period, the USSR appealed to those who looked with suspicion on America's overwhelming power and sought to restore some balance in international affairs. Some nations also preferred a socialist, or even communist, alternative to American capitalism. In addition, as a country with no overseas colonies, the USSR could easily position itself as a leader in the fight against colonialism.

The Cold War in Europe

Postwar agreements among the Allies provided some hope that the United States and the USSR would find a way to accommodate their different philosophies and compromise on their goals. Unfortunately, this did not happen. Agreements signed in the closing months of the war by Roosevelt, Churchill, and Stalin at Yalta, on the Black Sea, and at Potsdam, Germany (with President Harry Truman replacing Roosevelt, who had died just weeks before), gave the USSR latitude to expand its **sphere of influence** in Eastern Europe. Between 1945 and 1948 the USSR imposed communist governments, controlled from Moscow and backed by Soviet troops, on central and Eastern European nations, and then organized the economies of these satellite nations to serve its own needs. Despite its anti-imperial rhetoric, the Soviet Union had kept

What were the reasons for the Cold War between the USSR and the US?

21.1
21.2
21.3
21.4
21.5
21.6

KEY TERMS

Pax Americana Literally, "American peace," a Latin phrase derived by analogy from *Pax Romana* (the peace enforced within the boundaries of the Roman Empire by Roman rule) to designate the relative tranquility established within the American sphere of influence immediately after World War II.

Marshall Plan An American program of economic assistance for rebuilding non-communist Europe after World War II, proposed by US Secretary of State George Marshall.

sphere of influence The geopolitical region in which one external power is considered dominant and other powers keep their hands off.

21.1 What were the reasons for the Cold War between the USSR and the US?

21.2

21.3

21.4

21.5

21.6

The Yalta Conference, 1945. At Yalta in the Crimea in February 1945 Stalin (right), Roosevelt (center), and Churchill (left) planned their postwar positions in Europe. Misunderstandings between them later led to Cold War tensions and recriminations.

control of the tsar's land-based empire and was now adding to it. Observing the Soviet takeover of central Europe in 1946, Winston Churchill observed ruefully, "An **iron curtain** has descended across the continent."

📖 Read the **Document: Winston Churchill, from the Iron Curtain Speech (1946)** on **MyHistoryLab**

Moreover, in 1949, the communist revolution, which had been gestating in China through three decades of civil war, finally won control of that huge country. Americans, who had supported the opposition armies in that civil war, could hardly believe the news. America had "lost" China! The opposition was forced off the mainland to the island of Taiwan. The largest country in the world in terms of population had now joined the largest country in the world in terms of land area in a communist alliance against America in the Cold War.

Meanwhile, the Russians viewed America's actions around the world with equal apprehension. They judged American economic assistance to Western Europe and Japan as an attempt to form alliances against the USSR. American support to the Turkish government helped to keep Soviet troops out of that country. British and American assistance to the Greek government helped it to win its struggle against a communist guerrilla insurgency. In announcing its assistance to the Greek government, the US issued the Truman Doctrine (1947), offering "to help free people to maintain their institutions and their integrity against aggressive movements that seek to impose upon them totalitarian regimes." America was implementing a policy of **containment**, a policy of keeping the USSR bound within acceptable limits, short of confronting it in direct warfare. The Soviet Union correctly read all these American actions as attempts to restrict and encircle it. But would the United States stop short of war? This the Soviet Union could not predict. It did know, however, that at the end of World War II, America alone had the atomic bomb, and had used it. From the Soviet perspective, this made the United States the most dangerous nation on earth.

Each side feared and provoked the other. The first open test of will came in Germany. Following World War II, the Allies had divided Germany into four zones for administrative purposes. The United States, Britain, and France held three zones in the western sector, and the USSR held the east. The former capital, Berlin, was divided into the same four sectors, but geographically the city lay deep inside the

KEY TERMS

iron curtain Term introduced by Winston Churchill to describe the division of Europe by the Soviet Union spreading its areas of control in central and Eastern Europe and sealing it off from Western Europe.

containment The postwar policy of the United States, advocated by the diplomat George Kennan, to encircle and contain the Soviet Union within limits, through militant confrontation that would stop short of war. Containment advocated a balance of force.

Russian-held eastern sector, about 100 miles from the western sectors. Despite this distance, in 1948 the Western powers decided to integrate the economy of West Berlin more fully into the economy of West Germany. The Russians responded by blockading the access routes to West Berlin, challenging the ability of the Western powers to maintain control over their sectors of the city. The Americans and the British chose a creative response, short of war, by airlifting supplies and personnel into West Berlin round the clock until, almost a year and a half later, in September 1949, Russia gave up on its blockade. Nevertheless, Germany remained a divided country, and Berlin a divided city.

Nuclear weapons were the most terrifying arena of competition. Just as the Soviet Union had trembled when the United States exploded the world's first atomic bomb in 1945, so America reverberated in shock when the USSR followed with a bomb of its own in 1949. The American monopoly on nuclear weapons had lasted only four years. In 1952, the US thought it was once again gaining nuclear supremacy as it exploded the world's first hydrogen bomb, a weapon many hundreds or even thousands of times more lethal even than the atomic bomb, but, to America's consternation, the USSR matched this accomplishment in the very next year. In both cases, the Russians had attained this parity through the help of American spies, further shocking the Americans.

Driven by their mutual hostility, the two superpowers created military organizations of their allies. In 1949, with its Western European allies and Canada, the United States created the North Atlantic Treaty Organization (NATO), a military alliance that included democratic countries with capitalist, socialist, and mixed economies (see map of NATO and Warsaw Pact nations, "Postwar Europe," above). In response, the USSR formally established the Warsaw Pact in 1955 among the central and Eastern European nations that were under its control. Four decades of Cold War standoff had begun.

What were the reasons for the Cold War between the USSR and the US?

21.1
21.2
21.3
21.4
21.5
21.6

Russian postcard featuring Yuri Gagarin. Gagarin's *Vostok* spacecraft completed an orbit of the Earth on 12 April 1961, making him an instant hero throughout the world as the first human to reach outer space. Caught by surprise by Russia's accomplishment, US President Kennedy declared that America would have a man on the moon by the end of the decade. The space race was on.

731

Even the heavens became a field of contest. Here the Russians took an early lead, putting the first space satellite, the *Sputnik*, into orbit in 1957, and following it with the first manned satellite in 1961. Embarrassed, President John F. Kennedy vowed that America would be the first to land a man on the moon, within a decade, and in 1969 that mission was accomplished.

The Tail Wags the Dog: Client States Draw the Superpowers to War

The superpowers boasted of their technological dominance in bombs, missiles, Sputniks, and men on the moon, and of their political dominance over their dependent or **client states**. However, these dependent nations could also manipulate the superpowers for their own purposes. Consider first the example of the Korean War in 1950. Later in this chapter, we will consider superpower proxy wars in the Americas.

The Korean War, 1950–53. The Korean peninsula had been a colony of Japan from 1910 until 1945. At the end of World War II, control over the peninsula was at first divided at the Thirty-eighth parallel between the Soviets to the north and the Americans to the south, with the prospect of unification under Korean self-government left for future negotiations. On June 25, 1950, the armed forces of communist North Korea invaded South Korea. The North Koreans attacked with the approval of their two enormous communist neighbors, the USSR and China, and with some support in the form of training and equipment as well. North Korean armies drove all the way to the southernmost part of the peninsula before American troops, sent as part of a United Nations (UN) force, drove them back to North Korea by September, and then kept pushing them farther north, toward the border with China.

In response, China entered the war, sending in hundreds of thousands of troops in wave after wave of assaults, compensating with human numbers for what they lacked in equipment. In addition to their other weapons, the Americans and their allies deployed helicopters extensively to convoy troops, to stage aerial attacks, and to ferry wounded soldiers to mobile army surgical hospitals (MASH) units (later made famous by the long-running TV series *M*A*S*H* and film of the same name, 1972).

China crossed the border into the south, capturing the South Korean capital of Seoul for a second time, until additional US and UN forces pushed them back to the Thirty-eighth parallel. Here the military and political situation ground to a stalemate that continued, with battles and negotiations, until the border of 1950 was reimposed with some modifications to reflect the military lines of the armistice. By the end of the war, in 1953, some 37,000 American soldiers had died along with about 200,000 South Korean soldiers and upwards of half a million civilians. (North Korea did not release statistics, but estimates are approximately comparable.) China announced about 150,000 military dead, although the US gave an estimate of four times that number.

The Korean War increased the American feeling of threat from communism, since China was now involved. The war strengthened the reputation of the Chinese, who had held the mighty Americans to a military standoff. Mao repeated his charge that America was a "paper tiger" despite its nuclear weapons. He believed that, after Hiroshima and Nagasaki, America could never again use the arsenal of nuclear weapons that it possessed; the Korean War seemed to confirm his view. Ironically, the war poisoned the atmosphere between China and Russia as well, because Stalin had at first offered to support China if it went to war with America, and then withdrew the pledge. In the end, the USSR did lend some support, but Stalin's equivocation left the Chinese leadership feeling betrayed.

The war brought some prosperity to Japan, which served as a manufacturing base for United States war supplies and a prime location for rest-and-relaxation for US troops. Personal contact between Americans and Japanese, especially between GIs and Japanese women, increased, and the United States began to see Japan as its new

KEY TERM

client state A state that is economically, politically, or militarily dependent on another state.

ally in the Pacific. The United States terminated its occupation of Japan in 1952, and, reversing its earlier wish that Japan remain unarmed, encouraged that country to create some armed defense forces.

The Korean War drove a wedge between the United States and many of its European allies. These allies had supported the early war effort to repulse the North Korean attack, but felt that America's continuing push across the border into North Korea was unnecessarily belligerent and costly, and had provoked the Chinese response and the long, grinding years of war that followed. In addition, several European nations, which had so recently been at war with Germany, were apprehensive about America's new strategy of rearming its former enemy as a military ally in the fight against communism.

What were the reasons for the Cold War between the USSR and the US?

21.1
21.2
21.3
21.4
21.5
21.6

The Cold War and US Domestic Politics

The international struggle between the United States and the Soviet Union appeared to some as a struggle for land and empire, to others as an almost religious war between the ideologies of democracy and capitalism on one side and communism on the other. Everyone saw it as a bitter and consuming struggle. The international struggle overflowed into domestic policies as well.

McCarthyism and the Red Scare. Americans reacted badly when Russia, in 1949, broke the US monopoly on the atomic bomb. How had this happened? Spies were suspected—and found—in the government and the scientific community in the United States. In response, US Senator Joseph McCarthy (1908–57) unleashed a hunt for spies, communists, and fellow travelers—people sympathizing with communist perspectives—in a mixture of serious investigation and paranoia that threatened freedom of expression in the United States for several years. Public proclamations at this time also emphasized the importance of participation in organized religion in American life and contrasted it to the official atheism of the Soviet Union.

The success of the communist revolution in China in 1949, the Chinese commitment of millions of troops to the war in Korea in 1950, and America's inability to gain a clear victory in that war further fed American fears of communist power. This "Red Scare" and **McCarthyism** gained renewed strength in 1953, when Russia exploded a hydrogen bomb of its own. (The US had tested one the year before, as we have seen.) Many government bureaucrats, artists, film producers, writers, and university professors suspected of present or past membership of the Communist Party of the United States, or of expressing views considered overly critical of the United States, lost their jobs and were blacklisted. Investigations of such people were carried out by a Congressional committee called the House Un-American Activities Committee. This nibbling away at freedom of speech in America was not comparable to the almost complete suppression of it in the Soviet Union, but it did reflect a fear that pervaded America and threatened some of its core values of freedom of expression and of association.

The Military–Industrial Complex. In his farewell address as president of the United States in 1961, Dwight Eisenhower, a five-star general who had served as Supreme Commander of Allied Forces in Europe during World War II, warned his nation against the dangers of the "military–industrial complex," the combination of military and industrial leaders who might find it in their mutual interests to promote warfare:

> We must never let the weight of this combination endanger our liberties or democratic processes … Only an alert and knowledgeable citizenry can compel the proper meshing of the huge industrial and military machinery of defense with our peaceful methods and goals, so that security and liberty may prosper together.

KEY TERM

McCarthyism A strategy of attacking political opponents by labeling them unpatriotic or even treasonous, named for US Senator Joseph McCarthy, who employed this strategy in his campaign against alleged communists.

DEFENSE EXPENDITURE (in billions of current dollars)						
	US	USSR	China	Germany	UK	Japan
1930	0.699	0.722	–	0.162	0.512	0.218
1938	1.13	5.43	–	7.41	1.86	1.74
1950	14.5	15.5	2.5	–	2.3	–
1970	77.8	72.0	23.7	6.1	5.8	1.3
1987	293.2	274.7	13.4	34.1	31.5	24.2
1997	273.0	64 (Russia)	36.6	33.4	35.7	40.9

21.1

21.2

21.3

21.4

21.5

21.6

What were the reasons for the Cold War between the USSR and the US?

The financial costs of the military–technological competition of the Cold War were astronomical. In 1960, in peacetime, the governments of the world spent nearly $100 billion on military expenses. But Eisenhower's warning went unheeded. The military build-up continued, as did the confrontations between the US and the Soviet Union and its allies.

The United States and the Vietnam War. The 1959 comedy *The Mouse that Roared* made its lead actor, Peter Sellers, famous. The film's premise was that a tiny, impoverished nation would declare war on the United States in order to be defeated and then receive enough foreign aid to revive its economy and even flourish. As the satire unfolds, of course, the tiny nation wins the war. Audiences took it for a joke, but the film, and even its title, became the ironic symbol of small nations successfully embroiling large nations in their own affairs for their own benefit. The United States fell into this trap in Vietnam, as did the USSR in Afghanistan, as we shall see.

After World War II, the French attempted to reestablish their colonial rule in Vietnam. They met armed opposition and guerrilla warfare led by Ho Chi Minh, the leader of the communist Vietminh, or Independence League. The Vietminh had established themselves in 1939 to fight French colonialism. Then they fought the Japanese occupation. Now they were once again fighting the French, and this time they won. In May 1954 the French signed an armistice agreement with the Vietminh that partitioned the country at the Seventeenth parallel. The Vietminh governed the north. In the south, the French transferred full sovereignty to a new anticommunist government and withdrew their troops. Civil war engulfed the south. The north, under a communist government, called repeatedly for the reunification of the country and supported communist insurgents, the Vietcong, against the government of the south. America, tragically misreading this essentially nationalist civil war as a Cold War battle, and unskilled in fighting guerrilla warfare, committed increasing numbers of its own troops to supporting the government of the south in an ultimately doomed cause. American policymakers feared a **domino effect**: they believed that if South Vietnam fell to the communist north, other countries of the region would follow one after the other.

President Kennedy first committed American advisers to South Vietnam in 1961. President Lyndon Baines Johnson expanded the American commitment to full-scale warfare. By 1968, more than half a million US troops were fighting in support of South Vietnam. More than 58,000 American armed forces died in Vietnam during the war; 200,000 South Vietnamese military, more than a million South Vietnamese civilians, and 5,000 other allied forces also died. North Vietnam claimed 1,100,000 military deaths. Estimates of civilian deaths in the north were between one and two million. The war displaced more than six and a half million people in South Vietnam alone. The American effort failed.

The Vietnam War intruded deeply and divisively into US domestic life. In the 1960s and early 1970s, the civil rights and feminist movements coalesced with the nation-wide protest against the war in Vietnam, creating a vibrant, creative, colorful, shrill,

KEY TERM

domino effect The belief, held by many American policymakers, that if one country in a region became communist, others would follow, one after the other.

What were
the reasons for
the Cold War
between the
USSR and the
US?

21.1

21.2

21.3

21.4

21.5

21.6

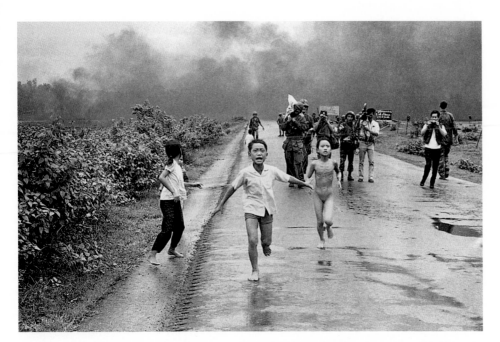

Children fleeing from Trang Bang, South Vietnam, June 8, 1972. The children were fleeing from a napalm attack ordered by the American military. This Pulitzer Prize-winning photograph, taken by photographer Nick Ut, became an instant antiwar plea and helped to turn American opinion against the war in Vietnam.

👁 **Watch** the **Video**: **Newsreel: Peace March, Thousands Oppose Vietnam War** on **MyHistoryLab**

and sometimes violent culture conflict that convulsed the country with its excesses on both sides (see section on "1968," below). Publicly and privately, within millions of families, citizens struggled with questions about the legitimacy of draft-dodging this unpopular war, the use of drugs, sexual freedom, and the appropriate limits of self expression and hair length. Johnson, buffeted by a failing war abroad and hostile antiwar protests at home, declined to run for a second term. His successor, Richard Milhous Nixon, could do no better against the Vietnamese guerrillas. America signed a peace agreement in 1973 and evacuated its last troops in ignominious defeat in 1975. Vietnam was reunified in 1976 under the rule and administration of the North Vietnamese.

The Soviet Union and the Cold War

The USSR was changing, too. Joseph Stalin, who had dominated the nation with tyrannical powers for three decades, died in 1953. At the Twentieth Party Congress in 1956, the general secretary of the Communist Party, Nikita Khrushchev (1894–1971), exposed the extent of Stalin's tyranny:

> Arbitrary behaviour by one person encouraged and permitted arbitrariness in others. Mass arrests and deportations of many thousands of people, executions without trial and without normal investigation created conditions of insecurity, fear, and even desperation. (cited in Kochan and Abraham, p. 447)

In the ensuing period of "de-Stalinization," Khrushchev released a number of political prisoners of conscience, permitted the publication of many politically banned works, and moderated Stalin's plans for heavy industrialization in favor of greater production of consumer goods. The Soviet government itself gradually began to portray Stalin as a political monster, as Khrushchev also began to open more of the record.

Alexander Solzhenitsyn: Reporting on the Gulag. In the new climate of openness, the Russian novelist Alexander Solzhenitsyn (1918–2008) was able to publish *A Day in the Life of Ivan Denisovich* (1962), a realistic novel depicting conditions in one of the Soviet prison labor camps. Khrushchev fell from power in 1964, however, and Solzhenitsyn's next two novels had to be smuggled out of the USSR. Internally, his writings circulated illegally in *samizdat* ("self-published"), privately copied formats. In 1970, he was awarded the Nobel Prize for Literature. He did not travel to Stockholm to receive the award, however, fearing that he would be denied reentry to the Russia he loved despite its political problems.

Solzhenitsyn courageously took his exposés beyond *Ivan Denisovich*. In the three volumes of his *Gulag Archipelago* (1973), he revealed the full extent of the **gulag**, the nationwide network of prison labor camps, most of them in cold, vast, remote Siberia. As many as eight million citizens were imprisoned at any given time, and some 20 million may have died in the camps through torture and harsh living conditions, which Solzhenitsyn described at length. After the publication of the *Gulag Archipelago* in 1973, Solzhenitsyn was stripped of his Soviet citizenship and exiled. For 15 years he lived in the United States, until the Soviet government restored his citizenship in 1990. He returned to Russia in 1994. When he died, in 2008, Russia's president attended his funeral.

The USSR under Khrushchev. Under Khrushchev, the Soviet Union continued to attempt to catch up to the west militarily and economically—and in some competitions even to surpass it, as it did with the *Sputnik* space satellite in 1957. Khrushchev tried, unsuccessfully, to develop more of the "virgin lands" of Kazakhstan and Siberia, but agriculture continued to lag. The USSR seemed on a par with the United States militarily and industrially, but it did not even attempt to keep up in the production of consumer goods. The two sides differed in their interpretation of the significance of consumer goods in the lives of their citizens.

KEY TERM

gulag The acronym of Glavnoye, Upravleniye Ispravitelno Trudovykh Lagerey, the "Chief Administration of Corrective Labor Camps," a department of the Soviet secret police founded in 1934 under Stalin. It ran a vast network of forced labor camps throughout the USSR to which millions of citizens accused of "crimes against the state" were sent for punishment.

Moscow power parade. At the height of the Cold War, the arms race against the West saw Russian leaders Khrushchev and Brezhnev pouring colossal sums of money into military hardware, trying to keep pace with the American military machine. This parade shows tanks moving through Red Square, Moscow, to mark the 66th anniversary of the 1917 October Revolution. Lenin keeps watch.

The "kitchen debate." In an astonishing, impromptu moment at an American exposition in Moscow in 1959, Khrushchev and American vice president Richard Nixon debated their nations' ability to provide butter as well as guns. While walking through a model of a middle-class American home, Nixon called Khrushchev's attention to some of the appliances—TV in the living room, dishwasher in the kitchen. These "make life more easy for our housewives," Nixon boasted. To which Khrushchev replied that the USSR did not have "the capitalist attitude toward women" and spoke of the "gadgets" as inconsequential.

This informal debate touched not only military and economic power, but also domestic life, gender relations, equality, and standards of living. American media regularly scoffed at the unfashionable, frumpy appearance of the wives of even the highest Soviet officials. The Soviets, on the other hand, stressed the strong representation of women in the professions, such as medicine and higher education (although not in high government positions). And while Americans praised the success of their system for the middle classes, Russian criticism pointed out America's racial and ethnic segregation, homelessness, and social inequities as the product of competitive capitalism. As Khrushchev argued in the "kitchen debate:" "In Russia all you have to do to get a house is to be born in the Soviet Union. You are entitled to housing … In America, if you don't have a dollar you have the right to choose between sleeping in a house or on the pavement."

Each side sought to win over the world's newly independent nations, as well, to its view of the appropriate life (discussed later in this chapter). But for how long could the relatively backward economy of the USSR continue to support its one-sided investment in heavy military industries, and restrict the production of consumer goods? The Soviet government saw no alternative. It felt surrounded and threatened by the United States and its allies, and saw no choice but to continue preparing its defenses—guns over butter—mirroring Stalin's defensive policies with regard to Germany in the 1930s.

In foreign affairs, Khrushchev was as aggressive as Stalin. He maintained the USSR's domination of Eastern Europe. He crushed the Hungarian uprising of 1956. He allowed the East Germans to build a wall through the heart of divided Berlin in 1961 in order to close escape routes to the West. And he stationed nuclear-tipped missiles in Cuba.

👁 **Watch** the **Video: Escaping the Berlin Wall** on **MyHistoryLab**

Confrontations in Cuba, 1961–62. The most frightening moment of the Cold War took place in 1962. In Cuba, an island nation only 90 miles off the coast of Florida, a revolution led by Fidel Castro (b. 1926) had overthrown the American-backed dictator Fulgencio Batista in 1959. Although Castro denied that he was a communist and did, for a time, try to negotiate agreements with the United States, he soon established close military and economic ties with the Soviet bloc, threatening America's hold over Latin America. In the Cold War environment of the time, the United States viewed Castro as a communist. When three multinational oil refineries refused to process oil brought to Cuba from the USSR, Castro expropriated the refineries. In response, the United States ended Cuban sugar imports to the US. In December 1961, Castro openly announced his allegiance to Marxism-Leninism. From that time, Cuba became dependent on the Soviet Union, reversing Batista's earlier dependence on the United States.

Castro then proceeded to expropriate or confiscate foreign assets, including $1 billion in North American property and investments in Cuba. He collectivized farms, thereby taking land away from peasants, and centralized control of the economy in the hands of the government. He took human development issues seriously, and devoted money and energies to health, education, and cultural activities. Education and all medical services were provided free to all citizens.

What were the reasons for the Cold War between the USSR and the US?

21.1

21.2

21.3

21.4

21.5

21.6

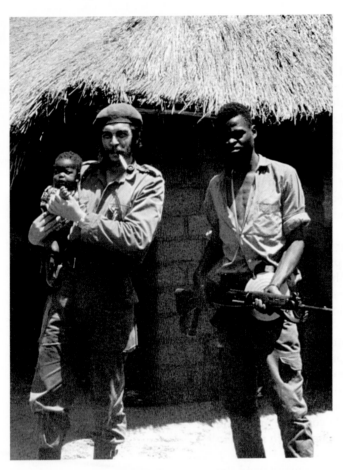

This 1965 archive photo depicts Cuban-Argentianian guerrilla fighter Ernesto "Che" Guevara (left) with an Afro-Cuban soldier in the Congo. Previously a medical student, "Che" joined Fidel Castro's guerrilla army fighting to overthrow the government of Cuba and went on to lead Cuban guerrillas in wars of national liberation in Latin America and Africa. His capture and execution in combat in Bolivia in 1967, aged 39, solidified his universal image as romantic, revolutionary theoretician, and fighter.

The living standards of most Cubans improved sharply. Nevertheless, most of the elites—hundreds of thousands of people, critical of Castro—fled, with the acquiescence of the government, which was pleased to have them gone. These exiles were received with open arms in the United States, where they formed a large community, centered in Miami, which lobbied heavily for the United States to take action against Castro. Meanwhile Castro and his close associate Ernesto "Che" Guevara dispatched advisers throughout Latin America and Africa to promote guerrilla wars against imperialism and **neocolonialism**.

Two confrontations between Cuba and the United States followed. The American government agreed to arm a group of about 1,500 Cuban exiles who planned to invade the island on the assumption that Cuba's people would join them, welcoming the opportunity to overthrow Castro. When the exiles did invade, on April 17, 1961, at the Bay of Pigs, they were met not by a popular uprising but by Cuban armed forces, who immediately defeated them.

In the next year, Cuba was the focus of the most direct confrontation of the Cold War between the United States and the Soviet Union. The Soviets had positioned nuclear missiles in Cuba. Although they denied the existence of these missiles, American reconnaissance aircraft obtained photographic evidence. President Kennedy demanded that the missiles be withdrawn, threatening nuclear war. As the world watched, terrified, in fear of imminent Armageddon, Khrushchev announced that the USSR would remove the missiles in exchange for American promises not to invade Cuba again and to remove its own missiles from Turkey.

Recent scholarship on the Cold War sees here also a confrontation between a superpower and a client state. In withdrawing the missiles, the USSR acted against the wishes of Castro, who was willing to push the nuclear challenge to the Americans even further to the brink. From this point onward, the two superpowers pulled back from such direct confrontation. The Soviet Party leadership, considering Khrushchev too reckless, removed him from power in 1964. He was followed by almost two decades of bureaucratic stagnation under Leonid Brezhnev (1906–82).

The Brezhnev Doctrine. In the spring of 1968, Czechoslovakia tried to escape Russian control and establish an independent government. Brezhnev ended the hopes of this **Prague Spring** by declaring that the Soviet Union would intervene in the affairs of its satellites to prevent counterrevolution, a policy later named the **Brezhnev Doctrine**. Soviet troops crushed the Czech revolt.

When Poland began to revolt in 1980, Brezhnev cracked down again. The Roman Catholic Church remained a powerful voice in Poland critical of communist rule, and when Karol Wojtyla, the Polish cardinal of Krakow, was elected pope in 1978, dissidents throughout Poland took heart. Millions turned out to welcome him on his visits back to Poland. Although their country, under communism, was officially atheistic, they now had a symbolic leader at the pinnacle of religious authority in Rome who could address their spiritual longings and provide a beacon of hope for independence from Soviet control. Lech Walesa (b. 1943), a shipyard worker in Gdansk, began to organize what ultimately became Solidarity, an independent trade union federation with a membership of more than ten million industrial and agricultural

What were
the reasons for
the Cold War
between the
USSR and the
US?

21.1

21.2

21.3

21.4

21.5

21.6

Pope John Paul II in the Vatican receiving Lech Walesa, the union leader of opposition to Soviet control of Poland, 1981. In electing John Paul, also a Pole, as pope the Roman Catholic Church was choosing to confront Soviet Cold War domination of Eastern and central Europe. Millions turned out to welcome the Pope on his visits to his native Polands, despite decades of anti-religious propaganda and suppression. The USSR was receiving yet again the answer to the classic, cynical question: "How many divisions does the pope have?"

workers. Solidarity demanded not only lower prices and higher wages, but also the right to strike, freedom for political prisoners, an end to censorship, and free elections. At Moscow's bidding, the Polish government jailed Walesa and other Solidarity leaders and declared martial law. The pope supported Solidarity, and the United States imposed economic sanctions on Poland, but Brezhnev remained unmoved. He found that he could implement his doctrine because, in effect, NATO and the Warsaw Pact powers had tacitly agreed to respect each other's spheres of influence. When the USSR crushed democratic revolts in East Germany (1953), Hungary (1956), Czechoslovakia (1968), and Poland (1981), NATO protested but did not intervene. In 1982, after Brezhnev died, martial law ended, and Walesa was freed. In 1983 he was awarded the Nobel Peace Prize. Demands for more freedom continued to build in Poland and throughout the Soviet Union.

The USSR in Afghanistan. In 1979, the USSR once again applied the Brezhnev Doctrine, invading Afghanistan to maintain its alliance. The invasion ultimately brought the USSR its own Vietnam.

In 1978, a pro-Soviet coup took over Afghanistan. In 1979 the USSR sent in troops and supplies to put down anticommunist, Islamic revolts against the new government, and sponsored a second coup in favor of an even more pro-Soviet government. More than 100,000 troops helped the new government to secure the cities, especially the capital, Kabul, but the Muslim rebels, with help from the United States, controlled the rural areas. (The rebels receiving aid from the US included a group of militant Muslims called the Taliban, and among them was a young Saudi guerrilla fighter named Osama bin Laden.)

The USSR lost some 15,000 soldiers in a decade of fighting in Afghanistan, which led to intense criticism of the Soviet government back home. The UN brokered a

KEY TERMS

neocolonialism The control of one country by another through economic rather than political-military domination, a method frequently employed after the end of formal, political colonization.

Prague Spring The period in the spring of 1968 when it appeared that Prague, and all of Czechoslovakia, would achieve greater freedom of expression and greater independence of control by the USSR. This hope was crushed by Soviet military intervention.

Brezhnev Doctrine In 1968, when Czechoslovakia sought independence, Leonid Brezhnev, head of the USSR government, declared that the USSR would intervene militarily to prevent any of its satellite countries from claiming independence.

SOURCE

Guerrilla Warfare

With the success of Mao's communist, agrarian revolution in China and Castro's in Cuba, and continuing peasant uprisings around the world, including Vietnam, the 1960s were especially alive with rural guerrilla warfare. Usually led by young, vigorous, brave, and single-minded revolutionaries, the guerrilla movements had a powerful mystique, and a number of successes. They demonstrated the potential of very simple conflict techniques against the most sophisticated modern weapons.

One of the most charismatic of the guerrilla warriors was Ernesto "Che" Guevara, who was born in Argentina in 1928 and was captured and killed while organizing a guerrilla movement in Bolivia in 1967. He participated in Castro's revolution in Cuba and was later appointed head of the national bank. But Guevara chose life as a full-time revolutionary, helping to establish guerrilla *focos*, revolutionary outposts, in many locations. His speeches and writings, like Mao's, were a bible to guerrilla warriors:

> Nuclei of relatively few persons choose places favorable for guerrilla warfare, sometimes with the intention of launching a counterattack or to weather a storm, and there they begin to take action. But the following must be made clear: At the

beginning, the relative weakness of the guerrilla fighters is such that they should endeavor to pay attention only to the terrain, in order to become acquainted with the surroundings, establish connections with the population, and fortify the places that eventually will be converted into bases. The guerrilla unit can survive only if it starts by basing its development on the three following conditions: constant mobility, constant vigilance, constant wariness …

We must carry the war into every corner the enemy happens to carry it—to his home, to his centers of entertainment: a total war. It is necessary to prevent him from having a moment of peace, a quiet moment outside his barracks or even inside; we must attack him wherever he may move …

Our every action is a battle cry against imperialism, and a battle hymn to the people's unity against the great enemy of mankind: the United States of America. Wherever death may surprise us, let it be welcome, provided that this, our battle cry, may have reached some receptive ear and another hand may be extended to wield our weapons and other men be ready to intone the funeral dirge with the staccato singing of the machine gun and new battle cries of war and victory.

(cited in Sigmund, pp. 370, 381)

---

peace agreement in 1988 that called for the withdrawal of all foreign troops, and the Russians went home discredited and in disarray. Afghanistan itself was thoroughly destabilized and descended into continuing civil war, with the Taliban generally taking command, but with no group firmly in control of the entire country. The military defeat in Afghanistan was the background against which Mikhail Gorbachev instituted his reforms of the Russian communist government and system (discussed later in this chapter).

1968: Revolt Against Authority

21.2 Why has "1968" become a shorthand for a time of cultural restlessness?

"1968" has become a shorthand designation for a series of revolts against authority that briefly shook established governments and institutions, and then seemed to dissipate, but ultimately transformed some of the most intimate aspects of life, as well as some of the cultural attitudes of a new generation. These revolts, cultural as well as political, penetrated deeply into the fabric of societies around the globe.

We have already encountered some of the manifestations of "1968." In Czechoslovakia in that year, cultural leaders such as Vaclav Havel (1936–2011) challenged the moral authority of the USSR, and the Soviets responded with a massive invasion of tanks and troops, and jail terms for the dissidents. In the United States, anti-Vietnam War protests brought the presidency of Lyndon Johnson to an end. Student revolts challenged the moral and academic authority of major universities. They seized college buildings and demanded changes in curriculum, in faculty–student relationships, and in student representation in university decisionmaking. College and high-school students experimented with drugs and new fashions in dress and personal style. Proclaiming "Make love, not war," young people expanded freedom of

21.1

21.2 Why has "1968" become a shorthand for a time of cultural restlessness?

21.3

21.4

21.5

21.6

expression in music, theater, and literature. The Beatles traveled to India to study meditation with Maharishi Mahesh Yogi, and young people from Canadians to Japanese followed suit. Leaders of third-world revolution, such as Mao Zedong of China and "Che" Guevara of Argentina (by birth) and Cuba (by choice), earned the reverence of irreverent youth around the world.

In Western Europe, too, 1968 brought revolt, beginning with student protests over a constricted, outdated, and unresponsive university establishment and continuing with massive strikes by millions of factory workers. The number of students in European universities multiplied in the postwar period, partly as a baby-boom generation came to university age, partly as more of them sought university education for the new age. West Germany had about 100,000 university students in 1950, and 400,000 by 1970; the number of university students in France by 1967 was about equal to the number of high-school students 12 years earlier (Judt, p. 394). University expansion did not keep up with the new demographic demands, not in buildings, nor in faculty, nor in curriculum. Students, perhaps inspired by other protests around the world, took their frustration onto the streets, especially in Paris, where in May 1968 they rioted and occupied the streets around the Sorbonne, the University of Paris. Soon factory workers joined in their own, much larger protests against their working conditions. In France, as many as ten million workers went on strike that month. In Italy the strikes came a little later, but were more sustained: 5.5 million workers on strike in the fall of 1969; 4.5 million in 1972; 6.1 million in 1973. In addition to the usual demands for shorter hours and more pay, the strikers wanted more say in the management of the factories.

Why has "1968" become a shorthand for a time of cultural restlessness?

21.1
21.2
21.3
21.4
21.5
21.6

Broadway show *Hair: The American Tribal Love-Rock Musical. Hair* opened off-Broadway in 1967, and on Broadway in 1968, at the height of the Vietnam War. It captured the American rebellious counterculture of peace movements, draft dodging, and hippie lifestyles expressed in long hair, colorful but tattered dress, indulgent sex, and illicit drugs. It celebrated the "make love not war" spirit of the time. In this scene, most of the hippies burn their draft cards. Claude, who does not, ultimately is sent to Vietnam and dies in the war. The Broadway revival in 2009 won numerous awards.

Governments in France and Italy, particularly, felt threatened—but only temporarily. Not all the citizenry was sympathetic to the revolts. Many felt that the protesters and strikers were asking for too much. Indeed, in subsequent elections, more conservative leaders won new mandates: Nixon in the United States and Charles de Gaulle in France in 1968; Giulio Andreotti in Italy in 1973. Some of the students' and workers' demands were met, others were not. Although many issues remained unresolved, the turmoil dissipated with the passage of time, the end of the Vietnam War, and, especially in Eastern Europe, with government repression.

The evaluation of "1968" has therefore been mixed. The most intense forms of cultural explosion passed relatively quickly, but from this time onward, cultural authority became more open and more flexible. Older rigidities of control, often viewed as stifling, had cracked open, and would not be put back together again.

Colonial Authority Overthrown: New Nations are Born

21.3   Why did decolonization take place so quickly, once it had begun?

The collapse of colonialism and the emergence of more than 80 new nations from colonial control to independence was in large part a legacy of the world wars and the global depression. These cataclysms, continuing for 30 years from 1914 to 1945, depleted the colonizers of manpower, financial resources, and moral authority. They no longer had the power to hold on to their colonies, especially as many of the colonies began to assert their right to independence. (Korea actually represented an early example of a country emerging from colonial control, finding itself caught between the conflicting claims of the US and the USSR, and charting a course of its own.) The colonized peoples, and many of the colonizers themselves, no longer believed in the "white man's burden" of civilizing the non-Western world. The almost unimaginable devastation of the wars exploded the myth of the superiority of the civilization of the colonizers.

Leaders of anticolonial movements had already been disillusioned once, when promises of self-government were broken at the end of World War I. By the time of World War II they no longer believed the word of their colonial masters. Famously, when the British offered to give India self-government at the end of World War II in exchange for India's participation in the war effort, Mohandas Gandhi declined, mocking the offer as "a postdated check on a failing bank." Following World War II, the demands for independence intensified throughout the colonial world. In the words of Kwame Nkrumah of Ghana,

> It is only when a people are politically free that other races can give them the respect that is due them. It is impossible to talk of equality of races in any other terms. No people without a government of their own can expect to be treated on the same level as peoples of independent sovereign states. It is far better to be free to govern or misgovern yourself than to be governed by anybody else. (Nkrumah, p. 9)

The anticolonial nationalists gained important new allies as the United States and the Soviet Union both added their voices. The Soviet Union had from its inception declared its opposition to overseas colonialism, although its holdings in central and Eastern Europe and central Asia looked like its own form of colonialism close to home. The United States, too, especially under presidents Roosevelt and Truman, spoke out for an end to colonialism. These anticolonial stands had some effect. Britain's Winston Churchill, for example, moderated his procolonial position, especially with regard to India, in deference to his wartime colleagues.

In the long run, Churchill's increased moderation was not enough. The British voted his party out of office at the end of the war. The voters felt that Churchill was the right man for the war, but not for the peace. They wanted new directions at home and abroad. They began to see British imperial holdings as economically and militarily costly in the face of renewed colonial resistance, and perhaps as morally inappropriate as well. They called for the termination of the imperial enterprise. The combination of increasingly resistant colonized nations and colonizing powers no longer able, or willing, to repress them led to the conferring of independence.

21.1

21.2

21.3

21.4

21.5

21.6

Why did decolonization take place so quickly, once it had begun?

The Middle East Breaks Free

The British- and French-mandated territories in the Middle East were the first to gain their freedom. Iraq had been granted formal independence from Britain in 1932, as a kingdom. British troops were called in, however, when coups attempted to overthrow the monarchy. In 1958, a leftist coup did succeed in overthrowing the king, breaking the ties to Britain and reorienting the country's foreign policy toward the USSR. Jordan gained independence in 1946 from Britain, as did Lebanon (1943) and Syria (1946) from France.

In 1947 the UN passed a resolution agreeing to partition the British-mandated land of Palestine between its bitterly antagonistic Jewish and Arab populations. In 1920, only about 60,000 Jews were living in Palestine, about one-tenth the number of Arabs. Jewish immigration and settlement increased between the two world wars, driven in part by the increasing persecution of Jews under the Nazis in Germany and its conquered territories. Arab resistance to this new stream of immigration from Europe led to repeated armed clashes between the two groups. To reduce tensions, the British severely restricted Jewish immigration. In the face of the Holocaust, however, the Jewish people felt a desperate need for a safe haven, and they continued to immigrate illegally.

In 1947, the UN declared its partition plan, and the British prepared to leave. Arabs and Jews armed for battle. David Ben-Gurion (1886–1973), as political head of the Jewish community, declared the establishment of the State of Israel in 1948, triggering an immediate armed attack from its neighbors. The new state survived the war, even expanding its borders slightly, but no peace treaties were signed, only agreements to cease fire. Since no new government had yet arisen to claim sovereignty over the Arab segments of Palestine, the king of Jordan asserted his country's control of that territory. The area was generally referred to as "the West Bank" of the Jordan River. The entire situation remained volatile.

Asian Nations Declare Independence

In Southeast Asia, the Japanese had driven out the European colonial powers during World War II. At the end of the war, when the Europeans tried to return, they faced nationalist opponents who wanted an end to colonialism. In Indonesia, the largest of these countries, Achmed Sukarno (1901–70), who had been imprisoned by the Dutch and freed by the Japanese, declared independence in 1945, before the Dutch tried to return. The Dutch did return the next year and, with the help of the British, attempted to reestablish their rule through force of arms. In 1949, however, after four years of fighting, and after the United States threatened to cut off Marshall Plan aid to the Dutch, they withdrew, recognizing Indonesian independence.

The Japanese had also seized Vietnam during World War II. When the French attempted to reestablish colonial rule, they met armed opposition and guerrilla warfare. As we have seen above, a sequence of military struggles—against the French; against the southerners, who tried to remain a separate nation; and against the United States—finally ended with the unification of independent Vietnam in 1976.

India, the largest of all the colonies, finally won its independence from Britain in 1947, although the subcontinent was partitioned on religious grounds into two nations, India and Pakistan. In China, the communist revolutionaries, fighting for two decades under the leadership of Mao Zedong, captured the government in

Ghana's independence. Prime minister (later president) Kwame Nkrumah waves to a celebrating crowd as the Gold Coast colony becomes the newly independent country of Ghana on March 6, 1957, the first colony in sub-Saharan Africa to gain its independence. Nkrumah formed a one-party state in 1964. His regime was ended by a military coup in 1966 during his absence on a trip to China.

1949, closed down the foreign holdings in the treaty ports, and asserted China's control over its own destiny. Because of their size and importance, these states will be discussed at greater length in the chapter "China and India."

African Struggles for Independence

Most African countries obtained independence between the end of World War II and the 1970s, in some cases after long struggles, in others quite abruptly. Although nominally independent since 1922, Egypt gained full sovereignty over the Suez Canal only in 1956. The following year, Ghana became the first black African country to win its independence, from Britain. Most of the French colonies gained their independence in 1960. Dozens more followed in the next decade.

The new nations faced many challenges. European colonizers had drawn the boundaries of their African colonies for their own convenience, without regard for tribal and ethnic differences. After independence, these differences came to the fore, often resulting in civil wars. In claiming independence, national leaders proclaimed such diverse ideologies as bourgeois democracy, workers' socialism, Islamic resurgence, and indigenous nationalism, in various combinations. These ideologies were often in conflict with one another. Most of all, the countries had not been prepared for independence by their colonial rulers, and they struggled to achieve stability. Their educational facilities, economic enterprises, and physical infrastructure were minimal. They were caught up in the Cold War struggles of the US and USSR. They were too weak to bargain effectively with the international businesses that came to exploit their natural resources. Their leaders often sold out to foreign political and economic interest groups.

📖 **Read** the **Document: Frantz Fanon, from The Wretched of the Earth** on **MyHistoryLab**

Egypt. In 1952, a group of Egyptian army officers, among them Gamal Abdel Nasser (1918–70), overthrew the government, forced King Farouk to abdicate, and asserted Egypt's independence from British control. In 1956, the British withdrew their troops from the Suez Canal and Egypt nationalized the waterway. Israel, which had been suffering guerrilla attacks across its border from Egypt, reached an agreement with Britain and France jointly to retake the canal, put an end to cross-border attacks, and change the governing policies of Egypt. At the end of October, Israeli forces attacked Egypt, and a few days later Britain and France bombed Egypt and airdropped troops to join the fighting. US President Eisenhower, blind-sided and infuriated by this neo-colonial aggression on the part of his own allies, put pressure on them to withdraw from Egypt and the canal. As a result, Nasser's reputation reached heroic heights throughout the Arab world as a man who had confronted the Western powers, divided them, and got rid of them.

In 1958, failing to reach an agreement with the United States, Nasser concluded one with the Soviet Union accepting its assistance in building the Aswan High Dam on the Nile River, one of the greatest engineering and hydroelectric projects of its time. Nasser died in 1970, and his successor, Anwar Sadat (1918–81), expelled all Soviet advisers, once again demonstrating that politics were mercurial in former colonies, and could cause problems for their former colonizers. Sadat was assassinated, but his

21.1
21.2
21.3 Why did decolonization take place so quickly, once it had begun?
21.4
21.5
21.6

successor, Hosni Mubarak (b. 1928), continued his policy of keeping the Soviet Union at a distance and maintaining collegial diplomatic relations with the United States.

Congo. The "Congo crisis" of 1960 demonstrated again the cross-cutting interests of the Cold War superpowers, international business groups, and the competitive regional and ethnic groups within a newly created nation. The Congo is rich in diamonds, copper, coffee, and crude oil. It has 70 percent of the world's known reserves of cobalt. In earlier days it was also known for its natural rubber, before the general use of the synthetic alternative. To reap the profits of these products, Leopold II, King of the Belgians, had first taken the Congo as his personal colony in 1885. Because of the extraordinary cruelty of his rule, the Belgian government itself took control in 1908, but violence and autocracy remained characteristic of Belgian rule. (See illustration of Congolese plantation workers in "Nationalism, Imperialism, and Resistance.")

Political devolution to limited self-rule began only in 1957. A small group of educated Congolese, who saw the preparations for independence in other African colonies, began to assert their own demands. Joseph Kasavubu (c. 1910–69) was an early advocate of independence, but his focus was primarily on his own ethnic group, the Bakongo people. Patrice Lumumba (1925–61) provided a more national and more militant leadership. Antigovernment rioting began in January 1959. In January 1960, Belgium convened a Round Table Conference in Brussels and, with breakneck, unrealistic speed, declared that the Congo would be independent on June 30, 1960.

Belgium had not prepared the country to function as an independent state. The nation had some 4,000 senior administrative posts to fill but only 30 university graduates. At the independence celebrations, Lumumba, the newly elected prime minister, delivered a bitter speech of deep-seated, festering rage toward the Belgians:

> We are no longer your monkeys ... We have known the back-breaking works exacted from us in exchange for salaries which permit us neither to eat enough to satisfy our hunger, nor to dress and lodge ourselves decently, nor to raise our children as the beloved creatures they are.
>
> We have known the mockery, the insults, the blows submitted to morning, noon, and night because we were nègres [blacks]. We have known that our lands were despoiled in the name of supposedly legal text which in reality recognized only the right of the stronger ... And, finally, who will forget the hangings or the firing squads where so many of our brothers perished, or the cells into which were brutally thrown those who escaped the soldiers' bullets—the soldiers whom the colonialists made the instruments of their domination? (cited in Andrea and Overfield, pp. 507–08)

Within days of independence, the army mutinied; Kasavubu, the new president, dismissed Lumumba; Lumumba, in turn, dismissed Kasavubu; Moise Tshombe (1919–69), a pro-Western political leader of Katanga, the Congo's richest region, declared that region independent under his leadership; the Belgians, eager to get their hands on the mineral wealth of Katanga, supported his move; and both Kasavubu and Lumumba appealed to the UN for assistance. Lumumba

21.1
21.2
21.3
21.4
21.5
21.6

Why did decolonization take place so quickly, once it had begun?

Patrice Lumumba, Congolese nationalist and first prime minister of the Congo after independence, 1960. Partly because of his anti-Belgian, anticolonial speech at the independence celebrations, Lumumba was viewed as a potential ally of the Soviet Union in the Cold War. As the Congo divided along tribal lines, and the wealthiest province seceded, the Congolese opposition, supported by Belgium and the United States, had Lumumba assassinated. The film made in 2000 by Haitian filmmaker Raoul Peck portrays Lumumba as a Cold War martyr whose spirit of independence and bravery live on.

21.1
21.2
21.3
21.4
21.5
21.6

wanted the UN peace-keeping force to bring Katanga, with its rich mineral wealth, back into the Congo, but Kasavubu did not. Their dispute paralyzed the UN forces. Lumumba called on the USSR for assistance, placing the Congo in the middle of the Cold War struggles. Lumumba was captured by Kasavubu, escaped, and was recaptured, turned over to the Katanga secessionists, and murdered, apparently with the complicity of the Belgian government and the assistance of the American Central Intelligence Agency (CIA). UN forces defeated Katanga and its mercenary armed forces only in 1963. By that time, however, other provinces of Congo also revolted against the central government and were subdued with the help of European mercenary troops. Most surprisingly, in the movement to restore the authority of the central government, Tshombe became prime minister.

Continuing disputes between Tshombe and President Kasavubu opened the way for a military coup led by Joseph Mobutu (1930–97; later Mobutu Sese Seko). With help from Morocco, France, and the United States, Mobutu held out against invasions and continuing attempts at secession. He ruled with dictatorial powers, changed the name of the country and its principal river from Congo to Zaire, and transferred much of the wealth earned by Congo's exports to his own overseas accounts—knowledgeable observers guessed their total value at $4–5 billion—until he was forced from office and into exile in 1997.

Congo is an especially stark example of the troubles of a weak new nation, rich in natural resources but underdeveloped economically and technologically, deeply divided among its various ethnic groups, caught up in the politics of the Cold War and the lure of the international marketplace, and ultimately captured by a kleptomaniac, tyrannical dictator for his own purposes.

Algeria. Algeria won independence in 1962 after a long and bitter struggle that threatened to plunge France itself into civil war. France had been the colonizing power in Morocco, Algeria, and Tunisia. Independence for Morocco and Tunisia came relatively easily and peacefully in 1956 through negotiations with France. Algeria won its independence, however, only through violence and civil war.

Algeria had the largest European settler community in North Africa. The French numbered one million, about 12 percent of the total population, but they held one-third of all the cultivable land. These settlers had become prosperous and comfortable. For them, Algeria was home. By the early 1950s, 80 percent of them had been born in Algeria. Constitutionally, Algeria was not a colony but an integral part of France, with official representation in the French National Assembly. In addition, through the 1930s, the Algerian elite were French-educated and saw themselves as more French than Algerian. By the 1940s, however, reformists were moving to create a more powerful Arab–Islamic nationalism, fostering social unity, a distinct national consciousness, and solidarity with other Arabs against European rule.

By the mid-1950s, an Algerian revolution against French rule was met by French repression. The two sides became increasingly entrenched. The violence ratcheted upward and spread not only throughout Algeria, but also to France. The governmental system of France, the Fourth Republic, was weak, and it fell as civil war seemed to threaten. In this time of crisis, the French government asked the hero and leader of the French resistance in World War II, Charles de Gaulle (1890–1970), to take over as president of France under a new constitution. Despite an apparent mandate to continue the war, de Gaulle surprised his supporters by choosing to negotiate a settlement that finally granted Algeria independence in 1962, but only after 300,000 Algerians and 20,000 French had been killed. Virtually all the one million European residents, many of whom had lived in the country for generations, left Algeria.

Of the Algerians, only 7,000 were in secondary school; in 1954, only 70 living, native Algerians had had a university education. The leaders of the new nation, hardened by their years of guerrilla warfare and ideologically committed to centralized

21.1

21.2

21.3

21.4

21.5

21.6

Why did
decolonization
take place so
quickly, once it
had begun?

Charles de Gaulle visits Algiers in June 1958. Algeria had been agitating for independence since 1954, and in 1956, Ben Bella, one of its leaders, was arrested. Two years later a political crisis in France, precipitated by continuing Algerian frustration and pressure for independence, put General de Gaulle, the commander of the free French forces during World War II, into office as the new president of the republic. De Gaulle maintained French rule in Algeria as long as possible, while he prepared the French people for the inevitable shift in power. Finally, in 1962, Algerians achieved independence and the French withdrew.

control, took over the tasks of development. They instituted a four-year plan in 1969, and nationalized the petroleum and natural gas resources that had been discovered in 1956. They devoted much of the new oil revenue to industrialization. They increased education's share of the national budget from 2.2 to 10 percent of the gross national product. The birth rate, however, remained very high. Rural migrants streamed toward the cities, and hundreds of thousands of Algerians emigrated to France in search of jobs.

Mozambique, Angola, and Guinea-Bissau. Portugal held on in Africa longer than any other major colonial power. Ruled by a dictator, Antonio Salazar, from 1932 to 1968, and then by Marcelo Caetano, Portugal was not about to give up control of its large African colonies of Angola and Mozambique, where many Portuguese had settled, nor even the much smaller colony of Guinea-Bissau. It governed harshly, with repressive labor policies that forced some 65,000–100,000 Mozambiquans to travel each year to work in the mines of South Africa. Each person had to keep an identification passbook at all times. The press was rigidly censored. The police were ruthless. Most of all, Portugal, alone among the European colonizers, believed that its current economy and its future greatness depended on continuing to control its African colonies. (Portugal was not even willing to cede its historic, but tiny, possession of Goa to India until, in 1961, the Indian government dispatched armed forces to seize the enclave.)

In the face of mounting international pressure against colonialism, Portugal maintained that Angola, Mozambique, and Guinea-Bissau were not colonies but "overseas provinces." In 1961, revolts broke out in all three. Supported by white-dominated South Africa, Portugal battled fiercely against anticolonial guerrilla fighters, but the warfare placed great strains on its economy and armed forces. Moreover, the three colonies were drawn into the Cold War as the USSR and Cuba dispatched troops to

21.1
21.2
21.3
21.4
21.5
21.6

Why did
decolonization
take place so
quickly, once it
had begun?

aid the guerrillas. Finally, in 1974, a military coup in Portugal captured the government and granted independence to all three colonies. Once again, resistance movements had triumphed over European colonial powers and, in the process, forced changes in the home government.

Even among the colonizers, colonialism was no longer considered an appropriate form of government, except in rare cases of geographically tiny dependencies, such as Caribbean or South Pacific islands. As new countries became independent, however, the two contesting blocs of the Cold War tried to win them over and often involved them in proxy wars, as we have seen, and will see further below. One reaction against such interference from the US and the USSR was the formation of a third bloc of nations, unaligned with either of the superpowers.

HOW DO WE KNOW?

Evaluating the Legacy of Colonialism

As the colonial era ended, historians divided sharply in assessing the impact of colonial rule. Leften Stavrianos, who spent most of his career at the University of California, San Diego, presented a Marxist, primarily economic, critical perspective. Colonial rule created "an unprecedented increase in productivity" in commerce and industry, but no corresponding increase in pay for the workers nor in distribution of wealth to the colony. In many colonies, white settlers and plantation owners seized the best lands. Rural communities were disrupted as

> private property arrangements displaced the former communal ownership and cultivation of land … Land now became a mere possession, food a mere commodity of exchange, neighbor a mere common property owner and labor a mere means of survival. (Stavrianos, p. 9)

As the Industrial Revolution matured into industrial capitalism, exploitation became more severe. The results were unfortunate and long-lasting:

> All these global economic trends combined to produce the present division of the world into the developed West as against the underdeveloped Third World. But underdevelopment did not mean nondevelopment; rather it meant distorted development—development designed to produce only one or two commodities needed by the Western markets rather than overall development to meet local needs. In short, it was the familiar Third World curse of economic growth without economic development. (p. 11)

Theodore Von Laue, on the other hand, who studied Westernization, said very little about economic inequality. Deeply influenced by Judeo-Christian perspectives, he emphasized the cultural upheaval of colonialism and the paradoxical introduction by force of Western values of freedom: "The world revolution of Westernization, in short, carried a double thrust. It was freedom, justice, and peace—the best of the European tradition—on the one hand; on the other hand (and rather unconsciously) raw power to reshape the world in one's own image" (Von Laue, p. 16). The transformation to Western values was not complete, however:

> Underneath the global universals of power and its most visible supporting skills—literacy, science and technology, large-scale

organization—the former diversities persist. The traditional cultures, though in mortal peril, linger under the ground floors of life. Rival political ideologies and ambitions clash head on. The world's major religions vie with each other as keenly as ever. Attitudes, values, life-styles from all continents mingle freely in the global marketplace, reducing in the intensified invidious comparison all former absolute truths to questionable hypotheses. (p. 7)

Von Laue looked forward to the day when all people "will be ready to fuse their personal egos with the egos of billions of other human beings, even in intimate matters like procreation and family size" (p. 9). It would appear that the common values on that day would be the Western values of the Enlightenment.

Dipesh Chakrabarty questioned this assumption that Western values would win out. Born in India after independence, trained in Australia and the United States, and later teaching there as well, Chakrabarty argued that the greatest (self-)deception of the colonizers was to project European values as the appropriate goals for the entire world, and to see history moving in that direction: "First in Europe, then elsewhere." He rejected the idea that the rest of the world exists in Europe's "waiting room." He did appreciate European, Enlightenment values, but he did not think they were the only valid ones, nor that they ought to or necessarily would become universal. Chakrabarty did not address economic issues. On cultural transformations brought by colonialism, however, he was not prepared to accept Von Laue's celebration of exclusively Western values, nor to look forward to the day when they alone would triumph.

- Which effects of colonialism do you think were more important, the economic and technological effects, or the cultural effects? Please be specific about the effects you are discussing.
- To the extent that the Cold War from the mid-1940s to the mid-1980s represents in part the values of the West, what values do you think colonized countries learned from the West?
- Do you think it is a good idea that some day the peoples of the world may share a similar set of values? Why or why not? If it is a good idea, then what should those values be? To what extent are they technological values?

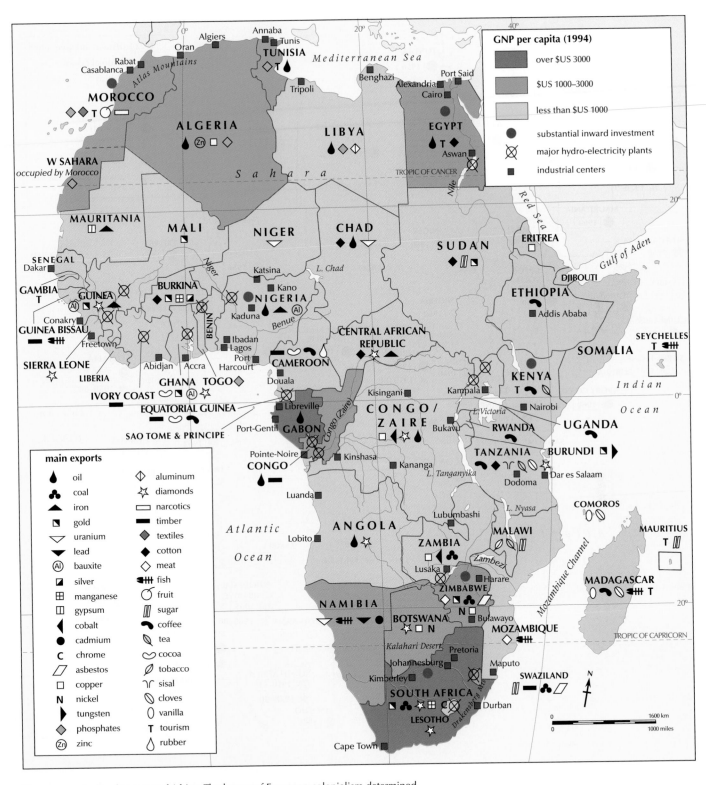

GNP per capita (1994)

- over $US 3000
- $US 1000–3000
- less than $US 1000
- substantial inward investment
- major hydro-electricity plants
- industrial centers

main exports

oil		aluminum	
coal		diamonds	
iron		narcotics	
gold		timber	
uranium		textiles	
lead		cotton	
bauxite		meat	
silver		fish	
manganese		fruit	
gypsum		sugar	
cobalt		coffee	
cadmium		tea	
chrome		cocoa	
asbestos		tobacco	
copper		sisal	
nickel		cloves	
tungsten		vanilla	
phosphates		tourism	
zinc		rubber	

The economic development of Africa. The legacy of European colonialism determined Africa's economic development, with a persistent reliance on primary products, mainly mineral wealth and cash crops. Both were widely exploited by multinational franchises, bringing little benefit to local economies. Political instability, corruption, disease, and natural disaster combined with low investment in education and health to create a general condition of underdevelopment. The northern Arab states and South Africa stand out as wealthier than the center of the continent.

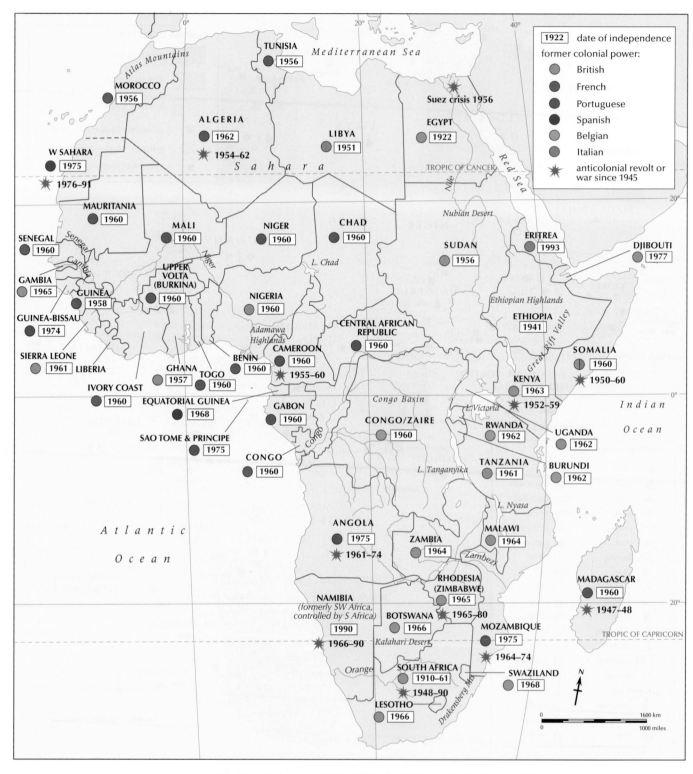

The decolonization of Africa. Ethiopia had been colonized only briefly by Italy, Liberia had been established as an independent state, and Egypt had nominal independence from 1922, but most African states gained their independence after World War II, first those in North Africa, and then, following Ghana in 1957, those of sub-Saharan Africa. Each colonial power had its own pattern for granting independence. The British and French hoped to establish amicable relations, generally, while the Portuguese and Belgians left in more bitter circumstances.

750

The Emergence of the Third World

21.1
21.2
21.3
21.4
21.5
21.6

21.4 Why did many "third-world" nations object to the pressures imposed on them by the Cold War?

Today the term "**third world**" is frequently used with a negative, and much resented, connotation to designate poor, technologically underdeveloped, inefficiently organized nations. When the term first came to be used in the 1950s, however, it carried more inspirational connotations.

The first and second worlds were bitterly and expensively polarized into two hostile, belligerent, heavily armed blocs, one led by the United States, the other by the USSR. Many of the newly independent nations wished to be **nonaligned**, to avoid taking sides. They felt that Europe and the United States regarded human life as cheap—as two world wars had demonstrated. These new nations urged disarmament, especially nuclear disarmament, at a time when the first two worlds were locked in an arms race. They advocated state investment in such basic human needs as food, clothing, shelter, medical care, and small, appropriate-scale technology, often through international assistance, not in the proliferation of weapons. They reminded the rest of the world that although they were "new nations" politically, many of them, such as India, Egypt, and Ethiopia, were ancient civilizations that took pride in millennia of traditional wisdom. And, although race was not usually mentioned overtly in third-world advocacy, almost all members of the third world were peoples of color, while the overwhelming majority of both first- and second-world groups were white. As they gained independence, these former colonies entered the UN, changing the size, complexion, and direction of that organization.

Third-World Countries Organize

In 1955, leaders of twenty nations of Africa and Asia—convened by Jawaharlal Nehru (1889–1964) of India, Gamal Abdel Nasser of Egypt, and Marshal Tito (Josip Broz, 1892–1980) of Yugoslavia—met to launch their collective entry into international politics, the first such meeting of third-world nations as a political bloc. In Bandung, Indonesia, they articulated a postcolonial agenda. They called for a global reduction in military expenditure and ideological confrontation, and an increase in expenditure for economic development, health, education, welfare, and housing.

The representatives at Bandung were not all from Africa and Asia: Tito, for example, represented Yugoslavia, a European, communist country. Nor were they all nonaligned: Zhou Enlai represented China at a time when his country was allied with the USSR. Nor did any permanent organization emerge. But for the first time, non-Western leaders assembled to articulate their own vision of a new world order. Further meetings of the nonaligned nations took place in Belgrade, Yugoslavia, in 1961; Cairo, Egypt, in 1964; and Lusaka, Zambia, in 1970.

An array of regional organizations also emerged to resolve regional problems and to present a united front in negotiations with other international organizations, such as NATO and the Warsaw Pact: the League of Arab States (1945); the Organization of American States (1948), although the OAS included the United States and was heavily influenced by it; the Organization of African Unity (1963); the Association of Southeast Asian Nations (1967); the Caribbean Community and Common Market (1973); and the South Asian Association for Regional Cooperation (1985).

In 1960 the Organization of the Petroleum Exporting Countries (OPEC) was created primarily by the oil-rich states of the Middle East, along with Venezuela, but it also came to include oil-producing states in Africa, Indonesia in Southeast Asia. OPEC's original goals were economic, but in the 1970s it also began actively to support the political goals of its member states in confrontations with Western countries, especially on issues involving Israel and the Arab states.

KEY TERMS

third world Today, generally refers to economically poor countries, often with ineffective governments. Historically the term referred to a group of newly independent countries that proposed strategies of development different from those of the US and its allies, the first world, and of the USSR and its allies, the second world.

nonaligned nations Those states, usually newly independent states, that chose not to take sides in the Cold War between the US and the USSR.

21.1
21.2
21.3
21.4
21.5
21.6

Why did many "third-world" nations object to the pressures imposed on them by the Cold War?

Despite their poverty and political weakness, third-world countries sometimes confronted the superpowers and won. In 1948, for example, Yugoslavia's Tito, who had led his guerrilla forces against the Nazis during World War II, turned against the USSR, even though his country was communist in its politics and economics. He expelled Soviet advisers, and, in turn, Yugoslavia was expelled from the Comintern.

In 1949, following their successful revolution, Chinese communist leaders signed a 30-year treaty of "friendship, alliance, and mutual assistance" with the Soviet Union. We have already seen the turmoil this caused in the United States: America refused to recognize the new government, and within a year China and the US were at war in Korea. But the Chinese revolutionaries ultimately had a falling-out with the Soviet Union as well. To the Chinese, the Soviets seemed far too restrained in their efforts to spread communism, and they refused to share their nuclear technology with China. In 1958, Mao Zedong expelled all his Soviet advisers, accusing them of arrogance. By 1960, the two communist titans were fighting in armed skirmishes over their mutual borders. The USSR cancelled its assistance to China, and China began to spread propaganda against the USSR.

Proxy Wars in the Americas

Some nations were able to play both sides diplomatically to get whatever benefits they could from the Cold War competition, but many more were entrapped by it. Between 1945 and 1983, some 20 million people were killed in more than a hundred wars and military conflicts, almost all of them in the third world. About a third to half of these conflicts were guerrilla wars, as peasants and urban workers fought armed struggles in small groups—often under the leadership of young intellectuals—against their exploitation by the rulers of their country. Frequently one superpower backed the government, the other the guerrillas. The superpowers sold or gave away their older weapons systems to their clients, and sometimes encouraged them to test the newer ones, but they themselves usually stood in the background and let others fight and kill on their behalf.

Many of these **proxy wars** were fought in Africa, as we have seen in the cases of Congo, Angola, and Mozambique—sometimes with Cuban troops fighting very far from home on behalf of the Soviet clients. In the Middle East, Israel was widely viewed as a client state of the US, and, in response, many Arab states turned to the USSR for economic aid and military assistance. In guerrilla wars in the Americas—in Nicaragua, Guatemala, and Chile—the United States and the USSR supported opposing parties, with Cuba often supplying training to communist guerrilla fighters.

Nicaragua, Guatemala, and Chile were not "new nations" in the 1960s. They had become formally independent a century and a half earlier, but they remained poor, divided by social and ethnic differences, and economically dependent on wealthier countries, especially the United States, which claimed the western hemisphere as its sphere of influence. They identified with the developmental problems of the third world.

📖 Read the **Document**: **Lourdes Arizpe Discusses the Silence of Peasant Women** on **MyHistoryLab**

Nicaragua. Strains in the relationship between the US and Nicaragua had deep roots. In 1909, the US dispatched Marines to encourage a revolt to overthrow the Nicaraguan government, because it had begun to grant economic concessions to governments other than that of the United States. The troops remained, with very few breaks, until 1933. One Nicaraguan army officer, Augusto Cesar Sandino (1893–1934), rejected American hegemony and for seven years, 1927–33, fought a guerrilla war against the US Marines and the Nicaraguan National Guard. During peace negotiations, Sandino was deceived, arrested, and murdered by officers of the guard

KEY TERM

proxy war A war waged between dependent, client states of larger, more powerful states that do not become directly involved in the fighting.

under Anastasio Somoza Garcia (1896–1956). Somoza subsequently seized control of the national government and, with the support of the United States, turned the presidency into a family dynasty for his two sons after him.

In the 1960s, a revolutionary movement, largely composed of students calling themselves Sandinistas in memory of Sandino, initiated an armed guerrilla revolt. As the Somoza government became more rapacious, the resistance expanded and intensified, finally driving the government into exile. By the time the Sandinistas came to power in 1979, however, some 50,000 people had been killed in guerrilla warfare.

American President Ronald Reagan with almost fanatic zeal, attempted to destabilize the Sandinista government. He authorized the creation of a paramilitary force against them, based across the border in Honduras, trained and supplied by the United States. He mined Nicaraguan harbors, violating the laws and treaties of the United States and earning the condemnation of the World Court, the primary judicial branch of the United Nations. When the American Congress refused to fund this clandestine war, the Reagan administration arranged to fund it secretly with the profits from equally secret arms sales to Iran, a country hostile to the United States at the time. An American Congressional investigation finally uncovered the double scandal.

Eventually, several Central American governments negotiated a settlement of the civil war in Nicaragua, including an end to foreign military involvement and a call for honest elections. For his initiative in this effort to negotiate an end to the Nicaraguan conflict, Costa Rican President Oscar Arias was awarded the Nobel Prize for Peace. The nine years of warfare, 1981 to 1990, had cost approximately 60,000 lives and another 28,000 casualties.

Guatemala. In Guatemala, the world's second largest producer of bananas, Jacobo Arbenz (1913–71) was elected president in 1951. (The term "**banana republic**" evolved to describe countries, such as Guatemala, that were economically dependent on a single crop that they sold primarily to a superpower, and helpless in the face of superpower political and military intervention.) At the time, the United Fruit Company, a private company owned mostly by citizens of the US, was Guatemala's largest landowner and held a monopoly on Guatemala's transportation infrastructure. To suppress banana production and keep prices high, the United Fruit Company left thousands of acres of arable land fallow. Arbenz proceeded to seize some 400,000 acres of this fallow land. He offered compensation according to the value of the land declared for tax purposes by the United Fruit Company itself, but the company found this insufficient. Arbenz also wanted to build a highway from his capital to the Atlantic Ocean, thus breaking the company's transportation monopoly, and to build a hydroelectric power plant, freeing Guatemala from its dependence on a foreign supply. Fearing an attack by exiles training in neighboring countries, Arbenz sought to buy arms from the United States. When the US turned him down, he bought from Poland, a communist country. Almost immediately, a small Guatemalan army-in-exile of some 150 soldiers, equipped by the United States, attacked from

An anti-American poster from the time of the Sandinista revolution, Nicaragua, 1979. Note the various drawings on the figure: military helicopters on the hat; a peace sign ("paz") among the little egghead representations of people massed together demonstrating; an ironic dollar bill with "In God we trust" on the leg. The final touch is the cowboy boot resting firmly on Uncle Sam's hat to keep him in check. Uncle Sam is a sickly gray color in contrast with the brightly colored cowboy.

KEY TERM

banana republic A country that is dependent economically on a single cash crop—such as bananas in Central America—and beholden politically to the company that controls the crop, and to the countries that buy it. Often applied to countries of Central America in their relationships with the United States.

Honduras. The Arbenz government fell, virtually without defenders, in 1954.

Arbenz's successor, Carlos Castillo Armas (1914–57), returned the lands taken from the United Fruit Company, abolished several political parties, disenfranchised all illiterates (about half the adult population), and had those who opposed him jailed, tortured, exiled, or executed. Castillo Armas was assassinated in mid-1957, and soon Guatemala plunged into a civil war in which 100,000 people died before a negotiated resolution was achieved in the 1990s. In 1999, United States President Bill Clinton (b. 1946), speaking in Guatemala, "apologized for US support of right-wing governments that killed tens of thousands of rebels and Mayan Indians in a 36-year civil war" (*The New York Times Almanac*, 2000, p. 16).

Chile. Chile began a program of agrarian reform and nationalized, with compensation, copper mines owned by American companies. The moderate government maintained good relations with the United States. In 1970, seeking more radical reform, the voters in Chile elected as president the socialist Salvador Allende (1908–73), although the United States government and major transnational corporations opposed him. Once in office, Allende confirmed their fears. He increased agrarian reform, purchased control of most banks, and continued the nationalization of the foreign-owned copper industry. Allende increased the salaries of government workers and expanded medical and housing programs, but he lacked the resources to pay for them, a circumstance that resulted in shortages and inflation. The United States government sharply reduced loans and aid to Allende's socialist government. The CIA, with a mandate to overthrow Allende, covertly financed opposition parties and labor strikes. Finally, the Chilean middle class, and especially housewives, who found the resulting chaos and economic instability intolerable, persuaded the military to act. In September 1973, they attacked and bombed the presidential palace, killing Allende.

General Augusto Pinochet (1915–2006), who headed the new government, jailed more than 100,000 Allende supporters, both men and women, and ultimately killed several thousand of them. Feared and hated for his violence toward the opposition, Pinochet was nevertheless effective in restoring the economy, with the aid of advisers from the United States. In a plebiscite in 1988, Pinochet was rejected by Chile's voters, and the government passed to the opposition. After 15 years of military rule, Chile returned to democracy.

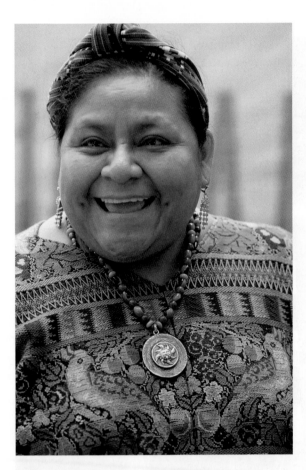

Rigoberta Menchú. Menchú, a Guatemalan Indian, won the Nobel Peace Prize in 1992. Her book *I, Rigoberta Menchú: An Indian Woman in Guatemala* was published in 1983 and became a best seller. Although some episodes were later challenged as exaggerated and "borrowed" from the lives of others, this autobiography presents an accurate account of Indian oppression and suffering.

21.1
21.2
21.3
21.4
21.5 How did the Soviet Union come to collapse and disintegrate?
21.6

The End of the Cold War: The Soviet Union Dissolves, 1989–91

21.5 How did the Soviet Union come to collapse and disintegrate?

The Soviet Union's Alternative Model

From the time of its establishment in 1917, the Soviet Union had offered alternative models to the capitalism, democracy, and individualism of Western Europe and the United States. Through the global depression, it had demonstrated that state planning could keep an economy—at least its industrial sectors—humming. In the

21.1
21.2
21.3
21.4
21.5
21.6

1930s, it alone had responded proactively to the dangers posed by the rise of Nazism by building up a strong military defense, and throughout World War II it held the eastern front at enormous cost in Soviet lives and wealth. During the Cold War, the Soviet Union alone provided a balance against the overwhelming military power of the United States, and offered an alternative path for newly independent nations emerging from colonialism. At the same time, the totalitarian power of its communist government, its gulag of prison camps, and its military occupation of central and Eastern Europe made the Soviet Union an imperial, and dreaded, neighbor.

For seven decades, individuals, institutions, states, and governments had looked to the Soviet Union as a model—some with hope, others with fear and apprehension. Then, in the space of just two years, between 1989 and 1991, the Soviet Union collapsed and disintegrated.

How did the
Soviet Union
come to collapse
and disintegrate?

Gorbachev's Reforms, 1985–91

In the Soviet Union, two men guided the process that brought the Soviet Union to its end: Mikhail Gorbachev and Boris Yeltsin. Gorbachev (b. 1931), who came to power in the USSR in 1985, assessed the country's problems directly and bluntly. Its economy was neither producing nor distributing goods effectively. In its haste to industrialize, it had allowed pollution to get out of control; the Aral Sea, for example, was drying up. The bureaucracy was bloated with doctrinaire Communist Party officials, while the growing professional classes protested restrictions on their freedom. The churches continued to seek greater freedom of religious expression. Not only in the satellite countries of Eastern Europe, such as Poland, but also in the non-Russian states of the USSR itself, nationalist groups sought greater independence—especially the Baltic states, which had long chafed under Russian control, and the Muslim-majority states of central Asia, which were culturally, linguistically, and religiously different from Russia. Finally, the Soviet Union was engaged in an arms race with the United States that it could no longer afford.

In response to these problems, Gorbachev introduced his policies of *glasnost* (political and cultural openness) and *perestroika* (economic restructuring). *Glasnost* meant, first of all, telling the truth about the communist state, and this included the truth about its past. Khrushchev had already revealed many of Stalin's atrocities; under Gorbachev, historians revealed even more: some 20 million people had been killed under Stalin and a similar number oppressed. In 1973, Solzhenitsyn had written: "It has always been impossible to learn the truth about anything in our country." Now the truth was coming out. *Glasnost* revealed the problems; *perestroika* looked for solutions. Gorbachev tried to reduce the size of the bureaucracy, to increase the efficiency of agriculture and industry, and to trim the military budget. He appointed reformers to important government offices. He planned and began a more competitive economic system, although one still under state control.

📖 **Read** the **Document**: **Mikhail Gorbachev on the Need for Economic Reform (1987)** on **MyHistoryLab**

Gorbachev was trapped by his own promises. Soon the reformers were criticizing him for moving too slowly to cut

Mikhail Gorbachev at the UN, 1988. From the time he became general secretary of the Communist Part of the Soviet Union, Gorbachev introduced domestic reforms in the economy (*perestroika*) and in politics and culture (*glasnost*). With his astonishing speech to the United Nations in 1988 he also declared himself in favor of an end to the arms race, cooperation instead of hostility among the world's most powerful countries, and dedication to solving such global problems as poverty and ecological destruction.

SOURCE

Gorbachev at the United Nations, December 7, 1988

Gorbachev left two contrasting legacies. At home, he failed in his practical attempts to bring *perestroika*, the restructuring of the Russian economy, politics, and society. On the other hand, his vision of the world's future inspired people everywhere. He dismantled the Soviet Union, its Communist Party, and its control over the satellite countries of central and Eastern Europe. He began to reduce the armed forces of the Soviet Union, especially its nuclear arsenal. The vision seemed utopian yet somehow, perhaps, achievable. Gorbachev's speech at the United Nations General Assembly in New York City on December 7, 1988, summarized his goals and aspirations. It called for global cooperation, tolerance for diverse social and political systems, protection for the globe's ecology, assistance for development in the poorer nations, and disarmament. This was quite a new agenda for the Soviet Union, and for the world. The speech drew enthusiastic, even ecstatic praise from statesmen and common people around the world.

Further world progress is now possible only through the search for a consensus of all mankind, in movement toward a new world order … It is a question of cooperation that could be more accurately called "co-creation" and "co-development." The formula of development "at another's expense" is becoming outdated. In light of present realities, genuine progress by infringing upon the rights and liberties of man and peoples, or at the expense of nature, is impossible …

It is evident, for example, that force and the threat of force can no longer be, and should not be instruments of foreign policy …

The variety of sociopolitical structures which has grown over the last decades from national liberation movements also demonstrates this. This objective fact presupposes respect for other people's views and stands, tolerance, a preparedness to see phenomena that are different as not necessarily bad or hostile, and an ability to learn to live side by side while remaining different and not agreeing with one another on every issue …

In the course of such sharing, each should prove the advantages of his own system, his own way of life and values, but not through words or propaganda alone, but through real deeds as well … Otherwise we simply will not be able to solve a single world problem; arrange broad, mutually advantageous and equitable cooperation between peoples; manage rationally the achievements of the scientific and technical revolution; transform world economic relations; protect the environment; overcome underdevelopment; or put an end to hunger, disease, illiteracy, and other mass ills. Finally, in that case, we will not manage to eliminate the nuclear threat and militarism.

Now about the most important topic, without which no problem of the coming century can be resolved: disarmament …

Today I can inform you of the following: The Soviet Union has made a decision on reducing its armed forces. In the next two years, their numerical strength will be reduced by 500,000 persons … The Soviet forces situated in those countries [of central and Eastern Europe] will be cut by 50,000 persons, and their arms by 5,000 tanks.

We would also like to draw the attention of the world community to another topical problem, the problem of changing over from an economy of armament to an economy of disarmament. Is the conversion of military production realistic? … We believe that it is, indeed, realistic … It is desirable that all states, primarily the major military powers, submit their national plans on this issue to the United Nations.

We are talking first and foremost about consistent progress toward concluding a treaty [with the United States] on a 50 percent reduction in strategic offensive weapons … about elaborating a convention on the elimination of chemical weapons—here, it seems to us, we have the preconditions for making 1989 the decisive year; and about talks on reducing conventional weapons and armed forces in Europe. We are also talking about economic, ecological, and humanitarian problems in the widest possible sense …

One would like to believe that our joint efforts to put an end to the era of wars, confrontation and regional conflicts, aggression against nature, the terror of hunger and poverty, as well as political terrorism, will be comparable with our hopes. This is our common goal, and it is only by acting together that we may attain it. Thank you.

free of discredited communist economics. Under *glasnost*, ethnic groups throughout the length and breadth of the highly diverse Soviet Union began to voice their grievances. Riots between them broke out in some areas, and full-scale independence movements began in the Baltic states. Others soon followed elsewhere. Meanwhile, the war in Afghanistan, initiated by Brezhnev in 1979, ground on. Some 2000 Russian soldiers were dying there every year, and there was no evidence of Soviet gains.

In 1988, Gorbachev allowed multi-candidate elections and began to give the Supreme Soviet increased powers. In February 1990, he announced that non-Party candidates could stand for office. Gorbachev announced that he was replacing the Brezhnev Doctrine of massive intervention in rebellious satellite countries with the (Frank) Sinatra Doctrine of "My Way," allowing them to break free of the Soviet

21.1
21.2
21.3
21.4
21.5 How did the Soviet Union come to collapse and disintegrate?
21.6

21.1
21.2
21.3
21.4
21.5
21.6

Union if they chose. Incredulous and ecstatic, Germans, using sledgehammers, pick-axes, and their bare hands, tore down the Berlin Wall, the symbol of their division into east and west. The date, November 9 (1989) became a new national holiday.

View the **Closer Look**: **Collapse of the Berlin Wall** on **MyHistoryLab**

With the removal of Soviet armies, all six satellite nations in Eastern and central Europe became independent: East Germany, Poland, Hungary, Czechoslova-kia (which, in 1993, divided into the Czech and Slovak republics), Bulgaria, and Romania. Divided at the end of World War II, East and West Germany reunited. At first, Gorbachev resisted the right of constituent republics of the USSR to declare their independence and leave the union, but many now simply defied his wishes: the Baltic states of Estonia, Latvia, and Lithuania; the Eastern European Slavic states of Belarus, Ukraine, and Moldova; the Caspian Sea states of Armenia, Georgia, and Azerbaijan; and the Muslim-majority states in central Asia: Turkmenistan, Uzbeki-stan, Tajikistan, Kyrgyzstan, and Kazakhstan. With government control uncertain, historic national and ethnic identities reemerged. These identities were sometimes hostile to one another, and violent clashes, as well as celebration, marked the end of the Soviet empire.

Gorbachev continued his negotiations for arms reductions with United States presidents Ronald Reagan and George H.W. Bush, and in December 1989, Gor-bachev and Bush formally announced the end of the Cold War. For the superpowers, it had remained mostly cold since World War II. Despite all the saber-rattling, all the expensive weaponry, all the conniving with client states, despite even the Cuban

> How did the
> Soviet Union
> come to collapse
> and disintegrate?

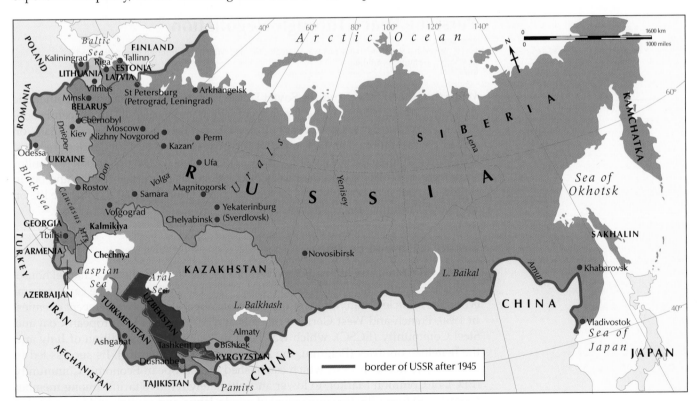

The break-up of the Soviet Union. The Soviet experiment with Marxist ideology crumbled, after 70 years, at the end of the 1980s. President Gorbachev's policy of *glasnost* (1985) allowed the nations of Eastern Europe to move, largely bloodlessly, toward independence and economic reform, but in the Caucasus Mountains and central Asia reform was often accompanied by an insurgence of nationalism, organized crime, and power struggles. In 1991, these nations also became independent—except for Chechnya, where fighting continued for years.

View the **Interactive Map**: **Break-up of the Soviet Union** on **MyHistoryLab**

21.1
21.2
21.3
21.4
21.5
21.6

What were the major postwar strategies for achieving peace through negotiation and institution-building?

Missile Crisis, the United States and the Soviet Union had always pulled back from nuclear war. Although they fought proxy wars, they did not confront each other in direct warfare. Some observers speculated that the investment in the threat of nuclear war—in Mutually Assured Destruction, or MAD—had provided a ritualized pose of macho strength on both sides that allowed the superpowers to avoid actual warfare. In retrospect it appeared that for 45 years they had created their own form of an international balance of power.

Yeltsin Preserves the Reforms. In August 1991, while Gorbachev was vacationing in the Crimea, die-hard communists mounted a coup against him. Boris Yeltsin, a reformer and the president of the Russian Federation, led public resistance to the coup, contacted political leaders across the country and around the world to gain support, and courageously went out into the streets and climbed atop an armored troop carrier to make his position clear. When the army refused to attack Yeltsin and his headquarters, the coup was finished. Gorbachev returned from the Crimea, but Yeltsin was the hero of the moment.

A few days later, Gorbachev resigned as general secretary of the Communist Party and moved to dissolve the Party altogether. On December 24, 1991, the USSR formally dissolved itself into 15 independent states. The new states joined in a loose Commonwealth of Independent States as a mechanism for continuing cooperation. The USSR was no more; the Communist Party was reduced to a shell; the global political landscape was transformed. The nation that Gorbachev had ruled no longer existed. Yeltsin's Russia was by far its largest surviving state.

Pursuing Peace Through Negotiation

21.6 What were the major postwar strategies for achieving peace through negotiation and institution-building?

While the United States and the Soviet Union were busy threatening each other, the nations of Western Europe and Japan were seeking new methods of peaceful cooperation. They were often critical of both the US and the USSR for their emphasis on armed confrontation. The UN, often at the behest of newly independent nations, sought to minimize the polarization of the superpowers. It also undertook to monitor the effects of technology on the health of the globe, as in climate change and ocean pollution. And numerous NGOs throughout the world also tried to improve life on the planet through peaceful means.

Toward a Unified Europe

In 1947, Winston Churchill had described Europe as "a rubble heap, a charnel house, a breeding ground for pestilence and hate." But out of the wreckage came several economic miracles, many of them the result of cooperation between recent enemies. In 1950, French and West German officials agreed to form the European Coal and Steel Community (ECSC), which was born in 1952 with the addition of Italy and the Benelux countries (Belgium, the Netherlands, Luxembourg). Its success led to the Treaty of Rome in 1957, which established the European Economic Community (EEC), or Common Market, to lower and ultimately remove tariffs among member countries; to foster the free movement of goods, labor, and capital; and to establish a single external tariff. The treaties also established Euratom to create common policies for the peaceful development of atomic energy.

In 1965, the Brussels Treaty merged the ECSC, the EEC, and Euratom to create the basis of a unified Western European economic administration. Additional nations were admitted, including Britain, Ireland, and Denmark in 1973, Greece in 1981, and Spain and Portugal in 1986. Western Europe was moving toward a new era, a

"Europe without borders," and its economy flourished. The economies of Western European nations experienced extraordinary growth. Germany called it a *wirtschaftswunder*, an economic miracle. Others referred to it as their "golden years."

The success rested on wide international cooperation outside Europe as well as within it. Part of the institutional base was prepared in 1944 in Bretton Woods, New Hampshire. Representatives of 40 nations gathered there to plan a new global economy for the postwar period that would escape the catastrophic depression that had followed World War I. They created three new institutions: the International Monetary Fund (IMF), the International Bank for Reconstruction and Development (World Bank), and the General Agreement on Tariffs and Trade (GATT). The IMF provided short-term loans to countries that were having difficulty meeting their balance of payment obligations. These were designed for moments of extreme, but short-term, crisis. The first goal of the World Bank was to provide capital for rebuilding war-torn nations. By the late 1960s and 1970s, as European nations had recovered from the economic devastation of the war, the bank increasingly turned to the developmental needs of the third world. The GATT was designed to promote world trade by reducing tariffs among all member nations.

Until the 1980s, all these organizations were generally praised for their achievements among the capitalist nations of the world. The communist bloc—both the European nations in the Soviet sphere and China after its communist revolution—refused to participate because they did not trust the open market as a means of economic decision-making. They rejected the capitalist laws of supply and demand in favor of state planning and therefore could not accept the Bretton Woods principles. Bretton Woods marked the division of the world into opposing blocs, even as it proved successful for the West.

Japan's Recovery

Just as startling as Europe's recovery after the war was the speed of Japan's recovery. Like Germany, Japan had the remains of an industrial infrastructure and a highly skilled workforce that could shift into production for peace. The US occupation of 1945–52 improved Japan's competitive position by redistributing land; breaking up the *zaibatsu* holding companies that had controlled the economy; encouraging the growth of labor unions (until some of them began to become communist); and restructuring the educational system, opening up high-school and college education for the first time to millions of Japanese students. The United States also encouraged Japan, as it had Germany, to join its Cold War struggle against the Soviet Union. Japan benefited from US economic investment, from the US purchase of supplies during the Korean War—and later during the Vietnam War—and from the military bases the US established in Japan.

Japan did not, however, participate in America's wars. Its postwar constitution forbade such overseas military action. Article Nine of the Japanese constitution states: "The Japanese people forever renounce war as a sovereign right of the nation and the threat or use of force as means of

21.1

21.2

21.3

21.4

21.5

21.6

What were the major postwar strategies for achieving peace through negotiation and institution-building?

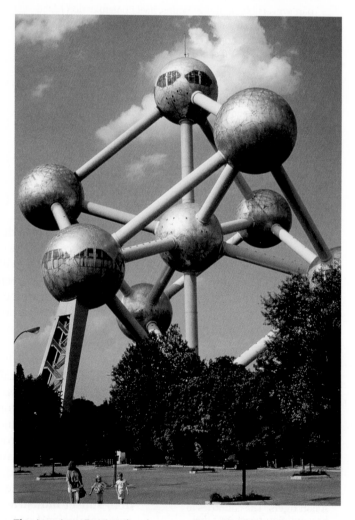

The Atomium, Euratom headquarters, Brussels. As European countries that had fought one another for centuries began to forge institutions of cooperation after 1945, collaboration in the peaceful development of atomic energy took on both practical and symbolic importance. The Treaty of Rome (1957), which established the European Economic Community, also created Euratom to create joint policies. The Atomium at the Euratom headquarters in Brussels symbolized this new commitment.

SOURCE

Rachel Carson's *Silent Spring*

The American biologist Rachel Carson's book *Silent Spring* (1962) exposed the devastating effects on humans, wildlife, and plants caused by the use of toxic chemicals—pesticides, fungicides, and herbicides—in everyday farming and insect control throughout the world. By virtue of its combination of scientific rigor and journalistic vividness, *Silent Spring* is frequently credited as the founding statement of the ecological movement in the twentieth century:

> The most alarming of all man's assaults on the environment is the contamination of air, earth, rivers, and sea with dangerous and even lethal materials. This pollution is for the most part irrecoverable; the chain of evil it initiates not only in the world that must support life but in living tissues is for the most part irreversible. In this now universal contamination of the environment, chemicals are the sinister and little recognized partners of radiation in changing the very nature of the world— the very nature of its life ... Chemicals sprayed on croplands or forests or gardens lie long in the soil, entering into living organisms, passing from one to another in a chain of poisoning and death. Or they pass mysteriously by underground streams until they emerge, and through the alchemy of air and sunlight, combine into new forms that kill vegetation, sicken cattle, and work unknown harm on those who drink from once-pure wells. (Carson, pp. 23–24)

Carson's powerful voice evoked responses. For example, after she revealed that DDT, one of the most powerful chemicals used to combat mosquitoes and, thus, malaria, was also poisonous to humans, governments throughout the world generally banned its use. "Green" parties, with strong platforms on ecological issues, began to organize in many countries, especially in Western Europe, and more mainstream parties began to adopt some of their programs. Citizens founded such organizations as the World Wildlife Fund and Greenpeace in order to protect the environment. Some farmers began to use natural means of pest control in place of chemicals, and consumers began to seek out "natural" or "organic" foods raised without the use of chemical fertilizers and pesticides.

As Carson pointed out, the political issues, and their implications for the standard of living in each country, were thornier than the technological:

> The Earth is one but the world is not. We all depend on one biosphere for sustaining our lives. Yet each community, each country strives for survival and prosperity with little regard for its impact on others. Some consume the Earth's resources at a rate that would leave little for future generations. Others, many more in number, consume far too little and live with the prospect of hunger, squalor, disease, and early death. (p. 28)

KEY TERMS

sunset industries Industries that are expected to be in decline in the near future.

sunrise industries Industries that are expected to be most profitable in the near future.

Asian tigers The countries in East and Southeast Asia that were doing extremely well economically in the last decades of the twentieth century. The list almost always includes South Korea, Taiwan, Singapore, and Hong Kong, and sometimes Indonesia and Thailand.

settling international disputes." It also outlawed the presence of nuclear weapons on Japanese territory. The constitution declared that "land, sea, and air forces, as well as other war potential, will never be maintained." Even so, in 1954 the Japanese parliament established the Self-Defense Forces, which by the early years of the twenty-first century came to number almost 250,000 armed troops. Nevertheless, Japan's military spending as a proportion of its total national budget was relatively small, as it put its faith in the American military shield and invested its money in productive economic enterprises.

Between 1950 and 1973, Japan's gross domestic product grew by 10.5 percent per year. By 1980, its per capita income, at almost $10,000 per year, rivaled America's at $11,400. Economists were beginning to speak of "Japan as Number 1" because of the efficiency and quality of its consumer products, especially its automobiles; its skill in overseas marketing; and its prospects for soon surpassing even the United States as the world's leading economy.

Japan's economic success also turned on its ability to bring together government advice and guidance with freely operating private enterprises. Its Ministry for International Trade and Industry successfully guided Japanese industries away from **sunset industries**, such as steel production, into **sunrise industries**, such as automobiles and computers, and helped them to find financial investments and marketing opportunities. Several countries of East and Southeast Asia—especially Korea and Taiwan, Japan's former colonies—adopted this model of state guidance and private enterprise with great success. These two nations, along with the city-states of Hong Kong and Singapore, were often referred to as the "**Asian tigers**" for their aggressive and successful economic development on the Japanese model.

AT A GLANCE: SOCIETY AND CULTURE

DATE	SOCIETY AND CULTURE
1950s	• American artists, writers, professors, filmmakers, and bureaucrats are blacklisted during the "Red Scare" (1950s) • Bandung Conference of (mostly) non-aligned nations (1955) • Contraceptive pill becomes available (late 1950s) • Soviet space program puts first satellite, *Sputnik*, into space (1957) • Ghana independent; Nkrumah in power (1957) • Revolution in Cuba; Castro in power (1959)
1960s	• Amnesty International founded (1961) • Alexander Solzhenitsyn, *A Day in the Life of Ivan Denisovich* (1962) • Rachel Carson, *Silent Spring* (1962) • Betty Friedan, *The Feminine Mystique* (1963) • Martin Luther King delivers "I Have a Dream" speech, Washington Mall (1963) • Stanley Kubrick, *Dr. Strangelove* (1964) • "Bullet train" (high-speed railway) inaugurated in Japan (1964) • Japan hosts Olympics (1964) • Malcolm X assassinated (1965) • *Hair* opens off-Broadway (1967) • Students and workers launch worldwide protests against authority (1968) • *Apollo II* lands on the moon (1969)
1970s	• Norman Borlaug, "the father of the green revolution," wins Nobel Peace Prize (1970) • United Nations conference on the Human Environment (1972) • Solzhenitsyn, *Gulag Archipelago* (1973) • E.F. Schumacher, *Small is Beautiful* (1973) • First World Conference on Women, Mexico City (1975) • Pope John Paul II visits Poland (1979) • Near meltdown of nuclear reactor at Three Mile Island, Pennsylvania (1979) • World Health Organization announces eradication of smallpox (1979)
1980s	• Meltdown in nuclear reactor at Chernobyl, Ukraine (1986) • World Wide Web created (1989)
1990s	• United Nations Earth Summit, Rio de Janeiro (1992) • Guatemalan Rigoberta Menchú wins Nobel Peace Prize for her work for social justice and the rights of indigenous peoples (1992) • Around ten percent of the US population is foreign-born (1997) • Internet connection worldwide rises from three million people in 1993 to 200 million in 1999 • Protests in Seattle, Washington, against the World Trade Organization (1999)

21.1

21.2

21.3

21.4

21.5

21.6 What were the major postwar strategies for achieving peace through negotiation and institution-building?

The UN: Growth and New Missions

Meanwhile, the UN was demonstrating some success as an arena for defusing international tension, providing peace-keeping missions to global trouble spots, and developing programs for international cooperation, including problems involving technology.

By the end of 1984, the membership of the UN had expanded to 159 sovereign states, the overwhelming majority of the world's nations. It provided a home in which the newly emerging nations could gain political recognition and representation. The diversity of states brought a diversity of ideologies, and UN decisions and activities were subjected to a constant stream of criticism from one point or another on the political spectrum. Yet within that highly politicized framework the organization went on with its work, providing a forum where nations could meet, discuss common goals, and negotiate agreements. It did not always succeed, but such a forum was invaluable. In the mid-1980s, the Soviet leader Mikhail Gorbachev called the UN a "unique instrument without which world politics would be inconceivable today," even though it lacked the sovereignty of a government and commanded only such powers as its members chose to vest in it. The UN helped to negotiate a

What were the major postwar strategies for achieving peace through negotiation and institution-building?

AT A GLANCE: THE SOVIET UNION DISSOLVES

1985	• Mikhail Gorbachev becomes president of USSR, introduces *glasnost* ("openness") and *perestroika* ("economic restructuring")
1988	• December: Gorbachev speaks to the United Nations, introduces his goals for democratization in satellite countries • Gorbachev allows multi-candidate elections
1989	• Gorbachev replaces the Brezhnev Doctrine with the Sinatra Doctrine ("My Way") • November 9: East and West Germans tear down the Berlin Wall • December: Gorbachev and the United States announce the end of the Cold War
1990	• Gorbachev announces that non-Communist Party candidates will be allowed to run for office • Gorbachev receives the Nobel Peace Prize
1991	• August: Boris Yeltsin, president of the Russian Federation, crushes an attempted coup against Gorbachev • December 24: The Soviet Union dissolves into 15 republics; Gorbachev resigns the next day

resolution of the Cuban Missile Crisis, the Arab–Israeli war of 1967, and the Iraq–Iran war of 1988. It called for a voluntary arms embargo against South Africa in 1963, in protest against that country's racist legal system (see "Apartheid in South Africa" in the chapter entitled "Contemporary History: Trade, Revolution, Technology, Identity"), and made it mandatory in 1972.

The UN dispatched "peace-keeping" armed forces, with military personnel drawn from many different countries, to police zones of potential conflict. These missions were not designed to fight wars, but to maintain the peace in cases in which antagonistic nations agreed that they would work for it but required an impartial "police force" to maintain it. UN peace-keeping forces were first sent to the Middle East in 1948 to monitor the ceasefire between the new state of Israel and its Arab neighbors. A small force was sent to Cyprus in 1964 to maintain a buffer between the Greek Cypriots and the Turkish Cypriots who had been fighting for control of the island. Peace-keepers were also sent to Kashmir in 1972 to monitor the Line of Control between India and Pakistan after the two countries signed peace agreements to end their warfare in 1971.

On a third level, the UN undertook many initiatives in organizing for the general welfare of the globe. In 1953 it coordinated the first global census, which found that the world's population had more than doubled from about 2.5 billion in 1950 to approaching six billion in 2000, with most of the increase coming in the poorer countries. Death rates were falling, leading to an increase also in the elderly population of the world, especially in the wealthier countries. People were moving steadily from rural to urban areas. Estimates suggested that in 1950 about 30 percent of the world's 2.5 billion people, about 750 million, lived in cities. By 1990, about 45 percent of the world's six billion people, 2.7 billion, lived in cities. (In 2007 the figure reached 50 percent.) By 1990, more people lived in cities than had lived in the entire world in 1900. The most rapidly growing cities, and most of the largest of them, were in the poorer, less industrialized areas of the world, with the fewest resources for responding to the requirements of such immense populations, for example, São Paulo, Brazil; Mexico City; Mumbai (Bombay) and Kolkata (Calcutta) in India; Shanghai and Beijing (Peking) in China. Each had upward of ten million inhabitants. To direct attention toward the needs of these enormous populations, and especially of their poorest citizens living in slums, the UN inaugurated its Habitat program in 1978.

Recognizing that most social and economic problems affect men and women differently, in 1975 the UN sponsored a "Decade for Women," opening with the first World Conference on Women, in Mexico City. Later women's conferences followed in Copenhagen in 1980, Nairobi in 1985, and Beijing in 1995. In 1976, the UN established UNIFEM to "provide financial and technical assistance to innovative programmes and strategies that promote women's human rights, political participation and economic security."

In 1979, the World Health Organization (WHO) declared that smallpox had been eradicated: every human being on earth had been inoculated against the disease. The WHO was only one of numerous international organizations working officially with the UN, many of them created by the UN itself. Others included the Food and Agriculture Organization, which works to increase the productivity of farms, forests, and fisheries; the International Atomic Energy Agency (IAEA), which monitors the nonproliferation of nuclear weapons and promotes the peaceful use of atomic energy; the International Labor Organization, which creates labor standards and promotes the welfare of workers everywhere; UNESCO, the UN's Educational, Scientific, and Cultural Organization, which promotes research, publication, and historic preservation; and the World Bank, which extends loans to help poor countries in their development tasks.

Finally, with the UN Conference on the Human Environment in Stockholm in 1972, the UN began a struggle against global ecological destruction. Many concerns dominated the agenda, but the main ones were the depletion of the ozone layer; global warming and greenhouse gasses; deforestation, especially in the tropics, where at least 25 million acres of trees are cut down yearly; acid rain, the pollution of the atmosphere with airborne chemical pollutants; and the destruction of the marine environment through ocean dumping, ship pollution, and the absorption of chemicals into the water table. The UN established the first laws regulating the sea, including those regulating ocean fishing (1970).

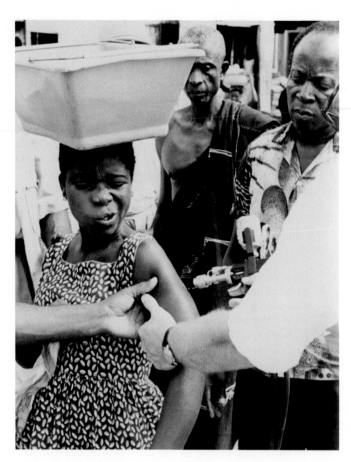

A girl is vaccinated against smallpox, Nigeria, 1969. In 1979, in one of the great triumphs of international humanitarian organization, the World Health Organization declared that smallpox had been eradicated. Every human being on earth had been inoculated against it.

Agreement was emerging on the need for international cooperation in a stronger UN environment program, but the UN lacked sovereign power. It could gather information, carry out research, make recommendations, hold conferences, and provide counsel, but it had no powers of enforcement. Implementation depended on the decisions of member nations.

NGOs and Transnational Organizations

The UN was perhaps the most important of all the organizations acting on a global scale that were not themselves actual governments. The second half of the twentieth century saw an enormous growth in the number and power of voluntary nongovernmental organizations (**NGOs**) devoted to more specific issues. These NGOs changed the way nations and economies carried out their work.

Normally, the term NGO does not include private businesses, but they too are in a sense NGOs, and, in the later years of the twentieth century, private businesses created not simply multinational corporations but even transnational corporations. Multinationals were companies headquartered in one nation but operating in several. By the late twentieth century, America alone had tens of thousands of such corporations. Transnational corporations also operated in many countries, but had no clear headquarters. Sometimes, for financial purposes (often to evade taxes), they

KEY TERM

NGO Nongovernmental organization. Broadly, any organization not controlled by the government, carrying out its own mission. Most commonly refers to voluntary organizations carrying out work of social and community service that the government cannot or does not do.

763

HOW DO WE KNOW?

The Social Setting of Technology

Even as the developed world created new products, established ever more efficient means of producing them, and designed advertising to convince people that these new products were necessary, a few people raised their voices to ask if this form of economic and technological development was "progress." One of the most prominent of these critics, E.F. Schumacher, published his sceptical evaluation in his classic book *Small Is Beautiful* (1973). Schumacher, a British economist, served for 20 years as head of planning at the British Coal Board, but his economic philosophy stressed the small-scale rather than the large. He wanted economics to be based in nature rather than in the subjugation of nature:

> In the excitement over the unfolding of his scientific and technical powers, modern man has built a system of production that ravishes nature and a type of society that mutilates man … The development of production and the acquisition of wealth have thus become the highest goals of the modern world in relation to which all other goals, no matter how much lip-service may still be paid to them, have come to take second place … This is the philosophy of materialism, and it is this philosophy—or metaphysic—which is being challenged by events … It is of little use trying to suppress terrorism if the production of deadly devices continues to be deemed a legitimate employment of man's creative powers … Equally, the chance of mitigating the rate of resource depletion or of bringing harmony into the relationships between those in possession of wealth and power and those without is non-existent as long as there is no idea anywhere of enough being good and more-than-enough being evil. (pp. 293–5)

Schumacher briefly explored the history of the economics profession to chart its transformation. The first professorship in political economy was endowed at the University of Oxford in 1825, and from the beginning philanthropists and economists alike asked what should be its scope; many, including Schumacher, argued that economics should be subservient to ethics. In 1969, the Nobel Prize for Economic Science was established, suggesting that this discipline would not rank second to any other. Schumacher, however, argued that the earlier evaluation was more appropriate.

Arnold Pacey, a British physicist who became a historian, also argued that technological developments were most effective when they fit the society that was adopting them. Pacey was not directly arguing for ethics, as Schumacher was, but his idea that inventions should fit the needs of society, and society's ability to absorb them, agreed with Schumacher's view that technological "development" should not proceed for its own sake, but rather for the sake of society. In an era of rapid technological development, when third-world nations frequently wanted the same technology for war and for peace as the first world had, the moral principles expressed directly by Schumacher and indirectly by Pacey set up a challenge: What would be the appropriate scale for the technology to be adopted? The argument for appropriate-scale technology was made forcefully, in practical terms, by Mohandas Gandhi of India, as we have seen in the chapter entitled "World War II," and shall see again in the chapter "China and India."

- Was Schumacher correct that technological "progress" is pursued, at least some of the time, simply for the purpose of making a profit, whether or not new technology is needed? Please explain, with examples.
- Can you provide examples of technology that seems appropriate for the people and societies that use it and examples of technology that seems inappropriate?
- How important do you think it is to ask about the appropriate scale of technology? Can you give an example of such a question in your own life?

placed much of their financial structure in small, relatively unregulated nations, such as the Cayman Islands or Curaçao. Regulating and policing the transnationals was not easy. Also, while multinational corporations might finally have to balance their desire for bottom-line profits against the need to live within the laws and values of their home country, transnationals had no allegiances other than their own profit.

At the same time, more conventional NGOs—much smaller, to be sure—also took shape. The World Wildlife Fund (WWF), for example, founded in the 1950s, grew to more than five million members working in more than a hundred countries. It became the world's largest privately financed conservation organization working to conserve the world's biological diversity, advocate for the use of renewable natural resources in sustainable fashion, and promote the reduction of pollution and wasteful consumption (see worldwildlife.org).

The WWF is just one example of the growing global concern for clean air, water, and food supplies, and for the protection of wilderness and diverse animal species—especially in the face of increasing global population and demands for energy and

UN AGENCIES

The primary focus of attention in the UN has been on peace and war, but its various programs and agencies, many concerned with technology, have provided forums for the resolution of other issues and the promotion of international welfare. Key agencies include:

- International Court of Justice (World Court): has dealt with such issues as territorial rights, territorial waters, rights of individuals to asylum, and territorial sovereignty

- Food and Agricultural Organization (FAO): monitors information for improving food supply and distribution

- World Trade Organization (WTO): oversees international trade, settles trade disputes, and negotiates trade liberalization

- World Bank: provides financial assistance to developing nations

- UNIFEM (since 2011 part of UN Women): dedicated to advancing women's rights and achieving gender equality

- United Nations Educational, Scientific, and Cultural Organization (UNESCO): sponsors research and publication

- United Nations Children's (Emergency) Fund (UNICEF): establishes programs for family welfare

- United Nations Human Settlements Programme (UN–HABITAT): the United Nations agency for human settlements

- World Health Organization (WHO): monitors and researches health conditions

- International Labor Organization (ILO): promotes employment and seeks to improve labor conditions and living standards

- World Intellectual Property Organization: protects the interests of the producers of literary, industrial, scientific, and artistic works

- United Nations Commission on Human Rights: gathers information and formulates policy on the rights of persons belonging to national, ethnic, religious, and linguistic minorities, including indigenous peoples

21.1
21.2
21.3
21.4
21.5
21.6

What were the major postwar strategies for achieving peace through negotiation and institution-building?

goods. Rachel Carson's book *Silent Spring* (1962; see Source box, above), a scientifically grounded, journalistically powerful account of the devastating effects on global ecology of the use of pesticides, fungicides, and herbicides in commercial farming, is often considered the founding document of this modern ecology movement.

Amnesty International also grew into a worldwide movement with over two million supporters dedicated to the protection and promotion of human rights. Amnesty took as its model the Universal Declaration of Human Rights. It acted to stop grave abuses of the rights of physical and mental integrity, freedom of conscience and expression, and freedom from discrimination. It campaigned to free prisoners of conscience, ensure fair trials for political prisoners, protect refugees, abolish the death penalty, and end political assassination and torture. It sought to bring to justice those responsible for human rights violations. It publicized its findings in order to bring public pressure to bear against governments and groups abusing human rights (see amnesty.org).

Oxfam, originally the Oxford Committee for Famine Relief, traces its origin to a group of Quaker intellectuals, social activists, and Oxford University academics who founded an organization to provide famine relief to Greece during World War II. In the years immediately after the war, it directed its attention to European needs, but in 1951 it extended famine relief to people in India, and in 1953, following the Korean War, to the homeless, hungry, and orphaned in that country. In the 1960s, Oxfam turned primarily to the needs of the third world. It focused less on famine relief and more on supplying the tools by which people could improve their living standards. Oxfam also prepared educational materials to explain to the first world

21.1
21.2
21.3
21.4
21.5
21.6

What were the major postwar strategies for achieving peace through negotiation and institution-building?

Amnesty International protest. Amnesty International is a worldwide movement of people who campaign for internationally recognized human rights for all. Founded in 1961, Amnesty now has more than 2.2 million members, supporters, and subscribers in over 150 countries and territories, in every region of the world. Amnesty campaigns to stop violence against women, abolish the death penalty, and free prisoners of conscience—people who have been jailed for exercising their right of freedom of speech.

the root causes of poverty and suffering, the connections between the first and third worlds, and the role that first-world people could play in improving the physical conditions of life in the third world (see oxfam.org).

These well-known organizations are only three of the thousands of multinational and transnational NGOs. Many of the larger ones are organizations of trade unionists, religious groups, sports enthusiasts, and artists. The Soviet Union dissolved, for example, in part because of international labor support for Lech Walesa's Solidarity movement and because the Polish Cardinal Wojtyla was elevated to the position of pope in the Roman Catholic Church.

Wealthy private foundations that carry out humanitarian work formed another cluster of NGOs. For example, the Rockefeller Foundation sponsored the work of agricultural scientists who discovered and disseminated new strains of wheat and other grains, increasing food productivity by as much as five times through the 1960s and 1970s. The **green revolution** they created saved the world from mass starvation in the face of continuing population growth. Norman Borlaug, who directed these efforts, won the Nobel Peace Prize in 1970 for his work.

Nevertheless, NGOs were frequently criticized for escaping full public scrutiny. For example, many political observers feared that the Rockefeller-financed green revolution, which did so much to increase food productivity, would ultimately create tension in society by making the rich richer and the poor poorer. The "miracle" seeds required new fertilizers and an abundance of irrigation water and pesticides. Richer farmers could afford these, but poorer farmers could not, and such farmers often lost their land. In addition, over time the chemical fertilizers reduced the fertility of the soil. In the short run, the world needed the green revolution to feed its people; in the long run the unforeseen consequences might be devastating. Short-run obvious benefits outweighed long-run potential problems, and the search for new hybrid, high-yield crops soon expanded from wheat to rice and other global staples.

KEY TERM

green revolution The revolution in agricultural production brought about by the use of new hybrid seeds, with increased use of irrigation, fertilizers, and pesticides.

Legacies of the Cold War, Decolonization, and Economic and Social Development:
What Difference Do They Make?

A healthy skepticism colors our perception of the transformations of the second half of the twentieth century. "Winners" gained more wealth, power, and convenience than had ever been known. Hundreds of millions of people, long colonized, won their political independence. Yet even the most fortunate often felt insecure, for the wars of the century were the bloodiest ever, and the weaponry the most powerful and frightening, carrying the potential to destroy all human life. Governments had shown the power not only to fight wartime enemies but also to attack, imprison, exile, and destroy masses of their own citizens. And while the Cold War balance of power had apparently kept nuclear weapons under control, local wars broke out constantly around the globe. Serious questions arose as to the ability of the earth and the seas to withstand the pressure of the new technology on planetary resources. Ecological **sustainability** became a new concern. Even for "winners," this was an age of anxiety.

For those less fortunate, poverty, servitude, ill-health, and hunger remained the common fate. Even though experts declared that new technologies provided the capacity to feed the entire, growing population of the earth, governmental policies, both national and international, did not provide the necessary legal and technological means of distribution.

The postwar years, however, seemed to favor the optimists over the pessimists. Global wars stopped. Despite proxy wars, the nuclear weapons of the Cold War remained unused. Almost all colonies gained their independence. The UN offered a global forum in which the peoples of the world could come together to address their common needs. The purview of the UN was continually extended to include not only conflict resolution, peace-keeping, and international law, but also education, child welfare, the condition of women, labor relations, human rights, ecology, settlement patterns, and appropriate technology. The world's economy—its production of food as well as of consumer goods—expanded more rapidly than its population. In retrospect, optimists could be justified in calling the postwar years of reconstruction, decolonization, economic expansion, and cultural regeneration, if not a golden era, at least an era of promise.

KEY TERM

sustainability A vague but very significant measurement usually applied to new technologies—for example new drugs or pesticides, or financial enterprises— concerning their compatibility with the ecological health of individuals and of the planet, and with social and economic equity among individuals and groups; at a minimum, assuring that these technologies do not deplete their own natural resource base.

CHAPTER REVIEW

THE COLD WAR: US VS. USSR

21.1 What were the reasons for the Cold War between the USSR and the US?

At the end of World War II, two nations, the Soviet Union and the United States, emerged as politically and militarily dominant. One espoused an ideology of communism in government and economics, the other democracy in government and capitalism in economics. Each sought to establish its supremacy. Through their alliances, they divided postwar Europe between them. They saw new nations emerging out of colonial control to political independence, or out of neocolonial control to economic independence, as a major new development in world politics, and as a source of allies. Both offered these new nations economic and military assistance. They urged the new nations to choose sides between them and their political ideologies. Some, like Cuba, chose the USSR, others, like South Korea, chose the US, still others, like India, chose to be non-aligned. Although the US and USSR never fought each other directly, they sometimes backed opposing sides in "proxy wars" among their allies.

1968: REVOLT AGAINST AUTHORITY

21.2 Why has "1968" become a shorthand for a time of cultural restlessness?

The culture shifted in the 1960s. In particular, 1968 was a watershed for youth rebellion, as European and American students protested the war in Vietnam, joined factory workers fighting for better working conditions, fought for reform in Iron Curtain countries like Czechoslovakia, and challenged authority on university campuses. In the US, in response to antiwar protests, President Lyndon Johnson decided not to run for reelection. In Czechoslovakia, liberal reforms were followed by a Soviet crackdown. Around the world, proclaiming "make love, not war," young people experimented with drugs and clothes, sex and music. Often they admired the heroes of third world revolution, like Che Guevara.

CHAPTER REVIEW (continued)

COLONIAL AUTHORITY OVERTHROWN: NEW NATIONS ARE BORN

21.3 Why did decolonization take place so quickly, once it had begun?

The gaining of independence by more than 50 European colonies was one of the great achievements of the postwar years. It was also a direct legacy of both world wars and the Great Depression, all of which were so cataclysmic that they exploded the myth of the moral superiority of the colonizing nations. Colonizing nations, especially Great Britain, began to see colonial holdings as costly, both morally and economically. Meanwhile, the US and the USSR, for different reasons, supported colonial nationalists' drives for independence. With colonized people eager for independence, and colonizing nations less eager and less able to continue to hold onto them, independence came quickly, once it started.

THE EMERGENCE OF THE THIRD WORLD

21.4 Why did many "third-world" nations object to the pressures imposed on them by the Cold War?

With the "first world" (consisting of the US and its allies) and the "second world" (consisting of the USSR and its allies) polarized into two hostile, belligerent, and heavily armed blocs, many of the world's newly independent nations sought to avoid taking sides. "Third-world" nations such as India, Egypt, and Ethiopia that were "new," politically, were actually ancient civilizations, and they were proud of their centuries of traditional knowledge. The devastation of two world wars, and the continuing arms race for nuclear weapons, provided clear evidence to them that in the first and second worlds, life was cheap. Representatives of the third world convened for the first time in 1955 to develop a postcolonial agenda. They called for an end to the superpowers' arms race, and for investment instead in such basic human needs as food, clothing, shelter, medical care, and small-scale technology.

THE END OF THE COLD WAR: THE SOVIET UNION DISSOLVES, 1989–91

21.5 How did the Soviet Union come to collapse and disintegrate?

For the West, the Soviet Union's collapse and disintegration in the space of two years was shocking. From its position as an overwhelming, and dreaded, totalitarian power, the USSR utterly dissolved into 15 independent states. The changes began in 1985 when Mikhail Gorbachev announced reforms: in response to the country's economic and social problems, which he bluntly (and surprisingly) identified, Gorbachev introduced the new policies of *glasnost* (openness) and *perestroika* (economic restructuring), and appointed reformers to government offices. From then on, Gorbachev was caught in his own promises, as reformers criticized him for moving too slowly, and ethnic groups began to state their complaints. In 1988, Gorbachev allowed multicandidate elections. In 1989, he announced that any Soviet satellite nations that wanted to break free, could—and they did. On November 9, 1989, the hated Wall between East and West Berlin was torn down, and in December, Gorbachev and US President George H. W. Bush announced the end of the Cold War. With Soviet armies gone, all six Soviet satellite nations became independent. Gorbachev at first resisted efforts by the republics of the Soviet Union to declare independence, but many of them simply declared it anyway. In August 1991, a few days after an attempted military coup against him was put down, Gorbachev resigned as president and dissolved the Communist Party. By the end of the year, the USSR was formally dissolved.

PURSUING PEACE THROUGH NEGOTIATION

21.6 What were the major postwar strategies for achieving peace through negotiation and institution-building?

While the USSR and the US threatened each other in a Cold War, and sometimes fought proxy wars, the nations of Western Europe and Japan sought to find new ways of peaceful cooperation after the wars of the first half of the century. The organizations they formed beginning in the 1950s created the basis of a unified European economic administration in the 1960s, a unification that would encourage cooperation, not war. In Japan, although the US encouraged the nation to become involved in its Cold War fight with the USSR, Japan's postwar constitution renounced war as a means of settling international disputes "forever."

Meanwhile, the United Nations worked to minimize the polarization of the superpowers, and it had some success as an arena for defusing tensions and providing peacekeeping missions. The UN also undertook to monitor global health, as in climate change and ocean pollution, and it enacted initiatives to support the poor, women's rights, the reduction of nuclear weapons, and the eradication of diseases. As well, many nongovernmental organizations (NGOs) throughout the world worked to supply the tools by which people could improve their lives (Oxfam) and to promote and protect human rights (Amnesty International).

Suggested Readings

PRINCIPAL SOURCES

Applebaum, Anne. *Gulag: A History* (New York: Doubleday Books, 2003). A comprehensive scholarly account, stressing the economic importance of the gulag and human relations inside it. Complements Solzhenitsyn's first-person, fictionalized account.

Bulliet, Richard W., ed. *The Columbia History of the 20th Century* (New York: Columbia University Press, 1998). Comprehensive and thoughtful collection of articles by theme rather than chronology.

Burns, E. Bradford, and Julie Charlip. *Latin America: A Concise Interpretive History* (Upper Saddle River, NJ: Prentice Hall, 2006). A standard text. Especially strong on Brazil.

Carson, Rachel. *Silent Spring* (New York: Penguin Books, 1965). An attack on the chemical and pesticide industries. The single most important book in launching the modern ecological movement.

Chakrabarty, Dipesh. *Provincializing Europe: Postcolonial Thought and Historical Difference* (Princeton, NJ: Princeton University Press,

2000). Sees Western history as following only one possible pattern. There are others.

Dower, John. *Embracing Defeat* (New York: W.W. Norton, 2000). A comprehensive, wonderfully readable story of America's occupation of Japan, 1945–52. Emphasizes the human contact more than the institutional changes.

Fieldhouse, D.K. *Black Africa 1945–1980* (London: Allen and Unwin, 1986). An attempt to understand what went wrong in independent Africa, and why.

Friedman, Thomas. *From Beirut to Jerusalem* (New York: Farrar, Straus and Giroux, 1989). Presentation of the continuing Israeli–Arab hostility by a leading *New York Times* reporter.

Goncharov, Sergei N., John W. Lewis, and Xue Litai. *Uncertain Partners: Stalin, Mao, and the Korean War* (Stanford, CA: Stanford University Press, 1993). Reveals the bargaining and, ultimately, the hostility between the communist leaders.

Harden, Blaine. *Dispatches from a Fragile Continent* (Boston, MA: Houghton Mifflin, 1990). *The Washington Post* bureau chief in sub-Saharan Africa calls it the way he sees it, and not much is very pleasant or elevating.

Hitchcock, William. *The Struggle for Europe* (New York: Anchor Books, 2003). Excellent, lucid history of postwar Europe, concentrating mostly on political history.

Immerman, Richard, and Petra Goedde, eds. *The Oxford Handbook of the Cold War* (New York: Oxford University Press, 2013). Interpretive essays by 36 leading scholars of the Cold War provide the most up-to-date insight based on newly opened archives and newly framed questions.

Judt, Tony. *Postwar: A History of Europe since 1945* (New York: Penguin Press, 2005). Comprehensive, masterly survey of the continent, 1945–2004.

Keen, Benjamin. *A History of Latin America* (Boston, MA: Houghton Mifflin, 9th ed., 2012). Good, standard comprehensive coverage. Now expanded into two volumes.

Kenez, Peter. *A History of the Soviet Union from the Beginning to the End* (Cambridge: Cambridge University Press, 1999). A study and evaluation of principal institutions and their impact. Thoughtful analyses and evaluations.

Kennedy, Paul. *The Rise and Fall of the Great Powers* (New York: Random House, 1987). Kennedy focuses on the balance between economic health and military preparedness.

Morris, Benny. *The Birth of the Palestinian Refugee Problem 1947–1949* (Cambridge: Cambridge University Press, 1988). A major revisionist historian indicts the Israelis for driving many Palestinians out of their homes.

——. *Righteous Victims: A History of the Zionist–Arab Conflict, 1881–1999* (New York; Knopf, 1999). Morris finds plenty of blame to go around for the continuing Arab–Israeli struggle.

Service, Robert. *A History of Twentieth-Century Russia* (Cambridge, MA: Harvard University Press, 1997). The story told largely through the actions and statements of Russia's leaders.

Sigmund, Paul, ed. *The Ideologies of the Developing Nations* (New York: Praeger Publishers, 2nd rev. ed., 1972). Excellent selection of observations, analyses, and manifestos by leaders from throughout the third world in its heyday.

Solzhenitsyn, Alexander. *The Gulag Archipelago*, 3 vols. (New York: Harper and Row, 1974–78). A terrifying revelation of the prison system at the base of the Soviet government's control of its citizens.

Stavrianos, Leften. *Global Rift* (New York: Morrow, 1981). A left-wing interpretation of the divisions between the rich and poor nations.

Vogel, Ezra. *The Four Little Dragons: The Spread of Industrialization in East Asia* (Cambridge, MA: Harvard University Press, 1991). Korea, Taiwan, Singapore, and Hong Kong demonstrated that countries could leap from the third world to the first. Vogel shows how they did it.

Von Laue, Theodore. *The World Revolution of Westernization* (New York, Oxford University Press, 1987). Sees the Western world as leading the way for everyone to modernization.

Westad, Odd Arne. *The Global Cold War: Third World Interventions and the Making of Our Times* (Cambridge: Cambridge University Press, 2005). Focuses on the destructive connections between Cold War politics and new nations.

ADDITIONAL SOURCES

Andrea, Alfred, and James H. Overfield, eds. *The Human Record*, vol. 2 (Florence, KY: Wadsworth Publishing Col, 6th ed., 2008). Excellent collection of primary documents.

Avishai, Bernard. *The Tragedy of Zionism* (New York: Farrar, Straus and Giroux, 1985). Covers the impact on the Arab world as well as the Jewish.

Black, Maggie. *A Cause for Our Time: Oxfam, the First Fifty Years* (Oxford: Oxford University Press, 1992). Recounts Oxfam's history, the tough decisions it has made, and its increasing influence in development planning.

Duus, Peter. *Modern Japan* (Boston, MA: Houghton Mifflin, 2nd ed., 1998). Excellent and comprehensive text.

Fanon, Frantz. *The Wretched of the Earth*, trans. Constance Farrington (New York: Grove Press, 1963). Classic statement of the psychological wounds of colonialism. Calls for anticolonial violence as a means of healing.

Hobsbawm, Eric. *The Age of Extremes: A History of the World, 1914–1991* (New York: Pantheon Books, 1994). Surveys the scene politically, economically, and culturally. Engagingly written.

International Institute for Environment and Development and the World Resources Institute. *World Resources* (New York: Basic Books, published annually). Basic report with abundant quantitative information.

Johnson, Hazel, and Henry Bernstein, eds. *Third World Lives of Struggle* (London: Heinemann Educational Books, 1982). Marvelous and touching selection of biographical and autobiographical sketches of people's lives with some poetry and interpretive articles as well.

Kochan, Lionel, and Richard Abraham. *The Making of Modern Russia* (London: Penguin Books, 1983). Useful on the Khrushchev and Brezhnev years.

Nkrumah, Kwame. *Ghana: The Autobiography of Kwame Nkrumah* (New York: Thomas Nelson and Sons, 1957). The leader of the first black African country to achieve independence from British rule tells his story, up to 1957.

Nugent, Neill. *The Government and Politics of the European Union* (New York: Palgrave Macmillan, 7th ed., 2010). Dry but comprehensive, thorough examination of the major institutions and their significance.

Power, Jonathan. *Like Water on Stone: The Story of Amnesty International* (Boston, MA: Northeastern University Press, 2001). Recounts the struggles of this preeminent international human rights organization.

Schumacher, E.F. *Economics as if People Mattered* (New York: Harper Perennial, 1989). Schumacher's essays in "humanistic economics" are concerned with the human effects of economic systems, and advocate for appropriate-scale technology.

FILMS

Battle of Algiers (1966; 2 hours 3 minutes). The classic film of the violent struggle for independence by a colony (Algeria) against a colonizer (France). Looks like a documentary, but is not. Remarkable views of Algiers, and there is humanity on both sides, through all the violence.

Dr. Strangelove, or: How I Learned to Stop Worrying and Love the Bomb (1964; 1 hour 33 minutes). Frightening, hilarious spoof on the use of nuclear weapons by renegade US military officer.

Fidel (2002; 2 hours 20 minutes). Biography of the leader, from his life as a lawyer for the poor to a guerrilla warrior who seized control of Cuba from Fulgencio Batista. Examines also his policies in governing Cuba after victory.

The Lives of Others (2006; 2 hours 17 minutes). Based on files of the East German secret police that became available at the end of the Cold War. Depicts the spying of one spy on another and all against civilians. Abuse of power is the main theme.

Lumumba (2001; 1 hour 55 minutes). Biography of the first prime minister of the independent Congo and his turbulent life in politics, up to his assassination as a result of the international political intrigue, and domestic infighting, over Congo's riches. Violent.

The Motorcycle Diaries (2004; 2 hours 8 minutes). We travel for some months with Che Guevara and his friends through many countries in South America. As we see the poverty through his eyes, we understand how the young medical student becomes a revolutionary.

One Day in the Life of Ivan Denisovich (1970; 1 hour 45 minutes). Bleak film about a bleak day in the life of a prisoner in a Soviet gulag prison in Siberia. Based on Alexander Solzhenitsyn's novel.

The Spy Who Came in from the Cold (1965; 1 hour 50 minutes). Film of John le Carré's spy novel set at the height of the Cold War. Surprisingly intimate presentation of the inner life of an aging British spy. Spying here is not romantic.

22 China and India

Into the Twenty-First Century

Home to some of the world's most ancient and influential civilizations, China and India are almost worlds in themselves. Both are vast and densely populated countries containing, together, more than a third of the world's population. Both were subject to European colonial domination in the nineteenth and early twentieth centuries, and both gained full political independence in the middle of the twentieth century. Both were predominantly agrarian countries (India still is: about 68 percent; China only about 50 percent). Nevertheless, they followed very different paths of development. Because of their sheer size, the similarity of many of their circumstances, and the contrast in their decisions on development, we devote a full chapter to them.

Jawaharlal Nehru and Zhou Enlai, 1954. Prime Minister Nehru (right), accompanied by Chinese foreign minister Zhou Enlai, is cheered by crowds as he arrives on a state visit to Red China.

LEARNING OBJECTIVES

22.1 ((•	22.2 ((•	22.3 ((•	22.4 ((•	22.5 ((•	22.6 ((•	22.7 ((•
Compare the political and economic paths of development of China since 1949 with India since 1947.	Explain ways in which the experiences of the Long March and the guerrilla war guided China's leaders after 1949.	Describe the revolutionary policies of the People's Republic of China.	Understand how the end of colonialism changed China's image of itself.	Describe Mohandas Gandhi's concept of civil disobedience and his role in India's struggle for independence.	Understand how the experiences of the independence movement guided the governance of India after 1947.	Explain the major policy issues addressed by independent India.

((• **Listen** on **MyHistoryLab**

China and India: A Comparison

22.1 How did China (since 1949) and India (since 1947) differ in their paths of economic and political development?

At the turn of the twentieth century, China, with 400 million people, contained about a quarter of the world's population. The India of the British Empire—which included today's Pakistan and Bangladesh—contained about one-sixth, about 285 million people. Both countries were overwhelmingly agricultural, with populations about 80 to 85 percent rural. Both were vast in territory and densely populated.

Politically, India was ruled as a colony of Britain until 1947. China was not administered directly by foreign powers, but Britain, France, Russia, Germany, and Japan had great economic and cultural control over the huge nation and directly ruled portions of it. Under British rule, India had a single central administration, despite its diverse ethnicities, languages, religions, castes, and local princes. China, on the other hand, was without an effective central government for most of the first half of the century, suffering both civil war and invasion from Japan.

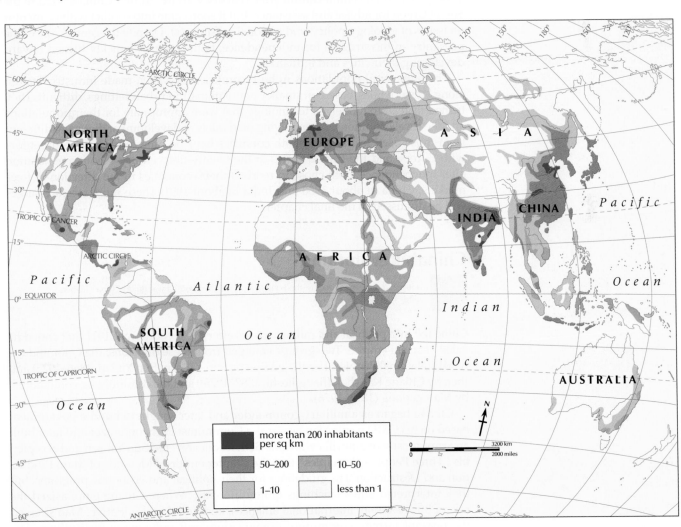

World population distribution, 2000. While the bulk of the world's population lives, as always, in coastal regions or along river valleys, the rapid rise in urbanism over the last century has created enormous imbalances as cities attract economic migrants from their hinterlands and from abroad. Some areas, such as Europe, are so urbanized that their entire surface has high densities; others, like China and India, are so packed that even rural areas house urban densities. The only low-density areas are those that are ecologically difficult for human life: deserts, mountains, and frozen regions.

Both countries sought independence from foreign control. Both began these struggles as protest movements from within their modern sectors, envisioning an industrialized, bureaucratized future, led by professional men trained in modern administrative, educational, journalistic, legal, and military skills. As they began to gain success, however, leaders of the struggle for independence in both countries found this urban- and professional-based organization inadequate. They turned instead to mass movements of the peasantry and common people, who formed the overwhelming majority of the population.

India and China attained independent statehood at about the same time. India won independence from Britain in 1947. In China, the communist revolution achieved victory in 1949 and unified almost the entire country (except for Taiwan, Hong Kong, and Macao) under its leadership. Then the two countries chose different strategies of development. Influenced by British colonial legacies and by its own heterogeneity, India chose democratic electoral politics and a mixed socialist–capitalist economy, with strong cultural ties to the Western democracies and some military links to the Soviet Union. In China, on the other hand, a victorious communist army asserted strong, dictatorial central control after years of warfare. At first China looked to the Soviet Union for advice and assistance, but it soon came into conflict with its mentor on issues of ideology, policy, and national self-interest. Despite the central role of the peasantry in the struggle for independence, both countries quickly turned toward developing their cities and industries.

The large rural populations in both countries, however, made industrialization along Western lines, based on smaller populations and urban settings, difficult. They turned instead to models of technology that were appropriate for their populations and the rural conditions. Often relying on models of development that were different from those used in the West, both countries have become formidable competitors with Europe and the United States in the twenty-first century. About a generation after independence, both chose to reorient their economies in the direction of freer markets, China in about 1980 and India in about 1991. These more recent changes will be discussed in the final chapters.

China's Revolutions

22.2 How did the experiences of the Long March and the guerrilla war guide China's leaders after 1949?

China fell into political and military chaos after the revolution of 1911 that ended its 2,000-year-old empire. Two groups emerged from these divisions: the Guomindang (GMD, National People's Party), led first by Sun Yat-sen (Sun Yixian, 1866–1925) and then by Chiang Kai-shek (Jiang Jieshi, 1887–1975); and the communists, commanded by Mao Zedong (1893–1976).

Chiang began as a military commander and later sought to build a government based on his GMD party. Mao began as a Communist Party organizer and later built an army, mostly of guerrilla warriors. Both leaders revered Sun Yat-sen and accepted his "Three People's Principles" (see the chapter entitled "Methods of Mass Production and Destruction") as guidelines for their political and economic programs, but they interpreted Sun's teachings quite differently. Where Chiang emphasized the role of businessmen, international alliances, and individual initiative, Mao stressed the peasant farmer, community organization, and indigenous institutions. The two men and their parties fought for control in a bitter civil war that festered for a quarter century after Sun's death in 1925. Both learned that "in a country ruled and plundered by marauding warlord armies, it was naked military power that was crucial in determining the direction of political events" (Meisner, p. 21). In Mao's blunt words: "Political power grows out of the barrel of a gun."

AT A GLANCE: CHINA AND INDIA

DATE	CHINA	INDIA
1900	• Boxer Rebellion against Western influence is suppressed by foreign troops (1900)	• Mohandas Karamchand Gandhi publishes *Hind Swaraj*, or *Indian Home Rule* (1909)
1910	• Revolution of 1911 ends Manchu dynasty and 2,000 years of imperial rule • Yuan Shihkai elected premier (1911); dies 1916 • Warlords battle throughout China • May Fourth Movement (1919)	• Gandhi returns from South Africa and establishes new *ashram* in Ahmedabad (1915) • Government of India Act creates dual British/Indian government (1919) • British crack down on freedom of the press and of assembly in the Rowlatt Acts (1919) • Amritsar (Jallianwala Bagh) massacre (1919)
1920	• Chinese Communist Party formed (1921) • Sun Yat-sen dies (1925) • Guomindang (GMD) and communists vie for power (1925–49) • Chiang Kai-shek captures Beijing (1927–28); rules from Nanjing • Mao's report on Hunan peasant movement (1927)	• Non-Cooperation campaign boycotts British interests (1920–22) • Gandhi fasts for 21 days to promote Hindu–Muslim unity (1924)
1930	• Mao Zedong leads communists on the Long March, from Jiangxi to Yan'an (1934) • Japanese seize Manchuria (1931) and go on to invade China proper (1937) • Communists kidnap Chiang to gain his cooperation in the war against Japan (1936)	• Salt March campaign (1930–32) • Gandhi outflanks socialists by persuading Jawaharlal Nehru to postpone land redistribution • Congress appoints National Planning Commission (1938)
1940	• Japan surrenders; civil war resumes (1945) • Foundation of the communist People's Republic of China (1949) • Foreigners expelled (1949)	• Quit India campaign (1942) • Independence from Great Britain is accompanied by partition of the subcontinent (1947) and Indo-Pakistan war over Kashmir (1947)
1950	• China invades and colonizes Tibet (1950) • Korean War (1950–53) • "Hundred Flowers" campaign briefly permits some freedom of expression (1956–57) • Mao initiates Great Leap Forward experiment (1958–60)	• Policy of protective discrimination reserves jobs for untouchable castes (1955) • Hindu Marriage Act (1955) and Hindu Succession Act (1956) increase rights for women; Muslims are not affected • India provides refuge to Dalai Lama escaping Tibet (1959)
1960	• Diplomatic relations with Russia are severed (1961) • Sino-Indian border war (1962) • Thousands of Chinese murdered in Indonesia (1965) • Cultural Revolution initiates party purges and reignites revolutionary zeal; formation of Red Guard (1966)	• Sino-Indian border war (1962) • Green revolution in agriculture (1960s–1970s) • Death of Nehru (1964) • War with Pakistan (1965)
1970	• China joins United Nations (1971) • Groundbreaking visit to China by President Nixon (1972) • Mao dies; "Gang of Four" arrested (1976) • Deng Xiaoping comes to power; economic liberalization (1979) • One family, one child policy (1979)	• Civil war leads to creation of Bangladesh on land of East Pakistan (1971) • Prime Minister Indira Gandhi asserts dictatorial powers during "Emergency Rule" (1975–77) • Policy of forced sterilization (1975–77)
1980	• China joins World Bank and the International Monetary Fund (1980) • Students demonstrating in Tiananmen Square are killed by soldiers (1989)	• Indira Gandhi assassinated (1984)

Chiang Kai-shek and the Guomindang

Chiang had studied in a Japanese military academy, fought in the revolution to overthrow the Manchu government in 1911, and rose to command China's own new Whampoa military academy near Guangzhou, established with Soviet financing. After Sun's death, he succeeded to the leadership of the GMD.

Chiang courted diverse, apparently contradictory constituencies. A staunch advocate of the neo-Confucian New Life movement in the 1930s, Chiang wrote

China's Destiny in 1943 to reaffirm the conservative virtues of China's indigenous, hierarchical, genteel culture. Yet he also became a Methodist, as Sun had. Also like Sun, Chiang married a Chinese Christian woman and valued the contributions of foreign Christians to China's economic modernization. He maintained a wide and diverse array of close personal, professional, and financial connections with Shanghai underworld figures, Soviet Comintern agents, Western businessmen, and Christian missionaries.

Foreign powers in the treaty ports monitored China's shifting fortunes with considerable self-interest. By 1931 foreigners had invested $3.25 billion in China. Foreign loans financed China's railways and heavy industry, and foreigners held 75 percent of all investments in shipping, almost 50 percent of the cotton spindles, and 80 to 90 percent of the coal mines. In the early 1920s, the politicization and unionization of industrial workers encouraged many strikes, to which the employers—many of them foreigners—responded violently. These employers wanted a compliant government that would help them to break the strikes and keep the workers in line. They believed Chiang to be their man and they provided large loans to keep his government afloat.

Christian missionaries and educational institutions also supported the GMD, attracted partly by Chiang's own Christian affiliation. The YMCA movement claimed 54,000 members in 1922. In the early 1920s some 12,000 Christian missionaries served in China. Christian and foreign colleges enrolled 4,000 of the 35,000 students in Chinese colleges in 1922. Nine percent of their students were women. China's universities incorporated the study of Western culture and literature, and Western academic luminaries (as well as the poet and Nobel laureate Rabindranath Tagore of India) toured and lectured widely.

With the support of Western business and cultural leaders, and of the Soviet Comintern as well, Chiang undertook to defeat the warlords and reestablish a viable central government under his own control. Through the great northern expedition from Guangzhou, Chiang captured Beijing in 1927–28, established his own capital in Nanjing on the lower Yangzi River, and began to consolidate GMD power over China.

Mao Zedong and Peasant Revolt

Mao Zedong, Sun's other principal successor, shared his goals of a strong, united, independent China and the improvement of the people's livelihood, but his background was quite different from Sun's and Chiang's.

First, even though Mao, too, participated in the revolution of 1911, it had ended by the time he was 18. Second, Mao's experience was limited to China. Although he read widely in Western as well as Chinese literature and philosophy, his first travel outside China, a visit to the Soviet Union, came only in 1949. Third, Mao had little experience of the Western business and missionary establishments in China. His own formative experiences were in the countryside and in formal educational institutions. Compared with both Sun and Chiang, Mao cared little for China's reputation in the West but much for the quality of life of the Chinese peasant. He had grown up on his father's farm in Hunan province, where he learned at first hand of the exploitation of the peasant. He viewed his father as one of the exploiters.

By 1919, Mao had come to study at Beijing (Peking) University, just as China's resentment against foreign imperialism was boiling over. The peace treaties of World War I assigned Germany's holdings in the Shandong Peninsula of north China to Japan rather than returning them to China. Enraged students created the May Fourth Movement, a powerful and enduring protest against China's international humiliation and the apparent disregard for its grand historical traditions. The movement helped to sow the seeds of the Chinese Communist Party (CCP), which came to fruition in 1921. At the time, Mao was a participant in the Marxist study group of Li Dazhao, chief librarian of Beijing University and one of the founders of the CCP. In a statement quite unusual for a Chinese intellectual, Li had already proclaimed

22.1
22.2
22.3
22.4
22.5
22.6
22.7

How did the experiences of the Long March and the guerrilla war guide China's leaders after 1949?

the importance of the peasantry and called on the university students to help them to mobilize: "Our China is a rural nation and most of the laboring class is made up of peasants. If they are not liberated then our whole nation will not be liberated. … Go out and develop them and cause them to … demand liberation" (cited in Spence, 1999, p. 308). When Mao first joined the party he began organizing workers in the industrial plants of the Wuhan region, but in 1925 he was reassigned to peasant organization in his native Hunan. Despite the orthodox Marxist doctrines of the CCP's Comintern advisers, in Hunan Mao came to see the rural peasantry, rather than the urban proletariat, as China's revolutionary vanguard. He abandoned the emphasis on large-scale industrial planning and sought instead local solutions to local problems through locally developed, appropriate rural technology. Mao's report of 1927 on the Hunan peasant movement updated Li's rural emphasis, adding large doses of communist rhetoric:

> The broad peasant masses have risen to fulfill their historic mission … the democratic forces in the rural areas have risen to overthrow the rural feudal power. The patriarchal-feudal class of local bullies, bad gentry, and lawless landlords has formed the basis of autocratic government for thousands of years, the cornerstone of imperialism, warlordism and corrupt officialdom. To overthrow this feudal power is the real objective of the national revolution … The leadership of the poor peasants is absolutely necessary. Without the poor peasants there can be no revolution. (cited in de Bary, *Chinese* ,1960, p. 869)

The peasants had to use their strength to overthrow the authority of the landlords. This revolution required violence.

While Mao was organizing rural peasants in the 1920s, Chiang was massacring the core of the revolutionary urban proletariat. As he completed the first stage of the northern expedition from Guangzhou to Nanjing, and consolidated his control over the warlords, he turned, in alliance with the international business community, and without excessive objection from the Soviet Comintern, to murdering thousands of communist workers in the industrialized cities of Shanghai, Wuhan, and Guangzhou in the spring of 1927. In Changsha, local military leaders joined with the GMD and local landlords to slaughter thousands of peasants who had recently expropriated the land they worked from its legal owners. By the summer of 1928, only 32,000 union members in all of China remained loyal to the Communist Party. By 1929, only three percent of party members were proletarians. Mao's peasant alternative was, of necessity, the communists' last resort.

When the GMD put down the Hunan Autumn Harvest Uprising in 1927, Mao's core group retreated to the border area between Hunan and Jiangzi. Other communist leaders, driven from the cities, joined them in this rural area. They instituted **soviets**, local communist governments that redistributed land, introduced improved farming methods, and instituted new educational systems to spread literacy along with political indoctrination. They recruited and trained a guerrilla army. Mao himself formulated its tactics: "The enemy advances, we retreat; the enemy camps, we harass; the enemy tires, we attack; the enemy retreats, we pursue" (cited in Spence, 1999, p. 375).

The guerrillas could exist only with the cooperation of the peasantry, whom they wished to mobilize. Mao therefore ordered them to treat the peasants with respect: "Be courteous and polite to the people and help them when you can … Be honest in all transactions with the peasants … Pay for all articles purchased" (cited in Snow, p. 176).

Gender Issues in the Revolution

Feminism had begun to flourish in China by the 1920s with the formation of such organizations as the Women's Suffrage Association and the Women's Rights League. Their constituency was mostly Western-influenced urban intellectuals. These women and men read magazines such as *New Youth*, which criticized Confucius for his

KEY TERM

soviet Chinese soviets, governing councils made up of peasants, were modeled in part on Russian examples, but they focused on rural, rather than urban, administration. Founded during the revolutionary movement, they also provided guerrilla warriors for the campaigns.

How did the experiences of the Long March and the guerrilla war guide China's leaders after 1949?

emphasis on patriarchy and obedience to authority. They translated and published Henrik Ibsen's feminist play *A Doll's House* in 1918. Ba Jinn's novel *Family*, one of the key works of China's reformist New Culture Movement, transplanted Ibsen's advocacy of women's equality and independence into a modern Chinese setting. Margaret Sanger, the American advocate of contraception, toured and lectured throughout China in 1922. There were also some 1.5 million women working outside their homes for pay in light industrial factories, mostly textiles, in China's cities. Women's rights were already advancing in China's coastal metropolises; Mao now refocused feminist attention onto the countryside and the peasantry as well:

> The authority of the husband … has always been comparatively weak among the poor peasants, because the poor peasant women, compelled for financial reasons to take more part in manual work than women of the wealthier classes, have obtained more right to speak and more power to make decisions in family affairs. In recent years the rural economy has become even more bankrupt and the basic condition for men's domination over women has already been undermined. And now, with the rise of the peasant movement, women in many places have set out immediately to organize the rural women's association; the opportunity has come for them to lift up their heads, and the authority of the husband is tottering more and more every day. (cited in de Bary, *Chinese*, 1960, p. 872)

Communist policies took two complementary directions. The first, and more effective, restructured the labor and military forces to give more scope and power to women. Building the Chinese soviets and fighting guerrilla battles required every available resource. While women did not usually participate in warfare directly, the increased need for production and personnel brought them out of the house into new jobs, effectively raising their status.

The Long March and the Communist Triumph

Chiang sent five successive military expeditions against the Jiangzi soviet, beginning with 100,000 men and leading up to one million. By 1934, the communists could no longer hold out. Mao led some 80,000 men and 35 women out of the siege and began the Long March, a 370-day, 6,000-mile strategic retreat, by foot, under constant bombardment and attack from Chiang's forces, across rivers, mountain ranges, marshes, and grasslands, to a new base camp in Yan'an. Some 20,000 men finally arrived in Yan'an, of whom about half had marched since the beginning; the rest had joined en route. The courage, comradeship, commitment, and idealism of this march, in the face of seemingly insurmountable natural obstacles and enemy harassment, were the formative experience of a generation of Chinese communist leaders. At the front, Mao now became the unquestioned leader of the movement, party, and army.

The Yan'an Soviet. In remote, impoverished Yan'an, Mao established his capital and rebuilt his soviet structure, nurturing his army and inducting its soldiers into agricultural assistance work; redistributing land; encouraging handicrafts; and establishing newspapers and schools, an arts and literature academy, and medical programs for training paramedical **barefoot doctors**. The Chinese communist program developed more fully here: a peasant-centered economy, administered and aided by guerrilla soldiers, capped by a dictatorial but comparatively benevolent communist leadership, encouraging literacy accompanied by indoctrination in communist ideology. Tension built up, however, between the advocates of ideological goals and the proponents of practical implementation, between being "Red" and being "expert."

Cooperation with the GMD. Meanwhile, Mao wished to join forces with Chiang to unite China against the foreigner. By comparison, Chiang seemed less nationalistic. He appeared willing to compromise with the Japanese, and more eager to pursue

KEY TERM

barefoot doctors Paramedical personnel trained in basic medicine and dispatched to work in rural areas, where virtually no professionally trained doctors chose to practice.

The Long March, 1934–35. The Long March, actually a strategic retreat of some 6,000 miles from communist headquarters in southeast China to a new base in northwest China, provided the founding legend of the Chinese communist movement, a tale of daring, resourcefulness, and guerrilla warfare. Along the route of the march, the leaders organized villagers into soviets, local government groups that redistributed land and set up educational and health facilities. Here, leaders of the march address their followers in Shensi Province, toward the end of the march.

22.1

How did the experiences of the Long March and the guerrilla war guide China's leaders after 1949?

22.2

22.3

22.4

22.5

22.6

22.7

the Chinese communists than to fight the foreign invaders. In the "Xi'an incident" of 1936, dissident generals kidnapped Chiang and threatened to kill him if he did not join more vigorously in the fight against the Japanese. Subsequently, Chiang moved toward temporary cooperation with the communists.

In 1937, the Japanese invaded China proper, launching World War II, although that was not clear at the time. At first, the Japanese hoped to rule China with the help of Chinese collaborators, as they had Manchuria, but their cruelty in the capture of Nanjing in December 1937 backfired. Instead of collapsing, the Chinese resistance became more resolute. The communists fought a rearguard guerrilla war from their northern base in Shaanxi, while Chiang led a **scorched-earth** retreat to a new headquarters far up the Yangzi River in Chongqing. Soldiers and civilians endured dreadful suffering.

The GMD Retreats to Taiwan. By the early 1940s, nationalist cooperation began to unravel as communists and GMD forces jockeyed for temporary power and future position. Following the defeat of Japan in 1945, full-scale civil war between the GMD and the communists resumed. The United States extended help to Chiang in training

KEY TERM

scorched-earth A strategy of defensive warfare, in which everything that might be of use to an invading army is destroyed by the defending army as it retreats.

777

The communist revolution in China. Chinese communists and nationalists (GMD) united briefly to subdue the warlord factions that emerged after the collapse of the Manchu (Qing) dynasty, and to consolidate a national government. After 1927, nationalist repression forced the communists to retreat to remote areas, focusing in the northwest (after the Long March of 1934–35), where guerrilla warfare continued. With the Japanese invasion of China proper in 1937, China was torn by both international and civil war. After Japan's defeat in 1945, the communists turned to defeating the GMD as well.

his troops, airlifting them to critical military locations, and delivering military supplies. The Soviet Union, fighting for its life against Germany, stayed out of the conflict against Japan until the final week of the war. Then it entered Manchuria, carrying off a great deal of that region's military and industrial equipment to the Soviet Union, while turning over some of it to the Chinese communists. As China's civil war continued after 1945, communist forces in many parts of the country, well disciplined and

CHAPTER TWENTY-TWO: CHINA AND INDIA

22.1
22.2
22.3
22.4
22.5
22.6
22.7

warmly supported by peasants, defeated the ill-disciplined and ill-provisioned GMD forces, whose rations and materials were often sold off for private profit, without ever reaching them. By the fall of 1949, the communists had driven the GMD completely out of mainland China to the island of Taiwan. Selfishly, the GMD occupied and took over houses and businesses of Taiwanese who already lived there. They claimed that their government in Taiwan was the true China. They dreamed of someday recapturing, reuniting with, and returning to the mainland.

What were the revolutionary policies of the People's Republic of China?

The People's Republic of China

22.3 What were the revolutionary policies of the People's Republic of China?

On the mainland, the new rulers surrounding Mao modeled much of their government on their experiences during the Long March and the Yan'an soviet. They returned to these experiences for inspiration in difficult times as long as they lived. Their principal fears were of foreign domination, internal chaos, and the lingering power of the wealthy urban classes and the large-scale rural landholders.

Revolutionary Policies

Mao's policy goals for the new government included the redistribution of land; protection of women's rights to hold land; implementation of appropriate technology; the production and equal distribution of basic necessities for all; and universal literacy. The government mobilized tightknit, local, social networks not only to suppress such vices as opium addiction and prostitution but also to enforce rigid political indoctrination and conformity. It encouraged family members to inform against one another in cases of opposition to the new government and it employed psychological coercion—"**brainwashing**"—to extract confessions of political deviance.

Land redistribution was a top priority. During this class revolution, perhaps half the peasantry of China received at least some benefits while as many as one million landlords were killed. The communist government at first invited the cooperation of businessmen, both Chinese and foreign.

Policies changed abruptly as China entered the Korean War in October 1950. Threats, expropriation, and accusations of espionage—sometimes justified—against businessmen and Christian missionaries forced almost all foreigners to leave China by the end of 1950. Numerous campaigns against counterrevolutionaries; the confiscation and redistribution of private property; thousands of executions; intensive public, group pressure to elicit confessions from those perceived as enemies of the revolution; and regular confrontations between workers and owners destroyed the capitalist sector in China. Pressured by the United States, many countries refused to recognize the new government. The government of the USSR, on the other hand, maintained a strong alliance.

KEY TERM

brainwashing The popular term used in the West at the time to refer to Chinese methods of group pressure and psychological coercion to extract confessions of political deviance.

Trial of a landlord. Most such trials ended with a confession and a promise to reform; some ended with a bullet for the accused. In its first moves toward collectivization, the communist government instituted a number of land reforms that gave the land to the peasants who worked it and did away with the landlords—literally.

View the **Closer Look**: **Trial of a Landlord** on **MyHistoryLab**

KEY TERM

**"Hundred Flowers"
campaign** An invitation by Mao
Zedong to the Chinese people
in 1956–57 to express their ideas
freely and openly. At first viewed
as an invitation to democracy;
later, after many who spoke out
were jailed and punished, it came
to be seen as a well-laid trap.

Communist policies on urbanization and industrialization were ambivalent. The communists had come to power as an anti-urban, peasant movement. The large cities, especially Shanghai, had fostered the foreign enclaves, extraterritorial law, and colonial behavior that flagrantly insulted the Chinese in their own country, but they also housed China's industrial base, military technology, administration, and cultural life. Although the government attempted to limit immigration to the cities, newcomers from the countryside continued to arrive steadily, if slowly. China's population, which had been 10.6 percent urban in 1949, reached 17.4 percent urban in 1976, an increase from 57 million (of a total of 550) to 163 (of a total of 920) million people.

Militarily, the communists extolled the spirit of the guerrilla warrior over the power of high-tech weaponry. They taunted America, the world's most heavily armed country, as unwilling or unable to deploy its vast arsenal, especially its nuclear weapons, in combat. Nevertheless, China also bought, produced, or purloined up-to-date military technology. In 1964, it exploded its first atomic bomb; in the mid-1970s it followed with hydrogen bombs; in 1980 it tested missiles with a range of 7,000 miles; and, in 1981, it launched three space satellites.

View the **Closer Look**: **Reporting Our Harvest to Chairman Mao** on **MyHistoryLab**

"Let a Hundred Flowers Bloom." Economically, China adopted a five-year plan based on the Soviet model (see the chapter entitled "Methods of Mass Production and Destruction"). It called for multiplying the value of industrial output between 1952

HOW DO WE KNOW?

A Journalist–Activist Responds to the "Hundred Flowers" Campaign

When Mao introduced the **"Hundred Flowers" campaign**, the journalist Liu Binyan praised him for his democracy. As he saw the reaction of the party, however, and the subsequent use of the campaign as a means of identifying and punishing critics of the government, Liu came to see the entire movement as a trap. Liu Binyan became one of the most prominent and active of the opponents of the communist government of China. Not all historians agree with this assessment of Mao's motives, although the results were clear.

I do not remember a moment in my life more exhilarating than when Mao Zedong's February 1957 speech to the State Council was released. My estimation of him soared to sublime heights. At *China Youth News* the response was equally enthusiastic; it seemed as if we were at the beginning of a new era in China … In that speech, Mao announced that dogmatism should not be mistaken for Marxism; he reiterated his policy of letting "a hundred flowers bloom and a hundred schools of thought contend"; he advocated open criticism and reiterated that senior party leaders should not be exempt from criticism. As for strikes by workers and students—unprecedented since the founding of the People's Republic and now taken seriously for the first time—he said the right way of dealing with them was not by force or coercion but by overcoming bureaucratism.

These issues were exactly the unspoken ones that had been weighing on me for the last few years—special privileges within Party ranks, bureaucratism, and dogmatic tendencies. Now my disquiet had been dispelled as if by magic. The political climate in Beijing cleared up; the mood of intellectuals brightened; everything seemed to take on a rosy hue. Mao was virtually

advocating more democracy and liberalization in matters of ideology; as a journalist and writer, I now felt I had a free hand in pursuing my vocation.

[Liu then describes meetings with local party officials that demonstrated that many did not interpret Mao's words as he did. They saw any approval of open expression to be very limited, at most.]

… Thirty years later, I reread Mao's speech (the original version, not the one revised for publication) and realized that at the time I had been too preoccupied with his main drift to detect hints of other tendencies hidden between the lines. For instance, he did not mince words over Stalin's dogmatism, but then insisted that Stalin must be assessed on the "three-seven" principle—that is, seven parts merit to three parts fault. Again Mao considered "democracy" as basically a tool to mobilize the people for the Party's own ends. (Liu, pp. 69–70)

Liu often criticized the communist government of China and paid a price, a total of some twenty years in detention and labor camps. He came to the United States in 1988 and lived there until his death in 2005.

- Which of Liu's points make his document a primary source document? Which of his points make it a secondary source document?
- Why did Liu find Mao's campaign to let a "hundred flowers bloom" surprising?
- What led Liu to change his mind in assessing the purpose of Mao's "Hundred Flowers" campaign?

22.1

22.2

22.3

22.4

22.5

22.6

22.7

What were the
revolutionary
policies of the
People's Republic
of China?

and 1957 almost two and a half times, and claimed at the end to have exceeded the target by 22 percent. By the end of the plan, even democracy seemed a possibility. In 1956–57, Mao's call, "Let a hundred flowers bloom, let a hundred schools of thought contend," opened the gates to public expression and even criticism of government. In Beijing, students and others posted their thoughts on what became known as Democracy Wall. By late 1957, however, fearing uncontrolled, growing protest, the government reversed its policies. It jailed protesters, sent them to labor camps, and exiled them to remote rural farms. Many observers felt the entire experiment had been a trap to expose and apprehend critics of the regime.

The Great Leap Forward. Increasingly threatened by an inability to feed its rapidly expanding urban populations, the government implemented the **Great Leap Forward**, "sending down" city people to work in villages, grouping almost all of rural China into communes, virtually shutting down whatever small private enterprises had survived, and attempting to downscale and disperse industry by establishing local, low-technology enterprises, referred to generically as "backyard steel mills." The idea was that committed communists could manufacture, in small-scale production units, goods normally produced only in large-scale factories. The enterprises generally failed. The Great Leap Forward, administered by powerful, distant government officials in an attempt to restructure the entire economy of the nation according to communist ideology, led to economic catastrophe, including millions of deaths by starvation.

The Cultural Revolution. In the face of these policy failures, Mao began to silence resistance. For a few years, the government had relaxed its economic and social controls, but in 1966 it reinstated even more extreme ideological and economic policies in the Great Proletarian **Cultural Revolution**. Mao sought through this revolution

Steel furnace, Shiu Shin, China, 1958. The French photographer Henri Cartier-Bresson traveled to Shiu Shin to capture and record the life of its communes. Some 310,000 inhabitants were divided into seven popular communes, or production units. Some were responsible for "backyard," very small-scale, local, steel furnaces. China's mobilization of its masses of rural population for undertaking industrial production was extraordinary, a continuation of the ethic of its communist, rural revolution, but the quality of the steel was low.

KEY TERMS

Great Leap Forward The policy of the Chinese communist government in the late 1950s of building China's economy on the basis of small-scale, localized production in rural communities.

Cultural Revolution The policy of the Chinese communist government, 1966–76, of basing its economy on rural productivity and quelling the intellectual and cultural life of the cities, subordinating freedom of thought completely in favor of communist ideology.

22.1

22.2

22.3   What were the
revolutionary
policies of the
People's Republic
of China?

22.4

22.5

22.6

22.7

to purge the party of time-serving bureaucrats and to reignite China's revolutionary fervor. Those who responded most enthusiastically were the armed forces and the students, who, with Mao's encouragement, organized themselves into the Red Guard. Students denounced their teachers and party officials squelched freedom of expression. Professors and intellectuals were exiled to remote villages and forced to undertake hard manual labor.

📖 **Read** the **Document**: **Decision Concerning the Great Proletarian Cultural Revolution** on **MyHistoryLab**

The Long March was now 30 years in the past, yet nostalgia for its ideological zeal continued to motivate China's aging leaders. Mao was venerated as their last hope of restoring the intensity of those early days of the revolution. Millions of copies of *The Quotations of Chairman Mao*, often called the "Little Red Book" because of its size and the color of its cover, were published. These were circulated and read publicly throughout the country to audiences who were forced to listen. Economic chaos and starvation on the one hand and the total stifling and destruction of intellectual and academic life on the other brought China's economic and cultural life to a standstill.

Recovery. As the damage became clearly visible, China reversed its policy in yet another example of *fang–zhou*, "loosening up–tightening down." The People's Liberation Army was given the task of suppressing the Red Guards, the youth and student cadres who had wreaked chaos in the name of Mao. The government sought new international recognition, most dramatically through the normalization of relations with the United States in 1972. Domestically, attention refocused on restoring industrial productivity. "Between 1950 and 1977 industrial output grew at an average annual rate of 13.5 percent … the highest rate of all developing or developed major nations of the world during the time, and a more rapid pace than achieved by any country during any comparable period of rapid industrialization in modern world history" (Meisner, pp. 436–37). By 1980, China was producing more steel than Britain or France.

On the other hand, agriculture was upended, collectivized, and relatively neglected in terms of investment. The agonizingly slow growth of agriculture could barely keep pace with population growth. By the time Mao died in 1976, China was ready for a dramatic change in leadership and policies.

Women in the People's Republic of China

Throughout the revolution, Mao had stressed the rights of women. After the communist victory in 1949, the new government issued a marriage law that forbade arranged marriages, prohibited marriage contracts for the purchase and sale of wives, and encouraged free choice of marriage partners. This law met strong resistance. Men who had already bought their wives objected; so did mothers-in-law, who ruled over each household's domestic labor force. The traditional Chinese family provided for old-age security, child-care, medical facilities, and the production and consumption of food, clothing, and shelter. The new communist marriage law seemed to threaten this structure without providing any alternative. It was not widely enforced. In addition, the leadership of the party remained conspicuously male.

Other laws in the new communist nation banned concubinage, footbinding, prostitution, and trafficking in women. A law of 1953 gave women the vote. Beginning in 1955, the government emphasized the importance of family planning; this led, in 1979, to a policy of limiting families, especially in urban areas, to only one child. Liberation of women was also seen as a means of expanding the labor force. In 1949 only 7 percent of the workforce was female; by 1982 the figure had reached 43 percent. About 70 percent of women worked (although in an overwhelmingly rural society, where women have always worked, all these official figures must be interpreted with caution). Declaring that "women hold up half the sky," the communist government set out to obliterate centuries of exploitation.

In practice, the task was not so simple. Historic patterns of male dominance persisted. The overwhelming majority of communist officials were men, and while they legislated better conditions for women, it was they, not the women, who formulated and promulgated the legislation. Decisions to end patriarchy were made patriarchally, and therefore had limited effect in practice. Men continued to feel that they should make the major decisions in the household, the workplace, and the political arena. Women in the workforce found that they now had the double burden of a day job outside the home and housework inside the home; this housework was not equally shared. Of the unemployed, 60–70 percent were women. In 1980, literacy among males had reached 78 percent; among females, it was 60 percent.

Most glaring of all the inequalities was the ratio of men to women, 108:100 in 1981. (It rose to 110:100 by 2000 and 118:100 in 2010.) In a situation where only one child was permitted, families were choosing to abort female fetuses, or to kill newborn female babies, or to allow young girls to perish through persistent neglect of their health needs, in preference to males.

The documentary film *Small Happiness*, directed by Carma Hinton and Richard Gordon in 1984, as one part of the *Long Bow Trilogy* on "One Village in China," presents perspectives on gender issues from just one village. Nevertheless, the conversations recorded among the women of the village provide profound insights. The oldest of them had her feet bound years before, but that procedure is now outlawed and defunct. Babies, whether male or female, are no longer killed, because there is now enough food for them. Contraception is practiced universally. Agriculture is becoming more of a female occupation, as many men travel to cities in search of work. The men who remain do not do housework. The old proverb still endures: "To give birth to a boy is considered a big happiness. To give birth to a girl is a small happiness."

Chinese woman with bound feet. From the early years of the twentieth century, urban women had begun to leave the confines of home to work in light industry. The move from home to workplace gave women higher status, which was further strengthened by the reforms of the communist government when it came to power. The abandonment of footbinding in all but the most outlying areas of China did much to enhance the freedom of women.

China's International Relations

In the first decade of communist rule, China's chief ally was the USSR, which helped the new communist state to design its five-year plan, train and provision its armed forces, and build factories, transportation facilities, urban neighborhoods, and administrative centers. But in the mid-1950s, the two countries quarreled bitterly over ideology. Replaying the scenario of 1927, China once again found the USSR becoming too moderate politically. The two giant countries even contested their mutual borders in central Asia in armed skirmishes. In 1961, they severed diplomatic relations. Only after 1985 were relations between the two countries normalized. Still, the two powers remained wary and armed across thousands of miles of shared borders.

The United States. China's relations with the United States began in cold hostility and hot war. For almost two decades after 1949, America lamented and resented its "loss" of China. America continued to support Chiang's forces on Taiwan after 1949, mostly because it wanted to combat communism. The United States lobbied to keep the People's Republic of China out of the UN; the government of Taiwan, the Americans asserted, represented the Chinese people. From 1950 to 1953, America and China fought each other for control of the Korean peninsula, America in alliance with the government of South Korea, China in alliance with that of North Korea. America suffered some 27,000 war dead; estimates of Chinese dead ranged from 150,000 to 600,000.

22.1

22.2

22.3

What were the revolutionary policies of the People's Republic of China?

22.4

22.5

22.6

22.7

22.1

22.2

22.3

22.4

22.5

22.6

22.7

What were the
revolutionary
policies of the
People's Republic
of China?

In the 1970s, however, the bitter hostility melted. Mao and his new advisers, retreating from the economic catastrophe of the Cultural Revolution, sought assistance from abroad. Meanwhile, the United States, favoring more pragmatic policies, did not stand in the way of China's joining the UN in 1971. In 1972, President Nixon visited China. Full diplomatic relations were established between the two countries in 1979.

China's Neighbors. Within its own area of the world, China for 2,000 years has viewed itself as the dominant, central power, and has sought that recognition from its neighbors, with mixed success. To many of these countries, China was a feared and resented neighbor, not an uncommon relationship for a regional superpower. China invaded Tibet in 1950 and forced the Dalai Lama, its most important spiritual and temporal leader, to flee and to seek refuge in India in 1959. In Cambodia, it backed the murderous Khmer Rouge party and its leader, Pol Pot, in vicious civil wars through the 1970s, even committing troops briefly to combat.

On the other hand, the astonishing economic recovery of Japan after World War II challenged China's leadership position. Japan was advancing rapidly to become the world's second largest economy while China lagged far behind. China's authorities were forced to rethink their economic policies.

Moreover, in several nearby states, Chinese minorities were viewed with suspicion as possible subversive infiltrators for the Chinese nation and the Communist Party. In 1965, as Indonesian nationalism turned against them, thousands of Chinese were murdered in Indonesia, and hundreds of thousands more were exiled.

President Nixon meets with Communist Party Chairman Mao Zedong in Beijing, during his groundbreaking 1972 visit to China. Alarmed by aggressive Soviet actions in Czechoslovakia, China and the United States took steps to improve their diplomatic relations. Four years after the Sino–Western rapprochement, begun in 1971, foreign trade with China had tripled, and by 1980, China had joined the IMF and the World Bank.

CHAPTER TWENTY-TWO: CHINA AND INDIA

22.1
22.2
22.3
22.4
22.5
22.6
22.7

How did the end
of colonialism
change China's
image of itself?

Ping-pong diplomacy. China's ping-pong team was invited to America by the United States National Ping-Pong Association in 1971. In this friendly match, a Chinese and an American ping-pong player are on the same side, a symbol of the new friendship between China and America.

India. China's relationship with India has been complex. When India became independent in 1947 and China completed its revolution in 1949, the two nations chose dramatically different social, political, and economic paths. At the Bandung Conference of nonaligned countries, in 1955, both offered leadership to nations newly emerging from colonialism. China became a model for agrarian guerrilla revolt throughout Southeast Asia and beyond, while India's nonviolent path inspired others, especially in black Africa.

India did not protest China's takeover of Tibet in 1950. It did, however, offer refuge to the Dalai Lama and his followers when hundreds of thousands of them fled a renewed communist crackdown in 1959. India consistently backed China's petition to enter the UN, even when differences over border demarcations led to open warfare in 1962. The Chinese decisively defeated Indian troops, penetrated through the mountain passes to within striking distance of India's heartland, and then withdrew voluntarily to the borders they had claimed. India's first test of nuclear devices in 1974 represented, in part, an attempt to catch up with the military power of her larger neighbor.

Postrevolutionary China

22.4 How did the end of colonialism change China's image of itself?

China demonstrated the inevitability of each huge nation of the world finding its own developmental path. China might for a time take guidance from one foreign ideology or another, and it might enter into alliances with various powers at one time or another, but finally it sought a path appropriate to its own size, geography, power, technology, and historical experience. Chinese at home and abroad, including many who disapproved of current government policies, took pride in the newfound unity, power, and independence of their nation. China might make mistakes, but they would be its own mistakes. Leaving behind a century of humiliating colonialism

22.1

22.2

22.3

22.4

22.5 What was
Mohandas
Gandhi's
22.6 concept of civil
disobedience,
22.7 and what was
his role in
India's fight for
independence?

and devastating international and civil war, China sought to establish stability and ideological purity. Soon it would seek a larger place in the world.

India's Struggle for Independence

 22.5 What was Mohandas Gandhi's concept of civil disobedience, and what was his role in India's fight for independence?

With the exception of the border war in 1962, India and China usually regarded each other as friendly rivals. Both were cautious in their approach to Western powers, their former imperial masters. Both set out to provide new models of development for countries emerging from colonial rule. These models differed because the countries' colonial experiences differed. Nevertheless, in India, as in China, the modern movement for independence began within the educated, intellectual, urban classes before expanding to include the peasantry. In India this expansion was led by Mohandas Gandhi, and focused primarily on the upper levels of peasantry.

First Steps Toward Self Rule

Established in 1885, at British initiative, as a vent for Indian nationalist criticism, the Indian National Congress led the resistance to British rule in the early twentieth century. Its leadership was concentrated in the hands of men who were educated in British ways, through British-run schools, sometimes in Britain itself. More than a third of its members were trained in the legal profession. In 1835, T.B. Macaulay, legal adviser to the British government of India, had declared the intent of the government's educational policy to create a class "Indian in blood and colour, but English in taste, in opinions, in morals, and in intellect" (cited in Hay, p. 31); the Congress leadership reflected the results. It approached government respectfully, proclaiming allegiance to the British monarchy, and framed its petitions—for representation on government councils, for example—in constitutional forms.

Early Congress leaders trusted British claims to be preparing India for democratic, responsible government. They welcomed a series of constitutional reforms establishing official councils with substantial Indian membership, elected by very limited elites, to advise the government. The Government of India Act, in 1919, expanded provincial and central legislatures and created a dual government, transferring powers over agriculture, public works, education, and local self-government to Indian elected legislators at the provincial level.

This halfway house proved unstable; Britain had trouble deciding whether it wished India to be a democracy or a colony. Each new problem revealed the contradiction. When Indian demands for political independence increased after World War I, the government responded with repression. Against the advice of all the elected Indians on the Imperial Legislative Council, in 1919 the government passed the Rowlatt Acts, which cracked down on freedom of the press and of assembly. When British troops shot point-blank into a peaceful crowd of protesters in Amritsar in the Punjab that year, killing 379 Indians and wounding 1,100, even Indian moderates could no longer justify British rule.

Mohandas Gandhi and Civil Disobedience

At this juncture, Mohandas Karamchand Gandhi (1869–1948) emerged as a leader offering new political direction, new moral perspective, and new programs of internal reform. Gandhi—called Mahatma, or "great soul," by his followers—inspired India to find strength and courage in its own village roots and spiritual traditions. His

INDIAN INDEPENDENCE—KEY FIGURES

22.1
22.2
22.3
22.4
22.5
22.6
22.7

Rabindranath Tagore (1861–1941)   Indian poet, painter, and musician from Bengal, who translated his own verse into English. He received the Nobel Prize for literature in 1913. An ardent nationalist and advocate of social reform, he resigned his knighthood (granted in 1918) in protest against British repression in India.

Mohandas Karamchand Gandhi (1869–1948)   Indian political and spiritual leader, who fought against anti-Indian discrimination in South Africa before returning to India in 1914. He became leader of the Indian National Congress in the 1920s, helping to unify its various factions. Gandhi maintained nonviolent ideals through campaigns of civil disobedience, and was imprisoned in 1922, 1932, 1933, and 1942 for anti-British activities. He played a crucial role in calming partition violence in Bengal.

Mohammed Ali Jinnah (1876–1948)   The founder of Pakistan. A member of the Indian National Congress, at first he advocated cooperation between Hindus and Muslims, but later he decided that Muslims would suffer as a minority in independent India. He transformed the Muslim League from a cultural to a political organization. In 1940, Jinnah demanded the partition of British India into separate Muslim and Hindu states. He achieved his goal, but he had to accept a smaller state than he had demanded. He became governor-general of Pakistan in 1947 and died in office.

Jawaharlal Nehru (1889–1964   Indian nationalist politician and prime minister, 1947–64. Before partition, he led the socialist wing of the Congress Party and was regarded as second only to Gandhi. Between 1921 and 1945, he was imprisoned by the British nine times for political activities. While in jail he wrote his autobiography, a history of India, and a history of the world. As prime minister he advocated nonalignment (neutrality toward the major powers), established an industrial base, and sustained a parliamentary democracy based on the rule of law.

Subhas Chandra Bose (1897–1945)   Indian nationalist leader (known as "Netaji"—"Respected Leader"). He led the left-wing opposition to Gandhi, advocating violence, class struggle, and immediate independence. He became president of the All-India Congress (1938–39). He supported the Axis Powers (Germany, Italy, and Japan) during World War II and became commander-in-chief of the Japanese-sponsored Indian National Army, made up of captured Indian soldiers. He was reported killed in a plane crash during his military career, adding to his stature as a martyr for his nation.

What was Mohandas Gandhi's concept of civil disobedience, and what was his role in India's fight for independence?

leadership had serious limitations, but virtually all political activity in India, almost until the present, would revolve around the Congress, which he now reconstructed into a mass movement.

📖 **Read** the **Document**: **Gandhi on Civil Disobedience (1910s)** on **MyHistoryLab**

Gandhi Develops Satyagraha in South Africa. Gandhi grew up in a prosperous middle-class family—his father was an administrator in local government—and, like many of the leaders of the National Congress, he studied law in Britain. In 1893, as a young lawyer, he left India to work for an Indian emigrant business firm in South Africa. There, apparently for the first time, Gandhi suffered racial persecution personally and repeatedly (see Source box, overleaf).

Most of the Indians in South Africa had come as indentured laborers. The South African government wanted them to return home at the end of their service, and instituted racist laws that made their long-term status untenable. Indians were required to carry identification cards at all times and to pay heavy head taxes. Most disturbing of all, in 1913, the government nullified all marriages not performed by Christian clergy, rendering illegitimate the children of almost all the Indian immigrants. Although he had arrived as the lawyer for a wealthy Indian Muslim client, Gandhi identified with the pain and humiliation of his less privileged countrymen and, indeed, suffered along with them. He was physically evicted from public facilities and threatened with beatings and even death for asserting his rights. Until that time a rather private person, Gandhi began to organize a protest movement.

SOURCE

Gandhi's First Experience with Racism in South Africa

Mahatma Gandhi published his autobiography originally as a series of newspaper articles. Many of the episodes also carried a moral message for readers. The story of his first encounter with racism in South Africa implies that he had never experienced such severe discrimination, neither in colonial India nor during his law-school days in London:

On the seventh or eighth day after my arrival, I left Durban. A first class seat was booked for me. … The train reached Maritzburg, the capital of Natal, at about 9 p.m. … A passenger came next, and looked me up and down. He saw that I was a "colored" man. This disturbed him. Out he went and came in again with one or two officials. They all kept quiet, when another official came to me and said, "Come along, you must go to the van compartment."

"But I have a first class ticket," said I.

"That doesn't matter," rejoined the other. "I tell you, you must go to the van compartment."

"I tell you, I was permitted to travel in this compartment at Durban, and I insist on going on in it."

"No you won't," said the official. "You must leave this compartment, or else I shall have to call a police constable to push you out."

"Yes, you may. I refuse to get out voluntarily."

The constable came. He took me by the hand and pushed me out. My luggage was also taken out. I refused to go to the other compartment and the train steamed away. I went and sat in the waiting room, keeping my hand bag with me, and leaving the other luggage where it was. …

It was winter, and winter in the higher regions of South Africa is severely cold. Maritzburg being at a high altitude, the cold was extremely bitter. My overcoat was in my luggage, but I did not dare to ask for it lest I should be insulted again, so I sat and shivered. There was no light in the room. A passenger came in at about midnight and possibly wanted to talk to me. But I was in no mood to talk.

I began to think of my duty. Should I fight for my rights or go back to India, or should I go on to Pretoria without minding the insults, and return to India after finishing the case? It would be cowardice to run back to India without fulfilling my obligation. The hardship to which I was subjected was superficial—only a symptom of the deep disease of color prejudice. I should try, if possible, to root out the disease and suffer hardships in the process. (cited in Jack, pp. 29–30)

Instead of leaving at the end of his year's employment, Gandhi remained in South Africa for 21 years, from 1893 to 1914, formulating new methods of resistance through civil disobedience. Some of his strategies were based directly on Indian religious and moral principles, some were his own creative responses. He began with the principle of *ahimsa*, "nonviolence"—a basic tenet of the Jain religion and of several branches of Hinduism—insisting that those who accepted his leadership must reject the use of violence. Then he formulated the new strategy of *satyagraha*, or "truth-force." (Gandhi coined this word, from the Hindi *satya*, truth, and *agraha*, force, to describe his strategy of militant, nonviolent civil disobedience.) *Satyagraha* called for peaceful, even self-sacrificing, opposition to oppression through methods designed to force the oppressors to recognize the immorality of their own position and to relieve the suffering of their victims.

Those who followed Gandhi's path of civil disobedience had to be prepared to suffer willingly the legal consequences, including imprisonment, and frequently the extra-legal consequences, such as beatings by thugs. Often they "courted arrest," convinced that their imprisonment would expose the perversity of the laws they were opposing. Gandhi established a headquarters, modeled on the Hindu religious *ashram* (the headquarters of a religious sect), and founded a publishing house next door for spreading the principles of his movement.

Gandhi first called his methods "passive resistance," but there was nothing passive about them; they were actually systems of militant nonviolence. (Later he renamed them "civil resistance.") These techniques were later adopted by leaders of resistance movements around the world, from Martin Luther King in the United States to Nelson Mandela in South Africa itself.

In 1909, Gandhi published *Hind Swaraj*, or *Indian Home Rule*. Banned in India, this short book championed India's own civilization, urged Indians to conquer the feelings of fear and inferiority that their colonial rulers had encouraged, and made a forthright attack on British cultural, economic, and political hegemony:

22.1

22.2

22.3

22.4

22.5 What was Mohandas Gandhi's concept of civil disobedience, and what was his role in India's fight for independence?

22.6

22.7

KEY TERMS

ahimsa Nonviolence; not causing injury or hurt. A basic tenet of Jainism and several sects of Hinduism.

satyagraha A word coined by Gandhi to mean truth-force, or militant nonviolence. Links two Hindi words: *satya* (truth) and *agraha* (force).

We have hitherto said nothing because we have been cowed down … it is our duty now to speak out boldly. We consider your schools and law courts to be useless. We want our own ancient schools and courts to be restored. The common language of India is not English but Hindi. You should, therefore, learn it. We can hold communication with you only in our national language …

We cannot tolerate the idea of your spending money on railways and the military. We see no occasion for either … We do not need any European cloth. We shall manage with articles produced and manufactured at home. You have great military resources … You may, if you like, cut us to pieces. You may shatter us at the cannon's mouth. If you act contrary to our will, we shall not help you; and without our help, we know that you cannot move one step forward. (cited in Jack, pp. 118–19)

Gandhi's success in South Africa was limited to short-term compromises with the government, but he earned the esteem of his countrymen in both South Africa and India. When he finally returned home and established a new *ashram* in Ahmedabad in 1915, his countrymen were eagerly awaiting his political initiatives for India itself. He did not disappoint them.

Gandhi and the Independence Movement

Gandhi soon demonstrated his organizational genius. Recognizing India's smoldering grass-roots anger against British rule, further inflamed by postwar economic hardship and political repression, Gandhi reconstituted the Congress from an organization of Western-educated elites into a mass organization with millions of dues-paying members from India's villages as well as its cities. He incorporated the vigor and boldness of such current leaders as the fiery journalist Bal Gangadhar Tilak (1856–1920), who proclaimed, "Freedom is my birthright, and I shall have it," and the milder-mannered lawyer Gopal Krishna Gokhale (1866–1915), who became Gandhi's political mentor in his first years back in India, as he was becoming reacquainted with his native land. Gandhi also mobilized India's enormous size and diversity by carefully cultivating personal and political alliances with a younger generation of regional leaders, including Rajendra Prasad (1884–1963) in Bihar, later the first president of independent India; Vallabhbhai Patel (1875–1950) in Gujarat, who became organizational "boss" of the entire Congress Party; and Jawaharlal Nehru (1889–1964) in Uttar Pradesh (then called United Provinces), who became the first prime minister of independent India. Gandhi adopted the nascent economic principle of *swadeshi*, the use of products of "one's own country," and organized nationwide boycotts of British imports. As he mobilized the nation in campaigns of mass civil disobedience, Gandhi included the poor and the **outcaste**—those outside India's caste system—in order to achieve not only independence from the British but also social reform at home.

Cultural, Social, and Economic Policies. Gandhi was not opposed to the general concept of the caste system, seeing differences among people, conferred by birth, as part of India's social reality, but he fought the designation of about 15 percent of the country's population as outcastes and "untouchables," those literally not permitted to touch or be touched by people of upper castes. Declaring, "It has always been a mystery to me how men can feel themselves honored by the humiliation of their fellow beings," Gandhi coined a new name for the untouchables: *harijan*, "children of God." He brought *harijans* into his movement and into his *ashram*.

In his drive for a free India, Gandhi rejected the use of English in India's public life and schools, and urged the development of India's regional languages and literature. His writings in Gujarati transformed the literature of that language, shifting the subject matter from the elites to the working people and poor.

22.1
22.2
22.3
22.4
22.5
22.6
22.7

What was Mohandas Gandhi's concept of civil disobedience, and what was his role in India's fight for independence?

KEY TERM

outcaste Refers to a person outside the caste system of India, usually also an outcast, rejected by the upper levels of society. Such people are now usually referred to as *dalits*, or oppressed persons.

22.1

22.2

22.3

22.4

22.5 What was Mohandas Gandhi's concept of civil disobedience, and what was his role in India's fight for independence?

22.6

22.7

Gandhi and Nehru. Mahatma Gandhi, wearing his customary *dhoti* (loincloth), and Jawaharlal Nehru are deep in conversation at the All-India Congress committee meeting in Bombay, July 6, 1946, where Nehru took office as president of the Congress. Gandhi and Nehru were the charismatic figures who led the Indian National Congress, a broad-based political organization that was the vehicle for the nationalist movement for independence.

Ascetic in his personal life, Gandhi led a temperance movement to ban alcoholic drinks. To identify with the poor and the villagers, he gave up his Western lawyer's suits in favor of the simplest loincloth, shawl, and sandals. Perhaps unintentionally, he became a kind of early patron saint of the "small is beautiful" movement, denouncing modern, highly- mechanized industry and arguing for small-scale, alternative technologies, such as the spinning wheel. His reasons were both economic and humanitarian:

> Hunger is the argument that is driving India to the spinning wheel ... We must think of millions who are today less than animals, who are almost in a dying state. The spinning wheel is the reviving draught for the millions of our dying countrymen and countrywomen ... I do want growth. I do want self-determination. I do want freedom, but I want all these for the soul ... A plea for the spinning wheel is a plea for recognizing the dignity of labor. (de Bary, *Indian*, p. 820.)

The Congress Party made the spinning wheel its emblem, handspun, handwoven cloth its dress, and the production of a daily quota of handspun yarn a requirement for membership.

Congress Campaigns for Independence. Gandhi led the Congress in three huge, nationwide *satyagraha* campaigns. These campaigns fell far short of winning independence, but they demonstrated to the world that masses of Indians wanted the British out. They undermined any remaining British claim to moral authority to rule. They announced that India was becoming a cohesive political entity, ready to rule itself.

The Non-Cooperation campaign of 1920–22 boycotted British colonial schools, law courts, administrative positions, manufactures, and imports. A decade later, in the Salt March campaign of 1930–32, Gandhi drew world attention to India's freedom

SOURCE

Gandhi and Labor Relations

Most famous for his advocacy of the spinning wheel and his condemnation of mechanized industry, Gandhi was actually very pragmatic in his approach to technology. He recognized that the mechanized Indian textile industry gave jobs to hundreds of thousands of workers and produced yarn and cloth that Indian consumers desperately needed. Cynics noted that the mill owners were among Gandhi's most generous financial supporters. Gandhi played a pivotal role in founding the Ahmedabad Textile Labour Association, one of India's most powerful labor unions, and he served as an adviser to several others. His advice to labor, and to management as well, reflected his view of the importance of harmony rather than conflict in industrial relationships, as in all human relationships. Communist labor leaders, of course, opposed Gandhi's principle of seeking harmony, rather than violence, or even strikes, between labor and management.

Two paths are open before India today, either to introduce the western principle of "Might is right," or to uphold the eastern principle that truth alone conquers, that truth knows no mishap, that the strong and the weak alike have a right to secure justice. The choice is to begin with the laboring class. Should the laborers obtain an increment in their wages by violence? Even if that be possible, they cannot resort to anything like violence, howsoever legitimate may be their claims. To use violence for securing rights may seem an easy path, but it proves to be thorny in the long run. Those who live by the sword die also by the sword …

If, on the other hand, they take their stand on pure justice and suffer in their person to secure it, not only will they always succeed but they will also reform their masters, develop industries and both master and men will be as members of one and the same family. A satisfactory solution of the condition of labor must include the following:

1. The hours of labor must leave the workmen some hours of leisure.
2. They must get facilities for their own education.
3. Provision should be made for an adequate supply of milk, clothing and necessary education for their children.
4. There should be sanitary dwellings for the workmen.
5. They should be in a position to save enough to maintain themselves during their old age.

None of these conditions is satisfied today. For this both the parties are responsible. The masters care only for the service they get. What becomes of the laborer does not concern them … The laborer, on the other hand, tries to hit upon all tricks whereby he can get maximum pay with minimum work.

A third party [the union] has sprung up between these two parties. It has become the laborer's friend. (from *Young India*, June 1, 1921, reprinted in Jack, pp. 157–59)

---

movement brilliantly by focusing on salt. He exposed the hardship created by the government's monopoly on the manufacture and sale of salt. Salt is necessary for life, even for the poorest person, but the British controlled its sale for their own profit. By marching to the sea and manufacturing salt from seawater, Gandhi demonstrated just how easy it is to extract salt from nature, for free, by anyone living along India's thousands of miles of coastline. By taking almost a month to march the 240 miles from his *ashram* to the seaside, Gandhi gave time for the news media of the world to cover the story. He shamed the British for forbidding this simple "manufacture" of salt, and for forcing people instead to buy their salt from a government monopoly. He put government officials in an awkward situation. If they arrested him for breaking the law, they looked stupid, and perhaps cruel. If they did not arrest him, they looked foolish and impotent. The government chose to enforce the law. It arrested tens of thousands of demonstrators at the seashore, and Gandhi himself a few days later. By extracting salt from the seawater, Gandhi had initiated a new nationwide campaign of civil disobedience. Once again he had challenged the moral authority of the colonial government in the eyes of most Indians and of the world. (*Time* magazine named Gandhi "Man of the Year" in 1931.)

Ten years later, the Quit India campaign of 1942 refused Indian political support to Britain's efforts in World War II until independence was granted. Most Indian leaders preferred the British over the Germans, but they refused to make a commitment to the war effort until their own country was granted its independence. (The Indian army, however, did fight loyally under British command.) By the time World War II ended, the British realized that they could no longer suppress Indian nationalism, certainly not at a cost they could afford. Almost 200 years after the Battle of Plassey made them a power in the country, the British prepared to leave India.

22.1

22.2

22.3

22.4

22.5

22.6

22.7

What was Mohandas Gandhi's concept of civil disobedience, and what was his role in India's fight for independence?

22.1
22.2
22.3
22.4
22.5
22.6
22.7

What was
Mohandas
Gandhi's
concept of civil
disobedience,
and what was
his role in
India's fight for
independence?

Gandhi's Leadership. Some readers, in common with some nationalist leaders of Gandhi's own era, may feel that this account overemphasizes Gandhi, his policies, and his techniques. In fact, Gandhi was not (entirely) successful. Despite his three nationwide campaigns, beginning in 1920, the British did not finally concede independence until 1947, only after they had been impoverished and exhausted by depression and world war and were no longer able to suppress the rebellious colony. Some Indian leaders, such as Subhas Chandra Bose (1897–1945) of Bengal, felt that violence would have achieved independence sooner. Many in Bose's socialist wing of the Congress found Gandhi too compromising with business and landlord interests as he consolidated his power. They opposed Gandhi's view that class conflict— between landowners and tenant peasants, between owners and workers—should be set aside until after independence was won. They lamented Gandhi's peaceful resistance as a sell-out.

Dr. B.R. Ambedkar (1891–1956), an untouchable who studied at Columbia University in New York City and went on to earn a law degree and a doctorate in London, clashed repeatedly with Gandhi. Ambedkar viewed the Mahatma as patronizing and much too willing to compromise away the demands of untouchables. He rejected Gandhi's term *"harijan"* as a designation for untouchables, preferring instead *"dalits,"* oppressed persons. Ambedkar's book *What Congress and Gandhi Have Done to the Untouchables* (1946) lays out the full indictment. By the 1930s, Ambedkar became recognized as the more authentic leader of the untouchables, and *dalit* won out. Ambedkar believed that persons accepting Hindu traditions, which Gandhi certainly did, would find it difficult ever to condemn fully its treatment of *dalits*. At the very end of his life, Ambedkar converted to Buddhism as a religion of Indian origin that nevertheless rejected caste.

Rabindranath Tagore (1861–1941), poet and man of letters, and the first Indian to win a Nobel Prize (for literature, in 1913) faulted Gandhi for excessive emphasis on the spinning wheel. According to Tagore, Gandhi's call to the nation was mostly

The Salt March. Mahatma Gandhi begins the symbolic 240-mile, 27-day march from Ahmedabad to Dandi on the coast, where the participants collected sea salt and thus technically broke the salt law—the government's monopoly on salt production. Civil disobedience did not win independence immediately, but it did discredit the moral and political authority of the colonial government.

"Spin and weave, spin and weave." Tagore professed his love of Gandhi, and he saw him clearly as the leader of the national movement for independence, but he hoped for a leader more attuned to cultural issues as well as social, economic, and political problems. Tagore was a poet, Gandhi a man of action.

Perhaps Gandhi's most serious failure, the one that left him most disappointed and distraught, was his inability to capture the majority of India's Muslims for the Congress. Mohammed Ali Jinnah (1876–1948) won their leadership. Also a British-trained lawyer, and a man of highly refined Western tastes, Jinnah was at first a devoted member of the Congress. But as independence came closer, and the Congress started to go it alone in provincial elections, without seeking to build coalitions with Muslims, Jinnah began to fear that after independence, Muslims would be left out politically. He began to advocate for a separate country for Muslims. Gandhi was not able to win his confidence, and Jinnah was successful in having the British divide India into two states, India and Pakistan, one secular but with a strong Hindu majority, and the other Muslim in population and constitution. This partition of India into two nations was the greatest failure of Gandhi and of the Congress.

In every one of these cases, and in others as well, however, Gandhi and the Congress held the organizational center of the national movement. Even when they failed, they were the foil against which others had to joust. Antagonists might or might not approve of the emphasis on nonviolence, on compromise among factions, on the use of Hindu symbols, on the economic plight of the poor, on Hindu–Muslim and Hindu–*dalit* unity, but they had to deal with it. Gandhi had created a political center, an enormous task in a country as fabulously diverse as India.

In addition, Gandhi restored to his colonized country and its people a renewed sense of pride and courage in the face of almost 200 years of British domination. He proclaimed that non-violence was the weapon of the strong, and that in the long run it was the only strategy that would not only win independence, but also provide a platform for peaceful self-government. His method of *satyagraha* not only made it impossible for Britain to continue to rule India, but also pointed Indians in the direction of their own internal social reform. In a century filled with violence and warfare, Gandhi inspired future world leaders such as Martin Luther King in the United States and Nelson Mandela in South Africa to search for alternatives.

📖 **Read** the **Document**: **Martin Luther King, Jr., Letter from Birmingham City Jail, 1963** on **MyHistoryLab**

Independence and Partition

22.6 To what degree did the experiences of the independence movement provide guidelines for governing India after 1947?

At independence in 1947, the subcontinent was partitioned into Hindu-majority India, an officially secular country, and Muslim-majority Pakistan, an officially Islamic country. The Indian National Congress transformed itself into the National Congress Party and assumed the responsibility of running the country until elections were held. Then, Jawaharlal Nehru was elected independent India's first prime minister, a position he held until his death in 1964. Mohammed Ali Jinnah became Pakistan's first governor-general.

Hindu–Muslim Separation/Partition

Pakistan's peculiar geography, with two "wings," east and west, separated by some 800 miles of hostile Indian territory, reflected the distribution of Muslim majorities in

22.1

22.2

22.3

22.4

22.5

22.6

22.7

To what degree did the experiences of the independence movement provide guidelines for governing India after 1947?

To what degree did the experiences of the independence movement provide guidelines for governing India after 1947?

Political change in south Asia after 1947. At independence in 1947, British India was partitioned into secular, but Hindu-majority, India and Muslim Pakistan amid enormous violence and migration. Disputes over Kashmir continue until today. In 1971, the east wing of Pakistan fought, with Indian assistance, a war of independence against the west and became Bangladesh.

the subcontinent. At partition, an estimated 12 million people shifted their homes. Six million Hindus and Sikhs from East and West Pakistan moved into India; six million Muslims from India transferred to Pakistan. The transfer of population was bloody; between 200,000 and one million people were murdered. Gandhi, too, was murdered at about this time—by a Hindu fanatic who thought he was too friendly to Muslims and their new state of Pakistan.

Most Indians rejected religion as the official basis of statehood. When East Pakistan revolted against the domination of West Pakistan and declared itself the independent state of Bangladesh in 1971, Indians rejoiced: their rival state was now broken in two, and they felt vindicated in their belief that religion alone should not, and could not, be the basis of national unity.

Few Hindus remained in Pakistan, but a sizeable Muslim minority, ten percent of India's population, remained in India. While Hindus and Muslims mostly cohabited peacefully under a secular constitution, tensions between them remained and were sometimes exploited by political leaders, with increasing frequency after 1990.

Mass migration. The partition of India at independence created an unprecedented transfer of population in two directions: most Hindus and Sikhs fled Pakistan for the safety of India, while many Muslims living in India struggled to get safely over the border into the newly established Islamic nation. This packed train, groaning with refugees from Pakistan, arrives in Amritsar, just over the Indian border, on October 16, 1947.

One of the continuing flashpoints has been the region of Kashmir, bordering—and claimed by—both Pakistan and India. Kashmir was one of the regions of India that had been ruled by the British indirectly, through a local *maharajah*, or prince. He was a Hindu and, at independence, he asked to join his state to India. However, the great majority of the population of Kashmir was Muslim, and they have never been given the opportunity to express their opinion in a vote. Several wars have been fought for control of Kashmir; the region is currently divided roughly along the line of the military cease-fires. No political resolution has been reached.

📖 **Read** the **Document**: **The Tandon Family at Partition (1947)** on **MyHistoryLab**

Unifying the Nation

At independence, the home minister Vallabhbhai Patel convinced and coerced India's 562 princes, local rulers under British colonial authority, to declare their merger with India, ending the fear of a break-up of the subcontinent into numerous, separate, small states. Linguistic fragmentation was also averted. Gandhi had organized the Congress by linguistic regions, different from the administrative units employed by the British. After independence, following several regional disputes, the Congress government agreed to draw up the new state borders in accordance with these linguistic borders. Some powerful regional separatist movements emerged—in Madras (now Tamilnadu) in the 1960s, in the Punjab in the 1970s and 1980s, in Kashmir regularly, and in several of the distant and ethnically Mongoloid northeastern states—but a combination of political bargaining and armed force has maintained the unity of the country.

22.1
22.2
22.3
22.4
22.5
22.6
22.7

To what degree did the experiences of the independence movement provide guidelines for governing India after 1947?

22.1
22.2
22.3
22.4
22.5
22.6
22.7

Democracy and its Challenges

22.7 What were the major policy issues addressed by independent India?

The democracy proposed by British rulers became a reality in India after independence. Except for two years of "Emergency Rule," from 1975 to 1977, India has functioned democratically and constitutionally as a union of some 30 states and territories, with universal adult franchise and guaranteed freedoms of press, assembly, speech, and religion, and an independent judiciary. Despite imperfections, India takes pride in being the world's largest democracy.

Indian Politics

Within the country's democratic framework, communist governments have also been elected in India's individual states. In 1957, the state of Kerala chose the first freely elected communist government anywhere in the world. Indians have not, however, given strong support to militant communism. The reasons for this may include: India's generally religious orientation; skepticism about a philosophy and organization tied to foreign governments; recognition of communism's origin as a proletarian rather than a peasant movement; and state repression of revolutionary organizations.

Until 1991, laissez-faire capitalism fared even less well. Indians, including much of the business community, seemed to view capitalism as excessively individualistic and materialistic, based on a philosophy of self-interest, often seen as greed, and associated with colonialism in the past and the return of a neocolonial economic dominance in the present. Despite a large free-enterprise sector in the economy, especially in agriculture, most major Indian parties advocated socialism, on the grounds of its stated concern for the common good. Nehru, in particular, espoused "a socialist pattern of development." His policy continued in force for a generation after his death, despite widespread criticism that it led to excessive power—and corruption—concentrated in the state and in the bureaucrats who controlled access to business licenses and investment capital. Many of these views changed in 1991 when India was forced by regulations of the IMF to move toward a more free-market economy.

Through the first four decades of independence, one party, the Congress, dominated India's democracy, and the party's leadership was dominated by one family, the Nehru dynasty. Jawaharlal Nehru was soon succeeded by his daughter Indira Gandhi (her name by marriage; she was not related to the Mahatma), who was prime minister 1967–77 and from 1980 until her assassination in 1984. She was followed by her son Rajiv in 1984–89. After he was assassinated in 1991, many Congress leaders asked his widow, the Italian-born Sonia Gandhi, to take his place as head of the party. Ultimately, she did.

Indira Gandhi. Indira Gandhi's reputation as a tough, determined leader grew when she ordered Indian troops to support East Pakistan in its civil war for independence from West Pakistan in 1971. Her support facilitated the creation of Bangladesh. In 1974, she ordered India's first underground test of an atomic bomb.

Her political manipulations, however, partially undermined India's democratic system. In 1975, facing the likely loss of political power, she had the president of India declare an "Emergency." She jailed the leaders of the opposition, curtailed freedom of speech and of the press, and set quotas of people to be rounded up for forcible reproductive sterilization, largely in response to India's large population. These dictatorial excesses alienated most Indians; when Gandhi restored elections in 1977, she was voted out of office.

After a brief period in jail for election irregularities, Gandhi was voted back to power in 1980. She continued her political manipulations, alienating many Sikhs in

CHAPTER TWENTY-TWO: CHINA AND INDIA

22.1
22.2
22.3
22.4
22.5
22.6
22.7

Indira Gandhi, prime minister of India, inspects the guard at an Independence Day celebration, August 23, 1967. Mahatma Gandhi did much to encourage women's participation in public life during the years leading to independence. Although many women are well educated, overall the literacy rate among females is only 65 percent (82 percent for males, according to the 2011 census).

the Punjab. Their opposition finally led to armed confrontation in which thousands died. Armed opposition leaders took refuge in the beautiful and sacred Sikh Golden Temple in the city of Amritsar. Gandhi ordered an army strike to dislodge them and the temple was badly damaged in the crossfire. In revenge, two Sikhs in Gandhi's bodyguard assassinated her in 1984.

Gender Issues

Indira Gandhi was only the most prominent example of women in Indian politics. Mahatma Gandhi had encouraged women's participation in the freedom movement, and many followed his call to come out of their homes into the public sphere for the first time. The poet Sarojini Naidu (1879–1949), who became president of the Indian National Congress, is the most famous. India instituted universal adult suffrage in 1950. In each national election approximately 55 percent of women voted, compared with about 60 percent of men. In 2005, women held 45 seats out of 542 in the lower house of parliament and 28 out of 242 in the upper, indicating a slowly increasing proportion from 1950. State government ratios were similar. New constitutional amendments, passed in 1993, created new electoral institutions for local government, and called for 33 percent of their seats to be held by women.

Read the Document: Women in Karimpur, India (1930s–1980s) on MyHistoryLab

Legal Changes. The Hindu Marriage Act of 1955 raised the age of marriage for Hindu women to 15 (18 for men) and assured Hindu women the right of divorce. The Hindu Succession Act of 1956 gave daughters equal rights with sons in inheriting their father's property. On the other hand, parliament did not legislate new personal law for non-Hindus, so other religious communities continued under their traditional systems of family law. This exclusion disturbed many feminists, but they trod lightly here; many Muslims, even feminist Muslims, did not want the secular state to interfere in the religious law of their community.

22.1

22.2

22.3

22.4

22.5

22.6

22.7

What were the
major policy
issues addressed
by independent
India?

Social Changes. Because family structures in India, especially north India, are both patrilineal and patrilocal—that is, inheritance and residence patterns follow the family of the male—the birth of a female child is often regarded as a financial and even emotional burden. Years of child-care and expense culminate in the girl's leaving home for marriage into another family, often somewhat distant and with limited ties to the family of origin.

The sex ratio in India in 2011, about 933 women to 1,000 men, is one of the lowest in the world, although not so low as China's. It suggests the systematic neglect of females, especially young girls. As amniocentesis and sonograms became more widely available, allowing parents to know the sex of unborn children, abortion of female fetuses seemed to result. Laws were passed to ban the use of these tests for this purpose, but the laws were widely disregarded. At the other end of the life cycle, women tend to outlive men, and widows are especially vulnerable if their children choose not to support them. Suicide rates for Indian women are comparatively high, and isolated cases of *sati* (suttee), in which a widow immolates herself on her husband's funeral pyre, continue. In 2001, the literacy rate among females was 54 percent as compared with 76 percent for males; but this was up from 8 percent and 25 percent respectively in 1951. The treatment of women in southern India is widely regarded as more egalitarian than in the north, perhaps because of different local traditions, including the influence in a few localities of matrilineal and matrilocal systems that follow the female line in inheritance and residence.

Economic Changes. Disconcerting results from an anthropological study in 1984 of a village near Delhi suggested that the position of poor, rural women was actually deteriorating as a result of increasing general prosperity in the new economic system and of increasing urbanization. Several factors were to blame. First, women who had worked in agriculture alongside their male kin were displaced when their husbands left field work to seek jobs in the cities. Second, women who traditionally worked in caste-based occupations as servants through *jajmani* (family patronage) systems could no longer find such jobs. Third, mechanization had replaced female labor in a variety of arenas. Finally, changes in cropping patterns had made female help in the fields less necessary. These factors all contributed to the marginalization of poor women, giving them less voice in their family and ultimately devaluing them (Wadley, in Wiser and Wiser, p. 287).

An encouraging contrary development has been the organization of working women into effective unions that provide both economic opportunity and political representation. In such cities as Mumbai, Madras, and Ahmedabad, voluntary organizations of tens of thousands of working women have begun to gain access to capital for working-class women who carry on their own small businesses; to form cooperatives, which help

New technology crosses gender lines. Power tillers provide a new technology more appropriate economically than either bullock-drawn plows or tractors in some areas of India. They are available through collaboration with Japan (Mitsubishi). In entering her new occupation, the driver has received financial and technical assistance from the Self-Employed Women's Association in Ahmedabad, one of India's most prominent organizations of poor, working-class women.

them to secure raw materials and market finished products; to lobby government for workers' safety, health, insurance, maternity, and job protection in nonunionized, small-scale shops; to develop new educational models for job training; and to create new systems of health-care delivery, especially for women. One of the most important of these organizations is the Self-Employed Women's Association (SEWA) in Ahmedabad, a daughter organization of the Textile Labour Union, which had been founded with the help of Mahatma Gandhi. (By 2012, SEWA claimed 1.6 million members across India.)

Economic and Technological Development

22.7
What were the major policy issues addressed by independent India?

At independence, 361 million people lived in India; by the mid-1980s, the population had more than doubled to three-quarters of a billion people; by 2000 it had reached one billion. During droughts in 1964–66, mass starvation was averted only by the import of 12 million tons of food grains each year, primarily from the United States. More recently, however, India has not only been able to feed itself, but also to sell food overseas (although millions of Indians do not receive adequate food even now).

Revolutions in Agriculture. A "green revolution" took root in India in the late 1960s. New strains of wheat, developed in Mexico under the auspices of the Rockefeller Foundation, increased India's productivity even faster than her population. Between the early 1960s and the late 1970s, rice production rose by more than 50 percent, and wheat production tripled. Total grain production rose from about 50 million tons per year at independence, to about 150 million tons in the mid-1980s, to about 190 million tons in 2008.

Meanwhile, a "white revolution" in dairy production and distribution was also taking place. Dairy cooperatives were formed throughout India, enabling village farmers to pool and ship their highly perishable products to urban markets—as fresh milk in refrigerated train cars, and as processed cheese and dairy products in conventional shipping—thus providing incentives for increasing production.

These revolutions in agriculture were not without their problems. First, ecologically, questions were raised about relying so exclusively on so few new strains of "miracle wheat." Were too many seeds coming from too few genetic baskets? Would the massive new quantities of chemical fertilizers needed to support the new seeds ultimately ruin the ecology? Would India's water resources prove adequate as the use of these water-intensive seeds expanded? Second, economic growth increased the disparities and tensions between haves and have-nots, and between those who worked more entrepreneurially and those who did not. The new productivity benefited most those who already had the economic resources to afford the new seeds, fertilizers, pesticides, and irrigation water. The rich were getting richer—although the poor did not seem to be getting poorer—and social tension increased. Similarly, the disparity between richer and poorer states grew.

Challenges of Population and Poverty. Government implementation of family planning, rejected overwhelmingly in the wake of Indira Gandhi's program of forced sterilization in 1975–77, has been soft-pedaled ever since. Nevertheless, birth rates fell from about 44 per thousand at independence to about 33 per thousand in 1985, to 20.6 in 2012, indicating great general interest in smaller, planned families. Life expectancy at birth rose from about 30 years at independence in 1947, to 56 in 1985, to 67 in 2012. On the other hand, in 2007, the government of India reported that 46 percent of Indian children under the age of three were underweight or severely underweight, and 18 percent were malnourished: "India is home to the highest number of undernourished people in the world. And we are working hard to fight that fact."

22.1
22.2
22.3
22.4
22.5
22.6
22.7

What were the major policy issues addressed by independent India?

Industrialization and Its Consequences. Industrial productivity increased, but the structure of the workforce did not change—exactly the process Mahatma Gandhi had feared. New machinery produced more goods more efficiently, but it did not provide proportionately more jobs. Although industrial production multiplied almost five times between 1951 and 1980, the percentage of workers in industry essentially stagnated, from about 10 percent in 1951 to about 13 percent in 1980 and back to 11 percent in 2000. Unemployment was reported steady at about 8 percent.

Until the 1980s, industrial policy derived from Gandhi's and Nehru's conflicting philosophies. Gandhi had urged austere consumption levels, handicraft production, spinning wheels, and national self-sufficiency through import substitution. Gandhi saw India's economy through the eyes of the poor. Nehru, who had been impressed by the rapid industrialization through state planning of the Soviet Union, implemented socialism, central planning, industrialization, government development of the "commanding heights" of the economy—energy, steel, petroleum, banking and finance—and regulation of the large-scale capitalist sector. Despite their strong differences on the importance of large-scale industry and modern technology, both Gandhi and Nehru stressed domestic self-sufficiency in production.

These policies were increasingly challenged by the new international political-economic wisdom of the 1980s, based on the economic successes of the East Asian countries and the political policies of the United States and Britain. Increased consumption spurred increased productivity, and a consumer society began to appear in India.

High-tech innovation for both home and foreign markets increased productivity, and India began to manufacture submarines, computer software (for which it had become a world center) and hardware, and machine tools, and even prepared to export nuclear power plants adapted to third-world conditions. Its impressive scientific and technological establishment had the capacity to adopt and adapt the newest technological advances.

In part, such technological success was possible because of an extraordinary imbalance in India's educational expenditure. The government strongly favored higher education while starving the primary schools. This policy, rooted in traditional hierarchical attitudes and interests, produced a skewed society in which the highly educated elite compared with the best anywhere in the world, but overall basic literacy was low, only about 65 percent even as late as 2000. Again, Gandhi's fears were coming true.

International Relations

India was the first major colony to win independence after World War II, and it served as a leader to other newly emerging countries. Nehru, in particular, provided articulate, innovative direction, and after independence India remained a model of democratic political stability and gradual economic growth in a society of unparalleled heterogeneity. Its international role, however, declined. It was defeated in a border war with China in 1962, after which it began to spend more on its armed forces. Military expenditure rose from $1.7 billion in 1960 to $9.8 billion in 1987 (in constant dollars, adjusted for inflation).

Decolonization throughout the world was virtually complete by the 1980s, and political colonialism was no longer a major global issue. The attention of new nations shifted to economic development. Japan and the highly successful "tigers" of East and Southeast Asia, with their more open, more liberalized, and more expansive economies, attracted them. More recently, China has been a model. In a world concerned with economic growth, the persistence of poverty and illiteracy made India a more problematic model for others. Its progress seemed too slow. It remained, however, a viable democracy and the dominant power in southern Asia. And, as its economy grew in the early 2000s, so did its international reputation.

HOW DO WE KNOW?

Technological Hazards and Questionable Accountability

Indian attitudes toward modern technology have fallen between the skepticism of Gandhi and the enthusiasm of Nehru. Some of the most biting critiques of India's technological policy on development came from a "modern intellectual," Ashis Nandy, who criticized the government for giving excessive power to the scientific-technological establishment. In particular, he focused on India's nuclear establishment in the mid-1980s:

> Nuclear scientists were freed from all financial constraints. The budget of the nuclear program ... was routinely pushed through parliament without any scrutiny whatsoever. And the expenditures ... were never publicly audited. All data on performance ... failures, unsafe technology and insufficient regard for human rights ... were protected by law from the public gaze. And all enquiries made from outside the nuclear establishment were preempted with the help of a special act that made it impossible to mount any informed, focused, data-based criticism of India's nuclear programme. (Nandy, p. 5)

Further skepticism concerning winners and losers in the quest for industrial modernization resulted from a tragedy of poison gas leakage in a Union Carbide insecticide plant in Bhopal in 1984, the worst industrial accident of its kind in the world up to that date. Compounding the tragedy for the victims, the American-owned corporation resisted payment of compensation:

> Dreadful tragedy struck central India's Bhopal ... in December 1984 ... Deadly invisible gas from Union Carbide's insecticide storage tanks had escaped through defective valves to be blown by ill-winds over the slumbering bodies of thousands of poor innocents outside that giant plant's walls, less than 400 miles south of New Delhi. Within hours, 2,000 people were dead and hundreds of thousands of others had been injured by the worst industrial accident of recent history. Union Carbide was still American-owned, one of the few multinationals in India that had not been taken over by a majority of Indian shareholders and management ...
>
> Though hundreds of billions of dollars in damages were quickly claimed in thousands of lawsuits filed both in India and America, virtually nothing was paid to any of the actual victims for seven full years after the tragedy devastated Bhopal. Legal snares and questions of jurisdiction plagued the process, serving to thwart justice instead of expediting its realization. (Wolpert, pp. 421–22)

- Why do you think India's nuclear development program had such independence of action without public political supervision? Do you approve of such secrecy in India? In the nuclear development programs in the United States? Why or why not?
- On what basis do you think Union Carbide resisted paying compensation to most of the victims of the leak? After you have made your guesses, you may wish to check Bhopal and Union Carbide on the web to see what answers you can find.
- In such an overwhelmingly agrarian, poor, rural society as India, what do you think is the proper place for modern industry? Peaceful use of atomic energy? Nuclear weapons?

Comparing China and India:
What Difference Does It Make?

At the end of World War I, India's demand for independence ignited a mass movement that bore many similarities to China's. With the vast majority of its population in rural areas, India, like China, was rooted in agriculture and the peasantry. Like Mao in China, so Gandhi in India mobilized this rural constituency. Both leaders created new social and economic institutions for greater equity and emphasized the need for new, simple technology appropriate to their agrarian, impoverished societies. Both regarded their methods and solutions as models for others to copy.

The differences between the two mammoth countries were at least equally significant. Unlike China, which had no functioning central government between 1912 and 1949, and had been carved into numerous European and Japanese spheres of influence, India had a central government, which was under British colonial control until independence in 1947. While China suffered decades of civil warfare, political disputes in India were addressed through generally peaceful, constitutional processes. India's nationalist leaders, unlike those of China, welcomed businessmen and professionals along with the peasantry in their struggle for independence. Unlike China, in its independence movement India pursued an extraordinary strategy of nonviolent mass civil resistance. It fought no civil war, nor did the battles of World War II significantly touch its borders. When independence came, relations with colonial Britain remained harmonious, and India retained membership in the Commonwealth of Nations, an association mostly of Britain's former colonies. Even the partition of the subcontinent into India and Pakistan in 1947 followed constitutional processes, although the subsequent transfers of population were enormously violent.

The creation in 1971 of the independent country of Bangladesh on the land of East Pakistan was the product of civil war, in which India aided Bangladesh against West Pakistan. Naxalite movements of communist, agricultural guerrilla warfare (named for the village of Naxalbari, the scene of their first revolt) broke out repeatedly, but mostly in somewhat remote eastern regions of *adivasi* populations of impoverished tribal peoples. Hindu–Muslim and high caste–low caste tensions sometimes also burst into violence, but the open violence of these confrontations was usually confined to local areas and short periods of time.

A generation after ending colonialism, both China and India could point to significant accomplishments, including cumulative and growing economic expansion (more rapid in China, slower in India); political cohesion; and social transformation in accord with their differing agendas. Both countries had moved from concentration on rural areas, a promise of their colonial struggles, to concern also with their cities and industries. They shared a similar challenge: How to maintain a coherent national agenda after the unifying enemy of colonialism had been defeated?

By the late twentieth century, both countries had chosen to shift economic policies dramatically, in the direction of deregulation and capitalism. Mao's principal successor, Deng Xiaoping, chose to abandon Mao's state-controlled communist programs centered on the domestic market, for free-market laissez-faire policies oriented toward international trade. The result was something new in world history: Communist Party-controlled politics coupled with a capitalist economy. The economic results were spectacular, with growth rates of ten percent per year for many years. In light of such economic expansion, no one knew the degree to which the political system could remain under party control.

India was slower and less dramatic in its policy changes, but its choice to open its economy moved in a similar direction. The transformation began in the late 1980s, under Prime Minister Rajiv Gandhi, and increased in speed after 1991 as a result of economic deregulation imposed by the IMF as a condition for granting India desperately needed loans. India's growth rate was not as high as China's, about five percent annually, but it was still much higher than it had been under previous state regulations.

India confronted enormous, persistent challenges from both its own social structure and its colonial heritage: hierarchical caste divisions, including especially severe discrimination against ex-untouchables; conflict between religious communities, especially Hindus and Muslims, but Sikhs as well in and around the Punjab; tension among regional and linguistic groups; renewed oppression of women; an economy of scarcity with widespread, persistent hunger and poverty; and continuing massive population growth. In these struggles, India followed policies of democratic political stability for development, including technological policies of great diversity.

Both China and India were aware of the technological and economic progress of Japan and the Asian tigers. For China this represented a galling challenge, since the Japanese powerhouse dominated the economics of East Asia, displacing China from her historic position. India did not see itself in competition with Japan, but it recognized that the smaller countries of Southeast Asia, which had previously trailed India, had now surpassed it economically and in consumer technology. India, too, saw this as a model and a challenge.

By the end of the twentieth century, economic, social, political, and cultural change was taking place so rapidly in both India and China that we devote renewed attention to these two giants in the final section of this book.

CHAPTER REVIEW

CHINA AND INDIA: A COMPARISON

22.1 How did China (since 1949) and India (since 1947) differ in their paths of political and economic development?

The two countries attained independence and statehood at about the same time, both out of struggles that began as protest movements, led by professional men. Both countries eventually turned to mass movements of the majority of their populations, which in each case were peasants and commoners. As new nations, China and India followed different development strategies. India was influenced by British colonial legacies, and chose democratic politics and a mixed socialist-capitalist economy. In China, the communist leadership asserted strong central, dictatorial control. China looked at first to the USSR for advice and assistance, but soon moved in its own direction. Both countries had difficulty industrializing along Western lines, and instead followed paths appropriate to their rural populations. Each became a model for some of the developing countries.

CHINA'S REVOLUTIONS

22.2 How did the experiences of the Long March and the guerrilla war guide China's leaders after 1949?

Threatened with annihilation by Chiang's armies, in 1934, the communists under Mao fled their base in Hunan Province and traveled some 6,000 miles in one year on foot over mountains and across rivers to a new base camp in China's northwest Yan'an Province. This long march, actually a strategic retreat, forged a camaraderie and toughness among the leaders that kept them in command for the next forty years. Their reliance upon the peasantry along the way solidified their commitment to guerrilla warfare and rural revolution until, and beyond, the success of their revolution in 1949.

THE PEOPLE'S REPUBLIC OF CHINA

22.3 What were the revolutionary policies of the People's Republic of China?

Mao's policy goals included primacy of the peasantry; the redistribution of land; protection of women's rights to hold land and to marry and divorce according to their own wishes; implementation of technology; the production and equal distribution of basic necessities for all; and universal literacy. The government organized local networks to suppress such vices as opium addiction and prostitution and to enforce rigid political indoctrination and conformity. It encouraged family members to inform against one another, and it employed "brainwashing" to extract confessions of political deviance. Mao also jailed protesters, sent them to labor camps, and exiled them to rural farms.

POSTREVOLUTIONARY CHINA

22.4 How did the end of colonialism change China's image of itself?

China, in the end, found its own path, one appropriate to its size, geography, and technology. As the Chinese surveyed their long history, the thread that the communists adopted was that of peasant revolution and they based their revolution on guerrilla warfare and their new economy on the primacy of agriculture. At the same time, the communist leadership kept centralized power in its own hands, much as the emperors had done before them. After years of international and civil war, China was ready to choose its own way.

INDIA'S STRUGGLE FOR INDEPENDENCE

22.5 What was Mohandas Gandhi's concept of civil disobedience, and what was his role in India's fight for independence?

Mohandas Gandhi was a leader of the Indian National Congress, the principal vehicle for India's nationalist movement for independence. Gandhi identified with the peasantry of India and reconstituted the Congress into a mass organization of paying members from India's villages as well as from its cities—comprising ordinary people as well as Western-educated elites. Gandhi led the Congress in three huge, nation-wide *satyagraha*, or "truth-force," campaigns, which demonstrated to the world a new way of non-violent struggle to force the British out of India. Gandhi's *satyagraha* campaigns called for peaceful opposition to oppression and were meant to show the oppressors—the British—the immorality of their position toward the Indians. Gandhi called his actions "civil resistance," but they were actually systems of militant nonviolence. His methods were later adopted by Martin Luther King, Jr. in the US, Nelson Mandela in South Africa, and other resistance movements around the world.

INDEPENDENCE AND PARTITION

22.6 To what degree did the experiences of the independence movement provide guidelines for governing India after 1947?

Under British rule, Indians had had opportunities, though limited, to vote in elections for responsible officials at almost all levels of government; this became the basis for a one-person-one vote electoral democracy. They used English as the link language for the country and preserved it in this status after independence. They built the Congress movement into an organization that could and did transform itself into a political party. They built the Congress into a mass movement, which brought the masses of the population into the political process. Festering antagonisms between Muslims and Hindus, however, led to partition of the country into India and Pakistan.

DEMOCRACY AND ITS CHALLENGES

22.7 What were the major policy issues addressed by independent India?

The openness of India's new democracy, with universal suffrage, at first brought a national government dedicated to a mixture of capitalism and socialism; two states freely elected communist governments. The declaration of an "Emergency," 1975–77, undercut democratic rule briefly, but otherwise regular elections have brought new opportunities especially for low caste and class groups who benefitted from the power of their numbers. The "green revolution" enabled India to grow adequate food for its entire population, but inequality and maldistribution remained problems, and poverty and malnutrition remained endemic. Industrialization, especially in information technology, brought new wealth and new jobs, although only to a minority. Hostility toward Pakistan, competition with China, and attempts at leadership of the third world were the cornerstones of foreign policy. India legislated new freedoms for women and raised the legal age of marriage to 18 years old. Female literacy went up; birth rates went down. Working women began to organize successfully. Yet a declining sex ratio of women to men showed that families still preferred boys to girls.

In general, a comparison of India after 1947 with China after 1949, shows democratic India moving more cautiously, with greater sensitivity to its voters; and communist China, with less need to consult its population, moving more dramatically and more abruptly in choosing, and changing, new directions.

Suggested Readings

CHINA

Andors, Phyllis. *The Unfinished Liberation of Chinese Women, 1949–1980* (Bloomington, IN: University of Indiana Press, 1983). Feminist, antipatriarchal ideology was central to the Chinese communist program. Andors captures the ideology and the degree of implementation.

Blunden, Caroline, and Mark Elvin. *Cultural Atlas of China* (New York: Facts on File, 1983). Another in the excellent Facts on File series. More than an atlas, it is a comprehensive approach to China, scholarly yet accessible.

de Bary, William Theodore, *et al.* comps. *Sources of Chinese Tradition* (New York: Columbia University Press, 1960). Original edition of this outstanding anthology of statements by China's intellectual and political leaders.

—— and Richard Lufrano, comps. *Sources of Chinese Tradition*, vol. 2 (New York: Columbia University Press, 2000). This revision in 2000 doubled the number of selections of the original.

Ebrey, Patricia Buckley, ed. *Chinese Civilization: A Sourcebook* (New York: The Free Press, 2nd ed., 1993). A very different selection from de Bary's, this one captures the lives of common people. Illuminating and excellent.

Meisner, Maurice. *Mao's China and After* (New York: The Free Press, 1986). A thoughtful, rather pro-Mao account of the revolution. A scholarly, accessible standard.

Schell, Orville, ed. *The China Reader*, 4 vols. (New York: Random House, 1967–74). Tells the story of China's revolution from the end of the colonial era until the end of Mao's years through an exceptional array of documents.

Snow, Edgar. *Red Star over China* (London: Victor Gollancz, 1968). Snow, a journalist, visited Mao in Yan'an and brought back to the West the first detailed knowledge of the man and the movement. Inspiring from a very pro-Maoist viewpoint.

Spence, Jonathan D. *The Search for Modern China* (New York: W.W. Norton & Company, 3rd ed., 2013). Clearly written, detailed yet highly accessible, excellent as an introduction to the subject and to further scholarly investigation.

——. *Mao Zedong* (New York: Viking/Penguin, 1999). Concise, readable, reasonably comprehensive biography.

INDIA

Bayly, Susan. *Caste, Society, and Politics in India from the Eighteenth Century to the Modern Age* (Cambridge: Cambridge University Press, 1999). Accessible, highly scholarly introduction to the phenomenon of caste, its changing meaning and its changing economic and political significance.

Brown, Judith M. *Modern India: The Origins of an Asian Democracy* (New York: Oxford University Press, 2nd ed., 1994). Stresses the constitutional processes in achieving independence, and in the negotiations between the British and the Congress. Brown sees India's postindependence democracy as a result of that process.

Chandra, Bipan. *India's Struggle for Independence, 1857–1947* (New York: Penguin Books, 1989). Chandra stresses the popular, revolutionary side of the struggle for independence, and sees Gandhi as the integrative force who encouraged it to take democratic directions.

Dalton, Dennis. *Mahatma Gandhi: Non-Violent Power in Action* (New York: Columbia University Press, 1993). Remarkably lucid account of Gandhi's theory and practice of *satyagraha*, and especially good on his fast in Calcutta in 1947.

de Bary, William Theodore, *et al.* comps. *Sources of Indian Tradition* (New York: Columbia University Press, 1958). Superb anthology of statements by India's intellectual and political leaders.

Forbes, Geraldine. *Women in Modern India* (Cambridge: Cambridge University Press, 1998). Useful survey of women in education, cultural and social life, and reform, the nationalist movement, the economy, and recent political action. Especially interesting for the shift from elite issues to the masses.

Guha, Ramchandra. *India after Gandhi* (London: Macmillan, 2007). Covers the challenges of independent India, with pride in its accomplishments and reservations about continuing problems.

Hay, Stephen, ed. *Sources of Indian Tradition*, vol. 2 (New York: Columbia University Press, 2nd ed., 1988). Excellent selection of statements by Indian political and cultural leaders. Stresses the elite.

Nehru, Jawaharlal. *The Discovery of India* (Bombay: Asia Publishing House, 1960). A personal history, Marxist in orientation, written from jail by the prime minister of India, illuminating of the nation's history and of Nehru's understanding of that history.

Panagariya, Arvind. *India: the Emerging Giant* (New York: Oxford University Press, 2008). A comprehensive, thorough overview of India's economy since independence.

Rothermund, Dietmar. *An Economic History of India: From Pre-Colonial Times to 1991* (London: Routledge, 1993). Clearly written, succinct introduction to the subject.

Rudolph, Lloyd I., and Susanne Hoeber Rudolph. *The Modernity of Tradition* (Chicago, IL: University of Chicago Press, 1967). Still the clearest introduction to the idea that tradition and modernity are not opposites, but interact in the hands of creative leaders, such as Gandhi and, later, caste leaders.

Wiser, William H., and Charlotte Viall Wiser. *Behind Mud Walls 1930–1960* (including Susan Wadley, "The Village in 1984," "The Village in 1998") (Berkeley, CA: University of California Press, 2000). The Wisers kept revisiting a north Indian village and writing down their observations. A fascinating, very readable review. Make sure to get the latest edition, as Susan Wadley continues to update the Wisers' work.

ADDITIONAL SOURCES

Bouton, Marshall M., and Philip Oldenburg, eds. *India Briefing: A Transformative Fifty Years* (Armonk, NY: M.E. Sharpe, 1999). Every year or two, Oldenburg and a co-editor bring together an excellent, scholarly set of interpretive essays on current events in India under the title *India Briefing*. This edition covered the entire period from independence.

Brass, Paul. *The Politics of India Since Independence* (Cambridge: Cambridge University Press, 2nd ed., 1994). Another in the Cambridge series of comprehensive introductions to India. Brass is comprehensive, thoughtful, and, appropriately, quite skeptical of official rhetoric.

Drèze, Jean, and Amartya Sen. *India's Economic Development and Social Opportunity* (Delhi: Oxford University Press, 1998). Sen won the Nobel Prize for economics in 1998 for his stress on the importance of education and health in development economics. Here he and Drèze bring that perspective to an analysis of India's record.

Fairbank, John King. *The Great Chinese Revolution: 1800–1985* (New York: Harper and Row, 1986). Fairbank was one of the masters of Chinese history. This book is now dated, but still very useful and interesting.

Frankel, Francine. *India's Political Economy, 1947–2004: The Gradual Revolution* (New York: Oxford University Press, 2005). To know how India said it was doing, and how it was actually doing in economic and political development after independence, this is a good place to begin.

Goldman, Merle, and Roderick MacFarquhar, eds. *The Paradox of China's Post-Mao Reforms* (Cambridge, MA: Harvard University Press, 1999). Although focused on China after Mao, the before-and-after contrast is illuminating.

Hardgrave, Robert L., and Stanley Kochanek. *India: Government and Politics in a Developing Nation* (Stamford, CT: Harcourt College Publishers, 1999). A standard introductory text, continuously revised for three decades.

Hardiman, David. *Gandhi in His Time and Ours: The Global Legacy of His Ideas* (New York: Columbia University Press, 2003). Bringing conflicting interest groups under his umbrella, Gandhi set an example to India and the world.

Jack, Homer, ed. *The Gandhi Reader* (New York: Grove Press, 1956). A comprehensive source book covering Gandhi's philosophies and activities in politics, economics, and moral life. Most sources are by Gandhi, some are about him.

Jayakar, Pupul. *Indira Gandhi* (New York: Viking, 1992). A friendly but critical biography by a friend and colleague.

Karlekar, Hiranmay, ed. *Independent India: The First Fifty Years* (Delhi: Oxford University Press and the Indian Council for Cultural Relations, 1998). A set of assessments of uneven quality, but many quite fascinating, of many aspects of India since independence. Written in India for Indians; may be somewhat dense for foreign readers.

Liang, Heng, and Judith Shapiro. *Son of the Revolution* (New York: Vintage Books, 1983). The biography of Liang, a young man who survived the Cultural Revolution but saw it destroy his parents, their marriage, his schooling, and his earlier belief that the revolution was benign.

Liu Binyan. *A Higher Kind of Loyalty* (New York: Pantheon, 1990). Exiled from China, the journalist Liu Binyan writes from America incisive, angry criticism of the actions of the government of the country that he loves.

MacFarquhar, Roderick Timothy Cheek, and Eugene Wu, eds. *The Secret Speeches of Chairman Mao* (Cambridge, MA: Council on East Asian Studies, 1989). Mao's policies in his own words.

Nandy, Ashis, ed. *Science, Hegemony and Violence* (Delhi: Oxford University Press, 1988). Nandy is an oddity: a prominent, Western-educated intellectual who is quite skeptical of Western influences in India, including those in science and technology.

Pa Chin. *Family* (Garden City, NY: Doubleday & Company, 1972). This novel of the 1910s and 1920s presented a new, feminist vision of what a family might be in modern China.

Ramusack, Barbara, *et al. Women in Asia: Restoring Women to History* (Bloomington, IN: Indiana University Press, 1999). Product of a decade-long project of the Organization of American Historians to provide perspectives and bibliographies on the study of women in the non-Western world. Other volumes treat sub-Saharan Africa, the Middle East, and Latin America.

Schell, Orville, and David Shambaugh, eds. *The China Reader: The Reform Era* (New York: Vintage Books, 1999). An excellent selection of essays and observations on the changes in China after Mao's death. Updates the earlier four volumes of *China Reader* noted above.

Weiner, Myron. *The Child and the State in India* (Princeton, NJ: Princeton University Press, 1991). In a very critical, down-to-earth assessment, Weiner asks why the literacy rate and school attendance are so low, and child labor so extensive, and argues that hierarchical values are a major culprit.

Wolf, Eric R. *Peasant Wars of the Twentieth Century* (New York: Harper and Row, 1969). A classic comparative study of the philosophy and strategy of modern guerrilla warfare. China figures prominently.

Wolpert, Stanley. *A New History of India* (New York: Oxford University Press, 8th ed., 2008). A useful, standard, sometimes rambling but highly readable text.

Wu, Harry. *Bitter Winds* (New York: John Wiley, 1994). One of the bitterest attacks on political repression in contemporary China.

FILMS

China

The Good Earth (1937; 2 hours 18 minutes). Based on Pearl Buck's Pulitzer Prize-winning novel. Shows how wretched rural life in China was for the peasantry.

The Last Emperor (1987; 2 hours 20 minutes). Puyi abdicated in 1912, ending the Chinese Empire; was later placed on the throne of Japanese-occupied Manchuria until 1945; was jailed as war criminal; and died in 1967. His life as represented in this award-winning film spans much of China's recent history.

The Long Bow Trilogy (1984; 2 hours 54 minutes). Three documentaries giving extraordinary insight into the life of village China in the early 1980s. Focus on one village, but representative of thousands. Especially good on women's lives.

The Manchurian Candidate (1962; 2 hours 6 minutes). The politics of "brainwashing" of American prisoners-of-war in Korea. Spying, thrilling, satirical. Gives a good idea of the fear of communist China in the United States.

Xiu Xiu: The Sent Down Girl (1997; 1 hour 39 minutes). Set during the Cultural Revolution of the 1960s. Xiu Xiu is "sent down" for hard labor to a remote part of Tibet. To get back home, she sells herself.

India

The Bandit Queen (1994; 1 hour 59 minutes) Based on the real life of Phulan Devi, a low-caste woman, gang-raped after her husband was murdered, who becomes the leader of a band of vengeful outlaws. She serves a jail term, but is ultimately elected to parliament.

Dadi's Family (1981; 50 minutes). Documentary set in a north Indian village. We watch the life of an extended family through the eyes of the grandmother/ mother-in-law who lives through and discusses the changes of her times.

Distant Thunder (1973; 1 hour 32 minutes). During World War II, the British government of India shipped grain out of Bengal to its troops, even though Bengalis were starving to death. Satyajit Ray's film captures the tragedy.

Earth (1998; 1 hour 41minutes). The violence and disasters of the partition of India and Pakistan in 1947 are captured through the experiences of a Punjabi family, and especially their young daughter. Directed and written by Deepa Mehta.

Gandhi (1982; 3 hours 8 minutes). This biography of Gandhi won eight Academy Awards. Presents the somewhat saintly Gandhi of Louis Fischer's biography (1954), but mostly accurate and very moving.

Kamala and Raji (1990; 50 minutes). Documentary of the lives of two working women, members of the Self Employed Women's Association (SEWA). Understand their work at the low end of the pay scale, their difficulties at home negotiating poverty and unsupportive husbands, and the help provided in their struggle by SEWA.

PART EIGHT

TURNING POINT: FROM PAST TO PRESENT TO FUTURE

1979–

We study history in order to understand the complexity of human life and affairs. Certain themes are always present, appearing and reappearing in various combinations and as turning points throughout the history of human life: the *evolution* that made us the humans we are; the *settlements* we develop and live in; the *political power* we assemble; the *religious systems* in which we may believe; the *movement* of people and products; industrial, political, and, especially, *social revolutions*; our mastery of *technological development*; and our search for *identity*, both personal and group. In the final section of this book, we explore the ways in which these themes help us to understand the world in its recent past and in its possible directions for the future. We find out how well a knowledge of the past helps us to understand our own identities in the present.

The opening unit dealt with the evolution of hominids into *Homo sapiens* and their very early social organization. We *Homo sapiens* have changed physically only imperceptibly, if at all, in the past 100,000 years. But cultural evolution showed such remarkable new developments about 35,000 years ago that we believe the brain must have experienced new evolution. It probably continues to develop today, but too slowly for us to confirm through direct observation.

In the 1950s, scientists discovered DNA (deoxyribonucleic acid), a chemical within the cells of each individual organism that carries the genetic instructions to make it what it is. DNA reaffirmed the scientific theory of evolution, and added information on genetic relationships among humans, between humans and animals, and even between humans and diseases, such as AIDS. Our understanding of DNA has also given us the capacity to intervene in nature in daring enterprises never before charted, for example in the cloning

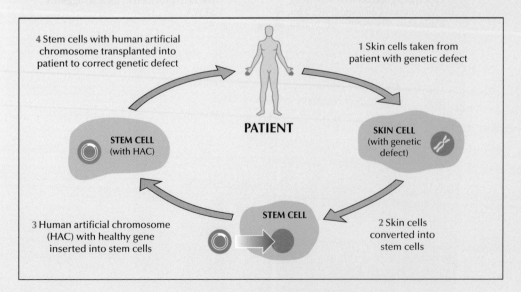

4 Stem cells with human artificial chromosome transplanted into patient to correct genetic defect

1 Skin cells taken from patient with genetic defect

PATIENT

STEM CELL (with HAC)

SKIN CELL (with genetic defect)

STEM CELL

3 Human artificial chromosome (HAC) with healthy gene inserted into stem cells

2 Skin cells converted into stem cells

Medical treatment using DNA processes. The discoveries of molecular biology were transforming the practice of medicine just as they were revising our understanding of human evolution. As they understood more about genes and DNA, basic building blocks of human life, doctors were beginning to replace conventional medicines designed to treat human disease in a shotgun approach, with new practices that targeted individuals, curing them one-by-one by manipulating and re-arranging their specific genes.

and genetic engineering of crops and animals. Medical research is showing new ways to identify and cure genetically based diseases. Such constant technological innovation reminds us that to create new technologies, even before the consequences can be evaluated, is human—and contentious.

Our second unit, dealing with settlement patterns, introduced themes concerning urbanization that have repeated throughout human history. Especially at the turning point of the Industrial Revolution, vast numbers of people left the countryside for industrial jobs in cities. In the past generation, the cityward migration has continued. By 2006, half the world's population lived in cities. Reading this history, Chinese leaders see urbanization as a means of modernizing the country and increasing its economic productivity. In 2013, they announced plans to move 250 million of China's population from villages to cities within fifteen years (Ian Johnson, "China's Great Uprooting: Moving 250 Million into Cities," *The New York Times*, June 15, 2013).

Our third theme, on politics in history, focused on the ancient empires of China, Rome, and India. The imperial theme remained critical, although at the end of the twentieth century the emphasis was on the fall of empires more than on their rise. The implosion of the Soviet Union in 1991 left the United States as "the sole superpower." But what did that mean? Twenty years later, America seemed to be reducing its global footprint. It was withdrawing from wars in Iraq and Afghanistan, without clearly achieving its goals in either; it fought its enemies with drone attacks from the air, rather than committing troops on the ground; its trade imbalances with the rest of the world continued to grow; and its economy sank into severe recession, from which it was recovering by 2013, but slowly.

Meanwhile, around the globe other nations were on the rise in power and prestige. China achieved economic growth rates of ten percent per year for three decades. Its global footprint was expanding, financed by the $3 trillion of cash reserves it had earned through international trade. India grew more slowly, but with one billion people, nuclear weapons, and software expertise, it, too, gained in importance. By the early years of the twenty-first century, Russia, developing its immense oil wealth, was asserting itself once again. The European Union brought peace and unprecedented prosperity to its members, although the recession of 2008 raised questions about the health of its economy. More countries adopted democratic systems of government, although others, most notably China, chose dictatorial forms, and Russia's leaders also seemed to be taking more power for themselves. All these countries and groupings saw themselves as peaceful rivals for global power.

Our fourth unit introduced the theme of religion in history, focusing largely on the five most ancient, widespread, scripture-based religions: Hinduism, Buddhism, Judaism, Christianity, and Islam. The skepticism of the French Revolution and the atheism of the Russian seemed to undercut organized religion as a force in modern history,

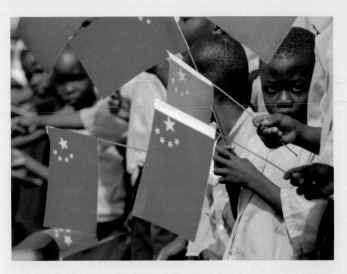

Liberian children hold Chinese flags awaiting the arrival of China's President Hu Jintao in Monrovia, 2007. As China's economy grew at a rate of about 10 per cent per year for three decades, the country began to seek overseas investments, especially in natural resources. The Chinese also sought to win friends and allies as they expanded, although they often encountered resentment for their policies, which ultimately were designed for China's interests.

but since the late twentieth century religion has reemerged as a powerful force in political life.

Revolution brought a theocracy to power in Iran in 1979 and ushered in an era of global Islamic political militancy. Most remarkably, in 2010, across North Africa and the Middle East, Arab countries exploded in political revolutions, which optimists called "The Arab Spring"; leaders of the revolutions, and their opponents, fought over the question of how much power Islam should have in government. Christianity continued to take on a new complexion as it expanded, especially in Asia, Africa, and Latin America. In 2013, the Roman Catholic Church elected its first Latin American pope, Francis I, from Argentina. The Orthodox Church revived in Russia after decades of communist suppression. Protestant evangelicals, firm in their emotional faith, attracted new followers and introduced their religious perspectives into political contests throughout the Americas. Religious differences often embittered political relations, for example, between Jews and Muslims in Israel/Palestine and between Hindus and Muslims in India. The Chinese communist government suppressed Buddhists in Tibet and Muslims in Xinjiang.

Trade, our fifth theme, rose to extraordinary importance. Truly global trade, initiated by the voyages of Columbus, da Gama, and Magellan, was in full swing by the turn of the twenty-first century. Containerization slashed the cost of shipping. New jobs were created, older ones terminated, and millions more transferred from high-wage countries to nations with lower labor costs. Britain and the United States deregulated large sectors of their economies in the 1980s. They encouraged the World Bank and the International

Monetary Fund to impose policies of free trade on many of the poorer countries of the world, many of which found the conditions too harsh for their fledgling economies. The fastest growing national economies—those of China and the Southeast and East Asian "tigers"—embraced free trade and prospered by fashioning export-based economies. In July 2013, the United States and the European Union began negotiations for a "Transatlantic Trade and Investment Partnership," a free-trade agreement that would include nearly half the world's economy. The World Trade Organization (WTO), the chief regulator of trade, became one of the most important institutions in international relations.

The victory for free markets in world trade, however, was far from total. The WTO was attacked by groups who believed that capitalistic competition produced inhumane economies. Poor countries suspected that free trade would put them at the mercy of more developed economies and turn them into virtual colonies. Even the United States, the staunchest advocate of free trade, wanted limits and regulations when its own economy seemed to be at risk.

Many of the social revolutions that were the theme of our sixth unit continued. In the aftermath of World War II, the United Nations promulgated an International Charter of Human Rights. High on the agenda were the rights of women, including: equal political and legal rights; equal pay for equal work; election to high political office; equal rights to be born and nurtured and not to be aborted or neglected in favor of male children; protection against genital mutilation and rape. Older cultural, religious, and sexual traditions concerning appropriate gender relations were reexamined and contested. Gays and lesbians fought against discrimination, often with considerable success. In the first decade of the twenty-first century the first laws recognizing same-sex marriage were passed; by mid-2013, thirteen countries recognized these marriages, with more in line to follow. Legal equality for transgendered people had begun to surface as an even newer public issue.

The struggle against racism was at least equally important, equally widespread, and it, too, won significant victories: the apartheid government of South Africa dissolved into a one-person-one-vote democracy; political mobilization against caste discrimination created a social revolution in India; America elected an African-American president. The migration of peoples continued with greater numbers than ever before, and virtually every large country in the world addressed the social and legal problems of migrant assimilation.

Around the globe millions of citizens organized themselves into nongovernmental organizations (NGOs) to fight for the rights of women, minorities, and political dissidents; to struggle against poverty; and to obtain food, water, shelter, health care, jobs, and other daily necessities for their constituents. Popular culture crossed national borders, creating a revolution of its own: "fusion" in food, music, and the arts.

Same-sex marriage, 2011. In the first year of the twenty-first century the first laws giving legal recognition to same-sex marriage were passed, in the Netherlands. By 2013, fourteen other countries had followed suit, as had several states in the United States and many regions within other countries. Supporters saw the new laws as establishing equality; opponents saw it as changing the meaning of marriage.

On the other hand, many people resisted social revolution from a desire to preserve their cultures and languages intact. Others resisted for the less noble motives of sexism, homophobia, racism, and a general antagonism toward "the other." Competition among cultures continued as part of the human condition.

The seventh unit, with its theme of technological change, connects smoothly with social revolution, since rapidly evolving technology inspired new opportunities and incited new turbulence. The rise of computerization and virtually instantaneous communication around the globe enabled revolutions of all sorts. The mass public assemblies of the "Arab Spring" revolutions, noted above, were convened in part through the use of Facebook and other social media.

The search for energy sources, however, grew increasingly problematic. Could the world continue to depend so heavily on fossil fuels? How long would they last? How much would they cost? How much of their pollution could the earth's environment tolerate before human life was endangered through climate change? What were the threats to animal and plant life, to the earth's biodiversity? Despite some progress in disarmament, nuclear weapons were still stockpiled by the thousands. Would any nation

Colombian singer (of Spanish, Italian, and Lebanese descent) Shakira performs during the opening celebration of the 2010 FIFA World Cup, Soweto, South Africa. Shakira has earned equal fame for her music—she has sold 125 million records worldwide, that is, over 70 million albums and 55 million singles—and for her humanitarian efforts, including the Barefoot Foundation (Pies Descalzos Foundation) which she founded in 1997 to help poor and impoverished children in Colombia, and her numerous performances in benefit concerts worldwide.

use them? Could terrorist organizations succeed in seizing any of them? As nations and commercial companies compiled vast stores of information, "big data," what was the danger to individual privacy? Or, as governments argued, what was the danger to national security if these data were not gathered?

The structure of this book suggests that individuals and groups are constantly confronting change originating from the many themes of human life, from new understanding of our evolution to a bewildering array of changing technologies. As we absorb new experiences and information, individually and collectively we modify our sense of self, our sense of where we are coming from and where we might (like to) be going. Usually the modifications are incremental and small, but sometimes they demand major transformation in attitude and behavior. Our study of major themes in human history is designed to help readers to see how others in the past negotiated their encounters with these themes, and thus seek conceptual frameworks for our own encounters.

Turning Point Questions

1. Do you agree that knowledge of the past is helpful in planning our future? Why or why not?
2. Choose one problem of today and suggest what kinds of knowledge of the past might be useful in confronting it. The problem may be personal, national, global, or of an institution or group of which you are a member.
3. Several of the events mentioned in this Turning Point are very recent, for example, the use of DNA in medical analysis and procedures, China's plan to relocate a quarter of a billion people, the Arab Spring, the election of a Latin American pope, the legalization of same-sex marriage, increasing climate change, leaks of classified information. Which of these seems to touch your own life most closely? How?

Kiribati, 2009. The beautiful South Pacific island of Kiribati is expected to be entirely underwater within 60 years. With the highest point of land just 2 yards above sea level, the entire population has been moved to Fiji.

23 Contemporary History

Evolution, Settlements, Politics, and Religion

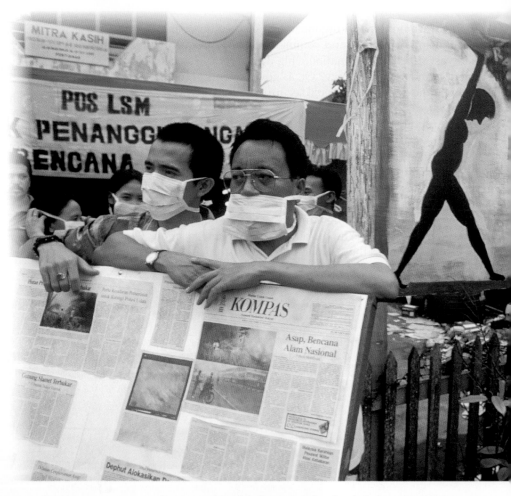

Contemporary history is hard to understand because we are living through it. Usually historians form their judgments only after they know how things turn out, but in the case of contemporary history we don't know yet. Who will win the war? Which candidate will win the election? How will his or her policies work out in the long run? Which styles in music, art, or fashion will endure and which will perish quickly as mere fads? How can we form definitive conclusions when we are still in the middle of events?

Protest against global warming, Pontianak, Indonesia, 2000. Because of forest fires that rage on unchecked, and urban congestion, Indonesia is one of the most polluted places on earth.

LEARNING OBJECTIVES

23.1 ((	23.2 ((	23.3 ((	23.4 ((
Discuss the ways in which the issues of evolution continue today.	Describe the changes in urban settlements in the early twenty-first century.	Discuss the realignments of global power in the early twenty-first century.	Describe the reemergence of religious groups as powerful political forces.

((Listen on MyHistoryLab

In contemporary history, the history of the last 35 years or so, the results are not clear. Leaders change their policies. Sports teams that are winning go into slumps; so do national and international economies. New inventions and ideas render older ones obsolete, eliminating long-standing industries and jobs while creating new ones. Unpredictable events erupt, totally altering our expectations.

So what do we do? It is the argument of this book that familiarity with the central themes of history helps us to grasp contemporary events. The themes do not tell us how current events will turn out—the past does not predict the future—but they alert us to possible outcomes, including some that we might not have considered. They enlarge our awareness of what is important to consider.

In this chapter we review the themes of the first four units—evolution, settlements, politics, and religion—and illustrate ways in which they continue to appear in our own time. In the process, we shall see how knowledge of the past enlarges our understanding of the present, and how being well informed in the present enriches our appreciation of the past.

How do the issues of evolution continue in contemporary times?

23.1
23.2
23.3
23.4

On Evolution

| 23.1 | How do the issues of evolution continue in contemporary times? |

Long before the scientific discoveries of the process of evolution, most major cultural and religious traditions of the world had mythological tales of the creation of the world and of humans. Those mythological explanations endure because they frequently show a profound understanding of human nature. But scientific methods of exploration, data collection, and evaluation have led to more systematic ways of understanding the emergence of human life. Scientists today believe that humans evolved from hominids, over millions of years, through biological processes that increased their adaptability, sophistication, and power. In the mid-nineteenth century, the British naturalist Charles Darwin formulated the biological hypothesis that a process of "natural selection" was responsible for the evolution of species. Since then, the entire record of fossil discoveries has supported the Darwinian argument, and, since the 1970s, the study of human DNA (deoxyribonucleic acid), the biological material that instructs all the cells within each individual, has added further confirmation.

In "The Dry Bones Speak," we also reviewed evidence for extensive cultural development, beginning with migration and adaptation to new geographical areas, increased capacity for speech and communication, and the fashioning and use of increasingly sophisticated tools. About 35,000 years ago, in quicker succession, came further cultural accomplishments: the creation of art, the domestication of plants and animals, and the association of humans in small bands for hunting, gathering, farming, and child-raising. It appears that further evolution of the human brain, although not of the rest of the body, made these later cultural developments possible.

The DNA Code and Its Discoveries

Our study of biological and cultural evolution makes us more sensitive to a number of scientific developments in our own time. Consider, for example, the discovery of DNA and its function. The unlocking of this secret of biological development, largely the work of Nobel laureates James D. Watson and Francis Crick in the 1950s, based on data provided by Rosalind Franklin, has opened many new doors. Most recently, for example, some scientists, reading the DNA of selected individuals from around the world, have argued that they see evolution continuing within historical time periods. Individuals within some groups show genetic change in specific brain cells that normally produce somewhat larger brains. The lead researcher, Bruce

23.1

23.2

23.3

23.4

How do the
issues of
evolution
continue in
contemporary
times?

Lahn at the University of Chicago, concluded, "the growth of brain size and complexity … is likely still going on" ("University Of Chicago Researchers Find Human Brain Still Evolving," *Science Daily*, September 9, 2005, http://www.sciencedaily.com/releases/2005/09/050909221043.htm [accessed October 2013]). Other scientists dispute these findings, partly because the test group is too small for statistical verification. But the subject of the speed of evolution is on the table as part of contemporary history.

In another development, stemming from the fact that the great apes and humans share 97 percent of their DNA, two philosophers, Peter Singer of Australia and Paolo Cavaliere of Italy, founded the Great Ape Project in 1993:

> The idea is founded upon undeniable scientific proof that non-human great apes share more than genetically similar DNA with their human counterparts. They enjoy a rich emotional and cultural existence in which they experience emotions such as fear, anxiety and happiness. They share the intellectual capacity to create and use tools, learn and teach other languages. They remember their past and plan for their future. … The Great Ape Project seeks to end the unconscionable treatment of our nearest living relatives by obtaining for non-human great apes the fundamental moral and legal protections of the right to life, the freedom from arbitrary deprivation of liberty, and protection from torture. (http://www.greatapeproject.org/)

In 2007 the project won a signal victory when the Spanish parliament conferred these three legal protections on great apes. Since 2011, the American National Institutes of Health has sharply reduced the use of chimpanzees in research and has begun to "retire" many of the 500 chimpanzees in its laboratories.

 Read the **Document: Jane Goodall, from "The Challenge Lies in All of Us"** on **MyHistoryLab**

Cloning and Genetic Engineering. Other new by-products of the cracking of the DNA genetic code have been the cloning of animals and the production of genetically modified foods. These processes, too, are subjects of contemporary history, for they are continuing day by day, acclaimed by some but opposed by others, both within and outside the scientific community. Genetic engineering has enabled scientists to make clones, genetically exact copies of living creatures. The first clone of a mammal, a sheep, was born in 1996. Cloned from a cell taken from a mammary gland, she was named Dolly, in honor of the singer Dolly Parton, and was a genetically exact copy of an existing sheep. She gave birth to six lambs, born naturally. But from the age of five she suffered from arthritis, and she died of a lung infection at age six, about half the usual life span of a sheep. Geneticists wonder if her biological age matched that of the sheep from whose cell she was cloned, rather than that of a conventional newborn. In addition, Dolly was the only sheep to survive out of 277 attempts at cloning up to that time. Subsequently, other mammals were cloned, including horses and bulls, but also with failure rates that bring into question the value of the technique.

The cloning of humans has been a subject of avid discussion and controversy. Cloning humans is illegal in most countries, both because the failure rate in cloning large, complicated animals is so high, and because the ethics are questionable. Should bereaved parents be allowed to clone a much-loved child who has died in an accident? Or is each individual unique and entitled to a unique genetic identity? Would you want to be cloned over and over again

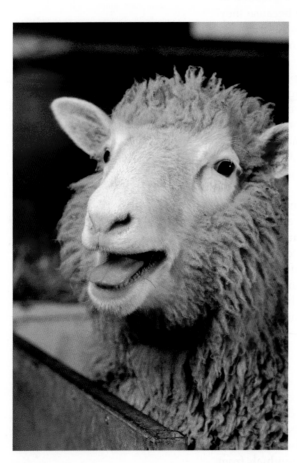

Dolly, the cloned sheep, 1997. Genetic engineering raised great hopes for increasing longevity, health, and food supplies, but it entered a new, unknown world of biological transformation that cannot be reversed.

for centuries to come? Consider also that no one knows what, if any, biological changes may be inserted into the hereditary chain through cloning; any such changes would be irreversible.

This question of unknown long-term effects has especially dogged the acceptance of genetically modified foodstuffs. Here, scientists mix genetic material, DNA, from different kinds of organisms to create new organisms that have never

How do the issues of evolution continue in contemporary times?

23.1
23.2
23.3
23.4

AT A GLANCE: EVOLUTION, SETTLEMENTS, POLITICS, RELIGION

DATE	EVOLUTION	SETTLEMENTS (CITIES)	POLITICS	RELIGION
1968–1970s			• 1978 Deng Xiaoping heads Chinese government	• 1968 Latin American Bishops' Conference supports Liberation Theology • 1979 Iranian revolution
1980s	• 1981 AIDS epidemic identified	• 1980 Shenzhen, China, designated Special Economic Zone (SEZ) • 1980s Sites and services programs for slum improvement	• 1989 Tiananmen massacre • 1989–91 Russia leaves Afghanistan; Soviet Union dissolves • 1983, 1993, 1995, 1996, 1998, 2000 Bombing attacks on US overseas military diplomatic posts	• 1989 *Fatwa* against Salman Rushdie
1990s	• 1993 Great Ape Project • 1996 Sheep (Dolly) cloned	• 1990s In-place, slum upgrading projects	• 1993 Formation of European Union (EU) • 1994 Chechnya declares independence from Russia • 1997 Hong Kong reverts to China • 1999, 2004, 2007–09 Former USSR satellites join NATO and the EU	• 1990s Pope John Paul II criticizes Liberation Theology • 1990 Latin American Evangelical Pentecostal Commission (CEPLA) established; 75 million Pentecostals in Latin America (2005) • 1992 Militant Hindus raze Babri Mosque • 1992–95 Civil war in Yugoslavia • 1992–98 Civil war in Algeria; 100,000 die • 1999 Chinese government bans Falun Gong
2000s	• 2002 Discovery of Toumai skull and (2005) teeth and jaw fragments	• 2005 Immigrant riots in suburban Paris • 2006 Fifty percent of world's population urban	• 2001 China admitted to World Trade Organization. Terrorist attacks in United States (September 11) • 2003 United States declares war on Iraq • 2005 Agreement in Northern Ireland for peaceful power sharing • 2008 China hosts Olympic Games • 2008 Barack Obama elected first African-American president of United States	• 2000s Christian–Muslim battles in Nigeria • 2002 Gujarat, India: Hindu–Muslim killing, leaving 2000 dead • 2009 Radical *jihadist* sect, Boko Haram, grows in power in Nigeria
2010s	• 2011 American National Institutes of Health begins to reduce sharply its use of chimpanzees in research	• 2012 One billion people around the world live in slums	• 2011 "Arab Spring" begins in Tunisia. Hosni Mubarak overthrown in Egypt • 2011 US Special Forces hunt down and kill Osama bin Laden • 2012 China becomes world's second largest oil importer, after the United States • 2012 Chinese complete Three Gorges Dam, the world's largest hydroelectric project • 2013 Summit meeting between Chinese and American presidents	• 2013 Election of first Latin American pope, Francis I

23.1

23.2 In what ways are the cities of the early twenty-first century different from those of the early twentieth?

23.3

23.4

existed before. One of the most prevalent examples is the creation of seeds resistant to specific plant diseases. These genetically modified seeds and plants have been widely accepted in the United States, but rejected in most parts of Europe. Trade battles over the issue continue a debate over the degree to which evolution is acceptable if it is human-made and artificially produces new organisms that could not form in nature. Once genetically modified organisms enter the breeding patterns of the natural world, they cannot be removed. Will they prove to be safe? Some scientists ask an opposing question: Without the increase in food production made possible by genetically modified plants, can the earth produce enough to feed the projected 50 percent population increase, to 10.5 billion people, over the next half-century?

The Evolution of Diseases

Evolution occurs not only in the world of humans, animals, and plants, but also in diseases. Some disease microbes prove resistant to today's medications; their genes will survive in new generations. For this reason, medications that are effective today will sooner or later prove inadequate to treat resistant strains of disease. Doctors caution that the overuse of antibiotic drugs will speed up the evolution of new forms of infection that the drugs will not be able to suppress. In this way, pharmacology becomes a race between the evolution of diseases and the creation of new medical remedies.

Additional diseases have ravaged human populations when an animal-borne disease, such as the bubonic plague, infected humans, who then infected one another (in contrast, for example, to malaria, which mosquitoes transmit to humans, but we do not transmit to one another). In recent years, the most lethal of these diseases that begin among animals but become infectious among humans was AIDS (Acquired Immunodeficiency Syndrome), which is believed to have crossed over from chimpanzees to humans in the mid-1900s in West Africa, perhaps transmitted by a bite or a cut or through the ingestion of chimpanzee meat. AIDS then spread among humans through sexual contact and the sharing of non-sterile injection needles, but it was identified as an epidemic only in 1981.

When HIV (Human Immunodeficiency Virus), the virus that causes AIDS, was first recognized as a health threat in the late 1970s, no drugs were available for treatment and the disease was deemed fatal. By 1996, however, a combination of drugs was found to be effective in inhibiting the development of HIV into AIDS, but the drugs are very expensive. In the developing world, where 95 percent of HIV cases occur—60 percent of them in sub-Saharan Africa—some drug manufacturers have negotiated somewhat lower prices. By the end of 2009, approximately 30 million people worldwide had died of AIDS, and in 2010 alone 2.5 million new cases of HIV were reported or estimated. Global spending on AIDS research, prevention, and treatment reached $11.7 billion in 2011, almost 40 times the spending in 1997.

On Settlements

23.2 In what ways are the cities of the early twenty-first century different from those of the early twentieth?

For twelve thousand years, people have been gathering together in fixed settlements, first in agricultural villages, later in cities. Then, beginning at the turning point of the Industrial Revolution (about 250 years ago), vast numbers of people left agriculture for industrial jobs, and cities began to absorb an ever-larger segment of the workforce. In the twentieth century, this process speeded up. Service jobs replaced industrial jobs as the primary urban occupation, and the population of cities multiplied. In 1900, about one person in six lived in a city, a total of about 260 million people worldwide. By 2000, some 47 percent of the world's population was urban, about three billion people worldwide. According to United Nations (UN) estimates, the 50 percent mark was reached in 2006.

The Growth of Cities

Individual cities grew to enormous size. By the end of the twentieth century, nineteen had become "megacities," with populations of ten million or more. They expanded geographically to breathtaking proportions. The Los Angeles metropolitan region, for example, held a population of 12 million, spanned a diameter of 120 miles, included five counties and 132 incorporated cities, and produced a gross annual economic output of nearly $250 billion.

During the twentieth century, the geographical distribution of cities shifted in an unexpected way. The link between economic growth and urbanization, which had once seemed so logical and natural, was broken. In earlier times, cities had mostly arisen in wealthier regions, where their presence seemed to reflect the "pull" of urban economic growth and job opportunities. In the late twentieth century, cities became more characteristic of poorer regions of the world, where their growth seemed to reflect the "push" from an overpopulated countryside that lacked jobs. In 1900, cities in the "economically developed world" held about 163 million people, and those in the "underdeveloped world" about 97 million. By 2012, the developed world held about one billion urbanites, and the underdeveloped world about 2.5 billion.

The key economic functions of cities changed equally dramatically. The large-scale industrial manufacture of commodities, such as steel in Pittsburgh, automobiles in Detroit, and textiles in Mumbai, gave way to service industries, such as information technology in California's Silicon Valley and India's Bangalore; the film industries

Shanghai skyscrapers. Much of China's economic success in raising hundreds of millions of its citizens out of poverty has been based on developing its cities. In 1960, just over 100 million Chinese lived in cities; by 2013, about 700 million. Some cities serve as flagships both for development and for show. Pudong, with its state-of-the-art skyscrapers, across the Huangpu River from the formerly colonial city center of Shanghai, is both: a designated growth center (Special Economic Zone) and an announcement to the world that the age of colonial control of China has long-since past.

815

23.1

23.2 In what ways are the cities of the early twenty-first century different from those of the early twentieth?

23.3

23.4

of Hollywood and Bollywood; the pleasure palaces of Las Vegas and the somewhat more risqué Bangkok and Manila; the theme parks of the Disney empire in Florida, California, Paris, Tokyo, and Hong Kong; and the tourism of such holiday destinations as Cancún, Rio de Janeiro, and Cape Town.

China was the great exception, demonstrating continuous growth in urban manufacturing. China also instituted four "special economic zones" (SEZ) to jump-start further development. The largest, the city and region of Shenzhen, contiguous to Hong Kong, grew from virtually no population in 1980 to 10 million in 2010. Manufacturing, trade, and services flourished, as did a huge container port. Another SEZ, Pudong, was built directly across the Huangpu River from Shanghai; by the early twenty-first century, it held some 10,000 financial, commercial, and trade institutions from over 60 countries in more than 100 high-rises, among them some of the world's tallest skyscrapers. China's urban population multiplied from 16 percent in 1960 (about 108 million people) to 19.6 percent in 1980 and then jumped sharply to 35.8 percent in 2000, and to 51 percent in 2012 (about 700 million people).

Recognizing the historical relationships between urbanization and economic growth, the Chinese government announced plans in 2013 to relocate 250 million of its citizens from the countryside to cities, most of them newly built, by the year 2025. This colossal project completely reversed the rural orientation of Mao's times, and in its magnitude was unprecedented in the history of the world (Ian Johnson, "China's Great Uprooting: Moving 250 Million into Cities," *The New York Times*, June 15, 2013, http://www.nytimes.com/2013/06/16/world/asia/chinas-great-uprooting-moving-250-million-into-cities.html [accessed October 2013]). In the same year, China announced the creation of a special free-trade zone on the edge of Shanghai.

Cities in other communist countries, which had been cut off from the global economy for decades, also adopted urban bourgeois styles of production and consumption. In Russian cities that had provided only minimal shopping facilities in the past, new shops began to open and private businesses to flourish, quickly giving the cities more life and color. Billboards proliferated. Business services, a sector of the economy virtually nonexistent under communist rule, employed almost 10 percent of Moscow's workforce by 2000. Many of the members of this new class were young, and just beginning to master the language, computer, and business skills of their new tasks. Often they arose from among former Communist Party bureaucrats, the people most experienced in administration and possessing the connections to buy the businesses, at bargain-basement prices, from the state, which was now withering away. Their prosperity inspired envy—and new commercial outlets to attract their disposable income. By 2013, Moscow was estimated to have 84 billionaires, more than any other city in the world (Ricardo Geromel, "Forbes Top 10 Billionaire Cities—Moscow Beats New York Again," *Forbes* online, March 14, 2013, http://www.forbes.com/sites/ricardogeromel/2013/03/14/forbes-top-10-billionaire-cities--moscow-beats-new-york-again [accessed October 2013]). Ethnic diversity in the major cities, especially Moscow, increased as Chechens and peoples from regions of the former Soviet Union, as well as immigrant Turks, Arabs, Chinese, and Vietnamese, arrived in search of work. Ethnic competition sometimes broke out in violence.

Nevertheless, urban centers in the capitalist world remained dominant in the world economy, and even increased their dominance. Sociologist Saskia Sassen noted the persistent influence of New York, London, and Tokyo over the international economy, referring to them—and only them—as "Global Cities."

So extraordinary were the size, technological transformation, and global integration of cities in the early twenty-first century that many observers viewed this combination as a fourth turning point in the history of human settlement patterns, following the creation of the agricultural village, the establishment of the first full-fledged cities, and the industrialization of cities.

Cities as Systems

High rates of economic growth in the global megacities, especially compared to rural areas, attracted high rates of diverse immigration. Third-world megacities attracted migrants from all parts of their nation and beyond. Abidjan in Ivory Coast drew from all of the West African Sahel; Mexico City from throughout Central America; Shanghai from the entire Yangzi River basin. Oil-rich cities of the Persian (Arabian) Gulf attracted migrants from the surrounding Arabian Sea periphery in Africa and Asia, and from Bangladesh and the Philippines as well. European cities had also received millions of migrants from their former colonies; Paris, for example, from North and West Africa; London from India, Pakistan, and the West Indies. Others came without any imperial connections, especially from Yugoslavia, Turkey, and southern Italy. Millions of migrants came from Islamic countries, introducing a new religious community into many European cities. By 2000, some 15 percent of Paris's population, 15–25 percent of the population of Frankfurt, Stuttgart, and Munich, and 50 percent of the population of Amsterdam was made up of international migrants.

The immigrants did not always find the jobs they were seeking, and their frustration fostered social and economic tension: "Large public housing projects in Paris and Amsterdam were increasingly populated by the structurally unemployed and their children, and—just as in their New York and London equivalents—violence was simmering just below the surface" (Hall, p. 459).

Not all violence was based on immigrant diversity. In many countries, electoral contests and sports competitions evoked periodic outbreaks of violence. Urban riots across India in the 1990s and early 2000s pitted Hindus and Muslims against one another as social upheaval, religious tension, and political grandstanding combined to inflame both spontaneous mobs and organized rioters (Brass). Violence among competing criminal gangs also flared up periodically in many cities.

A set of studies of large cities around the world concluded that in the process of globalization the spatial divisions among classes, ethnic groups, racial groups, and lifestyle groups within the city increased and "hardened, sometimes literally in the form of walls that function to protect the rich from the poor" (Marcuse and van Kempen, p. 250). Patterns of social segregation were common from city to city and from nation to nation. In all cities, people could live out their lives almost completely within geographically self-contained divisions, with residence, work, recreation, and socializing all included within their quarters of the city. These quarters were also separated from one another according to their political outlooks and self-interest.

Reactionary political parties, such as the Front National (National Front) of Jean-Marie Le Pen in France, campaigned on platforms urging bans on immigration and the expulsion of those immigrants already present. At street level, fights between immigrant and native youths became frequent, sometimes leading to firebombings. In many European cities, nativist youths shaved their heads and, as "skinheads," went out seeking "foreigners," even those who had been in place for a generation or more. In England the phenomenon earned its own name: "Paki[stani]-bashing." In 2005, rioting shook the immigrant, relatively poor, suburbs of Paris and spilled over into other cities in France and even into the Netherlands and Belgium. Beyond the immediate need to restore law and order, local and national political leaders appeared stymied as to what course to take economically, culturally, and politically.

Urban Slums. In the poorer countries of Asia, Africa, and South America, urban slums continued to expand in size and population. By 2012, about one billion people around the world lived in slums, many of them **squatters**. Because their settlements were often illegal, slum organizers had to negotiate deals with police and politicians. Squatters could maintain their toeholds in the city only through a combination of collective organization and payoffs to authorities.

In what ways are the cities of the early twenty-first century different from those of the early twentieth?

23.1
23.2
23.3
23.4

KEY TERM

squatter A person living on land, or in a residence, for which she or he does not pay and to which she or he has no legal title.

817

23.1

23.2   In what ways are
        the cities of the
23.3   early twenty-first
        century different
23.4   from those of the
        early twentieth?

Generations of squatters inhabit the Rocinha *favela* (shanty town, slum) neighborhood, the largest in Rio de Janeiro, Brazil, with about 70,000 residents. (Informal estimates are much higher.) Squatters migrate to cities in search of jobs and often temporarily settle in shacks. If they succeed in finding employment, they upgrade and expand their shacks into more conventional homes. On this hillside in Rio, several generations of squatters, acting collectively, have slowly improved their homes—most today are solidly built of brick and concrete, with basic plumbing and electricity—and have created thriving businesses as well. Some have gained legal status, many have not.

Cities and nations experimented with diverse strategies. Until the 1960s, most government plans in the developing world advocated the construction of public housing to accommodate new urban immigrants. The cost, however, was prohibitive. By the 1980s, programs of "sites and services" won favor. Governments would provide slum dwellers with space—a site marked off with individual plinths, or floors, often about 200–300 square feet—and the basic services of water, sewerage, and electricity, which householders could not provide for themselves individually. The recipients of the plots would then construct their own housing from their own resources. Even this strategy proved expensive, and it was difficult to decide which of the slum dwellers should receive the plots. In addition, after construction, the owner-builders often sold their new homes to middle-class buyers and returned to the slums, preferring the money to the home.

Despite such pessimistic accounts as Mike Davis's *Planet of Slums*, not all situations were dismal. In 1976 the UN sponsored the first Conference on Human Settlements, called Habitat I, in Vancouver, Canada. It was followed by Habitat II in Istanbul in 1996. Habitat III is scheduled for 2016. Urban research and study centers multiplied around the globe, some linked to government planning offices, some to universities, and some to NGOs. They addressed a wide spectrum of concerns, including physical planning, transportation, ecology, group relations, women's issues, youth organization, slum improvement, neighborhood planning, and the preservation of significant historic structures. Most important to the welfare of slums, however, was general economic progress as well as specific policies targeted at slum improvement. Cities whose economies were generally improving, as in much of East and Southeast Asia, and those that implemented specific policies to improve the lives of slum dwellers, as in much of Latin America, showed the most progress. Regions where the economy was generally lagging, such as sub-Saharan Africa, also lagged in reducing slum numbers and conditions—but even there some progress continued.

On Politics and Empire

23.3 How have power relationships between nations realigned in the early twenty-first century?

23.1

23.2

23.3

23.4

How have power
relationships
between nations
realigned in the
early twenty-first
century?

The early twenty-first century brought abrupt and astonishing realignments of global power. The Soviet Union had recently collapsed, leaving Russia in search of a new, more modest role commensurate with its reduced sphere of influence, but taking into account its enormous oil wealth, powerful armaments, and desire for recognition. America, despite its "superpower" status, soon found itself embroiled in two wars, and then saw its economy fall into the deepest recession in almost a century. Although the Cold War was over, new forms of guerrilla warfare—including terrorist attacks by suicide bombers, zealots willing to die in order to destroy their enemies—unleashed new uncertainty and fear. In response, America used new forms of aerial drone attack to counter some of the guerrilla warriors. The European Union was successfully expanding its membership, even though some of its members were experiencing severe economic difficulties. And China, riding the fastest economic expansion known in modern history, rose to new prominence and prestige.

The Former Soviet Union

President Mikhail Gorbachev, who presided over the dissolution of the USSR, won a reputation in the outside world for wisdom and courage, but inside the USSR many judged him a failure. His successor, Boris Yeltsin (in power 1991–99), kept the country afloat with foreign loans. Meanwhile, the transition from communism to capitalism funneled immense wealth into the pockets of a few insiders who managed to buy state-run enterprises at throwaway prices. Corruption was rampant. Inequality multiplied as the average worker lost the welfare protection formerly provided by the communist system. In addition to these domestic problems, the Muslim-majority republic of Chechnya declared its independence from Russia in 1994. Yeltsin put down the main revolt, after almost two years of fighting, but Chechen guerrillas continued the struggle, killing hundreds in numerous confrontations in Chechnya and within Russia itself, including attacks in theaters, schools, subways, and airplanes. The guerrilla warfare continues today.

Yeltsin's successor, Vladimir Putin—formerly a ranking officer in the Russian secret police, then president of Russia 2000–08, prime minister 2008–12, and president again from 2012—looked on his predecessors with scorn for their weakness and attempted to reassert the power of the Russian state. Putin's apparent thirst for power alienated many, leading to riots on the streets of Moscow before and after the 2012 elections. Journalists and wealthy businessmen who opposed Putin were jailed. Some fled Russia. Some were murdered.

Putin could carry a big stick based on the wealth of Russia's natural oil and gas deposits, some of the largest in the world, and the immense profits from their international sales. In 2012, oil and gas made up 58 percent of Russia's exports. The world recession in 2008 also hit the Russian economy, but it recovered its earlier growth trajectory faster than most to become once again one of the fastest

Theater siege, Moscow, 2002. In 1991, as the Soviet Union collapsed, Chechnya declared its independence. Russia responded with force and warfare followed, which continues sporadically until today (2013). Russia regained control of Chechnya, but only after tens of thousands were killed on both sides. Most of the fighting was in Chechnya itself, but Chechen rebels also attacked theaters, schools, subways, and airplanes in Russia. In 2002 Chechen guerrilla fighters—most of them women—seized a theater in Moscow and held some 800 people hostage for three days, until Russian troops recaptured the building.

How have power
relationships
between nations
realigned in the
early twenty-first
century?

growing in the world. At the time of writing, Putin has further asserted Russia's importance by intervening in a civil war in Syria. Nevertheless, America remained the sole superpower, able to project massive military, economic, and cultural power everywhere on the globe. At least, that was conventional wisdom. But what did it mean to be sole superpower?

The United States Stands Alone

In 1992, political scientist Francis Fukuyama argued in *The End of History* that the fall of Soviet communism had left just one viable political-economic system in the world, the capitalist-democratic system led by the United States. Even post-communist Russia was now moving toward accepting that model. The United States recovered from economic difficulties in the 1980s. Energized by innovations in communications technology and marketing, it entered a new phase of growth, one of the longest and steepest in its history.

Without the Soviet Union as an alternative, many nations turned to America for assistance or advice. Almost all the former satellites of the USSR chose to move toward free-market economic policies, and the Czech Republic, Hungary, and Poland joined NATO in 1999, with Russia's full consent. Six other former satellites joined in 2004, again with Russian consent. Middle Eastern nations, with no Russian alternative to choose, now aligned their foreign policies toward America and relied on America to mediate the Arab–Israeli dispute. India, which was already democratic politically, added a set of policy changes to reduce the role of the state in the national economy and to convert to greater reliance on free markets. In the Caribbean, communist Cuba's economy, already weak, virtually collapsed as the Soviet Union could no longer buy its sugar crop nor supply subsidies. The Caribbean island no longer had the capacity to send guerrilla troops to other parts of Latin America nor to parts of Africa where it had been deeply enmeshed: Angola, Mozambique, and Ethiopia.

These examples seemed to support Fukuyama's thesis, but there were other perspectives. Because it regarded itself as the lone superpower, America sometimes chose to act unilaterally, projecting an arrogance that alienated friends as well as enemies. It imposed sanctions on Iran and Cuba and forced many others to comply. It cut foreign aid, withheld dues to the UN and other international agencies, reduced State Department funding, and abolished the United States Information Agency. It declined to sign the Kyoto Protocol, an international agreement on the reduction of greenhouse gasses signed by 178 nations and it offered no alternative vision. In supporting Israel's assassination attacks on **Palestinian** guerrilla leaders, which often also killed innocent civilians, and in not confronting Israel over its construction of settlements in the occupied West Bank, in contravention of international law, America stood aloof from most of the rest of the world. Critics felt that America's unilateralism was making many important international problems worse.

KEY TERM

Palestinians Arab residents in the territories of the West Bank of the Jordan River and in the Gaza Strip of land along the Mediterranean coast conquered by Israel in the warfare of 1967. They do not have legal citizenship in Israel, nor in any other recognized state. Another group, Arab residents within the 1948 borders of Israel, are sometimes referred to as Palestinians, but more commonly as Arab Israelis or Israeli Arabs.

Terrorism. Terrorist attacks on the United States and its interests at home and overseas dispelled any further illusions that history had ended. One attack was from within, as Timothy McVeigh blew up the federal building in Oklahoma City in 1995, killing 168 people, in retaliation for the government's armed assault in 1993 on the Branch Davidians, a small religious sect based in Waco, Texas. This, however, was seen as an isolated incident.

More typically, terrorist attacks occurred overseas and were part of a violent dialogue with Islamic militancy. In 1983, a suicide car bomb destroyed the United States embassy in Beirut, Lebanon, killing 63 people. Later in the same year, suicide bombers exploded a truck bomb at US Marine headquarters in Beirut, killing 241 Marines and sailors. (Minutes later, another bomb killed 59 French paratroopers in their barracks, also in Beirut.) In 1993, a bomb delivered by Muslim terrorists exploded in a garage under the World Trade Center in New York, killing six. In Saudi Arabia, a bomb killed seven Americans at a military training installation in 1995, and another exploded at an American air force barracks in 1996, killing 19. In 1998, almost simultaneous explosions at US embassies in Kenya and Tanzania killed 220 people. In 2000, a small boat sailed alongside the USS *Cole*, a US Navy destroyer, in the harbor at Aden, Yemen, and bombed the ship, killing 17 sailors.

Terrorism is a strategy employed by the weak against the strong. It targets civilian noncombatants, in civilian locations, to terrify a general population into granting political concessions. It is not a new method of fighting. According to statistics compiled by the US Department of State, from 1981 to 1991, terrorist attacks worldwide averaged more than 500 a year. From 1991 to 2001 there were never fewer than the 274 attacks of 1998. In 2011 there were more than 10,000 terrorist attacks that killed at least one person; half of these took place in Iraq and Afghanistan, where conventional warfare was also raging.

Many countries had long experience with terrorism. The Irish Republican Army frequently launched attacks against civilians in Britain until 2005, when it agreed to give up its arms in favor of an official agreement on shared governance in Northern Ireland. During their war for independence, 1954–62, Algerian terrorist attacks in France and Algeria brought France to the brink of civil war. Since their founding in 1959, armed revolutionaries in the ETA movement, representing some of the Basque peoples in their quest for greater autonomy for their region of northern Spain, have killed some 800 Spaniards, about 350 of them civilians.

In the 1980s, Tamil rebels, beginning as terrorists seeking autonomy for their region of Sri Lanka, grew so numerous as to create a civil war that continued until 2009. Chechens in Russia and Uighurs in China also used methods of terror in their campaigns for autonomy.

By contrast, the American mainland had not been touched until the attacks of September 11, 2001, on the World Trade Center in New York City, the Pentagon in Washington, DC, and a thwarted attack, probably aimed at the Capitol Building or the White House in Washington. The attacks killed more than 3,000 people.

America's decision to strike back at Osama bin Laden, mastermind of the 9/11 attacks, and at the Taliban government who gave him shelter in Afghanistan seemed appropriate to observers abroad, especially those who had experienced terrorism in their own country. But the decision to launch a war against Iraq, in March 2003, drew massive international condemnation, for America could not demonstrate any credible connection between Iraq and Osama bin Laden. America's impatience in not waiting for the results of a UN investigation into the claim that Iraq possessed "weapons of mass destruction" was also widely criticized. Later, America's decision to place hundreds of captive "enemy combatants" in a special detention center in Guantanamo Bay, Cuba, without charge, without trial, without benefit of legal counsel, and without even notifying anyone in the outside world of their imprisonment—effectively suspending the centuries-old tradition of **habeas corpus**—and using torture in interrogating these prisoners was also widely condemned.

The American election of 2009 was in large part a referendum on this foreign policy. The new

Torture at Abu Ghraib, Iraq. Beginning in 2004, thanks to investigative reporting by the media, accounts of the torture of prisoners held in the Abu Ghraib prison in Iraq began to surface. Powerful photographic evidence of physical and psychological torture, sexual abuse, and homicide by American soldiers were published. This macabre photograph of a prisoner, hooded, forced to stand on a small platform, and being tortured with electric shocks, was one of the *less* repulsive examples. America's use of torture shocked American citizens and diminished the nation's reputation around the world.

President Barack Obama meets with Xi Jinping, vice president—and soon to be president—of the People's Republic of China, 2012. Thus far these two countries, with the two largest economies in the world, and the largest (China) and third largest (US) populations, have treated each other with wary caution and respect. Their intertwined economies suggest that competition between them will be tempered by self-interest in cooperation.

23.1

23.2

23.3 How have power relationships between nations realigned in the early twenty-first century?

23.4

KEY TERM

economic liberalism This term has had various meanings at different times. Today it usually refers to a free-market, capitalistic economy, with minimum government intervention. Often referred to as neo-liberalism.

president, Barack Obama, began reducing the number of American troops in Iraq, finally closing out the mission in mid-2010. He dispatched more troops to Afghanistan and then began gradually reducing the numbers, calling for a final exit from the country in 2014. Because of Congressional opposition, he could not close down the Guantanamo Bay Base.

The recession of 2008 imposed further limitations on America's imperial power. Many countries called for a military offensive in 2011 to oust Muammar Gaddafi, the ruler of Libya; Obama encouraged NATO and the French to take the lead. Similarly in 2013, when many called for American support for the opponents of Bashar al-Assad, president of Syria, Obama was reluctant to go to war and cautious even in supplying weapons to Assad's opponents. On the other hand, Obama authorized the mission of 2011 that killed Osama bin Laden, the man who had planned the 9/11 attacks. When Obama learned of the presence of guerrilla warriors in countries that would not give America permission to hunt them down on the ground, he used drone aircraft to attack and kill them from the air. He acted despite the hostility of the countries that gave shelter to the guerrillas, and despite the opposition of many civil libertarians in the United States who objected to the strikes as an example of extrajudicial execution. In response to Iran's apparent efforts to create nuclear weapons, Obama implemented severe economic sanctions, but he did not attempt a military response.

Under Obama's presidency, the United States appeared to be a "superpower" that was learning to live within economic, political, and military limits. Obama's willingness to work with Russia in seeking to rid Syria of chemical weapons, and perhaps to negotiate an end to civil war in that country, also demonstrated cautious restraint. His invitation to China's newly elected president, Xi Jinping, to summit discussions in 2013 symbolically suggested that the world's current sole superpower was welcoming, and assaying, the world's rising superpower.

China: An Emerging Superpower?

China's extraordinary economic progress after 1980 was turning that huge nation into another superpower, alongside America. The speed and scope of China's economic growth was unprecedented in the history of the world. The takeoff occurred only after Mao's death in 1976.

By the end of 1978, Deng Xiaoping (1904–97) and his allies had gained control of the Communist Party and its agenda. They remained in control for the next two decades. Deng advocated **economic liberalism**, operating with only limited government intervention but within a state firmly controlled by the party. By the time of his death, Deng and his colleagues had sold off about half of the state's economic holdings, leaving only 18 percent of the workforce in state employment, down from

90 percent in 1978. He welcomed foreign direct investment, which reached $42 billion in 1997 and tripled to about $120 billion in 2012. Deng also shifted more investment to agriculture, ended the failed policy of collectivization, and introduced a "private responsibility system," allotting land to private farmers for personal use and for market production. The growth rate of the economy averaged about 9.7 percent per year for 30 years, from 1978 to 2008. Per capita income quadrupled. The rate of poverty dropped from about 65 percent of the population to about 13 percent. Total adult literacy reached 90 percent. Young women were attending school at the same rate as men, and the rate of literacy for females aged 15–24 reached 99 percent.

After Deng's death, the transition of power occurred smoothly within the Communist Party-run government, with Jiang Zemin succeeding Deng as China's most important political leader, followed by Hu Jintao in 2002 and Xi Jinping in 2013. The

How have power relationships between nations realigned in the early twenty-first century?

HOW DO WE KNOW?

The Force Behind China's Economic Growth: Capitalism or Socialism?

As Chinese productivity grew at record rates in the 1980s, and even faster in the 1990s and early 2000s, almost all commentators attributed the economic expansion to the capitalistic reforms promoted by Deng Xiaoping. They usually contrasted Deng's success to the failed communist policies that he discarded. See, for example, this statement from a recent history of the twentieth century:

> The Chinese state had established a Soviet-style command economy in the 1950s by nationalizing industry and foreign trade, setting prices and collectivizing agriculture; inefficiency and low growth resulted … Living standards remained low, and most people lived in cramped, unmodernized housing …
>
> After Mao's death in 1976, reformers gained more power and began more active restructuring of the economy. Deng Xiaoping, a masterly politician who became head of the Central Advisory Commission, slowly moved the party toward economic reform. Once they were allowed to contract out of their agricultural communes, peasants deserted them in droves, working as family units and selling their surpluses in private markets. Output and rural incomes rose, stimulating rural industry. As trading companies under local control multiplied, foreign contacts expanded and foreign investment poured into the country. Overseas Chinese returned to invest. …
>
> A new private sector boomed in southern coastal areas … Wages rose and so did demand for consumer goods. (Crossley et al., p. 476)

The Nobel Prize-winning economist Amartya Sen might not disagree with the analysis of Deng's reforms, but he gives much more credit to the accomplishments of Mao's communist government in paving the way. His analysis of China's success comes as part of a discussion of the market-based economic policies that India began to adopt in 1991. Sen uses China's example to caution against the transition to capitalism before appropriate social policies have been set in place:

> While prereform China was deeply skeptical of markets, it was not skeptical of basic education and widely shared health care. When China turned to marketization in 1979, it already had a highly literate people, especially the young, with good schooling facilities across the bulk of the country. In this respect, China was not very far from the basic educational situation in South Korea or Taiwan, where too an educated population had played a major role in seizing the economic opportunities offered by a supportive market system. In contrast, India had a half-illiterate adult population when it turned to marketization in 1991, and the situation is not much improved today [1999].
>
> The health conditions in China were also much better than in India because of the social commitment of the prereform regime to health care as well as education. Oddly enough, that commitment, while totally unrelated to its helpful role in market-oriented economic growth, created social opportunities that could be brought into dynamic use after the country moved toward marketization … But the relevance of the radically different levels of social preparedness in China and India for widespread market-oriented development is worth noting even at this preliminary stage of the analysis. (Sen, pp. 42–43)

Sen does credit Indian democracy with other advantages for development that are lacking under China's communist government. In general, however, he seems to turn upside-down Marx's view of the triumph of communism arising out of a base constructed by capitalists. In China he sees capitalism arising out of a base constructed by communists.

- Is Sen's account of the achievements of Chinese communism inaccurate, or is he simply giving credit to a human-welfare achievement that others are overlooking? Why is he giving this emphasis? Is he right to stress the importance of human-welfare measures in economic development?
- According to Sen, why should Indian leaders be cautious in adopting for their own country the free-market policies that seem to work for China?
- To what degree should human welfare be considered in the assessment of the success of an economic system? Can an economic system be considered successful if education, health, and welfare standards of the general population are not rising?

23.1

23.2

23.3 How have power
relationships
between nations
realigned in the
early twenty-first
century?

23.4

new leaders continued with the same policies. In recognition of its position as a full participant in global trade, China was admitted to the World Trade Organization in November 2001.

Much of China's wealth came from its extraordinary success in manufacturing and world trade, a huge turnaround from the days of Mao, when agriculture was encouraged and foreign trade discouraged. China's exports in 2011 were $1.9 trillion, its imports $1.7 trillion, giving the country a trade surplus of $200 billion. In 2012, this once impoverished country held foreign reserves of $3.2 trillion and $688 billion in international investments, the largest amount in energy (see Heritage Foundation map: http://www.heritage.org/research/projects/china-global-investment-tracker--interactive-map). China has become the world's second-largest net importer of oil after the United States, and its oil ventures bring it into shared commercial enterprises in such countries as Saudi Arabia, Angola, Sudan, Kazakhstan, Russia, Iran, Canada, Indonesia, and Venezuela.

📖 **Read** the **Document**: **China's One-Child Family Policy (1970s)** on **MyHistoryLab**

Poverty. China's extraordinarily successful economy has lifted more than 600 million people above the poverty line, which is now estimated by the World Bank at $1.25/day. That still leaves 170 million people, or 13 percent of the total population, below the line, as of 2011. China's per capita income, at $4,940 per year, ranks 114th in the world, so the average Chinese is not wealthy by world standards. But some are. *Forbes* magazine reported 122 billionaires in China in 2013.

Although the poor are becoming less poor, the divisions between rich and poor have been growing. These divisions are regional, between the wealthier coastal areas and the more impoverished inland areas, and between the wealthier cities and the more impoverished villages; and they are gender-related, with women having less access to the better jobs. Especially in jeopardy are the villagers who come to the city to try their luck. These migrant workers have provided the low-cost labor for China's growing economy—when they can find jobs—but the conditions are harsh. Despite the current problems of unemployment for newcomers to the cities, as noted above the government is moving ahead with plans for the massive expansion of urbanization as a remedy for poverty.

📖 **Read** the **Document**: **China: A Farmer's Perspective, 2002** on **MyHistoryLab**

Corruption. At higher levels of the Chinese economy, white-collar crime and corruption became major problems. As the government liberalized economically, state assets were often sold to the Communist Party faithful at bargain prices, as had also happened in Russia (see above). The lure of new profits, a relaxation in law enforcement, and a rise in bribery created a new class of privately wealthy moguls. China witnessed a rapid growth of quasi-illegal nightspots, gangsterism, drug dealing, secret societies, prostitution, and gambling, much of it owned and operated by the police and the military. In 2011, China's central bank claimed that corrupt officials had smuggled more than $120 billion out of the country between the mid-1990s and 2008. Recognizing the damage to the national economy and to China's image in the eyes of its own citizens and of the world, the government began to crack down. Among the most conspicuous of its trials was that of Bo Xilai, powerful Communist Party chief of Chongqing, who was expelled from the party and charged with bribery, corruption, and abuse of power in 2013. His wife was sentenced to life in prison for the murder of a British businessman who had been working in Beijing for about a decade; the motive was not clear. Nevertheless, the United States and others also claimed that Chinese hackers were infiltrating United States security and commercial intelligence, stealing the designs for more than two dozen weapons systems and hundreds of billions of dollars worth of intellectual property. The

Chinese lodged counter-allegations against the United States, especially after security analyst Edward Snowden fled America and revealed secret information on spying by the United States government against its own citizens and those of other countries as well.

The Environment. Environmental degradation, including the pollution of air and water, has increased with China's industrialization. The rise of factories and cars and the use of artificial fertilizer have increased the pollution of land, air, and water. One of the most colossal projects is one of the largest offenders, but it is also a benefactor. The Three Gorges Dam on the upper Yangzi River, the largest hydroelectric project in the world, was completed in 2012 at a cost of about $30 billion, displacing 1.3 million residents. It also pours the industrial waste that has been emptied into the river through the years into the reservoir of water that will be drunk throughout central China. On the other hand, the dam's electricity generation will save China's air from the pollution that would otherwise have come through the coal-generation of electricity.

China's use of high-sulfur gasoline as a means of fueling its ever-increasing engines creates additional pollution. Sulfur levels in fuels are tightly regulated in the United States and Europe because of their high toxicity. China feels it cannot be so picky. High-sulfur gas is cheap and available. By 2012, China was the world's largest polluter in terms of emissions of carbon dioxide, the major greenhouse gas. Reports issue regularly from China's large cities of air too polluted to meet human health standards. On the other hand, China is the world's largest producer of solar panels and is a leader in seeking clean energy technology.

Population control. As its population topped one billion, China acted aggressively to limit population growth. Government programs for "small family happiness," beginning in 1974, culminated in 1980 in the policy of one family, one child. The party set maximum birth quotas for each county and city, established a nationwide system for

23.1

23.2

23.3

23.4

How have power relationships between nations realigned in the early twenty-first century?

The Three Gorges Dam, Hubei Province, China, 2012. By 10 a.m. each day at the dam site, the Yangzi River rises 114 meters above sea level. Despite criticism of the dam's impact on the ecology and residents of its region, the Chinese government views this as one of its most beneficial and spectacular technological accomplishments.

How have power
relationships
between nations
realigned in the
early twenty-first
century?

the distribution of contraceptive devices, enforced regulations against early marriage, and provided incentives for having only one child and disincentives for having more. The bureaucracy monitored pregnancies and births carefully, and abortions were frequently coerced (Rosenberg, p. 70). Fertility rates fell to 2.3 per hundred women in the 1980s, and 1.58 per hundred in 2011. The policy evoked widespread unrest and evasion—more easily accomplished in rural areas—and, in some cases, female infanticide, as couples preferred their one child to be male. As a result of widespread protest, at the time of this writing, the government began to issue new rules relaxing the "one child" ruling. The smaller families, however, encouraged greater freedom for women in the home and greater equality and participation in the workforce and in public life.

The Road to Democracy? In 1989, tens of thousands of demonstrators, mostly students, assembled in Tiananmen Square in central Beijing, demanding democracy as the antidote to a government ruled by old men, infested with corruption, and no longer in touch with the grass roots. The government called in the army to clear the square. Several hundred (some say as many as 5,000) demonstrators were killed, and more injured. China was not prepared for protest, transparency, and democracy.

In 1999 the government arrested thousands of members of the Falun Gong religious-meditation-exercise movement. Falun Gong combines elements of Buddhism, Taoism, and the martial arts. The group declared itself apolitical, but the government of China feared that any group of such size had political implications. Its membership of 70 million was larger than that of the Communist Party. In 1999, after 10,000 members of Falun Gong staged an unauthorized demonstration in Beijing, protesting government suppression of its activities, the government banned the sect entirely. Human rights reports claim that half of China's prison labor-camp population are members of Falun Gong and that they are regularly subjected to torture. Falun Gong has millions of practitioners outside China, and they demonstrate regularly on behalf of their colleagues inside the country.

Tiananmen Square, June 5, 1989. Tanks traveling down Changan Boulevard, in front of the Beijing Hotel, are confronted by a brave Chinese man who pleads for an end to the killing of students demonstrating for greater freedom of democratic expression. This photograph came to symbolize the struggle of the Chinese people to reassert their dignity and gain democracy in the face of the huge and powerful communist regime.

23.1

23.2

23.3

23.4

How have power
relationships
between nations
realigned in the
early twenty-first
century?

Transparency. China has been reluctant to admit the extent of its ecological and social problems. For example, when a SARS epidemic killed some 350 people in China in 2002, the government failed to report swiftly this previously unknown disease. It feared losing business and tourists. The World Health Organization and others censured China, which then began to release news about the epidemic promptly and widely.

In 2008, Sichuan Province suffered a massive earthquake, killing almost 70,000 people and leaving between five and ten million homeless. The Chinese seemed transparent in reporting the news, but later it appeared that some 7,000 schoolrooms had collapsed in the earthquake, burying thousands of students. The government tried, unsuccessfully, to cover up this news.

Global Recognition. The greatest test of Chinese openness came with the Olympic Games in Beijing in August 2008. The awarding of the games to China signaled recognition of the nation's coming of age. China had to pledge, however, to allow journalists and visitors to the Olympics to report on the country without censorship. These pledges were not fully honored. When Buddhists in Tibet (and their sympathizers around the world) used the games to gain world attention for their campaign for Tibetan autonomy, the protesters were beaten and some were killed. Nevertheless, the 2008 Olympics provided more access than had been available previously.

The spectacular opening ceremonies of the Olympics, watched by more than two billion people around the world, and China's athletes' excellence in winning more gold medals than any other country, revealed the accomplishments of authoritarian rule. A survey by the Washington-based Pew Research Center in 2013, of around 38,000 people in 39 countries, found that "China's economic power is on the rise, and many think it will eventually supplant the United States as the world's dominant superpower" (James T. Areddy, "US Seen Losing to China as World Leader," *Wall Street Journal*, July 19, 2013, http://online.wsj.com/article/SB1000142412788732426 3404578611623402415576.html [accessed October 2013]).

Tibetan protesters, 2008. China has often claimed Tibet as its own, and Tibet has always responded with claims of independent sovereignty. Most recently, in 1950, the Chinese government invaded and occupied Tibet, and in 1959, under immense pressure, Tibet's most venerated leader, the Dalai Lama, fled the country. Revolts against Chinese rule flare periodically. As world attention focused on China during the 2008 Olympics, Tibetans took the opportunity to demonstrate again their opposition to Chinese rule.

23.1

23.2

23.3

23.4

How have power
relationships
between nations
realigned in the
early twenty-first
century?

The Unification of Europe

In an astonishing reconciliation following two world wars, Western Europe had devoted itself to regional cooperation and, finally, unification. Constitutionally, a major step was taken in 1993 at Maastricht, the Netherlands, when all 12 of its members committed themselves to transforming the European Economic Community into the European Union (EU). They agreed to work toward formulating a common foreign policy, a common defense policy, guidelines toward similar social policies, and policies for assistance from the wealthier members for the poorer. They established common policies for agriculture, fisheries, and nuclear research projects. They also committed to creating a common currency. In 1998 they created a European Central Bank to monitor and coordinate financial activity, and by 2002, when the single currency, the euro, was adopted in most of its member states, the EU had become the world's largest integrated market.

The EU brought rapid economic growth, increased cultural creativity, and a more prominent voice in international affairs to most of its member states. Following the collapse of the USSR in 1991, many of the nations of central Europe applied to join the EU. In 2004, seven of them were admitted—Lithuania, Latvia, Estonia, the Czech Republic, Slovakia, Hungary, and Poland—along with the two island nations of Cyprus and Malta, and Slovenia, newly independent from the former Yugoslavia. In 2007, Romania and Bulgaria also joined, and Croatia followed in 2013, bringing the total EU membership to 28 nations. Europeans shared a common market, without internal tariffs, and with unrestricted movement throughout the Union of goods, services, capital, workers, and tourists. Citizens of most of the member nations could travel throughout the EU with only a basic identity card, for the most part encountering no customs formalities, and they could live wherever they chose within the EU.

The EU, however, is not a conventional, unified state. It has no collective military. It provides neither welfare nor basic educational functions to its inhabitants. It does, however, finance EU-wide programs in science and technology, culture, and the environment, and it supports efforts to raise the economic status of its poorer member states. It sets standards for health-and-safety regulations, social security and working conditions, and agriculture. The EU recognizes 23 official languages; in practice, however, English has become the most common language for commercial, political, and cultural exchange throughout the EU, as it has throughout the world.

Many questions about the further empowerment of the EU remain. Low voter turnouts in elections to the European parliament and rejections by voters in several countries of steps toward further unification leave in question the degree to which the EU will be consolidated.

An additional set of questions facing the EU concerns its reception of new applicants. The question of Turkey is the most pressing and problematic. Turkey's application has been pending since 1987. Officially, the EU is concerned with Turkey's compliance with EU standards for the administration of justice, economic regulations, and the resolution of a dispute with Greece over the sovereignty of the island of Cyprus. Beneath these official questions, however, are deeper issues: Should the EU add a nation that is geographically mostly in Asia, and which is religiously and culturally Islamic, although constitutionally secular? How far is the EU willing to push the geographic and cultural envelope of "European" identity?

A second problem for the EU is its stance regarding immigration. Since entry into any one of the nations gives access to almost all, EU member states demanded that the requirements for first entry be formidable and enforcement be strict. A series of agreements, named for Schengen, the town in Luxembourg where most were signed, established those common requirements. Serious friction has also arisen regarding immigration from one nation to another within the EU, especially from the poorer nations of southern and eastern Europe to the wealthier nations of the north and west. This issue of immigration from poorer regions to richer ones was a global one, and we

SOURCE

The Continuing Rationale for European Integration

In 1995, François Mitterrand (1916–96), past president of France and an elder statesman both of his own country and of the EU, spoke passionately to the EU Parliament, summarizing the EU's great accomplishments in binding up the physical, emotional, and economic wounds of war-devastated Europe. He looked forward to even greater achievements in formulating and enhancing its collective cultural identity. Mitterrand asserted that the success of the EU as a whole would also enhance the cultural identity and creativity of each of its member states, just as the collective success of its economic policies had benefited the economies of the individual member nations.

> Our Europe must be embodied in something more than simply balance sheets and freight tonnages. I would go as far as to say … that it needs a soul, so that it can give expression … to its culture, its ways of thinking, the intellectual make-up of its peoples, the fruits of the centuries of civilization of which we are the heirs. The expressions of Europe's many forms of genius are rich and diverse; and, as in the past, we must share with the whole world—while not seeking to impose them, somewhat differently from in the past—our ideas, our dreams, and, to the extent that they are of the right kind, our passions. …
>
> The cultural identity of nations is reinforced by the process of European integration. The Europe of cultures, ladies and gentlemen, is a Europe of nations as opposed to a Europe of nationalism. …
>
> I was born during the First World War and fought in the Second. I therefore spent my childhood in the surroundings of families torn apart, all of them mourning loved ones and feeling great bitterness, if not hatred, towards the recent enemy, the traditional enemy. …
>
> My generation has almost completed its work; it is carrying out its last public acts, and this will be one of my last. It is therefore vital for us to pass on our experience. Many of you will remember the teaching of your parents … will have felt the suffering of your countries, will have experienced the grief, the pain of separation, the presence of death—all as a result of the mutual enmity of the peoples of Europe. It is vital to pass on not this hatred but, on the contrary, the opportunity for reconciliation which we have, thanks—it must be said—to those who, after 1944–1945, themselves bloodstained and with their personal lives destroyed, had the courage to envisage a more radiant future which would be based on peace and reconciliation. That is what we have done.
>
> (*Official Journal of the European Communities: Debates of the European Parliament*, 1994–95 Session, no. 4–456, pp. 45–51, excerpted in Hunt, p. 343)

discuss it at greater length in the chapter "Trade, Revolution, Technology, Identity." In that same chapter, we shall also see that the global recession of 2008 put financial pressure on some of the poorer and less well-managed economies of the EU. So, on balance, the EU represented a very wealthy region with significant political unity, in temporary financial difficulties, and without a common, reliable military force.

On Religion

23.4 What might account for the reemergence of religious groups as powerful political forces?

One of the surprises of the later twentieth century was the reemergence of religious groups as powerful political forces. The skepticism of the scientific revolution, the secularism of the French Revolution, the atheism of the Russian Revolution, the ideal of the separation of church and state—all these intellectual and political transformations challenged the power of organized religion. The past 35 years, however, have provided abundant evidence of the power of religious faith to motivate public as well as private action. Many theories were suggested to explain the phenomenon. As the speed of change brought about by globalization threatened many people's sense of security, religious leaders promised faith and assurances to fill the void. Religious groups often sponsored social welfare programs and provided community support that governments did not. Followers came for the practical assistance and then stayed for the religious and political messages. This combination of practical help, community membership, and a message of comfort and cosmic acceptance has been a hallmark of organized religion since earliest times.

In the late twentieth century, this combination was especially prominent in Islam, which has been the fastest growing world religion in recent years. Although many

23.1

23.2

23.3

23.4

What might account for the reemergence of religious groups as powerful political forces?

23.1

23.2

23.3

23.4 What might account for the reemergence of religious groups as powerful political forces?

Westerners have come to see Islam as an aggressive and militant religion, especially after the 9/11 terrorist attacks in the United States (see below), most Muslims would argue that they are not the aggressors, but the attacked, and that Islam serves to sustain them in times of trouble. They assert that colonialism in the Middle East left in its wake underdeveloped economies and a history of personal insults and cultural disrespect. In Palestine, they claim that Israeli oppression is the cause of their economic stagnation and social disarray. In India, they argue that the Hindu majority restricts their opportunities and their civil rights. In Chechnya, they cite continuing Russian occupation and military intervention. A sharp divide has emerged between the Muslim self-image as an oppressed religious group prepared at last to reassert its dignity, and the views of some outsiders who see Muslims as potential terrorists.

Theocracy in Iran

In 1979 an Islamic revolution, led by **Ayatollah** Khomeini, overthrew the government of the shah of Iran and in its place established a Muslim **theocracy**. The new Iranian government also successfully challenged the power of the United States, which had supported the shah. It sought to avenge the American (and British) overthrow of the Iranian government in 1951. At that time, the increased development of Iran's oil resources had begun to bring new wealth to the kingdom and Prime Minister Muhammad Mussadeq (1880–1967) nationalized the Iranian oil industry, against the wishes of the shah. In response, Britain and the United States conspired with the Iranian army in a coup that overthrew Mussadeq.

Indebted to the West, the shah joined America in a Cold War military alliance against the Soviet Union. He invited additional Western oil investment, and proceeded to use Iran's oil wealth to fund deep and massive—but convulsive, erratic, and uneven—Westernization of the country. By the mid-1970s, about 150,000 foreigners had come to Iran to run the new high-technology industries and to live luxuriously in secluded residential communities. At the other extreme, local rural people were also flooding into the cities, putting great strain on the urban infrastructure. Shortages of food and other basic necessities resulted, and corruption permeated the shah's court, the government, the bureaucracy, and the business community. Opponents of the shah's system of forced modernization—including much of the student community—were pursued, jailed, and often tortured.

Such opponents included *ulama*, religious scholars, who lamented the suppression of traditional religion, along with many citizens who felt themselves squeezed economically and resented the loosening of what they saw as the moral foundations of society. In 1963, a Shi'ite Muslim religious leader, Ayatollah Ruhollah Khomeini (1902–89), led an abortive uprising against the shah. The army killed 15,000 of the rebels and exiled Khomeini. But, from Paris, the ayatollah kept in contact with dissidents

KEY TERMS

ayatollah Title of prestigious and powerful Muslim religious leaders in Iran.

theocracy A system of government based on religious beliefs and texts and headed by religious leaders.

The Ayatollah Khomeini returns to Iran, 1979. Exiled in 1963, Ayatollah Khomeini established himself in Paris but kept in touch with his supporters, opponents of the shah, back home in Iran. When popular resentment against the shah's policies of economic development undercut the ruler's power, Khomeini returned to the tumultuous welcome of millions of followers. In overthrowing the shah, Khomeini's revolution, based on Islam and on his own interpretation of the Quran, demonstrated the enduring power of religious principles as guiding motives in national affairs, at least in Iran.

in Iran via tape recordings and telephone, and in 1979 he returned to lead popular demonstrations of as many as five million people. He forced the shah into exile. Islamic government was introduced and Islamic law, the *shari'a*, became the law of the land. Khomeini declared:

> No others, no matter who they may be, have the right to legislate, nor has any person the right to govern on any basis other than the authority that has been conferred by God … It is the religious expert and no one else who should occupy himself with the affairs of the government. (Francis Robinson, *Atlas of the Islamic World Since 1500*, p. 171)

The religious fervor of the revolution astonished many Western observers who thought, mistakenly, that the Iranians had approved of the modernizing policies of the shah and that the man and his government were popular.

With its country strategically located, rich in oil, religiously militant, and internally secure, Khomeini's revolutionary government frightened its neighbors and wreaked havoc on many others more distant. In its first two years, it executed 800 people and exiled thousands. When America offered asylum to the exiled shah, who was suffering from cancer, Iranian students responded by seizing the American embassy in Tehran in November 1979 and holding 52 of its staff hostage. President Jimmy Carter failed to secure their release through negotiation. He then attempted a clandestine air rescue, which was aborted in humiliating failure. Carter's defeat in the presidential election of 1980 was caused in large part by this failure to cope with revolutionary Iran. (The hostages were finally released on January 20, 1981, the date on which Carter's term came to an end, 444 days after their capture.)

Khomeini's militancy increased instability in the Middle East. It inspired religious dissidents to attack the Great Mosque in Mecca during the *hajj* pilgrimage period in 1979, in an attempt to trigger a revolt against the Saudi Arabian government. Three hundred people were killed. In Egypt, in 1981, Islamic militants linked to Iran assassinated President Anwar Sadat. In 1989, following the publication of his novel *The Satanic Verses*, Iranian clerics proclaimed Britain's Indian-born, Muslim writer Salman Rushdie a heretic, and issued a *fatwa*, a religious decree, that marked him for execution. A bounty was placed on his head, and he was forced into hiding for several years under the protection of the British government. Fearing that Iran's Shi'ite religious revolution would spill across the border, Iraq, under Saddam Hussein, with the quiet support of the United States, attacked Iran, precipitating eight years of warfare and hundreds of thousands of deaths.

Legal restrictions on women, based on the interpretation of religious principles, continued in revolutionary Iran, calling for Islamic dress codes and Islamic legal authority over marriage, divorce, child custody, and the right to work. Most Iranian women accepted these restrictions willingly as a stand against Western culture and imperialism. Women's literacy rose to 80 percent by 2008, with 99 percent of girls of primary-school age attending classes. Birth rates dropped from 49 per thousand under the shah to 18 per thousand in 2012. The number of families using contraception rose from 23 to 73 percent in 2011 (UN data found via data.un.org). In mid-2012, Iran's supreme leader, Ayatollah Sayyid Ali Khameinei, declared that the time had come for Iranian families to have more children; at the time of writing, it was too soon to know the effect. Feminism, nationalism, and religion in Iran were intertwined in a unique configuration that did not fit into any stereotype.

For about a decade after Khomeini's death in 1989, more moderate leaders administered Iran. Then, in 2005, Mahmoud Ahmadinejad was elected president. Although the Iranian president's power is subordinate to the country's religious rulers, Ahmadinejad's public assertions denying the Holocaust, calling for Israel to be wiped off the map, and declaring that Iran would proceed with the development of its own nuclear power led to further tension with Western countries, especially the United States. In response, the United States and Israel both threatened preemptive

23.1

23.2

23.3

23.4

What might account for the reemergence of religious groups as powerful political forces?

What might account for the reemergence of religious groups as powerful political forces?

bombings of Iran's nuclear research facilities, and many countries agreed to impose economic sanctions against Iran. Following elections in 2013, a more moderate president, Hassan Rowhani, called for a quieter, calmer foreign policy, and Iran agreed to the destruction of its stores of chemical weapons. Iran began international discussions on restricting its nuclear capabilities.

Islamic Militants in Afghanistan

In the same year as the Iranian revolution, 1979, a resurgent Islam confronted a Soviet invasion in Afghanistan. The government of Afghanistan was allied with the Soviet Union, an officially atheist country. Large numbers of militant Muslim guerrilla fighters, called *mujahideen*, opposed this alliance. To support the government the Soviets dispatched more than 100,000 troops, along with tanks and aircraft. The war became a part of the Cold War, as the *mujahideen* drew support from several nations—the United States, Pakistan, Saudi Arabia, and other Islamic countries. (The United States boycotted the 1980 Olympics in Moscow to express its anger over the Russian invasion.) Many freelance guerrillas also came to Afghanistan to fight against the USSR. After a decade of warfare and having lost some 14,000 soldiers, the Russians withdrew in defeat in 1989. Islamic militants had confronted and repelled both of the world's superpowers, America in Iran, the USSR in Afghanistan.

The Russian withdrawal left Afghanistan in civil war, which was finally won by the *mujahideen* in 1992. Four years later, however, another Islamic militant group, the

The attack by al-Qaeda on the World Trade Center, New York, September 11, 2001. Along with a simultaneous attack on the Pentagon and a failed attack apparently targeted at government buildings in Washington, this announced to the world a new, more spectacular capacity for terrorism by nonstate-sponsored groups, with global reach both in recruiting and striking. America declared a war on terror, created the Department of Homeland Security, and went to war against Afghanistan, the apparent refuge of al-Qaeda leaders, especially Osama bin Laden, and against Iraq, which it accused, incorrectly, of complicity in the attack and of harboring weapons of mass destruction.

Taliban, seized control of the government of the country, and many private militias continued to operate outside its powers.

One of these was the private militia assembled by Osama bin Laden. Bin Laden had been born in Saudi Arabia in 1957, the seventeenth child and seventh son of a devout Sunni Muslim family that had become extremely wealthy in the construction business. He earned a degree in public administration in Jeddah in 1981. He had grown up in an atmosphere of militant **Wahabi** puritan interpretation of Sunni Islam, at a time when Islamic nationalism was growing, and he went to Afghanistan to join the struggle against Soviet occupation. He created **al-Qaeda** ("the base") to obtain and organize war supplies and to lead troops in the field. When the Soviets withdrew from Afghanistan, he returned to Saudi Arabia, committed to a militant, politicized vision of Islam.

Bin Laden was enraged by the Saudi cooperation with the Americans against Iraq, and especially by the stationing of American forces on Arabian soil, so close to Mecca. He relocated several times, finally settling in Afghanistan in 1996 where he established the World Islamic Front for the Jihad against Jews and Crusaders, a headquarters for radical Muslim movements. He issued a *fatwa*, stating that it was the duty of Muslims to kill American citizens and their allies. In his camps, he trained *jihadis* for these tasks. In a spectacular attack on September 11, 2001, al-Qaeda members hijacked four airplanes. Suicide pilots flew two of them into the World Trade Center twin towers in New York City, in the heart of the Wall Street area, the symbolic center of the capitalist world, destroying both towers and killing almost 3,000 people. Another flew a plane into the Pentagon, the symbolic center of American military power, destroying one wing of the building. One plane crashed in central Pennsylvania, failing in its apparent mission to attack the White House. Bin Laden's attack polarized the Islamic world. Although some approved, many Muslims, and several Muslim countries, including Saudi Arabia, condemned it as a terrorist murder of innocent civilians, which violated Islamic morality.

America returned to war in Afghanistan following the Bin Laden attack and became embroiled in the fighting among the various armed factions in that country. Following years of warfare, the United States proposed withdrawing in 2014; the terms of withdrawal were being negotiated with the president of Afghanistan.

📖 Read the **Document**: **Osama bin Laden World Islamic Front Statement, 1998** on **MyHistoryLab**

Islam, Secularism, and Christianity

Several Islamic-majority countries faced conflict between groups that wanted more theocratic governments, headed by religious authorities, and those that preferred more secular governments, with more of a separation between mosque and state. In Turkey and Algeria the armed forces, under the control of secular authorities, intervened in elections throughout the 1990s to prevent Islamic political parties from coming to power. In Algeria secular forces won out, but only after the country was plunged into all-out civil war, from 1992 to 2002, which killed at least 100,000 people, and continues to simmer today.

In some states of sub-Saharan Africa, armed conflicts broke out among followers of Islam, Christianity, and indigenous African religions who had usually coexisted peacefully. The trigger was often the attempt to impose Islamic legal systems on people who were not Muslims. Civil war broke out in 1966 in Chad, which is about 50 percent Muslim, mostly in the north, and 25 percent each Christian and followers of indigenous religions, mostly in the south. Since then, fighting has continued sporadically.

In neighboring Sudan, the people of the north, home to the 70 percent of Sudan's population that is Sunni Muslim and mostly Arab, have repeatedly attempted to impose Islamic law on the south, which is mostly black and mostly practices indigenous religions. The result has been protracted civil war in a country that is overwhelmingly poor and prone to famine. As many as two million people—mostly

KEY TERMS

Wahabi Wahabi Islam follows the very conservative teachings of Muhammad ibn Abd-al-Wahhab, an eighteenth-century scholar. It is the dominant form of Islam in Saudi Arabia.

al-Qaeda "The base." The militant Islamic group of guerrilla warriors mobilized by Osama bin Laden in Afghanistan, first to fight against Russian invaders, and later to attack the United States and its allies. Subsequently, a number of militant Islamic guerrilla groups in different parts of the world adopted the name al-Qaeda, some with ties to bin Laden's group, some without.

What might account for the reemergence of religious groups as powerful political forces?

southerners—have died in wars and famines, and millions more have been displaced from their homes. In 2004, forces in the north and south reached accommodations that seemed to allow peace and stability in the south.

By then, however, the people of the Darfur region of the western part of the country, claiming oppression, were at war with the central government and its local armed representatives, the Janjaweed. In Darfur, however, both groups were Muslim by religion. The problem seemed to be ethnic rather than religious, northern Arabs against western black Africans. The UN and several individual nations extended relief aid and considered military intervention to protect the people of Darfur. The situation became very complicated as China supported the government of Sudan while much of the rest of the world supported the Darfur refugees. But China had become increasingly influential, and it needed Sudan's oil. So Sudan got its way. The refugees of Darfur continued to suffer and their international advocates were powerless.

In Nigeria, too, the attempt to impose *shari'a* law precipitated violence. Nigeria is by far the most populous country in Africa, with 170 million people, about 45 percent of whom are Muslim, 45 percent Christian, and 10 percent followers of indigenous religions. In early 2000, some 2,000 people were killed in northern Nigeria when the regional government instituted *shari'a* law. In retaliation, several hundred Muslims were killed in the east and south, and many more fled to areas where their religious group was dominant. In May 2004, Christians attacked a Muslim market town in central Nigeria, leaving many people dead. Muslims and Christians fled areas in which they were minorities. In the north, Muslims forced 20,000 Christians out of their homes, and President Olusegun Obasanjo put the area under military command. Despite the hostility it engendered among non-Muslims, several additional northern states of Nigeria instituted *shari'a* law as the basis of their official legal codes.

The status of women in Islam brought further unwanted international attention to Nigeria. In 2002, a young woman accused of adultery was to be stoned to death under *shari'a* law, but she appealed the case and was acquitted in 2003. Also in 2002, the Miss World Pageant was scheduled to be held in Nigeria until Muslim leaders decried the spectacle of women parading in scanty bathing suits as incompatible with Islam. Riots broke out, killing more than a hundred people, and the pageant was moved to London.

Presidential elections in 2007 and 2011 provoked rioting between Muslims and Christians. An Islamic sect founded in 2001 transformed itself in 2009 into a more radical *jihadist* organization, usually referred to as Boko Haram ("western education is sinful"), and dedicated itself to transforming Nigeria into an Islamic state under *shari'a* law. It began to attack Christian churches and institutions and also allied itself with criminal gangs in Nigeria and neighboring states. Many Muslims condemned Boko Haram for its terrorism and attacks on civilians, and the government of Nigeria dispatched army forces to suppress the organization. Nevertheless, it is responsible for at least 1,000 deaths, possibly many times that number, and at the time of writing it remained a potent terrorist force.

Religious Strife in Yugoslavia

One of the worst examples of religious strife occurred in eastern Europe, in the Balkans, where civil war raged from 1992 to 1995 and continued to sputter afterward as well. Hundreds of thousands of people died and many more were made homeless in the worst warfare in Europe since World War II. Here, Eastern Orthodox Christians, Roman Catholics, and Muslims were involved, with Muslims suffering by far the greatest number of casualties.

The Balkans is a region of divisive nationalism in which religion plays an important part. The multiethnic state of Yugoslavia was created after World War I. After

KEY TERM

ethnic cleansing A euphemism for genocide. The act of exiling or murdering minority groups from a given territory.

World War II, ethnic hostility within Yugoslavia was suppressed by the nation's leader, Marshal Tito (Josip Broz), and even after his death the communist government of the country continued his policies. After the Soviet Union dissolved in 1989, however, Yugoslavia followed its example and splintered into several regions. Three of them—Serbia, Croatia, and Bosnia-Herzegovina—were soon locked in warfare. Even though Yugoslavs were not especially zealous in their religious observance, especially after half a century of communist rule, religion was one of the key elements in the division, and here Christians were the aggressors.

Serbs were generally Orthodox Christian (65 percent), while most Croatians were Roman Catholic (77 percent). Bosnians were the most mixed, with 40 percent Muslim, 31 percent Orthodox Christian, and 15 percent Roman Catholic. Until 1989, intermarriage between religious and national groups was not uncommon, but as Yugoslavia split apart, religious identity seemed to inspire horrendous violence.

Serbia's leaders attempted to keep Croatia and Bosnia-Herzegovina under its control. Civil war raged for three years, 1992–95, as Serbia undertook a policy of "**ethnic cleansing**," a euphemism for genocide, attempting to kill or drive out the Muslim and Croat populations, especially from Bosnia. Serbia employed rape and torture as instruments of policy. Hundreds of thousands of people died and many more were forced from their homes. The UN attempted repeatedly to broker a peace agreement, but each attempt was rejected or broken. Many observers faulted the EU, the United States, and the UN for their unwillingness to commit the military forces necessary to impose peace. In December 1995, however, a US-brokered peace agreement was signed in Paris by the presidents of Bosnia-Herzegovina, Croatia, and Serbia. The UN committed 60,000 peace-keeping troops to oversee the agreement.

None of the three new states was, however, internally homogeneous. Within the newly created nation of Serbia, one province, Kosovo, had a majority who were Albanian by ethnicity and Muslim by religion. In 1998, when the Albanian Muslims of Kosovo declared their intention to secede from Serbia and launched a guerrilla war, Serbia's president, Slobodan Milosevic, responded with fury, driving some 700,000 ethnic Albanians from their homes in Kosovo and resuming its policies of ethnic cleansing. After months of inaction, in 1999 NATO began a 72-day bombing campaign. Serbia surrendered and gave up its claim to Kosovo. Some 50,000 UN troops were dispatched as peace-keepers. Before the UN soldiers arrived, however, the remaining Albanian Muslim Kosovars and the returning refugees drove out the Serbian residents of Kosovo, implementing reverse ethnic cleansing. As peace was established and enforced, the Serbs were invited to return.

The next year, 2000, Milosevic was defeated in Serbian elections and the new government turned him over to the International War Crimes Tribunal in The Hague, the Netherlands, for trial as a war criminal for his actions in Kosovo. (The UN Security Council had established the Tribunal in 1993.) It was the first European invocation of such a trial since World War II. Milosevic died of a heart attack in 2006, before a verdict was reached.

The Tribunal also indicted eight men for sexual assault, the first time the systematic practice of rape had been condemned and prosecuted as a weapon of war and a "crime against humanity," and not just overlooked as "something that happens" during the stress of warfare.

23.1

23.2

23.3

23.4

What might account for the reemergence of religious groups as powerful political forces?

Ethnic map of Yugoslavia based on data from 1991 census. The death of Marshal Tito in 1980 and the example of the dissolution of the USSR in 1989–91 weakened forces that had kept the disparate peoples and territories of Yugoslavia together since 1918. After 1991, the country dissolved into several new nations, each with its own dominant ethnic group, several of which promptly went to war with one another. Tension continued, and became especially intense when Kosovo declared its independence from Serbia in 2008. Kosovo's population, given as Albanian by ethnicity, is predominantly Muslim by religion.

What might account for the reemergence of religious groups as powerful political forces?

Hinduism and Islam in India

At independence, India was partitioned into two new nations, India and Pakistan. Mahatma Gandhi, Jawaharlal Nehru, and the Congress Party they led declared themselves secular, but a substantial group of Hindus regarded Muslims as second-class citizens, or, at an extreme, even as alien descendants of foreign invaders. These militant Hindus formed the backbone of the Bharatiya Janata Party (Indian People's Party) or BJP, stressing "**Hindutva**," or "Hinduness." The BJP's goal has been to make Hindu identity the basis of national identity and thus to exclude non-Hindus from full membership in the Indian nation.

In the 1980s, the BJP began to capture more votes and, in 1990, L.K. Advani, its chief organizer, launched a religious pilgrimage/political campaign across northern India. Advani led the procession in a Toyota van decorated as a war chariot of Lord Rama. This pilgrimage was to climax at the north Indian town of Ayodhya, the home of a mosque built by the first Mughal emperor. The BJP claimed that the mosque had been built on the grounds of a Hindu temple, which marked the earthly birthplace of the Hindu Lord Rama, and which Muslims had destroyed. Advani's ultimate goal was to destroy the mosque and rebuild the temple. His pilgrimage instigated rioting between Hindus and Muslims throughout its journey, and hundreds of people, Hindus and Muslims, were killed. Advani was arrested and the pilgrimage halted far short of its goal.

Two years later, however, in defiance of the Indian government, and in violation of a pledge he had made, Advani instigated the destruction of the Ayodhya mosque. In response, even more serious riots broke out throughout India. In Mumbai 2,000 people were killed and bombs were exploded in the city's stock exchange. The BJP's electoral totals continued to climb from one election to the next; religious violence seemed to win victories at the ballot box. In 2002, religious riots in the state of Gujarat, with especially intense attacks on Muslims, were followed by an overwhelming victory by the BJP in state elections later that year. By the end of the decade, the BJP

Riots in Ahmedabad, Gujarat, 2002. Tensions between Hindus and Muslims flared into violence repeatedly before and after independence and the partition of India and Pakistan in 1947. Although the rhetoric was religious, the violence usually emerged around political issues. One major political party espoused Hindu supremacy for India, which had a 13 per cent Muslim population; Pakistan retained only a tiny Hindu minority. Especially severe attacks in the Indian state of Gujarat in 2002 left up to 2,000 dead, overwhelmingly Muslims. Some analysts blamed an apparent assault by Muslims on a train carrying Hindu pilgrims; others saw the savage revenge of Hindus as a strategy for winning Hindu votes in upcoming state elections.

KEY TERM

Hindutva A political–religious slogan calling for the merger of the Hindu religion with the power of the Indian state. It is the rallying cry of several militant Hindu organizations.

captured enough votes to elect a national governing coalition. In office, the BJP leadership continued to stress Hindutva. Wherever the BJP held power, school textbooks were rewritten to give prominence to stories of Hindu power and to depict Muslims as unpatriotic foreigners.

On the other hand, in the national elections of 2004 and 2009, the BJP was badly defeated. Moreover, the head of the triumphant Congress Party was Sonia Gandhi, the Italian-born Christian widow of the assassinated former prime minister Rajiv Gandhi; Manmohan Singh became the first Sikh prime minister; and the president of India, 2002–07, was a Muslim. Most Indians still seemed to appreciate the diversity of their composite identity. As national elections approached in 2014, the BJP itself stressed its pro-business economic policies rather than its Hindu religious origins.

23.1
23.2
23.3
23.4

What might account for the reemergence of religious groups as powerful political forces?

Buddhists in Tibet

Buddhism, suppressed in the early years of the communist revolution in China, reasserted itself in a challenge to government authority, especially in Tibet. In 2008, public protests by Tibetan Buddhists demanded independence from the Chinese government, which had seized control of the region in 1950, and had driven out its principal religious leader, the Dalai Lama, in 1959. Wanting no interference with the Olympic Games, which China was hosting in Beijing, the Chinese government cracked down on the protesters. Nevertheless, outside China, "Free Tibet" demonstrations followed the Olympic torch on its pre-Games journey around the world. Between 2009 and 2013, about 120 Tibetans burned themselves to death in protest against Chinese rule of their country, periodic protests in Tibet were suppressed by the police, and in Dharamsala, India, a Tibetan government-in-exile continued to call for independence.

Judaism

With the creation of the State of Israel in 1948, officially a Jewish state, Jews held sovereign power for the first time in almost 2,000 years, since the Roman Empire had conquered Judea and exiled its population. The new state was, however, surrounded by hostile neighbors. Jewish political philosophy seemed to alter accordingly. Previously, as weak, scattered, and dependent people, Jews had emphasized the Biblical concept that they would live "not by might and not by power," but by God's spirit. Now, surrounded by hostility, many came to believe that only military might would enable them to survive. They built the most powerful armed force in the Middle East, almost certainly including nuclear weapons, and brandished their weapons and power in ways that appeared restrained and unavoidable to the Israeli government, but excessively brutal to many others.

Despite the ever-present background threat of war, including the threat of nuclear attack from Iran, Israel was peaceful in the early 2010s, and this allowed tension to surface between the approximately 80 percent of the Jewish population who thought of themselves as secular, and the 20 percent who identified as religiously observant. More secular political parties called for an end to the subsidies for religious schools and the exemptions from the universal military draft for their students. In other parts of the world, differences in observance of Jewish tradition and law were a matter for personal choice; in Israel, where Judaism was the official religion of the state, the differences became the subject of legislation.

Christianity

Christianity is by far the world's largest religion, with two billion people professing the faith in Europe, Latin America, Africa, Asia, North America, and Oceania. The years of missionary proselytizing throughout the colonies of Europe had reaped an abundant harvest.

23.1
23.2
23.3
23.4

What might account for the reemergence of religious groups as powerful political forces?

Roman Catholicism. Half of this Christian population is Roman Catholic and the elections of the last three popes reflect its shifting geography. Polish cardinal Karol Josef Wojtyla (1920–2005) was elected by the College of Cardinals as Pope John Paul II in 1978, the first non-Italian pope since 1523. By elevating a cardinal from behind the "Iron Curtain," the Church gave inspiration and moral support to the people struggling against the control of the Soviet Union. (See the discussion in "The Brezhnev Doctrine" in the chapter "Cold War, New Nations, and Revolt Against Authority.")

John Paul II demonstrated his openness to the world by his remarkable record of travel—to Mexico, the United States, Turkey, India, China, Cuba, the Philippines, Haiti, Egypt, Israel, and some 30 countries in Africa—about 100 overseas trips in all. He traveled a greater distance than all previous popes combined. He reached out to non-Catholics and non-Christians, especially Jews and Muslims, in his trip to the Holy Land in March 2000 and in his meeting with the chief Sunni cleric, Sheikh al-Azhar, in Cairo. He called anti-Semitism a sin and referred to Jews as "our older brothers in faith." He visited Canterbury Cathedral in England, the most important cathedral in the Anglican faith, and Lutheran churches in Germany and Sweden.

This pope's positions were, however, quite complex. His opposition to abortion, birth control, the ordination of women as priests and homosexual behavior, and his insistence on clerical celibacy were conservative. (Nevertheless, Catholics around the world practiced birth control to about the same extent as their non-Catholic neighbors.) Meanwhile, other Christian groups were liberalizing their attitudes. For example, in 1994 the Church of England voted to ordain women as priests. The Episcopal Church in the United States ordained a female bishop for the first time in 1988 and the first openly gay bishop in 2003. In 2006 a woman was named head of the Episcopal Church in the United States.

John Paul II also took a conservative position on the means of combating poverty. In the late 1960s and 1970s a new school of thought, called **liberation theology**, took shape in Latin America. Identifying with Jesus' ministry to the poor, it established grass-roots communities in poor neighborhoods of cities and in rural pockets of poverty. These communities combined religious study and prayer with efforts to solve local problems, especially poverty. By the late 1970s, some observers estimated 80,000 such communities in Brazil alone.

Liberation theology confronted powerful forces of opposition. In March 1980, Archbishop Oscar Romero of El Salvador was assassinated as he was officiating at mass in a San Salvador chapel. Romero was only one of about 850 church leaders who were murdered after the assassination of Camilo Torres, a priest and sociologist in Colombia. An outstanding scholar and teacher, Torres gave up on peaceful reform and joined Colombia's communist-led guerrillas. He was killed in a battle with government forces in February 1966. In December 1980, three American nuns and a lay missionary who had gone to work with poor refugees in El Salvador were murdered by security officers of the state.

The advocates of liberation theology claimed to combine Christian ethics with Marxist politics. Pope John Paul II, raised in communist Poland, rejected this Marxist orientation. As new posts opened, he appointed mostly conservative priests, and as a result the clergy in Latin America were deeply split. About 20 percent aligned themselves with liberation theology, but the overwhelming majority, especially in Brazil, accepted the pope's orientation.

John Paul's successor, Pope Benedict XVI (r. 2005–2013), took more interest in theological issues and in Europe, than in poverty in the developing world. He, too, was not Italian, but German, and 78 years old at the time of his election. He saw that Islam was making inroads into historically Christian Europe, and he pushed back by stressing belief and adherence to ritual observance. He recognized that his conservatism might cause some, especially in Europe, to leave the Church, but those who remained, he felt, would be more sincere and more capable of challenging

KEY TERM

liberation theology A movement within the Catholic Church, especially in Latin America, especially in the 1960s and 1970s, combining some of the social concerns of Marxism with those of the Christian gospel, focusing on serving the needs of poor people, and organizing them for confrontations against governments when necessary.

Islamic inroads. In 2013 Benedict became the first pope in 600 years to retire from office.

The election of Francis I, the first Latin American pope, from Argentina, again reoriented the geographical and service priorities of the Church. Francis chose for his first international trip as pope a weeklong visit to Brazil, where he won overwhelming crowd adoration for his humble manner. In his final address, to some three million Catholics gathered at Copacabana Beach, Francis advocated for a Church close to the people and attentive to the needs of the poor.

📖 Read the Document: Address before the Puebla Conference (1979) Pope John Paul II on MyHistoryLab

Pope Francis I on World Youth Day in Rio de Janeiro, Brazil, 2013. The election in 2013 of Francis I as pope brought new initiatives to the Vatican. His predecessor, Pope Benedict XVI, was the first pope in 600 years to retire from the office, at age 85. Francis I, an Argentinean, was the first pope from Latin America. The new pope's desire to engage with and promote the welfare of the poor and downtrodden, and his suggestion that the Church should be less intrusive in issues concerning consensual sexuality among the clergy or the laity, suggested a re-orientation of the Vatican to the concerns and policies of Pope John XXIII in the 1960s.

Evangelical Christianity. Evangelical Christianity was giving a new face to the world's largest religion, especially in the Americas. In 1940 there were barely a million Protestants in all of Latin America; by 2010 there were some 60 million, 12 percent of the total population. The overwhelming majority were **Pentecostals**, appealing usually to the very poorest groups in society, and often to those who had been uprooted from rural areas. Pentecostals emphasize direct, personal experience of God and revelation, rather than the authority of scripture or of any Church hierarchy. Many Pentecostal groups are allied with North American churches. Pentecostal religion has a special appeal to women as it often refers to Jesus as a Divine Husband and Father, emphasizes male responsibility and chastity, and calls for a "reformation of machismo" in family relationships.

In the United States, as well, evangelical Christianity has been on the rise for the past generation. Many believing Christians resented the 1960s and 1970s "counter-culture" of antiwar protest, drugs, folk and protest music, provocative styles of dress and self-presentation, and freer sexual expression. They turned to their Bibles to rediscover the fundamentals of their faith, and decided that America was moving in the wrong direction. These fundamentalists began creating more of their own organizations and institutions. In 1979 a Gallup poll showed that one out of three American adults reported a "born-again" conversion, an experience of being touched and changed by a personal encounter with Jesus. Fifty percent believed that the Bible was an accurate account of history. Some 130 million people reported listening to and watching 1,300 evangelical Christian radio and television stations. Evangelicals were an important constituency in presidential elections, and powerful voices in challenging the right of women to obtain legal abortions.

Fundamentalism increased, but so did secularism and nonaffiliation. In the period 1990 to 2012, the percentage of adults who reported their religious identity as Christian dropped from 86 percent to 76 percent. The number of adults who did not subscribe to any religion almost doubled, from 8 percent to 15 percent of the total population. As religious attitudes polarized, commentators spoke of "culture wars."

New immigrants brought yet another, international dimension to American religious identity, increasing its diversity and cosmopolitanism. As Hindus and Sikhs

23.1

23.2

23.3

23.4

What might account for the reemergence of religious groups as powerful political forces?

KEY TERMS

evangelical Christianity Those forms of Protestant Christianity that emphasize the literal truth and authority of the Bible, and salvation through the personal acceptance of Jesus Christ.

Pentecostals Christians who stress a direct, personal experience of God, Jesus, and revelation, rather than the authority of scripture or of the Church hierarchy.

Perspectives on Religious Identity in the United States

Two recent studies of religious identity in the United States have painted contrasting pictures. Diana Eck celebrates an ever-increasing array of new and different religious communities. After noting the increasing diversity of their congregations and services in her Cambridge neighborhood, Eck sent her Harvard students to explore more systematically, first around Boston and then in their hometowns across America. In her book *A New Religious America* (1997), she reports the results of this Pluralism Project, exploring the extent to which "new" religions—especially Hinduism, Buddhism, and Islam—are appearing in America. She links her findings directly to the recent global migrations that are bringing about a million new immigrants to America every year:

> The immigrants of the last three decades … have expanded the diversity of our religious life dramatically, exponentially. Buddhists have come from Thailand, Vietnam, Cambodia, China, and Korea; Hindus from India, East Africa, and Trinidad; Muslims from Indonesia, Bangladesh, Pakistan, the Middle East, and Nigeria; Sikhs and Jains from India; and Zoroastrians from both India and Iran. Immigrants from Haiti and Cuba have brought Afro-Caribbean traditions, blending both African and Catholic symbols and images. New Jewish immigrants have come from Russia and the Ukraine, and the internal diversity of American Judaism is greater than ever before. The face of American Christianity has also changed with large Latino, Filipino, and Vietnamese Catholic communities; Chinese, Haitian, and Brazilian Pentecostal communities; Korean Presbyterians, Indian Mar Thomas, and Egyptian Copts. In every city in the land church signboards display the meeting times of Korean or Latino congregations that nest within the walls of old urban Protestant and Catholic churches.
> (Eck, pp. 3–4)

Karen Armstrong's crosscultural study of militant fundamentalist movements in Islam in Egypt and Iran, in Judaism in Israel, and in Christianity in the United States—*The Battle for God* (2000)—paints a very different picture. Armstrong spent seven years as a nun, then became a college professor, and during the past two decades she has become one of the most respected writers on religious history, especially on Christianity, Islam, and Judaism and their relationship to one another. Her reflections on fundamentalist Christianity in the United States suggest very little flexibility, compromise, or openness to new religious groups:

> Fundamentalism is not going to disappear. In America, religion has long shaped opposition to government. Its rise and fall has always been cyclical, and events of the last few years indicate that there is still a state of incipient warfare between conservatives and liberals which has occasionally become frighteningly explicit. In 1992, Jerry Falwell, who still adheres to the old-style fundamentalism, announced that with the election of Bill Clinton to the presidency, Satan had been let loose in the United States. Clinton, Falwell thundered, was about to destroy the military and the nation by letting "the gays" take over. Executive orders permitting abortion in federally funded clinics, research on fetal tissue, the official endorsement of homosexual rights, were all signs that America "had declared war on God." (Armstrong, p. 362)

How can we reconcile these very different perspectives on religious identity in contemporary America? Philip Jenkins, in his study of the global expansion of Christianity, suggests that we consider the demographics:

> The number of adherents of non-Christian religions in the United States is strikingly small. If we combine the plausible estimates for the numbers of American Jews, Buddhists, Muslims, and Hindus, then we are speaking of about 4 or 5 percent of the total population. (Jenkins, p. 132)

This proportion is not so different from Western Europe where non-Christians form about ten percent of the population of France, four percent of Britain, and five percent of Germany and the Netherlands. In many African and Asian nations, religious minorities make up 10 to 20 percent of the population, and in some cases even more. The same questions that attend religious diversity in many other countries of the world appear also in the United States.

So, Eck's celebratory report is restricted to a very small, and perhaps not quite so remarkable, proportion of the population. On the other hand, Armstrong's fundamentalists also do not make up an American majority. In a poll in 1984, only nine percent of Americans identified themselves as "fundamentalists," although "44 percent believed that salvation comes only through Jesus Christ."

Religious identity is important to most people in America. Both new immigration and "old-time religion" are having their effects on shaping it. The results of this amalgam are not yet clear. As Eck remarks, "diversity alone does not constitute pluralism … whether we are able to work together across the lines of religious difference to create a society in which we actually know one another remains to be seen."

- What other historical examples can you give of national religious identity changing under the influence of new immigrant groups?
- What other historical examples can you give of new religious identities clashing with older established ones?
- Do you think demographics is the main reason for the differences in perception about American religious life as represented by Eck and Armstrong? What other reasons can you suggest?

emigrated from India, Muslims from the Middle East and Pakistan, Buddhists from Southeast Asia, and other religious groups from elsewhere, American religious identity broadened. The new immigrants and their American-born children sometimes encountered xenophobia, but they enriched and extended religious and ethnic identity in the United States. They made up about four to five percent of the total population, and with their mosques, temples, sanctuaries, and church announcement boards in non-European languages, they added a highly visible new dimension to American religious identity.

The Thematic Approach: *What Difference Does It Make?*

Biological and cultural evolution, expanding urbanization, imperial projects, and religious devotion and conflict—themes around which we have structured this book from the beginning of human history—continue to serve as valuable touchstones for understanding the present. They are among the foundational building blocks of human society. By understanding them historically, we are better able to understand who we have been and who we are becoming.

In our final chapter we continue with the last three of our themes—trade, revolution, and technology. We then bring our study to a conclusion with a consideration of the formation of individual and collective identity.

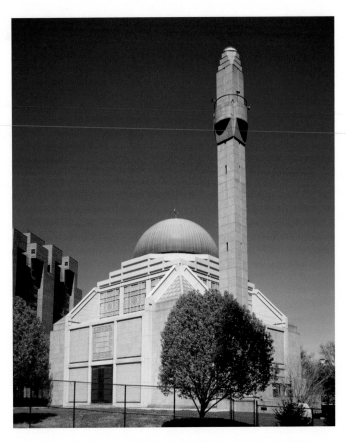

Islamic Cultural Center, New York City. Religions from around the world were finding new homes in America, often transplanted by new groups of immigrants and supplemented by native-born American converts.

CHAPTER REVIEW

ON EVOLUTION

23.1 How do the issues of evolution continue in contemporary times?

The discovery of DNA has opened many new doors, as scientists now work to clone animals and create genetically modified foods. Diseases continue to evolve, and some have proved resistant to treatment; doctors fear the overuse of antibiotic drugs will lead to more evolved and therefore more resistant strains of diseases. At the same time, medicine is increasingly studying individual human genomes to find personally tailored treatments for diseases. Scientists attribute more influence to genetic inheritance in determining individual human behavior. Debates about what behaviors and roles are biologically "natural" for women and men, in other words the product of evolution, may never be settled.

ON SETTLEMENTS

23.2 In what ways are the cities of the early twenty-first century different from those of the early twentieth?

The way we live has changed enormously in one hundred years. Today, more than 50 percent of the world's people live in cities. Some of those cities are huge—"megacities" of more than ten million people. And these cities are all firmly connected by new networks of regional and global exchange, provided by highways, shipping, and the internet. Cities' economic functions have changed tremendously, too. Instead of industrial jobs—textiles, automobiles—city workers primarily labor in the service industries: information technology, film and television, tourism, trade, and clerical occupations. China, in particular is an exception, as many manufacturers have relocated their facilities outside of urban areas and to poorer parts of the world, where labor costs are low. Meanwhile, inside the cities of the poorer countries of Asia, Africa, and South America, settlements of slums have grown to one-fourth of the total urban population. Governments and NGOs are developing programs to try to address the problems.

CHAPTER REVIEW (continued)

ON POLITICS AND EMPIRE

23.3 How have power relationships between nations realigned in the early twenty-first century?

The shifts in global power relations in the early twenty-first century are astonishing. The USSR is no more, although Russia still holds tremendous oil wealth and a huge stock of arms that give it international influence. The US remains the world's sole superpower in terms of its military capacity, but it became embroiled in two wars, which diminished its economic power and leadership. America's decisions to act on its own, as in its decisions to go to war, have alienated even some of its close allies. Meanwhile, China has risen steadily in international esteem, based on its steadily increasing economic power at home and overseas. Western Europe has unified as the European Union, with a common currency, and is expanding its membership, although its recovery from a severe global recession after 2008 has lagged.

ON RELIGION

23.4 What might account for the reemergence of religious groups as powerful political forces?

changes of globalization, and the speed at which life has changed, have threatened people's sense of security, which religious faith reassures. Also, religious groups often offer social welfare programs and community support that governments do not. Although the combination of practical assistance, community membership, and a message of comfort has been a hallmark of organized religion since its beginning, it is especially prominent in Islam, which has been the fastest growing world religion in recent years. While some Islamic-majority countries operate as Islamic theocracies, others struggle to reconcile conflicts between groups that want more theocratic government, headed by religious authorities, and those that prefer more secular government, with more of a separation between mosque and state. In India, tension between Muslims and Hindus has frequently emerged. In Israel, tensions continue between the majority secular Jewish population and the 20 percent who identify as religiously observant, not to speak of often strained relationships with the twenty percent of Israeli Arabs who are mostly Muslim, but also Christian. Christianity is the world's largest religion by far. About half are Roman Catholics who have seen their Church's policies change under a series of different popes. Evangelical Christianity also exerts a powerful influence on local and national politics in many countries. Religious groups reemerged in the late twentieth to early twenty-first century as powerful political forces. Theories vary on why this is so. Perhaps the intense

Suggested Readings

In this chapter we are moving into contemporary times, and even into current events. In addition to newspapers, and television and radio news programs, two publications are especially useful in tracking current events. The following serve an educated, but not specialized, readership:

The Economist, a weekly review published in London and providing extensive coverage of the United States and the entire world. Edited from a traditional liberal perspective—that is, favoring free markets and human rights as developed over the past centuries in Europe and the United States—*The Economist* covers the globe each week. The comprehensiveness and accessibility of its coverage is not matched in the English-speaking world.
The New York Review of Books, published bi-weekly, takes the form of a tabloid of book reviews, but its reviews are lengthy and extensive explorations of subject areas. The particular book under assessment serves as a springboard for wide-ranging, thoughtful, and careful discussions of the subject matter. The authors are leading scholars in their fields.

PRINCIPAL SOURCES

Ayres, Alyssa, and Philip Oldenburg, eds. *India Briefing: Takeoff at Last?* (Armonk, NY: M.E. Sharpe, 2005). The most recent of a series published every year or two,

of outstanding summary articles on developments in contemporary India. Various articles on politics, economics, social life, the arts, and culture.
Campanella, Thomas. *The Concrete Dragon: China's Urban Revolution and What It Means for the World* (Princeton: Princeton Architectural Press, 2008). Excellent introduction to the overall philosophy, process, and building, Highlights specific cases of individual cities.
Crossley, Pamela Kyle, Lynn Hollen Lees, and John W. Servos. *Global Society: The World Since 1900* (Boston, MA: Houghton Mifflin, 3rd ed., 2012). A fine, well-written history of the twentieth century, organized thematically rather than by nation or region. Special emphasis on technology and useful references to websites for further research.
Gilbert, Mark. *Surpassing Realism: The Politics of European Integration Since 1945* (Lanham, MD: Rowman and Littlefield, 2003). Step-by-step account of the building of the European Union with fascinating contemporary commentaries along the way.
Glenny, Misha. *The Balkans: Nationalism, War, and the Great Powers, 1804–1999* (New York: Viking, 2000). Comprehensive account of the Balkans and their somewhat unfortunate fate in the hands of the Great Powers, sometimes because of intervention, sometimes because of lack of intervention.

Human Development Report (New York: United Nations Development Program, annual). A survey of the nations of the world with an abundance of statistical tables and numerous, brief, specific topical discussions. Each year has a special focus on one broad issue.
Hunt, Michael H. *The World Transformed: 1945 to the Present: A Documentary Reader* (Boston, MA: Bedford/St. Martin's, 2004). An outstanding selection of primary documents with global scope and thematic breadth.
Jaffrelot, Christophe. *Hindu Nationalism: A Reader* (Princeton, NJ: Princeton University Press, 2007). Superb selections on the merger of religion and politics, covering almost 100 years.
——. *India's Silent Revolution: The Rise of the Lower Castes in North India* (London: Hurst and Company, 2003). Amazing, peaceful transformations in a hierarchical society.
——, ed. *A History of Pakistan and Its Origins* (New York: Anthem Press, 2004). Excellent selection of scholarly articles on the complexities of Pakistan.
Kishwar, Madhu. *Off the Beaten Track: Rethinking Gender Justice for Indian Women* (New Delhi: Oxford University Press, 1999). The editor of one of India's leading feminist journals, *Manushi*, discusses the evolution of her thought in light of the possible and the ideal.
Meredith, Robyn. *The Elephant and the Dragon: The Rise of India and China and*

What It Means for All of Us (New York: W.W. Norton, 2007). Chapter-by-chapter, point-by-point comparisons of the recent developments in these two giant nations.

Nafisi, Azar. *Reading* Lolita *in Tehran: A Memoir in Books* (New York: Random House, 2003). How an English professor and her students bucked the regime and studied literature as they chose.

Nugent, Neill. *The Government and Politics of the European Union* (Durham, NC: Duke University Press, 7th ed., 2010). Detailed exposition of the institutional workings of the EU, with very useful historical prelude and concluding perspectives on the future.

Rogel, Carole. *The Breakup of Yugoslavia and the War in Bosnia* (Westport, CN: Greenwood Press, 1998). Basic narrative supported by detailed chronology and primary documents to 1997. Critical of almost all participants, and of NATO and the United States for years of appeasement.

Sassen, Saskia. *The Global City: New York, London, Tokyo* (Princeton, NJ: Princeton University Press, 2001). Sassen demonstrates the significance of leading cities to global economic growth, and finds New York, London, and Tokyo the most significant of them.

Sen, Amartya. *Development as Freedom* (New York: Random House, 1999). Nobel Prize-winning economist stresses the significance of human development—health, education, and welfare—as the key issue in economic development, both as its cause and its result. Clearly and persuasively argued.

Tully, Mark. *Non-Stop India* (New Delhi: Penguin Books, 2011). Tully was the BBC's revered and respected correspondent from New Delhi for 25 years. He is perceptive and direct in his observations, especially as India enters uncharted territory.

Ullman, Richard H., ed. *The World and Yugoslavia's Wars* (New York: Council on Foreign Relations, 1996). Explores not only the wars but also the (lack of) response by the European Community, the United States, and the UN.

United Nations. *State of the World's Cities* (New York: Routledge, annual). Available online at http://www.unhabitat.org/pmss.

ADDITIONAL SOURCES

Armstrong, Karen. *The Battle for God* (New York: Knopf, 2000). Armstrong analyzes fundamentalist tendencies and groups within the world's major religions, historically and today.

Boo, Katherine. *Behind the Beautiful Forevers* (New York; Random House, 2012). Journalistic, realistic, heartrending account of life in a Mumbai slum in the shadow of a five-star hotel.

Brass, Paul. *The Production of Hindu-Muslim Violence in Contemporary India* (Seattle, WA: University of Washington Press, 2003). Sees violence between the groups as a result of cynical political manipulation.

Cavalieri, Paola, and Peter Singer, eds. *The Great Ape Project: Equality Beyond Humanity*

(New York: St. Martin's Press, 1994). The book that underlies the campaign.

China Development Brief. *250 Chinese NGOs: Civil Society in the Making* (unpublished report, 2001). Underlines the importance of NGOs to China's progress—economic as well as political—and outlines the mission and accomplishments of 250 of them.

Davis, Mike. *Planet of Slums* (New York: Verso, 2006). A pessimistic account of slums and their development, status today, and future.

Eck, Diana. *A New Religious America: How a "Christian Country" Has Become the World's Most Religiously Diverse Nation* (San Francisco: HarperSanFrancisco, 2001). Eck charts the rise in numbers and influence of non-Christians in America, mostly relatively new migrants.

Hall, Peter. *Cities of Tomorrow: An Intellectual History of Urban Planning and Design in the Twentieth Century* (Malden, MA: Blackwell, 3rd ed., 2002). Key developments in the history of urban planning in the twentieth century, with most, but not all, examples taken from Europe and the United States.

Hollinger, David. *After Cloven Tongues of Fire: Protestant Liberalism in Modern American History* (Princeton, NJ: Princeton University Press, 2013). Presents the accomplishments of liberal, mainstream Protestantism. A reply to those who argue that evangelicalism has been more central.

Huang, Shu-Min. *The Spiral Road* (Boulder, CO: Westview Press, 2nd ed., 1998). Changes in a Chinese village through the eyes of a Communist Party leader.

Jenkins, Philip. *The Next Christendom: The Coming of Global Christianity* (New York: Oxford University Press, 3rd ed., 2011). With quantitative and qualitative data, Jenkins highlights the growth of the Church especially in Latin America, Africa, and Asia.

Marcuse, Peter, and Ronald van Kempen, eds. *Globalizing Cities: A New Spatial Order* (Malden, MA: Blackwell, 2000). A set of coordinated research papers seeking—and finding—commonalities in the development of contemporary cities around the world.

Mistry, Rohinton. *A Fine Balance* (New York: Random House, 1995). Brilliant novelistic exposition of the fine balance between hope and despair that enables India's poor to endure.

Mohanty, Chandra Talpade, Ann Russo, and Lourdes Torres, eds. *Third World Women and the Politics of Feminism* (Bloomington, IN: Indiana University Press, 1991). The issues of feminism are different in different parts of the world, as this academic selection makes clear.

Nye, Joseph F. Jr.. "The Decline of America's Soft Power," *Foreign Affairs*, May/June 2004, vol. 83, no. 3, pp. 16–21. Brief, to-the-point exposition of the importance of soft power—that is—cultural power, in international relations.

Rosenberg, Rosalind. "The 'Woman Question,'" in Richard W. Bulliet, ed. *The Columbia History of the 20th Century* (New York: Columbia University Press, 1998).

Discusses the changing goals of women's movements around the world.

Satrapi, Marjane. *Persepolis* (New York: Pantheon, 2004). Autobiography in graphic-novel form of a young woman, from age 10 to 14, living through the Islamic revolution under Khomeini in Iran. The simplicity of the form makes the terror clearer and more striking.

Wickham, Kerry Rosefsky. *The Muslim Brotherhood: Evolution of an Islamist Movement* (Princeton, NJ: Princeton University Press, 2013). Traces the history of the Brotherhood since its inception in 1928, mostly in Egypt, but with some comparisons. Emphasizes the conflicting variety of philosophies in the Brotherhood.

Wu, Weiping, and Piper Gaubatz. *The Chinese City* (New York: Routledge, 2012). Comprehensive introduction to the history of Chinese urbanization, its modern forms and functions, including the impact of new philosophies and new interaction with the rest of the world.

FILMS

By the time we reach this period in contemporary history, abundant documentaries and news stories are available that touch on every aspect of historical change. Many are available on YouTube.

The Act of Killing (2012; 1 hour 55 minutes). During the revolution in Indonesia in 1965–66, half a million people, mostly Chinese, were murdered. Here, two of the murderers, half a century later, revel in the way they carried out the slaughter, enacting it as a movie in which they are the stars. Horrifying and thought-provoking.

Ai Weiwei: Never Sorry (2012; 1 hour 31 minutes). Documentary on the subversive art and filmmaking of the Chinese dissident Ai Weiwei, exposing the high-handedness of the Chinese government.

City of God (2002; 2 hours 10 minutes). Heart-wrenching story of children and youth trapped in the crime and violence of the slums of Rio de Janeiro. Beautiful and dismaying. The film influenced legislation for slum improvement in Brazil.

Persepolis (2007; 1 hour 36 minutes). Animated film based on the graphic-style autobiography of a young girl, from age 9 to 14, living through the Iranian revolution. Sent away for escape and schooling, she tries coming back, but ultimately cannot endure the dictatorship.

Slumdog Millionaire (2009; 2 hours). A boy from the Mumbai slums makes good on a quiz show and pays the price in a police beating. We get to watch the principal events in his young life. Feel-good ending, but lots of realistic images of the hardship of big-city slums.

Zero Dark Thirty (2012; 2 hours 37 minutes). Semi-fictionalized account of the ten-year search for and final apprehension of Osama bin Laden.

24 Contemporary History

Trade, Revolution, Technology, Identity

This final chapter reviews the last three themes of the text—trade, social revolution, and technology—and assesses their significance in understanding today's world. In conclusion, we introduce one final theme: identity. This theme explores the ways in which people, groups, and institutions define themselves in eras of continual change and constant spin—eras like our own. The theme of identity provides a conceptual viewpoint that helps us to integrate the past and present and even to anticipate the future. And with it, we close our study.

LEARNING OBJECTIVES

24.1 ((	24.2 ((	24.3 ((
Understand the significance of globalization and its goals in the twenty-first century.	Describe the key social revolutions of the early twenty-first century.	Discuss ecological technology and the world's response to climate change.

((**Listen** on **MyHistoryLab**

Israeli–Palestinian relations on the West Bank, 2000. An Israeli soldier is seen in discussion with two Palestinian women.

On Trade

24.1   Why is globalization significant? What are its goals?

Why is globalization significant? What are its goals?

24.1

24.2

24.3

Long-distance international trade is not new. Sumerians traded westward to Egypt and the Nile valley and eastward to India and the Indus valley. Later, silk routes facilitated trade between Han China, the ancient Roman Empire, and the empires of India. From the twelfth century onward, trade became a driving force in international relations. With improved navigation, trade networks became global; the oceans, no longer a barrier, became a bridge. Private merchant communities acquired influence in their home countries and internationally, separate from government, although intertwined with it. Merchants and trade came to rival political leaders and government in their power to determine the fate of nations.

In recent years, world trade has reached unprecedented levels. In 1990, the value of global trade totaled $22.8 trillion; in 2007, $53.3 trillion; and by 2011, despite the recession of 2008, it reached $72 trillion (or $82.5 trillion if we take into account the actual **purchasing power** of currencies in different countries). Global trade has been increasing by 10 percent per year. The increasing interaction in commercial trade—and in other kinds of international exchange—is often referred to as **globalization**. The term usually also signifies increasing communications technology, free-market capitalism, and decreasing government regulation. Globalization thrives on the new, inexpensive transportation and communications facilities of the later twentieth and early twenty-first centuries.

Globalization is more than just economics. Politically, it requires freedom of movement of goods, services, capital, knowledge, and people across borders. It creates new institutions for negotiating rules and regulations across international borders. It produces new and different social and cultural forms. Globalization brings increased travel and tourism, more world music and literature, and new dimensions of international economic investment.

Although many advocates of globalization claim that its home is the entire world and its benefits are equally accessible to everyone, more critical observers see its contemporary origins in the United States, spread not only by America's businesses but also by its effective control over global financial institutions. They see globalization as just one more measure of the superpower status of the United States. Since about 2000, however, the American role in the global economy has shrunk somewhat, and the roles of China and the European Union have increased. The leading countries of the developing world, sometimes represented in shorthand as the BRICS—Brazil, Russia, India, China, South Africa—have also done well. The process of globalization has become more fully global.

The Institutions of Globalization

The principal financial institutions that facilitate the expansion of globalization—the International Monetary Fund (IMF), the World Bank, and the General Agreement on Tariffs and Trade (GATT)—were put in place toward the end of World War II. In 1995, reflecting the growth in world trade, the GATT transformed itself into the World Trade Organization (WTO). By 2013, the WTO included 159 members. The member governments negotiate, sign, and implement agreements that form the legal ground rules for international trade. They are designed to enable producers, importers, and exporters—usually private businesses—to conduct business efficiently. Should disputes arise over interpretation of the agreements, they are adjudicated by the WTO, which can enforce its decisions by invoking sanctions against violators.

The Internet, the World Wide Web, and Containerization. The WTO has provided the institutional organization to facilitate the expansion of global trade. The internet, the

KEY TERMS

purchasing power parity (PPP) A statistical formulation based on the actual purchasing power of various currencies. For example, 100 Indian rupees may be officially equal to US$2, but in India it will buy far more in goods and services than US$2 will in the United States. The PPP statistic attempts to evaluate this actual purchasing power.

globalization The processes by which people, institutions, and nations are brought into unified networks of interaction around the globe. Most commonly the term refers to economic networks and integration, but cultural, political, and technological globalization also occurs.

24.1

24.2

24.3

Why is
globalization
significant? What
are its goals?

World Wide Web, and the improved transportation facilities of containerization have provided the technology.

In 1994, some three million people worldwide were connected to the internet; by 2013, that figure had increased to 2.4 billion. The largest national group, 568 million, was in China (42 percent of its total population); the second largest was in the United States, with 254 million users (81 percent of the American population). Other electronic communications media expanded similarly, with almost unbelievable speed. In 1990 there were 11 million cellular phone subscriptions worldwide; at the end of 2011 there were 6 billion, with the largest number, 481 million, in China. E-mail and texting have made instantaneous global communication available at nominal cost. Social media—Facebook, Twitter, Tumblr, LinkedIn, etc.—facilitated a new intensity of communication among existing groups and the formation of new groups online that had revolutionary potential for collective action.

Transportation played as large a role as communication. In his remarkable book *The Box: How the Shipping Container Made the World Smaller and the World Economy Bigger* (2006), Marc Levinson tells the story of the introduction, in 1956, of containers of standardized size that are sealed from shipper to receiver, even as they move among different modes of transportation—trucks, railway cars, and ships. These standardized containers have dramatically reduced the need for human labor in loading and unloading freight at each of the transfer points along the way. Huge cranes do the work. The sealed containers also cut the rate of pilferage and damage to goods. In 2012, some 1.5 billion tons of goods, the overwhelming bulk of shipping cargo, were carried in standardized shipping containers, at a cost that had become negligible. This reduced cost of shipping is one of the principal innovations that has helped to bring China, so distant from European and American markets, into the center of the world trade network: "In 1956, China was not the world's workshop. It was not routine for shoppers to find Brazilian shoes and Mexican vacuum cleaners

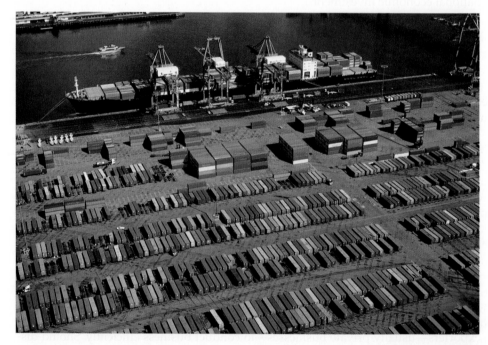

Shipping containers. Standard-size containers have been used in a limited way for centuries. In the late 1950s, however, greater standardization in containers was achieved, first by the transportation industry and then through the regulations of the International Organization for Standardization. With standardization of size, freight could be shipped from original expediter to final consumer relatively rapidly and cheaply, moving interchangeably from train to truck to ship, protected against pilferage. Containerization has facilitated the globalization of trade.

in stores in the middle of Kansas. Japanese families did not eat beef from cattle raised in Wyoming, and French clothing designers did not have their exclusive apparel cut and sewn in Turkey or Vietnam" (Levinson, p. 1).

Why is globalization significant? What are its goals?

24.1

24.2

24.3

Globalization and Its Critics

The constant development of new technology and the creation of new institutions make globalization appear inevitable and overwhelming. Perhaps that is why the process also has fierce opponents. In 1999, protesters gathered at a meeting of the WTO in Seattle, Washington, to demonstrate their apprehension at the increasing tempo of world trade. They feared that the quest for profit would eclipse humanitarian concerns. They demanded more regulation by national governments and by the United Nations (UN) to protect the environment, human rights, labor, and children's welfare. Many of the protesters also feared that globalization would homogenize the world's cultures into a single "McDonald's" culture and even replace its many languages with a single, dominant global language, English. They rejected the counterarguments of advocates of globalization, that new communications networks would allow small, niche cultures, languages, and organizations to flourish.

The globalization of communication also raised the specter of government and private surveillance and espionage via the internet. In 2010, Bradley Manning, a United States soldier with very high security clearance, leaked 250,000 diplomatic cables and 500,000 army reports concerning American military strikes that had killed civilians during the Iraqi and Afghan wars. Manning passed his information to WikiLeaks, a website run by Julian Assange, an Australian committed, he claimed, to keeping government activity transparent. Manning was sentenced to 35 years in prison for violating the Espionage Act and stealing government property. Assange found refuge in the Ecuadorian embassy in London. In 2013, Edward Snowden, a computer specialist working on United States surveillance operations, revealed that the US National Security Agency was gathering the raw data of every phone call made in the United States, as well as overseas calls. Fearing prosecution, Snowden fled the country. Russia granted him permission to stay, at least temporarily. In common with Manning and Assange, Snowden was viewed by some as a traitor, but by others as a hero who was trying to keep government accountable and internet activity private.

In 2001, an umbrella organization of protesters, the World Social Forum, held its first annual meeting in Porto Alegre, Brazil. Under its motto, "Another World is Possible," the forum sought alternative political and economic models to those that dominate the world today. The issues it raised were not new, but their massive representation at the global level, including participation by UNESCO, was. By the time of the fourth meeting, in 2004, in Mumbai, India, 100,000 people participated. At the seventh meeting, in Nairobi, Kenya, in 2007, attendees came from 110 countries. Since 2008, the usual pattern has been separate, more manageable, regional forums.

Globalization increases economic dislocation. The process confers great benefits on the winners and exacts costly consequences from the losers. Because of the competitive nature of the capitalist system—the order on which globalization rests—those who are prepared to take advantage of the new possibilities stand to reap enormous profits, while those who are not fall behind. Competition increases the speed of technological change, bringing new employment possibilities to some while eliminating many older jobs. This kind of economic innovation brings an overall increase in productivity, but at the cost—at least temporarily—of lost jobs and worker income.

Julian Assange, 2011. As digital communications created ever more comprehensive and dense networks of information, apprehensions multiplied concerning unwarranted surveillance and inappropriate secrecy, especially by governments. Julian Assange, an Australian editor and publicist, founded WikiLeaks as an online site for publishing news leaks and classified information that he felt to be in the public interest. Whistleblowers such as Bradley (Chelsea) Manning and Edward Snowden published tens of thousands of American government documents through WikiLeaks and through public newspapers that followed the activities of the site. At the time of writing, Manning is serving a 35-year jail sentence for espionage; Snowden is in Russia, evading American prosecution; Assange has been granted asylum in the Ecuadorean embassy in London in the face of a charge of sexual assault in Sweden.

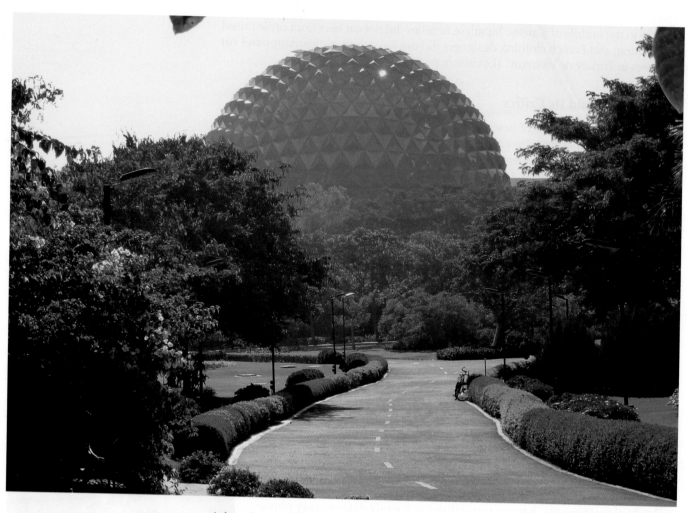

Infosys Campus, Mysore, India. By the 2000s, India had become a world leader in the development of software and in providing back-office support for companies based in America and Europe. Companies such as Infosys, Wipro, and Tata Consultancies built campuses for research, development, and training of new personnel. In the 200 classrooms on its 340-acre campus in Mysore, Infosys employs 500 instructors. It can train 12,000 employees at a time, with 3 batches of 4000 employees for 4 months each.

24.1 Why is globalization significant? What are its goals?

24.2

24.3

KEY TERM

outsourcing Buying goods and services, including personnel, from sources far away from the place where they are to be used, usually from overseas. A major example is the establishment of overseas call centers in countries where labor is cheap to service customers in places where labor is expensive.

Throughout the 1990s and 2000s, investors commonly regarded company layoffs of workers as moves toward efficiency. As firms let workers go, the share prices of their stock went up. The economist Joseph Schumpeter (1883–1950) famously remarked that capitalism was a system of "creative destruction." But those who benefited from the creativity and those who suffered from the destruction were usually different people. The total compensation package of Tim Cook, chief executive of Apple, for the year 2011 was $378 million, the highest in the world. *Forbes* magazine estimated 1,426 billionaires in the world in September 2013; the richest was Carlos Slim Helú and his family, of Mexico, possessing $73 billion. In 2012, the world's 13.8 million millionaires, a total of 0.9 percent of global households, owned 39 percent of the financial wealth of the planet (data from www.bcgperspectives.com).

Lagging regions do their best, but they have a very long way to go. The nations of Africa, for example, increased their usage of the internet by thirty-six times between 2000 and 2012. Even so, African nations, with 14 percent of the world's population, still have only 7 percent of the world's internet users. Meanwhile, technology research laboratories, especially in the United States, continue to attract talented, skilled persons, draining them from less technologically sophisticated nations.

Some poorer countries have benefitted from the possibility of new employment opportunities. New communications jobs in customer service and record-keeping are being **outsourced** to third-world countries where salaries are low. Almost 10 percent of the gross national product (GNP) of the Philippines—the world's leader in out-sourced jobs—comes from these jobs. At higher levels of skill and creativity, such

Why is globalization significant? What are its goals?

24.1

24.2

24.3

HOW DO WE KNOW?

Evaluating Globalization

Globalization—in the sense of global networks of economic, political, and cultural exchange—is not new. We have seen examples throughout this text going back thousands of years. The increasing sophistication of transportation and communication, especially the computer, the internet, and the World Wide Web, however, have given globalization far greater scope in the last two decades than ever before. As the power of globalization has increased over the past 15 years, our evaluation of it has become more careful and more nuanced.

Thomas Friedman, chief foreign political correspondent for *The New York Times*, introduced his highly influential book *The Lexus and the Olive Tree* (1999) with a sense of the inevitability of globalization:

I feel about globalization a lot like I feel about the dawn. Generally speaking, I think it's a good thing that the sun comes up every morning. It does more good than harm. But even if I didn't much care for the dawn there isn't much I could do about it. I didn't start globalization. I can't stop it—except at a huge cost to human development—and I'm not going to waste time trying. All I want to think about is how I can get the best out of this new system, and cushion the worst, for the most people. (Friedman, p. xviii)

Joseph Stiglitz, recipient of the Nobel Prize in Economics, served for a number of years as vice president and chief economist of the World Bank. He came away from the experience appalled by the failures of globalization and the hardship it often inflicted, especially on the poor. His powerful critique, *Globalization and Its Discontents* (2002), differs sharply from Friedman's general acceptance of the system:

I have written this book because while I was at the World Bank, I saw firsthand the devastating effect that globalization can have on developing countries, and especially the poor within those countries. I believe that globalization—the removal of the barriers to free trade and the closer integration of national economies—can be a force for good and that it has the potential to enrich everyone in the world, particularly the poor. But I also believe that if this is to be the case, the way globalization has been managed, including the international trade agreements that have played such a large role in removing those barriers and the policies that have been imposed on developing countries in the process of globalization, need to be radically rethought. (Stiglitz, pp. ix–x)

Today, few—apart from those with vested interests who benefit from keeping out the goods produced by the poor countries—defend the hypocrisy of pretending to help developing countries by forcing them to open up their markets to the goods of the advanced industrial countries while keeping their own markets protected, policies that make the rich richer and the poor more impoverished—and increasingly angry. (p. xv)

In 2008, the International Labor Organization of the United Nations (ILO) issued a report on income equality and inequality, *World of Work Report 2008: Income Inequalities in the Age of Financial Globalization*. With Stiglitz, it criticized excessive increases in inequality, but with Friedman, it felt that in the long run globalization would prove valuable:

Partly through the lack of proper regulation or an adequate supervisory framework, the frequency of financial crises has increased in both developed and emerging economies as a consequence of financial globalization. Worldwide, systemic banking crises have been 10 times more likely throughout the 1990s than during the late 1970s, which was hardly a period of calm economic activity. Such increased instability has come at a steep cost to inequality, as low-income households have been particularly affected by repeated boom-bust cycles. There is also evidence … that financial globalization is associated with higher unemployment. From a longer term perspective, however, and at least as regards economic growth, the benefits of financial liberalization outweigh the costs of crises. (p. 39)

Enigmatically, the ILO did not explain when or how it expected the long-run benefits to overcome the short-term losses. Much seemed to depend on policymakers around the world acting in the future with far greater wisdom and discretion than they had in the recent past.

By the beginning of 2009, a global recession of frightening proportions reinvigorated criticism of globalization.

- What experience has each author had in defining, evaluating, and implementing globalization?
- To what degree is each author dogmatic in his evaluation of globalization? What dogmas does he seem to accept or to reject?
- To what extent can you begin, on the bases of these authors' suggestions, to formulate your own values in evaluating globalization? On the bases of these introductions, which of the three evaluations do you think you would find most interesting? Most useful?

🔍 **View** the **Closer Look: Mexican Farmers Protest the North American Free Trade Agreement** on **MyHistoryLab**

24.1
24.2
24.3

Why is
globalization
significant? What
are its goals?

cities as Bangalore and Hyderabad in India have become miniature "Silicon Valleys" through the investment of multinational companies such as IBM, Texas Instruments, and Microsoft, and through the entrepreneurship of local information-technology experts who have started their own firms, such as Infosys, Wipro, and Tata Consultancy. In such cities, skilled personnel earn salaries far higher than most local jobs provide, although still substantially below those of the United States, the EU, and Japan. As a result, a well-educated person with a good job in India, for example, will be more similar in economic status to a colleague in Western Europe or the United States than to a fellow citizen of India with a poor education and a poor job.

Inequality among nations is actually decreasing, average living standards around the world have been improving, and the proportion of people living in absolute poverty is declining. China has set the pace. There, 600 million people had emerged from abject poverty by 2011. The proportion of undernourished people in developing regions decreased from 23.2 percent in 1990–92 to 14.9 percent in 2010–12. Although global recession in 2008 slowed growth, and sometimes reversed it, by 2010 the economies of the world's developing countries increased by 7.4 percent, in 2011 by 6.1 percent, and the estimate for 2012 was 5.3 percent.

Setting Goals for Globalization

By the early 2000s, the concern with global economic development shifted from achieving equality, or even **equity**, to reducing, and ultimately ending, poverty. Following a "Millennium Summit" convened by the UN in September 2000, 189 nations accepted eight "Millennium Development Goals" to be achieved by 2015. These are:

- eradicating (in progressive stages) extreme poverty and hunger;
- achieving universal primary education;
- promoting gender equality and empowering women;
- reducing child mortality;
- improving maternal health;
- combating HIV/AIDS, malaria, and other diseases;
- ensuring environmental sustainability; and
- developing a global partnership for development.

By 2013, two years early, the first stage in achieving the first goal had been reached and exceeded; the proportion of people living in extreme poverty had been halved. (Other goals have proved more elusive. For up-to-date information, see http://www.un.org/millenniumgoals.) In developing regions, the proportion of people living on less than $1.25 a day fell from 47 percent in 1990 to 22 percent in 2010. About 700 million fewer people lived in conditions of extreme poverty in 2010 than in 1990. Despite this impressive achievement, 1.2 billion people were still living in extreme poverty in 2013. More than a third of them were living in sub-Saharan Africa, according to the UN.

A UN report on extreme poverty (http://www.un.org/en/development/desa/policy/mdg_gap/mdg_gap2013/mdg_report_2013_en.pdf) laid much of the blame on the wealthier countries for failing to meet their commitments to provide aid to these poorest countries and to open their own markets more fully to the exports of these countries. In 2012, net aid disbursements from developed to developing countries totaled $126 billion, a drop of about 6 percent from 2010. This decline affected the least developed countries most of all. The United States contributed only about $30 billion, just 0.2 percent of its national income. Of this, $2.9 billion went to Afghanistan and $1.3 billion to Iraq, where America was fighting wars, and another $1.3 billion to Pakistan, where the US was also involved in military action.

The issue of market access was contentious. Wealthier countries in Europe and the United States often imposed **protectionist** policies, restricting access to their markets for the raw materials and finished manufactures of impoverished third-world countries.

KEY TERMS

equity A condition in which participants in a system believe that the system is fair and unbiased. Equity does not necessarily imply equality, a situation in which all participants have equivalent goods and rights, but it does require that participants share a sense of the justice and fairness of the system.

protectionism The policy of protecting domestic production from external competition by limiting or prohibiting imports from other countries.

Conditions were improving, however; by 2011 developed nations allowed duty-free access to their markets on more than 80 percent of the exports from poorer countries.

👁 **Watch** the **Video**: **Modernity's Pollution Problems (Andrew Jenks)** on **MyHistoryLab**

Why is globalization significant? What are its goals?

24.1

24.2

24.3

Hazards in the Trade System

Since the late 1990s, the world trade system has faced two serious malfunctions. The first began in East and Southeast Asia and spread to much of the rest of the world before it was contained by combined action on the part of several nations. The second crisis began in 2008 in the United States.

The countries of East and Southeast Asia experienced extraordinary growth between 1965 and 1996. While the average annual growth of the GNP for the world as a whole during these three decades was 3.1 percent, for East and Southeast Asian nations it averaged 6.8 percent. Then the currency of Thailand fell sharply, as investors recognized that the national economy was not expanding as rapidly as incoming investment and loans. The prices of land and industry on which the loans and investments had been based had been artificially inflated, in a "bubble," and when those prices collapsed and the bubble burst, so did the value of Thai currency. Investments stopped abruptly and loans were recalled, first from Thailand and then from neighboring countries with similar financial problems. In the space of a few months, entire national economies collapsed and others went into a deep recession. Japan, then the world's second largest economy, suffered financial bankruptcies and the devaluation of its stocks and bonds.

What had happened? The Asian economies had taken on more loans, especially short-term loans, than their productivity justified, and as collateral they had presented real estate that was unrealistically overpriced. Beyond this, their internal financial systems were not **transparent**. Corrupt politicians, bureaucrats, bankers, and leaders of organized crime were siphoning off investment capital for their own benefit, and covering up their actions. As investment money poured in from overseas, the funds were misused, pocketed, or poorly invested in speculation, until finally the economies collapsed.

The governments, which had been so helpful as their economies were growing, were now not strong enough to bail out the failing banks and industries. The system of government direction, which had produced economic miracles, now left a wake of recession and depression. The IMF came to the rescue of some of these countries with massive loans, but its very arrival frightened off private investors, who saw this as a sign of economic insolvency. In addition, the IMF seemed more concerned with recovering its loans and investments than with the economic health of the defaulting countries. It stipulated adherence to a collection of measures known as the "**Washington consensus**": opening the borders to international investment (although this was already in place and had caused some of the problems); lowering or removing tariffs against imports; **privatizing** government businesses; reducing government welfare programs; laying off government employees; and devaluing local currency. All these measures are the instruments of classical, conservative economic theory, although many economists argued that such measures had never been rigidly implemented in the economies of wealthy countries. The IMF virtually took over control of the economies of the defaulting countries. It imposed a regimen of economic austerity so severe that it jeopardized the health and welfare of the citizens of the country.

Capital markets had become global, but the national and international institutions for keeping them honest and transparent had not. Some regulation was needed at the international level. After several years of suffering and of economic restructuring, these countries mostly recovered their former economic health, and some, such as South Korea and Singapore, pushed far ahead. Their experience, however, highlighted the danger of unregulated global capital movement and of wishful thinking.

KEY TERMS

transparency The quality of making public and clear the (financial) transactions of government or of private enterprise. Increasingly, transparency is highly valued as a necessity for successful development.

"Washington consensus" A package of economic measures often required of governments by the International Monetary Fund (based in Washington) as a condition for receiving a loan. The measures included: permitting international investment; lowering or removing tariffs; privatizing government businesses; reducing welfare programs; reducing government employment; devaluing local currencies. Together they made government smaller and private business more important.

privatization The act of selling off government-owned enterprises to private businesses.

24.1
24.2
24.3

Why is
globalization
significant? What
are its goals?

A second malfunction began in 2008 in the United States and then spread internationally. Newer financial institutions had been permitted to issue mortgages without the regulations imposed on more traditional savings-and-loan associations. Home-buyers were tempted to take out mortgages larger than they could afford, on terms that they did not always understand, on houses that were overpriced and would soon drop in value. In late 2008, American home-buyers began to default. Inflated home prices began to come down and the companies that had issued the mortgages suffered huge losses. The repossessed homes were worth less than the mortgages.

The losses were spread widely because financial institutions in the US and abroad had bought hundreds of billions of dollars' worth of mortgages as securities. Some weaker banks and financial companies around the world began to fail. In the US, even the largest mortgage security companies of all, "Fannie Mae" (Federal National Mortgage Association) and "Freddy Mac" (Federal Home Loan Mortgage Corporation), which between them held $5.5 *trillion* dollars' worth of mortgages, were in danger of collapsing. These institutions, however, were "too big to be allowed to fail," and the United States government backed them up, first with loan securities, later with billions of dollars of actual loans, and finally by directly taking over the management of the failing companies. The US government provided a loan of $85 billion to AIG, the American International Group, an enormous insurance company that appeared to be on the verge of bankruptcy.

A few days later the government agreed to allocate up to $700 billion to buy up bad debts that were crippling major financial institutions. Otherwise, it appeared that lending for commercial and private purposes was drying up. If that happened, the economy of the United States, and of the world, would come to a halt. In essence, the government of the country that had been the world's leading apostle of private-enterprise capitalism was bailing out some immense corporations and picking up the debts of others to save them from failure.

These government interventions were necessary also to reassure overseas investors, for if the Chinese and the oil-rich states of the Middle East stopped investing in American securities, or, even worse, began to withdraw the trillions of dollars they had already invested, the American economy would collapse. The size of America's financial problems was unprecedented in the history of the world's economy, and sober observers were not sure what would come next.

In the 1990s, the United States had profited from globalization. Despite the complaint of labor unions that jobs were being lost, most Americans regarded globalization very favorably. A very few years later, they were much less sure. The years since 2000 had been difficult. Real wages had gone down, and jobs were less secure, in large part because of overseas competition and the offshoring of America's businesses, relocating them to other countries. America continued to buy overseas goods worth hundreds of billions of dollars more than it sold, running up colossal trade deficits, especially with China. In 2006, the United States ran a trade deficit of $817 billion with the rest of the world. Of that deficit, $233 billion was with China, and $88 billion with Japan. America could afford this only because China and Japan invested their profits back in American financial securities and business enterprises. China was slowly gaining control over these securities and enterprises, as Japan had done in the 1980s and early 1990s. American influence over the global economy diminished as others grew far faster. In 2000, US stock exchanges accounted for about half the value of global stock markets; at the beginning of 2008, they accounted for just 33 percent. Americans had one of the lowest savings rates in the world, and American businesses became increasingly reliant on foreigners for investment. Other countries were now applauding globalization while Americans were beginning to have second thoughts.

By 2013, the American economy and the global economy had largely recovered from the global recession of 2008, but not entirely. The New York Stock Exchange, which had dropped by about 50 percent in value, not only recovered but reached historic new highs. People with substantial investments were doing well. The economy began to grow at about 2 percent per year, and the housing market picked up, so the middle classes were also recovering. But unemployment continued at about 7.5 percent, and, as always, this hit hardest at the young, the minorities, and the least educated. Median household income in the United States declined by approximately 10 percent during the years of the great recession, from 2007 to 2012 (*The Economist*, September 21, 2013, p. 12). In addition, the rising cost of higher education far exceeded the general rate of inflation and threatened to choke off a critical route to upward mobility.

The eurozone, the 17 nations that had committed to the euro as a common currency, also fell into deep recession in 2008, partly because European financial institutions had bought from American banks and institutions securities that were not worth as much as they seemed. The securities were based on packages of mortgages that were priced at more than the value of the property they were written on. The American crisis had crossed the Atlantic.

In addition, European banks and national governments, especially in Greece, Portugal, Spain, Ireland, and Cyprus, had run up debts beyond their capacity to repay. They required help—bailouts—from the economically stronger economies in the eurozone, principally Germany. Some feared that the economically weaker countries of Europe would leave the eurozone. This triggered a major debate over the proper strategy for coping with the problem. Some economists counseled expanding the supply of money in order to stimulate spending and economic growth that would get the economies moving; the United States was implementing this policy in a restrained way. But the German chancellor, Angela Merkel, chose policies of greater austerity, making the struggling banks and nations pay off their debts, and cutting back on excessive government hiring and subsidies to the poor. She was applying a form of the "Washington Consensus." In charge of the most powerful economy in Europe, Merkel had her way. Her policy was buffered, however, by the European Central Bank, which did choose to expand the money supply and ease the austerity program.

The results were mixed. By mid-2013, the largest economies, notably those of Germany and France, were beginning to expand, although only slightly, while the economies of many other states were still contracting and unemployment rates were extremely high: 27 percent in Spain and Greece; 16 percent in Portugal; 12 percent overall. National elections would continue to turn on economic issues of expansion and contraction. But it appeared that the eurozone would stick together as the world's largest economic bloc.

Tax Havens. Globalization provided opportunities for new forms of international link, and some small nations—including the Cayman Islands, Bermuda, and Ireland—offered low tax rates to attract international businesses to register their offices there. These **tax havens** gained revenue without having to provide substantial services. The losers in this arrangement were the actual home offices of these companies; they lost substantial tax receipts. They complained, with reason, that they were supplying services to the companies in their principal places of business, but losing revenues to the tax havens in which they registered.

On Social Revolution

24.2 What have been the key social revolutions of the early twenty-first century?

In the late twentieth and early twenty-first centuries, nationalism, regionalism, and transnationalism all flowered anew, often pulling in contradictory directions. Massive new waves of immigration tested the abilities of governments around the globe to

KEY TERM

tax havens Legal jurisdictions offering low rates of tax to attract the offices of international businesses. While most of the business is actually done elsewhere, the tax haven provides a legal means to pay low taxes. The loser is the location in which the company does most of its business but pays little of its taxes.

24.1

24.2

24.3

What have been
the key social
revolutions of the
early twenty-first
century?

formulate effective policies. The feminist movement diversified as it reached around
the world. Gays and lesbians won increasing public acceptance, including the right
to marry in many nations. National struggles against racism advanced, for instance
in South Africa, aided by pressure from the international community. In a more conservative vein, widespread concern arose that local cultures might lose their integrity,
overwhelmed by larger, more powerful waves of global culture. This fear frequently
inspired cultural backlash.

📖 **Read** the **Document**: Towards a Green Europe, Towards a Green World on **MyHistoryLab**

Nationalism

In 1990, nationalism seemed to be on its way out. Communication, transportation,
business corporations, and NGOs all functioned transnationally. The nation seemed
less relevant with each passing year. As the future unfolded, however, nationalism
staged a comeback.

Already in 1990 Estonia and Lithuania declared their national independence,
helping to precipitate the dissolution of the USSR. Latvia, Russia, Ukraine, and
Belarus also soon declared theirs. The remaining 15 Soviet republics became independent states at the end of 1991 when the Soviet Union dissolved. Within Russia
itself, some citizens of the predominantly Muslim state of Chechnya began guerrilla
warfare in hopes of becoming an independent republic. Central European nations,
including Poland, Hungary, Bulgaria, and Romania, were equally jealous of their

Antiwar protesters march along Piccadilly, central London, 2004. Up to 100,000 people from across
the United Kingdom attended the march and rally, calling for troops to be removed from Iraq. The
Campaign for Nuclear Disarmament, the Stop the War Coalition, and the Muslim Association of Britain
organized the event. Hundreds of thousands also marched in Rome, New York, and other major cities
worldwide.

24.1

24.2

24.3

What have been
the key social
revolutions of the
early twenty-first
century?

independence. Czechoslovakia divided into two in 1993, as political leaders of both the Czech Republic and Slovakia chose to separate peacefully into two more homogeneous states, rather than continue as a single ethnically mixed one. The creation of these newly independent nations increased UN membership from 166 in 1991 to 193 in 2011. Moving in a reverse direction, East and West Germany reunited in 1990 after 45 years of Cold War division.

During the administration of President George W. Bush, especially, unilateralist nationalism was alive and well in the United States. America waged war against Iraq in 2003, despite massive antiwar protests around the world (and at home), and it did not join in several widely accepted international agreements, such as the Kyoto Protocol against global warming, and the establishment of the International Criminal Court in The Hague. Elsewhere, three states asserted their importance by testing nuclear weapons—India and Pakistan in 1998 and North Korea, on a more rudimentary level, in 2006. In 2013, Iran seemed poised to join this nuclear club, despite international opposition and sanctions.

As some nations reveled in the sovereignty of their already independent existence, other groups asserted their right to revolt, to free themselves from their current rulers, and to establish new independent states of their own. In the chapter entitled "Contemporary History: Evolution, Settlements, Politics, and Religion" we discussed the violent and bloody break-up of Yugoslavia and the continuing struggle of Chechnyans for independence from Russia and of Uighurs and Tibetans for independence from China. Other separatist movements included Basques in the north of Spain; Kurds in the north of Iraq, sometimes joined by other Kurds just across the borders in neighboring Turkey, Iran, and Syria; Tamils in Sri Lanka; French-speaking Canadians; and both the French-speaking Walloons and the Dutch-speaking Flemish in Belgium. The "host" countries feared the possibility of secession, and in many cases, they granted at least some degree of autonomy within the larger state.

Sometimes the desire for nationhood could lead to creative compromise, as in Northern Ireland. For decades the province was torn by violence between Protestants, most of them in favor of continued union with Great Britain, and Roman Catholics, who largely favored the creation of an independent Irish state. But in 2005 the Irish Republican Army, which had led the armed resistance to British rule, put down its arms, opening the way to power sharing in the elections of 2007. Northern Ireland became relatively peaceful with the legal agreement that "it is the birthright of all the people of Northern Ireland to identify themselves and be accepted as Irish or British, or both, as they may so choose." Scottish nationalists, more peacefully, also demanded greater autonomy from Britain. A Scottish parliament was created in 1999, with more control over Scotland's budget and the promise of a future vote on independence.

Many separatist movements grew up in Africa, where the borders that had been created by European colonial powers did not correspond to cultural realities on the ground. At independence in 1960, the province of Katanga broke away from the Congo, although it was forced back in 1963 through military force. The Igbo people in eastern Nigeria fought a failed war for an independent state for three years, 1967–70. More recently, Sudan waged devastating war against the breakaway region of Darfur. A peace agreement signed in 2006 was breached after 2010, and warfare continued. When South Sudan later demanded its independence, following two civil wars, that new state did emerge in 2011 and became the 193rd member of the UN. Battles for political power often included competition among religious groups. This amalgam of political and religious struggle appeared in Nigeria and Chad (as we saw in the previous chapter) and in Mali and Mauritania.

The Palestinian–Israeli Conflict. In 2013, Palestinians living under Israeli occupation in the West Bank of the Jordan River, and under Israeli domination in the Gaza Strip, continued to argue, and frequently to fight, for their own independent state. Their grievances went back to 1948, when the UN partitioned Palestine into two areas, one

What have been
the key social
revolutions of the
early twenty-first
century?

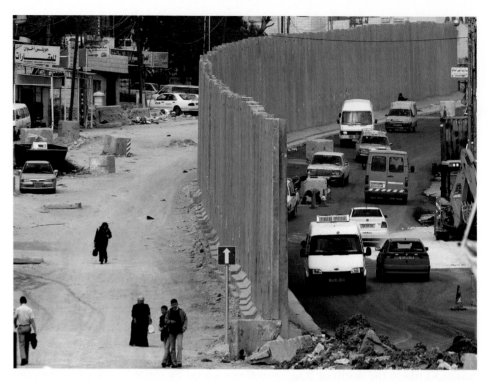

The Israeli–Palestinian separation wall. Construction of this wall began in 2002. Israelis claim to have
built it to stop terrorists from entering Israel, and call it a security fence; Palestinians say that Israelis built
it as a land-grab and an effort to separate Palestinians from their own lands, and call it an apartheid wall.
The concrete barrier, approximately 20 feet high, makes clear the line of separation between Israel and
the Palestinian territories, but it often runs on the Palestinian side of the prewar border of 1967. Debates
over the appropriateness of the wall therefore concern not only the reasons for its existence, but also its
geographical placement.

for Jews—which became the State of Israel—the other for Arabs, who did not accept
the partition. (See "The Middle East Breaks Free" in the chapter entitled "Cold War,
New Nations, and Revolt Against Authority.")

Continued attempts to resolve the conflict between the two sides over land and
sovereignty—often brokered by outside political groups—have thus far failed.
Extremists, although a minority on each side, have so far won the day. On the Israeli
side, "settlers" from Israel moved onto the lands of the West Bank and Gaza with
the support of the Israeli government, despite the ruling of the UN that occupation
of conquered lands is illegal. By 2013, about 200,000 settlers had staked out homes
in parts of Jerusalem that had been Arab, and another 350,000 had built homes in
other parts of the West Bank. The settlers have dominated these lands through often
inhumane treatment of their Arab owners. In 1987 and again in 2000, Palestinians
launched resistance movements, called **intifadas**, against Israeli occupation. Some
protested peacefully, some fired crude rockets into Israel from Gaza and Lebanon,
and a few suicide bombers delivered and detonated bombs to attack Israelis. These
tactics brought worldwide attention to Palestinian claims, but they often alienated
potential allies and certainly hardened the resistance of the Israelis.

Political scientist Samuel Huntington argued in 1996 that the world was wit-
nessing what he called a "clash of civilizations" among the major religious-cultural
groupings of the world: Christian, Muslim, Chinese, Japanese, and Indian. Martha
Nussbaum's book *The Clash Within: Democracy, Religious Violence, and India's Future*
(2007) argued, on the contrary, that some of the most difficult political struggles today
are not between opposing civilizations, but rather between the extremists and the
moderates on each side. The moderates, if left alone, might be able to find peaceful

KEY TERM

intifada Colloquial Arabic:
the act of shaking off; uprising,
rebellion.

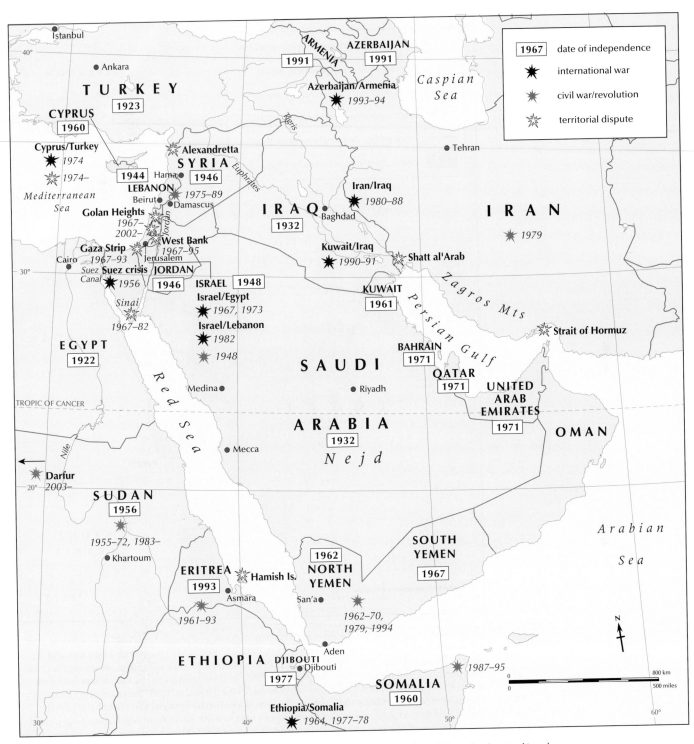

The Middle East since 1945. The presence of oil and gas reserves, the establishment of a Jewish homeland state of Israel in Palestine (1948), the intervention of outside states, and the emergence of militant, armed, political Islam have stirred the region. In addition to Arab–Israeli confrontation, an eight-year conflict between Iran and Iraq, a war over Iraq's invasion of Kuwait, the American invasion of Iraq in 2003, and civil war and revolution have kept the region in turmoil.

24.1

24.2

24.3

What have been the key social revolutions of the early twenty-first century?

compromise, but the extremists want victory and they sabotage attempts at compromise. This analysis holds especially clearly for the Israeli–Palestinian deadlock, in which the moderates on both sides appear to be more or less in agreement on a two-state solution, with Israel and Palestine existing side by side in peace, while

What have been
the key social
revolutions of the
early twenty-first
century?

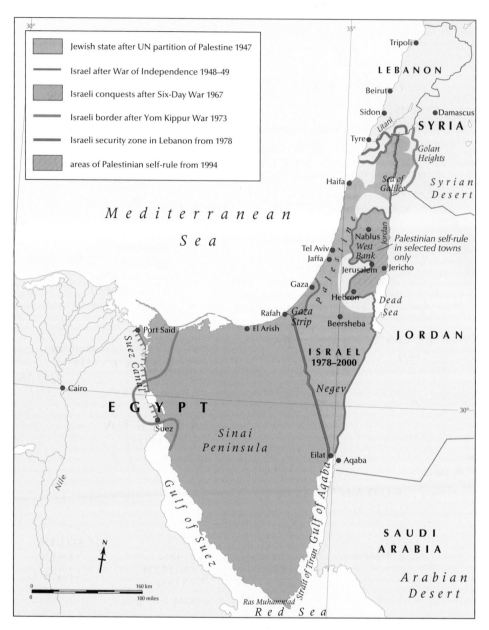

Israel and its neighbors. The creation, with Western support, of a Jewish homeland in Palestine in 1947 occurred at a time of increasing Arab nationalism. Israel's birth in 1948 was attended by a war, and more followed in 1956, 1967, 1973, and 1982. Peace treaties exist only with Egypt, which regained the Sinai peninsula, and Jordan (1994). Beginning in 1987, an intifada (uprising) by Palestinians forced more attention on Israeli–Palestinian relations—an extremely vexed issue. In 1993, the Palestinian Liberation Organization and Israel began negotiations that would return land to Palestinian control and perhaps lead to a Palestinian state, while recognizing Israel's right to exist. So far these negotiations have proved fruitless; a second intifada began in 2000. Meanwhile some 550,000 Jewish settlers have established homes in East Jerusalem and other sectors of the occupied West Bank, complicating any efforts to trade land for peace.

extremists on each side reject such compromise. Israeli and Arab leaders who sought peace were assassinated: Anwar Sadat, president of Egypt, in 1981; Yitzhak Rabin, prime minister of Israel, in 1995.

📖 **Read** the **Document: Israel-PLO Declaration of Principles on Interim Self-Government Arrangements (1993)** on **MyHistoryLab**

The Arab Spring

24.1

24.2

24.3

What have been the key social revolutions of the early twenty-first century?

On December 17, 2010, a street vendor in southern Tunisia, Mohamed Bouazizi, insulted by a local government official, set himself on fire in protest against government dictatorship, stunted economic prospects, and the harassment of ordinary citizens like himself. His protest ignited a fire that spread across much of the Arab world, where political power and wealth were held narrowly by a few families; where no real democracy was allowed; and where unemployment among those under the age of 30 ran as high as 60 percent. In most of these countries an unresolved religious-cultural struggle simmered below the surface between those who wanted somewhat more secular governments and those who wanted Islam to have a greater role in public life and government.

Mass protests spread across Tunisia until, in mid-January 2011, Zine El Abidine Ben Ali, president of Tunisia for 23 years, fled the country. Protests spread to Egypt, the most populous (85 million people) and culturally central of the Arab states. By February 12, the Egyptian president, Hosni Mubarak, agreed to give up power after 30 years of rule. Optimistic and imaginative journalists began to call these revolts "the Arab Spring," especially once they spread to Bahrain, Libya, Syria, and Yemen.

Excited and inspired by the popular revolts, people in the United States and Western Europe looked forward to the overthrow of the dictatorial governments that ruled most of the 19 countries of the Arab world, with their total population of some 350 million people. In fact, none of the revolts proved entirely successful. The most violent, the revolt in Syria, led to a civil war that was still continuing in 2013, with some 100,000 Syrians dead and one to two million refugees, mostly in nearby countries. In Egypt, the overthrow of Mubarak led to elections in which the Muslim Brotherhood, a previously banned religion-based party, came to power. Its emphasis

"Arab Spring" in Tahrir Square, Cairo, 2011. In December 2010, mass protests began against the dictatorial government of Tunisia. A month later the president resigned. Protests spread to other Arab states with oppressive governments in North Africa, the Gulf, and western Asia. Egyptians mounted the largest of the protests, centering on Tahrir Square in central Cairo. The president resigned and elections were held, but when the winners, the Muslim Brotherhood, appeared to exclude other representatives, the military ousted them, promising new elections. In Syria, the government held its ground and peaceful protests turned violent. The country dissolved in civil war with 100,000 people killed. "The Arab Spring," begun in hopes of democracy and economic progress, had spun out of control.

SOURCE

The "Arab Spring": First Journalistic Accounts

Journalism is sometimes called "the first draft of history." Here we look at four accounts of the "Arab Spring," and see how interpretation differs from one to the next. Part of the change comes from the different points of view of the writers; part from changes in the events that unfold.

1. Marc Lynch, "Obama's Arab Spring?," *Foreign Policy: The Middle East Channel*, 6 January 2011

> I don't expect these protests to bring down any regimes, but really who knows? It's an unpredictable moment. Many of these regimes are led by aging, fading leaders such as Hosni Mubarak and Zine El Abidine Ben Ali who could pass from the scene in a heartbeat—literally. Nor do I particularly know what to recommend that the Obama administration do. …What we are now seeing is the fruit of the failure to promote meaningful reform in the past, but that doesn't mean that doing so now would meet the challenge …
>
> Most everybody is carefully watching everyone else to see what's going to happen, with news traveling across borders and within countries through an ever-growing role for social media layered on top of (not replacing) satellite television and existing networks. I'm not hugely optimistic that we will see real change, given the power of these authoritarian regimes and their record of resilience. But still … interesting times.

2. Scott Peterson, "Egypt's Revolution Redefines What's Possible in the Arab World," *Christian Science Monitor*, February 11, 2011, http://www.csmonitor.com/World/Middle-East/2011/0211/Egypt-s-revolution-redefines-what-s-possible-in-the-Arab-world (accessed October 2013)

> The collapse in Egypt took just 18 days of bold protest, inspired by the overthrow of Tunisia's long-standing strongman just weeks before. For Arabs used to a heavy hand and little hope, Egypt's revolution has redefined the possible, before their very eyes …
>
> "On the psychological and symbolic level, it is a shattering moment," says Fawaz Gerges, director of the Middle East Centre at the London School of Economics. "Remember that Mubarak was the public face of political authoritarianism in the Arab world. He had built one of the most feared security apparatuses, employing five million personnel. … The model is millions of young Arabs, calling for open societies, for freedom, for transparent elections, for their voices to be heard … They have really Arabized democracy, and that is why it is such a powerful thing.

3. Susanne Koelbl, "It Will Not Stop: Syrian Uprising Continues Despite Crackdown," *Der Spiegel*, March 28, 2011, translated from the German by Josh Ward, http://www.spiegel.de/international/world/it-will-not-stop-syrian-uprising-continues-despite-crackdown-a-753517-druck.html (accessed October 2013)

> Now tightly controlled Syria has become the latest flashpoint for pro-democracy protests that have swept large parts of North Africa and the Middle East. Syria, of all places, Israel's autocratically ruled neighbor and a potential peace partner. A Syria that is an ally of Iran and funder of the Hezbollah militants in Lebanon. And also a country accused by United Nations atomic inspectors of trying to assemble a nuclear weapons program with North Korean assistance. But it is also the Syria that, at least in the eyes of the West, is a pivotal player in the region, a country leaders would like to woo away from the axis of hard-line states in the region.
>
> … the uprising in Syria broke out spontaneously, as happened in Tunisia months before. The uprising is spearheaded by Sunni tribal leaders from a region bordering Jordan, people who were minor political players in the past and considered loyal to the government.

4. Joseph Massad, Associate Professor of Modern Arab Politics and Intellectual History at Columbia University, "The 'Arab Spring' and Other American Seasons," *Al Jazeera* website, August 29, 2012, http://www.aljazeera.com/indepth/opinion/2012/08/201282972539153865.html (accessed October 2013)

> While the US and western media have tried to champion the professional, managerial and upper middle class elements that support neoliberal economics …, little attention has been paid to the massive strikes, slowdowns, work stoppages, marches, rallies and confrontations with police and army soldiers by workers, teachers, peasants and the unemployed poor across all five countries.
>
> The uprisings in Egypt and across the Arab world consist of wide class-coalitions, with differing and contradictory demands being advanced by the various classes: the upper-middle class professionals and executives want western-style rights to advance their class interests, while the lower classes, the workers, the teachers, the peasants and the impoverished urban and rural classes want both Soviet- and western-style [economic and political] rights.

- Use these four articles, plus other materials in this textbook, to present an integrated account of the first 20 months of the "Arab Spring."
- The articles suggest different leaders of the revolt at different times and in different places. Compare and contrast them.
- Some authors cite social media as important contributors to the revolts; others seem to give greater credit to existing organizations on the ground. Compare, contrast, and comment.
- What has happened to the "Arab Spring" subsequent to the events recorded here?

on religion in government alienated many, especially in the military, and within a year the army deposed the elected government, leading to new protests and military reprisals. Battles between the military and Muslim Brotherhood protesters left more than 1,000 people dead and the leadership of the Brotherhood in jail. Some journalists began to write of an "Arab Winter."

Gender Issues

Gender relationships within the family were transformed in the second half of the twentieth century. Marriage rates declined as more couples chose to live without a formal ceremony and other people chose not to pair off at all. Parents opted to have their children later in life, and to have fewer of them. Apart from the immediate post-World War II baby boom, birth rates generally declined throughout the world, including in majority-Catholic Latin America, majority-Hindu India, and the majority-Islamic Arab countries. Throughout the world, gender definitions—the expectation of the roles that men and women would fulfill—changed markedly, although it changed differently for different groups of women and men. The feminist movement, never monolithic, splintered into far more groups than ever before. In the Western world, some women wanted to retain, or reclaim, the lives of mothers and housewives, while others wanted to assert their right to a creative career. Many found themselves working outside the home because they, and their families, needed the money. The decisions by governments and employers on whether or not to provide maternity leave and child-care affected women's opportunities, and these issues became important targets of feminist campaigns.

One useful index of gender equality was the proportion of women elected to national government. According to statistics gathered by the Interparliamentary Union, the global average of seats in national governments held by women was nearly 21 percent in 2013. The variation ran from Rwanda with 56 percent, Andorra with 50 percent, and Cuba with 49 percent, to Iran with 3 percent, Egypt with 2 percent, and Qatar with none. On the plus side, in Saudi Arabia, where there had been no women in government, thanks to a royal decree in 2011 women held nearly 20 percent of seats in the consultative assembly in 2013. The United States ranked 77th in proportion of women in national government, with just under 18 percent (http://www.ipu.org/wmn-e/world.htm [accessed October 2013]).

A series of conferences on women hosted by the UN provided a forum for exploring gender issues from an international perspective. The first, in Mexico City in 1975, inaugurated the UN Decade for Women. Five years later a conference in Copenhagen marked the midpoint, and a decade-closing conference was held in Nairobi in 1985. Another conference followed in Beijing in 1995. These conferences led to commitments by the overwhelming majority of member nations to gathering data on women, helping to end their political and economic "invisibility," and working harder to insure their education, health, and employment was on an equal basis with those of men.

In addition to the governments, thousands of representatives of NGOs from around the world also participated. These representatives began to network, to seek solidarity, and to address problems they saw as common, sometimes for the first time. For example, many protested that the best new jobs in new fields went mostly to men. African representatives noted that when agriculture had been oriented to subsistence farming, to feed individual families, women played a major role, but when agriculture became commercialized as a money-making occupation, women were pushed out.

Sometimes new programs were created. Several different groups that had begun to extend **micro-finance** to women, providing them with small loans to start their own small businesses, began to share ideas for cooperation. The **micro-credit** movement, now worldwide, has usually been most attractive to and widespread among

KEY TERM

micro-finance or **micro-credit** The provision of very small loans, often equivalent to US$100 or even less, to very small-scale businessmen and women, people who would not usually have access to conventional commercial bank loans, because the banks do not deal in such small amounts, and because they would not usually recognize the relatively poor borrowers as "bankable." The loans are usually at below market rates, and are usually secured by the common bond among groups of borrowers that they will stand guaranty for one another.

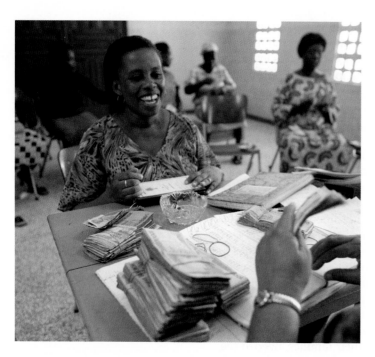

Micro-lending in Africa. Micro-lending, providing very small sums of money as business loans to relatively poor people, has proved very effective in helping the borrowers to start very small enterprises and thus to escape from poverty. Micro-lending has been especially effective with poor women, perhaps because they have been almost completely excluded from normal banking channels, perhaps because they have been especially effective at banding together to guarantee one another's loans, and thus secure lower interest rates. Here, members of Opportunity International's "Blessed Mary" Trust Group in Accra, Ghana, hold one of their weekly meetings to repay their loans and support one another.

24.1

24.2 What have been
the key social
24.3 revolutions of the
early twenty-first
century?

women, perhaps because they have had the most difficulty in accessing loans through normal commercial banks, and because they have proved especially creative and responsible in bonding together to insure one another's loans, and thus to secure lower interest rates. Muhammad Yunus of Bangladesh won the Nobel Peace Prize in 2006 for his establishment in 1976 of the Grameen Bank, the world's leading micro-lender, with 8.3 million borrowers (2011), about 96 percent of them women. Women's World Banking, headquartered in New York City, brings together professionals from 39 leading micro-finance institutions from 28 countries to create new credit, savings, and insurance products specifically designed for the unique needs of women. At present WWB claims that 14 million women worldwide benefit from their professional interventions.

Reproductive rights for women, and health standards for women and children, became another focus. India and China mounted campaigns against the abortion or infanticide of unwanted female babies, a difficult struggle against the deeply rooted preference for male children. In the Islamic world, many women's groups urged reinterpreting the Quran to discover and proclaim the profeminist viewpoints that can be found within the sacred scripture. Other Muslim women, however, proclaimed that in their view the classic Islamic texts were irreconcilably antifeminist and antidemocratic. For them, feminists would have to proceed in opposition to, rather than with the support of, the teachings of the Quran. In the United States, an increasing number of politicians at the state and national levels worked to reduce women's access to abortion, birth control, and other health care. Evangelical Christians usually supported these restrictions.

Sharp differences also emerged in prioritizing women's goals. Often women in developed, richer countries stressed the need for opening new categories of job, equal pay for equal work, child-care, and reproductive freedom of choice. In less wealthy nations, the issues might be the right to own property, to be free from the control of male relatives, and to have equal access to food, schooling, and medical care. Many third-world women felt that first-world women chose to concentrate on the wrong issues. Too often first-world women talked about the evils of veiling and of female genital mutilation (clitoridectomy, the surgical removal of the clitoris), as if third-world women had to be saved from the evils of their own societies. Many women from poorer countries believed that the most important problems were structural issues in the global economy and politics that kept them poor.

Gay Rights. Homosexuality, too, was seen differently in different locations. In many parts of the world, laws against it were abolished. Armed forces accepted "out" gays and lesbians, as did some national intelligence agencies that previously feared that gay and lesbian operatives would be subject to blackmail. Some governments in North America and Europe legalized same-sex marriage: the Netherlands was the first, in 2001, followed by Belgium, Canada, Norway, South Africa, and Spain. In the United States, in 2013, more than a dozen states recognized same-sex marriage. Many others, and some nations, such as Britain, Croatia, and Mexico, created legal unions for same-sex couples. On the other hand, some nations continued to pronounce homosexuality a shameful, if not sinful, orientation. In 2013, the president of

Russia signed a law authorizing the police to detain for up to 14 days any tourists or foreign nationals they suspect of being homosexual or "pro-gay."

24.1

What have been the key social revolutions of the early twenty-first century?

24.2

24.3

Racial and Caste Equality

Racism, like gender discrimination, seemed to be generally in retreat. South Africa's achievement in ridding itself of apartheid policies, through peaceful means, represented an astonishing victory. The quiet revolution of low castes and ex-untouchables in India drew less attention, but affected far more people. And in the United States, Barack Obama's election in 2008 as the first African-American president appeared as a triumph of progress in American race relations, although not as evidence of a post-racial society.

Apartheid in South Africa. Apartheid (segregation of the races) was established by law in South Africa in 1948. About 20 percent of the population was white, descended from Dutch and British settlers, and this minority controlled the government, most of the productive farmland, all industry, and the upper reaches of the economy. Black Africans had no political freedoms and were subject to severe restrictions on where they could live, work, and study.

Black African frustration, resentment, and anger at first expressed itself principally through independent Ethiopian churches as early as the 1870s and 1880s. The African National Congress (ANC) formed in 1912 as a constitutional party of protest, and grew steadily over several decades. In 1960, in the town of Sharpeville, the government confronted unarmed political protesters, massacring 69 black Africans and wounding many others. The ANC shifted to strikes and armed protests, although it renounced attacks on people, limiting itself to sabotage of property. The South African government continued to crack down. The ANC leader, Nelson Mandela (1918–2013), a brilliant and charismatic lawyer, was arrested, charged with plotting to overthrow the government, and eventually sentenced to life in prison. At his trial in 1964, Mandela declared his commitment to his country and his vision for its future:

I have fought against white domination. I have cherished the ideal of a democratic and free society in which all persons live together in harmony and with equal opportunities. It is an ideal which I hope to live for and to achieve. But if needs be, it is an ideal for which I am prepared to die. (Edelstein, p. 73)

As Zambia and Zimbabwe, Angola and Mozambique won independence and majority rule in the 1960s and 1970s, world attention focused on South Africa as the last bastion of white, minority rule. In addition, the newly independent nations bordering South Africa sheltered members of the ANC and other movements for majority rule, including some dedicated to guerrilla warfare. Many nations gradually adopted sanctions against South Africa, restricting or stopping trade; "disinvesting" or withdrawing economic investments; and ending diplomatic, cultural, and sports exchanges. Enforcing the sanctions proved difficult. Gradually, however, they did exact their toll. South Africa became a pariah nation.

In 1976, protests against government educational policy began in Soweto, a black township outside Pretoria, and led to nationwide riots in which 600 people were killed. Some liberalization was granted: black labor unions were legalized, the prohibition on interracial sex was abolished, and segregation in public transportation ended. Finally, in 1990, the new government of President F.W. de Klerk (b. 1936) lifted its ban against the ANC and freed Nelson Mandela. He had spent 27 years in prison. De Klerk's National Party repealed apartheid laws and began wary and difficult negotiations with the ANC for transition to majority rule. In 1993, Mandela was awarded the Nobel Peace Prize, and in the South African elections in 1994, open

24.1

24.2   What have been
        the key social
24.3   revolutions of the
        early twenty-first
        century?

equally to all races on the principle of one person, one vote, the ANC won 62 percent of the vote. Mandela was elected president.

📖 Read the Document: **A Liberal White Journalist on Apartheid (1970s–1980s)** on **MyHistoryLab**

📖 Read the Document: **Kwame Nkrumah on African Unity (1960s)** on **MyHistoryLab**

The Truth and Reconciliation Commission. South Africans confronted the problem of establishing a new political and cultural identity for themselves after the collapse of apartheid government. For the first time in their history, the blacks of South Africa counted as political equals to the whites. But unlike many other colonial situations in which most white colonizers left the newly independent colony, in South Africa the whites had been residents for centuries. This was their home, and most of them had no intention of leaving. Most had no other home to which to go. Thus 32 million mostly impoverished and until recently suppressed and persecuted blacks and eight million mostly wealthy and highly privileged whites had to find new ways of getting on. One of their highly imaginative solutions was the Truth and Reconciliation Commission, which functioned from 1996 to 1998 in an effort to clear the air for further interracial cooperation in the future.

The commission was initiated by President Mandela and chaired by Archbishop Desmond Tutu (b. 1931), the head of the Anglican Church in South Africa. The goal of the commission was to bring the peoples of South Africa together by exposing the bitter and violent events of the past and, through that exposure, enabling all its peoples to see themselves as part of a single nation. The commission heard cases of some 20,000 people who had suffered gross human-rights violations from the time of the Sharpeville massacre in 1960 until the first democratic election in 1994.

Thousands of people from all corners of the country stepped forward to testify. Thousands were granted some measure of reparation from the state treasury. Most

A democratic dawn for South Africa. South African president Nelson Mandela and second deputy president F.W. de Klerk address a huge crowd in front of the Union Building in Pretoria, after the inauguration ceremony on May 10, 1994. Only a few years earlier it would have been inconceivable that the imprisoned Mandela could ever attain high office in a country so firmly wedded to the policy of apartheid.

24.1

24.2

24.3

What have been
the key social
revolutions of the
early twenty-first
century?

whites, unable to state publicly that they had benefited from apartheid, did not initiate the act of admitting their crimes. Some did, however, helping in the process of reconciliation. Many others came because accusations of criminal activity had been brought against them; amnesty could be granted to those who could demonstrate that they were carrying out the political policies of the state, rather than their own agendas, and were acting without sadism. In his concluding remarks, Archbishop Tutu proclaimed the commission an exemplary success in healing South Africa's racial wounds and facilitating the emotional unification of the country and a new national identity:

> We have been privileged to help to heal a wounded people … When we look around us at some of the conflict areas of the world, it becomes increasingly clear that there

HOW DO WE KNOW?

South Africa's Truth and Reconciliation Commission

Many observers of the commission's proceedings raised serious criticisms. Some felt that the granting of amnesty came too easily to defendants in these noncriminal proceedings. Defendants could plead that they were simply following the orders of the government and that they had not acted sadistically, and receive amnesty. Dirk Coetzee, first commander of a counterinsurgency unit, and his team were convicted in criminal court for the murder of Griffiths Mxenge, a civil-rights lawyer, but subsequently the commission granted them amnesty because they were simply carrying out their duties as policemen engaged in the government's struggle against the liberation movement. Griffiths' brother was disgusted with this decision for amnesty: "My main objection is that amnesty promotes the interests of the perpetrators, as once they are granted amnesty they are not criminally liable and no civil action can be instituted against [them], and that is totally against the interests of the victims. It is totally unjust" (cited in Edelstein, p. 113). On the other hand, Josephine Msweli was more forgiving of the men who killed her sons:

> I want the people who killed my sons to come forward because this is a time for reconciliation. I want to forgive them and I also have a bit of my mind to tell them. I would be happy if they could come before me because I don't have [my] sons today … I want to speak to them before I forgive them. I want them to tell me who sent them to come and kill my sons. Maybe they are my enemies, maybe they are not. So I want to establish as to who they are and why they did what they did. (cited in Edelstein, p. 154)

One member of the commission, Pumla Gobodo-Madikizela, a clinical psychologist, reaffirmed the healing power of public disclosure by victim and perpetrator alike: "If a memory is kept alive in order to transcend hateful emotions, to free oneself or one's society from the burden of hatred, then remembering has the power to heal" (cited in Edelstein, p. 30). She lamented, however, the inability of most whites, despite the commission, to recognize that they had benefitted from the general violence of the system of inequality imposed by apartheid.

Despite its shortcomings, the commission brought truth to light, and most commentators believed that this truth allowed purification of the body politic. It allowed the true identity of the old state to be exposed so that a new identity could be formed.

Michael Ignatieff, director of the Carr Center for Human Rights Policy at the Kennedy School of Government, Harvard University, wrote: "Any society that allows its torturers to retire with medals and pensions inevitably pays the price. The price of lies is immobilized nostalgia for tyranny … you cannot create a culture of freedom unless you eliminate a specific range of impermissible lies … The Truth Commission had rendered some lies about the past simply impossible to repeat" (cited in Edelstein, pp. 20–21). Ignatieff concluded that the Truth and Reconciliation Commission made it impossible for white South Africans to deny the violence of their society. They could no longer deflect blame by saying that any problems were caused by only a few rotten apples, and that those were the exceptions rather than the rule. What the TRC uncovered was something very different indeed: "Not a few bad apples, not a few bad cops … but a system, a culture, a way of life that was organized around contempt and violence for other human beings. The truth, the cold core, of apartheid was the Sanlam building in Port Elizabeth where they threw you against radiators and beat you with wet towels. Every South African citizen was contaminated by the degradation, that deadness, that offence against the spirit" (cited in Edelstein, p. 21).

Knowing the painful truth, however, would ultimately set the society free.

- President Nelson Mandela inspired the creation of the commission and Archbishop Desmond Tutu was its chairman. Based on the concept and workings of the commission, how would you characterize the politics and ethics of these two men?
- How would you interpret the key goals of the commission? Were they realistic? Do you think they correspond to human nature as you understand it?
- Ignatieff argues that torture and violence against citizens were not an aberration caused by "a few rotten apples," but by "a system, a culture, a way of life that was organized around contempt and violence for other human beings." To what extent do you think his rhetoric and his description of consequences mirror the debate about torture carried out by Americans in the Abu Ghraib prison, and at the Guantanamo Bay detention camp, during and after the Iraq war?

24.1
24.2
24.3

What have been the key social revolutions of the early twenty-first century?

First-time voters, South Africa, 1994. Residents of the Western Transvaal queue to vote for the first time in South Africa's multiracial elections in 1994. After years of apartheid and oppression, black South Africans showed a respect and devotion to their new democracy that inspired citizens of democracies around the world who often took for granted their own right to vote and to participate in governance.

is not much of a future for them without forgiveness, without reconciliation. God has blessed us richly so that we might be a blessing to others. Quite improbably, we as South Africans have become a beacon of hope to others locked in deadly conflict that peace, that a just resolution, is possible. If it could happen in South Africa, then it can certainly happen anywhere else. Such is the exquisite divine sense of humor. (http://www.info.gov.za/otherdocs/2003/trc/foreword.pdf [accessed October 2013])

India's Social Revolution: The Mandal Commission. A similar movement against caste discrimination created a social revolution in India that transformed the status of tens of millions of people of the lowest rank, and of many more just somewhat above them. The Mandal Commission, named for its chairman, B.P. Mandal, was established in 1979 to deal with an economic and social problem that had bedeviled Indian politics for decades: caste discrimination. Many observers have compared caste discrimination to race discrimination, noting that a person's caste is an identity that comes by birth and situates him or her in hierarchical relation to members of other castes. Caste is not racial, and there are thousands of castes throughout India, so caste identification is less clear-cut than racial identity has been in the United States.

Those at the very bottom of the caste hierarchy, formerly called "untouchables" because they were forbidden to come into physical contact with upper-caste people, and now usually referred to as *dalits* ("oppressed people") were recognized almost universally as disadvantaged. These former untouchables were given special "reservations" or minimum quotas in public positions. This affirmative action program affected the fields of government jobs, elected offices, and education, and covered 15 percent of the population. Tribals, now more frequently called *adivasis*, or original settlers, usually lived in remote hilly and mountainous regions, outside the Hindu heartland and usually outside Hinduism. They formed about seven percent of the population and they also received preferential benefits, protected by India's constitution.

24.1

What have been
the key social
revolutions of the
early twenty-first
century?

24.2

24.3

The next levels up, usually referred to as the Other Backward Classes (OBCs), had also suffered severe discrimination on the basis of caste, although not quite so extreme. In 1980 the Mandal Commission's report argued that OBCs constituted about 52 percent of the nation's population and recommended that 27 percent of the positions in the central administration and in the public sector should be reserved for them. Although the "C" in OBC officially referred to class rather than caste, the commission argued that caste was the most significant indicator of class. The commission identified some 3,743 castes as OBCs and recommended them for benefits.

The road to implementation was often blocked by mass protests and riots by the upper castes. New political parties began to form around the issue of reservations, sometimes led by OBCs themselves, particularly at the state level, and sometimes by upper castes who were committed to ideals of equality, or who were seeking additional votes for themselves, or both.

In 1990, India's prime minister, V.P. Singh, brought the issue to a head by implementing the Mandal Commission's recommendations nationally. This and other of his reformist programs alienated many upper-class and upper-caste people, and Singh was forced from office in 1991. Nevertheless, a transformation was taking place. In the major north Indian states, from 1984 to 1999, the percentage of upper castes elected to the national parliament dropped by a third, from 47 percent to 31 percent, while the percentage of OBCs doubled, from 11 percent to 22 percent. India's two largest states, Uttar Pradesh and Bihar, were ruled by OBC parties headed by OBC leaders. Singh reflected, "A silent transfer of power is taking place in social terms" (Jaffrelot, p. 139).

Meanwhile, a protest movement, often violent, was taking root among the *adivasis* in the hilly, remote areas of India's eastern states. Named for the village of Naxalbari, where similar protests began, **naxalites** protested the displacement of *adivasis*

Medha Patkar heads protest against the Narmada River dam project, India, 2007. Economic "development" pushed hard against some of India's weakest communities. Private commercial development of natural resources and government dams for hydro-electric power and irrigation displaced them from heretofore-remote hilly areas of India's interior. They lost their homes, their lands, and their traditional occupations; their compensation was minimal. Beginning in the 1960s they began to fight back through "Naxalite" organizations in the eastern hills, and anti-dam protests in the west. Medha Patkar became the face of the movement against the dam and later, as displacement appeared inevitable, for appropriate compensation.

KEY TERM

naxalites A term used in India to designate rebels against the state or against exploitative businesses. Derived from the village of Naxalbari, where such rebellions began, they were at first organized by communist parties, but later became more often rebellions of exploited tribal peoples in remote areas.

What have been
the key social
revolutions of the
early twenty-first
century?

from their home territories, especially by business interests eager to exploit the raw materials—timber, metal, coal—of the hills in which they lived. Unlike the caste protests, which were nationwide, the *naxalite* revolts were more confined geographically, and did not generally touch the metropolitan areas of the country, but they posed a serious threat to local and state governments, which had to decide whether to accommodate the protests or to attempt to suppress them. Meanwhile Prime Minister Manmohan Singh declared repeatedly that "Naxalism remains the biggest internal security challenge facing our country."

America Elects an African-American President. In 2008, the election of Barack Obama as the first African-American president of the United States was hailed in America and around the world as a triumph of American democracy. The son of a Kenyan father, who left the boy's life when he was very young, and a white woman from Kansas, Obama spent his early years in Indonesia, after his mother remarried to an Indonesian, and then was raised in his teenage years largely by his maternal grandparents in Hawaii. His biography was international and transracial, and Obama introduced himself to the American electorate as a man whose "story" was quintessentially American, and impossible in any other country of the world. He was running not as a candidate primarily of black voters, as some previous African-American candidates (such as Jesse Jackson) had done, but as a representative of the entire population of America. Democratic Party voters, the first to weigh the man and his credentials, chose him in the primary elections over his rival, Hillary Clinton. The primary election itself was watched with intense interest throughout the world for its historic encounter between the most serious ever African-American candidate, and the most serious ever woman candidate. The vote in the end was close, with Clinton, who lost, drawing 18 million votes. One glass ceiling was cracking, but not yet shattered.

In the general election, Obama swept to victory with a margin of nearly eight million votes. Although he carried only 43 percent of the white votes, his margin of 2–1 among Hispanic voters and more than 9–1 among blacks gave him his substantial majority. The total white vote was only about 75 percent of the electorate. America was becoming more multiracial in its demography as well as in its attitude. Obama secured his reelection in 2012 by a margin of 5 million votes, with 93 percent of the black vote, 71 percent of the Hispanic, and 73 percent of the Asian.

Migration

From the time *Homo sapiens* emigrated from Africa, migration has been a staple of human life. In the most recent decades, migration continues to affect every region of the earth. The most common form of migration is that of poorer people in search of work in richer lands. The streams of migration frequently bring confrontation between those who are already in place and recent arrivals. The relationships are complicated because both groups need each other, yet they are wary. The poor need the jobs; the rich need the cheap labor; the poor fear legal and illegal attacks; the rich are often put off by the poverty and culture of the newcomers. One perspective on migration reveals its rural to urban dimension. Vast streams of immigrants relocate from rural to urban areas every year. By 2006 the world had become 50 percent urban (3.3 billion people), up from 13 percent in 1900 (220 million) and 29 percent in 1950 (736 million). Another perspective reveals its international dimensions.

United States. America permits more legal immigrants to enter each year than any other country in the world. Americans need immigrants from Mexico and other parts of Latin America to work as farm, construction, and domestic laborers at pay scales too low for already settled Americans to accept. Nevertheless, they may not want these new low-skilled migrants to stay after the work is over. They may not want them to avail themselves of the benefits of American workers, or costly medical care, and schooling for their children. So they write laws that make it difficult for low-income foreigners to gain access to the United States and almost impossible to stay legally. The migrants, desperate for better living conditions, sneak into the country by the millions and find jobs, but they live in fear of being caught and sent back to their home countries. In 2012, the United States government estimated 41 million foreign-born people legally resident in the country, 12 percent of the total population, and 11.6 million illegally resident. Mexicans comprised about 60 percent of the illegal residents. In recognition of the political significance of so many immigrants, the Congress of the United States began to give serious consideration to immigration reform.

Europe. European countries were not accustomed to large-scale immigration into the continent until the economic boom after World War II. Then the combination of war losses, low birth rates, and an expanding economy led them to welcome foreigners for their industrious hands, but not for their cultures. European governments did not want to grant them citizenship. Many of the new immigrants were citizens of the former colonies, a fact that sometimes conferred rights of migration. By 1990 Great Britain was home to about two million immigrants of color from south Asia and the Caribbean. By 2010, 12.9 per cent of the population of the United Kingdom was foreign born.

France had similar experiences with immigration from its former colonies. At first these immigrants were welcome, then they were restricted. By 1990 there were 615,000 from Algeria, 573,000 from Morocco, 206,000 from Tunisia, and about 100,000 from Senegal and Mali. Most were Muslims. Tension between the indigenous French and the new immigrants were threefold: class, racial, and religious/cultural. The new immigrants settled in French cities, in some of the worst urban housing. Fighting became common, with attacks coming from both sides, French against immigrants and immigrants against French. Nevertheless, migrants continued to come. In 2010, the estimated population of foreign-born immigrants in France was 7 million.

Germany had not held major colonies, but its economy expanded fastest of all the large European countries and it had the greatest need for workers. The government therefore agreed to accept immigrants from a wide variety of countries, but only for a set period. Access to legal citizenship was impossible. By 2010, Germany had accepted almost 10 million immigrants. About a third were from Turkey, and their difficulties were greater than most of the other immigrants since they were Asian and Muslim, and had no historic ties to Germany. Only after 1999 did it become legal for someone without a German ancestor to become a citizen, but even then the rules made citizenship difficult to obtain.

Historically, Italy had been a country of emigration, with some 25 million Italians emigrating between 1876 and 1965. After World War II, immigration was largely internal as Italians moved from the impoverished south of the country to the much more prosperous north. But with one of the lowest birth rates in the world, and an economy at last beginning to grow rapidly, Italy offered new opportunities for

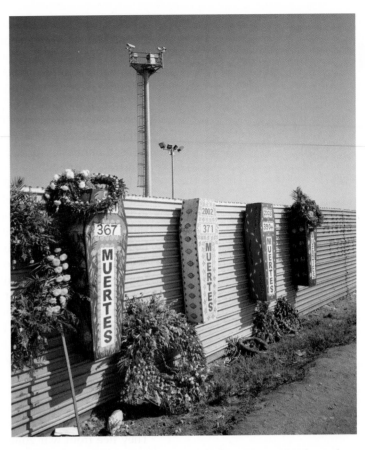

United States–Mexico border fence. As illegal Mexican immigration to the United States increased to an estimated 500,000 people per year, demands for barriers across the 2,000-mile-long border intensified in the United States. Fences, walls, and police patrols increased, making the attempt to cross into the United States more difficult and more dangerous. Images of coffins along the Mexico–California border memorialize four aspiring migrants who died attempting to enter the country illegally.

24.1

24.2

24.3

What have been the key social revolutions of the early twenty-first century?

869

What have been
the key social
revolutions of the
early twenty-first
century?

employment to millions of immigrants in the 1980s. By 2010, 8.8 per cent of Italy's population was foreign born, many of them having arrived by sea from North Africa.

With the tide of popular opinion running against immigrants, in 1990 many European nations implemented the **Schengen Agreement**, named for the town in Luxembourg where it was promulgated. Schengen addressed the problem created by the freedom of movement of people and goods inside the EU. Schengen was designed to insure that all member nations adopted and enforced equally strict limitations on immigration of people and importation of goods. Potential immigrants who were refused admission under the Schengen regulations denounced this new policy of "**Fortress Europe**."

In 2007, Romania and Bulgaria entered the EU. Their citizens now had the right of unrestricted travel throughout the bloc of 27 nations, but, because the income levels of these new entrants were far below many of the established EU members, their rights to work in many EU countries were restricted. Political parties often sought legislation restricting their access to jobs and benefits.

Immigrants came not only from poor countries to wealthy ones. They also came from extremely poor countries to countries that were somewhat less poor. India, for example, reported tens of millions of illegal immigrants from neighboring Bangladesh and an increasing but much smaller number from Africa. The Bangladeshis, ethnically identical to the Bengalis of India, could slip across the border rather easily, without detection. Many in India accepted them willingly, but others wanted them evicted, especially as they were Muslims in a Hindu-majority nation.

Refugees

Refugees are immigrants who are fleeing for their safety, and often for their lives. They flee from war zones and from political oppression. In the early years of the twenty-first century, the number of refugees worldwide has fluctuated between 15 and 20 million, about 80 percent of them women and children. In the 1990s, during

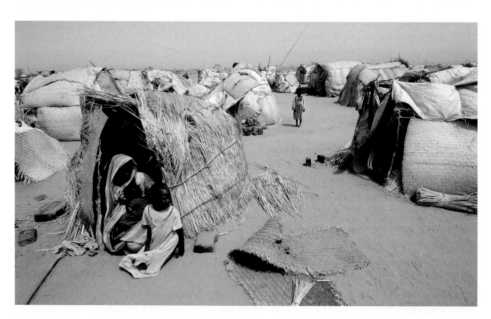

KEY TERMS

Schengen Agreement Set common, restrictive rules limiting immigration and the import of goods to signatory nations.

Fortress Europe The negative designation applied by potential immigrants who were denied entrance to the EU under the terms of the Schengen Agreement, implemented after 1990.

Refugee camp at Nyala, south Darfur, 2007. The Darfur region was added to the Sudan in 1916 during the period of British colonial rule, although it had been historically separate, populated by its own ethnic groups. After independence in 1956, the people of Darfur protested that they were not getting an equal share of the financial resources of the state, and in 2003 they began armed resistance to an oppressive state. The result was hundreds of thousands dead and up to two million displaced from their homes, most as refugees in neighboring Chad, many as internally displaced persons (IDP) in refugee camps within Darfur. Peace agreements have been signed, but violence continues and the situation is unstable.

24.1

24.2

24.3

What have been the key social revolutions of the early twenty-first century?

the wars between Hutus and Tutsis in Rwanda and Congo, two million refugees spilled over the border to Congo. In the 2000s, millions of citizens of Zimbabwe fled the country, seeking refuge from the brutal government of Robert Mugabe. According to UN estimates, more than two million Zimbabweans were living in South Africa, another two million in the United Kingdom, and as many as 45,000 in the United States. In 2007 and 2008, so many refugees from Zimbabwe crossed into South Africa that fighting broke out between the immigrants and the local population. The government of South Africa blocked new immigration and evicted thousands who had already arrived. Through the 2000s, millions of refugees from Darfur, in western Sudan, fled to Chad to escape the government-backed militias that attacked them.

More than two million refugees fled Iraq during the American-led war beginning in 2003, while another two million were displaced, although they remained in the country. Civil war in Syria, still raging in 2013, had produced two million refugees who fled the country and another four million who were displaced from the homes but still living within the national borders. In 1948, some 700,000 refugees fled Palestine. By 2010, the number of their patrilineal descendants had reached almost five million. In 2012, some 15 million refugees were displaced from their countries; another 29 million were displaced from their homes, but still living in their countries; and almost one million people were seeking permanent **political asylum**—in fear of persecution because of political positions they had proclaimed.

Cultural Expression

Globalization has transformed the arts, touching billions of people in their daily lives. Consider the singer-songwriter Shakira. She has sold more than 70 million albums worldwide and won two Grammy awards and ten Latin Grammy Awards. She is Colombian. Her mother is of Spanish and Italian ancestry, her father of Lebanese descent. Her fame is global. Consider reggae music, which came from the Caribbean, with African roots, to win popularity throughout the world, both as music and as protest, especially because of the political songs of the legendary Bob Marley of Jamaica. Consider just a few of the artists who have become musical presences around the world: Zakir Hussein of India, playing tabla, for example; or the late Nusrat Fateh Ali Khan of Pakistan, chanting the *qawwali* poetry of Sufi mysticism, sometimes fused with Western forms, in packed halls around the world. Youssou N'Dour, the singer and percussionist from Senegal, combines the songs of the *griot* storytellers of West Africa with Afro-Cuban rhythms, while Toumani Diabaté of Mali plays the kora—a 21-string harp/lute central to the classical traditions of West Africa. Diabaté has played with Taj Mahal, Peter Gabriel, Spain's flamenco-**fusion** band Ketama, the 52-piece Japanese/Malian Symmetric Orchestra, and jazz musicians who have come to work with him at his home in Bamako. Kiran Ahluwalia, born in India, raised in Canada, and now living in New York, composes and sings her own contemporary versions of Persian and Punjabi classical music. In 2012 she won a Juno, Canada's Grammy, for World Music album of the year. Websites such as afropop. org/wp carry the latest news on the worldwide varieties of popular music related to Africa, often with tracks and videos from current recordings and performances.

The Festival in the Desert (Festival au Désert), an annual event for world music in Mali, showcases especially the traditional music of North Africa's Tuareg peoples. The Tuareg band Tinariwen first came to international attention at the festival in 2001. In 2011 it won a Grammy for best World Music album of the year. The next year, the band suffered harassment and detention at the hands of Islamic fundamentalists in northern Mali. In 2013 the warfare in Mali, noted above, drove the festival itself into exile in neighboring Burkina Faso. Ouagadougou, the capital city of Burkina Faso, was already the showcase for African film. Every two years since 1969 it has hosted the Panafrican Film and TV Festival, the largest on the continent, attended by as many as a million people. In 2013, 170 films from across Africa were

KEY TERM

political asylum Asylum is normally applied for and granted, or refused, on the basis of individual cases brought by people who fear that if they return to their countries they will be persecuted, even murdered, because of their politics. Refugee status, by contrast, is usually a group phenomenon and does not imply any specific cause.

fusion In cultural terms, fusion refers to the mixing of different forms into new ones. Often used in terms of food recipes and presentation as well as musical and art forms. The term "hybridity" is used in a similar way, although "fusion" usually suggests a greater range of imagination in creating the final product.

What have been
the key social
revolutions of the
early twenty-first
century?

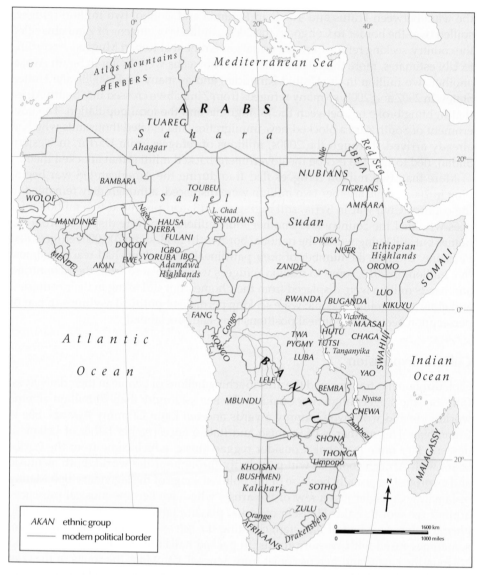

Ethnic groups in Africa. The insensitivity to local conditions of many European colonial administrators created territorial boundaries that failed to match the underlying cultural map of Africa and its peoples. The result of this was seen in postindependence internecine conflict between ethnic groups hemmed into artificial national territories: Congo (Zaire), Nigeria, Uganda, Angola, Zimbabwe, Sudan, and, more recently, Rwanda and Burundi are among those that have reaped this bitter harvest.

screened there. Cultural tourism has become a substantial business. Many countries and cities arrange special programming, highlighting their culture—history, music, art, drama—as attractions for tourists, and travel has been one of the largest and most rapidly growing industries.

The Nobel Prize for Literature, established in 1901, also charts the globalization of culture. The first non-European, non-American winner was Rabindranath Tagore of India in 1913. The second, Gabriela Mistral of Chile, came only in 1945. Over the next 45 years, only six winners came from outside the US or Europe, but in the 1990s there were four (from Mexico, South Africa, the West Indies, and Japan), and since 2000 there have been seven more, including the first from China (two) and Turkey. Tracking these international festivals, cultural exchanges, and awards, anthropologists spoke of **hybridization**, or cultural fusion, the mixing of cultures to produce new forms.

KEY TERM

hybridization Originally used in cultural anthropology, and now more widely, to refer to the mixing of cultures to produce new forms. Sometimes referred to as cultural fusion.

Many international artists have also "given back," participating in international relief work for the poor, the hungry, the dispossessed, and those suffering from natural disaster, and for the ecological health of the earth. The first of these major benefit concerts, the Concert for Bangladesh in New York City in 1971, raised money for the victims of a cyclone in that newly born country. It included performances by George Harrison of the Beatles and the Indian sitarist Ravi Shankar. In 2005, Live 8, a series of ten coordinated concerts around the world, was dedicated to urging governments to increase aid to poor countries. More than 1,000 musicians performed in the concerts, which were broadcast on 182 television networks and 2,000 radio networks. In 2007, the first Live Earth concert, organized by Nobel Prize-winner and former US Vice President Al Gore, and dedicated to raising awareness of global warming, took place in multiple locations: Sydney, Johannesburg, East Rutherford (New Jersey), Rio de Janeiro, Antarctica, Tokyo, Kyoto, Shanghai, London, Hamburg, Washington, DC, and Rome.

Chinese writer Mo Yan talks to the media after winning the 2012 Nobel Prize for literature. The Prize committee spoke of Mo's "hallucinatory realism [that] merges folk tales, history and the contemporary." Mo was only the second Chinese to win the literature prize; the first, Gao Xingjian, was a citizen of France, where he had resided for more than a decade, when he won in 2000. Mo Yan's award was quite controversial. Many criticized him for not supporting other Chinese artists and intellectuals who were censured, and sometimes jailed, by the state. He and his supporters countered that his writing was his message.

Many artists became almost as famous for their work against poverty and human suffering as for their music. Shakira, for example, performed at both Live 8 and Live Earth. In 2008 she and other Latin artists performed on behalf of the charity Latin America in Solidarity Action in Buenos Aires and in Mexico City. Perhaps most noteworthy of all has been Bono of the Irish band U2. Bono has participated in numerous benefit concerts, including the Live Aid concert in 1985. In 2002, he joined with others in organizing DATA (Debt, AIDS, Trade, Africa), dedicated to eradicating poverty and HIV/AIDS in Africa. He was also prominent in the worldwide Jubilee 2000 campaign to cancel the debts of some of Africa's poorest countries. In 2005 he joined with others to launch the clothing brand EDUN, dedicated to promoting trade with Africa. *Time* magazine named Bono, along with Bill and Melinda Gates, "persons of the year" in 2005. In 2008, the UN unveiled a $3 billion plan for eliminating malaria as a mass killer in Africa. Bono and, again, Bill Gates, joined the many heads of state and UN officials making the announcement.

Sometimes the music itself has been the gift. New recording labels, such as Putumayo and Rough Guides Music, sprang up, dedicated to producing music of the non-European world (as well as of Europe and the Americas). The TV channel MTV (Music Television), originally dedicated to popular music, began broadcasting in the United States in 1981. It generated spinoffs in other countries, in local languages, including MTV channels in the UK, Dubai (targeting markets from Cairo across Saudi Arabia to Bahrain), India, the Philippines, Turkey, Pakistan, Australia, and New Zealand.

Other TV channels, oriented toward news and features, were also reaching out to global audiences. By 2013, the British Broadcasting Corporation (BBC) was reaching about 330 million households in almost every country on earth. The America-based Cable News Network, CNN, and its related CNNI (International) now serve most of the nations of the world, reaching about half the number of people as the BBC.

24.1

24.2

24.3

What have been the key social revolutions of the early twenty-first century?

SOURCE

Bono's TED talk

TED (Technology, Entertainment, Design) talks began at a conference in 1990, as a venue for presenting new ideas of creative minds in lectures of no more than 18 minutes. By May 2013, more than 1,500 talks had been delivered and made available free online via YouTube.

In 2013, the musician Bono, leader of the band U2, delivered an inspirational TED talk urging people to contribute their voices politically and their money charitably to creating a better world. He emphasized issues of health and the continent of Africa. He began with victories:

> Since the year 2000 … there are eight million more AIDS patients getting life-saving antiretroviral drugs. Malaria: there are eight countries in sub-Saharan Africa that have their death rates cut by 75 percent. For kids under five, child mortality … is … down by 2.65 million a year. That's a rate of 7,256 children's lives saved each day. Wow. Wow. [Applause] … Have you read anything anywhere in the last week that is remotely as important as that number? Wow. Great news. It drives me nuts that most people don't seem to know this news … The Global Fund provides antiretroviral drugs that stop mothers from passing HIV to their kids. This fantastic news didn't happen by itself. It was fought for, it was campaigned for, it was innovated for. And this great news gives birth to even more great news, because the historic trend is this. The number of people living in back-breaking, soul-crushing extreme poverty has declined from 43 percent of the world's population in 1990 to 33 percent by 2000 and then to 21 percent by 2010.

Bono noted the external aid that helped to "unlock" the progress in Africa:

> Look at sub-Saharan Africa. There's a collection of 10 countries, some call them the lions, who in the last decade have had a combination of 100 percent debt cancellation, a tripling of aid, a tenfold increase in FDI—that's foreign direct investment— which has unlocked a quadrupling of domestic resources— that's local money—which, when spent wisely—that's good governance—cut childhood mortality by a third, doubled education completion rates, and they, too, halved extreme poverty, and at this rate, these 10 get to zero too. So the pride of lions is the proof of concept.

He urged citizens to get involved:

> Right now, today, in Oslo as it happens, oil companies are fighting to keep secret their payments to governments for extracting oil in developing countries. You can do something about that too. You can join the One Campaign, and leaders like Mo Ibrahim, the telecom entrepreneur. We're pushing for laws that make sure that at least some of the wealth under the ground ends up in the hands of the people living above it.
>
> And right now, we know that the biggest disease of all is not a disease. It's corruption. But there's a vaccine for that too. It's called transparency, open data sets, something the TED community is really on it [sic]. Daylight, you could call it, transparency. And technology is really turbocharging this. It's getting harder to hide if you're doing bad stuff.
>
> So let me tell you about the U-report, which I'm really excited about. It's 150,000 millennials all across Uganda, young people armed with 2G phones, an SMS social network exposing government corruption and demanding to know what's in the budget and how their money is being spent. This is exciting stuff.
>
> Look, once you have these tools, you can't not use them. Once you have this knowledge, you can't un-know it. You can't delete this data from your brain, but you can delete the clichéd image of supplicant, impoverished peoples not taking control of their own lives. You can erase that, you really can, because it's not true anymore. [Applause]

(http://www.ted.com/talks/bono_the_good_news_on_poverty_
yes_there_s_good_news.html)

- Bono and many other musicians and artists have used their celebrity status to promote political programs and charitable activities. How effective are their actions?
- Bono talks about "debt cancellation." What is this?
- Please give examples, beginning with examples from this textbook, of social media's importance in organizing mass political activity.

24.1
24.2
24.3

What have been the key social revolutions of the early twenty-first century?

Satellite Television for the Asian Region (STAR TV), based in Hong Kong and with programming offices in Australia, India, and other South Asian countries, claims to reach some 300 million viewers in 54 countries. Al Jazeera ("the [Arabian] Peninsula"), the first TV network headquartered in the Arab world (in Doha, Qatar), began operations in 1996 with a $150 million grant from the emir of Qatar. In 2013, it launched its own American cable channel, Al Jazeera America.

With so many networks, broadcasts could now reach hundreds of millions of people around the world in real time. The most common of these international broadcasts were sporting events, such as the World Cup soccer games, and news programming. According to Nielsen Media Research, 4.7 billion viewers worldwide, almost 75 percent of the population of the earth, tuned in to at least some parts of the

What are the
ecological
technology issues
of today?

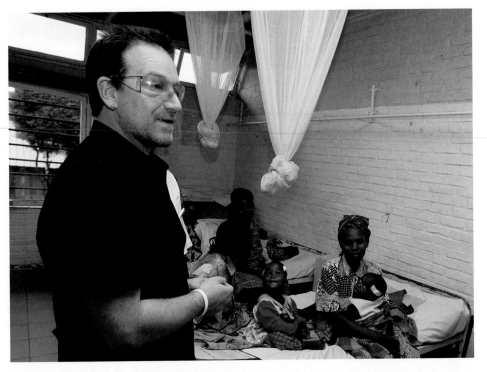

Irish rock star Bono, of the group U2, visits with malaria patients at the Kigali University Hospital, Rwanda. Bono, like Shakira, above, won international acclaim for his music and for his political and humanitarian activism. The group U2 has won 22 Grammy Awards and sold 150 million recordings. The U2 360° Tour from 2009–2011 was the highest-attended and highest-grossing concert tour in history. Meanwhile Bono has appeared in numerous global concerts for charitable causes, campaigned for debt forgiveness for African countries, and worked with Bill and Melinda Gates to eradicate malaria in Africa.

television coverage of the 2008 Olympic Games in Beijing. By 2012, television was only one of the viewing alternatives. Facebook, which in 2008 had 100 million profiles, had more than a billion in 2012; Twitter, which had 3 million users in 2008, now had 500 million users; and YouTube, which had made available 100 million videos a day, in 2012 showed 4 billion.

View the **Closer Look**: **Copenhagen Opera House** on **MyHistoryLab**

On Technology

24.3   What are the ecological technology issues of today?

We have already discussed the technology of communication and transportation, computers, the internet, and containerization, and genetic engineering and cloning. Here we look at two additional technologies. One, nanotechnology (technology based on organisms of molecular size and even smaller), is only beginning to come into its own. The other, ecological technology (technology to keep the globe's ecology intact for human life), is already perhaps the most critical for the world today.

Nanotechnology

Nanotechnology works with substances at the molecular, or even at atomic and subatomic, level. "Nano" refers to a substance one billionth of a meter in size. A nanometer is to a meter as the size of a marble is to the size of the planet Earth.

24.1

24.2

24.3 What are the
ecological
technology issues
of today?

Nanosubstances exist in nature, for example, in the enzymes of biological processes that allow the contraction of muscles; in the works of DNA molecules; and in the process of converting minerals and water into living cells. Experiments using and measuring nanosubstances began in the early 1900s, and in 1959 the Nobel laureate and physicist Richard Feynman brought the field to the attention of the world even outside the scientific community. Feynman noted that substances at atomic size exhibit properties different from those of the same substances at the scales at which we normally encounter them. For example, opaque substances become transparent (copper); stable materials become combustible (aluminum); solids turn into liquids at room temperature (gold); insulators become conductors (silicon). This last transformation has brought about the use of silicon as a conductor in computers. The term "nanotechnology" was used for the first time in 1974.

Making instruments that are capable of creating and working with such small substances posed problems, but by the 1980s and 1990s, scientists were beginning to create tools for reducing substances to such small dimensions. Some nanotechnology is already in place. Nanomaterials are seeded into materials of larger size, giving them new properties. For example, carbon at the nanoscale is used in some computer hard drives to increase their speed and capacity. Exciting possibilities for further use are under exploration; some seem practicable even now, while others appear more far-fetched. Nanomaterials might be seeded into cancerous cells to track or even destroy them. Carbon in nanoform could be used to create a fiber, or a wire, or a molecular coating. Nanosubstances might be used in desalinating and purifying water at minimal cost, in fuel cells, in controlling pollution, in the bioprocessing of food products. They also promise potential breakthroughs in the production of abundant, cheap, clean energy.

Research must proceed with care because substances at such small size may prove dangerous to human and animal life. If they enter the lungs and respiratory systems, they may destroy tissue. Because of their tiny size, they may also enter through the skin and, in effect, cut into internal organs. Experience with nanotechnology is new and limited. It requires, and commands, further attention.

Ecological Technology

The selection of Kenya's Waangari Maathai (1940–2011) for the Nobel Peace Prize in 2004 for her Green Belt movement, in which she motivated poor women in her country to plant some 30 million trees in 30 years, indicated the degree to which the struggle against "global warming" had become a priority for the world. Another indicator was the subsequent selection of Al Gore (b. 1948), a tireless campaigner for controlling climate change, for the Nobel Peace Prize in 2007. Gore's acceptance speech homed in on the global problem of carbon emissions:

> In the last few months, it has been harder and harder to misinterpret the signs that our world is spinning out of kilter. Major cities in North and South America, Asia and Australia are nearly out of water due to massive droughts and melting glaciers. Desperate farmers are losing their livelihoods. Peoples in the frozen Arctic and on low-lying Pacific islands are planning evacuations of places they have long called home. Unprecedented wildfires have forced a half million people from their homes in one country and caused a national emergency that almost brought down the government in another. Climate refugees have migrated into areas already inhabited by people with different cultures, religions, and traditions, increasing the potential for conflict. Stronger storms in the Pacific and Atlantic have threatened whole cities. Millions have been displaced by massive flooding in South Asia, Mexico, and 18 countries in Africa. As temperature extremes have increased, tens of thousands have lost their lives. We are recklessly burning and clearing our forests and driving more and more species into extinction. The very web of life on which we depend is being ripped and frayed.

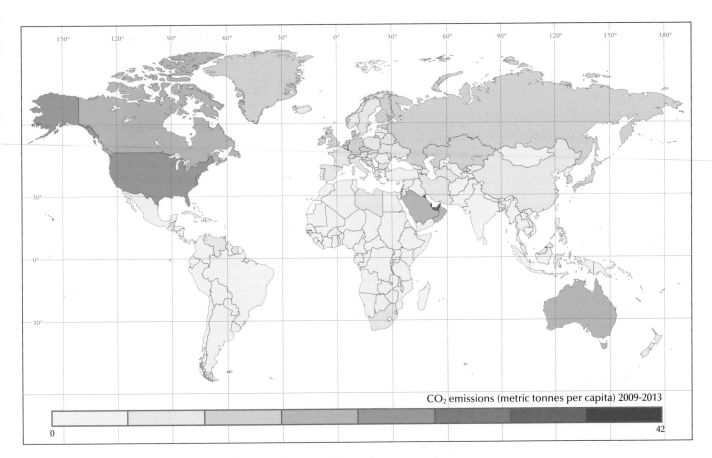

CO₂ emissions (metric tonnes per capita) 2009-2013

0   42

Greenhouse gas emissions, 2009–2013 As evidence of global warming and climate change became unmistakable, scientists measured more carefully the amount of greenhouse gas emissions, primarily carbon dioxide, CO_2. Here they are computed on a per capita basis, so that such countries as Canada, with a very cold climate and considerable use of coal and gas for heating, register very high, while China registers relatively low. Similar charts giving total emissions by country show China much higher, because of its immense population, and Canada much lower. The United States registers high in both per capita and total emissions. (Data from the World Bank)

24.1

24.2

What are the
ecological
technology issues
of today?

24.3

Gore called attention to the need for political leadership to solve the problem. He identified the need to limit global emissions of carbon dioxide, CO_2, and he identified the two largest national culprits creating those emissions: the United States and China. In 1980, the United States produced 4,754 million metric tons of CO_2 from fossil fuels; in 2011, that figure had increased by 14 percent to an estimated 5,420 million. Over the same period, China increased its emissions five times over, from 1,454 million metric tons to an estimated 9,700 million. Neither nation was willing to take the lead in solving the earth's climate problems.

Advocates of change, who proposed to limit consumption by raising the price of carbon fuels, met resistance from producers, automakers, and consumers, especially car drivers. Political leaders were reluctant to take the lead in proposing solutions that had such strong opposition. In many parts of the world—Saudi Arabia, Iran, Iraq, Russia, Venezuela—rulers who controlled petrofuels were dictators and could afford to be, since their "petrodollars" left them free to do as they wished. High levels of fossil-fuel consumption helped to keep them in power.

Gore and his colleagues around the world believed that technological innovation, economic planning, and political action were capable collectively of solving the problems of climate change, and that the process would be commercially rewarding

AT A GLANCE: TRADE, SOCIAL REVOLUTION, TECHNOLOGY

DATE	TRADE	SOCIAL REVOLUTION	TECHNOLOGY
1970s		• 1975 First UN Conference on Women	• 1973 Portable cellular phone invented • 1974 "Nanotechnology" term used for first time
1980s		• 1980 Mandal Commission Report on Other Backward Classes (India) • 1981 MTV begins broadcasting • 1985 Schengen Agreement; expanded 1997, 1999 • 1985 Live Aid concert • 1987 Palestinian intifada	• 1989 World Wide Web formalized
1990s	• 1994 North American Free Trade Agreement (NAFTA) • 1995 GATT becomes WTO; 153 members in 2008 • 1999 Anti-WTO protests	• 1994 One person one vote democratic elections in South Africa • 1996–98 Truth and Reconciliation Commission in South Africa • 1996 Al Jazeera begins broadcasting	• 1991 First digital cell-phone network; first text message
2000s	• 2000 UN Millennium Development Goals adopted • 2001 World Social Forum, first meeting • 2002 Euro currency adopted throughout most of EU • 2008 Global economic recession	• 2000 Second Palestinian intifada • 2001 The Netherlands legalizes same-sex marriage • 2004 c. 17 million refugees worldwide • 2008 Barack Obama elected President of the United States	• 2004 Waangari Maathai wins Nobel Peace Prize for Green Belt Movement • 2005 18 million containers make 200 million trips • 2006 2.6 billion cell-phone subscriptions • 2007 Al Gore wins Nobel Peace Prize for ecological advocacy • 2008 1.5 billion people connected to the internet
2010s	• 2011 Global trade increasing at rate of 10 percent per year; value reaches $72 trillion	• 2012 Barack Obama reelected • 2013 More than a dozen states in US legalize same-sex marriage	• 2010 WikiLeaks publishes United States diplomatic cables and other classified information • 2013 2.6 billion people connected to the internet

24.1

24.2

24.3 What are the ecological technology issues of today?

as well. Many companies reaped substantial profits by creating green solutions to energy problems through innovative design, equipment, and application. The production of wind power and solar power began to be economically competitive as pressure on the supply of petrofuels continued to raise oil prices.

Many technological initiatives were flawed: natural gas, a fossil fuel that burned more cleanly than coal, seemed to offer an alternative to coal. However, the method of extracting the gas from the earth—hydraulic fracturing, or "fracking," drilling and injecting fluid into the ground at high pressure in order to fracture shale rocks and release the gas—carried dangers of polluting local water supplies and of allowing the escape of methane gas. The United States permitted the process; France did not, and the rest of the European Union had it under consideration, urging the need for further research. Another apparent alternative to fossil fuels, nuclear power, seemed too dangerous after a nuclear reactor at Fukushima, Japan, was crippled by a combination of tsunami and earthquake in 2011 and leaked radiation, forcing the evacuation of 65,000 residents from surrounding areas. Even two years later, the reactor was leaking radioactive water into the sea, raising the question: Could nuclear waste be contained? Finally, an attempt to reduce the reliance on petrofuels, especially in the United States and Brazil, by devoting vast acreage of food crops to the production of ethanol, a corn-based fuel, removed that acreage from food production: the result was increased food costs, a burden that fell most heavily on the poor.

In some countries, especially in Europe, green political parties began to spring up, dedicated to fighting for ecologically healthy policies. The United Nations continued to keep ecological issues on the international agenda through its

Rio+20 conference in 2012, which brought together representatives—many of them heads of state—from 192 nations in Rio de Janeiro to continue discussions that had begun in the same city in 1992, and had continued in Johannesburg in 2002. Optimists cited the continuing dialogue; pessimists pointed out the difficulty of reaching workable solutions and compromises among so many nations and interest groups.

View the **Image: Earth at Night** on **MyHistoryLab**

On Identity:
What Difference Does It Make?

The world in 2013 was very different from the world of 1988. Consider it in terms of the themes of our text.

In terms of *evolution* and what it means to be a human being, the entire human genome had been mapped. Scientists learned to measure through DNA how truly related we are to the entire animal world, most closely to the great apes, with whom we share 97 percent similar DNA. The *urban population* of the world increased by 50 per cent, more than one billion people between 1990 (2.2 billion) and 2012 (3.5 billion). More than half of the world's population had become city dwellers. *Empires*, such as the USSR, collapsed, apparently leaving the United States as the world's lone superpower. By 2013, however, the United States had serious problems of unemployment, overstretched military, and diminished capacity to influence world events. From the time of the Iranian revolution of 1979, especially, *religion* resurfaced as a major factor not only in world culture, but also in world politics. Countries such as China and India, which had kept aloof from world trading systems, emerged as major powers in international finance and *trade*. Discrimination in terms of religion, gender, race, caste, nationality, and class was under attack as unworthy of civilized people, and was apparently receding as migration brought diverse groups together and schools created educational curricula for a world of diversity. No doubt, however, some peoples chose to reject *social change* as firmly as possible. New *technology* continued its promises and its threats to human life as it always had, but more pervasively.

So much was changing so swiftly that *identity* had become a key issue by the beginning of the twenty-first century. What does it mean to be a male, or a female; black or white; a villager or an urbanite or a suburbanite; a migrant or a local resident; an American, or a Kenyan, or a Brazilian, or a Chinese; a Christian, or a Muslim, or a Buddhist; an economic conservative or a liberal; a cultural traditionalist or a cosmopolitan; technologically savvy or primitive; wealthy or impoverished? What does a person stand for and against? What tasks are meaningful and important to undertake, and which seem less crucial?

Academic researchers ask these questions in formal and disciplined fashion. Historians, for example, trace the ways in which individuals and groups modify their sense of identity over time. But so do everyday people, in more colloquial ways, in conversation with friends and in internal conversation with themselves. It is our hope that this textbook has given its readers some guidelines for thinking about these issues of identity, by demonstrating that they have been with us forever, albeit with different levels of intensity at different times. We hope that readers will go away with the understanding that the study of history is the study of the context of our own lives and identities, individually and collectively. By knowing where we have come from in the past, and how we have come to the present, we will be better able to understand our choices, and our constraints, in determining where we might go in the future.

CHAPTER REVIEW

ON TRADE

24.1 Why is globalization significant? What are its goals?

Globalization thrives on the world's new, inexpensive transportation and communication facilities. It requires freedom of movement across borders of goods, services, capital, knowledge, and people. It also requires new institutions for negotiating rules and regulations across international borders. With globalization, and the internet, billions of dollars of investment capital can move around the globe at the stroke of a key. Globalization means increased trade among nations, as well as increased travel, more world art, music, and literature, and new dimensions of economic investment. New and different social and cultural forms have arisen. However, globalization has also led to increasing disparities of wealth between the rich and the poor, and this disparity has fostered movements opposing further globalization.

ON SOCIAL REVOLUTION

24.2 What have been the key social revolutions of the early twenty-first century?

Migration, both internal and international, continues to affect all regions of the globe as governments struggle to formulate effective policies to cope with huge waves of newcomers, while nationalists often fight to keep their state closed. Gender relationships within families have been transformed, and issues concerning gender roles and women's rights are universal. National struggles against racial discrimination are advancing, often aided by pressure from the international community. And the arts have gone truly global, as cultures mix to produce new forms of cultural fusion.

ON TECHNOLOGY

24.3 What are the ecological technology issues of today?

Technology that aims to keep the earth's ecology intact is most critical in the twenty-first century. In some countries, especially in Europe, "green" political parties have grown, their main goal to fight for ecologically healthy political and social programs. The United Nations has continued to keep ecological concerns on its agenda, and more and more people and governments around the world have accepted the need to address the dangers of climate change. There is much resistance, however: from companies that profit from dangerous carbon emissions; from consumers who do not want to pay more for "cleaner" fuel options; and from political leaders who are afraid to propose solutions for fear of a backlash from those same companies and consumers.

Suggested Readings

PRINCIPAL SOURCES

Carter, Jimmy. *We Can Have Peace in the Holy Land: A Plan that Will Work* (New York: Simon and Schuster, 2009). Carter advocates a two-state solution and calls for pressure to be exerted against Israelis and Palestinians to save them from themselves.

Chomsky, Noam. *Middle East Illusions* (Lanham, MD: Rowman and Littlefield, 2004). Chomsky takes to task everyone for failures in Middle East policy. He is especially critical of the United States for its uncritical support of Israel.

Crossley, Pamela Kyle, Lynn Hollen Lees, and John W. Servos. *Global Society: The World since 1900* (Boston, MA: Houghton Mifflin, 3rd ed., 2012). A fine, well-written history of the twentieth century, organized thematically rather than by nation or region. Special emphasis on technology and useful references to websites for further research.

Edelstein, Jillian. *Truth and Lies: Stories from the Truth and Reconciliation Commission in South Africa* (New York: The New Press, 2001). Portraits and testimony—often quite moving—from individuals who spoke to the commission.

French, Howard. *A Continent for the Taking: The Tragedy and Hope of Africa* (New York: Knopf, 2004). A senior writer for *The New York Times* places the blame for Africa's current difficulties on self-interested political leaders in both Africa and the West, showing that there is plenty of blame to go around.

Human Development (New York: United Nations Development Program, annual). A survey of the nations of the world with an abundance of statistical tables and numerous brief, specific topical discussions.

Jaffrelot, Christophe. *India's Silent Revolution: The Rise of the Lower Castes in North India* (London: Hurst and Company, 2003). Documents amazing, peaceful transformations in a hierarchical society.

Levinson, Marc. *The Box: How the Shipping Container Made the World Smaller and the World Economy Bigger* (Princeton, NJ: Princeton University Press, 2006). Describes the invention and application of containerized technology.

Nussbaum, Martha. *The Clash Within: Democracy, Religious Violence, and India's Future* (Cambridge, MA: Harvard University Press, 2007). Argues that

peaceful centrists must work together to defeat violent, radical extremists. The case study is India, but the argument is widely applicable.

Obama, Barack. *Dreams from My Father. A Story of Race and Inheritance* (New York: Three Rivers Press, 2004). Memoirs of America's first multiracial president. A splendid and insightful autobiography.

Preston, Julia, and Samuel Dillon. *Opening Mexico: The Making of a Democracy* (New York: Farrar, Straus and Giroux, 2004). Two *New York Times* reporters narrate the events that marked the contemporary "Opening of Mexico" from about 1968 to 2004. Thoughtful and engaged.

Rosenberg, Rosalind. "The 'Woman Question,'" in Richard W. Bulliet, ed. *The Columbia History of the 20th Century* (New York: Columbia University Press, 1998). Discusses the changing goals of women's movements around the world.

Saadawi, Nawal El. *The Nawal El Saadawi Reader* (New York: Zed Books, 1997). Important spokeswoman for third-world feminists. Explains how their issues differ from those of women in first-world countries.

Sassen, Saskia. *The Global City: New York, London, Tokyo* (Princeton, NJ: Princeton University Press, 2001). An analysis of the most important cities in the world economy, and of what makes them so important.

Truth and Reconciliation Commission of South Africa Report, http://www.info.gov.za/otherdocs/2003/trc/rep.pdf. The amazing account of the South African government's attempt to heal the breach between black and white, seeking understanding rather than reprisal.

United Nations. *The Millennium Development Goals Report, 2013.* Also available online at http://www.un.org/millenniumgoals/pdf/report-2013/mdg-report-2013-english.pdf. Provides updates on progress toward meeting the eight millennium goals set in 2000.

YaleGlobal Online. A useful website with information on global poverty and inequality. http://yaleglobal.yale.edu.

Yunus, Muhammad. *Creating a World Without Poverty: Social Business and the Future of Capitalism* (New York: Public Affairs, reprint edition, 2009). An account of his work by the Nobel Prize-winning advocate of micro-finance.

Zakaria, Fareed. *The Post-American World* (New York: W.W. Norton, 2008). Perceptive journalist analyzes current transformations in world economic and political power. America is still very important, but China and India are rising fast.

ADDITIONAL SOURCES

Acemoglu, Daron, and James Robinson. *Why Nations Fail: The Origins of Power, Prosperity, and Poverty* (New York: Crown Business, 2012). Praises democracy and free markets in reviewing the last several centuries of global development and underdevelopment.

Firebaugh, Glenn. *The New Geography of Global Income Inequality* (Cambridge, MA: Harvard University Press, 2003). Sociologist argues that while income inequality is increasing among people within countries, it is decreasing between nations, largely because of China's successful rise.

Foer, Franklin. *How Soccer Explains the World: An (Unlikely) Theory of Globalization* (New York: Harper Perennial, 2005). The subtitle is too grandiose, but this is a fun introduction to the craze of soccer around the world.

Friedman, Thomas L. *Hot, Flat, and Crowded: Why We Need a Green Revolution and How It Can Renew America* (New York: Farrar, Straus and Giroux, 2008). *New York Times* columnist urges America to attend to the problems of global warming, and sees economic benefits in new technology.

Gilbert, Mark, and Jonathan T. Reynolds. *Africa in World History: From Prehistory to the Present* (Upper Saddle River, NJ: Prentice Hall, 2nd ed., 2007). A useful survey.

Gourevitch, Philip. *We Wish to Inform You that Tomorrow We Will Be Killed with Our Families: Stories from Rwanda* (New York: Farrar, Straus and Giroux, 1998). Brilliant journalistic reporting from the killing fields of Rwanda. Attempts to understand and explain the differences between Tutsis and Hutus.

Hunt, Michael H. *The World Transformed: 1945 to the Present: A Documentary Reader* (Boston, MA: Bedford/St. Martin's, 2004). An outstanding selection of primary documents with global scope and thematic breadth.

Kishwar, Madhu. *Off the Beaten Track: Rethinking Gender Justice for Indian Women* (New Delhi: Oxford University Press, 1999). The editor of one of India's leading feminist journals, *Manushi*, discusses the evolution of her thought in light of the possible and the ideal.

Meade, Teresa. *A Brief History of Brazil* (New York: Checkmark Books, 2nd ed., 2009). Brief, incisive account, with many insights presented in sidebars. Especially interesting on culture, music, and sports. Well-chosen illustrations.

Milanovic, Branko. *Worlds Apart: Measuring International and Global Inequality* (Princeton, NJ: Princeton University Press, 2005). World Bank economist shows methods of evaluating inequality among nations and individuals, and sees little chance of greater equality in the near future.

Shavit, Ari. *My Promised Land: The Triumph and Tragedy of Israel* (New York: Spiegel and Grau, 2013). Widely acclaimed reassessment of the meaning and status of Zionism and Israel today.

Shulman, David. *Dark Hope: Working for Peace in Israel and Palestine* (Chicago, IL: University of Chicago Press, 2007). Personal, moving account of the actions of individual Israelis to bring humanitarian aid and justice for Palestinian Arabs.

Smick, David. *The World is Curved: Hidden Dangers in the Global Economy* (London and New York: Portfolio, 2008). Economist and businessman points out the hazards of globalization.

Stiglitz, Joseph, and Andrew Charlton. *Fair Trade for All: How Trade Can Promote Development* (New York: Oxford University Press, 2005). Argument for a level playing field among the participants in international trade; until now terms have favored the rich and powerful.

Wright, Donald. *The World and a Very Small Place in Africa: A History of Globalization in Niumi, The Gambia* (Armonk, NY: M.E. Sharpe, 2nd ed., 2004). Covers the period from the fifteenth century to the present. Fascinating conclusion on globalization and its dangers.

Zinsser, Judith P. "The United Nations Decade for Women: A Quiet Revolution," *The History Teacher,* vol. 24, no. 1 (November 1990), pp. 19–29. International organizations are helping women to organize globally to dream new dreams and work to achieve otherwise unattainable goals.

FILMS

Bamako (2006; 1 hour 57 minutes). A legal attack on the policies of the World Bank and the International Monetary Fund, unfolding in the courtyard of a family living its daily life in Bamako. Provocative juxtaposition.

Dadi and Her Family (1981; 58 minutes). Brilliant documentary of family life in rural northern India seen especially through the eyes of the grandmother/mother-in-law and her commitment to keeping the family together.

Waltz with Bashir (2008; 1 hour 31 minutes). Animated film in which a former Israeli soldier comes to grips with repressed memories of battle and killing during the occupation of Lebanon in 1982.

Hotel Rwanda (2005; 2 hours 2 minutes). A gripping account of the break-up of Rwanda, the slaughter of Tutsis, and the people who tried to save them.

Inside Job (2010; 2 hours). Academy Award-winning documentary view of the financial crisis of 2008. Through multiple interviews, gets at the stories behind the story.

Invictus (2009; 2 hours 14 minutes). An inspiring portrayal of Nelson Mandela's efforts to bring blacks and whites together, especially by promoting South Africa's sports teams as treasures of the entire nation.

The Last King of Scotland (2006; 2 hours 3 minutes). The story of the Scottish doctor who goes to work with Idi Amin of Uganda is fictional; Amin's dictatorial savagery is mostly fact.

Moolaadé (2005; 2 hours 4 minutes). "Sanctuary." Four girls facing ritual female genital mutilation (clitoridectomy) flee for sanctuary to a neighbor's home, evoking the fierce opposition to the practice. Ousmane Sembene's final film—an award-winner.

Too Big to Fail (2011; 1 hour 38 minutes). Made for HBO, an only lightly fictionalized presentation of the imminent collapse of Wall Street in 2008.

An Inconvenient Truth (2010; 1 hour 50 minutes). Al Gore's convincing, engaging, persuasive lecture-demonstration put to film, of all the consequences already evident in climate change, includes policy recommendations.

GLOSSARY

adivasis "Original inhabitants." The aboriginal peoples of the Indian subcontinent, who are outside the caste system and live somewhat separately from the rest of society, generally in remote places. Previously referred to as "tribals," they are today sometimes referred to as *vanvasis*, or forest dwellers.

agora A central feature of ancient Greek town planning. Its chief function was as a town market, but it also became the main social and political meeting-place. Together with the acropolis, it normally housed the most important buildings of the town. Later, the Roman forum fulfilled this function.

agronomy The systematic concern with field crop production and soil management. The term was first used in 1814.

ahimsa Nonviolence; not causing injury or hurt. A basic tenet of Jainism and several sects of Hinduism.

al-Qaeda "The base." The militant Islamic group of guerrilla warriors mobilized by Osama bin Laden in Afghanistan, first to fight against Russian invaders, and later to attack the United States and its allies. Subsequently, a number of militant Islamic guerrilla groups in different parts of the world adopted the name al-Qaeda, some with ties to bin Laden's group, some without.

Asian tigers The countries in East and Southeast Asia that were doing extremely well economically in the last decades of the twentieth century. The list almost always includes South Korea, Taiwan, Singapore, and Hong Kong, and sometimes Indonesia and Thailand.

asiento The right granted to England by Spain to carry all the slave cargoes from Africa to Spanish America, and the additional right to bring one goods ship each year to Panama.

assimilation The process by which different ethnic groups lose their distinctive cultural identity through contact with the dominant culture of a society, and gradually become absorbed and integrated into it.

asymmetrical warfare Warfare between groups armed and equipped very differently, and often using different strategies, usually between lightly armed guerrilla warriors and conventionally equipped armies of powerful states. Terror tactics and disinformation are also considered tactics of asymmetrical warfare. The term came into wide use in the 2000s, but it is also applicable to earlier guerrilla warfare.

atman The soul of each individual person, identical in its substance to Brahman, the universal power. Thus each individual soul is part of the great soul of the universe.

Ayatollah Title of prestigious and powerful Muslim religious leaders in Iran.

B.P. Before the Present. Archaeologists frequently use this notation, especially for dates before about 20,000 B.C.E.

balance of power In international relations, a policy that aims to secure peace by preventing any one state or alignment of states from becoming too dominant. Alliances are formed in order to build up a force equal or superior to that of the potential enemy.

banana republic A country that is dependent economically on a single cash crop—such as bananas in Central America—and beholden politically to the company that controls the crop, and to the countries that buy it. Often applied to countries of Central America in their relationships with the United States.

barbarians The Greeks first used the term "barbarous" to designate foreign and uncivilized peoples, those whose languages sounded to Greek ears like the sound *bar-bar*, rather than like Greek. Today, "barbarian" continues to refer to persons who are considered foreign and uncivilized, and may, in the extreme, also refer to people who are violent, uncontrolled, and, perhaps, uncontrollable.

barefoot doctors Paramedical personnel trained in basic medicine and dispatched to work in rural areas, where virtually no professionally trained doctors chose to practice.

bas-relief In sculpture, relief is a term for any work in which the forms stand out from the background. In bas- (or low) relief, the design projects only slightly from the background and the outlines are not undercut.

Bauhaus A movement in architecture arising in Germany between the world wars. It was characterized by an emphasis on streamlined forms and a rejection of ornamentation. It followed the motto "form follows function." Its work became controversial among political parties. When the Nazis took over Germany they destroyed the Bauhaus school, and most of its masters fled the country.

Berlin Conference Convened by Otto von Bismarck of Germany to settle peacefully European disputes over territory in Africa.

Bhakti Devotion to god; a personal dedication to and worship of god, often through meditation, music, chanting, dance—different from more formal rituals.

blood and iron Bismarck's policy of using warfare against enemies as a means of unifying his new nation. Subsequently the term has been used to designate the policy of any government committed to foreign warfare as a means of internal unification.

bodhisattva A "being of wisdom" worthy of entering *nirvana*, but who chooses to stay on earth, or be reborn, in order to help others. In Mahayana Buddhism, the Buddha himself is considered also to be one of the *bodhisattvas*.

bourgeoisie From the French word for town, *bourg*. Originally applied to the inhabitants of walled towns, who occupied a socio-economic position between the rural peasantry and the feudal aristocracy. With the development of industry, the bourgeoisie became identified more with employers, as well as with other members of the "middle class":

professionals, artisans, and shopkeepers who owned and directed the means of production. In Marxist thought, the bourgeoisie and the proletariat need each other, but are also always in conflict over the distribution of wealth.

bourse Another name for stock exchange, especially in Europe.

brainwashing The popular term used in the West at the time to refer to Chinese methods of group pressure and psychological coercion to extract confessions of political deviance.

bread and circuses Provision by the government of free food and entertainment, designed to divert the masses, and especially the poor masses, from engaging in political action.

Brezhnev Doctrine In 1968, when Czechoslovakia sought independence, Leonid Brezhnev, head of the USSR government, declared that the USSR would intervene militarily to prevent any of its satellite countries from claiming independence.

Caesar Augustus "Caesar" and "Augustus" are both titles of the emperor Octavian. Caesar means ruler or emperor, and the word comes down to the present in the title czar or tsar. Augustus means dignified, even majestic. It was sometimes used in place of Octavian's given name. The words could also be reversed as Augustus Caesar.

caliph The spiritual head and temporal ruler of the Muslim community.

capitalism An economic system characterized by private or corporate ownership of the means of production and by private control over decisions about prices, production, and distribution of goods in a free, competitive market of supply and demand.

cartel An association of independent producers or businessmen whose aim is to control the supply of a particular commodity or group of commodities in order to regulate or push up prices.

caste A hierarchical ordering of people into groups, fixed from birth, based on their inherited ritual status and determining whom they may marry and with whom they may eat.

caudillo A military leader who takes political power.

centuries The smallest units of the Roman army, each composed of some 100 foot soldiers and commanded by a *centurion*. A legion was made up of 60 centuries. Centuries also formed political divisions of Roman citizens.

client state A state that is economically, politically, or militarily dependent on another state.

concordat Agreement reached between the pope and Napoleon on the powers of the Church and the state in postrevolutionary France, 1801.

Congress of Vienna In 1815 the Congress brought together diplomats from the leading countries of Europe to resolve problems raised by the Napoleonic Wars and their aftermath. It redrew national borders, established a balance of power, and enshrined conservative government in Europe for about 30 years.

conquistadores The Spanish soldiers who invaded and conquered the kingdoms of the New World, especially in Mexico and Peru.

consul Under the Roman Republic, one of the two magistrates holding supreme civil and military authority.

containment The postwar policy of the United States, advocated by the diplomat George Kennan, to encircle and contain the Soviet Union within limits, through militant confrontation that would stop short of war. Containment advocated a balance of force.

Corn Laws Laws that restricted the import of food into England. These laws favored rural agricultural producers at the expense of urban consumers. Repealed in 1846.

Creole In the sixteenth to eighteenth centuries, a white person born in Spanish America of Spanish parents.

Cultural Revolution The policy of the Chinese communist government, 1966–76, of basing its economy on rural productivity and quelling the intellectual and cultural life of the cities, subordinating freedom of thought completely in favor of communist ideology.

cuneiform A writing system in use in the ancient Near East from around the end of the fourth millennium to the first century B.C.E. The earliest examples are in Sumerian. The name derives from the wedge-shaped marks (Latin: *cuneus*, a wedge) made by pressing the slanted edge of a stylus into soft clay.

D-Day Often used in the military as the day on which an important operation is to begin; more generally, signifies any date targeted for special action. Since the Normandy landing, June 6, 1944, the term "D-Day" has most often referred to that historic invasion.

daimyo The feudal lords of Japan, who, by the sixteenth century, controlled almost the entire country.

dar al-Islam The literal meaning of the Arabic words is "the abode of Islam." The term refers to the land of Islam, that is, territories in which Islam and its religious laws (*shari'a*) may be freely practiced. Some interpreters argue that the rulers themselves must be Muslims and that they must institute *shari'a* law, others argue that freedom for Muslims to follow Islamic practice is the only requirement. Also, sometimes, *dar as-Salam*, "the abode of peace."

deme A rural district or village in ancient Greece, or its members or inhabitants. The demes were a constituent part of the polis but had their own corporations with police powers, and their own cults, officials, and property.

demographics The study of human populations in quantitative terms, usually considered a sub-field of sociology. Demographers consider such data as birth and death rates, fertility and morbidity, and immigration and emigration, among many others.

dharma The duty of each person, determined in large part by his or her caste.

dhimmi Translates as "protected." A term applied to Jews, Christians, Zoroastrians, and others who were accepted as monotheists, like Muslims, and therefore eligible for protection that allowed them to practice their faith, but required them to pay a special tax.

diaspora A dispersion of peoples. Most commonly used to refer to the dispersion of Jews among the gentiles, which began with the Babylonian captivity of the sixth century B.C.E.

dictator In Roman times, a leader elected at a time of crisis by the Senate of Rome for a short term, usually six months, and vested with extraordinary powers to deal with the situation.

diffusion The spread of ideas, objects, or traits from one culture to another.

divide and rule A policy, usually unstated, by which a ruling power would encourage quarrels among its subjects so that they did not unite to challenge the ruling authority, and it could present itself as indispensable to keeping the peace. The rulers claimed that the divisions were inherent among the populations; anti-imperialists claimed the rulers created them for their own purposes.

divine right of kings A political doctrine influential in the sixteenth and seventeenth centuries which held that the monarch derived his authority from God and was therefore not accountable to earthly authority. James I of England (r. 1603–25) was a foremost exponent.

domesticity An ideal that valued the woman who stayed at home, raising children, keeping the home as comfortable as possible, and making it a safe haven to which her husband could return after his daily work earning a family wage.

dominance The imposition of alien government through force, as opposed to hegemony.

domino effect The belief, held by many American policymakers, that if one country in a region became communist, others would follow, one after the other.

double burden The burden on working women of combining their paid job with the unpaid tasks of housework and child-raising as well; implies that working men are not sharing the housework and child-care.

dual economy An economy of two largely unconnected tiers: one, usually small, tier of large-scale, modern, highly mechanized, highly capitalized businesses with large workforces in each unit, but since the total number of units is small, this is a relatively small proportion of the total workforce; the other of small-scale workshops with little capital, limited mechanization, and a small workforce in each unit, but since the total number of units is large, this is a relatively large proportion of the total workforce, usually producing traditional goods and services.

durbar A showy convocation of notables paying obeisance to, and receiving gifts from, the most powerful political leaders; a means of demonstrating and ratifying the relative position of each.

Eastern Ethics; Western Science The watchword of Sakuma Zozan in Japan, urging acceptance of Western science and technology, but rejecting Western culture and ethics in favor of those of Japan. This position was found in many countries colonized by Europeans.

economic liberalism This term has had various meanings at different times. Today it usually refers to a free-market, capitalistic economy, with minimum government intervention. Often referred to as neo-liberalism.

ecumene A Greek word referring to the inhabited world and designating a distinct cultural-historical community.

empiricism The theory that all knowledge originates in experience; the practice of relying on direct observation of events and experience to determine reality.

enclosure acts Laws passed in England between 1450 and 1640, and culminating in 1750–1860, which converted public lands held in common into parcels of land to be sold to private owners.

encomienda A concession from the Spanish crown to a colonist, giving the colonist permission to exact tribute from a specified number of Native Americans living in a particular area. Conditions were harsh and the Spanish attempted to convert the Indians to Christianity.

enlightened despotism A benevolent form of absolutism, a system of government in which the ruler has absolute rights over his or her subjects. The term implies that the ruler acts for the good of the people, not in self-interest.

equity A condition in which participants in a system believe that the system is fair and unbiased. Equity does not necessarily imply equality, a situation in which all participants have equivalent goods and rights, but it does require that participants share a sense of the justice and fairness of the system.

ethnic cleansing A euphemism for genocide. The act of exiling or murdering minority groups from a given territory.

Eucharist From the Greek *eucharistia*, "thanksgiving." The central sacrament and act of worship of the Catholic Church, culminating in Holy Communion, the eating of a sanctified wafer and drinking of sanctified wine as a reminder of Jesus' life, and, in Roman Catholicism, representing the actual act of partaking in his body and blood.

evangelical Christianity Those forms of Protestant Christianity that emphasize the literal truth and authority of the Bible, and salvation through the personal acceptance of Jesus Christ.

extraterritoriality Legal immunities enjoyed by the citizens of a sovereign state or international organization living within a foreign host country.

family wage A wage, usually earned by a male head of household, adequate to support a family. The concept suggested that a woman's place was in the home and that the male husband–father was the family breadwinner.

fascism A political philosophy, movement, or government that exalts the nation over the individual, the antithesis of liberal democracy. It advocates a centralized, autocratic government, often in alliance with major business leaders, led by a disciplined party and headed by a dictatorial, charismatic leader.

finance capital The capital necessary to finance the creation of new industry. The importance of finance capital marked the transition to an age of larger businesses than ever before and gave finance capitalists, who provided the investments, unprecedented power.

five-year plan A state-directed plan, frequently prepared by a communist government, to control the economy and to direct its growth. It contrasts with capitalist, laissez-faire, free-market economies, in which the government allows the forces of supply and demand to guide the market.

Fortress Europe The negative designation applied by potential immigrants who were denied entrance to the EU under the terms of the Schengen Agreement, implemented after 1990.

free-market economy An economic system in which the means of production are largely privately owned and there is little or no government control over the markets.

fusion In cultural terms, fusion refers to the mixing of different forms into new ones. Often used in terms of food recipes and presentation as well as musical and art forms. The term "hybridity" is used in a similar way, although "fusion" usually suggests a greater range of imagination in creating the final product.

garden city self-contained planned town combining work, residential, agricultural, and recreational facilities, and surrounded by a rural belt.

gender The social attributes of being male or female, in contrast to the biological attributes of sex. Thus, bearing children is an attribute of the female sex, but caring for children can be done by males or females. If females are expected to care for children, that is an attribute of gender, not sex, since both males and females are capable of doing it.

genocide The act of murdering an entire people. Originally used for the Nazi attempt to exterminate the Jewish people, it has been used since then to indicate the attempt to murder a substantial segment of a designated population.

ghetto The part of a city to which a particular group is confined for its living space. Named originally for an area adjacent to an iron foundry (in Italian, *ghetto*) in sixteenth-century Venice where Jews were segregated by government order, the term has been used most often to designate segregated Jewish living areas in European cities. It is also used, more broadly, to indicate any area where specific groups are segregated whether by law, by force, or by choice.

Girondins French revolutionary group formed largely from the middle classes, many of them originally from the Gironde region. Relatively moderate.

globalization The processes by which people, institutions, and nations are brought into unified networks of interaction around the globe. Most commonly the term refers to economic networks and integration, but cultural, political, and technological globalization also occurs.

good wives and wise mothers The stated goal of high-school education for girls in Japan. Women were expected to stay in the home (except, perhaps, for a few years before marriage).

Great Leap Forward The policy of the Chinese communist government in the late 1950s of building China's economy on the basis of small-scale, localized production in rural communities.

Great Trek Between 1834 and 1841 the Dutch settlers in the British Cape Colony left the British-dominated areas to the south to establish their own control in the north. The Dutch felt the British were too liberal in their treatment of blacks.

green revolution The revolution in agricultural production brought about by the use of new hybrid seeds, with increased use of irrigation, fertilizers, and pesticides.

guild A sworn association of people who gather for some common purpose, usually economic. Guilds of craftsmen or merchants were formed in order to protect and further the members' professional interests and for mutual aid.

gulag The acronym of Glavnoye, Upravleniye Ispravitelno Trudovykh Lagerey, the "Chief Administration of Corrective Labor Camps," a department of the Soviet secret police founded in 1934 under Stalin. It ran a vast network of forced labor camps throughout the USSR to which millions of citizens accused of "crimes against the state" were sent for punishment.

"guns vs butter" This refers to the budget decisions that governments have to make between military spending and domestic, often welfare, spending.

habeas corpus From the Latin, "you should have the body." A centuries-old principle requiring governments and their agents publicly to present an accused person, held in detention, and state the charges against him or her. It forbids holding a suspect without charge indefinitely.

hacienda A large rural estate in Spanish America, originating with Spanish colonization in the sixteenth century.

Usually controlled by one person or family giving shelter and protection to many dependent workers. The owner was called a *hacendado*.

hadith Traditional records of the deeds and utterances of the prophet Muhammad, and the basis, after the Quran, for Islamic theology and law.

han In Japan, a territory or feudal estate controlled by a feudal lord, or *daimyo*. *Han* were abolished in 1871.

hegemony The predominance of one unit over the others in a group, for example, one state in a confederation. It can also apply to the rule of an empire over its subject peoples, when the foreign government is exercised with their substantial consent.

heliocentric A system in which the sun is assumed to be at the center of the solar system—or of the universe—while Earth and the other planets move around it.

heresy A belief that is not in agreement with, or that even conflicts with, the official orthodoxy of its time and place. Heretics, those who espoused heresy, were often persecuted.

hieroglyphs The characters in a writing system based on the use of pictograms or ideograms. In ancient Egypt, hieroglyphics were largely used for monumental inscriptions. The symbols depict people, animals, and objects, which represent words, syllables, or sounds.

hijra The "migration" or flight of Muhammad from Mecca, where his life was in danger, to Medina (then called Yathrib), where he was welcomed as a potential leader in 622 C.E. The Islamic era (A.H.: After Hijra) is calculated from this date.

Hindutva A political–religious slogan calling for the merger of the Hindu religion with the power of the Indian state. It is the rallying cry of several militant Hindu organizations.

Hominid Any of a family (Hominidae) of erect bipedal (two-legged) primate mammals, which includes humans and humanlike species.

Homo erectus The most widespread of all prehistoric hominids, and the most similar to humans. Evolved about two million years ago and became extinct 100,000 years ago.

Homo sapiens Homo, "human," is the genus in which modern humans are placed; sapiens means "wise."

Homo sapiens sapiens The first human being of the modern type.

hoplite A heavily armed foot soldier of ancient Greece, whose function was to

fight in close formation, usually in ranks of eight men. Each soldier carried a heavy bronze shield, a short iron sword, and a long spear for thrusting.

humanism Cultural movement initiated in Western Europe in the fourteenth century deriving from the rediscovery and study of Greek and Roman literary texts. Most humanists continued to believe in God, but emphasized the study of humans.

"Hundred Flowers" campaign An invitation by Mao Zedong to the Chinese people in 1956–57 to express their ideas freely and openly. At first viewed as an invitation to democracy; later, after many who spoke out were jailed and punished, it came to be seen as a well-laid trap.

hybridization Originally used in cultural anthropology, and now more widely, to refer to the mixing of cultures to produce new forms. Sometimes referred to as cultural fusion.

iconoclast An "image-breaker," or a person who rejects the veneration of icons, on the grounds that the practice is idolatrous.

ideogram (alternative: ideograph) A character or figure in a writing system in which the idea of a thing is represented rather than its name. Languages such as Chinese use ideograms.

ijtihad A method of Quranic interpretation based on text, local custom, and the personal judgment of the *qadi*, or judge.

imam In Islam, a title for a person whose religious leadership or example is to be followed.

indentured labor Labor performed under signed indenture, or contract, which binds the laborer to work for a specific employer, for a specified time (usually years), often in a distant place, in exchange for transportation and maintenance.

Indo–Aryan A subgroup of the Indo-Iranian branch of the Indo-European group of languages, also called Indic, and spoken in India, Sri Lanka, Bangladesh, and Pakistan. The Indo–Aryan languages are descended from Sanskrit, the sacred language of Hinduism.

indulgences In the Roman Catholic Church, the remission from the punishments of sin, obtainable through good works or special prayers and granted by the Church through the merits of Christ and the saints. In the sixteenth century, the Church began to sell indulgences, precipitating the reforms of Martin Luther.

Industrial Revolution Once defined primarily in terms of new technology in Britain and Europe, now recognized also as a global phenomenon of unprecedented transformation in social organization and political/military power.

innovation The explanation that similar cultural traits, techniques, or objects found among different groups of people were invented independently rather than spread from one group to another.

intifada Colloquial Arabic: the act of shaking off; uprising, rebellion.

iron curtain Term introduced by Winston Churchill to describe the division of Europe by the Soviet Union spreading its areas of control in central and Eastern Europe and sealing it off from Western Europe.

iron law of wages The belief that as incomes increased people would choose to have more children. By 1900, this "iron law" reversed: as incomes increased, people chose to have fewer children.

Jacobins A French revolutionary party founded in 1789. It later became the most radical party of the revolution, responsible for implementing the Reign of Terror and executing the king (1793).

janapada A large political district in India, beginning about 700 B.C.E.

janissaries The elite corps of the Ottoman armies. Captured or bought as children from Christian families, usually in the Balkans, these soldiers were converted to Islam and trained.

kami In Japanese thought, the powers and spirits inherent in nature.

karma The doctrine that actions have their own appropriate consequences. A person's actions carry their own rewards (or punishments) because they set the directions of his or her life.

kulak A prosperous peasant in late tsarist and early Soviet Russia. The leaders of local agricultural communities, kulaks often owned sizeable farms and could afford to hire labor.

kulturkampf German for "struggle over culture" or "culture war." The struggle among proponents of different views of culture for recognition and for control over state policies. Such struggles are normal in any society, but in Germany between the world wars they became intense. They were waged philosophically and physically, and, ultimately, by banishing from the nation unwelcome cultural ideas, and those who held them.

laissez-faire (French for "let it be") An economic philosophy that calls for minimal (or no) interference by government in the workings of the economy. Often equated with the basic principles of capitalism.

lateen sail A triangular sail affixed to a long yard or crossbar at an angle of about 45 degrees to the mast, with the other free corner secured near the stern. The sail was capable of tacking against the wind on either side. Lateen sails were so named when they appeared in the Mediterranean, where they were associated with Latin culture, although their origin was actually far away.

Lebensraum In German, "room for living." The claim was that Germany needed to expand and take over the land of its neighbors because its own land was overcrowded. Similar claims on neighbors' lands have been issued by many nations throughout history.

Legalism A school of Chinese philosophy that came into prominence during the Period of the Warring States and had great influence on the policies of the Qin dynasty. Legalists took a pessimistic view of human nature and believed that social harmony could be attained only through strong government control and the imposition of strict laws, enforced absolutely.

liberation theology A movement within the Catholic Church, especially in Latin America, especially in the 1960s and 1970s, combining some of the social concerns of Marxism with those of the Christian gospel, focusing on serving the needs of poor people, and organizing them for confrontations against governments when necessary.

libertador Literally "liberator." Term applied to leaders of the independence revolts against Spanish rule in Latin America. Especially applied to Simón Bolívar.

Lost Ten Tribes Ten tribes of Israel were exiled from their homeland in 721 B.C.E. They totally assimilated into their new surroundings, lost their Jewish identity, and were lost to history. Periodically, groups in remote areas today claim that they are the Lost Ten Tribes.

made the trains run on time The boast of Mussolini—that he made the trains run on time—became the criticism of his democratic opponents. Both he and they saw the force of the police and military as the means of this accomplishment. For Mussolini it evoked pride; for his critics, despair and even ridicule. For the critics, the cure—excessive state police power—was greater than the problem: inefficiency. Nowadays the phrase is normally used to caricature a government eager to achieve efficiency but unconcerned about the effect on individual freedom.

magistrate An official elected by the Senate of Rome to administer the Republic under the supervision of the Senate. There were many different ranks of magistrate, serving different functions. At the end of their term of office they became senators themselves.

mahdi According to Islamic tradition, this messianic leader will appear to restore justice, truth, and religion for a brief period before the universal Day of Judgment.

Malthusian constraints The British scholar Thomas Malthus (1766–1834) believed that population would always grow faster than the food supply, leading to famine and death that would limit excess population.

mandala A symbolic circular diagram of complex geometric design used as an instrument of meditation or in the performance of sacred rites in Hinduism and Buddhism.

Mandate of Heaven A concept in China: the ruler had moral authority so long as the heavenly powers granted it to him on the basis of his good character. A well-functioning government was evidence that the ruler possessed the Mandate of Heaven. A poorly functioning government, especially when accompanied by such natural disasters as flood or drought, showed that the Mandate had passed away.

mantra A formula of words and sounds that are believed to possess spiritual power, a practice of both Hinduism and Buddhism.

maroon An escaped slave who fled to remote, often hilly areas, and joined with others to create small, free colonies. The process of flight followed by community building is called **maroonage**.

Marshall Plan An American program of economic assistance for rebuilding non-communist Europe after World War II, proposed by US Secretary of State George Marshall.

mastaba A low, rectangular, benchlike structure that covered a grave. The architectural forerunner of the pyramid.

master narrative The conventional, widely accepted view of the historical record.

maya Illusion. The manifest world in which we appear to live is only illusion; there is a reality beyond what we experience here on earth.

mazombo An American-born direct descendant of Portuguese settlers.

McCarthyism A strategy of attacking political opponents by labeling them unpatriotic or even treasonous, named for US Senator Joseph McCarthy, who employed this strategy in his campaign against alleged communists.

medieval The "middle period." Europeans of the Renaissance period, who felt that they were, at last, reconnecting with the glories of ancient Greece and Rome, called the ten centuries between the end of the Western Roman Empire and the beginning of the Renaissance "the medieval period." They used the term pejoratively. More recent scholars see that very long period as far more complicated and diverse, and analyze it by specific geographical regions and into much smaller periods of time.

Meiji restoration The reforms effected in Japan in the name of the emperor Mutsuhito (r. 1867–1912), who was known as the Meiji emperor. During his reign, constitutional changes restored the emperor to full power, displacing the militarily powerful shogun, and Japan adopted many Western innovations as it became a modern, industrial, militarized state.

mercantilism An economic policy pursued by many European nations between the sixteenth and eighteenth centuries. It aimed to strengthen an individual nation's economic power at the expense of its rivals by stockpiling reserves of bullion, which involved government regulations of trade.

mestizo A person of mixed race. In Central and South America it usually denotes a person of combined Indian and European descent.

mfecane Literally "time of troubles," the period in southern Africa from about 1816, when Shaka took control of the Zulu kingdom, until about 1841, when the Dutch completed their Great Trek. The expansion of the Zulus and the migration of the Dutch dislodged local kingdoms and peoples, increasing political instability throughout the region.

micro-finance or **micro-credit** The provision of very small loans, often equivalent to US$100 or even less, to very small-scale businessmen and women, people who would not usually have access to conventional commercial bank loans, because the banks do not deal in such small amounts, and because they would not usually recognize the relatively poor borrowers as "bankable." The loans are usually at below market rates, and are usually secured by the common bond among groups of borrowers that they will stand guaranty for one another.

millet **system** The Ottoman Empire's system of rule through religious communities. Legal issues among members of individual *millets*, or religious groups, were administered by the group itself, and taxes were also collected by the *millets* on behalf of the empire. *Millets* kept in close contact with their coreligionists in other countries, sometimes undermining the power of the Ottoman government.

mit'a A system of forced labor in Peru, begun under Inca rule, by which indigenous communities were required to contribute a set number of laborers for public works for a given period. Conditions were virtually those of slavery.

monoculture An agricultural economy focused on a single crop, usually a cash crop for export, at the expense of others, including food crops.

Montagnards Members of a radical French revolutionary party, closely associated with the Jacobins and supported by the artisans, shopkeepers, and sansculottes. They opposed the more moderate Girondins.

moral economy An economy whose goal is providing basic necessities for all members of a society before allowing any particular members to take profits; in contrast to a free-market economy.

mudra A hand gesture with specific meaning or significance in Indian classical sculpture and dance. One specific *mudra*, for example, indicates teaching, another fearlessness, another revelation, etc.

mulatto In the Americas, a person of mixed race, usually with parents of European and African origin.

myth An interpretive story of the past that cannot be verified historically but may have a deep moral message.

nabob A corruption of the title "Nawab," for an Indian Muslim ruler, nabob referred to a British trader or administrator who grew rich in India. Often used sarcastically.

nation-state A state occupying geographic territory, with its own government, and having a population with a widely shared language, religion, history, and ethnicity. The nation-state defines itself, in part, by its uniqueness and its separation from other nation-states.

nationalism A positive feeling of belonging to a particular nation, often including a desire to serve the nation, based on such elements as birth and ancestry, later choice and naturalization, anticipation of a common future, and/or material and cultural benefits of membership in the nation. In a negative form nationalism may lead to suppression of difference at home, and warfare against others abroad.

naxalites A term used in India to designate rebels against the state or against exploitative businesses. Derived from the village of Naxalbari, where such rebellions began, they were at first organized by communist parties, but later became more often rebellions of exploited tribal peoples in remote areas.

neocolonialism The control of one country by another through economic rather than political-military domination, a method frequently employed after the end of formal, political colonization.

Neolithic "New Stone Age," the last division of the Stone Age, immediately preceding the development of metallurgy and corresponding to the ninth to fifth millennia B.C.E. it was characterized by the increasing domestication of animals and cultivation of crops, established agricultural communities, and the appearance of such crafts as pottery and weaving.

Neoplatonic A philosophical system founded by Plotinus (205–70 C.E.) and influenced by Plato's theory of ideas. It emphasizes the transcendent, impersonal, and indefinable "One" as the ground of all existence and the source of an eternal world of goodness, beauty, and order, of which material existence is but a feeble copy.

New Europes The lands explored, conquered, and settled by Europeans, who brought with them European institutions and ways of life. New Europes include North and South America, Australia, New Zealand, and South Africa.

NGO Nongovernmental organization. Broadly, any organization not controlled by the government, carrying out its own mission. Most commonly refers to voluntary organizations carrying out work of social and community service that the government cannot or does not do.

nirvana In Theravada Buddhism, the blissful nothingness into which a soul that had lived properly entered after death, and from which there would be no further rebirth. In Mahayana Buddhism, *nirvana* became an abode of more active bliss, a kind of heaven, filled with heavenly activities.

nome An administrative district in ancient Egypt.

nonaligned nations Those states, usually newly independent states, that chose not to take sides in the Cold War between the US and the USSR.

original sin First understood as the disobedience of Adam and Eve in the Garden of Eden as they ate the forbidden fruit of the Tree of Knowledge. Later understood as the sexual relations between Adam and Eve. In Christian belief, Jesus' death atoned for these sins—for those who believed in him.

outcaste Refers to a person outside the caste system of India, usually also an outcast, rejected by the upper levels of society. Such people are now usually referred to as *dalits*, or oppressed persons.

outsourcing Buying goods and services, including personnel, from sources far away from the place where they are to be used, usually from overseas. A major example is the establishment of overseas call centers in countries where labor is cheap to service customers in places where labor is expensive.

paleoanthropology The study of the earliest humans and their environments.

Palestinians Arab residents in the territories of the West Bank of the Jordan River and in the Gaza Strip of land along the Mediterranean coast conquered by Israel in the warfare of 1967. They do not have legal citizenship in Israel, nor in any other recognized state. Another group, Arab residents within the 1948 borders of Israel, are sometimes referred to as Palestinians, but more commonly as Arab Israelis or Israeli Arabs.

paper tiger The mocking comment of the Chinese toward the Americans, who had vast arrays of conventional and nuclear weaponry, but could not cope with simply armed warriors, often guerrillas, fighting for their homelands in Korea, Vietnam, and elsewhere.

Parsis ("from Persia") Those followers of the teachings of Zoroaster who fled Persia around the tenth century in the face of persecution by Muslim invaders.

partisans Partisan fighters, or partisans, are guerrilla warriors fighting in the resistance against occupying armies. The term is used especially for the resistance against the Germans and Italians in World War II, and against Franco in Spain.

paterfamilias The head of a family or household in Roman law—always a male—and the only member to have full legal rights. The *paterfamilias* had absolute power over his family, extending to life and death.

patrician Born to a family with long-standing residence and prominence in Rome, a patrician was an aristocrat. About seven to ten percent of Rome's population were patricians.

patron–client relationship In a patron–client relationship, the patron offers protection and, often, employment, while the client offers obedience, labor, and services in exchange. Sometimes these relationships are formalized under law. More frequently they exist in place of law, in situations where legal structures are weak or nonexistent. Patron–client relationships are common throughout world history.

Pax Americana Literally, "American peace," a Latin phrase derived by analogy from *Pax Romana* (the peace enforced within the boundaries of the Roman Empire by Roman rule) to designate the relative tranquility established within the American sphere of influence immediately after World War II.

Pax Romana The "Roman peace," that is, the state of comparative concord prevailing within the boundaries of the Roman Empire from the reign of Augustus (r. 27 B.C.E.–14 C.E.) to that of Marcus Aurelius (r. 161–180 C.E.), enforced by Roman political and military control.

Pentecostals Christians who stress a direct, personal experience of God, Jesus, and revelation, rather than the authority of scripture or of the Church hierarchy.

philosophes A group of eighteenth-century writers and philosophers, mostly French, who emphasized human reason as the key to progress. They advocated freedom of expression and social, economic, and political reform.

pictogram (alternative: pictograph) A pictorial symbol or sign representing an object or concept.

plebeian A citizen of ancient Rome who was not a member of the privileged patrician class. Beginning in the later Republican period, the term "plebeian" implied low social class.

pogrom A murderous attack on a group of people—usually based on their ethnicity or religion—that is sanctioned by the government, either officially or unofficially.

political asylum Asylum is normally applied for and granted, or refused, on the basis of individual cases brought by people who fear that if they return to their countries they will be persecuted, even murdered, because of their politics. Refugee status, by contrast, is usually a group phenomenon and does not imply any specific cause.

praetor In ancient Rome, the term was originally applied to the consul as leader of an army. In 366 B.C.E. a further praetor was elected with special responsibility for the administration of justice in Rome, with the right of military command. Further praetors were subsequently appointed to administer the increasing number of provinces.

Prague Spring The period in the spring of 1968 when it appeared that Prague, and all of Czechoslovakia, would achieve greater freedom of expression and greater independence of control by the USSR. This hope was crushed by Soviet military intervention.

prehistory Everything that occurred before the invention of writing.

presbyter In early Christian usage, a member of the governing body of a church.

price revolution The massive inflation in Europe from the late 1400s to the early 1600s, caused in large part by the influx of silver and gold from the New World, but also by increased mining of precious metals in Europe, general population increase, and, in particular, increases in urban populations. The inflation tended to help urban entrepreneurs but to harm farmers and landholders.

privatization The act of selling off government-owned enterprises to private businesses.

proletariat A collective noun designating the working class that produces wealth. The singular is "proletarian."

protectionism The policy of protecting domestic production from external competition by limiting or prohibiting imports from other countries.

Protestant Reformation The movement, in sixteenth-century Europe, in which Luther, Calvin, Henry VIII, and others broke away from the Catholic Church.

proxy war A war waged between dependent, client states of larger, more powerful states that do not become directly involved in the fighting.

publicans or **tax farmers** Collected taxes on behalf of the government, paying in an agreed sum but keeping for themselves any surplus they could extort. The system was extremely oppressive to those who were taxed.

purchasing power parity (PPP) A statistical formulation based on the actual purchasing power of various currencies. For example, 100 Indian rupees may be officially equal to US$2, but in India it will buy far more in goods and services than US$2 will in the United States. The PPP statistic attempts to evaluate this actual purchasing power.

Putsch (German) An attempt to seize control of the government, often by the military. A coup d'etat.

putting-out system In this system, employers provide employees with raw materials and the orders for turning them into finished products, which they then buy on completion. The employees carry out the work at home, thus reducing the production cost for the employer.

qadi A judge in Islamic legal practice.

Red Scare The fear that communists would take over the United States, especially powerful in the years just after the Communist Revolution in Russia, 1917.

Renaissance From the French for "rebirth," a period of cultural and intellectual creativity in Western Europe between 1300 and 1570. The artists and intellectuals who created the movement saw themselves reconnecting with the traditions of ancient Greece and Rome, thus giving a "rebirth" to European culture. The cultural rebirth was accompanied by an expanding urban economy, another rebirth.

repartimiento A system by which the Spanish crown allowed colonists to employ Indians for forced labor, in conditions of virtual slavery.

republic A state that is ruled not by a hereditary leader (as in a monarchy) but by a person or persons appointed under the constitution.

Revere the Emperor; Expel the Barbarian A much more conservative position than "Eastern Ethics; Western Science," urging rejection of almost everything coming from Western colonization.

Roma (gypsies) An itinerant people, probably originally from northern India, now usually resident in south and southwest Asia, Europe, and the Americas. "Gypsy" is today usually considered a derogatory term; "Roma" is more formal and more polite.

sacrament In Christian theology, a rite or ritual that is an outward sign of a spiritual grace conveyed on the believer by Christ through the ministry of the Church.

samsara The process and cycle of living, dying, and being reborn.

samurai The hereditary warrior-aristocrats of Japanese society, known for their codes of honor and loyalty. Only *samurai* were permitted to wear swords in their everyday dress.

sansculottes From the French, "without breeches." Members of the militant, generally poorer classes of Paris, so called because they wore trousers rather than the knee breeches of affluent society.

satrapy A province or colony in the Achaemenid or Persian Empire ruled by a satrap or governor. Darius I completed the division of the Empire into provinces, and established 20 satrapies with their annual tributes. The term "satrapy" can also refer to the period of rule of a satrap.

satyagraha A word coined by Gandhi to mean truth-force, or militant nonviolence. Links two Hindi words: *satya* (truth) and *agraha* (force).

Schengen Agreement Set common, restrictive rules limiting immigration and the import of goods to signatory nations.

scorched earth A strategy of defensive warfare, in which everything that might be of use to an invading army is destroyed by the defending army as it retreats.

scramble for Africa The rush of European nations to colonize the parts of Africa that were assigned to them in the international negotiations at the Berlin Conference.

see The geographical home of a Church authority: the Vatican in Roman Catholicism, four separate locations for the Eastern Christian churches.

serf An agricultural worker or peasant bound to the land and legally dependent on the lord. Serfs had their own homes, plots, and livestock, but they owed the lord labor, dues, and services. These services could be commuted to rent, but serfs remained chattels of the lord unless they were emancipated, or escaped. Serfdom declined in Western Europe in the late medieval period, but persisted in parts of eastern Europe until the nineteenth century.

shaman In the religious beliefs of some African, Asian and American tribal societies, a person capable of entering into trances and believed to be endowed with supernatural powers, with the ability to cure the sick, find lost or stolen property, predict the future, and protect the community from evil spirits. A shaman may act as judge or ruler, and, as a priest, a shaman directs communal sacrifices and escorts the souls of the dead to the next world.

Shi'a Short form for *shiat Ali*, "follower of Ali." In choosing a successor to Muhammad, the shi'a argued for Ali, his cousin/son-in-law, his closest male relative. From that time on, they remained a separate sect within Islam, representing about 20 percent of all

Muslims worldwide, and a majority in countries such as Iran and Iraq.

shogun The military dictator of Japan, a hereditary title held by three families between 1192 and 1867. Although they were legally subservient to the emperor, their military power gave them effective control of the country.

Sikh Member of a religious community founded in the Punjab region of northern India by Guru Nanak in the sixteenth century. Sikhism combines *bhakti*, devotional Hinduism, with Islamic Sufism. In the face of the militant opposition of their neighbors, Sikhs also became a militant armed people.

silk route The set of rough roads or transportation links across central Asia carrying trade and cultural exchange as far as China, India, and the eastern Mediterranean.

sinicization The adoption and absorption by foreign peoples of Chinese language, customs, and culture.

social contract A mythical, unwritten agreement among early people in a "state of nature" to establish some form of government. This "contract" generally defines the rights and obligations of the individuals and of the government.

social Darwinism A theory popularized by Herbert Spencer, based on a misreading of Charles Darwin's theory of the survival of the fittest. Darwin argued that those plants and animals best suited to a particular environment survived best in that environment. Spencer took this to mean that whichever creatures were dominant ought to be dominant. For example, among humans the rich and powerful deserved to be rich and powerful; conversely, the poor and powerless deserved their low status.

socialist Socialists believed that too much wealth was going into the hands of the owners of property and industry, and too little to the workers who actually produced the wealth. They were divided sharply, however, about the precise definition of the problem and the appropriate paths of struggle for change.

sophist An itinerant professor of higher education in ancient Greece, who gave instruction for a fee. The subjects taught, which included oratory, grammar, ethics, mathematics, and literature, had the practical aim of equipping pupils for successful careers. The sophist professor taught his students to argue all sides of every question, regardless of their merit. **Sophistry** is this kind of clever argumentation, regardless of merit.

889

soviet A council of workers, the primary unit of government in the Soviet Union at local, regional, and national levels, also adopted by other communist regimes. Chinese soviets, governing councils made up of peasants, were modeled in part on Russian examples, but they focused on rural, rather than urban, administration. Founded during the revolutionary movement, they also provided guerrilla warriors for the campaigns.

Spanish Inquisition A court established with the consent of the Vatican to search out and punish Jews who claimed to have converted to Christianity but were still secretly practicing the Jewish religion, which had been outlawed in Spain in 1492. Subsequently the Inquisition, which was not bound by civil law and which employed torture, also turned against Christians who were not properly observant.

speaking in tongues A mode of praying and preaching emphasizing ecstasy and even an entering into trances, such that the words of prayer and preaching may not be understood, but are meaningful nonetheless.

sphere of influence The geopolitical region in which one external power is considered dominant and other powers keep their hands off.

squatter A person living on land, or in a residence, for which she or he does not pay and to which she or he has no legal title.

state of nature The mythical situation in which people lived without any legal codes or contracts, each free to do exactly as he or she pleased, without the restrictions of law and society, but also without the protection of law and society.

state Several definitions; sometimes used for the total political organization of a group of people controlling their own territory.

Sufi In Islam, a member of one of the orders practicing mystical forms of worship that first arose in the eighth and ninth centuries C.E. Some Muslims see Sufis as fulfilling the mission of Islam; others criticize them as not adhering strictly enough to the formal laws and practices of Islam.

Sunni From the Arabic *sunna*, the words and acts of Muhammad, as recorded in *hadiths*. The Sunni are the majority group in Islam, representing just over 80 percent of the total. They differed from the Shi'a in choosing Uthman as the first successor of Muhammad, and argued that they were following the wish and example of the Prophet.

sunrise industries Industries that are expected to be most profitable in the near future.

sunset industries Industries that are expected to be in decline in the near future.

superpower The term ascribed to both the US and the USSR in recognition of their power, especially their military power, far greater than that of any other country in the world at the time.

supply and **demand** In economics, the relationship between the amount of a commodity that producers are able and willing to sell (supply) and the quantity that consumers can afford and wish to buy (demand).

sustainability A vague but very significant measurement usually applied to new technologies—for example new drugs or pesticides, or financial enterprises—concerning their compatibility with the ecological health of individuals and of the planet, and with social and economic equity among individuals and groups; at a minimum, assuring that these technologies do not deplete their own natural resource base.

syllabary A writing system in which each symbol represents the syllable of a word, in contrast to ideogram.

syncretism refers to the merging of different traditions from different origins into a single unified practice. The term is also used to refer to hybridity in other areas, such as art, music, philosophy, and religion.

TaNaKh A Hebrew term for the books of the Bible that are written in Hebrew. The word is composed of the initial letters of the words Torah (first five books of the Bible, traditionally attributed to Moses), Nevi'im (the books of the Prophets), and Ketuvim (additional historical, poetic, and philosophic writings). These are the three sections of the Hebrew Bible.

tariqa In Islam, a generic term meaning "path," referring to the doctrines and methods of mysticism and esoterism. The word also refers to schools or brotherhoods of mystics, which were often situated at a mosque or the tomb of a Muslim saint.

tax farmer An official entrusted with collecting taxes. The total amount to be collected was fixed by the government, and any collection exceeding that amount belonged to the tax farmer. The system encouraged exploitation of the taxpayer.

tax havens Legal jurisdictions offering low rates of tax to attract the offices of international businesses. While most of the business is actually done elsewhere, the tax haven provides a legal means to pay low taxes. The loser is the location in which the company does most of its business but pays little of its taxes.

teleology The philosophical study of final causes or purposes. Teleology refers especially to any system that interprets nature or the universe as having design or purpose. It has been used to provide evidence for the existence of God.

the big lie A propaganda technique, defined by Hitler as a lie so colossal that no one would believe the liar would dare to say it if it were not true.

the cultivation system A system of Dutch rule over Indonesian agriculture that forced peasants to devote 20 percent of their land to cash crops for export. This policy took away the peasant's right to determine his use of his own fields, and diminished the production of food.

the other Using the term "the other" establishes a relationship between two individuals or groups that define themselves in terms of contrast with each other. Normally the definition implies that one has most of the virtues, and "the other" has most of the vices. Occasionally the word is used in verb form, "othering," meaning the process of defining "the other" in negative terms, and oneself in terms of positive virtues.

theme A theme was originally a military unit stationed in one of the provinces of the Byzantine Empire, but it later applied to the large military districts that formed buffer zones in the areas most vulnerable to Muslim invasion.

theocracy A system of government based on religious beliefs and texts and headed by religious leaders.

third world Today, generally refers to economically poor countries, often with ineffective governments. Historically the term referred to a group of newly independent countries that proposed strategies of development different from those of the US and its allies, the first world, and of the USSR and its allies, the second world.

totalitarianism A totalitarian state is one that seeks total control of the economy, politics, media, and culture of the state, under a single dictator or party. It does away with individual rights, proclaiming the rights of the state—as defined by its dictator—superior to those of any individual or group.

trade diaspora A diaspora is a dispersion over far-flung territories of a group of people who have a common bond. Usually this is an ancestral bond, such as in the Jewish diaspora and the African diaspora. A trade diaspora refers to the network of international traders who relate to one another through the bonds of their trade.

transhumance The practice of shifting residence and livestock between mountains and valleys according to the season of the year, or more generally a pattern of seasonal migration.

transparency The quality of making public and clear the (financial) transactions of government or of private enterprise. Increasingly, transparency is highly valued as a necessity for successful development.

tribune In ancient Rome, a plebeian officer elected by the plebeians and charged to protect their lives and properties, with a right of veto against legislative proposals of the Senate.

tributary status The relationship of a low-ranking state to a more powerful one, recognized formally by the regular payment of tribute.

triumvirate Literally, an association of three strong men. An unofficial coalition of Julius Caesar, Pompey, and Crassus formed in 60 B.C.E. After Caesar's murder in 44 B.C.E., a triumvirate including his heir Octavian (later Augustus), Mark Antony, and Marcus Lepidus was appointed to maintain public order.

Turkic/Turkish Turkic languages are a family of related languages spoken by peoples of central Asia and their descendants. The most widely spoken of these languages is Turkish.

tyrant A ruler with absolute power, sometimes granted through election in times of crisis, sometimes seized through force of arms.

ulama The theologians and legal experts of Islam.

umma The community of believers in Islam, which transcends ethnic and political boundaries.

USSR Union of Soviet Socialist Republics. The country formed from the union of Russia and some fifteen other nations under a single communist government, 1917–91.

value added An economist's term for the increase in value from the cost of raw materials to the cost of finished products. It is the value added to the raw material by processing, manufacture, and marketing.

vassal A low-ranking political ruler or state that is subordinate and pays homage to a more powerful one.

vodoun (**voodoo**) A religion of the Caribbean region which blended religious practices brought from Africa with those of Catholicism brought from Europe.

Wahabi Wahabi Islam follows the very conservative teachings of Muhammad ibn Abd-al-Wahhab, an eighteenth-century scholar. It is the dominant form of Islam in Saudi Arabia.

"Washington consensus" A package of economic measures often required of governments by the International Monetary Fund (based in Washington) as a condition for receiving a loan. The measures included: permitting international investment; lowering or removing tariffs; privatizing government businesses; reducing welfare programs; reducing government employment; devaluing local currencies. Together they made government smaller and private business more important.

Weimar The constitution of the new German government after World War I was written in the city of Weimar. That government espoused democracy and cultural creativity, but was attacked from communists on the left and Nazis on the right, and was taken over by Nazis in 1933. Since then, "Weimar" has stood for a government that is democratic and idealistic, but weak and fragile.

welfare state A government that assumes responsibilities for the welfare of its citizens, including such necessities as education, old-age pensions, health care, and unemployment benefits. A more capitalist state leaves these responsibilities to private initiative.

White Man's Burden A concept, based on the title of a poem by Rudyard Kipling, that white men were superior to people of color, and that it was the duty of the former to rule over, serve, and improve the latter. The concept was often invoked, sometimes self-righteously, sometimes sarcastically, to justify a colonial system that was, in fact, hugely exploitative, a situation not mentioned in the poem.

white-collar jobs Professional and clerical jobs; office work; clean work. This kind of occupation became more prevalent as the Industrial Revolution also created these kinds of urban, service job.

world system A theory held by some social scientists concerning the political and economic organization of the world in modern times. It posits that a few countries, the "core," dominated most of the others, "the periphery," and exploited them. During the period of imperialism this dominance was both political and economic. Afterward it was mostly economic, taking the form of neocolonialism.

yurt A portable dwelling used by the nomadic peoples of central Asia, consisting of a tentlike structure of skin, felt, or handwoven textiles arranged over wooden poles, simply furnished with rugs.

ziggurat A temple tower of ancient Mesopotamia, constructed of square or rectangular terraces of diminishing size, usually with a shrine on top built of blue enamel bricks, the color of the sky.

zimbabwe (zim-bahb-way) Stone-walled enclosure or building built during the African Iron Age in the region of modern Zimbabwe and Mozambique. The structures were the courts of local rulers. They have been associated with foreign trade, integrated farming and animal husbandry, and gold production. The Great Zimbabwe is the ruins of the former capital of the Monomatapa Empire, situated in Zimbabwe and occupied from around the thirteenth to the sixteenth century C.E.

PICTURE AND LITERARY CREDITS

Picture credits

Private collection; **533** YUAG Open Access; **534** Bridgeman Art Library/Capitol Collection, Washington DC; **538** Bridgeman Art Library/Musée Carnavalet, Paris; **540** Topfoto/The Granger Collection; **541** Bridgeman Art Library/Bibliothèque Nationale, Paris; **542** Château de Versailles, France/Giraudon/Bridgeman Art Library; **546** Topfoto/The Granger Collection; **551** Getty/Hulton Archive; **553** AKG Images/Bibliothèque Nationale, Paris; **558** Hulton Deutsch Collection/Corbis; **560** Mary Evans Picture Library; **562** AKG Images/Stedelijk Museum, Leiden; **563** Mary Evans Picture Library; **565** Bridgeman Art Library/Guildhall Library, Corporation of London; **566** Universal History Archive/UIG/Bridgeman Art Library; **568** Coo-ee Historical Picture Library; **569** Corbis/Schenectady Museum; Hall of Electrical History Foundation; **573** Private collection, London; **575** Mary Evans Picture Library; **576** Bridgeman Art Library/© Manchester Art Gallery; **577** Getty/Hulton Archive; **578** Library of Congress; **580** Alamy/Michael Jenner; **582** Bridgeman Art Library/Museum Folkwang, Essen; **585** Corbis; **587** Private collection; **588** Scala, Florence/White Images; **590** Library of Congress; **594** Corbis/Bettmann; **598** Private collection; **602** Musée d'Art et d'Histoire, Saint-Denis, France/Giraudon/Bridgeman Art Library; **603** Scala, Florence; **604** Getty Images/Leemage/UIG; **605** Château de Versailles, France/Giraudon/Bridgeman Art Library; **611** AKG Images/Ullstein Bild; **615** National Maritime Museum, London; **616** Bridgeman Art Library/Private Collection/Archives Charmet; **617** Library of Congress, Washington DC; **619, 623** Private collection, London; **626** AKG Images/Ullstein Bild; **628** Bridgeman Art Library/Taylor Gallery, London; **629** British Library, London; **630** Getty Images/Rischgitz; **635** Arthur M. Sackler Gallery, Smithsonian Institution, USA/Gift of Ambassador and Mrs. William Leonhart/Bridgeman Art Library; **636** Corbis/Underwood & Underwood; **638** Old Japan Picture Library; **644** Corbis/Bettmann; **645** Corbis/Underwood & Underwood; **646, 647, 648** Corbis/Bettmann; **650** Scala, Florence/Art Resource/The Philadelphia Museum of Art. © 2013 Artists Rights Society (ARS), New York/ADAGP, Paris; **652** Universal History Archive/UIG/The Bridgeman Art Library; **654** From *Ahmedabad: The Life of a City in India* by Howard Spodek, cinematographer Norris Brock; **656** Corbis/Hulton-Deutsch Collection; **659** Private Collection/The Stapleton Collection/Bridgeman Art Library; **660** Mary Evans Picture Library; **664** Imperial War Museum, London; **666, 667** Corbis/Bettmann; **669** Special Collections Department, W.E.B. Du Bois Library, University of Massachusetts, Amherst; **673** David King Collection; **675** Ronald Grant Archive; **676, 678** David King Collection; **680** Getty Images/Hulton Archive; **681, 686** Corbis; **690** AKG Images/Ullstein Bild; **693** Schenectady Museum; Hall of Electrical History Foundation/Corbis; **694** Getty Images/Hulton Archive/Felice Beato; **698** © 2013 Estate of Pablo Picasso/Artists Rights Society (ARS), New York; **702** Corbis/Reuters/China Daily; **704** Topfoto/Novosti; **705** Imperial War Museum, London; **706** Corbis/Bettmann; **709** Topfoto/The Granger Collection; **711** Topfoto/Ullsteinbild; **712** D.O.D. & U.S.A.F.; **715** © Richard Kalvar/Magnum Photos; **721** © Fabrizio Bensch/Reuters/Corbis; **722** Getty Images/Hedrich-Blessing Photographers/Chicago Historical Society/UIG; **723** Topfoto/Jean Pierre Couderc/Roger-Viollet; **726** © Corbis/Bettmann; **730** AKG Images; **731** © Corbis/Rykoff Collection; **735** © Corbis/Bettmann/U.P.I.; **736** Rex Features; **738** Getty Images/AFP; **739** Getty Images/Gamma-Keystone; **741** © 2009 Josh Gerritsen Photography http://www.joshgerritsen.com; **744** © Corbis/Bettmann/U.P.I.; **745** Ronald Grant Archive/Zeitgeist Films/Photofest; **747** © Nicolas Tikhomiroff/Magnum Photos; **753** Alamy/Vespasian; **754** Getty Images/Orlando Sierra/AFP; **755** Getty Images/AFP/Don Emmert; **759** Rex Features; **763** © Corbis/Bettmann; **766** Getty

Images/AFP/Robyn Beck; **770** © Corbis/Bettmann; **777** Corbis/Hulton-Deutsch Collection; **779** © Corbis/Bettmann; **781** © Magnum Photos/Cartier-Bresson; **783** Topfoto; **784** The National Archives, Washington; **785** Getty Images/AFP; **790** Getty Images/Hulton Archive/Central Press; **792** Getty Images/Gamma-Keystone; **795** Topfoto; **797** © Corbis/Bettmann; **798** Howard Spodek; **807** © Corbis/Reuters/Christopher Herwig; **808** © Corbis/Zuma Press/Julia Cumes; **809 (top)** Getty Images/AFP/Gianluigi Guercia; **809 (bottom)** Panos Pictures/Jocelyn Carlin; **810** © Panos Pictures/Paul Lowe; **812** © Najlah Feanny/Corbis/Saba; **815** © Corbis/Reuters/HO; **818** © Corbis/Paulo Fridman; **819** Rex Features/Sipa Press; **821** Rex Features; **822** © Corbis/Martin H. Simon; **825** Getty Images/ChinaFotoPress; **826** © Corbis/AP; **827** © Corbis/Kapoor Baldev/Sygma; **830** © Corbis/Michel Setboun; **832** © Corbis/Sean Adair/Reuters; **836** Getty Images/AFP/Sebastian D'Souza; **839** © Corbis/Demotix/Vito Di Stefano; **841** Alamy/Russell Kord; **844** © Corbis/Peter Turnley; **846** © Gerry Penny/epa/Corbis; **847** © Corbis/Demotix/Alex Milan Tracy; **848** Howard Spodek; **854** Getty Images/Scott Barbour; **856** © Goran Tomasevic/Reuters/Corbis; **859** Getty Images/AFP/Pedro Ugarte; **862** Opportunity Organisation/Ron Londen; **864** © Corbis/Reuters/Juda Ngwenya; **866** Rex Features; **867** Getty Images/AFP/Raveendran; **869** Getty Images/Diane Cook and Len Jenshel; **870** Panos Pictures/Sven Torfinn; **873** © Corbis/Reuters/China Daily; **875** © Corbis/Reuters/Antony Njuguna.

Literary credits

For permission to reprint copyright material the publishers gratefully acknowledge the following:

Introduction
(p. I-19): from *Christianizing the Roman Empire (A.D. 100–400)* by Ramsay MacMullen (New Haven, CT: Yale University Press, 1984).

Chapter Two
(pp. 57–58): from *The Epic of Gilgamesh*, translated with an introduction by N.K. Sandars (Penguin Classics, 1960, Third Edition 1972), Copyright © N. K. Sandars, 1960, 1964, 1972, reproduced by permission of Penguin Books Ltd; **(p. 60):** from *The Sumerians: Their History, Culture, and Character* (Chicago, IL: University of Chicago Press, published 1963), by Samuel Noah Kramer. Copyright © 1963 by The University of Chicago. All rights reserved. Reprinted by permission of University of Chicago Press.

Chapter Three
(pp. 65, 70): "Hymn to the Nile," and "The Harper's Song for Inherkhawy," both from *Ancient Egyptian Literature: An Anthology*, translated by John L. Foster (University of Texas Press, 2001), copyright © 2001, by permission of the author and the University of Texas Press; **(p. 73):** "The Egyptian Book of the Dead and the 'Negative Confession'," from *Ancient Near Eastern Texts Relating to the Old Testament*, Third Edition With Supplement, edited by James B. Pritchard (Princeton University Press, 1969) © 1950, 1955, 1969, renewed 1978 by Princeton University Press, reprinted by permission of Princeton University Press; **(p. 77):** "Si-nuhe," from *Ancient Near Eastern Texts Relating to the Old Testament*, Third Edition With Supplement, edited by James B. Pritchard (Princeton University Press, 1969) © 1950, 1955, 1969, renewed 1978 by Princeton University Press, reprinted by permission of Princeton University Press.

Chapter Four
(p. 93): from *The Book of Songs*, translated by Arthur Waley (London: George Allen & Unwin, 1936), copyright © by permission of The Arthur Waley

Estate; **(p. 106):** "Great-Jaguar-Paw: Mayan King of Tikal" from *A Forest of Kings: The Untold Story of the Ancient Maya*, edited by Linda Schele and David Freidel (William Morrow, 1990), © 1990 by Linda Schele and David Freidel; **(p. 108):** from *Popul Vuh: Sacred Book of the Quiché Maya People* (Norman: University of Oklahoma Press, 2007), translation and commentary by Allen J. Christenson. Reprinted by permission of University of Oklahoma Press and O Books, John Hunt Publishing.

Chapter Five
(p. 140): "Hector Returns to Troy", from *The Iliad* by Homer, translated by Robert Fagles, translation copyright © 1990 by Robert Fagles. Used by permission of Viking Penguin, a division of Penguin Group (USA) LLC; **(p. 140):** "Book 22: Slaughter in the Hall", "Book 23: The Great Rooted Bed" from *The Odyssey* by Homer, translated by Robert Fagles, translation copyright © 1996 by Robert Fagles. Used by permission of Viking Penguin, a division of Penguin Group (USA) LLC; **(p. 145):** from *The History of the Peloponnesian War* by Thucydides, translated by Rex Warner, with an introduction and notes by M. I. Finley (Penguin Classics 1954, Revised edition 1972). Translation copyright © Rex Warner, 1954. Introduction and appendices copyright © M. I. Finley, 1972. Reprinted by permission of Penguin Books Limited. Reproduced with permission of Curtis Brown Group Limited, London on behalf of The Estate of Rex Warner. Copyright © Rex Warner, 1954; **(pp. 146, 148):** from *The Collected Dialogues of Plato*, Including the Letters, by Edith Hamilton. © 1961 Princeton University Press, 1989 renewed. Reprinted by permission of Princeton University Press; **(p. 150):** from *The Reign of the Phallus: Sexual Politics in Ancient Athens* by Eva C. Keuls. Reprinted by permission of University of California Press; **(pp. 150–151):** from *Worshiping Women: Ritual and Reality in Classical Athens*, edited by Nikolaos Kaltsas and Alan Shapiro (Alexander S. Onassis Public Benefit Foundation (in collaboration with National Archaeological Museum, Athens, 2008). Reprinted with permission; **(p. 156):** from *Alexander of Macedon* by Peter Green (Berkeley, CA: University of California Press, 1991). Reprinted by permission of University of California Press.

Chapter Six
(pp. 185): from *The Aeneid* by Virgil, translated by Rolphe Humphries (Charles Scribner's Sons, 1951) © 1951 Charles Scribner's Sons, reprinted by permission of Pearson Education Inc; **(p. 193):** Sima Qian, from *First Emperor: Selections from the Historical Records*, translated by Raymond Dawson (2007). By permission of Oxford University Press.

Chapter Seven
(p. 205): from *The Book of Songs*, translated by Arthur Waley (London: George Allen & Unwin, 1936), copyright © by permission of The Arthur Waley Estate; **(pp. 210, 211, 212, 220):** from *Sources of Chinese Tradition* Volume I, Second Edition, edited by William Theodore de Bary and Irene Bloom (Copyright © Columbia University Press, 1999), reprinted by permission of the publisher; **(pp. 210–211, 213, 220):** Sima Qian, from *First Emperor: Selections from the Historical Records*, translated by Raymond Dawson (2007). By permission of Oxford University Press; **(p. 217):** "A Woman's Hundred Years" from *Chinese Civilization: A Sourcebook*, Second Edition, edited by Patricia Buckley Ebrey (The Free Press, 1993), copyright (1993) by Patricia Buckley Ebrey, reprinted by permission of The Free Press, a division of Simon & Schuster, Inc. **(p. 229):** Du Fu, "Autumn Meditation" from *The Selected Poems of Du Fu*, translated by Burton Watson (Copyright © Columbia University Press, 2002), reprinted by permission of the publisher; **(p. 231):** Du Fu, "Ballad of the Army Carts" from *Three Chinese Poets: Translations of Poems by Wang Wei, Li Bai, and Du Fu*, edited by Vikram Seth (HarperCollins Publishers, 1993), translation

copyright © 1992 by Vikram Seth, reprinted by permission of the publisher and Irene Skolnick Literary Agency.

Chapter Eight

(p. 249): from *Asoka and the Decline of the Mauryas* by Romila Thapar (1998). By permission of Oxford University Press, USA; **(p. 254):** "A King's Double Nature" and "Harvest of War" from *Poems of Love and War: From the Eight Anthologies and Ten Long Poems of Classical Tamil*, translated by A.K. Ramanujan (Columbia University Press, 1985) © 1985 by Columbia University Press, reprinted by permission of the publisher.

Chapter Nine

(p. 272): from *Sources of Indian Tradition* Vol. I (From the Beginning to 1800), edited by Ainslee Embree (New York: Columbia University Press, 2nd ed., 1988) (translations of *The Rigveda*). Copyright © 1988 Columbia University Press, reprinted by permission of the publisher; **(p. 276):** from *Bhagavad-Gita*, translated by Barbara Stoler Miller (Bantam Books, 1986), translation copyright © 1986 by Barbara Stoler Miller, used by permission of Bantam Books, a division of Random House, Inc.; **(pp. 280, 281):** from *The Wonder that Was India* by A. L. Basham (New York: Grove Press, 1954), St Martin's Press; **(p. 288):** "A Woman's Hundred Years" from *Chinese Civilization: A Sourcebook*, Second Edition, edited by Patricia Buckley Ebrey (The Free Press, 1993), copyright (1993) by Patricia Buckley Ebrey, reprinted by permission of The Free Press, a division of Simon & Schuster, Inc.

Chapter Ten

(p. 325): from *Who Are the People of God? Early Christian Models of Community* by Howard Clark Kee (New Haven, CT: Yale University Press, 1995); **(pp. 326, 327):** from *The City of God* by Augustine (New York: Modern Library, 1950); **(p. 335):** from *Two Lives of Charlemagne* by Einhard and Nokter the Stammerer, translated with an introduction by Professor Lewis Thorpe (Penguin Classics, 1969). Copyright © Professor Lewis Thorpe, 1969.

Chapter Eleven

(pp. 343, 346–347, 348): from *The Koran* (With a Parallel Arabic Text), translated with notes by N.J. Dawood (London: Penguin Books, 1990). Copyright © N.J. Dawood, 1956, 1959, 1966, 1968, 1974, 1990; **(p. 347):** from *The Islamic World*, edited by William H. McNeill and Marilyn Robinson Waldman (Chicago, IL: University of Chicago Press, 1983) (OUP); **(p. 348):** from *The Koran*, translated by M. Pickthall (New York: Alfred A. Knopf, 1930).

Chapter Twelve

(p. 393): Ibn Battuta, from *Travels in Asia and Africa 1325–1354*, translated and edited by H.A.R. Gibb (The Hakluyt Society, 1958). By permission of David Higham Associates; **(pp. 397, 398, 404):** from *The Travels of Marco Polo*, translated with an introduction by Ronald Latham (Penguin Classics, 1958), Copyright © Ronald Latham, 1958, reprinted by permission of Penguin Books Ltd; **(pp. 397, 403):** from *The Mongols: A Very Short Introduction* by Morris Rossabi (2012). By permission of Oxford University Press, USA.

Chapter Thirteen

(p. 423): from *The Decameron* by Giovanni Boccaccio, translated by Frances Winwar (New York: Modern Library, 1955). Reprinted by permission of MBI Inc.

Chapter Fourteen

(p. 457): from *Religion and the Rise of Capitalism* by R.H. Tawney (New York: Harcourt, Brace, & Co., 1926); **(p. 460):** from *Introduction to Contemporary Civilization in the West*, 2 vols. (New York: Columbia University Press, 2nd ed., 1954; 3rd ed. 1960). Copyright © 1960 Columbia University Press, reprinted by permission of the publisher.

Chapter Fifteen

(p. 506): from *An Arab Philosophy of History* by Ibn Khaldun, translated by Charles Issawi (London: John Murray, 1950).

Chapter Sixteen

(p. 530): from *Introduction to Contemporary Civilization in the West*, 2 vols. (New York: Columbia University Press, 2nd ed., 1954; 3rd ed. 1960). Copyright © 1960 Columbia University Press, reprinted by permission of the publisher; **(p. 553):** from *Canto General* by Pablo Neruda, translated by Jack Schmitt (University of California Press, 1991), © 1991 by the Fundación Pablo Neruda and the Regents of the University of California, by permission of University of California Press.

Chapter Seventeen

(p. 584): from *Pandita Ramabai's American Encounter: The Peoples of the United States* by Pandita Sarasvati Ramabai, translated and edited by Meera Kosambi, 0-253-34190-6 Copyright © Indiana University Press, 2003. Reprinted with permission of Indiana University Press.

Chapter Eighteen

(p. 597): from "What is a Nation?" by Joseph-Ernest Renan in *The Poetry of the Celtic Races*, trans. William G. Hutchison, The Walter Scott Publishing Co., Ltd. 1896; **(p. 600):** from *Introduction to Contemporary Civilization in the West*, 2 vols. (New York: Columbia University Press, 2nd ed., 1954; 3rd ed. 1960). Copyright © 1960 Columbia University Press, reprinted by permission of the publisher; **(p. 633):** from *The Autobiography of Yukichi Fukuzawa*, translated by Eiichi Kiyooka. (New York: Columbia University Press, 1966). Copyright © 1966 Columbia University Press, reprinted by permission of the publisher and Keio University, Tokyo.

Chapter Nineteen

(pp. 645, 683): "The Century's Decline," from *View with a Grain of Sand* (Harcourt Brace, 1995), copyright © 1993 by Wislawa Szymborska, English translation by Stanislaw Baranczak and Clare Cavanagh copyright © 1995 by Houghton Mifflin Harcourt Publishing Company, reprinted by permission of the publisher. Published in the UK by Faber & Faber Limited; **(p. 656):** From *Sources of Chinese Tradition*, vol. 2. by William Theodore de Bary and Richard Lufrano. (New York: Columbia University Press, 2000). Copyright © 2000 Columbia University Press, reprinted by permission of the publisher.

Chapter Twenty

(p. 710): from *Comfort Women Speak: Testimony by Sex Slaves of the Japanese Military*, edited by Sangmie Choi Schellstede (New York: Holmes and Meier, 2000); **(p. 713):** from Hind Swaraj or Indian Home Rule by Mohandas Karamchand Gandhi, from *The Gandhi Reader*, edited by Homer Jack (Grove Press, 1956); **(p. 714):** from "The Waste Land" by T.S. Eliot, in *Collected Poems 1909–1962* (New York: Harcourt Brace Jovanovich, 1936). Published by Faber and Faber Limited; **(pp. 714, 715):** from *Night* by Elie Wiesel (New York: Bantam Books, 1962), Farrar Straus & Giroux; **(p. 723):** from "Prayers to Masks" by Leopold Sedar Senghor, from *Leopold Sedar Selected Poems*, translated by Reed & Wake (1964). By permission of Oxford University Press and the University of Virginia Press.

Chapter Twenty-one

(p. 760): from *Silent Spring* by Rachel Carson (New York: Penguin Books, 1965). Houghton Mifflin Harcourt Publishing Company.

Chapter Twenty-two

(p. 780): from *A Higher Kind of Loyalty* by Liu Binyan. (Pantheon Books, 1990) translation copyright © 1990 by Random House, Inc., used by permission of Pantheon Books, a division of Random House, Inc.; **(pp. 788, 789, 791):** from Hind Swaraj or Indian Home Rule, and Young India, June 1, 1921, by Gandhi, from *The Gandhi Reader*, edited by Homer Jack (Grove Press, 1956); **(p. 790):** from *Sources of Indian Tradition* by William Theodore de Bary. (New York: Columbia University Press, 1958.) Copyright © 1958 Columbia University Press, reprinted by permission of the publisher.

Chapter Twenty-three

(p. 823): from *Global Society: The World Since 1900* by Pamela Kyle Crossley, Lynn Hollen Lees, and John W. Servos (Boston, MA: Houghton Mifflin, 3rd ed., 2012); **(p. 823):** from *Development as Freedom* by Amartya Sen (New York: Random House, 1999).

Chapter Twenty-four

(pp. 863, 865): from *Truth and Lies: Stories from the Truth and Reconciliation Commission in South Africa* by Jillian Edelstein (The New Press, 2001).

Every effort has been made to obtain permission from all copyright holders, but in some cases this has not proved possible. The publishers therefore wish to thank all authors or copyright holders who are included without acknowledgment. Pearson Education Inc./Laurence King Publishing Ltd apologizes for any errors or omissions in the above list and would be pleased to incorporate any corrections in the next edition.

INDEX